Council for Exceptional Children CEC

CEC Content Standards for All Beginning Special Education Teachers

The Council for Exceptional Children has established a comprehensive set of ten content standards for the preparation of all special education teachers. All newly prepared special educators are expected to develop a professional portfolio that includes evidence of their knowledge and skills across each of the ten domains.

Special Education Content Standard 1:
FOUNDATIONS

Special educators understand the field as an evolving and changing discipline based on philosophies, evidence-based **principles and theories**, relevant **laws and policies**, diverse and **historical** points of view, and **human issues** that have historically influenced and continue to influence the field of special education and the education and treatment of individuals with exceptional needs both in school and society. Special educators understand how these **influence professional practice**, including assessment, instructional planning, implementation, and program evaluation. Special educators understand how **issues of human diversity** can impact families, cultures, and schools, and how these complex human issues can interact with issues in the delivery of special education services. They understand the **relationships of organizations of special education** to the organizations and functions of schools, school systems, and other agencies. Special educators use this knowledge as a ground upon which to construct their own personal understandings and philosophies of special education.

Special Education Content Standard 2:
DEVELOPMENT AND CHARACTERISTICS OF LEARNERS

Special educators know and **demonstrate respect** for their students first as unique human beings. Special educators understand the **similarities and differences in human development** and characteristics between and among individuals with and without exceptional learning needs (ELN). Moreover, special educators understand how **exceptional conditions** can interact with the domains of human development and they **use this knowledge to respond to the varying abilities and behaviors of individuals** with ELN. Special educators understand how the experiences of individuals with ELN can impact families, as well as the individuals' ability to learn, interact socially, and live as fulfilled contributing members of the community.

Special Education Content Standard 3:
INDIVIDUAL LEARNING DIFFERENCES

Special educators understand the **effects that an exceptional condition** can have **on an individual's learning** in school and throughout life. Special educators understand that the beliefs, traditions, and values across and within cultures can affect relationships among and between students, their families, and the school community. Moreover, special educators **are active and resourceful in seeking to understand how primary language, culture, and familial backgrounds interact with the individual's exceptional condition** to impact the individual's academic and social abilities, attitudes, values, interests, and career options. The understanding of these learning differences and their possible interactions **provides the foundation** upon which **special educators individualize instruction** to provide meaningful and challenging learning for individuals with ELN.

Special Education Content Standard 4:
INSTRUCTIONAL STRATEGIES

Special educators possess a repertoire of evidence-based **instructional strategies to individualize instruction** for individuals with ELN. Special educators select, adapt, and use these instructional strategies to promote **positive learning results in general and special curricula** and to appropriately **modify learning environments** for individuals with ELN. They enhance the **learning of critical thinking, problem solving, and performance skills** of individuals with ELN, and increase their self-awareness, self-management, self-control, self-reliance, and self-esteem. Moreover, special educators emphasize the **development, maintenance, and generalization** of knowledge and skills across environments, settings, and the lifespan.

Special Education Content Standard 5:
LEARNING ENVIRONMENTS AND SOCIAL INTERACTIONS

Special educators actively **create learning environments** for individuals with ELN that foster cultural understanding, safety and emotional well-being, positive social interactions, and **active engagement** of individuals with ELN. In addition, special educators **foster environments in which diversity is valued** and individuals are taught to live harmoniously and productively in a culturally diverse world. Special educators shape **environments to encourage the independence**, self-motivation, self-direction, personal empowerment, and self-advocacy of individuals with ELN. Special educators **help their general education colleagues integrate individuals** with ELN in regular environments and engage them in meaningful learning activities and interactions. Special educators use **direct motivational and instructional interventions** with individuals with ELN to teach them to respond effectively to current expectations. When necessary, special educators can safely **intervene with individuals with ELN in crisis**. Special educators coordinate all these efforts and provide **guidance and direction to paraeducators and others**, such as classroom volunteers and tutors.

(continued in the back)

D0026688

ELEVENTH EDITION

Human Exceptionality

School, Community, and Family

MICHAEL L. HARDMAN

CLIFFORD J. DREW

M. WINSTON EGAN

WADSWORTH
CENGAGE Learning

Australia • Brazil • Japan • Korea • Mexico • Singapore • Spain • United Kingdom • United States

WADSWORTH
CENGAGE Learning·

Human Exceptionality: School, Community, and Family, Eleventh Edition
Michael L. Hardman, Clifford J. Drew and M. Winston Egan

Editor-in-Chief: Linda Ganster

Executive Editor: Mark Kerr

Managing Development Editor: Lisa Mafrici

Development Editor: Kassi Radomski

Editorial Assistant: Greta Lindquist

Media Editor: Elizabeth Momb

Brand Manager: Melissa Larmon

Senior Market Development Manager: Kara Kindstrom

Content Project Manager: Samen Iqbal

Art Director: Jennifer Wahi

Manufacturing Planner: Doug Bertke

Rights Acquisitions Specialist: Tom McDonough

Production Service: Jill Traut, MPS Limited

Photo Researcher: Tim McDonough/Janice Yi

Text Researcher: Pablo D'Stair

Copy Editor: Heather McElwain

Designer: Kathleen Cunningham

Cover Image: GATEWAY ARTS

Compositor: MPS Limited

For product information and technology assistance, contact us at **Cengage Learning Customer & Sales Support, 1-800-354-9706**

For permission to use material from this text or product, submit all requests online at **www.cengage.com/permissions**
Further permissions questions can be e-mailed to **permissionrequest@cengage.com**

Library of Congress Control Number: 2012938473

Student Edition:
ISBN-13: 978-1-133-58983-9
ISBN-10: 1-133-58983-9

Loose-leaf Edition:
ISBN-13: 978-1-133-96437-7
ISBN-10: 1-133-96437-0

Wadsworth
20 Davis Drive
Belmont, CA 94002-3098
USA

Cengage Learning is a leading provider of customized learning solutions with office locations around the globe, including Singapore, the United Kingdom, Australia, Mexico, Brazil, and Japan. Locate your local office at **www.cengage.com/global**

Cengage Learning products are represented in Canada by Nelson Education, Ltd.

To learn more about Wadsworth, visit **www.cengage.com/wadsworth**

Purchase any of our products at your local college store or at our preferred online store **www.CengageBrain.com**

Printed in Canada
1 2 3 4 5 6 7 16 15 14 13 12

Dedication

This book is dedicated to people with differences everywhere, who have risen to the challenge of living in a society that is sometimes nurturing, but all too often ambivalent.

To our spouses, Monica, Linda, and Linda, our loving appreciation for being so patient and caring during the writing of this 11th edition and the 30 years of writing, rewriting, and revising this text. Your insightful contributions have been invaluable to the quality and success of our work.

MLH
CJD
MWE

Brief Contents

Contents

PART IV
Exceptional Gifts and Talents 403

Guide to Selected Features

About the Authors

MICHAEL L. HARDMAN is currently the interim senior vice president for academic affairs (provost) at the University of Utah. In assuming this leadership role, he is on administrative leave as dean from the college of education and professor of special education. Dr. Hardman is also past chair of the department of special education and the department of teaching and learning. In the 2004–2005 school year, Dr. Hardman was appointed the Matthew J. Guglielmo Endowed Chair at California State University, Los Angeles, and the Governor's Representative to the California Advisory Commission on Special Education. In addition, Dr. Hardman is also senior education advisor to the Joseph P. Kennedy, Jr. Foundation in Washington, D.C., past president of the Higher Education Consortium for Special Education, a member of the board of directors for Best Buddies International, and a former member of the board of directors for the Council for Exceptional Children. He has directed or consulted on several international projects on school improvement for U.S. AID, the Organization for Economic Cooperation and Development, and UNICEF.

Dr. Hardman has numerous publications in national and international journals throughout the field of education and has authored several college textbooks, of which *Human Exceptionality: School, Community, and Family* is now in its 11th edition, and *Intellectual Disabilities across the Lifespan* is in its 9th edition. Prior to the release of the 11th edition of *Human Exceptionality*, his two newest texts are *Research and Inquiry in Education* (2007) and *Successful Transition Programs* (2009). As a researcher, he has directed international and national demonstration projects in the areas of educational policy and reform, developmental disabilities, professional development, inclusive education, transition from school to adult life, and preparing tomorrow's leaders in special education.

CLIFFORD J. DREW has served as associate dean for research and outreach in the college of education, and as director of academic outreach and continuing education at the University of Utah. He is currently a professor in the special education and educational psychology departments. Dr. Drew came to the University of Utah in 1971, after serving on the faculties of the University of Texas at Austin and Kent State University. He received his master's degree from the University of Illinois and his PhD from the University of Oregon. He has published numerous articles in education and related areas including intellectual disabilities, research design, statistics, diagnostic assessment, cognition, evaluation related to the law, and information technology. His most recent book is *Adolescent Online Social Communication and Behavior* (IGI Global, 2010). His professional interests include research methods in education and psychology, human development and disabilities, applications of information technology, and outreach in higher education.

M. WINSTON EGAN is professor emeritus and past chair of the teacher education department at the David O. McKay School of Education, Brigham Young University. Dr. Egan has taught children of all ages, preschool through high school. He began his special education career at Utah Boys Ranch. His writings appear in *Behavior Disorders, Journal of Teacher Education, Teacher Education and Special Education, American Journal of Distance Education, Journal of Special Education, Rural Special Education Quarterly,* and *Teaching and Teacher Education.* He has been honored with several university teaching awards including Professor of the Year, Blue Key National Honor Society, Brigham Young University; and Excellence in Teaching Award, College of Education, University of Utah. He has also been honored as an associate for the National Network for Education Renewal (NNER). His interests include youth development, teacher socialization, education for democracy, and emotional/behavior disorders.

Preface

The realization that we are all basically the same human beings, who seek happiness and try to avoid suffering, is very helpful in developing a sense of brotherhood and sisterhood; a warm feeling of love and compassion for others.

— Dalai Lama

Welcome to *Human Exceptionality: School, Community, and Family!* In this, our 11th edition, we are very pleased to continue as part of the Cengage Learning family of college textbooks. As authors in a partnership with Cengage Learning, we aspire to our publisher's mission and vision of being "a respected and innovative source of teaching, learning, and research solutions." In doing so, our goal in writing this new 30th anniversary edition is to provide you, our readers, with a textbook that is current, informative, relevant, user-friendly, and meaningful in both your professional and personal life—a book that rises to the Cengage vision of fostering academic excellence and professional development, as well as provides measurable learning outcomes to you the reader.

For some of you, this book is the beginning of your journey into the lives of people who are exceptional, their families, and the schools and communities in which they live. This text is first and foremost about people—people with many different needs, desires, characteristics, challenges and lifestyles—people who for one reason or another are described as *exceptional*. What does the word *exceptional* mean to you? For that matter, what do the words *disabled, challenged, or different* mean to you? Who or what influenced your knowledge and attitudes toward people with differences and labels we often use to describe them? You are most influenced by your life experiences. You may have a family member, friend, or casual acquaintance who is exceptional. It may be that you are a person who is exceptional in some way. Then again, you may be approaching a study of human exceptionality with little or no background. In reading and interacting with this book, we believe you will find that the study of human exceptionality is the study of being human. Perhaps you will come to understand yourself better in the process. As suggested by the novelist Louis Bromfield,

There is a rhythm in life, a certain beauty which operates by a variation of lights and shadows, happiness alternating with sorrow, content with discontent, distilling in this process of contrast a sense of satisfaction, of richness that can be captured and pinned down only by those who possess the gift of awareness.

About This Edition

Organization

We have thoughtfully listened to the needs of our current adopters, the faculty instructors and students who use our book week in and week out. In doing so, we have taken their recommendations to divide the chapters into four distinct parts (rather than five) and to maintain the same number of chapters (15) as in the 10th edition. This organization easily coordinates with a 15-week semester, a common time frame for many university and college courses. Additionally, the **new** four-part organization can easily be taught within a 10-week period, with each part addressed over a two-week period, which better accommodates those at a university or college that follows a quarter system.

The four parts reflect the major themes of the book, beginning with a focus on understanding exceptionality through the lifespan and from the perspective of many different disciplines. Part II looks into the meaning of diversity and the role of family, and is followed by, Part III, a study of individuals who are identified as exceptional. Our new edition concludes with an in-depth discussion on people with exceptional gifts and talents. In responding to the needs and desires of our audience of students and adopters who are currently using this text, as well as those who are considering adopting it for future use, we have completely rewritten and updated three chapters in Parts II and III: "Cultural and Linguistic Diversity" (Chapter 5), "Learning Disabilities" (Chapter 7), and "Autism Spectrum Disorders" (Chapter 11).

New and Updated Features

- In this edition, you will find that each chapter begins with the heading *A Changing Era in the Lives of People Who are Exceptional* and concludes with *Looking toward a Bright Future*. The narratives within these headings begin and end each chapter on a positive note on the past, present, and future, while acknowledging the challenges that people with differences are facing and will continue to face in the years to come.

- Many chapters in the 11th edition now include Teach-Source Video boxes, which direct readers to videos on the Education CourseMate website. These videos highlight a major theme in the chapter and create an opportunity for interactive in-class and/or online discussion and reflection on current topics drawn from today's headlines and the daily lives of people who are exceptional.

- We are pleased to announce the new feature, *Learning through Social Media.* As access to social media on the Internet becomes more than a personal convenience and moves into the realm of a necessity in every student's learning experience, this new feature provides interesting and informative online blogs, social media sites by and for people who are exceptional, and the use of this technology to promote inclusion in school, family, and society.

- The features that have been so popular with our readers in past editions, including *Reflect on This, Case Study, Assistive Technology,* and *Debate Forum*, continue to appear in the 11th edition and many have been updated and expanded. These features are now even more interactive, with the inclusion of questions for reflection and application and connections to features on the Education Course-Mate website for *Human Exceptionality*, 11th edition.

- We continue to update our unique topical coverage of multidisciplinary and collaborative approaches to education, health care, and social services with the *Inclusion and Collaboration through the Lifespan* boxes that you'll find in Chapters 7 through 15.

- As in the previous edition, the contents of this edition correspond with the Council for Exceptional Children (CEC) Standards, and icons in the margins highlight these. In this edition, a **new** Standards Correlation Chart at the end of the book details where specific standards are addressed in the book.

- We are also very proud of the fact that the 11th edition contains over *1,500 citations* from sources that have been published since the year 2004, and many of which have been published within the last two years. As authors, we are very comfortable in saying to you, our readers, that the 11th edition of *Human Exceptionality* is one of the most current sources available on the lives of people who are exceptional.

Pedagogical Features and Student Learning System

In addition to providing you with current and informative content, we are committed to making your experience with this textbook informative, interesting, enjoyable, and productive. To this end, each chapter in this 11th edition contains new and continuing features that will significantly enhance your desire to learn more about human exceptionality.

Focus Preview, Focus Concepts and Questions, and Focus Review

At the beginning of each chapter, we have provided tools to assist you in locating and more effectively learning key content. **Focus Preview** serves as an advanced organizer for your reading. It lists each of the **focus concepts and questions** that also occur next to major headings in the margins throughout the chapter, which helps to highlight important information within the chapter. Each chapter concludes with a **Focus Review** that reiterates and summarizes the focus concepts and questions.

FOCUS 2
Identify three approaches to describe human differences.

FOCUS REVIEW

FOCUS 1 What are the three components of the TASH definition of severe disabilities?
- The relationship of the individual within the environment (adaptive fit)
- The inclusion of people of all ages

- Physical and health needs are common, involving conditions such as congenital heart disease, epilepsy, respiratory problems, spasticity, athetosis, and hypotonia. Vision and hearing loss are also common.

FOCUS 5 Identify three types of educational assessments for

...ce on standardized ...tifying people with

...romote independ- ...s are referred to as ...ent.

...e in statewide and ...or the school must ...priate for the child. ...these assessments ...disabilities are ex- ...essments are con-

...ervices and ...e disabilities

FOCUS PREVIEW

As you read the chapter, focus on these key concepts:

1 Why do we continue to apply labels to people even when we know they may have a negative effect on an individual?

2 Identify three approaches to describe human differences.

3 How have societal views on people with disabilities changed from widespread discrimination to an era of inclusion and support in the 21st century?

4 What is the Americans with Disabilities Act?

5 Describe the role of health care, psychology, and social services professionals in meeting the needs of people with disabilities.

6 What services and supports must be available to ensure a bright future for people with disabilities?

Snapshot

Snapshot features are personal insights into the lives of real people. These insights may come from the teachers, family members, friends, peers, and professionals, as well as from the person who is exceptional. Each chapter in the 11th edition opens with a narrative *Snapshot* of people who are exceptional, their family members, or teachers. We believe you will find *Snapshots* to be one of the most enriching aspects of your introduction to human exceptionality. For example, you'll learn about:

- Martha Cleveland's "education for all" approach to teaching (Chapter 2)
- Rebecca's and Ben's experiences in inclusive classrooms (Chapter 3)
- Jennifer and Linea and their unique mental health challenges (Chapter 8)
- Actress Lauren Potter from TV's *Glee* (Chapter 9)
- Olympic gold medalist Vonetta Flowers (Chapter 10)
- Diagnosing Kaysen (Chapter 11)

Inclusion and Collaboration through the Lifespan

Another feature in this new edition is *Inclusion and Collaboration through the Lifespan.* This feature provides helpful information on ways to interact with, include, communicate with, or teach people who are exceptional across a variety of settings (home, school, and community) and age spans (early childhood through the adult years). Hopefully, these ideas provide stimulus for further thinking about ways to fully include these individuals as family members, school peers, friends, or neighbors, as well as collaborate with other professionals concerned with improving the lives of people who are exceptional.

Reflect on This

Every chapter includes one or more *Reflect on This* boxes. Each box highlights additional interesting and relevant information beyond the chapter narrative that will add to your learning and enjoyment of the topic, such as:

- "What's My Role on the Multidisciplinary Schoolwide Assistance Team?" (Chapter 3)
- "Redefining Learning Disabilities Using a Response to Intervention Model" (Chapter 7)

SNAPSHOT
"Disabled or Differently Abled"

A BLOG BY JOE DOLSON

Courtesy Joe Dolson

Many of those who could be considered disabled would not choose to self-identify as disabled. *Disability* is a label, and like any label, the members of the labeled group are diverse and may exhibit the label in unexpected ways. How many people with color blindness self-identify as disabled? How many people with children in strollers are unable to climb stairs with their child—would they self-identify as disabled? How many left-handed people struggle with right-handed scissors? Is this disability? An issue may appear trivial, but that makes the problem no less frustrating when encountered.

What Is Disability?
Disability, at some level, affects every part of our day-to-day existence. Disability is nothing more than an inability to make use of a particular resource as it is presented to you. This is how disability is particularly dif-

ferent... their children and stroller up the stairs; others may not. An elevator, moving walkway, or escalator platform can resolve the problem. Some left-handed people can successfully switch to the right hand, or at least manipulate right-handed scissors in such a manner as to successfully cut

That's right ... I forgot. Everybody has a different and independent capability to perform tasks. Some people are impaired when it comes to math; others, art. Some people don't run very fast; others can't walk. These disabilities will always affect one's life. The degree to which disability affects one's life is highly variable. People who are classically considered disabled tend to have limitations that are severe enough to affect their life every day.

What is commonly called "normal" is truly just an abstract concept that we apply to our personal experience: Whether by attributing it to ourselves or to others, it is relative to our own perceptions and our environments.

The Web has a great power to reduce that effect. It's commonly remarked that people behave differently on the Web. This is because the Web divorces them from their mundane routine—and this is true

---

INCLUSION AND COLLABORATION THROUGH THE LIFESPAN
PEOPLE WITH AUTISM SPECTRUM DISORDERS

EARLY CHILDHOOD YEARS

Tips for the Family

- Seek out and read information regarding autism spectrum disorders, and become knowledgeable about not just possible limitations, but strengths too.
- Be an active partner in the treatment of your child. Collaborate proactively in the multidisciplinary team for your child, facilitating communication and coordinating interventions.
- Learn about the simple applications of positive behavior support in a home environment, perhaps by enrolling in a parent training class.
- When working with your child, concentrate on one behavior at a time as the target for change; emphasize increasing positive, appropriate behaviors rather than focusing solely on inappropriate behavior.
- Involve all family members in learning about your child's strengths, interests,

Use pictures or photographs to facilitate understanding.
- Pair physical cues with verbal cues to begin teaching verbal compliance.
- Limit instruction to one item at a time; focus on what is concrete rather than abstract.
- Avoid verbal overload by using short, direct sentences.
- Encourage the development of programs where older children model good behavior and interact intensely with children with ASD.
- Initiate and maintain communication with the child's parents to enhance the information flow and to promote consistent collaboration across environments.
- Promote ongoing collaborative relationships between the preschool and medical personnel who can provide advice and assistance for children with ASD.

- Consistently follow through with the basic principles of your child's treatment program at home. This may mean taking more workshops or training on various topics to effectively collaborate as part of the intervention team.
- Provide siblings with information and opportunities to discuss the issues they are concerned about. Provide them with appropriate levels of support and attention, particularly if they feel neglected, embarrassed, or jealous of the sibling with ASD.
- It may be necessary to take safety precautions in the home (e.g., installing locks on all doors).

Tips for the General Education Classroom Teacher

- Help with collaborative organizational strategies, assisting the student with autism spectrum disorders regarding matters that are difficult for him or her (e.g., remembering where to turn in homework).

REFLECT ON THIS
ONE CITY'S RESPONSE TO ADA

© Jose Carrillo/Photo Edit

BUILDING A BARRIER-FREE COMMUNITY FOR 10-YEAR-OLD BRITTANY AND HER FRIENDS

Fernandina Beach, Florida, a resort community of 8,800 residents on Amelia Island between the Atlantic Ocean and the Amelia River, is Florida's second oldest city and the state's first resort area. With its 50-block downtown historic district, golf courses, parks and nature areas, beaches, and a resident shrimping fleet, the community welcomes visitors and vacationers from all corners of the country. And recently, Fernandina Beach became an even more welcoming place for people with disabilities.

The city of Fernandina Beach made a decision—and a commitment—to go above and beyond the minimum ADA requirements and to make the city as usable and accessible as possible for everyone. To do this, city officials and residents worked together to find new approaches to accessibility, an experience they found both gratifying and exciting.

She no longer has to lift her daughter onto the play equipment and can happily watch as Brittany and her buddy go down the slide together. "What's really good is that Brittany now can play longer because she's not as tired from trudging to the playground. She also can play on pretty much all the equipment and play together with her friends; she's not being excluded now." Ten-year-old Brittany, who uses crutches and sometimes a wheelchair to get around, agrees. "I like the rope things that go round and round and I like the slide with the bumps and I liked the three of us sliding together!" In addition to creating accessible playgrounds, the city installed an accessible route to the picnic pavilions in each of its city parks and accessible picnic tables in every pavilion. The city constructed a beach walkover at the Main Beach and constructed an accessible viewing area connected to the accessible beach path,

Park Beaches to give wheelchair users access to the beach nearest them. The city also purchased two beach wheelchairs for those who wish to join family and friends near the water on the sandy beach. It has plans to buy more.

Question for Reflection

Can you identify examples of how your city or town has removed physical barriers for people with disabilities from parks, restaurants, schools, universities, or government buildings in order to facilitate every person's full participation

Assistive Technology

The 11th edition offers new information on the expanding use of technology for people who are exceptional. *Assistive Technology* features highlight important innovations in computers, biomedical engineering, and instructional systems. The following are examples of *Assistive Technology* features:

- "Assistive Technology for People with Intellectual Disabilities" (Chapter 9)
- "Apps for Autism" (Chapter 11)
- "VGo: The Ultimate School-Based Robot" (Chapter 14)
- "From Science Fiction to Reality: Ekso Exoskeletons" (Chapter 14)
- "Renzulli Learning: Differentiation Engine" (Chapter 15)

Debate Forum

Every chapter includes a *Debate Forum* to broaden your view of issues that affect the lives of people with differences. For each topic, a position is taken (*point*) and an alternative to that position (*counterpoint*) is given. The purpose of the *Debate Forum* is not to establish right or wrong answers, but to better understand the diversity of issues concerning individuals who are exceptional. Students can also take advantage of the opportunity to participate in and learn from the "What Do You Think?" interactive feature on the Education CourseMate website for *Human Exceptionality,* 11th edition. Various current issues are addressed, such as:

- "English-Only or Dual-Language Education?" (Chapter 5)
- "Emergency Rooms: The Best Place for Routine Care of Children and Youth with Mental Illnesses?" (Chapter 8)
- "Why is Using the 'R' Word Such a Big Deal? It's Only a Word." (Chapter 9)
- "Can Special Schools for Students with Severe and Multiple Disabilities Be Justified?" (Chapter 12)
- "Should We Protect Our Children and Youth from Firearm Violence?" (Chapter 14)

Case Study

Each chapter includes a *Case Study* feature, which is an in-depth look at a personal story of exceptionality. Each *Case Study* also includes Application Questions to extend your knowledge and apply what you learned from each vignette. You'll find a variety of stories, such as:

- Nathan, a first-grader from an impoverished and abusive home environment where English language usage is limited (Chapter 5)
- Ten-year-old Toby's challenging day as a boy with emotional/behavioral disorders (Chapter 8)
- Donald T., the first child to be diagnosed with autism (Chapter 11)
- The Weld County School District's program for preschool through 12th-grade students who are deaf or hard of hearing, and its relationship with professors from the deaf education program at the University of Northern Colorado (Chapter 13)

ASSISTIVE TECHNOLOGY
THE STRATEGY TUTOR

The World Wide Web is an engaging, information-rich learning environment—but it also can present significant challenges for struggling learners. Unlike textbooks, which are laid out to help learn a specific curriculum, websites are created for a wide range of purposes and by a varied and often unknown group of authors. As a result, the Internet can be a challenging environment for students who struggle with reading.

Strategy Tutor, developed by the Center for Applied Special Technology and funded by the Carnegie Corporation of New York, is an instructional tool that supports students and their teachers in getting the most out of information-rich web pages. The program helps teachers implement reading strategy instruction while guiding students through specific online research projects. Teachers can add prompts and interactive features that will, through the Strategy Tutor interface, be displayed as part of websites they have preselected. On sites not customized by the teacher, Strategy Tutor gives generic tips intended to guide students through the process of web research, teaching strategies that will serve them well even without the Strategy Tutor interface. For more information on Strategy Tutor, visit http://cst .cast.org.

SOURCE: *Center for Applied Special Technology*. (2012). *Carnegie Strategy Tutor*. Retrieved January 15, 2012, from www.cast.org/research/projects/tutor.html (Coyne, P., & Dalton, B., Project Directors).

DEBATE FORUM
CASEY'S STORY: THEN AND NOW

Casey Martin was born with a very rare congenital disorder (Klippel-Trenaunay-Weber syndrome), a condition with no known cure. The disorder is degenerative and causes serious blood circulation problems in Casey's right leg and foot. His right leg is about half the size of his left, and when forced to walk on it, Casey experiences excruciating pain and swelling. Obviously, this condition would be difficult and very painful under any circumstances, but Casey's occupation is professional golf and he is a member of the Professional Golfers' Association (PGA). Unfortunately, Casey reached the point where he could no longer walk a golf course; he had to use a cart to get around. The PGA did not permit the use of a golf cart during *competitions*. Casey requested an exemption that would allow him to ride rather than walk. The PGA refused his request, and Casey took the matter to court, claiming discrimination on the basis of the Americans with Disabilities Act. The debate escalated over whether Casey was given an advantage over his fellow professional golfers by being able to ride a golf cart when others must walk. Is riding a cart an advantage for Casey or does the golf cart simply level the "playing field" as intended in the ADA? What do you think of the following "for and against" arguments:

POINT

The PGA's attempt to disallow Casey Martin's use of a golf cart was an act of discrimination against a person with a disability. The PGA is a public entity, and golf courses are places of public accommodation under the Americans with Disabilities Act. Therefore, the PGA must provide *reasonable accommodations* for someone with a permanent disability. As the Supreme Court ruling notes, Casey met all the ADA requirements. He has a permanent disability, and without a reasonable accommodation (riding in a golf cart), he could not participate in his chosen profession. The PGA argued that riding in a cart creates an advantage for Casey. The PGA also argued that it should have the right to determine its own rules for competitions. Fine! Change the rules to allow Casey and any other golfer with disabilities to use a cart. In the end, if letting Casey Martin ride means that the PGA must allow every golfer to use a cart, so be it. Isn't the PGA's motto "anything is possible"?

COUNTERPOINT

One cannot help but express admiration for the grit and determination of Casey Martin. However, the U.S. Congress never intended for ADA to require an organization such as the PGA to change its basic rules of operation and, thus, create an advantage for one golfer over another. Physical requirements, including walking up to five miles on any given day in unfavorable weather, is an *essential element* of golf at its highest level. Any golfer who is allowed to ride in a cart will have an unfair advantage over other competitors. If the PGA allows this for one player, it will create hardship for others, which is exactly what ADA did not want. Players in the highest levels of competition must walk the course as part of the test of their skills. One set of rules must apply to all players.

Update: Whatever your point of view, a U.S. magistrate found in Casey's favor in 1998. Casey played the events on the Nike tour throughout 1998 and 1999,

qualifying for his first PGA tour event in January 2000. Meanwhile, the PGA appealed the decision to allow Casey to ride a cart, and in a 7-to-2 decision in 2001, the U.S. Supreme Court ruled that Casey must be allowed to ride a cart during competition. The Court ruled that allowing Casey access to the cart would not "fundamentally alter" the game of golf nor give him any advantage over other golfers on the course.

Casey left the pro tour in 2005, and in May 2006, he was named head coach of the University of Oregon's men's golf team. Casey Martin is the cofounder of a social networking golf community website: www.the10thgreen.com.

 What Do You Think? Please visit the Education CourseMate website for Human Exceptionality, 11th edition, to access and respond to questions related to the Debate Forum.

CASE STUDY SARINA

Over the past several years, many changes have occurred in Sarina's life. After spending most of her life in a large institution, Sarina, now in her late 30s, moved into an apartment with two other women, both of whom have a disability. She receives assistance from a local supported-living program in developing skills that will allow her to make her own decisions and become more independent in the community.

Over the years, Sarina has had many labels describing her disability, including mental retardation, epilepsy, autism, physical disability, chronic health problems, and serious emotional disturbance. She is very much challenged both mentally and physically. Medical problems associated with epilepsy necessitate the use of medications that affect Sarina's behavior (motivation, attitude, and so on) and her physical well-being. During her early 20s, while walking up a long flight of stairs, Sarina had a seizure that resulted in a fall and a broken neck. The long-term impact from the fall was a paralyzed right hand and limited use of her left leg.

Sarina's life goal has been to work in a real job, make money, and have choices about how she spends her money. For most of her life, the goal has been out of reach. Her only jobs have been in sheltered workshops, where she worked for next to nothing, doing piecemeal work such as sorting envelopes, putting together cardboard boxes, or folding laundry. Whereas most of the focus in the past has been on what Sarina "can't do" (can't read, can't get along with supervisors, can't handle the physical requirements of a job), her family and the professionals on her support team are looking more at her very strong desire to succeed in a community job.

About three miles from Sarina's apartment, a job has opened up for a stock clerk at a local video store. The store manager is willing to pay minimum wage for someone to work four to six hours a day stocking the shelves with videos and handling some basic tasks (such as cleaning floors, washing windows, and dusting furniture). Sarina loves movies and is really interested in this job. With the support of family and her professional team, she has applied for the job.

APPLICATION QUESTIONS

1. As Sarina's potential employer, what are some of the issues you would raise about her capability to perform the essential functions of the job?

2. What would you see as the "reasonable accommodations" necessary to help Sarina succeed at this job if she were hired?

Learning through Social Media

As is mentioned earlier, the *Learning through Social Media* boxes provide interesting and informative online blogs, social media sites by and for people who are exceptional, and the use of this technology to promote inclusion in school, family, and society. Examples of *Learning through Social Media* boxes include:

- "Edutopia on Culturally Responsive Teaching" (Chapter 5)
- "KIDZ: Finding Joy in Having Children with Special Needs" (Chapter 6)
- "BringChange2Mind" (Chapter 8)
- "Opening up the World for People with Disabilities" (Chapter 12)
- "Experiences of People with Sensory Impairments" (Chapter 13)
- "Through My Eyes: My Life With Cerebral Palsy" (Chapter 14)

TeachSource Videos

Most chapters in this new edition feature a *TeachSource Video* box, which suggests a video from the Education CourseMate website, includes a brief narrative summarizing the video, as well as discussion questions to enhance student and instructor engagement with the key concepts in the video. (CourseMate can be bundled with the student text. Instructors, please contact your Cengage sales representative for information on getting access to CourseMate.)

End-of-Chapter Features

In addition to the Focus Review concepts mentioned earlier, other end-of-chapter features include a list of Council for Exceptional Children standards addressed in the chapter and Mastery Activities and Assignments, many of which are also available on the Education CourseMate website.

Student Supplements
Education CourseMate for *Human Exceptionality*

For students, Cengage Learning's Education CourseMate brings course concepts to life with interactive learning, study, and exam preparation tools that support the printed textbook. Access an integrated eBook as well as learning tools including flash cards, quizzes, the award-winning TeachSource Video Cases, WebQuests, Portfolio Activities, and more in your Education CourseMate. Go to CengageBrain.com to register or purchase access.

Instructor Supplements: A Complete Instructional Package

A variety of teaching tools are available to assist instructors in organizing lectures, planning evaluations, and ensuring student comprehension.

LEARNING THROUGH SOCIAL MEDIA
"SPREAD THE WORD TO END THE WORD!"

A national campaign is under way to encourage everyone to pledge to stop using the word retard. Here are just a few blog excerpts on why this is so important:

"The R-word is hurtful to people with intellectual disabilities and their families and friends. However, many people do not recognize the dehumanizing effects of the word and use it frequently in casual conversation. Whether intentional or not, the R-word conjures up a painful stereotype of people with intellectual and developmental disabilities."
—From Diana Z on *Disability Blog*, (Retrieved March 10, 2010, from http://blog.govdelivery.com/usodep/2010/03/spread-the-word-to-end-the-word-awareness-day.html)

"I pledge and support the elimination of the derogatory use of the r-word from everyday speech and promote the acceptance and inclusion of people with intellectual disabilities. I want my students to become socially aware of the importance of acceptance and tolerance. It starts with our words and

actions. It starts with me being a positive role model for them."
—From Missy Cervantez, middle school coordinator, on "R-Word: Take the Pledge to Spread the Word to End the Word" (Retrieved August 19, 2011, from www.r-word.org/)

"It's disappointing that people need to be told so directly that the R-word is an unacceptable slur. You'd like to think that, with so many other hateful words having been recognized and removed, it would only make sense to extend the same respect to people with intellectual disabilities. Yet time and again, we see people treating the R-word as something fun and harmless, free speech rather than hate speech. Perhaps putting it just this bluntly is what it takes to make the connection. Do you hate hearing those slurs coming out of your TV? Do they sting your ears and make your heart race? Good. Feel the same way about the R-word."
—From Terri Mauro, mom and author on "R-Word: Spread the Word to End the Word" (Retrieved August 20, 2011, from www.r-word.org/r-word-not-acceptable-psa.aspx)

". . . We are trying to awaken the world to the need for a new civil rights movement—of the heart. We seek to educate people that a crushing prejudice against people with intellectual disabilities is rampant—a prejudice that assumes that people with significant learning challenges are stupid or hapless or somehow just not worth much. They're, um, *retarded*. And that attitude is not funny or nuanced or satirical. It's horrific."
—From Tim Shriver, Chairman and Chief Executive of Special Olympics on "The Bigotry Behind the Word 'Retarded'" (Retrieved February 15, 2010, from www.washingtonpost.com/wp-dyn/content/article/2010/02/14/AR2010021402893.html)

Question for Reflection

What can you do to get involved in "Spread the Word to End the Word?" Taking the pledge may be an important first step, but what else do you think is essential if the language of discrimination is to end? To take the pledge, go to www.r-word.org/.

TEACHSOURCE VIDEO RESPONSE TO INTERVENTION (RTI): THE THREE-TIERED MODEL IN A PRESCHOOL ENVIRONMENT

Please visit the Education CourseMate website for *Human Exceptionality*, 11th edition, at CengageBrain.com to access this chapter's TeachSource video. Response to intervention (RtI) is a multitiered system of support in which schools seek to identify and help students at risk for poor learning outcomes. In this system, teachers assess students and then review student data to determine who requires what type of educational intervention. Then teachers provide evidence-based interventions and adjust the intensity

and nature of those interventions depending on a student's responsiveness. If a student does not respond to these interventions over an appropriate period of time, the school will seek to determine if the student has a disability so that appropriate and further intervention can be made. Although this video is set in the preschool classroom, the principles apply to elementary classrooms in general. Watch this video to see RtI in action and respond to the following questions:

1. How is response to intervention used in this classroom?
2. What instructional information is collected on each child, and how is it used in planning a program that will meet individual needs?
3. How does classroom teacher Jessica Cruz use the information from the RtI process to enhance her teaching and more effectively meet the needs of the students in her class?

Education CourseMate for *Human Exceptionality*

For instructors, Cengage Learning's Education CourseMate includes access to Engagement-Tracker, a first-of-its-kind tool that monitors student engagement in the course. The accompanying instructor website, available through www.cengage.com, offers access to password-protected resources including the Instructor's Manual, Test Bank files, and PowerPoint® slides. CourseMate can be bundled with the student text. Contact your Cengage sales representative for information on getting access to CourseMate.

WebTutor

Jump-start your course with customizable, rich, text-specific content within your Course Management System. Whether you want to Web-enable your class or put an entire course online, WebTutor™ delivers. WebTutor™ offers a wide array of resources, including access to the eBook, flash cards, quizzes, videos, and more.

Online Instructor's Resource Manual and Test Bank

The *Human Exceptionality Instructor's Manual* (IM) includes a wealth of interesting ideas and activities designed to help instructors teach the course. Each chapter in the IM includes at-a-glance grids, chapter outlines introducing the chapter, lecture outlines, related discussion/activities, case study feedback, related media, and handout masters. For assessment support, the Test Bank includes challenging essay, multiple-choice, true/false, short answer, and case study questions for every chapter. Page number references, suggested answers, and skill level are included with each question to better help instructors create and evaluate student tests.

Online ExamView Test Bank

Available for download from the instructor website, ExamView® testing software includes all the test items from the Test Bank in electronic format, enabling you to create customized tests in print or online.

PowerPoint® Presentation

The ready-to-use Microsoft® PowerPoint® lecture slides provided to instructors are ideal for lecture presentations or student handouts. The PowerPoint® presentation created for each chapter of this text includes graphics and illustrations from the text.

Acknowledgments

We begin with a very big thank you to our colleagues from across the country and around the world who provided such in-depth and constructive feedback on the 11th edition of *Human Exceptionality,* including the following:

Alida Adams, American University
Michael Benhar, Suffolk County Community College
Jocelyn Carter, DePaul University
Robert Cimera, Kent State University
Robert Egbert, Walla Walla University
Karla Henderson, Ivy Tech Community College
Jack Hourcade, Boise State University
Alvin House, Illinois State University
Kathy-Anne Jordan, Mercy College
Samantha Loetman, Nassau Community College
Brenda-Jean Tyler, Radford University
Denise Uitto, The University of Akron Wayne College
Andrew Wiley, Kent State University
Barbara Wilson, Bloomsburg University of Pennsylvania
Mark Zablocki, University of Maryland

Special thanks to the people with disabilities and their families who participated in the Snapshot, Case Study, and Assistive Technology features for this book. These are the people who make up the heart of what this book is all about. Throughout the writing and production of this book, they made us keenly aware that this book is first and foremost about people.

For the first time in the 30-year history of *Human Exceptionality*, we added three new and outstanding co-authors for completely rewritten and updated chapters on cultural and linguistic diversity, learning disabilities, and autism spectrum disorders. Our deep gratitude to chapter co-authors Tina Dyches, Gordon Gibb, and Carol Solomon of Brigham Young University for their major contributions to this new 11th edition. Each of these co-authors is also acknowledged in the text's table of contents.

We also extend our gratitude to Dr. Shirley Dawson for her first-rate effort in taking the lead in revising the supplements for the book. Shirley spent untold hours developing and editing lecture notes, creating related activities, and locating the most current and informative media available in the area of exceptionality. She produced an easy-to-use and high-quality PowerPoint® presentation for every chapter in the book. Shirley was always on time with a high-quality product. We also extend our appreciation to the faculty and students at the University of Utah and Brigham Young University who continue to teach us a great deal about writing textbooks. Many of the changes incorporated into this 11th edition are a direct result of critiques from university colleagues and students in our classes.

As authors, we are certainly grateful for the commitment and expertise of the Cengage editorial and production team in bringing to fruition the highest-quality text possible. This team has sought to consistently improve the readability, utility, and appearance of this book. We want to especially thank Executive Editor Mark D. Kerr. This is our first opportunity to work with Mark and we appreciate his vision, insights, and patience with us while consistently supporting this text and its enhanced narrative and features. Thanks also to Genevieve Allen for coordinating the supplements, and Ashley Cronin for her expertise on all media matters, particularly the Education CourseMate website.

We want to especially acknowledge our opportunity to work with Kassi Radomski, freelance development editor, who worked with this text's authors and chapter co-authors for the first time. Kassi handled the editorial development of the text and has been wonderful to work with, attending not only to the quality of the content but also ensuring that the book maintains its strong, user-friendly approach to instruction. Kassi's careful and in-depth editing of the manuscript has been critical in presenting a new edition of which we are all very proud. Our thanks to Jill Traut, Project Manager for MPS, for her patience and expertise in leading the process for reviewing the copyedited pages, as well as the final page proofs for this text. The photo researcher for this book, Tim McDonough, did an outstanding job of locating photos that brought to life the text's printed word. Under Tim's direction, we have included the most recent photographs from general education classes, including school systems throughout the country that work with the inclusion model, and current photos of families with children and adults with disabilities.

To those professors who have chosen this book for adoption, and to those students who will be using this book as their first information source on people with differences, we hope our 11th edition of *Human Exceptionality* meets your expectations.

A loving thank you to our families who have always been there during the past three decades of writing and rewriting this text. We have strived "oh so hard" to produce a book of which you can be proud.

Michael L. Hardman
Clifford J. Drew
M. Winston Egan

Through the Lifespan

Stephen Simpson

As we move through the second decade of the 21st century, we have come a long way in our understanding of diversity in today's society—that is, everyone is *unique* in some way.

For some of you, this book is the beginning of your journey into the past, present, and future of people who are exceptional. It is a journey about those with diverse needs, desires, interests, backgrounds, characteristics, and lifestyles. What does the word *exceptional* mean to you? Who or what influenced your knowledge, attitudes, and behavior toward people, and the words you use to describe them? You may have a family member, friend, or casual acquaintance who is exceptional in some way—or you may be a person who has at one time or another been described as "different." The purpose of this book is to put forward a critical premise for the 21st century. That is, understanding human exceptionality is to understand *ourselves*.

PART I CHAPTER OVERVIEWS

Our journey into the lives of people with differences begins with four chapters that encompass the life span in family, school, and community living, moving through the early childhood years into elementary school and on to adolescence, high school, and the challenging transition to becoming an adult with disabilities in a complex and changing world.

> *"Diversity is not about how we differ. Diversity is about embracing one another's uniqueness."*
>
> —Olayinka Joseph, Nigerian-born author and motivational speaker

- Chapter 1, "Understanding Exceptionalities in the 21st Century," begins with a close look into a changing era for people with disabilities, a period in time that has its beginnings in a long and demeaning history of discrimination. We examine the meaning of derogatory language, such as *retard* and *cripple,* and the current movement to a "people-first" view on human exceptionality. "People-first" is the language of individuality, dignity, and respect. For example, people-first language emphasizes that Marianne, a 10-year-old child diagnosed with autism spectrum disorder, is first and foremost an individual—a child who also happens to have a disability. Chapter 1 also focuses on the desegregation of people with disabilities and the road to inclusion. Inclusion is at the forefront of the Americans with Disabilities Act in the United States and has resulted in many positive changes around the world. Chapter 1 concludes with the critical role played by the many different fields of study that are involved in the lives of people with disabilities and their families, including health care, psychology, and social services. As we do in each chapter throughout this text, we look closely at what society must do in partnership with people with disabilities and their families to create a bright future—one of hope and equality.

- Chapter 2, "Education for All," provides an introduction to the field of education in a 21st century world.

From the origins of special education to the Individuals with Disabilities Act, we examine the critical distinction between schooling for the *privileged* and the right of every child to a free and appropriate education. Characteristics of effective special education practice are discussed, including the hallmarks of the field (individualization, intensive instruction, and the explicit teaching of skills), as well as the critical elements of appropriate instruction, including multitiered systems of support (Response to Intervention), universal design for learning, access to the general education curriculum, and greater accountability for student achievement.

- Chapter 3, "Inclusion and Multidisciplinary Collaboration in the Early Childhood and Elementary School Years," introduces principles of effective inclusion and collaboration practices in early childhood, and within education programs and schools. Some of the most recent approaches to evidence-based education are addressed, including *differentiated and direct instruction, assistive technology, and curriculum-based assessment.*

- Part I concludes with Chapter 4, "Secondary Education and Transition Planning," focusing on students with disabilities moving from school and into adult life. Critical issues, such as self-determination, preparation for college and employment, and the importance of family and community are explored in depth.

CHAPTER 1

Understanding Exceptionalities in the 21st Century

AP Photo/Peter DeJong

FOCUS PREVIEW

As you read the chapter, focus on these key concepts:

1 Why do we continue to apply labels to people even when we know they may have a negative effect on an individual?

2 Identify three approaches to describe human differences.

3 How have societal views on people with disabilities changed from widespread discrimination to an era of inclusion and support in the 21st century?

4 What is the Americans with Disabilities Act?

5 Describe the role of health care, psychology, and social services professionals in meeting the needs of people with disabilities.

6 What services and supports must be available to ensure a bright future for people with disabilities?

*"Dis*abled or *Differently* Abled*"*

A BLOG BY JOE DOLSON

Many of those who could be considered disabled would not choose to self-identify as disabled. *Disability* is a label, and like any label, the members of the labeled group are diverse and may exhibit the label in unexpected ways. How many people with color blindness self-identify as disabled? How many people with children in strollers are unable to climb stairs with their child—would they self-identify as disabled? How many left-handed people struggle with right-handed scissors? Is this disability? An issue may appear trivial, but that makes the problem no less frustrating when encountered.

What Is Disability?

Disability, at some level, affects every part of our day-to-day existence. Disability is nothing more than an inability to make use of a particular resource as it is presented to you. This is how disability is particularly differentiated from usability: With disability, you *cannot* use the resource on your own. If a resource has poor usability, you are *able* to use it, albeit with difficulty.

This is why disability is not an absolute. Disability only prevents you from using tools if alternatives are not made available to you in a manner that you *are* able to use. The blind can "see" if an object or action is described well enough.

The previous examples are situations that may only disable the person in certain circumstances. People with color blindness are disabled when a circumstance requires them to distinguish red from green with no other clarifying indicators. Some people may be able to carry

Courtesy Joe Dolson

their children and stroller up the stairs; others may not. An elevator, moving walkway, or escalator platform can resolve the problem. Some left-handed people can successfully switch to the right hand, or at least manipulate right-handed scissors in such a manner as to successfully cut paper—but can many switch hands to write a letter?

Physical strength or handedness are not classically considered disabilities, but there can be no question that they affect one's ability to accomplish certain tasks.

But Some People Really Are "Normal"

Oh, yes, of course. I mean, *I'm* normal. But *you*? Well, I have some doubts.

I mean, there are tons of things that I can do that you can't. Doesn't that mean you're disabled? No? It just means that you have a different set of abilities than I do. Or, alternatively, a different set of *disabilities*. **Neither of us is necessarily disabled; but we are "differently abled."**

That's right … I forgot. Everybody has a different and independent capability to perform tasks. Some people are impaired when it comes to math; others, art. Some people don't run very fast; others can't walk. These disabilities will always affect one's life. The degree to which disability affects one's life is highly variable. People who are classically considered disabled tend to have limitations that are severe enough to affect their life every day.

What is commonly called "normal" is truly just an abstract concept that we apply to our personal experience: Whether by attributing it to ourselves or to others, it is relative to our own perceptions and our environments.

The Web has a great power to reduce that effect. It's commonly remarked that people behave differently on the Web. This is because the Web divorces them from their mundane routine—and this is true for everybody. On the Web, with a well-designed and accessible website, people with disabilities such as cerebral palsy, sight impairment, or hearing impairment can have an experience fundamentally equal to the experience of the so-called "normal" user.

In any context, people with a disability are disabled not because of an inherent inability to compensate, but because they are in an environment that requires tasks they are unable to perform. If we change the environment, we can remove the disability.

A Changing Era in the Lives of People with Disabilities

FOCUS 1

Why do we continue to apply labels to people even when we know they may have a negative effect on an individual?

Disorder
A disturbance in normal functioning (mental, physical, or psychological).

Disability
A condition resulting from a loss of physical functioning; or, difficulties in learning and social adjustment that significantly interfere with normal growth and development.

Handicap
A limitation imposed on a person by the environment and the person's capacity to cope with that limitation.

Exceptional
An individual whose physical, mental, or behavioral performance deviates so substantially from the average (higher or lower) that additional support is required to meet the individual's needs.

Gifts and talents
Extraordinary abilities in one or more areas.

Learning disabilities
A condition in which one or more of an individual's basic psychological processes in understanding or using language are deficient.

Intellectual disabilities
Substantial limitations in functioning, characterized by significantly subaverage intellectual functioning concurrent with related limitations in two or more adaptive skills. Intellectual disability is manifested prior to age 18.

Deaf
Individuals who have hearing losses greater than 75 to 80 dB, have vision as their primary input, and cannot understand speech through the ear.

In our opening snapshot, Joe Dolson, an Internet accessibility consultant, emphasizes the point that "disability is not an absolute." Yet, for good or bad, labeling is the fundamental way society chooses to describe human difference. The purpose of a label is to communicate specific differences in people who vary significantly from what is considered "typical or normal." Sociologists use labels to describe people who do not follow society's expectations (e.g., *sociopath*); educators and psychologists use labels to identify and provide services for students with learning, physical, and behavioral differences (e.g., *autistic*); and physicians use labels to distinguish the sick from the healthy (e.g., *diabetic*). Governments label people to identify who is eligible for, or entitled to, publicly funded services and supports (e.g., *disabled*).

We use many labels, including *disorder, disability,* and *handicap,* to describe people who are different. These terms are not synonymous. **Disorder**, the broadest of the three terms, refers to a general abnormality in mental, physical, or psychological functioning. A **disability** is more specific than a disorder and is associated with a loss of physical functioning (e.g., loss of sight, hearing, or mobility), or a challenge in learning and social adjustment that significantly interferes with typical growth and development. A **handicap** is a limitation imposed on the individual by the demands in the environment and is related to the individual's ability to adapt or adjust to those demands. For example, Franklin Roosevelt, the 32nd president of the United States, used a wheelchair because of a physical disability that resulted from having polio as a child—the inability to walk. He was dependent on the wheelchair to move from place to place. When the environment didn't accommodate his wheelchair (such as a building without ramps that was accessible only by stairs), his disability became a handicap. Historically, *handicap* has taken on a very negative connotation and is seldom used in today's society. The word *handicapped* literally means "cap in hand"; it originates from a time when people with disabilities were forced to beg in the streets merely to survive. For President Roosevelt, his advisors took great pains to disavow his "handicap" because many people in the 1930s and 1940s viewed it as a sign of weakness. However, there is hope that such negative attitudes are changing in the United States today. The national monument in Washington, D.C. that honors President Roosevelt includes a life-size bronze statue of him sitting in a wheelchair.

Exceptional is a comprehensive label. It describes an individual whose physical, intellectual, or behavioral performance differs substantially from what is typical (or normal), either higher or lower. People described as exceptional include those with extraordinary abilities (such as **gifts and talents**) and/or disabilities (such as **learning disabilities** or **intellectual disabilities**). People who are exceptional, whether gifted or disabled, benefit from individualized assistance, support, or accommodations in school and community settings.

Labels are only rough approximations of characteristics. Some labels, such as **deaf**, might describe a permanent characteristic—loss of hearing; others, such as *overweight*, describe what is often a temporary condition. Some labels are positive, and others are negative. Labels communicate whether a person meets the expectations of the culture. A given culture establishes criteria that are easily exceeded by some but are unreachable for others. For example, one society may value creativity, innovation, and imagination, and will reward those who have such attributes with positive labels, such as *bright, intelligent,* or *gifted*. Another society, however, may brand anyone whose ideas significantly exceed the limits of conformity with negative labels, such as *radical, extremist,* or *rebel*.

Moreover, the same label may have different meanings within a culture. Let's take the example of Ellen who is labeled by her high school teachers as a *conformist* because she always follows the rules. From the teachers' point of view, this is a positive characteristic, but to Ellen's peer group, it is negative. She is described by her high school classmates as a *brownnoser* or *teacher's pet*.

As emphasized in our opening Snapshot, labels are not absolutes and are often based on perception and not fact. As such, what are the possible consequences of using labels to describe people? Although labels have always been the basis for developing and providing services to people, they have also promoted stereotyping, discrimination, and exclusion. Some researchers suggest that the practice of labeling people has perpetuated and reinforced both the label and the stereotypical behaviors associated with it (Hardman & McDonnell, 2008; Hardman & Nagle, 2004; Mooney, 2007).

If labels may have negative consequences, why is labeling used so extensively? One reason is that many social services and educational programs for people who are exceptional require the use of labels to distinguish who is eligible for services and who is not. Discussing the need to label students with special educational needs, Woolfolk (2009) suggested that labeling may actually help protect a child with learning differences from a class bully who, knowing the child is "intellectually disabled," may be more willing to accept the learning differences. Others (Hardman & McDonnell, 2008; Rock, Thead, Gable, Hardman, & Van Acker, 2006) argue that labeling a child often has just the opposite effect—the child becomes more vulnerable to discrimination and abuse.

As Woolfolk, suggests, however, the fact remains that being "labeled" in today's society still opens doors to special programs, useful information, special technology and equipment, or financial assistance. To illustrate, Antonio, a child with a hearing loss, must be assessed and labeled as "hearing impaired" before specialized educational or social services can be made available to him in his school. Another reason for the continued use of labels is the "useful information" they provide to professionals in communicating effectively with one another; they also provide a common ground for evaluating research findings. Labeling helps to identify the specific needs of a particular group of people. Labeling can also help to determine degrees of needs or to set priorities for services when societal resources are limited.

When Someone Doesn't Conform to the Norm

Significant physical, behavioral, and learning differences are found in every society. Most people conform to what is expected of them. Conformity—acting as we are "supposed" to act, or looking the way we are "supposed" to look—is the rule for most of us, most of the time (Baron, Branscombe, & Byrne, 2008). Usually, we look the way we are expected to look, behave the way we are expected to behave, and learn the way we are expected to learn. When a person differs substantially from the norm, three approaches may be used to describe the nature and extent of these differences (see Figure 1.1).

A Developmental Approach

To understand human differences, we must first establish the definition of typical development or what is often described as "normal." According to the developmental approach, typical development can be described by using statistics (and milestones)—that is, observing in large numbers of individuals those characteristics that occur most frequently at a specific age. For example, when stating that the average 3-month-old infant is able to follow a moving object visually, *average* is a statistical term based on observations of the behavior of 3-month-old infants. When comparing an individual child's growth to that group average, differences in development (either advanced or delayed) are labeled accordingly.

A Cultural Approach

From a cultural view, "typical" is defined by what any given society values. Whereas a developmental approach considers only the frequency of behaviors to define differences, a cultural view suggests that differences can be explained to a large extent by examining the *values* inherent within a society. What constitutes a significant difference changes over time, from culture to culture, and among the various social classes within a culture. People are considered *different* (sometimes deviant) when they do something that is disapproved of by other members within the dominant culture. For example, in some cultures, intelligence is described in terms of how well someone scores on a test measuring a broad

CEC

Standard 1
Foundations

FOCUS 2
Identify three approaches to describe human differences.

Figure 1.1 *Three Approaches to Describing Human Differences*.
Copyright © 2014 Cengage Learning

Developmental Approach

KidStock/Jupiterimages

Cultural View

Self-Labeling

range of cognitive abilities; in other cultures, intelligence relates much more to how skillful someone is at hunting or fishing. The idea that people are the products of their cultures has received its greatest thrust from anthropology, which emphasizes the diversity and arbitrary nature of cultural rules regarding dress, eating habits, sexual habits, politics, and religion.

Self-Labeling

Everyone engages in a process of self-labeling that may not be recognized by others with whom they interact. Thus, self-imposed labels reflect how we perceive ourselves, not how others see us. Conversely, a person may be labeled by society as different, but the individual does not recognize or accept the label. Such was the case with Thomas Edison. In school, young Thomas Edison was described as "addled," unable to focus, terrible at mathematics, a behavior problem, dyslexic, and unable to express himself in a coherent manner (difficulty with speech). Although the schools imposed many negative labels on young Thomas Edison, he eventually recognized that he was an individualist, ignored the labels, and pursued his own interests as an inventor. (See the nearby Reflect on This feature, and take a quiz on other famous people with disabilities.)

The Effects of Being Labeled

Reactions to a label differ greatly from one person to another but can often be negative (Hardman & McDonnell, 2008; Rock et al., 2006; Woolfolk, 2009). In a study of the reactions of family members, professionals, and the general public to the commonly used label *mental retardation,* researchers found the label generated a more negative reaction than the newer terminology of "intellectual disabilities" (see Chapter 9) (Schroeder, Gerry, Gertz, & Velazquez, 2002).

LEARNING THROUGH SOCIAL MEDIA
"SPREAD THE WORD TO END THE WORD!"

A national campaign is under way to encourage everyone to pledge to stop using the word retard. *Here are just a few blog excerpts on why this is so important:*

"The R-word is hurtful to people with intellectual disabilities and their families and friends. However, many people do not recognize the dehumanizing effects of the word and use it frequently in casual conversation. Whether intentional or not, the R-word conjures up a painful stereotype of people with intellectual and developmental disabilities."

—From Diana Z on *Disability Blog*, (Retrieved March 10, 2010, from http://blog.govdelivery. com/usodep/2010/03/spread-the-word-to-end-the-word-awareness-day.html)

"I pledge and support the elimination of the derogatory use of the r-word from everyday speech and promote the acceptance and inclusion of people with intellectual disabilities. I want my students to become socially aware of the importance of acceptance and tolerance. It starts with our words and actions. It starts with me being a positive role model for them."

—From Missy Cervantez, middle school coordinator, on "R-Word: Take the Pledge to Spread the Word to End the Word" (Retrieved August 19, 2011, from www.r-word.org/)

"It's disappointing that people need to be told so directly that the R-word is an unacceptable slur. You'd like to think that, with so many other hateful words having been recognized and removed, it would only make sense to extend the same respect to people with intellectual disabilities. Yet time and again, we see people treating the R-word as something fun and harmless, free speech rather than hate speech. Perhaps putting it just this bluntly is what it takes to make the connection. Do you hate hearing those slurs coming out of your TV? Do they sting your ears and make your heart race? Good. Feel the same way about the R-word."

—From Terri Mauro, mom and author on "R-Word: Spread the Word to End the Word" (Retrieved August 20, 2011, from www.r-word. org/r-word-not-acceptable-psa.aspx)

"... We are trying to awaken the world to the need for a new civil rights movement—of the heart. We seek to educate people that a crushing prejudice against people with intellectual disabilities is rampant—a prejudice that assumes that people with significant learning challenges are stupid or hapless or somehow just not worth much. They're, um, *retarded*. And that attitude is not funny or nuanced or satirical. It's horrific."

—From Tim Shriver, Chairman and Chief Executive of Special Olympics on "The Bigotry Behind the Word 'Retarded'" (Retrieved February 15, 2010, from www.washingtonpost.com/wp-dyn /content/article/2010/02/14/AR2010021402893 .html)

Question for Reflection

What can you do to get involved in "Spread the Word to End the Word?" Taking the pledge may be an important first step, but what else do you think is essential if the language of discrimination is to end? To take the pledge, go to www.r-word.org/.

Separating the Person and the Label Once a label has been affixed to an individual, the two may become inseparable. For example, Becky has been labeled as mentally retarded. The tendency is to refer to Becky and her condition as one in the same—Becky is retarded. She is described by a negative label, causing people to lose sight of the fact that she is first and foremost a person, and that her exceptional characteristics (intellectual and social differences) are only a small part of who she is as an individual. To treat Becky as a label rather than someone who is differently abled is discrimination, and an injustice, not only to Becky, but to everyone else as well.

Environmental Bias The environment in which we view someone can clearly influence our perceptions of that person. For example, it can be said that if you are in a mental hospital, you must be insane. In a classic study from 1973, psychologist David Rosenhan investigated this premise by having himself and seven other "sane" individuals admitted to a number of state mental hospitals across the United States. Once in the mental hospitals, these subjects behaved normally. The question was whether the staff would perceive them as people who were healthy instead of as patients who were mentally ill. Rosenhan reported that the eight pseudopatients were never detected by the hospital staff but were recognized as imposters by several of the real patients. Throughout their hospital stays, the pseudopatients were incorrectly labeled and treated as schizophrenics. Rosenhan's investigation demonstrated that the environment in which the observations are made could bias the perception of what is normal.

a. Albert Einstein

b. Sarah Bernhardt

c. Stephen Hawking

d. Whoopi Goldberg

e. Walt Disney

f. Tom Cruise

g. James Earl Jones

h. Jay Leno

i. Julia Roberts

REFLECT ON THIS A FEW FAMOUS PEOPLE WHO ARE DIFFERENTLY ABLED (YET LABELED AS HAVING A DISABILITY)

MATCH THE NAMES TO THE DESCRIPTIONS:

____ 1. He was diagnosed with amyotrophic lateral sclerosis (ALS-Lou Gehrig's disease) at the age of 21. He must use a wheelchair and have round-the-clock nursing care. His speech has been severely affected, and he communicates through a computer by selecting words from a screen that are expressed through a speech synthesizer. Acknowledged as one of the greatest physicists in history, he developed a theory on black holes that provided new insights into the origin of the universe. Currently, he is professor of mathematics at Cambridge University, a post once held by Sir Isaac Newton.

____ 2. She was disabled by an accident in 1914, and eventually had to have part of her leg amputated. Regarded as one of the greatest French actresses in history, she continued her career on stage until her death in 1923.

____ 3. A well-known, tireless humanitarian advocate for children, the homeless, human rights, and also involved in the battles against substance abuse and AIDS, this Oscar-winning actress and Grammy winner is a high school dropout with an acknowledged reading disability.

____ 4. He is the voice of Darth Vader and the most in-demand narrator in Hollywood. Virtually mute as a child, he stuttered throughout most of his youth. With the help of his high school English teacher, he overcame stuttering by reading Shakespeare aloud to himself and then to audiences. He went on to debating and finally to stage and screen acting.

____ 5. He was regarded as a slow learner during his school years and never had much success in public education. Later, he became the best-known cartoonist in history, producing the first full-length animated motion picture.

____ 6. He did not speak until the age of 3. Even as an adult he found that searching for words was laborious. Schoolwork, especially math, was difficult for him, and he was unable to express himself in written language. He was thought to be "simple-minded" (retarded) until he discovered that he could achieve through visualizing rather than the use of oral language. His theory of relativity, which revolutionized modern physics, was developed in his spare time. *Time* magazine named him the most important person of the 20th century.

____ 7. He didn't learn to read while in school due to severe dyslexia and was unable to finish high school. Today he is regarded as one of most accomplished actors of his time. Although unable to read early in his career, he could memorize his lines from a cassette tape or someone reading to him. He later learned to read as an adult.

____ 8. He is an American stand-up comedian and television host. From 1992 to 2009, he was the host of NBC's *The Tonight Show*, and is again as of 2012. He grew up in Andover, Massachusetts, and has confirmed that he is dyslexic. Although his high school guidance counselor recommended that he drop out of high school because of his grades, he not only graduated but also went on to receive a bachelor's degree in speech therapy from Emerson College, in 1973. He also attended Bentley College in Waltham, Massachusetts.

____ 9. She is an Academy Award–winning American film actress and former fashion model. She became the highest paid actress in the world, topping the annual power list of top-earning female stars for four consecutive years (2002 to 2005). She acknowledged that she stuttered when she was child, but with therapy, she now speaks fluidly.

Question for Reflection

Select two of these famous people, or another famous person with a disability that you know about, and write a short essay on how their disability has had a positive influence on their lives. Can you describe someone with a disability that you know and how he or she has met the challenges of being a person who is "differently abled"?

SOURCE: The original source of the information contained in this quiz is unknown.

First. © Topham/The Image Works. Second. © Bettmann/Corbis. Third. AP Photo/Banks. Fourth. AP Photo/Lisa Bul. Fifth. © Bettmann/Corbis. Sixth. © Stephane Cardinale/Sygma/Corbis. Seventh. AP Photo/Bob Galbraith. Eighth. Featureflash/Shutterstock.com. Ninth. Featureflash/Shutterstock.com

Answers: 1(c), 2(b), 3(d), 4(g), 5(e), 6(a), 7(f), 8(h), 9(i)

Historical Perspectives on Disability

In the fourth century B.C., the Greek philosopher Aristotle openly declared, "As to the exposure and rearing of children, let there be a law that no deformed child shall live. . . ."

Aristotle's stark statement is inconceivable in a 21st-century world, but from the beginning of recorded time, children with disabilities were vulnerable to practices such as infanticide, slavery, physical abuse, and abandonment. Many civilizations accepted infanticide as a necessary means of controlling population growth and ensuring that only the strongest would survive in societies highly dependent on "living off the land." Early Greek and Roman patriarchies practiced selected eugenics—the belief in the possibility of improving the human species by discouraging the reproduction of people having genetic defects or inheritable "undesirable" traits. Although there are notable exceptions to the barbarism that marked early history, such as the ancient Egyptians who viewed infanticide as a crime, many early civilizations viewed "deformed children" as a sign of weakness, shame, and an unnecessary burden on society. Such views continued well into the 20th century. In Nazi Germany, genocide had come full circle from early Greek and Roman history to reach its pinnacle in 1939, with the planned extermination of "the mentally and physically disabled" under Operation T4. In the Hitler era, people with disabilities were openly targeted for the "final solution." The German government actively terminated the lives of people with disabilities as a means to purify the human race and put these individuals whose "life wasn't worthy of life" out of their misery (United States Holocaust Memorial Museum, 2011).

The 20th century was an era of marked contradictions in societal and government support for people with disabilities and their families. On one hand, treatment and education that had been denied for centuries were becoming more accessible. Schools were offering special classes for slow learners, children with physical disabilities, and those who were deaf and blind. In contrast, the societal view became increasingly more negative and accusatory. Parents were blamed for both the genetic inferiority of their children and were held responsible for not being able to take care of their needs without additional government support. The fear grew that many disabilities were passed on from generation to generation, and that eventually these "defectives" would defile the human race (Braddock & Parish, 2002). The following quote from Spratting in 1912 (cited in Wolfensberger, 1975) describes this phenomenon:

> We must come to recognize feeblemindedness, idiocy, imbecility and insanity as largely communicable conditions or diseases, just as the physician recognizes smallpox, diphtheria, etc. as communicable.

In the United States, the response to this fear was the enforcement of 17th-century blue laws (such as the Connecticut Code of 1650) that prohibited "mental and moral defectives" from marrying. Eventually the legislation was expanded to include **sterilization**. For most countries throughout the world, this eugenics scare of the 20th century evolved from laws about marriage and sterilization to planned social isolation rather than extermination. The emphasis on keeping families together at all costs changed to a perspective that removing the child with disabilities from the family into a controlled, large congregate living facility would be in the best interests of society, the family, and the child. Such isolation would prevent the further spread of genetic and social deviance, as well as protect society from the defective person.

Large congregate living facilities for people with disabilities were subsumed under many different labels, such as institution, hospital, colony, prison, school, or asylum. The move away from treatment to isolation increased over a period of 50 years as these large institutions grew in size. Families faced the dilemma of either keeping the child at home, often with no medical, educational, or social supports, or giving children over to professionals to live in an institution where they could be with others of "their own kind." This situation remained virtually unchanged for nearly five decades and declined even further

Library of Congress Prints and Photographs Division Washington, D.C. 20540 USA

FOCUS 3

How have societal views on people with disabilities changed from widespread discrimination to an era of inclusion and support in the 21st century?

Early institutions were human warehouses intended to prevent the spread of genetic and social deviance, as well as protect society from a "defective" person.

Sterilization
The process of making an individual unable to reproduce, usually done surgically.

during the Depression of the 1930s and 1940s, when funds and human resources were in short supply. By the 1950s, more than a million people in the United States had been committed to mental hospitals and institutions.

Parental Involvement and Advocacy

Throughout the 20th century, parents, people with disabilities, and their families struggled with a society that, in the best of times, was apathetic to their needs and, in the worst of times, was downright discriminatory. In response to the apathy and discrimination that permeated their lives, new parent groups advocating for the rights of children with disabilities began to organize on a national level around 1950. The United Cerebral Palsy (UCP) was founded in 1949, and the National Association for Retarded Children[1] (NARC) began in 1950. These organizations had similar goals. Both were concerned with providing accurate information to the public regarding the people they represented; both wanted to ensure the rights of full citizenship for people with disabilities through access to medical treatment, social services, and education. Other parent groups followed the lead of these two landmark organizations, including the National Society for Autistic Children (1961) and the Association for Children with Learning Disabilities[2] (1964).

The advent of parent organizations as advocates for people with disabilities coincided with the civil rights movement in the 1950s. As courts throughout the country reaffirmed the civil rights of ethnic minorities, parent organizations seized the opportunity to lay a foundation for stronger federal and state roles in meeting the needs of individuals with disabilities. In 1956—only two years after the landmark U.S. Supreme Court decision in *Brown v. The Board of Education* of *Topeka, Kansas* declared that separate education for people of color was inherently unequal—the NARC presented a call to action for the federal government to expand teaching and research in the education of children with mental retardation. Other parent and professional organizations followed suit. By 1960, the Congress and state legislatures were actively engaged with both parents and professionals concerned with improving the lives of people with disabilities.

Parents and professionals received a major boost in 1961, with the election of President John F. Kennedy. Through the strong encouragement of his sister Eunice Kennedy Shriver, who passed away in August 2009, and out of a strong family commitment to his sister Rosemary (who had an intellectual disability), President Kennedy elevated the needs of people with disabilities to a major national concern. The first-ever President's Committee on Mental Retardation (now the President's Committee for People with Intellectual Disabilities) was formed, and legislation that eventually resulted in many federal initiatives on behalf of people with disabilities was passed. President Kennedy was also a strong advocate for institutional reform:

We as a nation have long neglected the mentally ill and mentally retarded. This neglect must end. … We must act … to stimulate improvements in the level of care given the mentally disabled in our state and private institutions, and to reorient those programs to a community centered approach. (Kennedy, 1963)

Spurred on by an emerging federal role in services for people with disabilities and the expanding civil rights movement in the United States, parents moved to the courts to fight discrimination. In 1972, parents of institutionalized people in Alabama filed a lawsuit claiming that people with mental retardation were being deprived of the right to treatment that would provide the skills to live in a community and family setting. The court described the institution as a human warehouse steeped in an atmosphere of psychological and physical deprivation. The state was ordered to ensure that people residing in the institution had a therapeutic environment. The *Wyatt v. Stickney* case led to the development of federal standards for institutions across the country that mandated specific rights for people with disabilities, including privacy, management of their own affairs, freedom from physical restraint and isolation, and adequate medical programs. The *Wyatt v. Stickney* case was followed by several

[1] The National Association for Retarded Children became the National Association for Retarded Citizens in 1974. It is now known as the ARC of the United States.
[2] The Association for Children with Learning Disabilities is now known as the Learning Disabilities Association (LDA).

© Wally McNamee/CORBIS

Parents, family members and advocacy organizations led the way in the effort to ensure full citizenship for people with disabilities.

other landmark decisions on institutional reform, such as *Halderman v. Pennhurst State School and Hospital*, *Youngberg v. Romeo*, and *Homeward Bound v. Hissom Memorial Center*.

Parents were equally active in their efforts to reform education. In 1971, parents from the Pennsylvania Association for Retarded Citizens (PARC) filed a class-action suit (*PARC v. Commonwealth of Pennsylvania*), claiming that their children were being denied the right to a free and appropriate public education on the basis of mental retardation. The court ordered Pennsylvania schools to provide a free public education to all children with mental retardation between the ages of 6 and 21. Later that same year, the Pennsylvania decision was expanded to include all children with disabilities in the case of *Mills v. Board of Education of the District of Columbia*. The Pennsylvania and Mills cases were catalysts for several court cases and legislation in the years that followed, culminating in the passage of federal legislation in 1975 mandating a free and appropriate public education for all students with disabilities. The passage of Public Law 94-142[3] brought together all of the various pieces of state and federal legislation into a national law requiring parent involvement in the education of their children, multidisciplinary and nondiscriminatory testing, education in the least restrictive environment, and the development of an individualized education plan for every student.

Today, the rights of people with disabilities have come full circle from the early history of genocide, to an era of rights and family support. The humanitarian reforms of the past four decades have resulted in significant changes in the lives of people with disabilities and their families. The culmination of parent and professional advocacy on behalf of 43 million people with disabilities in the United States was the passage of the Americans with Disabilities Act (ADA) in 1990.

The Americans with Disabilities Act (ADA)

A precursor to the Americans with Disabilities Act and the national movement to end discrimination against people with disabilities came with the passage of **Section 504** of the Vocational Rehabilitation Act in 1973. Section 504 stated:

> *No otherwise qualified person with a disability … shall, solely on the basis of disability, be denied access to, or the benefits of, or be subjected to discrimination under any program or activity provided by any entity/institution that receives federal financial assistance.*

[3] Public Law 94-142, the Education for All Handicapped Children Act, was renamed the Individuals with Disabilities Education Act (IDEA) in 1990.

FOCUS 4
What is the Americans with Disabilities Act?

Section 504
Provision with the Vocational Rehabilitation Act of 1973 that prohibits discrimination against people with disabilities in federally assisted programs and activities.

Americans with Disabilities Act (ADA)
Civil rights legislation that provides a mandate to end discrimination against people with disabilities in private-sector employment, all public services, public accommodations, transportation, and telecommunications.

Civil Rights Act of 1964
U.S. legislation that prohibits discrimination on the basis of race, sex, religion, or national origin.

Section 504 of the Vocational Rehabilitation Act set the stage for passage of the **Americans with Disabilities Act (ADA)** of 1990, the most sweeping civil rights legislation in the United States since the **Civil Rights Act of 1964**. The purpose of ADA is to prevent discrimination on the basis of disability in employment, programs, and services provided by state and local governments, goods and services provided by private companies, and commercial facilities. (See the nearby Reflect on This feature, "One City's Response to ADA.")

In the past, people with disabilities had to contend with the reality that learning to live independently did not guarantee access to community services or jobs. Access to public restrooms, restaurants, and successful employment have often eluded people with disabilities, due to architectural and attitudinal barriers. The purpose of ADA was to change this discrimination and affirm the rights of more than 50 million Americans with disabilities to participate in the life of their community. Much as the Civil Rights Act of 1964 removed barriers to the African American struggle for equality, the ADA promised to do the same for those with disabilities. Its success in eliminating fears and prejudices remains to be seen, but the need for this legislation was obvious.

REFLECT ON THIS
ONE CITY'S RESPONSE TO ADA

BUILDING A BARRIER-FREE COMMUNITY FOR 10-YEAR-OLD BRITTANY AND HER FRIENDS

Fernandina Beach, Florida, a resort community of 8,800 residents on Amelia Island between the Atlantic Ocean and the Amelia River, is Florida's second oldest city and the state's first resort area. With its 50-block downtown historic district, golf courses, parks and nature areas, beaches, and a resident shrimping fleet, the community welcomes visitors and vacationers from all corners of the country. And recently, Fernandina Beach became an even more welcoming place for people with disabilities.

The city of Fernandina Beach made a decision—and a commitment—to go above and beyond the minimum ADA requirements and to make the city as usable and accessible as possible for everyone. To do this, city officials and residents worked together to find new approaches to accessibility, an experience they found both gratifying and exciting.

The city is working to make all its playgrounds accessible. Each city playground will have new accessible equipment, accessible playground surfaces, and accessible paths to the playground equipment. Cheri Fisher is thrilled with the changes.

She no longer has to lift her daughter onto the play equipment and can happily watch as Brittany and her buddy go down the slide together. "What's really good is that Brittany now can play longer because she's not as tired from trudging to the playground. She also can play on pretty much all the equipment and play together with her friends; she's not being excluded now." Ten-year-old Brittany, who uses crutches and sometimes a wheelchair to get around, agrees. "I like the rope things that go round and round and I like the slide with the bumps and I liked the three of us sliding together!" In addition to creating accessible playgrounds, the city installed an accessible route to the picnic pavilions in each of its city parks and accessible picnic tables in every pavilion. The city constructed a beach walkover at the Main Beach and constructed an accessible viewing area connected to the accessible beach path, allowing as many as eight people using wheelchairs to sit together on the beach and enjoy an unobstructed view of the surf. The city plans to construct two additional walkovers at opposite ends of the city at the North Park and Seaside

© James Shaffer/Photo Edit

© Jose Carillo/Photo Edit

Park Beaches to give wheelchair users access to the beach nearest them. The city also purchased two beach wheelchairs for those who wish to join family and friends near the water on the sandy beach. It has plans to buy more.

Question for Reflection

Can you identify examples of how your city or town has removed physical barriers for people with disabilities from parks, restaurants, schools, universities, or government buildings in order to facilitate every person's full participation in the life of the community?

SOURCE: United States Department of Justice. (2011). "A Resort Community Improves Access to City Programs and Services for Residents and Vacationers." Retrieved August 25, 2011, from www.usdoj.gov/crt/ada/fernstor.htm.

First, people with disabilities faced discrimination in employment, access to public and private accommodations (e.g., hotels, theaters, restaurants, grocery stores), and services offered through state and local governments (Kessler Foundation and the National Organization on Disability, 2010; NOD/Harris & Associates, 2004). Second, because the historic Civil Rights Act of 1964 did not even mention people with disabilities, they had no federal protection against discrimination. As stated by the United States Department of Justice (2011):

> Barriers to employment, transportation, public accommodations, public services, and telecommunications have imposed staggering economic and social costs on American society and have undermined our well-intentioned efforts to educate, rehabilitate, and employ individuals with disabilities. The Americans with Disabilities Act gives civil rights protections to individuals with disabilities similar to those provided to individuals on the basis of race, color, sex, national origin, age, and religion. It guarantees equal opportunity for individuals with disabilities in public accommodations, employment, transportation, state and local government services, and telecommunications.

In 2010, the Kessler Foundation and National Organization on Disability (NOD) released the results of a survey on the quality of life of people with disabilities and the gaps in employment, services, and supports between people with and without disabilities. A summary of the survey results of more than 1,000 adults with disabilities and 788 adults without disabilities are found in the nearby Reflect on This feature, "The ADA: 20 Years Later."

CEC

Standard 2
Development and Characteristics of Learners

CEC

Standard 1
Foundations

REFLECT ON THIS
THE ADA: 20 YEARS LATER

- Although there has been substantial improvement reported in education attainment and political participation since 1986, large gaps still exist between people with and without disabilities with regard to employment, household income, access to transportation, health care, socializing, going to restaurants, and satisfaction with life. In some instances, the gaps have actually worsened since the inception of the first NOD survey.

- Employment remains the largest gap between people with and without disabilities. Of all working-age people with disabilities, only 21 percent indicated that they are employed, compared to 59 percent of people without disabilities—a gap of 38 percentage points.

- As was true in 1990, people with disabilities living in the second decade of the 21st century remain more likely to be living in poverty and less likely than those without disabilities to socialize with friends, relatives, or neighbors. The survey suggests that significant barriers remain to participation in leisure activities for those with disabilities.

- The second-largest gap between people with and without disabilities is Internet access. Of those surveyed, 85 percent of adults without disabilities access the Internet, whereas only 54 percent of adults with disabilities report doing so—a gap of 31 percentage points.

- The 2010 survey continues to emphasize that there is no single indicator of the quality of lives of people with disabilities. They face a range of challenges, and have varied experiences and aspirations. This diversity is characterized not only by a broad spectrum of disability characteristics, specifically type and severity, but also by a range of personal characteristics and circumstances. Understanding this heterogeneity is crucial in our understanding of how to support people with disabilities with the tools, skills, and opportunities they need to succeed.

Question for Reflection

Although ADA accomplished a great deal on behalf of people with disabilities in the past two decades, much remains to be done. Identify and discuss three key areas where you see more attention is needed from policy makers, businesses, and the community if we are truly to improve the quality of life for children and adults with disabilities.

SOURCE: Kessler Foundation and the National Organization on Disability. (2010). *Survey of Americans with Disabilities*. New York: Author.

The ADA Definition of Disability

The original ADA passed by the U.S. Congress in 1990 defines a person with a disability as (1) having a physical or mental impairment that substantially limits him or her in some major life activity, and (2) having experienced discrimination resulting from this physical or mental impairment. Federal regulations define a physical or mental impairment as:

1. any physiological disorder, or condition, cosmetic disfigurement, or anatomical loss affecting one or more of the following body systems: neurological, musculoskeletal, special sense organs, respiratory (including speech organs), cardiovascular, reproductive, digestive, genitourinary, hemic and lymphatic, skin, and endocrine; or

2. any mental or psychological disorder, such as mental retardation, organic brain syndrome, emotional or mental illness, and specific learning disabilities. (29 C.F.R. § 1630.2[h])

In 2008, Congress expanded the ADA definition of disability with the passage of the American with Disabilities Act Amendments Act (ADAAA). The new legislation is intended to clarify the standard for what constitutes a "disability." The ADAAA states that a person will have to show only that he or she was discriminated against because of an actual or *perceived* impairment, even if the impairment doesn't limit or isn't perceived to limit a major life activity. Under the original ADA definition, an individual had to prove that an employer regarded the employee as being substantially limited in a major life activity because of a qualified disability. The amendments to ADA (ADAAA) require individuals to demonstrate that the employer believed they have a mental or physical impairment.

Major Provisions of ADA

ADA mandates protections for people with disabilities in public and private-sector employment, all public services, and public accommodations, transportation, and telecommunications. The U.S. Department of Justice is charged with the responsibility of ensuring that these provisions are enforced on behalf of all people with disabilities. The intent of ADA is to create a "fair and level playing field" for eligible people with disabilities. To do so, the law specifies that **reasonable accommodations** need to be made that take into account each person's needs resulting from his or her disabilities. As defined in law, the principal test for a reasonable accommodation is its effectiveness: Does the accommodation provide an opportunity for a person with a disability to achieve the same level of performance and to enjoy benefits equal to those of an average, similarly situated person without a disability? See nearby feature, Debate Forum, "Casey's Story: Then and Now."

The major provisions of the ADA include:

- *Employment*. ADA mandates that employers may not discriminate in any employment practices, including job application procedures, hiring, firing, advancement, compensation, training, and other terms, conditions, and privileges of employment. It applies to recruitment, advertising, tenure, layoff, leave, fringe benefits, and all other employment-related activities. The law applies to any business with 15 or more employees.

- *Transportation*. ADA requires that all new public transit buses, bus and train stations, and rail systems must be accessible to people with disabilities. Transit authorities must provide transportation services to individuals with disabilities who cannot use fixed-route bus services. All Amtrak stations are now accessible to people with disabilities. Discrimination by air carriers in areas other than employment is not covered by the ADA, but rather by the Air Carrier Access Act (49 U.S.C. §1374 [c]).

- *Public accommodations*. Restaurants, hotels, and retail stores may not discriminate against individuals with disabilities. Physical barriers in existing facilities must be removed, if removal is readily achievable. If not, alternative methods of providing the services must be offered. All new construction and alterations of facilities must be accessible.

- *Government*. State and local agencies may not discriminate against qualified individuals with disabilities. All government facilities, services, and communications must be accessible to people with disabilities.

Reasonable accommodations
Requirements within ADA to ensure that a person with a disability has an equal chance of participation. The intent is to create a "fair and level playing field" for the person with a disability. A reasonable accommodation takes into account each person's needs resulting from their disability. Accommodations may be arranged in the areas of employment, transportation, or telecommunications.

DEBATE FORUM
CASEY'S STORY: THEN AND NOW

ZUMA Press/Newscom

Casey Martin was born with a very rare congenital disorder (Klippel-Trenaunay-Weber syndrome), a condition with no known cure. The disorder is degenerative and causes serious blood circulation problems in Casey's right leg and foot. His right leg is about half the size of his left, and when forced to walk on it, Casey experiences excruciating pain and swelling. Obviously, this condition would be difficult and very painful under any circumstances, but Casey's occupation is professional golf and he is a member of the Professional Golfers' Association (PGA). Unfortunately, Casey reached the point where he could no longer walk a golf course; he had to use a cart to get around. The PGA did not permit the use of a golf cart during *competitions*. Casey requested an exemption that would allow him to ride rather than walk. The PGA refused his request, and Casey took the matter to court, claiming discrimination on the basis of the Americans with Disabilities Act. The debate escalated over whether Casey was given an advantage over his fellow professional golfers by being able to ride a golf cart when others must walk. Is riding a cart an advantage for Casey or does the golf cart simply level the "playing field" as intended in the ADA? What do you think of the following "for and against" arguments:

POINT

The PGA's attempt to disallow Casey Martin's use of a golf cart was an act of discrimination against a person with a disability. The PGA is a public entity, and golf courses are places of public accommodation under the Americans with Disabilities Act. Therefore, the PGA must provide *reasonable accommodations* for someone with a permanent disability. As the Supreme Court ruling notes, Casey met all the ADA requirements. He has a permanent disability, and without a reasonable accommodation (riding in a golf cart), he could not participate in his chosen profession. The PGA argued that riding in a cart creates an advantage for Casey. The PGA also argued that it should have the right to determine its own rules for competitions. Fine! Change the rules to allow Casey and any other golfer with disabilities to use a cart. In the end, if letting Casey Martin ride means that the PGA must allow every golfer to use a cart, so be it. Isn't the PGA's motto "anything is possible"?

COUNTERPOINT

One cannot help but express admiration for the grit and determination of Casey Martin. However, the U.S. Congress never intended for ADA to require an organization such as the PGA to change its basic rules of operation and, thus, create an advantage for one golfer over another. Physical requirements, including walking up to five miles on any given day in unfavorable weather, is an *essential element* of golf at its highest level. Any golfer who is allowed to ride in a cart will have an unfair advantage over other competitors. If the PGA allows this for one player, it will create hardship for others, which is exactly what ADA did not want. Players in the highest levels of competition must walk the course as part of the test of their skills. One set of rules must apply to all players.

Update: Whatever your point of view, a U.S. magistrate found in Casey's favor in 1998. Casey played the events on the Nike tour throughout 1998 and 1999,

qualifying for his first PGA tour event in January 2000. Meanwhile, the PGA appealed the decision to allow Casey to ride a cart, and in a 7-to-2 decision in 2001, the U.S. Supreme Court ruled that Casey must be allowed to ride a cart during competition. The Court ruled that allowing Casey access to the cart would not "fundamentally alter" the game of golf nor give him any advantage over other golfers on the course.

Casey left the pro tour in 2005, and in May 2006, he was named head coach of the University of Oregon's men's golf team. Casey Martin is the cofounder of a social networking golf community website: www.the10thgreen.com.

What Do You Think? Please visit the Education CourseMate website for Human Exceptionality, *11th edition, to access and respond to questions related to the Debate Forum.*

- *Telecommunications*. ADA requires that all companies offering telephone service to the general public must offer telephone relay services to individuals with hearing loss who use telecommunication devices or similar equipment.

Multidisciplinary Roles and Responsibilities

FOCUS 5

Describe the role of health care, psychology, and social services professionals in meeting the needs of people with disabilities.

This chapter continues with an initial discussion of three disciplines concerned with supporting people with disabilities and their families in community settings: health care, psychology, and social services. (Education is the focus of Chapter 2 in this text.) Each discipline is unique in its understanding of, and approach to, people with disabilities. Figure 1.2 provides the common terminology associated with each field.

The Role of Health Care Professionals

Medical model

Model by which human development is viewed according to two dimensions: normal and pathological. Normal refers to the absence of biological problems; pathological refers to alterations in the organism caused by disease.

Pathology

Alterations in an organism that are caused by disease.

The **medical model** has two dimensions: normalcy and pathology. *Normalcy* is defined as the absence of a biological problem. **Pathology** is defined as alterations in an organism caused by disease, resulting in a state of ill health that interferes with or destroys the integrity of the organism. The medical model, often referred to as the *disease model*, focuses primarily on biological problems and on defining the nature of the disease and its pathological effects on the individual. The model is universal and does not have values that are culturally relative. It is based on the premise that being healthy is better than being sick, regardless of the culture in which one lives.

When diagnosing a problem, a physician carefully follows a definite pattern of procedures that includes questioning the patient to obtain a history of the problem, conducting a physical examination and laboratory studies, and in some cases, performing surgical explorations. The person who has a biological problem is labeled the *patient*, and the deficits are then described as the *patient's disease*.

We must go back more than 200 years to find the first documented attempts to personalize health care to serve the needs of people with differences. In 1799, as a young physician and authority on diseases of the ear and education of those with hearing loss, Jean-Marc Itard (1775–1838) believed that the environment, in conjunction with physiological stimulation, could contribute to the learning potential of any human being. Itard was influenced by the earlier work of Philippe Pinel (1745–1826), a French physician concerned with mental illness, and John Locke (1632–1704), an English philosopher. Pinel advocated that people characterized as insane or idiots needed to be treated humanely, but his teachings emphasized that they were essentially incurable and that any treatment to remedy their disabilities would be fruitless. Locke, in contrast, described the mind as a "blank

Figure 1.2 *Common Terminology in Medicine, Psychology, and Sociology.*

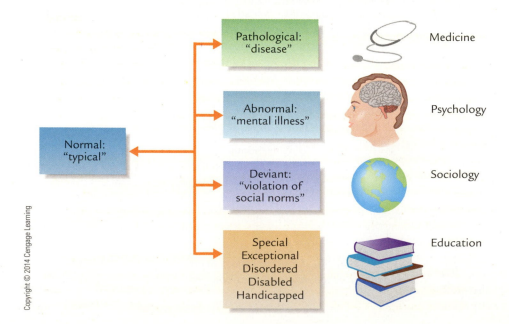

Copyright © 2014 Cengage Learning

slate" that could be opened to all kinds of new stimuli. The positions of Pinel and Locke represent the classic controversy of **nature versus nurture:** What are the roles of heredity and environment in determining a person's capabilities?

Itard tested the theories of Pinel and Locke in his work with Victor, the so-called wild boy of Aveyron. Victor was 12 years old when hunters found him in the woods. He had not developed any language, and his behavior was virtually uncontrollable, described as savage or animallike. Ignoring Pinel's diagnosis that the child was an incurable idiot, Itard took responsibility for Victor and put him through a program of sensory stimulation that was intended to cure his condition. After five years, Victor developed some verbal language and became more socialized as he grew accustomed to his new environment. Itard's work with Victor documented for the first time that learning is possible even for individuals that most professionals describe as totally helpless.

Health care services for people with disabilities have evolved considerably since Itard's groundbreaking work. The focus today is directly on the individual in family and community settings. In many cases, the physician is the first professional with whom parents have contact concerning their child's disability, particularly when the child's challenges are identifiable immediately after birth or during the early childhood years. The physician is the family adviser and communicates with parents regarding the medical prognosis and recommendations for treatment. However, too often physicians assume that they are the family's only counseling resource (Drew & Hardman, 2007). Physicians should be aware of additional resources within the community, including other parents, social workers, mental health professionals, and educators.

Health care services are often taken for granted simply because they are readily available to most people. This is not true, however, for many people with disabilities. It is not uncommon for a pediatrician to suggest that parents seek treatment elsewhere for their child with a disability, even when the problem is a common illness such as a cold or a sore throat.

It would be unfair to stereotype health care professionals as unresponsive to the needs of people with disabilities. On the contrary, medical technology has prevented many disabilities from occurring and has enhanced the quality of life for many people. However, to ensure that people with disabilities receive comprehensive health care services in a community setting, several factors must be considered. The physician in community practice (e.g., the general practitioner, pediatrician) must receive more training in the medical, psychological, and educational aspects of disability conditions. This training could include instruction regarding developmental milestones; attitudes toward children with disabilities; disabling conditions; prevention; screening, diagnosis, and assessment; interdisciplinary collaboration; effective communication with parents; long-term health care and social treatment programs; and community resources.

Health care professionals must also be willing to treat people with disabilities for common illnesses when the treatment is irrelevant to the patient's disability. Physicians need not become disability specialists, but they must have enough knowledge to refer patients to appropriate specialists when necessary. For instance, physicians must be aware of and willing to refer patients to other community resources, such as social workers, educators, and psychologists.

The health care profession must continue to support physicians and other allied health personnel who are well equipped to work with people with disabilities. These specialized health professionals include **geneticists** and **genetic counselors**, **physical therapists** and **occupational therapists**, public health nurses, and nutritional and dietary consultants.

Nature versus nurture
Controversy concerning how much of a person's ability is related to sociocultural influences (nurture) as opposed to genetic factors (nature).

Steve McAlister/Riser/Getty Images

Physicians in community practice must be willing to provide medical care to people with disabilities. What additional training do you think is needed in order for physicians to care for people with disabilities?

Geneticist
A professional who specializes in the study of heredity.

Genetic counselor
A specially trained professional who counsels people about their chances of producing a seriously ill infant, in reference to their genetic history.

Physical therapist
A professional who provides services that help restore function, improve mobility, relieve pain, and prevent or limit permanent physical disabilities. They help restore, maintain, and promote overall fitness and health for people of all ages.

Occupational therapist
A professional who specializes in developing self-care, work, and play activities to increase independent function and quality of life, enhance development, and prevent disability.

The Role of Psychologists

Psychology is the science of human and animal behavior, the study of the acts and mental events that can be observed and evaluated. Broadly viewed, psychology is concerned with every behavior of an individual. Behavior is the focus of psychology, and when the behavior of an individual does not meet the criteria of normalcy, it is labeled *abnormal* and the person is labeled. Labels describing abnormal behavior include emotional disturbance, behavior disorders, psychosis, neurosis, and so on.

Psychology, as we know it today, is more than 125 years old. In 1879, Wilhelm Wundt (1832–1920) defined psychology as the science of conscious experience. His definition was based on the *principle of introspection*—looking into oneself to analyze experiences. William James (1842–1910) expanded Wundt's conception of conscious experience in his treatise, *The Principles of Psychology* (James, 1890), to include learning, motivation, and emotions. In 1913, John B. Watson (1878–1958) shifted the focus of psychology from conscious experience to observable behavior and mental events.

We cannot live in today's world without encountering the dynamics of abnormal behavior. The media are replete with stories of murder, suicide, sexual aberration, burglary, robbery, embezzlement, child abuse, and other incidents that display abnormal behavior. Each case represents a point on the continuum of *abnormal behavior* that exists in society. Levels of emotional and behavioral challenges range from actions that are slightly deviant or eccentric (but still within the confines of normal human experience) to **neurotic disorders** (partial disorganization characterized by combinations of anxieties, compulsions, obsessions, and phobias) to **psychotic disorders** (severe disorganization resulting in loss of contact with reality and characterized by delusions, hallucinations, and illusions).

The study of abnormal behavior historically has been based in philosophy and religion in Western culture. Until the Middle Ages, the disturbed or mad person was thought to have made a "pact with the devil," and the psychological affliction was believed to be a result of divine punishment or the work of devils, witches, or demons residing within the person. The earliest known treatment for mental disorders, called *trephining,* involved drilling holes in a person's skull to permit evil spirits to leave (Carlson, Miller, Heth, Donahoe, & Martin, 2009).

Today, psychologists play a critical role in the treatment of many individuals with disabilities. Depending upon their training and philosophy, psychologists provide treatments that include behavior therapy, rational-emotive therapy, group psychotherapy, family therapy, or client-centered therapy. According to Carlson et al. (2009), the majority of psychologists describe their therapeutic philosophy as eclectic. They choose from many different approaches in determining the best way to work with an individual in need of psychological help, including **neuropsychological assessments**.

The Role of Social Services Professionals

Whereas psychology focuses primarily on the behavior of the individual, social services professionals are concerned with modern cultures, group behaviors, societal institutions, and intergroup relationships. These professionals view individuals in relation to their physical and social environments. When individuals meet the social norms of the group, they are considered normal. When individuals are unable to adapt to social roles or to establish appropriate interpersonal relationships, their behaviors are labeled **deviant**. Unlike medical pathology, social differences cannot be defined in universal terms. Instead, they are defined within the context of the culture, in any way the culture chooses to define them.

Even within the same society, different social groups often define human differences in myriad ways. Groups of people who share the same norms and values will develop their own rules about what is and what is not acceptable social behavior. Four principles serve as guidelines in determining who will be labeled socially different:

1. Normal behavior must meet societal, cultural, or group expectations. Difference is defined as a violation of social norms.

2. Social differences are not necessarily illnesses as defined by the medical model. Failure to conform to societal norms does not imply that the individual has pathological or biological deficits.

Neurotic disorders
Behavior characterized by combinations of anxieties, compulsions, obsessions, and phobias.

Psychotic disorders
Serious behavior disorders resulting in a loss of contact with reality and characterized by delusions, hallucinations, or illusions.

Neuropsychological assessments
Comprehensive examinations that assess several critical areas of how an individual is functioning, including, but not limited to, the level of consciousness, cranial nerves function, movement, sensation, and reflexes.

Deviant
A term used to describe the behavior of individuals who are unable to adapt to social roles or to establish appropriate interpersonal relationships.

3. Each culture determines the range of behaviors that are defined as normal or deviant and then enforces these norms. Those people with the greatest power within the culture can impose their criteria for normalcy on those who are less powerful.

4. Social differences may be caused by the interaction of several factors, including genetic makeup and individual experiences within the social environment.

Today, many different kinds of social service professionals specialize across more than 50 subfields and specialties. Within each specialty area, these professionals undertake a systematic study of social groups, organizations, cultures, and societies on individual and group behavior. The social services professionals provide information about social behavior (including disability) in the context of the society as a whole. The following are just a few examples of specialties that may include an emphasis on disability: sociology, social work, gerontology (aging), criminology and criminal justice, and family and marriage. This chapter has examined many different perspectives on people with disabilities, including common terminology used to describe these individuals, bringing about social change and inclusion through the Americans with Disabilities Act, and understanding people with disabilities from the disciplines of medicine, psychology, and sociology.

Looking toward a Bright Future

The ADA seeks to ensure that comprehensive services (e.g., employment, housing, educational programs, public transportation, restaurant access, and religious activities) are available to all individuals with disabilities within or as close as possible to their families and communities. In 1999, the U.S. Supreme Court ruled in *Olmstead v. L.C. & E.W.* (now known as the *Olmstead Decision*) that it is a violation of the ADA to discriminate against people with disabilities by providing services only in institutions when they could be served in a community-based setting. This historic decision encouraged policy makers to reevaluate how they deliver publicly funded services and supports to

FOCUS 6
What services and supports must be available to ensure a bright future for people with disabilities?

© Mika/Corbis

As a result of ADA, people with disabilities and their families have opportunities to experience living in their neighborhood communities, paid employment, access to public transportation, and schooling that were not available even 20 years ago.

people with disabilities. Communities must have (1) a comprehensive, effective working plan for placing qualified people in less restrictive settings, and (2) a waiting list for community-based services that ensures people can receive services and be moved off the list at a reasonable pace.

As a result of the ADA, federal and state support for community living is being redirected from isolated large congregate care settings to small, community-based residences located within local neighborhoods. Although the unemployment rate of people with disabilities is the highest of any group of people in the world, antidiscrimination legislation, such as ADA, is expanding the traditional sheltered work model for people with disabilities to an emphasis on real jobs, earning wages, and working side by side with those who are not disabled. For families, there has been an expansion in services, such as respite care and in-home assistance, to provide help in coping with everyday stress. People with disabilities and their families are also experiencing a stronger emphasis on person-centered supports. Through individualized program planning, myriad agencies (such as social services, vocational rehabilitation, health care, Social Security) are brought together with adults with disabilities and their families to plan, develop, and implement the supports necessary for individuals to participate in the life of their communities.

To ensure a bright future, people with disabilities need access to their local community services, such as education, health care, transportation, recreation, and life insurance. Access to these supports creates the opportunity to be included in community life. Successful inclusion is based on the individual's ability, with appropriate education and training, to adapt to community expectations, and the willingness of the community to adapt to and accommodate individuals with differences.

Access to adequate housing and a barrier-free environment are essential for people with disabilities. **Barrier-free facilities** are created by requiring that buildings and public transportation incorporate barrier-free designs. People with disabilities need entrance ramps to and within public buildings; accessibility to public telephones, vending machines, and restrooms; and lifts for public transportation vehicles. Community living options should include apartments, small group homes, foster homes, and home ownership.

The availability of recreation and leisure experiences within the community vary substantially depending upon age and severity of disability. Many people with a disability may not have access to the arts and sports activities that are generally available to others within the community. Similar challenges exist for children, adolescents, and adults with disabilities, many of whom have limited opportunities for recreation and leisure experiences beyond watching television.

Recreational programs must be developed to assist individuals in accessing leisure activities of their choice and creating more satisfying lifestyles. Therapeutic recreation is a profession concerned specifically with this goal: use recreation to help people adapt their physical, emotional, or social characteristics to take advantage of leisure activities more independently in a community setting.

Work is essential to the creation of successful lifestyles for all adults, including those with disabilities. Yet many individuals with disabilities are unable to gain employment during their adult years. A poll conducted by the Kessler Foundation and the National Organization on Disability (NOD; 2010) found significant gaps between the employment rates of people with disabilities in comparison with their peers who were not disabled. Only 35 percent of people with disabilities (ages 18 to 64) work full- or part-time, compared with 78 percent of people who are not disabled. A comparison of working and nonworking individuals with disabilities revealed that working individuals were more satisfied with life, had more money, and were less likely to blame their disability for preventing them from reaching their potential. For more insight into the employment of a person with disabilities, see the nearby Case Study, "Sarina."

Many of the changes in the last three decades have had a positive and dramatic impact on the lives of people with disabilities and their families. However, much remains to be done. As people with disabilities and their families engage in life in the 21st century, it will be critical to carefully listen to and support their individual needs and preferences.

CEC

Standard 5
Learning Environments and Social Interactions

Barrier-free facility
A building or structure without architectural obstructions that allows people with mobility disabilities (such as those in wheelchairs) to move freely through all areas.

CASE STUDY SARINA

Over the past several years, many changes have occurred in Sarina's life. After spending most of her life in a large institution, Sarina, now in her late 30s, moved into an apartment with two other women, both of whom have a disability. She receives assistance from a local supported-living program in developing skills that will allow her to make her own decisions and become more independent in the community.

Over the years, Sarina has had many labels describing her disability, including mental retardation, epilepsy, autism, physical disability, chronic health problems, and serious emotional disturbance. She is very much challenged both mentally and physically. Medical problems associated with epilepsy necessitate the use of medications that affect Sarina's behavior (motivation, attitude, and so on) and her physical

well-being. During her early 20s, while walking up a long flight of stairs, Sarina had a seizure that resulted in a fall and a broken neck. The long-term impact from the fall was a paralyzed right hand and limited use of her left leg.

Sarina's life goal has been to work in a real job, make money, and have choices about how she spends her money. For most of her life, the goal has been out of reach. Her only jobs have been in sheltered workshops, where she worked for next to nothing, doing piecemeal work such as sorting envelopes, putting together cardboard boxes, or folding laundry. Whereas most of the focus in the past has been on what Sarina "can't do" (can't read, can't get along with supervisors, can't handle the physical requirements of a job), her family and the professionals on her support team are looking more at her very strong desire to succeed in a community job.

About three miles from Sarina's apartment, a job has opened up for a stock clerk at a local video store. The store manager is willing to pay minimum wage for someone to work four to six hours a day stocking the shelves with videos and handling some basic tasks (such as cleaning floors, washing windows, and dusting furniture). Sarina loves movies and is really interested in this job. With the support of family and her professional team, she has applied for the job.

APPLICATION QUESTIONS

1. As Sarina's potential employer, what are some of the issues you would raise about her capability to perform the essential functions of the job?

2. What would you see as the "reasonable accommodations" necessary to help Sarina succeed at this job if she were hired?

As suggested by the Center for Human Policy at Syracuse University (2011), support for people with disabilities should:

- be based on the principle "whatever it takes." Services should be flexible, individualized, and designed to meet the diverse needs of the individual and the family.
- build on existing social networks and natural sources.
- maximize each person's control over his or her services.
- be based on the assumption that the individual and the family, rather than governments and agencies, are in the best position to determine needs.
- encourage the inclusion of people with disabilities into the life of the family and community.

FOCUS REVIEW

FOCUS 1 Why do we continue to apply labels to people even when we know they may have a negative effect on an individual?

- Labels are an attempt to describe, identify, and distinguish one person from another.

- Many medical, psychological, social, and educational services require that an individual be labeled in order to determine who is eligible to receive special services.
- Labels help professionals communicate more effectively with one another and provide a common ground for evaluating research findings.

- Labels enable professionals to differentiate more clearly the needs of one group of people from those of another.

FOCUS 2 Identify three approaches to describe human differences.

- The developmental approach is based on differences in the course of human development from what is considered normal physical, social, and intellectual growth. Human differences are the result of interaction between biological and environmental factors. Observing large numbers of individuals and looking for characteristics that occur most frequently at any given age can explain normal growth.
- The cultural approach defines *normal* according to established cultural standards. Human differences can be explained by examining the values of any given society. What is considered normal will change over time and from culture to culture.
- Self-labeling reflects how we perceive ourselves, although those perceptions may not be consistent with how others see us.

FOCUS 3 How have societal views on people with disabilities changed from widespread discrimination to an era of inclusion and support in the 21st century?

- People with disabilities have historically been viewed as a burden to families and society. Discrimination has been prevalent since early civilizations.
- The 20th century brought about positive changes in societal and government support for people with disabilities and their families. Treatment and education that had been denied for centuries became more accessible. By 1960, the Congress and state legislatures were actively engaged with both parents and professionals concerned with improving the lives of people with disabilities.
- With the passage of the Americans with Disabilities Act in 1990, the rights of people with disabilities came full circle, from the early history of genocide to an era of rights and family support in the 21st century.

FOCUS 4 What is the Americans with Disabilities Act?

- ADA is a U.S. federal law that provides a national mandate to end discrimination against individuals with disabilities in private-sector employment, in all public services, and in public accommodations, transportation, and telecommunications.

FOCUS 5 Describe the role of health care, psychology, and social services professionals in meeting the needs of people with disabilities.

- Health care professionals are focused directly on the individual in family and community settings. In many cases, the physician is the first professional with whom parents have contact concerning their child's disability, particularly when the child's challenges are identifiable immediately after birth or during early childhood. The physician is the family adviser and communicates with parents regarding the medical prognosis and recommendations for treatment.
- Psychologists use many different approaches in the treatment of mental health challenges, including behavior therapy, rational-emotive therapy, group psychotherapy, family therapy, or client-centered therapy.
- Whereas psychology focuses primarily on the behavior of the individual, social services professionals are concerned with modern cultures, group behaviors, societal institutions, and intergroup relationships. They view the individual in relation to the physical and social environment.

FOCUS 6 What services and supports must be available to ensure a bright future for people with disabilities?

- To ensure a bright future, people with disabilities must have access to community services, such as education, health care, transportation, recreation, and life insurance. Access to these supports creates the opportunity to be included in community life. Successful inclusion is based on the individual's ability, with appropriate education and training, to adapt to community expectations, and the willingness of the community to adapt to and accommodate individuals with differences.

Council for Exceptional Children (CEC) Standards to Accompany Chapter 1

 If you are thinking about a career in special education, you should know that many states use national standards developed by the Council for Exceptional Children (CEC) to assess a teacher candidate's knowledge and skills for working with students with disabilities. See a complete listing of the 10 CEC Content Standards on the inside back cover of this text.

CEC Content Standards Addressed in Chapter 1:
1 Foundations
2 Development and Characteristics of Learners
5 Learning Environments and Social Interactions
9 Professional and Ethical Practice

Mastery Activities and Assignments

To master the content within this chapter, complete the following activities and assignments. Online and interactive versions of these activities are also available on the accompanying Education CourseMate website, where you may also access TeachSource videos, chapter web links, interactive quizzes, portfolio activities, flash cards, an integrated eBook, and much more!

1. Complete a written test of the chapter's content. If your instructor requires a written test of your content knowledge for this chapter, keep a copy for your portfolio. A practice test on the information covered in this chapter is available through the Education CourseMate website.

2. Review the Case Study, "Sarina," and respond in writing to the Application Questions. Keep a copy of the case study and your written response for your portfolio.

3. Complete the "Take a Stand" activities for Debate Forum, "Casey's Story: Then and Now." Read the Debate Forum in this chapter and then visit the CourseMate website to complete the activity, "Take a Stand." Keep a copy of this activity for your portfolio.

4. Participate in a community service learning activity. Service learning is a valuable way to enhance your learning experience. Visit the Education CourseMate website for suggested community service learning activities that correspond to the information presented in this chapter. Develop a reflective journal of the service learning experience for your portfolio.

CHAPTER 2

Education for All

Purestock/Jupiter Images

FOCUS PREVIEW

As you read the chapter, focus on these key concepts:

1 What educational services were available for students with disabilities during most of the 20th century?

2 Identify the principal issues in the right-to-education cases that led to eventual passage of the national mandate to educate students with disabilities.

3 Identify five major provisions of the Individuals with Disabilities Education Act (IDEA).

4 Discuss the special education referral, assessment, planning, and placement process.

5 Identify three principles that are intended to assure that schools across the nation are accountable for student learning. Under IDEA 2004, what must a student's IEP include to ensure access to the general curriculum?

6 Distinguish between students with disabilities eligible for services under Section 504/ADA and those eligible under IDEA.

SNAPSHOT
Meet Martha Cleveland and Her "Educaton for All" Approach to Teaching

In today's schools, teachers must be able to use multiple teaching strategies to address the needs of all children, including those with disabilities. Yet understanding how to meet every child's needs—educationally, socially, and emotionally—requires continuously keeping abreast of new evidence-based teaching techniques, such as differentiating instruction, focusing on the development of a student's organizational abilities, and structuring an individualized learning environment. Each day veteran elementary teacher Martha Cleveland

Copyright 2014 Cengage Learning

accommodates the learning needs of each student in her classroom. She brings her unwavering belief that all children can be successful learners into a learning environment where her students receive individual attention, have access to the latest instructional technology, feel safe, and are valued.

 To see Martha Cleveland in action, please visit the Education CourseMate website and view the video, "Including Students with High Incidence Disabilities: Strategies for Success."

A Changing Era in the Lives of Students with Disabilities

Educating children with disabilities around the world has historically focused on caring for each student in a segregated setting away from nondisabled peers, or not providing any schooling at all. Today, many nations are acknowledging the importance of an education for these children as a critical factor in promoting independence in family and community settings. The view that children with disabilities should be excluded from school is being replaced with the call to provide an educational opportunity for every child. An example of this worldwide call to educate children with disabilities is seen in the 1994 Salamanca Statement issued by the United Nations (UN) with the support of 92 different countries. The Salamanca Statement affirms that:

- Every child has unique characteristics, interests, abilities, and learning needs.
- Education systems should be designed, and educational programs should be implemented to take into account the wide diversity of characteristics and needs.
- Those with special educational needs must have access to regular [general education] schools that should accommodate them within a child-centered instructional program.
- Regular schools with this inclusive orientation are the most effective means of combating discriminatory attitudes, creating welcoming communities, building an inclusive society and achieving education for all. (United Nations Education, Scientific and Cultural Organization [UNESCO], 1994)

The UN further strengthened its strong view on *education for all* during the World Summit for Children (UNESCO, 2001), calling for schools to promote access to education for every child with a disability. To meet this call, schools are expected to provide students with the opportunity to learn and apply the necessary skills for a successful transition to adult life.

In the United States, access to education is a basic value, reflecting the expectation that all children should have an opportunity to learn and develop to the best of their ability. Schools are responsible for every student, from the most academically capable to those in need of specialized services and supports. All Martha Cleveland from our opening snapshot wants for her students is the opportunity for them to learn the skills that would facilitate success in school, family, and community. As a teacher, Martha's dream is no different than what each of us wants for our nation's children: an appropriate education that truly values personal fulfillment while teaching the critical skills needed to succeed in a very complex and changing world.

Origins of Special Education in the United States

FOCUS 1
What educational services were available for students with disabilities during most of the 20th century?

The goal of *education for all* is full participation for everyone—regardless of race, cultural background, socioeconomic status, physical disability, or intellectual challenges. It wasn't until 1975, however, that this value was translated into practice for all students with disabilities in the United States. The following section describes the beginnings of special education; a view from some professionals and national leaders that education is a privilege and not a right for students with disabilities; and the expanding role of the U.S. government in educating these students.

Early Special Education Programs

Throughout most of the last three centuries, many families who had a child with a disability were unable to get help for their most basic needs, such as medical and dental care, social services, or education. In the 18th and 19th centuries, educational services consisted of programs that were usually separate from the public schools, established mainly for children who were described as "slow learners" or had hearing or sight loss. These students were usually placed in separate classrooms in a public school building or in separate schools. Special education meant segregated education. Moreover, students with very substantial learning and behavior differences were excluded from public education entirely.

CEC

Standard 1
Foundations

Education as a Privilege but Not a Right

From 1920 to 1960, most states merely allowed for special education; they did not mandate it. Educational services to children with mild emotional disorders (e.g., discipline problems or inappropriate behavior) were initiated in the early 1930s, but mental hospitals continued to be the only alternative for most children with severe emotional problems. Special classes for children with physical disabilities expanded in the 1930s; separate schools for these children became very popular during the late 1950s, with specially designed elevators, ramps, and modified doors, toilets, and desks.

During the 1940s, special school versus general education class placement emerged as an issue in the education of students with disabilities. Educators and parents began to advocate that these students be educated in a school setting that would promote social interaction with "typical" (nondisabled) peers.

By the 1950s, many countries around the world sought to expand educational programs for students with disabilities in special schools and classes. Additionally, many health care and social services professionals were advocating on behalf of individuals with disabilities, thus enriching our knowledge regarding effective programs and services. For the most part, children with disabilities continued to be educated in a school setting that isolated them from peers without disabilities. Researchers and families continuously called into question the validity of these segregated programs. Several studies in the 1950s and 1960s (e.g., Cassidy & Stanton, 1959; Johnson, 1961; Jordan & deCharms, 1959; Thurstone,

Special Education Schooling throughout History

1959) examined the value of special classes. This research resulted in the development of a new model (*mainstreaming*) in which a child could remain in the general class program for the majority, if not all, of the school day, receiving special education when and where it was needed.

John F. Kennedy and the Expanding Role of National Government

The 1960s brought significant changes in the education of students with disabilities. President John F. Kennedy expanded the role of the U.S. government, providing financial support to university programs for the preparation of special education teachers. The Bureau of Education for the Handicapped (BEH) in the Office of Education (now the Office of Special Education and Rehabilitative Services in the U.S. Department of Education) was created as a clearinghouse for information at the federal level. New projects were funded nationwide to meet the educational needs of students with disabilities in the public schools.

The Right to Education

The right to education for children with disabilities came about as a part of a larger social issue in the United States: the civil rights of people from differing ethnic and racial backgrounds. The civil rights movement of the 1950s and 1960s awakened the public to the issues of discrimination in employment, housing, access to public facilities (e.g., restaurants and transportation), and public education.

Education was reaffirmed as a right and not a privilege by the U.S. Supreme Court in the landmark case of *Brown v. Board of Education* of *Topeka, Kansas* (1954). In its decision, the Court ruled that education must be made available to everyone on an equal basis. A unanimous Supreme Court stated, "In these days, it is doubtful that any child may reasonably be expected to succeed in life if he is denied the opportunity of an education. Such an opportunity, where the state has undertaken to provide it, is a right which must be made available to all on equal terms" (*Brown v. Board of Education of Topeka, Kansas,* 1954). Although usually heralded for striking down racial segregation, this decision also set a precedent for the right to education for students with disabilities. Yet, it was nearly 20 years later before federal courts confronted the issue of a free and appropriate education for these students.

The 1970s have often been described as a decade of revolution in the education of students with disabilities. Many of the landmark cases were brought before the courts to address the right to education for students with disabilities. Additionally, major pieces of state and federal legislation were enacted to reaffirm the right of students with disabilities to a free public education.

FOCUS 2

Identify the principal issues in the right-to-education cases that led to eventual passage of the national mandate to educate students with disabilities.

CEC
Standard 1
Foundations

Table 2.1 Major Court Cases and Federal Legislation Focusing on the Right to Education for Individuals with Disabilities

Court Cases and Federal Legislation	Precedents Established
Brown v. Board of Education of *Topeka, Kansas* (1954)	Segregation of students by race is held unconstitutional. Education is a right that must be available to all on equal terms.
Pennsylvania Association for Retarded Citizens v. Commonwealth of Pennsylvania (1971)	Pennsylvania schools must provide a free public education to all school-age children with mental retardation.
Mills v. Board of Education of the District of Columbia (1972)	Exclusion of individuals with disabilities from free, appropriate public education is a violation of the due process and equal protection clauses of the 14th Amendment to the Constitution. Public schools in the District of Columbia must provide free education to all children with disabilities regardless of their functional level or ability to adapt to the present educational system.
Public Law 93-112, Vocational Rehabilitation Act of 1973, Section 504 (1973)	Individuals with disabilities cannot be excluded from participation in, denied benefits of, or subjected to discrimination under any benefit or activity receiving federal financial assistance.
Public Law 94-142, Part B of the Education for All Handicapped Children Act (1975)	A free and appropriate public education must be provided for all children with disabilities in the United States. (Those up through age 5 may be excluded in some states.)
Board of Education of the Hendrick Hudson School District v. Rowley (1982)	The U.S. Supreme Court held that in order for special education and related services to be appropriate, they must be reasonably calculated to enable the student to receive educational benefits.
Public Law 99-457, Education of the Handicapped Act Amendments (1986)	A new authority extends free and appropriate education to all children with disabilities aged 3 to 5, and provides a new early intervention program for infants and toddlers.
Public Law 101-336, Americans with Disabilities Act (1990)	Civil rights protections are provided for people with disabilities in private-sector employment, all public services, and public accommodations, transportation, and telecommunications.
Public Law 101-476, Individuals with Disabilities Education Act (1990)	The Education for All Handicapped Children Act Amendments are renamed the Individuals with Disabilities Education Act (IDEA). Two new categories of disability are added: autism and traumatic brain injury. IDEA requires that an individualized transition plan be developed no later than age 16 as a component of the IEP process. Rehabilitation and social work services are included as related services.
Public Law 105-17, Amendments to the Individuals with Disabilities Education Act (1997) (commonly referred to as IDEA 97)	IDEA 97 expands the emphasis for students with disabilities from public school access to improving individual outcomes (results). The 1997 amendments modify eligibility requirements, IEP requirements, public and private placements, disciplining of students, and procedural safeguards.
Public Law 108-446, Individuals with Disabilities Education Improvement Act of 2004	IDEA 2004 eliminates IEP short-term objectives for most students; establishes new state programs for multiyear IEPs and paperwork reduction; and establishes qualifications to become a highly qualified special education teacher.

Table 2.1 summarizes court cases and legislation addressing the right to education for students with disabilities.

FOCUS 3

Identify five major provisions of the Individuals with Disabilities Education Act (IDEA).

The Individuals with Disabilities Education Act (IDEA)

In 1975, the U.S. Congress brought together various pieces of state and federal legislation into one comprehensive national law. **The Education for All Handicapped Children Act (Public Law 94-142)** made available a free and appropriate public education to nearly four million U.S. school-age students with disabilities between the ages of 6 and 21. The law included provisions for an individualized education program, procedural safeguards to protect the rights of students and their parents, nondiscriminatory and multidisciplinary assessment, and education with nondisabled peers to the maximum extent appropriate (aka "the least restrictive environment"). Each of these provisions is discussed in depth later in this chapter.

In 1986, Congress amended the Education for All Handicapped Children Act to make available a free and appropriate public education for preschool-age students. **Public Law 99-457** extended all the rights and protections of school-age children (ages 6 through 21) to preschoolers ages 3 through 5. PL 99-457 also established a program for infants and toddlers up through 2 years old. Infants and toddlers with developmental delays became eligible for services that included a *multidisciplinary* assessment and an **individualized family service plan (IFSP)**. Although this provision did not mandate that states provide services to all infants and toddlers with developmental delays, it did establish financial incentives for state participation. (The IFSP and other provisions of PL 99-457 are discussed in depth in Chapter 3.)

In 1990, the same year that the Americans with Disabilities Act was signed into law, Congress renamed the Education of All Handicapped Children Act (Public Law 94-142) the **Individuals with Disabilities Education Act (IDEA; Public Law 101-476)**. The purpose of this name change was to reflect "people-first" language and promote the use of the term *disabilities* rather than handicapped.

What Are Special Education and Related Services?

Referred to as the **zero-exclusion principle**, IDEA requires that public schools provide special education and related services to meet the individual needs of all eligible students, regardless of the extent or type of their disability. **Special education** means specially designed instruction provided at no cost to parents in all settings (such as the classroom, physical education facilities, the home, and hospitals or institutions). IDEA also stipulates that students with disabilities receive any related services necessary to ensure that they benefit from their educational experience. **Related services** include the following:

> *transportation, and such developmental, corrective, and other supportive services (including speech-language pathology and audiology services, interpreting services, psychological services, physical and occupational therapy, recreation, including therapeutic recreation, social work services, school nurse services designed to enable a child with a disability to receive a free appropriate public education as described in the individualized education program of the child, counseling services, including rehabilitation counseling, orientation and mobility services, and medical services, except that such medical services shall be for diagnostic and evaluation purposes only) as may be required to assist a child with a disability to benefit from special education, and includes the early identification and assessment of disabling conditions in children. (Exception: The term does not include a medical device that is surgically implanted, or the replacement of such device.) (IDEA, 2004, PL 108-446, Sec. 602[26])*

Who Is Eligible for Special Education and Related Services?

For a student to receive the specialized services available under IDEA, two criteria must be met: First, the student must be identified as having one of the disability conditions identified in federal law, or a corresponding condition defined in a state's special education rules and regulations. These conditions include mental retardation (herein referred to as intellectual disabilities), hearing impairments (including deafness), speech or language impairments, visual impairments (including blindness), serious emotional disturbance,

The Education for All Handicapped Children Act (Public Law 94-142)
This federal law made a free and appropriate public education available to all eligible students regardless of the extent or type of handicap (disability). Eligible students must receive special education and related services necessary to meet their individual needs.

Public Law 99-457
Extended the rights and protections of Public Law 94-142 to children ages 3 through 5. The law also established an optional state program for infants and toddlers with disabilities.

Individualized family service plan (IFSP)
A plan of services for infants and toddlers and their families. It includes statements regarding the child's present development level, the family's strengths and needs, the major outcomes of the plan, specific interventions systems to accomplish outcomes, dates of initiation and duration of services, and a plan for transition into public schools.

Individuals with Disabilities Education Act (IDEA; Public Law 101-476)
The new name for the Education of All Handicapped Children Act (Public Law 94-142) as per the 1990 amendments to the law.

Zero-exclusion principle
Advocates that no person with a disability can be rejected for a service regardless of the nature or extent of the disabling condition.

Special education
Specially designed instruction provided at no cost to parents in all settings (such as the classroom, physical education facilities, the home, and hospitals or institutions).

Related services
Those services necessary to ensure that students with disabilities benefit from their educational experience. Related services may include special transportation, speech pathology, psychological services, physical and occupational therapy, recreation, rehabilitation counseling, social work, and medical services.

Standard 1
Foundations

Standard 2
Development and Characteristics of Learners

orthopedic impairments, **autism**, **traumatic brain injury**, multiple disabilities, other health impairments, or specific learning disabilities (IDEA, 2004, PL 108-446, Sec. 602[3][A][i]). Each disability will be defined and described in depth in subsequent chapters of this text.

In the 1997 amendments to IDEA, states and school districts/agencies were given the option of eliminating categories of disability (such as serious emotional disturbance or specific learning disabilities) for children ages 3 through 9. For this age group, a state or school district may define a child with a disability as

> *experiencing developmental delays, as defined by the State and as measured by appropriate diagnostic instruments and procedures, in one or more of the following areas: physical development; cognitive development; communication development; social or emotional development; or adaptive development. (IDEA, 2004, PL 108-446, Sec. 602[3][b][i][ii])*

The second criterion for special education eligibility is the student's demonstrated need for specialized instruction and related services in order to receive an appropriate education. This need is determined by a team of professionals and parents. Both criteria for eligibility must be met. If this is not the case, it is possible for a student to be identified as disabled but not be eligible to receive special education and related services under IDEA. These students may still be entitled to accommodations or modifications in their educational program. (See heading "Section 504/ADA and Reasonable Accommodations" later in this chapter.)

Major Provisions of IDEA

The five major provisions of IDEA are:

1. All students with disabilities are entitled to a free and appropriate public education designed to meet their unique needs and prepare them for employment and independent living.

2. Schools must use nondiscriminatory and multidisciplinary assessments in determining a student's educational needs.

3. Parents have the right to be involved in decisions regarding their son's or daughter's special education program.

4. Every student must have an individualized education program (IEP).

5. Every student has the right to receive an education with nondisabled peers to the maximum extent appropriate.

A Free and Appropriate Public Education (FAPE)   IDEA is based on the value that every student can learn. As such, all students with disabilities are entitled to a **free and appropriate public education** (FAPE) designed to meet their unique needs. Schools must provide special education and related services at no cost to parents. The IDEA provisions related to FAPE are based on the 14th Amendment to the U.S. Constitution guaranteeing equal protection of the law. No student with a disability can be excluded from a public education based on a disability (the zero-exclusion principle). A major interpretation of FAPE was handed down by the U.S. Supreme Court in *Board of Education of the Hendrick Hudson School District v. Rowley* (1982). The Supreme Court declared that an appropriate education consists of "specially designed instruction and related services" that are "individually designed" to provide "educational benefit." Often referred to as the "some educational benefit" standard, the ruling mandates that a state need not provide an ideal education, but must provide a beneficial one for students with disabilities.

Nondiscriminatory and Multidisciplinary Assessment   IDEA incorporated several provisions related to the use of nondiscriminatory testing procedures in labeling and placing students for special education services. Among those provisions are the following:

- The testing of students in their native or primary language, whenever possible
- The use of evaluation procedures selected and administered to prevent cultural or racial discrimination
- Validation of assessment tools for the purpose for which they are being used

- Assessment by a team of school professionals, using several pieces of information to formulate a placement decision

Historically, students with disabilities were too often placed in special education programs on the basis of inadequate or invalid assessment information. This resulted in a disproportionate number of children from differing ethnic backgrounds, as well as those from disadvantaged backgrounds (e.g., living in poverty), being inappropriately placed in special education.

Parental Safeguards and Involvement
IDEA granted parents the following rights in the education of their children:

- To give consent in writing before the child is initially assessed to determine eligibility for special education and related services
- To give consent in writing as to the educational setting in which the child will receive special education and related services
- To request an independent educational assessment if the parents believe the school's assessment is inappropriate
- To request an educational assessment at public expense if the parent disagrees with the school's assessment and recommendations
- To participate on the committee that considers the assessment of, placement of, and programming for the child
- To inspect and review educational records and challenge information believed to be inaccurate, misleading, or in violation of the privacy or other rights of the child
- To request a copy of information from the child's educational record
- To request a due process hearing concerning the school's proposal or refusal to initiate or change the identification, educational assessment, or placement of the child or the provision of a free and appropriate public education

Standard 3
Individual Learning Differences

Standard 7
Instructional Planning

Standard 9
Professional and Ethical Practice

The intent of these safeguards is twofold: first, to create an opportunity for parents to be more involved in decisions regarding their child's education program; and second, to protect the student and family from decisions that could adversely affect the child's education. Families thus can be secure in the knowledge that every reasonable attempt is being made to educate their child appropriately.

Some professionals and parents have argued that IDEA's promise for a parent and professional partnership has never been fully realized (Berry, 2009; Drew & Hardman, 2007). Several challenges may exist between the school and the home, including poor communication, a lack of trust, and inadequate service coordination (Friend & Bursuck, 2012; Schaller, Ynag, & Chang, 2004). Byrnes (2011) suggested that schools must go beyond the procedural due process requirements in IDEA and assure that parents are actively involved in their child's education. As such, every attempt should be made to prevent adversarial relationships, such as those that often occur in due process hearings. Such hearings may lead to mistrust and long-term problems. IDEA responds to the need for a mediation process to resolve any conflict between parents and school personnel and to prevent long-term adversarial relationships. The law requires states to establish a mediation system in which parents and schools voluntarily participate. In such a system, an impartial individual would listen to parents and school personnel and attempt to work out a mutually agreeable arrangement in the best interest of the student with a disability. Although mediation is intended to facilitate the parent and professional partnership, it must not be used to deny or delay the parents' right to a due process hearing.

The development of the IEP is a collaborative process, involving parents, educators, and students. Why is it important for parents to participate in the development of the IEP?

Standard 3
Individual Learning Differences

Standard 7
Instructional Planning

The Individualized Education Program (IEP)
The individualized education program (IEP) is a written statement that is the framework for delivering a free and appropriate public education to every eligible student with a disability. The IEP provides an opportunity for parents and professionals to join together in developing and delivering specially designed instruction to meet student needs.

Individualized education program (IEP)
A written framework for delivering appropriate and free education to every eligible disabled student.

Among Friends is a one-stop portal into the world of people with special needs and the people who love them. Sponsored by the Friendship Circle of Michigan, *Among Friends* is a nonprofit social media site with online learning and social media blogs to and from parents, siblings, volunteers, supporters, and even those with special needs themselves. (For more information, go to http://blog.friendshipcircle.org/.)

The following is a blog written by Rebecca Zusel, a licensed master social worker (LMSW), mother of three, practicing therapist, previous school social worker and active advocate, representing children with special needs and their families.

THE INDIVIDUALIZED EDUCATION PROGRAM: GETTING THE BEST FOR YOUR CHILD

A Blog by Rebecca Zusel

What happens when we disagree? A look at parents and educators getting together at school meetings…

Not often, but sometimes, when we gather a team together of parents and professionals to discuss the educational needs of a child, we don't always agree. You can be meeting at your child's school to discuss any number of things:

- Discovery of findings from a full scale evaluation
- Goal setting and accommodations
- Placement changes for Special Education
- Re-evaluation or termination from Special Education

These are just a few examples of what the "team" (psychologist, social worker, special education director, principal, teachers, other professional specialists . . .) may be discussing at a meeting. So what happens when either the parents or one of the school's team members don't agree? We want to go in with an open mind that everyone has the best interest of the child in mind. That being said, sometimes certain things are difficult for parents to hear from the professionals. It's often hard for parents to swallow the information they are hearing about their child for the first time in this meeting. And sometimes, both parents don't feel the same way. For example, I recently attended a meeting to determine a child's eligibility for special education. The findings spoke for themselves; the child had an undisputed learning disability, and thus had been struggling in school. It seemed straightforward, but it wasn't.

As the educators started discussing goals and accommodations, the mother started crying and the father started saying that he didn't want "his kid to be different." Dad felt that the child was "getting by" well enough that he really didn't need to be in "special ed." I could see where this was going and I started to get concerned; the direction of this meeting needed to stay on topic. This boy needed to be educated in the best way *he* is capable of learning. There is a lot of stigma associated with special education; it is very real for parents and children, especially the ones who are diagnosed at older ages.

Now let's look at another perspective: What if the school feels one way and the parents feel another? This can present itself in so many ways that we can't get too in depth about it. Ultimately, there are two things you should know as the parent. One, if the district feels you are not acting in the best interest of your child and that you are keeping services from the child, they can take you to court. Second, YOU have a right to fight for services and accommodations you feel your child needs if you feel they are being denied!

Here is the bottom line on this topic: We really want to work together as a "team." We want to have a good working relationship with the school district we live in and send our child to. That doesn't always happen so easily. Being in a team meeting can be extremely overwhelming when you are surrounded by a bunch of professionals and educators. Do yourself a favor. Bring someone along who can help you stay focused, unemotional, and on top of things! That person can be a friend, an outside therapist, or an advocate. It's only natural to be emotional and a little defensive when entering into one of these meetings. So, don't beat yourself up for having these feelings and don't question yourself if you find you disagree with the school's team. Everyone is trying to have your child's best interests at heart and get his/her needs met.

A neutral, nonemotional person who speaks and acts solely on the behalf of the child is a valuable tool in a team meeting. They can explain things to you in a gentler, kinder way. They can make suggestions that the team may not think of because they don't work for the district. It is just a different perspective.

SOURCE: Zusel, R. (2011). The Individualized Education Program: Getting the Most for Your Child. Retrieved December 23, 2011, from http://blog.friendshipcircle.org/2010/12/20/individualized-education-program-getting-the-best-for-your-child/.

The team responsible for developing the IEP consists of the student's parents; at least one special education teacher; at least one general education teacher if the child is, or may be, participating in the general education environment; and a school district representative. The school district representative must be qualified to provide, or supervise the provision of, specially designed instruction to meet the unique needs of children with disabilities. This educator must also be knowledgeable about the **general curriculum** and the availability of resources within the school. The IEP team must also include a professional(s) who can interpret the eligibility and instructional implications of the various assessment results. When appropriate, other professionals who have knowledge or special expertise regarding the child (including related services personnel) as well as the student with a disability may be included on the team at the discretion of the parents or school district.

General curriculum
Instructional content that all students are expected to learn in school. Specific content and performance standards for student achievement are set by individual states or local districts.

The purpose of the IEP process is to ensure continuity in the delivery of special education services and supports for each student on a daily and annual basis. The IEP is also intended to promote more effective communication between school personnel and the child's family. IDEA 2004 requires that each child's IEP must include:

- a statement of the child's present levels of academic achievement and functional performance, including how the child's disability affects the child's involvement and progress in the general education curriculum; for preschool children, as appropriate, also a statement of how the disability affects the child's participation in appropriate activities.

- a statement of measurable annual goals, including academic and functional goals, designed to meet the child's needs that result from the child's disability to enable the child to be involved in and make progress in the general education curriculum; and meet each of the child's other educational needs that result from the child's disability; for children with disabilities who take *alternate assessments* aligned to alternate achievement standards, include a description of benchmarks or short-term objectives.

- a description of how the child's progress toward meeting the annual goals described will be measured and when periodic reports on the progress the child is making toward meeting the annual goals will be provided.

- a statement of the special education and related services and supplementary aids and services, based on peer-reviewed research to the extent practicable, to be provided to the child, or on behalf of the child, and a statement of the program modifications or supports for school personnel that will be provided for the child to (a) advance appropriately toward attaining the annual goals, (b) be involved in and make progress in the general education curriculum and to participate in extracurricular and other nonacademic activities, and (c) be educated and participate with other children with disabilities and nondisabled children.

- an explanation of the extent, if any, to which the child will not participate with nondisabled children in the regular [general education] class.

- a statement of any individual appropriate accommodations that are necessary to measure the academic achievement and functional performance of the child on state and district-wide assessments, or if the IEP team determines that the child shall take an alternate assessment of student achievement, a statement of why the child cannot participate in the regular assessment; and the particular alternate assessment selected as appropriate for the child (IDEA, 2004, PL 108-446, Sec. 614[d]).

Education in the Least Restrictive Environment

All students with disabilities have the right to learn in an environment consistent with their academic, social, and physical needs—the **least restrictive environment (LRE)**. IDEA mandated that:

> To the maximum extent appropriate, children with disabilities, including children in public or private institutions or other care facilities, are educated with children who are not disabled, and that special classes, separate schooling, or other removal of children

Least restrictive environment (LRE)
Students with disabilities are to be educated with their peers without disabilities to the maximum extent appropriate.

with disabilities from the regular [general] education environment occurs only when the nature or severity of the disability is such that education in regular classes with the use of supplementary aids and services cannot be achieved satisfactorily. (IDEA, 2004, PL 108-446, Sec. 614[d])

CEC

Standard 3
Individual Learning
Differences

To be certain that schools meet this mandate, federal regulations required districts to develop a continuum of educational placements based on the individual needs of students. The continuum may range from placement in a general classroom with support services to homebound and hospital programs. Placement in a setting along this continuum is based on the premise that this is the most appropriate environment to implement a student's individualized program as developed by the IEP team. An educational services model depicting seven levels on the continuum of placements is presented in Figure 2.1.

Some parents and professionals have criticized the concept of "a continuum of placements" in recent years. The concern is that, despite IDEA's strong preference for students with disabilities to be educated with their peers who are not disabled, the continuum has legitimized and supported the need for more restrictive, segregated settings. Additionally, the continuum has created the perception that students with disabilities must "go to" services, rather than having services come to them. In other words, as students move farther from the general education class, the resources available to meet their needs increase concomitantly. Of the more than six million students with disabilities in U.S. schools, ages 6 to 21, 4 percent receive their education in separate schools, residential facilities, and homebound programs (U.S. Department of Education, 2011). For a closer look at who is being served in special education programs, and where, see Figure 2.2.

Figure 2.1 *Educational Service Options for Students with Disabilities.*

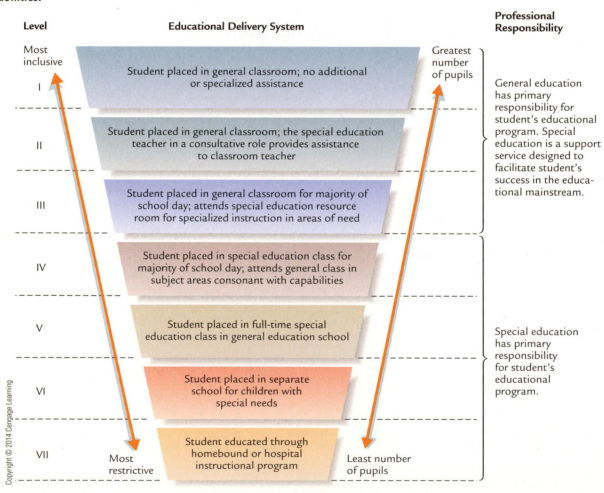

Copyright © 2014 Cengage Learning

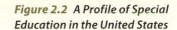
Figure 2.2 *A Profile of Special Education in the United States*

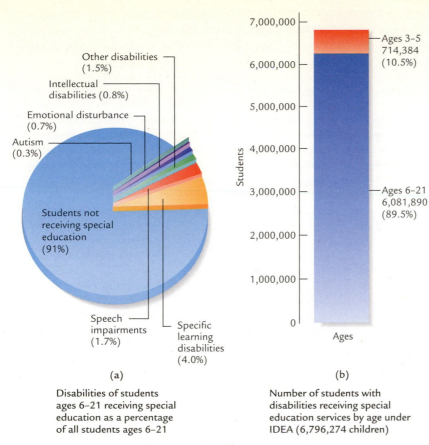

(a)

Disabilities of students ages 6–21 receiving special education as a percentage of all students ages 6–21

(b)

Number of students with disabilities receiving special education services by age under IDEA (6,796,274 children)

SOURCE: U.S. Department of Education. (2011). The Thirtieth Annual Report to Congress on the Implementation of the Individuals with Disabilities Education Act 2008. Washington, D.C.: U.S. Government Printing Office.

The Special Education Referral, Assessment, Planning, and Placement Process

The purpose of special education, as mandated in IDEA, is to ensure that all eligible students with disabilities have the opportunity to receive a free and appropriate public education. The process involves four sequential phases: (1) initiating the referral, (2) assessing student eligibility and educational need, (3) developing the individualized education program (IEP), and (4) determining the student's educational placement in the least restrictive environment. (See Table 2.2.)

FOCUS 4

Discuss the special education referral, assessment, planning, and placement process.

Phase I: Initiating the Referral

The referral process begins with a request to the school's *special services committee or child-study team* for an assessment to determine whether the student qualifies for special education services. Once the team receives the referral, it may choose one of two steps: (1) attempt to modify current instruction in the general education class through **coordinated early intervening services,** or (2) conduct a formal evaluation to determine the student's eligibility for special education services.

The first step, coordinated early intervening services, involves instructional adaptations, modifications, or accommodations designed to provide additional support to children who are at risk for educational failure prior to referring them for special education services. Adaptations may vary according to student need but most often involve modifying curriculum, changing a seating arrangement, changing the length and difficulty of homework or classroom assignments, using peer tutors or volunteer parents to assist with instructional programs, or implementing a behavior management program. It is the responsibility of the general education teacher to implement the modified instruction and

Coordinated early intervening services
The provision of services and supports for students who have not yet been identified as needing special education and related services but who need extra academic and behavior support to succeed in the general education classroom.

Table 2.2   The Special Education Referral, Assessment, Planning, and Placement Process

Phase 1 Initiating the Referral	Phase 2 Assessing Student Eligibility and Educational Need	Phase 3 Developing the Individualized Education Program (IEP)	Phase 4 Determining the Least Restrictive Environment (LRE)
• School personnel or parents indicate concern about student's learning, behavior, or overall development. • If referral is made by school personnel, parents are notified of concerns. • Child-study team decides to provide additional support services and adapt student's instructional program prior to initiating formal assessment for eligibility. (This step may be bypassed, and team may choose to immediately seek parental permission to evaluate the student's eligibility for special education.) • School seeks and receives parents' permission to evaluate student's eligibility for special education services. (This will occur if the additional support services and adaptive instruction are unsuccessful OR if the team has chosen to move directly to a formal evaluation to determine student eligibility.)	• Multidisciplinary and non-discriminatory assessment tools and strategies are used to evaluate student's eligibility for special education services. • Child-study team reviews assessment information to determine (1) whether student meets eligibility requirements for special education services under one of 12 disability classifications or meets the definition of developmentally delayed (for students between ages 3 and 9), and (2) whether student requires special education services. • If team agrees that the student is eligible for and needs special education services, then the process moves to Phase 3: developing the IEP.	• Appropriate professionals to serve on an IEP team are identified. A team coordinator is appointed. • Parents (and student when appropriate) participate as equal members of the team and are provided with written copies of all assessment information. • Team meets and agrees upon the essential elements of the student's individualized education program plan: • Measurable annual goals • Skill areas needing special education and related services • People responsible for providing services and supports to meet student's identified needs • Criteria/evaluation procedures to assess progress • Student's access to the general education curriculum • Student's participation in statewide or school district assessments • Beginning and end dates for special education services • A process for reporting to parents on student's progress toward annual goals • Positive behavioral intervention plan if needed	• Identify potential educational placements based on student's annual goals and special education services to be provided. • Adhering to the principle that students with disabilities are to be educated with their peers without disabilities to the maximum extent appropriate, justify any removal of the child from the general education classroom. • With parents involved in the decision-making process, determine student's appropriate educational placement. • Document, on the student's IEP, justification for any removal from the general education classroom. • Team members agree in writing to the essential elements of the IEP and to the educational placement where special education and related services are to be provided. • As members of the IEP team, parents must consent in writing to the agreed-upon educational placement for their child.

to assess the student's progress over a predetermined period of time. If the modifications are successful, a referral for special education is not necessary.

Should the team determine that the student's educational progress is not satisfactory, even with the use of early intervening services, a formal referral for special education may be initiated. The formal referral begins with the team's analysis of the information provided by education professionals and parents in order to further understand the child's educational needs. Documentation may include results from achievement tests, classroom performance tests, samples of student work, behavioral observations, or anecdotal notes (such as teacher journal entries). The team must also decide whether additional assessment information is needed to determine the child's eligibility for special education. At this time, a written notice must be provided to parents that includes all of the following:

- A full explanation of the safeguards available to the parents
- A description of the action proposed or refused by the school, why the school proposes or refuses to take the action, and a description of any options the school considered and the reasons why those options were rejected

© JLP/Jose L. Pelaez/Corbis

Early intervening services involve adapting instruction to the need of the student before initiating a referral for special education services. What are some early intervening strategies that teachers can use in their classroom?

- A description of each evaluation procedure, test, record, or report the school used as a basis for the proposal or refusal
- A description of any other factors relevant to the school's proposal or refusal to take action

Following a written notice, the school must seek written parental consent to move ahead with further evaluation. Informed consent means that parents

- have been fully informed of all information relevant to the activity for which consent is sought, in their native language or other mode of communication;
- understand and agree in writing to the carrying out of the activity for which his or her consent is sought; the consent describes that activity and lists the record (if any) that will be released and to whom; and
- understand that the granting of consent is voluntary on the part of the parent and may be revoked at any time.

Phase 2: Assessing Student Eligibility and Educational Need

Once parents give written consent to evaluate, the school child-study team moves ahead to assess the student's eligibility for special education services under IDEA. The assessment should include the student's performance in both school and home environments. When the assessment process is complete, a decision is made regarding the student's eligibility for special education and his or her disability classification (such as specific learning disabilities, autism, and so on).

Phase 3: Developing the Individualized Education Program (IEP)

The IEP is a cornerstone of a free and appropriate public education (Huefner, 2012; National Information Center for Children and Youth with Disabilities, 2011). Once it has been determined that the student is eligible for special education services under IDEA, the next step is to establish an IEP team. At a minimum, this team consists of the student's parents, the student (when appropriate), a special education teacher, a general education teacher (if the student is participating in the general education environment), and a representative of the local education agency (LEA). As stated in IDEA, the LEA representative must be qualified to provide, or supervise the provision of, specially designed instruction to meet the unique needs of children with disabilities; be knowledgeable about the general education curriculum; and be knowledgeable about the availability of resources of the local educational agency (IDEA, 2004, PL 108-446, Sec. 614[b][D][iv]). Additionally, IDEA requires that someone must be available (either a current team member or someone from

CEC
Standard 3
Individual Learning Differences

CEC
Standard 3
Individual Learning Differences

Standard 8
Assessment

outside of the team, such as a school psychologist) to interpret each student's assessment results. At the discretion of the parents or school district, other individuals with knowledge or special expertise, including related services specialists, may also be invited to participate on the IEP team.

Each IEP team should have a coordinator (such as the special education teacher, school psychologist, or school principal) who serves as liaison between the school and the family. The coordinator has the responsibility to (1) inform parents and respond to any concerns they may have regarding the IEP process, (2) assist parents in developing specific goals they would like to see their child achieve, (3) schedule IEP meetings that are mutually convenient for both team members and parents, and (4) lead the IEP meetings. Prior to the initial IEP meeting, parents should be provided with written copies of all assessment information on their child. Individual conferences with members of the IEP team or a full team meeting may be necessary prior to developing the IEP. This will further assist parents in understanding and interpreting assessment information. Analysis of the assessment information should include a summary of the child's strengths as well as areas in which the child may require special education or related services.

Once there is mutual agreement between educators and parents on the interpretation of the assessment results, the team coordinator organizes and leads the IEP meeting(s). Such meetings are meant to achieve the following purposes:

- Document each student's present levels of performance.
- Agree upon measurable annual goals (and objectives/benchmarks for children with disabilities who take alternate assessments aligned to alternate achievement standards).
- Identify skill areas needing special education (including physical education) and related services, the people responsible for delivering these services, and the criteria/evaluation procedures to assess progress.
- Document student access to the general curriculum.
- Document student participation in state- and district-wide assessment programs with individual modifications or adaptations made, as necessary, in how the tests are administered. For children who cannot participate in regular assessments, the team must document use of state-developed **alternate assessments**.
- Establish beginning and end dates for special education services.
- Determine a process for reporting to parents on student progress toward annual goals.

See Figure 2.3, a sample individualized education program for Diane, an elementary-age student with disabilities.

Alternate assessments
Assessments mandated in IDEA 1997 for students who are unable to participate in required state- or district-wide assessments. They ensure that all students, regardless of the severity of their disabilities, are included in the state's accountability system.

Standard 3
Individual Learning Differences

Phase 4: Determining the Student's Educational Placement in the Least Restrictive Environment

The decision regarding placement is based on the answers to two questions: First, what is the appropriate placement for the student, given his or her annual goals? Second, which of the placement alternatives under consideration is consistent with the least restrictive environment? As stated in IDEA, the student is to be educated to the maximum extent appropriate with peers who are not disabled. To ensure that this principle is applied in making placement decisions, IDEA begins with the premise that the general education classroom is where all children belong. As such, any movement away from the general education class must be justified and documented on the student's IEP. The IEP must be the result of a collaborative process that reflects the views of both the school and the family. For more information on the special education referral, assessment, planning, and placement process, see the nearby TeachSource Video, "Students with Special Needs: The Referral and Evaluation Process."

Once the school team has determined that a student is eligible for special education services, educators, related services personnel, parents, and students must consider many important issues in the development of IEP goals and objectives as well as determine the most appropriate educational placement. For a more in-depth look into these considerations, see the nearby Case Study, "Jerald."

Figure 2.3 A Sample Individualized Education Program (IEP) for Diane: An Elementary-Age Student with Disabilities.

STUDENT'S PRIMARY CLASSIFICATION: SERIOUS EMOTIONAL DISTURBANCE
SECONDARY CLASSIFICATION: NONE

Student Name   _Diane_

Date of Birth   _5-3-98_

Primary Language:
   HOME   _English_   Student   _English_

Date of IEP Meeting   _April 27, 2011_

Entry Date to Program   _April 27, 2011_

Projected Duration of Services   _One school year_

Required   _Specify amount of time in educational and/or related services per day or week_

General Education Class   _4 to 5 hours/day_

Resource Room   _1 to 2 hours/day_

Special Ed Consultation in General Ed Classroom   _Co-teaching and consultation with general education teacher in the areas of academic and adaptive skills as indicated in annual goals_

Self-Contained   _None_

Related Services   _Group counseling sessions twice weekly with guidance counselor. Counseling to focus on adaptive skill development as described in annual goals and short-term objectives_

P.E. Program   _45 minutes daily in general ed PE class with support from adapted PE teacher as necessary_

Assessment

Intellectual   _WISC R_

Educational   _Key Math Woodcock Reading_

Behavioral/Adaptive   _Burks_

Speech/Language

Other

Vision   _Within normal limits_

Hearing   _Within normal limits_

Classroom Observation Done

Dates   _1/15-2/25/2011_

Personnel Conducting Observation   _School Psychologist, Special Education Teacher, General Education Teacher_

Present Level of Performance Strengths

1. Polite to teachers and peers
2. Helpful and cooperative in the classroom
3. Good grooming skills
4. Good in sports activities

Access to General Education Curriculum

Diane will participate in all content areas within the general education curriculum. Special education supports and services will be provided in the areas of math, reading, and social skills development.

Effect of Disability on Access to General Education Curriculum

Emotional disabilities make it difficult for Diane to achieve at expected grade-level performance in general education curriculum in the areas of reading and math. It is expected that this will further impact her access to the general education curriculum in other content areas (such as history, biology, English) as she enters junior high school.

Participation in Statewide or District Assessments

Diane will participate in all state and district-wide assessments of achievement. No adaptations or modifications required for participation.

Justification for Removal from General Education Classroom

Diane's objectives require that she be placed in a general education classroom with support from a special education teacher for the majority of the school day. Based on adaptive behavior assessment and observations, Diane will receive instruction in a resource room for approximately 1 to 2 hours per day in the areas of social skills development.

Reports to Parents on Progress toward Annual Goals

Parents will be informed of Diane's progress through weekly reports of progress on short-term goals, monthly phone calls from general ed teachers, special education teachers, and school psychologist, as well as regularly scheduled report cards at the end of each term.

Figure 2.3 *A Sample Individualized Education Program (IEP) for Diane: An Elementary-Age Student with Disabilities. (continued)*

Areas Needing Specialized Instruction and Support

1. Adaptive Skills

- *Limited interaction skills with peers and adults*
- *Excessive facial tics and grimaces*
- *Difficulty staying on task in content subjects, especially reading and math*
- *Difficulty expressing feelings, needs, and interests*

2. Academic Skills

- *Significantly below grade level in math—3.9*
- *Significantly below grade level in reading—4.3*

Annual Review: _____ Date: _____

Comments/Recommendations

_____

_____

_____

_____

_____

STUDENT'S PRIMARY CLASSIFICATION: SERIOUS EMOTIONAL DISTURBANCE

SECONDARY CLASSIFICATION: NONE

Team Signatures   IEP Review Date _____

LEA Rep. _____

Parent _____

Sp Ed Teacher _____

Gen Ed Teacher _____

School Psych _____

Student (as appropriate) _____

Related Services Personnel (as appropriate) _____

Objective Criteria and Evaluation Procedures _____

Please visit the Education CourseMate website for *Human Exceptionality*, 11th edition, at CengageBrain.com to access this TeachSource Video. The student referral process is extremely complex, requiring the teacher to give careful consideration to a student's past history and learning challenges before approaching the referral team. In this video, you'll see how fourth-grade teacher Mike Costello approaches the referral process on behalf of a student he is concerned about. Mike first goes through a pre-referral stage and implements the team's recommendations before advocating that his student be tested by specialists in a variety of domains. You'll hear Mike's commentary on his student's strengths and weaknesses, and why he believes further evaluation will be in his student's best interest.

Respond to the following questions:

1. What reasons did teacher, Mike Costello, indicate as the need to bring Caitlin for referral to the school assessment team?

2. What does Mr. Costello identify as Caitlin's educational strengths as well as areas in which she is struggling and needs additional instructional modifications and support?

3. Describe the school's pre-referral process known as "the Teacher Assistance Team (TAG)" in assisting students prior to a formal referral for special education services.

4. Based on the pre-referral assessment of Caitlin's educational progress and instructional needs, Mr. Costello and the Teacher Assistance Team recommend moving forward with a formal referral to assess and evaluate Caitlin's eligibility for special education services. What are the steps as described by the team in completing this formal referral process? What is the parents' role in referral? Identify the responsibilities for each member of the team in assessing Caitlin's need for specialized instructional services. What are the two primary criteria that the team is looking for in determining whether Caitlin is eligible for special education services?

Educating Students with Disabilities in the 21st Century: From Access to Accountability

The education of students with disabilities has gone through many changes during the past three decades. In this section, we take a closer look at 21st-century U.S. schools and the national policies that impact each student's opportunity for a free and appropriate public education. The rallying cry in today's schools is "higher expectations for all students."

A Standards-Based Approach to Improving Student Achievement

National education policy under the Elementary and Secondary Education Act (as amended in 2001) uses a **standards-based approach** as the basis for improving the quality of U.S. schools. That is, schools must set high standards for what should be taught and how student performance should be measured based on these standards. Three principles that characterize a standards-based approach to school accountability are:

1. A focus on student achievement as the primary measure of school success

2. An emphasis on challenging academic standards that specify the knowledge and skills students should acquire and the levels at which they should demonstrate these skills in getting ready for college or beginning a career

3. A desire to extend the standards to all students, including those for whom expectations have been traditionally low (U.S. Department of Education, 2011)

Federal involvement has been, and continues to be, a strong influence on the reform of educational programs and services for students with disabilities. Prior to the

FOCUS 5
Identify three principles that are intended to assure that schools across the nation are accountable for student learning. Under IDEA 2004, What must a student's IEP include to ensure access to the general curriculum?

Standards-based approach
Instruction emphasizes challenging academic standards of knowledge and skills, and the levels at which students should demonstrate mastery of them.

Standard 1
Foundations

AP Photo/Rusty Kennedy

Students with disabilities must have access to the general curriculum and be included in statewide testing programs when appropriate. Do you think participation in the general curriculum results in higher academic achievement for students with disabilities?

congressional reauthorizations of IDEA in 1997 and 2004, federal policy concentrated on ensuring *access* to a free and appropriate public education (FAPE). In clarifying the definition of FAPE, the courts required schools to make available individualized, specially designed instruction and related services resulting in "some educational benefit." Eventually, the "some educational benefit standard" was further expanded to ensure meaningful progress that could be measured for each student.

Many advocates for educational reform have strongly emphasized the importance of including students with disabilities in a state and school district accountability system (Huefner, 2012). However, as much of the policy research suggests, the participation of students with disabilities in the general curriculum and statewide assessments of student performance varied considerably from state to state and district to district (Hardman & Mulder, 2004; Hardman & Dawson, 2008). Hehir (2002) suggests that "one of the reasons students with disabilities [were] not performing better is that they have not had sufficient access to the general curriculum" (p. 6). States and school districts were keeping students with disabilities out of their accountability systems because fears that they would pull down scores.

In response to these concerns, IDEA 2004 requires that a student's IEP must describe how the disability affects the child's involvement and progress *in the general curriculum*. The law requires an explanation of any individual modifications in the administration of state- or district-wide assessment of student achievement that are needed for the child to participate.

The promise of IDEA 2004 is straightforward—all students can and will learn more than they are currently learning, and all students will succeed if schools expect the highest academic standards. If students don't succeed, then public schools must be held accountable for their failure. The definition of success is determined by student proficiency on content specified by the state and as measured by state performance standards. The promise of "all means all" includes students with disabilities. Therefore, students with disabilities must be assured access to (1) "highly qualified and effective" teachers who are knowledgeable in the subject matter area(s) being taught; (2) a curriculum upon which the standards are based; (3) assessments that measure performance on the standards; and (4) inclusion in the reported results that determine how well a school is meeting the established performance criteria. During the past two decades, the promise that every student will learn and succeed has been translated into public policy. Although public policy provides the impetus for every student to learn and succeed, the critical issue is whether the promise becomes reality.

For a more in-depth look at contrasting perspectives on the inclusion of students with disabilities in a standards-driven system as mandated in IDEA 2004, see the nearby Debate Forum, "Educational Accountability for Students with Disabilities: High Academic Achievement or Inevitable Failure?"

Section 504/ADA and Reasonable Accommodations

FOCUS 6

Distinguish between students with disabilities eligible for services under Section 504/ADA and those eligible under IDEA.

U.S. schools must provide supports and services to two groups of students with disabilities. One group qualifies for special education services under IDEA because their disability limits their access to an appropriate education. Another group, not viewed as educationally limited

CASE STUDY JERALD

Jerald is finishing up his last two months in a second-grade classroom at Robert F. Kennedy Elementary School. Kennedy is a large urban school with a number of students from low economic and culturally diverse backgrounds. Many of its students are described as "disadvantaged" and at significant risk of school failure. Next year, Jerald will move to third grade, and his parents and teachers have expressed some concerns. "Jerry is an outgoing kid who loves to talk about anything to anyone at any time," says his mother. His current second-grade teacher, Miss Robins, complains that he is "hyperactive, inattentive, and a behavior problem." His mom, his dad, and his teacher agree that Jerald has a great deal of difficulty with controlling his emotions.

MOTHER: I just wish he wasn't so easily frustrated at home when things aren't going his way.

MISS ROBINS: He's always in a state of fight or flight. When he is in a fighting mode, he hits, teases, and screams at me or the other students. When in a state of "flight," he withdraws and refuses to comply with any requests. He may even put his head on his desk and openly cry to vent his frustrations.

During second grade, Jerald's "fight" behavior has increased considerably. Miss Robins reported that "he has made very little progress and is uncontrollable—a very disruptive influence on the other children in the class." With permission from Jerald's parents, she initiated a referral to the school's child-study team to assess his eligibility for special education services. His overall assessment indicated that he was falling further behind in reading (word-decoding skills at grade level 1.5; reading comprehension at grade level 1.0) and math (grade level 1.9).

Behaviorally, Jerald has difficulty expressing his feelings in an appropriate manner. He is impulsive, easily distracted, and not well liked by his peers. After determining his eligibility for special education services, the school IEP team developed Jerald's third-grade annual goals and objectives:

1. Improve Jerald's reading and math achievement by ensuring access to general curriculum with specialized academic instruction and support— Jerald is to be included in the district and state testing program.

2. Teach Jerald the skills to (a) manage his own behavior when faced with difficult or frustrating situations, and (b) improve daily interactions with teachers and peers—the activities for these goals will be included on the IEP as components of Jerald's *behavioral intervention plan*.

Once the team had agreed on annual goals for Jerald, they discussed various classroom and school settings that would be appropriate to his needs as described in the IEP. Miss Robins and the school principal were concerned that his disruptive behavior would be too difficult to control in a general education classroom. They wanted to place him in a special self-contained class for emotionally disturbed students. They were concerned not only about Jerald's education but also about his negative effect on his classroom peers. Miss Robins reported that she had to spend a disproportionate amount of her time dealing with Jerald's inappropriate behavior.

Taking into account the views of Jerald's teachers and the school principal, the team is considering placement in a special education class for students with serious behavior problems. Such a class is not available at his home school,

so Jerald would have to be transported to a special education program in another location. Ms. Beckman, the special education consulting teacher, has an alternative point of view. She proposes that Jerald stay at Kennedy Elementary and that his behavioral intervention plan and specialized academic instruction be implemented in next year's third-grade classroom. Working in collaboration with Jerald's general education teacher and other members of the school's assistance team, Ms. Beckman suggests using cooperative learning techniques, co-teaching among the general and special education teachers, and ongoing support from the school psychologist.

Jerald's parents, although they recognize that his disruptive behavior is increasing and that he is falling further behind academically, are reluctant to have him transferred to another school. They feel it would remove him from his family and neighborhood supports. His brother, who will be in the fifth grade, also goes to Kennedy Elementary.

APPLICATION

1. What do you see as the important issues for the team to consider in deciding what educational setting would be most appropriate to meet Jerald's needs?

2. In addition to the recommendations made by Ms. Beckman, the special education resource room teacher, what suggestions would you have to adapt Jerald's academic and behavioral program if he were to remain in his third-grade class at Kennedy Elementary?

3. Should he remain in his third-grade class at Kennedy Elementary?

DEBATE FORUM EDUCATIONAL ACCOUNTABILITY FOR STUDENTS WITH DISABILITIES: HIGH ACADEMIC ACHIEVEMENT OR INEVITABLE FAILURE?

Standards-based educational reform is based on the premise that improving student achievement is highly correlated with an accountability system that is inclusive of all students. However, this premise has generated considerable debate within the field of education. In the following Debate Forum, we examine contrasting perspectives on including students with disabilities in a standards-driven system with high-stakes accountability.

POINT

Proponents of including students with disabilities in a system that focuses on "educating all children" argue that doing so enables these students to experience a wider variety of subjects at a deeper level. This exposes students with disabilities to higher-order thinking skills such as problem solving, enables them to develop collaborative skills, and engenders responsibility and self-esteem (Florian, 2007; McLaughlin & Tilstone, 2000). An inclusive educational system built on common standards for all students promotes more collaboration among special and general educators, requiring them to develop more challenging learner goals and raise expectations for students with disabilities.

Proponents also argue that if students know their promotion to a higher grade level or high school graduation is dependent on their attainment of a particular standard, they will be motivated to achieve at a higher performance level. Traditionally, special education students have not been held accountable to meeting their IEP goals. This sometimes results in a lowering of individual expectations and a failure to learn essential skills. As a corollary, special educators have not been accountable for the poor performance of their students; they often regard the IEP as paper compliance rather than an accountability tool (Riddell, 2007; Sebba, Thurlow, & Goertz, 2000). Including students in a standards-driven system forces teachers to use the IEP as an accountability blueprint, altering goals and objectives to ensure student progress in the general curriculum.

Some educators accept the premise that standards-based reform should apply to all students, but they are uneasy about including test scores from students with disabilities in the accountability system. Educators are also concerned about the impact on teachers. Teachers and principals may become anxious about the consequences of published low scores. They may fear that students with disabilities will negatively affect publicly available scores and that schools will blame them.

COUNTERPOINT

Opponents of the standards-based approach raise several concerns. First, they maintain, failure is inevitable because there is insufficient instructional time and resources to meet the educational needs of students with disabilities. Second, there is no evidence that a standards-driven system will actually lead to sustained higher levels of achievement among students with disabilities, and no indication "whether the skills gained through this curriculum are the ones that will prove necessary for successful transition from school" (McLaughlin & Tilstone, 2000, p. 62).

Establishing content standards for students with disabilities at the state level is inconsistent with the concept of individualization; it is not in the best interests of disabled students or their nondisabled peers. A fear exists that if all students are expected to reach the same standard, then the bar will be lowered to accommodate those with less ability. If the bar isn't lowered, then students with disabilities will routinely fail to meet the standard. Teachers may feel powerless because they believe it is not possible for all students to reach the required standards.

Another issue is that including students with disabilities within a standards-driven system will affect their rate of high school graduation. The failure to graduate has serious repercussions in today's society. Students who continually fail to reach required standards won't receive a high school diploma in a high-stakes system. One reason for ensuring student access to the general curriculum was the need to improve results. Ironically, it is possible that the requirement of high standards in the general curriculum may instead further compromise the graduation rate for students with disabilities.

Some educators believe that inclusion in a standards-driven system will damage the self-esteem of students with disabilities if they do not perform well. Valuable instruction time would be spent teaching content in academic areas, rather than concentrating on the acquisition of critical functional skills. To facilitate a student's mastery of academic skills, teachers could be forced to remove students from the

by their disability and therefore ineligible for special education, are protected against discrimination under Section 504 of the Vocational Rehabilitation Act and the Americans with Disabilities Act (ADA). Together, Section 504 and ADA address issues of nondiscrimination and equal opportunity for students with disabilities

Students with disabilities eligible under Section 504/ADA are entitled to have a *written plan* that ensures access to an education comparable to that of students who are not disabled. A **504/ADA plan** is different from an IEP in its scope and intent. Whereas an IEP is concerned with ensuring access to a free and appropriate education designed to provide educational benefit, a 504 plan provides for reasonable accommodations or modifications as a means to "create a fair and level playing field" for the student. For example, a student who uses as wheelchair, but does not require special education services may still need a written 504/ADA plan to assure access to adapted transportation or physical therapy (Huefner, 2012). Table 2.3 provides a comparison of IDEA and 504/ADA provisions.

504/ADA plan
Provides for reasonable accommodations or modifications in assessment and instruction to "create a fair and level playing field" for students who qualify as disabled under Section 504 of the Vocational Rehabilitation Act and the Americans with Disabilities Act.

Many professionals and parents of students with disabilities are concerned that if schools allow a cessation of services, IDEA's zero-exclusion principle would be undermined. Others argue that students with disabilities should be treated no differently than students without disabilities when the individual is likely to cause injury to others and themselves.

In dealing with this controversial issue, IDEA 2004 reiterated that a free and appropriate public education must be available to all students with disabilities and that there should be no cessation of services. Schools must seek to employ instructional alternatives to expulsion—that is, helping children to learn decision-making and problem-solving skills that promote acceptable behavior.

Looking Toward a Bright Future

This chapter has briefly discussed a history of special education services within the overall context of educational reform in the United States. Over the last four decades, national policy in the United States has reaffirmed the rights of students with disabilities who are eligible for special education services to a free and appropriate public education (FAPE). In doing so, the Individuals with Disabilities Education Act established five basic tenets to assure every eligible student's access to FAPE. In looking to the future, it is certainly appropriate to say that "much has been accomplished and much remains to be done." As suggested by the President's Commission on Excellence in Special Education (2002):

> *Four decades ago, [the U.S.] Congress began to lend the resources of the federal government to the task of educating children with disabilities. Since then, special education has become one of the most important symbols of American compassion, inclusion, and educational opportunity. Over the years, what has become known as the Individuals with Disabilities Education Act has moved children with disabilities from institutions into classrooms, from the outskirts of society to the center of class*

Table 2.3 A Comparison of the Purposes and Provisions of IDEA and Section 504/ADA

	IDEA	Section 504/ADA
General Purpose	Provides financial aid to states in their efforts to ensure adequate and appropriate services for children and youth with disabilities.	Prevents discrimination on the basis of disability in employment, programs, and services provided by state and local governments, goods and services provided by private companies, and commercial facilities.
Definition of Disability	Identifies 12 categories of disability conditions. However, the law also allows states and school districts the option of eliminating categories for children ages 3 through 9 and defining them as developmentally delayed.	Identifies students as disabled if they meet the definition of a qualified handicapped (disabled) person (i.e., student has or has had a physical or mental impairment that substantially limits a major life activity, or student is regarded as disabled by others).
Responsibility to Provide a Free and Appropriate Public Education (FAPE)	Both statutes require the provision of a free and appropriate education, including individually designed instruction, to students covered under specific eligibility criteria.	
	Requires a written IEP document.	Does not require a written IEP document but does require a written plan.
	"Appropriate education" means a program designed to provide "educational benefit."	"Appropriate" means an education comparable to the education provided to students who are not disabled.
Special Education or General Education	Student is eligible to receive IDEA services only if the child-study team determines that the student is disabled under one of the 12 qualifying conditions and requires special education. Eligible students receive special education and related services.	Eligible student meets the definition of a qualified person with a disability: one who currently has or has had a physical or mental impairment that substantially limits a major life activity or who is regarded as disabled by others. The student is not required to need special education to be protected.
Funding	Provides additional funding if a student is eligible.	Does not provide additional funds.
Accessibility	Requires that modifications be made, if necessary, to provide access to a free and appropriate education.	Includes regulations regarding building and program accessibility.
Notice Safeguards	Both statutes require notice to the parent or guardian with respect to identification, evaluation, and/or placement.	
	Requires written notice.	Does not require written notice, but a district would be wise to provide it.
	Delineates required components of written notice.	Particular components are not delineated.
	Requires written notices prior to *any* change in placement.	Requires notice only before a "significant change" in placement.
Evaluations	Requires consent before an initial evaluation is conducted.	Does not require consent but does require notice.
	Requires reevaluations at least every three years.	Requires periodic reevaluations.
	Requires an update and/or review before *any* change in placement.	Requires reevaluation before a significant change in placement.
	Provides for independent educational evaluations.	Independent educational evaluations are not mentioned.

Table 2.3	A Comparison of the Purposes and Provisions of IDEA and Section 504/ADA *(continued)*	
Due Process	Both statutes require districts to provide impartial hearings for parents or guardians who disagree with the identification, evaluation, or placement of a student with disabilities.	
	Specific requirements are detailed in IDEA.	Requires that the parent have an opportunity to participate and be represented by counsel. Other details are left to the discretion of the local school district. These should be covered in school district policy.
Enforcement	Enforced by the Office of Special Education Programs in the Department of Education.	Enforced by the Office for Civil Rights in the Department of Justice.

instruction. Children who were once ignored are now protected by the law and given unprecedented access to a "free and appropriate public education." But America's special education system presents new and continuing challenges. . . . Hundreds of thousands of parents have seen the benefit of America's inclusive education system. But many more see room for improvement. . . . Although it is true that special education has created a base of civil rights and legal protections, children with disabilities remain those most at risk of being left behind. (President's Commission on Excellence in Special Education, 2002)

Today, a number of important questions are yet to be answered. A formidable challenge lies ahead if educators and families are able to come together and ensure that every student has the opportunity to learn. The mantra of "education for all" remains more a promise than a reality in today's schools. Although there is considerable agreement with the intent of IDEA 2004 to improve student learning, the means to achieve the goal are controversial. Clearly, research is needed to directly support or refute the assumption within national policy that a standards-based education system will improve results for all students, including those with disabilities. Without such evidence, educators will continue to operate in a vacuum of opinion. Finally, it will be critical that all general and special educators have the knowledge and skills to work collaboratively in partnership with families to provide an education experience that consistently reflects the stated value of an *education for all*.

FOCUS REVIEW

FOCUS 1 What educational services were available for students with disabilities during most of the 20th century?

- Educational programs at the beginning of the 20th century were provided primarily in separate, special schools.
- For the first 75 years of the 20th century, the availability of educational programs for students with disabilities was sporadic and selective. Special education was allowed in many states but required in only a few.
- Research on the efficacy of special classes for students with mild disabilities suggested that there was little or no benefit in removing students from general education classrooms.

FOCUS 2 Identify the principal issues in the right-to-education cases that led to eventual passage of the national mandate to educate students with disabilities.

- The U.S. Supreme Court reaffirmed education as a right and not a privilege.
- In Pennsylvania, the court ordered the schools to provide a free public education to all children with mental retardation of ages 6 to 21.
- The *Mills* case extended the right to a free public education to all school-age children with disabilities.

FOCUS 3 Identify five major provisions of the Individuals with Disabilities Education Act (IDEA).

- The labeling and placement of students with disabilities in educational programs required the use of nondiscriminatory and multidisciplinary assessment.
- Parental safeguards and involvement in the educational process included consent for testing and placement, and participation as a team member in the development of an IEP.
- Procedural safeguards (e.g., due process) were included to protect the child and family from decisions that could adversely affect their lives.
- Every student with a disability is entitled to a free and appropriate public education.
- The delivery of an appropriate education occurs through an individualized education program (IEP).
- All children have the right to learn in an environment consistent with their academic, social, and physical needs. The law mandated that children with disabilities receive their education with peers without disabilities to the maximum extent appropriate.

FOCUS 4 Discuss the special education referral, assessment, planning, and placement process.

- Initiating the referral: A student is referred for an assessment to determine whether he or she qualifies for special education services. Once the school's child-study team receives the referral, it may try to modify or adapt instruction in the general education classroom or conduct a formal assessment to determine whether the student is eligible for special education.
- Assessing student eligibility and educational need: A multidisciplinary team of professionals conducts a nondiscriminatory assessment of the student's needs, including performance in both school and home environments, to determine eligibility for special education.
- Developing the individualized education program (IEP): An IEP team is established that includes professionals and parents. This team is responsible for documenting the student's present level of performance; agreeing on measurable annual goals; identifying skill areas where special education

and related services are needed; documenting access to the general curriculum and participation in state- and district-wide assessments; establishing beginning and ending dates for special education services; and determining a process for reporting to parents on student progress in meeting annual goals.

- Determining the least restrictive environment: Once the IEP team has agreed upon annual goals, a decision is made regarding the most appropriate educational placement to meet the student's individual needs.

FOCUS 5 Identify three principles that are intended to assure that schools across the nation are accountable for student learning. Under IDEA 2004, What must a student's IEP include to ensure access to the general curriculum?

- The three principles include:
  1. A focus on student achievement as the primary measure of school success
  2. An emphasis on challenging academic standards that specify the knowledge and skills students should acquire and the levels at which they should demonstrate mastery of that knowledge
  3. A desire to extend the standards to all students, including those for whom expectations have been traditionally low
- IDEA 2004 requires that a student's IEP must describe how the disability affects the child's involvement and progress in the general curriculum. IEP goals must enable the child to access the general curriculum when appropriate.

FOCUS 6 Distinguish between students with disabilities eligible for services under Section 504/ADA and those eligible under IDEA.

- Students eligible under ADA are entitled to accommodations and/or modifications to their educational program that will ensure that they receive an appropriate education comparable to that of their peers without disabilities.
- Students eligible under IDEA are entitled to special education and related services to ensure they receive a free and appropriate education.

Council for Exceptional Children (CEC) Standards to Accompany Chapter 2

 If you are thinking about a career in special education, you should know that many states use national standards developed by the Council for Exceptional Children (CEC) to assess a teacher candidate's knowledge and skills for working with students with disabilities. See a complete listing of the 10 CEC Content Standards on the inside back cover of this text.

1 Foundations
2 Development and Characteristics of Learners
3 Individual Learning Differences
7 Instructional Planning
8 Assessment
9 Professional and Ethical Practice

Mastery Activities and Assignments

To master the content within this chapter, complete the following activities and assignments. Online and interactive versions of these activities are also available on the accompanying Education CourseMate website, where you may also access TeachSource videos, chapter web links, interactive quizzes, portfolio activities, flash cards, an integrated eBook, and much more!

1. Complete a written test of the chapter's content. If your instructor requires a written test of your content knowledge for this chapter, keep a copy for your portfolio. A practice test on the information covered in this chapter is available through the Education CourseMate website.

2. Review the Case Study, "Jerald," and respond in writing to the Application Questions. Keep a copy of the case study and your written response for your portfolio.

3. Read the Debate Forum, "Educational Accountability for Students with Disabilities: High Academic Achievement or Inevitable Failure?" in this chapter and then visit the Education CourseMate website to complete the activity, "Take a Stand." Keep a copy of this activity for your portfolio.

4. Participate in a community service learning activity. Service learning is a valuable way to enhance your learning experience. Visit the Education CourseMate website for suggested community service learning activities that correspond to the information presented in this chapter. Develop a reflective journal of the service learning experience for your portfolio.

Inclusion and Multidisciplinary Collaboration in the Early Childhood and Elementary School Years

© Robin Nelson/ZUMA Press/Corbis

FOCUS PREVIEW

As you read the chapter, focus on these key concepts:

1 Define inclusive education.

2 Describe the characteristics of evidence-based inclusive schools.

3 Define multidisciplinary collaboration and identify its key characteristics.

4 Why is it so important to provide early intervention services as soon as possible to young children at risk?

5 Identify the purposes of Part C of IDEA and the components of the individualized family service plan (IFSP).

6 Identify evidence-based instructional approaches for preschool-age children with disabilities.

7 Describe the roles of special education and general education teachers in an inclusive classroom setting.

8 Identify the characteristics of evidence-based instruction that enhance learning opportunities for all students, including those with disabilities. What approaches to assessment and instruction are considered evidence-based practice in an inclusive elementary school classroom?

Rebecca and Ben

LEARNING IN AN INCLUSIVE CLASSROOM

Rebecca is a student with autism in a first-grade inclusive classroom. On the Education CourseMate

website, you can view the video in which you'll see Rebecca's classroom teacher working in collaboration with her learning support teacher to accommodate Rebecca's

learning and behavior challenges, including difficulties in coping with changes. The video demonstrates the many different instructional strategies Rebecca's teachers use to meet her individual needs in an inclusive classroom setting. Ben is a 12-year-old with **Asperger's syndrome** who loves to draw and build things, but has challenges with social skills development. In the Education CourseMate website for *Human Exceptionality*, 11th edition, you can view how Ben's teachers use role playing along with other evidence-based instruction to facilitate Ben's learning of age-appropriate social skills.

A Changing Era in the Lives of Children with Disabilities

This chapter explores inclusive education, collaboration, instructional programs, and services in the early childhood and elementary school years. For infants, toddlers, and preschool-age children, the world is defined primarily through family and a small group of same-age peers. As children progress in age and development, their world expands to include their neighborhood, school, and the larger community. For Rebecca in our opening Snapshot, learning takes place with "typical" peers in a first-grade inclusion classroom where the focus is on assuring the success of "all children." Rebecca's behavior could clearly distract other students in this classroom setting, but her teachers are skilled in using effective strategies that will not only support Rebecca's interactions with the other students, but also assure that every student in the class is learning and successful. As Rebecca gets older, the skills she is learning and applying in the early elementary years will be critical to her participation and success in developing friendships within her neighborhood and eventually living and working in a community setting.

Ben, who is 12 years old and a seventh grader, experiences many of the same challenges as Rebecca. He has difficulty interacting with his "typical" peers and avoids social situations. His teachers are effectively using "role playing" as a means to help Ben learn and use the skills needed to participate with other adults and children and enhance his academic learning. As is true with Rebecca, the skills that Ben learns in role playing transfer to real-life situations in his family, school, and community life.

Asperger's syndrome
A condition that shares certain unusual social interaction and behaviors with autism, but typically does not include general language delay.

Standard 3
Individual Learning Differences

Standard 5
Learning Environments and Social Interactions

Inclusive Education

FOCUS 1

Define inclusive education.

The history of education has seen continuous evolution in the terms used to describe the concept of educating students with disabilities in a general education setting, side by side with their peers without disabilities. The most common terms are *mainstreaming, least restrictive environment,* and *inclusive education.* We discussed the least restrictive environment in the context of IDEA in Chapter 2. The expression *mainstreaming* dates back to the very beginnings of the field of special education. It didn't come into widespread use until the 1960s, however, with the growth of public school classes for children with disabilities, most of which separated students with disabilities from their peers without disabilities.

At that time, some professionals called into question the validity of separate programs. Dunn (1968) charged that classes for children with mild retardation could not be justified: "Let us stop being pressured into continuing and expanding a special education program that we know now to be undesirable for many of the children we are dedicated to serve" (p. 225). Dunn, among others, called for a placement model whereby students with disabilities could remain in the general education class program for at least some portion of the school day and receive special education when and where needed. This model became widely known as **mainstreaming**. Although mainstreaming implied that students with disabilities would receive individual planning and support from both general and special educators, this did not always happen in actual practice. In fact, the term *mainstreaming* fell from favor when it became associated with placing students with disabilities in general education classes without providing additional support, as a means to save money and limit the number of students who could receive additional specialized services. (Such practices gave rise to the term *maindumping* as an alternative to mainstreaming.) However, the term *mainstreaming* remains in some use today as one way to describe educating students with disabilities in general education settings.

Mainstreaming
Placement of students with disabilities into general education classrooms for some or all of the school day.

Inclusive education
Students with disabilities receive the services and supports appropriate to their individual needs within the general education setting.

Full inclusion
Students with disabilities receive all instruction in a general education classroom; support services come to the student.

Partial inclusion
Students with disabilities receive some of their instruction in a general education classroom with *"pull-out"* to another instructional setting when appropriate to their needs.

The terms *mainstreaming* and *inclusive education,* although often used interchangeably, are not synonymous. Whereas mainstreaming implies the physical placement of students with disabilities in the same school or classroom as students without disabilities, inclusive education suggests that placement alone is not enough. **Inclusive education** means students with disabilities receive the services and supports appropriate to their individual needs within the general education setting. This concept may be described as "push-in" services. Whereas, the traditional model for special education "pulls the student out of the general education class to receive support," inclusive education focuses on "pushing services and supports into" the general education setting for both students and teachers.

Inclusive education may also be defined by the extent of the student's access to, and participation in, the general education classroom. **Full inclusion** is an approach whereby students with disabilities receive all instruction in a general education classroom; support services come to the student. **Partial inclusion** involves students with disabilities receiving some of their instruction in a general education classroom as well as relocation to another instructional setting when appropriate to their individual needs. The success of full and partial inclusion depends on several factors, including a strong belief in the value of inclusion on the part of professionals and parents. Equally important is the availability of a support network of general and special education educators along with related services professionals (speech and language specialists, school psychologists,

Inclusive classrooms promote diversity, acceptance, and belonging for all children. What are the responsibilities of professionals to ensure a successful inclusive program?

AP Photo/Journal Times, Mark Hertzberg

physical or occupational therapists, social workers, nurses, and so on), working together to assure each student's access to programs and services that meet individual needs.

A number of educators have argued that in spite of certain accomplishments, pull-out programs have caused negative effects or obstacles to the appropriate education of students with disabilities (Holzberg, 2012; Lipsky & Gartner, 2002; Shapiro-Barnard et al., 2002). On the other hand, proponents of pull-out programs have argued that the available research doesn't support the premise that full-time placement in a general education classroom is superior to special education classes for all students with disabilities (Dorn & Fuchs, 2004; Leafstedt et al., 2007; Worrell, 2008). For a more in-depth look at the differing perspectives on full inclusion, see the nearby Debate Forum, "Perspectives on Full Inclusion."

Characteristics of Evidence-Based Inclusive Schools

The No Child Left Behind Act of 2001 and IDEA 2004 launched a great deal of discussion and controversy about which characteristics, taken together, constitute an evidence-based school and classroom for all students. There seems to be considerable agreement that schools are most effective in promoting student achievement and valued post-school outcomes when they

- promote the values of diversity, acceptance, and belonging.
- ensure the availability of formal and natural supports within the general education setting.
- provide services and supports in age-appropriate classrooms in neighborhood schools.
- ensure access to the general curriculum while meeting the individualized needs of each student.
- provide a multidisciplinary school-wide support system to meet the needs of all students.

Diversity, Acceptance, and Belonging

An evidence-based inclusive school promotes acceptance and belonging within a diverse culture (Gollnick & Chinn, 2009; Hollins & Guzman, 2005; Sapon-Shevin, 2008). Wade and Zone (2000) described this value as "building community and affirming diversity.... [S]truggling learners can be actively involved, socially accepted, and motivated to achieve the best of their individual and multiple abilities" (p. 22). These authors further suggested that the responsibility for ensuring a successful inclusive program lies with adults who create learning through individualized and appropriate educational instruction consistent with each student's abilities and interests.

Formal and Natural Supports

Within an effective inclusive school, students with disabilities must have access to both formal and natural support networks (Friend & Bursuck, 2012; Hogansen et al., 2008; McDonnell & Hardman, 2009). **Formal supports** are those available through the public school system. They include highly effective teachers, related services personnel, para-professionals, and access to instructional materials designed for, or adapted to, individual need. **Natural supports** consist of the student's family and classmates. These individuals constitute a support network of mutual caring that promotes greater inclusion within the classroom and school, access to effective instruction, and the development of social relationships (friendships). Through these networks, students with disabilities achieve success within an inclusive environment. High-quality formal supports are the key to each student's opportunity to learn valued instructional content. Through the natural support network, students are able to bond with others who will listen, understand, and support them as they attempt to meet the challenges of being in an inclusive setting.

FOCUS 2
Describe the characteristics of evidence-based inclusive schools.

Standard 3
Individual Learning Differences

Standard 9
Professional and Ethical Practice

Formal supports
Educational supports provided by, and funded through, the public school system. They include qualified teachers, paraprofessionals, and access to instructional materials designed for, or adapted to, individual needs.

Natural supports
The student's family and classmates; these individuals comprise a support network of mutual caring that promotes greater inclusion within the classroom and school, access to effective instruction, and the development of social relationships (friendships).

TEACHSOURCE VIDEO INCLUSION: GROUPING STRATEGIES FOR INCLUSIVE CLASSROOMS

Please visit the Education CourseMate website for *Human Exceptionality,* 11th edition at CengageBrain.com, to access this chapter's TeachSource video.

In this fourth- and fifth-grade inclusion classroom, you'll see how teacher Sheryl Cebula works with an inclusion specialist and other school support staff to assure that each child has the opportunity to succeed. The curricular topic in this video is the Caribbean area. Sheryl assigns each student to one of four groups: maps, food, music, and flags. Through an interview, Sheryl reflects on how she created her groups and her expectations for all students.

1. How does Ms. Cebula use learning centers as means to engage all students in the instructional activity on the Caribbean?

2. Are student interests considered as the four learning groups are organized? How?

3. What are the organizers (guidelines) that Ms. Cebula provides to the students and how do they facilitate student learning?

4. What is the role of the inclusion specialist in this classroom activity?

DEBATE FORUM
PERSPECTIVES ON FULL INCLUSION

Full inclusion: Students are placed in a general education classroom for the entire school day. The supports and services necessary to ensure an appropriate education come to the student in the general education class; the student is not "pulled out" into a special education classroom for instruction.

POINT

We must rethink our current approach to the educational placement of students with disabilities. Pulling these students out of general education classrooms and placing them into separate settings does not make sense in today's schools from the standpoint of both a "moral imperative" and "what works." As a moral imperative, inclusion is the right thing to do:

> Inclusion goes beyond returning students who have been in separate placements to the general education classroom. It incorporates an end to labeling students and shunting them out of the regular [general education] classroom to obtain needed services. It responds to … the call for "neverstreaming" by establishing a refashioned mainstream, a restructured and unified school system that serves all students together. (Lipsky & Gartner, 2002, p. 203)

The reality is that traditional special education has failed; it does not work (Peterson & Hittie, 2010). Setting aside the values inherent in the inclusion of all students, let's look at the reality:

COUNTERPOINT

No one is questioning the value of children belonging, of their being a part of society. However, it is not necessarily true that removing a child with a disability from the general education classroom is a denial of human rights. Is it a denial of human rights to remove a student with a disability from a setting where that child receives inadequate academic support to meet his or her instructional needs? Isn't it a denial of human rights to leave a child in a classroom where she or he is socially isolated? We must separate the vision from the reality. General education does not have the inclination or the expertise to meet the diverse needs of all students with disabilities. General education is already overburdened with the increasing number of at-risk students, large class sizes, and an inadequate support system.

There is always a flip side to the research coin. What about the following research findings?

- Research doesn't support the premise that full-time placement in a general education classroom is superior to special education pull-out programs for all students with disabilities (Leafstedt et al., 2007; Worrell, 2008).

- People with disabilities are more likely to be living in poverty and less likely than those without disabilities to socialize with friends, relatives, or neighbors.

- There is a significant gap between people with and without disabilities in Internet access. Eight of ten adults without disabilities access the Internet, whereas only five of ten adults with disabilities report doing so.

- People with disabilities remain twice as likely to drop out of high school (21 percent versus 10 percent).

- Not surprisingly given the persistence of these gaps, life satisfaction for people with disabilities also trails. Only 34 percent say they are very satisfied, compared with 61 percent of those without disabilities (Kessler Foundation/NOD, 2012; National Organization on Disability [NOD]/Harris Survey, 2004).

Positive and successful experiences in school, including interactions with peers who are not disabled, put students with disabilities on a better trajectory toward successful transition into adult life. Falvey et al. (2006) noted that there is no evidence that pulling students with disabilities out of general education classrooms benefits them.

The goal behind full inclusion is to educate students with disabilities with their typical peers (students without disabilities) in a general education class, as a means to increase their access to, and participation in, all natural settings. The general education classroom is a microcosm of the larger society. As educators, we must ask: "What are the barriers to full participation, and how do we work to break them down?" A partnership between general and special education is a good beginning to breaking down these barriers. This unified approach to instruction will provide teachers with the opportunity to work across disciplines and gain a broader understanding of the diversity in all children. Pull-out programs result in a fragmented approach to instruction, with little cooperation between general and special education.

Finally, students in pull-out programs are much more likely to be stigmatized. Separate education on the basis of a child's learning or behavioral characteristics is inherently unequal.

- General education teachers have little expertise in assisting students with learning and behavioral difficulties and are already overburdened with large class sizes and inadequate support services (Mastropieri & Scruggs, 2007).

- Special educators have been specifically trained to individualize instruction, develop instructional strategies, and use proven techniques that facilitate learning for students with disabilities (Hallahan, 2002).

Given that 96 percent of all students with disabilities are spending at least a portion of their day in general classes, shouldn't we be looking at the system as a whole, not just special education, in trying to deal with student failure?

The conclusions from researchers that special education has failed can be countered by other investigators who offer a very different interpretation (Dorn & Fuchs, 2004; Lane, Hoffmeister, & Bahan, 2002). These researchers, although calling for improvements in special education, don't support its abolition.

Finally, students in pull-out programs are much more likely to be stigmatized. Separate education on the basis of a child's learning or behavioral characteristics is inherently unequal.

The value of full inclusion is a laudable goal, but nevertheless one that is not achievable, or even desirable, for many students with disabilities. The reality is that specialized academic and social instruction can best be provided, at least for some students, in a pull-out setting. These more restricted settings *are* the least restrictive environment for some students. A move to full inclusion will result in the loss of special education personnel who have been trained to work with students who have diverse needs. The result will be dumping these students into an environment that will not meet their needs.

 What Do You Think? Please visit the Education CourseMate website for Human Exceptionality, *11th edition, to access and respond to questions related to the Debate Forum.*

Age-Appropriate Classrooms in a Neighborhood School

Evidence-based inclusive schools provide services and support to students with disabilities in age-appropriate classrooms within a neighborhood school. The National Association of School Psychologists (2012) defines inclusive education as the opportunity for students with disabilities to attend the same school they would attend if they were not disabled.

Inclusive programs are those in which students, regardless of the severity of their disability, receive appropriate specialized instruction and related services within an age-appropriate general education classroom in the school that they would attend if they did not have a disability.

Access to the General Curriculum
Access to the general curriculum for students with disabilities is a critical provision of IDEA 2004. As suggested within the law, "[more than] 30 years of research and experience has demonstrated that the education of children with disabilities can be made more effective by having high expectations for such children and ensuring their access in the general curriculum to the maximum extent possible" (IDEA, 2004, PL 108-446, Sec. 682[C][5]). A student's IEP must describe how the disability affects the child's involvement and progress in the general curriculum. An evidence-based inclusive school promotes meaningful participation for each student within the subject matter content areas identified in the general curriculum (e.g., reading, mathematics, science, etc.). Meaningful participation in the general curriculum will necessitate the development and use of effective teaching strategies, such as universally designed curriculum, instructional adaptations, a **multitiered system of support** (aka **response to intervention** [RtI]), assistive technology, and cooperative learning. Each of these strategies is discussed in detail later in this chapter.

School-Wide Instructional Support
Evidence-based inclusive schools are characterized by a school-wide support system that uses both general and special education resources in combination to benefit all students in the school (Humphrey, 2008; Lewis & Norwich, 2005; Mastropieri & Scruggs, 2007; Murawski, 2008; Peterson & Hittie, 2010). The leadership of the school principal is vital. The principal should openly support the inclusion of all students in the activities of the school, advocate for the necessary resources to meet student needs, and strongly encourage cooperative learning and peer support programs (Friend & Cook, 2010; Grenier, Rogers, & Iarusso, 2008; Tan & Cheung, 2008). Inclusive classrooms are characterized by a philosophy that celebrates diversity, rewards collaboration among professionals, and teaches students how to help and support one another. In the next section, we discuss the essential elements of school-wide collaboration, why it is an important concept within an inclusive school, and who must be involved for it to be effective.

Multidisciplinary Collaboration

Multidisciplinary collaboration is defined as professionals from across different disciplines, parents, and students *working together* to achieve the mutual goal of delivering an evidence-based educational program designed to meet individual need and access to the general curriculum. It should always be viewed as a cooperative, not a competitive, endeavor. As suggested by Friend and Bursuck (2010), collaboration is not *what* those involved do, it is *how* they do it. This process can be described as a *collaborative ethic,* in which everyone works together as a multidisciplinary team to meet the needs of all students, including those with disabilities. The team focuses on mastering the process of collaboration as well as cultivating the professional values and skills necessary to work effectively as part of a team.

In an inclusive school, effective multidisciplinary collaboration has several key characteristics:

- Parents are viewed as active partners in the education of their children.
- Team members from various disciplines (such as education, health care, and psychological and social services) share responsibility; individual roles are clearly understood and valued.
- Team members promote peer support and cooperative learning.

Parents as Valued Partners
Inclusive schools are most effective when they value families and establish positive and frequent relationships with parents. A strong relationship between home and school is characterized by a clear understanding of the philosophical and practical approaches to

---

Multitiered system of support (MTSS)
A system-wide approach to providing evidence-based instruction using a three-tiered model based on the needs of each child. It involves continuous monitoring of student progress in making decisions regarding the frequency and intensity of instruction.

Response to intervention (RtI)
Synonymous with MTSS. Also a process used to determine whether students have specific learning disabilities (see Chapter 7).

FOCUS 3
Define multidisciplinary collaboration and identify its key characteristics.

Multidisciplinary collaboration
Professionals, parents, and students *working together* to achieve the mutual goal of delivering an effective educational program designed to meet individual needs.

CEC
Standard 10
Collaboration

meeting the needs of the student with a disability within the general education setting. Collaboration among parents and professionals is most effective when everyone

- acknowledges and respects each other's differences in values and culture.
- listens openly and attentively to the other's concerns.
- values opinions and ideas.
- discusses issues openly and in an atmosphere of trust.
- shares in the responsibility and consequences for making a decision (Berry, 2009; Drew & Hardman, 2007; McDonnell & Hardman, 2009).

When parents feel valued as equal members of the team, they are more likely to develop a positive attitude toward school professionals. Consequently, educators are able to work more closely with parents to understand each student's needs and functioning level. Home–school collaboration will work only if communication is a two-way process where everyone feels respected.

Sharing the Responsibility

An inclusive school is effective when professionals from across the disciplines work together to achieve a common goal: a free and appropriate education for students with disabilities. Unfortunately, professional isolation was the norm for teachers of students with disabilities for more than a century. Special education meant separate education. However, in the late 1980s, some parents and professionals questioned whether it was in the best interest of students with disabilities to be taught solely by special education teachers in separate classrooms or schools. A merger of general and special education was proposed to ensure that these students would have access to qualified professionals from both disciplines. The proposed merger became known as the **regular education initiative** (REI). The goal of REI was for general and special education teachers to share responsibility in ensuring an appropriate educational experience for students with disabilities. Ultimately, the separate special education system would be eliminated. Although some viewed REI as an attempt on the part of the federal government to reduce the number of students with mild disabilities receiving special education, and thus ultimately to reduce the cost of special education, it did result in a reexamination of the roles of general and special educators within the inclusive school. "Shared responsibility" became the means by which students with disabilities could receive both the formal and the natural supports necessary for them to participate in the general curriculum and in the inclusive classroom.

Regular education initiative A merger of general and special education proposed to ensure all educators would share responsibility in ensuring appropriate education for students with disabilities.

Multidisciplinary School-Wide Assistance Teams
To meet the needs of a diverse group of students, including those with disabilities, schools have developed support networks that facilitate collaboration among professionals. **Multidisciplinary school-wide assistance teams**, sometimes referred to as teacher assistance teams (TATs), involve groups of professionals from several different disciplines, students, and/or parents working together to solve problems, develop instructional strategies, and support classroom teachers. The team uses a variety of strategies to assist teachers in making appropriate referrals for students who may need specialized services, to adapt instruction or develop accommodations consistent with individual student needs, to involve parents in planning and instruction, and to coordinate services across the various team members.

Multidisciplinary school-wide assistance teams Groups of professionals, students, and/or parents working together to solve problems, develop instructional strategies, and support classroom teachers.

Working Together as a Professional and Parent Team
Students with disabilities have very diverse needs, ranging from academic and behavioral support to functional life skills, communication, and motor development. These needs require that students have access to many different education and related services professionals who work together in delivering instruction and providing appropriate resources.

Multidisciplinary collaborative teaming involves bringing key specialists together to develop an instructional program that views the student from a holistic perspective. All members of the team work together to integrate instructional strategies and therapy

A team is a group of professionals, parents, and students who join together to plan and implement an appropriate educational program for a student at risk or with a disability. Team members may be trained in different areas of study, including education, health services, speech and language, school administration, and so on. In the team approach, these individuals, regardless of where or how they were trained, sit down together and coordinate their efforts to help the student. For this approach to work, all team members must clearly understand their roles and responsibilities as members of the team. Let's visit with some team members and explore their roles in working with a student.

SPECIAL EDUCATION TEACHER

It's my responsibility to coordinate the student's individualized education program. I work with each member of the team to assist in selecting, administering, and interpreting appropriate assessment information. I maintain ongoing communication with each team member to ensure that we are all working together to help the student. It's my responsibility to compile, organize, and maintain good, accurate records on each student. I propose instructional alternatives for the student and work with others in the implementation of the recommended instruction. To carry this out, I locate or develop the necessary materials to meet each student's specific needs. I work directly with the student's parents to ensure that they are familiar with what is being taught at school and can reinforce school learning experiences at home.

PARENTS

We work with each team member to ensure that our child is involved in an appropriate educational program. We give the team information about our child's life outside school and suggest experiences that might be relevant to the home and the community. We also work with our child at home to reinforce what is learned in school. As members of the team, we give our written consent for any evaluations of our child and any changes in our child's educational placement.

SCHOOL PSYCHOLOGIST

I select, administer, and interpret appropriate psychological, educational, and behavioral assessment instruments. I consult directly with team members regarding the student's overall educational development. It is also my responsibility to directly observe the student's performance in the classroom and assist in the design of appropriate behavioral management programs in the school and at home.

SCHOOL ADMINISTRATOR

As the school district's representative, I work with the team to ensure that the resources of my school and district are used appropriately in providing services to the student. I am ultimately responsible for ensuring that the team's decisions are implemented properly.

GENERAL EDUCATION CLASSROOM TEACHER

I work with the team to develop and implement appropriate educational experiences for the student during the time that he or she spends in my classroom. I ensure that the student's experiences outside my classroom are consistent with the instruction he or she receives from me. In carrying out my responsibilities, I keep an accurate and continuous record of the student's progress. I am also responsible for referring any other students in my classroom who are at risk and may need specialized services to the school district for an evaluation of their needs.

ADAPTED PHYSICAL EDUCATION TEACHER

I am an adapted physical education specialist who works with the team to determine whether the student needs adapted physical education services as a component of his or her individualized education program.

RELATED SERVICES SPECIALIST

I may be a speech and language specialist, social worker, school counselor, school nurse, occupational or physical therapist, juvenile court authority, physician, or school technology coordinator. I provide any additional services necessary to ensure that the student receives an appropriate educational experience.

Question for Reflection

What suggestions do you have for the members of the school's multidisciplinary team that would help them to collaborate more effectively in meeting the needs of children with disabilities?

concurrently within the classroom—and to evaluate the effectiveness of their individual roles in meeting the needs of each student.

Collaborative teaming is advantageous in an inclusive setting, but it may be difficult to implement because of differing philosophical orientations on the part of team members.

If a professional believes that only he or she is qualified to provide instruction or support in a particular area of need (e.g., communication or motor development), then efforts to share successful strategies are inhibited (McDonnell & Hardman, 2009; Vaughn, Bos, & Schumm, 2011). To overcome this barrier, several strategies could be used to facilitate successful multidisciplinary collaborative teaming:

- Always focus on the needs of the student first, rather than on the individual philosophy or expertise of each professional.

- View team members as collaborators rather than experts. Understand what each professional has to offer in planning, implementing, integrating, and evaluating instructional strategies in an inclusive setting.

- Openly communicate the value of each professional's role in meeting student needs. Maintain an open and positive attitude toward other professionals' philosophy and practices.

- Meet regularly and consult one another on how the student is progressing. Identify what is working, what barriers to progress exist, and what steps will be taken next in furthering the student's learning and development (Spencer, 2005).

Peer Support and Cooperative Learning

Peers may serve as powerful natural supports for students with disabilities in both academic and social areas (Tannock, 2009). They often have more influence on their classmates' behavior than the teacher does. Peer support programs may range from simply creating opportunities for students with disabilities to interact socially with peers without disabilities to highly structured programs of peer-mediated instruction. **Peer-mediated instruction** involves a structured interaction between two or more students under the direct supervision of a classroom teacher. The instruction may use peer and cross-age tutoring and/or cooperative learning. **Peer and cross-age tutoring** emphasize individual student learning, whereas **cooperative learning** emphasizes the simultaneous learning of students as they seek to achieve group goals. Although they are

Rebecca Emery/Getty Images

In addition to being effective teaching strategies, peer support and cooperative learning build self-esteem and increase the acceptance of students with disabilities in inclusive classrooms. Why do you think these strategies are often underutilized in general education classrooms?

Peer-mediated instruction
Structured interaction between two or more students under direct supervision of a classroom teacher. Peers assist in teaching skills to other students.

Peer tutoring
An instructional method whereby one student provides instruction and/or support to another student or group of students.

Cross-age tutoring
An instructional method that pairs older students with younger students to facilitate learning.

Cooperative learning
Emphasizes the simultaneous learning of students as they work together to achieve group goals.

often an underrated and underused resource in general education, peers are very reliable and effective in implementing both academic and social programs with students who have disabilities (Mastropieri, Scruggs, & Berkeley, 2007). In addition, cooperative learning is beneficial to all students, from the highest achievers to those at risk of school failure. Cooperative learning builds self-esteem, strengthens peer relationships, and increases the acceptance of students with disabilities in inclusive classrooms. The effectiveness of peers, however, is dependent on carefully managing the program so that students both with and without disabilities benefit. It is important for teachers to carefully select, train, and monitor the performance of students working as peer tutors. Cooperative learning appears to be most effective when it includes goals for the group as a whole, as well as for individual members (Eggen & Kauchak, 2010; Guralnick et al., 2008; Vaughn, Bos, & Schumm, 2011).

Standard 4
Instructional Strategies

LEARNING THROUGH SOCIAL MEDIA WHAT DOES IT MEAN FOR STUDENTS WITH DISABILITIES?

Just a few years ago, social media—blogging, text messaging, wikis, and Facebook—were on the fringes, the domain of early adopters. Today, they've gone mainstream. ... We are witnessing a fundamental shift in the ways and means that people communicate, connect and engage with each other. Fueling this profound shift are emerging technologies that have spawned an explosion of online communication and collaboration tools from text messaging, to blogging, to social networking sites like Facebook and LinkedIn that facilitate the growth of online communities of interest.

What does this mean for young people with disabilities, the educators who teach them, and the developers of technologies for this market? [It means] an exciting new world of opportunities that should and must be seized. For young people with disabilities, "social media" offers ways to learn about and connect with the world in ways that have not been possible before. For the assistive technology field, social media offers opportunities to make better products and to get those products to the marketplace more easily on a global scale. As social media and the underlying technologies continue to grow, the market will expand as well. There is an unprecedented opportunity before the field of assistive and learning technologies. There are also numerous barriers. Educators and leaders from the assistive and learning technologies field must come together to address these barriers to take advantage of the opportunities of social media... . Unfortunately, not enough young people with disabilities have been able to participate in the use of social media.... Millions of youth with disabilities have less access to Internet resources at home than their peers without disabilities.

SOURCE: Reprinted by permission from National Center for Technology Innovation. (2012). *The Power of Social Media to Promote Assistive and Learning Technologies*. Retrieved January 16, 2012, from www.nationaltechcenter.org/documents/power_of_social_media.pdf.

The Early Childhood Years

FOCUS 4

Why is it so important to provide early intervention services as soon as possible to young children at risk?

The past two decades have seen a growing recognition of the educational, social, and health needs of young children with disabilities. This is certainly true for Yvonne from the nearby Snapshot. Yvonne was born with cerebral palsy, requiring immediate services and supports from many different professionals. Yvonne's early learning experiences provided a foundation for her future learning, growth, and development. Early intervention was also crucial to the family's understanding of Yvonne's needs and of the importance of a strong parent–professional partnership.

The first years of life are critical to the overall development of children, including those at risk for disabilities. Moreover, classic studies in the behavioral sciences from the 1960s and 1970s indicated that early stimulation is critical to the later development of language, intelligence, personality, and a sense of self-worth (Bloom, 1964; Hunt, 1961; Piaget, 1970; White, 1975).

Early intervention
Comprehensive services for infants and toddlers who are disabled or at risk of acquiring a disability.

Advocates of **early intervention** for children at risk for disabilities believe that intervention should begin as early as possible in an environment free of traditional disability labels (such as "intellectual disabilities" and "emotionally disturbed"). Carefully selected services and supports can reduce the long-term impact of the disability and counteract any negative effects of waiting to intervene. The postponement of services may, in fact, undermine a child's overall development, as well as his or her acquisition of specific skills (Batshaw, Pellegrino, & Rozien, 2008; Berk, 2011).

Bringing about Change for Young Children with Disabilities

FOCUS 5

Identify the purposes of Part C of IDEA and the components of the individualized family service plan (IFSP).

For most of the 20th century, comprehensive educational and social services for young children with disabilities were nonexistent or were provided sporadically at best. For families of children with more severe disabilities, often the only option outside of the

Yvonne: The Early Childhood Years

Anita was elated. She had just learned during an ultrasound that she was going to have twin girls. As the delivery date neared, she thought about how much fun it would be to take them on long summer walks in the new double stroller. Two weeks after her estimated delivery date, she was in the hospital, giving birth to her twins. The first little girl arrived without a problem. Unfortunately, this was not the case for the second.

There was something different about her; it became obvious almost immediately after the birth. Yvonne just didn't seem to have the same body tone as her sister. Within a couple of days, Yvonne was diagnosed as having cerebral palsy. Her head and the left side of her body seemed to be affected most seriously. The pediatrician calmly told the family that Yvonne would undoubtedly have learning and physical problems throughout her life. She referred the parents to a division of the state health agency responsible for assisting families with children who have disabilities. Further testing was done, and Yvonne was placed in an early intervention program for infants with developmental disabilities. When Yvonne reached the age of 3, her parents enrolled her in a preschool program where she would have the opportunity to learn communication and social skills, while interacting with children of her own age with and without disabilities. Because neither of the parents had any direct experience with a child with disabilities, they were uncertain how to help Yvonne. Would this program really help her that much, or should they work with her only at home? It was hard for them to see this little girl go to school so very early in her life.

family home was institutionalization. As recently as the 1950s, many parents were advised to institutionalize a child immediately after birth if he or she had a recognizable physical condition associated with a disability (such as Down's syndrome). By doing so, the family would not become attached to the child in the hospital or after returning home.

CEC
Standard 1
Foundations

The efforts of parents and professionals to gain national support to develop and implement community services for young children at risk began in 1968 with the passage of Public Law (PL) 90-538, the Handicapped Children's Early Education Program (HCEEP). The documented success of HCEEP eventually culminated in the passage of PL 99-457, in the form of amendments to the Education of the Handicapped Act, passed in 1986. The most important piece of legislation ever enacted on behalf of infants and preschool-age children with disabilities, PL 99-457 opened up a new era of services for young children with disabilities. It required that all states ensure a free and appropriate public education to every eligible child with a disability between 3 and 5 years of age. For infants and toddlers (birth to 2 years of age), a new program, Part H (changed to Part C in the 1997 amendments to IDEA), was established to help states develop and implement programs for early intervention services. Part C has the following purposes:

1. To enhance the development of infants and toddlers with disabilities, to minimize their potential for developmental delay, and to recognize the significant brain development that occurs during a child's first three years of life;

2. To reduce the educational costs to our society, including our nation's schools, by minimizing the need for special education and related services after infants and toddlers with disabilities reach school age;

3. To maximize the potential for individuals with disabilities to live independently in society;

4. To enhance the capacity of families to meet the special needs of their infants and toddlers with disabilities; and

5. To enhance the capacity of state and local agencies and service providers to identify, evaluate, and meet the needs of all children, particularly minority, low-income, inner-city,

and rural children, and infants and toddlers in foster care (IDEA, 2004, PL 108-446, Part C Sec. 631[a]).

Although states are not *required* to participate, every state provides at least some services under Part C of IDEA.

Early Intervention Programs and Services

Early intervention focuses on the identification and provision of education, health care, and social services as a means to enhance learning and development, reduce the effects of a disability, and prevent the occurrence of future difficulties for young children. IDEA 2004 defines eligible infants and toddlers as those under age 3 who need early intervention services for one of two reasons: (1) There is a developmental delay in one or more of the areas of cognitive development, physical development, communication development, social or emotional development, and adaptive development; or (2) there is a diagnosis of a physical or mental condition that has a high probability of resulting in a developmental delay.

Timing is critical in the delivery of early intervention services. The maxim, "the earlier, the better," says it all. Moreover, early intervention may be less costly and more effective than providing services later in the individual's life (Crane & Winser, 2008; Leppert & Rosier, 2008; Lipkin & Schertz, 2008). Effective early intervention services are directed not only to young children with a disability but also to family members (McDonnell et al., 2003; Neal, 2008). All early intervention services must be designed and delivered within the framework of informing and empowering family members. Comprehensive early intervention is broad in scope, as illustrated in the listing of IDEA, Part C services found in Figure 3.1.

Individualized family service plan (IFSP)
Service plan written to ensure that infants and toddlers receive appropriate services under Part C of IDEA; broadens the IEP's focus to include all family members.

The services under Part C of IDEA that are needed for the child and the family are identified through the development of an **individualized family service plan** (IFSP). The IFSP is structured much like the individualized education program (IEP), but it broadens the focus to include all members of the family. Figure 3.2 lists the required components of the IFSP.

Evidence-Based Early Intervention

This section examines evidence-based models for delivering services and supports to infants and toddlers, including developmentally supportive care in hospitals, and center-based and family-centered programs. For these models to be effective, services and supports should focus on individualization, intense interventions, and a comprehensive approach to meeting the needs of each child and that child's family.

Intensive care specialists
Health care professionals trained specifically to treat newborns who are seriously ill, disabled, or at risk of serious medical problems; also referred to as *neonatal specialists*.

Developmentally supportive care
Approach to care that views the infant as "an active collaborator" in determining what services are necessary to enhance survival.

Service Delivery Advancements in health care have increased the number of at-risk infants who survive birth. **Intensive care specialists,** working with sophisticated medical technologies in newborn intensive care units and providing developmentally supportive care, are able to save the lives of infants who years ago would have died in the first days or weeks of life. **Developmentally supportive care** views the infant as "an active collaborator" in determining what services are necessary to enhance survival. With

Figure 3.1 *Services Provided to Infants and Toddlers under Part C of IDEA.*

- Special instruction
- Speech and language instruction
- Occupational and physical therapy
- Psychological testing and counseling
- Service coordination
- Diagnostic and evaluative medical services
- Social work services
- Sign language and cued speech services

- Assistive technology devices and services
- Family training, counseling, and home visits
- Early identification, screening, and assessment
- Health services necessary to enable the infant or toddler to benefit from the other early intervention services
- Transportation and related costs as necessary to ensure that the infant or toddler and the family receive appropriate services

Figure 3.2 *Required Components of the IFSP*

1. Infant's or toddler's present levels of physical development, cognitive development, communication development, social or emotional development, and adaptive development, based on objective criteria;

2. Family's resources, priorities, and concerns related to enhancing the development of the family's infant or toddler with a disability;

3. Measurable results or outcomes expected to be achieved for the infant or toddler and the family, including preliteracy and language skills, as developmentally appropriate for the child, and the criteria, procedures, and timelines used to determine the degree to which progress toward achieving the results or outcomes is being made and whether modifications or revisions of the results or outcomes or services are necessary;

4. Specific early intervention services based on peer-reviewed research, to the extent practicable, necessary to meet the unique needs of the infant or toddler and the family, including the frequency, intensity, and method of delivering services;

5. Natural environments in which early intervention services will appropriately be provided, including a justification of the extent, if any, to which the services will not be provided in a natural environment;

6. Projected dates for initiation of services and the anticipated length, duration, and frequency of the services;

7. Identification of the service coordinator from the profession most immediately relevant to the infant's or toddler's or family's needs who will be responsible for the implementation of the plan and coordination with other agencies and people, including transition services; and

8. Steps to be taken to support the transition of the toddler with a disability to preschool or other appropriate services.

SOURCE: DEA, 2004, PL 108-446, Sec. 636[d]

this approach, infant behavior is carefully observed to determine what strategies (such as responding to light, noise, or touch) the infant is using to try to survive. Specially trained developmental specialists then focus on understanding the infant's "developmental agenda" to provide appropriate supports and services to enhance the infant's further growth and development.

In addition to the critical services provided in hospital newborn intensive care units, early intervention may be delivered through center-based and family-based programs or a combination of the two (Frankel & Gold, 2007). The center-based model requires families to take their child from the home to a setting where comprehensive services are provided. These sites may be hospitals, churches, schools, or other community facilities. The centers use various instructional approaches, including both developmental and therapeutic models, to meet the needs of infants and toddlers. Center-based programs tend to look like hospitals or health care facilities in which the primary orientation is therapy. In contrast to the center-based model, a family-centered program provides services to the child and family in their natural living environment. Using the natural resources of the home, professionals address the needs of the child in terms of individual family values and lifestyles.

Finally, early intervention may be provided through a combination of services at both a center and the home. Infants or toddlers may spend some time in a center-based program, receiving instruction and therapy in individual or group settings, and also receive in-home family-centered services to promote learning and generalization in their natural environment.

Standard 5
Learning Environments and Social Interactions

Individualized, Intensive, and Comprehensive Services Early intervention programs for infants and toddlers should be based on individual need, and they should be intensive over time and comprehensive. Intensity reflects the frequency and amount of time an infant or child is engaged in intervention activities. An intensive approach requires that the child participate in intervention activities that involve two to three hours of contact each day, at least four or five times a week. Until the 1980s, this child-centered model of service delivery placed parents in the role of trainers who provided direct instruction to the child and helped him or her transfer the learning activities from the therapeutic setting to the home environment. The model of parents as trainers eventually was questioned by many professionals and family members. Families were dropping out of programs; many parents either did not use the intervention techniques effectively with their children or they simply preferred to be parents, not trainers (McDonnell, Hardman, & McGuire, 2007). With the passage of PL 99-457 in 1986 (now IDEA), early intervention evolved into a more family-centered approach in which individual family needs and strengths became the basis for determining program goals, supports needed, and services to be provided.

Providing the breadth of services necessary to meet the individual needs of an infant or toddler within the family constellation requires a *multidisciplinary intervention team*. It should include professionals with varied experiential backgrounds—such as speech and language therapy, physical therapy, health care, and education—and the parents or guardian. The multidisciplinary team should review the IFSP at least annually and issue progress updates to the parents every six months. Coordination of early intervention services across disciplines and with the family is crucial if the goals of the program are to be realized.

The traditional academic-year programming (lasting approximately nine months) that is common to many public school programs is not in the best interests of infants and toddlers who are at risk or have disabilities. Year-round continuity is essential. Services and supports must be provided throughout the early years without lengthy interruptions.

Preschool Services: Referral, Assessment, and IEP Development

Four-year old Matt from the nearby Snapshot began receiving preschool services as soon as he came out of a coma that resulted from being hit by a car. Although he suffered severe head trauma and still has to wear a helmet and use a walker, Matt is doing well in his kindergarten class. Preschool services for Matt began with a referral to his local school to assess the type and extent of his perceived delays relative to same-age peers without disabilities. Once Matt's needs were identified and the multidisciplinary team determined his eligibility for preschool special education services, appropriate developmental and age-appropriate instructional strategies were implemented in a school-based classroom.

Referral Programs
Referral programs for preschool-age children with disabilities have several important components. First, a **child-find system** is set up in each state to locate preschool-age (ages 3 to 5) children at risk and to make referrals to the local education agency. Referrals may come from parents, the family physician, health care or social service agencies, or the child's day care or preschool teacher. Referrals for preschool services may be based on a child's perceived delays in physical development (such as not walking by age 2), speech and language delays (such as nonverbal by age 3), excessive inappropriate behavior (such as frequent temper tantrums, violent behavior, extreme shyness, or excessive crying), or sensory difficulties (unresponsive to sounds or unable to visually track objects in the environment).

Multidisciplinary Assessment
Following a referral, a child-study team initiates assessments to determine whether the child is eligible for preschool special education services under IDEA 2004. Preschool-age children with disabilities are eligible if they meet both of the following requirements. First, developmental delays are evident as measured by appropriate diagnostic instruments and procedures, in one or more of the following areas: physical development, cognitive development, communication development, social or emotional development, or adaptive development. Second, as a result of these delays, the child needs special education and related services (IDEA, 2004, PL 108-446, Sec. 602[3]).

Standard 4
Instructional Strategies

Child-find system
A system within a state or local area that attempts to identify all children who are disabled or at risk in order to refer them for appropriate support services.

Standard 7
Instructional Planning

Standard 4
Instructional Strategies

One day, 4-year-old Matt was playing across the street from his house. As he crossed the street to return home, he was hit by a car. Matt suffered a severe trauma as a result of the accident and was in a coma for more than two months. Now he's in school and is doing well.

Matt wears a helmet to protect his head, and he uses a walker in his general education kindergarten class in the morning and special education class in the afternoon. The general education kindergarten children sing songs together and work on handwriting, before they work at centers in the classroom. Matt's favorite center is the block area. He spends most of his time there. Recently, however, he has become interested in the computer and math centers.

He is working on his fine motor skills and speech skills so he can learn to write and use a pencil again. The focus of his academic learning is mastering the alphabet, learning how to count, and recognizing numbers. He also receives regular speech therapy. He speaks in sentences, but it is very difficult for others to understand what he is saying.

Matt is well liked by his classmates. His teacher enjoys seeing his progress: "Well, it's our hope that he'll be integrated with the other kids eventually, and through the activities we do in the classroom here (in special education) and in the kindergarten, we hope the kids will get to know him and interact with him and that this will help pull up his skills to the level where he can go back to the general education classroom for all his schoolwork."

Developing an IEP for Preschool-Age Children

If a child is eligible, an individualized education program (IEP) is developed. Specialists from several disciplines—including physical therapy, occupational therapy, speech and language therapy, pediatrics, social work, and special education—participate in the development and implementation of IEPs for preschool-age children. The purpose of preschool programs for young children with disabilities is to assist them in living in and adapting to a variety of environmental settings, including home, neighborhood, and school. Depending on individual needs, preschool programs may focus on developing skills in communication, social and emotional learning, physical well-being, self-care, early academics, and coping (Raver, 2010). The decision regarding which skill areas are to be taught should be based on a **functional assessment** of the child and of the setting where he or she spends time. Functional assessments determine the child's skills, the characteristics of the setting, and the family's needs, resources, expectations, and aspirations (Harvey et al., 2008; Horner et al., 2006). Through a functional assessment, professionals and parents come together to plan a program that supports the preschool-age child in meeting the demands of the home, school, or community setting.

This section reviews the concept of developmentally appropriate practice (DAP) for preschool-age children and explains how it serves as a foundation to meet the individual needs of young children with disabilities in age-appropriate placements. We also examine the importance of teaching functional skills in inclusive preschool settings.

Functional assessment
Assessments to determine the child's skills, the characteristics of the setting, and the family's needs, resources, expectations, and aspirations.

FOCUS 6
Identify evidence-based instructional approaches for preschool-age students with disabilities.

Developmentally Appropriate Practice

Early child educators share the conviction that programs for young children should be based on **developmentally appropriate practice** (DAP). DAP is grounded in the belief that there has been too much emphasis on preparing preschool-age children for academic learning and not enough on activities that are initiated by the child, such as play, exploration, social interaction, and inquiry. As suggested by the National Association for the Education of Young Children (NAEYC, 2012), "high-quality early childhood programs do much more than help children learn numbers, shapes, and colors. Good programs help children learn how to learn: to question why and discover alternative

Developmentally appropriate practices (DAP)
Instructional approaches that use curriculum and learning environments consistent with the child's developmental level.

- *Create a caring community of learners.* Developmentally appropriate practices occur within a context that supports the development of relationships between adults and children, among children, among teachers, and between teachers and families.

- *Teach to enhance development and learning.* Adults are responsible for ensuring children's healthy development and learning. From birth, relationships with adults are critical determinants of children's healthy social and emotional development, and they also serve as mediators of language and intellectual development.

- *Construct an appropriate curriculum.* The content of the early childhood curriculum is determined by many factors, including the subject matter of the disciplines, social or cultural values, and parental input. In developmentally appropriate programs, decisions about curriculum content also take into consideration the age and experience of the learners.

- *Assess children's learning and development.* Assessment of individual children's development and learning is essential for planning and implementing an appropriate curriculum. In developmentally appropriate programs, assessment and curriculum are integrated, with teachers continually engaging in observational assessment for the purpose of improving teaching and learning.

- *Establish reciprocal relationships with families.* Developmentally appropriate practices derive from deep knowledge of individual children and of the context within which they develop and learn. The younger the child, the more important it is for professionals to acquire this knowledge through relationships with the child's family.

SOURCE: Adapted from National Association for the Education of Young Children (2009). NAEYC position statement. Retrieved February 28, 2009, from www.naeyc.org/about/positions/pdf/PSDAP98.PDF.

answers; to get along with others; and to use their developing language, thinking, and motor skills."

DAP is viewed as culturally sensitive because it emphasizes interaction between children and adults. Adults become "guides" for student learning rather than controlling what, where, and how students acquire knowledge. DAP is strongly advocated by the NAEYC, the largest national organization for professionals in early childhood education. NAEYC has developed several guiding principles for the use of DAP; these are illustrated in Figure 3.3.

Age-Appropriate Placement

As we have noted, DAP is widely accepted throughout the early childhood community, but many special education teachers and related services personnel (such as speech and language pathologists and physical therapists) see DAP as a base or foundation to build on in order to meet the individual needs of young children with disabilities. These professionals indicate that early childhood programs for students with disabilities must also take into account age-appropriate placements and functional skill learning.

Age-appropriate placements emphasize the child's chronological age over developmental level. Thus, a 2-year-old with developmental delays is first and foremost a 2-year-old, regardless of whether he or she has disabilities. A young child with disabilities should be exposed to the same instructional opportunities and settings as a nondisabled peer of the same chronological age. Age-appropriate learning prepares children to live and learn in inclusive environments with same-age peers. Arguing that DAP and age-appropriate practice are compatible, McDonnell et al. (2003) and Widerstrom (2005) suggested that there are many ways to create learning experiences for young children that are both developmentally appropriate and age-appropriate. The following is one example:

> Mark is a 5-year-old with limited gross and fine motor movement and control. His cognitive development is similar to a typically developing 11-month-old. Mark is learning to use

Age-appropriate placement
Educational placement based on instructional programs consistent with chronological age rather than developmental level.

adaptive switches to activate toys and a radio or [CD] player. Mark enjoys listening to music and toys that make noise and move simultaneously. Mark would also enjoy the lullabies and battery-operated lamb and giraffe toys that might usually be purchased for an 11-month-old. However, he also enjoys Raffi songs and songs from Disney movies, as well as automated racetracks and battery-operated dinosaurs and robots. The latter selection of music and toys would also interest other children of his age ... and could provide some familiar and pleasurable experiences for Mark to enjoy in classroom and play settings with typical peers. (McDonnell et al., 2003, p. 239)

Teaching Functional Life Skills

Consistent with the individualized needs of the child and the expectations of the family, teaching functional life skills facilitates the young child's learning in the natural setting (such as home and family). Functional skill development helps the child adapt to the demands of a given environment—that is, it creates an **adaptive fit** between the child and the setting in which he or she must learn to function. Functional skills focus on teaching and assisting the child to become more independent and to interact appropriately with family, friends, and professionals. In fact, it may be more important for some children to be able to dress themselves, brush their teeth, comb their hair, and take care of other personal hygiene needs than to be able to name six breeds of dogs.

Adaptive fit
Compatibility between demands of a task or setting and a student's instructional needs and abilities.

Inclusive Preschool Classrooms

In the evidence-based inclusive classroom, young children with disabilities receive their educational program side by side with peers without disabilities in a regular preschool or day care program. Effective programs are staffed by child care providers, special education preschool teachers in a co-teaching or consultant role, paraprofessionals, and other related services personnel as needed by the children. Figure 3.4 describes the values that are at the foundation of an evidence-based inclusion preschool program, and the multidisciplinary resources that are essential to implement it.

In a study of child care providers, Devore and Hanley-Maxwell (2000) identified five critical factors that contributed to successfully serving young children with disabilities in inclusive, community-based child care settings: (1) a willingness on the part of the child care provider to make inclusion work; (2) a realistic balance between the resources available in the program and the needs of the student; (3) continual problem solving with parents; (4) access to emotional support and technical assistance from special educators and early intervention therapists; and (5) access to other supports, such as other child care providers, respite care providers, and houses of worship.

There are many reasons for the increasing number of inclusive classrooms for preschool students with disabilities. Inclusive classrooms create opportunities for social interaction and for the development of friendships among children with disabilities and same-age peers without disabilities. The social development skills learned in inclusive settings are applied at home and community as well as in future educational and social settings. Preschool-age children without disabilities learn to value and accept diversity (Drew & Hardman, 2007).

Fotosearch/Getty Images

Evidence-based inclusive preschool classrooms are staffed by highly-trained professionals in both child care and special education. What other indicators of quality should we look for in an inclusive preschool classroom?

CEC
Standard 5
Learning Environments and Social Interactions

Figure 3.4 *Indicators of Quality in an Inclusive Preschool Program*

- Inclusion, as a value, supports the right of all children, regardless of abilities, to participate actively in natural settings within their communities. Natural settings are those in which the child would spend time if he or she did not have a disability. These settings include (but are not limited to) home, preschool, nursery schools, Head Start programs, kindergartens, neighborhood school classrooms, child care, places of worship, recreational venues (such as community playgrounds and community events), and other settings that all children and families enjoy.

- Young children and their families have full and successful access to health, social, educational, and other support services that promote full participation in family and community life. The cultural, economic, and educational diversity of families is valued and supported as a process for identifying a program of services.

- As young children participate in group settings (such as preschool, play groups, child care, and kindergarten), their active participation should be guided by developmentally and individually appropriate curricula. Access to and participation in the age-appropriate general curriculum become central to the identification and provision of specialized support services.

- To implement inclusive practices, there must be
  - the continued development, implementation, evaluation, and dissemination of full inclusion supports, services, and systems that are of high quality for all children;
  - the development of preservice and in-service training programs that prepare families, services providers, and administrators to develop and work within inclusive settings;
  - collaboration among key stakeholders to implement flexible fiscal and administrative procedures in support of inclusion;
  - research that contributes to our knowledge of recommended practice; and
  - the restructuring and unification of social, educational, health, and intervention supports and services to make them more responsive to the needs of all children and families.

SOURCE: Adapted from Division for Early Childhood, Council for Exceptional Children and the National Association for the Education of Young Children. (2012). *Position statement on inclusion [online]*. Retrieved January 10, 2012, from www.dec-sped.org/uploads/docs/about_dec/position_concept_papers/PositionStatement _Inclusion_Joint_updated_May2009.pdf.

Head Start
Federally funded preschool program for economically disadvantaged children.

Head Start, the nation's largest federally funded early childhood program, was enacted into law in 1965, and has served over 27 million children. The program was developed around a strong research base suggesting that early enrichment experiences for children with economic disadvantages would better prepare them for elementary school (Bierman et al., 2008; Phillips & Cabrera, 2006; U.S. Department of Health and Human Services, 2012). Although the original legislation did not include children with disabilities, the law was eventually expanded in 1982 to require that at least 10 percent of Head Start enrollment be reserved for these children. The U.S. Department of Health and Human Services (2012) reported that of the more than 900,000 children in Head Start programs, children with disabilities accounted for 11.5 percent of this population. Head Start has been hailed through the years as a major breakthrough in federal support for early childhood education.

Federal regulations under Head Start have been expanded to ensure that a disabilities service plan be developed to meet the needs of all children with disabilities and their families, that the programs designate a coordinator of services for children with disabilities, and that the necessary special education and related services be provided for children who are designated as disabled under IDEA.

Transition from Preschool to Elementary School

Transitions, although a natural and ongoing part of everyone's life, are often difficult under the best of circumstances. For preschool-age children with disabilities and their families, the transition from early childhood programs to kindergarten can be very stressful. Early childhood programs for preschool-age children with disabilities commonly employ many adults (both professional and paraprofessional). In contrast, kindergarten programs are often not able to offer the same level of staff support, particularly in more inclusive educational settings. Therefore, it is important for preschool professionals responsible for transition planning to attend not only to the needs and skills of the individual students, but also to how they can match the performance demands of the elementary school and classroom setting. Guralnick et al. (2008) indicated that successful transition from preschool to elementary programs is a critical factor in inclusion. Sainato and Morrison (2001) make several suggestions for professionals engaged in the transition process:

- The child's skill level is viewed as the predictor of the potential for success.
- Kindergarten teachers identify functional, social, and behavioral skills as more important for successful transition than academic skills.
- Readiness skills, language competence, self-care skills, appropriate social behavior, and independent performance during group activities are identified as prerequisites to inclusive placements in elementary school programs.
- Focusing on the prerequisite skills that are likely to increase the child's success in inclusive elementary settings is important, but it must not be used to prevent young children from participating in inclusive placements.

To identify the skills needed in the elementary school environment, a preschool transition plan should begin at least one to two years before the child's actual move. This move is facilitated when the early intervention specialist, the child's future kindergarten teacher, and the parents engage in a careful planning process that recognizes the significant changes that the child and the family will go through as they enter a new and unknown situation (DeVore & Russell, 2007; Rosenkoetter et al., 2001).

In summary, early childhood programs for children with disabilities focus on teaching skills that will improve a child's opportunities for living a rich life and on preparing the child to function successfully in family, school, and neighborhood environments. Young children with disabilities are prepared as early as possible to share meaningful experiences with same-age peers. Additionally, early childhood programs lessen the impact of conditions that may deteriorate or become more severe without timely and adequate intervention and that may prevent children from developing other, secondary disabling conditions. The intended outcomes of these programs will not, however, be accomplished without consistent family participation and professional collaboration.

CEC
Standard 7
Instructional Planning

The Elementary School Years

In the elementary school years, the focus is on supporting children as they attempt to meet the expectations of the general education curriculum. The degree to which a child is able to cope with these expectations depends on how effectively the school accommodates individual needs and provides evidence-based instructional programs. For Ricardo in the nearby Case Study, the school's expectations were a challenge, and he fell significantly behind his classmates in reading and language. His third-grade teacher decided to initiate a referral to evaluate Ricardo's eligibility for special education services. Once it was determined that Ricardo qualified as a student with a learning disability, a multidisciplinary team of special educators, general educators, related services personnel, and his parents worked together to develop his individualized education program (IEP) and meet his reading and language needs.

FOCUS 7
Describe the roles of special education and general education teachers in an inclusive classroom setting.

Meeting Student Needs through a General Education/ Special Education Partnership

Today's teachers are charged with preparing the next generation of students for a changing and diverse world. The growing student diversity includes increasing numbers from ethnically diverse backgrounds, those with disabilities, and children at risk of educational failure. Each of these factors contributes to the critical need for general education and special education teachers to work together in preparing all students for the many challenges of the next century, while at the same time not losing sight of individual learning needs, styles, and preferences.

The current wave of reform in U.S. schools, as mandated in federal law, is focused on finding new and more effective ways to increase student achievement by establishing high standards for *what* should be taught and *how* performance will be measured. Accountability for meeting high standards rests at several levels, but the ultimate test of success is what happens between teacher and student in the day-to-day classroom.

Increasing student diversity in the schools will require general educators to teach students whose needs exceed those of the traditionally defined "typical child." Correspondingly, special education teachers must have the specialized skills to meet the needs of students with disabilities, and will be called upon to apply this expertise to a much broader group of high-risk and disadvantaged students in a collaborative educational environment. The combination of these factors makes a very strong case for a partnership between general education and special education.

The Many Roles of the Special Education Teacher

In an inclusive school, special educators are called upon to fill multiple roles often referred to as the three Cs: collaboration, consultation, and coordination. In the role of *collaborator,* special educators

- work with school personnel (such as general educators, the school principal, related services personnel) and parents to identify the educational needs of students with disabilities;
- link student assessment information to the development of the IEP and access to the general curriculum;
- determine appropriate student accommodations and instructional adaptations; and
- deliver intensive instruction using specialized teaching methods.

CEC

Standard 10
Collaboration

Special educators provide instruction and support in academic, behavioral, and/or adaptive/functional areas, as well as fostering student self-determination and self-management skills. As collaborators, special education teachers use effective problem-solving strategies to facilitate student learning, co-teach with general educators, and apply effective accountability measures to evaluate individual students' progress and long-term results.

In the role of *consultant,* the special education teacher must be able to serve as a resource to general educators and parents on effective instructional practices for students with disabilities. Expertise may be provided in content areas (such as effective approaches to teaching reading to students with special needs) and/or problem-solving skills (such as strategies to motivate students to participate in class activities).

In the role of *coordinator,* the special education teacher takes the lead responsibility for organizing the activities of the school team in developing, implementing, and evaluating student IEPs. He or she also may be responsible for organizing school resources to best meet the needs of students with disabilities; initiating professional development activities for school team members; supervising paraprofessionals, peer support, and volunteers; and facilitating positive communication with parents.

The General Education Teacher: Meeting the Challenge to Educate All Students

The Study of Personnel Needs in Special Education (SPeNSE, 2006) reported that 95 percent of all general education teachers are currently working directly with students with disabilities in their classrooms, with an average caseload of 3.5 students. General education teachers must continually meet the challenges of achieving increased academic excellence, as well as responding to students with many different backgrounds and instructional needs coming together in a common environment. The inclusion of students with disabilities in general education classes need not be met with teacher frustration, anger, or refusal. These reactions are merely symptomatic of the confusion surrounding

Ricardo, a third-grader at Bloomington Hill Elementary School, has recently been referred by his teacher, Ms. Thompson, to the school's pre-referral team for an evaluation. During the first four months of school, Ricardo has continued to fall further behind in reading and language. He entered third grade with some skills in letter and sound recognition but had difficulty reading and comprehending material beyond a first-grade level. It was clear to Ms. Thompson that Ricardo's language development was delayed as well. He had a very limited expressive vocabulary and had some difficulty following directions if more than one or two steps were involved.

Ms. Thompson contacted Ricardo's mother, Maria Galleghos (a single parent), to inform her that she would like to refer Ricardo for an in-depth evaluation of his reading and language skills. A representative from the school would be calling her to explain what the evaluation meant and to get her approval for the necessary testing. The school psychologist, Jean Andreas, made the call to Ms. Galleghos. During the phone conversation, Ms. Galleghos reminded the school psychologist that the primary language spoken in the home was Spanish, even though Ricardo, his parents, and his siblings spoke English, too. Ms. Andreas indicated that the assessment would be conducted in both Spanish and English to determine whether Ricardo's problems were related to a disability in reading or perhaps to problems with English as a second language.

Having received written approval from Ricardo's mother, the school's pre-referral team conducted an evaluation of Ricardo's academic performance. The formal evaluation included achievement tests, classroom performance tests, samples of Ricardo's work, behavioral observations, and anecdotal notes from Ms. Thompson. An interview with Mrs. Galleghos was conducted as part of the process to gain her perceptions of Ricardo's strengths and problem areas and to give her an opportunity to relate pertinent family history.

The evaluation confirmed his teacher's concerns. Ricardo was more than two years below what was expected for a child his age in both reading and language development. Ricardo's difficulties in these areas did not seem to be related to his being bilingual, but the issue of English as a second language would need to be taken into careful consideration in developing an appropriate learning experience.

The team determined that Ricardo qualified for special education services as a student with a specific learning disability. Once again, Ms. Andreas contacted Ms. Galleghos with the results, indicating that Ricardo qualified for special education services in reading and language. Ms. Andreas pointed out that, as a parent of a student with an identified disability, Ms. Galleghos had some specific legal rights that would be further explained to her both in writing and orally.

One of those rights is the right to participate as a partner in the development of Ricardo's individualized education program (IEP). Ms. Andreas further explained that a meeting would be set up at a mutually convenient time to develop a plan to assist Ricardo over the next year.

APPLICATION

1. Prior to the meeting, what could Ricardo's teachers do to help his mother feel valued as a member of the IEP team and to better understand her role in developing the IEP?

2. What additional information could Ricardo's mother provide that would help the team better understand his needs and interests, particularly in the areas of reading and language development?

3. What do you see as important for Ricardo to learn in school?

inclusive education. Huefner (2012) suggested that the IDEA 2004 requirement for general educators to be members of the IEP team gives them leverage to obtain the supports they need to be more effective with special education students and to work more collaboratively with special education teachers. As members of the IEP team, general educators are in a better position to share their knowledge and insight on individual students and to provide important information on how the student will fare in the general education curriculum and the classroom setting.

Specific roles for general educators in working collaboratively with special education and related services personnel include

- identifying and referring students who may be in need of additional support to succeed in an inclusive setting;

- understanding each student's individual strengths and limitations, and the effects on learning;
- implementing an appropriate individualized education program that is focused on supporting student success in the general education curriculum; and
- initiating and maintaining ongoing communication with parents.

Unfortunately, inclusive education is sometimes synonymous with dumping a student with disabilities into a general education class without the necessary supports to the teacher or to the student, and at the expense of others in the class. Teachers may experience many different needs and challenges, such as disruptive students who must learn social and behavioral skills to succeed in a general education setting. General education teachers may need support from a special education teacher or other school personnel (speech and language specialist, occupational therapist, social worker, nurse), and access to appropriate instructional adaptations necessary to meet the needs of students with disabilities.

However, in a review of the literature on the attitudes and beliefs of general educators regarding students with disabilities, Pugach (2005) suggested that the discussion has shifted away from focusing on the barriers to inclusion to what it is that teachers need to know, and what they can do, to meet the needs of these students. To address these needs, Pugach further asserts,

> it will be crucial to take advantage of the natural progression [in universities] toward collaborative [teacher education] programs ... conducted in a joint fashion, teams comprised of teacher educators from special and general teacher education, across content areas and multicultural education... . By joining forces in this manner we can begin to provide answers to a new generation of questions about how best to achieve the goal of delivering instruction of the highest quality to students with disabilities. (p. 578)

The role of the general education teacher extends not only to working with students with mild disabilities, but also to involvement with those with more severe disabilities. Success in a general education class for students with severe disabilities depends critically on the cooperative relationship among the general education teacher, the special education teacher, and the school support team. The general educator works with the team to create opportunities to include students with more severe disabilities. Inclusion may be achieved by having the general education class serve as a homeroom for the student; by developing opportunities for students with severe disabilities to be with their peers without disabilities as often as possible both within the general education class and in school activities such as recess, lunch, and assemblies; by developing a peer support program; and by using effective practices, such as multitiered systems of support (RtI), universal design for learning, differentiated instruction, assistive technology, and curriculum-based measurement.

Evidenced-Based Practices in Inclusive Elementary School Programs

FOCUS 8
Identify the characteristics of evidence-based instruction that enhance learning opportunities for all students, including those with disabilities. What approaches to assessment and instruction are considered evidence-based practice in an inclusive elementary school classroom?

Ensuring appropriate and effective educational learning experiences for all students, including those with disabilities, is dependent upon the provision of evidence-based educational services and supports. Characteristics of evidence-based instruction that enhance learning opportunities for students of all ages and across multiple settings include:

- *Individualization*: A student-centered approach to instructional decision making
- *Intensive instruction*: Frequent instructional experiences of significant duration
- An *"education for all" approach to teaching and learning*: Developing and adapting instruction to meet the needs of every student (Hardman & Dawson, 2008; Hardman & Mulder, 2004)

Individualization

The defining hallmark of special education has always been **individualization**—developing and implementing an appropriate educational experience based on the individual needs of each student. Research indicates that fundamental differences have characterized the ways in which special educators approach instruction, distinguishing them from their general education colleagues. Traditionally, instruction in general education has most often centered on the curriculum (content knowledge). Although general education has traditionally been guided by a utilitarian approach (the greatest good for the greatest number), special education practice is driven by individually referenced decision making. It is designed to meet the unique needs of every student, regardless of educational need or ability. Using an individually referenced approach to decision making, special education teachers continually plan and adjust curriculum and instruction in response to the student. However, the fact is that *all* teachers must have at their disposal multiple ways to adapt curriculum, modify their instructional approaches, and motivate every student to learn (Peterson & Hittie, 2010; Vaughn, Bos, & Schumm, 2011). Hardman and McDonnell (2008) suggested that the vast majority of teachers, whether in general or special education, unfortunately do not have this broad expertise in both the subject matter (content area) and in adapting curriculum and instruction (pedagogy) necessary to meet individual student needs. Thus, together, general and special educators must acquire a core of knowledge and skills, as well as the ability to work collaboratively to facilitate their effectiveness in providing evidence-based instruction to all students.

Intensive Instruction

Intensive instruction involves (1) actively engaging students in their learning by requiring high rates of appropriate response to the material presented, (2) carefully matching instruction to student ability and skill level, (3) providing instructional cues and prompts to support learning and then fading them when appropriate, and (4) providing detailed feedback that is directly focused on the task the student is expected to complete. Intensive instruction may involve both group and one-to-one learning. Research suggests that intensive instruction can significantly improve both academic achievement and the student's life skills (Mastropieri & Scruggs, 2007; Vaughn, Bos, & Schumm, 2011). For all students, including those with disabilities, intensive instruction provided consistently over time and by qualified and effective teachers can result in significant gains in academic achievement and life skill learning.

An "Educational for All" Approach to Teaching and Learning

Learning is a continual process of adaptation for all students as they attempt to meet the demands of school (Friend & Bursuck, 2012; Peterson & Hittie, 2010). Not every student learns in the same way or at the same rate. Some students do not learn as quickly or as efficiently as their classmates and are constantly fighting a battle against time and failure. Despite these challenges, however, all students, including those with disabilities, can learn the required skills that will orient them toward striving for success rather than fighting against failure. Success can be achieved only when educators remain flexible, constantly adjusting to meet the needs of their students. For example, an "education for all approach" to instruction in core academic areas (e.g., reading, math, science) stresses that students must learn a specified set of sequenced skills, each a prerequisite to the next. This process can be illustrated by briefly analyzing the teaching of reading. When learning to read, students must acquire many individual skills and then be able to link them together as a whole. The students then have the ability to decode abstract information and turn it into meaningful content. When one of the separate skills required for reading is not learned, the entire process may break down. Teaching core academic skills, whether in reading or any other content area, lays the groundwork for further development and higher levels of functioning. Vaughn, et al. (2011) suggested that reading instruction is *appropriate* and *intensive* when:

- students have a clear understanding of teacher expectations and the goals of instruction;
- the reader's instructional reading level and needs match the instruction provided;

Standard 3
Individual Learning Differences

Individualization
A student-centered approach to instructional decision making.

Intensive Instruction
An instructional approach that involves (1) actively engaging students in their learning by requiring high rates of appropriate response; (2) carefully matching instruction to student ability and skill level; (3) providing instructional cues and prompts to support learning and then fading them when appropriate; and (4) providing detailed feedback directly focused on the task the student is expected to complete.

- instruction is *explicit* and direct in the skills and strategies the reader needs to become more proficient and more independent;
- students are grouped appropriately, which includes ability-level grouping;
- instruction includes frequent opportunities for responding with feedback and ongoing progress monitoring; and
- teachers and peers support the students when necessary.

Not all children are able to learn core academic skills within the time frame dictated by schools. The degree to which a student is able to cope with the requirements of a school setting and the extent to which the school recognizes and accommodates individual diversity are known as adaptive fit. This fit is dynamic and constantly changes in the negotiations between the individual and the environment.

For students with a disability, adaptive fit may involve learning and applying various strategies that will facilitate the ability to meet the expectations of a learning environment. Such students may find that the requirements for success within a general education classroom are beyond their adaptive capabilities and that the system is unwilling to accommodate academic, behavioral, physical, sensory, or communicative differences. As a result, students develop negative attitudes toward school. Imagine yourself in a setting that constantly disapproves of how you act and what you do, a place in which activities are difficult and overwhelming, a setting in which your least desirable qualities are emphasized. What would you think about spending more than 1,000 hours a year in such a place?

Over the years, educators have responded in several ways to mismatches between the needs of students and the demands of the learning environment. Using the first alternative, the traditional approach, students remain in the negative situation and nothing is done until inevitable failure occurs. This changed with the second alternative—the advent of special education and the continuum of placements whereby students are pulled out of a setting and moved to a classroom or school more conducive to individual needs. In this approach, no attempt is made to modify the students' current environment.

For some time, the general classroom teacher has had to work with students who have disabilities without the assistance of any effective support. This is no longer the case in many of today's schools. The emergence of inclusive education programs in elementary schools throughout the United States has strengthened collaborative efforts between the general education classroom teacher and the network of supports available in the school.

In U.S. schools today, we see a greater emphasis on access to the general curriculum and on accountability for student learning. What does access to the general curriculum mean for students with disabilities? How can schools make the curriculum accessible to all students in an inclusive setting? What approaches are needed to measure student progress effectively? In the next section, we take a closer look at several evidence-based instructional approaches that have proved effective in creating access to the general education curriculum and facilitating student learning in an inclusive setting.

Multitiered System of Support (aka RtI)

A multitiered system of support (MTSS), often used synonymously with "the three-tiered model of assessment and instruction" or "response to intervention" (RtI), has its origins in the research on school-wide positive behavioral supports (PBS) (Horner, Sugai, & Anderson, 2010; Sugai & Horner, 2010). See Chapter 8 for more discussion on PBS. MTSS is based on a system-wide approach to providing evidence-based instruction using a three-tiered model based on the instructional and behavioral needs of each child. It involves continuous monitoring of student progress in making decisions regarding the frequency and intensity of instruction. Data are used to guide instruction, appropriate intervention and practice, parent involvement, and other evidence-based practices (Vaughn, et al., 2011). As described by Gargiulo and Metcalf (2013), "an RtI [MTSS] framework represents a conceptual shift in thinking from a 'wait to fail' approach to one that emphasizes early intervention and possibly prevention …" (p. 58).

The MTSS framework is most often described in terms of three assessment and instructional tiers. *Tier I* focuses on core classroom instruction that is provided to all students using evidence-based practices to teach the critical elements within a core curriculum. The general education teacher and special education teacher in conjunction with a school-wide support team provide instruction to students who are at various levels of development in critical academic and/or behavior skills. Most students will demonstrate proficiency with effective Tier I instruction. These students are able to acquire skills through the core instruction provided by the teacher, whereas others require more intensive instruction in specific skill areas. The use of universal design for learning, differentiated instruction (see the following section on differentiated instruction), and the targeting of specific skill development provide classroom teachers, in conjunction with the school-wide support team, with the tools to meet the needs of most students.

Tier II provides supplemental targeted instruction in addition to evidence-based practices taught at the Tier I level. For some students, core classroom instruction in the general classroom is not enough for them to demonstrate proficiency. These students require targeted supplemental instruction in addition to the skills taught through core instruction. Tier II meets the needs of these students by giving them additional time for intensive small-group instruction daily. The goal is to support and reinforce skills being taught by the general and special education teachers as well as the school-wide support team at the Tier I level. At this level of intervention, data-based monitoring is used to ensure adequate progress is being made on target skills. The frequency, intensity, and duration of this instruction vary for each student depending on the assessment and progress monitoring data.

A small number of students who receive targeted supplemental instruction (Tier II) continue to have difficulty becoming proficient in necessary content skills. *Tier III* provides intensive targeted instruction to the most at-risk learners who have not adequately responded to evidence-based practices. These students require instruction and/or behavioral intervention that is more explicit, more intensive, and specifically designed to meet their individual educational needs. Additional sessions of specialized one-to-one or small-group instruction are provided with progress monitoring of specific skills.

In summary, the key components of MTSS are (1) the use of evidence-based instruction designed to meet the needs of students at each level, and (2) assessment and progress-monitoring procedures that measure current skills and growth over time and that are used to provide new instruction to individual students. For additional information, see the related TeachSource Video box, "Response to Intervention: The Three-Tiered Model in a Preschool Environment."

Universal Design for Learning and Adaptive Instruction

Universal design as an applied concept began in the field of architecture where its initial focus was to create accessibility to a physical space (e.g., building and/or landscape) that would meet the needs of every individual without having to adapt or alter the critical elements of the space over time. As applied to architecture, the purpose of universal design is to accommodate everyone, including people in wheelchairs, people with low vision, people with children, and people who are elderly. In schools, **universal design for learning** shares with architecture the primary goal of assuring "accessibility." In education, however, the concept of "accessibility" is focused on developing common (universal) approaches to teaching and learning that are intended to meet the needs of all students within a collaborative learning environment and without adaptation or modification.

Compared to universal design for learning, **adaptive instruction** seeks to enhance student performance in a given content area (e.g., reading) by modifying the way in which instruction is delivered and by changing the environment where the learning takes place. This approach uses a variety of instructional procedures, materials, and alternative learning sequences in the classroom setting to help students master content consistent with their needs, abilities, and interests (Wood, 2006). For example, a student who is unable

Universal design for learning
Instructional programs that work for all students to the greatest extent possible without the needs for adaption or specialized design.

Adaptive instruction
Instruction that modified the learning environment to accommodate unique learner characteristics.

In a UDL curriculum ...

- *Goals* provide an appropriate challenge for all students.
- *Materials* have a flexible format, supporting transformation between media and multiple representations of content to support all students' learning.
- *Methods* are flexible and diverse enough to provide appropriate learning experiences, challenges, and supports for all students.
- *Assessment* is sufficiently flexible to provide accurate, ongoing information that helps teachers adjust instruction and maximize learning.

Teaching Math Using UDL

Suppose a math teacher uses the UDL approach to convey the critical features of a right triangle. With software that supports graphics and hyperlinks, a document is prepared that shows:

- Multiple examples of right triangles in different orientations and sizes, with the right angle and the three points highlighted.
- An animation of the right triangle morphing into an isosceles triangle or into a rectangle, with voice and on-screen text to highlight the differences.
- Links to reviews on the characteristics of triangles and of right angles.
- Links to examples of right triangles in various real-world contexts.
- Links to pages that students can go to on their own for review or enrichment on the subject.
- The teacher could then project the documentation onto a large screen in front of the class. Thus, the teacher would present the concept not simply by explaining it verbally or by assigning a textbook chapter or workbook page, but by using many modalities and with options for extra support or extra enrichment.

SOURCE: From Hitchcock, C., Meyer, A., Rose, D., & Jackson, R. (2002, November/December). Providing new access to the general curriculum: Universal design for learning. *Teaching Exceptional Children 8, 13*.

to memorize multiplication tables may be taught to use a calculator to complete the task. Learning to use the calculator would likely not take place in a large group setting but in a one-to-one or small-group situation. The degree of difficulty for the task is modified to fit with the capability of the student; the alteration within the learning environment allows the student to be taught the skill through intensive instruction.

Universal design for learning goes one step beyond adaptive instruction, creating instructional programs and environments that work for all students, to the greatest extent possible, without the need for adaptation or specialized design.

As is true for adaptive instruction, the basic premise of universal design for learning is to make the curriculum accessible and applicable to all students, regardless of their abilities or learning styles. A range of options is available to each student that supports access to and engagement with the learning materials (Bender, 2008; Bolt & Roach, 2009; Ketterlin-Geller, 2008; Kotering, McClannon, & Braziel, 2008; Rose & Meyer, 2002). Figure 3.5 describes the basic principles of the universal design curriculum and provides an example of its application in the teaching of mathematics.

Differentiated Instruction

Today's classrooms include children with many different needs and abilities. Haager and Klinger (2005) describe what it is like for teachers to face the challenges of a mixed-ability class:

Mrs. Ryan [an elementary special education teacher] co-teaches in Mrs. Crawford's fourth-grade class during language arts time. Today Mrs. Crawford is explaining an assignment after reading aloud a chapter of a literature book. The students have their own copies of the literature book to use as a reference. The assignment is to write each vocabulary word written on the board, draw an illustration of the word, and write a sentence demonstrating its meaning. The students are using the class dictionaries and will complete any work they do not finish in class for homework. They will also write an entry in their reading journals for homework. Mrs. Ryan observes Marcel and Tomika, two students on her special education roster, during the reading time and makes some notes in her consultation log regarding Marcel's approved attention. He has refrained from talking aloud during reading, one of his goals. When the students begin their seat work, [Mrs. Ryan] implements adaptations for both students. They will both do only half of the words, and she and the teacher [Mrs. Crawford] have rearranged which words are most critical. Marcel and Tomika will do journal entries later with Mrs. Ryan's assistance. Mrs. Ryan quietly explains the modifications to Marcel and Tomika and directs them to begin with the assignment, reminding them that they should spell the vocabulary words correctly since they are copying them, but they need not worry about spelling all the words right in their sentences; the important thing is getting their ideas down. (pp. 54–55)

CEC

Standard 4
Instructional Strategies

In a mixed-ability class, students of the same age are clearly not alike in *how* they learn or in their *rate* of acquiring new knowledge. Therefore, teachers must use **differentiated instruction**, a teaching technique in which a variety of instructional approaches within the same curriculum are used to meet individual instructional need. At its most basic level, differentiated instruction provides students with many different ways to access and learn content within the general education curriculum. Peterson and Hittie (2010) describe differentiated instruction as "designing for diversity" and suggest several strategies for its implementation:

Differentiated instruction
Provides students with many different ways to access and learn content within the general education curriculum.

- Design lessons at multiple levels.
- Challenge students at their own level.
- Provide support to push children ahead to their next level of learning.
- Engage children in learning via activities related to the real world—to their lives at home and in the community.
- Engage the **multiple intelligences** and learning styles of children so that many pathways for learning and demonstrating achievement are available.
- Involve students in collaborative pair or group work in which children draw on each other's strengths (p. 46).

Multiple intelligences
A theory that human intelligence spans several domains: linguistic, logical-mathematical, spatial, musical, bodily-kinesthetic, interpersonal, intrapersonal, and naturalistic.

TEACHSOURCE VIDEO RESPONSE TO INTERVENTION (RTI): THE THREE-TIERED MODEL IN A PRESCHOOL ENVIRONMENT

Please visit the Education CourseMate website for *Human Exceptionality,* 11th edition, at CengageBrain.com to access this chapter's TeachSource video. Response to intervention (RtI) is a multitiered system of support in which schools seek to identify and help students at risk for poor learning outcomes. In this system, teachers assess students and then review student data to determine who requires what type of educational intervention. Then teachers provide evidence-based interventions and adjust the intensity and nature of those interventions depending on a student's responsiveness. If a student does not respond to these interventions over an appropriate period of time, the school will seek to determine if the student has a disability so that appropriate and further intervention can be made. Although this video is set in the preschool classroom, the principles apply to elementary classrooms in general. Watch this video to see RtI in action and respond to the following questions:

1. How is response to intervention used in this classroom?

2. What instructional information is collected on each child, and how is it used in planning a program that will meet individual needs?

3. How does classroom teacher Jessica Cruz use the information from the RtI process to enhance her teaching and more effectively meet the needs of the students in her class?

Universal design for learning helps make the curriculum accessible and applicable to all students, regardless of their abilities or learning styles. Here students are using a digital talking textbook. What are some other ways in which universal design for learning can help students with disabilities in an inclusive classroom?

Recording for the Blind and Dyslexic

To be effective, differentiated instruction requires that general and special education teachers work together to ensure access to the curriculum for all children in the class, while at the same time accepting individual goals for each child (Gartin et al., 2002; Haager & Klinger, 2005; Hammeken, 2007; Karen, 2007). Together with related services, these teachers use many different instructional strategies that are consistent with a student's level and rate of learning. Finally, students are able to demonstrate progress in many different ways (such as orally instead of in writing).

Assistive Technology

Have you ever watched a program with closed-captioning or a foreign movie with subtitles? Do you turn on your television and open your garage door with a remote control device? Do you use speed dial or a digital address book on your cell phone? If so, you use assistive technology. **Assistive technology** is "any item, piece of equipment, or product system, whether acquired commercially off the shelf, modified, or customized, that is used to increase, maintain, or improve the functional capabilities of a child with disabilities" (Technology Related Assistance for Individuals with Disabilities Act, 20 U.S.C. 1401[1]).

Assistive technology can take many forms (high-tech or low-tech) and can be helpful to students with disabilities in several different ways. For students with reading problems, a high-tech digital textbook could assist with decoding and comprehending text. Students who have difficulty in verbally communicating with others might use a low-tech language board on which they point to pictures cut from magazines to indicate what they would like for lunch. Students with motor difficulties could learn to operate a joystick so they can move their power wheelchair in any direction.

Assistive technology
An item or product used to increase, maintain, or improve the functional capabilities of a child with disabilities.

ASSISTIVE TECHNOLOGY
THE STRATEGY TUTOR

The World Wide Web is an engaging, information-rich learning environment—but it also can present significant challenges for struggling learners. Unlike textbooks, which are laid out to help learn a specific curriculum, websites are created for a wide range of purposes and by a varied and often unknown group of authors. As a result, the Internet can be a challenging environment for students who struggle with reading.

Strategy Tutor, developed by the Center for Applied Special Technology and funded by the Carnegie Corporation of New York, is an instructional tool that supports students and their teachers in getting the most out of information-rich web pages. The program helps teachers implement reading strategy instruction while guiding students through specific online research projects. Teachers can add prompts and interactive features that will, through the Strategy Tutor interface, be displayed as part of websites they have preselected. On sites not customized by the teacher, Strategy Tutor gives generic tips intended to guide students through the process of web research, teaching strategies that will serve them well even without the Strategy Tutor interface. For more information on Strategy Tutor, visit http://cst.cast.org.

SOURCE: Center for Applied Special Technology. (2012). *Carnegie Strategy Tutor.* Retrieved January 15, 2012, from www.cast.org/research/projects/tutor.html (Coyne, P., & Dalton, B., Project Directors).

Curriculum-Based Assessment/Measurement

In this era of accountability, developing *assessments* that reliably *measure* student learning is an essential component of instruction (Arthur-Kelly et al., 2008; Hosp & Hosp, 2003; Lund & Veal, 2008). As Howell and Nolet (2000) put it, "Assessment is the process of collecting information by reviewing the products of student work, interviewing, observing, or testing" (p. 3). Educators assess students for the purpose of deciding whether they are making adequate progress and, if not, what additional or different services and supports are needed.

The hallmarks of any good assessment are its accuracy, fairness, and utility. Traditional standardized tests (such as intelligence quotient [IQ] or achievement tests) compare one student with another to determine how each individual compares with the overall average. For example, an average score on the Stanford-Binet Intelligence Test is 100. Any score (higher or lower) would be described as deviating from the average. Significantly higher scores may lead to the use of such descriptors as *gifted* or *talented*. Significantly lower scores may result in the label *intellectually disabled*.

Traditional assessments may be useful in determining a student's eligibility for special education (comparing the student with the average performance of peers), but many educators question their use in planning for instruction and measuring day-to-day student learning. An alternative approach to traditional assessment is the use of **curriculum-based assessments** (CBAs) and **curriculum-based measurements** (CBMs). CBAs include "any procedure that evaluates student performance in relation to the school curriculum, such as weekly spelling tests," whereas CBMs are the "frequent, direct measurements of critical school behaviors, which could include timed (1–5 minute) tests of performance on reading, math, and writing skills" (Mastropieri & Scruggs, 2007, p. 271).

Curriculum-based assessments (CBAs) Procedure that evaluates student performance in relation to the school curriculum.

Curriculum-based measurements (CBMs) Frequent, direct measurements of critical school behaviors, which could include timed (1- to 5-minute) tests of performance.

Looking Toward a Bright Future

In the nearly four decades since the passage of the Individuals with Disabilities Education Act, we have been witness to the most significant and positive improvements in educational services and supports for students with disabilities in our history. From isolation to inclusion and from research to practice, much has been accomplished to create access to appropriate schooling and improve the quality of education for these children. As we now move through the second decade of the 21st century, the future looks bright. The future will become even brighter if we continue to pay attention to what we know about best practices and use them in preparing our new and highly qualified teachers, focusing on quality professional development for practicing teachers, and providing the critical resources that schools must have to meet the individual needs of all students. It will be essential for general and special education teachers to find new and innovative ways to work together along with their related services colleagues to use evidence-based instruction that will create access to the general curriculum and increase student learning and achievement. We know what works, including differentiated instruction, universal design for learning, direct instruction, assistive technology, and curriculum-based assessment/measurement. A bright future will depend on our willingness and ability to use these practices with each child, all day, and in every school.

FOCUS REVIEW

FOCUS 1 Define inclusive education.

- Inclusive education may be defined as placing students with disabilities in a general education setting within their home or neighborhood school while making available both formal and natural supports to ensure an appropriate educational experience.
- Full inclusion occurs when students with a disability receive all instruction and support within the general education classroom.

Partial inclusion occurs when students with a disability receive most instruction within the general education classroom but are "pulled out" for specialized services part of the school day.

FOCUS 2 Describe the characteristics of evidence-based inclusive schools.

Evidence-based inclusive schools

- promote the values of diversity, acceptance, and belonging.

- ensure the availability of formal and natural supports within the general education setting.
- provide services and supports in age-appropriate classrooms in neighborhood schools.
- ensure access to the general curriculum while meeting the individualized needs of each student.
- provide a school-wide support system to meet the needs of all students.

FOCUS 3 Define multidisciplinary collaboration and identify its key characteristics.

- Collaboration is defined as professionals, parents, and students *working together* to achieve the mutual goal of delivering an effective educational program designed to meet individual needs. Collaboration is not what those involved do; it is how they do it.
- In an inclusive school, effective collaboration has several key characteristics:
  - Parents are viewed as active partners in the education of their children.
  - Team members share responsibility; individual roles are clearly understood and valued.
  - Team members promote peer support and cooperative learning.

FOCUS 4 Why is it so important to provide early intervention services as soon as possible to young children at risk?

- The first years of life are critical to the overall development of all children—normal, at-risk, and disabled.
- Early stimulation is crucial to the later development of language, intelligence, personality, and self-worth.
- Early intervention may prevent or reduce the overall impact of disabilities, as well as counteract the negative effects of delayed intervention.
- Early intervention may in the long run be less costly and more effective than providing services later in an individual's life.

FOCUS 5 Identify the purposes of Part C of IDEA and the components of the individualized family service plan (IFSP).

- Part C of IDEA has several purposes, including
  - enhancing the development of infants and toddlers with disabilities to minimize their potential for developmental delay, and recognizing the significant brain development that occurs during a child's first three years of life;
  - reducing the educational costs to our society by minimizing the need for special education and related services when infants and toddlers with reach school age;
  - maximizing the potential for individuals with disabilities to live independently in society;
  - enhancing the capacity of families to meet the special needs of their infants and toddlers with disabilities; and
  - enhancing the capacity of state and local agencies and service providers to identify, evaluate, and meet the needs of all children, particularly minority, low-income, inner-city, and rural children, and infants and toddlers in foster care.

- The components of the individualized family service plan include
  - the infant's or toddler's present levels of physical development, cognitive development, communication development, social or emotional development, and adaptive development;
  - family resources, priorities, and concerns related to enhancing the development of their child;
  - major outcomes to be achieved for the infant or toddler and the family, and the criteria, procedures, and timelines used to determine progress toward achieving those outcomes;
  - early intervention services necessary to meet the unique needs of the infant or toddler and the family; the natural environments in which early intervention services are to be provided; the projected dates for initiation of services and the anticipated duration of the services;
  - identification of the service coordinator; and
  - steps to be taken to support the transition of the toddler with a disability to preschool or other appropriate services.

FOCUS 6 Identify evidence-based instructional approaches for preschool-age children with disabilities.

Evidence-based instructional instructional approaches for preschoolers with disabilities include:

- A child-find system in each state to locate young children at risk and make referrals to appropriate agencies for preschool services
- An individualized education program (IEP) that involves specialists across several disciplines
- Instruction that reflects developmentally appropriate practice, age-appropriate practice, and the teaching of functional skills
- Inclusive preschool classrooms where young children with disabilities are educated side by side with peers without disabilities

FOCUS 7 Describe the roles of special education and general education teachers in an inclusive classroom setting.

- Special education teachers have multiple roles that may be referred to as the "three Cs": collaborator, consultant, and coordinator.
- In the role of *collaborator,* special educators work with a school to assess student needs, develop the IEP, determine appropriate accommodations and instructional adaptations, and deliver intensive instruction in academic, behavioral, and/or adaptive functional areas. Special education teachers use effective problem-solving strategies to facilitate student learning, co-teach with general educators, and apply effective accountability measures to evaluate individual student progress and long-term results.
- In the role of *consultant,* the special education teacher serves as a resource to general educators and parents on effective instructional practices for students with disabilities.
- In the role of *coordinator,* the special education teacher takes the lead responsibility for organizing the activities of the school team in developing, implementing, and evaluating student IEPs. Special education teachers may also be responsible for organizing school resources; spearheading professional development activities; supervising paraprofessionals, peer support, and volunteers; and facilitating positive communication with parents.

- General educators must be able to identify and refer students who may be in need of additional support; understand each student's individual strengths and limitations, and the effects on learning; implement an appropriate individualized instructional program that is focused on supporting student success in the general education curriculum; and initiate and maintain ongoing communication with parents.

FOCUS 8 Identify the characteristics of evidence-based instruction that enhance learning opportunities for all students, including those with disabilities. What approaches to assessment and instruction are considered evidence-based practice in an inclusive elementary school classroom?

- The characteristics of evidence-based instruction for all students are *individualization:* (student-centered approach to instructional decision making); *intensive instruction* (frequent instructional experiences of significant duration); and *an "education for all" approach to teaching and learning* (developing and adapting instruction to meet the needs of every student).
- Multitiered systems of support (MTSS) (aka response to intervention [RtI]) are based on a system-wide approach to providing evidence-based instruction using a three-tiered model based on the instructional and behavioral needs of each child.

- Universal design for learning goes one step beyond multilevel instruction, creating instructional programs and environments that work for all students, to the greatest extent possible, without the need for adaptation or specialized design.
- Students of the same age are clearly not alike in how they learn or in their rate of learning. For this reason, teachers must use *differentiated instruction* in which multiple teaching approaches within the same curriculum are *adapted* to individual need and functioning level.
- Assistive technology can take many forms and can be helpful to students with disabilities in several different ways (examples include a high-tech digital textbook, a low-tech language board, and a joystick to guide a power wheelchair).
- Although traditional assessments may be useful in determining a student's eligibility for special education, many educators question their use in planning for instruction and measuring day-to-day student learning. An alternative to traditional tests is the use of curriculum-based assessments (CBAs) and curriculum-based measurements (CBMs). CBAs include any procedure that evaluates student performance in relation to the school curriculum. CBMs are frequent, direct measurements of critical school behaviors, which could include timed (1- to 5-minute) tests of performance.

Council for Exceptional Children (CEC) Standards to Accompany Chapter 3

 If you are thinking about a career in special education, you should know that many states use national standards developed by the Council for Exceptional Children (CEC) to assess a teacher candidate's knowledge and skills for working with students with disabilities. See a complete listing of the 10 CEC Content Standards on the inside back cover of this text.

1 Foundations
3 Individual Learning Differences
4 Instructional Strategies
5 Learning Environments and Social Interactions
7 Instructional Planning
9 Professional and Ethical Practice
10 Collaboration

Mastery Activities and Assignments

 To master the content within this chapter, complete the following activities and assignments. Online and interactive versions of these activities are also available on the accompanying Education CourseMate website, where you may also access TeachSource videos, chapter web links, interactive quizzes, portfolio activities, flash cards, an integrated eBook, and much more!

1. Complete a written test of the chapter's content. If your instructor requires a written test of your content knowledge for this chapter, keep a copy for your portfolio. A practice test on the information covered in this chapter is available through the Education CourseMate website and the Student Study Guide.

2. Review the Case Study, "Ricardo," and respond in writing to the Application Questions. Keep a copy of the Case Study and of your written response for your portfolio.
3. Read the Debate Forum in this chapter and then visit the Education CourseMate website to complete the activity, "Take a Stand." Keep a copy of this activity for your portfolio.
4. Participate in a community service learning activity. Community service is a valuable way to enhance your learning experience. Visit the Education CourseMate website for suggested community service learning activities that correspond to the information presented in this chapter. Develop a reflective journal of the service learning experience for your portfolio.

CHAPTER 4

Secondary Education and Transition Planning

Spencer Grant/Getty Images

FOCUS PREVIEW

As you read the chapter, focus on these key concepts:

1 What do we know about lives of people with disabilities after they leave school?

2 What are the requirements for transition planning in IDEA?

3 Identify the purpose of person-centered transition planning and the basic steps in its formulation.

4 Why is it important for students with disabilities to receive instruction in self-determination, academics, adaptive and functional life skills, and employment preparation during the secondary school years?

Meet Ellie and Kari and Their "Educaton for All" Approach to Teaching Math in a High School Classroom

Ellie Goldberg is a general education high school math teacher. Kari Abdal-Khallaq is a special education teacher who specializes in math-related learning problems for high school students with disabilities. Each day Ellie and Kari come together in an inclusive high school classroom to provide math instruction for students who have varying ranges of abilities, learning styles, behavioral challenges, and instructional needs. Together, these teachers use many different strategies to assure

Copyright 2014 Cengage Learning

every student is focused and on task during instructional time, including classroom rules and expectations, large- and small-group instruction, individual tutoring, tactile activities, written and oral feedback, and extended instructional time.

 To see Ellie and Kari in action, watch "Managing an Inclusive Classroom: High School Math Instruction" on the Education CourseMate website for Human Exceptionality, 11th edition.

A Changing Era in the Lives of People with Disabilities

In the 21st century, our expectations for students leaving school and moving into adult life are college or career readiness. Early adulthood begins a new era in life. It is a time of change—a transition from dependence on the family to increasing responsibilities. Young adults are concerned with furthering their education, earning a living, establishing their pathways through life, and creating social networks. As an adolescent leaves high school, decisions need to be made. Each of us may reflect on several questions: What kind of career or job do I desire? Should I further my education to increase my career choices? Where shall I live and with whom shall I live? How shall I spend my money? With whom do I choose to spend time? Who will be my friends?

Although most young people face these choices as a natural part of growing into adult life, the challenges confronting individuals with disabilities and their families may be different. For many, the choice may be to disappear into the fabric of society and try to make it on their own without the supports and services that were so much a part of their experience growing up. Others may choose to go to college, seeking the needed accommodations (such as more time to take tests, large-print books, or interpreters) that will give them a fighting chance to succeed in an academic world. Still others will need continuing supports to find and keep a job and to live successfully in the community.

Given the expectations for adult life, the school's responsibility is to teach the skills that will assist each individual with disabilities to access valued postschool outcomes. Much has been done to improve the quality of life for adults with disabilities and much more remains to be done to ensure that every person with a disability is able to access the services or supports necessary for success following graduation from school.

Standard 1
Foundations

Standard 9
Professional and Ethical Practice

Research on the Lives of Adults with Disabilities

FOCUS 1

What do we know about lives of people with disabilities after they leave school?

One measure of the effectiveness of a school program is the success of its graduates. Nearly four decades have passed since the passage of the federal mandate to provide a free and appropriate public education to all students with disabilities. The educational opportunities afforded by this landmark legislation have not yet led to full participation of special education graduates in the social and economic mainstream of their local communities (Kessler Foundation and the National Organization on Disability [N.O.D.], 2010). However, there have been some very positive changes. Whereas follow-up studies of special education graduates in the 1990s suggested that these individuals had higher unemployment rates, lower rates of participation in postsecondary education, and less extensive support networks than their peers without disabilities (Hasazi, Furney, & Destefano, 1999; Wagner & Blackorby, 1996), the National Longitudinal Transition Study-2 (Wagner, Newman, Cameto, & Levine, 2005) reported that progress had been made in several areas (high school completion, living arrangements, social involvement, further education, and employment rates). The nearby Reflect on This, "Changes Over Time in the Postschool Outcomes of Young Adults with Disabilities," highlights some of the positive changes, as reported by Wagner and her colleagues.

High School Completion and Access to Valued Postschool Outcomes

CEC

Standard 5
Learning Environments and Social Interactions

The increasing emphasis on the transition from school to adult life has altered many earlier perceptions about people with disabilities. Without question, the potential of adults with disabilities has been significantly underestimated. In recent years, professionals and parents have begun to address some of the crucial issues facing students with disabilities as the students prepare to leave school and face life as adults in their local communities. More than 400,000 students with disabilities exit school each year, but the drop-out rate for these students is nearly twice that of their typical nondisabled peers (Thurlow, Sinclair, & Johnson, 2009). Of the students with disabilities exiting school (ages 14 to 21), only 56.5 percent leave with a high school diploma, compared with 90 percent of their peers without disabilities (U.S. Department of Education, 2011). Although there has been improvement, as evidenced by the results of the National Longitudinal Transition Study-2 (Wagner et al., 2005), too many of the current graduates from special education programs are not adequately prepared for employment and have difficulty accessing further education. They are also unable to locate the critical programs and services necessary for success as adults in their local communities (Kessler and N.O.D., 2010; Wehman, 2011). For people with more severe disabilities, long waiting lists for employment and housing services prove frustrating (Crockett & Hardman, 2009). Prouty, Smith, and Lakin (2001) reported that nearly 72,000 adults with severe disabilities were on waiting lists for residential, day treatment, or family support services. Furthermore, individuals with disabilities who enroll in postsecondary education often find that the supports and services they need to achieve success in college are also not available (Babbitt & White, 2002; McDonnell, Kiuhara, & Collier, 2009).

Employment

The U.S. Department of Education's National Longitudinal Transition Study-2 (NLTS-2) (Wagner et al., 2005) reported that the *probability* of young adults with disabilities working for pay at some time during the first few years out of high school had increased significantly (from 55 percent to 70 percent) between 1987 and 2003. However, the rate of employment for young adults with disabilities lagged significantly behind that of same-age peers without disabilities in 2003 (41 percent versus 63 percent). Worse yet, the employment rate Wagner et al. reported in 2005 was significantly higher than the findings of the 2010 Kessler and N.O.D. poll, in which only 21 percent of the people with disabilities indicated that they were employed.

From 1985 to 2003, two studies documented the changes that young adults with disabilities have experienced after they exited high school. The National Longitudinal Transition Study (NLTS) followed up on students with disabilities who had been receiving special education services in 1985, and the National Longitudinal Transition Study-2 (NLTS2) assessed the status of young adults with disabilities who exited school some 25 years later at the beginning of the 21st century. The following presents highlights of comparisons between these two studies.

SCHOOL COMPLETION

- The school completion rate of young adults with disabilities increased, and the drop-out rate decreased by 17 percent between 1987 and 2003.

COMMUNITY LIVING AND SOCIAL ACTIVITIES

- The living arrangements of young adults with disabilities have been stable over time. Two years after exiting high school, approximately 75 percent of young adults with disabilities from both studies lived with their parents, 3 percent lived in a residential facility or institution, and one in eight lived independently.

- Of young adults with disabilities from the 1987 and 2003 studies, 90 percent were single. However, membership in organized community groups (such as hobby clubs, community sports, and performing groups) more than doubled, such that 28 percent of young adults with disabilities from the 2003 study belonged to a group.

- Between 1987 and 2003, there was a large increase in adults with disabilities who had ever been subject to disciplinary action at school, fired from a job, or arrested. More than 50 percent of the young adults with disabilities from the 2003 study had negative consequences for their behavior, compared with 33 percent from the 1987 study.

ENGAGEMENT IN SCHOOL AND WORK, OR PREPARATION FOR WORK

- Overall engagement in school, work, and job training increased only slightly (from 70 percent to 75 percent) between 1987 and 2003. Although their overall rate of engagement in these activities did not increase markedly over time, the modes of engagement did change.

- Engagement in the combination of postsecondary education and paid employment nearly quadrupled, rising to 22 percent for students in the 2003 study.

- There was a significant increase in employment (11 percent) from 1987 to 2003.

EMPLOYMENT

- In 2003, 70 percent of young adults with disabilities who had been out of school up to two years had worked for pay at some time since leaving high school; only 55 percent had done so in 1987. However, 18 percent of young adults in the 2003 study were less likely than those in the 1987 study to be working full-time in their current job. Approximately 39 percent of the young adults in the 2003 study were employed full-time.

- Over time, considerably more young adults with disabilities earned more than the federal minimum wage (70 percent in 1987 versus 85 percent in 2003). Yet the average hourly wage did not increase when adjusted for inflation; earnings averaged $7.30 an hour in 2003.

Question for Reflection

Of the areas studied by NLTS, where did the most changes occur for young adults with disabilities over time? Which of the areas had the most positive change? Most negative change?

SOURCE: Wagner, M., Newman, L., Cameto, R., & Levine, P. (2005). *Changes over time in the early postschool outcomes of youth with disabilities.* A report from the National Longitudinal Transition Study (NLTS) and the National Longitudinal Transition Study-2 (NLTS2) (pp. ES-1–ES-3). Menlo Park, CA: SRI International.

Closing the Gap: Transition Planning and Services

Standard 7
Instructional Planning

The transition from school to adult life is a complex and dynamic process. Transition planning should culminate with the transfer of support from the school to an adult service agency, access to postsecondary education, or life as an independent adult. The planning process involves a series of choices about which experiences in their remaining school years will best prepare students with disabilities for what lies ahead in the adult world. A successful transition from school to the adult years requires both formal (government-funded) and natural supports (Muller, Schuler, & Yates, 2008; Steere, Rose, & Cavaiuolo, 2007; Wehman, 2011). Historically, providing *formal supports*, such as health care, employment preparation, and supported living, has been emphasized. Only recently has society begun to understand the importance of the family and other *natural support* networks in preparing adolescents with a disability for adult life. Research suggests that the family unit may be the single most powerful force in preparing an adolescent with a disability for the adult years (Drew & Hardman, 2007).

The principal components of an effective transition system include:

- Effective middle (junior high) and high school programs that link instruction to further education (such as college or trade schools) and to valued postschool outcomes (such as employment, independent living, and recreation/leisure activities).

- A cooperative system of transition planning that involves public education, adult services, and an array of natural supports (family and friends) to ensure access to valued postschool outcomes.

- The availability of formal government-funded programs following school that meet the unique educational, employment, residential, and leisure needs of people with disabilities in a community setting.

IDEA Transition Planning Requirements

FOCUS 2

What are the requirements for transition planning in IDEA?

Transition services
Coordinated activities designed to help disabled students move from school to employment, further education, vocational training, independent living, and community participation.

IDEA requires that every student with a disability receives transition services. **Transition services** are a coordinated set of activities for students with disabilities that are designed to facilitate the move from school to employment, further education, vocational training, independent living, and community participation. To be more specific, transition services should possess the following attributes:

- They are designed to be within a results-oriented process—that is, focused on improving the academic and functional achievement of the child with a disability to facilitate the child's movement from school to postschool activities, including postsecondary education, vocational education, integrated employment (including supported employment), continuing and adult education, adult services, independent living, and community participation.

- They are based on the individual child's needs, taking into account the child's strengths, preferences, and interests.

- They are designed to include instruction, related services, community experiences, the development of employment and other postschool adult living objectives, and, when appropriate, acquisition of daily living skills and functional vocational evaluation (IDEA, 2004, PL 108–446, Sec. 602[34]).

Standard 1
Foundations

IDEA requires that, beginning at age 16 and updated annually, a student's individualized education program (IEP) should include measurable postsecondary goals based on age-appropriate transition assessments related to training, education, employment, and, where appropriate, independent living skills. The IEP must include a statement of transition services related to various courses of study (such as participation in advanced placement courses or a vocational education program) that will assist the student in reaching her or his goals (IDEA, 2004, PL 108–446, Sec. 614[d]).

Other Federal Laws Linked to IDEA and Transition Planning

Five other pieces of federal legislation are linked directly to the IDEA transition requirements to facilitate an effective transition planning process. They are the Vocational Rehabilitation Act, the Carl D. Perkins Vocational and Applied Technology Education Act, the Americans with Disabilities Act (ADA), the School-to-Work Opportunities Act, and the Ticket to Work and Work Incentives Improvement Act. The Vocational Rehabilitation Act provides services through rehabilitation counselors in several areas (such as guidance counseling, vocational evaluation, vocational training and job placement, transportation, family services, interpreter services, and telecommunication aids and devices). Amendments to the act have encouraged stronger collaboration and outreach between the schools and the rehabilitation counselors in transition planning.

Greater connections between education and vocational rehabilitation are expected to help students with disabilities to move on to postsecondary education or obtain employment. The Carl D. Perkins Vocational and Applied Technology Education Act provides students with disabilities greater access to vocational education services. ADA addresses equal access to public accommodations, employment, transportation, and telecommunication services following the school transition years (see Chapter 1). Such services are often directly targeted as a part of the student's transition plan.

The School-to-Work Opportunities Act provides all students in the public schools with education and training to prepare them for first jobs in high-skill, high-wage careers, and for further education following high school. Students with disabilities are specifically identified as a target population of the act. The Ticket to Work and Work Incentives Improvement Act provides people with disabilities greater opportunities for employment by allowing them to work and still keep critical health care coverage. Prior to the passage of this act, many people with disabilities were not able to work because federal Social Security laws put them at risk of losing Medicaid and Medicare coverage if they accrued any significant earnings. Thus, there was little incentive for people with disabilities to work because they could not access health insurance. The Work Incentives Improvement Act made health insurance available and affordable when a person with a disability went to work or developed a significant disability while working (for more information, see www.socialsecurity.gov).

CEC

Standard 7
Instructional Planning

FOCUS 3
Identify the purpose of person-centered transition planning and the basic steps in its formulation.

Person-centered transition planning
Planning process based on a commitment to each student's needs and preferences, and developed and implemented within each student's IEP.

Person-Centered Transition Planning

Transition involves more than the mere transfer of administrative responsibility from the school to an adult service agency. **Person-centered transition planning** is based on an understanding of and commitment to each student's needs and preferences, and must be developed and implemented within each student's IEP. The process includes access to the general education curriculum and a focus on the adaptive and functional skills that will facilitate life in the community following school (Bakken & Obiakor, 2008; Steere, Rose, & Cavaiuolo, 2007; Wehman, 2011).

CASE STUDY MARIA

Maria is 19 years old and leaving high school to begin her adult life. For most of her high school years, she was in special education classes for reading and math, because she was about three grade levels behind her peers without disabilities. During the last term of high school, she attended a class on exploring possible careers and finding and keeping a job. The class was required for graduation, but it didn't make much sense to Maria because she had never had any experience with this area before. It just didn't seem to be related to her other schoolwork.

Although Maria wants to get a job in a retail store (such as stocking clothing or shoes), she isn't having much success. She doesn't have a driver's license, and her parents don't have time to run her around to apply for various jobs. The businesses she approached are close by her home and know her well, but they keep telling her she isn't *qualified* for the jobs available. She has never had any on-the-job training in the community. Maria's parents are not very enthusiastic about her finding employment because they are afraid she might lose some of her government-funded medical benefits.

APPLICATION

1. In retrospect, what transition planning services would you have recommended for Maria during her last years of high school?

2. How would you help Maria now? Do you see the Americans with Disabilities Act playing a role in Maria's story?

3. Whose responsibility is it to work with potential employers to explore "the reasonable accommodations" that would facilitate the opportunity for Maria to succeed in a community job?

Figure 4.1 Illustrative Transition Planning Form in the Area of Employment

Student: *Robert Brown*

Meeting Date: *January 20, 2010*

Graduation Date: *June, 2011*

IEP/Transition Planning Team Members: *Robert Brown (student), Mrs. Brown (parent), Jill Green (teacher), Mike Weatherby (Vocational Education), Dick Rose (Rehabilitation), Susan Marr (MR/DD)*

TRANSITION PLANNING AREA: *Employment*

Student Preferences and
Desired Postschool Goals: *Robert would like to work in a grocery store as a produce stocker.*

Present Levels of Performance: *Robert has held several work experience placements in local grocery stores (see attached work placement summaries). He requires a self-management checklist using symbols to complete assigned work tasks. His rate of task completion is below the expected employer levels.*

Needed Transition Services: *Robert will require job placement, training, and follow-along services from an employment specialist. In addition, he needs bus training to get to his job.*

ANNUAL GOAL: *Robert will work Monday through Friday from 1:00 to 4:00 p.m. at Safeway's Food Center as a produce stocker, completing all assigned tasks without assistance from the employment specialist on ten consecutive weekly performance probes.*

Benchmarks Aligned with Alternate Achievement Standards:

1. When given his bus pass, Robert will independently take the number 5 outbound bus to Safeway's Food Center on five consecutive daily performance probes.

2. When given his bus pass, Robert will independently take the number 11 inbound bus to the Mill Hollow bus stop on five consecutive daily performance probes.

3. When given a self-management checklist using symbols, Robert will initiate all assigned tasks without prompts from the employment specialist on five consecutive daily performance probes.

4. During break, Robert will purchase a drink and snack from the deli without prompts from the employment specialist on five consecutive daily performance probes.

Activities	Person	Completion Date
1. Place Robert on the state-supported employment waiting list.	Susan Marr	May 1, 2010
2. Obtain a monthly bus pass.	Mrs. Brown	February 1, 2011
3. Schedule Robert for employee orientation training.		February 16, 2011

SOURCE: Adapted from Polychronis, S., & McDonnell, J. (2009). Developing IEPs/transition plans. In J. McDonnell & M.L. Hardman (Eds.), *Successful transition programs* (pp. 81–100). Los Angeles: Sage Publishing Co.

See Figure 4.1 for an illustration of person-centered transition planning in the area of employment preparation. The purpose of the transition statement is to (1) identify the type and range of transitional services and supports, and (2) establish timelines and personnel responsible for completing the plan. Wehman (2011) identifies six basic steps in the person-centered transition planning process. These are listed in Figure 4.2.

Facilitating Student and Parent Involvement

Standard 9
Professional and Ethical Practice

In the transition from school to adult life, many students and parents receive quite a shock. Once they leave school, students may not receive any further assistance from government programs or, at the least, they may be placed on long waiting lists for employment training, housing, or education assistance. Thus, the person with a disability may experience a significant loss in services at a crucial time. Many students and their parents know little, if anything, about what life may bring during the adult years.

1. Convene IEP teams, individualized to reflect the wants and needs of each transition-age student.

- Identify all transition-age students.
- Identify appropriate school service personnel.
- Identify appropriate adult service agencies.
- Identify appropriate members of the student's networks.

2. Review assessment data and conduct additional assessment activities.

- Meet with transition-age student and a small circle of friends, family members, co-workers, neighbors, church members, and/or staff to establish the individual's needs and preferences for adult life.

3. Teams develop IEPs/Transition IEPs.

- Schedule the IEP meeting.
- Conduct the IEP meeting.
- Open the IEP/transition IEP meeting.

4. Implement the IEP or transition IEP.

- Operate according to guidelines defined in interagency agreements.
- Use the Circle of friends/Circle of support: a group of individuals who meet regularly to work on behalf of and support a person with disabilities. These circles work to "open doors" to new opportunities for the person with disabilities, including establishing new friendships.

5. Update the IEP/transition IEP annually and implement follow-up procedures.

- Phase out involvement of school personnel, while increasing involvement of adult service agencies.
- Contact people responsible for completion of IEP/transition IEP goals to monitor progress.

6. Hold an exit meeting.

- Ensure most appropriate employment outcome or access to further education.
- Ensure most appropriate community living and recreation outcome.
- Ensure referrals to all appropriate adult agencies and support services.

SOURCE: Wehman, P. (2006). Individualized transition planning. In P. Wehman (Ed.), *Life beyond the classroom: Transition strategies for young people with disabilities,* 4th ed. (pp. 78–95). Baltimore: Paul H. Brookes.

To fully prepare for the transition from school, students and parents must be educated about critical components of adult service systems, including the characteristics of service agencies and what constitutes a good program, as well as current and potential opportunities for employment, independent living, or further education (Margolis & Prichard, 2008; Payne-Christiansen & Sitlington, 2008; Winn & Hay, 2009). Schools can use several strategies to facilitate family involvement in the transition process. These include the adoption of a person-centered approach to transition planning, where the student is at the core of the planning process and the school works with parents to identify the student's preferences and expectations.

Working with Adult Services

In addition to the student, parents, and school personnel, professionals from adult service agencies (such as vocational rehabilitation counselors, representatives from university or college centers

Terry Vine/Getty Images

Schools have many roles in the transition planning process. What do you think are a school's most important responsibilities in facilitating a successful transition from school to adult life?

LEARNING THROUGH SOCIAL MEDIA REFLECTIONS ON INCLUSIVE EDUCATION AND PARENT INVOLVEMENT AT THE SECONDARY LEVEL

A BLOG BY LISA DIECKER AND SELMA POWELL

Dr. Lisa Diecker is a parent of a student with a disability as well as a professor and Lockheed Martin Eminent Scholar at the University of Central Florida. Selma Powell is a doctoral candidate at the University of Central Florida.

To include or not to include? That is the question every parent has to struggle with as his or her child progresses through the school; issues related to placement options for students with disabilities are challenging. This question is a complex one for parents, teachers, administrators, and even students to answer, as grade point averages become more and more important for college admissions or future career options. Therefore, what *is* the least restrictive environment for all students? That is a question that becomes even more complex as students enter middle and high school.

As an educator and a parent of a student with a disability, I (Lisa Dieker) can share that our family has had these same struggles. Compound the parent role with what both of us (Lisa and Selma) know about secondary schools and we will share some of the reasons the struggle at the secondary level exists. Many parents struggle with the right balance between their child participating in inclusive settings and closing gaps that might still exist for stu-

dents as they progress in grade level. In addition, parents must consider a range of service delivery options when GPAs count, and there are few instances of general and special educators teaching together. Not only are students transforming intellectually, emotionally, sexually, and socially, but also teachers' identities seem to change from foregrounding children to foregrounding discipline knowledge. In this blog, we share what we have seen that works for secondary schools that develop successful inclusive education contexts.

We both have worked with students, families, teachers, and administrators in the roles of special educator, general educator, administrator, and researcher in secondary schools. We want to celebrate the great secondary schools we have seen that have successfully included students with disabilities to the maximum extent possible and appropriate, a decision we believe can only be made by students with disabilities and their parents/guardians. So what do these successful secondary schools look like? From visiting hundreds of schools at this level, we have seen common themes to what works . . .

- Technology use and adoption: Schools provided students with disabilities with tools that they were taught to use to meet their unique needs to become successful independent learners.

- Self-advocacy preparation: Students were aware of their disability and how to advocate for their own needs.

- Grading: Grading was discussed across schools and teams as a way to report to parents student progress (e.g., standard-based report cards, portfolios).

- Homework: Teachers coordinated efforts across the school and teams to provide a logical structure to when homework was assigned and was due.

- Teams: Teachers (both general and special education) were aligned by content teams, grade-level teams, or professional learning communities to work together toward the success of all students.

- Collaborative teaching: Teachers were in classrooms working together with special educators, general educators, English as a second language teachers, reading specialists, and speech therapists.

- Behavior: Schools had discussed the need for similar rules and consequences, with many using positive behavioral intervention support models.

- Active learning: Students were not in rows, but actively engaged in cooperative learning or peer support groups.

SOURCE: Reprinted with permission from Diecker, L., & Powell, S. (2012). Reflection on inclusive practices at the secondary level. Retrieved February 19, 2012 from www.niusileadscape.org/bl/?p=762# more-762.

Adult service agencies
Agencies that provide services and supports to assist people with disabilities to become more independent as adults.

for students with disabilities, and the state developmental disability agency) may also be involved in transition planning. **Adult service agencies** assist individuals with a disability in accessing postsecondary education, employment, supported living, and/or leisure activities.

Agencies may provide support in vocational rehabilitation, social services, and mental health. Examples of supports include career, education, or mental health counseling, job training and support (such as a job coach), further education (college or trade school), attendant services, and interpreter services. Adult service agencies should become involved early in transition planning to begin targeting the services that will be necessary once the student leaves school. Adult service professionals should collaborate with the school in establishing transition goals and identifying appropriate activities for the student during the final school years. Additionally, adult service professionals must be involved in developing information systems that can effectively track students as they leave school, and should monitor the availability and appropriateness of services to be provided during adulthood (Wehman, 2011).

Preparing Students for Adult Life: The Role of Secondary Schools

Successful transition begins with a solid foundation—the school. Secondary schools have many roles in the transition process: assessing individual needs; helping each student develop an IEP/transition plan; coordinating transition planning with adult service agencies; participating with parents and students in the planning process; and providing experiences to facilitate access to community services and employment. For one student, these experiences may include learning to shop in a neighborhood grocery store and training for a job in the community. For another student with a disability who has different needs and abilities, the activities may be more academically oriented to prepare the student for college.

Several outcomes are expected for students with disabilities as they enter adulthood. First, they should be able to function as independently as possible in their daily lives; their reliance on others to meet their needs should be minimized. As students with disabilities leave school, they should be able to make choices about where they will live, how they will spend their free time, and whether they will be employed in the community or go on to college. For students with disabilities considering college, Babbitt and White (2002) devised a process to help them to identify their readiness for further education.

Secondary schools are in the unique position of being able to coordinate activities that enhance student participation in the community and link students with needed programs and services. Several instructional practices are at the core of evidence-based secondary programs for students with disabilities. These include teaching self-determination, academic skills, adaptive and functional life skills, and employment preparation (McDonnell, Hardman, & McGuire, 2007).

FOCUS 4
Why is it important for students with disabilities to receive instruction in self-determination, academics, adaptive and functional life skills, and employment preparation during the secondary school years?

Teaching Self-Determination

Self-determination plays a critical role in the successful transition from school to adult life (Bremer, Kachgal, & Schoeller, 2003; Pierson, Carter, Lane, & Glaeser, 2008; Getzel & Thoma, 2008; Wehmeyer, Gragoudas, & Shogren, 2006). Definitions of self-determination focus on a person's ability to consider options and make appropriate decisions and to exercise free will, independence, and individual responsibility (University of Illinois at Chicago National Research and Training Center, 2009). The need for secondary schools to teach self-determination skills is evident from research on positive transition outcomes. Wehmeyer et al. (2006) indicate that "teaching effective decision-making and problem-solving skills has been shown to enhance positive transition outcomes for youth and young adults" (p. 45). These include the reduction of problem behaviors, improved outcomes in community-based instruction, and the promotion of choice-making opportunities in vocational tasks. Teaching self-determination skills to students with disabilities helps them become more efficient in acquiring knowledge and solving problems (Agran, Wehmeyer, Cavin, & Palmer, 2008; Bambara, Browder, & Kroger, 2006; Finn, Getzel, & McManus, 2008; Smith, Beyer, Polloway, Smith, & Patton, 2008). Students grow better able to achieve goals that will facilitate their transition out of school and become aware of the specific challenges they will face in the adult years. Ultimately, the student leaves school with a more highly developed sense of personal worth and social responsibility and with better problem-solving skills.

Creating opportunities for individual choice and decision making is an important element in the transition from school to adult life. Each individual must be able to consider options and make appropriate choices. This means less problem solving and decision making on the part of service providers and family members and a greater focus on teaching and promoting choice. The planning process associated with the development of a student's IEP is an excellent opportunity to promote self-determination. Unfortunately, very few adolescents with disabilities attend their IEP meetings, and even fewer actively participate (Wehman, 2011).

CEC
Standard 4
Instructional Strategies

Standard 3
Individual Learning Differences

TEACHSOURCE VIDEO TEACHER PERSPECTIVES: MANAGING FLEXIBILITY THROUGH TECHNOLOGY

Please visit the Education CourseMate website for *Human Exceptionality*, 11th edition, to access this chapter's TeachSource Video. Differentiating instruction and providing students opportunities for choice in their learning requires a good bit of flexibility on the part of the teacher. Yet, managing students with different learning preferences with varied levels of content and technology skills all in the same classroom may seem daunting. These teachers describe strategies they use for managing flexibility in terms of technology use and learning in their classrooms.

Respond to the following questions:

1. Describe how each of the teachers in this video creates flexibility through technology to enhance their students' learning.

2. Why is it important for students on various learning levels to be able to work at their own pace?

Teaching Academic Skills and Access to the General Curriculum

Research suggests that students with disabilities are not faring as well as they could be in the academic content of high school programs or in postsecondary education (U.S. Department of Education, 2011). These students have higher school drop-out rates and lower academic achievement than their peers without disabilities. However, the research also suggests that students with mild disabilities, particularly those with learning disabilities, can achieve in academic content beyond their current performance (Friend & Bursuck, 2006; Lock & Layton, 2008). Getzel and Gugerty (2001) propose that high school programs for students with mild disabilities must

Standard 2
Development and Characteristics of Learners

Standard 4
Instructional Strategies

- develop teaching strategies based on the unique learning characteristics of each student;

- take into account the cultural background of each student and its effect on learning;

- determine each student's strongest learning modes (visual, auditory, and/or tactile) and adapt instruction accordingly;

- use assistive technology (e.g., laptop computers, personal data managers, pocket-size spell-checkers, etc.) to help students capitalize on their strengths (see nearby Teach-Source Video, "Teacher Perspectives: Managing Flexibility through Technology"); and

- create positive learning environments to enable students to feel motivated and build their self-esteem.

For students with moderate to severe disabilities, the purpose of academic learning may be more functional and compensatory—to teach skills that have immediate and frequent use in the student's environment (McDonnell & Copeland, 2011). Instruction concentrates on skills needed in the student's daily living routine. For example, safety skills may include reading street signs, railroad crossings, entrance/exit signs, or product labels. Information skills may include reading job application forms, classified ads, maps, telephone directories, or catalogs.

With an increasing emphasis on academics and increasing access to the general curriculum, there is a growing concern about students with disabilities and the opportunity to earn a high school diploma. Because employers view the high school diploma as a minimum requirement signaling competence, what does this mean for students with disabilities who are unable to meet academic criteria? Many students with disabilities do not receive the same high school diploma as their peers without disabilities. Some states and local school districts have adopted graduation requirements that specify successful completion of a number of credits in order to receive a diploma. Students with disabilities must meet the same requirements as their peers to receive a "regular" high school diploma. If a student with a disability fails to meet graduation requirements, he or she may be awarded an "IEP diploma," marking progress toward annual goals, or a certificate of high school completion (or attendance). IEP diplomas and certificates of completion communicate that a student was unable to meet the requirements to obtain a standard diploma.

Other states award students with disabilities the standard high school diploma based on modified criteria that are individually referenced, reflecting the successful completion of IEP goals and objectives as determined by a multidisciplinary team of professionals and the student's parents. For more insight into the controversy surrounding this issue, see the nearby Debate Forum, "Students with Disabilities and the Meaning of a High School Diploma."

Fuse/Jupiterimages

In many school districts, students with disabilities must meet the same requirements as their peers without disabilities in order to receive a high school diploma. Do you think students with disabilities should be held to the same academic standard as those who are not disabled?

Teaching Adaptive and Functional Life Skills

Students with disabilities in the secondary school years need access to social activities. Adaptive and functional life skills training may include accessing socialization activities in and outside school and learning to manage one's personal affairs. It may be important to provide basic instruction on how to develop positive interpersonal relationships and the behaviors that are conducive to successfully participating in community settings (Allen, Ciancio,

---

REFLECT ON THIS TIPS AND STRATEGIES FOR CO-TEACHING AT THE SECONDARY LEVEL

Co-teaching can be a powerful in tool in meeting the needs of all students, including those with disabilities in middle and high school settings. However, the success of a co-teaching experience is dependent upon many factors, including but certainly not limited to:

- Clearly defined roles for both the general and special education teacher in regard to teaching instructional content and pedagogical approaches to learning.

- Taking advantage of the unique teaching styles of both the general and special education teacher;

- Instruction in subject matter areas that is focused on access to the general education curriculum while at the same time meeting the individualized needs of students with disabilities;

- Continuous progress monitoring of student learning within and across subject matter areas.

- Strong administrative support for instructional planning time, scheduling, and on-going professional development.

Murawski and Dieker (2004) suggest several strategies for general and special education teachers at the secondary level to consider in developing a co-teaching model:

- Involve an administrator. How is the district addressing the least restrictive environment (LRE) mandate and and the inclusive [education] movement?

- Would our school site be willing to be proactive by including co-teaching?

- What discipline [subject matter] areas will we target first?

- Do we both have the same level of acquaintance with the curriculum and expertise in instructing students with disabilities?

- How shall we ensure that we both are actively involved and that neither feels over- or underutilized?

- What feedback structure can we create to assist in our regular communication?

- How often will co-teaching occur (daily, a few times a week, for a specific unit)?

- What schedule would best meet the needs of the class and of both instructors?

- How can we ensure that this schedule will be maintained consistently so that both co-teachers can trust it?

Question for Reflection

Several tips strategies for enhancing the success of co-teaching at the secondary level are presented in this feature. What additional tips would you offer to general and special education teachers who are just beginning to work together in a co-teaching situation?

DEBATE FORUM STUDENTS WITH DISABILITIES AND THE MEANING OF A HIGH SCHOOL DIPLOMA

Should students with disabilities be required to demonstrate the same academic competence as their peers without disabilities to receive a high school diploma? Or, if they are unable to meet graduation requirements, should they receive an IEP diploma or certificate of completion?

POINT

The purpose of a high school diploma is to communicate to employers, colleges, and society in general that an individual has acquired a specified set of knowledge and skills that prepares him or her to leave school and enter postsecondary education or the world of work. All students must be held to the same standards, or the diploma will have no meaning as a "signal" of competence and will make no impression on employers or colleges. For those students with disabilities who cannot meet graduation requirements, there is certainly a need to signal what the individual has achieved during high school, even though it is not to the same performance level as those who are awarded the diploma. This can be accomplished through a certificate of completion with modified criteria for graduation. What is most important is not to devalue the high school diploma by lowering the requirements for earning it. Otherwise, employers and colleges will continue to lose faith in public education as a credible system for preparing students for the future.

COUNTERPOINT

Although the move to hold all students to specific requirements (or standards) is to be applauded, it is discriminatory to expect all students to meet the same standards to receive a high school diploma. The purpose of a high school diploma is to communicate that the individual has demonstrated a "personal best" while in school, thus acquiring knowledge and a set of skills consistent with his or her ability. I would also support the viewpoint that students with disabilities can achieve at much higher levels than they do now, and expectations should be raised. However, some will never be able to satisfy the graduation requirements now in place in many states and school districts. Students with disabilities who cannot perform at the level mandated in graduation requirements should still be awarded a standard diploma based on their having met requirements consistent with their individual needs and abilities. This is the basis of a free and appropriate public education for students with disabilities. If a standard diploma is not awarded, students with disabilities will be immediately singled out as incompetent and will be at a major disadvantage with employers, regardless of the skills they possess.

What Do You Think? Please visit the Education CourseMate website for Human Exceptionality, *11th Edition, to access and respond to questions related to the Debate Forum.*

Rutkowski, 2008; Hansen & Morgan, 2008; Harchik & Ladew, 2008; Joseph & Konrad, 2009; Manley, Collins, Stenhoff, & Kleinert, 2008; McDonnell, 2009; Wehman, 2011). Instruction may include co-teaching among general and special education teachers, as well as the use of peer tutors to both model and teach appropriate social skills in community settings such as restaurants, theaters, or shopping malls. See the nearby Reflect on This, "Tips and Strategies for Co-Teaching at the Secondary Level."

Employment Preparation

People with disabilities are often characterized as consumers of society's resources rather than as contributors, but employment goes a long way toward dispelling this idea. Paid employment means earning wages, through which individuals can buy material goods and enhance their quality of life; it also contributes to personal identity and status (Crockett & Hardman, 2009; Drew & Hardman, 2007).

In the past, high schools have been somewhat passive in their approach to employment training, focusing primarily on teaching vocational readiness through simulations in a classroom setting. More recently, high schools have begun to emphasize employment preparation for students with disabilities through work experience, career education, and community-referenced instruction. In a work experience program, the student spends a portion of the school day in classroom settings (which may emphasize academic and/or vocational skills) and the rest of the day at an off-campus site receiving on-the-job training. The responsibility for the training may be shared among the high school special education teacher, vocational rehabilitation counselor, and vocational education teacher.

CEC

Standard 4
Instructional Strategies

Career education includes training in social skills development as well as general occupational skills. Career education programs usually concentrate on developing an awareness of various career choices, exploring occupational opportunities, and developing appropriate attitudes, social skills, and work habits.

Whereas career education is oriented to developing an awareness of various occupations, community-referenced instruction involves direct training and ongoing support, as necessary, in a community employment site. The demands of the work setting and the functioning level, interests, and wishes of each individual determine the goals and objectives of the training. The most notable difference between community-referenced instruction and work experience programs is that the former focuses on the activities to be accomplished at the work site rather than on the development of isolated skills in the classroom. An employment training program based on a community-referenced approach includes the following elements:

- Primary focus on student and family needs and preferences
- A balance between time spent in inclusive general education classrooms and in placement and employment preparation at least until age 18
- A curriculum that reflects the job opportunities available in the local community
- An employment training program that takes place at actual job sites
- Training designed to sample the student's performance across a variety of economically viable alternatives
- Ongoing opportunities for students to interact with peers without disabilities in a work setting
- Training that culminates in employment placement
- Job placement linked to comprehensive transition planning, which focuses on establishing interagency agreements that support the student's full participation in the community (Drew & Hardman, 2007)

For more insight into employment preparation during the high school years, see the Case Study, "Maria," earlier in this chapter.

Looking Toward a Bright Future

During the middle and high school years, the challenges associated with receiving quality services and supports for students with disabilities are ever-changing, varied, and complex. For middle and high school-age students, there are clear expectations that they must achieve the same high academic standards as their peers without disabilities in general education classrooms. This expectation will become reality only when there is positive and ongoing communication between educators and families, as well as new and innovative approaches to address diverse learning needs across the curriculum (Murawski & Dieker, 2004; Stenhoff, Davey, & Lignugaris/Kraft, 2008; Worrell, 2008).

As students with disabilities transition from school to adult life, these young adults must be able to participate in a coordinated system of services and supports that will help them find work, housing, or recreational and leisure activities. Many will find jobs or go on to postsecondary education if they have been taught the academic, technical, and social skills necessary to find and/or maintain employment. The transition requirements of the IDEA are designed to help students successfully leave school to live and work within the community or go on to further education. Today, more students with disabilities are participating in postsecondary education than ever before. Nearly 10 percent of these students go on to a college, university, or applied technical school (Higbee & Goff, 2008; Murray, Flannery, & Wren, 2008; Murray, Wren, & Keys, 2008; Schnee, 2008; Tiedemann, 2008).

This concludes Part I of this text, "Through the Lifespan." As we begin Part II, our discussion moves to understanding diversity, equity, and access in the education of students with disabilities, particularly those students and families who come from differing cultural and linguistic backgrounds. Part II concludes with a chapter on the important role that the family plays in working with professionals to meet the unique needs of children and adults with disabilities.

FOCUS REVIEW

FOCUS 1 What do we know about lives of people with disabilities after they leave school?

The educational opportunities afforded under IDEA have not yet led to full participation of special education graduates in the social and economic mainstream of their local communities.

- However, there has been considerable improvement. The National Longitudinal Transition Study-2 reports that progress has been made in several areas (high school completion, living arrangements, social involvement, further education, and employment rates).
- Adult service systems do not have the resources to meet the needs of students with disabilities following the school years.
- The capabilities of adults with disabilities are often underestimated.

FOCUS 2 What are the requirements for transition planning in IDEA?

- IDEA requires that every student with a disability receive transition services.
- Transition planning is designed to be a results-oriented process focused on improving the academic and functional achievement of a child with a disability to facilitate the child's movement from school to postschool activities.
- Transition services must be based on the individual student's needs, taking into account the student's preferences and interests.
- Transition services must include a focus on postsecondary education, vocational education, integrated employment (including supported employment), continuing and adult education, adult services, independent living, and/or community participation.
- IDEA requires that, beginning at age 16 and updated annually, a student's individualized education program (IEP) should include measurable postsecondary goals based on age-appropriate transition assessments related to training, education, employment, and, where appropriate, independent living skills.
- The IEP must include a statement of transition services related to various courses of study (such as participation in advanced placement courses or a vocational education program) that will assist the student in reaching her or his goals.

FOCUS 3 Identify the purpose of person-centered transition planning and the basic steps in its formulation.

- Person-centered transition planning is based on an understanding of and commitment to each student's needs and preferences; it must be developed and implemented within each student's IEP.
- It is a process that ensures each student's access to the general education curriculum and/or a focus on the adaptive and functional skills that will facilitate life in the community following school. The basic steps in person-centered transition planning include
  - Convening the IEP team organized in terms of the preferences and needs of each student
  - Reviewing assessment data and conducting additional assessment activities
  - Developing IEPs/transition IEPs
  - Implementing the IEP or transition IEP
  - Updating the IEP/transition IEP annually and implementing follow-up procedures
  - Holding an exit meeting

FOCUS 4 Why is it important for students with disabilities to receive instruction in self-determination, academics, adaptive and functional life skills, and employment preparation during the secondary school years?

- Self-determination skills help students to solve problems, consider options, and make appropriate choices as they transition into adult life.
- Academic skills are essential in meeting high school graduation requirements and preparing students with disabilities for college. A functional academic program helps students learn applied skills in daily living, leisure activities, and employment preparation.
- Adaptive and functional life skills help students learn how to socialize with others, maintain personal appearance, and make choices about how to spend free time.
- Employment preparation during high school increases the probability of success on the job during the adult years and places the person with a disability in the role of a contributor to society.

Council for Exceptional Children (CEC) Standards to Accompany Chapter 4

 If you are thinking about a career in special education, you should know that many states use national standards developed by the Council for Exceptional Children (CEC) to assess a teacher candidate's knowledge and skills for working with students with disabilities. See a complete listing of the 10 CEC Content Standards on the inside back cover of this text.

1 Foundations
2 Development and Characteristics of Learners
3 Individual Learning Differences
4 Instructional Strategies
5 Learning Environments and Social Interactions
7 Instructional Planning
9 Professional and Ethical Practice

Mastery Activities and Assignments

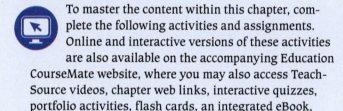 To master the content within this chapter, complete the following activities and assignments. Online and interactive versions of these activities are also available on the accompanying Education CourseMate website, where you may also access Teach-Source videos, chapter web links, interactive quizzes, portfolio activities, flash cards, an integrated eBook, and much more!

1. Complete a written test of the chapter's content. If your instructor requires a written test of your content knowledge for this chapter, keep a copy for your portfolio. A practice test on the information covered in this chapter is available through the Education CourseMate website for *Human Exceptionality*.

2. Review the Case Study, "Maria," and respond in writing to the Application Questions. Keep a copy of the Case Study and of your written response for your portfolio.

3. Read the Debate Forum in this chapter and then visit the Education CourseMate website to complete the activity "Take a Stand." Keep a copy of this activity for your portfolio.

4. Participate in a community service learning activity. Community service is a valuable way to enhance your learning experience. Visit our CourseMate website for suggested community service learning activities that correspond to the information presented in this chapter. Develop a reflective journal of the service learning experience for your portfolio.

Perspectives on Diversity and the Family

Jose Luis Pelaez, Inc./Corbis

> *We all should know that diversity makes for a rich tapestry, and we must understand that all the threads of the tapestry are equal in value no matter what their color.*
>
> — Maya Angelou

Increasingly, diversity permeates every aspect of our lives. This is especially true when we speak of children, youth, and their families. If you have recently visited one or several of the public schools in your community, you will have seen firsthand what is taking place across the nation. Public schools are places where *all* children come together to learn, to develop trust in one another, to reach their potential, and to become contributing community members.

The opportunities and challenges of preparing the young for active participation in our democracy and other vital roles in our communities are both exciting and daunting. Diversity by definition connotes a very broad span of talents, needs, interests, and desires. Attending to all of these aforementioned elements across different cultures, languages, and belief systems is remarkably challenging.

Diversity involves language, values, beliefs, individual and family aspirations, religious preferences and practices, dress, traditions, and different ways of thinking about life and its purposes.

Part 2 of this book examines the importance of understanding families and diversity—coming to understand how you as future professionals and community members may respond in responsible and caring ways to children, youth, and adults with disabilities and their families.

To support and nurture others, we must be able to communicate with one another. We must come to know each other. We must trust each other. We must have a sense of empathy—a connectedness with others that allows us to move beyond personal convenience, to reach out to others, to put others' interests and well-being above our own.

As you come to understand and embrace the content in these chapters, think carefully about the opportunities and challenges that lie ahead as you pursue a career in health, education, social services, business, or other pursuits.

PART 2 CHAPTER OVERVIEWS

Chapter 5, "Cultural and Linguistic Diversity," begins with a compelling story about Pedro and his family. This brief Snapshot introduces you to many of the opportunities and challenges associated with preparing Pedro for full participation in society, readying him to be a full-fledged participant in our democracy. Moreover, Pedro's story sets the stage for helping you understand the issues surrounding how and where he should be served in the public schools. Is he truly a child with a disability? Or is he a child with unique learning needs—much in part because of his language and cultural assets or differences?

You will discover the inherent tensions and inconsistencies that exist in labeling children who are linguistically and culturally diverse—particularly if the intent is to assure needed services and support that children or youth without "a label" would not otherwise receive. In this regard, language competence plays a significant role in how professionals experience the range of abilities in these children. When a child like Pedro is not thriving academically or socially, professionals face heart-wrenching challenges in making decisions and selecting appropriate instruction, interventions, and school placements.

How does special education compare to multicultural education? How are they similar? How are they different? How do we fairly identify children with disabilities who are also culturally and linguistically diverse? What is the role of our public schools in relation to sustaining our democracy?

By the end of Chapter 5, you will understand the importance of collaboration, particularly in addressing the needs of children and families from diverse cultural and linguistic backgrounds. You will also see that we still have much to learn about effectively serving children who are culturally and linguistically diverse and who may also be exceptional in some fashion.

Chapter 6, "Exceptionalities and Families," begins with a personal reflection of a mother about her daughter Teela. She shares her initial reactions to the birth of Teela, talks about her other children, and tells us how her family works together to meet the needs of every member of the family.

Cultural and Linguistic Diversity

iStockphoto.com/andres balcazar

FOCUS PREVIEW

As you read the chapter, focus on these key questions:

1 In what three ways do the purposes and approaches to general education, multicultural education, and special education differ in the United States?

2 Describe population trends among culturally and linguistically diverse (CLD) groups in the United States. How do these changes affect the educational system?

3 Identify four ways in which culturally and linguistically responsive collaboration might decrease the disproportionality of students from CLD backgrounds in special education programs.

4 Cite three ways in which differing sociocultural customs may affect the manner in which parents become involved in the educational process.

5 Indicate two areas that require particular attention in the development of an individualized education program (IEP) for a student from a CLD background; identify one challenge in serving children from CLD backgrounds in the least restrictive environment.

6 Identify three ways in which poverty and migrancy may contribute to the academic difficulties of children with CLD backgrounds, often resulting in their referral to special education.

7 Cite two conceptual differences between using a culturally and linguistically responsive model versus a deficit model.

SNAPSHOT
Pedro, a Profile of a Diverse Learner, his Family, School, and Community

PEDRO AND HIS FAMILY

Six-year-old Pedro entered first grade at a small rural elementary school. He lived with his mother and four of his seven siblings. His 24-year-old mother had dropped out of high school early. His grandparents came to the United States from Mexico with the hope of a better life for their family. The family speaks both English and Spanish in the home; however, the language level is only conversational and not academically oriented in either language. Spanish is often used for telling or maintaining family secrets, especially in front of English speakers. The children do not have access to books in their home. Their mother does not read to the children or spend much time talking to them or helping them with their homework.

Pedro's mother uses her knowledge of government systems, the street, and resources available from family and friends (e.g., temporary shelter, transportation, food) to house, feed, and clothe her children. Although she loves her children, she struggles to meet the expectations of the school and community in regard to their physical and

© Ellen B. Senisi/The Image Works.

school needs. The school health nurse and other community agencies unsuccessfully tried to provide various types of support to the family. The school principal also made home visits and sometimes picked up the children for school when they had missed the bus. Unfortunately, the problems continued.

The year Pedro entered first grade, the socioeconomic status (SES) in the school was lowered because the school boundaries were changed to include a

low-income housing unit in which he lived. This move upset the local community, which once consisted of all white children of local farmers and businessmen. Community members actively voiced their opinions and sought to stop the district decision.

Although Pedro's third- and fifth-grade sisters seemed to manage their academic work well enough, Pedro struggled. Because he missed most of his kindergarten year, the school decided that he should participate in a transition program. He attended kindergarten readiness classes in the morning and his regular first grade in the afternoon. He made progress in his literacy and math, but at a much slower rate than his peers. Pedro's first-grade teacher felt that this lack of expected progress indicated that he had a learning disability. Though his kindergarten teacher did not agree entirely, the first-grade teacher made the request. Before testing could be done, the family suffered an additional blow when their mother was arrested, and the children were moved to the care of relatives and friends outside the district boundaries.

A Changing Era in the Lives of Students with Disabilities from Cultural and Linguistically Diverse Backgrounds

In this chapter, we will examine many complex issues related to cultural and linguistic diversity; their impact on children in schools and public education.

Educational reformers identify two particular groups of students who have been underserved in the education community—in one case, because of their disabilities and in the other because of their cultural, linguistic, or racial background. Special education evolved

Barry Chin/The Boston Globe via Getty Images

Preventing dispro-portionality of children from CLD backgrounds being placed into special education settings is a team effort.

Multicultural education
An education movement that promotes the concept that cultures (race, religion, gender, ethnicity, and social class) are important and vibrant parts of the fabric of the United States.

FOCUS 1

In what three ways do the purposes and approaches to general education, multicultural education, and special education differ in the United States?

from the lack of appropriate instructional programs that met the needs of students who were not learning at the same rate or in the same way as their peers.

Similarly, **multicultural education** evolved from a belief that the needs of children whose cultural or linguistic backgrounds differed from those of the majority were not being appropriately met. The societal unrest in the early 1960s related to racial discrimination fueled this belief.

To understand multiculturalism and diversity, we will first explore the basic purpose of general education and the conventional approaches used to achieve this purpose. We will also compare the underlying purposes and approaches of special education and multicultural education and discuss the connections between them. After building this foundation, we will examine multicultural and diversity issues in the context of this book's focus: human exceptionality in society, school, and family. This process will highlight an interesting perspective on collaboration among general and special educators. In the context of multicultural and diversity issues, collaboration becomes more complex. Professionals and advocates in multicultural education face a troubling reality. Although not all children from CLD backgrounds need special education, specialized instruction and services through general education may meet important needs for many of them.

Purposes and Approaches to Education

The fundamental purpose of education according to the Declaration of Independence and the U.S. Constitution is to produce literate and economically productive citizens who can preserve "life, liberty and pursuit of happiness". . . . The term "*citizen*" incorporates the concepts of collaboration between individuals and the skills and resources they possess, which create vibrant, viable, and sustainable communities. However, it was not until 2001 that this concept was fully realized through changes in federal law. Even with all its challenges, the reauthorization of the Elementary and Secondary Education Act (ESEA) of 2001, which became known as No Child Left Behind (NCLB), acknowledged for the first time in U.S. education that all children are to have access to education from kindergarten through 12th grade. To explore this idea further, we review the roles of three distinct approaches to education, general education, multicultural education, and special education.

General Education

A major purpose of general education is to provide education for all students and to help them achieve academically and socially. This goal is implemented by teaching students according to chronological age and evaluating their performance on the basis of what society expects children of a specific age to achieve. Society looks at what students of each age are typically able to learn as its yardstick for assessing progress. Thus, U.S. education is aimed at the masses, and performance is judged in terms of an average. Through this system, schools attempt to bring most students to a similar level of knowledge.

Although federal requirements for adequate yearly progress (AYP) have created a tension in schools to find ways that more effectively meet the educational needs of all students, some children continue to lag behind. These include students who are from CLD backgrounds, are economically disadvantaged, and those identified with disabilities—another challenge for public education and how to provide opportunities for all students to learn to be accepting of the changing culture within the United States.

Multicultural Education and Its Role

Understanding diverse cultures and the impact of collective culture on each individual is an ongoing challenge for professionals in the social sciences (Carpenter, Zarate, & Garza, 2007; Deaux, Reid, & Martin, 2006). Multicultural education seeks to change how schools think about children from diverse backgrounds and how to develop curriculum to support their learning (Banks, 2008; Moule, 2012). Multicultural education values and promotes **cultural pluralism** or the cultural or linguistic differences of individuals and how those differences work together to create a richer society. The idea of a **modified cultural pluralism** approach to multicultural education, as defined by William Newman in Sleeter and Grant (2009), encourages the idea of cultural groups retaining their unique characteristics but also building relationships across cultures. This theory encourages the perception of U.S. society as a "tossed salad," rather than a "melting pot," which promotes assimilation or homogenization into the dominant culture, or the theory of building walls either by a specific culture or by others outside that culture to maintain distinct identities that separate one culture from the dominant culture. This concept is referred to as the "class of civilizations" (Banks, 2008; Grant & Sleeter, 2009; Gollnick & Chinn, 2009; Pieterse, 2009). Salvadore (2012) frames this concept as, "We're all hyphenated Americans really. It's the way we identify our backgrounds and that's fine. If, however, identification by self or others becomes a way to maintain separation, well, that's not fine" (p. xxx). Modified cultural pluralism incorporates the idea of **social capital**, which is made up of two kinds of social interactions: (a) bonding capital that strengthens the cultural characteristics within a group such as a family, a particular religion, or a specific ethnic group; and (b) bridging capital that promotes more formal social ties across cultures to create mutual interests that strengthen the shared society, be it local, state, or national (Flora, 2011). This model for cultural pluralism allows the teaching about cultural diversity and how it functions in a culturally pluralistic society; thus, it is not exclusively aimed at students from culturally or linguistically diverse backgrounds (Ornstein & Moses, 2005; Riad, 2007). Asserting that multicultural education is a concept that addresses cultural diversity, Gollnick and Chinn (2009) cited six beliefs and assumptions on which it is based:

1. Cultural differences have strength and value.

2. Schools should be models for the expression of human rights and respect for cultural differences.

3. Social justice and equal access for all people should be of paramount importance in the design and delivery of curricula.

4. Attitudes and values necessary for the continuation of a democratic society can be promoted in schools.

5. Schooling can provide the knowledge, skills, and dispositions—and the values, attitudes, and commitments—to help students from diverse groups learn.

6. Educators working with families and communities can create an environment that is supportive of multiculturalism. (p. 4)

This perspective opposes the once-prevalent view that schools should minimize cultural differences (Baldwin, Faulkner, & Hecht, 2006). Further, this notion of cultural pluralism/multiculturalism/diversity promotes the philosophy that collaboration among multiple cultures creates a stronger, more unified citizenry that can contribute both socially and economically.

Multicultural education is intended to not only reduce discrimination, but also to provide the tools necessary to maintain student cultural identities, and navigate among diverse cultures as well as within the majority culture (Banks, 2008; Sleeter & Grant, 2009). Young people develop many of their enduring attitudes and a significant knowledge base, including their thoughts and feelings about diverse cultures, in the classroom. Incomplete information and stereotypical presentations about different cultures detract from students' understanding of the variety of people that characterizes our world (Arredondo & Perez, 2006; Vasquez, Lott, & Garcia-Vazquez, 2006).

As a country, the United States has made progress, but we must make a stronger effort to create an awareness of how members of different cultural groups have contributed to major developments in U.S. history. To illustrate, during World War II, some members of the Navajo tribe from the southwestern United States became known as "Code Talkers" as they served in critical communications roles by transmitting classified messages in their native language, which could not be decoded by Axis forces (Bruchac, 2005.) Japanese Americans volunteered for critical assignments serving the United States with distinction

Cultural pluralism
The cultural or linguistic differences of individuals and how those differences work together to create a richer society.

Modified cultural pluralism
Multiple cultural subgroups living together in a manner that preserves the characteristics (traditions, culture, language) of the group and promotes the interaction between groups to create vibrant, viable, and sustainable communities.

Social capital
Made up of two kinds of social interactions, bonding capital that strengthens the cultural characteristics within a group, and bridging capital that promotes more formal social ties across cultures to create mutual interests that strengthen the shared society.

TEACHSOURCE VIDEO
DIVERSITY: TEACHING IN A MULTIETHNIC CLASSROOM

Please visit the Education CourseMate website for *Human Exceptionality*, 11th edition, to access this TeachSource Video. In this video, you will see how one teacher develops the idea of collaboration among her students who speak English and Japanese as she develops a lesson using a Japanese cultural language arts structure to help every student have a multicultural learning experience. Respond to the following questions:

1. What does the teacher do to engage her English- and Japanese-speaking students collaboratively in this activity?

2. How does the teacher develop the lesson on Japanese culture to include language development that might be found in the core curriculum (hint: think of reading, writing, speaking, and listening)?

3. Do you think this learning activity is an effective multicultural experience for all of the children?

during World War II, despite the degrading abuse inflicted on them (Hosokawa, Mukoyama, Oshiki, Takahashi, & Tsutsumida, 2001). Such stories need to be told to create a complete education that includes recognition, respect, and appreciation for the roles of the many people who have shaped or will shape our country and the world.

Special Education and Its Role

The basic purpose of special education is to provide opportunities for each child with a disability to learn and develop. Special education focuses on individual learning differences by providing individually designed instruction and related services to help students benefit from the general education curriculum. This individualized approach is important because many students in special education have difficulties learning through instruction that is directed at large groups. Evaluation is based, at least in part, on individual attainment of a specified mastery level, not entirely on comparison with **norm-based averages**. This is especially true since the introduction of multitiered systems of support (MTSS, also known as response to intervention, as discussed in Chapter 3) now being used across the country (Jimerson, Burns, & VanDerHeyden, 2007; NICHCY, 2010; Reschly, 2009).

Important differences exist between the fundamental purposes of general education, multicultural education, and special education. The differences among the goals and approaches of general, special, and multicultural education often create challenges within school systems and among educators as they struggle with policies, high performance demands, and effective academic strategies and supports that will make the difference in the lives of all students.

Norm-based averages
Comparison of a person's performance with the average performance scores of age-mates.

Multiculturalism/Diversity and Special Education

An uneasy interface exists between multicultural and special education, involving special education's role of serving children who are failing in the general education classroom. Unfortunately, a disproportionate number of students placed in special education are from specific CLD backgrounds that are not being successful in the regular classroom (Ferri & Connor, 2005; Waitoller, Artiles, & Cheney, 2010). For example, in 2008, the National Education Association (NEA) issued a brief indicating that African American males were overrepresented in special education programs for emotional disabilities, whereas Asian/Pacific Islander students where underrepresented in special education, but overrepresented in gifted and talented programs (National Education Association (NEA), 2008). These issues continue to surface (Erevelles, Kanga, & Middleton, 2006; Skiba, Poloni-Staudinger, & Simmons, 2005; Spinelli, 2006), fueling suspicion that special education has been used as a tool of discrimination (Connor & Ferri, 2010).

FOCUS 2
Describe population trends among culturally and linguistically diverse (CLD) groups in the United States. How do these changes affect the educational system?

Our discussion of special and multicultural education will focus on the prevalence of students from CLD backgrounds in special education, along with five major elements of the Individuals with Disabilities Education Act (IDEA, presented in Chapter 2):

1. Nondiscriminatory and multidisciplinary assessment
2. Parental involvement in developing each child's educational program
3. A free and appropriate public education (FAPE)
4. Delivery through an individualized education program (IEP)
5. Implementation in the least restrictive environment (LRE)

Prevalence and Disproportionality of Students from Culturally and Linguistically Diverse Backgrounds

The term *prevalence* refers to the number of people in a given population who exhibit a condition or are placed in a particular category, such as those who have a hearing loss, speak Spanish, or are a specific gender. Prevalence is determined by counting how often something occurs. In this section, we will examine prevalence by certain factors relevant to the relationship between human exceptionality and multicultural issues.

We will also examine the **disproportionality** of students from CLD backgrounds in special education. Disproportionality is the over- or underrepresentation of a specific cultural group within a specified setting when compared to the percentage of their representation or prevalence in the general population. For instance, African American male children are overrepresented in being identified as having emotional and behavior disorders. Asian and Pacific Islander students are underrepresented in special education. The opposite is true in gifted and talented programs where Asian students are overrepresented and black American children are underrepresented (Artiles, Kozleski, Trent, Osher, & Ortiz, 2010; Gollnick & Chinn, 2009; NEA Brief, 2008; Sullivan, 2011). On the other hand, English language learners (ELLs) can be both underrepresented and overrepresented in special education (Keller-Allen, 2008; Sullivan, 2011). For instance, if the number of ELL students in a district (local education agency) is small, the chances of receiving special education services are greater than in a district with a larger number of ELL students (NEA Brief, 2008). One explanation could be that the increased number of ELL students generates more funding and the ability of the school district to provide more appropriate resources.

Prevalence
The number of people in a given population who exhibit a condition or particular state; it is determined by counting how often it occurs (the number of people who speak Spanish or who are identified for special education).

Disproportionality
Disproportionality is the over- or underrepresentation of a specific cultural group represented within a specified setting when compared to the percentage of their representation in the general population.

© Will Hart/Photo Edit

Some students from culturally and linguistically diverse backgrounds may be inappropriately identified for placement or non-placement into special education, resulting in disproportionality.

Prevalence: The Changing Population in the United States

Richard Rodriguez (Salam, 2011) has dubbed the changing population as the "browning of America" because of the significant increase in Hispanic people since 1990 (Johnson & Kasarda, 2011; Salam, 2011; Stavans, 2002). This change includes both cultural and linguistic diversity and affects education and the workforce.

Ethnic and Cultural Diversity
Ethnic and culturally diverse groups, such as Latinos, African Americans, and others represent substantial portions of the U.S. population. For example, in the 2010 U.S. census, Hispanic people represented 19.2 percent of the total population, up significantly from 15.1 percent in 2000 (U.S. Census Bureau, 2000, 2010a).

Figure 5.1 *Percentage of Population by Race: 1990 to 2010.*

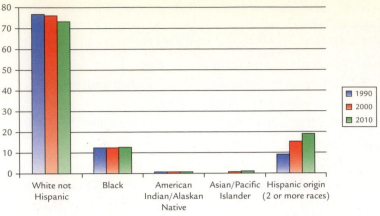

SOURCE: From Day, J. C. (1995); U.S. Census Bureau (2000); U.S. Census Bureau (2010b).

Bilingual
The ability to speak in two or more languages.

Limited English proficiency (LEP)
A child whose native language is other than English and whose ability to speak, read, write, or understand English may deny the child the ability to successfully achieve in classrooms or state assessments where English is the language of instruction or the opportunity to participate fully in society.

Specially designed academic instruction in English (SDAIE) or sheltered instruction
Instruction offered to English learners that includes realia, manipulatives, visuals, graphic organizers, and planned interactions for cooperative learning to support academic development along with English language learning.

English as a second language (ESL)
Language instruction programs provided in English only to children learning English as a second language.

Dual language or dual immersion
A variety of language instruction programs provided in two languages, English and a target language directed at either English learners to strengthen their native language and develop their English language, or for English speakers learning a target language such as Spanish or Chinese; another term for bilingual education.

Basic interpersonal communication skills
Basic language used in simple social conversations with friends and to survive in English (e.g., "you play me?"; "Everyone understand me, I not need help."; "You play my house, I show."; "You help get milk me?").

Several culturally or ethnically diverse groups of people are growing rapidly, in some cases at twice the rate of growth of the white population because of increasing birthrates and immigration levels. Young Hispanics are having children at a much higher rate than their white peers (Perlich, 2011; U.S. Census Bureau, 2012). Figure 5.1 graphically portrays the U.S. population growth rates of five races between the years of 1990 and 2010. The increase of culturally and linguistically diverse groups will have a profound impact on education, presenting diverse needs that demand a broader spectrum of educational services.

Language Diversity People with diverse language backgrounds constitute a rapidly growing sector of the U.S. population. Between 1990 and 2000, the number of children between 5 and 17 who were **bilingual** increased by 54.6 percent, and of those speaking English not well or not at all, the percentage grew by 45.7 percent. This represented about 1.33 million children in 2000 (Glimpse, 2012). By 2007, that number had increased by 5 percent according to the American Community Survey (Skinner, Wight, Aratani, Cooper, & Thampi, 2010). This has had a major impact on school systems (Barnum-Martin, Mehta, Fletcher, Carlson, Ortiz, Carlo, & Frances, 2006; Nippold, 2006; Wiese, 2006) because the number of students with **limited English proficiency (LEP)** is growing more rapidly than the numbers of other groups of students (Barrera, 2006; Solarsh & Alant, 2006). Schools increasingly need to provide linguistically appropriate assessments and instruction in classrooms through such programs as **specially designed academic instruction in English** (SDAIE; or sheltered English), **English as a second language (ESL)**, or **dual language or immersion**. Not all of these students will need special supports or programs, though many will require a substantial amount of supplementary assistance. Many linguistically diverse students come from academically and experience-rich backgrounds, which enable them to achieve in school based primarily on their knowledge of the English language. Students with different language backgrounds will have varying levels of skill with academic language, which is the language being used for instruction. Academic language ranges from

- not having any understanding of the language at all;
- being able to communicate in informal social settings with friends due to **basic interpersonal communication skills** (BICS); and
- being able to succeed academically due to their cognitive/academic language proficiency (CALP).

This alters the overall school environment because extraordinary instructional adaptation is necessary for students with limited English proficiency, including those who need a more intense focus due to disabilities. The broad range of educational curricula requires reevaluation if we are to provide optimal learning opportunities for these students (Edelsky, 2006; Vaughn, et al., 2006).

DEBATE FORUM
ENGLISH-ONLY OR DUAL-LANGUAGE EDUCATION?

Some lawmakers have supported declaring English as the official language of the United States at several levels during the past few years, and as recently as 2011 (Kasperowicz, 2011). Initiatives to promote such legislation at the state level are fluid and politically volatile. The same is true nationally with legislators passing such legislation, and at the same time arguing about whether it has racist overtones (Grant & Sleeter, 2009; Sullivan, 2011). Yet English is not the primary language for many Americans. Students from culturally diverse backgrounds represent a very large proportion of the school enrollment across the country and carry with them common underlying language proficiency in their heritage language that can support context learning in their new language (¡Colorín Colorado!, 2011; Goldenberg, 2008; Rodriguez, 2005). Even when they are not maneuvering for political position, critics claim that dual-language education places an unacceptable burden on the educational system, compromising its ability to provide specialized educational services to meet students' needs. There is a significant cost involved, and added to this are the various components of different integration models that are needed to meet individual student needs and the lack of teacher training to adequately provide dual-language instruction (Collier, 2004; Rodriguez, 2005).

POINT

English has always been the primary language in the United States and immigrants know that they must speak the language of the majority to fit into their new communities. Having a common language promotes unity and gives everyone a fair shake at the American dream. Children from different cultures must have this opportunity to survive and succeed in the world of the cultural majority. They must develop the skills necessary to be contributing members in English-speaking communities and workplaces. The best way to prepare them for becoming a part of their communities and to hold good jobs is for them to be taught by immersing them in English. This knowledge will prepare them for success and will more efficiently utilize the limited funds available, because specialized culturally sensitive services will not be required.

COUNTERPOINT

Children from cultures different from that of the majority must have an equal opportunity to learn in the most effective manner possible to become successful and contributing citizens. To expect students who are linguistically diverse to use English adequately to attain academic achievement in a short period of time is also an example of misinformation about how language is developed. Research shows that strengthening the native language while also teaching English supports successful academic development in both languages more effectively.

As the U.S. economy becomes more global, the idea of having citizens with strong dual-language abilities is an economically sound investment. One group that must be recognized with potential for meeting this demand is the English language learner community that already has a first language useful in international trade. If we consider English language learners as resources to be developed, and that the dollars spent on the investment of developing both the native language and English, we will see a very positive return on that investment.

For additional opportunities to participate in this Debate Forum, please visit the Education CourseMate website for Human Exceptionality, 11th edition.

The importance of linguistically appropriate instruction is magnified considerably when we consider other multicultural factors, such as the need for a careful examination of educational goals and the methods used to achieve them (Barrera, 2006; Rodriguez, 2005; Rueda & Yaden, 2006). However, these issues become politicized and complex as legislators enact laws that dictate matters of language (see the nearby Debate Forum, "English-Only or Dual-Language Education?").

Disproportionality of Culturally Diverse Children in Special Education

Several factors are associated with students at risk for academic failure. They include diverse cultural backgrounds, limited background in speaking English, and poverty. It is important to emphasize that these factors indicate risk for challenges in school, but do not predestine a student for special education placement. Yet a continuing concern is the disproportionate number (both over- and underrepresentation) of special education students who come from cultural backgrounds that differ from the white majority (Artiles et al., 2010; Harry & Klingner, 2006; Skiba, Poloni-Staudinger, & Simmons, 2005). The concern for disproportionality has been around for almost 40 years since the inception of special education (Artiles et al., 2010; Reschly, 2009; Waitoller, Artiles, & Cheney, 2010). The complexity of this concern should not be underestimated. As we shall see, a tangled web of issues related to school funding, assessment bias and misdiagnosis, poverty, discrimination (intended or unintended), ELL language acquisition, inequity in education, behavior management, levels of teacher competency in providing appropriate culturally responsive strategies for students from CLD backgrounds, pressure to make adequate yearly progress (AYP), interpretation of statistical data, high school completion rates, and changing populations by age, race, and language all feed into the challenges that schools face in addressing this issue (Artiles et al., 2008; Skiba, Poloni-Staudinger, & Simmons, 2005).

When carefully looking at the data collected over the past 20 years, we find that progress is being made, but we have a long way to go on issues surrounding disproportionality. We will discuss assessment, placement, high school completion, and English language learners to better understand the complexity of disproportionality.

The National Association for the Education of African American Children with Learning Disabilities (AACLD) is an example of the effort to increase awareness of diverse children who learn differently through parent advocacy.

© iStockphoto.com/Daniel Laflor

Assessment and Placement
Decisions regarding school placements in special education and other educational services are heavily influenced by assessment and academic context (Artiles et al., 2008; Erevelles, Kanga, & Middleton, 2006; Spinelli, 2006). Some professionals contend that these circumstances, along with sociocultural factors, play a significant role in shaping definitions, diagnoses, and resulting intervention or treatment (August & Shanahan, 2006; Rueda & Yaden, 2006). In the past, the mainstream culture has largely determined the definitions, diagnoses, and treatments that result in more nonmainstream children than expected being misidentified for specialized education.

Even so, the evidence is mixed. Some research indicates that people of color and some other ethnicities are equally represented, or are underrepresented compared with their Caucasian counterparts in disability categories, such as mood and anxiety disorders (Cuffe,

McKeown, Addy, & Garrison, 2005; Ferrell, Beidel, & Turner, 2004). These mixed results may be due to the number of students from CLD backgrounds in a school district, the level of training on the use of nonbiased assessment techniques, the level of teacher training in implementing appropriate instruction, and the intended or unintended biases of professionals involved.

High School Completion

Due to the increase in technical jobs requiring higher levels of education and the staggering costs to the nation from those who do not complete high school (estimated at $200 to $300 billion), high school completion rates have become increasingly important (Melville, 2006; National Center for Education Statistics [NCES], 2002). There are differing opinions on how to collect and interpret the data (see Education Week, 2010; NCES, 2010). What is clear in the existing data is the troubling disproportionality of CLD and low-income students completing high school (Melville, 2006). The NCES recently reported the 2008 national completion rates for ages 18 through 24, with 94.2 percent of white non-Hispanics, 86.9 percent of black non-Hispanics, and 78.5 percent of Hispanics completing high school (NCES, 2011). High school completion rates also correlate closely with family school history and vary across income groups (Banks, 2008; Stearns & Glennie, 2006). For example, the population with the highest high school drop-out rate is our lowest income group at 8.7 percent (13.8 percent of the total population ages 15 to 24) compared to that of 2 percent for our highest income group.

Some researchers view poverty as a threat to academic performance (Berliner, 2006; Hauser-Cram, Warfield, Stadler, & Sirin, 2006). In an outcome related to poverty and school completion, 10th- through 12th-grade students living in poverty were 4.5 times more likely to drop out of school than their peers from higher incomes (Chapman, Laird, & KewalRamani, 2010).

English Language Learners (ELLs)

Language differences often contribute to academic difficulties for students from diverse backgrounds who are educated in a system designed by the cultural majority (Luykx, Okhee, Mahotiere, Lester, Hart, & Deaktor, 2007; Prasad, 2008; Vaughn et al., 2006). Census data indicate that over 21 million people 5 years of age or older speak English less than "very well" (U.S. Census Bureau, 2010a). This represents nearly 18 percent of the total population in this age range and has an enormous impact on schools in general. Particular challenges arise when youngsters have a disability and also have limited English skills.

Disproportionality for students who are ELLs is of great concern to the educational community and among advocacy groups. Research indicates that ELLs with low proficiencies in both English and their native language are more likely to be identified for services under the special education category of specific learning disability when the population of English language learners in a district is substantial. However, if the ELL population in general is lower, they tend to be underrepresented in special education. Other studies show that ELLs identified for special education services are underrepresented in lower grades and overrepresented in grades three and up. For ELL students who are identified for special education, placement in more restrictive educational environments is significantly more likely than for other students receiving such services (Artiles et al., 2008; Sullivan, 2011). There are three major reasons for these phenomena: First, there is a lack of test reliability and validity for English language learners. Second, there is confusion about the difference between what is common for language acquisition and a language disability. Third, there is insufficient training of teachers in providing appropriate instruction for students who are ELLs (Fujiki, & Brinton, 2010; Rodriguez, 2005; Sullivan, 2011). Another significant issue according to Artiles et al. (2008) is that English language learners who are receiving all their education in English are more likely to be placed in special education settings than ELL students who have received dual-language support in their native language (p. 283). This is a clear example of the need to carefully consider a child's access to the most effective educational interventions and placements (Ferri & Connor, 2005).

Standard 2
Development and Characteristics of Learners

Standard 3
Individual Learning Differences

Multidisciplinary collaboration
Collaboration between parents and professionals with different expertise such as the classroom teacher, assessment specialist, disability specialist, ESL specialist, and school administrator in planning for the individual learning needs of a child.

Nondiscriminatory and Multidisciplinary Collaboration

FOCUS 3

Identify four ways in which culturally and linguistically responsive collaboration might decrease the disproportionality of students from CLD backgrounds in special education programs.

CEC

Standard 8
Assessment

Nondiscriminatory assessment
Testing done in a child's native language without cultural or racial discrimination through the use of validated assessment tools.

Multidisciplinary collaboration that is culturally responsive should include high levels of parent involvement and is essential to nearly every area of instruction for students with disabilities. Such collaboration is crucial in addressing the needs of culturally and linguistically diverse (CLD) students (Dettmer, Thurston, & Dyck, 2005; Friend & Cook, 2007), and is needed in areas of assessment, professional preparation, language diversity, and culturally responsive teaching.

Nondiscriminatory Assessment

Assessment has two main purposes in schools: first, to provide teachers with accurate information to develop meaningful instructional interventions that are understandable and meaningful to the child and promote measurable progressive academic development of that child (Teemant, Smith, & Pinnegar, 2003); and second, as a general measure, which the public uses to understand how schools are performing in the preparation of students for lives as productive citizens and competitive employees in our ever-complex and changing workforce. The history of assessment for children from diverse backgrounds raises serious issues of accuracy, fairness, and the ability to provide appropriate services to children based on those assessments.

Perhaps nowhere is the interface between special and multicultural education more prominent than in issues of **nondiscriminatory assessment**. As noted earlier, disproportionate numbers of students from cultural and linguistically diverse backgrounds are found in special education classes (Artiles et al., 2010; Sullivan, 2011). Decisions regarding referral and placement in these classes are based on a psychological assessment, which is typically based on standardized evaluations of intellectual and social functioning. Using assessments constructed with a specific language or content that favors the majority culture often leads to discrimination, or bias against children from culturally and linguistically diverse backgrounds.

Additionally, this can lead to inaccurate results that are detrimental to the child (Moule, 2012; Wright, 2007). Professionals who are not properly trained to interpret results for the child from a culturally and linguistically diverse background may lead to misdiagnosis and inappropriate academic or social intervention (Rodriguez, 2006). In several early cases, courts determined that reliance on academic and psychological assessments discriminated against Latino students (*Diana v. State Board of Education*, 1970, 1973) and African American students (*Larry P. v. Riles*, 1972, 1979). Assessment and instruction for Asian American children were addressed in the case of *Lau v. Nichols* (1974). These California cases had a national impact and greatly influenced the drafting of the reauthorization of IDEA.

Two prominent precedents in IDEA, for example, were established in the case of *Diana v. State Board of Education*: (1) Children tested for potential placement in special education must be assessed in their native or primary language, and (2) children cannot be placed in special classes on the basis of culturally biased tests. Finally, IDEA also mandates that evaluation involve a multidisciplinary team using several sources of information in making a placement decision. To put these safeguards in context, it is necessary to examine the assessment process and how cultural bias can occur.

Test bias
A test or testing procedure that creates a disadvantage for one group as a consequence of factors unrelated to ability, such as culture, linguistic or racial background, or gender.

Measurement bias
An unfairness or inaccuracy of test results or their interpretation that is related to cultural or linguistic background, gender, or race.

Test Bias, Assessment Errors, and Measurement Bias
Bias in psychological assessment has been recognized as a problem for many years and continues to concern professionals (Artiles et al., 2010; Gregory, 2007; Moule, 2012; Sullivan, 2011). Some assessment procedures simply fail to document the same level of performance by individuals from mainstream and diverse cultural backgrounds, even if they have similar abilities. This phenomenon is referred to as **test bias**. **Measurement bias** produces error during testing, leading to unfair or inaccurate test results that do not reflect the student's actual mental abilities or skills (Harry & Klingner, 2006; Hays, 2008).

In many cases, cultural bias taints both the construction and development of assessment instruments and their use (Gregory, 2007; Reynolds, Livingston, & Willson, 2006). Standardized, norm-referenced instruments have been particularly criticized because the performance of children from different cultures is often compared with norms developed on the basis of other populations. Under these testing conditions, children from more diverse backgrounds often appear disadvantaged due to cultural differences (Erevelles, Kanga, & Middleton, 2006; McMillan, 2007; Spinelli, 2006). For example, a second-grader being assessed for learning disabilities using a commonly used intelligence test as part of the evaluation was asked to name the four seasons of the year. After thinking about it for a few minutes, he responded, "fishing season, deer season, duck season and," pausing to think, "rabbit season?" Although the answer did not fit the pattern required by the standardization of the test, it was a reasonable answer given this child's background and provides important insight into the language and experiences of this child. Another example is a Navajo child who may not respond to questions about snakes in a testing situation because the cultural custom is not to speak of such matters. If the test administrator assumes this lack of response means the child does not know the answer, it may be classified as an error on the test without providing the context for the nonresponse.

Professional Judgment

Professional Judgment These examples raise the issue of **professional judgment**, which is an informed opinion based on training that bridges the gap between quantitative data and qualitative information gathered about a child. For all children being evaluated for high-incidence disabilities, such as learning disabilities, intellectual delays, and emotional disturbance, professional judgment in evaluating the data collected in an evaluation is absolutely necessary. However, too often bias on the part of the assessor or members of the multidisciplinary team plays a prejudicial role in interpreting the outcome of that evaluation (Artiles et al., 2010).

Nondiscriminatory Assessment Tools

Nondiscriminatory Assessment Tools Considerable effort has been expended to develop tests that are culture-free or culture-fair. This effort was rooted in the belief that the test itself contributed to bias or unfairness. But this simplistic perspective was flawed because it focused solely on the test instrument itself and did not adequately address bias in the use of an instrument or the interpretation of data. The following are other questions raised about test bias: What and how do we measure academic achievement accurately for students from CLD backgrounds? Should this be different than for other students? What are the academic achievement goals we expect of *all* children?

Over the years, however, this effort led to some improvement in areas where cultural bias was involved in instrument construction and to some procedural adaptations. Changes in assessment tools minimized the most glaring problems by reducing both the amount of culture-specific content (e.g., naming items more familiar to middle-class white students than to others) and the culture-specific language proficiency required to perform test tasks (e.g., using language more commonly heard in middle-class, English-speaking homes). Refinements to test instruments have limited effectiveness when the use of the test and the interpretation of results are not appropriate and conceptually sound. Recent attention has led to a more balanced focus on procedures the evaluator uses as well as on the test instruments themselves (see the discussion under "Professional Preparation") (Butcher, Cabiya, Lucio, & Garrido, 2007; Downing & Haladyna, 2006; Smith, Lane, & Llorente, 2008).

Language Diversity

Assessment of non-English-speaking children has often been biased, providing an inaccurate reflection of those children's abilities (Gregory, 2007; Solarsh & Alant, 2006). The issue is two-sided. ELL students may be thought to have speech or language disorders or may be disregarded for consideration because of their lack of English proficiency. If language diversity is not considered during assessment and educational planning, a child may receive an inappropriate educational placement (Butcher et al., 2007; Cohen &

Professional judgment
An informed opinion based on specialized training in the area being evaluated that bridges the gap between quantitative data and qualitative information when making decisions.

CEC

Standard 2
Development and Characteristics of Learners

Standard 3
Individual Learning Differences

Spenciner, 2007; Harrington & Brisk, 2006). Sometimes a child's native language may appear to be English because of conversational fluency at school, but the child may not be proficient enough to engage in academic work in English.

A particularly difficult situation exists for students with limited English proficiency and a language disorder, such as delayed language development (Salvia, Ysseldyke, & Bolt, 2007; Trawick-Smith, 2006). Determining the degree to which each factor contributes to academic deficiency is difficult. In fact, it may not be important to assign a certain proportion of performance deficit to language differences and another proportion to intellectual, language, or academic ability. What may be vitally important, however, is identifying students with language differences and finding appropriate educational services, other than special education, to help them. Deciding whether such a child should be placed in special education may be difficult. It is important to keep in mind that language differences may not necessarily mean that the child speaks a language other than English or that the English spoken is not the English of the middle class as is seen in the nearby Case Study, "Nathan."

Special education placement will surely raise questions about whether such placement is occurring because the child is linguistically diverse as a consequence of the child's cultural background or is linguistically deficient for developmental reasons. Although these questions are not easily answered, the field is enormously strengthened because such questions are now being asked and addressed (Brinton & Fujiki, 2010; Cohen & Spenciner, 2007; Salvia, Ysseldyke, & Bolt, 2007).

As indicated earlier, census data show a substantially increasing number of children in the U.S. educational system who speak languages other than English (Nippold, 2006; U.S. Census Bureau, 2010b; Wiese, 2006). Therefore, all teachers, related education personnel, social workers, psychologists, and administrators must become aware of the challenges in conducting appropriate educational assessments of students with language diversity (Cohen & Spenciner, 2007; Sullivan, 2011). In many cases, this means that specific, focused training must be included in professional preparation programs (Ralabate, 2007; Rodriguez, 2005).

One of the seemingly positive safeguards in IDEA, requiring assessment of a child in his or her native language, also raises questions. Although this law represents a positive step toward fair treatment of students from linguistically diverse backgrounds, some difficulties have emerged in its implementation. Specifically, the legislation defines *native language* as the language used in the home, yet a regulation implementing IDEA defines it as "[t]he language normally used by that individual, or, in the case of a child, the language normally used by the parents of the child (except as provided below); In all direct contact with a child (including his or her evaluation), the language normally used by the child in the home or learning environment." For children with limited English proficiency (LEP), this has been clarified to mean, "in all direct contact with a child (including his or her evaluation), the language normally used by the child in the home or learning environment" (Office of Special Education Programs [OSEP], 2002).

This latter definition may present problems for a dual-language student who has achieved a conversational fluency in English. However, the student's proficiency may not be adequate to sustain academic work. In addition, parents may be reticent to identify a home language other than English and seldom understand the difference between the language level required for general conversation and academic achievement. For instance, Maria and Rosa were identified for services in special education for learning disabilities as well as for intellectual delays. The girls and their mother both insisted that the girls only spoke English. However, at a back-to-school night, they were heard speaking happily together in Spanish. The question arises about the IEP team's lack of knowledge about the girls' language and how that might have affected their identification and services. In essence, because of language differences, academic or psychological assessment may inaccurately represent a child's ability when the team does not adequately understand or have access to correct information about a child's language acquisition levels.

Professional Preparation

Effective training of professionals in culturally and linguistically responsive practices is one of the best ways to assure appropriate use of professional judgment in the interpretation of test results and implementation of interventions when working with children from diverse backgrounds. This is particularly important in achieving effective collaboration for all students with disabilities (Dettmer, Thurston, & Dyck, 2005; Friend & Cook, 2007; Ralabate, 2007). Such models are often not addressed successfully in programs in psychology, teacher education, and a number of related areas (Alvarez, 2007; Gimbert, Cristol, & Sene, 2007; Ralabate, 2007; Rodriguez, 2005). Culturally and linguistically responsive teacher preparation trains professionals to be constantly aware of potential bias due to cultural and language differences as well as other factors that may mask students' true abilities (Merrell, 2007; O'Hara & Pritchard, 2008; Reynolds, Livingston, & Willson, 2006). Learning how to gather information about what a child knows from their home life and other environments, their funds of knowledge, matters. It can provide valuable insight to aid evaluators and instructors in administering assessment, interpreting results, and providing interventions. That gathering of information includes what languages are spoken in the household and by whom, who the child's caregivers are (parents and others), how much time the child spends with caregivers, and what types of activities (e.g., cooking, gardening, religion, carpentry, bowling, baseball, Kiwanis) the family and child know about and participate in and with whom.

As universities and colleges train teacher candidates in special education and regular education, specific attention must be given to understanding how to choose and use assessments that are nonbiased and do not discriminate. This training must include **authentic assessment** that involves teachers and parents in the consideration of where students are in their learning journey, and then linking assessment information socially, cognitively, and linguistically to goals, strategies, and tools that best support the students in the learning process (Mueller, 2011; Sleeter & Grant, 2009; Teemant, Smith, & Pinnegar, 2003). Such preparation is essential for professionals to obtain accurate data for development of effective instructional strategies and to minimize misinterpretations that may lead to disproportionality (Artiles et al., 2010; Gregory, 2007; Merrell, 2007).

Culturally and Linguistically Responsive Teaching

It is vitally important to understand the child in the context of the family (De Von Figueroa-Moseley, Ramey, & Keltner, 2006; González, Moll, & Amanti, 2005; Rodriguez, 2005). **Culturally and linguistically responsive teaching** focuses on the strengths, prior knowledge, and experiences of the learner and the family to create an effective learning environment. The concept of **funds of knowledge** encompasses the belief that all families are competent and have knowledge based on their life experiences, and that they use this knowledge to develop social relationships and connections necessary for the survival of their families and to make sense of their everyday experiences (González, Moll, & Amanti, 2005). One of the most important elements in providing successful interventions is gathering information in a culturally responsive way by learning who the family and child are without prejudice. Gay (2002) describes this process as:

- Recognizing and understanding personal attitudes and behaviors toward differing cultural groups.

- Understanding and using students' strengths, background knowledge, and previous experience to enhance instruction in a way that will strengthen new learning experiences.

- Creating an inviting and caring classroom community that supports the development of interdependence and collaboration.

- Building strong relationships with and among students and their families.

- Holding students highly accountable for their own learning.

Authentic assessment
Performance-based assessment of real tasks carried out by the student and usually evaluated with a rubric.

Standard 1
Foundations

Standard 8
Assessment

Standard 9
Professional and Ethical Practice

Culturally and linguistically responsive (CRT) teaching
Culturally and linguistically responsive teaching focuses on the strengths, prior knowledge, and experiences of the learner to create an effective learning environment.

Funds of knowledge
The belief that all families are competent and have knowledge based on their life experiences; and that they use this knowledge to develop social relationships and connections necessary for the survival of their family and to make sense of their everyday experiences.

Edutopia is a nonprofit social media site sponsored through the What Works in Education, George Lucas Educational Foundation. Here you will find resources and interactive networking for teachers working in K–12 classrooms that support general, special education, and multicultural instruction. Along with resources are examples of innovative school programs. For more information, you can visit www.edutopia.org.

The following is a portion of a blog from the Edutopia website written by Diane Demee-Benoit:

> I consider myself multicultural: born in Hong Kong of multicultural parents (a mix of Chinese, Portuguese, French, and Italian). I understand two "native" languages, but only speak one (English). I began my formal schooling in the United States, and I almost didn't "graduate" from kindergarten.

Here's the deal. At the end of my kindergarten year, my mother was called in for a parent–teacher meeting because the school thought I might have a learning disability or a hearing problem. My teacher said I couldn't pass the alphabet test, which is required if you want to graduate from kindergarten.

After some hearing and cognitive tests, and still much confusion about what was wrong, the problem was finally identified! The real problem turned out to be a difference in how British and Americans pronounce the letter "z." . . . I still remember the alphabet debacle from my kindergarten days as being quite stressful.

Forty years later, I don't think most teachers have been prepared any better for dealing with diversity. It's not only the English language issue; it's also the differences in sociocultural norms that need to be addressed. Students from culturally and linguistically diverse backgrounds are too often erroneously placed in special education classes or deemed "lower achievers" because they learn differently.

The good news is that people are trying to correct the problem. The National Center for Culturally Responsive Educational Systems (NCCRESt), funded by the U.S. Department of Education, grew from collaboration among researchers who were studying trends in special education over time. . . . [T]hey noticed that many more children of color are in special ed and wondered whether this stemmed from problems within the educational system. Guess what?

SOURCE: Demee-Benoit, D. (2006). Culturally responsive education. Retrieved from www.edutopia.org/culturally-responsive-education.

Examples of models for culturally and linguistically responsive teaching methods can be found at the University of California, Berkeley's Center for Research on Education, Diversity and Excellence, and Arizona State University's National Center for Culturally Responsive Educational Systems (www.nccrest.org or www.equityallianceatasu.org/).

Multidisciplinary collaboration is a very important tool in education, particularly in special and multicultural education. Effective collaboration requires that all of the professionals have a student- and family-centered focus, remembering this includes knowing their funds of knowledge and building a relationship with them. With these culturally responsive tools in hand, the team can effectively bridge the need of the child with the purposes of education itself.

FOCUS 4

Cite three ways in which differing sociocultural customs may affect the manner in which parents become involved in the educational process.

Parents from Different Cultures and Involvement in Special Education

Parental involvement in the education of students with disabilities is required by IDEA. Parent rights, however, are based on certain assumptions. One fundamental assumption is that parents are consistently proactive and will challenge the school if their child is not being treated properly. This assumption is true of some but not for all. Parents from some cultural backgrounds may be reluctant to take an active role in the educational system because of fear of what people will think, or because institutions or agencies may have mistreated them in the past, or most commonly, they simply do not understand their expected role in the process. The manner in which parents are involved is important to achieving maximum benefit (Arias, Morillo-Campbell, 2008; De Von Figueroa-Moseley, Ramey, & Keltner, 2006; Epstein, 2011). Building a relationship with the family, knowing who they are, learning what their funds of knowledge are, and what they believe can be critical to an IEP team in the development of educational support for the child.

Families can support multicultural education by working with children on school projects that are focused on their cultural heritage.

Gary S Chapman/Getty Images

The acceptance of a child's disability is not easy for any parent. Parents from some cultural backgrounds may view special assistance differently than educational institutions do. They may have perspectives and beliefs regarding illness, disability, and specialized services that differ from those of the majority culture. For example, although all cultures recognize intellectual disability, its conceptualization, social interpretation, and treatment are culture-specific (Baca & Cervantes, 2004; Drew & Hardman, 2007; Skinner & Weisner, 2007). Certain behaviors that may suggest a disabling condition that calls for special education assistance are viewed as normal in some cultures. Some cultures have great difficulty accepting disabilities because of religious beliefs and values. And in some cultures, the condition may be regarded as a punishment visited on the family or may be viewed as a blessing, for instance.

Parents of children with disabilities who are from lower socioeconomic levels, have an ethnically diverse background, and speak a primary language other than English face enormous disadvantages in interacting with the special education system and the educational system in general (Arias & Morillo-Campbell, 2008). The language barrier and lack of knowledge about these systems may make it difficult for parents to fully understand the process, thus impacting their right to fully participate. The Internet now offers many helpful sites (e.g., National Association for the Education of African American Children with Learning Disabilities (AACLD, www.aacld.org; Utah Parent Center, www.utahparentcenter.org/; Recursos en Español, www.ncld.org/recursos-en-espanol) for parents and schools to support better understanding of the issues, responsibilities, and available supports. These resources may help bridge a gap in building the relationships, and having appropriate supports in place for the parents to participate knowledgably (e.g., a specially trained interpreter) is critical to the process.

Sensitivity in interpersonal communication is very important when professionals deliver services to children of families who are culturally diverse (Arias & Morillo-Campbell, 2008; De Von Figueroa-Moseley, Ramey, & Keltner, 2006). Professionals need to be aware of the meaning and interpretation of certain facial expressions; the expression of emotions, manners, and behaviors denoting respect and interpersonal matters vary greatly among cultures. Moreover, illegal immigration status of some families, although this constitutes a pragmatic consideration rather than a cultural difference, may cause them to avoid or be very cautious in interacting with an educational system.

U.S. public education predominantly reflects the philosophy of the cultural majority; the social customs of the diverse subcultures may continue to flourish in private and often emerge in individual interactions and behaviors (Collier, 2004; Gollnick & Chinn, 2009; Skinner & Weisner, 2007). Such differences surface in discussions of disabilities. Understanding that some level of cultural bias and insensitivity is present in our professional work is important when providing services in a society characterized by cultural pluralism. Keep in mind that the key to bridging these challenges is developing relationships with the families and their children (Banks, 2008; Deaux, Reid, & Martin, 2006; Díaz-Rico & Weed, 2010; Sleeter & Grant, 2009).

Standard 5
Learning Environments and Social Interactions

Standard 5
Learning Environments and Social Interactions

Special Education Considerations for Culturally Diverse Students

FOCUS 5

Indicate two areas that require particular attention in the development of an individualized education program (IEP) for a student from a CLD background; identify one challenge in serving children from CLD backgrounds in the least restrictive environment.

The IDEA requires developing an individualized education program (IEP) and determining the subsequent placement in the LRE for each student with a disability. Most school districts have considerable experience in this process, but in meeting the needs of a child from a CLD background, additional considerations must be kept in mind (Hendrick & Weissman, 2007; Morrison, 2007). Depending on the student's background, the IEP team must consider cultural factors, such as language differences, as well as learning and behavior needs based both on the disability and the cultural and linguistic differences. Although collaboration among a variety of trained professionals in special education programs is always the case, making sure to include team members with training and background in the student's culture and language and in the specialized skills needed to remediate disabilities is essential. Coordination of different services and professional personnel with training in culturally responsive techniques becomes crucial (Baca & Cervantes, 2004; Gollnick & Chinn, 2009).

Individualized Education

For all children, including children from CLD backgrounds, the first consideration in developing an IEP is the educational need of the child established by the team in context of the general curriculum. Although there is clear, researched evidence to indicate that established instructional interventions work for all children with special needs, for children from CLD backgrounds, IEP development includes instructional interventions, and related services provided in a culturally and linguistically responsive manner. Education professionals should avoid making stereotypical assumptions about a child's cultural background, which means that getting to know the child and the family is critical. When specific cultural content is included in instruction, content must be relevant to the required general curriculum and the student's identified learning needs, and activities must be specifically accurate, not just uninformed generalizations about a religious celebration or folk dance, but rather actually related to the student's experience to make new learning more effective. Selection of culturally responsive practices requires a knowledge base that is beyond that of many educational professionals, which suggests that culturally responsive practices be included in teacher preparation programs (Kauffman, Conroy, Gardner, & Oswald, 2008).

Language Acquisition Attending to language acquisition for children who are culturally and linguistically diverse in special education programs is especially important. Because all language acquisition is based on development stages and experience, it is important for instructional providers to have training in language acquisition to understand the language development levels of their students (Krashen, 2002). To assume that all English language learners lack language acquisition can be a costly mistake. A child who enters the classroom speaking only Spanish may have highly developed levels of academic language because of the language level of the parents and the background knowledge developed through the life experiences of the child, providing a solid foundation for learning. On the other hand, a child speaking only English but who comes from a language-impoverished environment with little access to experiences that enhance academic language environment will not have the same academic language foundation for learning new concepts. Making sure that appropriate related services for language acquisition as well as language-rich instructional interventions are included in the IEP are critical to the progress a student from a CLD background will make toward achieving academic goals established by the team.

IEPs written for children from culturally diverse backgrounds and the systematic monitoring of language and academic progress must truly be developed in an individualized fashion, perhaps even more so than for children with disabilities who come from the cultural majority. Keep in mind the child's cultural and linguistic experiences that may be useful in strengthening their individual academic performance in the general curriculum and functional performance in the school environment.

The Least Restrictive Environment

Informed decisions regarding appropriate placement in the least restrictive environment (see Chapter 2) for a student with a disability is crucial. In the case of students from CLD backgrounds, school staffs often lack sufficient training to make appropriately informed decisions, and this lack rather than the child's needs might influence placement decisions. The guiding principle is that instruction for students with disabilities should take place in an environment as similar to that of the educational mainstream as possible and alongside peers without disabilities to the greatest extent appropriate. However, supplemental cultural or language instruction may be needed in addition to general and special education instruction, making inclusion in the educational mainstream more difficult.

CEC
Standard 1
Foundations

In all cases, settings must be culturally and linguistically responsive, sensitive to family and cultural differences. When possible, these cultural differences may be used as instructional tools or enhancements to the general curriculum, usually in the child's regular classroom. For example, the teacher recognizing the collaborative learning style of her Hispanic students, and having gathered information about family and student funds of knowledge prepares a lesson from the core curriculum on listening and speaking. Youngsters are asked to orally share and then discuss likes and differences of a specific family cultural trait.

The teacher might prepare an example for class gathered ahead of time from a child from a CLD background. This is an example of how a teacher in the least restrictive environment of the regular classroom can combine general education, multicultural education, and possibly ESL and specially designed instruction defined in an IEP.

Bob Daemmrich/PhotoEdit

The goal is to have many or most of the students functioning academically at the same level with their peers irrespective of their cultural or racial background.

Although children with exceptionalities who have language differences may also receive assistance from English as a second language or dual-language education staff, language instruction should be incorporated across learning environments (August & Shanahan, 2006; Harrington & Brisk, 2006; Hellerman & Vergun, 2007). In situations where the disability is more severe or the language difference is extreme (perhaps the child has little or no English proficiency), the student may be placed in a separate setting for a portion of instructional time, with the staff carefully monitoring the acquisition of skills so that the child can be moved into more inclusive settings as soon as possible for optimum learning opportunities.

Cultural and language instruction will vary with the child's needs, according to the model used in a given school district. For example, if the student needs total assistance to interact and is in a *very* early stage of language development, this child may be provided inclusive instruction with targeted pull-out programs to provide very focused assistance.

Programming options for LRE vary along the continuum of needs and levels of fluency with a goal of totally inclusive instruction. This model allows consideration of language development and bilingual students' needs and represents an important framework for factoring in potential disability needs as well as language diversity status. Although this concept is logical, Collier (2004) noted "there is still considerable debate concerning how and where the bilingual exceptional child should be served" (p. 305). It is important to keep in mind that, even at the beginning stages of second-language acquisition, many children can progress quite nicely in inclusive environments such as the regular classroom with proper instructional strategies. We saw earlier that Collier's statement is multifaceted. It involves overrepresentation and political components, and deciding how best to serve students with maximum effectiveness throughout this complex set of influences.

Other Diversity Considerations

FOCUS 6

Identify three ways in which poverty and migrancy may contribute to the academic difficulties of children from culturally diverse backgrounds, often resulting in their referral to special education.

Many influences come into play as we consider multicultural and diversity issues in education. It is important to note that the study of culture and associated variables is seldom well served by attempts to identify simplistic causal relationships. Research on race and culture involves complex and interacting variables that defy simple conclusions (Emerson & Hatton, 2007; Newell & Kratochwill, 2007; Ram, 2005). However, we will discuss two variables—poverty and migrancy—that are constantly on the minds of educators, and how they intersect with cultural and linguistic diversity.

Children Living in Poverty

Census data published in 2010 indicated that 27.4 percent of all African Americans and 26.6 percent of Latinos lived below the poverty level, compared with 9 percent of the non-Hispanic white population. Of all children 18 and younger, 22 percent were considered to be living below the poverty level. This is an overall increase of 3.4 percent since 2001 (U.S. Census Bureau, 2010d).

Poverty is found more often in CLD populations than in mainstream populations; poverty is also associated with academic risk. Figure 5.2 summarizes poverty rates across several characteristics (Bratter & Eschbach, 2005; Evans & Kim, 2007; Feldman, 2005; Skiba, Poloni-Staudinger, & Simmons, 2005). Because of environmental factors (e.g., pre- and postnatal nutrition, potential exposure to risk, limited health care), a child from an impoverished environment may be destined for special education even before birth (Emerson & Hatton, 2007; McDonough, Sacker, & Wiggins, 2005). In addition, new

Figure 5.2 *Poverty Rates for People and Families with Selected Characteristics: 2010*

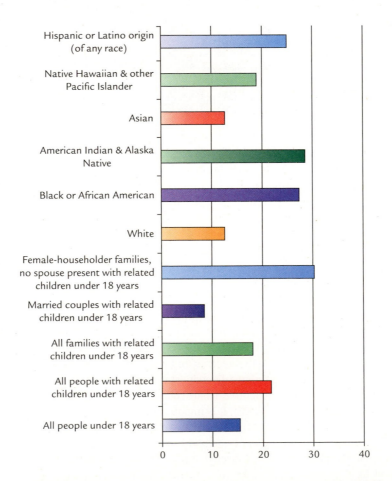

SOURCE: From Bishaw, A., & Iceland, J. (2009). Poverty: 1999, census 2000 brief. Washington, DC: U.S. Government Printing Office. U.S. Bureau of the Census.

research indicates increased risk in children from low socioeconomic-status families for proper brain development in areas affecting school success such as attention, problem-solving skills, vocabulary, and language development (Kishiyama, Boyce, Jimenez, Perry, & Knight, 2008). The effects of impoverished environments continue to cast the shadow of health risk beyond childhood and often over a lifetime, which frequently includes shortened life expectancy, more chronic health problems, neurological problems, and stress (Drew & Hardman, 2007; Hallerod & Larsson, 2008; McDonough, Sacker, & Wiggins, 2005; Kishiyama et al., 2008; Skiba, Poloni-Staudinger, & Simmons, 2005).

Because all learning is language-based, vocabulary knowledge is a critical element of the language development of young children. Subsequently, another major risk factor prevalent in poverty is that children's language interaction (mainly listening and speaking) with parents and caregivers is more likely to be inadequate. In the 1995 seminal longitudinal study conducted by Hart and Risely, language interactions or talking between parents and their young children was measured. Findings in this and subsequent studies indicate that the amount and type of language interactions is a strong predictor of children's cognitive ability and school success. The amount and type of vocabulary used with young children is critical. Vocabulary-rich homes and child care settings increase children's exposure to a quantity of different words and a quality of words (Lucchese, & Tamis-LeMonda, 2007). By the time these children are 6 years of age, this vocabulary disparity is significant, with 2,000 known words for low-SES children compared to 4,000 for middle-income and 6,000 for high-SES children (reading.uoregon.edu/big_ideas/voc/voc_what.php). This translates into the number of words children are prepared to use in developing skills in listening, speaking, reading,

CASE STUDY NATHAN

Nathan was a slightly built, dark-haired little boy with a ready smile and willingness to learn. Born in the Ozarks, he traveled with his grandmother, parents, and sister to a small rural town on the West Coast. Granny is the matriarch of the family and oversees all aspects of home life. She is also very involved in volunteering at the local school where Nathan is a first-grader, but his parents are not involved at all. At home, Nathan helps gather wood for the potbelly stove, mows the lawn with a push mower, and helps his granny with the garden. He helps with the household chores like making his bed, sweeping, and cooking. He also goes hunting with his dad. Granny reads to him from the "Good Book" and expects him to follow its precepts. One cold day at recess, he excitedly ran to Mr. Washington; he had found a "dead" ladybug and had picked it up, holding it lovingly in his closed hand. "Mr. Washington, Mr. Washington," he said, "Look! I said a prayer and now it's alive!"

He had been identified in kindergarten for services in speech/language; his academic progress was so slow that his first-grade teacher and the principal, a well-trained special education teacher, were concerned that he may be intellectually delayed. Nathan came from a very impoverished and abusive home environment where language used, though English, was limited in scope. However, school personnel used culturally and linguistically responsive practices such as home visits, engaging Granny in the school environment, trying to engage the parents though not successful. The information gathered was used as part of the assessment process. The completed assessment found him to be of average intelligence. It was further determined that though speech and language issues continued, much of the learning problem for this child was due to inadequate language acquisition.

APPLICATION

1. What funds of knowledge might you assume are present in Nathan's family? What connections did school personnel use to engage the family and Nathan in the school?

2. What culturally responsive practices did the school use to gather information about the family and Nathan? How do you think this information supported an accurate interpretation of the test results?

3. What types of services might be helpful to Nathan in supporting his language development? What else might you suggest the multidisciplinary team might have done or might continue to do to support Nathan's learning journey?

and writing in a middle-class school setting. This gap persists, and by the time these children are in sixth grade, many children in poverty are so far behind that they lack the skills needed to comprehend more complex reading and writing tasks (Moats, 2011). This difference can put children with few words at risk throughout their educational careers (Blachowicz, Fisher, & Watts-Taffe, 2005; Marulis, & Neuman, 2010). Now consider the exponential challenges and consequences that children from poverty who are also English language learners face in learning adequate vocabulary to be successful at literacy tasks throughout their school careers.

Poverty does not exert a simple, singular influence; rather, it is accompanied by a complex set of other influences, including detrimental physical elements of the environment, the children's assessment of their own abilities, teachers' judgments of the children's performance, and other environmental influences (Evans & Kim, 2007; Hallerod & Larsson, 2008). Research evidence indicates that thoughtfully developed, culturally responsive early intervention programs provided by well-trained professionals have beneficial effects on poor children's academic performance, cognitive development, and general health (Coll-Black, Bhushan, & Fritsch, 2007; Emerson & Hatton, 2007; Kline & Huff, 2008; MacFarlane, 2007; Reschly, 2009). Family assistance such as home visitation programs, nutrition assistance, and health care along with guidance in accessing these programs generally has very positive outcomes.

Children from Migrant Families

Immigration
The movement of people entering a new country to live.

In-migration
The movement of people from one state to another usually for the purpose of work.

The United States is the top migrant destination in the world. Immigrants make up 13.79 percent of the U.S. population, with migration from Mexico leading the way (Peoplemovin, 2010). Our recent surge of **immigration** is the largest since the early 1990s (Banks, 2008; Perlich, 2010). A new term, **in-migration**, has immerged to explain the increasing movement between states (Perlich, 2010). This moving is usually for the purpose of securing employment with the hope of permanence (Gollnick & Chinn, 2009). The proportion of migrant workers from diverse backgrounds varies geographically and often involves seasonal or migrant work throughout the nation; for example, over 80 percent of the farm laborers in California and other western states are recent immigrants from Mexico (Barranti, 2005; Drew & Hardman, 2007).

In many cases, the circumstances of migrancy are associated with economic disadvantage as well as cultural and linguistic differences, creating social and physical isolation from much of the larger community. Migrancy can become an impediment in academic achievement for children in this population. Forces that interrupt the continuity of schooling have an impact on learning, teacher and peer relationships, and general academic progress (Clare & Garcia, 2007; Levin, 2006). For example, children who move three or four times each year may begin the school year in one reading program and finish only a lesson or two before moving to another school that uses a totally different program and approach to the topic. They may also have little access to services because of short-term enrollment, and it is quite possible for children with a need for educational interventions to be in each school for such a short time that they are never identified or referred as needing specialized instructional assistance. Migrant Education Programs are available to support districts and schools and provide extended learning opportunities for migrant children, but determining the programs' success is difficult because of these children's mobility (U.S. Department of Education, 2012).

Multicultural Issues and Specialized Instruction

Specialized instruction for students with disabilities who come from culturally diverse backgrounds must be based on individual need. The IEP must include specific cultural considerations that are relevant for a particular child, addressing language dominance and language proficiency in terms of both conversational and academic skills and what they already know, their funds of knowledge. An IEP may need to address the type of language intervention needed (e.g., enrichment, either in a native language or in English). Instruction may target language enhancement through a strategy integrated with existing curriculum material, such as children's literature or that includes activities that the child may have learned in the home environment.

These are only examples of the considerations that may need attention, and they are issues related primarily to language diversity. Environmental conditions, such as extreme poverty and developmental deprivation, may dictate that services and supports focus on environmental stimulation that was lacking in the child's early learning (Blachowicz, Fisher, & Watts-Taffe, 2005; Emerson & Hatton, 2007; Hendrick & Weissman, 2007). Keep in mind that the child has had a variety of experiences, though different from middle-class peers and teachers, and that these experiences may be useful for supporting instruction. Individual strategies are as varied as the factors that make up a child's background.

It is also important to note that most children from culturally diverse backgrounds do not require special education. Although the factors discussed here may place such students at risk for special education referral, general instruction may meet their needs. When this is possible, it is a mistake to label such students as disabled. Table 5.1 outlines points that educators should consider as they address various elements of the referral process for children from diverse backgrounds.

Table 5.1   **Process Checklist for Serving Children from Diverse Backgrounds**

This checklist provides professionals with points to consider in the process of educating children from culturally diverse backgrounds. These matters should be considered during each of the following: referral, testing, or diagnostic assessment; classification, labeling, or class assignment change; and teacher conferences or home communication.

Process	Issues	Question to be Asked
Referral, Testing, or Diagnostic	Language issues	Is the native language different from the language in which the child is being taught, and should this be considered in the assessment process? What is the home language? What is the normal conversational language? In what language can the student be successfully taught or assessed (academic language)?
	Cultural issues	What are the views toward schooling of the culture from which the child comes? Do differences exist in expectations between the school and family for the child's schooling goals? What are the cultural views toward illness or disability?
	Home issues	What is the family constellation, and who are the family members? What is the family's economic status?
Classification, Labeling, or Class Assignment Change	Language issues	Does the proposed placement change account for any language differences that are relevant, particularly academic language?
	Cultural issues	Does the proposed placement change consider any unique cultural views regarding schooling?
	Home issues	Does the proposed change consider pertinent family matters?
Teacher Conferences or Home Communication	Language issues	Is the communication to parents or other family members in a language they understand?
	Cultural issues	Do cultural views influence communication between family members and the schools as a formal governmental organization? Is there a cultural reluctance of family members to come to the school? Are home visits a desirable alternative? Is communication from teachers viewed positively?
	Home issues	Is the family constellation such that communication with the schools is possible and positive? Are family members positioned economically and otherwise to respond to communication from the schools in a productive manner? If the family is of low socioeconomic status, is transportation a problem for conferences?

Using a Culturally and Linguistically Responsive Model versus a Deficit Model

FOCUS 7

Cite two conceptual differences between using a culturally and linguistically responsive model versus a deficit model.

A number of other factors link special and multicultural education. Some of them raise serious concerns about the placements and effective interventions for diverse children in special education. Special education is primarily seen as a deficit model, focusing on learning and social skills different from the norm. Another model that must be considered when working with all children is to view them from what they already know or from their funds of knowledge. This is especially important when working with children from CLD and poverty environments because they may have very different but very relevant funds of knowledge than their peers or teachers from middle-class families.

What if the student comes from a CLD background, as does Pedro in the opening Snapshot? What are Pedro's funds of knowledge, his strengths? Have his teachers considered his funds of knowledge and how they might be used to support his learning? Should Pedro be considered disabled because of his academic performance or because of his CLD background? This question may not have a clear answer because contributing factors may be so intertwined that they may be difficult to separate and weigh in a meaningful manner. Pedro might have been inappropriately considered for specialized education as long as his performance was primarily a language and cultural matter, and it could be argued that the reason for Pedro receiving special help is irrelevant as long as he received that extra help. This perspective may have intuitive appeal, but it is not a satisfactory position for professionals involved in multicultural education. If Pedro received special education because of his cultural and language background, not primarily because he was disabled, he would have been labeled and placed inappropriately. Unfortunately, children can often become "the label," thus impeding their progress. The concept of the self-fulfilling prophecy resulting in youngsters becoming what they are labeled has been discussed for many years and continues to receive attention in a variety of contexts, from marketing to education (Snyder, Shorey, & Rand, 2006; Spangenberg & Sprott, 2006; Trouilloud, Sarrazin, & Bressoux, 2006).

Further, special education carries a stigma. Many people, including peers and professionals, infer that children in special education are somehow inferior to those who do not require such instruction. Some parents are more comfortable with having their child placed in the general education classes—even if the child might do better in special education. And for Pedro, will this early assistance place him at a disadvantage later? How would viewing him from his strengths improve his chances for success?

An additional problem may occur if a child's special education placement is not culturally responsive. As noted earlier, designing appropriate instructional programs for children from CLD backgrounds is complex and is likely to involve a number of different specialists operating as a team. Such culturally responsive instruction should consider the strengths and knowledge the student has. It may also require some adaptations in the organization of the educational system and accommodations to the instruction so that these children may progress satisfactorily through the academic material (Gollnick & Chinn, 2009; Morrison, 2007).

These factors warrant particular attention as we study multicultural issues and specialized instruction. Seeing Pedro as he is, a successful learner and possessor of knowledge and skills, might change perceptions of him as a capable learner by his school, his family, and himself.

Looking Toward a Bright Future

Cultural and linguistic diversity are more transparent now than they have been in the past and continue to be integral parts of our daily lives in the United States. We are in the midst of a revolution for school change. We are scrutinizing how we look at assessment from its construction to how we gather information generally and individually on student learning.

We are examining in depth our instructional practice. We have become a data-driven society. And although many question the efficacy of this practice, it has provided a catalyst to challenge current practices in education. The number of children from CLD and poverty backgrounds and those identified for services in special education leaving the school systems too early and unprepared to participate fully and successfully in our democratic society is unacceptable. We are a creative people and recognize the value of these students; if we educate them right, they have great potential to contribute and strengthen their communities.

How do we do that? We have already started. We have seen in this chapter a new and challenging juncture between diversity and disability. We find that cultural and language matters present significant challenges for the educational system that can be solved. Consider the following points:

- The purposes and approaches for general education have an altered trajectory.

- As educators, we have a pressing need to avoid taking one single-minded approach to understanding cultural diversity.

- We must understand data simply as markers along the way, but we must also understand the connections between practice and data so that we can determine which practices are effective.

- As we refocus on individual progress, instruction will likewise focus on individual needs. The response to intervention (RTI) framework can be helpful in offering support for both disability and diversity as it reflects an educational system that is culturally and linguistically responsive.

- We need to use our best and most effective means of developing academic language so that children have the most effective educational preparation for the future (Ornstein & Moses, 2005; Riad, 2007).

- Universities and schools must recognize the need to train teachers in culturally and linguistically responsive practices that build relationships and use the funds of knowledge that children and their families bring with them to the school environment.

- We must focus on the future of the individual child, something that disability education has moved toward over the past decades. As educators made their case for specialized instruction for those with intellectual disabilities, the field of education went through several approaches, from pull-out programs to integrated instruction for many (Gollnick & Chinn, 2009).

Both ability and diversity become drivers for change in the educational system. Cultural and linguistic diversity will certainly overlap with disability instruction as we move forward.

FOCUS REVIEW

FOCUS 1 In what three ways do the purposes and approaches to general education, multicultural education, and special education differ in the United States?

- A major purpose of general education is to provide education for everyone and to bring all students to a similar level of performance.

- Multicultural education values and promotes cultural pluralism or the cultural or linguistic differences of individuals.

- Special education focuses on individual learning differences.

FOCUS 2 Describe population trends among culturally and linguistically diverse (CLD) groups in the United States. How do these changes affect the educational system?

- Ethnically and culturally diverse groups such as Latinos, African Americans, and others represent substantial portions of the U.S. population.

- Several culturally or ethnically diverse populations are growing rapidly—in some cases, at twice the rate of growth of the white population because of increasing birthrates and immigration levels.

- Increased demands for services will be placed on the educational system as growth continues among culturally diverse populations.

FOCUS 3 Identify four ways in which culturally and linguistically responsive collaboration might decrease the disproportionality of students from CLD backgrounds in special education programs.

- Use team assessment instruments that are designed and constructed to be nonbiased and including authentic assessments of what a child can do in real settings.
- Understanding children's real academic language fluency in their native tongue and in English allows more accurate decisions about assessments to use and interpretation of results.
- Gathering information from the child and the family about their funds of knowledge in culturally responsive ways supports making successful decisions for assessment and intervention.
- Proper training of professionals in culturally responsive practices increases appropriate interpretation of results and implementation of interventions.

FOCUS 4 Cite three ways in which differing sociocultural customs may affect the manner in which parents become involved in the educational process.

- Parents from some cultural backgrounds may view special assistance differently than educational institutions do.
- They may be afraid to interact with the educational system because institutions or agencies may have mistreated them in the past or they simply do not understand their expected role in the process.
- Certain behaviors that may suggest a disabling condition that calls for special education assistance are viewed as normal in some cultures; parents from those cultures may not see them as problematic.

FOCUS 5 Indicate two areas that require particular attention in the development of an individualized education program

(IEP) for a student from a CLD background; identify one challenge in serving children from CLD backgrounds in the least restrictive environment.

- Coordination of different services and professional personnel with training in culturally responsive techniques becomes crucial.
- IEP development, instructional interventions, and related services should be provided in a culturally and linguistically responsive manner.
- Supplemental cultural or language instruction may be needed in addition to other general and special education instruction teaching, making inclusion in the educational mainstream more difficult.

FOCUS 6 Identify three ways in which poverty and migrancy may contribute to the academic difficulties of children from CLD backgrounds, often resulting in their referral to special education.

- Environmental circumstances that place children at risk, such as inadequate health care or malnutrition, are found most frequently in impoverished households; poverty is often found among culturally and linguistically diverse populations.
- Language interaction (listening and speaking) with parents and caregivers is inadequate to develop the language skills necessary for academic learning and school success.
- Children experience limited continuity and considerable inconsistency in educational programming.

FOCUS 7 Cite two conceptual differences between using a culturally and linguistically responsive model versus a deficit model.

- A deficit teaching model looks at what the child does not know compared to the child's peers.
- A culturally and linguistically responsive teaching model starts by gathering the funds of knowledge the child and the family already have, and then using that information to support learning new skills.

Council for Exceptional Children (CEC) Standards to Accompany Chapter 5

 If you are thinking about a career in special education, you should know that many states use national standards developed by the Council for Exceptional Children (CEC) to assess a teacher candidate's knowledge about and skills for working with students with disabilities. See a complete listing of the 10 CEC Content Standards on the inside back cover of this text.

1 Foundations
2 Development and Characteristics of Learners
3 Individual Learning Differences
5 Learning Environments and Social Interactions
8 Assessment
9 Professional and Ethical Practice

Mastery Activities and Assignments

To master the content within this chapter, complete the following activities and assignments. Online and interactive versions of these activities are also available on the accompanying Education CourseMate website, where you may also access TeachSource videos, chapter web links, interactive quizzes, portfolio activities, flash cards, an integrated eBook, and much more!

1. Complete a written test of the chapter's content. If your instructor requires a written test of your content knowledge for this chapter, keep a copy for your portfolio. A practice test on the information covered in this chapter is available through the Education CourseMate website.

2. Review the Case Study, "Nathan," and respond in writing to the Application Questions. Keep a copy of the Case Study and of your written response for your portfolio.

3. Read the Debate Forum in this chapter and visit the Education CourseMate website to complete the activity "Take a Stand." Keep a copy of this activity for your portfolio.

4. Participate in a community service learning activity. Community service is a valuable way to enhance your learning experience. Visit the Education CourseMate website for suggested community service learning activities that correspond to the information presented in this chapter. Develop a reflective journal of the service learning experience for your portfolio.

CHAPTER 6

Exceptionalities and Families

© Paul Barton/Corbis

FOCUS PREVIEW

As you read the chapter, focus on these key concepts:

1 Identify five factors that influence the ways in which families respond to an infant with a birth defect or disability.

2 Identify three ways in which a newborn child with a disability influences the family social/ecological system.

3 Identify three aspects of raising a child with a disability that contribute to spousal stress.

4 Identify four factors that influence the relationship that develops between an infant with a disability and his or her mother.

5 Identify three ways in which a father may respond to his child with a disability.

6 Identify four ways in which siblings respond to a brother or sister with a disability.

7 Identify three types of support grandparents and other extended family members may render to families that include children with a disability.

8 Describe five behaviors that skilled and competent professionals exhibit when interacting with and relating to families that include children with disabilities.

Teela is a beautiful, fun, 16-year-old young lady who happens to be severely disabled. When she was born, doctors didn't realize that there was anything wrong. By the time she was a year old, it was very apparent that Teela was not the perfect baby I had planned on. This realization was so devastating to me that I honestly believed I could never be happy again for the rest of my life. While the ensuing years have certainly had disappointments and heartache, I have also had a lot of joy from Teela, and my family and I have learned that happiness is indeed still possible.

Teela has two younger siblings—Marissa is 14 and Travis is 9. When asked what kind of an effect Teela has had on our family, both replied that it isn't really a good or bad effect, it's just what our family is and they can't imagine anything else. They don't feel like they've missed out on anything by having Teela as a sibling. Marissa even suggested that other families miss out on our experiences by not having a special needs member. As their mother, I put a lot of effort into making sure we have "normal" family activities. This means researching and planning carefully and making

Courtesy of Ellen Burkett

adaptations, but we have great times together and our efforts to include Teela help to unify us. We love to participate in outdoor activities such as camping and walking. We always make sure to go places where Teela can also go in her "Teela-mobile"—this is what we call her stroller because teenagers don't ride in strollers.

Caring for Teela and keeping her safe from the multiple seizures she suffers every day is also a family effort. Everyone helps with opening doors, physical therapy, and other small tasks. I do have to be careful to not ask too much of her siblings in order to avoid feelings of resentment. I worry that the extra time I spend

with Teela could cause the rest of my family to feel neglected. I am always conscious of this and try to make sure that they are also getting enough of my time and attention. This puts a lot of pressure on me. I feel responsible for holding my family together and making sure their needs are all met while also meeting the special needs of Teela. It's an overwhelming task that I have to just take one day at a time. I have noticed that the way I treat Teela has a huge influence on how my other kids perceive her. When I'm feeling frustrated with her, they tend to also have negative feelings about her. I have had to work very hard to develop coping skills so that we can be a happy family. As I have learned to appreciate Teela and focus more on the positive, my family has followed suit.

Being the mother of a child with disabilities is by far the biggest challenge of my life but by no means has it ruined my life. This isn't exactly the family life I had envisioned, but we have all learned from Teela and have grown closer together because of her.

SOURCE: Burkett, Personal Communication, September 19, 2011

A Changing Era in the Lives of People with Disabilities

As revealed in the first Snapshot, "Teela," families play essential roles in caring for and nurturing children, particularly families who have children with disabilities. Increasingly, care providers who work with families and children with disabilities seek to understand their needs and aspirations. Moreover, professionals are becoming more inclusive in the ways they partner with, care for, and build rewarding relationships with families.

Professionals understand more completely that family members are the primary caregivers, the most constant sources of ongoing support, and powerful repositories of knowledge about their children and youth with disabilities. Moreover, professionals are now more adept in providing assistance and interventions that are home- and family-based, helping parents and siblings deal with the often challenging behaviors presented by their children with disabilities, providing increased access to respite care, and giving material and emotional assistance when needed.

Understanding Families

FOCUS 1

Identify five factors that influence the ways in which families respond to an infant with a birth defect or disability.

Nowhere is the impact of exceptionalities felt as strongly as in families (Hauser-Cram, 2006; Strohm, 2005). The discovery that your infant or child is disabled can be heart wrenching. Carefully think about Teela's mother and how she felt when she realized her little one-year-old girl was not the "perfect baby" she had anticipated.

The discovery or birth of an infant with a disability affects a family as a social unit in many ways. Parents may react with disappointment, anger, depression, guilt, confusion, or other related feelings (Hastings, Daley, Burns, & Beck, 2006; Nagler, 2011; Rummel-Hudson, 2008; Strohm, 2005). Moreover, youth with disabilities who evidence pronounced demanding, destructive, disruptive, and/or aggressive behaviors pose special challenges to the well-being and coping capacities of their parents and often their siblings (Abbeduto et al., 2004; Lach et al., 2009; McCarthy, Cuskelly, van Kraayenoord, & Cohen, 2006). However, many parents and siblings over time develop coping skills that enhance their sense of well-being and their capacity to deal with the demands of caring for a child, youth, or adult with a disability (Baskin & Fawcett, 2006; Gray, 2002; Hauser-Cram, 2006; Pipp-Siegel, Sedey, & Yoshinaga-Itano, 2002). Many families become resilient and adapt well to having a child with a disability (Hastings & Taunt, 2002; Poston et al., 2003; Raver, 2005; Snow, 2001). For some families, humor plays an important role in releasing negative emotions, remedying stress, connecting in unique ways with family members, and moving away from "terminal seriousness," a malady no one wants or needs (Rieger & Scotti, 2004).

Unique and Diverse Challenges

CEC

Standard 1
Foundations

Children with physical, intellectual, or behavioral disabilities present unique and diverse challenges for families (Orgassa, 2005). In one instance, the child may hurl the family into crisis, precipitating major conflicts among its members. Family relationships may be weakened by added and unexpected physical, emotional, and financial demands. Or the child with the disability may be a source of unity that bonds family members together and strengthens their relationships (Ferguson, 2002; Snow, 2001). Many factors influence the reactions of families, including the emotional stability of the family, religious values and beliefs, cultural perspectives and values, socioeconomic status, as well as the severity and type of the child's disability (Gaventa, 2008; Ong-Dean, 2009; Poston & Turnbull, 2004; Turnbull & Turnbull, 2002).

In the United States, 28 percent of children with disabilities live in poverty (Fujiuara & Yamaki, 2000; Park, Turnbull, & Turnbull, 2002). They and their families experience hunger, housing instability, greatly diminished access to health care, and a host of other problems (Parish et al., 2008).

A Social/Ecological Approach

Social/ecological system
A system that provides structure for understanding human interactions, defining roles, establishing goals for behavior, and specifying responsibilities in a social environment.

Ecocultural
A descriptive term that combines ecological and cultural elements to identify factors that influence family functioning, such as unemployment, the family's primary language, the country-of-origin traditions, and so on.

In this chapter, we discuss how raising children with disabilities influences parents, siblings, grandparents, and other extended family members. We also explore the family as a **social/ecological system** defined by a set of purposes, cultural and societal beliefs and aspirations, parent and child roles, expectations, and family socioeconomic conditions (Jackson & Turnbull, 2004; Keen, 2007; Mallory, 2010; Ortiz, 2006; Turnbull & Turnbull, 2002). A social/ecological approach examines how each family member fulfills roles consistent with expectations established by discussion, traditions, cultures, beliefs, or other means (see Figure 6.1). In the process, each family member functions interdependently with other family members to achieve collective and individual goals (Poston et al., 2003). This approach also examines the **ecocultural** and socioeconomic factors that impinge on children with disabilities and their families (Turnbull & Turnbull, 2002). For example, a family that has experienced substantial income loss because of layoffs or a family with parents who are

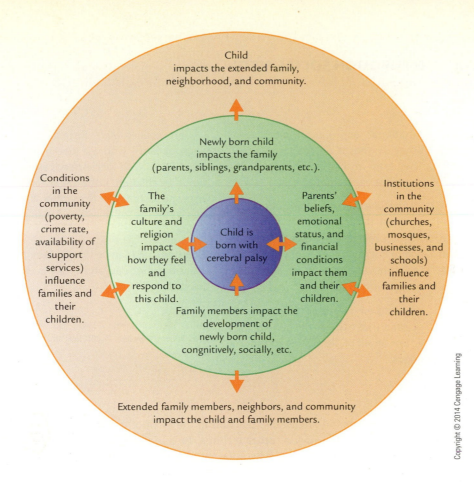

Copyright © 2014 Cengage Learning

Figure 6.1 *Social Ecological Model: Spheres of Influence.*

drug abusers will not be as effective, resilient, or resourceful in responding to an infant, child, youth, or adult with a disability.

A social/ecological framework makes it easy for us to see how changes in one family member can affect every other member and, consequently, the entire family (Ferguson, 2002; Fox, Vaughn, Wyatte, & Dunlap, 2002; Hauser-Cram, Warfield, Shonkoff, & Krauss, 2001). Furthermore, we touch on the ways in which children with disabilities influence the general quality of life experienced by families.

In general, families that include children with a disability experience greater stress and more intense concerns about quality of life issues than families without disabled children (Baker-Ericzén, Brookman-Frazee, & Stahmer, 2005; Griffith et al., 2011; McCarthy et al., 2006). These concerns relate to such factors as financial well-being, emotional health, social well-being, family interaction, parenting skills, and the presence of other co-occuring disabilities in their children, particulary behavior problems (Lach et al., 2009; Neece, Blacher, & Baker, 2010; Poston et al., 2003; Senal, 2010; Stoneman, 2007).

The birth of an infant with an identifiable disability has a profound impact on the family (MacInnes, 2008). The expected or fantasized child whom the parents and other family members had anticipated does not arrive; generally parents are thrown into a state of emotional shock or disequilibrium. Such was the case with Teela's mother. Interestingly, most diagnoses of disabilities occur well after a child's birth, in most cases several years later.

Determining a Diagnosis

Some conditions, such as **spina bifida**, **Down syndrome**, and other physical anomalies are often apparent at or before birth, whereas others, such as hearing impairments and learning disabilities, are not immediately detectable. Even if attending physicians and other professionals suspect the presence of a disabling condition, they may be unable to give a firm diagnosis without the passage of some time and further testing. When parents suspect something is wrong, waiting for a diagnosis or confirmation can be agonizing (Fox & Dunlap, 2002; Frost, 2002; Siklos, & Kerns, 2007).

Spina bifida
A developmental defect of the spinal column.

Down syndrome
A condition caused by a chromosomal abnormality that results in unique physical characteristics and varying degrees of mental retardation.

LEARNING THROUGH SOCIAL MEDIA
KIDZ: FINDING JOY IN HAVING CHILDREN WITH SPECIAL NEEDS

A Utah mom is trying to be a positive voice in what can be a discouraging time for parents. She runs a blog dedicated to finding the positive and the joy of having children with special needs.

When Tara Bennett's daughter was diagnosed with cerebral palsy, her doctor told her not to Google it. She did anyway and found so much negativity and heartache.

So she started *Kidz*, a blog dedicated to the positive and encouraging.

"A lot of the things I share and write are for parents who just got a diagnosis because for me, that was so hard," she said.

Additional contributors now cover other diagnoses on the blog as well. They hope to help people cope with challenges and enjoy life.

"Sure some things are hard, but we can do hard things," Bennett said. "(It's) helping me to be present in my life, and to not put off my happy life. To just really enjoy every moment, and not regret or wish or compare."

Besides being a support network, the site also tries to make the general public less afraid of disabilities and special needs.

Bennett spelled *Kidz* (http://kidzorg. blogspot.com/) with a z because she says children with special needs are just like other children, just a bit different. Since she started it in November 2008, she says the site has thrived and changed her life.

"I learned that I can do this, and tomorrow is a better day, and today is OK," she said.

SOURCE: Adapted from *Kidz: A Special Place for Special Needs*. Retrieved September 29, 2011 from http://kidzorg. blogspot.com/.

The most immediate and predictable reaction to the birth of a child with a disability is shock, characterized by a host of other feelings, including disappointment, sadness, loneliness, fear, anger, frustration, devastation, numbness, uncertainty, and a sense of being trapped. Courtney, the mother of a preschooler with a disability, put it this way: "I really think I am on the verge of getting lost. Well, I probably am lost. Things that used to be important issues in my daily life—like weight, clothes, and all that material stuff—seem so senseless now" (Baskin & Fawcett, 2006, p. 97). Another reaction is depression, often exhibited in the form of grief or mourning (Parentlink, 2011). Some parents describe such emotions as very much like those suffered after the death of a loved one. Recurrent sorrow and frequent feelings of inadequacy are emotions that parents may experience as they gradually adjust to having an infant or child with a disability (Lee, Strauss, Wittman, Jackson, & Carstens 2001). These ongoing feelings may be triggered by health or behavior challenges presented by the child, challenging care demands, the child's inability to meet developmental milestones (walking, talking, etc.), and the insensitivity of extended family and/or community members (Gray, 2002; Lee et al., 2001). Consider this statement made by a sister of a child with a disability who later had a child of her own who became disabled:

> I felt my mother's deep sorrow inside me, and there was nothing I could do for her. Later in my life, I would feel that same helpless grief when one of my own children became blind and I couldn't stop it from happening. There is nothing more terrible than not being able to keep harm away from your child. And for a sibling, there is nothing more painful than watching your mother's heart break because one of her children is wounded. (McHugh, 2003, p. 6)

Although parents of children with disabilities share many of the same feelings and reactions, their responses to specific challenges and related time periods as well as their eventual adjustments vary immensely (Poston et al., 2003; Turnbull & Turnbull, 2002). There is no consistent path or sequence of specific stages of adjustment through which all parents move (Hauser-Cram, 2006). The stage approach simply helps us think about the ways in which parents and others might respond to an infant or child with a disability over time. Emotions associated with one stage may overlap and resurface during another period. Some parents may go through distinct periods of adjustment, whereas others may adjust without passing through any identifiable stages. The process of adjustment for parents is continuous and uniquely individual (Baxter, Cummins, & Yiolitis, 2000; Fine & Nissenbaum, 2000; Ulrich, 2003).

Consider this revealing reflection of a mother of a child with autism:

But I could not stay in denial long. I reread every single book and highlighted paragraphs that supported Rocky's autism diagnosis, this time in neon yellow. By the end of my research, my books were suffering from severe jaundice.

I showed the diseased pages to my doubting spouse. Together we conceded defeat in the battle against the dreaded label.

After sobering up from the intoxication of denial, grief and despair overwhelmed me. I sank into a deep depression. Friends urged me to get help, so I reluctantly went to a support group. . . . (Mara, 2010, p. 17)

Some parents, siblings, and even relatives of children with disabilities employ a kind of cognitive coping that enables them to think about the child, sibling, or grandchild with a disability in ways that enhance their sense of well-being and increase their capacity for responding positively to the child (Baskin & Fawcett, 2006; Chapadjiev, 2009). For example, consider the following account of one mother concerning her response to the birth of a child with a disability:

Brian, my husband, was so completely calm and supportive, he comforted me (and still does) many a many a many a time! We believed that God would show us miracles—maybe not in the way of miraculously having a "normal" baby, but that all would be well and His will, and that we would be HAPPY. Things changed. I started looking at life differently and noticing what was really important. Earlier challenges seemed so trivial now. I had my faith in God, my family, and an active baby boy growing inside of me.

I was grateful for each kick and bump I felt the baby make, as well as the bond that mama and baby were creating. I wrote a special song and sang it to him often. Pregnancy is so amazing. (Bree, 2011)

This mother was able to interpret the birth and subsequent events in a positive manner. Her thinking or cognitive coping helped her reduce or successfully manage potential feelings of shock, distress, and depression. Additionally, her positive interpretation of this event aided her adjustment and contributed to her capacity to respond effectively to her child's needs.

Experiencing Shock

The initial response to the birth of an infant with a disability is generally shock, distinguished variously by feelings of anxiety, guilt, numbness, confusion, helplessness, anger, disbelief, denial, and despair. Parents sometimes have feelings of grief, detachment, bewilderment, or bereavement. At this time, when many parents are most in need of support, the least amount of help may be available.

The ways in which parents react during this period depend on the nature of their psychological makeup, the types of support available, their cultural beliefs, and the type and severity of the disability. Over time, many parents move from being victims to being survivors of the trauma (Gray, 2002).

During the initial period of shock, parents may be unable to process or comprehend information provided by medical and other health care personnel. For this reason, information may need to be communicated later to parents—even several times in loving and understandable ways. Moreover, parents may experience major assaults to their self-worth and belief systems during this period. They may blame themselves for their child's disability and may seriously question their once positive views of themselves. Likewise, they may be forced to reassess the meaning of their lives, the reasons for their present challenges, and how they will move forward.

Coming to a Realization

The stage of realization is characterized by several types of parental behavior. Parents may be anxious or fearful about their ability to cope with the demands of caring for a child with unique needs. They may be easily irritated or upset and spend considerable time in self-accusation, self-pity, or self-hatred. They may continue to reject or deny information provided by care providers and medical personnel. During this stage, however, parents do come to understand the actual demands and constraints that will come with raising a child or youth with a disability (Lee et al., 2001). For example, one parent wrote:

"It's probably Cerebral Palsy," said the Early Intervention therapist. Rachel was only four months old during this initial evaluation. She couldn't hold her head up, roll over, sit up, or crawl. She couldn't even lift her arms or legs. She had no eye contact, cried constantly, and never slept. I knew something was wrong and feared she would never bond with me.

I remember starting to cry. The grandmothers looked on, tried to hold back their tears, but they couldn't. My perfect child was officially not perfect. After collecting my thoughts and trying to shed the feeling of devastation, I tried to think of the positives. As long as it's CP, I thought, this diagnosis meant that she would be physically disabled, but her mental faculties would be intact. We called to make an appointment with a neurologist within 10 minutes of the initial CP diagnosis. (Epstein & Bessell, 2002, p. 56)

Moving Away from Retreat

During defensive retreat stage, parents attempt to avoid dealing with the anxiety-producing realities of their child's condition. Some try to solve their dilemma by seeking placement for the child in a clinic or residential setting. Other parents disappear for a while or retreat to safer and less demanding environments. One mother, on returning home from the hospital with her infant with Down syndrome, quickly packed her suitcase and left with her infant in the family car, not knowing what her destination would be. She simply did not want to face her immediate family or relatives. After driving around for several hours, she decided to return home. Within several months, she adapted well to her daughter's needs and began to provide the stimulation and support necessary for growth.

Coming to Acknowledgment

Acknowledgment is the stage in which parents mobilize their strengths and skills to confront the conditions created by having a child with a disability. At this time, parents begin to involve themselves more fully in interventions and treatments. They are also better able to comprehend information or directions provided by care providers. Some parents join advocacy groups that address their child's needs. Parents begin to accept the child with the disability (Capitani, 2007; Friend & Cook, 2003). During this stage, parents begin to direct their energies and inherent abilities to address their children's challenges and capitalize on their strengths.

Family Characteristics and Roles

FOCUS 2

Identify three ways in which a newborn child with a disability influences the family social/ecological system.

The birth of a child with a disability and its continued presence strongly influence how family members respond to one another, particularly if the child is severely disabled or has multiple disabilities. In many families, the mother experiences the greatest amount of trauma and strain. In caring for such a child, she may no longer be able to do many of the tasks she once did, and her attention to other family members may be greatly altered. Providing ongoing care for multiple children with disabilities can be especially challenging, potentially giving rise to more pronounced symptoms of depression and anxiety, as well as reduced family cohesion and adaptability (Orsmond, Lin, & Seltzer, 2007).

When mothers are drawn away from the tasks they once performed, other family members—usually daughters—often must assume more responsibility and new roles (Laman & Shaughnessy, 2007). Adjusting to new roles and routines may be difficult for some family members.

Cultures and Disability Perspectives

Responses of siblings and other extended family members vary according to their cultural backgrounds and related beliefs about children with disabilities (Banks, 2003; Bui & Turnbull, 2003; Frankland, Turnbull, Wehmeyer, & Blackmountain, 2004). We are just beginning to understand the influence of various cultures on the ways in which children with disabilities are viewed, treated, and reared by their parents and families (Banks, 2003; Boscardin, Brown-Chidsey, & Gonzalez-Martinez, 2001; McHatton & Correa, 2005).

Teachers and other care providers need to be sensitive to issues related to child-rearing practices, family religious beliefs, cultural perspectives, and family views about the role of education (Chapadjiev, 2009; McHatton & Correa, 2005; Poston & Turnbull, 2004; Rivers, 2000; Zhang & Bennett, 2001). Professionals also need to be aware of the different meanings that parents assign to disabilities (Banks, 2003). Furthermore, greater efforts must be directed at finding well-trained interpreters who play essential roles in helping parents and educators understand one another as they develop *individualized family service plans* (IFSPs) and *individualized education plans* (IEPs) for children and youth with disabilities. Moreover, teachers and other care providers need to become skilled in cross-cultural communication: learning how to do home visits and becoming proficient in connecting with diverse families and communities (Matuszny, Banda, & Coleman, 2007; McHatton, 2007).

Working with All Families

Many children with disabilities are being raised by foster parents, single parents, parents of blended families, and grandparents, as well as by lesbian and gay couples. Furthermore, about a half million children are cared for through various state social services organizations and agencies (Fish, 2000). It is clear that all child care professionals need to work effectively and respectfully with all families, learning about their unique needs, and responding with family-sensitive programs and interventions (Dunst & Dempsey, 2007; McKie, 2006; Ulrich, 2003).

The nature of families may vary, but one common factor is the presence of a child with a disability. This child deserves the attention and support of school personnel and other professionals—regardless of the type of family unit to which he or she belongs. The people who serve as primary caregivers or legal guardians of the child should be invited to participate fully in all programs and support services (Fish, 2000).

Spousal Relationships

Research related to spousal relationships is often contradictory (Lach et al., 2009; McCarthy et al., 2006; Stoneman & Gavidia-Payne, 2006). Some families experience extreme spousal turmoil, often culminating in separation and eventually divorce, yet others experience the usual joys and challenges of being married and serving as parents (McCarthy et al., 2006). Recent research suggests that there "is a detectable overall negative impact on marital adjustment, but this impact is small and much lower than would be expected given earlier assumptions about the supposed inevitability of damaging impacts of children with disabilities on family well-being" (Risdal & Singer, 2004, p. 101).

Achieving Balance

The following statement illustrates the interactions and outcomes that a couple may experience in living with a child that has a disability:

> You have not forgotten how your husband (who is no longer your husband . . .) would finally come throttling down the stairs, squinting at the two of you as if he were near-sighted. How he'd open his mouth and close it a few times as [the baby] wailed on, finally saying, in a low, clenched voice, "Do you realize that I have to get up at five o'clock in the morning?" (the "o" sounding like a strangled moan). How your eyes would fill and you would begin a monologue of your helplessness. . . . (Segal, 2010, p. 50)

An infant with a chronic health condition or disability may require more immediate and prolonged attention from the mother for feeding, treatment, and general care. Thus, her attention may become riveted on the life of the child with a disability. The balance that once existed between being a mother and being a spouse no longer exists. The mother may become so involved with caring for the child that other relationships lose their quality and intensity. Feelings of loss, neglect, and dissatisfaction are typical for some fathers. Other fathers have the opposite reaction. Some may become excessively involved with their disabled children's lives, causing their partners to feel neglected.

FOCUS 3
Identify three aspects of raising a child with a disability that contribute to spousal stress.

Parents of children with disabilities need time to be together. This is often made possible through respite care.

Monkey Business Images/Shutterstock.com

Husband Support and Involvement

Mothers deeply involved in caregiving often feel over-worked, overwhelmed, and in need of a break. They may wonder why their spouses are not more helpful and understanding. Husbands who assist with the burdens of caring serve as a buffer, contributing to their part-ner's well-being and resilience. Day-to-day physical and psychological support provided by husbands is invalu-able to mothers of children with disabilities (Rummel-Hudson, 2008; Simmerman, Blacher, & Baker, 2001). This support is also predictive of couple-centered sat-isfaction and contentment (ibid., 2001). Moreover, hus-bands who effectively employ problem-focused coping, actively confronting stressful problems associated with rearing a child with disabilities, contribute to higher marital adjustment and greater life satisfaction in their spouses (Stoneman & Gavidia-Payne, 2006).

Stress

Respite care
Assistance provided by individuals outside of the immediate family to give parents and other children time away from the child with a disability.

Fear, anger, guilt, and resentment often interfere with a couple's capacity to communicate and seek realistic solutions. Fatigue itself profoundly affects how couples function and communicate. As a result, some parents of children with disabilities join together to create **respite care** programs, which give them opportunities to get away from the demands and

REFLECT ON THIS
FRIDAY'S KIDS RESPITE

Friday's Kids Respite (www.fridayskids .org/) is a totally unique service for families. Simply expressed, it delivers high-quality respite care—allowing parents and family members a reprieve from the demands of caring for an in-fant or child with a disability. As mir-rored in its name, Friday is the night on which parents and others can be free for several hours to be with each other, knowing their child with simple or profound needs will be fully cared for while having a fun and even stimu-lating evening with caring volunteers and well-trained professionals.

One of Friday's Kids Respite's most unique features is its capacity to care for children with unique medical or other needs. Children with all kinds of conditions and disabilities are gladly accepted. Feeding, medical regimens, and medications—all factors are

attended to in providing the respite care.

The program strengthens families and communities by giving parents and other caregivers opportunities to catch their breath, to enjoy an evening out, or to give some concentrated attention to their other children in family-centered activities. Children with disabilities re-ceive one-on-one attention in a safe and yet stimulating environment with caring youth, adults, and medical pro-fessionals who attend to their unique needs and capacities.

Concerned individuals can play wonder-ful roles in their communities by volun-teering once a month to give respite care.

Locating a youth or adult who is willing and able to provide quality care for an evening or weekend is extremely dif-ficult. In some areas of the country,

however, enterprising teenagers have developed babysitting businesses that specialize in tending children with dis-abilities. Frequently, local disability associations and parent-to-parent programs help families find quali-fied babysitters or other respite care providers.

Questions for Reflection

1. Now that you are familiar with the concept of respite care, what are the skills and dispositions you would need to participate fully and effec-tively in a program such as Friday's Kids Respite?

2. What would motivate you as a health care provider to give a Friday each month to this kind of enterprise?

SOURCE: Adapted from Friday's Kids, retrieved September 29, 2011 from www.fridayskids.org/app/?page=home.

stress of child rearing. These programs give couples opportunities to relax, renew, and sustain their relationships (Baskin & Fawcett, 2006).

Other factors also contribute to stress: unusually heavy financial burdens for medical treatment or therapy; frequent visits to treatment facilities; forgone time in couple-related activities; lost sleep and fatigue, particularly in the early years of the child's life; and social isolation from relatives and friends.

Time away from the child with a disability or serious illness gives parents and siblings a chance to meet some of their own needs (Chan & Sigafoos, 2000). (See the related Reflect on This, "Friday's Kids Respite.") Parents can recharge themselves for demanding regimens, and siblings can use the exclusive attention of their parents to reaffirm their importance and their value as family members. When parents cannot take a break, the added stress of caring for a child with a disability continues to grow. The nearby Case Study, "Rita," describes this situation.

CEC

Standard 3
Individual Learning Differences

Mother–Child Relationships

Mothers play significant roles in the lives of their children, especially children with disabilities. In most cases, if a child's impairment is readily apparent at birth, the mother often becomes responsible for relating to the child and attending to his or her needs. If the infant is born prematurely or needs extensive, early medical assistance, the mother may be prevented from engaging in the typical feeding and caregiving routines that bring about attachment and provide the foundation for vitally important bonding. Moreover, mothers responsible for caring for multiple children with disabilities are likely to experience "greater challenges to their personal well-being and family functioning" (Orsmond, Lin, & Seltzer, 2007, p. 264).

FOCUS 4

Identify four factors that influence the relationship that develops between an infant with a disability and his or her mother.

Dyadic Relationships

Mothers often develop strong **dyadic relationships** with their children with disabilities (Hauser-Cram, 2006). Dyadic relationships are characterized by very close ties between these children and their mothers.

Dyadic relationships
Relationships involving two individuals who develop and maintain a significant affiliation over time.

CASE STUDY RITA

Please review this brief description of Rita's activities as a single parent of two children with disabilities. As you read through the case, think about what you might do if you were approached to identify ways in which the community, neighbors, service providers, and others might be helpful to her in caring for her children and herself:

My weekdays start about 4:45 in the morning. I get up, take my shower, get everything ready for the day. Pull their snack packs, put their ice packs in there, put them by the door—just get it organized. Around 6:30–6:45 in the morning I wake them up. I usually dress them—at least once because they will take something off and throw it around the house. I come downstairs

and we normally eat breakfast. We are out of the house somewhere around 7:30, if I'm lucky....

[We] get home around 6:45–7:00 in the evening.... [N]ormally on the weekend I cook enough so I just pull out a portion; defrost it in the microwave and heat it up. That's their first meal of the night.

I put them down initially for bedtime around 8:30, but they have difficulty going to sleep at night so between 8:30 and 11:00 they are constantly up, walking down(stairs); I put them back to bed—they'll come down, put them back to bed; they'll come down. I'll put them back to bed. There's usually another snack in there. Up, down, back to bed. Around 11:00 at night that's when I get

a chance to finish my ironing—finishing their snack packs for the next day and their lunches. That's all set up in the fridge. I just line it all up in there and it's ready to go. Put all the clothes out for the next day before I get to bed. I normally don't get more than about five hours of sleep a night. If I'm lucky, five. (Segal, 2004, p. 337)

APPLICATION

1. What could you do as a neighbor to be helpful to Rita?

2. What family-centered services might be useful to Rita?

3. How might grandparents and other family members be involved in a meaningful fashion?

Rather than communicating with all members of the family, a child may use his or her mother as the exclusive channel for communicating needs and making requests. Dyadic relationships may also develop between other members of the family. Certain siblings may turn to each other for support and nurturing. Older siblings, particularly daughters, may take on the role of parent substitutes as a result of their new caregiving responsibilities, and their younger siblings may develop strong relationships with them.

Overprotectiveness

Mothers, who develop very close relationships with their children who have disabilities, often walk a variety of tightropes (Larson, 2000). In their desire to protect their children, they may be overprotective and, thus deny their children of opportunities to practice the skills and participate in the activities that ultimately lead to independence. Mothers may also underestimate their children's capacities and may be reluctant to allow them to engage in challenging activities. In contrast, other mothers may neglect their children with disabilities and not provide the stimulation so critical to their most favorable development.

The mother's long-term vision for her child with a disability dramatically influences her behavior in preparing her son or daughter for adulthood and appropriate independence. For many mothers, conquering the tendency to be overprotective is extremely difficult, but it can be accomplished with help from other parents who have already experienced and overcome this particular challenge. If the mother or other care providers continue to be overprotective, the results can be counterproductive, especially when the child reaches late adolescence and is unprepared for entry into adulthood or semi-independent living.

Father–Child Relationships

FOCUS 5

Identify three ways in which a father may respond to his child with a disability.

Research about fathers of children with disabilities is limited (Parette, Meadan, & Doubet, 2010). What information we have about fathers is drawn generally from case studies, websites, magazine articles, and books (Dollahite, 2001; Meyer, 1995; Rummel-Hudson, 2008).

Responses of Fathers

Some research suggests that the involvement of fathers with children who have disabilities is not significantly different from that of fathers of other children (Turbiville, 1997; Young & Roopnarine, 1994). Moreover, fathers are generally more reserved and guarded in expressing

Supportive fathers contribute to the happiness of their children and their spouses by being available for child care and other home-centered support.

their feelings in contrast to other family members (Lamb & Meyer, 1991). Fathers are more likely to internalize their feelings. Research suggests that fathers respond differently than mothers to the challenges and stressors associated with caring for and rearing a child with a disability, particularly sons who display behavior problems (McCarthy et al., 2006). Unfortunately, some fathers are treated as "afterthoughts" by program providers and related professionals (Parette, Meadan, & Doubet, 2010, p. 382).

Fathers of children with mental retardation are typically more concerned than mothers about their children's social development and eventual educational status, particularly if they are boys (Turbiville, 1997). Likewise, fathers are more affected than mothers by the visibility and severity of their children's conditions (Lamb & Meyer, 1991; Turbiville, 1997; Wang et al., 2004). Often fathers of children with severe disabilities spend less time interacting with them, playing with them, and engaging in school-related tasks.

Fathers are more likely to be involved with their children with disabilities if the children are able to speak or interact with words and phrases.

The relationships that emerge between fathers and their children with disabilities are influenced by the same factors as mother–child relationships. One important factor may be the gender of the child (Turbiville, 1997). If the child is male and if the father had idealized the role he would eventually assume in interacting with a son, the adjustment for the father can be very hard. The father may have had hopes of playing football with the child, of the son eventually becoming a business partner, or of participating with his son in a variety of recreational activities. Many of these hopes may not be realized with a son who has a severe disability.

Preferences of Fathers

Fathers of children with disabilities prefer events and learning activities that are directed at the whole family, not just themselves (Turbiville & Marquis, 2001). They want to learn with other family members about encouraging learning, fostering language development, and promoting other skills (Johnson, 2000). Service providers sometimes neglect fathers, not realizing the important contributions they are capable of making. Fathers prefer programs that clearly address their preferences and priorities—programs that focus on their needs (Turbiville & Marquis, 2001). Children whose fathers are involved in their education perform better in school, evidence better social skills, are more highly motivated to succeed in school, and are less likely to exhibit violent or delinquent behavior later on in their lives (Johnson, 2000; Turbiville, 1997).

Sibling Relationships

About 6.5 million children in the United States have a sibling with a disability (Laman & Shaughnessy, 2007). The vast majority of siblings of children with a disability are essentially identical to siblings in families without disabilities (Neece, Blacher, & Baker, 2010). Having a sister or a brother with a disability does not cause or promote psychological problems per se (Hastings, 2006). Across a spectrum of behaviors and attributes (self-concept, perceived ability, and so on), siblings of children with a disability are remarkably similar to siblings of families without disabilities (Stoneman, 2005; Verté, Hebbrecht, & Roeyers, 2006). However, recent research affirms a strong relationship between the presence of behavior problems and negative impacts on siblings as well as parents, especially if behavior problems co-occur with other disabilities in a child or youth (Lach et al., 2009; Neece, Blacher, & Baker, 2010; Pinkham, 2010).

FOCUS 6

Identify four ways in which siblings respond to a brother or sister with a disability.

Common Questions

Responses of siblings to a sister or brother with a disability vary (Brown, 2004; Laman & Shaughnessy, 2007; McHugh, 2003; Meyer, 2005; Skotko & Levine, 2009; Strohm, 2005). Upon learning that a brother or sister has a disability, siblings may be burdened with different kinds of concerns. A number of questions are commonly asked: "Why did this happen?" "Is my brother contagious?" "Can I catch what he has?" "What am I going to say to my friends?" "Am I going to have to take care of him all of my life?" "Will I have children who are disabled too?" "How will I later meet my responsibilities to my brother with a disability and also meet the needs of my future wife and children?"

Like their parents, siblings generally want to know and understand as much as they can about the disability of their siblings. They want to know how they should respond and how their lives may be different as a result of having a brother or sister with a disability. If these concerns can be adequately addressed, the prospects for positive involvement with the brother or sister with a disability are much better (Brown, 2004; Darley, Porter, Werner, & Eberly, 2002).

Rhea Anna/Aurora Photos

Siblings may play many roles in nurturing a brother or sister with a disability.

What follows are comments made by siblings of children with disabilities. These comments give you a sense for the perceptions and feelings of youth regarding their siblings (Meyer, 2005, p. 72–73): "You get more clothes because she doesn't care about them" (Lydia Q., 13, Massachusetts). "If my sister wasn't a part of my life, I would be so ignorant about people who have disabilities" (Margaret C., 14, Illinois). "It gives you a different outlook on life. You don't take anything in life for granted. Jeremy helps me to slow down and just take a moment to relax and love life" (Lindsay D., 17, North Carolina). "One thing is that we have a handicap sticker for parking. She also brings happiness to our family" (Katelyn C., 16, Virginia). "You become sensitive to other people's needs and more understanding and accepting of people's differences. You also get to be part of special groups like Sibshops" (Erin G., 14, Alberta). "I think David's made me a better person. Definitely a less judgmental one" (Katie J., 19, Illinois).

Parents' Attitudes and Behaviors

Parents' attitudes and behaviors significantly affect their children's views of a sibling with a disability (Grissom & Borkowski, 2002; Stoneman, 2005). Don Meyer, a specialist in sibling relationships, expressed it this way:

> If parents perceive their child's disability as this life-searing tragedy from which there's no escape, they shouldn't be a bit surprised to find that their typically developing kids perceive it that way as well. On the other hand, if they perceive it as being a series of challenges that they have little choice but to meet with as much grace and humor as they can muster, then they have every reason to believe that their typically developing kids will face it that way as well. (Laman & Shaughnessy, 2007, p. 46)

If parents are optimistic and realistic in their views toward the child with a disability, then siblings are likely to mirror these attitudes and related behaviors.

Positive Feelings and Related Impacts

Generally, siblings have positive feelings about having a sister or brother with a disability and believe that their experiences with this sibling with a disability made them better individuals (Chambers, 2007; Connors & Stalker, 2003; McHugh, 2003; Stoneman, 2005). Siblings who are kindly disposed toward assisting the child with a disability can be a real source of support (Brown, 2004; Harland & Cuskelly, 2000). One mother of an 11-year-old son put it this way:

> In the past he has said, "I wish I had a regular brother, I wish I had someone to play with." And there are really some hard, sad things like that. But over the years, he has been such a support, and he will help in any way that we ask. I'm pleased with the qualities that I see in him. (Darley et al., 2002, pp. 34–35)

Many siblings play a crucial role in fostering the intellectual, social, and cognitive development of a brother or sister with a disability. Some even become special educators and care providers in part because of their experiences in growing up with a sibling with a disability (Chambers, 2007; Marks, Matson, & Barraza, 2005).

Sibling Support Groups

Support groups for siblings of children with disabilities can be particularly helpful to adolescents (Laman & Shaughnessy, 2007). These groups introduce youth to the important aspects of having a sibling with a disability. They assist in setting appropriate expectations and discussing questions siblings may be hesitant to ask in family settings. These groups also provide helpful means for analyzing problems and identifying practical solutions (McHugh, 2003).

Impact of Inclusion

With increased inclusion of students with disabilities in neighborhood schools and other general education settings, siblings are often "called into action." They may be asked to explain their brother or sister's behavior, to give ongoing support or modeling, and to respond to questions teachers and others might ask. Furthermore, they may be subject to teasing and related behaviors. Because of these and other factors, some siblings are at greater risk for developing behavior problems.

Some siblings resent the time and attention parents devote to their sister or brother with a disability. This resentment may also take the form of jealousy. Some siblings feel emotionally neglected, convinced that their parents are unaware of their needs for attention and emotional support (McHugh, 2003). For some siblings, the predominant feeling is one of bitter resentment or even rage. For others, the predominant attitude is to feel deprived, believing that their social, educational, and recreational pursuits have been seriously limited.

The following statements are examples of such feelings: "We never went on a family vacation because of my brother, Steven." "How could I invite a friend over? I never knew how my autistic brother would behave." "How do you explain to a date that you have a sister who is retarded?" "Many of my friends stopped coming to my house because they didn't know how to handle my brother, Mike, who is deaf. They simply could not understand him." "I was always shackled with the responsibilities of tending my little sister. I didn't have time to have fun with my friends." "I want a real brother, not a retarded one."

Siblings of children with disabilities may also believe they must compensate for their parents' disappointment about having a child with a disability (McHugh, 2003). They may feel an undue amount of pressure to excel or to be successful in a particular academic or artistic pursuit.

Extended Family Relationships

The term *extended family* is frequently used to describe a household in which an immediate (nuclear) family lives with/along with relatives. In this section, this term is used to refer to close relatives or friends with whom the immediate family has regular and frequent contact, even though they do not necessarily live in the same household. These individuals may include grandparents, uncles, aunts, cousins, close neighbors, or friends.

FOCUS 7
Identify three types of support grandparents and other extended family members may render to families that include children with a disability.

Grandparents

When a grandchild with a disability is born, the joy of the birth event may dissipate. Like parents, grandparents are hurled into a crisis that necessitates reevaluation and reorientation (Scherman, Gardner, & Brown, 1995; Seligman & Darling, 1989). They must decide not only how they will respond to their child, who is now a parent, but also how they will relate to the new grandchild. Many grandparents, having grown up in a time when deviation from the norm was barely tolerated, much less understood, enter the adjustment process without much prior understanding.

Photodisc/Getty Images

Grandparents or other close relatives may be very helpful in providing respite care.

However, things are changing with the inclusion of children with disabilities in general education classrooms and schools. Many yet-to-be parents and grandparents will have had many experiences with children and youth with disabilities because of their elementary and secondary school experiences.

Responses of Grandparents and Others

Research indicates that grandparents, particularly during the disability identification process, are influential in how their children—the new parents—respond to the child with a disability. If grandparents and others show understanding, offer emotional support, and provide good role models of effective coping, they may positively impact the struggling mother and father. If grandparents are critical and nonresponsive, they may add to the parents' burdens and worsen an already challenging situation (Lee & Gardner, 2010; Seligman & Darling, 1989).

On a positive note, grandparents and other family members may contribute a great deal to the primary family unit and increase its overall happiness (Baskin & Fawcett, 2006; Darley et al., 2002; Fox et al., 2002; Luckner & Velaski, 2004). The correlation between grandparent support and positive paternal adjustment is significant (Sandler, Warren, & Raver, 1995). One mother of a child with a disability described a grandmother's actions in this way: "She would play with my son and make a big game out of things that the therapist wanted him to practice. I believe because of her . . . [my son] is able to walk today" (Baranowski & Schilmoeller, 1999, p. 441). If grandparents or other relatives live near the family, they may become integral parts of the support network and, as such, may be able to provide assistance before the energies and resources of their children are so severely depleted that they require additional costly help. To be of assistance, grandparents must be prepared and informed, which can be achieved in a variety of ways. They must have an opportunity to voice their questions, feelings, and concerns about the disability and its complications. Also, they must have meaningful opportunities to become informed. Parents can aid in this process by sharing with their own parents and siblings the pamphlets, materials, and books suggested by health, advocacy, medical, and educational support groups.

Grandparent Support

Grandparents may be helpful in providing much-needed respite care and sometimes financial assistance in the form of a "special needs" trust for long-term support of a grandchild (Bertelli, Silverman, & Talbot, 2009; Carpenter, 2000). Furthermore, they may be able to give parents a weekend reprieve from the pressures of maintaining the household and assist with transportation or babysitting. Grandparents may often serve as third-party evaluators, providing solutions to seemingly irresolvable problems. The child with a disability profits from the unique attention that only grandparents can provide. This attention can be a natural part of special occasions such as birthdays, outings, and other traditional family activities.

Interestingly, millions of children with disabilities now live with their grandparents who are their primary caregivers. These grandparents struggle with many of the same issues and challenges as other parents, including depression, stress, and anxiety—often related to finances and housing. They, like other parents, need access to respite care and support services. Additionally, some of their needs are greater because of their own heightened physical and emotional circumstances. The needs of grandparents may be more pronounced if they are less culturally assimilated; if they have limited English skills; or if they have no legal custody of their grandchildren (Cox, 2008), thus limiting the role they can play in formal deliberations related to IEPs and placements.

Standard 5
Learning Environments and Social Interactions

Family Support throughout the Life Cycle

The relationships between parents and children with disabilities are a function of many factors. Some of the most crucial factors include the child's age and gender; the family's socioeconomic status; the family's culture, coping strength, and composition (one-parent family, two-parent family, or blended family); and the nature and seriousness of the disability. Families go through developmental phases in responding to the needs and nuances of caring for children with disabilities:

1. The time at which parents learn about or suspect a disability in their child
2. The period in which the parents make plans regarding the child's education
3. The point at which the individual with a disability has completed his or her education
4. The period when the parents are older and may be unable to care for their adult offspring (Knox & Bigby, 2007; Turner, 2000)

The nature and severity of the disability and the willingness of the parents to adapt and educate themselves regarding their roles in helping their children move through these phases have an appreciable influence on the parent–child relationships that eventually emerge.

Family-Centered Support, Services, and Programs

Family-centered support, services, and programs encourage families to take the lead in establishing and pursuing their priorities (Brown, 2004; Dempsey & Keen, 2008; Epley, et al., 2010; see Figure 6.2). Professionals who embrace a family-centered philosophy focus on the strengths and capabilities of families, not their deficits (Muscott, 2002; Raver, 2005; Ulrich, 2003). These professionals move away from a "fix and serve" framework to seeing individuals with disabilities as children, youth, and adults with unique kinds of practical knowledge that can be strengthened and actualized through participation in family-centered support services. Furthermore, family-centered services and support are directed at the entire family, not just the mother and the child or youth with a disability (Keen, 2007; Lach, et al., 2009).

Patterns of family-centered support vary as a function of the life cycle of the family, including the changing needs of parents, children with disabilities, and their siblings (Dunst, 2002; Turnbull & Turnbull, 2002; Vacca & Feinberg, 2000). Family support during the early childhood years focuses on delivering appropriate services in natural settings and on helping family members develop an understanding of the child's disability. Support may also center on addressing child behavior problems, becoming knowledgeable about legal rights, learning how to deal with ongoing challenges, and learning how to communicate and work effectively with caregivers and school personnel (Bruder, 2000; Gallagher, Rhodes, & Darling, 2004; Hauser-Cram et al., 2001; Raver, 2005; Shelden & Rush, 2001).

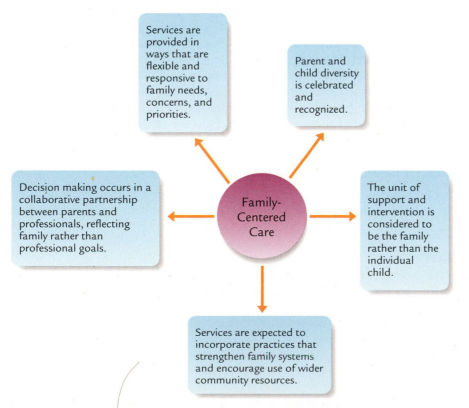

Figure 6.2 *Attributes of Family-Centered Care*

SOURCE: Adapted from Brown, G. (2004). Family-centered care, mothers occupations of caregiving and home therapy programs. In S. A. Esdaile & J. A. Olson (Eds.), *Mothering occupations: Challenge, agency, and participations* (pp. 346–371, esp. p. 349). Philadelphia: F.A. Davis.

Figure 6.3 *Quiet Mice Get Something Nice : Behavioral Incentive Chart.*

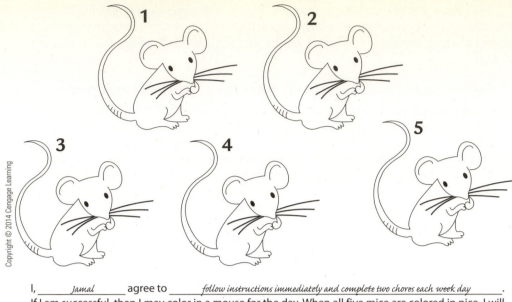

I, _____Jamal_____ agree to _____follow instructions immediately and complete two chores each week day_____. If I am successful, then I may color in a mouse for the day. When all five mice are colored in nice, I will get:

_____a Saturday afternoon with Dad doing something of my choice (movie, shooting baskets, trip to favorite fast-food, etc.)_____

Date: _____March 12_____
Child: _____Jamal_____
Parent: _____Dad_____

Family support may focus on helping parents create effective home rules; develop family routines for dinner, bedtime, and study/homework times; use daily report cards; build behavior monitoring devices; establish effective incentive systems; and create simple contracts. See Figure 6.3 for an example of a behavioral incentive chart designed to help the child and the family.

Family-centered, home-based services delivered by educational and social services professionals are directed at fostering appropriate motor development, promoting speech and language development, assisting with toilet training, and encouraging cognitive development. Other assistance may be targeted at helping parents address specific physical or health conditions that may require special diets, medications, or therapy regimens. The thrust of these services is to enhance capacity and build competence (Raver, 2005).

Elementary School Years

During the elementary school years, parents become increasingly concerned about their children's academic achievement and social relationships. With the movement in many school systems to more inclusionary programs, parents may be particularly anxious about their children's social acceptance by peers without disabilities and about the intensity and appropriateness of instructional programs delivered in general education settings. Overall, parents seem to be pleased with inclusion, particularly its social aspects. Intervention efforts during this period are based on the individualized education program (IEP).

Consistent collaboration between parents and various multidisciplinary team members is crucial to the actual achievement of IEP goals and objectives. Unfortunaetly, many parents find the IEP process intimidating, confusing, and discouraging (Gallagher & Konjoian, 2010). Many parents would like to be more fully involved in the IEP-related decision-making processes, but feel unskilled in representing their views or conclude they will not be taken seriously if they speak out. Others have been taught by their cultures to respect authority, to defer to those above them; thus they rely on the judgments of others, the more educated, in determining the specifics of their child's IEP. These individuals are merely passive participants in the creation of their child's IEP (Ong-Dean, 2009).

Secondary School Years

The secondary school years frequently pose significant challenges for adolescents with disabilities, their parents, and their families. Judith, the mother of a teenager with several disabilities put it this way:

> I am very worried about her future. We have joined the local Arc trust, but otherwise haven't made many plans for the future with her. I am hoping that she will be able to live in a supported setting as an adult, and that we might regain a little freedom, although that might be overly optimistic. (Baskin & Fawcett, 2006, p. 205)

Like their peers, adolescents with disabilities confront significant physical and psychological issues, including learning how to deal with their emerging sexuality, how to develop satisfactory relationships with individuals outside of the home environment, and how to become appropriately independent. Parents of adolescents with disabilities agree that academic achievement is vitally important; nevertheless, they want their sons and daughters to develop essential social skills and other behaviors associated with empathy, perseverance, and character (Geisthardt, Brotherson, & Cook, 2002; Kolb & Hanley-Maxwell, 2003). Other issues must also be addressed during these years, including preparation for employment, development of appropriate self-regulation, provision of instruction in how to access adult services, and development of community living skills.

During their children's adolescence, parents often experience less compliance with their requests and greater resistance to their authority. Parents who are attuned to the unique challenges and opportunities work closely with education and other support personnel to develop IEPs that address these issues and prepare the adolescent with disabilities for entry into adulthood. As appropriate, youth with disabilities are now actively prepared for and often participate in IEP meetings with parents and professionals (Martin et al., 2006).

Transition to the Adult Years

The transition from high school to community and adult life can be achieved successfully by adolescents with disabilities if parents and professionals of disciplines plan for this transition (Levinson, McKee, & DeMatteo, 2000). Transition planning is mandated by IDEA and is achieved primarily through the IEP planning process. IEP goals during this period are directed at providing instruction that is specifically related to succeeding in the community, using public transportation, and functioning as an adult. These adult skills include behaviors related to self-regulation, self-realization, and autonomy. The challenge for parents and care providers is to help adolescents with disabilities achieve as much independence as possible, given their unique strengths and challenges. Some research suggests that parents are often the greatest impediments to adults with disabilities in achieving their own independence and autonomy (Steeves, 2006).

Standard 10
Collaboration

Parents, Families, and Partnerships

The interaction among professionals, parents, and families is often marked by confusion, dissatisfaction, disappointment, and anger (Blue-Banning et al., 2004; Keen, 2007). Consider this father's expressed concern:

FOCUS 8

Describe five behaviors that skilled and competent professionals exhibit when interacting with and relating to families that include children with disabilities.

> When the physician walked in to deliver the message that day, he looked squarely into my wife's eyes. Even though my wife and I were sitting side by side on a chair-turned-hospital-bed, his eyes never made contact with mine. I surely can empathize with the physician, who clearly recognized the pain in my beautiful wife's eyes. But I too was in a state of complete emotional collapse. This physician's body language seemed to convey one of two messages—either that I was not hurting, or that I should simply "take it like a man."
>
> I have to believe that this extremely capable doctor did not treat me this way with any degree of premeditation. Rather, he avoided both eye contact and dialogue out of conditioning. While the mother-child relationship is undeniably powerful, health care providers have been slow to recognize the equally powerful bonds between father and child. I have spent countless nights with grieving fathers over seemingly endless cups of coffee; many of my brothers are hurting and have few outlets to express their emotions. (Fischer, 1994)

Available research and other new developments have led many observers to believe that partnerships and relationships among parents, families, and professionals can be significantly improved (Dunst & Dempsey, 2007; Keen, 2007). One parent described the emotional support she received in this way:

> Every time I talk to him he'll give me words of encouragement. He'll say something like, "You know you are Devante's primary caretaker and the best thing you can do for him is to love him." I mean, this is regardless of if I bring him in for a scraped knee or ear infection, it's always something about just loving him and being there for him and understanding. (Fox et al., 2002, p. 444)

Strengthening Family Supports

The primacy of the family in contributing to the well-being of all children is obvious. Research indicates that family members provide one another with the most lasting, and often the most meaningful, support (Dunlap & Fox, 2007; Raver, 2005; Turnbull & Turnbull, 2002). Much of what has been done to assist children with disabilities, however, has supplanted rather than supported families in their efforts to care and provide for their children. Historically, monies and resources have been directed at services and supports outside the family or even beyond the neighborhood or community in which the family lives.

Funding Challenges

Another related challenge in partnering with medical and other health care personnel are the inherent costs of funding various therapies, medications, surgeries, adaptive devices, and equipment—expenses that exceed the financial means of many families (Parish, et al., 2008). It is beyond the scope of this chapter to address the particulars of these issues, but government representatives have proposed universal health care for all. Consider the nearby Debate Forum to determine where you might stand.

Positive Behavior Support

Indeed, progress has been made in helping professionals partner and relate more effectively and compassionately to parents, families, and others responsible for children and youth with disabilities (Dunst & Dempsey, 2007; Keen, 2007). This is particularly true in the preparation of special educators and others who serve as direct and indirect service providers in family-, school-, and community-based programs (Correa, Hudson, & Hayes, 2004; Rupiper & Marvin, 2004).

One such partnering approach is positive behavior support (PBS) (Bambara & Knoster, 2009; Fox & Dunlap, 2002; Frankland, Edmonson, & Turnbull, 2001; Lee, Poston, & Poston, 2007; Young, Calderella, Richardson, & Young, 2011). This approach focuses on changing disruptive behaviors and supporting behaviors that are valued and naturally supported by parents, neighbors, teachers, and other community members. In effect, all important players in the child's or youth's life become interveners, working together to achieve highly functional positive behaviors—behaviors that are valued and supported in family, school, and community settings (Dunlap & Fox, 2007). These may include skills related to making and keeping friends, replacing loud vocalizations with more appropriately toned speech and language, making requests, expressing appreciation, and developing new ways of responding to events that normally produce aggression or property destruction. Again, the primary focus of PBS is to develop behaviors that are useful and highly valued at home, at school, and in the community—behaviors that "facilitate and promote comprehensive lifestyle changes for enhancing [the] quality of life of both the individual and his or her family" (Lee, Poston, & Poston, 2007, p. 418).

Elements of Successful Partnerships

Effective professional partners and care providers strive to establish trust and respect, empower families, create supportive environments, demonstrate sensitivity to family issues, affirm the positive features of the child with a disability, share valuable information, contribute to the parent's confidence, clarify expectations, and listen well (Blue-Banning

DEBATE FORUM UNIVERSAL HEALTH CARE: SHOULD IT BE A REALITY FOR ALL—EVEN CHILDREN WITH DISABILITIES?

WHAT IS IT?

Universal health care is a health care system in which all residents of a geographic or political entity have their health care paid for by the government, regardless of medical condition.

WHAT WOULD BE COVERED?

Universal health care systems vary in what services are covered completely, covered partially, or not covered at all. Some of these services may include medically necessary services from physicians, physical therapy, occupational therapy, mammography screenings, immunization services, treatment of sexually transmitted diseases, HIV testing, optometry and vision services, alcohol and drug abuse treatment and rehabilitation services, mental health services, gambling addiction services, dentistry services, prescription drugs, medical supplies and appliances, podiatry services, chiropractic services, emergency medical transportation, nursing home care, and home care services.

HOW WOULD IT BE FUNDED?

The majority of universal health care systems are funded primarily by tax revenue.

WHAT IS A "SINGLE-PAYER" SYSTEM?

The term *single-payer* refers to a health care system in which only one entity is billed for all medical costs, typically a government-run universal health care agency or department. Instead of billing the patient directly, government agencies (such as Medicare or the Department of Social and Health Services [DSHS]), and any number of private insurance companies, a doctor or pharmacist need only bill the universal health care agency. This service is also offered in the private sector by entities known as "cash flow companies" in the medical billing industry. Such entities provide the benefit of a single-payer system, including reduced paperwork and guaranteed payment. However, these benefits are often neutralized by the fees associated with employing a cash flow company's services. Such fees typically would not exist in a government-run universal health care system, because a government agency does not need to concern itself with turning a profit.

POINT

- Health care is a right.
- There are 45 million uninsured individuals in the United States.
- Universal health care provides coverage to all citizens regardless of ability to pay.
- Wasteful inefficiencies in medical care could be eliminated.
- Health care becomes increasingly unaffordable for businesses and individuals.
- Universal health care provides for uninsured adults who may forgo treatment needed for chronic health conditions.
- A centralized national database makes diagnosis and treatment easier for doctors.
- Health care professionals would be able to concentrate on treating patients rather than focusing on administrative duties.
- Universal health care would encourage patients to seek preventive care, enabling problems to be detected and treated earlier, preventing more severe expressions of the diseases.
- The profit motive in the current health care system adversely affects the cost and quality of health care.

COUNTERPOINT

- Health care is not a right.
- Universal health care would increase waiting times for medical treatments.
- Universal health care would lessen the overall quality of health care.
- Unequal access and health disparities still exist in some universal health care systems.
- Government agencies are less efficient due to bureaucracy.
- Citizens may not curb their drug costs and doctor visits, thus increasing costs.
- Universal health care must be funded with higher taxes and/or spending cuts in other areas.
- Profit motives, competition, and individual ingenuity lead to greater cost control and effectiveness in providing health care.
- Uninsured citizens can sometimes still receive health and emergency care from alternative sources such as nonprofits and government-run hospitals.
- Government-mandated procedures reduce doctor flexibility and lead to poor patient care.
- Healthy people who take care of themselves have to pay for the burden of those who smoke, are obese, and so on.

- Some systems have banned physicians from selling services outside the system, forcing universal compliance with one system, which some say violates human liberties.

- Loss of private practice options and possible reduced pay may dissuade many would-be doctors from pursuing the profession.

- Implementation of universal health care would cause losses in insurance industry jobs and set the stage for other business closures in the private sector.

SOURCE: Adapted from "Universal Health Care." Wikipedia. Retrieved September 28, 2011 from http://en.wikipedia.org/wiki/Universal_health_care; and "Should the Government Provide Free Universal Health Care for All Americans?" Retrieved September 28, 2011 from www.balancedpolitics.org/universal_health_care.htm.

 *What Do You Think? Please visit the Education CourseMate website for* Human Exceptionality, *11th edition, to access and respond to questions related to the Debate Forum.*

Standard 5
Learning Environments and Social Interactions

et al., 2004; Dunst & Dempsey, 2007; Keen, 2007; Luckner & Velaski, 2004). Care providers seek to understand the family, its ecology, and its culture, taking the time to listen and to build trusting and nurturing relationships, as indicated earlier (Dunlap & Fox, 2007; Frankland et al., 2004; Zhang & Bennett, 2001).

Healthy, well-functioning families of children with disabilities contribute greatly to the well-being of all family members. The same is true of marriages that are cohesive and strong. On the other hand, family tension and disorganization may negatively affect siblings of children with disabilities, heightening their chances for developing behavior problems, lessening their social competence, and diminishing their capacity for developing important problem-solving skills (Lobato, Kao, & Plante, 2005; Stoneman, 2005). Fortunately parent-to-parent programs, communities of practice—groups of people who share common concerns and frequently interact with one another and other family support programs—are directed at helping families function more optimally, thus contributing positively to the development of the child with a disability and other children within the family (Gotto, Beauchamp, & Simpson, 2007; Lucyshyn, Dunlap, & Albin, 2002; Santelli, Ginsberg, Sullivan, & Niederhauser, 2002).

Superb family support programs keep families together, enhancing their capacity to meet the needs of the individual with a disability, reducing the need for out-of-home placement, and giving families access to typical social and recreational activities (Heiman & Berger, 2008). The following statement expresses a parent's wonderment at the effectiveness of family-centered support:

> They never give up. I am just astounded by the many creative ways they keep coming up with to help him. Oftentimes they do not understand him, but they never give up. At one point I had to ask myself: Are these people for real? . . . I cannot believe how genuine and real they really are. (Worthington, Hernandez, Friedman, & Uzzell, 2001, p. 77)

Increasingly, policy makers and program providers are realizing the importance of the family, emphasizing its crucial role in the development and ongoing care of a child with a disability. Services are now being directed at the family as a whole, rather than just at the child with the disability (Raver, 2005). This support is particularly evident in the individualized family service plan (IFSP), as discussed earlier in this chapter and in Chapter 3. Such an orientation honors the distinctive and essential roles of parents, siblings, and other extended family members as primary caregivers, nurturers, and teachers (Heiman & Berger, 2008). Additionally, these services provide parents and siblings with opportunities to engage in other respite-related activities that are important to their physical, emotional, and social well-being.

Please visit the Education CourseMate website for *Human Exceptionality*, 11th edition, at CengageBrain.com to access this TeachSource Video.

As you are beginning to learn, collaboration is essential to meeting the needs of children and youth with disabilities. Family–school connections greatly contribute to the success of students with disabilities. The synergy that can and does emanate from successful teacher–family collaborations is tangible and beneficial for students, classrooms, schools, and families. Improvements may come in the form of improved behavior, greater academic achievement, enhanced self-regulation, better social skills, and a greater sense of self—a more positive academic and/or social identity. In this video, Sophia Boyer speaks to us about her initial expectations and goals in working with her students and their families, and how she had to alter or adjust some of her notions and beliefs.

Given what you've learned in this video and in this chapter, what will you need to do as a professional in collaborating effectively and caringly with parents and families?

Because of family support services and parent-to-parent programs, many children and youth with disabilities enjoy relationships and activities that are a natural part of living in their own homes, neighborhoods, and communities. These services allow children and youth with disabilities to truly be a part of their neighborhoods and communities.

Standard 10
Collaboration

Training for Parents, Families, and Professionals

Parent training is an essential part of most early intervention programs for children with disabilities. As part of IDEA, parent training is directed at helping parents acquire the essential skills that assist them in implementing their child's IEP or IFSP (Tynan & Wornian, 2002; Whitbread, Bruder, Fleming, & Park, 2007). No longer is the child viewed as the primary recipient of services; instead, services and training are directed at the complex and varied needs of each family and its members. Much of the training is conducted by experienced and skilled parents of children with disabilities, who volunteer their time as part of their affiliation with an advocacy or support group. These support groups are invaluable in helping parents, other family members, neighbors, and friends respond effectively to the child or youth with a disability (Gallagher & Konjoian, 2010). In describing her experiences with parent training, one mother made the following observations:

> Oh yes, she [the parent trainer] was excellent. Our third child was a 29 weeker. We didn't know any of that stuff. . . . I enjoyed finding out what was going on and knowing the signals, because if he's going to throw up a red flag to me, I want to know how to react. . . . I couldn't believe all the stuff that she told me that I didn't know. . . . [S]he related to all members of the family. . . . I appreciated what she did. (Ward, Cronin, Renfro, Lowman, & Cooper, 2000)

Training may be focused on feeding techniques, language development, toilet training programs, challenging behaviors, motor development, or other related issues important to parents (Buschbacher, Fox, & Clarke, 2004; Kazdin, 2005; Tynan & Wornian, 2002). For parents of youth or adults with disabilities, the training may be directed at accessing adult services, using functional assessment and positive behavior support, accessing recreational programs, finding postsecondary vocational programs, locating appropriate housing, qualifying for Social Security benefits, or legal planning for guardianship (Brooke & McDonough, 2008; Chambers, Hughes, & Carter, 2004; Russell & Grant, 2005). In some instances, the training and preparation center on giving parents meaningful information about their legal rights, preparing them to participate effectively in IEP meetings, helping them understand the nature of their child's disability, making them aware of recreational programs in their communities, or alerting them to specific funding opportunities. Through these training programs, parents learn how to engage effectively in problem solving and conflict resolution and, thus, are empowered and prepared to advocate for their children and themselves. Parent involvement with the education of their children with disabilities significantly benefits their children's learning and overall school performance.

Training for Siblings, Grandparents, and Others

Training may also be directed at siblings, grandparents, and other relatives. It may even involve close neighbors or caring friends who wish to contribute to the well-being of the family. Often these are individuals who are tied to the family through religious affiliations or long-standing friendships (Poston & Turnbull, 2004).

Siblings of children with disabilities need information about the nature and possible course of disabilities affecting their brother or sister (Chambers, Hughes, & Carter, 2004). Furthermore, they need social and emotional support, including acknowledgment of their own needs for nurturing, attention, and affirmation. Some research suggests that many siblings know very little about their brother or sister's disability, its manifestations, and its consequences. Siblings need to understand that they are not responsible for a particular condition or disability. Other questions also need addressing. These questions deal with the heritability of the disability, the siblings' future role in providing care, the ways in which siblings might explain the disability to their friends, and the ways the presence of the brother or sister with a disability will affect their family and themselves.

In most instances, the training of siblings occurs through support groups or workshops sometimes referred to as "Sibshops," as indicated earlier (Laman & Shaughnessy, 2007). These groups are age-specific so that siblings can express feelings, vent frustrations, and learn from others. They may also get advice on how to deal with predictable situations—that is, what to say or how to respond. Some learn how to use sign language, how to complete simple medical procedures, how to manage misbehavior, or how to use certain incentive systems. In some cases, siblings may become prepared for the eventual death of a brother or sister who has a life-threatening condition.

Training of grandparents, other relatives, neighbors, and friends is also crucial. They, like the siblings of children with disabilities, must be informed, must have opportunities to express feelings, must be able to ask pertinent questions, and must receive training that is tailored to their needs. If they are informed and well trained, they often provide the only consistent respite care that is available to families. Also, they may contribute invaluable transportation, recreational activities, babysitting, critical emotional support, and/or short-term and long-term financial assistance (Gorman, 2004).

CEC

Standard 9
Professional and Ethical
Practice

Training for Professionals

Collaborative training involves professionals, such as educators, social workers, psychologists, and health care professionals. This training focuses primarily on building relationships, collaborating, understanding cross-cultural matters, and providing meaningful instruction. Training is also aimed at helping professionals understand the complex nature of family cultures, structures, functions, and interactions, as well as at encouraging them to take a close look at their own attitudes, feelings, values, and perceptions about families that include children, youth, and adults with disabilities (Gorman, 2004; Stone, 2005; Turnbull & Turnbull, 2002).

Some professionals may be insensitive to the daily demands inherent in caring for a child, youth, or adult who presents persistent challenging behaviors (Alonzo, Bushey, Gardner, Hasazi, Johnston, & Miller, 2006). As a consequence, they may use vocabulary that is unfamiliar to parents, may speak a language that is foreign to parents, may not give parents enough time to express their feelings and perceptions, and may be insensitive to cultural variations in relating and communicating with parents. Hence, the skills that are stressed in training for professionals include effective communication, cultural awareness, problem-solving strategies, negotiation, and conflict resolution (Ortiz, 2006).

Looking Toward a Bright Future

As we know, families play vitally important roles in the development and well-being of all children—this is particularly true of children and youth with disabilities. Now more than ever, educational, medical, social, and other health care professionals seek to understand the needs, concerns, and aspirations of families of children with a disability. Increasingly, the preparation of physicians, nurses, school administrators, and other care providers includes experiences about and with these families. Professionals are becoming more inclusive and innovative in the ways they connect with, care for, and build rewarding partnerships and relationships with families.

Professionals now understand more completely that family members are the primary nurturers, the first and most consistent teachers, the crucial providers of care, and powerful sources of knowledge about children and youth with disabilities. Increasingly, professionals are listening more, giving more of themselves and their expertise, and providing services and interventions that were often reserved for children and youth without disabilities. Moreover, professionals are much more skilled in providing assistance that is home- and family-based, helping parents and siblings deal with real and often challenging behaviors their children present, providing increased access to respite care, and giving material and emotional assistance when needed.

Families, siblings, grandparents, and other family members, particularly fathers, now have vastly improved access to support groups, social networks, and systems of care, each of which is designed to benefit not only the child with disabilities, but also the family and its constituent members.

We are also beginning to understand the role of culture in working with families with children who have a disability, becoming sensitive to the unique perspectives of parents and other family members about disabilities. More and more, talented clinicians and other professionals are involving interpreters and other community members in meaningful ways, genuinely seeking to understand and respond to diverse families in respectful, sensitive, and supportive ways.

We can all contribute to this bright future for families with children who have a disability as we seek to inform ourselves, to alter our attitudes, and to commit to new levels of involvement and service. Our contributions might include providing respite care for a family in our neighborhood, actively recruiting and preparing individuals with a disability for employment, being more inclusive in our social and recreational activities, and expressing care and regard in our communications.

FOCUS REVIEW

FOCUS 1 Identify five factors that influence the ways in which families respond to an infant with a birth defect or disability.

- The emotional stability of each family member
- Religious and cultural values and beliefs
- Socioeconomic status
- The severity of the disability
- The type of disability

FOCUS 2 Identify three ways in which a newborn child with a disability influences the family social/ecological system.

- The communication patterns within the family may change.
- The power structure within the family may be altered.
- The roles and responsibilities assumed by various family members may be modified.

FOCUS 3 Identify three aspects of raising a child with a disability that contribute to spousal stress.

- A decrease in the amount of time available for the couple's activities
- Heavy financial burdens
- Fatigue

FOCUS 4 Identify four factors that influence the relationship that develops between an infant with a disability and his or her mother.

- The mother may be unable to engage in typical feeding and caregiving activities because of the intensive medical care being provided.
- Some mothers may have difficulty bonding to children with whom they have little physical and social interaction.

- Some mothers are given little direction in becoming involved with their children. Without minimal involvement, some mothers become estranged from their children and find it difficult to begin the caring and bonding process.
- The expectations that mothers have about their children and their own functions in nurturing them play a significant role in the relationship that develops.

FOCUS 5 Identify three ways in which a father may respond to his child with a disability.

- Fathers are more likely to internalize their feelings than are mothers.
- Fathers often respond to a son with a disability differently from the way they respond to a daughter.
- Fathers may resent the time their wives spend in caring for their children with a disability.

FOCUS 6 Identify four ways in which siblings respond to a brother or sister with a disability.

- Siblings tend to mirror the attitudes and behaviors of their parents toward a child with disability.
- Siblings may play a crucial role in fostering the intellectual, social, and affective development of the child with a disability.

- Some siblings may attempt to compensate for their parents' disappointment by excelling in an academic or artistic pursuit.
- Some siblings respond with feelings of resentment or deprivation.

FOCUS 7 Identify three types of support grandparents and other extended family members may render to families that include children with a disability.

- They may provide their own children with weekend respite from the pressures of the home environment.
- They may assist occasionally with babysitting or transportation.
- They may support their children in times of crisis by listening and helping them deal with seemingly irresolvable problems and by providing short-term and long-term financial assistance.

FOCUS 8 Describe five behaviors that skilled and competent professionals exhibit when interacting with and relating to families that include children with disabilities.

- They establish rapport.
- They create supportive environments.
- The demonstrate sensitivity to the needs of these families and seek to understand the culture and ecology of each family.
- They share valuable information.
- They listen well.

Council for Exceptional Children (CEC) Standards to Accompany Chapter 6

 If you are thinking about a career in special education, you should know that many states use national standards developed by the Council for Exceptional Children (CEC) to assess a teacher candidate's knowledge and skills for working with students with disabilities. See a complete listing of the 10 CEC Content Standards on the inside back cover of this text.

1 Foundations
3 Individual Learning Differences
5 Learning Environments and Social Interactions
9 Professional and Ethical Practice
10 Collaboration

Mastery Activities and Assignments

 To master the content within this chapter, you may wish to complete the following activities and assignments. Online and interactive versions of these activities are also available on the accompanying Education CourseMate website, where you may also access TeachSource videos, chapter web links, interactive quizzes, portfolio activities, flash cards, an integrated eBook, and much more!

1. Complete a written test of the chapter's content. If your instructor requires a written test of your content knowledge for this chapter, keep a copy for your portfolio. A practice test on the information covered in this chapter is available through the Education CourseMate website.

2. Review the Case Study, "Rita," and respond in writing to the Application Questions. Keep a copy of the Case Study and your written response for your portfolio.

3. Read the Debate Forum, "Universal Health Care: Should it be a Reality for All—Even Children with Disabilities?," and then visit the CourseMate website to complete the activity "Take a Stand." Keep a copy of this activity for your portfolio.

4. Participate in a community service learning activity. Community service is a valuable way to enhance your learning experience. Visit the Education CourseMate website for suggested community service learning activities that correspond to the information presented in this chapter. Develop a reflective journal of the service learning experience for your portfolio.

People Who Are Exceptional

PART 3

HIGH INCIDENCE EXCEPTIONALITIES

More than 90 percent of students with disabilities receiving special education services in the United States are identified as having learning disabilities, emotional and behavior disorders, intellectual disabilities, communication disorders, or autism spectrum disorders. Of these students, 95 percent are receiving their education in inclusive programs in general education schools and classrooms for all or part of the day (U.S. Department of Education, 2011a).

Every educator has taught students who can be described as having a "high-incidence" exceptionality. These individuals share academic, behavioral, and communication challenges that are often initially identified and evident within a school and family setting. For most individuals identified as having a high-incidence exceptionality, the cause of their disability is unknown; different biological (genetic predisposition) and environmental issues (such as poverty and inadequate instructional practices) may contribute to their learning, behavior, and communication challenges.

Educational instruction for students with high-incidence exceptionalities includes both academic and social programs that are framed around one fundamental question: Are the educational needs of these students more alike than different?

Today, students identified in these high-incidence categories are often placed in inclusive education classrooms, working side by side with "typical students" and supported by general and special education teachers as well as related service professionals, including speech and language pathologists and school psychologists. Part III of this text explores the definitions, characteristics, and multidisciplinary approaches used to meet the instructional, social, and health care needs across each of the five categories associated with high-incidence disabilities.

PART III CHAPTER OVERVIEWS

Part III opens with Chapter 7, "Learning Disabilities." Students with learning disabilities comprise about 42 percent of students with disabilities. These students may exhibit educational challenges in academic subjects (reading, mathematics, science), as well as in language, attention, and memory.

Chapter 8 introduces people with emotional disturbance and behavior disorders, described as "serious emotional disturbance" in federal law under IDEA. These students face many behavioral challenges in educational, family, and community settings, including being able to adapt to school and community behavioral standards, social relationships, as well as emotional difficulties with anxiety or depression.

Chapter 9 explores students with intellectual and developmental disabilities. As a "label," *intellectual disabilities* is a relatively new category that replaces terms such as *mental retardation* and *feebleminded*. Individuals with intellectual disabilities are characterized

by intellectual deficits (most often measured by intelligence quotient [IQ] tests) and difficulty in adapting to school, family, or community environments. Intellectual disabilities are considered "developmental disorders" because, by definition, they must be identified during the childhood and adolescent years.

Chapter 10 examines people with communication disorders. These individuals may present challenges with speech and/or language. Speech disorders include difficulties with voice, articulation, or fluency, whereas language disorders involve difficulties with phonology, morphology, syntax, semantics, or pragmatics of language use.

Part III concludes with the newest category to be included as a high-incidence exceptionality: autism spectrum disorders. Chapter 11 focuses on autism, one of the most visible and discussed disability categories of the 21st century. Although autism has a more than 60-year history as a disability label and is included as a category within IDEA, *autism spectrum disorders* is a broad term that encompasses autism as well as other conditions (such as Asperger's Syndrome) with a range of characteristics regarding a person's ability to communicate and language, intelligence, and social interaction skills.

As you now begin your exploration of high-incidence disabilities, remember the many different perspectives associated with this term. The vast majority of individuals classified with high-incidence disabilities are now receiving their education within general education settings.

© Elizabeth Crews/Photo Edit

Learning Disabilities

© Bill Aron/Photo Edit

FOCUS PREVIEW

As you read the chapter, focus on these key concepts:

1 Cite four reasons why definitions of learning disabilities have varied.

2 Identify seven characteristics attributed to those with learning disabilities, and explain why it is difficult to characterize this group.

3 List four causes thought to be involved in learning disabilities.

4 Compare and contrast the purpose of assessments used for screening and progress monitoring.

5 Identify five types of interventions or supports used with people who have learning disabilities, including two that use assistive technology.

6 Explain how behavior and emotion can affect the achievement of students with learning disabilities, and describe two strategies for addressing these concerns.

7 Compare learning disabilities in childhood and adolescence by listing four challenges that individuals experience as they move into secondary school and beyond.

8 Cite three areas in which general education teachers may not feel prepared to collaborate for inclusion.

Note: The following is an excerpt from a statement prepared by an upper-division psychology undergraduate student who has learning disabilities. Mathew tells his story in his own words, recounting some of his school experiences, his diagnosis, and how his learning disabilities affect his academic efforts.

Imagine having the inability to memorize times tables, not being able to "tell time" until the ninth grade, and taking several days to read a simple chapter from a school textbook.

In elementary and high school, I was terrified of math classes for several reasons. First, it did not matter how many times I practiced my times tables or other numerical combinations relating to division, subtraction, and addition. I could not remember them. Second, I dreaded the class time itself for inevitably the teacher would call on me for an answer to a "simple" problem. Multiplication was the worst! Since I had to count on my fingers to do multiplication, it would take a lot of time and effort. Do you know how long it takes to calculate 9×7 or 9×9 on your fingers? Suffice it to say, too long, especially if the teacher and the rest of the class are waiting.

When I was a sophomore at a junior college, I discovered important information about myself. After two days of clinical cognitive testing, I learned that my brain is wired differently than most individuals. That is, I think, perceive, and process information differently. They discovered several "wiring jobs" which are called learning disabilities. First, I have a problem with processing speed. The ability to bring information from long-term memory to consciousness (into short-term memory) takes me a long time. Second, I have a deficit with my short-term memory. This means that I cannot hold information there very long. When new information is learned, it must be put into long-term memory. This is an arduous process requiring the information to be rehearsed several times. Third, I have a significant problem with fluid reasoning. Fluid reasoning is the ability to go from A to G without having to go through B, C, D, E, and F. It also includes drawing inferences, coming up with creative solutions to problems, solving unique problems, and the ability to transfer information and generalize. Hence, my math and numerical difficulties . . . .

With all of this knowledge, I was able to use specific strategies that will help me in compensating for these neurological wiring patterns. Now I tape all lectures rather than trying to keep up taking notes. I take tests in a room by myself and they are not timed. Anytime I need to do mathematical calculations I use a calculator. . . .

SOURCE: From Gelfand, D. M., & Drew, C. J. (2003). *Understanding child behavior disorders*, 4th ed. (p. 238). Belmont, CA: Wadsworth. Used with permission.

A Changing Era in the Lives of People with Disabilities

Learning disabilities have likely always been a part of the human condition, but it is only since the latter half of the 20th century that we have focused on this particular area of disorder. Often called one of the invisible disabilities, **learning disabilities** affect people of all ages and walks of life but cannot be detected simply by appearance, dress, or behavior. In the opening Snapshot, Mathew did not learn the reasons for his struggles until he was in college, yet learning disabilities affected his entire school experience.

Mathew's case is not altogether unusual. Although parents, educators, and other professionals in the field have learned much about recognizing the condition, some people do not learn the reasons for their academic or social struggles until high school or college or beyond. Still, it is most common to see indicators of possible learning disabilities in the early years of school. The cognitively complex activities of learning to read, write, and do math usually bring concerns to the fore when knowledgeable teachers and parents notice a student's lack of progress compared to other children.

Learning disability
A condition in which one or more of the basic psychological processes involved in understanding or using language are deficient.

We are fortunate to live at a time of great progress in assessing, affirming, planning for, and instructing individuals with learning disabilities. However, this is not to say that we have all the answers; the field continues to evolve. This chapter discusses the continuing debate over the definition of learning disabilities and estimates of the prevalence of the disorder. It then presents the characteristics and possible causes of learning disabilities, and explores the current understanding of appropriate learning disabilities practice and effective interventions.

Definitions and Classifications

FOCUS 1

Cite four reasons why definitions of learning disabilities have varied.

The field of learning disabilities was virtually unrecognized prior to the 1960s. These disabilities are often considered mild because people with learning disabilities usually have average or near-average intelligence, although learning disabilities can occur at all intelligence levels. People with learning disabilities achieve at unexpectedly low levels, particularly in reading and mathematics. The term *learning disabilities* has become a generic label representing a very heterogeneous group of conditions that range from mild to severe in intensity (Bender, 2008a; Buttner & Hasselhorn, 2011). Individuals with learning disabilities exhibit a highly variable and complex set of characteristics and needs. Consequently, they present a substantial challenge to family members and professionals. This set of challenges, however, is repeatedly met with significant success, as evidenced by many stories of outstanding achievement by adults who have histories of learning disabilities in childhood.

Confusion, controversy, and polarization have been associated with learning disabilities as long as they have been recognized as a family of disabilities. In the past, many children now identified as having specific learning disabilities would have been labeled remedial readers, remedial learners, emotionally disturbed, or even children with intellectual disabilities. Delayed academic performance is a major element in most current definitions of learning disabilities (Kavale, Spaulding, & Beam, 2009; Waber, 2010). Today, services related to learning disabilities represent the largest single program for exceptional children in the United States. Those with learning disabilities represented about 25 percent of all students with disabilities in 1975, but that figure had grown to 42 percent in 2010 (U.S. Department of Education, 2011b).

CEC

Standard 1
Foundations

Definitions

The definitions of learning disabilities vary considerably. This inconsistency may be due to the field's unique evolution, rapid growth, and strong interdisciplinary nature. The involvement of multiple disciplines (such as medicine, psychology, speech and language, and education) has also contributed to confusing terminology (Buttner & Hasselhorn, 2011; Kavale, Spaulding, & Beam, 2009). A child with a brain injury is described as having an organic impairment resulting in perceptual problems, thinking disorders, and emotional instability. A child with minimal brain dysfunction manifests similar challenges but often shows evidence of difficulties in language, memory, motor skills, and impulse control.

The Individuals with Disabilities Education Act (IDEA) of 2004 stated that:

> *"Specific learning disability" means a disorder in one or more of the basic psychological processes involved in understanding or in using language, spoken or written, which may manifest itself in an imperfect ability to listen, think, speak, read, write, spell, or to do mathematical calculations. The term includes such conditions as perceptual disabilities, brain injury, minimal brain dysfunction, dyslexia, and developmental aphasia. The term does not include children who have learning challenges which are primarily the result of visual, hearing, or motor disabilities, of [intellectual disabilities], of emotional disturbance, or of environmental, cultural, or economic disadvantage. (IDEA, 2004, PL 108-446, Sec. 602[30])*

This definition codified into federal law many of the concepts found in earlier descriptions. It also furnished a legal focus for the provision of services in the public schools. Service guidelines through the IDEA definition matured over the years with criteria from the companion "Rules and Regulations." Figure 7.1 summarizes the criteria, published in the *Federal Register* in 2006, used for identifying a specific learning disability. These criteria are consistent with the IDEA definition presented earlier.

Figure 7.1 Criteria for Identifying a Specific Learning Disability

1. A team may determine that a child has a specific learning disability if the child does not achieve adequately for the child's age or meet state-approved grade-level standards in one or more of the following seven areas, when provided with learning experiences and instruction appropriate for the child's age or state-approved grade-level standards. Criteria adopted by a state must permit the use of a process based on the child's response to research-based intervention and cannot prohibit the use of a severe discrepancy between intellectual ability and achievement:

   i. Oral expression

   ii. Listening comprehension

   iii. Written expression

   iv. Basic reading skill

   v. Reading comprehension

   vi. Mathematical calculation

   vii. Mathematical reasoning

2. The team may not identify a child as having a specific learning disability if the lack of achievement is primarily the result of:

   i. A visual, hearing, or motor impairment,

   ii. [Intellectual disabilities],

   iii. Limited English proficiency,

   iv. Emotional disturbance,

   v. Environmental, cultural, or economic disadvantage, or

   vi. Lack of instruction

SOURCE: Adapted from Rules and regulations. (2006, August 14). *Federal Register*, section [300.541, p. 12,457] (b).

The IDEA definition and the guidelines in Figure 7.1 primarily describe conditions that are *not* learning disabilities and give little substantive explanation of what *does* constitute a learning disability (i.e., a discrepancy between achievement and ability in areas of oral expression, listening, written expression, and so on). This use of exclusionary criteria still surfaces in a variety of circumstances (e.g., Hoover, 2010; Kavale, Spaulding, & Beam, 2009). The IDEA definition is also somewhat ambiguous because it prescribes no clear way to measure a learning disability.

This definition is important to our discussion for several reasons. First, it describes *learning disabilities* as a generic term that refers to a heterogeneous group of disorders. Second, a person with learning disabilities must manifest significant difficulties. The word *significant* is used in an effort to remove the connotation that a learning disability constitutes a mild problem. Finally, this definition makes it clear that learning disabilities are lifelong challenges and places them in a context of other disabilities and cultural differences.

Varying definitions and terminology related to learning disabilities emerged partly because of different theoretical views of the condition. For example, perceptual-motor theories emphasize an interaction between various channels of perception and motor activity. Children with learning disabilities are seen as having unreliable and unstable perceptual-motor abilities, which present challenges when such children encounter activities that require an understanding of time and space. Language disability theories, on the other hand, concentrate on a child's reception or production of language (Berninger & May, 2011; Troia, 2011). Because language is so important in learning, these theories emphasize the relationship between learning disabilities and language deficiencies.

Still another view of learning disabilities has emerged in the past several years. Some researchers have suggested that many different, specific disorders have been grouped under one term. They see *learning disabilities* as a general umbrella term that includes both academic and behavioral problems; they have developed terminology to describe particular conditions falling within the broad category of learning disabilities. Some of these terms refer to particular areas of functional academic difficulty (such as math, spelling, and reading), whereas others reflect difficulties that are behavioral in nature. This perspective was adopted by the American Psychiatric

Association in the fourth edition of its *Diagnostic and Statistical Manual of Mental Disorders* (American Psychiatric Association, 2000). This manual uses the term *learning disorders* to refer specifically to disorders in areas such as reading, mathematics, and written expression.

Research on learning disabilities also reflects the difficulties inherent when attempting to define a specific disability. The wide range of characteristics associated with children who have learning disabilities, along with various methodological challenges (such as heterogeneous populations and measurement error), has caused many difficulties in conducting research on learning disabilities (Gall, Gall, & Borg, 2007; Jitendra, Burgess, & Gajria, 2011).

The notion of severity has largely been ignored in earlier definitions and concepts related to learning disabilities. Although this has changed somewhat, severity still receives only limited attention (see Pierangelo & Giuliani, 2006; Porter, 2005). Learning disabilities have probably been defined in more ways by more disciplines and professional groups than any other type of disability (Buttner & Hasselhorn, 2011; Kavale, Spaulding, & Beam, 2009). See the nearby Reflect on This, "Redefining Learning Disabilities Using a Response to Intervention Model," for one perspective.

Classification

Learning disabilities is a term applied to a complex constellation of behaviors and symptoms. Many of these symptoms or characteristics have been used for classification purposes at one time or another. Three major elements have a substantial history of being employed in classifying learning disabilities: discrepancy, heterogeneity, and exclusion—all points that we noted earlier. Discrepancy approaches to classification are based on the notion that there is an identifiable gap between intelligence and achievement in particular areas, such as reading, math, and language. Heterogeneity classification addresses the differing array of academic domains where these children often demonstrate performance problems (as in the seven areas noted in Figure 7.1). The exclusion approach reflects the idea that the learning disabilities cannot be due to selected other conditions. The evidence supporting the use of discrepancy and exclusion as classification parameters is not strong, whereas heterogeneity seems to be supported (Hoover, 2010; National Joint Committee on Learning Disabilities, 2011b).

Reference to severity appears in the literature on learning disabilities fairly often, even though it is not accounted for in most definitions (Swanson, 2011a; Waesche, Shatschneider, Maner, Ahmed, & Wagner, 2011). Prior to 2004, IDEA mandated that any criterion for classifying a child as having learning disabilities must be based on a preexisting severe discrepancy between intellectual capacity and achievement. A child's learning disability must be determined on an individual basis, and there must be a severe discrepancy between achievement and intellectual ability in one or more of the following areas: oral expression, listening comprehension, written expression, basic reading skill, reading comprehension, mathematical calculation, or mathematical reasoning. The determination of referral for special services and type of educational placement was related to the following criteria:

1. Whether a child achieves commensurate with his or her age and ability when provided with appropriate educational experiences

2. Whether the child has a severe discrepancy between achievement and intellectual ability in one or more of seven areas related to communication skills and mathematical abilities

The meaning of the term *severe discrepancy* is debated among professionals (e.g., Buttner & Hasselhorn, 2011; Maehler & Schuchardt, 2011). Although it is often stipulated as a classification parameter, there is no broadly accepted way to measure it. What is an "acceptable" discrepancy between a child's achievement and what is expected at his or her grade level? 25 percent? 35 percent? 50 percent? Research on discrepancy classifications, particularly in reading, reveals that the discrepancy concept has mixed empirical support, particularly in field applications (Aaron, Joshi, Gooden, & Bentum, 2008; McKenzie, 2009).

In recognizing the controversy surrounding the use of a "discrepancy formula" as the only criterion for determining eligibility for special education services, current IDEA regulations no longer *require* that school districts determine whether a child has a severe discrepancy between intellectual ability and achievement. Schools now have the option of

REFLECT ON THIS REDEFINING LEARNING DISABILITIES USING A RESPONSE TO INTERVENTION MODEL

Response to intervention, or RTI, is a strategy for addressing the individual learning and behavior needs of all students within a school. Rather than waiting for students to fail before finding a way to help them, RTI employs assessment and data-based decisions to identify students that need extra help and then provides individualized and intensive interventions to help those who are not progressing adequately.

Referred to as a multitiered system, RTI begins with primary prevention, or general classroom instruction for all students. This must be effective, evidence-based practice that provides the primary prevention of failure for most students. Those who do not respond adequately to good primary instruction may be served in secondary prevention with moderately intensive interventions to remediate learning difficulties. A very small percentage of students who do not respond to secondary prevention may then be served at the tertiary level, with very intensive individual or small-group interventions to address specific needs. RTI success depends on effective instruction at each level and progress monitoring to determine each student's progress.

RTI is developing as a way to identify learning disabilities in lieu of the traditional discrepancy approach. As noted earlier in the chapter, educators and psychologists are challenging the use of discrepancy between aptitude and achievement to identify learning disabilities. Within an RTI approach, progress monitoring data can be combined with other valid assessments to ensure that students are not being identified with learning disabilities when the real cause of difficulty is inappropriate learning opportunities. For those who do have learning disabilities, RTI data can be used to help make the determination of eligibility for special education services. Though not yet universal, several states either require or allow the use of RTI to determine whether students have specific learning disabilities. As yet, there is no one accepted method for doing so, but the steady increase in the knowledge base about RTI and its usefulness for determining learning disabilities will no doubt inform the future of this approach.

Questions for Reflection

How does RTI provide a proactive approach to addressing student needs? How does RTI promote inclusion for instruction?

SOURCE: Adapted from National Center on Response to Intervention. (2010). *Essential Components of RTI—A Closer Look at Response to Intervention*. Retrieved from www.rti4success.org/pdf/rtiessentialcomponents_042710.pdf.

using a process that determines a child's response to intervention (RTI), which is aimed at evidence-based decisions and is research-based (National Center on Response to Intervention, 2010). The basic concept of RTI is empirically based decision making—that is, determining intervention success on the basis of data reflecting the student's performance. This approach has considerable appeal for several reasons. In particular, RTI is focused on the child's academic response to specific instruction, and it is also another perspective for assessing children with learning disabilities. This latter rationale is very useful for some children who are struggling with early academic work but may not evidence a severe discrepancy. RTI is attracting increased interest generally—and particularly regarding children with learning disabilities (Bender & Waller, 2011; Searle, 2010; Zirkel & Thomas, 2010). The Reflect on This box summarizes key elements of the RTI model.

Lack of agreement about concepts basic to the field has caused difficulties in both research and treatment for those with learning disabilities. Nonetheless, many people who display the challenging characteristics of learning disabilities are successful in life and have become leaders in their fields (an example is Charles "Pete" Conrad, Jr., who became an astronaut in the 1960s).

Response to intervention (RTI)
A student's response to instructional interventions that have been determined to be effective through scientifically based research.

Prevalence and Characteristics

Challenges in determining the numbers of people with learning disabilities are amplified by differing definitions, theoretical views, and assessment procedures. Prevalence estimates are highly variable, ranging from 2.7 percent to 30 percent of the school-age population (McLeskey, Landers, Hoppey, & Williamson, 2011; National Joint Committee on Learning Disabilities, 2011a). The most reasonable estimates range from 5 percent to 10 percent, as shown in Figure 7.2.

FOCUS 2

Identify seven characteristics attributed to those with learning disabilities, and explain why it is difficult to characterize this group.

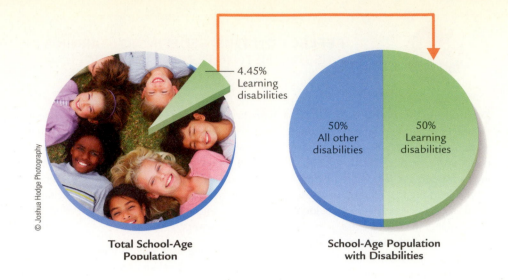

Figure 7.2 The Prevalence of Learning Disabilities for Students 6–21 Years of Age.

SOURCE: U.S. Department of Education, 2000a.

4.45% Learning disabilities

50% All other disabilities

50% Learning disabilities

© Joshua Hodge Photography

Total School-Age Population

School-Age Population with Disabilities

Because learning disabilities emerged as a category, their prevalence has been high compared with other exceptionalities. Learning disabilities are among the most common of all reported causes of disability. However, it is difficult to find one prevalent figure upon which all involved in the field agree. In 2010, over 5,822,800 children with disabilities were served under IDEA in the United States. Of that number, over 2,415,500 were classified as having learning disabilities, a figure that represents about 42 percent of the population with disabilities being served (U.S. Department of Education, National Center for Education Statistics, 2011b). Although there was a drop in learning disabilities from 1998 to 2009, it was a fluctuation mirrored by variations in other disability areas and probably can be accounted for by data collection and child count procedures.

Professionals and parents involved with other disability groups often question the high prevalence of learning disabilities. Some are concerned that the learning disabilities category is being overused to avoid the stigma associated with other labels or because of misdiagnosis, which may result in inappropriate treatment. And the heavy use of the learning disabilities label in referrals for services continues to grow, as illustrated in Table 7.1.

Although discrepancies in prevalence estimates occur in all fields of exceptionality, the area of learning disabilities seems more variable than most. This can be partly attributed to the different procedures used by those who do the counting and estimating (e.g., Buttner & Hasselhorn, 2011; MacKay, 2009). Another source of discrepancy may be differing or vague definitions of learning disabilities. Prevalence figures gathered through various studies are unlikely to match when different definitions determine what is counted.

Comorbidity
The occurrence together of multiple medical conditions or disabilities.

Many students with learning disabilities have difficulties with word recognition, word knowledge, and the use of context in learning to read.

Characteristics

Although specific learning disabilities are often characterized as representing mild disorders, few attempts have been made to validate this premise empirically. Identification of subgroups, subtypes, or severity levels in this heterogeneous population was largely neglected in the past. However, some attempts have been made in recent years to address these issues (Buttner & Hasselhorn, 2011; Davis & Broitman, 2011). Subtype and **comorbidity** research are appearing in the current literature at increasing rates (Hain, Hale, & Kendorski, 2009; Mangina & Beuzeron-Mangina, 2009). Subtype research investigates the characteristics of youngsters to identify

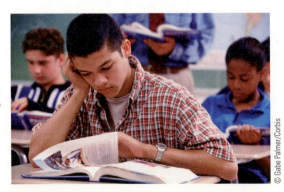

© Gabe Palmer/Corbis

Table 7.1	Changes in Number of Students Ages 6 through 21 Served under IDEA by Disability Category, 1998 and 2009		
Disability	**1998**	**2009**	**Change in Number**
Specific learning disabilities	2,790,000	2,476,000	–314,000
Speech or language impairments	1,068,000	1,426,000	358,000
Intellectual disability	597,000	478,000	–119,000
Emotional disturbance	462,000	420,000	–42,000
Hearing impairments	70,000	78,000	8,000
Orthopedic impairments	69,000	70,000	1,000
Other health impairments	220,000	659,000	439,000
Visual impairments	26,000	29,000	3,000
Multiple disabilities	106,000	130,000	24,000
Deafness/blindness	2,000	2,000	0
Autism	53,000	336,000	283,000
Traumatic brain injury	13,000	26,000	13,000
Developmental delay[1]	12,000	354,000	342,000
All disabilities	6, 056,000	6, 483,000	427,000

[1]Beginning in 1997, states had the option of reporting children aged 3 through 9 in the developmental delay category.

SOURCE: U.S. Department of Education, National Center for Education Statistics. (2011). *Digest of Education Statistics*, 2010 (NCES 2011-015), Chapter 2.

distinctive groups within the broad umbrella of learning disabilities. Comorbidity research investigates the degree to which youngsters exhibit evidence of multiple disabilities or conditions (such as learning disabilities and communication disorders, or personality disorders) (Fasmer et al., 2011; McGillivray & Baker, 2009).

Researchers have investigated a broad array of subgroups ranging from people with reading problems to those with hyperactivity (e.g., Hain, Hale, & Kendorski, 2009; Mangina & Beuzeron-Mangina, 2009). Attention deficit/hyperactivity disorder (ADHD) is a condition often associated with learning disabilities, with some estimates as high as 25 percent (McGillivray & Baker, 2009; Willcutt, et al., 2010).

Academic Achievement

Problems and inconsistencies in academic achievement largely prompted the recognition of learning disabilities as an area of exceptionality. Individuals with learning disabilities, though generally of average or near-average intelligence, seem to have many academic challenges. These challenges usually persist from the primary grades through the end of formal schooling, including college (Goldstein, 2011; Waber, 2010). Researchers are suggesting that educational planning for students with learning disabilities should offer a variety of long-range alternatives, including options and academic preparation for post-secondary education (Barron & Hassiotis, 2008; Grigal, Hart, & Migliore, 2011).

Reading Reading problems are found among students with learning disabilities more often than in any other area of academic performance. Historically, as the learning disabilities category began to take shape, it was applied to youngsters who had earlier been identified as remedial reading students. Estimates have suggested that as many as 60 to 90 percent

Standard 2
Development and Characteristics of Learners

Standard 3
Individual Learning Differences

Dyslexia
Dyslexia is a severe type of learning disability that impairs the ability to read.

of students with learning disabilities have reading difficulties (Bender, 2008a). Clearly, difficulties with the reading process are prevalent among students identified as having learning disabilities (Judge & Bell, 2011; McNamara, Scissons, & Gutknecth, 2011). However, the specific challenges that they have in reading vary as much as the many components of the reading process. (See the nearby Reflect on This, "Dyslexia: Searching for Causes.")

Both word knowledge and word recognition are vitally important parts of reading skill, and they both cause a challenge for people with learning disabilities (Janse, de Bree, & Brouwer, 2010; Sheehy, 2009; Taub, 2011). When most of us encounter a word that we know, we recall its meaning from our "mental dictionary," but for unfamiliar words, we must "sound out" the letters and pronounce the words by drawing on our knowledge of typical spelling patterns and pronunciation rules. This ability is important, both because we cannot memorize all words and because we constantly encounter new ones.

Students must also be able to generalize letter patterns and draw analogies with considerable flexibility. Good readers usually accomplish this task rather easily, quite quickly, and almost automatically after a little practice (Deacon, Leblanc, & Sabourin, 2011). Students with reading disabilities, however, experience substantial difficulty with this process, and when they can, they do it only slowly and laboriously. Such students need training and practice in strategies that help them succeed at recognizing words (Morris & Gaffney, 2011; O'Brien, Wolf, & Miller, 2011).

Some students with learning disabilities focus on minor details within a text, without distinguishing the important ideas from those of less significance. A specific focus on learning strategies can help these students. Teaching them skills like organizing and summarizing, using mnemonics, problem solving, and relational thinking can help them avoid these difficulties and enhance academic performance (Berkeley, Mastropieri, & Scruggs, 2011; Harris, Schumaker, & Deshler, 2011; Rosenzweig, Krawec, & Montague, 2011).

Reading involves many skills (e.g., an ability to remember and an ability to focus on important, rather than irrelevant, aspects of a task) that also affect performance in other subjects (Cerdan, Gilabert, & Vidal-Arbaca, 2011; Swanson, 2011b). Some difficulties experienced by people with learning disabilities emerge in more than one area. For example, does a child with reading disabilities have attention difficulties or working memory deficits? The problem could be caused by either disability or by a combination of the two.

Specific instruction may improve performance, but if the focus of the training is too narrow, the student may not generalize it to other relevant areas. Instruction that combines different methods (e.g., using both phonological awareness and instruction in specific skills) may serve students with reading disabilities better than applying a single method (Berkeley, Mastropieri, & Scruggs, 2011; Staudt, 2009; Stothers & Klein, 2010).

Writing and Spelling Children with learning disabilities often exhibit quite different writing performance than their peers without disabilities. This problem affects their academic achievement and frequently persists into adulthood. Difficulties may occur in handwriting (slow writing, spacing problems, poor formation of letters), spelling, and composition or general written expression (Gardner, 2011; Overvelde & Hulstijn, 2011; Viel-Ruma, Houchins, Jolivett, Fredrick, & Gama, 2010). Some children are poor at handwriting because they have not mastered basic developmental skills required for the process, such as grasping a pen or pencil. Handwriting also involves understanding spatial concepts, such as up, down, top, bottom, and letter alignment. These abilities frequently are less developed in youngsters with learning disabilities than their peers without disabilities (Kushki, Schwellnus, & Ilyas, 2011; Overvelde & Hulstijn, 2011). Some children with rather mild handwriting problems exhibit slowness in development that will improve as they grow older, receive instruction, and practice. However, in more severe cases, age and practice may not result in mastery of handwriting skills. Several such difficulties are found in Figure 7.3.

Some researchers view the handwriting, writing, and composition skills of students with learning disabilities as closely related to their reading ability. A number of processes, ranging from basic skills to strategies employed, seem to contribute significantly to writing problems among students with learning disabilities (Gardner, 2011; Mason, Harris, & Graham, 2011). Letter reversals, and in severe cases, **mirror writing** have been used as illustrations of poor handwriting. However, it is questionable whether children with learning disabilities make these types of errors more often than their peers without disabilities at the same reading level.

Mirror writing
Writing backward from right to left, making letters that look like ordinary writing seen in a mirror.

Poor spelling (evident in Figure 7.3) is often a problem among students with learning disabilities. Research indicates that spelling problems are associated with other linguistic shortcomings. Limitations in overall language abilities often give rise to difficulties with spelling for students with learning disabilities. These children frequently omit letters or add incorrect ones. Their spelling may also show evidence of letter-order confusion and developmentally immature pronunciation (Friend & Olson, 2008; Kohnen, Nickels, &

Figure 7.3 *Writing Samples of a College Freshman with a Learning Disability.*

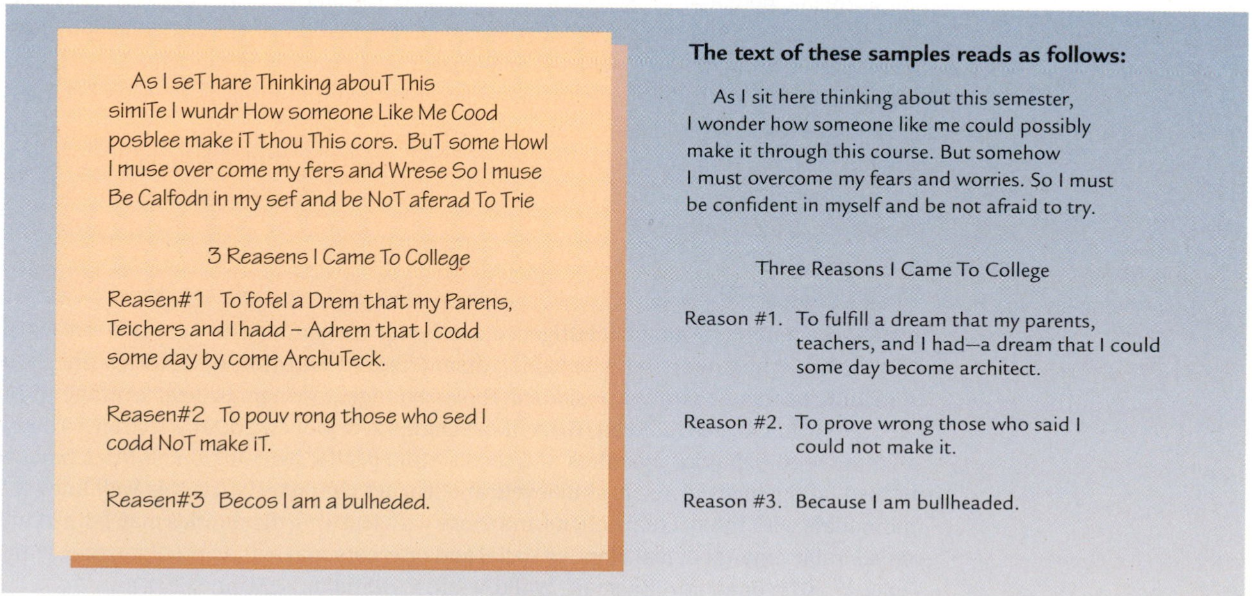

As I seT hare Thinking abouT This simiTe I wundr How someone Like Me Cood posblee make iT thou This cors. BuT some Howl I muse over come my fers and Wrese So I muse Be Calfodn in my sef and be NoT aferad To Trie

3 Reasens I Came To College

Reasen#1 To fofel a Drem that my Parens, Teichers and I hadd — Adrem that I codd some day by come ArchuTeck.

Reasen#2 To pouv rong those who sed I codd NoT make iT.

Reasen#3 Becos I am a bulheded.

The text of these samples reads as follows:

As I sit here thinking about this semester, I wonder how someone like me could possibly make it through this course. But somehow I must overcome my fears and worries. So I must be confident in myself and be not afraid to try.

Three Reasons I Came To College

Reason #1. To fulfill a dream that my parents, teachers, and I had—a dream that I could some day become architect.

Reason #2. To prove wrong those who said I could not make it.

Reason #3. Because I am bullheaded.

Coltheart, 2010; Moats, 2009). Some studies have shown promise in the remediation of spelling difficulties. Encoding instruction (Weiser & Mathis, 2011), error self-correction (Viel-Ruma, Houchins, & Fredrick, 2007), using mnemonics for difficult irregular words (Schmalzl & Nickles, 2006), and explicit instruction with feedback provided by the teacher or a peer accompanied by immediate practice (Sayeski, 2011) all resulted in significant gains for spellers with learning disabilities. Recent literature suggests that the spelling skills of students with learning disabilities follow developmental patterns similar to those of their peers without disabilities but that they are delayed (Bender, 2008a; Sayeski, 2011).

Mathematics Arithmetic is another academic area that causes individuals with learning disabilities considerable difficulty. Such individuals often have trouble with counting, writing numbers, and mastering other simple math concepts (Desoete, Ceulemans, & Roeyers, 2009; Mammarella, Lucangeli, & Cornoldi, 2010; Stock, Desoete, & Roeyers, 2010). Counting objects is perhaps the most fundamental mathematics skill and is a foundation for development of the more advanced, yet still basic, skills of addition and subtraction. Some youngsters omit numbers when counting sequences aloud (e.g., 1, 2, 3, 5, 7, 9), and others can count correctly but do not understand the relative values of numbers. Students with arithmetic learning disabilities have difficulties when asked to count beyond 9, which requires the use of more than one digit. This skill is somewhat more advanced than single-digit counting and involves knowledge about place value.

Place value, a function of base-10 understanding, is a more complex concept than the counting of objects and is fundamental to understanding addition and subtraction. Many students with learning disabilities in math have problems understanding the base-10 principle of place value, particularly that the same digit (such as 6) represents different values according to its position in a written number (as in 16, 61, and 632). Research has shown that early place value misunderstanding can predict later difficulties with math understanding and procedures (Moeller, Pixner, & Zuber, 2011). Such complexities require strategic problem solving, which presents particular difficulties for students with learning disabilities (Montague, Enders, & Dietz, 2011; Powell, 2011). Research on the provision of math problem-solving instruction indicates significant success at both elementary and middle school levels (Jitendra & Star, 2011; Xin et al., 2011). Some of these math difficulties are often major obstacles in the academic paths of students with learning disabilities; they frequently continue to cause challenges through high school and into the college years (Morris, Schraufnagel, Chudnow, & Weinberg, 2009).

Achievement Discrepancy Students with learning disabilities perform below expectations based on their measured potential, in addition to scoring below their peers in overall achievement. Attempts to quantify the discrepancy between academic achievement and academic potential for students with learning disabilities have appeared in the literature, but the field still lacks a broadly accepted explanation of the phenomenon (Kavale, Spaulding, & Beam, 2009; Maehler & Schuchardt, 2011). Early in the school years, youngsters with learning disabilities may find themselves two to four or more years behind their peers in academic achievement; many fall even further behind as they continue in the educational system. This discouraging pattern often results in students dropping out of high school or graduating without proficiency in basic reading, writing, or math skills (U.S. Department of Education, 2008).

Intelligence

Certain assumptions about intelligence are being reexamined in research on learning disabilities. Populations with behavior disorders and learning disabilities are thought to include people generally considered above average, average, or near average in intelligence (Swanson, 2011a; Kebir, Grizenko, Sengupta, & Joober, 2009). Differences between students with behavior disorders and those with specific learning disabilities have been defined on the basis of social skill levels and learner characteristics. It is well known that individuals with intellectual deficits and those with learning disabilities may both exhibit a considerable amount of maladaptive social and interpersonal behavior (Algozzine, Wang, & Violette, 2011; Semrud-Clikeman, Walkowiak, Wilkinson, & Minne, 2010).

These insights have affected ideas about the distinctions between learning disabilities and intellectual disabilities. Marked discrepancy between measured intelligence and academic performance has long been viewed as a defining characteristic of people with learning disabilities (Dunn, 2010; Machek & Nelson, 2010). Also, descriptions of learning disabilities have often emphasized great intraindividual differences between skill areas. For example, a youngster may exhibit very low performance in reading but not in arithmetic. However, intraindividual variability is sometimes evident in students with intellectual disabilities and those with behavior disorders. Further, intraindividual variability in students with learning disabilities does not always appear; here again, the research evidence is mixed (Dean, Burns, & Grialou, 2006; Sabornie, Cullinan, & Osborne, 2005).

Cognition and Information Processing

People with learning disabilities have certain characteristics related to **cognition**, or **information processing**, the way a person acquires, retains, and manipulates information (e.g., Geary, Hoard, Nugent, & Bailey, 2011; Maehler & Shurchardt, 2009). These processes often emerge as challenges for individuals with learning disabilities. For example, teachers have long complained that such children have poor memory function. In many cases, these students seem to learn material one day but cannot recall it the next. Memory function is also centrally involved in language skill and development, a challenging area for many children with learning disabilities (Baird, Dworzynski, Slonims, & Simonoff, 2010; Passolunghi, 2011).

Attention problems have also been associated with learning disabilities. Such problems have often been characterized as short attention span. Parents and teachers note that their children with learning disabilities cannot sustain attention for more than a very short time and that some of them exhibit considerable daydreaming and high distractibility. Some researchers have observed **short attention spans** in these children while others indicate that they have difficulty in certain types of attention problems and, in some cases, attend selectively (Bender, 2008a; Obrzut & Mahoney, 2011). **Selective attention** problems make it difficult to focus on centrally important tasks or information rather than on peripheral or less relevant stimuli. Attention problems remain in the spotlight as the information-processing problems of children with learning disabilities are investigated (e.g., Iseman & Naglieri, 2011; Shiran & Breznitz, 2011).

Learning Characteristics

The study of perceptual problems had a significant role early in the history of learning disabilities although interest in this topic has declined. Some researchers, however, continue to view perception difficulties as important. Perception difficulties in people with learning disabilities represent a constellation of behavior anomalies, rather than a single characteristic. Descriptions of these problems have referred to the visual, auditory, and **haptic** sensory systems. Difficulty in visual perception has been closely associated with learning disabilities. This type of abnormality can cause a child to see a visual stimulus as unrelated parts rather than as an integrated pattern; for example, a child may not be able to identify a letter in the alphabet because he or she perceives only unrelated lines, rather than the letter as a meaningful whole (Bender, 2008a). Visual perception problems may emerge in **figure–ground discrimination**, the process of distinguishing an object from the background. Most of us have little difficulty with figure–ground discrimination, but children with learning disabilities may have trouble focusing on a word or sentence in a textbook because they cannot distinguish it from the rest of the page.

Other discrimination difficulties have also surfaced in descriptions of people with learning disabilities. Individuals with difficulties in **visual discrimination** may be unable to distinguish one visual stimulus from another (they cannot tell the difference between words such as *sit* and *sat*, for example, or between letters such as V and W, and they commonly reverse letters such as b and d). This type of error is common among young children, causing great concern for parents. Yet most youngsters overcome this problem in the course of normal development, and by about 7 or 8 years of age, show few reversal or rotation errors with visual image. Children who make frequent errors beyond that age might be viewed as potential problem learners and may need additional instruction specifically aimed at improving such skills.

Cognition
The act of thinking, knowing, or processing information.

Information processing
A model used to study the way people acquire, remember, and manipulate information.

Short attention span
An inability to focus one's attention on a task for more than a few seconds or minutes.

Selective attention
Attention that often does not focus on centrally important tasks or information.

Haptic
Related to the sensation of touch and to information transmitted through body movement or position.

Figure–ground discrimination
The process of distinguishing an object from its background.

Visual discrimination
Distinguishing one visual stimulus from another.

Auditory perception problems have historically been associated with learning disabilities. The current discussion in the field addresses **auditory processing disorder** as a condition resulting in difficulties distinguishing the sounds of language, but not with general understanding or use of language. As described by the American Speech and Hearing Association, this condition can result in difficulties isolating one sound in a blend, discriminating similar sounds, and recognizing sound patterns—all of which are important for processing spoken language (American Speech-Language- Hearing Association, 2005; Kamhia, 2011). Affected children may be unable to distinguish /ch/ from /sh/, hear the difference between /b/ and /d/, or recognize the identical sound endings in *stone* and *own*. At this time there is no generally agreed-upon definition of auditory processing disorder, and debate continues about appropriate and effective interventions (Fey et. al., 2011; Moore, 2011).

Another area of perceptual difficulty long associated with learning disabilities involves haptic perception (touch, body movement, and position sensation). For example, handwriting requires haptic perception, because tactile information about the grasp of a pen or pencil must be transmitted to the brain. In addition, **kinesthetic** information regarding hand and arm movements is transmitted as one writes. Children with learning disabilities have often been described by teachers as having poor handwriting and difficulties in spacing letters and staying on the lines of the paper (Cahill, 2009; Overvelde & Hulstijn, 2011). Figure 7.3 shows examples of writing by a college freshman with learning disabilities. The two samples in this figure were from consecutive days, each in a 40-minute period. The note beside the samples translates what was written.

Social and Emotional Characteristics

Children and adolescents with learning disabilities often have emotional and interpersonal difficulties that are quite serious and highly resistant to treatment (Cowden, 2010b). Because of their learning challenges, they frequently have low self-esteem and a negative emotional status (Bloom & Heath, 2010; Semrud-Clikeman et al., 2010). They may not be able to interact effectively with others because they misunderstand social cues or cannot discriminate among, or interpret the subtleties of, typical interpersonal associations. For some with learning disabilities, social life poses greater challenges than their academic deficits.

Hyperactivity

Hyperactivity has commonly been linked to children labeled as having learning disabilities (Harrison, Vannest, & Reynolds, 2011; Knowles, 2010). Also termed **hyperkinetic behavior**, **hyperactivity** is typically defined as a general excess of activity. Not all children with learning disabilities are hyperactive, and not all hyperactive children have learning disabilities.

Causation

Researchers have theorized about a number of possible causes for learning disabilities. There are probably many different causes of learning disabilities, and in some cases, a specific type of learning disability may have multiple causes (Buttner & Hasselhorn, 2011; Kaufman, 2008; Miller & McCardle, 2011). Also, a single cause may underlie multiple disorders, such as learning disabilities and hyperactivity, in the same child (Mangina & Beuzeron-Mangina, 2009; Stothers, & Cardy, 2012). Because it is imperative to help affected students even though we do not yet fully understand the cause of learning disabilities, the practical issues of assessment and intervention have frequently taken priority in research so that specialized instruction can be offered to such students (Bender, 2008b; National Joint Committee on Learning Disabilities, 2011b).

Neurological Factors

For many years, some have viewed the cause of learning disabilities as structural neurological damage, abnormal neurological development, or some type of abnormality in neurological function (e.g., Bender, 2008a; Miller & McCardle, 2011). Neurological damage associated with learning disabilities can occur in many ways. Damage may occur in the neurological system at birth by conditions such as anoxia (a lack of oxygen), low birth weight, or abnormal fetal positioning during delivery (Taylor, Espy, & Anderson, 2009). Infections may also cause neurological damage and learning disabilities, as can certain types of physical injury. However, magnetic resonance imaging (MRI) is generating research that supports some unusual neurological functioning in these children (Cleary & Scott, 2011; Goswami, 2008).

Maturational Delay

In many ways, the behavior and performance of children with learning disabilities resemble those of much younger individuals (Lerner & Kline, 2006). They often exhibit delays in skills maturation, such as slower development of language skills and problems in the visual-motor area and several academic areas, as already noted. Although maturational delay is probably not a causative factor in all types of learning disabilities, there is evidence that it contributes to some (Pierangelo & Giuliani, 2006).

Genetic Factors

Genetic abnormalities, which are inherited, are thought to cause or contribute to one or more of the challenges categorized as learning disabilities (Goswami, 2008; Miller & McCardle, 2011). Some research, including studies of **identical twins** and **fraternal twins**, has suggested that such disorders may be inherited (Davis, Haworth, & Plomin, 2009; Haworth et al., 2009). These findings must be viewed cautiously because of difficulty in separating the influences of heredity and environment, but selected evidence supports the idea that some learning disabilities are inherited (Kovas & Plomin, 2007; Scerri & Schulte-Korne, 2010).

Identical twins
Twins from a single fertilized egg and a single placental sac. Such twins are of the same sex and usually resemble one another closely.

Fraternal twins
Twins from two fertilized eggs and two placental sacs. Such twins do not resemble each other closely.

Environmental Factors

The search for the causes of learning disabilities has also implicated certain environmental influences: Dietary inadequacies, food additives, radiation stress, fluorescent lighting, unshielded television tubes, alcohol consumption, drug consumption, and inappropriate school instruction have all been investigated at one time or another (Loomis, 2006; Walker & Plomin, 2005). Some environmental factors, such as irradiation, lead ingestion, maternal smoking, illicit drugs, and family stress, are known to have negative effects on development (Anderko, Braun, & Auinger, 2010; Dufault et al., 2009; U.S. Department of Education, 2011a).

Standard 8
Assessment

Assessment

Assessment, or the evaluation of individuals with learning disabilities, has several purposes. The ultimate goal is to provide an appropriate intervention, if warranted, for the child or adult being evaluated. Assessment and intervention involve a series of related steps, which include screening, identification, placement, and delivery of specialized assistance. Deciding how to meet an individual student's needs requires data obtained through specialized assessment procedures (Rosenblum, Larochette, Harrison, & Armstrong, 2010; Sze, 2009).

FOCUS 4
Compare and contrast the purpose of assessments used for screening and progress monitoring.

Formal and Informal Assessment

Formal versus informal assessment has come to mean standardized tests versus teacher-made tests or techniques. Standardized instruments, such as intelligence tests and achievement tests, are published and distributed commercially. Teacher-made techniques or instruments (or those devised by any professional) are ones that are not commercially available. These may be constructed for specific assessment purposes and are often quite formal, in that great care is taken in the evaluation process (Beirne-Smith & Riley, 2009; Miller, 2009).

Norm-referenced assessment compares an individual's skills or performance with that of others, such as peers, usually on the basis of national average scores. Thus, a student's counting performance might be compared with that of his or her classmates, with that of others in the school district of the same age, or with state or national average scores. In contrast, **criterion-referenced assessment** does not compare an individual's skills with a norm but with a desired performance level (criterion) or a specific goal. For example, the goal may involve counting to 100 with no errors by the end of the school year. One application of criterion-referenced assessment, **curriculum-based assessment**, has received attention recently. It uses a student's

Norm-referenced assessment
Assessment wherein a person's performance is compared with the average of a larger group.

Criterion-referenced assessment
Assessment that compares a person's performance with a specific established level (the criterion). This performance is not compared with that of other people.

Curriculum-based assessment
Assessment in which the objectives of a student's curriculum are used as the criteria against which progress is evaluated.

By comparing a student's skill level with a criterion-based assessment, a teacher is able to make a specific instruction plan for the student.

John Nordell/Getty Images

curriculum objectives as the criteria by which progress is evaluated (McMaster, Du, & Yeo, 2011; Seethaler & Fuchs, 2011). Curriculum-based assessment used to screen students for individual strengths and needs is sometimes contrasted with ongoing curriculum-based *measurement* as used for progress monitoring (monitoring a student's progress), or repetitive measures given over time to monitor students' progress toward learning goals (Jenkins & Terjeson, 2011; Luckner & Bowen, 2010). The relationship between evaluation and instructional objectives makes instruction planning and assessment more efficient. The purpose of measuring from the students' curriculum is to determine the effectiveness of instruction and make changes as needed to ensure student success.

Both norm- and criterion-referenced assessments are useful for working with students with learning disabilities. Norm-referenced assessment is used for administrative purposes, such as compiling census data on how many students achieve at or above the state or national average. Criterion-referenced assessment is helpful for specific instructional purposes and planning. These two assessments do not require separate types of assessment instruments or procedures. Depending on how a technique, instrument, or procedure is employed, it may be used in a norm-referenced or a criterion-referenced manner. Some areas, such as intelligence, are more typically evaluated using norm-referenced procedures. However, even a standardized intelligence test can be scored and used in a criterion-referenced fashion. Assessment should always be undertaken with careful attention to the purpose and future use of the evaluation (Keeley, 2011; Yeh, 2010).

Screening

Screening of students who have learning disabilities has always been an important facet of assessment. Screening occurs prior to determining eligibility or treatment of the student, although clinicians or others (e.g., parents) often suspect that a problem exists. Assessment for potential learning disabilities most often takes place during the school years. This is partly because the types of performance that are most problematic for these children are not usually required until the child goes to school and partly because one of the important markers for learning disabilities (a discrepancy between ability and achievement) does not seem to show as well very early.

The role of screening is to "raise a red flag," or suggest that investigation is needed. Four questions are relevant at this point: (1) Is there a reason to investigate the abilities of the child more fully? (2) Is there a reason to suspect that the child in any way has disabilities? (3) If the child appears to have disabilities, what are their characteristics, and what sort of intervention is appropriate? (4) How should we plan for the future of the individual? Answers to these questions might point to a variety of needs such as further classification of the disability, planning of intervention services such as psychological treatment or individualized instruction, or ongoing evaluation of progress. For students with learning disabilities, assessment is not a simple, isolated event resulting in a single diagnosis. Rather, it is a complex process with many different steps (Lindstrom, Tuckwiller, & Hallahan, 2008; National Joint Committee on Learning Disabilities, 2011b).

Intelligence

For the most part, individuals with learning disabilities are described as having average or near-average intelligence, although they experience many challenges in school that are typical of students with lower intelligence levels. In many cases, measures of intelligence may be inaccurate because of specific visual, auditory, or other limitations that may affect

Screening
A preliminary assessment to decide if further study of a child's functioning level is necessary. Screening raises "a red flag" if a problem is indicated.

the student's performance (Dean, Burns, & Grialou, 2006; Sabornie, Cullinan, & Osborne, 2005). However, intelligence remains an important matter for individuals with learning disabilities; assessment of intelligence is often done with a standardized instrument such as an intelligence test. Where measured intelligence fits into the definition of learning disabilities is somewhat controversial (Dunn, 2010; Maehler & Schuchardt, 2011).

Adaptive Skills

People with learning disabilities are frequently described as exhibiting poor adaptive skills—that is, they lack a sense of what constitutes appropriate behavior in a particular environment. Such descriptions have appeared primarily in clinical reports, though evaluation of adaptive skills has not historically been a routine part of assessment of learning disabilities to the same degree as in other areas of exceptionality. However, some work has been undertaken to address adaptive and social skills and their assessment for individuals with learning disabilities (e.g., Bender, 2008b; Ditterline, Banner, & Oakland, 2008; Firth, Frydenberg, & Greaves, 2008).

Academic Achievement

Academic achievement has always been a major problem for students with learning disabilities. Assessment of academic achievement helps evaluate the student's level of functioning in one or more specific academic areas. Instruments have been developed and used to diagnose specific academic challenges. For example, a number of reading tests, including the Woodcock Reading Mastery Tests, the Diagnostic Reading Scales, and the Stanford Diagnostic Reading Test, determine the nature of reading problems. Likewise, mathematics assessment employs instruments such as the Key Math Diagnostic Arithmetic Test and the Stanford Diagnostic Mathematics Test (Gronlund & Waugh, 2009).

Academic assessment for students with learning disabilities is very important. Assessment techniques resemble those used in other areas of exceptionality, because deficits in academic achievement are a common problem among students with a variety of disabilities. Diagnosis of deficits in specific skills, however, has a more prominent history in learning disabilities and has prompted the development of focused, skills-oriented assessment of academic achievement in other disability areas as well.

The Elementary School Years

FOCUS 5

Identify five types of interventions or supports used with people who have learning disabilities, including two that use assistive technology.

Services and supports for children with learning disabilities have changed over time as professionals have come to view learning disabilities as a constellation of specific individualized needs. Specific disabilities, such as cognitive learning problems, attention

SNAPSHOT
Alice

Alice found herself very frustrated with school. She was in the fourth grade, and her grades were very bad. She had worked hard, but many of the things that were required just didn't seem to make sense.

History was a perfect example. Alice had looked forward to learning more about history; it was so interesting when her grandfather told his stories. Alice thought it would have been fun to live back then, when all the kids got to ride horses. But history in school was not fun, and it didn't make any sense at all. Alice had been reading last night, supposedly about a girl who was her age and was moving west with a wagon train. As Alice looked at the book, she read strange things.

One passage said, "Mary pelieveb that things would get detter. What they hab left Missouri they hab enough foob dut now there was darely enough for one meal a bay. Surely the wagon-master woulb finb a wet to solve the brodlem." Alice knew that she would fail the test, and she cried quietly in her room as she dressed for school.

Figure 7.4 *RTI Model for Instruction and Service Delivery.*

Tier Three Intervention: Most specialized, intense instruction, needed by about 5% of the students.

Tier Two Intervention: More intensive and supplemental intervention enhancing progress for 10–15% of the students.

Tier One Intervention: Comprehensive, well-designed curriculum serving most students (80–85%) who are making adequate academic progress.

CEC

Standard 5
Learning Environments and Social Interactions

Standard 7
Instructional Planning

deficit and hyperactivity, social and emotional difficulties, and problems with spoken language, reading, writing, spelling, and mathematics, are all receiving research attention (e.g., Berninger & May, 2011; Harrison, Vannest, & Reynolds, 2011; Montague, Enders, & Dietz, 2011). This approach has resulted in services and supports focused on individual need. Greater attention is being paid to social skills instruction for children with learning disabilities and to the effective use of tutors and peer tutors (Dettmer, Knackendoffel, Thurston, & Sellberg, 2009; Scheeler, Macluckie, & Albright, 2010).

An overarching concept for this approach to intervention is the RTI model for making decisions about instructional focus. RTI tends to be associated with assessment because of its prominent and ongoing measurement components (Barrera & Liu, 2010; Wixson & Valencia, 2011). Although the assessment element is important, the comprehensive RTI concept also includes other important components related to evidence-based decisions about interventions (Fuchs, Compton, & Fuchs, 2011; Wagner & Compton, 2011). As indicated in Figure 7.4, the three-tiered service triangle involves a carefully designed comprehensive academic core to which a very large proportion of students with learning disabilities will respond—perhaps as high as 80 to 85 percent. In tier two, more intensive or supplemental instruction is undertaken to help the next 10 to 15 percent make progress. Tier three involves even more specialized and intense instruction needed by about 5 percent of students with the most serious academic challenges. Of course, these proportions are rough estimates and will vary (Klingner & Edwards, 2006; Wilber & Cushman, 2006). A balanced RTI concept focuses on both the assessment and intervention elements of the evidence-based decision making that is crucial for both general and special education.

Services and supports for adolescents or adults with learning disabilities may differ from those for children. Some changes in approach are due to shifting goals as individuals grow older (e.g., the acquisition of basic counting skills versus instruction in preparation for college). Individuals from varied professions must function as a team and also as unique contributors to create well-balanced programs for students with learning disabilities (Dettmer et al., 2009; Lembke, Garman, Deno, & Stecker, 2010; Mahdavi & Beebe-Frankenberger, 2009).

Academic Instruction and Support

A wide variety of instructional approaches have been used over the years for children with learning disabilities. These include strategies to develop cognition, attention, spoken language, and skill in reading, writing, and mathematics (McLeskey & Waldron, 2011; Volpe, Anastasio, & DuPaul, 2011). Even within each area, a whole array of instructional procedures has been used to address specific prolems. For example, cognitive training has incorporated problem solving, strategies for attacking problems, and instruction in social competence (Jitendra, Burgess, & Gajria, 2011; Montague, Enders, & Dietz, 2011).

Various approaches to cognitive instruction are needed to teach the heterogeneous population of children with learning disabilities. Such strategies or tactics are often customized or reconfigured to individualize the program and target a student's specific needs. For example, if a youngster exhibits adaptive skills deficits that interfere with inclusion in general education, such skills may form an instructional focus. Flexible and multiple services or supports may make inclusion possible, providing a well-defined instructional environment, teaching the child important skills, and addressing interpersonal or social-emotional needs (Abbott, McConkey, & Dobbins, 2011; McLeskey & Waldron, 2011).

Mathematics Students with learning disabilities often have difficulties with four foundational math skills: counting, memorizing and retrieving math facts, base-10 understanding, and problem solving (Becker, McLaughlin, Weber, & Gower, 2009; Fischer, Kongeter, & Hartnegg, 2008; Montague, Enders, & Dietz, 2011; Swanson, Jerman, & Zheng, 2009). Counting may be most effectively taught with manipulative objects. Repetitive experience with counting buttons, marbles, or any such objects provides practice in counting, as well as exposure to the concepts of magnitude associated with numbers. Counting and grouping sets of 10 objects can help children begin to grasp rudimentary place-value concepts. These activities must often be quite structured for students with learning disabilities (Fischer, Köngeter, & Hartnegg, 2008; Kamawar, LeFevre, & Bisanz, 2010). Effective strategies for memorizing and retrieving math facts depend on consistent oral and written rehearsal with immediate corrective feedback and practice to mastery, as used in the cover, copy, and compare approach (Becker et al., 2009). Teaching base-10 understanding involves helping students understand that multidigit numbers are made up of groups of ones, tens, and hundreds rather than numerals in a certain place or position. This can be taught by having students manipulate units, tens, and hundreds using counting sticks or base-10 blocks (Cooper & Tomayko, 2011; Swanson, Jerman, & Zheng, 2009). Recent research on teaching problem solving indicates that cognitive strategy instruction increases achievement for students with learning disabilities (Iseman & Naglieri, 2011; Montague, Enders, & Dietz, 2011).

Information and communication technology have replaced much traditional seat and board work for teaching students with learning disabilities. Laptop computers, tablet computers, and interactive whiteboards are commonly used for a variety of teaching and learning activities in general and special education classrooms. These devices allow teachers and students to engage in interactive teaching and learning just as they would with pencils, paper, books, or math manipulatives. Downloadable web applications provide almost unlimited strategies for teaching and learning with tablet computers. Math applications ranging from basic counting, sorting, and classifying activities to algebra and geometry make it possible for teachers to customize practice for students with learning disabilities. (Banister, 2010; Olsen, LeMire, & Baker, 2011; Waters, 2010). The only drawback to using new technologies for these purposes seems to be inadequate teacher preparation for keeping up with quickly evolving possibilities (Blue & Tirotta, 2011; Obudo, 2008).

Reading It has long been recognized that students with learning disabilities have great difficulty with reading. Because of this, many different strategies have been developed to address the problem (Dexter & Hughes, 2011; Stetter & Hughes, 2010; Swanson, Kehler, & Jerman, 2010). Each procedure has succeeded with certain children, but none with all. Research on particular types of skill instruction has produced significant improvements for students with learning disabilities (see Berkeley, Mastropieri, & Scruggs, 2010; Jitendra, Burgess, & Gajria, 2011).

LEARNING THROUGH SOCIAL MEDIA
TEEN USE OF SOCIAL MEDIA ON THE RISE

Teen use of social media is nearly ubiquitous. Quickly replacing blogging as the preferred way to update status and communicate with others, the use of social networking increased from 55 percent of teens in 2006 to 73 percent in 2010. Facebook and Twitter are the current preferred group forums for communicating with friends, building relationships, and sharing social comment, but text messaging is still the most used form of digital communication other than voice. Current data indicate that older kids are more likely to use Twitter than younger ones, and high school girls are more likely to use Twitter than any other school-aged group (Lenhart, Purcell, Smith, & Zickuhr, 2010).

Are there useful applications for social media in the classroom? Many writers answer in the affirmative. Teachers are exploring student use of Twitter for taking and sharing notes, and encouraging students to use Facebook to work together on shared assignments. Others are helping students prepare and produce podcasts that are then used to mentor younger students using iPads or smartphones (Koenig, 2011). For some, answering class questions using Twitter proves to be less threatening than traditional oral responses. Out-of-class sharing and peer-to-peer homework help are now accomplished largely through social media (Jackson, 2011).

There is little research on the use of social media to specifically address the needs of students with learning disabilities, but technology-savvy teachers are finding ways to use the latest devices and applications to empower this population. The challenges that those with learning disabilities have with reading textbooks or literature, expressing themselves in writing, or using math in appropriate and functional ways present opportunities for creative teachers to explore applications of social media in and out of the classroom.

The largest-ever analysis of reading research, conducted by the National Reading Panel (2000), found that all readers must master five fundamental skills to read fluently and with comprehension: phonemic awareness, phonics, fluency, vocabulary, and text comprehension. Phonemic awareness is the ability to hear, discriminate, and manipulate the sounds of language. Phonics refers to the alphabetic principle, or the system of representing sounds with letters. Fluent reading is the ability to read with speed, accuracy, and correct intonation. Vocabulary refers to the number and variety of words that children can read and speak. Text comprehension is the ability to understand and enjoy what one reads without relying on illustrations or other images (Armbruster, Lehr, & Osborn, 2006).

Students can be classified as having learning disabilities in either basic reading skills or in reading comprehension, or both (Ritchey, 2011). Helping children with learning disabilities master the skills of reading is best accomplished by teaching practices with strong research support, or evidence-based practice (practice that is based on evidence or data). Explicit, intensive, and systematic instruction is integral to one evidence-based class of instructional practices, whether for teaching basic skills or helping students master strategies for specific types of comprehension (Coyne et al., 2009; Ritchey, 2011; Rupley, Blair, & Nichols, 2009; Stockard, 2010). Explicit instruction is exemplified by specific learning objectives, teacher modeling, high rates of students responding with affirmative and corrective feedback, praise for success, and practice to mastery (Kim & Axelrod, 2005; Stein, Carnine, & Dixon, 1998). Effective strategies for improving reading beyond the basic level include self-monitoring for comprehension, cognitive strategy instruction, attribution retraining, and computer-assisted instruction (Berkeley, Mastropieri, & Scruggs, 2011; Jitendra, Burgess, & Gajria, 2011; Joseph & Eveleigh, 2011; Stetter & Hughes, 2011). It is important to note that focusing on isolated skills is not effective for overall reading improvement. Instead, teachers must engage students in consistent application of the complete reading process through reading, discussing, and making meaning from what is read (Berkeley, Mastropieri, & Scruggs, 2011; Hollenbeck, 2011).

Computer-assisted instruction has successfully enhanced the reading skills of students with learning disabilities. Researchers have studied computer instruction for phonemic awareness, phonics, fluency, vocabulary acquisition, and text comprehension, all of which

Writing has long been recognized as an academic area that presents considerable difficulty for children with learning disabilities. Advances in educational applications of technology, especially the development of new computer software, have the potential to assist children with writing problems (Moorman, Boon, & Keller-Bell, 2010; Stetter & Hughes, 2011). An example of such software is Starter Paragraph Punch©, used in elementary schools to help students master basic paragraph writing by guiding them through the topic sentence, body, and conclusion. It includes a teaching monitoring system and comes in both CD software and web versions (Merit, 2011). Grammar Fitness© is a companion program that includes a speak-aloud text talker to guide students while learning to identify and correct errors in punctuation, usage, and tenses.

WriteOnline© is another program for guiding student writing in upper elementary and secondary schools (Crick, 2011). The program includes a word processor, a word-prediction feature that uses word bars to present word choices to the writer, a speech function, and a system to help teachers analyze student writing. Teachers can choose either the CD software or online versions for use in their classrooms.

The proliferation of tablet computers such as the Apple iPad makes interactive teaching and learning readily available to individual students. Downloadable web applications ("apps") are available for just about any educational purpose with more coming available at a dizzying rate. Several current apps apply specifically to a variety of language arts skills, including writing. One such is StoryBuilder© for beginning writers (Northwest Kinematics, 2010). The program uses audio recording to capture a student's spoken story and then replays the audio clips to form a complete narrative. The idea is that students can learn to form and present their ideas as spoken stories before committing them to text.

Another is My Writing Spot©, developed for students with special needs. The program lets students write in portrait or landscape, tracks word count, has a dictionary/thesaurus, and emails documents (PT Software, 2010). The autosave function ensures that students do not lose their work between sessions.

Many state offices of education and school district websites are adding lists of approved or recommended downloadable apps. These and other resources can help teachers as they address specific needs for students with learning disabilities (Kendall, Nino, & Stewart, 2010).

have shown promise (Macaruso, & Rodman, 2011; Stetter & Hughes, 2011; Torgesen, Wagner, & Rashotte, 2010). Whether on a desktop computer, a smartphone, or a tablet computer, students can learn and practice skills ranging from letter names and sounds to text comprehension using a wide variety of software and apps (King-Sears, Swanson, & Mainzer, 2011). Teachers should be careful to evaluate the actual instructional effectiveness of any program before adopting it for the classroom. Studies of software design show that many lack helpful features, such as tracking student performance and providing timely feedback to users (Lovell & Phillips, 2009).

Progress monitoring for reading is an important strategy to help teachers make decisions regarding the effectiveness of particular instruction for student achievement. As mentioned previously, frequent systematic measurement of student progress toward learning goals and objectives provides the data needed to either continue a particular strategy or change to something more effective (Fuchs & Fuchs, 2011; Jenkins & Terjeson, 2011). Good teachers also monitor other important factors of the classroom learning environment, including student grouping, behavior management, access to materials, the emotional climate, and physical appearance. Such attention to the whole child and common human needs can greatly enhance motivation, emotional health, and achievement (Gettinger, Schieneback, Seigel, & Vollmer, 2011).

Behavioral Interventions

Distinctions between behavioral and academic interventions are not always sharp and definitive. Both involve students in learning skills and changing behavior. Behavioral interventions, however, generally use practical applications of learning principles such as

FOCUS 6

Explain how behavior and emotion can affect the achievement of students with learning disabilities, and describe two strategies for addressing these concerns.

reinforcement. Behavioral interventions, such as the structured presentation of stimuli (e.g., letters or words), reinforcement for correct responses, and self-monitoring of behavior and performance, are used in many instructional approaches (Joseph & Eveleigh, 2011; Stockard, 2010).

Some students with learning disabilities who experience repeated academic failure, despite their great effort, become frustrated and depressed (e.g., Nelson & Harwood, 2011b; Toland & Boyle, 2008). They may not understand why their classmates without disabilities seem to do little more than they do and yet achieve more success. These students with learning disabilities may withdraw or express frustration and anxiety by acting out or becoming aggressive. When this type of behavior emerges, it may be difficult to distinguish individuals with learning difficulties from those with behavior disorders as a primary disability (e.g., Al-Yagon, 2009; Langberg, Vaughn, Brinkman, Froehlich, & Epstein, 2010). Social and behavioral difficulties of students with learning disabilities are receiving increasing attention (Cowden, 2010a; Semrud-Clikeman et al., 2010).

Behavioral contracts are one type of intervention that is often used to change undesirable behavior. Using this approach, a teacher, behavior therapist, or parent establishes a contract with the child that provides him or her with reinforcement for appropriate behavior. Such contracts are either written or spoken, usually focus on a specific behavior, and reward the child with something that she or he really likes and considers worth striving for (such as going to the library or using the class computer). It is important that the pupil understand clearly what is expected and that the event or consequence be appealing to the child. Behavioral contracts have considerable appeal because they give students some responsibility for their own behavior (Accardo, 2008; Lane, Menzies, & Bruhn, 2010).

Token reinforcement systems represent another behavioral intervention often used with youngsters experiencing learning difficulties. **Token reinforcement systems** allow students to earn tokens for appropriate behavior and to exchange them eventually for a reward of value to them (Accardo, 2008; Hackenberg, 2009). Token systems resemble the work-for-pay lives of most adults, and therefore, can be generalized to later life experiences.

Behavioral interventions are based on fundamental principles of learning largely developed from early research in experimental psychology. These principles have been widely applied in many settings for students with learning disabilities as well as other exceptionalities. One of their main strengths is that once the basic theory is understood, behavioral interventions can be modified to suit a wide variety of needs and circumstances.

Behavioral contract
An agreement, written or oral, stating that if one party behaves in a certain manner, the other will provide a specific reward.

Token reinforcement system
A system in which students, by exhibiting positive behavior changes, may earn plastic chips, marbles, or other tangible items that they can exchange for rewards.

The Adolescent Years

FOCUS 7
Compare learning disabilities in childhood and adolescence by listing four challenges that individuals could experience as they move into secondary school and beyond.

Services and supports for adolescents and young adults with learning disabilities differ from those used for children. New issues emerge during the teen years; assistance appropriate for a young child will not typically work for a preteen or teenager. Adolescents and young adults with learning disabilities may, like their peers without such disabilities, become involved in alcohol use, drug use, gambling, and sexual activity (McNamara & Willoughby, 2010; McNamara, Vervaeke, & Willoughby, 2008). Although teens have peer pressures and temptations to behave like their friends, they are also influenced by their parents' expectations of them. Effective services and supports for adolescents with learning disabilities must be individually designed to be age-appropriate.

Academic Instruction and Support

Research suggests that the educational system often fails adolescents with learning disabilities. These students have lower school completion rates than their peers without learning disabilities, as well as higher unemployment rates (U.S. Department of Education, 2011a). Often these adolescents still need to develop basic academic survival skills; they may also lack social skills and comfortable interpersonal relationships (Cowden, 2010a; Semrud-Clikeman et al., 2010). Adolescents with learning disabilities are attending college in greater numbers than ever, but they also tend to drop out at higher rates than their peers without disabilities (U.S. Department of Education, 2011a). A comprehensive model needs to be developed to address a broad spectrum of needs for adolescents and young adults with learning disabilities (Elias & Leverett, 2011; Waber, 2010).

Relatively speaking, adolescents with learning disabilities have received considerably less attention than their younger counterparts. Academic deficits that first appeared during the younger years tend to grow more marked as students face progressively more challenging schoolwork; by the time many students with learning disabilities reach secondary school or adolescence, they may be further behind academically than they were in the early grades (McDonald, Keys, & Balcazar, 2009; Morris et al., 2009). Problems with motivation, self-reliance, learning strategies, social competence, and skill generalization all emerge related to adolescents and young adults (e.g., Farmer, Hall, & Weiss, 2011; O'Brien, 2006).

Time constraints represent one difficulty that confronts teachers of adolescents with learning disabilities. In some areas, high school students may not have progressed beyond the fifth-grade level academically, and they may have only a rudimentary grasp of some academic topics (Bender, 2008a). Yet they are reaching an age at which life grows more complex. A broad array of issues must be addressed, including possible college plans (an increasingly frequent goal for students with learning disabilities), employment goals, and preparation for social and interpersonal life during the adult years. In many areas, instead of building and expanding on a firm foundation of knowledge, many adolescents with learning disabilities are operating only at a beginning to intermediate level.

The challenge of time constraints has led researchers to seek alternatives to traditional teaching of academic content to students with learning disabilities. Even with the press of time, each individual requires specific instructional planning. For example, evidence suggests that direct instruction may also be effective when focused on key areas such as writing skills (Viel-Ruma et al., 2010). However, in other cases, learning strategies may be the focus of instruction. Teaching learning strategies to students is one widely used approach that focuses on the learning process. Learning strategies instruction often employs mnemonic acronyms that help the student remember steps for the strategy process.

Secondary school instruction for adolescents with learning disabilities may also involve teaching compensatory skills to make up for those not acquired earlier. For example, audio recording may be used in class to offset difficulties in note taking during lectures, and thus, compensate for a listening (auditory input) problem. For some individuals, personal problems related to disabilities require counseling or other mental health assistance. And to complicate matters further, hormonal changes with strong effects on interpersonal behavior come into play during adolescence. Research results are beginning to emerge on such issues for adolescents with learning disabilities (Leichtentritt & Schechtman, 2010; Sin, Francis, & Cook, 2010).

Transition from School to Adult Life

Many of the difficulties that adolescents with learning disabilities experience do not disappear as they grow older; specialized services are often needed throughout adolescence and perhaps into adulthood (Cumella, 2009; Devine, Taggart, & McLornian, 2010). The National Research Center on Learning Disabilities emphasized this developmental need, noting that "specific learning disabilities are frequently experienced across the life span with manifestations varying as a function of developmental stage and environmental demands" (NRCLD, 2007, p. 2). We may find that this period of life is characterized by some unique challenges, just as it is for young people with other disabilities (Bond & Hurst, 2010; Ferguson, Jarrett, & Terras, 2011).

Transition Services

The transition from school to adult life is a central concern for planning and instruction in secondary settings for students with learning disabilities. Preparing students for post–school life usually involves a combination of high school classes directed toward adult skills and/or preparation for postsecondary education, and supervised opportunities to

Standard 5
Learning Environments and Social Interactions

Standard 7
Instructional Planning

CASE STUDY ALICE REVISITED

Remember Alice, who we met in the last Snapshot? When we last saw her, Alice was in the fourth grade and was extremely frustrated with school. Unfortunately, she failed the history test for which she was preparing. She could not obtain enough information from the narrative and consequently could not answer the questions on the test. The exam was a paper-and-pencil test, which to Alice, looked like the book that she was supposed to read about the family who was moving west with the wagon train. When she received her graded test, Alice broke into tears. This was not the first time she had wept about her schoolwork, but it was the first time her teacher had observed it.

Alice's teacher, Mr. Dunlap, was worried about her. She was not a troublesome child in class, and she seemed attentive. But she could not do the work. On this occasion, Mr. Dunlap consoled Alice and asked her to stay after school briefly to chat with him about the test. He was astonished when they sat together and he determined that Alice

could not even read the questions. If she could not read the questions, he thought, then she undoubtedly cannot read the book. But he was fairly certain that she was not lacking in basic intelligence. Her conversations simply didn't indicate such a problem.

Mr. Dunlap sent her home and then contacted her parents. He knew a little about exceptional children and the referral process. He set that process in motion, meeting with the parents, the school psychologist, and the principal, who also sat in on all the team meetings at this school. After a diagnostic evaluation, the team met again to examine the psychologist's report. Miss Burns, the psychologist, had tested Alice and found that her scores fell in the average range in intelligence (with a full-scale WISC-III score of 114). Miss Burns had also assessed Alice's abilities with a comprehensive structural analysis of reading skills; she concluded that Alice had a rather severe form of dyslexia, which interfered substantially with her ability to read.

Alice's parents expressed a strong desire for her to remain in Mr. Dunlap's class. This was viewed as a desirable choice by each member of the team, and the next step was to determine how an intervention could be undertaken to work with Alice while she remained in her regular class as much as possible. All team members, including Alice's parents, understood that effectively meeting Alice's educational and social needs would be challenging for everyone. However, they all agreed that they were working toward the same objectives—a very positive first step.

APPLICATION

Placing yourself in the role of Mr. Dunlap, and given the information that you now have about Alice, respond to the following questions:

1. How could you facilitate Alice's social needs, particularly her relationships with classmates?

2. Who should be a part of this broad educational planning?

3. Should you talk with Alice about it?

---

experience work, service, and other aspects of adult living through collaboration with community agencies (Carter, Trainor, & Ditchman, 2011; Cobb & Alwell, 2009; O'Connor, 2009). IDEA 2004 requires IEP teams to begin transition planning no later than a student's 16th birthday, but effective practices have been slow to evolve. Programs that show promise have turned their focus to providing as much mainstream academic course work as possible and to enhancing students' self-determination skills as they consider their interests and goals for the future (Daviso, Denney, & Baer, 2011; Pierson, Carter, & Lane, 2008). Students who actively participate in their own transition planning report higher levels of satisfaction with the process and the outcomes (Woods, Sylvester, & Martin, 2010).

Those who are planning transition programs for adolescents with learning disabilities must consider that these adolescents' life goals may approximate those of adolescents without disabilities. Some students look forward to employment that will not require education beyond high school. Some plan to continue their schooling in vocational and trade schools (Daviso, Denney, & Baer, 2011; Grigal, Hart, & Migliore, 2011). Employment preparation activities—occupational awareness programs, work experience, career and vocational assessment, development of job-related academic skills, and interpersonal skills—should all be part of transition plans and should benefit these students. In addition, professionals may need to negotiate with employers to secure some accommodations at work for young adults with learning disabilities.

College Bound As we have noted, growing numbers of young people with learning disabilities plan to attend a college or university (Hadley, 2011; Milsom & Dietz, 2009; U.S. Department of Education, 2011a). There is little question that they will encounter difficulties and that careful transition planning is essential to their success. It is also clear that with some additional academic assistance, they not only will survive but also can be competitive college students (Cowden, 2010b; Holzer, Madaus, Bray, & Kehle, 2009; Kirby, Allingham, Parrila, & LaFave, 2008). But there is considerable difference between the relatively controlled setting of high school and the more unstructured environment of college. In their preparation for this transition, students profit from focused assistance, planning, and goal setting (e.g., Abreu-Ellis, Ells, & Hayes, 2009; Milsom & Dietz, 2009).

College-bound students with learning disabilities may find that many of their specific needs are related to basic survival skills in higher education. It is assumed that students can already take notes and digest lecture information auditorily and that they have adequate writing skills, reading ability, and study habits. Transition programs must strengthen these abilities as much as possible (Cobb & Alwell, 2009; Daviso, Denney, & Baer, 2011). Students with reading disabilities can obtain the help of readers who audio record the content of textbooks so that they can listen to the material, rather than making painfully slow progress if reading is difficult and time-consuming. College students with learning disabilities must seek out educational support services and social support networks to offset emotional immaturity and personality traits that may impede college achievement (DaDeppo, 2009; Reed, Kennett, & Lewis, 2011).

Perhaps the most helpful survival technique that can be taught to an adolescent with learning disabilities is actually more than a specific skill; it is a way of thinking about survival—an overall attitude of resourcefulness and a confident approach to solving problems. Recall Mathew, the psychology student in one of this chapter's first Snapshots.

DEBATE FORUM REASONABLE ACCOMMODATION VERSUS UNREASONABLE COSTS

No concept seems more likely to be accepted—even embraced—by most people than that of a "fair and level playing field" for all. Yet the notion of reasonable accommodation in providing services for students with disabilities continues to be controversial, especially in institutions of higher education.

POINT

Accessing services for students with learning disabilities often involves requests for reasonable accommodations in order to take into account students' needs resulting from their disability. For students with learning disabilities, such requests may involve extensions of time during exams, oral instead of written exams, or modification of homework assignments. In some cases, providing accommodations is easily accomplished; in others, it is more difficult and creates significant challenges for the teacher and even the educational institution. It is the law, however, and such requests must be honored.

COUNTERPOINT

Many educators do not know or have a good grasp of what is involved in reasonable accommodation. As individuals, their sources of information may be rumor or faculty department meetings in colleges or universities. It is probably prudent to consider all requests, but the notion that all requests must be honored is faulty. For example, students often make requests of their professors, implying that they have a learning disability but offering no evidence. There must be solid evidence, such as a diagnostic review by a campus center for disabilities. Documentation is required by the institution's legal department.

What Do You Think? Please visit the Education CourseMate website for Human Exceptionality, *11th edition to access and respond to questions related to the Debate Forum.*

Mathew has an amazing array of techniques that he uses to acquire knowledge while compensating for the specific areas where he has deficits.

Another key transition element involves establishing a support network. Students with learning disabilities should be taught how to establish an interpersonal network of helpers and advocates. An advocate on the faculty can often be more successful than the student in requesting special testing arrangements or other accommodations (at least to begin with). However, faculty are bombarded with student complaints and requests, and many assertions are not based on extreme needs. Consequently, many faculty are wary of granting special considerations. However, an appeal from a faculty colleague may carry more weight and enhance the credibility of a student's request.

Concern about the accommodations requested by students who claim to have learning disabilities is genuine and growing. Because learning disabilities are invisible, they are hard to understand; there is much room for abuse in students' requests for accommodations due to a disability. Such requests have increased dramatically, and many faculty are skeptical about their legitimacy. Although the Americans with Disabilities Act clearly mandates accommodation, college students with learning disabilities should be aware that many higher-education faculty are skeptical about the merits of this mandate; the process of getting special arrangements approved is not simple (Bolt, Decker, & Lloyd, 2011; Marshak, Van Wieren, & Ferrell, 2010). Providing clear diagnostic evidence of a learning disability will enhance the credibility of a request for accommodation. The accompanying Debate Forum, "Reasonable Accommodataion versus Unreasonable Costs," illustrates some elements of these issues.

Students with learning disabilities can lead productive, even distinguished, adult lives. But some literature suggests that even after they complete a college education, adults with learning disabilities have limited career choices (Bender, 2008a). We know that notable individuals have been identified as having learning disabilities. They include scientist and inventor Thomas Edison, former U.S. president Woodrow Wilson, scientist Albert Einstein, and former vice president of the United States and former governor of New York Nelson Rockefeller. We also know that the young man whose writing we saw in Figure 7.3 became a successful architect. Such achievements are not accomplished without considerable effort, but they show that the outlook for people with learning disabilities is very promising.

Multidisciplinary Collaboration: Education and Other Services

FOCUS 8

Cite three areas in which general education teachers may not feel prepared to collaborate for inclusion.

Multidisciplinary collaboration is particularly crucial for those with learning disabilities because of the wide range of characteristics that may emerge in these individuals. Providing effective inclusive education and the full range of other services requires a wide variety of professionals (Pugach, Blanton, & Correa, 2011). There is an enormous heterogeneity of ability and disability configurations that emerge and evolve at various ages in those with learning disabilities (Nelson & Harwood, 2011a; Rubinsten & Henik, 2009).

Collaboration on Inclusive Education

Definitions and descriptions of various approaches to inclusive education were introduced in earlier chapters. A very large proportion of students with learning disabilities receive educational services in settings that are either fully or partially inclusive (McLeskey & Waldron, 2011). In 2008, less than 9 percent of students with learning disabilities from 6 to 21 years of age were served mostly outside the regular classroom. The U.S. Department of Education defines this service pattern as being more than 60 percent of the time outside the regular class (U.S. Department of Education, 2010).

Inclusive approaches have received increasing attention in the learning disability literature, which has prompted thought-provoking debate about appropriate formats and the advantages and limitations of placing students with learning disabilities in fully inclusive educational environments (McLeskey & Waldron, 2011; Zigmond, Kloo, & Volonino, 2009). To be successful, inclusive education requires commitment to collaboration among general and special educators and other team members. Individualized educational programs (IEPs) at this stage evolve with a student's chronological age and as his or her skills develop. The academic focus may be on a reading problem or on difficulties in some content area. Social and behavioral issues may emerge in the inclusive environment; related interventions may form part of the spectrum of services and supports (Carnaby, Roberts, Lang, & Nielson, 2011; Mowat, 2009).

Teacher attitudes about inclusive education are very influential. Some evidence suggests that general education teachers feel unprepared to teach students with disabilities, to collaborate with special educators, and to make academic adaptations or accommodations. Adequate teacher preparation requires a significant collaborative partnership between general education and special education teacher education programs. In addition to teachers' curriculum and instructional skills, their personal attitudes toward inclusive education are vitally important. General education teachers often have less positive attitudes toward and perceptions of inclusive education than special education teachers do (Gal, Schreur, & Engel-Yeger, 2010; Hills, 2011).

Successful inclusion requires much more than just placing students with learning disabilities in the same classroom with their peers without disabilities. Some researchers have noted that successful inclusion might better be described as *supported* inclusion. Inclusive education must be undertaken only after careful planning of the instructional approach, services, and supports (Eisenman, Pleet, & Wandry, 2011; Murawski & Hughes, 2009).

Collaboration on Health and Other Services

A variety of other services may be marshaled for students and adults with learning disabilities, and here again, collaboration and communication are essential. Collaboration between educators, speech and language specialists, physical therapists, and occupational therapists is essential for a smoothly functioning personal plan (Bock, Michalak, & Brownlee, 2011; Kochhar-Bryant & Heishman, 2010). One area that often receives attention for those with learning disabilities involves health care professionals. Medical personnel are sometimes involved in the diagnosis of learning disabilities and in prescribing medications used in treating conditions that may coexist with learning disabilities.

Childhood
Physicians often diagnose a child's abnormal or delayed development in the areas of language, behavior, and motor functions. Physicians may have early involvement with a child with learning disabilities because of the nature of the problem, such as serious developmental delay or hyperactivity. More often, a medical professional sees the young child first because he or she has not yet entered school; the family physician becomes a primary adviser for parents (Pennington, 2009; Schneiderman, Leslie, & Arnold-Clark, 2011).

One example of medical service appropriate for some children with disabilities involves controlling hyperactivity and other challenging behaviors. Many children with learning disabilities receive medication such as Ritalin to control hyperactivity (generic name, methylphenidate). Although their action is not completely understood, such psychostimulants appear to result in general improvement for a large proportion of children with hyperactivity (Buitelaar, Wilens, Shuyu, Yu, & Feldman, 2009; DuPaul, 2008; Holmes, Gathercole, Place, Dunning, Hilton, & Elliott, 2010). Some researchers have expressed caution about such treatment, however, focusing on matters of effectiveness, overprescription, and side effects (e.g., Hoekstra, 2011; Setlik, Bond, & Ho, 2009). Uncertainty regarding medications and dosage levels, and the fact that high doses may have toxic effects, add to the confusion. Although there are benefits to medication, it may be overprescribed (Graziano, Geffken, & Lall, 2011; Kalikow, 2011).

Adolescence
As in other treatment areas, medical services for adolescents and young adults with learning disabilities differ somewhat from those for children. In some cases, psychiatric treatment may be involved either through interactive therapy or antidepressant medication. Additonally, efforts are under way to improve the assessment of medical, developmental, functional, and growth variables for those with learning difficulties (e.g., Logan, Catanese, & Coakley, 2007; Nelson & Harwood, 2011a; Shaw & McCabe, 2007).

Some adolescents receiving medication to control hyperactivity may have been taking it for a number of years. Many physician assessments are made during the childhood years of the learning disabled patients; as a result, medications are prescribed when these patients are still children. On the other hand, some treatments are of rather short duration and may terminate within two years (DuPaul, 2008; Powell, Thomsen, & Frydenberg, 2011).

Looking Toward a Bright Future

Nearly 50 years ago, "learning disabilities" became a formally recognized category within the disability field. Over the years, there have been many different perspectives on what constitutes a learning disability, and the idea that students with learning disabilities can be effectively taught in general education settings with children who were not disabled is still evolving (Litvack, Ritchie, & Shore, 2011; McLeskey et al., 2011). Today, learning disabilities are central to our understanding of effective instructional approaches for all children, as reflected through emerging approaches such as with response to intervention (RTI) (Bender & Waller, 2011; Searle, 2010; Zirkel & Thomas, 2010). As a concept, RTI focuses on the individual needs of each child within an inclusive educational setting. This means that educational assessments must focus on each child's strengths and challenges for educators to prescribe effective academic instruction (Swanson, 2011a). In doing so, research suggests that we will find that children with learning disabilities have a great deal more variability in their skill levels across academic subject areas than their nondisabled peers. These students may have difficulty focusing on specific academic tasks and appear to be overly active in certain circumstances (Graziano, Geffken, & Lall, 2011).

In teaching students with learning disabilities, it will be important for educators to collaborate with other disciplines, such as behavior and language specialists, health care providers, and school psychologists. With the individual as the focal point, and the support of family members, we may find that medical intervention in conjunction with new and innovative approaches to learning will be effective in meeting the needs of students with learning disabilities. This can only be determined in a consultative manner with other professions, including health care (for assessment and prescriptions), educational professionals (for assessment and instructional planning), school psychologists and counseling professionals, and family members (for information, assessment, and planning for the future) (Gross, 2011; Kibby, 2009; National Joint Committee on Learning Disabilities, 2011a). Through the use of evidence-based instruction, students with learning disabilities can and will learn to survive and thrive in our complex world. This represents a promising future for those with learning disabilities.

FOCUS REVIEW

FOCUS 1 Cite four reasons why definitions of learning disabilities have varied.

- *Learning disabilities* is a broad, generic term that encompasses many different specific problems.
- The study of learning disabilities has been undertaken by a variety of different disciplines.
- The field of learning disabilities per se has existed for only a relatively short period of time and is therefore relatively immature with respect to conceptual development and terminology.
- The field of learning disabilities has grown at a very rapid pace.

FOCUS 2 Identify seven characteristics attributed to those with learning disabilities, and explain why it is difficult to characterize this group.

- Typically, of above-average or near-average intelligence
- Uneven skill levels in various areas
- Hyperactivity
- Perceptual problems
- Problems with visual and auditory discrimination

- Cognition deficits, such as in memory
- Attention problems
- The individuals included under the umbrella term *learning disabilities* are so varied that they defy simple characterization in terms of a single concept or label.

FOCUS 3 List four causes thought to be involved in learning disabilities.

- Neurological damage or malfunction
- Maturational delay of the neurological system
- Genetic abnormality
- Environmental factors

FOCUS 4 Compare and contrast the purpose of assessments used for screening and progress monitoring.

- Both are used for determining what is best for the individual student.
- Screening occurs prior to determining eligibility or treatment of the student, when clinicians or others (e.g., parents) suspect that a problem exists.

- Progress monitoring uses curriculum-based measurement as repetitive measures given over time to monitor students' progress toward learning goals.

FOCUS 5 Identify five types of interventions or supports used with people who have learning disabilities, including two that use assistive technology.

- Medical treatment, in some circumstances involving medication to control hyperactivity
- Academic instruction and support in a wide variety of areas that are specifically aimed at building particular skills
- Behavioral interventions aimed at improving social skills or remediating problems in this area (behavioral procedures may also be a part of academic instruction)
- Interactive whiteboards for small- or large-group instruction
- Laptop and tablet computer apps for teaching and practice

FOCUS 6 Explain how behavior and emotion can affect the achievement of students with learning disabilities, and describe two strategies for addressing these concerns.

- Become anxious, frustrated, or depressed; withdraw or act out
- Behavior contracts, token reinforcement systems

FOCUS 7 Compare learning disabilities in childhood and adolescence by listing four challenges that individuals experience as they move into secondary school and beyond.

- Involvement in alcohol or drug abuse, gambling, sexual activity
- Worsening academic deficits
- Failure to graduate
- Problems with motivation, social competence, and skill generalization

FOCUS 8 Cite three areas in which general education teachers may not feel prepared to collaborate for inclusion.

- Teaching students with learning disabilities
- Collaborating with special educators
- Making academic adaptations or accommodations

Council for Exceptional Children (CEC) Standards to Accompany Chapter 7

 If you are thinking about a career in special education, you should know that many states use national standards developed by the Council for Exceptional Children (CEC) to assess a teacher candidate's knowledge about and skills for working with students with disabilities. See a complete listing of the 10 CEC Content Standards on the inside back cover of this text.

1 Foundations
2 Development and Characteristics of Learners
3 Individual Learning Differences
5 Learning Environments and Social Interactions
7 Instructional Planning
8 Assessment

Mastery Activities and Assignments

 To master the content within this chapter, complete the following activities and assignments. Online and interactive versions of these activities are also available on the accompanying Education Course-Mate website, where you may also access TeachSource videos, chapter web links, interactive quizzes, portfolio activities, flash cards, an integrated eBook, and much more!

1. Complete a written test of the chapter's content. If your instructor requires a written test of your content knowledge for this chapter, keep a copy for your portfolio. A practice test on the information covered in this chapter is available through the Education CourseMate website.
2. Review the Case Study, "Alice Revisited," and respond in writing to the Application Questions. Keep a copy of the Case Study and of your written response for your portfolio.

3. Read the Debate Forum in this chapter and visit the Education CourseMate website to complete the activity "Take a Stand." Keep a copy of this activity for your portfolio.
4. Participate in a community service learning activity. Community service is a valuable way to enhance your learning experience. Visit our Education CourseMate website for suggested community service learning activities that correspond to the information presented in this chapter. Develop a reflective journal of the service learning experience for your portfolio.

CHAPTER 8

Emotional/Behavioral Disorders

Petri Artturi Asikainen/Gorilla Creative Images/Getty Images

FOCUS PREVIEW

As you read the chapter, focus on these key concepts:

1 Identify six essential features of the federal definition for emotional/behavioral disorders (EBD).

2 What four statements can be made about prevalence figures and identification rates for children and youth with EBD?

3 Identify five general characteristics of children and youth with EBD.

4 What can accurately be said about the causes of EBD?

5 Cite three reasons why classification systems are important to professionals who identify, treat, and educate individuals with EBD.

6 Identify five essential elements and goals of the assessment process and related practices.

7 What five guiding principles are associated with systems of care?

"[My] mother always said, 'There must be nothing worse than losing a child.'" Patty never understood what her mother meant until she had a child of her own, and thought she might lose her, though in a different way.

What are we doing here? Patty wondered to herself. *This can't be happening! She had, after all, led a happy, normal childhood. . . . Now she was leaving her 11-year-old daughter, Jennifer, in a real hospital. A mental hospital.*

At that moment, Patty wasn't sure if she had lost her daughter forever. But the truth was, she had been losing Jennifer for a few years.

She actually knew something was terribly wrong when Jennifer was just 8. Patty and her family were on a dream family vacation in Disney World—"the Happiest Place on Earth."

The evening parade had just ended. Mickey, Minnie, and the gang had floated away into the sunset, leaving Patty's family and her favorite characters. . . . behind. Patty couldn't help but smile as she looked up and down the colorful streets at all the families grinning from mouse ear to mouse ear.

That is, until she was interrupted by an all-too-familiar and painful screech.

"Why do they have to leave? Why!" shouted 8-year-old Jennifer, who was sitting on the curb, hugging the Minnie Mouse on her sweatshirt and flailing her legs.

"Oh that's just great! It's even happening here!" muttered Patty, helplessly realizing that the Magic Kingdom, the place where "dreams come true," was about to turn into her personal nightmare.

It really shouldn't have surprised her. Over the past few months, Jennifer's moods had become increasingly

Courtesy of Jenn & Patricia Konjoian

unpredictable. She would cry for hours and become violent about the smallest things.

"Why? Why can't I wear my jelly shoes?"

"Because, Jenns, it's 30 degrees outside and snowing."

"WAAAAAHHHH! I hate you!"

She was also becoming alarmingly destructive.

"Jennifer Marie! What are you doing with my scissors and the family picture?"

"I'm cutting myself out. I don't want to be part of this family anymore."

And during that dream vacation to Disney—the one Jennifer had been excited about for months ("How many days till we go, Mom? Tell me! Tell me!")—her moods were just as unpredictable. Somehow Patty had actually thought Jenn's problems would disappear, but instead of seeing Snow White, Patty saw her daughter magically transform into Grumpy, Saddy, and Angry (Gallagher & Konjorian, 2010, p. 15–17).

Linea (excerpted from her high school journal)

I was numb, a smile plastered on my face like the one I wore every day. I couldn't feel anything. The pills prescribed to me after witnessing my best friend slash open her arms kept me from the pain of sadness. They also robbed me of the euphoria of joy. I was at an even keel all the time. My life was bland while all my outside interaction and activities suggested excitement, adventure, and pride.

As I developed new and increasingly dangerous coping methods such as self-mutilation, and drug and alcohol use, I began to question myself as a perfectionist. I began seeing myself as a perfectionist. I began seeing myself in a dualist view, the stable productive side as the "good" me and the unstable often incontrollable side as the "bad" me. . . . What I truly needed was a comforting voice outside my loving family, to tell me that it was okay if I failed, or even broke a few rules.

My training as a perfectionist in high school taught me to hide my feelings. I found ways to act like nothing had changed and found ways to make myself appear happy to the average population. And though I did a good job of feigning composure to the general population, the people I saw daily, friends, boyfriend, and teachers, should have been aware of my changing interaction with the world.

I believe had I even one teacher who knew me well enough to see the stress and pain that came from my endless search for perfection, I would have felt more comfortable confronting my feelings earlier. It is so important for teachers and educational professionals to be aware of their students' patterns and personalities

SOURCE: Adapted from Johnson, C., Eva, A. L., Johnson, L., & Walker, B. (2011). Don't turn away: Empowering teachers to support students' mental health. *The Clearing House: A Journal of Educational Strategies, Issues and Ideas, 84(1),* 9–11.

in order to help the students trust themselves and others when it comes to emotional crises. By fearing that my emotions would ruin my reputation as a good student and mature young adult, I let myself get to increasingly dangerous levels of depression.

A Changing Era in the Lives of People with Disabilities

Emotional disorders
Behavior problems, frequently internal, exhibited by difficulties in expressing emotions evoked in normal everyday experiences.

Behavior disorders
Conditions in which the emotional or behavioral responses of individuals significantly differ from those of their peers and seriously impact their relationships.

Individuals with **emotional and behavioral disorders** (EBD)—such as Jennifer and Linea in the opening Snapshot—may experience great difficulties in relating appropriately to peers, siblings, parents, teachers, and other adults. However, recent advances in intervention approaches are making a difference for many children and youth with EBD, allowing them to be served in integrated settings—regular classrooms, neighborhood schools, and in other community-based programs.

As you might guess, many children and youth with EBD have difficulty responding to academic and social tasks that are essential parts of their schooling (Lane, Barton-Arwood, Nelson, & Wehby, 2008). Generally, they are deficient in vitally important academic and social behaviors. This chapter explores issues and opportunities related to EBD in greater detail, giving you a framework for understanding these children and youth.

FOCUS 1

Identify six essential features of the federal definition for emotional/behavioral disorders.

CEC

Standard 1
Foundations

Definitions

As you will see, several terms have been developed to describe individuals with EBD. Think about Jennifer and Linea as you move through this section. These terms include *emotionally disturbed*, *conduct disordered*, *behavior disordered*, and *socially maladjusted*. In reading this chapter, think about the labels you have used over time to describe peers, relatives, classmates, or other acquaintances who frequently exhibited atypical behaviors. Use the experiences you have had with others as reference points for thinking about and coming to understand children and youth with EBD. How are your experiences similar to those revealed by Jennifer's mother and Linea?

The IDEA Definition

Emotional disturbance is defined in the Individuals with Disabilities Education Act (IDEA) as:

(I) A condition exhibiting one or more of the following characteristics over a long period of time and to a marked degree, which adversely affects educational performance:
   (A) An inability to learn which cannot be explained by intellectual, sensory, or health factors;
   (B) An inability to build or maintain satisfactory relationships with peers and teachers;
   (C) Inappropriate types of behavior or feelings under normal circumstances;
   (D) A general pervasive mood of unhappiness or depression; or
   (E) A tendency to develop physical symptoms or fears associated with personal or school problems.
(II) The term does not include children who are socially maladjusted, unless it is determined that they are seriously emotionally disturbed.

This definition of severe emotional disturbance, or EBD, was adapted from an earlier definition created by Bower (1959). The IDEA definition for EBD has been criticized for its lack of clarity, for its incompleteness, and for its exclusion of individuals described as *socially maladjusted*—sometimes referred to as juvenile delinquents (Cullinan, 2004; Merrell & Walker, 2004; U.S. Department of Education, 2006). Furthermore, this definition mandates that assessment personnel—teachers, special educators, and school psychologists—demonstrate that the EBD adversely impact students' school performance and achievement. In some cases, students with serious EBD—such as eating disorders, mood disorders (depression and bipolar disorder), suicidal tendencies, and social withdrawal—do not receive appropriate care and treatment, merely because their academic achievement in school appears to be normal or above average (Crundwell & Killu, 2007; Johnson, Johnson, & Walker, 2011). This is also true for young preschool children who do not manifest "substantial deficits in academic achievement," but evidence high levels of aggressive and antisocial behaviors (Maag & Katsiyannis, 2010, p. 472).

Youth with EBD often engage in destructive behaviors directed at themselves or others.

Identifying Normal Behavior

Many factors influence the ways in which we perceive the behaviors of others. Our perceptions of behavior are significantly influenced by our personal beliefs, standards, and values about what constitutes normal behavior. Our range of tolerance varies greatly, depending on the behavior and the related context. What some may view as normal, others may view as abnormal.

The context in which behaviors occur also dramatically influences our view of their appropriateness. For example, teachers and parents expect children to behave reasonably well in settings where they have interesting things to do or where children are doing things they seem to enjoy. Often children with EBD misbehave in these settings. At times, they seem to be oblivious to the settings in which they find themselves.

CEC

Standard 1
Foundations

Major Contributing Factors

Many factors influence the types of behaviors that children and youth exhibit or suppress: (1) the parents' and teachers' management/discipline approaches, (2) school or home environments, (3) the social and cultural values of the family, (4) the social and economic conditions of the community, (5) the expectations and responses of peers and siblings, and (6) the biological, intellectual, and social-emotional temperaments of the individuals.

Prevalence

Estimates of the prevalence of EBD vary greatly from one study to the next, ranging from 2 percent to 20 percent (Harry, Hart, Klinger, & Cramer, 2009; Kauffman, Simpson, & Mock, 2009; Young, Sabbah, Young, Reiser, & Richardson, 2010). A sensible estimate is 3 to 6 percent (Kauffman & Landrum, 2009). Sadly, during the past ten plus years in the United States, less than 1 percent of children and youth 3 to 21 years of age have been identified and served as exhibiting EBD (National Center for Education Statistics, 2006; U.S. Department of Education, 2011).

Unfortunately, significant numbers of children and youth with EBD remain unidentified and do not receive the therapeutic care or special education they need to succeed (Johnson, Johnson, & Walker, 2011; Kauffman, et al., 2009). Equally distressing is the disproportionate number of young African American males who are identified as having EBD, vastly exceeding the percentage that would be expected in the general population of school-age students (Kauffman, Mock, & Simpson, 2007; Osher et al., 2004; U.S. Department of Education, 2005).

FOCUS 2

What four statements can be made about prevalence figures and identification rates for children and youth with EBD?

CEC

Standard 1
Foundations

FOCUS 3

Identify five general
characteristics of children
and youth with EBD.

Characteristics

If you had to describe children or youth with EBD, what would you say about their intellectual capacity, their behavior, their academic performance, and their long-term prospects for employment and success? How many males are identified? How many females? This section provides answers to some of these questions. However, note that the figures introduced here represent averages. We must view each child or youth with EBD individually, focusing on his or her strengths and potential for growth and achievement.

Intelligence

Researchers from a variety of disciplines have studied the intellectual capacity of individuals with EBD. Recent research suggests that children and youth with EBD tend to have average to below-average IQs compared with their peers (Algozzine, Serna, & Patton, 2001; Coleman & Webber, 2002; Seifert, 2000).

What impact does intelligence have on the educational and social-adaptive performance of children with EBD? Is the intellectual capacity of a child with EBD a good predictor of other types of achievement and social behavior? The answer is yes. The IQs of students with EBD are the best predictors of future academic and social achievement (Kauffman, 2005). The below-average IQs of many of these children contribute to the challenges they experience in mastering academic content and developing other important school-related social skills.

Social and Adaptive Behavior

Children and youth with EBD exhibit a variety of problems in adapting to their home, school, and community environments (Bradley, Henderson, & Monfore, 2004; Wicks-Nelson & Israel, 2006). Furthermore, they usually exhibit difficulties in relating socially and responsibly to peers, parents, teachers, and other authority figures. In short, students with EBD are generally difficult to teach and to parent. In contrast to their peers who generally follow rules and respond well to their teachers and parents, children and youth with EBD often defy their parents and teachers, disturb others, are aggressive with others, and behave in ways that invite rejection by those around them. Children and youth with EBD experience the highest rate of suspensions from school. Moreover, they have the highest rate of "interim alternative placements" for drug or weapon offenses that occur in school settings (U.S. Department of Education, 2011).

Socially, children and youth with EBD have difficulties sharing, playing typical age-appropriate games, and apologizing for actions that hurt others. They may be unable to deal appropriately with situations that produce strong feelings, such as anger and frustration. Problem solving, self-control, accepting consequences for misbehavior, negotiating, expressing affection, and reacting appropriately to failure are social skills that are generally underdeveloped or absent in these children and youth. Because these children and youth have deficits in these social-adaptive behaviors, they frequently experience difficulties in meeting the demands of the classrooms and other social environments in which they participate (Hansen & Lignugaris-Kraft, 2005; Polsgrove & Smith, 2004; Vazsonyi & Huang, 2010).

Several studies shed considerable light on the social difficulties these children experience. Researchers have found that about three out of four children with EBD show clinically significant language deficits (Cross, 2004; Forness, 2004; Mattison, Hooper, & Carlson, 2006; Nungesser & Watkins, 2005). These include problems related to processing and understanding verbal communication and using language to communicate (Benner, Nelson, & Epstein, 2002). These researchers also found that one out of two children with language deficits is identified as having EBD. These language deficits contribute to the social problems these children experience.

Children and adolescents who are anxious and withdrawn frequently exhibit behaviors such as seclusiveness and shyness. They may find it extremely difficult to interact with others in typical social settings. They tend to avoid contact with others and may often be found daydreaming. In the extreme, some of these youth begin to avoid school or refuse to attend (Graczyk, Connolly, & Corapci, 2005). Their school avoidance or refusal is marked by persistent fear of social situations that might arise in school or related settings. These youth fear being humiliated or embarrassed. Their anxiety may be expressed in tantrums, crying, and other bodily complaints (stomachaches, sickness, etc.).

Other children and youth with EBD may struggle with mood disorders (Ialongo, Poduska, Werthamer, & Kellam, 2001; Roberts & Bishop, 2005). These may include depression and bipolar disorder (National Institute of Mental Health, 2008). Left untreated, these individuals are at risk for suicide, poor school performance, and relationship problems with peers, siblings, parents, teachers, and spouses. Manifestations of depression in children and youth include sleep disturbance (nightmares, night terrors, and so on), fatigue or loss of energy, excessive feelings of guilt or worthlessness, inability to concentrate, and suicidal thoughts.

Bipolar disorders are characterized by episodes of manic behavior and depression. Manic behaviors may include defiance of authority, agitation, distractibility, sleeping very little, strong frequent cravings, inappropriate sexual behavior, unrealistic beliefs about abilities, impaired judgment, racing thoughts, destructive rages, and other related behaviors.

Depressive behaviors may include sleeping too much, extreme sadness, lack of interest in play or highly preferred activities, crying spells, persistent thoughts of death or suicide, irritability, and inability to concentrate (Child and Adolescent Bipolar Foundation, 2009). Jennifer, identified in the opening Snapshot, is challenged with this disorder.

Youth gang activities, drug abuse, truancy, violence toward others, and other delinquent acts characterize children and adolescents who are often identified as being "socially maladjusted" or having a conduct disorder (see Figure 8.1). Serious conduct problems in children and youth often foreshadow poor adult adjustment—substance abuse, spousal and friendship violence, and serious criminal activity (Capaldi & Eddy, 2005).

Adolescents with conduct problems are often seen as impulsive, hyperactive, irritable, and excessively stubborn. Furthermore, many students with EBD engage in behaviors that draw attention to themselves. Other behaviors associated with this condition include cruelty to others, drug trafficking, and participation in other illegal activities (Capaldi & Eddy, 2005). It is easy to see how the behaviors associated with these categories are maladaptive and interfere with youths' opportunities for success in schools, families, communities, and employment settings.

Academic Achievement

As we have noted, students with EBD experience significant difficulties and deficits in academic subject areas, and rarely catch up academically (Allen-DeBoer, Malmgren, & Glass, 2006; Griffith, Trout, Hagaman, & Harper, 2009; Johnson, McGue, & Iacono, 2009; Kostewicz & Kubina, 2008; Lane et al., 2008). In contrast to other students with high-incidence disabilities such as learning disabilities, students with EBD exhibit the "poorest academic outcomes" (Shriner & Wehby, 2004, p. 216). Some attribute these poor outcomes to the preparation of the teachers who work with these students and to the poor quality of the academic instruction these students often receive (Gable, 2004; Lane, 2004; Shriner & Wehby, 2004). Additionally, interventions for students with EBD have often been directed primarily at controlling behavior and developing social competence rather than building academic skills and promoting achievement (Ryan, Reid, & Epstein, 2004). Thus, many, if not most, students with EBD are not prepared to perform well on state- or federally mandated tests or on other measures of academic achievement (Carter et al., 2005).

The drop-out and graduation rates for students with EBD are staggering (Maag & Katsiyannis, 2006). About 51 to 70 percent of these students drop out of school—most before they finish the tenth grade—a greater percentage than for any other disability group (Sitlington & Neubert, 2004; U.S. Department of Education, 2010). Students with EBD consistently have the lowest graduation rates in contrast to other disability groups (25 to 29 percent) (U.S. Department of Education, 2005). Only one in five youth with EBD participate in postsecondary schooling (Wagner et al., 2005).

Figure 8.1 Diagnostic Criteria for Conduct Disorder

A. A repetitive and persistent pattern of behavior in which the basic rights of others or major age-appropriate societal norms or rules are violated, as manifested by the presence of three (or more) of the following criteria in the past 12 months, with at least one criterion present in the past 6 months:

Aggression to People and Animals

(1) Often bullies, threatens, or intimidates others

(2) Often initiates physical fights

(3) Has used a weapon that can cause serious physical harm to others (e.g., a bat, brick, broken bottle, knife, gun)

(4) Has been physically cruel to people

(5) Has been physically cruel to animals

(6) Has stolen while confronting a victim (e.g., mugging, purse snatching, extortion, armed robbery)

Destruction of Property

(7) Has deliberately engaged in fire setting with the intention of causing serious damage

(8) Has deliberately destroyed others' property (other than by setting fire)

Deceitfulness or Theft

(9) Has broken into someone else's house, building, or car

(10) Often lies to obtain goods or favors or to avoid obligation (i.e., "cons" others)

(11) Has stolen items of nontrivial value without confronting a victim (e.g., shoplifting, but without breaking and entering; forgery)

Serious Violations of Rules

(12) Often stays out at night despite parental prohibitions, beginning before age 13 years

(13) Has run away from home overnight at least twice while living in parental or parental surrogate home (or once without returning for a lengthy period)

(14) Is often truant from school, beginning before age 13 years

B. The disturbance in behavior causes clinically significant impairment in social, academic, or occupational functioning.

C. If the individual is age 18 years or older, criteria are not met for antisocial personality disorder.

SOURCE: Reprinted with permission from the *Diagnostic and Statistical Manual of Mental Disorders,* 4th ed., Text (rev. pp. 98–99), Copyright 2000 American Psychiatric Association.

Studies dealing with employment rates of students after high school are frankly disheartening (Bullis, 2001; Carter & Wehby, 2003; Sitlington & Neubert, 2004). Only 41 percent of students with EBD who have exited high school are employed two years later, compared with 59 percent of typical adolescents who have left or completed high school. Three to five years later, the contrasts are even stronger: Of students without disabilities, 69 percent are employed, compared with 42 to 70 percent of students with EBD. Significant challenges persist in preparing young people with EBD for meaningful employment and involvement in our communities (Bullis, 2001; Carter & Wehby, 2003).

The postsecondary school years for youth with EBD are often tragic. Many are incarcerated, some are involved in domestic abuse, and many or most are unemployed or underemployed (Kauffman & Landrum, 2009; Menzies & Lane, 2011). Later on in this chapter, we highlight collaborative approaches to intervention that are designed to address the social, educational, transition, and employment challenges of youth and adults with EBD.

Causation

What causes children and youth to develop EBD? As you read this section, think about your own patterns of behavior. How would you explain these patterns? What has given rise to them?

FOCUS 4
What can accurately be said about the causes of EBD?

Throughout history, philosophers, psychologists, and others have attempted to explain why people behave as they do. Historically, people who were mentally ill were viewed as being possessed by evil spirits. The treatment of choice was religious in nature. Later, Sigmund Freud (1856–1939) and others advanced the notion that behavior could be explained in terms of subconscious phenomena and/or early traumatic experiences. More recently, researchers have attributed disordered behaviors to inappropriate learning and complex interactions among factors such as native temperament, family environment, poverty, health care, and so on (Ensor, Marks, Jacobs, & Hughes, 2010; Rutter, 2006). Others, approaching the issue from a biological perspective, suggest that aberrant behaviors are caused by certain biochemical substances (Haltigan et al., 2011), brain abnormalities or injuries, chromosomal irregularities, and other inherited genetic factors (Forsman, Lichtenstein, Andershed, & Larsson, 2010; Johnson, McGue, & Iacono, 2009; Vazsonyi & Huang, 2010).

With such a wealth of explanations, it is easy to see why practitioners might select different approaches in identifying, treating, and preventing EBD. As you will see, the causes of behavioral disorders are multifaceted and often complex (Burt, 2009; Burt & Neiderhiser, 2009; Heilbrun, 2004; Rutter, 2006).

Clearly, many factors contribute to the emergence of EBD (Crews, Bender, Cook, Gresham, Kern, & Vanderwood, 2007). Family and home environments play critical roles (Barber, Stolz, & Olsen, 2005; Murray, Irving, Farrington, Colman, & Bloxsom, 2010; Whitted, 2011). Economic stress, involvement of primary caregivers with drugs and alcohol, child abuse and neglect, malnutrition, dysfunctional family environments, family discord, and inept parenting have a profound impact on the behaviors that emerge in children and adolescents (Burt, 2009; Conroy & Brown, 2004; Wicks-Nelson & Israel, 2006; Murray et al., 2010). For example, "minimal rules in the home, poor monitoring of children, and inconsistent rewards and punishments create an environment in which behavior problems flourish" (Sampers, Anderson, Hartung, & Scambler, 2001, p. 94).

Peggy Barnett

Children who have been abused are at risk for the development of emotional/behavior disorders.

Children reared in low-income families and communities bear increased risks for wide-ranging challenges, including low cognitive stimulation, deficient school achievement, and high rates of EBD. Antisocial behaviors often emerge in children whose family poverty is accompanied by other stressors, such as homelessness, the death of a parent, maternal depression, placement in foster care, or persistent child abuse or neglect (Murray et al., 2010).

Family discord also plays a role in the development of EBD in some children. Extended marital conflict and distress are associated with several serious child outcomes, including aggressive behavior, difficulty with schoolwork, depression, health problems, and lower social competence (Wicks-Nelson & Israel, 2006).

Procedures used in child management and discipline also play important roles in the development of EBD (Nelson, Stage, Duppong-Hurley, Synhorst, & Epstein, 2007). However, the way in which child management may trigger EBD is highly complex. Parents who are extremely permissive, who are overly restrictive, or who use highly aggressive discipline approaches often produce children with conduct disorders (Vieno, Nation, Pastore, & Santinello, 2009). Again, home environments that are devoid of consistent rules and consequences for negative behaviors, that lack parental supervision, that reinforce aggressive behavior, and that use aggressive child-management practices produce children who are very much at risk for developing conduct disorders (see Figure 8.1; Barker, Oliver, Viding, Salekin, & Maughan, 2011; Wicks-Nelson & Israel, 2006).

Child abuse plays a major role in the development of aggression and other problematic behaviors in children and adolescents. Effects of child abuse on young children include withdrawal, noncompliance, aggression, enuresis (bed-wetting), and physical complaints. Physically abused children exhibit high rates of adjustment problems of all kinds (Wicks-Nelson & Israel, 2006). Neglected children often experience difficulty in academic subjects and receive below-average grades. Children who have been sexually abused manifest an array of problems, including inappropriate, premature sexual behavior; poor peer relationships; and serious mental health problems. Similar difficulties are evident in adolescents who have been abused. These include low self-esteem, depression, poor peer relationships and school problems, and self-injurious and suicidal behaviors.

The pathways to EBD are multidimensional. However, the more we learn about these pathways, the greater our opportunities are to prevent EBD or to lessen its overall impact (Eivers, Brendgen, & Borge, 2010). Much can be done for children, at-risk youth, and their families if appropriate preventive measures, protective factors, and interventions are actively pursued and put in place (Adelman & Taylor, 2006; Crews et al., 2007; Hester, Baltodano, Hendrickson, Tonelson, Conroy, & Gable, 2004; Quinn & Poirier, 2004; Whitted, 2011).

Classification Systems

FOCUS 5

Cite three reasons why classification systems are important to professionals who identify, treat, and educate individuals with EBD.

We use classification systems to describe various groups and kinds of challenging behaviors. These systems serve several purposes for professionals. First, they provide professionals with a shared means for describing various types of behavior problems in children and youth. Second, they provide professionals with common terms for communicating with one another (Cullinan, 2004). Third, physicians and other mental health specialists use these characteristics and other information as a basis for diagnosing and treating individuals. Unfortunately, "[c]lassifications as yet have limited validity for the most important purpose of classification: specifying interventions [and treatments] that are best suited to improve any particular form of EBD" (Cullinan, 2004, p. 41).

The field of EBD is broad and includes many different types of problems, so it is not surprising that many approaches have been used to classify these individuals. Some classification systems describe individuals according to statistically derived categories—patterns of strongly related behaviors are identified through sophisticated statistical techniques. Other classification systems are clinically oriented; they are derived from the experiences of physicians and other mental health specialists who work directly with children, youth, and adults with EBD.

Statistically Derived Classification System

For a number of years, researchers have collected information about children with EBD using parent and teacher questionnaires, interviews, and behavior rating scales. Applying sophisticated statistical techniques, two broad categories of behavior have been identified from these sources: externalizing symptoms (disruptive, hyperactive, and aggressive behaviors) and internalizing symptoms. The latter category refers to behaviors that are directed more at the self than at others (Johnson, Johnson, & Walker, 2011). Withdrawal, depression, shyness, and phobias are examples of internalized behaviors; some clinicians would describe individuals with these conditions as *emotionally disturbed*. The average ratio of males to females referred for internalized behaviors is 2:1 (Young et al., 2010).

Children or youth who exhibit externalizing disorders may be described as engaging in behaviors that are directed more at others than at themselves. These behaviors could be characterized as aggressive, noncompliant, defiant, resistive, disruptive, and dangerous. These behaviors significantly affect parents, families, siblings, classmates, teachers, and neighbors. The average ratio of males to females referred for externalizing behaviors is 5:1 (Young et al., 2010).

Clinically Derived Classification Systems

Although several clinically derived classification systems have been developed, the system primarily used by medical and psychological professionals is that contained in the *DSM-IV-TR, Mental Disorders: Diagnosis, Etiology and Treatment* (First & Tasman, 2004). This and previous editions were developed by groups of psychiatric, psychological, and health care clinicians—hence, the term *clinically derived classifications.* Professionals in each of these groups included people who worked closely with children, adolescents, and adults with mental disorders, or using our terminology, emotional and behavioral disorders (EBD).

The categories and subcategories of *DSM-IV-TR, Mental Disorders: Diagnosis, Etiology and Treatment* (First & Tasman, 2004) were developed after years of investigation and field testing. These psychiatric categories are not used by school personnel in identifying children or adolescents for special education services. However, school personnel and other care providers should be familiar with these categories as they often work with medical specialists and clinicians in hospitals, clinics, and residential settings with young people with EDB.

The current manual identifies nine major groups of childhood disorders that may be exhibited by infants, children, or adolescents. Again, not all of these disorders are included within the IDEA definition of EBD. Some of the *DSM-IV-TR* disorders are related to other special education designations such as intellectual disabilities and learning disabilities. The *DSM-IV-TR* disorders include (1) mental retardation; (2) learning and motor skills disorders; (3) communication disorders; (4) pervasive developmental disorders; (5) attention-deficit and disruptive behavior disorders; (6) feeding and eating disorders of infancy or early childhood; (7) tic disorders; (8) elimination disorders and childhood anxiety disorders; and (9) reactive attachment disorders of infancy or early childhood. As indicated earlier, this classification system is not used in schools or by school psychologists for identifying and classifying children and youth with EBD. What follows are brief descriptions of emotional and behavior disorders drawn from this clinical classification system.

Attention-Deficit and Disruptive Behavior Disorders

Children with these disorders manifest a variety of symptoms. For example, children with attention deficits have difficulty responding well to typical academic and social tasks. Moreover, they experience challenges in controlling their level of physical activity. Often their activity appears to be very random or purposeless in nature. (See Chapter 14 for more information on attention-deficit disorders.)

Children with disruptive behavior disorders frequently cause physical harm to other individuals or to animals, often engage in behaviors destructive to others' property, repeatedly participate in theft and deceitful activities, and regularly violate rules and other social conventions. In some instances, children with these disorders are highly oppositional. They exhibit a pattern of recurrent negativism, opposition to authority, and loss of temper. Other typical behaviors include disobeying, arguing, blaming others for problems and mistakes, and being spiteful. Most of the students with EBD who are served in special education through IDEA manifest conduct disorders or are oppositionally defiant.

Feeding and Eating Disorders

The disorder known as pica consists of the persistent eating of nonnutritive materials for at least one month. Materials consumed may be cloth, string, hair, plaster, or even paint. Often children with pervasive developmental disorders manifest pica.

Anorexia and bulimia are common eating disorders evidenced by gross disturbances in eating behavior (Levitt, Sansone, & Cohn, 2004). In the case of anorexia nervosa, the most distinguishing feature is body weight that is 15 percent below the norm (Smolak, 2005). These individuals are intensely afraid of weight gain and exhibit grossly distorted perceptions of their bodies. Bulimia is characterized by repeated episodes of bingeing, followed by self-induced vomiting or other extreme measures to prevent weight gain. Both anorexia nervosa and bulimia may result in depressed mood, social withdrawal, irritability, and

Anorexia and bulimia may lead to very serious medical problems.

© john angerson/Alamy

other serious medical conditions. Rumination disorder is characterized by repeated regurgitation and rechewing of food. Of the girls and women receiving treatment for anorexia and bulimia, 5 to 10 percent will die from complications of these conditions (Smolak, 2005).

Tic Disorders Tic disorders involve movements or vocalizations that are involuntary, rapid, and recurrent over time. Tics may take the form of excessive eye blinking, facial gestures, sniffing, snorting, repeating certain words or phrases, or grunting. Stress often exacerbates the nature and frequency of tics. These disorders include Tourette's syndrome, chronic motor or vocal tic disorder, and transient tic disorder.

Elimination Disorders and Childhood Anxiety Disorders Elimination disorders entail soiling (encopresis) and wetting (enuresis) in older children. Children who continue to have consistent problems with bowel and bladder control past their fourth or fifth birthday may be diagnosed as having an elimination disorder, particularly if the condition is not a function of any physical problem.

Children and youth with anxiety disorders have difficulty dealing with fear-provoking situations and with separating themselves from parents or other attachment figures (e.g., close friends, teachers, coaches). Unrealistic worries about future events, concern about achievement, excessive need for reassurance, and somatic complaints are characteristic of young people who exhibit anxiety disorders. Behaviors indicative of this disorder include persistent refusal to go to school, excessive worry about personal harm or injury to themselves or other family members, reluctance to go to sleep, and repeated complaints about headaches, stomachaches, nausea, and other related conditions.

The last condition included within this subset of disorders is selective mutism. Young children with this condition are able to speak but do not speak in specific social situations. Most commonly, this disorder appears in the first days or weeks of attending school or participating in a new social environment. These children are able to talk and do speak at home with their parents or other care providers, but they are verbally silent in school and other social settings.

Reactive Attachment Disorder Reactive attachment disorder of infancy or early childhood is represented by noticeably abnormal and developmentally inept social relatedness. This disorder appears as a result of grossly inadequate care—such as physical or emotional neglect, frequent changes in major caregivers, and other abuse. Behaviors common to this disorder include extreme inhibitions, inability to form appropriate attachments, complete lack of ability to respond to or instigate social interaction with others, and hypervigilance or complete absence of attention to surrounding social opportunities.

Childhood Schizophrenia Childhood schizophrenia is a chronic condition characterized by hallucinations, delusions, irrational behavior, strange thinking, and other severe behaviors. Less than 1 in 10,000 preadolescents develop this serious illness. Often referred to as childhood-onset schizophrenia, its impacts are profound. Causes of the condition seem to be combinatorial: genetic, environmental, and biochemical. Early medical and educational treatments and interventions are essential to the well-being of these children.

Again, these clinically derived classifications of behavior disorders are primarily used by psychiatric and other related personnel who work in hospital and clinical settings.

LEARNING THROUGH SOCIAL MEDIA
BRING CHANGE 2 MIND

Bring Change 2 Mind, a nonprofit organization, seeks to counter the prevailing myths, misconceptions, and misinformation about mental illness. It was launched by Glenn Close and other organizations interested in changing public opinion about children, youth, and adults with emotional and behavioral disorders. Glenn's interests were spawned by her own interactions with her sister and nephew who are individuals with mental illnesses.

What follows are some recent story entries on the Bring Change 2 Mind website.

Community Story: Barb

My name is Barb Devine, and I was diagnosed as bipolar when I was 28. I'm now 46, and medication has greatly helped me manage my illness, but I understand everyone who has attempted suicide or is a cutter, as I've experienced both. But (and this a big but), those things are in the past, and I am so thankful that I can now enjoy life so fully.

That's my message, first and foremost—life is so worth living, and you can be bipolar and have a wonderful life. We have so much to share with the world, and it's so important that we educate others about the illness. WE ARE AMAZING PEOPLE!!!!!!!

Community Story: Lisa

I am a 39-year-old woman with bipolar disorder. I am a daughter, sister, wife, and mother. Being diagnosed with bipolar disorder was a blessing and in some ways a curse at first. I was young, 19 when I was diagnosed, my parents took me to a psychiatrist because I had spent over $5,000.00 in less than a month and couldn't tell them where or what I had bought. This was not the only reason they took me, but it was the capper to a long list of behaviors they knew were not normal and that were becoming increasingly out of control. After my diagnosis and the first cocktail of medications were prescribed, I spent much of the next 15 years fighting and self-sabotaging to believe everyone else was wrong and that I was in control of my mind and body. The only person that was wrong was me.

I now have faced the fact that there is only one way to be in control: through surrender. When I began to really be in a therapeutic relationship with my doctor and medication, it felt like the world "slowed down" and it is very often frustrating not be able to do five or six things all at the same time. Even with these small sacrifices I have found that the payoff of staying "level" is well worth it. I want people to know that with a good doctor, medication, and family support bipolar, people can be functional and productive members of society.

SOURCE: Bring Change 2 Mind (2012). *Barb* and *Lisa*. Retrieved June 20, 2012 from http://www.bringchange2mind .org/stories/entry/community-story-barb and http:// www.bringchange2mind.org/stories/entry/ community-story-lisa

Question for Reflection

What have you learned from these brief personal reflections about individuals with mental illnesses that is useful for you?

Assessment

Screening is the first step in the assessment process. It is designed to identify children and youth who may or may not present EBD. Once these children and youth are identified, teachers and other support personnel may provide targeted pre-referral interventions. These interventions are designed to address the presenting problems, often using **positive behavior support** (PBS) strategies without formally labeling the child or youth as having EBD (Vincent & Tobin, 2011). If the child or youth is unresponsive to these carefully conceived and applied interventions over time, a referral would be made for further observations and testing, thus potentially qualifying the child or youth for more intensive services and potential placements. We will speak more about PSB in the next section.

Screening, Pre-Referral Interventions, and Referral

Screening is based on the belief that early identification leads to early treatment, which may reduce the overall impact of the EBD on the individual, family, and community (Davis, Young, Hardman, & Winters, 2011; Eivers, Brendgen, & Borge, 2010). As suggested earlier in this chapter, significant numbers of children and youth with EBD are not identified, and thus do not receive appropriate services and interventions.

FOCUS 6

Identify five essential elements and goals of the assessment process and related practices.

Standard 8
Assessment

Positive behavior support (PBS)
A school-wide approach to supporting all children in developing highly functional social and academic skills supported by all teachers and school personnel through clearly stated expectations and powerful incentives.

Screening approaches are multiagent and multigated; that is, they do not rely on one professional, one method, or one observation for assessing a child or youth when EBD are suspected (Conroy, Hendrickson, & Hester, 2004). Screeners move through successive "gates" to identify children or youth for more intensive assessment and pre-referral interventions.

One such approach is systematic screening for behavior disorders (SSBD; see Walker & Severson, 1992). This approach has been very effective in identifying young children who need interventions and other services before being seriously considered for formal referrals for special education services. SSBD is a three-stage process, beginning with nominations by a general education teacher. Teachers think about the children in their classes and then group them according to various behavior patterns, some of which mirror the characteristics of children with EBD. Once the children have been grouped, each child is ranked within the group according to the severity and frequency of his or her behaviors. The last step is a series of systematic observations conducted in classrooms and in other school environments to see how the children, who were ranked most severely, behave in these environments. As children are progressively and systematically identified through this multiple-gating process, assessment team members determine which children ought to be considered for pre-referral interventions or other more intensive assessments.

Standard 10
Collaboration

Response to intervention (RTI)
A problem-solving structure to identify and address student difficulties using research-based instruction and interventions monitored over time.

Collaboration Pre-referral interventions are designed to address students' identified behavioral and academic problems and to reduce the likelihood of further, more restrictive placements. These interventions are applied generally when the academic and behavior challenges of children are more amenable to change and amelioration (Lane, 2007). Often these interventions are developed, planned, and implemented under the direction of multidisciplinary collaborative teams. Many states now require the application of scientifically based interventions specifically tailored to the needs of all students experiencing learning or behavior problems based on informal and formal assessments. Commonly referred to as the **response to intervention** (RTI), regular and special educators join together with other professionals in conducting ongoing assessments and applying carefully selected, evidence-based interventions in working with *all* children (Kurns & Tilly, 2008; Ryan, Pierce, & Mooney, 2008). These interventions and practices, often referred to as positive behavior support (PBS), hold great promise for helping students from diverse backgrounds and those with challenging behaviors remain and succeed in general education classrooms and in other less restrictive settings (Arter, 2007; Reinke, Herman & Tucker, 2006). PBS "is a systems approach for establishing a continuum of proactive, positive discipline procedures for all students and staff members in all types of school settings" (Eber, Sugai, Smith, & Scott, 2002, p. 171).

Instead of treating the symptom(s) and ignoring the underlying problems, the thrust of PBS is to address all the features and factors that may be related to a child's or youth's negative behaviors or academic challenges. The primary goals of PBS systems are improved behaviors for all children and youth at home, at school, and in the community; enhanced academic performance; and the prevention of serious violent, aggressive, or destructive behaviors (Lane, Kalberg, & Menzies, 2009).

Schools in which PBS systems are evident define school-wide expectations and rules; actively and regularly build social competence through active and intense teaching of social skills; provide rewards for targeted, prosocial behaviors; and make decisions on the basis of frequently collected, pertinent data (Gresham, Van, & Cook, 2006; Miller, Lane, & Wehby, 2005; Reinke, Herman, & Tucker, 2006; Meadows & Stevens, 2004). Additionally, collaborative teams of professionals develop and put into action individually tailored plans for students who present chronic, challenging behaviors. These plans evolve from carefully completed functional behavior assessments conducted by key individuals in the students' school, home, and community settings (Young, Calderella, Richardson, & Young, 2011).

Several response to intervention cycles using PBS would be applied before school administrators seriously considered any student for referral for special education services. In effect, RTI and PBS efforts are both proactive and preventive; that is, they are focused on helping any child or youth who is not succeeding in school as soon as possible and lessening the emergence of more serious learning or behavior problems.

The actual submission of a referral for a student is generally preceded by several parent–teacher conferences. These conferences help teachers and parents determine what actions should to be taken. For example, the student's difficulties may be symptomatic of family problems such as a parent's extended illness, marital difficulties, or severe financial challenges. If the parents and concerned teachers continue to be perplexed by a child's or youth's behavior, a referral may be initiated. Referrals are generally processed by school principals who review them, consult with parents, and then forward the referred families to a licensed psychologist or other qualified professionals.

Once a referral has been appropriately processed and a parent's or guardian's permission for testing and evaluation has been obtained, assessment team members carefully observe and assess the child's present levels of performance: intellectually, socially, academically, and emotionally. Their task is to determine whether the child has EBD and whether he or she qualifies for special education services.

Assessment Factors As we noted earlier in this chapter, emotional and behavioral disorders have many causes. Likewise, the behaviors of children and youth being assessed for EBD serve many throw a functions. In other words, behaviors are purposeful. For example, a young child may throw a tantrum to avoid schoolwork that is too difficult. Or a youth may engage in destructive behavior to gain attention that he or she does not otherwise derive from peers or parents.

Behavior is also a function of interactions with environmental factors. Some conditions set off negative behaviors, and other conditions reward or reinforce these same behaviors. Interpersonal factors—such as depression, anxiety, or erroneous interpretations of environment events—may contribute to a child's or youth's problems. If a child or youth is showing behaviors that are highly problematic, teachers and other professionals have an obligation to look at them from a functional point of view—that is, to see what purposes these behaviors serve and what conditions give rise to them.

Current IDEA regulations require assessment team members to conduct functional behavioral assessments and to document the impact of the EBD on the child's or youth's academic achievement (U.S. Department of Education, 2006; Witt, VanDerHeyden, & Gilbertson, 2004). Simply defined, "Function assessment is a collection of methods for obtaining information about antecedents [things a child experiences before the behavior of concern], behaviors [what the child does], and consequences [what the child experiences after the behavior of concern]. The purpose is to identify potential reasons for the behavior and to use the information to develop strategies that will support positive student performance while reducing the behaviors that interfere with the child's successful functioning" (Witt, Daly, & Noell, 2000, p. 3). The purpose of completing a function assessment is to identify the roles and purposes of a student's behavior in relationship to various school, home, or community settings (Scott & Kamps, 2007).

Assessment team members collect information through interviews, make careful observations, and examine the effects of probes or experimental manipulations over a period of several days. Through these procedures, team members, general education teachers, and parents discover reliable relationships among specific problem behaviors, the settings or events that give rise to these behaviors, and their consequences for the child or youth.

If the functional behavioral assessment is done well, it provides grounding for the development of behavior intervention plans (BIPs) that may be used to assist the child or youth in developing new, more useful behaviors for school and home (Arter, 2007; Etscheidt, 2006; Lane et al., 2007; Maag & Katsiyannis, 2006). Additionally, the BIP may include new curricular or instructional approaches tailored to the student's learning needs and preferences. The BIP may also identify changes to be implemented in the school setting or home. These might include peer and paraprofessional support, use of conflict resolution specialists, home-based specialists and programs, and other carefully selected interventions. In the end, BIPs seek to prevent problem behaviors, and in their place, build useful, functional behaviors that advance the youth's social, emotional, and academic development using evidence-based practices (Maag & Katsiyannis, 2006).

Assessment Techniques

Several techniques and procedures are used to identify children with EBD. As we have seen, the identification and classification of a child or youth with EBD is preceded by screening

CEC

Standard 8

Assessment

			0 = Not True (as far as you know) 1 = Somewhat or Sometimes True 2 = Very True or Often True
0	1	2	1. Acts too young for his/her age
0	1	2	5. There is very little he/she enjoys
0	1	2	10. Can't sit still, restless, or hyperactive
0	1	2	15. Cruel to animals
0	1	2	20. Destroys his/her own things
0	1	2	25. Doesn't get along with other kids
0	1	2	30. Fears going to school
0	1	2	35. Feels worthless or inferior
0	1	2	40. Hears sounds or voices that aren't there (describe):
0	1	2	45. Nervous, high strung, or tense
0	1	2	50. Too fearful or anxious

SOURCE: From Achenbach, 1. M., & Rescorla, L. A. *Manual for the ASEBA school-age forms and profiles.* Burlington, VT: University of Vermont, Research Center for Children, Youth, and Families. Copyright 2001 by L. M. Achenbach. Reproduced by permission.

When completing behavioral assessments, parents are asked to assess their child's behavior at home, such as how well the child interacts with siblings.

procedures accompanied by a functional behavior assessment, motivational assessments, teacher and parent interviews, diagnostic academic assessments, behavior checklists, a variety of sociometric devices (e.g., peer ratings), and the use of teacher and parent rating scales (Conroy & Brown, 2004; Cunningham & O'Neill, 2007; Rosenberg, Wilson, Maheady, & Sindelar, 2004).

Typically, parents and teachers are asked to respond to a variety of rating-scale items that describe behaviors related to various classifications of EBD. The number of items marked and the rating given to each item contribute to the behavior profiles generated from the ratings (see Figure 8.2). In making their assessments, parents and professionals are asked to consider the child's behavior during the past several months.

Strength-based assessment Assessment that rates a child's strengths and uses this information to develop a strength-centered individualized education program.

A positive development in assessing children and youth for EBD is **strength-based assessment** (Donovan & Nickerson, 2007; Epstein, 1998). In contrast to deficit-oriented instruments, this approach focuses on the child's or youth's strengths. One such instrument is the *Behavioral and Emotional Rating Scale—Second Edition* (BERS-2) (Epstein & Sharma, 1997). Using this instrument, parents, teachers, and other caregivers rate the child's or youth's strengths in several important areas, including interpersonal strength, involvement with family, intrapersonal assets, school functioning, and affective or emotional strengths. Clinicians use the BERS and other similar approaches to develop strength-centered, rather than deficit-centered, IEPs for children and youth with EBD (see Figure 8.3).

Once the screening process has been concluded, specialists or consultants—including psychologists, special educators, and social workers—complete in-depth assessments of the child's academic and social-emotional strengths and weaknesses in various settings. The assessment team may analyze the child with EBD in classroom and playground interactions

Figure 8.3 *Representative Items from the Behavioral and Emotional Rating Scale, Second Edition (BERS 2)*

0 = Not at all like the child		2 = Like the child		
1 = Not much like the child		3 = Very much like the child		

0	1	2	3	1. Demonstrates a sense of belonging to family
0	1	2	3	3. Accepts a hug
0	1	2	3	6. Acknowledges painful feelings
0	1	2	3	10. Uses anger management skills
0	1	2	3	15. Interacts positively with parents
0	1	2	3	30. Loses a game gracefully
0	1	2	3	34. Expresses affection for others
0	1	2	3	39. Pays attention in class

SOURCE: From the Epstein, M. H., & Sharma, J. (2004). *BERS-2 (Behavioral and Emotional Rating Scale)* 2nd ed. Austin, TX: Pro-Ed, Inc. Used with permission.

with peers, using functional behavioral assessment techniques; may administer various tests to evaluate personality, achievement, and intellectual factors; and may interview the parents and the child. Additionally, the assessment team may observe the child at home, again making use of functional behavioral assessment procedures.

A particularly complex problem for clinicians is the assessment of children and youth who have limited English proficiency and/or are culturally diverse (Goh, 2004; Obiakor et al., 2004). Unfortunately, many of these children and youth are disproportionately represented in special education settings for students with EBD (Osher et al., 2004). Some hope for optimism is merited, especially as practitioners collaborate and use functional behavioral assessment and related procedures, pre-referral interventions, and positive behavioral support (PBS) for all students (Lane, Kalberg, & Menzies, 2009).

CEC

Standard 4
Instructional Strategies

Standard 5
Learning Environments and Social Interactions

Standard 10
Collaboration

CASE STUDY TOBY

Toby is 10. Toby's day usually starts out with arguing with his parents about what he can and cannot bring to school.

Toby does not go to school on the bus. He gets teased and then retaliates immediately.

At the beginning of the school year he would flip desks, swear at the teacher, tear up his work, and refuse to do most things. Looking back, the reasons seem so trivial. He was not allowed to go to the bathroom, so he flipped his desk. He was told to stop tapping his pencil, so he swore at the teacher.

Recess is still the hardest time. Toby tells everyone that he has lots of friends, but if you watch what goes on in the lunchroom or on the playground, it is hard to figure out who they are. Some kids avoid him, but most would give him a chance if he wasn't so bossy. The playground supervisor tries to get him involved in a field hockey game every day. He isn't bad at it, but he will not pass the ball, so no one really wants him on his team.

At home, Toby asks his mom every day at about 4:30 if she will help him with a model or play a game. Each day she tells him she cannot right now as she is making supper. Each day he screams out that she doesn't ever do anything with him, slams the door, and goes in the other room and usually turns on the TV very loud. She comes up, tells him to turn it down three times. He doesn't and is sent to his room.

After supper Toby's dad takes over and they play some games together and usually it goes fine for about an hour. Then it usually ends in screaming.

SOURCE: Adapted from *ODD plus ADHD: Case Studies: Elementary School Toby—*, www.difficultstudents.com/2010/01/odd-plus-adhd-case-studies.html.

APPLICATION

1. What would you do as a teacher for and with Toby, if he were in your classroom?

2. Where would you go for help as his teacher?

3. Given what you have learned in this chapter, what are some recommendations that you would make to Toby's parents?

Interventions

CEC

Standard 3
Individual Learning Differences

Standard 4
Instructional Strategies

Standard 5
Learning Environments and Social Interactions

Standard 10
Collaboration

Wraparound approach (WRAP)
An intensive, complete, team/community approach of involving children and youth and their families so that they can thrive in their homes, local schools, and communities and develop the skills and behaviors needed for successful living and learning.

Cognitive-behavior therapy
Therapy that focuses on the role of thinking and language and how they influence behavior(s) and related feelings.

Historically, most children and youth with EBD received treatments and interventions in isolation from their families, homes, neighborhoods, and communities. These treatments and interventions were based on the assumption that students' problems were primarily of their own making. Services, if they were delivered at all, were rarely coordinated. Fragmentation was the rule (Eber & Keenan, 2004).

Multidisciplinary Collaboration: Systems of Care

Increasingly, care providers for children and youth with EBD are establishing systems of care (Adelman & Taylor, 2006; National Mental Health Information Center, 2006). One very promising practice is the **wraparound approach (WRAP)** (Eber, Breen, Rose, Unizycki, & London, 2008). "Wraparound is not a service or set of services; it is a [collaborative] planning process. This process is used to build consensus within a team of professionals, family members, and natural support providers to improve the effectiveness, efficiency, and relevance of supports and services developed for children and their families" (Eber et al., 2002, p. 173). We will have more to say about the wraparound process in subsequent sections of this chapter.

Community-based and family-centered systems for delivering services to children and youth with EBD are also emerging. In these systems, educational, medical, and community care providers are beginning to pay greater attention to youth with EBD and their families, as well as to the communities in which they live (see Figure 8.4). This new approach is based on several core values and guiding principles (see Figure 8.5). One of the basic features of the systems of care concept is that it does not represent a prescribed structure for assembling a network of services and agencies. Rather, it reflects a philosophy about the way in which services should be delivered to children, youth, and their families. The child and family become the focus of the delivery system, with vital services surrounding them. These services might include home-based interventions, special class placement, therapeutic foster care, financial assistance, primary health care, outpatient treatment, career education, after-school programs, and carefully tailored family support.

An integral part of the systems of care is school-wide primary prevention (Adelman & Taylor, 2006; Eber et al., 2008). Interventions associated with this kind of prevention include systems for positive behavior support (PBS), response to intervention (RTI) practices as identified earlier, multidisciplinary collaboration, teaching conflict resolution, emotional literacy, **cognitive-behavioral therapy**, and anger management for all students in the school—not just to those identified with EBD (Guerra, Boxer, & Kim, 2005; Mayer, Lochman, & Van Acker, 2005; Powell et al., 2011; Robinson, 2007; Ryan, Pierce, & Mooney, 2008). These kinds of interventions can prevent 75 to 85 percent of student adjustment and behavior problems.

Figure 8.4 The System of Care Framework

Figure 8.5 *Core Values and Guiding Principles of Systems of Care*

Core Values

1. The system of care should be child-centered and family-focused, with the needs of the child and family dictating the types and mix of services provided.

2. The system of care should be community-based, with the locus of services as well as management and decision-making responsibility resting at the community level.

3. The system of care should be culturally competent, with agencies, programs, and services that are responsive to the cultural, racial, and ethnic differences of the population they serve.

Guiding Principles

1. Children with emotional disturbances should have access to a comprehensive array of services that address physical, emotional, social, and educational needs.

2. Children with emotional disturbances should receive individualized services in accordance with the unique needs and potentials of each child and guided by an individualized service plan.

3. Children with emotional disturbances should receive services within the least restrictive, most normative environment that is clinically appropriate.

4. The families and surrogate families of children with emotional disturbances should be full participants in all aspects of the planning and delivery of services.

5. Children with emotional disturbances should receive services that are integrated, with linkages between child-serving agencies and programs and mechanisms for planning, developing, and coordinating services.

6. Children with emotional disturbances should be provided with case management or similar mechanisms to ensure that multiple services are delivered in a coordinated and therapeutic manner and that they can move through the system of services in accordance with their changing needs.

7. Early identification and intervention for children with emotional disturbances should be promoted by the system of care to enhance the likelihood of positive outcomes.

8. Children with emotional disturbances should be ensured smooth transitions to the adult service system as they reach maturity.

9. The rights of children with emotional disturbances should be protected, and effective advocacy efforts for children and youth with emotional disturbances should be promoted.

10. Children with emotional disturbances should receive services without regard to race, religion, national origin, sex, physical disability, or other characteristics, and services should be sensitive and responsive to cultural differences and special needs.

SOURCE: From Stroul, B., & Friedman, R. M. (1986). *A system of care for children and adolescents with severe emotional disturbances.* rev. ed. (p. xxiv). Washington, D.C.: Georgetown University Child Development Center, National Technical Assistance Center for Children's Mental Health. Copyright 1986 by B. Stroul and R. M. Friedman, Reprinted by permission.

The Early Childhood Years: Multidisciplinary/ Multiagency Collaboration

Standard 4
Instructional Strategies

Standard 6
Communication

Standard 7
Instructional Planning

Standard 8
Assessment

Standard 10
Collaboration

"Increasingly, it is understood that serious and persistent challenging behaviors in early childhood are associated with subsequent problems in socialization, school adjustment, school success, and educational and vocational adaptation in adolescence and adulthood" (Dunlap et al., 2006, p. 29). The early childhood years are vitally important for all children; but they are particularly crucial for young children with EBD—young children who are consistently noncompliant, defiant, oppositional, destructive, aggressive, and so on (Whitted, 2011). Recent research suggests that EBD can be successfully prevented and ameliorated by developing within young children the skills and dispositions needed for successful schooling, relationships, and community connections (Maag & Katsiyannis, 2010). Many children would not develop serious EBD if they and their families received early, child-centered, intensive, community-based, and family-focused services and interventions. Moreover, the cost of delivering these prevention services would be far less than that of providing services to these same individuals as teens, young adults, and adults. Society seems unwilling to make investments that would yield remarkable financial, social, and emotional dividends for us, our children, and our communities (Lopes, 2005). Key elements of the prevention process include early identification, family-driven needs assessment, home-based and community-based interventions, parent training, and collaboration with an array of educational and community agencies (Dunlap et al., 2006; Hester et al., 2004; Kendziora, 2004).

Interventions for young children with EBD are child-, family-, and home-centered. Often they are directed at reducing the impacts of the EBD, replacing challenging behaviors with more functional ones, and preventing more serious emotional and behavioral problems from developing (Dunlap et al., 2006; Joseph & Strain, 2003; Kendziora, 2004). Thus, the goals associated with individualized family service plans (IFSPs) go well beyond the typical educational goals found in individualized education programs (IEPs) for older children. Interventions for young children with EBD include teaching them to manage their feelings; developing empathy skills (how to read and interpret others' behaviors); problem solving (how to take turns and ask for help, and to develop self-control); and learning how to manage impulses, how to delay gratification, and how to deal with anger (Whitted, 2011). Additionally, interventions are directed at building positive replacement behaviors for challenging behaviors, promoting appropriate social interactions with peers and others, and creating positive behavioral supports across a child's natural environments (Essa, 2003; Hester et al., 2004; Powell et al., 2011).

CEC

Standard 6
Communication

Children with emotional/behavior disorders can pose challenges for general education teachers.

Family-centered interventions focus on respite care; parent training directed at managing the young child with EBD at home and in other community settings; the delivery of family, marital, or drug therapy; treatment for maternal depression; and the provision of specialized day care or day treatment. The nature, intensity, and duration of these multiagency services and interventions are determined by the needs of the families and the

Catherine Ledner/Stone+/Getty Images

speed with which they develop new skills and coping strategies. The interventions are delivered in multiple contexts—the places where children, family members, and others play, work, learn, and associate.

Often the interventions for young children with EBD are directed at functional communication skills—learning how to get attention, learning how to make a request, or recruiting praise; developing appropriate social interaction with siblings, parents, and peers; learning targeted and useful social skills; and mastering developmentally appropriate tasks. Also, in keeping with the movement toward inclusion, family intervention and transition specialists are focused on preparing young children for successful participation in less restrictive environments (Kennedy et al., 2001).

The Elementary School Years

CEC

Standard 4
Instructional Strategies

Standard 5
Learning Environments and Social Interaction

Standard 8
Assessment

Standard 10
Collaboration

Elementary children with EBD often present overlapping behavioral problems. These problems center on accepting appropriate consequences, building appropriate academic skills, interacting successfully with others, using self control, following directions, and expressing strong feelings appropriately. Such behaviors become the focus of intervention efforts. With the assistance of parents, IEP team members strive to construct a complete picture of each child, determining his or her present levels of intellectual, social, emotional, and academic performance and the contexts that give rise to and support these behaviors (Beard & Sugai, 2004). These levels of performance and the outcomes derived from the functional behavioral assessment become the basis for identifying important goals for the child's IEP and for developing behavior intervention plans (Lewis, Lewis-Palmer, Newcomer, & Stichter, 2004).

EARLY CHILDHOOD YEARS

Tips for the Family

- Become involved with parent training and other community support services.
- Work collaboratively with multidisciplinary personnel (educators, social workers, health care professionals, and parent–group volunteers) in developing effective child management strategies.
- Use the same evidence-based intervention strategies at home that are applied in the preschool settings.
- Establish family routines, schedules, and incentive systems that reward and build positive behaviors.
- Participate actively in advocacy or parent–support groups.
- Understand your rights regarding health care, education, and social services benefits.

Tips for the Preschool Teacher

- Work collaboratively with the multidisciplinary professionals in your preschool (the director, psychologist, social worker, parent trainers, special educators, and health care professionals) to identify evidence-based instructional strategies.
- Establish clear schedules, class routines, rules, and positive consequences for all children in your classroom.
- Create a learning and social environment that is nurturing for everyone.
- Explicitly teach social behaviors (e.g., following directions, greeting other children, sharing toys, using words to express anger, etc.) to all children.
- Ask for help from the multidisciplinary teacher support team—remember collaboration is the key to success.

Tips for Preschool Personnel

- Engage older socially competent peers to assist with academic readiness and social skills training.
- Help others (teaching assistants, aides, volunteers, etc.) know what to do in managing children with challenging behaviors.
- Make every effort to involve children with EBD in school-wide activities and special performances.
- Orient and teach preschool children without disabilities about how to appropriately respond to classmates with challenging behaviors such as ignoring, walking away, getting help from the teacher, and so on.
- Collaborate with parents in using the same management systems and strategies in your preschool classroom as those used in the home.

Tips for Neighbors and Friends

- Become familiar with the things you can do as a neighbor or friend in responding to the challenging behaviors of a neighborhood child with EBD.
- Be patient with parents who are attempting to cope with their child's temper tantrums or other challenging behaviors in community settings (such as at a grocery store, in the mall, etc.).
- Assist parents who would benefit from some time away from their preschooler by offering respite care for short periods of time.
- Involve the neighborhood child with EBD in your family activities.
- Encourage parents to involve their child in neighborhood and community events (e.g., parades, holiday celebrations, and birthday parties).

ELEMENTARY YEARS

Tips for the Family

- Use the effective management techniques that are being applied in your child's classroom in your home environment.
- Establish clear rules, set routines, and consequences that are consistent with your child's developmental age and interests.
- Obtain counseling when appropriate for yourself, your other children, and your spouse from community mental health agencies or other public or private sources.
- Help your other children and their friends understand the things they can do to support your child with EBD.

Tips for General Education Classroom Teacher

- Provide a positive, structured classroom/learning environment (e.g., clearly stated rules, helpful positive and negative consequences, well-conceived classroom schedules, carefully taught classroom routines, and solid relationship building activities).
- Teach social skills (dealing with bullying, accepting criticism, etc.) to all of the children with the help of members of the school's multidisciplinary teacher assistance team.
- Teach self-management skills (goal selection, self-monitoring, self-reinforcement, etc.) to all children with the aid of members of the school's multidisciplinary teacher assistance team.
- Promote the positive peer interaction that develops positive relationships among students.
- Ask for targeted help from members of your school's multidisciplinary teacher assistance team or the youth's parents.

Tips for School Personnel

- Use same-age or cross-age peers to provide tutoring, coaching, and other kinds of assistance in developing the academic and social skills of children with EBD.
- Establish school-wide management programs and positive behavioral supports that reinforce individual and group accomplishments.
- Work closely and collaboratively with members of the multidisciplinary teacher assistance team to create a school environment that is positive and caring.
- Use collaborative problem-solving techniques in dealing with difficult or

persistent behavior problems—work with your school multidisciplinary teacher assistance team.

- Help all children in the school develop an understanding of how to appropriately respond to students with challenging behaviors.

Tips for Neighbors and Friends

- Involve the child with EBD in appropriate after-school activities (recreational events, informal sports, etc.).

- Invite the child to spend time with your family in appropriate excursions and recreational activities (swimming, hiking, boating, etc.).

- Teach your children how to support appropriate behaviors and how to ignore inappropriate behaviors when they occur.

- As a youth leader, coach, or recreational specialist, get to know each child with behavior disorders well so that you can respond with confidence when providing support and potential corrections/consequences.

SECONDARY AND TRANSITION YEARS

Tips for the Family

- Continue your efforts to focus on the positive behaviors of your child with EBD.

- Assist your child in understanding and selecting appropriate postsecondary training, education, and/or employment.

- Give yourself a regular break from the task of being a parent and engage in activities that are totally enjoyable for you.

- Seek help from community mental health services, clergy, or a close friend when you are feeling overwhelmed or stressed.

- Consult regularly with support personnel to monitor progress and develop ideas for maintaining the behavioral and academic gains made by your child.

- Maintain involvement in advocacy and parent–support groups.

Tips for General Education Classroom Teacher

- Create positive relationships within your classroom with cooperative learning teams and group-oriented assignments.

- Engage all students in creating standards for conduct as well as consequences for positive and negative behaviors.

- Provide relevant/engaging instruction.

- Incorporate your students' interests and strengths.

- Focus your efforts on developing a positive relationship with students with EBD by greeting them regularly in your class, informally talking with them at appropriate times, attending to improvements in their performance, and becoming aware of their interests and concerns.

- Promote the positive peer interactions that develop positive relationships among students.

- Work closely with the members of the school multidisciplinary teacher assistance team to be aware of teacher behaviors that may positively or adversely affect the student's performance.

- Understand that changes in behavior often occur very gradually with periods of regression and sometimes tumult.

Tips for School Personnel

- Create a school climate that is positive and supportive.

- Provide students with an understanding of their roles and responsibilities in responding to peers with disabilities.

- Engage peers in providing social skills training, job coaching, and academic tutoring.

- Engage members of the school multidisciplinary teacher assistance team to help you deal with crisis situations and to provide other supportive therapies and interventions.

- Establish school-wide procedures for dealing quickly and efficiently with particularly difficult behaviors.

Tips for Neighbors, Friends, and Potential Employers

- If you have some expertise in a content area (such as math, English, history, etc.), offer to provide assistance with homework or other related school assignments for students with EBD.

- Provide opportunities for students with EBD to be employed in your business.

- Give parents an occasional respite by inviting the adolescent with EBD to join your family for a cookout, movie night, or other family-oriented activities.

- Encourage other children and adolescents to volunteer as peer partners, job coaches, and social skills trainers.

- Do not allow others to tease, harass, or ridicule an adolescent with behavior disorders in your presence.

ADULT YEARS

Tips for the Family

- Build on efforts to develop appropriate independence and interdependence.

- Maintain contact with appropriate multidisciplinary personnel (health care professionals and social services personnel), particularly if the adult with EBD is on medication or receiving counseling.

- Work collaboratively with appropriate adult service agencies that are required by law to assist with your adult child's employment, housing, and recreation.

- Prepare your other children or other caregivers as appropriate to assume the responsibilities that you may be unable to assume over time.

Tips for Neighbors, Friends, and Employers

- As an employer, be willing to make sensible and reasonable adjustments in the work environments.

- Understand adjustments that may need to take place with new medications or treatment regimens.

- Get to know the individual as a person—his/her likes or dislikes, who they admire, and preferred leisure activities.

- Be willing to involve the individual in appropriate holiday and special occasion events such as birthdays, athletic activities, and other social gatherings.

- Understand what might be irritating or uncomfortable to the individual.

- Be available to communicate with others who may be responsible for the individual's well-being—a job coach, an independent living specialist, and others.

Typically, programs for children with EBD focus on replacing maladaptive with adaptive behaviors, increasing self-regulation, building appropriate academic skills and dispositions, increasing self-awareness, increasing cooperative behavior, and acquiring age-appropriate self-control (Lane, Kalberg, & Menzies, 2009). Children need these skills and behaviors to succeed in their classrooms, homes, and communities.

In the past, many programs for children with EBD were restrictive, controlling, and punitive in nature. Rather than teaching new behaviors, these programs focused on controlling the behaviors of children and youth. These programs employed the **curriculum of control** (Knitzer, Steinberg, & Fleisch, 1990) or the *curriculum of noninstruction* (Shores & Wehby, 1999, p. 196). Rather than developing replacement behaviors or new behaviors, children and youth in many of these programs languished or regressed. Even today, many children and youth with behavior disorders are served in settings that remove them from natural interactions with students without disabilities. Some of these programs are boot camp–like in nature (Jeter, 2010). Most young people with EBD have friends that are neighborhood-based rather than school-centered—just the opposite of young people without disabilities.

Curriculum of control
Classroom routines, structures, and instructional strategies focused on controlling children rather than teaching them success-related behaviors.

Collaboration: Wraparound Services

New systems of care for children and adolescents with EBD have emerged (Eber & Keenan, 2004; Eber, Hyde, & Suter, 2011). As mentioned earlier, these systems deliver wraparound services to children and youth with EBD and their families (Eber et al., 2008) (see Reflect on This, "Henry: Wraparound"). As is implied by the word *wraparound*, children, youth, and their families receive the support they need to address the problems uncovered through carefully conducted assessments. Preliminary research regarding the provision of these services is very positive for youth with complex and challenging EBD. Results include successfully living at home, positive emotional and behavioral growth, reduced recidivism rates for delinquent-related behaviors, and better performance at school as evidenced in improved attendance and grades (Eber, Hyde, & Suter, 2011).

Services may include in-home child management training, employment assistance, and family therapy—whatever is needed to help families become successful. Figure 8.6 reveals essential phases of wraparound systems and related programs.

Again, at the heart of many new programs is positive behavioral support (PBS). Instead of trying to exclusively control behaviors, teachers, parents, and clinicians collaborate, working together to build new replacement behaviors—behaviors that are highly regarded and especially functional in school, home, and community settings.

As highlighted in the assessment section of this chapter, professionals use functional behavioral assessment to determine the patterns and functions of certain behaviors. Once these patterns and functions are well understood, teachers, parents, and others help children and youth with EBD develop new behaviors, grow academically, achieve worthwhile goals, and learn how to deal with their thoughts and feelings in positive ways (Beard & Sugai, 2004).

Children who exhibit moderate to severe EBD may be served in special classes (see Reflect on This, "Henry: Wraparound"). In some school systems, special classes are found in elementary, middle, and high schools. They may be grouped in small clusters of two to three classes in selected buildings. Other special classes may be found within hospital units, special schools, residential programs, juvenile units, and other specialized treatment facilities.

Most special classes for children with moderate to severe disorders share certain characteristics. The first is a high degree of structure and specialized instruction: In other words, rules are clear and consistently enforced; helpful routines are in place; high-quality academic and social instruction is provided; and both adult–child relationships and child–child relationships are fostered and developed (Kauffman, Bantz, & McCullough, 2002; Rorie, Gottfredson, Cross, Wilson, & Connell, 2011). Other features include close teacher monitoring of student performance, frequent feedback, and reinforcement based on students' academic and social behaviors. Students learn how to express themselves, how to address individual and group problems, and how to deal effectively with very strong feelings and emotions. Often point systems or token economies are used, although some concerns have been raised about these systems. These systems provide students with a specific number of points or tokens when they maintain certain behaviors or achieve certain goals. The points can be exchanged for various rewards, such as treats, school supplies, or activities that students enjoy. Furthermore, all members of special classes are well informed about behavioral and academic expectations (see Figure 8.7). One

Standard 5
Learning Environments and Social Interactions

Standard 10
Collaboration

Standard 8
Assessment

Standard 4
Instructional Strategies
Standard 5
Learning Environments and Social Interactions

Figure 8.6 *Phases of the Wraparound Process*

Phase I: Engagement and Team Preparation
Facilitator . . .

- Meets with family and key team members to gather their perspectives.
- Guides family to generate a strengths list (multiple settings and perspectives) and a list of needs.
- Generates a team member list, which includes natural supports, with the family.
- Documents and shares baseline data about student's strengths/needs.

Phase II: Initial Plan Development
Team . . .

- Begins regular meeting schedule.
- Documents and reviews strengths and needs data (home/school/community).
- Chooses a few needs for team to focus action planning, with special priority assigned to family concerns.
- Develops an intervention plan (including function-based behavior supports as needed) to respond to home, school, and community strengths/needs.
- Assesses community supports/resources available to meet needs identified by family.

Phase III: Plan Implementation and Refinement
Team . . .

- Documents accomplishments of student and team at each meeting.
- Meets frequently, checking follow-through and assessing progress of different interventions.
- Receives regular documentation including data and plan updates.
- Facilitates ongoing communication among those providing interventions in home, school, and community.

Phase IV: Transition Team . . .

- Discusses transitioning out of wraparound.
- Considers the concerns of all team members in transition planning.
- Communicates methods for future access to services to all team members.
- Negotiates methods of introducing student and family to future teachers or providers.

SOURCE: Adapted from Eber, L., Breen, K., Rose, J., Unizycki, R. M., & London, T. H. (2008, July/August). Wraparound as a tertiary level intervention for students with emotional/behavioral needs. *Teaching Exceptional Children*, *40*(6), p. 19. Copyright © 2008 Council for Exceptional Children (CEC)

TEACHSOURCE VIDEO
CLASSROOM MANAGEMENT

Please visit the Education CourseMate website for *Human Exceptionality*, 11th edition, at CengageBrain.com to access this chapter's TeachSource video, "Classroom Management: Handling a Student with Behavior Problems." You have just returned to your classroom. Outside the classroom you see Peter, one of your students. You use your best skills to have him reenter the classroom. He refuses verbally and physically to respond to your request. Ellen Henry, a student support coach, provides us with some powerful commentary on how she handled the situation and how her actions played out with Peter. Give some thought to the skills and dispositions you will need to be an inclusive teacher, helping children and youth with behavior disorders grow if not thrive in your classroom or other comparable settings.

1. Do you agree with how Ellen Henry handled this situation with Peter? How might you have handled it differently?

2. Who is available to help you when your best efforts are ineffective?

3. What do you think would really help Peter in these moments of stark resistance and intense emotions?

Figure 8.7 *Point Card for IEP Goals*

Name: _____ Date: _____ September 25 _____

1. My IEP goal today is: Raising my hand to get teacher help, to answer questions, or to participate in class discussions:

Goal "Positives"	Goal " Negative"		Percent "Positives"
///	//		8/10 = 80%

2. Returned Daily Home Note: Yes _X_   No ___   Points Earned on Daily Home Note __10__

3. Bus Report: Poor __X__   Good _____   Excellent _____   Points Earned on Bus Report __3__

DEBATE FORUM EMERGENCY ROOMS: THE BEST PLACE FOR ROUTINE CARE OF CHILDREN AND YOUTH WITH MENTAL ILLNESSES?

Estimates of hospital emergency department use by children and youth with mental health problems range from 200,000 to over 825,000 visits annually. Mental health–related emergency department visits range from 2 percent to 5 percent of all pediatric hospital emergency department visits. In rural areas, 5 percent of all pediatric emergency department visits and 10 percent of all psychiatric-related emergency department visits are from children and youth with mental health problems. Despite the small number of national studies that comprehensively examine this issue, various local and statewide studies provide a portrait of the escalating increases in the use of hospital emergency departments by children and youth for mental health treatment:

- Over a four-year period, one emergency department experienced a 59 percent increase in mental health–related visits to the emergency department compared to a 20 percent increase in nonpsychiatric-related visits over the same time period.

- Over a six-year period in Connecticut, emergency departments witnessed a 110 percent increase in child mental health–related emergencies.

- A six-year study showed that overall hospital emergency department visits grew by 43 percent, with pediatric and pediatric mental health–related visits increasing by 72 percent and 102 percent, respectively.

Adapted from the National Center for Children in Poverty, *Child and Youth Emergency Mental Health Care (Unclaimed Children Revisited*, Issue Brief No. 1, June 1, 2010).

POINT

Affordable, community-based, mental health care should be available to all children and youth. The emergency room should not be the primary or sole option for mental health care. Children, youth, and families experiencing profound needs for mental health care and services should not be pushed to emergency rooms for needed care. Access to quality mental health care should be considered a basic human right, not a privilege of the financially able. Emergency rooms should be used for emergency care, not as a substitute for community-based mental health care and related services.

COUNTERPOINT

Universal health care, including mental health care, is not a fundamental right. It is a personal responsibility of each family to provide. Establishing a universal health care system would reward individuals who are unwilling to take responsibility for their own well-being and would undermine self-reliance. Also, government-run systems are far less effective financially than private-sector systems in delivering quality care. The focus on mental health care ought to be prevention not treatment.

What Do You Think? Please visit the Education CourseMate website for Human Exceptionality, *11th edition, to access and respond to questions related to the Debate Forum.*

REFLECT ON THIS
HENRY: WRAPAROUND

"Henry," a student at Sunnyside Elementary School, had extremely poor attendance, failing grades, and poor homework completion. He had experienced trouble with the law in the community, which resulted in a court-assigned probation officer and a mandated Department of Children and Family Services (DCFS) counselor.

FIRST PHASE

During the first phase of wraparound, engagement and team preparation, Henry's family was introduced to the wraparound program. When Henry's mother shared a pamphlet she had been given for a short-term residential treatment center, the school social worker started the conversation by offering Henry's mother the opportunity to develop a comprehensive support plan so Henry could experience success in his own home, school, and community settings.

SECOND PHASE

In the second phase of wraparound, initial plan development, the team identified and documented Henry's strengths and needs. Henry's strengths included a good relationship with his teacher, responsiveness to positive attention from adults he liked, leadership among his peers, and effective self-advocacy. The school social worker helped the team identify two big needs for Henry: (1) "Henry needs to feel as if he fits in with the other kids at school," and (2) "Henry needs to feel successful at school." By focusing on needs rather than problems, Henry's team changed the tone of both meetings and interventions from reactive to proactive. Rather than using pre-existing interventions or services that are more deficit-oriented, the team designed interventions to respond to Henry's unique strengths and needs.

Because Henry had a positive relationship with his teacher, he was included in the check-and-connect intervention being delivered to other students in the school, some of whom were not on wraparound plans. Henry's teacher would greet him each morning by saying, "Thank you for coming; I am so glad you are here today." Henry and his teacher would talk about the individual behavior goals listed on his daily point card. This intervention was selected because Henry's expected behavior could be "corrected" in advance and positive behavior encouraged in other settings, with extra support or reminders as needed.

Henry's plan included strategies that he selected along with his family and teachers and that were based on his expressed strengths and needs. For example, he joined the school safety patrol, with the goal of acting as a positive role model; this helped him monitor and improve his own behavior in the hallways.

THIRD PHASE

In the third phase of wraparound, plan implementation and refinement, the team focused on (1) regularly using data for decision making; (2) checking with the family, student, and teacher(s) to ensure that the plan was working; (3) adjusting the wraparound plan based on feedback from team members; and (4) addressing additional needs that may have been identified but were not priorities at the onset of the wraparound process. . . .

Classroom interventions included homework adjustments, fewer spelling words, checking that Henry understood directions and extra reading support in class from the Title I teacher. In addition, the team designed unique progress criteria for Henry so he could be eligible for the school-wide Student of the Month recognition. His classroom duties included putting stickers on the homework chart for everyone in class. The school also referred Henry and his family to a local interagency network so they could receive financial support to participate in community recreation activities.

FOURTH PHASE

During the fourth phase, transition, Henry's accomplishments will continue to be reviewed and celebrated. The team will develop a transition plan to ensure success as it adjusts to less frequent team meetings and/or moves to natural supports without the ongoing wraparound team. As Henry's school performance improved, the team had to plan for increasing the use of natural supports and for ensuring successes during and after summer breaks.

Questions for Reflection

- What are the advantages of helping Henry succeed in his own home setting and neighborhood rather than treating him in a residential treatment center?

- How do we help students like Henry feel successful at school when they may not naturally have some of the necessary social skills for making and sustaining friendships?

- Given what you know about the wraparound process, what are the natural supports in a child's life? How can they be strengthened?

SOURCE: Adapted From Eber, L., Breen, K., Rose, J., Unizycki, R. M., & London, T. H. (2008). Wraparound: A tertiary level intervention for students with emotional/behavioral needs. *Teaching Exceptional Children*, 40(6), 18–21.

of the greatest challenges in teaching and treating students with EBD is treatment intensity and generalization—having them use their newly learned knowledge and social skills outside their "treatment" environments or special class settings—at home, in the community, and in the workplace (Maag, 2006; Gresham, Van, & Cook, 2006).

In addition to behaviorally oriented interventions, students may also receive individual counseling or group and family therapy (Wicks-Nelson & Israel, 2006). Also, many children with EBD profit from carefully prescribed and monitored drug therapies and regimens— about 50 percent of the youth identified with behavior disorders take medications for their conditions (Konopasek & Forness, 2004; Shoenfeld & Konopasek, 2007; U.S. Department of Education, 2005). These medications help students who struggle with depression, hyperactivity, impaired attention, and mood variations. These medications may be prescribed by a psychiatrist, pediatrician, or primary-care physician.

The Adolescent Years

Individually and collectively, adolescents with EBD pose significant challenges for parents, teachers, and other care providers. These problems include violent exchanges with parents and others, delinquency, school refusal, bullying, fighting, withdrawal, substance abuse, and other difficult behaviors. In the past, interventions and programs for adolescents with EBD, like those created for elementary children, were often punitive, controlling, and negative.

Multidisciplinary Collaboration

Fortunately, perspectives and practices are changing. Professionals in education, medicine, social work, and mental health are developing systems of care. Again, these systems of care are characterized by family-friendly, multidisciplinary collaborations (Kendziora, Bruns, Osher, Pacchiano, & Mejia, 2001; Woodruff et al., 1999). Ideally, the care is community-based, family-driven, individualized, based on strengths rather than weaknesses, sensitive to diversity, and team-based. In these systems, the knowledge and views of parents and family members are taken very seriously. Parents and key providers help design, shape, and assess interventions and transition programs (Sitlington & Neubert, 2004). If a family needs parent training, family therapy, and employment assistance, the agencies and school work together to provide these services. If the youth needs services beyond those typically delivered in a school, they are secured.

Another approach that is beginning to gather momentum is **individualized care (IC)**. IC is also linked to the wraparound approach (WRAP). As you recall, WRAP focuses on improving the outcomes for children and adolescents with EBD through coordinated, flexible

Standard 4
Instructional Strategies

Standard 5
Learning Environments and Social Interactions

Standard 8
Assessment

Standard 10
Collaboration

Standard 10
Collaboration

Individualized care (IC)
Improving the outcomes for children and adolescents with EBD through coordinated, flexible approaches to integrated, family-centered care.

ASSISTIVE TECHNOLOGY
EASYCHILD: ENCOURAGEMENT SYSTEM

EasyChild is a wonderful piece of software that provides parents with excellent tools for encouraging and supporting positive behaviors in their children and students. After entering basic information about the child, parents may produce weekly behavior charts, token incentive systems, graphic summaries of performance, privileges charts, and management and encouragement-support materials. Charts and graphs are easily produced

EasyChild Software, 2009. Encourage Software

for refrigerator placement and for monitoring the child's ongoing behavior. The software also provides a means for parents to handle major incidents with advance planning, and establishing appropriate rules and consequences (EasyChild Software, 2006).

approaches to integrated, family-centered care. Rather than being provided to students in school settings or at a mental health agency exclusively, these services are delivered to children and adolescents, their parents, and families where they are needed—frequently in their homes. Henry's case provides powerful examples of IC and WRAP in action (see Reflect on This, "Henry: Wraparound").

Increasingly, mental health professionals are readying young people with EBD for additional education, employment, and fuller participation in our neighborhoods and communities (Benitez, Lattimore, & Wehmeyer, 2005). With recent advances in psychotropic medications and other innovative interventions, entry into meaningful schooling and employment for youth with behavior disorders is now a greater reality. Features associated with successful programs include program locations that are unique and separate from adult program sites, a focus on strengths and assets of each respective youth, access to a range of transitional housing options, and individually tailored, youth-friendly interventions (Woolsey & Katz-Leavey, 2008).

Gangs

In the United States, youth gangs represent the largest segment of criminally active, peer-centered groups. Prominent researchers view gang affiliation as a developmental phenomenon emanating from a variety of family, neighborhood, and other contextual variables, some of which include access and exposure to deviant peers and relatives, nonintact families, unsafe neighborhoods, availability and access to drugs, high community crime rates, and poor schools (Dodge, Dishion, & Lansford, 2006; Howell & Egley, 2005, 2008; Short & Hughes, 2006). As indicated earlier in this chapter, 42 percent of youth in correctional facilities are young people with identified EBD, often referred to as socially maladjusted or delinquent (Burrell & Warboys, 2000).

The primary age range for gang members is 12 to 24 years of age. The peak range for gang activity and involvement is 15 to 16 years of age. Adolescents who are chronically delinquent or who are found guilty of felony offenses (e.g., physical assault, armed robbery) present considerable challenges for parents and community members. Additionally, the proliferation of gangs in many communities poses serious problems for schools, teachers, law enforcement officers, and gang members themselves (Borg & Dalla, 2005).

Youth join gangs for a variety of reasons. Many join for social reasons—wanting to be around friends and family, siblings or cousins who are already members of gangs. Others join gangs for protection, believing gang membership will protect them from others who might hurt them. And some join gangs for the financial benefits derived from selling drugs and engaging in other related activities (National Gang Center, 2011a).

A variety of community conditions give rise to gangs, including economically challenged neighborhoods—where essential social institutions operate feebly, including poorly functioning schools, families, and economic support systems. Parents and families may be largely unsuccessful in their attempts to socialize their children. In some instances, parents push away or alienate their children, thus losing their capacity to socialize and positively impact them. Also, many youth in these neighborhoods have a great deal of discretionary time that is devoid of adult supervision or mentoring. Often gangs are intergenerational, in part because of limited access to standard attractive career paths such as solid adult employment (National Gang Center, 2011b).

Standard 2
Development and
Characteristics of Learners

Many youth involved in gangs mirror the characteristics and behaviors associated with conduct disorders discussed earlier in the classification section of this chapter. As early as first grade, antisocial behaviors and learning failure are significant predictors of potential gang involvement. Again, family factors related to gang involvement include minimal or no parental support or supervision, alcohol and drug abuse, poverty, abuse and neglect, and single or no-parent families (youth being raised by grandparents or others). Availability of drugs, unsafe neighborhoods, low-quality schools, inconsistent or negative social norms—all of these community factors contribute to gang membership and related behaviors (Howell & Egley, 2008).

Generally speaking, gang prevention, boot camps, and suppression programs have not been particularly effective (Borg & Dalla, 2005; Jeter, 2010; Thornberry, Krohn, Lizotte, Smith, & Tobin, 2003). In part, this lack of success is clearly a reflection of the inherent challenges in addressing larger societal issues such as poverty, racism, and discrimination.

Inclusive Education

The term **full inclusion** is generally defined as the delivery of appropriate, specialized services to children or adolescents with EBD or other disabilities in general education settings. These services are usually directed at improving students' social skills, helping them develop satisfactory relationships with peers and teachers, building targeted academic skills, and improving the attitudes of peers without disabilities.

Another aspect of the full-inclusion movement is that some professionals have recommended elimination of the present delivery systems. These options would be replaced by a model in which all students, regardless of disabling condition, would be educated in their neighborhood schools. These schools would serve all students with disabilities, including those with EBD; thus, special schools, special classes, and other placements associated with the typical continuum of placements would no longer be available. Despite the emphasis on inclusion, many students with EBD are served in settings separated from general education classrooms. In fact, students with EBD are far more likely to be served in special schools and separate facilities than students with learning disabilities, mental retardation, and hearing impairments (U.S. Department of Education, 2011). About 17 percent of all students identified as having EBD are served in separated environments—settings removed from regular education settings (U.S. Department of Education, 2007).

Inclusion of students with EBD in general education settings should be determined ultimately by what the child or adolescent with EBD genuinely needs and the safety of other students (Kauffman, Bantz, & McCullough, 2002). These needs are established through the thoughtful deliberations of parents, professionals, and, as appropriate, the child or adolescent, via the IEP process. This process creates the basis for determining the services and supports required to address the child's or adolescent's needs, both present and anticipated. If the identified services and supports can be delivered with appropriate intensity in the general education environment without adversely affecting the learning and safety of other students, placement in this environment should occur (Carrell & Hoekstra, 2008; Figlio, 2007; McCarthy & Soodak, 2007). However, if the needs of the student cannot be successfully met in the general education setting, other placement alternatives should be explored and selected.

Inclusion of students with EBD is greatly enhanced when school personnel develop school-wide structures that support inclusion—positive behavior support (PBS), when collaborative teaching is fostered, and when general education personnel receive targeted preparation and training, timely consultation, and appropriate in-class and out-of-class support for students with EBD.

CEC

Standard 1
Foundations

Full inclusion
The delivery of appropriate specialized services to children or adolescents with EBD or other disabilities in general education settings.

Looking Toward a Bright Future

As we anticipate the future for children and youth with behavior disorders and their families, there is room for optimism. This optimism is centered in having professionals and others actively apply evidenced-based practices—practices that are supported by rigorous research. Also, the movement to family-sensitive and family-responsive interventions is a step in the right direction. Listening to families, focusing on their assets and strengths, and giving families the support they need to nurture and connect with their children in healthy and productive ways are causes for hope and positive anticipation.

Systems of care—often delivered in the form of wraparound programs—are being embraced by communities, schools, and other mental health agencies. These systems give rise to new ways of thinking about and responding to children and youth with behavior disorders. Rather than a deficit orientation, these programs focus on the strengths, possibilities, and assets of children and youth, their families, and their communities. Also, these systems present possibilities for being appropriately sensitive to cultural and ethnic concerns of families and communities.

Progressively, we are seeing the development of early intervention programs for young children who are at risk for serious behavior and other problems. Although relatively few in number, these programs focus on providing nurturing and supportive environments for young children, giving parents the skills and dispositions needed for developing feelings of competence, self-determination, and connectedness in their children, and fostering a sense of community and increased personal capacity in all participants.

More and more schools are embracing and applying school-wide, positive behavioral support systems for all children. These systems give rise to thriving school communities where the primary goals are solid learning and growth for every child. Such schools generate the protective buffers children need to sustain themselves and grow into healthy citizens and adults. These schools spawn safe and caring environments, positive relationships with peers, and strong bonds with caring teachers and adults.

Finally, well-respected leaders on every level are challenging and expecting all parents to play more significant roles in nurturing and caring for their children—turning off their televisions, listening to their children read, helping children with homework, and engaging in relationship-forming activities. There are many challenges in serving children and youth with emotional and behavior disorders, but there is cause for hope and optimism on many fronts.

FOCUS REVIEW

FOCUS 1 Identify six essential features of the federal definition for emotional/behavioral disorders.

- The behaviors in question must be exhibited to a marked extent.
- Learning problems that are not attributable to intellectual, sensory, or health deficits are common.
- Satisfactory relationships with parents, teachers, siblings, and others are few.
- Behaviors that occur in many settings and under normal circumstances are considered inappropriate.
- Children with EBD frequently display pervasive unhappiness or depression.
- Physical symptoms or fears associated with the demands of school are common in some children.

FOCUS 2 What four statements can be made about prevalence figures and identification rates for children and youth with EBD?

- EBD prevalence figures vary greatly, from 1 percent to 33.5 percent.
- Conservative estimates for the prevalence of EDB are 3 to 6 percent.
- Less than 1 percent of the children/youth in the United States are formally identified as presenting EBD.
- Many children and youth with EBD are not identified, thus limiting their access to appropriate treatments and support services.

FOCUS 3 Identify five general characteristics of children and youth with EBD.

- Children and youth with EBD tend to have average to below-average IQs compared to their normal peers.
- Children and youth with EBD have difficulties in relating socially and responsibly to peers, parents, teachers, and other authority figures.

- Three out of four children with EBD show clinically significant-language deficits.
- More than 40 percent of the youth with disabilities in correctional facilities are youngsters with identified EBD.
- Compared to other students with disabilities, students with EBD are absent more often, fail more classes, are retained more frequently, and are less successful in passing minimum competency examinations.

FOCUS 4 What can accurately be said about the causes of EBD?

- Continuously interacting biological, genetic, cognitive, social, emotional, environmental, and cultural variables contribute to development of EBD in children and youth.

FOCUS 5 Cite three reasons why classification systems are important to professionals who identify, treat, and educate individuals with EBD.

- They provide a means of describing and identifying various types of EBD.
- They provide a common language for communicating about various types and subtypes of EBD.
- They sometimes provide a basis for treating a disorder and making predictions about treatment outcomes.

FOCUS 6 Identify five essential elements and goals of the assessment process and related practices.

- Screening is designed to identify children or youth who potentially display EBD.
- Children and youth identified through screening receive pre-referral interventions that provide *positive behavior support* for developing appropriate social, emotional, and academic achievement.
- *Response to intervention* procedures provide a means for precisely monitoring the success of carefully selected interventions.

- If these interventions are unsuccessful, further observations and assessments will be done to see if the child or youth should be formally identified and receive more intensive services.
- If the functional behavioral assessment and other assessment procedures are well done, they provide the basis for developing behavior interventions plans to develop useful and desirable behaviors for school, home, and community settings.

FOCUS 7 What five guiding principles are associated with systems of care?

- Children with emotional disturbances have access to services that address physical, emotional, social, and educational needs.
- Children receive individualized services based on unique needs and strengths, which are guided by an individualized service plan.
- Children receive services within the least restrictive environment that is appropriate.
- Families are full participants in all aspects of the planning and delivery of services.
- Children receive integrated services with connections between child-serving agencies and programs and mechanisms for planning, developing, and coordinating services.

Council for Exceptional Children (CEC) Standards to Accompany Chapter 8

 If you are thinking about a career in special education, you should know that many states use national standards developed by the Council for Exceptional Children (CEC) to assess a teacher candidate's knowledge and skills for working with students with disabilities. See a complete listing of the 10 CEC Content Standards on the inside back cover of this text.

1 Foundations
2 Development and Characteristics of Learners
3 Individual Learning Differences
4 Instructional Strategies
5 Learning Environments and Social Interactions
6 Communication
7 Instructional Planning
8 Assessment
10 Collaboration

Mastery Activities and Assignments

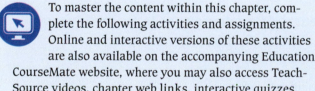 To master the content within this chapter, complete the following activities and assignments. Online and interactive versions of these activities are also available on the accompanying Education CourseMate website, where you may also access Teach-Source videos, chapter web links, interactive quizzes, portfolio activities, flash cards, an integrated eBook, and much more!

1. Complete a written test of the chapter's content. If your instructor requires a written test of your content knowledge for this chapter, keep a copy for your portfolio. A practice test on the information covered in this chapter is available through the CourseMate website.

2. Respond in writing to the Application Questions for the Case Study, "Toby." Keep a copy of the case study and your written response for your portfolio.

3. Read the Debate Forum, "Emergency Rooms: The Best Place for Routine Care of Children and Youth with Mental Illnesses?" and then visit the Education CourseMate website to complete the activity "Take a Stand." Keep a copy of this activity for your portfolio.

4. Participate in a community service learning activity. Community service is a valuable way to enhance your learning experience. Visit the Education CourseMate website for suggested community service learning activities that correspond to the information presented in this chapter. Develop a reflective journal of the service learning experience for your portfolio.

CHAPTER 9

Intellectual and Developmental Disabilities

RICHARD HUTCHINGS/Getty Images

FOCUS PREVIEW

As you read the chapter, focus on these key concepts:

1 Identify the major components of the American Association on Intellectual and Developmental Disabilities (AAIDD) definition and classification system for people with intellectual and developmental disabilities.

2 What is the prevalence of intellectual disabilities?

3 Identify intellectual, self-regulation, and adaptive skills characteristics of individuals with intellectual disabilities.

4 Identify the academic, motivational, speech and language, and physical characteristics of children with intellectual disabilities.

5 Identify the causes of intellectual disabilities.

6 Why are early intervention services for children with intellectual disabilities so important?

7 Identify five skill areas that should be addressed in programs for elementary-age children with intellectual disabilities.

8 Identify four educational goals for adolescents with intellectual disabilities.

9 Why is the inclusion of students with intellectual disabilities in general education settings important to an appropriate educational experience?

Actress Lauren Potter

The Press-Enterprise

Riverside [California] has a new prime-time star . . . Poly High School graduate Lauren Potter (Lauren costars in the popular Fox TV series *Glee*). Lauren has Down's syndrome and is a member of the Down Syndrome Association of Los Angeles, a nonprofit agency that offers programs, resources, education, counseling, and more. The association has an in-house talent agency, Hearts and Hands, which casting directors can contact when searching for an actor with Down's syndrome. Lauren was contacted when the part came up. Lauren Potter practiced her lines for *Glee* with her mother, Robin Sinkhorn. "She memorizes easily . . . you never have to feed her lines," Sinkhorn said. "I'm shocked because she really hasn't had any formal training."

"She and 13 others from various agencies auditioned for the part," said Lauren's mother. "She then got the callback, then got the role."

This is Lauren's second role; her first was in the feature film *Mr. Blue Sky*, which was in theaters in 2007. She played a 10-year-old girl with Down's syndrome who falls in love with a boy who has no disability: "It was great filming it, and it was a lot of fun," Lauren said. "I love *Glee*, and it was a great experience meeting all the characters." Lauren, 19, plays the character Becky Johnson, a 16-year-old sophomore at McKinley High School who tries out for the cheerleading squad. The coach is really tough on her, but she makes the squad.

"It was kind of ironic because Lauren tried out for Poly cheerleading this year," Sinkhorn said. "She didn't make it. She was really heartbroken.

Then here comes this role and in it she wears a cheerleading outfit and makes the team. . . ."

Lauren enjoyed the two-day shoot but said it bothered her that when people looked at her, they first saw the Down's syndrome. "It's really hard for me when people see me as a Down's syndrome kid," she said. "I want them to see me as typical. . . ."

Lauren has a lot of plans for the future, now that she has graduated. She'll be going into Riverside School District's Project Team, which is a transition program for students with mental or physical disabilities, that offers job training and self-sufficiency basics. She has also recently tapped into another artistic talent—cooking—and wants to take some classes in that subject as well. And she plans to keep working in TV and film. "I really love performing and acting," Lauren said (Dean, 2011).

SOURCE: From Jennifer Dean, "Riverside teen to co-star on 'Glee' episode," *The Press Enterprise*, June 15, 2009. Copyright © 2009 Enterprise Media. Reprinted by permission.

A Changing Era in the Lives of People with Disabilities

This chapter is about people whose intellectual and social capabilities may differ significantly from what is considered "typical." Their growth and development depend on the educational, social, and medical supports made available throughout life. Lauren from our opening Snapshot is a teenager with intellectual disabilities who has drive, talent, and a wonderful support network of family, friends, and teachers. As she moves into her adult years, she is achieving the dream of being an actress, but still longs for being viewed first and foremost as "Lauren," a typical person who just happens to have Down's syndrome.

Lauren is also a person with **intellectual disabilities**, but she is not necessarily representative of the wide range of ability that characterizes people who have this condition. For example, this wide range of ability may include 6-year-old Juliana, described as having mild intellectual disabilities who may be no more than one or two years behind the normal

Intellectual Disabilities
Limited ability to reason, plan, solve problems, think abstractly, comprehend complex ideas, learn quickly, and learn from experience.

development of academic and social skills. Many children with mild intellectual disabilities are not identified until they enter elementary school at age 5 or 6, because they may not exhibit physical or learning delays that are readily identifiable during the early childhood years. As these children enter school, developmental delays become more apparent. During early primary grades, it is not uncommon for the cognitive and social differences of children with intellectual disabilities to be attributed to immaturity. However, within a few years, educators recognize the need for specialized services to support the child's development in the natural settings of school, neighborhood, and home.

People with moderate to severe intellectual disabilities have challenges that transcend the classroom. Some have significant, multiple disabling conditions, including sensory, physical, and emotional problems. People with moderate intellectual disabilities are capable of learning adaptive skills that allow a degree of independence, with ongoing support. These skills include the abilities to dress and feed themselves, to meet their own personal care and health needs, and to develop safety skills that enable them to move without fear wherever they go. These individuals have some means of communication. Most can develop spoken language skills; others may be able to learn manual communication (signing). Their social interaction skills are often limited, which makes it a challenge for them to interact spontaneously to others.

People with profound intellectual disabilities, such as Thomas, often depend on others to maintain even their most basic life functions, including eating, hygiene, and dressing. Thomas will need ongoing support with self-care and the development of functional communication skills. This certainly does not mean that education and treatment beyond routine care and maintenance are not beneficial. The extent of profound disabilities is one reason why Thomas was excluded from the public schools for so long. Exclusion was often justified on the basis that schools did not have the resources, facilities, or trained professionals to deal with the needs of these students.

FÔCUS 1

Identify the major components of the AAIDD definition and classification system for people with intellectual and developmental disabilities.

Standard 1
Foundations

American Association on Mental Retardation (AAMR)
Professionals involved in the study and treatment of intellectual disabilities. Became the American Association on Intellectual and Developmental Disabilities in 2006.

American Association on Intellectual and Developmental Disabilities (AAIDD)
See definition of **AAMR**.

Definitions and Classification

People with intellectual disabilities have been labeled with pejorative terms for centuries. They have often been stereotyped with one of the most derogatory terms in the English language—*retard*. As suggested by Corum (2003), the term *retard* remains with us, even today in what should be a much more enlightened 21st century:

> Retard! *My ninth-grade students toss this word around as if its meaning is clear . . . someone who is slow and stupid. "You retard!" Sometimes I quietly ask them not to call one another names. But some days I feel like making a point, so I just quietly mention that my youngest son, Thomas, is retarded [has intellectual disabilities]. Their faces reveal embarrassment, and I wonder if they know the musical meaning of the word. I hear the music that is Thomas—slow down to a different pace . . . ritard.*

Evolving Terminology

Varying perspectives exist on the use of the label *intellectual disabilities*. In the United States, *feebleminded* was the most common term used in the 19th century, and *mental retardation* was in use for most of the 20th century and into the early 21st century. In the first decade of the 21st century, many individuals, family members, and professionals questioned the continued use of *mental retardation*. In 2006, members of the **American Association on Mental Retardation (AAMR)**, the most widely known professional association in the United States whose mission is progressive policies, sound research, effective practices, and universal human rights, officially changed its name to the **American Association on Intellectual and Developmental Disabilities** (AAIDD).

Definition

In this section, we address six major dimensions of the AAIDD definition: (1) intellectual abilities; (2) adaptive behavior; (3) participation, interactions, and social roles; (4) physical and mental health; (5) environmental context; and (6) age of onset.

DEBATE FORUM WHY IS USING THE "R" WORD SUCH A BIG DEAL? IT'S ONLY A WORD

POINT

"WORDS HURT. And the pain stays and even grows, and I took it in silence. But I shouldn't have had to. No one should have to. I support this cause ["Spread the Word to End the Word"] because it's giving back to us the faith in ourselves that we've lost. It's what gives us the power to beat bullying and stop it from happening to others. It's empowering, and it gives me hope. Imagine a world without bullies. . . . "

—Student [with intellectual and developmental disabilities], age 16

As young children, we're taught that "sticks and stones may break my bones, but words will never hurt me." We repeated this phrase to ourselves whenever we were teased by other kids. As we grow older, though, we start to realize the truth: Words can hurt. Many times, they leave emotional scars that—unlike broken bones—don't always heal easily with time. Sometimes, words that aren't necessarily meant to offend can still be painful. In fact, many words exist that young people—and even adults—use regularly that have the power to perpetuate stereotypes and hurt others' feelings. One of these words is the "r-word." As the mother of a son with Down's syndrome, I can't bring myself to use that word here. I need to abbreviate it in an attempt to lessen my own painful reaction to its use. So, for the purposes of this blog, let's just say this word begins with an R, has six letters, and rhymes with "yard." At any given school, peers carelessly toss this word around without giving it a second thought. For many young people, it's just another expression, part of their lingo. But this word has a derogatory connotation. Consider its use in these sentences: "That's so r-word-ed," or, "You're such an r-word." Many young people probably don't even realize that this word sends the message that it's okay to make fun of students with disabilities, or—worse yet—to disregard them completely.

SOURCE: Adapted from Hertzog, 2011.

COUNTERPOINT

How does a word, such as *retarded*, take on such a negative connotation? If we stopped using the word, wouldn't it just be replaced by other negative words, such *stupid*, *dumb*, *idiot*, or *imbecile*? Using words to label people for good or bad is a part of who we are as society and is used extensively by government, in our schools, and throughout our communities So, if using a word, such as *retarded*, to label a person has such negative consequences, why do we keep doing it? The reason is simple. The problem isn't with the word *retarded*, or any other controversial word for that matter, it is the intent behind the use of the word. Sure, you can eliminate *retarded* from your vocabulary, but it will just be replaced by another word that will take on an equally negative value unless we eliminate the intent. In fact, this has been exactly the case throughout history. The chronology of the word *retarded* began with *feebleminded* and then evolved to *idiot*, *imbecile*, and *moron*. These are all words that are now considered as pejorative and inappropriate in today's society. So, what will be the next word to replace *retarded*? Or will we finally realize that it isn't the word that hurts? It's the power we give the word.

 What Do You Think? Please visit the Education CourseMate website for Human Exceptionality, *11th edition, to access and respond to questions related to the Debate Forum.*

The most widely accepted definition of intellectual disabilities is that of the AAIDD:

Intellectual disability [is] characterized by significant limitations both in intellectual functioning and in adaptive behavior as expressed in conceptual, social, and practical adaptive skills. This disability originates before age 18. (AAIDD, 2009)

The AAIDD definition has evolved through years of effort to more clearly reflect the ever-changing perception of intellectual disabilities. Historically, definitions of intellectual disabilities were based solely on the measurement of intellect, emphasizing routine care and maintenance rather than treatment and education. In recent years, the concept of adaptive behavior has played an increasingly important role in defining and classifying people with intellectual disabilities.

Intellectual Abilities Intellectual abilities include reasoning, planning, solving problems, thinking abstractly, comprehending complex ideas, learning quickly, and learning from experience (AAIDD, 2009). These abilities are assessed by a standardized intelligence test in which a person's score is compared with the average of other people who have taken the same test (referred to as a *normative sample*). The statistical average for an intelligence test is generally set at 100. We state this by saying that the person has an intelligence quotient (IQ) of 100. Psychologists use a mathematical concept called the **standard deviation** to determine the extent to which any given individual's score deviates from this average of 100. An individual who scores more than two standard deviations below 100 on an intelligence test meets AAIDD's definition of subaverage general intellectual functioning. This means that people with IQs of approximately 70 to 75 and lower would be considered as having intellectual disabilities.

Adaptive Behavior AAIDD defines **adaptive behavior** as a collection of conceptual, social, and practical skills that have been learned by people in order to function in their everyday lives. (Figure 9.1 provides several examples of adaptive behavior.) If a person has limitations in these adaptive skills, he or she may need some additional assistance or supports to participate more fully in both family and community life.

As is true with intelligence, adaptive skills also may be measured by standardized tests. These tests, most often referred to as *adaptive behavior scales*, generally use structured interviews or direct observations to obtain information. Adaptive behavior scales measure the individual's ability to take care of personal needs (such as hygiene) and to relate appropriately to others in social situations. Adaptive skills may also be assessed through informal appraisal, such as observations by family members or professionals who are familiar with the individual, or through anecdotal records.

Standard deviation
A statistical measure of the amount that an individual score deviates from the average.

Adaptive behavior
Conceptual, social, and practical skills that people have learned to function in their everyday lives.

Standard 2
Development and Characteristics of Learners

Figure 9.1 Examples of Conceptual, Social, and Practical Adaptive Skills

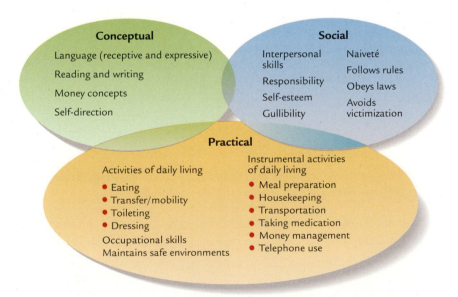

SOURCE: Adapted from AAIDD (AAMR) Ad Hoc Committee on Terminology and Classification. (2002). *Intellectual disabilities: Definition, classification, and systems of support* (10th ed., p. 42). Washington, DC: American Association on Intellectual and Developmental Disabilities.

Participation, Interactions, and Social Roles AAIDD emphasizes the importance of a positive environment for fostering growth, development, and individual well-being. Thus, a person's participation and interaction within the environment are indicators of adaptive functioning. The more an individual engages in valued activities, the more likely that an "adaptive fit" exists between the person and his or her environment. (Valued activities may include appropriate education, living arrangements, employment settings, and community participation.)

The idea of people's ability to participate in valued activities was introduced by Bengt Nirje from Sweden over three decades ago through the **principle of normalization**. This principle emphasizes the need to make available to the person with intellectual disabilities the patterns and conditions of everyday life that are as close to the norms and patterns of mainstream society as possible (Nirje, 1970). Normalization goes far beyond the mere physical inclusion of the individual in a community. It also promotes the availability of needed supports, such as education and supervision, without which the individual with intellectual disabilities may not be prepared to meet the demands of community life.

> **Principle of normalization**
> Making the patterns and conditions of everyday life and of mainstream society available to people with disabilities.

Physical and Mental Health The physical and mental health of an individual influences his or her overall intellectual and adaptive functioning. AAIDD indicates that the functioning level for people with intellectual disabilities is significantly affected (facilitated or inhibited) by the effects of physical and mental health. "Some individuals [with intellectual disabilities] enjoy robust good health with no significant activity limitations. . . . On the other hand, some individuals have a variety of significant health limitations, such as epilepsy or cerebral palsy, that could impair body functioning and severely restrict personal activities and social participation" (AAIDD, 2009).

Environmental Context *Environmental context* is the term for the interrelated conditions in which people live their lives. Context is based on an environmental perspective with three different levels: (1) the immediate social setting that includes the person and her or his family, (2) the broader neighborhood, community, or organizations that provide services and supports (such as public education), and (3) the overarching patterns of culture and society. The various levels are important to people with mental intellectual disabilities because they provide differing opportunities and can foster well-being.

Age of Onset The AAIDD defines the age of onset for intellectual disabilities as prior to 18 years. The reason for choosing age 18 as a cutoff point is that intellectual disabilities belong to a family of conditions referred to as developmental disabilities. **Developmental disabilities** are mental and/or physical impairments that are diagnosed at birth or during the childhood and adolescent years. A developmental disability results in substantial functional limitations in at least three areas of major life activity (such areas include self-care, language, learning, mobility, self-direction, capacity for independent living, and economic self-sufficiency).

> **Developmental disabilities**
> Mental and/or physical impairments that limit substantial functioning in at least three areas of major life activity.

Putting the Definition into Practice There are five criteria that professionals should apply as they put the definition into practice:

1. Limitations in a person's present functioning must be considered within the context of community environments typical of the individual's age, peers, and culture.

2. Valid assessment considers cultural and linguistic diversity as well as differences in communication, sensory, motor, and behavioral factors.

3. Within an individual, limitations often coexist with strengths.

4. An important purpose of describing limitations is to develop a profile of needed supports.

5. With appropriate personalized supports over a sustained period, the life functioning of the person with [intellectual disabilities] generally will improve (AAIDD, 2009).

Classification

To more clearly understand the diversity of people with intellectual disabilities, several classification systems have been developed. Each classification method reflects an attempt by a particular discipline (such as medicine or education) to better understand

and respond to the needs of individuals with intellectual disabilities. We will discuss four of these methods.

Severity of the Condition

Severity of the Condition The extent to which a person's intellectual capabilities and adaptive skills differ from what is considered "normal" can be described by using terms such as *mild*, *moderate*, *severe*, or *profound*. *Mild* describes the highest level of performance; *profound* describes the lowest level. Distinctions between severity levels associated with intellectual disabilities are determined by scores on intelligence tests and by limitations in adaptive skills. A person's adaptive skills can also be categorized by severity. Adaptive skill limitations can be described in terms of the degree to which an individual's performance differs from what is expected for his or her chronological age.

CEC

Standard 3
Individual Learning Differences

Educability Expectations

Educability Expectations To distinguish among the many needs of students with intellectual disabilities, the field of education developed its own classification system. As implied by the word *expectations*, students with intellectual disabilities have been classified according to how well they are expected to achieve in a classroom situation. The specific descriptors used vary greatly from state to state, but they most often indicate an approximate IQ range and a statement of predicted achievement:

- *Educable* (IQ 55 to about 70). Second- to fifth-grade achievement in school academic areas. Social adjustment skills will result in independence with intermittent or limited support in the community. Partial or total self-support in a paid community job is a strong possibility.

- *Trainable* (IQ 40 to 55). Learning primarily in the area of self-care skills; some achievement in functional academics. A range of more extensive support will be needed to help the student adapt to community environments. Opportunities for paid work include supported employment in a community job.

The classification criterion for educability expectation was originally developed to determine who would be able to benefit from school and who would not. The term *educable* implied that the child could cope with at least some of the academic demands of the classroom, meaning that the child could learn basic reading, writing, and arithmetic skills. The term *trainable* indicated that the student was not educable and was capable only of being trained in settings outside the public school. In fact, until the passage of PL 94–142 in 1975 (now IDEA, 2004), many children who were labeled trainable could not get a free public education. In some school systems, the terms *educable* and *trainable* have been replaced by symptom-severity classifications (mild through severe intellectual disabilities).

Medical Descriptors

Medical Descriptors Intellectual disabilities may be classified on the basis of the biological origin of the condition. A classification system that uses the cause of the condition to differentiate people with intellectual disabilities is often referred to as a *medical classification* system because it emerged primarily from the field of medicine. Common medical descriptors include fetal alcohol syndrome, chromosomal abnormalities (e.g., Down's syndrome), metabolic disorders (e.g., phenylketonuria, thyroid dysfunction), and infections (e.g., syphilis, rubella). These medical conditions will be discussed more thoroughly in the section on causation.

Classification Based on Needed Support

Classification Based on Needed Support Today, AAIDD uses a classification system based on the type and extent of the support that the individual requires to function in the natural settings of home and community. Four levels of support are recommended:

- *Intermittent*. Supports are provided on an "as-needed basis." These supports may be (1) episodic—that is, the person does not always need assistance; or (2) short-term, occurring during lifespan transitions (e.g., job loss or acute medical crisis). Intermittent supports may be of high or low intensity.

- *Limited*. Supports are characterized by consistency; the time required may be limited, but the need is not intermittent. Fewer staff may be required, and costs may be lower than those associated with more intensive levels of support (examples include time-limited employment training and supports during transition from school to adulthood).

Robert Burke/Getty Images

School and community programs are moving away from pejorative classification categories (such as "trainable") to descriptions of the individual based on type and extent of support needed to function in natural settings.

- *Extensive*. Supports are characterized by regular involvement (e.g., daily) in at least some environments, such as work or home; supports are not time-limited (e.g., long-term job and home-living support will be necessary).

- *Pervasive*. Supports must be constant and of high intensity. They have to be provided across multiple environments and may be life-sustaining in nature. Pervasive supports typically involve more staff and are more intrusive than extensive or time-limited supports.

The AAIDD's emphasis on classifying people with intellectual disabilities on the basis of needed support is an important departure from the more restrictive perspectives of the traditional approaches. Supports may be described not only in terms of the level of assistance needed, but also by type—that is, as formal or natural support systems. Formal supports may be funded through government programs, such as income maintenance, health care, education, housing, or employment. Another type of formal support is the advocacy organization (e.g., **The ARC of the United States** that lobbies on behalf of people with intellectual disabilities for improved and expanded services, as well as for providing family members a place to interact and support one another. **Natural supports** differ from formal supports in that they are provided not by agencies or organizations, but by the nuclear and extended family members, friends, or neighbors. Natural supports are often more effective than formal supports in helping people with intellectual disabilities access and participate in a community setting. Research suggests that adults with intellectual disabilities who are successfully employed following school find more jobs through their natural support network of friends and family than through formal support systems (Crockett & Hardman, 2009).

The ARC of the United States
A national organization that works to enhance the quality of life for people with intellectual disabilities.

Natural supports
Supports for people with disabilities that are provided by family, friends, and peers.

Prevalence

The prevalence of intellectual disabilities worldwide and across all ages is estimated at 1 percent of the total population (Maulik, Mascarenhas, Mathers, Dua, & Saxena, 2011). For school-age children between ages 6 and 21, the most recent annual report from the U.S. Department of Education (2011) reported that approximately 600,000 students were labeled as having intellectual disabilities and were receiving services under IDEA. Approximately 10 percent of all students with disabilities between the ages of 6 and 21 have intellectual disabilities (see Figure 9.2).

The President's Committee for People with Intellectual Disabilities (2011) estimates that approximately seven to eight million Americans of all ages have intellectual disabilities. Intellectual disabilities affect about one in ten families in the United States. Note that we are able only to estimate prevalence, because no one has actually counted the number of people with intellectual disabilities.

FOCUS 2
What is the prevalence of intellectual disabilities?

Figure 9.2 *Prevalence of Intellectual Disabilities*

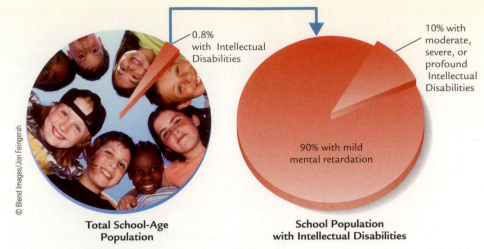

0.8% with Intellectual Disabilities

10% with moderate, severe, or profound Intellectual Disabilities

90% with mild mental retardation

© Blend Images/Jon Feingersh

Total School-Age Population

School Population with Intellectual Disabilities

SOURCE: U.S. Department of Education. (2011). To Assure the Free Appropriate Public Education of All Children with Disabilities. *Thirtieth Annual Report to Congress on the Implementation of the Individuals with Disabilities Education Act.* Washington, DC: U.S. Government Printing Office.

FOCUS 3

Identify intellectual, self-regulation, and adaptive skills characteristics of individuals with intellectual disabilities.

CEC

Standard 2
Development and Characteristics of Learners

Characteristics

We now examine the myriad characteristics of people with intellectual disabilities that can affect their academic learning, as well as their ability to adapt to home, school, and community environments.

Learning and Memory

Intelligence is the ability to acquire, remember, and use knowledge. A primary characteristic of intellectual disabilities is diminished intellectual ability that translates into a difference in the rate and efficiency with which the person acquires, remembers, and uses new knowledge, compared to the general population.

The learning and memory capabilities of people with intellectual disabilities are significantly below average in comparison to peers without disabilities. Children with intellectual disabilities, as a group, are less able to grasp abstract, as opposed to concrete, concepts. Accordingly, they benefit from instruction that is meaningful and useful, and they learn more from contact with real objects than they do from representations or symbols.

Intelligence is also associated with learning how to learn and with the ability to apply what is learned to new experiences. This process is known as establishing learning sets and generalizing them to new situations. Children and adults with intellectual disabilities develop

LEARNING THROUGH SOCIAL MEDIA
E-BUDDIES

Best Buddies International, founded by Anthony K. Shriver (son of Sargent and Eunice Kennedy Shriver), offers a social media program called e-Buddies, which provides opportunities for Internet friendships among people with intellectual and developmental disabilities and people who do not have a disability. The e-Buddies program has proven to be a fun and safe way for people with intellectual disabilities to make new friends. E-mail matches are made on the basis of similar age, gender, geography, and shared interests. The e-Buddies program provides individuals with an intellectual disability an opportunity to develop new friendships through social media while also acquiring computer skills. For people without disabilities, e-Buddies is a unique opportunity to change a life and make a friend. (For more information, go to www.e-buddies.org.)

learning sets at a slower pace than peers without disabilities, and they are deficient in relating information to new situations (Beirne-Smith, Patton, & Hill, 2010). **Generalization** happens "when a child applies previously learned content or skills to a situation in which the information has not been taught" (Drew & Hardman, 2007). The greater the severity of intellectual deficit, the greater the difficulties with memory. Memory problems in children with intellectual disabilities have been attributed to several factors. People with intellectual disabilities have trouble focusing on relevant stimuli in learning and in real-life situations, sometimes attending to the wrong things (Kittler, Krinsky-McHale, & Devenny, 2004; Westling & Fox, 2009).

Self-Regulation

People with intellectual disabilities do not appear to develop efficient learning strategies, such as the ability to rehearse a task (to practice a new concept, either out loud or to themselves, over and over). The ability to rehearse a task is related to a broad concept known as **self-regulation** (Beirne-Smith, Patton, & Hill, 2009). Whereas most people will rehearse to try to remember, individuals with intellectual disabilities do not appear to be able to apply this skill.

Some researchers have begun to focus on **information-processing theories** to better understand learning differences in people with intellectual disabilities. Information-processing theorists study how a person processes information from sensory stimuli to motoric output (Sternberg, 2008). In information-processing theory, the learning differences in people with intellectual disabilities are seen as the underdevelopment of metacognitive processes. Metacognitive processes help the person plan how to solve a problem. First, the person decides which strategy he or she thinks will solve a problem. Then the strategy is implemented. During implementation, the person monitors whether the strategy is working and makes any adaptations necessary. Finally, the results of the strategy are evaluated in terms of whether the problem has been solved and how the strategy could be used in other situations (Sternberg, 2008). Even though children with intellectual disabilities may be unable to use the best strategy when confronted with new learning situations, they can be taught ways to do so.

Adaptive Skills

The abilities to adapt to the demands of the environment, relate to others, and take care of personal needs are all important aspects of an independent lifestyle. In the school setting, adaptive behavior is defined as the ability to apply skills learned in a classroom to daily activities in natural settings.

The adaptive skills of people with intellectual disabilities are often not comparable to those of their peers without disabilities. A child with intellectual disabilities may have difficulty in both learning and applying skills for a number of reasons, including a higher level of distractibility, inattentiveness, failure to read social cues, and impulsive behavior. Thus, these children will need to be taught appropriate reasoning, judgment, and social skills that lead to more positive social relationships and personal competence. Adaptive skill differences for people with intellectual disabilities may also be associated with a lower self-image and a greater expectancy for failure in both academic and social situations. Lee, Yoo, and Bak (2003) investigated the quality of social relationships among children with mild intellectual disabilities and peers who were not disabled. They found that the children without disabilities did perceive their classmates with intellectual disabilities as friends. However, the nondisabled students had concerns that limitations in communication and some behavior problems would make it difficult to maintain a friendship with a child who had an intellectual disability.

Academic Achievement

Research on the academic achievement of children with mild to moderate intellectual disabilities has suggested that they will experience significant delays in the areas of literacy and mathematics. Reading comprehension is usually considered the weakest area of learning. In general, students with mild intellectual disabilities are better at decoding words than comprehending their meaning (Drew & Hardman, 2007), and they read below their own mental-age level (Katims, 2000; Partnership for Accessible Reading Assessment, 2011).

FOCUS 4
Identify the academic, motivational, speech and language, and physical characteristics of children with intellectual disabilities.

The academic performance of children with intellectual disabilities varies greatly, depending on the level of intellectual ability and adaptive skills. Many children with mild intellectual disabilities may learn to read, though at a slower rate, whereas those with moderate intellectual disabilities benefit from a functional academic program.

© Bob Daemmrich/Photo Edit

Children with intellectual disabilities also perform poorly on mathematical computations, although their performance may be closer to what is typical for their mental age. These children may be able to learn basic computations but may be unable to apply concepts appropriately in a problem-solving situation (Beirne-Smith, Patton, & Hill, 2010; Partnership, for Accessible Reading Assessment, 2011).

A growing body of research has indicated that children with moderate or severe intellectual disabilities can be taught academics as a means to gain information, participate in social settings, increase their orientation and mobility, and make choices (Browder, Ahlgrim-Delzell, Courtade-Little, & Snell, 2011; Browder & Spooner, 2011). Reading helps students develop a useful vocabulary that will facilitate their inclusion in school and community settings (Browder et al., 2011). These children may be able to recognize their names and those of significant others in their lives, as well as common survival words, including *help*, *hurt*, *danger*, and *stop*. Math assists students in learning such skills as how to tell time, how to add and subtract small sums to manage finances (such as balancing a checkbook), and how to appropriately exchange money for products in community settings (e.g., grocery stores, movie theaters, and vending machines).

Motivation

People with intellectual disabilities are often described as lacking motivation, or outer-directed behavior. They may seem unwilling or unable to complete tasks, take responsibility, and be self-directed. Although people with intellectual disabilities may appear to be less motivated than their peers without disabilities, such behavior may be attributable to the way they have learned to avoid certain situations because of a fear of failure. A child with intellectual disabilities may have a history of failure, particularly in school, and may be afraid to take risks or participate in new situations. The result of failure is often **learned helplessness:** "No matter what I do or how hard I try, I will not succeed." To overcome a child's feelings of learned helplessness, professionals and family members should focus on providing experiences that have high probabilities for success. The opportunity to strive for success, rather than to avoid failure, is a very important learning experience for these children.

Learned helplessness
Refusal or unwillingness to take on new tasks or challenges, resulting from repeated failures or control by others.

Speech and Language

One of the most serious and obvious characteristics of individuals with intellectual disabilities is delayed speech and language development. The most common speech difficulties involve **articulation problems**, **voice problems,** and **stuttering**. Language problems are generally associated with delays in language development rather than with a bizarre use of language (Beirne-Smith, Patton, & Hill, 2010; Moore & Montgomery, 2008). Kaiser (2000) emphasized that "the overriding goal of language intervention is to increase the functional communication of students" (p. 457).

There is considerable variation in the language skills of people with intellectual disabilities. In general, the severity of the speech and language problems is positively correlated with the cause and severity of the intellectual disabilities: The milder the intellectual disabilities, the less pervasive the language difficulty (Moore & Montgomery, 2008). Speech and language difficulties may range from minor speech defects, such as articulation problems, to the complete absence of expressive language. Speech and language pathologists are able to correct minor speech differences for most students with intellectual disabilities.

Articulation problems
Speech problems such as omissions, substitutions, additions, and distortions of words.

Voice problems
Abnormal acoustical qualities in a person's speech.

Stuttering
A speech problem involving abnormal repetitions, prolongations, and hesitations as one speaks.

Physical Development

The physical appearance of most children with intellectual disabilities does not differ from that of same-age children who are not disabled. However, a relationship exists between the severity of the intellectual disabilities and the extent of physical differences for the individual (Beirne-Smith, Patton, & Hill et al., 2010; Drew & Hardman, 2007). For people with severe intellectual disabilities, there is a significant probability of related physical challenges; genetic factors are likely to underlie both disabilities. Individuals with mild intellectual disabilities, in contrast, may exhibit no physical differences because the intellectual disabilities may be associated with environmental, not genetic, factors.

The majority of children with severe and profound intellectual disabilities have multiple disabilities that often affect nearly every aspect of their intellectual and physical development (Westling & Fox, 2009). Increasing health problems for children with intellectual disabilities may be associated with genetic or environmental factors. For example, people with Down's syndrome have a higher incidence of congenital heart defects and respiratory

REFLECT ON THIS EUNICE KENNEDY SHRIVER: A CELEBRATION OF AN EXTRAORDINARY LIFE DEDICATED TO PEOPLE WITH INTELLECTUAL DISABILITIES

As founder and honorary chairperson of Special Olympics and executive vice president of the Joseph P. Kennedy, Jr. Foundation, Eunice Kennedy Shriver was a leader in the worldwide struggle to improve and enhance the lives of individuals with intellectual disabilities for more than five decades. Born in Brookline, Massachusetts, the fifth of nine children of Joseph P. and Rose Fitzgerald Kennedy and sister to President John F. Kennedy, she received a bachelor of arts degree in sociology from Stanford University....

In 1957, Eunice Shriver took over the direction of the Joseph P. Kennedy, Jr. Foundation. The foundation, established in 1946 as a memorial to Joseph P. Kennedy, Jr.—the family's eldest son, who was killed in World War II—has two major objectives: to seek the prevention of intellectual disabilities by identifying its causes, and to improve the means by which society deals with citizens who have intellectual disabilities. Under Eunice Shriver's leadership, the foundation has helped achieve many significant advances, including the establishment by President Kennedy of the President's Committee on Mental Retardation in 1961 (now called the President's Committee for People with Intellectual Disabilities);

development of the National Institute of Child Health and Human Development (NICHD) in 1962 (now the Eunice Kennedy Shriver NIHCD); the establishment of a network of university-affiliated facilities and mental retardation [intellectual disabilities] research centers at major medical schools across the United States in 1967; the establishment of Special Olympics in 1968; the creation of major centers for the study of medical ethics at Harvard and Georgetown Universities in 1971; the founding of the "Community of Caring" for the reduction of intellectual disabilities among babies of teenagers in 1981 . . . and the establishment of "Community of Caring" programs in 1,200 public and private schools (now the Eunice Kennedy Shriver National Center for Community of Caring at the University of Utah).

Recognized throughout the world for her efforts on behalf of people with intellectual disabilities, Shriver received many honors and awards, including the Presidential Medal of Freedom, the Legion of Honor Award, the Prix de la Couronne Francaise, the Mary Lasker Award, the Philip Murray-William Green Award (presented to Eunice and Sargent Shriver by the AFL-CIO), the American Association on Mental Deficiency

(AAMD) Humanitarian Award, the Laetare Medal of the University of Notre Dame, the Order of the Smile of Polish Children, the Franklin D. Roosevelt Four Freedoms Freedom from Want Award, the National Women's Hall of Fame, the Laureus Sports Award, the National Collegiate Athletics Association (NCAA) Theodore Roosevelt Award, and the International Olympic Committee Award....

In 1984, U.S. President Reagan awarded Eunice Shriver the Presidential Medal of Freedom, the nation's highest civilian award, for her work on behalf of people with intellectual disabilities, and in 2005, she was honored for her work with Special Olympics as one of the first recipients of a sidewalk medallion on The Extra Mile Point of Light Pathway in Washington, DC. To learn more about Eunice Kennedy Shriver, visit www.eunicekennedyshriver.org or www.specialolympics.org.

Question for Reflection

Eunice Kennedy Shriver is an example of how one very special person can make a profound difference. How have you made a difference in the lives of people with intellectual disabilities? Volunteering for Special Olympics, Best Buddies, or the Community of Caring schools where you live?

problems directly linked to their genetic condition. On the other hand, some children with intellectual disabilities experience health problems because of their living conditions. A significantly higher percentage of children with intellectual disabilities come from low socioeconomic backgrounds in comparison to peers without disabilities. Children who do not receive proper nutrition and are exposed to inadequate sanitation have a greater susceptibility to infections (Drew & Hardman, 2007). Health services for families in these situations may be minimal or nonexistent, depending on whether they are able to access government medical support, so children with intellectual disabilities may become ill more often than those who do not have disabilities. Consequently, children with intellectual disabilities may miss more school or not get involved in healthy activities, such as sports and recreation.

In the area of health and physical fitness, one individual truly stands alone as recognizing the importance of engaging people with intellectual disabilities in fitness activities, particularly sports. This person was Eunice Kennedy Shriver, founder of the Special Olympics, and sister of President John F. Kennedy. More than any other notable figure in history, Eunice Shriver changed society's perceptions of what is possible for people with intellectual disabilities. For more information on the unparalleled accomplishments of Eunice Shriver, see the nearby Reflect on This feature, "Eunice Kennedy Shriver: A Celebration of an Extraordinary Life Dedicated to People with Intellectual Disabilities."

Causation

FOCUS 5

Identify the causes of intellectual disabilities.

CEC

Standard 2
Development and Characteristics of Learners

Standard 8
Assessment

Nature versus nurture
Controversy concerning how much of a person's ability is related to sociocultural influences (nurture) as opposed to genetic factors (nature).

Cultural-familial intellectual disabilities
Intellectual disabilities that may be attributable to both sociocultural and genetic factors.

Biomedical factors
Biologic processes, such as genetic disorders or nutrition, which can cause intellectual disabilities or other disabilities.

Intellectual disabilities result from multiple causes, some known, many unknown (The ARC, 2011a). Possible known causes of intellectual disabilities include sociocultural influences, biomedical factors, behavioral factors, and unknown prenatal influences.

Sociocultural Causes

For individuals with mild intellectual disabilities, the cause of the problem is not generally apparent. A significant number of these individuals come from families of low socioeconomic status and diverse cultural backgrounds; their home situations often offer few opportunities for learning, which only further contributes to their challenges at school. Additionally, because these high-risk children live in such adverse economic conditions, they generally do not receive proper nutritional care. In addition to poor nutrition, high-risk groups are in greater jeopardy of receiving poor medical care and living in unstable families (Children's Defense Fund, 2011).

An important question to be addressed concerning people who have grown up in adverse sociocultural situations is this: How much of the person's ability is related to sociocultural influences, and how much to genetic factors? This issue is referred to as the **nature versus nurture** controversy. Numerous studies over the years have focused on the degree to which heredity and environment contribute to intelligence. These studies show that although we are reaching a better understanding of the interactive effects of both heredity and environment, the exact contribution of each to intellectual growth remains unknown.

The term used to describe intellectual disabilities that may be attributable to both sociocultural and genetic factors is **cultural-familial intellectual disabilities**. People with this condition are often described as (1) having mild intellectual disabilities, (2) having no known biological cause for the condition, (3) having at least one parent or sibling who has mild intellectual disabilities, and (4) growing up in a low socioeconomic status (low SES) home environment.

Biomedical Causes

For the majority of people with more severe intellectual disabilities, problems are evident at birth. As defined by the AAIDD, **biomedical factors** "relate to biologic processes, such as genetic disorders or nutrition" (AAIDD, 2002, p. 126).

Many biomedical factors are associated with intellectual disabilities. In this section, we will discuss three major influences: chromosomal abnormalities, metabolism and nutrition, and postnatal brain disease.

Chromosomal Abnormalities Chromosomes are thread-like bodies that carry the genes that play the critical role in determining inherited characteristics. Defects resulting from **chromosomal abnormalities** are typically severe and visually evident. Fortunately, genetically caused defects are relatively rare. The vast majority of humans has normal cell structures (46 chromosomes arranged in 23 pairs) and develops without accident. Aberrations in chromosomal arrangement, either before fertilization or during early cell division, can result in a variety of abnormal characteristics.

One of the most widely recognized types of intellectual disabilities, Down's syndrome, results from chromosomal abnormality. About 3,000 to 5,000 children are born with this disorder each year in the United States (about one in every 800 to one in every 1,100 live births; The ARC, 2011a). Physical characteristics of a person with Down's syndrome include slanting eyes with folds of skin at the inner corners (epicanthal folds); excessive ability to extend the joints; short, broad hands with a single crease across the palm on one or both hands; broad feet with short toes; a flat bridge of the nose; short, low-set ears; a short neck; a small head; a small oral cavity; and/or short, high-pitched cries in infancy.

Down's syndrome has received widespread attention from medical, education, and social services professionals for many years. Part of this attention is due to the ability to identify a cause with some degree of certainty. The cause of such genetic errors has become increasingly associated with the age of both the mother and the father. The most common type of Down's syndrome is **trisomy 21**. In about 25 percent of the cases associated with trisomy 21, the age of the father (particularly when he is over 55 years old) is also a factor.

Other chromosomal abnormalities associated with intellectual disabilities include **Williams syndrome** and **fragile X syndrome**. Williams syndrome, a rare genetic disease that occurs in about 1 in every 20,000 births, is characterized by an absence of genetic materials on the seventh pair of chromosomes. Most people with Williams syndrome have some degree of intellectual disabilities and associated medical problems (such as heart and blood vessel abnormalities, low weight gain, dental abnormalities, kidney abnormalities, hypersensitive hearing, musculoskeletal problems, and elevated blood calcium levels). While exhibiting deficits in academic learning and spatial ability typical of people with intellectual disabilities, they are often described as highly personable and verbal, exhibiting unique abilities in spoken language.

Fragile X syndrome is a common hereditary cause of intellectual disabilities associated with genetic anomalies in the 23rd pair of chromosomes. Males are usually more severely affected than females because they have an X and a Y chromosome. Females have more protection because they have two X chromosomes; one X contains the normal functioning version of the gene and the other is nonfunctioning. The normal gene partially compensates for the nonfunctioning gene. The term *fragile X* refers to the fact that this gene is pinched off in some blood cells. For those affected with fragile X, intellectual differences can range from mild learning disabilities and a normal IQ to severe intellectual disabilities and autism. Physical features may include a large head and flat ears; a long, narrow face with a broad nose; a large forehead; a squared-off chin; prominent testicles; and large hands. People with fragile X are also characterized by speech and language delays or deficiencies and by behavioral problems. Some people with fragile X are socially engaging and friendly, but others have autistic-like characteristics (poor eye contact, hand flapping, hand biting, and a fascination with spinning objects) and may be aggressive. Males may also exhibit hyperactivity.

Chromosomal abnormalities
Defects or damage in chromosomes that carry genetic material and play a central role in inherited characteristics.

Trisomy 21
The most common type of Down's syndrome in which the chromosomal pairs on the 21st pair have an extra chromosome; also called *nondisjunction*.

Williams syndrome
A rare genetic disease that occurs once in every 20,000 births and is characterized by an absence of genetic materials on the seventh pair of chromosomes.

Fragile X syndrome
A condition involving damage to the chromosome structure, which appears as a breaking or splitting at the end of the X chromosome.

Aurora Photos

The most common cause of Down syndrome is a chromosomal abnormality known as trisomy 21, in which the 21st chromosomal pair carries one extra chromosome.

Metabolic disorders
The body's inability to process (metabolize) substances that can become poisonous and damage the central nervous system.

Phenylketonuria (PKU)
A disorder in which an infant cannot digest a substance found in many foods, including milk; may cause intellectual disabilities if left untreated.

Galactosemia
A disorder causing an infant to have difficulty in processing lactose. The disorder may cause intellectual disabilities and other problems.

Neurofibromatosis
An inherited disorder resulting in tumors of the skin and other tissue (such as the brain).

Tuberous sclerosis
Birth defect related to intellectual disabilities in about 66 percent of the cases and characterized by tumors on many organs.

Fetal alcohol syndrome (FAS)
Damage caused to the fetus by the mother's consumption of alcohol.

Behavioral factors
Behaviors, such as dangerous activities or maternal substance abuse, which can cause intellectual disabilities or other disabilities.

Maternal infection
Infection in a mother during pregnancy, sometimes having the potential to injure the unborn child.

Congenital rubella
German measles contracted by a mother during pregnancy, which can cause intellectual disabilities, deafness, blindness, and other neurological problems.

Human immunodeficiency virus (HIV)
A virus that reduces immune system function and has been linked to AIDS.

Toxoplasmosis
An infection caused by protozoa carried in raw meat and fecal material.

Metabolism and Nutrition **Metabolic disorders** are characterized by the body's inability to process (metabolize) certain substances that can then become poisonous and damage tissue in the central nervous system. With **phenylketonuria** (PKU), one such inherited metabolic disorder, the baby is not able to process phenylalanine, a substance found in many foods, including the milk ingested by infants. The inability to process phenylalanine results in an accumulation of poisonous substances in the body. If it goes untreated or is not treated promptly (mostly through dietary restrictions), PKU causes varying degrees of intellectual disabilities, ranging from moderate to severe deficits. If treatment is promptly instituted, however, damage may be largely prevented or at least reduced. For this reason, most states now require mandatory screening for all infants to treat the condition as early as possible and prevent lifelong problems.

Milk also presents a problem for infants affected by another metabolic disorder. With **galactosemia**, the child is unable to properly process lactose, which is the primary sugar in milk and is also found in other foods. If galactosemia remains untreated, serious damage results, such as cataracts, heightened susceptibility to infection, and reduced intellectual functioning. Dietary controls must be undertaken to eliminate milk and other foods containing lactose from the child's diet.

Postnatal Brain Disease Some disorders are associated with gross postnatal brain disease. **Neurofibromatosis**, for example, is an inherited disorder that results in multiple tumors in the skin, peripheral nerve tissue, and other areas such as the brain. Intellectual disability does not occur in all cases, although it may be evident in a small percentage of patients. The severity of intellectual disabilities and other problems resulting from neurofibromatosis seems to be related to the location of the tumors (e.g., in the cerebral tissue) and to their size and pattern of growth. Severe disorders due to postnatal brain disease occur with a variety of other conditions, including **tuberous sclerosis**, which also involves tumors in the central nervous system tissue and degeneration of cerebral white matter.

Behavioral Causes

Intellectual disabilities may result from behavioral factors that are not genetically based. Behavioral causes of intellectual disabilities include infection and intoxication (such as HIV and **fetal alcohol syndrome** as well as traumas and physical accidents). As defined by AAIDD, **behavioral factors** are "potentially causal behaviors, such as dangerous (injurious) activities or maternal substance abuse" (AAIDD, 2009, p. 126).

Infection and Intoxication Several types of **maternal infections** may result in difficulties for an unborn child. In some cases, the outcome is spontaneous abortion of the fetus; in others, it may be a severe birth defect. The probability of damage is particularly high if the infection occurs during the first three months of pregnancy. **Congenital rubella** (German measles) causes a variety of conditions, including intellectual disabilities, deafness, blindness, cerebral palsy, cardiac problems, seizures, and a variety of other neurological problems. The widespread administration of a rubella vaccine is one major reason why the incidence of intellectual disabilities as an outcome of rubella has declined significantly in recent years.

Another infection associated with intellectual disabilities is the **human immunodeficiency virus** (HIV). When transmitted from the mother to an unborn child, HIV can result in significant intellectual deficits. The virus actually crosses the placenta and infects the fetus, damaging the infant's immune system. HIV is a major cause of preventable infectious intellectual disabilities (Gargiulo, 2011).

Several prenatal infections can result in other severe disorders. **Toxoplasmosis**, an infection carried by raw meat and fecal material, can result in intellectual disabilities and other problems, such as blindness and convulsions. Toxoplasmosis is primarily a threat if the mother is exposed during pregnancy, whereas infection prior to conception seems to cause minimal danger to an unborn child.

Intoxication is cerebral damage that results from an excessive level of some toxic agent in the mother–fetus system. Excessive maternal use of alcohol or drugs or exposure to certain environmental hazards, such as X-rays or insecticides, can damage the child.

Damage to the fetus from maternal alcohol consumption is characterized by facial abnormalities, heart problems, low birth weight, small brain size, and intellectual disabilities. The terms *fetal alcohol syndrome (FAS)* and *fetal alcohol effects (FAE)* (a lesser number of the same symptoms associated with FAS) refer to a group of physical and mental birth defects resulting from a woman's drinking alcohol during pregnancy. FAS is recognized as a leading preventable cause of intellectual disabilities. The National Organization on Fetal Alcohol Syndrome (2011) estimated that one in every 100 live births involves FAS and that more than 40,000 babies with alcohol-related

© David H. Wells/Corbis

Fetal alcohol syndrome is a leading cause of preventable intellectual disabilities.

problems are born in the United States each year. Similarly, pregnant women who smoke are at greater risk of having a premature baby with complicating developmental problems such as intellectual disabilities (Centers for Disease Control and Prevention 2011). The use of drugs during pregnancy has varying effects on an infant, depending on frequency of use and drug type. Drugs known to produce serious fetal damage include LSD, heroin, morphine, and cocaine. Prescription drugs such as **anticonvulsants** and antibiotics have also been associated with infant malformations.

Maternal substance abuse is also associated with gestation disorders involving prematurity and low birth weight. **Prematurity** refers to infants delivered before 37 weeks from the first day of the last menstrual period. **Low birth weight** characterizes babies that weigh 2,500 grams (5.5 pounds) or less at birth. Prematurity and low birth weight significantly increase the risk of serious problems at birth, including intellectual disabilities.

Another factor that can seriously affect an unborn baby is blood-type incompatibility between the mother and the fetus. The most widely known form of this problem occurs when the mother's blood is Rh-negative, whereas the fetus has Rh-positive blood. In this situation, the mother's system may become sensitized to the incompatible blood type and produce defensive antibodies that damage the fetus. Medical technology can now prevent this condition through the use of a drug known as Rhogam.

Intellectual disabilities can also occur as a result of postnatal infections and toxic excess. For example, **encephalitis** may damage the central nervous system following certain types of childhood infections (e.g., measles or mumps). Reactions to certain toxic substances—such as lead, carbon monoxide, and drugs—can also damage the central nervous system.

Traumas or Physical Accidents

Traumas or physical accidents can occur prior to birth (e.g., exposure to excessive radiation), during delivery, or after the baby is born. The continuing supply of oxygen and nutrients to the baby is a critical factor during delivery. One threat to these processes involves the position of the fetus. Normal fetal position places the baby with the head toward the cervix and the face toward the mother's back. Certain other positions may result in damage to the fetus as delivery proceeds. The baby's oxygen supply may be reduced for a period of time until the head is expelled and the lungs begin to function; this lack of oxygen may result in damage to the brain. Such a condition is known as **anoxia** (oxygen deprivation).

Unknown Prenatal Influences

Several conditions associated with unknown prenatal influences can result in severe disorders. One such condition involves malformations of cerebral tissue. The most dramatic of these malformations is **anencephaly**, a condition in which the individual has a partial or even complete absence of cerebral tissue. In some cases, portions of the brain appear to develop and then degenerate. In **hydrocephalus**, which also has unknown origins, an

Anticonvulsants
Medication prescribed to control seizures (convulsions).

Prematurity
Infants delivered before 37 weeks from the first day of the mother's last menstrual period.

Low birth weight
A weight of 5½ pounds (2,500 grams) or less at birth.

Encephalitis
An inflammation of brain tissue that may damage the central nervous system.

Anoxia
A lack of oxygen that may result in permanent damage to the brain.

Anencephaly
A condition in which the person has a partial or complete absence of cerebral tissue.

Hydrocephalus
An excess of cerebrospinal fluid, often resulting in enlargement of the head and pressure on the brain, which may cause intellectual disabilities.

excess of cerebrospinal fluid accumulates in the skull and results in potentially damaging pressure on cerebral tissue. Hydrocephalus may involve an enlarged head and cause decreased intellectual functioning. If surgical intervention occurs early, the damage may be slight because the pressure will not have been serious or prolonged.

Although we have presented a number of possible causal factors associated with intellectual disabilities, the cause is unknown and undeterminable in many cases. Additionally, many conditions associated with intellectual disabilities are due to the interaction of hereditary and environmental factors. Although we cannot always identify the causes of intellectual disabilities, measures can be taken to prevent their occurrence.

We now turn our attention to educating students with intellectual disabilities from early childhood through the transition from school to adult life. The provision of appropriate services and supports for individuals with intellectual disabilities is a lifelong process. For children with mild intellectual disabilities, educational services may not begin until they are in elementary school. However, for those with more severe intellectual disabilities, services and supports will begin at birth and may continue into the adult years.

Educational Services and Supports: The Early Childhood Years

FOCUS 6
Why are early intervention services for children with intellectual disabilities so important?

Children with mild intellectual disabilities may exhibit subtle developmental delays in comparison to age mates, but parents may not view these discrepancies as significant enough to seek intervention during the preschool years. Even if parents are concerned and seek help for their child prior to elementary school, they are often confronted with professionals who are apathetic toward early childhood education. Some professionals believe that early childhood services may actually create problems, rather than remedy them, because the child may not be mature enough to cope with the pressures of structured learning in an educational environment. Simply stated, the maturation philosophy means that before entering school, a child should reach a level of growth at which he or she is ready to learn certain skills. Unfortunately, this philosophy has kept many children out of the public schools for years.

The antithesis of the maturation philosophy is the prevention of further problems in learning and behavior through intervention. **Head Start**, funded as a federal preschool program for students from low-income families, is a prevention program that attempts to identify and instruct at-risk children before they enter public school. Although Head Start did not have the results that were initially anticipated (the virtual elimination of school adjustment problems for students from low-income families), it has represented a significant move forward and continues to receive widespread support from parents and professionals alike. The rationale for early education is widely accepted in the field of special education and is an important part of the IDEA mandate.

Head Start
A federally funded preschool program for students with disadvantages to give them "a head start" prior to elementary school.

Intervention based on normal patterns of growth is referred to as *developmental milestones* because it seeks to develop, remedy, or adapt learner skills based on the child's variation from what is considered normal. This progression of skills continues as the child ages chronologically; rate of progress depends on the severity of the condition. Some children with profound intellectual disabilities may never exceed a developmental age of 6 months. Those with moderate intellectual disabilities may develop to a level that will enable them to lead fulfilling lives as adults, with varying levels of support.

Standard 3
Individual Learning Differences

Standard 7
Instructional Planning

The importance of early intervention cannot be overstated. Significant advances have been made in the area of early intervention, including improved assessment, curricula, and instructional technologies; increasing numbers of children receiving services; and appreciation of the need to individualize services for families as well as children (Batshaw, Pellegrino, & Rozien, 2007; Berk, 2005; Guralnick, 2001). Early intervention techniques, such as **infant stimulation** programs, focus on the acquisition of sensorimotor skills and intellectual development. Infant stimulation involves learning simple reflex activities and equilibrium reactions. Subsequent intervention then expands into all areas of human growth and development.

Infant stimulation
An array of visual, auditory, and physical stimuli programs to promote infant development.

Educational Services and Supports: Elementary School Years

Public education is a relatively new concept as it relates to students with intellectual disabilities, particularly those with more severe characteristics. Historically, many of these students were defined as *noneducable* by the public schools because they did not fit the programs offered by general education. Because such programs were built on a foundation of academic learning that emphasized reading, writing, and arithmetic, students with intellectual disabilities could not meet the academic standards set by the schools and, thus, were excluded. Public schools were not expected to adapt to the needs of students with intellectual disabilities; rather, the students were expected to adapt to the schools.

With the passage of Public Law 94-142 (now IDEA), schools that excluded these children for so long now face the challenge of providing an appropriate education for all children with intellectual disabilities. Education has been redefined on the basis of a new set of values. Instruction and support for children of elementary school age with intellectual disabilities focus on decreasing dependence on others, while concurrently teaching adaptation to the environment. Therefore, instruction must concentrate on those skills that facilitate the child's interaction with others and emphasize independence in the community. Instruction for children with intellectual disabilities generally includes development of motor skills, self-help skills, social skills, communication skills, and academic skills.

FOCUS 7
Identify five skill areas that should be addressed in programs for elementary-age children with intellectual disabilities.

Motor Skills

The acquisition of motor skills is fundamental to the developmental process and a prerequisite to successful learning in other content areas, including self-help and social skills. Gross motor development involves general mobility, including the interaction of the body with the environment. Gross motor skills are developed in a sequence, ranging from movements that make balance possible to higher-order locomotor patterns. Locomotor patterns are intended to move the person freely through the environment. Gross motor movements include controlling the head and neck, rolling, body righting, sitting, crawling, standing, walking, running, jumping, and skipping.

Fine motor development requires more precision and steadiness than the skills developed in the gross motor area. The development of fine motor skills, including reaching, grasping, and manipulating objects, is initially dependent on the ability of the child to visually fix on an object and visually track a moving target. Coordination of the eye and hand is an integral factor in many skill areas, as well as in fine motor development. Eye-hand coordination is the basis of social and leisure activities and is essential to the development of the object-control skills required in employment.

CEC
Standard 7
Instructional Planning
Standard 8
Assessment

Self-Help Skills

The development of self-help skills is critical to a child's progression toward independence from caregivers. Self-help skills include eating, dressing, and maintaining personal hygiene. Eating skills range from finger feeding and drinking from a cup to using proper table behaviors (such as employing utensils and napkins), serving food, and following rules of etiquette. Dressing skills include buttoning, zipping, buckling, lacing, and tying. Personal hygiene skills are developed in an age-appropriate context. Basic hygiene skills include toileting, face and hand washing, bathing, tooth brushing, hair combing, and shampooing. Skills associated with adolescent and adult years include skin care, shaving, hair setting, and the use of deodorants and cosmetics.

Social Skills

Social skills training emphasizes the importance of learning problem-solving and decision-making skills and of using appropriate communication in a social context. Difficulty with problem solving and decision making have been barriers to the success of people with

CEC
Standard 5
Learning Environments and Social Interactions

Figure 9.3 *Instructional Targets in Social Skills Training*

Establish eye contact.	Make requests.
Establish appropriate proximity.	Respond to requests.
Maintain appropriate body posture during conversation.	Ask for information.
Speak with appropriate volume, rate, and expression.	Provide information.
Maintain attention during exchange.	Ask for clarification.
Initiate greetings.	Respond to requests for clarification.
Respond to greetings.	Extend social invitation.
Initiate partings.	Deliver refusals.
Respond to partings.	Respond to refusals.
Discriminate appropriate times to greet or part.	Use social courtesies (please, thank you, apology).
Answer questions.	Maintain topic.
Ask questions.	Initiate a new topic.

SOURCE: From Westling, D., & Fox, L. (2009). *Teaching students with severe disabilities*. Upper Saddle River, NJ: Merrill.

intellectual disabilities in community and school settings. Students with intellectual disabilities will not learn these skills through observation but must be specifically taught how to solve problems.

Westling and Fox (2009) suggested several learning outcomes for students in the use of appropriate communication in a social context. They must be able to initiate and maintain a conversation (verbal, signed, or pictorial) while using appropriate social conventions and courtesies (e.g., staying on topic, not interrupting the speaker, using appropriate body posture). These authors suggested a list of social skills that are important instructional targets for students with intellectual disabilities (see Figure 9.3).

INCLUSION AND COLLABORATION THROUGH THE LIFESPAN
PEOPLE WITH INTELLECTUAL DISABILITIES

EARLY CHILDHOOD YEARS

Tips for the Family

- Promote family learning about the diversity of all people in the context of understanding the child with intellectual differences.

- Create opportunities for friendships to develop between your child and children without disabilities, in preschool and in family and neighborhood settings.

- Help facilitate your child's opportunities and access to neighborhood preschools by actively participating in the education planning process and collaborating with professionals with multidisciplinary backgrounds (health care, social services, education, etc.). Become familiar with the individualized family service plan (IFSP) and how it can serve as a planning tool to support the inclusion of your child in preschool programs that involve students without disabilities.

Tips for the General Education Preschool Teacher

- Focus on the child's individual abilities first. Whatever labels have been placed on the child (e.g., "mentally retarded") will have little to do with instructional needs.

- When teaching the child, focus on presenting each component of a task clearly while reducing outside stimuli that may distract the child from learning.

- Begin with simple tasks, and move to more complex ones as the child masters each skill.

- Verbally label stimuli, such as objects or people, as often as possible to provide the child with both auditory and visual input.

- Provide a lot of practice in initial learning phases, using short but frequent sessions to ensure that the child has mastered the skill before moving on to more complex tasks.

- Create success experiences by rewarding correct responses to tasks as well as appropriate behavior with peers who are not disabled.

- Help young children with intellectual disabilities to be able to transfer learning from school to the home and neighborhood. Facilitate such transfer by providing information that is meaningful to the child and noting how the initial and transfer tasks are similar.

Tips for Preschool Personnel

- Support the inclusion of young children with intellectual disabilities in classrooms and programs.

- Collaborate with the team of multidisciplinary professionals, including teachers, staff, related services professionals (such as speech and language pathologists), and volunteers as they attempt to create success experiences for the child in the preschool setting.

- Integrate families as well as children into the preschool programs. Offer parents as many opportunities as possible to be part of the program (e.g., advisory boards, volunteer experiences).

Tips for Neighbors and Friends

- Look for opportunities for young neighborhood children who are not disabled to interact during playtimes with a child who has an intellectual disability.

- Provide a supportive community environment for the family of a young child who has an intellectual disability. Encourage the family, including the child, to participate in neighborhood activities (e.g., outings, barbecues, outdoor yard and street cleanups, crime watches).

- Try to understand how a young child with intellectual disabilities is similar rather than different to other children in the neighborhood. Focus on those similarities in your interactions with other neighbors and children in your community.

ELEMENTARY YEARS

Tips for the Family

- Actively participate with the multidisciplinary team in the development of your son or daughter's individualized education program (IEP). Through active participation, advocate for those goals that you would like to see on the IEP that will focus on your child's developing social interaction and communication skills in natural settings (e.g., the general education classroom).

- To help facilitate your son's or daughter's inclusion in the neighborhood elementary school, help the multidisciplinary team of professionals to better understand the importance of inclusion with peers who are not disabled (e.g., riding on the same school bus, going to recess and lunch at the same time, participating in school-wide assemblies).

- Participate in as many school functions for parents (e.g., PTA, parent advisory groups, volunteering) as is reasonable, to connect your family to the mainstream of the school.

- Create opportunities for your child to make friends with same-age children without disabilities.

Tips for the General Education Classroom Teacher

- View children with intellectual disabilities as children, first and foremost. Focus on their similarities to other children rather than on their differences.

- Recognize children with intellectual disabilities for their own accomplishments within the classroom, rather than comparing them to those of peers without disabilities.

- Employ cooperative learning strategies wherever possible to promote effective learning by all students. Use peers without disabilities as support for students with intellectual disabilities. This may include establishing peer–buddy programs or peer and cross-age tutoring.

- Consider all members of the classroom when you organize the physical environment. Find ways to meet the individual needs of each child (e.g., establishing aisles that will accommodate a wheelchair and organizing desks to facilitate tutoring on assigned tasks).

Tips for School Personnel

- Integrate the multidisciplinary resources within the school to meet the needs of all children.

- Wherever possible, help general classroom teachers access the collaborative and multidisciplinary resources necessary to meet the needs of students with intellectual disabilities. Make available instructional materials and programs to whoever needs them, not just to those identified as being in special education.

- Help general and special education teachers to develop peer–partner and support networks for students with intellectual disabilities.

- Promote the heterogeneous grouping of students. Avoid clustering large numbers of students with intellectual disabilities in a single general education classroom. Integrate no more than two in each elementary classroom.

- Maintain the same schedules for students with intellectual disabilities as for all other students in the building. Recess, lunch, school assemblies, and bus arrival and departure schedules should be identical for all students.

- Create opportunities for the multidisciplinary personnel in the school to collaborate in the development and implementation of instructional programs for individual children.

Tips for Neighbors and Friends

- Support families who are seeking to have their child with intellectual disabilities educated with children who are not disabled. This will give children with intellectual disabilities more opportunities for interacting with children who are not disabled, both in school and in the local community.

SECONDARY AND TRANSITION YEARS

Tips for the Family

- Create opportunities for your son or daughter to participate in activities that are of interest to him or her, beyond the school day, with same-age peers who are not disabled, including high school clubs, sports, or just hanging out in the local mall.

- Promote opportunities for students from your son's or daughter's high school to visit your home. Help arrange get-togethers or parties involving students from the neighborhood and/or school.

- Become actively involved in the development of the individualized education and transition program. Explore with the high school's team of advisers what should be done to assist your son or daughter in the transition from school to adult life.

Tips for the General Education Classroom Teacher

- Collaborate with the school's multidisciplinary team (special educators, related services personnel, administrators, paraeducators) to adapt subject matter in your classroom (e.g., science, math, or physical education) to the individual needs of students with intellectual disabilities.

- Let students without disabilities know that students with intellectual disabilities belong in their classroom. The goals and activities of these students may be different from those of other students, but with support, students with intellectual disabilities will benefit from working with you and the other students in the class.

- Support students with intellectual disabilities in becoming involved in extracurricular activities. If you are the faculty sponsor of a club or organization, explore whether these students are interested and how they could get involved.

Tips for School Personnel

- Advocate for parents of high school–age students with intellectual disabilities to participate in the activities of the school (e.g., committees and PTA).

- Help facilitate parental collaboration in the IEP process during the high school years by helping the school's multidisciplinary team value parental input that focuses on a desire to include their child in the mainstream of the school. Parents will be more active when school personnel have general and positive contact with the family.

- Provide human and material support to high school special education or vocational teachers seeking to develop community-based instruction programs that focus on students learning and applying skills in actual community settings (e.g., grocery stores, malls, theaters, parks, and work sites).

Tips for Neighbors, Friends, and Potential Employers

- Work with the family and school personnel to create opportunities for students with intellectual disabilities to participate in community activities (such as going to the movies, "hanging out" with peers without disabilities in the neighborhood mall, and going to high school sports events).

- As a potential employer, work with the high school to locate and establish community-based employment training sites for students with intellectual disabilities.

ADULT YEARS

Tips for the Family

- Become aware of what life will be like for your son or daughter in the local community during the adult years. What formal supports (government-funded advocacy organizations) from various disciplines (such as health care and social services) and informal supports are available in your community? What are the characteristics of adult service programs? Explore adult support systems in the local community in the areas of supported living, employment, and recreation and leisure.

Tips for Neighbors, Friends, and Potential Employers

- Seek ways to become part of the community support network for individuals with intellectual disabilities. Be alert to ways in which these individuals can become and remain actively involved in community employment, neighborhood recreational activities, and functions at a local house of worship.

- As potential employers in the community, seek information on employment of people with intellectual disabilities. Find out about programs (e.g., supported employment) that focus on arranging work for people with intellectual disabilities while meeting your needs as an employer.

Communication Skills

The ability to communicate with others is an essential component of growth and development. Without communication, there can be no interaction. Communication systems for children with intellectual disabilities take three general forms: verbal language, augmentative communication (including sign language and language boards), and a combination of the verbal and augmentative approaches. The approach used depends on the child's capability. A child who can develop the requisite skills for spoken language will have greatly enhanced everyday interactive skills. For a child unable to develop verbal skills as an effective means of communication, manual communication must be considered. Such children must develop some form of communication that will facilitate inclusion with peers and family members throughout their lives. For some specific tips

HOW DO PEOPLE WITH INTELLECTUAL DISABILITIES USE TECHNOLOGY?

Communication. For individuals who cannot communicate vocally, technology can help them communicate. Augmentative and alternative communication (ACC) may involve technology ranging from low-tech message boards to computerized voice output communication aids and synthesized speech.

Mobility. Simple to sophisticated computer-controlled wheelchairs and mobility aids are available. Technology may be used to aid in finding directions, guiding users to destinations. Computerized cueing systems and robots have also been used to guide users with intellectual disabilities.

Environmental control. Assistive technology can help people with severe or multiple disabilities to control electrical appliances, operate audio/video equipment such as home entertainment systems, or perform basic tasks such as locking and unlocking doors.

Activities of daily living. Technology is assisting people with disabilities to successfully complete everyday tasks of self-care:

- Automated and computerized dining devices allow an individual who needs assistance at mealtime to eat more independently.

- Audio prompting devices can assist a person with memory difficulties to complete a task or to follow a sequence of steps from start to finish in such activities as making a bed or taking medication.

- Video-based instructional materials can help people learn functional life skills such as grocery shopping, writing a check, paying the bills, or using the ATM.

Education. Technology is used in education to aid communication, support activities of daily living, and to enhance learning. Computer-assisted instruction can help in many areas, including word recognition, math, spelling, and even social skills. Computers have also been found to promote interaction with nondisabled peers.

Employment. Technology, such as video-assisted training, is being used for job training and job skill development and to teach complex skills for appropriate job behavior and social interaction. Prompting systems using digital recorders and computer-based prompting devices have been used to help workers stay on task. Computerized prompting systems can help people manage their time in scheduling job activities.

Sports and recreation. Toys can be adapted with switches and other technologies to facilitate play for children. Computer or video games provide age-appropriate social opportunities and help children learn cognitive and eye–hand coordination skills. Specially designed Internet-access software can help people with intellectual disabilities access the World Wide Web. Exercise and physical fitness can be supported by video-based technology.

WHAT BARRIERS TO TECHNOLOGY USE WILL PEOPLE WITH INTELLECTUAL DISABILITIES ENCOUNTER?

Even though it is the goal of most technology development efforts to incorporate the principles of universal design, cognitive access is not carefully considered. Universal design ensures that the technology may be used by all people without adaptation. An example of cognitive access can be found in computer use—if someone with a disability is using a computer, the onscreen messages should last long enough or provide enough wait time to allow a disabled person to consider whether to press a computer key. Or the time should be sufficient between making a phone call and pressing the numbers to complete the call using a rechargeable phone card as payment. Because individuals with intellectual disabilities have a range of learning and processing abilities, it is difficult to develop assistive technology solutions that are appropriate for all skill levels.

DO SCHOOLS HAVE TO PROVIDE ASSISTIVE TECHNOLOGY TO STUDENTS WHO NEED IT?

IDEA requires that the need for assistive technology be considered for all students when developing individualized education programs. The intention of the special education law is this: If a student with disabilities needs technology to be able to learn, the school district will (1) evaluate the student's technology needs; (2) acquire the necessary technology; (3) coordinate technology use with other therapies and interventions; and (4) provide training for the individual, the individual's family, and the school staff in the effective use of the technology. If a student's individualized education program specifies assistive technology is needed for home use to ensure appropriate education, the school must provide it. If the school purchases an assistive technology device for use by a student, the school owns it. The student cannot take it when moving to another school or when leaving school.

SOURCE: From "Technology for people with intellectual disabilities," Copyright © 2009 The Arc. Reprinted with permission from The Arc, www.thearc.org <http://www.thearc.org> (1825 K St. NW Suite 1200 Washington, DC 20006)

on effective ways to include people with intellectual disabilities from early childhood through the adult years, see the nearby Inclusion and Collaboration through the Lifespan feature, "People with Intellectual Disabilities."

Some students with intellectual disabilities benefit from the use of **assistive technology** and communication aids. Assistive technology may involve a variety of communication approaches that aid people with intellectual disabilities who have limited speech ability. These approaches may be low-tech (a language board with pictures) or high-tech (a laptop computer with voice output). Regardless of the approach, a communication aid can be a valuable tool in helping people with intellectual disabilities communicate with others. For more information, see the nearby feature, "Assistive Technology for People with Intellectual Disabilities."

Assistive technology
Devices such as computers, hearing aids, wheelchairs, and other equipment that help individuals adapt to the natural settings of home, school, and family.

Academic Skills

Students with intellectual disabilities can benefit from instruction in basic or functional academic programs. In the area of literacy, students with mild intellectual disabilities will require a systematic instructional program that allows for differences in the rate of learning, but they will learn to read when given rich, intensive, and extensive literary experiences. In fact, these students may achieve as high as a fourth- or fifth-grade level in reading. The Partnership for Accessible Reading Assessment (2011) emphasized that students with intellectual disabilities can make significant progress in literacy programs that emphasize **direct instruction** (the direct teaching of letters, words, and syntactic, phonetic, and semantic analysis) in conjunction with written literature that is meaningful to the student or that draws on the student's own writings.

Direct instruction
Teaching academic subjects through precisely sequenced lessons involving drill, practice, and immediate feedback.

A significant relationship exists between measured IQ and reading achievement: Students with intellectual disabilities read well below the level of nondisabled students of the same age. This relationship seems to suggest that reading instruction should be limited to higher-functioning students with intellectual disabilities. A growing body of research, however, indicates that students with more severe intellectual disabilities can learn academic skills. According to Browder and colleagues (2011), "The emerging research shows that students with severe disabilities can master academic skills. However, educators continue to have substantial work ahead to demonstrate effective practices for teaching them the wide range of academic skills typical of the general curriculum" (p. 493).

A functional reading program uses materials that are a part of a person's normal routines in work, everyday living, and leisure activities. For example, functional reading involves words that are frequently encountered in the environment, such as those used on labels or signs in public places; words that warn of possible risks; and symbols such as the skull and crossbones to denote poisonous substances.

Students with intellectual disabilities also have challenges in developing math skills, but the majority of those with mild intellectual disabilities can learn basic addition and subtraction. However, these children will have significant difficulty in the areas of mathematical reasoning and problem-solving tasks (Beirne-Smith, Patton, & Hill, 2010). Math skills are taught most efficiently through the use of money concepts. For example, functional math involves activities such as learning to use a checkbook, shopping in a grocery store, or using a vending machine. The immediate practical application motivates the student. Regardless of the approach used, arithmetic instruction must be concrete and practical to compensate for the child's deficiencies in reasoning ability.

Transitioning from School to Adult Life

FOCUS 8
Identify four educational goals for adolescents with intellectual disabilities.

The goals of an educational program for adolescents with intellectual disabilities are to increase personal independence, enhance opportunities for participation in the local community, prepare for employment, and facilitate a successful transition to the adult years.

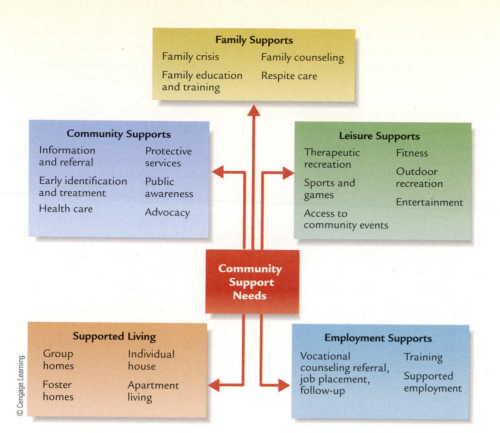

Figure 9.4 *Categories of Supports Needed During the Adult Years*

Family Supports
Family crisis · Family counseling
Family education and training · Respite care

Community Supports
Information and referral · Protective services
Early identification and treatment · Public awareness
Health care · Advocacy

Leisure Supports
Therapeutic recreation · Fitness
Sports and games · Outdoor recreation
Access to community events · Entertainment

Community Support Needs

Supported Living
Group homes · Individual house
Foster homes · Apartment living

Employment Supports
Vocational counseling referral, job placement, follow-up · Training · Supported employment

© Cengage Learning

Personal Independence and Participation in the Community

The term *independence* refers to the development and application of skills that lead to greater self-sufficiency in daily personal life, including personal care, self-help, and appropriate leisure activities. Participation in the community includes access to programs, facilities (grocery stores, shopping malls, restaurants, theaters, and parks), and services that people without disabilities often take for granted. Adolescents with intellectual disabilities need opportunities for interaction with peers without disabilities (other than caregivers), access to community events, sustained social relationships, and involvement in choices that affect their lives. An illustration of the range of community services and supports that can facilitate the transition of an adolescent with intellectual disabilities into the adult years is shown in Figure 9.4.

CEC

Standard 1
Foundations

Sheltered workshop
A segregated vocational training and employment setting for people with disabilities.

Employment Preparation

Work is a crucial measure of any person's success during adulthood, providing the primary opportunity for social interaction, a basis for personal identity and status, and a chance to contribute to the community. These needs are basic to adults who have intellectual disabilities, just as they are for their peers without disabilities.

Fortunately, employment training for students with intellectual disabilities is shifting from the isolation and "getting ready" orientation of a **sheltered workshop** to activities accomplished in community employment. Goals and objectives are developed according to the demands of the community work setting and

© Robin Nelson/Photo Edit

For adolescents with moderate and severe intellectual disabilities, employment preparation during high school is shifting away from segregated sheltered workshops to supported employment in inclusive community settings.

the functioning level of the individual. The focus is on helping each person to learn and apply skills in a job setting while receiving the support necessary to succeed. Providing ongoing assistance to the individual on the job is the basis of an approach known as supported employment. **Supported employment** is work in an inclusive setting for individuals with disabilities (including those with intellectual disabilities) who are expected to need continuous support services and for whom competitive employment has traditionally not been possible.

Research indicates that people with intellectual disabilities can work in community employment if adequate training and support are provided (Crockett & Hardman, 2009; Wehman, 2011). Following are some suggested guidelines in developing a comprehensive employment training program for students with intellectual disabilities:

- The student should have the opportunity to make informed choices about what jobs he or she wants to do and where he or she wants to work.
- The student should receive employment training in community settings prior to graduation from high school.
- Employment training should focus on work opportunities present in the local area where the individual currently lives.
- The focus of the employment training should be on specific job training as the student approaches graduation.
- Collaboration between the school and adult service agencies must be part of the employment-training program (Drew & Hardman, 2007).

Supported employment
Jobs for the severely disabled who will need continuous support, and for whom competitive jobs have traditionally not been possible.

CASE STUDY   DESIGNING A ROAD MAP FOR THE FUTURE

ELLA

When Ella was 4 years old, she had a near-drowning incident that resulted in [a significant brain injury]. Now Ella is a 15-year-old student at Mountain High School. She enjoys school but often struggles to understand instructions given to her by teachers and has difficulty concentrating for long periods. The special education team at Mountain High has been committed to supporting Ella in the general education curriculum and has helped her develop coping skills when she feels overwhelmed and frustrated. Ella gets very excited when discussing her future plans for adulthood because she has wanted to be an actress since she was a small child. . . .

Ella will be 16 years old at the beginning of next year and has begun preparing for her first transition planning meeting. She sits down with Mr. Allen, the special educator, and discusses her personal vision for her future, as well

as possible accommodations she feels will help her succeed. Ella would like to move to the city when she graduates and enroll in a small acting school. During the planning session, Ella's parents express concerns regarding her judgment of new people, as well as her problem-solving skills in dealing with stressful situations. Her parents are clearly apprehensive about Ella's plans to live on her own in an apartment in the city and attend acting school.

So the planning team works together to discuss possible coordinated activities that will prepare Ella for the transition to adulthood and help her work toward her personal goals. For the remainder of the school year, Mr. Allen and Ella work to complete various skill inventories and assessment to gather more information about her needs and interests. Over the summer, Ella and her parents attend a recruitment event at the acting college and look into various living arrangements and supports in the city.

When school begins in the fall, Mr. Allen works with the school faculty to determine which general educators will be teaching the classes that Ella will be taking so [these teachers] can attend the meeting. When the transition planning meeting is held, the entire team is able to use the report from the planning team to establish a coordinated set of activities and support services that will lead Ella to achieving the postschool goals she envisioned for herself! (adapted from Polychronis & McDonnell, 2009, p. 82).

APPLICATION

1. Why is it so important to begin transition planning for Ella at age 15 when she may not leave school until she is 22 years old?

2. How did Mr. Allen deal with the differing views between Ella and her parents regarding Ella's future desire to go to acting school?

Inclusive Education

Historically, special education for students with intellectual disabilities meant segregated education. Today, however, the focus is on including these students in general education schools and classrooms. Some students with intellectual disabilities are included for only a part of the school day and attend only those general education classes that their individualized education program (IEP) teams consider consistent with their needs and functioning levels (such as physical education, industrial arts, or home economics). Other students with intellectual disabilities attend general education classes for all or the majority of the school day. For these students, special education consists primarily of services and supports intended to facilitate their opportunities and success in the general education classroom. Placement information from the U.S. Department of Education (2011) indicated that approximately 94 percent of students with intellectual disabilities between the ages of 6 and 21 were placed in general education schools for the entire day. Of these students, about 11 percent were served in a general education class for at least 80 percent of the time, and 53 percent spent more than half of their time outside the general education class. For more information on the effectiveness of academic and social inclusive education programs for students with intellectual disabilities, see the nearby TeachSource Video, "Bobby: Serving a Student with Special Needs in an Inclusive Elementary Classroom."

Another placement option for students with disabilities is the special school. Special schools are defined as facilities exclusively for students with intellectual disabilities or other disabilities. Approximately 4.1 percent of students with intellectual disabilities were found to attend public special schools, and less than one percent attended private special schools (U.S. Department of Education, 2007). In this era of inclusion, considerable controversy exists as to whether there is *any* justification for placing students with intellectual disabilities in special schools.

FÓCUS 9

Why is the inclusion of students with intellectual disabilities in general education settings important to an appropriate educational experience?

Standard 5
Learning Environments and Social Interactions

Looking Toward a Bright Future

Historically, services for people with intellectual disabilities have been primarily focused on isolating and caring for the individual rather than facilitating their access and participation in school, family, and community life. With the passage of civil rights and federal education legislation in the late 20th century, the promise of autonomy, choice, and independence for people with intellectual disabilities has become a reality for some but remains a dream for others. Even today, more than 100,000 people with intellectual and developmental disabilities remain institutionalized in the United States. Others, although not institutionalized, have little control over where, with whom, and how they live in their communities (Lakin, 2005). And then there are the Troy Daniels of this world. Troy, a young man with Down's syndrome who uses a wheelchair, was selected to stand and deliver the senior speech before his graduating class at Northfield High School in Vermont. Here is what Troy had to say to friends, family, and neighbors on that special day:

> Not long ago people with disabilities could not go to school with other kids; they had to go to special schools. They could not have real friends; they call people like me "retard." That breaks my heart. . . . The law says that I can come to school but no law can make me have friends. But then some kids started to think that I was okay, first just one or two kids were nice to me. . . . Others started to hang out with me and they found out we could be friends. I cared about them and they cared about me. . . . I want all people to know and see that these students I call my friends are the real teachers of life.

FOCUS REVIEW

FOCUS 1 Identify the major components of the American Association on Intellectual and Developmental Disabilities (AAIDD) definition and classification system for people with intellectual and developmental disabilities.

- There are significant limitations in intellectual abilities.
- There are significant limitations in adaptive behavior as expressed in conceptual, social, and practical adaptive skills.
- Disability originates before the age of 18.
- The severity of the condition is tempered by the individual's participation, interactions, and social roles within the community; by her or his overall physical and mental health; and by the environmental context.
- Classification for severity of the condition may be described in terms of mild, moderate, severe, or profound intellectual disabilities.
- Educability expectations as a classification are designated for groups of children who are educable and children who are trainable.
- Medical descriptors classify intellectual disabilities on the basis of the origin of the condition (e.g., infection, intoxication, trauma, chromosomal abnormality).
- Classification based on the type and extent of support needed categorizes people with intellectual disabilities as having intermittent, limited, extensive, or pervasive needs for support to function in natural settings.

FOCUS 2 What is the prevalence of intellectual disabilities?

- The prevalence of intellectual disabilities world-wide and across all ages is estimated at 1 percent of the total population.
- There are approximately 600,000 students between the ages of 6 and 21 labeled as having intellectual disabilities and receiving service under IDEA. Approximately 10 percent of all students with disabilities between the ages of 6 and 21 have intellectual disabilities.
- Overall, students with intellectual disabilities constitute about 0.88 percent of the total school population.

FOCUS 3 Identify intellectual, self-regulation, and adaptive skills characteristics of individuals with intellectual disabilities.

- Intellectual characteristics may include learning and memory deficiencies, difficulties in establishing learning sets, and inefficient rehearsal strategies.
- Self-regulation characteristics include difficulty in mediating or regulating behavior.
- Adaptive skills characteristics may include difficulties in coping with the demands of the environment, developing interpersonal relationships, developing language skills, and taking care of personal needs.

FOCUS 4 Identify the academic, motivational, speech and language, and physical characteristics of children with intellectual disabilities.

- Students with intellectual disabilities exhibit significant deficits in the areas of reading and mathematics.
- Students with mild intellectual disabilities have poor reading mechanics and comprehension, compared to their same-age peers.
- Students with intellectual disabilities may be able to learn basic computations but be unable to apply concepts appropriately in a problem-solving situation.
- Motivational difficulties may reflect learned helplessness— "No matter what I do or how hard I try, I will not succeed."
- The most common speech difficulties involve articulation problems, voice problems, and stuttering.
- Language differences are generally associated with delays in language development rather than with the bizarre use of language.
- Physical differences generally are not evident for individuals with mild intellectual disabilities because these intellectual disabilities are usually not associated with genetic factors.
- The more severe the intellectual disabilities, the greater the probability of genetic causation and of compounding physiological problems.

FOCUS 5 Identify the causes of intellectual disabilities.

- Intellectual disabilities are the result of multiple causes, some known, and many unknown. The cause of intellectual disabilities is generally not known for individuals with mild intellectual disabilities.
- Causes associated with moderate to profound intellectual disabilities include sociocultural influences, biomedical factors, behavioral factors, and unknown prenatal influences.

FOCUS 6 Why are early intervention services for children with intellectual disabilities so important?

- Early intervention services are needed to provide a stimulating environment for children to enhance growth and development.
- Early intervention programs focus on the development of communication skills, social interaction, and readiness for formal instruction.

FOCUS 7 Identify five skill areas that should be addressed in programs for elementary-age children with intellectual disabilities.

- Motor development skills
- Self-help skills
- Social skills
- Communication skills
- Academic skills

FOCUS 8 Identify four educational goals for adolescents with intellectual disabilities.

- To increase the individual's personal independence
- To enhance opportunities for participation in the local community
- To prepare for employment
- To facilitate a successful transition to the adult years

FOCUS 9 Why is the inclusion of students with intellectual disabilities in general education settings important to an appropriate educational experience?

- Regardless of the severity of their condition, students with intellectual disabilities benefit from placement in general education environments where opportunities for inclusion with nondisabled peers are systematically planned and implemented.

Council for Exceptional Children (CEC) Standards to Accompany Chapter 9

 If you are thinking about a career in special education, you should know that many states use national standards developed by the Council for Exceptional Children (CEC) to assess a teacher candidate's knowledge and skills for working with students with disabilities. See a complete listing of the 10 CEC Content Standards on the inside back cover of this text.

1 Foundations
2 Development and Characteristics of Learners
3 Individual Learning Differences
5 Learning Environments and Social Interactions
7 Instructional Planning
8 Assessment

Mastery Activities and Assignments

 To master the content within this chapter, complete the following activities and assignments. Online and interactive versions of these activities are also available on the accompanying Education CourseMate website, where you may also access TeachSource videos, chapter web links, interactive quizzes, portfolio activities, flash cards, an integrated eBook, and much more!

1. Complete a written test of the chapter's content. If your instructor requires a written test of your content knowledge for this chapter, keep a copy for your portfolio. A practice test on the information covered in this chapter is available through the Education CourseMate Website.
2. Review the Case Study, "Designing a Road Map for the Future," and respond in writing to the Application Questions. Keep a copy of the case study and your written response for your portfolio.
3. Read the Debate Forum, "Why is Using the 'R' Word Such a Big Deal? It's Only a Word," in this chapter and then visit the Education CourseMate website to complete the activity, "Take a Stand." Keep a copy of this activity for your portfolio.
4. Participate in a community service learning activity. Service learning is a valuable way to enhance your learning experience. Visit this book's Education CourseMate website for suggested community service learning activities that correspond to the information presented in this chapter. Develop a reflective journal of the service learning experience for your portfolio.

CHAPTER 10

Communication Disorders

© Ted Foxx/Alamy

FOCUS PREVIEW

As you read the chapter, focus on these key concepts:

1 Identify four ways in which speech, language, and communication are interrelated.

2 Explain how language delay and language disorder differ.

3 Identify three factors that are thought to cause language disorders.

4 Describe how treatment approaches for language disorders generally differ for children and for adults.

5 Cite three factors that are thought to cause stuttering.

6 Identify two ways in which learning theory and home environments are related to delayed speech.

7 Identify two reasons why some professionals are reluctant to treat functional articulation disorders in young schoolchildren.

Vonetta Flowers

This presentation was made by Olympic gold medalist Vonetta Flowers when she received the "Hearing Hear-o-Award":

Tonight I stand before you as a parent of a child who has a hearing loss. . . . I accept the "Hearing Hear-o-Award" on behalf of all the people who have been touched by your medical advancements in technology, your financial contributions, and the life-changing devices that have enabled our kids to hear. Just a few years ago I knew nothing about the deaf community. I thought I had the perfect life. My teammate and I won the gold at the 2002 Winter Olympics, my husband and I were pregnant with twins and all we needed was a dog, a white picket fence, and we would have our chance at living the American Dream. . . .

We never imagined that at 30 weeks, I would deliver twin boys, who weighed two pounds, nine ounces and three pounds, eight ounces . . . that they would have to spend six to seven weeks in the hospitals' NCIU . . . that one of our sons would be born with a profound hearing loss and that we would have to learn sign language in order to communicate with him. We sought the advice of specialists; we

REUTERS/Fabrizio Bensch/Landov

researched the Internet and felt like we had to become experts overnight. Each day we found ourselves trying to understand what level of hearing, if any, our son had. We tried the Baha or the bone conduction hearing aid . . . which didn't work. We inquired about the cochlear implant, but since he was born without hearing nerves, he didn't qualify for this type of device.

After speaking with doctors in California, New York, and Alabama, we were introduced to a new procedure called the ABI. . . . The auditory brainstem implant had been successfully implanted in adults in the U.S., but it had not been approved by the FDA

for kids under 12. Finding this option gave us a new enthusiasm and helped us to keep our dream alive . . . of Jorden hearing our voices and eventually learning to speak.

Jorden's life did not turn out the way we planned it, and that's okay, because he has already impacted more lives than we'd ever expected. . . . Over the past few years he's taught us how to be more thankful, he's helped us to be more appreciative of each gift that God has given us, and encouraged us to fight for issues that affect our community. No, our life isn't the way we planned it, but we couldn't imagine it any other way. . . . Jorden became the first child in the U.S. and the eighteenth child in the world to have the ABI surgery. His success and our petition to the FDA will depend on how well he responds to the device over the next few years.

For years, I took my hearing for granted and now each day I pray for the day when my son will say "mom" or respond to me by saying, "I can hear you now."

SOURCE: Adapted from Hear Our Voices, The Children's Hearing Institute. Retrieved March 2, 2012, www .childrenshearing.org/custom/personal_stories.html.

A Changing Era in the Lives of People with Communication Disorders

Communication is one of the most complicated activities we undertake and one that receives the least attention. We communicate many times each day. We order food in a restaurant, thank a friend for doing a favor, ask a question in class, call for help in an emergency, follow instructions regarding the assembly of a piece of furniture, or give directions to someone who is lost. Our lives revolve around communication in many crucial ways, but communication rarely gets much attention unless we have a problem with it. Fortunately,

FOCUS 1

Identify four ways in which speech, language, and communication are interrelated.

Phonology
The system of speech sounds that an individual utters.

Syntax
The rules governing sentence structure, the way sequences of words are combined into phrases and sentences.

Morphology
The form and internal structure of words.

Semantics
The understanding of language, the component most directly concerned with meaning.

Pragmatics
A component of language that represents the rules that govern the reason(s) for communicating.

Figure 10.1 *A Conceptual Model of Communication, Language, and Speech*

record keeping in education has improved vastly with the addition of computers and tablet devices to the arsenal of tools teachers have at their disposal. This allows an accurate delivery of many services that were not possible before.

Speech, Language, and Communication

As we noted before, communication is one of the most complicated processes we undertake. Communication is the exchange of ideas, opinions, or facts between senders and receivers. It requires that a sender (an individual or group) compose and transmit a message, and that a receiver decode and understand the message (Bernstein, 2009; Pfeiffer & Adkins, 2012). The sender and receiver are therefore partners in the communication process.

Two highly interrelated components of communication are speech and language (see Figure 10.1). However, although they are related, they are not the same thing. Speech is the audible representation of language. It is one means of expressing language but not the only means. Language represents the message contained in speech. It is possible to have language without speech, such as sign language used by people who are deaf, and speech without language, such as the speech of birds that are trained to talk. Speech is often thought of as a part of language, although language may exist without speech. Figure 10.1 illustrates the interrelationship of speech, language, and communication.

Language consists of several major components, including phonology, syntax, morphology, semantics, and pragmatics. **Phonology** is the system of speech sounds that an individual utters—that is, rules regarding how sounds can be used and combined (Owens, Metz, & Farinella, 2011; Pfeiffer & Adkins, 2012). For example, the word *cat* has three phonemes, C-A-T. **Syntax** involves the rules governing sentence structure, the way sequences of words are combined into phrases and sentences. For example, the sentence *Will you help Janice?* changes in meaning when the order of the words is changed to *You will help Janice*. **Morphology** is concerned with the form and internal structure of words—that is, the transformations of words in terms of areas such as tense (e.g., present to past tense) and number (singular to plural), and so on. When we add an *s* to *cat*, we have produced the plural form, *cats*, with two morphemes, or units of meaning: the concept of cat and the concept of plural. Such transformations involve prefixes, suffixes, and inflections (Owens, 2008; Plante & Beeson, 2013). Grammar is constituted from a combination of syntax and morphology. **Semantics** represents the understanding of language, the component most directly concerned with meaning. Semantics addresses whether the speaker's intended message is conveyed by the words and their combinations in an age-appropriate manner.

Pragmatics is a component of language that is receiving increased attention in recent literature (e.g., Ryder, Leinonen, & Schulz, 2008; Schwartz, 2009). It represents the "rules

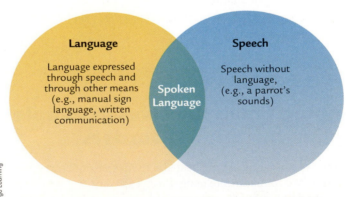

Language can exist without speech (left), and not all speech constitutes language (right), but spoken language (center) is one outcome of typical human development. Communication is the broad umbrella concept that includes speech and language. Although communication can be achieved without these components, it is greatly enhanced by them.

that govern the reason(s) for communicating (called *communicative functions* or *intentions*) as well as the rules that govern the choice of codes to be used when communicating" (Bernstein, 2009, p. 9). Pragmatics can be illustrated by the fact that teachers talk differently depending on whether they are providing direct instruction, making a point in a faculty meeting, or chatting at a party. Pragmatics includes processes such as turn taking and the initiating, maintaining, and ending of a conversation.

Zelick Nagel/Taxi/Getty Images

Language can exist without speech and not all speech includes language. Spoken language is one outcome of typical human development.

Language Development

In a vast percentage of cases, children develop language in a normal fashion, without significant delays or disruptions to the process. It is important to understand this typical developmental process as we examine and describe language characteristics that differ from the norm and interfere with the effectiveness of communication.

The development of language is a complex process. It is also one of the most fascinating to observe, as parents of infants know well. Young children normally advance through several stages in acquiring language, from a preverbal stage to the use of words in sentences. An infant's initial verbal output is primarily limited to crying and, hence, is usually associated with discomfort (from hunger, pain, or being soiled or wet). Before long (around 2 months), babies begin to coo as well as cry, verbally expressing reactions to pleasure as well as discomfort. At about 3 to 6 months of age, they begin to babble, which involves making some consonant and vowel sounds. At this point, babies often make sounds repeatedly when they are alone, seemingly experimenting with their sound making and not necessarily trying to communicate with anyone (Fogle, 2013; Owens, 2008). They may also babble when their parents or others are playing with or otherwise handling them.

A baby's first word is a momentous, long-anticipated event. In fact, eager parents often interpret as "words" sounds that probably have no meaning to the child. What usually happens is that the baby begins to string together sounds that occasionally resemble words. To the parents' delight, these sounds frequently include utterances such as "Da-Da" and "Ma-Ma," which, of course, are echoed, repeated, and reinforced greatly by the parents. As the baby actually begins to listen to the speech of adults, exchanges, or "conversations," seem to occur, where the youngster responds by saying "Da-Da" when a parent says that sound. Although this type of interchange sounds like a conversation, the child's vocal productions may be understood only by those close to him or her (such as parents or siblings); people other than immediate family members may not be able to interpret their meaning at all. The baby also begins to use different tones and vocal intensity, which makes his or her vocalization vaguely resemble adult speech. The interactions between babies and their parents can do much to enhance babies' developing language at this time. Parents often provide a great deal of reinforcement, such as praise in excited tones, or hugs, for word approximations. They also provide stimulus sounds and words for the baby to mimic, giving the youngster considerable directed practice.

CEC

Standard 2
Development and Characteristics of Learners

Standard 6
Communication

Language is made up of several components, such as phonology, syntax, morphology, symantics and pragmatics. These will vary as the children mature and grow in their ability to communicate, and as they learn from interacting with others.

© Robin Sachs/Photo Edit

CEC

Standard 3
Individual Learning
Differences

The timing of a baby's actual first word is open to interpretation, although it usually happens between 9 and 14 months. These words often involve echoing (repeating what has been heard) or mimicking responses based on verbalizations of those nearby. At first the words may have little or no meaning, although they soon become attached to people or objects in the child's immediate environment, such as Daddy, Mommy, or milk. Before long, these words begin to have more perceptible intent, as the child uses them for requests and as a means of pleasing parents. Strings of two and three words that resemble sentences typically begin between 18 and 24 months of age. At this stage, meaning is usually unmistakable because the child can clearly indicate that he or she wants something. The child uses fairly accurate syntax, with word order generally consisting of subject-verb-object.

Most children with normally developing language are able to use all the basic syntactical structures by 3 to 4 years of age. By 5 years, they have progressed to using six-word sentences, on the average. Children who are developing language at a normal pace articulate nearly all speech sounds correctly, and in context, somewhere between 4 and 8 years of age. These illustrations are couched in terms of when children produce language—that is, in terms of expressive language development. However, some observations suggest that children's receptive skills precede their abilities to express language. Thus, children are able to understand a great deal more than they can express. Most children show some understanding of language as early as 6 to 9 months, often responding first to commands such as "no-no" and their names (Owens, 2008; Vinson, 2012; Williams, 2011).

Variable age ranges are used for each milestone in outlining normal language development, some with rather broad approximations. Several factors contribute to this variability. For one thing, even children who are developing normally exhibit substantial differences in their rates of development. Some variations are due to a child's general health and vitality, others to inheritance, and still others to environmental influences, such as the amount and type of interaction with parents and siblings (Gleason & Ratner, 2009; Vinson, 2012). Note also that age ranges become wider in more advanced stages of development (e.g., 3 to 6 months for babbling; 18 to 24 months for two- and three-word strings). Therefore, observation of when they first occur is perhaps less accurate. Table 10.1 summarizes general milestones of normal language and prelanguage development. A link to Kimberly Powell's article, "Speech and Language: Causes, Milestones and Suggestions" can be found on the Education CourseMate website for *Human Exceptionality*. Considerable variability also occurs with abnormal language and speaking ability. In some cases, the same factors that contribute to variability in normal language are considered disorders if they result in extreme performance deviations. In other cases, the definitions differ and characteristics vary among people—the same variability we have encountered with other disorders.

Multidisciplinary Collaboration

A wide range of topics will be addressed as we discuss the details of communication disorders. These extend from developmental delays to physical characteristics, all factors that may influence a person's ability to communicate. Some of these may have genetic causes, whereas others are influenced primarily by environmental factors. Thus the communication features are widely varied, and effective intervention components must reflect that variation to adequately serve the needs of the individual (Schwartz, 2012). As we discuss these various communication challenges and their assessment and treatment, it is important to return to a recurring theme: multidisciplinary collaboration. Such cooperation is crucial for students with communication disorders because of the broad array of challenges that fall into the purview of different disciplines ranging from medical and health-related specialties to those involving teaching and behavior modification.

Interventions for all communication disorders must consider multiple elements: the nature of the problem, the impact on the individual, and the availability and delivery of services (Fogle, 2013; Pfeiffer & Adkins, 2012). It is also important to consider cultural and linguistic background as an intervention is being planned (Payne, 2011). The influences of different cultures and linguistic circumstances have been noted as significant in previous chapters, but it is their direct impact on communication that is especially clear. Assessment and intervention are an individualized undertaking, just as with other types of disorders (Chabon & Cohn, 2011; Schwartz, 2011). Some causes are easily identified and may or may not be remedied by mechanical or medical intervention (see the opening Snapshot about Vonetta Flowers).

As we have seen with other disabilities, referrals may come from several stakeholders, notably parents and teachers or other educational personnel (Fogle, 2013; Seden, 2008; Shaw, Heyman, Reynolds, Davies, & Godin, 2007). Parents play a significant role in initial identification of a potential problem, because their child's communication, and sometimes her or his communication disability, develop during the early years. Such initial assessments are likely to emerge when the child's communication performance attracts someone's attention. Parents working with speech and language pathologists become key leaders in coordinating multidisciplinary team collaboration, although they often acquire knowledge about services from professionals in health and educational fields (Pfeiffer & Adkins, 2012; Shapiro, Prinz, & Sanders, 2008). Referrals, screening procedures, diagnoses, and interventions will follow trajectories that are mapped specifically on the features of a child's communication disability and other contextual matters, such as family circumstances (Moore & Montgomery, 2008).

CEC

Standard 4
Instructional Strategies

Standard 5
Learning Environments and Social Interactions

Language Disorders

History has witnessed language in many different forms. Some early Native Americans communicated using systems of clucking or clicking sounds made with the tongue and teeth. These sounds were also used in combination with hand signs and spoken language that often differed greatly between tribes. Such differing language systems have been described extensively in a variety of historical documents and continue to be of interest (e.g., Engstrom, 2008; Fogle, 2013).

Current definitions of language reflect the breadth necessary to encompass diverse communication systems. For the most part, these definitions refer to the systems of rules and symbols that people use to communicate, including matters of phonology, syntax, morphology, and semantics (Freed, 2012; Greenwood, Grassly, Hickin, & Best, 2010; Owens, 2008). In these definitions of language, considerable attention is given to meaning and understanding. For example, Bernstein (2009) defined language as encompassing the "complex rules that govern sounds, words, sentences, meaning, and use. These rules underlie an individual's ability to understand language (language comprehension) and his or her ability to formulate language (language production)" (pp. 5–6).

Speech disorders include problems related to verbal production—that is, vocal expression. Language disorders represent serious difficulties in the ability to understand or express ideas in the communication system being used. The distinction between speech

FOCUS 2
Explain how language delay and language disorder differ.

CEC

Standard 6
Communication

disorders and language disorders is like the difference between the sound of a word and the meaning of a word. As we examine language disorders, we will discuss both difficulties in expressing meaning and difficulties in receiving it. A language impairment may result in a variety of behaviors which are observable to the teacher or aide with primary instructional responsibility. For example, it may be evident that the child mispronounces words, sounds, or partial words such as tenses. The child might also overuse or misuse words or sounds in a manner that is suggestive of a youngster that is immature. He or she may encounter difficulty in recalling the correct word for use in a sentence and consequently overuse certain sounds or words. All of these matters may combine to suggest a child that has difficulty using language or is somewhat behind his or her peers in language development.

The child may encounter difficulty with using the proper tense, using conjunctions, or presenting a word order that is proper and consistent with peers who are progressing properly with language development. The child may have difficulty in relating events sequentially or following directions. Their questions may be somewhat vague, their answers may be off topic from that being addressed by the teacher. These children are fundamentally encountering challenges as they interact with adults although their peers may be able to interpret meanings from their language. They may encounter challenges as they attempt to express their needs, greet others, or exchange information in verbal formats. They may become frustrated as they attempt to express their emotions or subtle more nuanced interactions.

These children may not interact in certain situations and may limit their language output to certain locations or audiences. They often present an overall lower language skill set which influences their social interaction. They may not seem to be attending to the listener and show a variety of difficulties in academic areas like reading and writing. Challenges can be rather subtle in some situations and yet explosive in others, depending on the child's emotional make-up and the individuals around him or her. As we examine language disorders, we will discuss both difficulties in expressing meaning and difficulties in receiving information.

Definition

A serious disruption of the language acquisition process may result in language disorders. Such irregular developments may involve comprehension (understanding) or expression in

Interactions between individuals are complex and may reflect language maturation challenges in the child.

written or spoken language (Klammler & Schneider, 2011; Pfeiffer & Adkins, 2012). Such malfunctions may occur in one or more of the components of language. Because language is one of the most complex sets of behaviors exhibited by humans, language disorders are complex and present perplexing assessment problems. Language involves memory, learning, message reception and processing, and expressive skills. An individual with a language disorder may have deficits in any of these areas, and it may be difficult to identify the nature of the problem (Bernstein & Levey, 2009; Klammler & Schneider, 2011; Owens et al., 2007). In addition, language problems may arise in the form of language delays.

Language delay occurs when the normal rate of developmental progress is interrupted but the systematic sequence of development remains essentially intact. For youngsters with a language delay, the development follows a normal pattern or course of growth but is substantially slower than in most children of the same age. In language disorders, by contrast, language acquisition is not systematic and/or sequential. The term language disorder is used in a general sense to refer to several types of behaviors.

CEC

Standard 2
Development and
Characteristics of Learners

Classification

The terminology applied to the processes involved in language, and to disorders in those processes, varies widely. In many cases, language disorders are classified according to their causes, which may be known or only suspected (Anderson & Shames, 2011; Owens et al., 2007). In other cases, specific labels are used. One useful approach to viewing language disorders is in terms of receptive and expressive problems (Freed, 2012; Justice, Mashburn, Pence, & Wiggins, 2008). We will examine both of these categories.

Receptive Language Disorders

People with **receptive language disorders** have difficulty comprehending what others say. In many cases, receptive language problems in children are noticed when they do not follow an adult's instructions. These children may seem inattentive, as though they do not listen to directions, or they may be very slow to respond. Individuals with receptive language disorders have great difficulty understanding other people's messages and may process only part of what is being said to them (Owens et al., 2007; Pfeiffer & Adkins, 2012). They have a problem in language processing, which is basically half of language (the other part being language production). Language processing is essentially listening to and interpreting spoken language.

It is not uncommon for receptive language problems to appear in students with learning disabilities (Fogle, 2013). Such language deficits contribute significantly to problems with academic performance and to difficulties in social interactions for these students. Receptive language disorders appear as high-risk indicators of other disabilities (Freed, 2012).

Receptive language disorders
Difficulties in comprehending what others say.

Expressive Language Disorders

Individuals with **expressive language disorders** have difficulty in language production, or formulating and using spoken or written language. Those with expressive language disorders may have limited vocabularies and use the same array of words regardless of the situation. Expressive language disorders may appear as immature speech, often resulting in interaction difficulties (Freed, 2012; Justice et al., 2008; McGowan et al., 2008). People with expressive disorders also use hand signals and facial expressions to communicate.

Expressive language disorders
Difficulties in producing language.

Aphasia

Aphasia involves a loss of the ability to speak or comprehend because of an injury or developmental abnormality in the brain. Aphasia most often affects those in whom a specific brain injury has resulted in impairment of language comprehension, formulation, and use. Thus, definitions of aphasia commonly link the disorder to brain injury, through either mechanical accidents or other damage, such as that caused by a stroke. Many types of aphasia and/or conditions associated with aphasia have been identified (Bastiaanse & Thompson, 2012; Martin, 2009; Vukovic, Vuksanovic, & Vukovic, 2008). Aphasic language disturbances have also been classified in terms of receptive and expressive problems.

Aphasia may be found both during childhood and in the adult years. The term *developmental aphasia* has been widely used for children, despite the long-standing association of aphasia with neurological damage. Children with aphasia often begin to use words at age 2 or later and to use phrases at age 4. The link between aphasia and neurological

Aphasia
An acquired language disorder caused by brain damage and characterized by complete or partial impairment of language comprehension, formulation, and use.

Aphasia treatment using social media tools varies as widely as the causes. This speech problem may respond to repetitive practice that can be prompted by one or several computer applications (apps) that are specifically tailored for aphasia (for specific apps, see http:// buyersguide.asha.org/). In many cases, computer programs are designed to help an individual with aphasia rehearse sounds or words that are problematic. Within the context of aphasia, the goals of social media include auditory assessment, augmentative/ alternative communication, speech and language swallowing treatments, and many others. This is a growing field that offers many treatment tools and aids that will only continue to expand.

abnormalities in children is of interest to researchers; some evidence suggests a connection. In many cases of aphasia in children, however, objective evidence of neurological dysfunction has been difficult to acquire.

Adult aphasia typically is linked to accidents or injuries likely to occur during this part of the lifespan, such as gunshot wounds, motorcycle and auto accidents, and strokes. For this group, it is clear why terms such as *acquired language disorder* emerge. These disorders are typically acquired through specific injury. Current research suggests that different symptoms result from damage to different parts of the brain (e.g., Bastiaanse & Thompson, 2012; Owens et al., 2007). Those with injury to the front part of the brain often can comprehend better than they can speak; they also have considerable difficulty finding words, have poor articulation with labored and slow speech, omit small words such as *of* and *the*, and generally have reduced verbal production. Individuals with aphasia resulting from injury to the back part of the brain seem to have more fluent speech, but it lacks content. The speech of these individuals appears to reflect impaired comprehension (Martin, 2009).

Causes of Language Disorders

FOCUS 3

Identify three factors that are thought to cause language disorders.

Standard 2
Development and Characteristics of Learners

Standard 6
Communication

Pinpointing the causes of different language disorders can be difficult. We do not know precisely how normal language acquisition occurs or how malfunctions influence language disorders. We do know that certain sensory and other physiological systems must be intact and developing normally for language processes to develop normally. For example, impaired vision or hearing may result in a language deficit (Freed, 2012; Reed, 2012). Likewise, serious brain damage may inhibit normal language functioning. Learning must also progress in a systematic, sequential fashion for language to develop appropriately (Bernstein & Levey, 2009).

Many physiological problems may cause language difficulties. Neurological damage that may affect language functioning can occur prenatally, during birth, or any time throughout life (Berko Gleason & Bernstein Ratner, 2009; Williams, 2011). For example, language problems clearly can result from oxygen deprivation before or during birth. Likewise, a serious accident later in life can disrupt a person's language. Serious emotional disorders may accompany language disturbances if an individual's perception of the world is substantially distorted (Freed, 2012; Owens et al., 2007).

Language disorders may also occur if learning opportunities are seriously deficient or are otherwise disrupted. As with speech, children may not learn language if the environment is not conducive to such learning (Froemling, Grice, & Skinner, 2011). Modeling in the home may be so infrequent that a child cannot learn language in a normal fashion. This might be the case in a family where no speaking occurs because the parents have hearing impairments, even though the children hear normally. Such circumstances are rare, but when they do occur, a language delay may result.

Language Differences: We Didn't Know They Were Different

My name is Cy, and I am one of the four brothers. Both of my parents were deaf from a very early age; they never learned to speak. When you ask me how we learned speech, I can't really answer, knowing what I now know about how important those very early years are in this area. When we were really young, we didn't even know our parents were deaf or different (except for Dad's active sense of humor). Naturally, we didn't talk; we just signed. We lived way out in the country and didn't have other playmates. Grandma and

Grandpa lived close by, and I spent a lot of time with them. That is when I began to know something was different. We probably began learning to talk there.

When we were about ready to start school, we moved into town. My first memory related to school is sitting in a sandbox. We had some troubles in school, but they were fairly minor as I recall. I couldn't talk or pronounce words very well. I was tested on an IQ test in the third grade and they said I had an IQ of 67. Both Mom and Dad worked, so we were all sort of

out on our own with friends, which probably helped language. I wonder why those kids didn't stay away from us because we were a bit different. Probably the saving grace is that all four of us seemed to have pretty well-developed social intelligence. We did get in some fights with kids, and people sometimes called us the "dummies' kids." One thing is for certain: I would not trade those parents for any others in the world. Whatever they did, they certainly did right.

Cy, PhD

Learning outcomes are highly variable. In situations that seem normal, we may find a child with serious language difficulty. In circumstances that seem lacking, we may find a child whose language facility is normal. The Snapshot presents an example involving four brothers with normal hearing raised by parents who both had severe hearing impairments and no spoken-language facility. The brothers distinguished themselves in various ways, earning PhDs and MDs (one holds both degrees) to other achievements (one became a millionaire with patents). Although the Snapshot represents rare circumstances, it illustrates how variable language learning is.

Distinctions between speech problems and language problems are blurred because they overlap as much as the two functions of speech and language overlap. Receptive and expressive language disorders are as intertwined as speech and language. When someone does not express language well, does he or she have a receptive problem or an expressive problem? These disorders are not easily separated.

Treatment Approaches

As outlined in our discussion of multidisciplinary collaboration, treatments of language disorders must account for many elements as a plan is developed (Payne & Taylor, 2006; Pfeiffer & Adkins, 2012). Interventions are individualized, and significant planning is required (Meinzen-Derr, Wiley, Grether, & Choo, 2011; Schwartz, 2012).

Individualized Language Plans

A number of integrated steps are involved in effective language training. They include identification, assessment, development of instructional objectives, development of a language intervention program, implementation of the intervention program, reassessment of the child, and reteaching, if necessary. These steps are similar to the general stages of specialized educational interventions that are outlined in IDEA. Specific programs of intervention may also involve other activities aimed at individualized intervention (see, e.g., Moore & Montgomery, 2008). Collaboration among professionals reflects the federal

FOCUS 4

Describe how treatment approaches for language disorders generally differ for children and for adults.

Standard 4
Instructional Strategies

Standard 7
Instructional Planning

law and is also one of our important recurring themes. Programs of language training are tailored to an individual's strengths and limitations. In fact, current terminology labels them individualized language plans (ILPs), similar in concept to the individualized education plans (IEPs) mandated by IDEA (Tiegerman-Farber, 2009). These intervention plans include several components:

- Long-range goals (annual)
- Short-range and specific behavioral objectives
- A statement of the resources to be used in achieving the objectives
- A description of evaluation methods
- Program beginning and ending dates
- Evaluation of the individual's generalization of skills

For young children, interventions often focus on beginning language stimulation. Treatment is intended to mirror the conditions under which children normally learn language, but the stimulation may be intensified and more systematic.

Many different approaches have been used for instruction in language, although consistent and verifiable results have been slow to emerge. Intervention typically involves the development of an individual's profile of strengths, limitations, age, and developmental level, monolingual or bilingual background, and literacy, as well as considerations regarding temperament that may affect therapy. From such a profile, an individualized treatment plan can be designed (Bastiaanse & Thompson, 2012; Marion, Hussmann, Bay, Christoph, Piefke, Willmes, & Huber, 2008).

Several questions immediately arise, including what to teach or remediate first and whether teaching should focus on an individual's strong or weak areas. These questions have been raised with respect to many disorders. Teaching exclusively to a child's weak areas may result in more failure than is either necessary or helpful to his or her progress. That is, the child may experience so little success and receive so little reinforcement that he or she becomes discouraged. Good clinical judgment needs to be exercised in deciding how to divide one's attention between the aphasic child's strengths and his or her weaknesses. Intervention programs include the collaborative participation of parents and other family members, as well as any other professionals who may be involved with the overall treatment of the youngster (Murdoch, 2010; Tiegerman-Farber, 2009).

The perspective for remediation of adults with aphasia begins from a point different from that for children, because it involves relearning or reacquiring language function. Views regarding treatment have varied over the years. Strengths and limitations must both receive attention when an individualized remediation program is being planned. However, development of an aphasic adult's profile of strengths and deficits may involve some areas different from those that apply to children. For example, social, linguistic, and vocational readjustments are three broad areas that need attention for most adults with aphasia. Furthermore, the notion of readjustment differs substantially from initial skill acquisition. Language learning treatment (relearning) is often employed in a way that focuses on the individual's needs and is practical in terms of service delivery (Chilosi et al., 2008; Bastiaanse & Thompson, 2012). Some individuals with aphasia are effectively treated in group settings, whereas individual therapy works well for others (e.g., Faroqi-Shah, 2008; Vukovic, Vuksanovic, & Vukovic, 2008). Advances in technology are often used in diagnosis and treatment (Fogle, 2013; Johnston, Reichle, Feeley, & Jones, 2012); see the nearby Assistive Technology feature about a person who has had multiple cochlear implants and her views on particular technology devices.

An individualized treatment plan for adults with aphasia also involves evaluation, profile development, and teaching/therapy in specific areas within each of the broad domains (Chabon & Cohn, 2011; Owens et al., 2007). Such training should begin as soon as possible, depending on the person's condition. Some spontaneous recovery may occur during the first 6 months after an incident resulting in aphasia, but waiting beyond 2 months to begin treatment may seriously delay the degree of recovery possible.

ASSISTIVE TECHNOLOGY ASSISTIVE TECHNOLOGY DEVICES HELP LEVEL THE PLAYING FIELD

Susan Cheffo had her first cochlear implant when she was 51 years old. Now she serves as the educational services coordinator for the Beth Israel/New York Eye and Ear Cochlear Implant Center where her main function is to help others learn to hear. She shared her views on certain cell phones now available in "Hear Our Voices" on The Children's Hearing Institute website (www.childrenshearing.org/custom/personal_stories.html):

I was glad to find out that some models of cell phones were now T-coil–compatible. . . . I went to my local Verizon store to listen to various T-coil–compatible cell phones and was quite impressed with the quality. . . . Since my present cell phone contract did not allow me an upgrade yet, I spoke to Verizon customer service. After much explaining about my cochlear implant and the need for a T-coil–compatible cell phone, I was told to send a let-

ter from my doctor (audiologist) and I would receive an authorization for an early upgrade. After waiting 10 days for the authorization, I became impatient. I went to the Verizon main store in the mall and explained my situation to a salesperson. This young man was extremely helpful and authorized my upgrade on the spot! I also explained that I was in the car a great deal and could not use a hands-free device. He suggested that I purchase the car charger/speaker combination that was compatible with my new Samsung cell phone. It also came with a microphone that clipped onto the overhead sun visor. He explained that the quality from the speaker was quite good as reported by other customers. I purchased it along with my new phone and ran to my car to try out the new system. I was extremely impressed

with the clarity from the speaker, and that people that I called could hear my voice easily. I even tested the system on the highway, where background noise is most prevalent and found that I could understand and be understood with almost no difficulty. I went back to the Verizon store to thank the salesperson and explained how successful this system was. He responded by letting me know that I helped him direct future customers who were hearing aid/cochlear implant users. What a great attitude.

Assistive devices help to level playing field and can be key to productive life and individual self-esteem.

SOURCE: Adapted from Horiuchi, V. (1999, April 10). Assistive devices help to level playing field: Machines can be key to productive life and individual self-esteem. Salt Lake Tribune, p. D8.

Augmentative Communication

Some individuals require intervention through communication other than oral language. In some cases, the person may be incapable of speaking because of a severe physical or cognitive disability, so a nonspeech means of communication must be designed and implemented. Known variably as assistive, alternative, and **augmentative communication**,

Augmentative communication
Forms of communication that employ nonspeech alternatives.

TEACHSOURCE VIDEO ASSISTIVE TECHNOLOGY IN THE INCLUSIVE CLASSROOM: BEST PRACTICES

Please visit the Education CourseMate website for *Human Exceptionality*, 11th edition, at CengageBrain.com to access this TeachSource Video. Assistive technology can be used effectively for children with communication disorders in a general education setting. In this

video, observe how assistive technology is shown as one of the best practices in an inclusive classroom, and then answer the following questions:

1. How does Jamie's speech output device allow her to work in the class?

2. How do four buttons on Jamie's device help her to work the speech output device?

3. Why is it important for Jamie to work with people who know her well as inclusive aides?

these strategies may involve a variety of approaches, some employing new technological developments. Augmentative communication strategies have received increasing attention in the past few years, partly because of the development of technology applications in unusual settings and partly because of coverage in the popular press (Law, McBean, & Rush, 2011). Applications include a range of circumstances and disability conditions, such as intellectual disabilities, autism, and multiple disabilities that are often in the severe functioning range (Johnston et al., 2012). These strategies must also be individualized to meet the specific needs of those being treated and to take into account their strengths and limitations in operating the technology. Augmentative communication strategies are providing therapists with important new alternatives for intervention with individuals who have language disorders. Research results suggest that carefully chosen techniques and devices can be quite effective (e.g., Fogle, 2013; Johnston et al., 2012). Two examples of specific devices are communication boards with graphics or symbols and electronic appliances that simulate speech sounds. Other approaches include systems of manual communication (such as gestures and signs) that do not depend on mechanical or electronic aids. See the nearby Assistive Technology feature, "Assistive Technology Devices Help Level the Playing Field."

CEC

Standard 6
Communication

Some approaches to augmentative or assistive communication have come from the field of technology directly. Examples include the rather broad use of tablet devices (iPads, other tablet mechanisms). These have been used as direct communicators in terms of symbols or letters being included, or have at other times been used as display devices for wireless networks where videos or slide shows are projected to the user. In some cases these are used by teachers whereas in other cases they are employed directly by students with disabilities. As used by teachers these devices become much like laptop computers which may be written on (the keyboard is often disappearing like the smart phone). They may have variable levels of memory so messages can be saved and sent at another time or in some low-cost devices the message may be sent immediately. The type with a memory is definitely preferred because it provides much more flexibility. In either case the device may be used rather quickly and easily by the teacher or student with disabilities.

iPads or similar technology devices may be used effectively for children as they learn to name items, speak to others when the pads are programmed in this fashion, or flexibly as both with different applications installed.

Klaus Vedfelt/Riser/Getty Images

Speech Disorders: Fluency

Speech disorders involve deviations sufficient to interfere with communication. Such speaking patterns are so divergent from what is typical and expected that they draw attention to the speaking act, thereby distracting the hearer's attention from the meaning of the message being sent. Such deviant speaking behavior can negatively affect the listener, the speaker, or both.

Speech is very important in contemporary society. Speaking ability can influence a person's success or failure in personal/social and professional arenas. Most people are about average in speaking ability, and they may envy those who are unusually articulate and pity those who have a difficult time with speech. What is it like to have a serious deficit in speaking ability? It is different for each individual, depending on the circumstances in which he or she operates and the severity of the deficit.

People often carry strong emotional reactions to their speech that may significantly alter their behavior. Speech is so critical to functioning in society that speech disorders often have a significant impact on affected individuals. It is not difficult to imagine the impact that stuttering, for example, may have in classroom settings or in social encounters. Children may be ridiculed by peers, begin to feel inadequate, and suffer emotional stress. And that stress may continue into adulthood, limiting these individuals' social lives and influencing their vocational choices.

There are many different speech disorders and many theories about causes and treatment. In this chapter, we will discuss fluency disorders, delayed speech, articulation disorders, and voice disorders.

In typical speech, we are accustomed to a reasonably smooth flow of words and sentences. For the most part, speech has a rhythm that is steady, regular, and rapid. Most of us also have times when we pause to think about what we are saying, either because we have made a mistake or because we want to mentally edit what we are about to say. However, these interruptions are infrequent and do not disturb the ongoing flow of our speaking. Our speech is generally fluent in speed and continuity.

Speech flow is a serious problem for people with a fluency disorder. Their speech is characterized by repeated interruptions, hesitations, or repetitions that interrupt the flow of communication. Some people have a fluency disorder known as cluttered speech, or **cluttering**, which is characterized by overly rapid speech that is disorganized, and occasionally filled with unnecessary words (Ward & Scott, 2011). However, the most recognized fluency disorder is stuttering.

Stuttering

Stuttering occurs when the flow of speech is abnormally interrupted by repetitions, blocking, or prolongations of sounds, syllables, words, or phrases (Fogle, 2013; Owens et al., 2007). Although stuttering is a familiar concept to most people, it occurs rather infrequently, in 1 percent to 5 percent of the general population, and has one of the lowest prevalence rates among all speech disorders (e.g., Owens et al., 2007; Ramig & Dodge, 2010). For example, articulation disorders (e.g., omitting, adding, or distorting certain sounds) occur in about 2 percent of 6- and 7-year-old children in the United States (American Psychiatric Association, 2000).

The high awareness of stuttering comes partly from the nature of the behavior involved. Interruptions in speech flow are very

FOCUS 5
Cite three factors that are thought to cause stuttering.

Cluttering
A speech disorder characterized by excessively rapid, disorganized speaking, often including words or phrases unrelated to the topic.

Stuttering
A speech disorder that occurs when the flow of speech is abnormally interrupted by repetitions, blocking, or prolongations of sounds, syllables, words, or phrases.

The way in which parents speak greatly affects their child's speech patterns.

Elena Kouptsova-Vasic/Shutterstock.com

evident to both speaker and listener, are perhaps more disruptive to communication than any other type of speech disorder. Listeners often grow uncomfortable and may try to assist the stuttering speaker by providing missing or incomplete words (Van Borsel & Eeckhout, 2008; Weber-Fox & Hampton, 2008). The speaker's discomfort may be magnified by physical movements, gestures, or facial distortions that often accompany stuttering.

Parents often become concerned about stuttering as their children learn to talk. Anxiety is usually unnecessary; most children exhibit some normal nonfluencies that diminish and cease with maturation. However, these normal nonfluencies have historically played a role in some theories about the causes of stuttering.

Causation Current thinking suggests that stuttering may have a variety of causes (e.g., Fogle, 2013; Manning, 2010; Weber-Fox & Hampton, 2008); most behavioral scientists have abandoned the search for a single cause. Theories regarding causes for stuttering follow three basic perspectives: Stuttering is a symptom of some emotional disturbance; it is a result of biological makeup or some neurological problem; or it is a learned behavior.

Some investigations of emotional problems have explored psychosocial factors emerging from the parent–child interaction, although this work is somewhat fragmentary. The emotional component has been included in many descriptions of contributors to stuttering, including speculation that stuttering may be caused by an individual's capacity being exceeded by demands. Such theories, however, often consider a person's cognitive, linguistic, and motor capacities as other contributors. Research on the relationship of stuttering to emotion continues only sporadically (Bloodstein & Ratner, 2008; Onslow, Packman, & Payne, 2007). Many professionals have become less interested in emotional theories of the causation of stuttering. Investigation of this perspective is difficult because of problems with research methodology (e.g., Bernstein & Levey, 2009).

Investigators continue to explore biological causes in a number of different areas. Limited evidence indicates that the brains or neurological structures of some who stutter may be organized or function differently than those of people without fluency disorders, although the nature of such differences remains unclear (Bloodstein & Ratner, 2008; Manning, 2010; Ramig & Dodge, 2010). Some research also suggests that individuals who stutter use different sections of the brain to process information than do their counterparts with fluent speech. Some researchers also suggest that nervous system damage, such as from an injury, can result in stuttering (Freed, 2012). Other theories imply that a variety of problems may disrupt the person's precise timing ability, coordination, or capacity for synchrony, all of which are important elements in speech production (Owens, Metz, & Farinella, 2011).

It has long been theorized that stuttering is learned behavior. According to this perspective, learned stuttering emerges from the normal nonfluency evident in early speech development. Language develops rapidly from 2 to 5 years of age, and stuttering often emerges in that general time frame as well—between 3 and 5 years of age (e.g., Owens et al., 2007; Ramig & Dodge, 2010). From a learning causation point of view, a typical child may become a stuttering child if considerable attention is focused on normal disfluencies at that stage of development. The disfluency of early stuttering may be further magnified by negative feelings about the self, as well as by anxiety (e.g., Bloodstein & Ratner, 2008; Manning, 2010). Interest in this theory persists, although, like others, it has its critics (e.g., Carey, O'Brian, Onslow, Block, Jones, & Packman, 2010; Onslow, Packman, & Payne, 2007).

Theories about the causes of stuttering have also included the role of heredity (Froemling, Grice, & Skinner, 2011; Weber-Fox & Hampton, 2008). Although this hypothesis remains speculative, some evidence suggests that stuttering may be gender-related, because males who stutter outnumber females about 4 to 1. Heredity has also been of interest because of the high incidence of stuttering and other speech disorders within certain families, as well as in twins (Fogle, 2012; Owens, Metz, & Farinella, 2011). However, it is very hard to separate hereditary and environmental influences—a ubiquitous problem for research in human development (DeThorne et al., 2008; Drew & Hardman, 2007).

Causation has been an especially elusive and perplexing matter for workers in speech pathology. Some recent literature has raised questions about definitions, assessment, and some of the theoretical logic related to stuttering. Researchers and clinicians continue their search for a cause, seeking more effective treatment and prevention (e.g., Ramig & Dodge, 2010).

Intervention Many approaches have been used to treat stuttering over the years, with mixed results. Interventions such as modeling, self-monitoring, counseling, and the involvement of support group assistance have all been studied and shown to be somewhat useful for children who stutter (e.g., Ramig & Dodge, 2010; Reed, 2012). Some research on medication treatment has shown improvements, although pharmacological intervention has not been widely employed (Yairi & Seery, 2011). Hypnosis has been used to treat some cases of stuttering, but its success has been limited. Speech rhythm has been the focus of some therapy, as has developing the naturalness of speaking patterns. Relaxation therapy and biofeedback have also been used, because tension and anxiety are often observed in people who stutter (Fogle, 2012; Owens, Metz, & Farinella, 2011). In all the techniques noted, outcomes are mixed, and people who stutter are likely to try several approaches (Fogle, 2012; Weber-Fox & Hampton, 2008). The inability of any one treatment or cluster of treatments consistently to help people who stutter demonstrates the ongoing need for research in this area. There is also need for research on effective timing for intervention (e.g., Onslow, Packman, & Payne, 2007). Early intervention has long been popular in many exceptionality areas. However, it does carry a risk associated with labeling: that a child may become what he or she is labeled (Yairi & Seery, 2011).

For several years, treatment models have increasingly focused on direct behavioral therapy—that is, attempting to teach children who stutter to use fluent speech patterns (e.g., Carey et al., 2010). In some cases, children are taught to monitor and manage their stuttering by speaking more slowly or rhythmically. Using this model, they are also taught to reward themselves for increasing periods of fluency. Some behavioral therapies include information regarding physical factors (such as regulating breathing) and direct instruction about correct speaking behaviors. The overall therapy combines several dimensions, such as an interview regarding the inconvenience of stuttering, behavior modification training, and follow-up. Because stuttering is a complex problem, effective interventions are likely to be complicated.

Standard 4
Instructional Strategies

Standard 7
Instructional Planning

Fluency Disorders: Delayed Speech

Delayed speech is a deficit in communication ability in which the individual speaks like a much younger person. From a developmental point of view, this problem involves delayed speech and language development. Delayed speech may occur for many reasons and take various forms. Assessment and treatment differ accordingly (Kaderavek, 2011).

Delayed speech is often associated with other maturational delays and it may be associated with a hearing impairment, intellectual disabilities, emotional disturbance, or brain injury (e.g., Drew & Hardman, 2007; Froemling, Grice, & Skinner, 2011). Young children can typically communicate, at least to some degree, before they learn verbal behaviors. They use gestures, gazing or eye contact, facial expressions, other physical movements, and nonspeech vocalizations, such as grunts or squeals. This early development illustrates the relationship among communication, language, and speech. Children with delayed speech often have few or no verbalizations that can be interpreted as conventional speech. Some communicate solely through physical gestures. Others may use a combination of gestures and vocal sounds that are not approximations of words. Although some may speak, but in a very limited manner, perhaps using single words (typically nouns without auxiliary words, such as *ball* instead of *my ball*), they often have fewer syllables per word, or primitive sentences like "Get ball" rather than "Would you get the ball?" (Kaderavek, 2011). Such communication is normal for infants and very young children, but it is abnormal for children beyond the age when most have at least a partially fluent speech (Weber-Fox & Hampton, 2008).

FOCUS 6
Identify two ways in which learning theory and home environments are related to delayed speech.

Delayed speech
A deficit in speaking proficiency whereby the individual performs like someone much younger.

Differences between stuttering and delayed speech are obvious, but the distinction between delayed speech and articulation disorders is less clear (Baker, Hipp, & Alessio, 2008; Kaderavek, 2011). In fact, children with delayed speech usually make many articulation errors in their speaking patterns. However, their major problems lie in grammatical and vocabulary deficits, which are more matters of developmental delay. The current prevalence of delayed speech is not clear; government estimates do not even regularly provide data on the provision of services for delayed speech (U.S. Department of Education, 2011).

Causation

Because there are a variety of forms of delayed speech, the causes of these problems also vary greatly. Environmental deprivation can contribute to delayed speech. For example, partial or complete hearing loss may seriously limit an individual's sensory experience and, hence, cause serious delays in speech development (e.g., Owens, 2011; Radziewicz & Antonellis, 2009). For those with normal hearing, the broader environment may also contribute to delayed speech (e.g., Bernstein & Levey, 2009). For example, in some children's homes, there is minimal conversation, little chance for the child to speak, and, thus, little opportunity to learn speech. Other problems, such as cerebral palsy and emotional disturbance, may also contribute to delayed speech.

Negativism may be one cause of delayed speech. Negativism involves a conflict between parents' expectations and a child's ability to perform; such a conflict often occurs as children develop speech. Considerable pressure is placed on children during the period when they normally develop their speaking skills: to go to bed when told, to control urination and defecation properly, and to learn appropriate eating skills, among other things. The demands are great, and they may exceed a child's performance ability. Viewing negativism from another angle, children may be punished even to the point of abuse for talking in some situations. Parents may be irritated by a child's attempt to communicate. A child may speak too loudly or at inappropriate times, such as when adults are reading, watching television, resting, or talking with other adults (even more rules to learn at such a tender age). Delayed speech may occur in extreme cases of prolonged negativism related to talking (Bernstein & Levey, 2009; Owens, 2010).

Such unpleasant environments may raise concerns about the amount of love and caring in such a situation and the role that emotional health plays in learning to speak (e.g., Gee, 2008; Schwartz, 2009). But delayed speech can also occur in families that exhibit great love and caring. In some environments, a child may have little need to learn speech. Most parents are concerned about satisfying their child's needs or desires. However, carrying this ambition to the extreme, a "superparent" may anticipate the child's wants (e.g., toys, water, or food) and provide them even before the child makes a verbal request. Learning to speak is much more complex and demanding than making simple movements or facial grimaces. When gesturing is rewarded, speaking is less likely to be learned properly.

Intervention

Treatment approaches for delayed speech are as varied as its causes. Whatever the cause, an effective treatment should teach the child appropriate speaking proficiency for his or her age level. In some cases, matters other than just defective learning, such as hearing impairments, must be considered in the treatment procedures (Owens, 2010; Radziewicz & Antonellis, 2009). Such cases may involve surgery and prosthetic appliances such as hearing aids, as well as specially designed instructional techniques aimed at teaching speech.

Treatment is likely to focus on the basic principles of learned behavior if defective learning is the primary cause of delayed speech. In this situation, the stimulus and reinforcement patterns that are contributing to delayed speech must be changed so that appropriate speaking behaviors can be learned (Froemling, Grice, & Skinner, 2011). Some success has been achieved through direct instruction, as well as through other procedures aimed at increasing spontaneous speech. Such instruction emphasizes

DEBATE FORUM
TO TREAT OR NOT TO TREAT?

Articulation problems represent about 80 percent of all speech disorders that speech clinicians encounter, making this type of difficulty the most prevalent of all communication disorders. It is also well known that young children normally make a number of articulation errors during the process of maturation as they are learning to talk. A substantial portion do not conquer all the rules of language and produce all the speech sounds correctly until they are 8 or 9 years old, yet they eventually develop normal speech and articulate properly. In lay terminology, they seem to "grow out of" early articulation problems. This maturation outcome and the prevalence of articulation problems raise serious questions about treatment in the early years.

POINT

Some school administrators are reluctant to treat young children who display articulation errors because the resources of school districts are in very short supply and budgets are extremely tight. If a substantial proportion of young children's articulation problems will correct themselves through maturation, then shouldn't the precious resources of school districts be directed to other problems? Articulation problems should not be treated unless they persist beyond the age of 10 or 11.

COUNTERPOINT

Although articulation does improve with maturation, delaying intervention is a mistake. The longer such problems persist, the more difficult treatment will be. Even the claim of financial savings is an invalid one. If all articulation difficulties are allowed to continue, those children who do not outgrow such problems will be more difficult to treat later, requiring more intense and expensive intervention than they would have needed if treated early. Early intervention for articulation problems is vitally important.

What Do You Think? Please visit the Education CourseMate website for Human Exceptionality, *11 edition, to access and respond to questions related to the Debate Forum.*

positive reinforcement of speaking to shape the child's behavior in the direction of more normal speech. Other interventions involve the collaborative efforts of speech clinicians, teachers, and parents to focus on modifying the child's speech and the family environment that contributed to the problem (Tiegerman-Farber, 2009; Turner & Whitworth, 2006; Weiss, 2009).

Speech Disorders: Articulation

Articulation disorders represent the largest category of all speech problems, which are termed phonological disorders in *DSM-IV* and in much of the speech and language research (American Psychiatric Association, 2000; Kaderavek, 2011; Plante & Beeson, 2013). For most people with this type of difficulty, the label **functional articulation disorders** is used. This term refers to articulation problems that are *not* due to structural physiological defects, such as cleft palate and neurological problems, but rather are likely to have resulted from environmental or psychological influences.

Articulation disorders are characterized by abnormal production of speech sounds, resulting in the inaccurate or otherwise inappropriate execution of speaking. This category of problems often includes omissions, substitutions, additions, and distortions of certain sounds (Hartmann, 2008; Owens et al., 2007). Omissions most frequently involve dropping consonants from the ends of words (e.g., *los* for *lost*), although omissions may occur in any position in a word. Substitutions frequently include saying *w* for *r* (e.g., *wight* for *right*), *w* for *l* (e.g., *fowo* for *follow*), and *th* for *s* (e.g., *thtop* for *stop*, and *thoup* for *soup*). Articulation errors may also involve transitional lisps, where a *th* sound precedes or follows an *s* (e.g., *sthoup* for *soup* or *yeths* for *yes*) (Plante & Beeson, 2013).

FOCUS 7

Identify two reasons why some professionals are reluctant to treat functional articulation disorders in young schoolchildren.

Functional articulation disorders
Articulation problems that are likely the result of environmental or psychological influences.

Articulation disorders are a rather prevalent type of speech problem. Research suggests that most problems encountered by speech clinicians involve articulation disorders (e.g., American Psychiatric Association, 2000; Owens et al., 2007). Although the vast majority of these difficulties are functional, some articulation problems may be attributed to physiological abnormalities.

Causation

Articulation disorders develop for many reasons. Some are caused by physical malformations, such as abnormal mouth, jaw, or teeth structures, and others result from nerve injury or brain damage (e.g., Plante & Beeson, 2013; Raposa & Perlman, 2012). Functional articulation disorders are often seen as caused by defective learning of the speaking act. However, such categories of causation overlap in practice, and even the line between functional and structural articulation disorders is indistinct. Function and structure, though often related, are not perfectly correlated: Some people with physical malformations that "should" result in articulation problems do not have such problems, and vice versa.

Despite this qualifying note, we will examine the causes of articulation performance deficits in terms of two general categories: those due to physical oral malformations and those that seem functional because there is no physical deformity. These distinctions remain useful for instructional purposes because it is the unusual individual who overcomes a physical abnormality and articulates satisfactorily.

In addition to physical abnormalities of the oral cavity, other types of physical defects, such as an abnormal or absent larynx, can affect articulation performance. Many different physical structures influence speech formulation, and all must be synchronized with learned muscle and tissue movements, auditory feedback, and a multitude of other factors. These coordinated functions are almost never perfect, but for most people they occur in a remarkably successful manner. Oral structure malformations alter the manner in which coordinated movements must take place, and sometimes they make normal or accurate production of sounds extremely difficult, if not impossible.

Cleft palate
A gap in the soft palate and roof of the mouth, sometimes extending through the upper lip.

One faulty oral formation recognized by most people is the cleft palate, which speech pathologists often refer to as clefts of the lip or palate or both. The **cleft palate** is a gap in the soft palate and roof of the mouth, sometimes extending through the upper lip. The roof of the mouth serves an important function in accurate sound production. A cleft palate reduces the division between the nasal and mouth cavities, influencing the movement of air that is so important to articulation performance (Klinto, Salameh, Svensson, & Lohmander, 2011). Clefts are congenital defects that occur in about one of every 700 births and may take any of several forms (e.g., Owens, Metz, & Farinella, 2011; Raposa & Perlman, 2012). Figure 10.2 nearby shows a normal palate in part (a) and unilateral and bilateral cleft palates in parts (b) and (c), respectively; it is easy to see how articulation would be impaired. These problems are caused by prenatal developmental difficulties and are often corrected by surgery.

Articulation performance is also significantly influenced by a person's dental structure. Because the tongue and lips work together with the teeth to form many sounds, dental

Figure 10.2 *Normal and Cleft Palate Configuration*

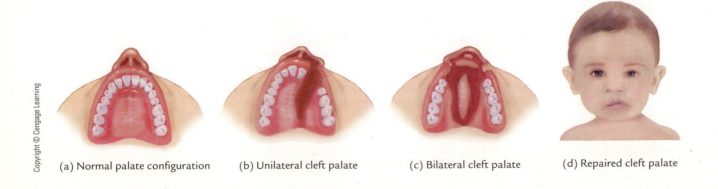

Copyright © Cengage Learning

(a) Normal palate configuration   (b) Unilateral cleft palate   (c) Bilateral cleft palate   (d) Repaired cleft palate

Figure 10.3 *Normal and Abnormal Dental Occlustion*

(a) Normal dental occlusion   (b) Overbite malocclusion   (c) Underbite malocclusion

abnormalities may result in serious articulation disorders. Some dental malformations are side effects of cleft palates, as shown in parts (b) and (c) of Figure 10.2, but other dental deformities not associated with clefts also cause articulation difficulties.

The natural meshing of the teeth in the upper and lower jaws is important to speech production. The general term used for the closure and fitting together of dental structures is **occlusion**, or dental occlusion. When the fit is abnormal, the condition is known as **malocclusion**. Occlusion involves several factors, including the biting height of the teeth when the jaws are closed, the alignment of teeth in the upper and lower jaws, the nature of curves in upper and lower jaws, and teeth positioning. A normal adult occlusion is illustrated in part (a) of nearby Figure 10.3. The upper teeth normally extend slightly beyond those of the lower jaw, and the bite overlap of those on the bottom is about one-third for the top front teeth when the jaw is closed.

Occlusion abnormalities take many forms, although we will discuss only two. When the overbite of the top teeth is unusually large, normal difference between the lower and upper dental structures is exaggerated. Such conditions may be due to the positioning of the upper and lower jaws, as illustrated in part (b) of Figure 10.3. In other cases, nearly the opposite occurs, as illustrated in part (c) of Figure 10.3, forming another kind of jaw misalignment. Exaggerated overbites and underbites may result from atypical teeth positions or angles as well as from atypical jaw alignment. All can cause articulation difficulties.

Many disorders are thought to be due to faulty language learning or functional articulation disorders. The sources of defective speech learning are often unknown or difficult to identify precisely (Robinson & Robb, 2009; Snowling & Hulme, 2012). Like other articulation problems, those of a functional nature have numerous specific causes. For example, interactions between children and their adult caretakers (parents and others) make a major contribution to language acquisition (Bernstein & Levey, 2009; Williams, 2011). In some cases, existing stimulus and reinforcement patterns may not support accurate articulation. For example, parents may be inconsistent in encouraging and prompting accurate articulation. Urging their children to speak properly may not be high on their priority list. However, such encouragement is important, particularly if misarticulation begins to emerge as a problem.

Also, adults may unthinkingly view some normal inaccuracies of speech in young children as cute or amusing. "Baby talk," for example, may be powerfully reinforced by parents asking the young child to say a particular word in the presence of grandparents or other guests and rewarding him or her with laughter and hugs and kisses. Such potent rewards can result in misarticulations that linger long beyond the time when normal maturation would diminish or eliminate them. Related defective learning may come from modeling. Parents (or other adults) may model and, thus, reinforce articulation disorders when they imitate the baby talk of young children or substantially change their manner of speaking in what has been called "parentese" (Owens, 2008). Modeling is a potent tool in shaping learned behavior. Although the negative influence of baby talk between parents and children has been questioned, modeling and imitation are used in interventions and are thought to influence natural verbal development (Aarts, Demir, & Vallen, 2011; Syrja, 2011).

Occlusion
The closing and fitting together of dental structures.

Malocclusion
An abnormal fit between the upper and lower dental structures.

Intervention

Many types of treatment exist for articulation disorders. Clearly, the treatment for disorders due to physical abnormalities differs from that for functional disorders. In many cases, however, treatment may include a combination of procedures. The treatment of articulation disorders has also been somewhat controversial, partly because of the large number that are functional in nature. A predictable developmental progression occurs in a substantial number of functional articulation disorders. In such cases, articulation problems diminish and may even cease to exist as the child matures. For instance, the *r*, *s*, and *th* problems disappear for many children after the age of 5. Thus, many school administrators are reluctant to treat functional articulation disorders in younger students. In other words, if a significant proportion of articulation disorders is likely to be corrected as the child continues to develop, why expend precious resources on early treatment? This logic has a certain appeal, particularly in times when there is a shortage of educational resources and their use is constantly questioned (see the nearby Debate Forum, "To Treat or Not to Treat"). However, this argument must be applied with considerable caution. In general, improvement of articulation performance continues until a child is about 9 or 10 years old (see the nearby Reflect on This feature to hear from 7½-year-old Timothy). If articulation problems persist beyond this age, they are unlikely to improve without intense intervention. Furthermore, the longer such problems are allowed to continue, the more difficult treatment will become and the less likely it is to be successful. Although some researchers suggest that the impact of articulation difficulties is ultimately minimal, others believe that affected individuals may still have residual indications of the disorder many years later (e.g., Owens, Metz, & Farinella, 2011; Plante & Beeson, 2013).

Deciding whether to treat articulation problems in young children is not easy; interventions can be complex. One option is to combine articulation training with other instruction for all very young children. This approach may serve as an interim measure for those who have continuing problems, by facilitating the development of articulation for others and not overly taxing school resources. It does, however, require some training for teachers of young children.

Considerable progress has been made over the years in various types of surgical repair for cleft palates. Current research addresses a number of related matters, such as complex patient assessment before and after intervention (Chabon & Cohn, 2011; Reed, 2012). The surgical procedures may be intricate because of the dramatic nature of the structural defect. Some such interventions include Teflon implants in the hard portion of the palate, as well as stretching and stitching together the fleshy tissue. As nearby Figure 10.4 suggests, surgery is often required for the upper lip and nose structures, and corrective dental work may be undertaken as well. It may also be necessary to train or retrain the individual in articulation and to assess his or her emotional status insofar as it is related to appearance or speech skills, depending on the child's age at the time of surgery (Snowling & Hulme, 2012). A child's continued development may introduce new problems later; for example, the physical growth of the jaw or mouth may create difficulties for someone who underwent surgery at a very young age. Although early correction results in successful healing and speech for a very high percentage of treated cases, the permanence of such results is uncertain in light of later growth spurts.

Treatment of cleft palate may involve the use of prosthetic appliances as well. For example, a prosthesis that basically serves as the upper palate or at least covers the fissures may be employed. Such an appliance may be attached to the teeth to hold it in position; it resembles the palate portion of artificial dentures.

Dental malformations other than those associated with clefts can also be corrected. Surgery can alter jaw structure and alignment. In some cases, orthodontic treatment may involve the repositioning of teeth through extractions and the use of braces. Prosthetic appliances, such as full or partial artificial dentures, may also be used. As in other challenges, the articulation patient who has orthodontic treatment often requires speech therapy to learn proper speech performance.

Treatment of functional articulation disorders often focuses on relearning the speaking act; in some cases, muscle control and usage are the focus. Specific causes of defective learning are difficult to identify precisely, but the basic assumption is that an inappropriate

CEC

Standard 4
Instructional Strategies

Standard 7
Instructional Planning

stimulus and reinforcement situation was present in the environment during speech development (Owens, Metz, & Farinella, 2011; Plante & Beeson, 2013). Accordingly, treatment includes an attempt to correct that set of circumstances so that accurate articulation can be learned. Several behavior modification procedures have been employed successfully in treating functional articulation disorders. In all cases, treatment techniques are difficult to implement because interventions must teach proper articulation, must be tailored to the individual, and must promote generalization of the new learning to a variety of word configurations and diverse environments beyond the treatment setting (Owens, Metz, & Farinella, 2011). Some call for improving the measurement and research methods employed in this and other areas of communication disorders (Johnston, et. al., 2012; Pfeiffer & Adkins, 2012).

It should also be noted that differences in language and dialect can create some interesting issues regarding treatment. When a child's first language is other than English or involves an ethnic dialect, that youngster may demonstrate a distinctiveness of articulation that makes his or her speech different and perhaps hard to understand (Aarts, Demir, & Vallen, 2011; Battle, 2009; Snowling & Hulme, 2012). Does this circumstance require an intervention similar to that applied for articulation disorders? Such a question involves cultural, social, and political implications beyond those typically considered by communication professionals.

- Be proactive in collaborating and communicating across different professions to coordinate the child's services. Family members, especially parents or guardians, may play a central coordination role for the child's interactions and services with professionals.

Tips for the Preschool Teacher

- Encourage collaborative parent involvement in all dimensions of the program, including systematic speech and language stimulation at home.
- Consider all situations and events as opportunities to teach speech and language, perhaps initially focusing on concrete objects and later moving to the more abstract, depending on the individual child's functioning level.
- Ask "wh" questions, such as what, who, when, and where, giving the child many opportunities to practice speaking as well as thinking.
- Practice with the child the use of the prepositions *in, on, out*, and so forth.
- Use all occasions possible to increase the child's vocabulary.

Tips for Preschool Personnel

- Communicate with the young child and all of those who are interacting with him or her. Collaborate in either direct or indirect communication instruction, but do so in collaboration with the child's teacher and parent. Many times the informal communication in the hallway is more important than we think.

Tips for Neighbors and Friends

- Interact with young children with communication disorders as you would with any others, speaking to them normally and directly modeling appropriate communication.
- Intervene if you encounter other children ridiculing the speech and language of these youngsters, encourage sensitivity to individual differences among your own children and other neighborhood children.

ELEMENTARY YEARS

Tips for the Family

- Stay proactively involved in your child's educational program through active participation with the school.
- Work in collaboration with the child's teacher on speaking practice, blending it naturally into family and individual activities.
- Communicate naturally with the child; avoid "talking down" and thereby modeling the use of "simpler language."

Tips for the General Education Classroom Teacher

- Continue collaborating with and promoting parents' involvement in their child's intervention program in whatever manner they can participate.
- Encourage the child with communication disorders to talk about events and things in his or her environment and to describe experiences in as much detail as possible.
- Use all situations possible to provide practice for the child's development of speech and language skills.
- Promote vocabulary enhancement for the child in different topic areas.

Tips for School Personnel

- Promote an environment where all who are available and in contact with the child are involved in communication instruction, if not directly then indirectly through interaction and modeling.
- Encourage student involvement in a wide array of activities that can also be used to promote speech and language development.

Tips for Neighbors and Friends

- Interact with children with communication disorders normally; do not focus on the speaking difficulties that may be evident.
- As a neighbor or friend, provide support for the child's parents, who may be struggling with difficult feelings about their child's communication skills.

SECONDARY AND TRANSITION YEARS

Tips for the Family

- Children who still exhibit communication problems at this level are likely to perform on a lower cognitive level. In such cases, communication may focus on functional matters such as grooming, feeding, and so on.
- For some children, communication may involve limited verbalization; consider other means of interacting.
- Interact with your child as much and as normally as possible.

Tips for the General Education Classroom Teacher

- Embed communication instruction in the context of functional areas (e.g., social interactions, requests for assistance, choice making).
- Consider adding augmented communication devices or procedures to the student's curriculum.

Tips for School Personnel

- Develop school activities that will encourage use of a broad variety of skill levels in speaking (i.e., not just the debate club).
- Collaborate and communicate with others in the school to find the best way you can contribute to the child's language or speech growth. Informal communication about daily activities may represent a very important growth and practice opportunity for the child.
- Promote school activities that permit participation through communication modes other than speaking (being careful to ensure that these efforts are consistent with therapy goals).

Tips for Neighbors and Friends

- To the degree that you are comfortable doing so, interact with children using alternative communication approaches (e.g., signs, gesturing, pantomiming).

Speech Disorders: Voice

Voice disorders involve unusual or abnormal acoustical qualities in the sounds made when a person speaks. All voices differ significantly in pitch, loudness, and other features from the voices of others of the same gender, cultural group, and age. However, voice disorders involve acoustical qualities that are so different that they are noticeable and divert attention away from the content.

Relatively little attention has been paid to voice disorders in the research literature for several reasons. First, the determination of voice normalcy involves a great deal of subjective judgment. Moreover, what is normal varies considerably with the circumstances (e.g., football games, barroom conversation, or seminar discussion) and with geographical location (e.g., the West, a rural area, New England, or the Deep South). Another factor that complicates analysis of voice disorders is related to the acceptable ranges of normal voice. Most individuals' voices fall within acceptable ranges. Children with voice disorders are often not referred for help, and untreated problems may be persistent (Ferrand, 2012; Portone, Johns, & Hapner, 2008).

Children with voice disorders often speak with an unusual nasality, hoarseness, or breathiness. Nasality involves either too little resonance from the nasal passages (**hyponasality** or **denasality**), which dulls the resonance of consonants and sounds as though the child has a continual cold or stuffy nose, or too much sound coming through the nose (**hypernasality**), which causes a twang in the speech. People with voice disorders of hoarseness have a constant husky sound to their speech, as though they had strained their

voices by yelling. Breathiness is a voice disorder with very low volume, like a whisper; it sounds as though not enough air is flowing through the vocal cords. Other voice disorders include overly loud or soft speaking and pitch abnormalities (such as monotone speech).

Like so many speech problems, the nature of voice disorders varies greatly. Our description provides considerable latitude, but also outlines

Voice disorder
A condition in which an individual habitually speaks with a voice that differs in pitch, loudness, or quality from the voices of his or her peer group.

Hyponasality
A voice resonance disorder whereby too little air passes through the nasal cavity; also known as denasality.

Denasality
A voice resonance problem that occurs when too little air passes through the nasal cavity; also known as hyponasality.

Hypernasality
A voice resonance disorder that occurs when excessive air passes through the nasal cavity, often resulting in an unpleasant twang.

Copyright © Mary Kate Denny/Photo Edit

Factors in voice disorders that interfere with communication are pitch, loudness, and quality. A voice disorder exists when these factors, singly or in combination, cause the listener to focus on the sounds being made rather than the message to be communicated.

general parameters of voice disorders often dismissed in the literature: pitch, loudness, and quality. An individual with a voice disorder may exhibit problems with one or more of these factors, and they may interfere with communication (Boone, McFarlane, Von Berg, & Zraick, 2010; Ferrand, 2012).

Causation

An appropriate voice pitch is efficient and is suited to the situation and the speech content as well as to the speaker's laryngeal structure. Correct voice pitch permits inflection without voice breaks or excessive strain. Appropriate pitch varies as emotion and meaning change and should not distract attention from the message. The acoustical characteristics of voice quality include such factors as nasality, breathy speech, and hoarse-sounding speech. As for the other element of voice, loudness is subjective. A normal voice is not habitually characterized by undue loudness or unusual softness. The typical level of loudness depends greatly on circumstances.

Pitch disorders take several forms. The person's voice may have an abnormally high or low pitch, may be characterized by pitch breaks or a restricted pitch range, or may be monotonal or monopitched. Many individuals experience pitch breaks as they progress through adolescence. Although more commonly associated with young males, pitch breaks also occur in females. Such pitch breaks are a normal part of development, but if they persist much beyond adolescence, they may signal laryngeal difficulties. They may be learned through imitation, as when a young boy attempts to sound like his older brother or father. They may also be learned from certain circumstances, as when a person in a position of authority believes a lower voice pitch evokes the image of power. Organic conditions, such as a hormone imbalance, may result in abnormally high- or low-pitched voices.

Voice disorders involving volume also have varied causes. Voices that are excessively loud or soft may be learned through imitation, perceptions and characteristics of the environment, and even aging (Ferrand, 2012; Portone, Johns, & Hapner, 2008). An example is mimicking the soft speaking of a female movie star. Other cases of abnormal vocal intensity occur because an individual has not learned to monitor loudness. Organic problems may result from problems such as paralysis of vocal cords, laryngeal trauma (e.g., larynx surgery for cancer, damage through accident or disease), and pulmonary diseases like asthma or emphysema (e.g., Chavira, Garland, Daley, & Hough, 2008; Richardson, Russo, Lozano, McCauley, & Katon, 2008). Loud speech may be related to hearing impairments or brain damage.

Voice disorders related to the quality of speech include production deviances such as those of abnormal nasality. Hypernasality occurs essentially because the soft palate does not move upward and back to close off the airstream through the nose properly. Such conditions can be due to improper tissue movement in the speech mechanism, or they may result from physical flaws such as an imperfectly repaired cleft palate (Sweeney & Sell, 2008). Excessive hypernasality may also be learned, as in the case of country music or certain rural dialects. Hyponasality or denasality is the type of voice quality experienced during a head cold or hay fever. In some cases, however, denasality is a result of learning or of abnormal physical structures, rather than these more common problems (Ferrand, 2012).

Intervention

The approach to treatment for a voice disorder depends on its cause. In cases where abnormal tissue development and/or dental structures result in unusual voice production, surgical intervention may be necessary. Surgery may also be part of the intervention plan if removal of the larynx is required. Such an intervention will also involve relearning communication through alternative mechanisms, including prostheses, and learning communication techniques to replace laryngeal verbalizations (Hardin-Jones & Chapman, 2008; Sweeney & Sell, 2008). In some situations, treatment may include direct instruction to enhance the affected individual's learning or relearning of acceptable voice production. These efforts are more difficult if the behavior has been long-standing and is well ingrained.

Voice disorders are seldom the focus of referral and treatment in the United States. However, some researchers have argued that voice disorders should be treated more aggressively (Portone, Johns, & Hapner, 2008; Sapienza & Hicks, 2006). One important element in planning interventions for voice disorders is clear and open communication with the person seeking treatment (Ferrand, 2012). It is important to avoid setting unrealistic expectations about outcomes and to remember that those being treated are the ultimate arbiters of that treatment's success.

Prevalence

We have already noted the difficulties involved in estimating the prevalence of other disorders: Many arise from differences in definitions and data collection procedures. The field of speech disorders is also vulnerable to these problems, so prevalence estimates vary considerably. It is typically claimed that speech disorders affect between 5 percent and 10 percent of the population. Yet, in 2009, 22 percent of all children (ages 3 to 21) who were served in programs for those with disabilities were categorized as having speech or language impairments (U.S. Department of Education, 2011). These figures do not deviate greatly from other estimates, although some data have suggested substantial geographical differences (e.g., significantly higher percentages in some areas of California than in parts of the Midwest). These figures themselves present a problem when we consider the 12 percent ceiling for services to all students with disabilities, as specified in the Individuals with Disabilities Education Act (IDEA). Obviously, individuals with speech disorders of a mild nature cannot be eligible for federally funded services. However, the 30th Annual Report to Congress on the Implementation of IDEA cited speech or language impairments as the second most frequently occurring disability (next to learning disabilities) to receive special services during the 2008–2009 school year (U.S. Department of Education, 2011). Occurrences of speech problems diminish in the population as age increases. Speech disorders are identified in more children in kindergarten through the middle grades, but decline as age increases. Thus, age and development diminish speech disorders considerably, though more so with certain types of problems (e.g., articulation difficulties) than with others.

Looking Toward a Bright Future

Communication disorders have a very long history in terms of attention as a disability area. It is clear that challenges presented through communication disorders represent extremely central functioning to affected individuals as well as those around them. Accurate and fluid speaking is very important to us in nearly every aspect of life. Because our society places such an emphasis on interpersonal interaction, the challenges people with communication disorders face are paramount and have a significant impact. And yet the future of science, understanding, and intervention is very promising.

Professionals working in this specialty have made significant progress over the years and have adopted and adapted technology in serving those with disabilities that are studied in this area. In those specialties where technology plays a central role, the profession has made enormous use of what is offered and has participated actively in the invention process. Where technology can be adapted to fit the specific needs of particular individuals, such adaptations have been made and continue to impress the field.

The emphasis on science, understanding, and intervention in communication areas is important and should be embraced, both by the family and by the education system. As shown by topics in this chapter, each area of challenge has its own set of implications and its own set of intervention approaches that differ significantly. As we have with other disability areas, progress in communication disorders provides individuals with the very best opportunity for a positive outcome that could possibly be imagined. The understanding of language delay generates an intervention leading to enhanced learning, whether the specific causation is known or only suspected. In circumstances where malformations of the jaw or the dental structure lead to faulty articulation, surgery may correct the unusual structures and then the individual may be taught to speak. Although the process may be time-consuming, it can lead to a successful outcome that enhances communication accuracy and results in an individual who no longer stands out in the crowd.

FOCUS REVIEW

FOCUS 1 Identify four ways in which speech, language, and communication are interrelated.

- Both speech and language form part, but not all, of communication.
- Some components of communication involve language but not speech.
- Some speech does not involve language.
- The development of communication—language and speech—overlap to some degree.

FOCUS 2 Explain how language delay and language disorder differ.

- In language delay, the sequence of development is intact, but the rate is interrupted.
- In language disorder, the sequence of development is interrupted.

FOCUS 3 Identify three factors that are thought to cause language disorders.

- Defective or deficient sensory systems
- Neurological damage occurring through physical trauma or accident
- Deficient or disrupted learning opportunities during language development

FOCUS 4 Describe how treatment approaches for language disorders generally differ for children and for adults.

- Treatment for children generally addresses initial acquisition or learning of language.

- Treatment for adults involves relearning or reacquiring language function.

FOCUS 5 Cite three factors that are thought to cause stuttering.

- Learned behavior, emotional problems, and neurological problems can contribute to stuttering.
- Some research has suggested that brain organization differs in people who stutter.
- People who stutter may learn their speech patterns as an outgrowth of the normal nonfluency evident when speech development first occurs.

FOCUS 6 Identify two ways in which learning theory and home environments are related to delayed speech.

- The home environment may provide little opportunity to learn speech.
- The home environment may interfere with speech development, as when speaking is punished.

FOCUS 7 Identify two reasons why some professionals are reluctant to treat functional articulation disorders in young schoolchildren.

- Many articulation problems evident in young children are developmental in nature, so speech may improve "naturally" with age.
- Articulation problems are quite frequent among young children, and treatment resources are limited.

Council for Exceptional Children (CEC) Standards to Accompany Chapter 10

 If you are thinking about a career in special education, you should know that many states use national standards developed by the Council for Exceptional Children (CEC) to assess a teacher candidate's knowledge and skills for working with students with disabilities. See a complete listing of the 10 CEC Content Standards on the inside back cover of this text.

1 Foundations
2 Development and Characteristics of Learners
3 Individual Learning Differences
4 Instructional Strategies
5 Learning Environments and Social Interactions
6 Communication
7 Instructional Planning

Mastery Activities and Assignments

To master the content within this chapter, complete the following activities and assignments. Online and interactive versions of these activities are also available on the accompanying Education CourseMate website, where you may also access TeachSource videos, chapter web links, interactive quizzes, portfolio activities, flash cards, an integrated eBook, and much more!

1. Complete a written test of the chapter's content. If your instructor requires a written test of your content knowledge for this chapter, keep a copy for your portfolio. A practice test on the information covered in this chapter is available through the Education CourseMate website.

2. Read the Debate Forum in this chapter and visit the Education CourseMate website to complete the activity "Take a Stand." Keep a copy of this activity for your portfolio.

3. Participate in a community service learning activity. Community service is a valuable way to enhance your learning experience. Visit the Education CourseMate website for suggested community service learning activities that correspond to the information presented in this chapter. Develop a reflective journal of the service learning experience for your portfolio.

CHAPTER 11

Autism Spectrum Disorders

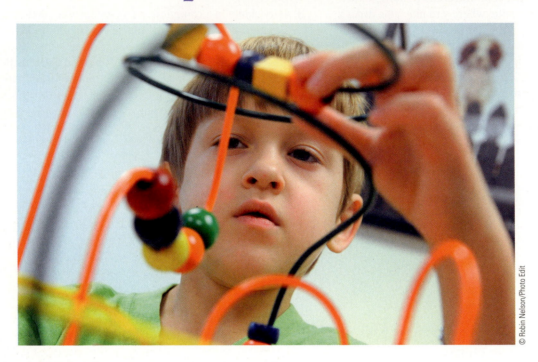

© Robin Nelson/Photo Edit

FOCUS PREVIEW

As you read the chapter, focus on these key concepts:

1 Describe the variability and severity of characteristics within the autism spectrum.

2 Identify the primary impairments present in children with autism spectrum disorders.

3 What are the current prevalence estimates for autism spectrum disorders?

4 Identify factors related to the biological theoretical view regarding the causes of autism spectrum disorders.

5 Identify the major approaches to the treatment of autism spectrum disorders.

6 How are families impacted when raising a child with autism spectrum disorders?

Diagnosing Kaysen

Kala Reynolds

We had a very difficult time with the diagnosis process. When my son Kaysen started kindergarten he was "uncontrollable," as his teachers put it. He was first diagnosed as having ADHD [attention deficit/hyperactivity disorder], but soon it became very obvious that the only time he was hyperactive was when he was not on his normal schedule or when he was being switched from a task he was focused on. As we watched him, we noticed other things about his behaviors and how they were a little bit different than most kids.

I have a close family friend that works with kids with autism and she watched him and pointed out the behaviors that could be due to autism. After speaking with her we started talking to the pediatrician about the possibility of Asperger's syndrome. The pediatrician referred us to have Kaysen go through neuropsychological testing. However, the office that would accept our insurance was not easy to get into.

Kala Reynolds

It took about six months to get a call back to set up an appointment for the testing he needed. Yet, when we did get an appointment scheduled, the testing occurred right away and at age 7, Kaysen was diagnosed with autism and obsessive-compulsive disorder.

In the meantime, his school had not been following what we found to work when he was in kindergarten, things which were also listed on his IEP. Because his diagnosis was undetermined, we hit block walls trying to get him extra help in school. The teacher and the principal said that he just needed to be disciplined more often and that taking him out of the class when he had a meltdown was the best way to help everybody. So Kaysen spent many school hours sitting in the sick room. Without being in class, he began to fall further behind in his studies. He also started to become more withdrawn and sad. Students teased him for having meltdowns. He was unable to eat lunch or breakfast at school; he was unable to play on the playground with the rest of his class. It seemed that the teacher and the principal both believed that Kaysen was not a child with a disability, but a very misbehaved child. We now try to meet Kaysen's needs by homeschooling him with an online program.

A Changing Era in the Lives of People with Autism Spectrum Disorders

Autism spectrum disorders are among the most complicated disabilities in our field. Periodically we hear about this disability in that the prevalence is reassessed, recounted, or remeasured. There is no question that we have improved our assessment techniques and we have also improved our treatment. Today's assessment is far more comprehensive than what we used over the years. Likewise our placement and treatment have improved along with the monitoring of progress. Autism is now openly viewed on a spectrum that has emerged rather recently. Before this, we didn't openly speak of the disability in such terms. Likewise, we now know for certain that growth and maturation for many of these children are evident and can be observed. It is truly a changing era in the field of autism, and this has emerged to the forefront of the field.

Autism
A pervasive developmental disorder with onset prior to age 3, characterized by qualitatively impaired social interactive and social communicative skills along with restricted and repetitive repertoire of behavior, interests, and activities.

CEC
Standard 1
Foundations

Autism has received widespread media attention over the past few years, partially due to celebrities like Jenny McCarthy.

Savant syndrome
A rare and extraordinary condition in which unusual skills are performed, usually in one of five areas: music, art, calculating, mathematics, and mechanical or spatial skills, characterized by obsessive preoccupation with specific items or memorization of facts, trivia, sequences, or patterns that are in stark contrast to the developmental level of the individual, ranging from splinter skills to prodigious savant skills.

Asperger's syndrome
A condition that shares unusual social interactions and behaviors with autism, but historically has included no general language delay.

Autism spectrum disorders
A range of functioning among many dimensions related to social communicative and social interactive functioning, with impairments in repertoire of behavior. Typically considered to be autism; Asperger's syndrome; and pervasive developmental disorder, not otherwise specified.

CEC
Standard 8
Assessment

Definition and History

The term **autism** comes from the Greek word *autos* meaning "self," and was first used in the early 1900s to describe unique behavioral symptoms of patients with schizophrenia who had extreme difficulties in the social world (Dyches, 2010). Although autism is thought to have been described first in the early 1800s (Volkmar & Wiesner 2009), it did not gain much attention until Johns Hopkins University psychiatrist Leo Kanner wrote his seminal paper describing children with "autistic disturbances of affective contact" (Kanner, 1943). Research conducted during subsequent decades focused on etiology, and in some cases blaming "cold, refrigerator mothers" for causing their child's autism (Bettelheim, 1967).

In the 1970s, however, the focus shifted toward education for individuals with autism. With the passage of the Education for All Handicapped Children Act of 1975, children with autism were permitted a free and appropriate public education, but because autism was not a distinct educational category, these students were likely served under disability labels that were then called mental retardation and seriously emotionally disturbed. The term *autism* became more widely known after federal law recognized autism as a disability category in the Individuals with Disabilities Education Act of 1990 (IDEA). But the popular media, most notably the 1988 movie *Rain Man*, starring Dustin Hoffman as an institutionalized adult with autism, raised awareness beyond the research and educational communities. *Autism* became a household word.

In the 1980s and early 1990s, autism began to be viewed as encompassing a broader range of functioning than in the past, including those with **savant syndrome** (Treffert, 2009), extraordinarily focus and gifted skills such as those displayed in *Rain Man*. The 1981 English translation of Hans Asperger's 1944 paper describing a condition later to be named Asperger's disorder (or **Asperger's syndrome**) brought greater awareness of the wide variability of symptoms in autism (Dyches, 2010).

Paul Morig/WireImage/Getty Images

Today, autism and Asperger's syndrome are considered to be **autism spectrum disorders (ASD)**, and have received significant attention from both researchers and the public media. More than ever, popular novels and picture books include depictions of individuals with ASD (Dyches, Prater, & Leininger, 2009). Also popular in Hollywood, big-screen films such as *Dear John*, made-for-TV movies such as *Temple Grandin*, film documentaries such as *The Horse Boy*, and television shows such as *American Idol* and *Parenthood* include individuals with ASD. Other shows include characters who appear to function along the autism spectrum, but have not been identified as such (e.g., Jim Parsons on *Big Bang Theory* and Temperance Brennan on *Bones*).

Furthermore, many celebrities have become spokespeople, organizers for charities, and other types of supporters for raising awareness about ASD. Although many of the more public portrayals of ASD in many cases neglect the severity of the condition, they educate and capture the interest of a considerable segment of the public.

Evaluation

Because no biologic markers exist for ASD, identification is made by a team of professionals that uses direct assessment, questionnaires, observational techniques, and interviews to evaluate the presence of autistic symptoms and developmental functioning.

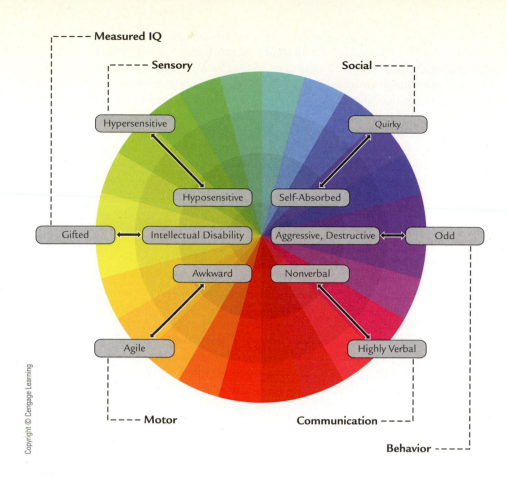

Figure 11.1 *The Autism Spectrum*

Such evaluations are complex and can be imprecise due to many factors, including the changing definition of ASD over time. Early descriptions of autism implied a seriously reduced level of functioning, yet current understanding indicates a broad range of capacity occurs, from severe to mild impairments. Acknowledgment of this has led to the concept of autism spectrum disorders, which includes a range of impairments in areas that are significant and pervasive: social communication and social interaction skills, and restricted, repetitive patterns of behavior, interests, or activities. Additionally, many individuals with ASD have skills and disabilities along a spectrum of other characteristics such as gross and fine motor skills, measured IQ, and sensory sensitivities. For example, while one child with ASD might be highly verbal, socially quirky, intellectually gifted, awkward in physical movements, hypersensitive, and engages in repetitive self-calming behavior, another child might be nonverbal, socially self-absorbed, physically agile, hyposensitive, destructive to self and others, with a low IQ. Many different combinations of characteristics within the spectrum are possible. Figure 11.1 illustrates this concept of the autism spectrum.

Standard 2
Development and Characteristics of Learners

Diagnostic Criteria

The terms *autism spectrum disorder*, *autistic spectrum disorder*, and *pervasive developmental disorder* are often used interchangeably to describe the variable differences in severity and changes of autistic characteristics in individuals over time. However, historically these terms have not been formally used when an individual is diagnosed. More specific diagnoses are typically warranted, and these usually occur based upon evaluations that employ the *Diagnostic and Statistical Manual of Mental Disorders* (*DSM*; American Psychiatric Association, 2000). The *DSM* is the authoritative text by which a medical professional such as a psychologist or psychiatrist diagnoses individuals with ASD in the United States.

This manual has undergone several revisions since its first edition in 1952. Initially, autism was incorrectly associated with childhood schizophrenia; it was not mentioned as a separate diagnosis until 1980. The fourth revision of the *DSM* uses the umbrella term **pervasive developmental disorders** (PDD) to characterize those with similar autistic-like conditions, including autistic disorder; Asperger's syndrome; childhood disintegrative disorder; Rett syndrome; and pervasive developmental disorder, not otherwise specified (PDD-NOS) (American Psychiatric Association, 2000). Those with the triad of impairments in social, communication, and behavioral skills have historically been considered to have "classic autism." According to the fourth revision of the *DSM*, Asperger's syndrome is characterized by deficits in both social interaction and repetitive and idiosyncratic behavior, but there is no clinically significant language delay. Although those with Asperger's may not communicate in a socially normative fashion, they do not have language delays. Those diagnosed as having PDD-NOS have severe and pervasive deficits, but not to the degree that would qualify them as having any of the other PDDs (American Psychiatric Association, 2000). They are often considered to have "atypical autism" or be "autistic-like."

The proposed changes to the fifth edition of *Diagnostic and Statistical Manual of Mental Disorders* (*DSM-V*), which are still being debated in 2012, will change the terminology of the general condition, autism spectrum disorder, to reflect the variability within the diagnosis and because distinctions among most of the pervasive developmental disorders have been inconsistent over time. It is characterized by the early presence of persistent deficits in social communication and social interaction as well as restrictive, repetitive patterns of behavior, interests, or activities. These deficits together must limit and impair everyday functioning. Autism spectrum disorder includes the previous designations of autistic disorder; Asperger's syndrome; childhood disintegrative disorder; and pervasive developmental disorder, not otherwise specified. Table 11.1 includes the various names used over time to describe autism according to the *DSM*.

Due to the spectrum nature of the disorder, it is not clear what differentiates low-functioning from high-functioning individuals, although narrow interpretations set the cutoff at an IQ of below 70, a standard used to indicate intellectual disability (Kanai

Table 11.1	Diagnostic Terms Used to Describe Autism Spectrum Disorders	
Edition	**Year**	**Diagnostic Labels**
I	1952	Schizophrenic reaction, childhood type
II	1968	Schizophrenia, childhood type
III	1980	Infantile autism
III-R	1987	Autistic disorder
IV	1994	Pervasive developmental disorders 1. Autistic disorder 2. Rett's disorder 3. Childhood disintegrative disorder 4. Asperger's syndrome 5. Pervasive developmental disorder, not otherwise specified
V	Proposed, not adopted as of 2012	Autism spectrum disorder 1. Autistic disorder 2. Childhood disintegrative disorder 3. Asperger's syndrome 4. Pervasive developmental disorder, not otherwise specified

et al., 2012). A broader interpretation considers many characteristics, and posits that the higher the performance and verbal IQ, communicative abilities, adaptation skills, and decreased manifestation of symptoms, the higher functioning the individual is perceived to be. However, the level of functioning rarely translates to programmatic decisions—a more adaptive approach is to describe the level and intensity of supports needed for the affected individual to succeed in inclusionary and preferred environments.

As knowledge increases, the need to better define conditions arises, yet this is not without much debate and concern. Such is the case with the fifth revision of the *DSM*, primarily over the issue of accurately diagnosing Asperger's syndrome and high-functioning autism. Some researchers argue that Asperger's syndrome is a distinct disorder; others contend it is a higher-functioning version of autism spectrum disorders (Blakemore et al., 2006; Matson & Wilkins, 2008; Minshew & Meyer, 2006). Although this argument continues unresolved, the notion of a spectrum of disability severity has grown in acceptance and allows students and parents to begin to receive services (Baron-Cohen & Klin, 2006; Beaumont & Newcombe, 2006; McConachie & Robinson, 2006). Also, there does not appear to be a need for different treatments for those with high-functioning autism and those with Asperger's syndrome, and in practice, similar interventions are typically offered.

Educational Classification

Although medical diagnoses are important for families to obtain appropriate services and available insurance coverage, school personnel are not required to rely on *DSM* diagnoses to serve students with ASD. If a child is suspected of having ASD, the multidisciplinary team must evaluate that child to determine if he or she has a disability that adversely impacts the student's progress in the general curriculum and by reason thereof requires special education. It is important to note that, depending on the state in which the family lives, the child may not need to have a medical diagnosis to qualify for an educational classification of autism (MacFarlane & Kanaya, 2009). Conversely, when students diagnosed with ASD are experiencing success in school so that their educational progress is not significantly impacted, they may not qualify for special education services. Such students may be served with an accommodation plan, also called a 504 plan, with services provided by the general, rather than the special education teacher. The Snapshot of Kaysen illustrates the difficulties in diagnosing students with ASD.

The law governing classification of students with ASD, the Individuals with Disabilities Education Improvement Act (IDEA), employs the following definition of autism:

> Autism means a developmental disability significantly affecting verbal and nonverbal communication and social interaction, generally evident before age three, that adversely affects educational performance. Other characteristics often associated with autism are engagement in repetitive activities and stereotyped movements, resistance to environmental change or change in daily routines, and unusual responses to sensory experiences. (34 C.F.R. 300.8(c)(1))

The IDEA definition is based largely upon the *DSM* criteria; however, because it is stated generally, there is great variability from state to state and district to district in how students along the autism spectrum are classified (MacFarlane & Kanaya, 2009). It is the responsibility of the multidisciplinary team to determine if students qualify for services under the educational classification of autism or another category.

Characteristics

Symptoms of autism spectrum disorders emerge very early in a child's life, with behavioral symptoms becoming evident before the age of 3 (Centers for Disease Control and Prevention, 2009); in some cases, abnormal brain development has been found in infants (Ozonoff et al., 2010; Wolff, et. al., 2012). Many are diagnosed around the age of 5 (Centers for Disease Control and Prevention, 2009). However, those with Asperger's syndrome and high-functioning autism are often diagnosed later than those with ASD who have lower IQs (Levy, et al., 2010; Shattuck et al., 2009), and they may have been previously misdiagnosed with

FOCUS 2
Identify the primary impairments present in children with autism spectrum disorders.

conditions such as ADHD, conduct disorder, pragmatic language disorder, attachment disorder, or obsessive-compulsive disorder (Fombonne, 2009; Mandell, Ittenbach, Levy, & Pinto-Martin, 2007). Also, those who are from low socioeconomic status are diagnosed later than those from higher socioeconomic status (Fountain, King, & Bearman, 2011; Levy et al., 2010).

The primary impairments that constitute autism spectrum disorders are social communication and social interaction skills, and the presence of restricted, repetitive patterns of behavior, interests, or activities. These impairments are present early in a child's life and limit and impede everyday functioning. Autism Speaks, an advocacy organization, has developed a glossary that highlights side-by-side videos of typically developing children (usually toddlers) and videos of children with autistic behavior. These videos give parents and practitioners examples of the "red flags" they may see in children suspected of having ASD. These videos can be found on the Autism Speaks website at www.autismspeaks.org. See Table 11.2 for profiles of several school-aged children within the autism spectrum.

Social Communication and Social Interaction Skills

Children with autism spectrum disorders have persistent deficits in social skills involving communication and interactions with others. These social impairments are hallmark features of individuals with ASD.

Social Communication
Social communication includes nonverbal as well as verbal elements required for shared understanding. Nonverbal elements include the use of gestures and facial expressions, which are often difficult for children with ASD. For example, while other students respond readily to the "teacher look" when they are misbehaving, a child with ASD is likely to have difficulty understanding the interpretation of this emotional means of communication.

Speech is an element of verbal communication that may be impaired in children with ASD. The variation of speech abilities in those with ASD ranges from being completely

Table 11.2   Social and Communication Skills Associated with Behaviors, Interests, and Activities

Social Communication and Social Interaction Skills	Restricted, Repetitive Patterns of Behavior, Interests, or Activities
Six-year-old Alex uses both immediate and delayed echolalia. When asked, "What do you want?" he replies, "What do you want?" He often sings jingles from TV commercials.	Six-year-old Alex bites his wrist to the point of bleeding when he is prevented from getting what he wants. He doesn't appear to feel any pain.
Eight-year-old Colton can say *please*, *cookie*, and *want*, and uses sign language to communicate about other wants and needs.	Eight-year-old Colton rocks back and forth for long periods of time if he is not redirected. He also toe walks and flaps his hands out to his side when he is excited.
Ten-year-old Devaun uses the paraeducator's hand as a tool to get a desired object rather than reaching for the object herself.	Ten-year-old Devaun doesn't appear to notice when her peer tutor approaches her desk. Devaun continues to watch the spinning Frisbee she brought in from recess.
Eleven-year-old Willis does not speak, but uses an iPad with special software to communicate his wants, needs, ideas, tell jokes, interact with friends, and do his homework. He is on grade level in all subjects.	Eleven-year-old Willis becomes anxious when his classmates touch him on the shoulder and ask him to play. He averts his eyes from their gaze and responds to them by typing on his iPad.
Fourteen-year-old Ivan tries to engage his friends in conversations by telling them facts about his special interests, such as "Did you know that Saturn is known as the 'jewel of the solar system' and that it is nothing like our very own planet Earth?"	Fourteen-year-old Ivan demands that his friends play the same games at recess in the same order as the previous day. When they refuse, he goes inside to squeeze himself into his locker to "get away from those ignorant fools."
Sixteen-year-old Keisha refers to herself in the third person. She often uses phrases such as, "Keisha wants to go home now."	Sixteen-year-old Keisha becomes anxious when she has a substitute bus driver, teacher, or paraeducator. Agitated, she paces the room and repeats, "Keisha wants the regular people."

absent, to having limited functional speech, and to having overly formal speech with difficulties managing topics, reciprocity, and intonation (Paul, Orlovski, Marcinko, & Volkmar, 2009). Approximately 25 percent of those with autism do not develop functional speech (Tiegerman-Farber, 2009). Many who do speak often engage in strange language and speaking behavior, such as **echolalia**, where they repeat or "echo back" what has been said to them, or what they have heard previously, such as lines from a favorite movie. Additionally, the tonal quality of their speech is often unusual or flat with little variation in pitch or volume; in some cases, their speech appears to serve the purpose of self-stimulation rather than communication.

Language skills are another aspect of verbal ability that is often impaired in children with ASD. They may exhibit an uneven level of development between their cognitive abilities and their receptive and expressive language skills, and fail to use pronouns in speech directed at other people (Tiegerman-Farber, 2009; Weismer, Lord, & Esler, 2010), preferring to call people by their names, and sometimes their full names, even when they know them quite well. These children seem to differ from their peers in failing to grasp grammatical complexity and making little use of semantics in sentence structure (e.g., Perkins, Dobbinson, Boucher, Bol, & Bloom, 2006).

Those with Asperger's syndrome and high-functioning autism have difficulties primarily with the social components of using language, specifically related to social-emotional reciprocity. They may engage in inappropriate turn taking, make poor judgments about how much or how little to say, struggle with taking another person's perspective, and ask inappropriate questions during conversations (Paul, Orlovski, Marcinko, & Volkmar, 2009). Often considered to be "little professors," students with Asperger's syndrome use high-level or awkward vocabulary rather than the slang or common language their peers use (e.g., a teenage boy saying "I am very pleased to meet you," rather than "Wazzup?").

Verbal children with ASD find it difficult to initiate verbal interactions to express their feelings, or to interpret the feelings or facial expressions of others. Also, they tend to use and understand language that is concrete and literal. Words that depend upon contextual factors for understanding meaning such as homonyms (e.g., *which* for *witch*), pronouns, jokes, sarcasm, and figurative language are often difficult to interpret. The Snapshot on Krista illustrates how an individual with Asperger's syndrome literally interprets language.

Echolalia
Imitation or repetition of words that have been spoken, either immediate or delayed.

Social Interaction Skills
Another component of social communication is the development and maintenance of relationships. Although some individuals with ASD avoid social contact, others yearn for friends and interactions but are challenged by initiating and maintaining rewarding relationships. They may have a significantly abnormal social approach with limited or no initiation of social interactions or sharing of interests with others. Many have abnormal or infrequent eye contact with others (American Psychiatric Association, 2000). Clearly, children with ASD interact with their environment in ways that are not typical of their same-age peers, as though they have difficulty making sense of the world around them.

Restricted, Repetitive Patterns of Behavior, Interests, or Activities

In addition to social impairments, individuals with ASD exhibit restricted or repetitive patterns of behavior, interests, or activities. This is another hallmark feature and can include repetitive speech, motor movements, and use of objects; certain rituals and routines; and restricted, fixated movements.

Repetitive Speech, Motor Movements, or Use of Objects
Children with ASD engage in patterns of behaviors, interests, and activities that are limited and repetitive. These patterns can occur across speech, motor movements, and use of objects. For example, children who are echolalic may say the same words, phrases, or scripts redundantly. Other children may use idiosyncratic language, or language that has particular meaning to themselves, but which may not be known to others except for knowledgeable communicative

Krista: A Girl with Asperger's Syndrome

Everything is literal to my daughter, Krista. When she was 5, I said that she had "rats" in her hair. She began screaming, "Get them out!" I explained that people say that when you have knots in your hair. A few days later she asked me to get the knots out of her hair, but one knot was really bad. When I told her I couldn't get the knot out, she informed me that the knot must be "double-knotted."

When she was 8, my husband said, "I have a backache." She began to argue with him, informing him that he didn't have a backache. The argument was getting pretty heated, so I asked

Jennifer Fletcher

my husband to stop and see what she meant. I asked her why she thought Dad didn't have a backache. She grabbed his hands and said, "Look, there is nothing in his hands!" To her,

"to have" meant that your hands had to be holding an object. She didn't understand a more abstract meaning of "have," where your body could possess something such as a backache.

Moments like these continue, even though she is now 15. She was visiting a friend and was told to come home at 6:30. The rest of the family got home at 7:00 and she wasn't there. When we asked her about it she said, "But I did come home at 6:30! Then I went back."

partners. For example, a child may say "Wanna push?" to indicate "I want to go on the swing." Still others may be preoccupied with certain sounds, words, phrases, or ideas, and may say them repeatedly, having difficulty switching their attention to other topics.

Typical motor repetitions include flicking hands in front of their faces, flapping hands, rocking, and spinning (Bruns & Thompson, 2012). These repetitive behaviors are sometimes termed **stereotypic behavior** or **self-stimulation** and may continue for a few seconds or if unattended, for hours. Some behaviors that seem to start as stereotypy or self-stimulation may worsen or take different forms and create the potential for injury to the child. Examples include hair pulling, face slapping, biting, and head banging (e.g., Cannon, Kenworthy, Alexander, Werner, & Anthony, 2011). Behavior that becomes self-injurious is more often found in low-functioning children and can understandably cause concern and stress for parents and others around them.

Although the purposes and origins of stereotypic behavior are not well understood, for some, such activity may provide sensory input whereas for others it may provide a sense of organization. Stereotypic behavior is one area, among others, where autobiographic material written by high-functioning individuals with autism spectrum disorders may significantly enhance our understanding (Koegel & Koegel, 2012).

Individuals with ASD may use objects in a stereotypic way, such as spinning objects, lining up items, and playing with objects in an unusual and repetitive manner. For example, when given a toy truck to play with, instead of pushing the truck along the ground, a child with ASD may turn the truck upside down and spin the wheels for long periods of time.

Rituals and Routines Intense and rigid adherence to routines, ritualized patterns of verbal or nonverbal behavior, or excessive resistance to change are characteristic of children with ASD. Occurring among a spectrum of severity, a mild case might include repetitive questioning (e.g., "Is the fire drill today?"), distress at small changes (e.g., substitute teacher, change in the arrangement of desks, unannounced school assembly), or insistence on a particular food for a given meal (e.g., pizza for school lunch only on Fridays). Extreme adherence to rituals and routines may lead to "meltdowns" or uncontrollable tantrums if a familiar routine is disrupted.

Stereotypic behavior
Behavior or stereotypy involving repetitive movements such as rocking, hand flicking, or object manipulation.

Self-Stimulation
Repetitive body movements used to stimulate one's senses. Often colloquially referred to as "stimming."

Often, items must be arranged in a symmetrical or orderly fashion to seem proper to children with an autism spectrum disorder. They may line up their toys in a particular way or keep items in their desk in an organized fashion, becoming distraught or panicked if their items are moved or disrupted. They may wash themselves, collect certain items, and demand sameness in a manner reminiscent of those with obsessive-compulsive disorder (Zandt, 2007). However, autism spectrum disorders and obsessive-compulsive disorder are two distinct conditions and require different treatment protocols (see Leininger, Dyches, Prater, & Heath, 2010).

Such obsessive, ritualistic behaviors create numerous problems, as one might expect, particularly if an effort is made to integrate the child into daily life. For example, most people pay little attention to the exact route they take when driving to the grocery store, or to the precise pattern of moving through the store once they arrive. For parents who take their child with ASD along, however, minor deviations may cause a serious crisis for the child as well as the parent. One mother indicated that while being out in the community with her child, she "grew immune to the stares and thoughtless comments from casual observers, such as, 'That girl is evil' or 'Your child is so rude'" (Smith, 2007, p. 324).

Restricted, Fixated Interests Children with ASD have restricted interests that are fixated on certain topics, objects, or activities. These interests are abnormally intense and can be all-consuming. Some have an unusually strong attachment to or preoccupation with certain objects such as trains, string, or maps. They may have a preoccupation with parts of objects such as the wheels on a toy car or the blades of a toy helicopter.

Others may have excessively narrow interests that they continue to explore or discuss. Such extreme focus on these circumscribed interests is often called **perseveration**. For example, verbal children with ASD may investigate with great intensity and perseverance the train schedule in their city, and attempt to share their specialized knowledge with anyone who will listen.

Perseveration
An extreme focus on circumscribed interests, topics, or activities.

These restricted, repetitive patterns of behavior, interests, or activities may be associated with the sensory-processing difficulties many children with ASD exhibit. These sensory-processing responses can be manifest in any sensory area: sight, hearing, smell and taste, touch, balance, body position/awareness, and pain. Children may react to stimuli with hyporesponsiveness, hyperresponsiveness, and sensory-seeking behaviors (Watson et al., 2011). Those who are hyporesponsive do not exhibit the typical response to a stimulus, such as a teacher calling the child's name. Some may appear to be indifferent to pain, heat, or cold. Hypersensitive children with ASD have an exaggerated reaction to a stimulus, such as covering one's ears when the school bell rings, when a vacuum is turned on, or when a toilet is flushed. Some textures may bother them, leading them to wear only certain articles of clothing, or demanding that the tags from their shirts be removed. They may also be bothered by physical touch. Sensory-seeking behaviors are actions that make a sensory experience more intense, such as sniffing shoes in the locker room, or watching water drip from the faucet (Watson et al., 2011).

Other Conditions Associated with Autism Spectrum Disorders

Many children with autism spectrum disorders have other conditions that impact their daily functioning, commonly described as "comorbid" conditions. This term implies a condition separate from the primary diagnosis, but in the case of ASD, this may not be true. Some of these conditions can be considered to be features of ASD and thereby "co-occurring" conditions. Typically these include developmental, mental health, neurological, and genetic disorders. Approximately four out of five young children with ASD have at least one other condition, making accurate diagnosis difficult (Levy et al., 2010).

Developmental disorders are the most frequently co-occurring condition with ASD. Most commonly, these include language disorders, ADHD, and intellectual disabilities (Levy, et al., 2010; Nicholas, Charles, Carpenter, King, Jenner, & Spratt, 2008). Intellectual ability varies among children with autism spectrum disorders, and high-functioning individuals may test at a normal level. Others may have a tested IQ in the gifted range (Koegel & Koegel, 2012).

For children within the autism spectrum, approximately 40 to 60 percent have been shown to have intellectual disabilities, with uneven learning profiles rather than across-the-board delays (Centers for Disease Control and Prevention, 2009; Nicholas et al., 2008). However, IQ testing may not be reliable for these children, as the verbal and reasoning skills required in intelligence testing pose particular difficulties for them.

Mental health or psychiatric disorders are found among children with ASD. Young children may be diagnosed with conditions such as oppositional defiant disorder, anxiety disorder, emotional disturbance, obsessive-compulsive disorder, among other conditions (Levy et al., 2010). Children and adolescents with ASD are at an increased risk for depression and anxiety symptoms (Strang et al., 2012). It appears that the greater the autism severity, the more likely the child will have somatic complaints, mood disturbance, and social problems (Mayes, Calhoun, Murray, & Zahid, 2011).

Neurological and other medical conditions also occur in children with ASD. Most common is epilepsy. Although relatively rare, conditions such as fragile X syndrome, tuberous sclerosis, and 15q duplication syndrome have also been found in children with ASD (Abrahams & Geschwind, 2008; Levy, 2010).

Families of children with ASD who have other co-occurring conditions may be at increased risk for accessing appropriate care and services. This may create additional financial burden, stress, and mental health issues for such families (Kogan, Strickland, Blumberg, Singh, Perrin, & van Dyck, 2008).

Unique Strengths

A unique characteristic of ASD is the "odd mixture of cognitive strengths and weaknesses" (Wallace, 2008). The strengths of children with autism spectrum disorders are frequently different from those of their normally developing peers and may present interesting educational challenges. The abilities of children with autism spectrum disorders frequently develop unevenly, both within and among skill areas.

Some individuals with ASD have areas of ability in which levels of performance are unexpectedly high compared with those of other domains of functioning. For instance, students with autism may perform unusually well at figuring mathematical calculations "in their heads" or drawing detailed pictures of horses, but have serious deficiencies in language skills and abstract reasoning. Approximately 10 percent of those with ASD exhibit splinter skills or have savant syndrome, usually in one of five areas: music, art, calculating, mathematics, and mechanical or spatial skills (Heaton, Williams, Cummins & Happe, 2008; Treffert, 2009). For example, Stephen Wiltshire, who has ASD, creates architectural drawings accurately and with minute detail after a brief flight over a city such as Rome; he now has his own gallery in London (Treffert, 2007).

For parents of such students, these savant skills create enormous confusion. Although most parents realize very early that their child has exceptionalities, they also hope that he or she is developmentally healthy. These hopes may be fueled by the child's demonstration of unusually precocious skills.

Parents and teachers are strongly recommended to "train the talent" rather than to suppress or eliminate these unusual skills (Treffert, 2009, p. 1,335). Instead of viewing the student's intense fascination with a narrow topic as perseveration that is annoying or bothersome, create learning activities in which the student can demonstrate "perseverance" in meeting the learning objectives. Strategies to capitalize on strengths, interests, and talents associated with these focused fascinations do not demand much time, but do require creative thinking and student input (see Lanou, Hough, & Powell, 2012). These highly focused skills can become a means toward achieving normalization, socialization, and independence.

Also, although "everyday memory" or the use of memory for daily purposes appears to be impaired in individuals with ASD (Jones, et al., 2011), others seem to have relatively strong, specific long-term memory skills, particularly for factual information like names, numbers, and dates (Koegel & Koegel, 2012). Once these students have learned a piece of information, they may not forget it. Their long-term memory skills may equal or exceed those of their normally developing peers. The juxtaposition of unique skills with difficulty in social interactions is highlighted in the description of Donald T. in the nearby Reflect on This box.

Young Donald's behavior was perplexing to his parents. While he seemed slow and backward in some areas, he also displayed sparks of brilliance. At age 1, Donald could hum and sing tunes accurately; at age 2, he could name the U.S. presidents, along with many of his ancestors and relatives. Later he could recite short poems, the 23rd Psalm, and 25 questions and answers from the Presbyterian catechism. However, at age 3, Donald did not feed himself and exhibited problematic behaviors, and his mother believed that he was "hopelessly insane."

Following the recommendations of the family physician, Donald's parents had him institutionalized in a Mississippi town aptly named Sanatorium. Yet after one year of institutionalization, minimal progress, and a diagnosis of "some glandular disease," his parents took him home. Two months later, in October 1938, 5-year old Donald was examined by Austrian American psychiatrist Leo Kanner, who observed him not to be feebleminded, insane, or affected with schizophrenia. Donald, along with 10 other children, was described in the now-famous 1943 report as having a condition that "differs so markedly and uniquely from anything reported so far," something Kanner called "autistic disturbance of affective contact" (Kanner, 1943, p. 217).

Donald T., as he was known in the report, was the first child reported to have autism. His parents and Dr. Kanner noted Donald's triad of impairments that have typically characterized a diagnosis of autism—qualitative impairments in both social interaction and communication; and patterns of behavior, activities, and interests that are restricted, repetitive, and stereotyped. When examined at age 5, Donald was described as being happiest when left alone, oblivious to his social environment, and having no apparent affection to others. Although he could enunciate words clearly, he asked questions only in single words, parroted words and phrases from others, and repetitively made irrelevant utterances such as "chrysanthemum," "dahlia, dahlia, dahlia," and "Through the dark clouds shining." He jumped up and down jubilantly while watching blocks, pans, and other round objects spin, had temper tantrums when interrupted, and had unusual body movements with his fingers and head.

Seventy-two years after being examined by Leo Kanner, the identity of "Case 1: Donald T." was discovered in Forest, Mississippi. Donald Gray Triplett, then 77 years old, grew up in a community of approximately 3,000 where he was educated, included, and accepted decades before the term *autism* became a household word. Today, Donald is an avid golfer and world traveler. He lives alone in the home he grew up in and enjoys his morning ritual of drinking coffee with his friends, going for a walk, watching *Bonanza* reruns, then driving to the golf course for a round of golf, preferring to play by himself. He has dinner with his brother and sister-in-law every Sunday night. Still showing signs of autism, Donald's life is tranquil, familiar, stable, and secure, particularly for a man with autism, and most notably for the first person diagnosed with autism.

Questions for Reflection

1. What are some of the characteristics of autism that Donald exhibited when he was a young child and as a grown man?

2. How can misdiagnosis affect individuals with autism?

3. What types of adult outcomes are possible for those diagnosed with autism today?

SOURCES: Donovan, J. & Zucker, C. (2010, October). Autism's first child. *The Atlantic*. Retrieved February 25, 2012, www.theatlantic.com/magazine/archive/2010/10/autism-8217-s-first-child/8227/; Kanner, L. (1943). Autistic disturbances of affective contact. *Nervous Child*, 2, 217–250.

TEACHSOURCE VIDEO REBECCA AND BEN: CREATING STRUCTURED EDUCATIONAL PROGRAMS FOR STUDENTS WITH AUTISM

Please visit the Education CourseMate website for *Human Exceptionality*, 11th edition, to access this chapter's TeachSource Video. In this clip, you will be introduced to two students, Rebecca and Ben. Rebecca is a first-grader with autism in an inclusive classroom. Watch for the strategies her teachers use to help Rebecca adapt to a deviation in her daily routine. Ben is 12 years old and has Asperger's syndrome. Ben's mom and teachers discuss the progress he has made in learning appropriate social skills.

1. What are the different instructional tactics used with the two children?

2. What are the similarities?

Prevalence

FOCUS 3

What are the current prevalence estimates for autism spectrum disorders?

CEC

Standard 3
Individual Learning Differences

Despite widespread claims of an "autism epidemic," and compared with other conditions, autism is relatively rare. However, there appears to be a real increase in prevalence across the United States and in other countries. Although prevalence rates vary from study to study, a thorough analysis of recent epidemiological surveys estimates the prevalence of autism to be 22 per 10,000, and 70 per 10,000 for all those with pervasive developmental disorders (Saracino, Noseworthy, Steiman, Reisinger, & Fombonne, 2010). For the spectrum of PDDs, this translates to approximately 1 child out of 143 diagnosed with an autism spectrum disorder.

The most recent report from the Centers for Disease Control and Prevention (2012) has gained much media attention, citing the prevalence of ASD in 14 U.S. sites as one out of every 88 children and one out of every 54 boys. Because studies like this do not comprise nationally representative samples, the CDC cautions that this prevalence rate cannot be generalized to the United States as a whole. Nevertheless, it sounds out a warning cry to the public of an autism "epidemic." Also, when citizens hear these statistics in the media, they may picture individuals with the most significant of autistic symptoms. Yet, due to the broad definition of ASD, many individuals with ASD are not severely affected.

The variation in prevalence rates is likely due to a number of factors. Current knowledge points to changes in diagnostic criteria, case identification, and reporting over time; variations in measurement; earlier identification; heightened awareness among parents and professionals; additional policies and services; and a true increase in the population (Centers for Disease Control and Prevention, 2009; Kogan et al., 2008; Parner, Schendel, & Thorsen, 2008; Saracino et al., 2010). The wide range in prevalence may diminish over time as greater consensus about what constitutes autism spectrum disorders is achieved.

Gender differences are evident in autism; males outnumber females substantially. Estimates of these prevalence differences are typically reported to be around 4 to 1 (Centers for Disease Control and Prevention, 2009; Giarelli, Wiggins, Rice, Levy, Kirby, Pinto-Martin, & Mandell, 2010). Some researchers attribute this gender difference to girls with autism being less socially aberrant than males, "camouflaging" their symptoms and making a diagnoses more difficult, although girls with autism often have less intellectual ability (Centers for Disease Control and Prevention, 2009; Nicholas et al., 2008; Lai et al., 2011).

Identification of ASD has been shown to vary by race and ethnicity. Some reports indicate greater prevalence among non-Hispanic white children than among non-Hispanic black children and Hispanic children (Centers for Disease Control and Prevention, 2009).

It is clear that the debate over accurately determining prevalence of ASD is not ending in the near future. What is most important to teachers, however, is that there are more children with ASD being served in public schools than ever before. These increases necessitate better preparation of both pre-service and in-service teachers to serve students with ASD in appropriate environments and with evidence-based strategies.

Causation

FOCUS 4

Identify factors related to the biological theoretical view regarding the causes of autism spectrum disorders.

Etiology
The cause or reason a condition occurs.

CEC

Standard 1
Foundations

The cause or **etiology** of autism has been a topic that has been a concern since Leo Kanner first described it in 1943. Although Kanner noted that a biological component might be involved, later theories implicated parents, in particular, mothers, who were described as being cold and indifferent to their children (Bettelheim, 1967), resulting in the child withdrawing from this rejection and erecting defenses against psychological pain. In so doing, the child retreats to an inner world and essentially does not interact with the outside environment that involves people. This psychodynamic theory has largely been refuted, although some "failure to bond" theories occasionally gain attention.

 Current research points to an integrated etiology. It is well accepted that neither is there one cause nor one cure for ASD. Rather, autism spectrum disorders appear to be an assortment of symptoms that will require varied treatments. Possible contributors to the cause of ASD include genetic, infectious, neurologic, metabolic, and immunologic factors.

Widespread media attention has led many to believe that vaccinations cause autism, theorizing that repeated stimulation of the immune system with a series of vaccinations results in damage to the developing brain, thereby causing abnormal neural pathway development that leads to autism. However, little empirical evidence exists to support this claim. Nevertheless, the autism–vaccination link continues to be explored (Blaylock, 2008).

Clearly, various causes of autism spectrum disorders remain unsolved puzzles in the face of ongoing research and widespread interest in the condition. Accumulated evidence has strongly implicated biological factors. Some biological malfunctions may be related to environmental influences, although evidence is only suggestive at this point (Karmiloff-Smith, 2009).

As with many areas of disability, an understanding of causation is important as we attempt to improve treatment. Research continues to unravel the sources of this perplexing disability, and improved research methodology is vital for further progress in the investigation of autism spectrum disorders.

Multidisciplinary Collaboration: Diagnosis and Intervention

Throughout this book, we have discussed collaboration between multiple disciplines as we have examined other disabilities. In each case, the discussion has involved different features and varying professional fields as the most prominent characteristics of the disability have shaped the context. This is also the case with autism spectrum disorders. Because of the wide variation of characteristics presented in this spectrum of disorders, the diversity of the collaboration team is quite broad, and may include professionals from the fields of medicine, psychology, education, speech-language pathology, occupational pathology, physical therapy, social work, counseling, and other fields, depending on the student's needs (Cannon et al., 2011; Margetts, LeCouteur, & Croom, 2006).

As we saw in the definition, the diagnosis of autism spectrum disorders emerges quite early in a child's life. Because of this relatively young age, parents often have an ongoing relationship with their pediatrician, which puts the medical profession on the multidisciplinary team collaboration very early, preferably by 18 months for the child's universal screening or at the 24- or 33-month screening (Kogan et al., 2008).

As the child's evaluation is begun, assessment is typically undertaken in multiple skill areas, including communication and language, intelligence, and social interaction (Anckarsater, 2006). Following the assessment process, this multidisciplinary collaboration moves forward to plan, deliver, and evaluate the interventions. From the parents' perspective, the important outcome of this collaboration is to allow their child to receive effective and individualized service in appropriate environments (White, Scahill, Klin, Koenig, & Volkmar, 2007). Although the nature of the multidisciplinary collaboration evolves over time as circumstances change, the need for collaboration on assessments and interventions will continue as the child grows older, reaches adolescence, and transitions into adulthood (Henault, 2006). A primary goal of these multidisciplinary teams is to facilitate post-school outcomes, such as appropriate social outlets, recreation, employment, education, housing, finances, and respite care for the family, that the person with ASD and his family values (Billstedt, Gillberg, & Gillberg, 2011; Eaves & Ho, 2008).

Attempts to identify causes of autism spectrum disorders have gone hand in hand with efforts to discover effective treatments. For decades, there have been a wide variety of treatments, some of which have little to no empirical evidence, yet are still popular with families and in schools. Different approaches have been based on theories of causation, while others have focused on specific observable behaviors, but empirical evidence supporting effectiveness is important in all cases (National Autism Center, 2009). Significant progress has been made in successful interventions for people with autism spectrum disorders, although investigators continually emphasize the importance of further systematic research on the effectiveness of various treatment strategies.

FOCUS 5
Identify the major approaches to the treatment of autism spectrum disorders.

CEC
Standard 4
Instructional Strategies

Educational and Therapeutic Interventions

The characteristics of autism spectrum disorders and the severity of specific problem areas vary significantly from individual to individual. Consequently, a wide variety of instructional options are required for the effective education of these children, which makes multidisciplinary collaboration fluid between individuals and across ages (Henault, 2006).

Services for Toddlers and Preschoolers
Early intervention is critical in the treatment of disabling characteristics related to ASD. Research is replete with evidence that early, intense treatments have long-lasting positive effects in the lives of individuals with ASD, particularly in the areas of measured IQ, expressive and receptive language, and adaptive behavior (Peters-Scheffer, Didden, Korzilius, & Sturmey, 2011). To help parents and practitioners understand various treatment options, Autism Speaks has developed a Video Glossary of more than 100 video clips from actual therapy sessions with young children with ASD. The therapy sessions illustrate more than 20 treatments that focus on building skills, connecting with peers and family, and reducing challenging behaviors.

When children with ASD are identified before the age of 3, they can receive early intervention through a provider of services to children with disabilities or delays ages newborn to 3. Some parents choose to supplement these services, or even replace them, with in-home therapy. At age 3, children with ASD may qualify for early childhood special education, and can range from a typical preschool program with specialized support, to a program designed specifically for students with ASD. Along with specialized instruction, most preschoolers with ASD receive speech therapy, occupational therapy, behavior management programs, learning strategies, and study skills assistance (Bitterman, Daley, Misra, Carlson, & Markowitz, 2008).

Services for School-Aged Students
By age 5, children with ASD who qualify for special education will receive services as determined on their IEP. Each IEP should include statements of short- and long-term goals that relate to the core deficits of the disorder (social communication/interaction and restrictive, repetitive behavior). IEPs and instructional plans should focus on individual strengths, interests, and talents required for maximum independence (Lanou, Hough, & Powell, 2012).

The type and amount of services, as well as location of these services, are determined by the child's IEP team. The type of services provided often includes special education, and related services such as speech, physical, and occupational therapy. Location can range along a continuum from inclusion in general education classes, to spending part of the day in general classes, to being self-contained in the general school or in a school designed for students with ASD. Some students receive instruction at the home, hospital, or institution, depending upon the decision the IEP team makes (Gibb & Dyches, 2007). The current literature, however, has emphasized educational integration to the maximum extent appropriate, with educational placement and instructional programming dependent on the student's age and functioning level (White et al., 2007). The ultimate goal is to prepare all students, and not just those who have high-functioning ASD, to live a high-quality life in their home communities.

Students with high-functioning autism or Asperger's syndrome may not qualify for special education in some circumstances because their disability does not significantly impact their progress in the general curriculum. These students may be served in general education settings with adaptations and accommodations provided according to a 504 plan. Other students may not be served with any special services, or may be in gifted and talented education programs.

Evidence-Based Practices

To facilitate the success of students with ASD, multidisciplinary teams have the professional responsibility to use evidence-based practices. Unfortunately, the field is filled with so many interventions claiming to be effective for students with ASD that parents and professionals may be confused and frustrated in selecting the most appropriate treatments. They may rely upon what is currently available or, alternatively, invest in treatments that claim to cure the child, but have little or no empirical support. It is the professionals' responsibility to know the current research regarding effective treatments, and to verify the evidence base by analyzing student progress data. Although it is nearly impossible for practicing teachers to review the thousands of research articles on treatments for students with ASD, it is not unreasonable to access recent comprehensive reviews or meta-analyses of research.

One such recent report by the National Autism Center (2009) thoroughly examined the current empirical literature regarding treatments for ASD. Using specific and stringent guidelines, they compiled a comprehensive report of the level of scientific evidence for many current educational and behavioral treatments. They found only 11 treatments to have sufficient evidence to be considered "established," 22 treatments that are "emerging," 5 that are "unestablished," and no qualified reports of treatments were found to be ineffective or harmful to students with ASD. See Table 11.3 for a list of these treatments.

Most educational interventions for students with ASD include elements of collaborative communication services; applied behavior analysis (ABA); visual structure and support; enhancing positive social relationships; and functional skills development.

Collaborative Communication Services

The most critical and frequently used therapeutic approach in schools is the collaborative provision of communication services for students with ASD. It is not solely the work of the speech-language therapist to provide students with access to appropriate communication devices, aides, and strategies. The classroom teacher, special education teacher, and others who serve the child with ASD will see fewer communicative breakdowns, tantrums, and other maladaptive behavior when they use evidence-based communication practices designed to meet individual students' needs. Furthermore, the use of **augmentative and alternative communication** strategies is likely to increase rather than suppress speech production (Schlosser & Wendt, 2008), and naturalistic language interventions that are guided by the child's interest are more effective than contrived interventions (Kane, Connell, & Pellecchia, 2010).

One frequently used intervention for students with ASD who are nonverbal or who have little to no communicative initiation skills is the Picture Exchange Communication System, or PECS. This system teaches children to initiate a communicative exchange with a partner by using pictures. Research indicates that the use of PECS enhances the communication skills of children with ASD, but few gains are made in speech (Flippin, Reszka, & Watson, 2010).

Applied Behavior Analysis

Many educational and therapeutic approaches are based upon principles of applied behavior analysis in that they break a large task into small, manageable parts and reinforce successive approximations to the goal. For example, instead of expecting a student with ASD to sit quietly in his chair for a 30-minute language arts lesson, the child may be allowed to hold a favorite "comfort toy" while sitting and is praised every 10 minutes for sitting and participating. Another student may be reinforced with praise and a favorite item for her attempts to speak. Instead of waiting for the child to say, "I want a

CEC

Standard 6
Language

Augmentative and alternative communication
The use of aided and unaided strategies (such as a communication device, sign language, gestures, written language) to communicate wants and needs and to transfer information.

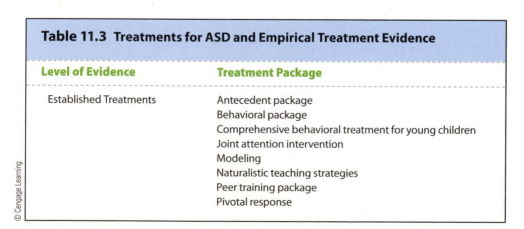

Table 11.3 Treatments for ASD and Empirical Treatment Evidence	
Level of Evidence	**Treatment Package**
Established Treatments	Antecedent package
	Behavioral package
	Comprehensive behavioral treatment for young children
	Joint attention intervention
	Modeling
	Naturalistic teaching strategies
	Peer training package
	Pivotal response

Table 11.3	(continued)	
	Schedules Self-management Story-based intervention package	
Emerging Treatments	Augmentative and alternative communication device Cognitive behavioral intervention package Developmental relationship-based treatment Exercise Exposure package Imitation-based interaction Initiation training Language training (production) Language training (production and understanding) Massage/touch therapy Multicomponent package Music therapy Peer-mediated instructional arrangement Picture Exchange Communication System Reductive package Scripting Sign instruction Social communication intervention Social skills package Structured teaching Technology-based treatment Theory of mind training	
Unestablished Treatments	Academic interventions Auditory integration training Facilitated communication Gluten- and casein-free diet Sensory integrative package	
Harmful/Ineffective Treatments	None reported	

cookie," the teacher reinforces the child for saying "cook," an approximation of the word, *cookie*. Common strategies and programs such as discrete trial training, PECS, pivotal response treatment, positive behavior intervention and support, among many others, are based upon ABA principles (National Autism Center, 2009). Decades of research support the efficacy of ABA strategies.

Visual Structure and Support Providing visual structure and support is another strategy to set up the environment in such a way that capitalizes on the student's visual strengths. Teachers who establish visually structured classrooms post their class rules/expectations in a prominent place along with consequences for maintaining or not maintaining those expectations. They teach the expectations to the students, reteach as necessary, and reinforce frequently. Also, these teachers have the daily schedule posted and refer to it often. Some students may need individualized schedules, either in writing, or accompanied with pictures (see Figures 11.2 and 11.3). This helps students with ASD know what to predict for their school day, which decreases their anxiety. Effective teachers also prevent problems during transition times by providing structured verbal and visual cues to smooth these transitions (Bondy & Frost, 2008). To facilitate a predictable environment, teachers establish logical routines that are taught and reinforced throughout the year (e.g., what to do upon entering the classroom, where to put completed work, what to do if students finish work early, when students are allowed to leave their seats). They also establish areas in the class designated for certain activities or items (e.g., a quiet zone, a one-on-one instructional area

Tina Dyches

Figure 11.2 *Portable Picture Schedule Made from Potato Chip Container*

with teacher or paraeducator, specific locations to keep various instructional items). Labeling the areas in the room with written words, photographs, or pictures and referring to these labels is one strategy to reinforce the concepts and to increase literacy skills. For some students, color-coding facilitates understanding. For example, Noah, who is currently unable to understand the meaning of pictures and written words, has his items labeled in his favorite color—yellow. His desk is labeled with his name on a yellow card, as is his desk, his coat hook, and his storage bin with his personal calming and reinforcement items.

CEC

Standard 5
Learning Environments and Social Interactions

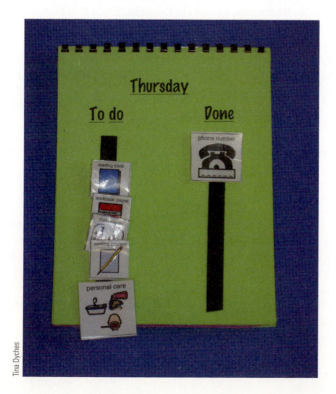

Tina Dyches

Figure 11.3 *Daily Picture Schedule with "To Do" and "Done" Velcro Strips*

Visual supports can also be provided via technological means. One common strategy is to use video modeling, where a student with ASD watches himself or another person perform a target behavior that has previously been videotaped. Any prompts or errors that were made during the video shoot are edited out, so the student can view an error-less execution of the skill. After viewing the video, the student then practices the skill. Video modeling is often used to teach language, self-help, and daily living skills (Bellini & Akullian, 2007; LeBlanc, 2010).

Enhancing Positive Social Relationships
Interventions that focus on enhancing positive social relationships are based upon developmental theory, and can be delivered in a variety of settings. Examples include programs such as the Denver model, floortime therapy, relationship developmental intervention, and responsive teaching. These treatments are considered to be "emerging" (National Autism Center, 2009), and continued research may find greater evidence for the effectiveness of these relatively new treatments.

Programs that focus on the development of social skills target a primary core deficit of children with ASD. Examples of programs or strategies include joint attention intervention, peer training, pivotal response treatment, and story-based interventions, and these particular programs have an established level of scientific support (National Autism Center, 2009). Social skills can be taught as in a variety of settings such as during class activities, friendship groups, buddy or mentoring programs, social skill groups, or individualized instruction. Common strategies to teach social skills are direct instruction, role playing, modeling, social stories, peer practice, and constructive feedback (Toth & King, 2008).

Teaching social skills to students with ASD is critical because they are likely targets for bullying (Cappadocia, Weiss, & Pepler, 2012). When students with ASD have serious concerns about their school achievement, self-esteem, stress and coping, difficulties learning, and being bullied, then their quality of life is decreased (Lee, Harrington, Louie, & Newschaffer, 2008).

Functional Skills
Functional skills and knowledge will vary among individuals. For some children, functional instruction will mean intense use of language training, augmentative and alternative communication, and social, self-help, and self-protection skills (Koegel & Koegel, 2006; Legoff & Sherman, 2006). For others, functional instruction will focus on traditional academic subjects, as well as subjects not always included in general education curricula, such as sex education; other topics may be those of special concern to the children's parents (Dale, Jahoda, & Knott, 2006; Harrington, Patrick, & Edwards, 2006; U.S. Department of Education, 2011). Educational interventions for children with autism spectrum disorders and other disabilities are also beginning to include greater use of technology enhancements in the teaching process (LeBlanc, 2010). Additional research on the effectiveness of such technology presents intriguing possibilities as hardware, software, and applications continue to mature.

LEARNING THROUGH SOCIAL MEDIA
ASSESSING AND TREATING ASD

There are many different interventions that are aimed at teaching those on the autism spectrum. After reviewing evidence-based practices, one has to experiment with individual interventions to determine particular treatment(s) that will facilitate the most growth for the person. Autism Internet Modules are available and may be reviewed to learn how to accurately assess students with ASD, and how to teach children with ASD at home, school, the workplace, and in the community. Many instructional strategies are described in text and video, shown in photographs, and demonstrated with case studies (www.autisminternetmodules.org). This set of modules includes a large number of particular applications that may be modified to fit a child's or adult's needs for social interaction with others, academic instruction, or skill acquisition to build or offset problems or promote growth.

ASSISTIVE TECHNOLOGY
APPS FOR AUTISM

The phenomenal success of tablets such as the iPad with the general public has spawned hundreds of applications for individuals with autism spectrum disorders, many of which are free or low in cost. Having strong visual skills, students with autism are motivated to participate in learning activities presented on tablet computers. Some apps are designed for individuals without disabilities (e.g., academic programs such as names of the U.S. presidents, math flash cards, spelling, graphic organizers), while other apps are designed specifically for individuals with disabilities such as ASD (e.g., social skills, eye contact, visual timers, sign language). Apps that have the greatest impact on nonverbal students are those that can be used for augmentative and alternative communication (AAC). Typical electronic AAC devices are expensive, but apps for tablets provide similar functionality at a lower price and with greater portability.

One app that has gained much attention recently is Proloquo2go, an AAC application that allows non- or low-verbal users to communicate single words, phrases, and sentences, or even compose essays by touching pictures or typing on an on-screen keyboard. This app has natural sounding text-to-speech voices, approximately 8,000 symbols, and is accessed with the touch of a finger. It has the potential to help many individuals who use AAC to not only communicate better, but also to gain access to the general curriculum and be more fully integrated with their same-age peers.

Providing Positive and Creative Educational Services Creative, innovative, and positive teachers are particularly important in providing effective education for students with autism spectrum disorders (e.g., Willis, 2009). As noted earlier, these children present some unique challenges for instruction. Some seemingly insignificant actions by teachers can create great difficulties for students who have autism spectrum disorders—difficulties that can easily be avoided if teachers are informed and receive training. For example, many high-functioning individuals with autism spectrum disorders who have some language skills may interpret speech literally, so it is important to avoid using slang, idioms, and sarcasm. An individual with an autism spectrum disorder might take such phrases literally and learn something very different from what was intended. The Snapshot by Taylor Crowe illustrates how teachers can be more effective with students with autism spectrum disorders.

To capitalize on the unique characteristics of students with ASD, teachers need to plan in advance. These four steps offer structure to follow: (1) List the students' strengths, interests, and talents; (2) identify whether the student's specific area of need is behavioral, academic, social, or emotional; (3) consider and select evidence-based strategies to teach the student; and (4) pair the strategy with a strength, interest, or talent (Lanou, Hough, & Powell, 2012). For example, Kahner has a fascination with Superman. He has a collection of Superman comics and has memorized facts from the movies. However, he does not initiate conversation with his classmates, so his teacher decided to use direct instruction and role playing to teach Kahner how to initiate a conversation. She then chose the power card strategy (Gagnon, 2001) to help Kahner perform the skill more frequently with peers. Using his special interest in Superman, she created a story and a power card with Superman, encouraging Kahner to talk to his friends. See Figure 11.4 for an example of the story and a power card.

Parental participation in preparing children with autism spectrum disorders for school and other aspects of life is critical (Ashbaker, Dyches, Prater, & Sileo, 2012; Dyches, Carter, & Prater, 2011). Such preparation can include objectives like instilling a positive attitude in the child, helping him or her with scheduling, and teaching him or her how to find the way around in school. Also helpful is identifying a "safe" place and a "safe" person to seek out should the child become confused or encounter a particularly upsetting event.

CEC

Standard 4
Instructional Strategies

My Thoughts About the Education of High-Functioning Individuals with Autism

Taylor Crowe

My name is Taylor Crowe, and I have autism. As I write this, I am 30 years old. I am a graduate of the California Institute of the Arts, where I studied character animation. Like many students with special needs in the United States, I attended public school until just before my 21st birthday.

After undergoing extreme behavioral changes and losing almost all of my language skills at age 3, I was diagnosed with severe autism one year later. From those earliest days, my parents worked to surround me with other children who knew me, and who, as we grew older, accepted me and understood that my autism shouldn't be a barrier to our friendships. In a very real sense, those neurotypical kids taught me how to be a kid, and were some of the best "teachers" I ever had. I've come to learn that a wonderful side effect of these relationships was that teasing and bullying were never a serious problem for me because my friends protected me from those things. Unlike many kids with special needs, my memories of school and childhood are very pleasant.

My parents arranged for a speech therapist to give me language therapy beginning at age 4½. I worked with her for 15 years, slowly building language skills and learning to use language. My mom and dad say that as my ability to communicate started to develop, my "meltdowns" decreased, probably because I was able to communicate what I was thinking and wasn't as frustrated as I was when I couldn't speak.

After two years of kindergarten to build my social skills, I was "mainstreamed" in first grade, but that didn't work very well because I couldn't keep up with my classmates. I couldn't communicate very well and I was easily overwhelmed, both verbally and socially. I was placed in a special needs classroom in the second grade, attending the "regular ed" classroom only for art and music class. During these years, my teachers worked to facilitate my friendships with the other kids in school, so I never felt isolated.

I've learned that early on in school, a lot of focus was placed on survival language skills and community-based education. This created lots of opportunities to meet other people and created a lot of "real-world" social challenges for me. It also helped a lot of people in our community get to know me and understand more about autism.

Something I think all teachers should know is that most people with autism are visual learners: In my case, *seeing* something and learning from it visually meant a lot more to me than hearing something and trying to learn. Language was very confusing to me. It often still is.

Idioms and figures of speech were very hard for me to figure out. I spent years in language therapy slowly learning about these very difficult parts of language. If you believe exactly what you hear, what does "It's raining cats and dogs" mean? What about "Keep your eye on the ball," "Ants in your pants," or "Bite the hand that feeds you"? If you interpret everything literally, things like this can be very confusing or upsetting.

All teachers should be very careful not to tease or exaggerate when working with individuals who have autism. I once had a teacher who told me I couldn't go home until I finished a worksheet and that if I didn't finish it, I'd just have to spend the night in school. I believed her and thought she wanted to kidnap me, so I was absolutely terrified! I remained scared of her for years.

My best teachers were the ones who treated me as if I was their own child and went out of their way to help me. My seventh-grade mainstream English teacher discovered that I was really good at spelling. Every week, when it was time to work on spelling in her class, she'd have me come down from the special needs classroom to take part in a spelling exercise. She said I was as good or better than anyone else in the class in spelling, and she wanted all the other kids to see what I was capable of. She did this on her own, because she wanted to; no one told her to do it.

Early in my school years, teachers discovered my interests in art. They encouraged those interests, not just to help me become a better artist, but also to create social situations for me in an environment in which I was comfortable. Those opportunities enhanced my social skills and helped me get to where I am today.

Having good teachers and friends who cared about me has had a huge impact on my life. Those relationships gave me levels of freedom that no one believed I was capable of when I was a preschooler.

Superman is good at talking to friends. When Superman wants to be friendly, he finds a person to talk to, says "Hey," and their name, and then asks them a question. He waits for them to answer the question before saying something else. When Superman does this, he makes a new friend, and they have fun together. Superman likes talking to his friends!

Figure 11.4 *Superman Talks to Friends*

Superman wants you to talk to your friends! He knows that when you do this, you will have a lot of fun. It will make you happy and it will make others happy to be your friend.

Superman wants you to remember these four steps when you are making friends:

1. Find a person to talk to.
2. Say "Hey" and the person's name.
3. Ask the person a question.
4. Wait for the person to answer before asking another question.

Psychological and Medical Interventions

As mentioned earlier, the multidisciplinary collaboration for individuals with autism spectrum disorders will include psychological and medical professions, often from the very early stages of the child's life. Support from these professionals will most often continue in various forms throughout the individual's lifespan, depending on needs and specific contextual circumstances.

Various medical treatments have been used for individuals with ASD, but the primary purpose is not to cure the autism, but to alleviate or eliminate symptoms. In particular, parents may consider medicating their child due to challenging behaviors such as hyperactivity, impulsivity, aggression, tantrums, repetitive thoughts, anxiety, and depression. Parents should make informed decisions when they are investigating the possible benefits and costs of medicating their child. Some benefits include the possibility of having reduced symptoms, the child might function better, sleep better, and fit in better with peers. Some costs include financial burden, side effects, and the possibility that the medicine will not work. Parents should also be informed that medication is not likely to solve problems related to the child not following directions, learning slowly, not talking, and poor social skills (Autism Speaks, 2011).

Medications Medications have been used in the past with individuals with autism for certain conditions. For example, stimulant medications such as Ritalin and Adderall have been used to treat hyperactivity, short attention span, and impulsive behavior. Antianxiety medications such as Prozac, Luvox, and Zoloft have been used to treat depression, anxiety, and repetitive thoughts and behaviors. Second-generation/atypical antipsychotics such as Risperdal and Zyprexa have been used to treat irritability, aggression, and sleep problems. Certain medications such as Tegretol and Depakote have been used to treat seizures and mood problems. A simple toolkit is available at www.autismspeaks.com to aid parents in making informed decisions (Autism Speaks, 2011).

Generally, medication has shown some promise in the treatment of autism spectrum disorders. There appears to be potential for improvement, but such treatment should be used thoughtfully in conjunction with a multicomponent, comprehensive treatment plan.

Behavioral Interventions

As noted earlier, applied behavior analysis (ABA) represents a broad intervention strategy that has become multidisciplinary over the past several decades. This model of intervention has been used in a wide array of circumstances within education, psychology, medicine, and family therapy. Interventions using behavioral treatment for children with autism spectrum disorders are undertaken without concern for the underlying cause(s) of the disability; rather, it focuses on enhancing appropriate behaviors and reducing inappropriate or maladaptive behaviors.

An outgrowth of ABA is the field of positive behavior intervention and support (PBIS), which aims to analyze the function of a challenging behavior and create structures and supports that reduce the barriers for engaging in more appropriate behaviors. The presence of a problem behavior does not lie within the individual, because it represents a mismatch between the individual and the environment. PBIS requires research and intervention to be conducted in natural settings, is family-centered, avoids using punishment strategies, uses a collaborative, assessment-based approach, and results in multicomponent support plans (Carr et al., 2002; Lucyshyn, Dunlap, & Albin, 2002).

In the PBIS model, the individual receiving support is the most important decision maker in the behavior-change process. The individual's preferences are used to make data-based decisions, and those who are valued by the target individual give their perspectives regarding developing interventions and support plans (Dunlap, Carr, Horner, Zarcone, & Schwartz, 2008).

Behavioral interventions may focus on challenging behavior such as self-stimulation, tantrum episodes, or self-inflicted injury, and have substantially reduced or eliminated these problem behaviors in many cases (Northey, 2009). Behavioral interventions have also been effective in remediating deficiencies in fundamental social skills and language development, as well as in facilitating community integration for children with autism spectrum disorders (Bauminger, Solomon, Aviezer, Heung, Brown, & Rogers, 2008). Furthermore,

DEBATE FORUM
SELF-STIMULATION AS A REINFORCER?

Reinforcers as behavioral treatments are sometimes difficult to find for some children who have autism. Teachers must often take what the student gives them to work with and remain flexible in designing an intervention program.

Many individuals with autism do not respond to the same types of rewards that others do; social rewards may not provide reinforcement or have any effect on these children, at least in the initial stages of a treatment program. Research has also shown that, in some cases, tangible reinforcers may produce desired results, but they often seem to lose their power for individuals with autism. Given these circumstances, some researchers have suggested that self-stimulation, which appears to be a powerful and durable reinforcer, should be used to assist in teaching appropriate behavior. Self-stimulation is very different for each child and may involve manipulation of items such as strings, keys, and twigs.

POINT

Because reinforcers are often difficult to identify for children with autism, it is important to use whatever is available and practical in teaching these youngsters. Self-stimulation has been recognized as providing strong reinforcement for those who engage in it. Although typically viewed as an inappropriate behavior, self-stimulation may be very useful in teaching the beginning phases of more adaptive behavior and other skill acquisition. For some children with autism, it may be the most efficient reinforcer available, so why not use it, at least initially?

COUNTERPOINT

Using inappropriate behavior as a reinforcer carries with it certain serious problems and, in fact, may be unethical. The use of self-stimulation as a reinforcer may cause an increase in this behavior, making it an even more pronounced part of the child's inappropriate demeanor. Should this occur, it may make self-stimulation more difficult to eliminate later.

What Do You Think? Please visit the Education CourseMate website for Human Exceptionality, *11th edition, to access and respond to questions related to the Debate Forum.*

parental involvement in behavioral interventions has shown promising results. Research has demonstrated that certain students with autism spectrum disorders can be effectively taught to employ self-directed behavior management, which further enhances efficiency (Blacher & McIntyre, 2006; Rogers & Ozonoff, 2006). However, finding reinforcers to use in behavioral treatments is sometimes difficult, as suggested in the nearby Debate Forum, "Self-Stimulation as a Reinforcer?"

Although there is some evidence that implementing an early and intensive program based upon ABA principles can drastically reduce or even eliminate symptoms of autism, the results of this type of treatment differ for individual children. This approach seems effective for many children with autism spectrum disorders, prompting decreases in problem behaviors and potential improvement of survival skills (e.g., Cohen, Amerine-Dickens, & Smith, 2006). Such gains constitute a significant step toward normalization for both the children and their families.

Impact on the Family

The impact of raising children with ASD on families is enormous and presents significant challenges to parents and family members (Hall & Graff, 2010; Stuart & McGrew, 2009). Obviously, the more significantly the child is impacted with symptoms of autism, the greater challenges families will face (Johnson, Frenn, Feetham, & Simpson, 2001; Stuart & McGrew, 2009). Parents are often challenged by the intense caregiving responsibilities associated with raising their child, the personal emotional and physical challenges they experience, their efforts to maintain a healthy marital relationship, their attempts to attend to the needs of their other children, and the need to seek for and obtain effective services.

FOCUS 6

How are families impacted when raising a child with autism spectrum disorders?

Caregiving Responsibilities

Parents raising children with ASD have increased caregiver burden than other families, often resulting in leaving their jobs due to child care issues (Lee et al., 2008). Needing to provide constant care often isolates parents from their extended families and neighborhood communities (Conroy, Asmus, Boyd, Ladwig, & Sellers, 2007; Dillenburger, Keenan, Doherty, Byme, & Gallagher, 2010; Lee et al., 2008).

Caregiving responsibilities are not limited to daytime hours, however, nor are they temporary. A child with autism may sleep only a few hours each night and spend many waking hours engaged in self-abusive or disruptive behavior. It is easy to see how parents may feel as though they are running a marathon, 24 hours a day, 7 days a week, with no respite. Not only is the family routine interrupted, but the constant demands are also physically and emotionally draining, resulting in a number of problems for family members, such as extremely high stress levels and depression (Brobst, Clopton, & Hendrick, 2009; Conroy et al., 2007; Hoffman, Sweeney, Hodge, Lopez-Wagner, & Looney, 2009; Hoffman, Sweeney, Hodge, Nam, & Botts, 2008). And, as we have noted, the situation may be especially confusing for family members if the child with ASD also has savant-like skills.

Parental Emotional and Physical Challenges

Parents of children with ASD are likely to be challenged with maintaining their emotional and physical health. Parents of children with ASD may experience symptoms of parenting stress, depression, and other psychopathology (Gau, et al., 2012; Ingersoll & Hambrick, 2011). Their ability to cope and advocate for their child will be significantly affected if they neglect their personal well-being (Johnson et al., 2001; Pottie & Ingram, 2008).

Families with a child with ASD frequently experience lower marital satisfaction than other families (Gau et al., 2012; Ingersoll & Hambrick, 2011; Parker, Mandleco, Roper, Freeborn, & Dyches, 2011); however, recent research indicates these families are not more likely to experience divorce than are families who are not raising children with ASD, despite the incorrect and frequently cited statistic of an 80 percent divorce rate (Freedman, Kalb, Zablotsky, & Stuart, 2012).

Frequently, parents must turn to multiple sources for assistance and information, and relations between professionals and parents are not simple or easy (Brookman-Frazee, Baker-Ericzen, Stadnick, & Taylor, 2011; McConachie & Robinson, 2006; Montes, Halterman, & Magyar, 2009). Parents may find that they have to become assertive and vocal in their search for services from various agencies (Goin-Kochel, Mackintosh, & Myers, 2006; McConachie & Robinson, 2006).

Parents may be concerned about their family's cohesion, adaptability, and the well-being of their other children (Cannon, Kenworthy, Alexander, Werner, & Anthony, 2011). Siblings of children with ASD may experience a number of challenges, particularly during the early years. They may have difficulty understanding their parents' distress regarding their brother or sister and the level of attention afforded this child, and they may manifest stress, anxiety, behavioral problems, or depression (Orsmond & Seltzer, 2007; Petalas, Hastings, Nash, Lloyd, & Dowey, 2009; Schaaf, Toth-Cohen, Johnson, Outten, & Benevides, 2011). Siblings may also have difficulty accepting the emotional detachment of the child with ASD, who may seem not to care for them at all (Orsmond & Seltzer, 2007). Like the siblings of children with other disabilities, brothers and sisters of a child with autism spectrum disorders may be embarrassed and reluctant to bring friends home. However, if they can become informed and move beyond the social embarrassment, siblings can be a significant resource in assisting parents, and may be a strength and resource to the child with ASD. Some research suggests fairly positive adjustment with high levels of self-concept and social competence among siblings of children with ASD (Meadan, Stoner, & Angell, 2010; Nielson, Mandleco, Roper, Cox, Dyches, & Marshall, 2012; Rivers & Stoneman, 2008). Several resources exist for helping siblings of children with disabilities. See Table 11.4 for examples of such resources.

Obtaining Services and Support

To cope with the challenges associated with raising a child with ASD, parents may need multiple levels of support. School personnel can provide support in some ways. First, by openly communicating with the parents, teachers are more likely to gain parents' trust and confidence. Find a system of regular communication that fits the needs of both school and home. Second, realize that parents of children with ASD may be overloaded with many social, emotional, and physical demands, and attending just one more meeting at school may

Table 11.4   Resources for Siblings of Children with Disabilities

Sibling Support Project (www.siblingsupport.org)	Provides published curricula and children's books that assist agencies in starting Sibshops. They sponsor listservs for young and adult siblings.
Sibshops	Provides fun, interactive workshops that help siblings of children with special needs to get support in a recreational and educational context.
SibNet (www.siblingsupport.org)	Hosts an online discussion group for young adult and adult brothers and sisters of people with disabilities and other health needs.
Sib Kids (www.siblingsupport.org)	Similar to SibNet but for younger brothers and sisters of people with mental, emotional, and physical needs.
Autism Siblings (www.autismsiblings.org)	Shares stories and provides support for siblings of children with autism.
Sibling Leadership Network	Advances causes important to the millions of siblings of people who have disabilities.
The Arc's National Sibling Council	Fosters the active involvement of siblings of individuals with intellectual and developmental disabilities (I/DD) to impact policy, service delivery, and the quality of life for millions of Americans with I/DD through specialized programming, events, and opportunities to connect.

Autism in the Family

Christie Allred

My qualifications to speak to you on autism do not stem from a formal education, but rather, from two of my six children being diagnosed on different quadrants of the autism spectrum. Our story begins over 26 years ago, with the birth of my oldest son, Andrew, who has Asperger's syndrome, and continues through the birth of my youngest daughter, Mariah, who was diagnosed with high-functioning autism 10 years later. This story also reaches across two generations, with my grandson being diagnosed with autism five years ago and with one other grandchild, still too young to be diagnosed, showing those all-too-familiar symptoms of the disorder.

When I started my parenting years, *autism* was not a familiar term. Teachers interacting with Andrew referred to him as "unteachable" and an "odd duck." In fact, one middle school principal stated that Andrew brought the bullying on himself by playing the constant victim.

However, for us, Andrew stood out with his gentle disposition and extremely focused individual play. Most of the time, he created his own world.

When given numbers to add, he never used his fingers or counted individual items. Even as early as 3 years old, he could add large numbers in his head, immediately knowing the answer. His brilliance was just beginning to show through his blank, and often emotionless, face.

With greater understanding in later years, our family became closer and stronger, building up a defensive wall against the outside world. Siblings, who were once resentful, now stuck together to protect their autistic brother from those who would try to tease or single him out.

The diagnosis finally came for Andrew when he was 17, way too late to stop the painful years of suffering from bullies, overmedication, misdiagnosis, and hospitalization. He continues to need assistance with the basic needs in his life. His intellect, however, is as bright as ever. He is currently a senior at a university, majoring in mathematics and physics.

In stark contrast to Andrew's early school years, Mariah now has the benefit of increased educational focus on the social and behavioral challenges of autistic children. Mariah

was diagnosed at age 11, and was allowed special accommodations that helped her to succeed in school. With education on how to teach students with autism, teachers provided Mariah a positive and creative learning experience, specially developed to meet her needs.

My grandson was diagnosed with severe autism. At the age of 2, he would not communicate or acknowledge anyone when called. He wears a tracking device on his ankle to provide security in case he wanders away. Today, he is thriving, with positive experiences of early intervention at home and school. The school district was providing speech therapy and developmental classes to help him succeed by the time he was 3 years old. Now he is included in a classroom two grade levels above his age group.

As time passes, we have grown to understand that autism is not just a disability of children, but is a lifelong family commitment, as autistic children become autistic adults. Even so, we continue to feel blessed to have these special individuals as part of our family.

not be their priority. Third, provide child care if possible, during important school meetings such as IEP meetings, so the parents might be more available to attend. Finally, serve as a resource for parents to connect them with the community. Parents may need respite time and care from a number of sources—from the family as a whole and from knowledgeable and supportive agencies (Eaton, 2008). Interventions to help different families and family members need to be tailored to the specific circumstances and individuals involved. Perhaps most difficult is realizing that there are no clear-cut answers to many of the questions they have. The Snapshot by Christie Allred highlights some of the issues families face when raising more than one child with ASD.

The tips found in this chapter's Inclusion and Collaboration through the Lifespan illustrate how varied and complicated the overall environment is in terms of the various influences on individuals with autism spectrum disorders.

EARLY CHILDHOOD YEARS

Tips for the Family

- Seek out and read information regarding autism spectrum disorders, and become knowledgeable about not just possible limitations, but strengths too.

- Be an active partner in the treatment of your child. Collaborate proactively in the multidisciplinary team for your child, facilitating communication and coordinating interventions.

- Learn about the simple applications of positive behavior support in a home environment, perhaps by enrolling in a parent training class.

- When working with your child, concentrate on one behavior at a time as the target for change; emphasize increasing positive, appropriate behaviors rather than focusing solely on inappropriate behavior.

- Involve all family members in learning about your child's strengths, interests, and talents as well as her weaknesses.

- Protect your own health by obtaining respite care when you need a rest or a break. You may need to devise a family schedule that allows adequate time for ongoing sleep and respite. Plan ahead for respite; otherwise, when you need it most, you may be too exhausted to find it.

- Help prepare your child for school by instilling a positive attitude about it; help him or her with the idea of a school schedule and how to find a "safe" place and a "safe" person at school.

Tips for Preschool Personnel

- Depending on the child's level of functioning, you may have to use physical cues or clear visual modeling to encourage her to do something; children with autism may not respond naturally to social cues.

- Establish, teach, and reinforce class expectations/consequences and natural routines throughout the school day.

Use pictures or photographs to facilitate understanding.

- Pair physical cues with verbal cues to begin teaching verbal compliance.

- Limit instruction to one item at a time; focus on what is concrete rather than abstract.

- Avoid verbal overload by using short, direct sentences.

- Encourage the development of programs where older children model good behavior and interact intensely with children with ASD.

- Initiate and maintain communication with the child's parents to enhance the information flow and to promote consistent collaboration across environments.

- Promote ongoing collaborative relationships between the preschool and medical personnel who can provide advice and assistance for children with ASD.

- Promote the appropriate collaborative involvement of nonteaching staff through workshops that provide information and awareness.

Tips for Neighbors and Friends

- Be supportive of the parents and siblings of a child with autism spectrum disorders. They may be under a high level of stress and need moral support.

- Be positive with the parents. They may receive information that places blame on them, which should not be magnified by their friends.

- Offer parents a respite to the degree that you're comfortable; you may give them a short but important time away to go to the store.

ELEMENTARY YEARS

Tips for the Family

- Be active in community efforts for children with autism spectrum disorders; join local or national parent groups to provide and gain support from others.

- Consistently follow through with the basic principles of your child's treatment program at home. This may mean taking more workshops or training on various topics to effectively collaborate as part of the intervention team.

- Provide siblings with information and opportunities to discuss the issues they are concerned about. Provide them with appropriate levels of support and attention, particularly if they feel neglected, embarrassed, or jealous of the sibling with ASD.

- It may be necessary to take safety precautions in the home (e.g., installing locks on all doors).

Tips for the General Education Classroom Teacher

- Help with collaborative organizational strategies, assisting the student with autism spectrum disorders regarding matters that are difficult for him or her (e.g., remembering where to turn in homework).

- Avoid abstract ideas as much as possible unless they are necessary in instruction. Be as concrete as possible.

- Communicate with specific directions or questions, not vague or open-ended statements.

- If the child becomes agitated or upset, help him identify his emotions by using a visual scale, similar to a pain scale found in doctor's offices. Depending on the child's emotional level, he may need to change activities or go to a place in the room that is "safe" for a period of time.

- Together with the child, create a self-monitoring chart to track appropriate behavior. This can serve as a "home note" to celebrate the child's daily success.

- Collaborate with parents and other school personnel to determine classroom expectations/consequences and schedules. Explicitly teach students so they understand what is expected of them. Accompany the written expectations and schedules with pictures to enhance comprehension.

- Begin preparing the child with an autism spectrum disorder for a more variable environment by teaching adaption to changes in routine. Involve the child in planning for the changes, mapping out what they might be.

Tips for School Personnel

- Promote an environment throughout the school where children model appropriate behavior and receive reinforcement for it. Proactively collaborate with all members of the team, including parents.
- Develop peer assistance programs, where older students can help tutor and model appropriate behavior for children with autism spectrum disorders.
- Encourage the development of strong, ongoing collaborative school–parent relationships and support groups working together to meet the child's needs.
- Find a reliable way to communicate with parents. Some students with ASD may not be able to take messages home with them, as the notes may get lost.

Tips for Neighbors and Friends

- As possible, ignore trivial disruptions or misbehaviors; focus on positive behaviors.
- Don't take misbehaviors personally; the child is not trying to make your life difficult or to manipulate you.
- Avoid sarcasm and idiomatic expressions, such as "beating around the bush." These children may not understand and may interpret what you say literally.

SECONDARY AND TRANSITION YEARS

Tips for the Family

- Be alert to developmental and behavioral changes as the child grows older, watching for any changing effects of a medication.
- Continue as a proactive collaborative partner in your child's educational and treatment program, planning for the transition to adulthood.
- Begin acquainting yourself with the adult services that will be available when your child leaves school. If

appropriate, consider or plan for adult living out of the family home.

Tips for the General Education Classroom Teacher

- Gradually increase the level of abstraction in teaching, remaining aware of the individual limitations a child with an autism spectrum disorder has.
- Continue preparing the student for an increasingly variable environment through specific instruction and example.
- Focus increasingly on matters of vital importance to the student as he or she matures (e.g., social awareness and interpersonal issues between the sexes).
- Teach the student with an eye toward post-school community participation, including matters such as navigating the community, recreational and social activities, and employment. Teach the student about interacting with police in the community, because they require responses different from those appropriate for other strangers.

Tips for School Personnel

- To the degree possible for children with autism spectrum disorders, promote involvement in social activities and clubs that enhance interpersonal interaction.
- Encourage the development of functional academic programs that are combined with transition planning and programs for students with ASD.
- Consider and encourage participation in gifted or other programs that facilitate unique interests and skills.
- Promote a continuing collaborative relationship with parents, other school staff, and agency personnel who might be involved in the student's overall treatment program (e.g., health care providers, social service agencies, and others).
- Work with other agencies that may encounter the child in the community (e.g., law enforcement). Provide workshops, if possible, to inform officers regarding behavioral characteristics of people with autism.

Tips for Neighbors and Friends

- Encourage a positive understanding of people with autism spectrum disorders

among other neighbors and friends who may be in contact with the child; help them to provide environmentally appropriate interaction.

- Promote the positive understanding of people with autism spectrum disorders by community agencies that may encounter these individuals at this stage of life (e.g., law enforcement officials, fire department personnel).
- Support the parents as they consider the issues of adulthood for their child. Topics such as guardianship and community living may be difficult for parents to discuss.

THE ADULT YEARS

Tips for the Family

- Continue to be alert for behavioral or developmental changes that may occur as the individual matures. Continued biological maturation may require medication adjustments as well as adjustments in behavioral intervention programming.
- Continue to seek out adult services that are available to individuals with disabilities.
- Seek legal advice regarding plans for the future when you are no longer able to care for the family member with an autism spectrum disorder. Plan for financial arrangements and other needs that are appropriate, such as naming an advocate. Backup plans should be made; do not always count on the youngster's siblings. Consider guardianship by other people or agencies.

Tips for Therapists or Other Professionals

- Remain cognizant of the maturity level of the individual with whom you are working. Despite the presence of an autism spectrum disorder, some individuals have mature interests and inclinations. Do not treat the person as a child.
- Proactively promote collaboration between appropriate adult service agencies to provide the most comprehensive services.

SOURCE: A portion of this material is adapted from A. Spek, T. Schatorje, E. Scholte, and I. van Berckerlaer-Onnes. (2009). Verbal fluency in adults with high-functioning autism or Asperger's syndrome. *Neuropsychologia, 47,* 652–656.

Looking Toward a Bright Future

Autism spectrum disorder (ASD) has received substantial attention in the popular press during the past decade. A brighter picture is emerging due to this media attention. As recent as 40 years ago, the picture of autism was bleak—most were denied a free and appropriate public education, those with severe behavioral challenges were institutionalized, most had intellectual disabilities, and few lived enviable lives. However, today, the diagnosis of an autism spectrum disorder can bring unexpected joys as well as challenges. As we move forward, we can take several points from this chapter that both guide us and present a bright future for those having ASD.

FOCUS REVIEW

FOCUS 1 Describe the variability and severity of characteristics within the autism spectrum.

- Individuals within the autism spectrum may have autism, Asperger's syndrome, pervasive developmental disorder, not otherwise specified, and have daily functioning among various dimensions, such as social communication, social interaction, behaviors, intellect, motor skills, and sensory processing.

FOCUS 2 Identify the primary impairments present in children with autism spectrum disorders.

- Individuals with ASD have two primary impairments that are pervasive and significantly affect their functioning:
  - Social communicative and social interactive functioning
  - Restrictive, repetitive repertoire of behavior, interests, and activities

FOCUS 3 What are the current prevalence estimates for autism spectrum disorders?

- Most accurate prevalence of autism spectrum disorders ranges from approximately 22 cases per 10,000 to 70 cases per 10,000, or 1 out of every 143 children.
- The most recent report from the Centers for Disease Control and Prevention (2012) has gained much media attention, citing the prevalence of ASD in 14 U.S. sites as one out of every 88 children.

FOCUS 4 Identify factors related to the biological theoretical view regarding the causes of autism spectrum disorders.

- ASD is likely caused by genetic, infectious, neurologic, metabolic, and immunologic factors.

FOCUS 5 Identify the major approaches to the treatment of autism spectrum disorders.

- Educational and therapeutic interventions occur across a range of environments and are intended to address the core deficits of ASD through special education, adaptations and accommodations, or group or individual therapy.
- Medical and psychological treatment often involves the use of medication.
- Behavioral interventions focus on enhancing specific appropriate behaviors or on reducing inappropriate behaviors.

FOCUS 6 How are families impacted when raising a child with autism spectrum disorders?

- Parents are often challenged by increased caregiving responsibilities.
- Parents may struggle with maintaining their emotional and physical health.
- Parents of children with ASD frequently experience lower marital satisfaction than other couples.
- Although siblings can experience social and emotional difficulties with a child with ASD, they also can be sources of strength and a resource.
- Parents need multiple levels of support to cope with the challenges associated with raising a child with ASD.

Council for Exceptional Children (CEC) Standards to Accompany Chapter 11

CEC If you are thinking about a career in special education, you should know that many states use national standards developed by the Council for Exceptional Children (CEC) to assess a teacher candidate's knowledge and skills for working with students with disabilities. See a complete listing of the 10 CEC Content Standards on the inside back cover of this text.

1 Foundations
2 Development and Characteristics of Learners
3 Individual Learning Differences
4 Instructional Strategies
5 Learning Environments and Social Interactions
6 Language
8 Assessment

Mastery Activities and Assignments

To master the content within this chapter, complete the following activities and assignments. Online and interactive versions of these activities are also available on the accompanying Education CourseMate website, where you may also access TeachSource videos, chapter web links, interactive quizzes, portfolio activities, flash cards, an integrated eBook, and much more!

1. Complete a written test of the chapter's content. If your instructor requires a written test of your content knowledge for this chapter, keep a copy for your portfolio. A practice test on the information covered in this chapter is available through the Education CourseMate website.

2. Read the Debate Forum in this chapter and visit the Education CourseMate website to complete the activity "Take a Stand." Keep a copy of this activity for your portfolio.

3. Participate in a community service learning activity. Community service is a valuable way to enhance your learning experience. Visit the Education CourseMate website for suggested community service learning activities that correspond to the information presented in this chapter. Develop a reflective journal of the service learning experience for your portfolio.

CHAPTER 12

Severe and Multiple Disabilities

Fotosearch/Jupiterimages

FOCUS PREVIEW

As you read the chapter, focus on these key concepts:

1 What are the three components of the TASH definition of severe disabilities?

2 Define the terms *multiple disabilities* and *deaf–blindness* as described in the Individuals with Disabilities Education Act (IDEA).

3 Identify the estimated prevalence and causes of severe and multiple disabilities.

4 What are the characteristics of people with severe and multiple disabilities?

5 Identify three types of educational assessments for students with severe and multiple disabilities.

6 Identify the features of effective services and supports for children with severe and multiple disabilities during the early childhood years.

7 Identify the features of effective services and supports for children with severe and multiple disabilities during the elementary school years.

8 Describe four outcomes that are important in planning for the transition from school to adult life for adolescents with severe and multiple disabilities.

9 Describe three features that characterize successful inclusive education for students with severe and multiple disabilities.

Sarina never had the opportunity to go to preschool and didn't begin her formal education in the public schools until the age of 6. She is now 15 years old and goes to Eastmont Junior High, her neighborhood school. Sarina does not verbally speak, walk, hear, or see. Professionals have used several labels to describe her, including *severely disabled, severely multiply handicapped, deaf–blind,* and *profoundly mentally retarded.* Her teenage classmates at Eastmont call her Sarina.

Throughout the day, Sarina has a support team of administrators, teachers, paraprofessionals, and peers who work together to meet her instructional, physical, and medical needs. And she has many, many needs. Sarina requires some level of support in everything she does, ranging from eating and taking care of personal hygiene to communicating with others. In the last few years, she has learned to express herself through the use of assistive technology. Sarina has a personal communication board with picture symbols that keeps her in constant contact with teachers, friends, and family. Through the use of an electronic wheelchair and her ability to use various switches, Sarina is able to maneuver her way through just about any obstacle in her environment. She is also learning to feed herself independently.

Sarina lives at home with her family, including three older brothers. Her parents, siblings, and grandparents are very supportive, always looking for ways to help facilitate Sarina's participation in school, family, and community activities. What she loves to do most is go shopping with her mom at the local mall, eat with friends at a fast-food restaurant, relax on the lawn in the neighborhood park, and play miniature golf at Mulligan's Pitch and Putt.

A Changing Era in the Lives of People with Disabilities

Sarina, in the opening Snapshot, is a person with **severe and multiple disabilities**. In one way or another, she will require services and support in nearly every facet of her life. Some people with severe disabilities have significant intellectual, learning, and behavioral differences; others are physically disabled with vision and hearing loss. Many also have significant, multiple disabilities. Sarina has multiple needs, one of which is communication. Yet, although she is unable to communicate verbally, she is able to express herself through the use of an assistive communication device, a language board. Thus, in many circumstances, a disability may be described as severe, but through today's technology and our understanding of how to adapt the environment, individuals with severe disabilities are able to lead constructive, happy, and productive lives in school, family, and community.

This chapter is about *people* with severe and multiple disabilities. These individuals are often described and labeled by the severity of their disability. Yet, they bring unique personalities, characteristics, and life experiences to this world. We begin our discussion of the various definitions and characteristics associated with severe disabilities. Sarina from our opening window is a 15-year-old teenager. Instead of initially describing Sarina as a teenager with green eyes and a beautiful smile who loves to listen to Coldplay with her brothers and attends Eastmont High School, she is too often described solely by her deficits: severely multiply disabled with profound retardation, blindness, or physical impairments. In this chapter, regardless of whether we are talking about definitions, characteristics, or causation, the language will be "people first." As such, Sarina is a teenager who also happens to have severe disabilities.

Severe and multiple disabilities
Disabilities that involve significant physical, sensory, intellectual, and/or social-interpersonal performance deficits.

Definitions of People with Severe Disabilities

FOCUS 1

What are the three components of the TASH definition of severe disabilities?

CEC

Standard 1
Foundations

The needs of people with severe disabilities cannot be met by one professional. The nature of their disabilities extends equally into the fields of education, medicine, psychology, and social services. Because these individuals present such diverse characteristics and require the attention of several professionals, it is not surprising that numerous definitions have been used to describe them.

Throughout history, terminology associated with severe disabilities has communicated a sense of hopelessness and despair. The condition was described as "extremely debilitating," "inflexibly incapacitating," or "uncompromisingly crippling." In the 1970s, Abt Associates (1974) described individuals with severe handicaps as unable "to attend to even the most pronounced social stimuli, including failure to respond to invitations from peers or adults, or loss of contact with reality" (p. v). The definition went on to use terms such as *self-mutilation* (e.g., head banging, body scratching, and hair pulling), *ritualistic behaviors* (e.g., rocking and pacing), and *self-stimulation* (e.g., masturbation, stroking, and patting). The Abt definition focused almost exclusively on the individual's deficits and negative behavioral characteristics.

Justen (1976) proposed a definition that moved away from negative terminology to descriptions of the individual's developmental characteristics. "The 'severely handicapped' refers to those individuals . . . who are functioning at a general development level of half or less than the level which would be expected on the basis of chronological age and who manifest learning and/or behavior problems of such magnitude and significance that they require extensive structure in learning situations" (p. 5).

Whereas Justen emphasized a discrepancy between normal and atypical development, Sailor and Haring (1977) proposed a definition that was oriented to the educational needs of each individual:

> A child should be assigned to a program for the severely/multiply handicapped according to whether the primary service needs of the child are basic or academic. . . . If the diagnosis and assessment process determines that a child with multiple handicaps needs academic instruction, the child should not be referred to the severely handicapped program. If the child's service need is basic skill development, the referral to the severely/multiply handicapped program is appropriate. (p. 68)

In the 1990s, Snell (1991) further elaborated on the importance of defining severe disabilities on the basis of educational need, suggesting that the emphasis be on supporting the individual in inclusive classroom settings. The Association for Persons with Severe Handicaps (now TASH), agreeing in principle with Snell, proposed a definition that focused on inclusion in *all* natural settings: family, community, and school (Meyer, Peck, & Brown, 1991).

TASH is an association of people with disabilities, their family members, other advocates, and professionals who promote full inclusion into family, school, and community life. "TASH advocates for human rights and inclusion for people with significant disabilities and support needs—those most vulnerable to segregation, abuse, neglect, and institutionalization. TASH works to advance inclusive communities through advocacy, research, professional development, policy, and information and resources for parents, families, and self-advocates" (TASH, 2012a).

TASH describes the individuals it serves as follows:

> People with significant disabilities and support needs who are most at risk for being excluded from society; perceived by traditional service systems as most challenging; most likely to have their rights abridged; most likely to be at risk for living, working, playing, and learning in segregated environments; least likely to have the tools and opportunities necessary to advocate on their behalf; and are most likely to need ongoing, individualized supports to participate in inclusive communities and enjoy a quality of life similar to that available to all people. (TASH, 2012b)

TASH focuses on the relationship of the individual within the environment (adaptive fit), the need to include people of all ages, and "ongoing support" in life activities. The adaptive fit between the person and the environment is a two-way proposition. First, it is important to determine the capability of the individual to cope with the requirements of family, school, and community environments. Second, the extent to which these various environments recognize and accommodate the need of the person with severe disabilities is vital. The adaptive fit of the individual within the environment is a dynamic process requiring continuous adjustment that fosters a mutually supportive coexistence. The TASH definition suggests that an adaptive fit can be created only when there is ongoing support (formal and/or natural) for each person as he or she moves through various life activities, including social interactions, taking care of personal needs, and making choices about lifestyle, working, and moving from place to place.

The IDEA Definitions of Severe and Multiple Disabilities

The Individuals with Disabilities Education Act (IDEA) does not include the term *severe disabilities* as one of the categorical definitions of disability identified in federal regulation. Individuals with severe disabilities may be subsumed under any one of IDEA's categories, such as intellectual disabilities, autism, serious emotional disturbance, speech and language impairments, and so on. (These disability conditions are discussed in other chapters in this text.) Although *severe disabilities* is not a category within IDEA, *multiple disabilities* and *deaf–blindness* are categories in federal regulation.

Multiple Disabilities

As defined in IDEA federal regulations, *multiple disabilities* means:

> *concomitant impairments (such as intellectual disabilities–blindness, intellectual disabilities–orthopedic impairment, etc.), the combination of which causes such severe educational needs that they cannot be accommodated in special education programs solely for one of the impairments. The term does not include deaf–blindness. (34 C.F.R. 300.8(c)(7), August 14, 2006)*

This definition includes multiple conditions that can occur in any of several combinations. One such combination is described by the term **dual diagnosis** and involves people who have serious emotional disturbance or who present challenging behaviors in conjunction with severe intellectual disabilities. Estimates of the percentage of people with intellectual disabilities who also have serious challenging behaviors vary, ranging from 5 percent to 15 percent of those living in the community to a much higher percentage for people living in institutions (Beirne-Smith, Patton, & Hill, 2011). Why do people with intellectual disabilities and other developmental disabilities often have higher rates of challenging behaviors? These individuals are more likely to live in situations that are restrictive, are prejudicial, limit their independence, and result in victimization. For more insight into the life of a person with multiple disabilities, see the nearby Reflect on This, "Mat's Story."

Deaf–Blindness

For some with multiple disabilities, intellectual disabilities may not be a primary symptom. One such condition is deaf–blindness. The concomitant vision and hearing difficulties (sometimes referred to as **dual sensory impairments**) exhibited by people with **deaf–blindness** result in severe communication deficits as well as in developmental and educational difficulties that require extensive support across several professional disciplines. IDEA defines deaf–blindness in federal regulation as:

> *concomitant hearing and visual impairments, the combination of which causes such severe communication and other developmental and educational needs that they cannot be accommodated in special education programs solely for children with deafness or children with blindness. (34 C.F.R. 300.8(c)(2), August 14, 2006)*

The impact of both vision and hearing loss on the educational needs of the student is a matter of debate among professionals. One perspective on deaf–blindness is that individuals have such severe intellectual disabilities that both vision and hearing are also affected.

FOCUS 2
Define the terms *multiple disabilities* and *deaf–blindness* as described in Individuals with Disabilities Education Act (IDEA).

CEC
Standard 1
Foundations
Standard 2
Development and Characteristics of Learners

Dual diagnosis
Identification of both serious emotional problems and intellectual disabilities in the same individual.

Dual sensory impairments
A condition, characterized by both vision and hearing sensory impairments (deaf–blindness), which can result in severe communication problems.

Deaf–blindness
A disorder involving simultaneous vision and hearing impairments.

Another view is that they have average intelligence and lost their hearing and sight after they acquired language. Intellectual functioning for people with deaf–blindness may range from normal or gifted to severe intellectual disabilities. All people with deaf–blindness experience challenges in learning to communicate, access information, and comfortably move through their environment. These individuals may also have physical and behavioral disabilities. However, the specific needs of each person will vary enormously, depending on age, age at onset, and type of deaf–blindness.

REFLECT ON THIS
MAT'S STORY: JOINING THE COMMUNITY

Mat is a 23-year-old man with severe and multiple disabilities (including autism and intellectual disabilities). He lives in a home with one roommate and holds two jobs. One job involves cleaning at a local bar and restaurant for an hour each morning. The second job is delivering a weekly advertiser to 170 homes in his neighborhood. In addition to working in the community, Mat goes shopping, takes walks around a nearby lake, goes to the movies, attends concerts and special events, and eats at a fast-food restaurant where he uses a wallet-sized communication picture board to order his meal, independently.

Mat hasn't always been so integrated into his local community. In the past he engaged in a number of challenging behaviors, including removing pictures from the wall, taking down drapes and ripping them, dismantling his bed, ripping his clothing, breaking windows, smearing his bowel movements on objects, urinating on his clothing, hurting others, stripping naked, and similar behaviors. For almost one entire year, Mat refused to wear clothing and spent most of his time wrapped in a blanket. He would often cover his head with the blanket and lie on the couch for hours. He frequently stripped in community settings, on those few occasions when staff were able to coax him to go out. After this had continued for months, the assistance of a behavioral analyst was sought. An analysis of the function that the behaviors served revealed that Mat's stripping and subsequent refusal to wear clothing were the result of his attempt to exert control over his environment, primarily to escape or avoid undesirable events. For this reason, the behavior analyst suggested not focusing directly on the issue of wearing clothing but, rather, addressing the development of a communication system for Mat.

Mat was reported to know over 200 signs, but he was rarely observed to use the signs spontaneously. When he did sign, others in his environment were unable to interpret his signing. Consequently, the behavior analyst and a consultant in augmentative and alternative communication suggested that a communication system using pictures or symbols be implemented to supplement his existing system.

The support program that was developed for Mat had two main components. The first was to enhance his communication and choice-making skills; the second was to provide opportunities for him to participate in activities that were motivating and required him to wear clothing. To address communication and choice-making skills, several photographs were taken of people Mat knew and had worked with, activities he liked or was required to engage in (e.g., watching MTV, going to McDonald's, shaving, taking a shower), and a variety of objects (e.g., lotion, pop, cookies). Then, a minimum of four times each hour, Mat was presented with a choice. Mat would then pick one of the pictures, and staff would help him complete whatever activity he had chosen. Soon he had over 130 photographs in his communication system.

The photographs were mounted on hooks in the hallway of the house where he lived, ensuring that he had easy access to them. Staff reported that over time, Mat began spontaneously using some of the pictures to request items. He would, for example, bring staff the photo of a Diet Pepsi to request a Diet Pepsi. Thus, the communication served to enhance his ability to make his wants and needs known, as well as to help him understand choices presented to him.

While Mat's communication system was being developed, staff was also trying to address indirectly his refusal to wear clothes by capitalizing on the fact that he seemed to genuinely like to go out into the community. Staff would periodically encourage Mat to dress. On those occasions when he would dress, he was able to participate in a community activity that was reinforcing for him. The length of these outings was gradually increased.

Questions for Reflection

1. Why do you believe the two components of Mat's community support program were so effective in helping him to participate more in community activities?

2. What ideas do you have for supporting Mat's opportunities to "join the community"?

SOURCE: Hewitt, A., & O'Nell, S. (2009). I am who I am. A little help from my friends. Washington, DC: President's Committee on Intellectual Disabilities. Adapted from Piche, L., Krage, P., & Wiczek, C. (1991). Joining the community. IMPACT, 4(1), 3, 18. Retrieved May 5, 2009, from www.acf. hhs.gov/programs/pcpid/pcpid_help.html.

Prevalence and Causation

People with severe and multiple disabilities constitute a very small percentage of the general population. Even if we consider the multitude of conditions, prevalence is no more than 0.1 percent to 1.0 percent. Approximately 4 out of every 1,000 people have severe disabilities where the primary symptom is intellectual disabilities. The U.S. Department of Education (2011) reported that more than 130,000 students between the ages of 6 and 21 were served in the public schools under the label *multiple disabilities*. These students account for about 2 percent of the over 7 million students considered eligible for services under IDEA. The Department of Education also reported that more than 1,600 students between the ages of 6 and 21 were labeled as deaf–blind. These students account for 0.0002 percent of students with disabilities served under IDEA. Overall, about 14,000 individuals in the United States are identified as deaf–blind.

© Myrleen Ferguson Cate/Photo Edit

Multiple disabilities result from multiple causes. For the vast majority of people with severe and multiple disabilities, the differences are evident at birth. Severe disabilities may be the result of genetic or metabolic disorders, including chromosomal abnormalities, phenylketonuria, or Rh incompatibility. (See Chapter 9 for more in-depth information on these disorders.) Most identifiable causes of severe intellectual disabilities and related developmental disabilities are genetic in origin (The ARC, 2012a). Other causes include prenatal conditions: poor maternal health during pregnancy, drug abuse, infectious diseases (e.g., HIV), radiation exposure, venereal disease, and advanced maternal age. Severe and multiple disabilities can also result from incidents or conditions that occur later in life, such as poisoning, accidents, malnutrition, physical and emotional neglect, and disease.

FOCUS 3

Identify the estimated prevalence and causes of severe and multiple disabilities.

CEC

Standard 2
Development and Characteristics of Learners

Students with deaf–blindness require extensive support to meet their educational needs, particularly in the area of communication.

Characteristics

The multitude of characteristics exhibited by people with severe and multiple disabilities is mirrored by the numerous definitions associated with these conditions. A close analysis of these definitions reveals a consistent focus on people whose life needs cannot be met without substantial support from others, including family, friends, and society. With this support, however, people with severe and multiple disabilities have a much greater probability of escaping the stereotype that depicts them as totally dependent consumers of societal resources. People with severe disabilities can become contributing members of families and communities.

Giangreco (2011) suggests that "inclusion-oriented people seek to establish an ethic that welcomes all children into their local schools and simultaneously pursues a range of individually meaningful learning outcomes through effective education practices" (p. 4). For Sarina, in the opening Snapshot, this would mean concentrating on educational outcomes that will decrease her dependence on others in her environment and create opportunities to enhance her participation at home, at school, and in the community. Instruction would be developed with these outcomes in mind, rather than on the basis of a set of general characteristics associated with the label *severely disabled*.

FOCUS 4

What are the characteristics of people with severe and multiple disabilities?

CEC

Standard 2
Development and Characteristics of Learners

Intelligence and Academic Achievement

Most people with severe and multiple disabilities have intellectual disabilities as a primary condition. Thus, their learning and memory capabilities are diminished. The greater the intellectual disabilities, the more difficulty the individual will have in learning, retaining, and applying information. People with severe and multiple disabilities will require specialized and intensive instruction to acquire and use new skills across a number of settings.

Given the diminished intellectual capability of many people with severe and multiple disabilities, academic learning is often a low instructional priority. The vast majority of students with severe disabilities are unable to learn from basic academic programs in reading, writing, and mathematics. Instruction in functional academic skills that facilitate access to the general curriculum is the most effective approach to academic learning. Basic academic subjects are taught in the context of daily living. For example, functional reading focuses on those words that facilitate a child's access to the environment (*restroom, danger, exit,* and the like). Functional math skill development involves developing strategies for telling time or the consumer's use of money. A more in-depth discussion on teaching functional skills to students with severe disabilities appears later in this chapter.

Adaptive Skills

Adaptive skills
Conceptual, social, and practical skills that facilitate an individual's ability to function in community, family, and school settings.

The learning of **adaptive skills** is critical to success in natural settings. These skills involve both personal independence and social interaction. Personal independence skills range from the ability to take care of one's basic needs—eating, dressing, and hygiene—to living on one's own in the community (including getting and keeping a job, managing money, and finding ways to get around in the environment). Social interaction skills involve being able to communicate one's needs and preferences, as well as listening and appropriately responding to others. People with severe and multiple disabilities often do not have age-appropriate adaptive skills; they need ongoing services and supports to facilitate learning and application in this area. We do know that when given the opportunity to learn adaptive skills through participation in inclusive settings with peers without disabilities, children with severe disabilities have a higher probability of maintaining and meaningfully applying this learning over time (Snell & Brown, 2011; Westling & Fox, 2009).

Epilepsy
A condition that produces brief disturbances in brain function, resulting in seizures of varying intensity.

Spasticity
A condition that involves involuntary contractions of various muscle groups.

Athetosis
A condition characterized by constant, contorted twisting motions in the wrists and fingers.

Hypotonia
Poor muscle tone.

Catheterization
The process of introducing a hollow tube (catheter) into body cavities to drain fluid, such as introducing a tube into an individual's bladder to drain urine.

Gastronomy tube feeding
The process of feeding a person through a rubber tube that is inserted into the stomach.

Respiratory ventilation
Use of a mechanical aid (ventilator) to supply oxygen to an individual with respiratory problems.

Speech and Language

People with severe and multiple disabilities generally have significant deficits and delays in speech and language skills, ranging from articulation and fluency disorders to an absence of any expressive oral language (Westling & Fox, 2009). Speech and language deficits and delays are positively correlated with the severity of intellectual disabilities (Moore- & Montgomery, 2008). As is true for adaptive skill learning, people with severe and multiple disabilities will acquire and use appropriate speech and language if these skills are taught and applied in natural settings. Functional communication systems (such as signing, picture cards, communication boards, and gesturing) are also an integral part of instruction. Regardless of the communication system(s) used to teach speech and language skills, they must be applied across multiple settings. For example, if picture cards are used in the classroom, they must also be a part of the communication system used at home and in other environments.

Physical and Health

People with severe and multiple disabilities have significant physical and health care needs. For instance, these individuals have a higher incidence of congenital heart disease, **epilepsy**, respiratory problems, diabetes, and metabolic disorders. They also exhibit poor muscle tone and often have conditions such as **spasticity**, **athetosis**, and **hypotonia**. Such conditions require that professionals in the schools and other service agencies know how to administer medications, **catheterization**, **gastronomy tube feeding**, and **respiratory ventilation** (Rues, Graff, Ault, & Holvoet, 2006).

Vision and Hearing

Although the prevalence of vision and hearing loss is not well documented among people with severe disabilities, sensory impairments do occur more frequently in people with severe disabilities than in the general population (Drew & Hardman, 2007). Some individuals, particularly those described as deaf–blind, have significant vision and hearing disorders that require services and supports beyond those for a person with blindness *or* deafness.

Educational Assessments

The axiom "the earlier, the better" is certainly applicable to educational assessments and supports for children with severe and multiple disabilities. Such services must begin at birth and continue throughout the lifespan. Traditionally, there has been a heavy reliance on standardized assessments, particularly IQ tests, in identifying people with severe and multiple disabilities, particularly when the primary condition is intellectual disabilities (see Chapter 9). Some professionals (Bishop, 2005; Brown & Snell, 2011) have suggested that standardized tests, particularly the IQ test, do not provide information useful in either diagnosing the disability or providing instruction to individuals with severe disabilities. Others (McDonnell, Hardman, & McDonnell, 2003) believe that standardized tests may be appropriate as one tool in a battery of multidisciplinary assessments to determine eligibility for special education services, but that they provide no meaningful information for making curriculum decisions such as what and how to teach.

Assessments that focus on valued skills to promote independence and quality of life in natural settings are referred to as functional, ecological, or **authentic assessment** (Horner, Albin, Sprague, & Todd, 2006; McDonnell, Hardman, & McDonnell, 2003). These assessments focus on the match between the needs of the individual and the demands of the environment (adaptive fit). The purpose of the assessment is to determine what supports are necessary to achieve the intended outcomes of access and participation in natural settings. Skills are never taught in isolation from actual performance demands. Additionally, the individual does not "get ready" to participate in the community through a sequence of readiness stages as in the developmental model but, rather, learns and uses skills in the setting where the behavior is expected to occur.

During the past decade, there has been increasing emphasis on holding schools more accountable for student learning and progress. States are setting educational standards and then assessing how students progress toward the intended goals. A major challenge for education is to demonstrate accountability for all students, including those with the most significant disabilities:

> *Regardless of one's perspective on the wisdom and implications of this [accountability] movement, it promises to have a significant effect on curricular guidance and foci for students with [severe] disabilities. . . . A major question facing educators and parents is how can those concerned with the education of students with significant disabilities ensure a continued and focused emphasis on full membership and meaningful outcomes during this era? (Ford, Davern, and Schnorr, 2001, p. 215)*

IDEA requires that schools must include students with disabilities in district-wide or statewide assessments of achievement or provide a statement of why that assessment is not appropriate for the child. The law also requires that individual modifications in the administration of statewide or district-wide assessments be provided as appropriate for the child to participate. Examples of student accommodations include large-print text, testing in a separate setting, and extended time. Ysseldyke, Olsen, and Thurlow (2012) estimate that about 85 percent of students with disabilities have mild or moderate disabilities and can take state or district assessments, either with or without accommodations. For many students with severe disabilities, these assessments are inappropriate; such students are excluded from taking them. Schools are still accountable, however, for the progress of these students. IDEA mandated that states conduct **alternate assessments** to ensure that all students are included in the state's accountability system. Quenemoen and Thurlow (2012) identified five characteristics of good alternate assessments:

- There have been careful stakeholder and policy-maker development and definition of desired student outcomes for the population, reflecting the best understanding of research and practice.

- Assessment methods have been carefully developed, tested, and refined.

- Professionally accepted standards are used to score evidence (e.g., adequate training, dual-scoring third-party tiebreakers, reliability tests, and rechecks of scorer competence).

FOCUS 5

Identify three types of educational assessments for students with severe and multiple disabilities.

CEC

Standard 8
Assessment

Authentic assessment
An alternative basis used to measure student progress. Assessment is based on student progress in meaningful learning activities.

Alternate assessments
Assessments mandated in IDEA for students who are unable to participate in required state- or district-wide assessments. It ensures that all students, regardless of the severity of their disabilities, are included in the state's accountability system.

- An accepted standards-setting process has been used so that results can be included in reporting and accountability.
- The assessment process is continuously reviewed and improved.

Alternate assessment systems should include as key criteria the extent to which the system provides the supports and adaptations needed and trains the student to use them.

Alternate assessments may involve either normative or absolute performance standards (Ysseldyke & Olsen, 2012). If a normative assessment is used, then a student's performance is compared to that of peers (other students of comparable age or ability participating in the alternate assessment). If an absolute standard is used, then a student's performance is compared against a set criterion, such as being able to cross the street when the "walk" sign is flashing 100 percent of the time without assistance.

The Early Childhood Years

FOCUS 6

Identify the features of effective services and supports for children with severe and multiple disabilities during the early childhood years.

Effective early intervention services that start when the child is born are critical to the prevention and amelioration of social, medical, and educational problems that can occur throughout the life of the individual (Batshaw, Pellegrino, & Rozien, 2008; Berk, 2005). During the early childhood years, services and supports are concentrated on two age groups: infants and toddlers, and preschool-age children.

Services and Supports for Infants and Toddlers

Effective programs for infants and toddlers with severe and multiple disabilities are both child- and family-centered. A child-centered approach focuses on identifying and meeting individual needs. Services begin with infant stimulation programs intended to elicit in newborns the sensory, cognitive, and physical responses that will connect them with their environment. As the child develops, health care, physical therapy, occupational therapy, and speech and language services may become integral components of a child-centered program.

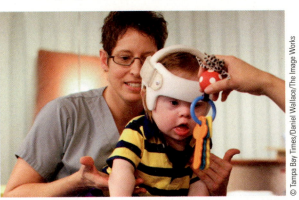

Effective programs for infants and toddlers with severe and multiple disabilities are both child- and family-centered. Therapists work closely with the infant and the family to promote early learning and development.

© Tampa Bay Times/Daniel Wallace/The Image Works

Family-centered early intervention focuses on a holistic approach that involves the child as a member of the family unit. The needs, structure, and preferences of the family drive the delivery of services and supports. The overall purpose of family-centered intervention is to enable family members first to cope with the birth of a child with a severe disability and eventually to grow together and support one another. Family-centered approaches build on and increase family strengths, address the needs of every family member, and support mutually enjoyable family relationships. Supports for families may include parent-training programs, counseling, and **respite care**.

Respite care
Assistance provided by individuals that allows parents and other children within the family time away from the child with a disability.

Services and Supports for Preschool-Age Children

Preschool programs for young children with severe and multiple disabilities continue the emphasis on family involvement while extending the life space of the child to a school setting. McDonnell, Hardman, & McDonnell (2003) suggest four goals for preschool programs serving children with severe disabilities:

1. Maximize the child's development in a variety of important developmental areas. These include social communication, motor skills, cognitive skills, preacademic skills, self-care, play, and personal management.

2. Develop the child's social interaction and classroom participation skills. Focus should be on teaching the child to follow adult directions while developing peer relationships, responding to classroom routines, and becoming self-directed (that is, completing classroom activities without constant adult supervision).

Standard 3
Individual Learning Differences

Standard 4
Instructional Strategies

Standard 7
Instructional Planning

3. Increase community participation through support to family members and other care-givers. Work to identify alternative caregivers so that the family has a broader base of support and more flexibility to pursue other interests. Help the family to identify activities within the neighborhood that their preschooler would enjoy to provide the child with opportunities to interact with same-age peers. Activities may involve swimming or dancing lessons, joining a soccer team, attending a house of worship, and so on.

4. Prepare the child for inclusive school placements, and provide support for the transition to elementary school. The transition out of preschool will be facilitated if educators from the receiving elementary school work collaboratively with the family and preschool personnel.

To meet these goals, preschool programs for children with severe disabilities blend the principles and elements of developmentally appropriate practices (DAP), multicultural education, and special education. DAP was developed by the National Association for the Education of Young Children as an alternative to an academic curriculum for preschoolers. It emphasizes age-appropriate child exploration and play activities that are consistent with individual needs. Multicultural education emphasizes acceptance of people from different cultural and ethnic backgrounds within and across the preschool curriculum. Successful culturally

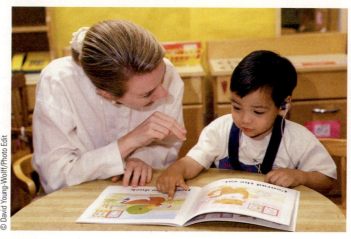

© David Young-Wolff/Photo Edit

Culturally inclusive preschool programs blend the principles and practices that guide special education, inclusive education, and multicultural education.

inclusive programs blend principles and practices that guide special education, inclusive education, and multicultural education (Gollnick & Chinn, 2012). Special education focuses on assessing individual needs, providing intensive instruction, and teaching explicit skills within the context of an individualized education program (IEP). Families, educators, and other professionals committed to DAP, multicultural education, and special education work together to provide a quality experience for preschool-age children with severe disabilities.

The Elementary School Years

Historically, services and supports for students with severe and multiple disabilities have been oriented to protection and care. The objective was to protect the individual from society, and society from the individual. This philosophy resulted in programs that isolated the individual and provided physical care rather than preparation for life in a heterogeneous world. Today, educators working together with parents are concentrating their efforts on preparing students with severe and multiple disabilities to participate actively in the life of the family, school, and community. Given the emphasis on lifelong learning and living in natural settings, educators have identified several features that characterize quality programs for elementary-age students with severe and multiple disabilities:

- Self-determination is important—student preferences and needs are taken into account in developing educational objectives.
- The school values and supports parental involvement.
- Instruction focuses on frequently used functional skills related to everyday life activities.
- Assistive technology and augmentative communication are available to maintain or increase the functional capabilities of the student with severe and multiple disabilities.

FOCUS 7

Identify the features of effective services and supports for children with severe and multiple disabilities during the elementary school years.

Standard 4
Instructional Strategies

Standard 7
Instructional Planning

LEARNING THROUGH SOCIAL MEDIA
OPENING UP THE WORLD FOR PEOPLE WITH DISABILITIES

Social media is developing into more than a pastime for [people who are] . . . elderly or disabled. If implemented properly, it could become their social lifeline. For some residents at Davis Health Care Center and Champions Assisted Living in Porters Neck [North Carolina], this is already the case. Davis recently installed computer stations equipped with Skype, a free software that allows users to "call" and see anyone around the world using a webcam. Twenty-three people of varying abilities . . . have full access to computers. Staff hope to improve this figure through the installation of wireless Internet in all rooms when they remodel the facility later this year.

Not everyone at Davis has the capabilities to use a standard system, but that hardly stops them from accessing the information superhighway. . . . Edsel Odom . . . uses a wheelchair and clicks a mouse with his single functioning thumb. To type, he uses an infrared device mounted on a baseball cap. Odom uses all types of social media, including Facebook, Twitter, MySpace, and blogs. Social media is about more than just family and friends for Odom. "I want to share my message with the world!" he said.

Others, like Laura Still . . . just want to have fun. Still was involved in a serious car accident 16 years ago that left her with brain damage. Within the past five years, her true technological abilities have surfaced. She uses a fully functioning Macintosh computer set up in her room to play games, draft e-mail, and listen to her favorite tunes. Her message to others with disabilities is, "Never give up!" As more and more people with disabilities enter the social media arena, disability resources and organizations have to stay one step ahead. For example, information from the website disability.gov, which provides resources on topics such as traveling with a disability or how to apply for benefits, can now be found on Facebook as well as Twitter.

Bethany Ferguson, a sociology instructor at Cape Fear Community College, emphasized the importance of awareness about these tools. Now more than ever as society transitions into the postindustrial technology era, people must find ways to remain connected, she said. "Social media provides isolated individuals of any age group with a socializing outlet. It is not uncommon for the elderly in our society to feel as if they have lost their social voice, and the use of social media restores this voice, oftentimes from the comfort of one's home. The value in maintaining this voice for the elderly individual is undeniable," Ferguson said.

A person's age and work status might be barriers to that technology, said Eleanor Covan, professor of gerontology and sociology at the University of North Carolina, Wilmington (UNCW). Covan said people become used to the technology with which they grow up.

"Once people leave the workforce, they tend not to learn new elements of technology, and that is one reason why the oldest old are not likely to be on Facebook," Covan said.

"This is the population that prefers reading a newspaper, rather than an electronic news report, no matter who authored the article," she said.

At Davis Health Care Center, Vel Evans and Edsel Odom are among the exceptions, joining the 38 percent of those 65 and older who use the Web, according to 2009 Internet trend data from the Pew Research Center.

SOURCE: From Morrison, D. (2010). Social media opens social world to elderly disabled. *Star News Online*. Retrieved March 2, 2012, from www.starnewsonline.com/article/20100126/articles/100129756?p=1&tc=pg.

Self-Determination

People with severe and multiple disabilities, like everyone else, must be in a position to make their own life choices as much as possible. School programs that promote self-determination enhance each student's opportunity to become more independent in the life of the family and in the larger community. Providing students with severe disabilities the opportunity to communicate their needs and preferences enhances autonomy, problem-solving skills, adaptability, and self-efficacy expectations (Bremer, Kachgal, & Schoeller, 2003; Wehmeyer, Gragoudas, & Shogren, 2006).

Parental Involvement

Schools are more successful in meeting the needs of students when they establish positive relationships with the family. The important role parents play during the early childhood years must continue and be supported during elementary school. Parents who actively participate in their child's educational program promote the development and implementation of instruction that is consistent with individual needs and preferences. Parental involvement can be a powerful predictor of postschool adjustment for students with severe and multiple disabilities. A strong home–school partnership requires that parents and educators acknowledge and respect each other's differences in values and culture, listen openly and attentively to one another's concerns, value varying opinions and ideas, discuss issues openly and in an atmosphere of trust, and share in the responsibility and consequences of making a decision.

Teaching Functional Skills

Effective educational programs focus on the functional skills that students with severe and multiple disabilities need to live successfully in the natural settings of family, school, and community. A functional skill is one that will have frequent and meaningful use across multiple environments. Instruction should involve the following elements:

- Many different people
- A variety of settings within the community
- Varied materials that will interest the learner and match performance demands

If the student with severe disabilities is to learn how to cross a street safely, shop in a grocery store, play a video game, or eat in a local restaurant, the necessary skills should be taught in the actual setting where the behavior is to be performed. It should not be assumed that a skill learned in a classroom will simply transfer to a setting outside of the school. Instruction in a more natural environment can ensure that the skill will be useful and will be maintained over time.

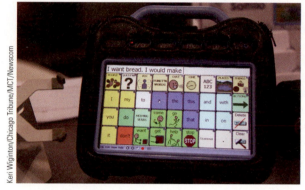
Keri Wiginton/Chicago Tribune/MCT/Newscom

An assistive device, such as this computerized touch screen language board, helps students who are nonverbal to communicate with parents, teachers, and friends.

As suggested by Drew and Hardman (2007), a functional approach teaches academic skills in the context of environmental cues. The learning of new skills is always paired directly with environmental stimuli. Snell and Brown (2011) stressed that the teacher must use instructional materials that are real and meaningful to the student. Traditional materials, such as workbooks, basal readers, and flash cards, do not work for students with severe disabilities. Students must be taught using *real objects in real situations* in the home or community setting. For example, when teaching the word *exit*, pair it with an actual exit sign in a movie theater. Or when teaching the word *stop*, pair it with a stop sign on a street corner.

Assistive Technology and Augmentative Communication

Assistive technology is any item, piece of equipment, or product system that can be used to increase, maintain, or improve the functional capabilities of students with disabilities (The Technology-Related Assistance for Individuals with Disabilities Act, PL 100-407, [20 U.S.C. Sec. 140(25)]). An assistive technology service "directly assists an individual with a disability in the selection, acquisition, or use of an assistive technology device" (20 U.S.C. Sec 140(26)). Johnston (2003) identified several types of assistive technology:

- Aids for daily living (such as nonslip placement to hold a bowl, utensils with built-up handles to provide a better gripping surface, and two-handed mugs to allow for two-handed grasping)
- Communication aids (computers with voice output, hearing aids)
- Aids for working, learning, and playing (braces, artificial limbs, prosthetic hands)
- Mobility aids (wheelchairs, lifts, walkers)
- Positioning aids (cushions, pelvic strips or hip guides, head supports on a wheelchair)

ASSISTIVE TECHNOLOGY
MEET ASHLEY

In the vignette that follows, Kimberly Voss describes how she taught her daughter Ashley, a child born with Down's syndrome and severe disabilities, to learn reading through the use of assistive technology. Kimberly describes Ashley's odyssey through life as one of "getting Ashley out":

Trapped inside a body that does not always do what she asks it to do, we have had to invent and create from scratch numerous methods that allow her to emerge. Her medical diagnosis and developmental label have not been an accurate measure of her human potential. Unwilling to accept "can't" as an option, we have focused on "what if." Ashley's determination, as well as mine, has been our key to unlocking door after door, every day revealing more of Ashley's abilities and character. While she lives with many challenging and complex disabilities, Ashley has emerged as an assertive, independent, loving, and spirited young woman with a zest for life and wonderfully keen sense of humor. She will face adversity throughout her life, but we will face it, as we have all the changes that came before, one day and one creative solution at a time (from Voss, 2005, pp. 9–10).

TEACHING ASHLEY TO READ USING ASSISTIVE TECHNOLOGY

When Ashley was quite young, I had the good fortune to attend a workshop Patricia Oelwein gave before her 1995 book, *Teaching Reading to Children with Down Syndrome* was published. Her technique began by following a three-step progression (matching, selecting, and naming) and was very visual, initially teaching sight words rather than phonics or text decoding. Pat suggested starting off by playing simplified matching-type games, matching text to text—for example, putting the word "Daddy" on "Daddy." After that was mastered, Pat suggested matching text to an image and then selecting the correct word from a set of different word choices. We would ask, "Give me the card that says 'Daddy.'" This approach worked very well for Ashley.

For Ashley, teaching sight words held real potential. Because of her complex speech problems, Ashley could not verbally describe what letters she was seeing or what words she was reading, making it even more of a challenge to teach her to read. But Pat's approach of matching words and selecting words

required no speech at all. Using these methods, Ashley was quickly able to learn to read a number of meaningful sight words, matching text to text, matching text to image, and then selecting a requested word from a set. Over time, she significantly increased her sight word vocabulary and eventually completed the final step of naming: expressively communicating her identification of many words using sign language. As she began to read and sign, lo and behold, along came speech.

Sight word cards really show the advantages of designing the materials by computer, including the opportunity to customize the word choices and to keep it constantly fresh and new. And the computer enables uniformity. If the words are to be matched, it is best if they are an exact copy of one another (so that they are truly visually the same), which they cannot be if handwritten. It is quick and easy to accomplish this using a computer.

SOURCE: Voss, K. S. (2005). *Teaching by design.* Bethesda, MD: Woodbine House (pp. 9, 215).

TEACHSOURCE VIDEO TYLER: AUGMENTATIVE COMMUNICATION TECHNIQUES FOR A KINDERGARTEN STUDENT WITH AUTISM AND LANGUAGE ISSUES

Please visit the Education CourseMate website for *Human Exceptionality*, 11th edition, at CengageBrain.com to access this TeachSource video. Tyler is a kindergarten student who began the school year with no verbal skills and was content to sit by himself in the corner with no interactions with other students. Tyler is now in an inclusion classroom where Whitney

Meade, his learning support teacher, uses a variety of strategies to develop and enhance Tyler's learning and social skills.

Respond to the following questions:

1. Describe the picture exchange communication system (PECS) and how it is used to teach social skills to Tyler.

2. Describe Tyler's language and social skills now that he is in an inclusion classroom.

3. What strategies does Becky Paden, speech and language pathologist, recommend for teachers who are working with students who have significant challenges in language delay, social skills development, and academic learning?

Students with severe and multiple disabilities benefit from any one or more of these assistive devices or activities. For students with severe disabilities who are unable to use speech and need an additional communication mode, **augmentative communication** will nearly always be an integral component of their individualized education program. Augmentative communication involves adapting existing vocal or gestural abilities into meaningful communication; teaching manual signing (such as American Sign Language), static symbols, or icons (such as **Blissymbols**), and using manual or electronic communication devices (such as electric communication boards, picture cues, or synthetic speech; Westling & Fox, 2009). For more insight into the use of assistive technology for a student with severe disabilities, see the nearby Assistive Technology, "Meet Ashley" and the TeachSource Video, "Tyler."

The Adolescent Years

Societal perceptions about the capabilities of people with severe and multiple disabilities have changed a great deal over the past several years. Until very recently, the potential of these individuals to learn, live, and work in community settings was significantly

Augmentative communication
Communication systems that involve adapting existing vocal or gestural abilities into meaningful communication, or using manual or electronic devices.

Blissymbols
A system developed by C. K. Bliss that ties a specific symbol to a word in one of four categories: pictographic, ideographic, relational, and abstract.

Standard 1
Foundations

 DEBATE FORUM CAN SPECIAL SCHOOLS FOR STUDENTS WITH SEVERE AND MULTIPLE DISABILITES BE JUSTIFIED?

The debate regarding what constitutes an appropriate educational placement for students with severe disabilities has been a major point of disagreement among professional and parents since the passage of the federal law mandating the education of students with disabilities in public schools. Some professionals and parents argue that there will always be a need for special schools and that they are the least restrictive environment for a number of children with severe disabilities. Others contend that special schools are never the least restrictive environment. On the contrary, all students with severe disabilities benefit from placement in general education classes and schools where opportunities for interaction with students who are not disabled are systematically planned and implemented (Drew & Hardman, 2007). This debate forum highlights some of the major points of contention in this ongoing and unresolved issue.

POINT

Although inclusion may be appropriate for many students with severe disabilities, special schools are the least restrictive environment for a small number of children who require intensive instruction and support that cannot be provided in a general education school or classroom. Special schools provide for greater homogeneity in grouping and programming. Teachers can specialize in particular areas such as art, language, physical education, and music. Teaching materials can be centralized and, thus, used more effectively with larger numbers of students. A special school more efficiently uses available resources. In addition, some parents of students with severe disabilities believe that their children will be happier in a special school that "protects" them.

COUNTERPOINT

Inclusive education for students with severe disabilities embodies a variety of opportunities, both within the general education classroom and throughout the school. Besides interaction in a classroom setting, ongoing inclusion occurs in the halls, on the playground, in the cafeteria, and at school assemblies. Special schools generally offer little, if any, opportunity for interaction with normal peers and deprive the child of valuable learning and socialization experiences. Special schools cannot be financially or ideologically justified. Public school administrators must now plan to include children with severe disabilities in existing general education schools and classes.

 What Do You Think? Please visit the Education CourseMate website for Human Exceptionality, *11th Edition to access and respond to questions related to the Debate Forum.*

CEC

Standard 5
Learning Environments and
Social Interactions

FOCUS 8

Describe four outcomes that are
important in planning for the
transition from school to adult
life for adolescents with severe
and multiple disabilities.

FOCUS 9

Describe three features that
characterize successful inclusive
education for students with
severe and multiple disabilities.

underestimated. People with severe and multiple disabilities can become active participants in the lives of their community and family. This realization has prompted professionals and parents to seek significant changes in the ways that schools prepare students for the transition to adult life.

In a review of the research on successful community living for people with severe disabilities, Crockett and Hardman (2009a) address four tasks that are important in planning for the transition to adult life:

- Establish a network of friends and acquaintances.
- Develop the ability to use community resources on a regular basis.
- Secure a paid job that supports the use of community resources and interaction with peers.
- Establish independence and autonomy in making lifestyle choices.

Inclusive Education

The provision of services and supports in an inclusive educational setting is widely viewed as a critical factor in delivering a quality program for students with severe and multiple disabilities (The ARC, 2012b). Effective educational programs include continual opportunities for interaction between students with severe disabilities and peers without disabilities. Frequent and age-appropriate interactions between students with disabilities and their

---

CASE STUDY DAVID

David is a 16-year-old sophomore with Down's syndrome at Valley High School. His IEP targets his participation in content-area classes in the school, participation in a community leisure routine, and employment training in community settings. His special education teacher collaborated with the school counselor to schedule David's content-area classes in the morning. Following lunch, David leaves school to receive instruction on his community-based goals.

David's schedule fits with the schedules of his peers without disabilities at Valley High School. The school has adopted a flexible schedule for students. For example, classes are offered throughout the day and into the evening. Many students split their classes between the high school and the local community college. Many others combine part-time work with classes at the high school.

On Monday, Wednesday, and Friday afternoons, David goes to his work ex-

perience at the neighborhood public library. He completes a number of tasks including sorting returned books, rewinding videos, and many others. A paraprofessional staff member from the high school provides instruction and support to David in completing his job. His instruction focuses on riding the bus to and from the library, completing job tasks, self-monitoring job assignments, and social interactions with peers. The instruction is designed to gradually fade the assistance provided to David by the paraprofessional.

On Tuesday and Thursday afternoons, David is learning to go swimming or use the workout room at the local community recreation center. With the assistance of Steve, a peer tutor, David chooses the activities that he wants to complete, travels to and from the recreational center, dresses appropriately for the selected activity, and uses the facilities and equipment appropriately. In addition to providing instructional

support to David, Steve completes the routine with David and as a result, Steve and David have become good friends. Their friendship has evolved to the point where they do things together on weekends.

APPLICATION QUESTIONS

1. Why is it important for David to receive instruction in both his content-area classes (e.g., math and science) as well as community settings?

2. What are the skills David is learning while participating in community settings? Why is instruction in life skills important?

3. Who is Steve and why is he an important part of David's life outside of school?

Source: Crockett, M., & Hardman, M. L. (2009b). The role of secondary education in transition. In J. McDonnell & M. L. Hardman, *Successful transition programs* (p. 44). Los Angeles: Sage Publishing Company.

peers without disabilities can enhance opportunities for successful participation in the community during the adult years. Social interaction can be enhanced by creating opportunities for these students to associate both during and after the school day. Successful inclusion efforts are characterized by the following features:

- Physical placement of students with severe and multiple disabilities in the general education schools and classes they would attend if they didn't have disabilities

- Systematic organization of opportunities for interaction between students with severe and multiple disabilities and students without disabilities

- Specific instruction in valued post-school outcomes that will increase the competence of students with severe and multiple disabilities in the natural settings of family, school, and community

One of the most important characteristics of the natural settings in which students ultimately must function is frequent interaction with people without disabilities. Consequently, it is logical to plan educational programs that duplicate this feature of the environment and that actively build skills required for successful inclusion. For more insight into the importance of instruction in natural settings and friendships for students with severe disabilities, see the nearby Case Study, "David."

As students with severe and multiple disabilities are included in general education schools and classrooms, it is important to find ways to encourage social interactions between these students and students who are not disabled. Planned opportunities for interaction may include the use of in-class peer supports (tutors, circles of friends) as well as access to everyday school activities such as assemblies, recess, lunch, and field trips. For more tips on supporting people with severe and multiple disabilities in natural settings, see this chapter's Inclusion and Collaboration through the Lifespan.

INCLUSION AND COLLABORATION THROUGH THE LIFESPAN
PEOPLE WITH SEVERE AND MULTIPLE DISABILITIES

EARLY CHILDHOOD YEARS

Tips for the Family

- During the infant and toddler years, seek out family-centered programs that focus on communication and the building of positive relationships among all individual members.

- Seek supports and services for your preschool-age child that promote communication and play activities with same-age peers without disabilities.

- Seek opportunities for friendships to develop between your child and children without disabilities in family and neighborhood settings.

- Use the individualized family service plan and the individualized education plan as a means for the multidisciplinary team to establish goals that develop your child's social interaction and classroom participation skills.

Tips for the Preschool Teacher

- Establish a classroom environment that promotes and supports diversity.

- Use a child-centered approach to instruction that acknowledges and values every child's strengths, preferences, and individual needs.

- Ignore whatever labels have been used to describe the child with severe and multiple disabilities. There is no relationship between the label and the instruction needed by the child to succeed in natural settings.

- Create opportunities for ongoing communication and play activities among children with severe disabilities and their same-age peers without disabilities. Nurture interactive peer relationships across a variety of instructional areas and settings.

Tips for Preschool Personnel

- Support the inclusion of young children with severe and multiple disabilities in all preschool classrooms and programs.

- Always refer to children by name, not label. If you must employ a label, use "child-first language." For example say, "children with severe disabilities," not "severely disabled children."

- Communicate genuine respect and support for all teachers, staff, and volunteers who look for ways to include children with severe disabilities in preschool classrooms and collaborative school-wide activities.

- Welcome families into the preschool programs. Listen to what parents have to say about the importance of, or concerns about, including their child in school programs and activities.
- Create opportunities for parents to become involved in their child's program through collaborative projects with school personnel, including volunteering, school governance, and the like.

Tips for Neighbors and Friends

- Most importantly, see the child with severe disabilities as an individual who has needs, preferences, strengths, and weaknesses. Avoid the pitfalls of stereotyping and "self-fulfilling prophecies."
- Support opportunities for your children and those of friends and neighbors to interact and play with a child who has severe and multiple disabilities.
- Help children without disabilities build friendships with children who have severe and multiple disabilities, rather than merely playing caregiving roles.
- Provide a supportive and collaborative community environment for the family of a young child with severe and multiple disabilities. Encourage the family, including the child, to participate in neighborhood activities.

ELEMENTARY YEARS

Tips for the Family

- Actively collaborate with the multidisciplinary team in the development of your son's or daughter's IEP. Write down the priorities and educational goals that you see as important for your child in the natural settings of home, school, and community.
- Follow up at home on activities that the school suggests are important for helping your child generalize skills learned at school to other natural settings.
- Actively collaborate with school personnel, whether it be in your child's classroom or in extracurricular

activities. Demonstrate your appreciation and support for administrators, teachers, and staff who openly value and support the inclusion of your child in the school and classroom.
- Continually collaborate with administrators and teachers on the importance of children with severe disabilities being included with peers without disabilities during classroom and school-wide activities (such as riding on the same school bus, going to recess and lunch at the same time, and participating in school-wide assemblies).

Tips for the General Education Classroom Teacher

- See children with severe and multiple disabilities as individuals, not labels. Focus on their similarities with other children rather than on their differences.
- Openly value and support diversity and collaboration in your classroom. Set individualized goals and objectives for all children.
- Develop a classroom environment and instructional program that recognize multiple needs and abilities.
- Become part of a team that continually collaborates to meet the needs of all children in your classroom. View the special education teacher as a resource who can assist you in developing an effective instructional program for the child with severe and multiple disabilities.

Tips for School Personnel

- Communicate that diversity is strength in your school. Openly value diversity by providing the resources necessary for teachers to work with students who have a range of needs and come from differing backgrounds.
- Integrate school resources as well as children. Develop school-wide teacher-assistance or teacher-support teams that work collaboratively to meet the needs of every student.
- Collaborate with general and special education teachers in the development of peer-partner and support

networks for students with severe and multiple disabilities.
- Include all students in the programs and activities of the school.

Tips for Neighbors and Friends

- Openly communicate to school personnel, friends, and neighbors your support of families who are seeking to have their child with severe and multiple disabilities be a part of an inclusive school setting.
- Communicate to your children and those of friends and neighbors the value of collaboration and inclusion. Demonstrate this value by creating opportunities for children with severe disabilities and their families to play an active role in the life of the community.

SECONDARY AND TRANSITION YEARS

Tips for the Family

- Seek opportunities for students from your son's or daughter's high school to visit your home. Help arrange get-togethers or parties involving students from the neighborhood and/or school.
- Communicate to the school what you see as priorities for your son or daughter as they transition from school into adult life. Suggest goals and objectives that promote and support social interaction and community-based activities with peers who are not disabled. Collaborate with the school to translate your goals into an individualized education plan that includes transition activities from school to adult life.

Tips for the General Education Classroom Teacher

- Become part of a school-wide team that collaborates to meet the needs of all students in high school. Value the role of the special educator as teacher, collaborator, and consultant who can serve as a valuable resource in planning for the instructional needs of students with severe disabilities. Collaborate with special education teachers and other specialists to adapt subject matter in your classroom (e.g., science, math, or physical education) to the individual needs of students with severe and multiple disabilities.

- Communicate the importance of students with severe disabilities being included in school programs and activities. Although the goals and activities of this student may be different from those of other students, with support, she or he will benefit from working with you and other students in the class.

- Encourage the student with severe disabilities to become involved in extracurricular high school activities. If you are the faculty sponsor of a club or organization, explore whether this student is interested and how he or she could get involved.

Tips for School Personnel

- Advocate for parents of high school–age students with severe and multiple disabilities to participate in the activities and governance of the school.

- Collaborate with parents in the transition-planning process during the high school years by listening to parent input that focuses on a desire for their son or daughter to be included as a valued member of the high school community.

- Support high school special education or vocational teachers seeking to develop community-based instruction programs that focus on students learning and applying skills in actual community settings (e.g., grocery stores, malls, theaters, parks, work sites).

Tips for Neighbors, Friends, and Potential Employers

- Collaborate with the family and school personnel to create opportunities for students with severe and multiple disabilities to participate in community activities (such as going to the movies, "hanging out" with peers who are not disabled in the neighborhood mall, and going to high school sporting events) as often as possible.

- As a potential employer, collaborate with the high school to locate and establish community-based employment training sites for students with severe and multiple disabilities.

ADULT YEARS

Tips for the Family

- Develop an understanding of life after school during your son's or daughter's adult years. What are the formal (government-funded or parent organizations) and informal supports (family and friends) available in your community? What are the characteristics of adult service programs? Explore adult support systems in the local community in the areas of supported living, employment, and recreation/leisure.

Tips for Neighbors, Friends, and Potential Employers

- Become part of the community support network for the individual with severe and multiple disabilities. Be alert to ways in which this individual can become and remain actively involved in community employment, neighborhood recreational activities, and local church functions.

- As a potential employer in the community, seek information on employment of people with severe and multiple disabilities. Find out about programs (such as supported employment) that focus on establishing work for people with mental retardation while meeting your needs as an employer.

Looking Toward a Bright Future

Throughout history, individuals with severe and multiple disabilities have been forgotten and neglected people, often being denied opportunities for education, social services, and health care. Today, these individuals are receiving more services and supports than ever before, although there is much left to do to assure their full access to and participation in school, family, and community life. As such suggested by TASH (2012c):

Children and adults with disabilities should have opportunities to develop relationships with neighbors, classmates, co-workers, and community members. Adults, whether married or single, should make decisions about where and with whom they live. The preferences of each individual should be honored in regards to their decisions on community life and participation. Individuals with disabilities and families must be entitled to quality educational supports, decent and affordable housing, financial security, recreation, and employment.

The attitudes and progressive policies of the 21st century bring considerable hope to the lives of people with severe and multiple disabilities. Inclusive education is increasing in our schools; opportunities to live and work in the community are no longer just a dream; and every day the critical support that is needed from family, friends, neighbors, and professionals becomes more and more a natural part of the lives of people with severe disabilities.

FOCUS REVIEW

FOCUS 1 What are the three components of the TASH definition of severe disabilities?

- The relationship of the individual within the environment (adaptive fit)
- The inclusion of people of all ages
- The necessity of extensive ongoing support in life activities

FOCUS 2 Define the terms *multiple disabilities* and *deaf–blindness* as described in Individuals with Disabilities Education Act (IDEA).

- The term *multiple disabilities* refers to concomitant impairments (such as intellectual disabilities and orthopedic impairments). The combination causes educational problems so severe that they cannot be accommodated in special education programs designed solely for one impairment. One such combination is "dual diagnosis," a condition characterized by serious emotional disturbance (challenging behaviors) in conjunction with severe intellectual disabilities.
- *Deaf–blindness* involves concomitant hearing and visual impairments. The combination causes communication and other developmental and educational problems so severe that they cannot be accommodated in special education programs designed solely for children who are deaf or blind.

FOCUS 3 Identify the estimated prevalence and causes of severe and multiple disabilities.

- Prevalence estimates generally range from 0.1 percent to 1 percent of the general population.
- Students with multiple disabilities recently accounted for about 2 percent of the 7 million students with disabilities served in the public schools. Approximately 0.0002 percent of students with disabilities were labeled deaf–blind.
- Many possible causes of severe and multiple disabilities exist. Most severe and multiple disabilities are evident at birth. Birth defects may be the result of genetic or metabolic problems. Most identifiable causes of severe intellectual disabilities and related developmental disabilities are genetic in origin. Factors associated with poisoning, accidents, malnutrition, physical and emotional neglect, and disease are also known causes.

FOCUS 4 What are the characteristics of people with severe and multiple disabilities?

- Having intellectual disabilities is often a primary condition.
- Most children will not benefit from basic academic instruction in literacy and mathematics. Instruction in functional academics is the most effective approach to learning academic skills.
- People with severe and multiple disabilities often do not have age-appropriate adaptive skills and need ongoing services and supports to facilitate learning in this area.
- Significant speech and language deficits and delays are a primary characteristic.

- Physical and health needs are common, involving conditions such as congenital heart disease, epilepsy, respiratory problems, spasticity, athetosis, and hypotonia. Vision and hearing loss are also common.

FOCUS 5 Identify three types of educational assessments for students with severe and multiple disabilities.

- Traditionally, there has been a heavy reliance on standardized assessments, particularly the IQ test, in identifying people with severe and multiple disabilities.
- Assessments that focus on valued skills to promote independence and quality of life in natural settings are referred to as *functional, ecological,* or *authentic assessment.*
- Students with disabilities must participate in statewide and district-wide assessments of achievement, or the school must explain why that assessment is not appropriate for the child. For many students with severe disabilities, these assessments are inappropriate, and the students with disabilities are excluded from taking them. Alternate assessments are conducted instead.

FOCUS 6 Identify the features of effective services and supports for children with severe and multiple disabilities during the early childhood years.

- Services and supports must begin at birth.
- Programs for infants and toddlers are both child- and family-centered.
- The goals for preschool programs are to maximize development across several developmental areas, to develop social interaction and classroom participation skills, to increase community participation through support to family and caregivers, and to prepare the child for inclusive school placement.
- Effective and inclusive preschool programs have a holistic view of the child, see the classroom as a community of learners, base the program on a collaborative ethic, use authentic assessment, create a heterogeneous environment, make available a range of individualized supports and services, engage educators in reflective teaching, and emphasize multiple ways of teaching and learning.

FOCUS 7 Identify the features of effective services and supports for children with severe and multiple disabilities during the elementary school years.

- Self-determination is important—student preferences and needs are taken into account in developing educational objectives.
- The school values and supports parental involvement.
- Instruction focuses on frequently used functional skills related to everyday life activities.
- Assistive technology and augmentative communication are available to maintain or increase the functional capabilities of the student with severe and multiple disabilities.

FOCUS 8 Describe four outcomes that are important in planning for the transition from school to adult life for adolescents with severe and multiple disabilities.

- Establishing a network of friends and acquaintances
- Developing the ability to use community resources on a regular basis
- Securing a paid job that supports the use of community resources and interaction with peers
- Establishing independence and autonomy in making lifestyle choices

FOCUS 9 Describe three features that characterize successful inclusive education for students with severe and multiple disabilities.

- Physical placement of students with severe and multiple disabilities in the general education schools and classes they would attend if they didn't have disabilities
- Systematic organization of opportunities for interaction between students with severe and multiple disabilities and students without disabilities
- Specific instruction in valued postschool outcomes that will increase the competence of students with severe and multiple disabilities in the natural settings of family, school, and community

Council for Exceptional Children (CEC) Standards to Accompany Chapter 12

 If you are thinking about a career in special education, you should know that many states use national standards developed by the Council for Exceptional Children (CEC) to assess a teacher candidate's knowledge and skills for working with students with disabilities. See a complete listing of the 10 CEC Content Standards on the inside back cover of this text.

1 Foundations
2 Development and Characteristics of Learners
3 Individual Learning Differences
4 Instructional Strategies
5 Learning Environments and Social Interactions
7 Instructional Planning
8 Assessment

Mastery Activities and Assignments

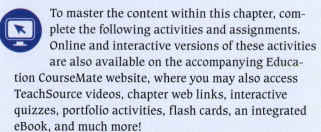 To master the content within this chapter, complete the following activities and assignments. Online and interactive versions of these activities are also available on the accompanying Education CourseMate website, where you may also access TeachSource videos, chapter web links, interactive quizzes, portfolio activities, flash cards, an integrated eBook, and much more!

1. Complete a written test of the chapter's content. If your instructor requires a written test of your content knowledge for this chapter, keep a copy for your portfolio. A practice test on the information covered in this chapter is available through the Education CourseMate website.

2. Review the Case Study, "David," and respond in writing to the Application Questions. Keep a copy of the case study and your written response for your portfolio.

3. Read the Debate Forum, "Can Special Schools for Students with Severe and Multiple Disabilities Be Justified?," in this chapter and then visit the Education CourseMate website to complete the activity "Take a Stand." Keep a copy of this activity for your portfolio.

4. Participate in a community service learning activity. Service learning is a valuable way to enhance your learning experience. Visit the Education CourseMate website for suggested community service learning activities that correspond to the information presented in this chapter. Develop a reflective journal of the service learning experience for your portfolio.

CHAPTER 13

Sensory Disabilities: Hearing and Vision Loss

© The Star-Ledger/John Munson/The Image Works

FOCUS PREVIEW

As you read the chapter, focus on these key concepts:

1 Describe how sound is transmitted through the human ear.

2 Distinguish between the terms *deaf* and *hard of hearing*.

3 What are the estimated prevalence, causes, and characteristics of hearing loss?

4 Identify four approaches to teaching communication skills to people with a hearing loss.

5 Why is early detection of hearing loss so important?

6 Distinguish between the terms *blind* and *partially sighted*.

7 What are the distinctive features of refractive eye problems, muscle disorders of the eye, and receptive eye problems?

8 What are the estimated prevalence, causes, and characteristics of vision loss?

9 Describe two content areas that should be included in educational programs for students with vision loss.

10 Why is the availability of appropriate health care and social services important for people with vision loss?

Tamika

Tamika Catchings is the all-star forward for the WNBA's Indiana Fever and two-time Olympic gold medalist. . . . She proudly admits to being an organization freak—in high school she would plan her outfits a month in advance. [Tamika] speaks with a slight speech impediment, as if she hadn't quite come out from under a shot of Novocain. She was born with fairly severe hearing loss in both ears, so she cannot hear certain tones, pitches, or sounds, like "ch" and "th," even in her own voice, an impairment that for years she tried, quite successfully, to hide from anyone outside her family. In third grade, fed up with the abuse from classmates, she tossed her hearing aids into a field and refused to wear new ones.

[Tamika's] hearing problem forced her to learn to read lips, which has left her with the habit of looking intently at anyone who is speaking to her (except while driving). For a professional athlete who was a four-time all-American in both high school and college, she can be surprisingly deferential. When Van Chancellor, the coach of the United States national women's basketball team, chewed out Catchings in practice by informing her that great players have to back on defense, Catchings wrote him a letter thanking him for thinking of her as a great player.

Almost every program in the country recruited her, and Catchings wrote thank-you notes to each of the 200 schools that contacted her. ("For me not to say anything would have been selfish," she says.) But she had wanted to go to [the University of] Tennessee since eighth grade, when she caught a glimpse of the Lady Vols

© Pat Lovell/Cal Sport Media/Newscom

coach, Pat Summitt, on TV. Summitt is perhaps the one on-court presence in basketball who is more intense than [Tamika]—she has been known to dent her rings by pounding her hands on the hardwood during a particularly trying game. She also demands that her players buy daily planners and schedule their days in minute increments.

SOURCE: Adams, M. (2003). Elevated: Tamika Catchings will not let her niceness, or her deafness, prevent her from becoming the best player in the W.N.B.A. *New York Times Magazine*, May 25, pp. 26–29. Copyright © 2003, Mark Adams.

Update on Tamika from 2004–2012

In 2004, Tamika was named a three-time WNBA Community Assist Award winner for her outstanding involvement in the community. During August 2004, Catchings was a starter on the USA women's basketball team and helped bring home the gold after a perfect performance in Athens, Greece. In 2006, Tamika's community contributions earned her the honor of being a finalist for the Coach John Wooden Citizenship

Cup award, awarded by Athletes for a Better World. She is the Indiana Fever's first 2,000-point scorer and is among the WNBA's top career leaders in several categories. During the 2007 season, she was named an All-Star starter for the sixth time in her career. Tamika became the first recipient of the Dawn Staley Community Leadership Award for her commitment to being a positive role model and bettering the community. Following a season-ending injury during the 2007 season, she bounced back to rejoin the Indiana Fever and was able to help Team USA win consecutive gold medals at the Beijing Olympics. In 2009, the WNBA's MVP runner-up led the team in rebounds, steals, and assists. She won her third WNBA Defensive Player of the Year and was named to the All-WNBA First Team. A WNBA MVP runner-up for the second straight season, Catchings posted perhaps her finest year in 2010. She led the WNBA in steals (77) for the fourth time and recorded a season-high 30 points over eventual East champion Atlanta. In addition to being named to the All-WNBA First Team and WNBA All-Defensive Team, she received the league's Kim Perrot Sportsmanship Award. In 2011, the WNBA awarded Tamika with the MVP Award as she led the Fever to the playoffs. One of her future goals is to open a full-service community center with basketball courts, fitness equipment, computer rooms, and a reading corner.

SOURCE: The Official Website of Tamika Catchings. (2012). Retrieved March 12, 2012, from www.catchin24.com/bio/.

A Changing Era in the Lives of People with Sensory Impairments

In a world controlled by sight and sound, the ability to see and hear is a critical link to our overall development and perspectives on the world. Children who can hear learn to talk by listening to those around them. Everyday communication systems depend on sound. What, then, would it be like to live in a world that is silent? People talk, but you hear nothing. The television and movie screens are lit up with moving pictures, but you can't hear and understand what is going on. Your friends talk about their favorite music and hum tunes that have no meaning to you. A fire engine's siren wails as it moves through traffic, but you are oblivious to its warning. To people with hearing, the thought of such a world can be very frightening. To those without hearing, it is quite simply their world—a place that can be lonely, frustrating, and downright discriminatory. Persons with a hearing loss may live in isolation from everyday interactions that make life enjoyable. They may feel alienated from friends, family, and the community, and this alienation can evolve into a strong sense of fear and a need to avoid the hearing world.

The frustration of a hearing loss may be felt not only by the person experiencing the loss, but by those who are close to the individual. This is exemplified by siblings who often feel they are being ignored because their brother or sister with a hearing loss does not respond when called from another room or when their back is turned. Since hearing loss is an "invisible disability", people who are able to hear often forget to make needed accommodations. It is all too common for a person with who can hear accuse the person with a hearing loss of "selectively listening" –that is choosing what they do or don't want to hear.

Yet, the most common emotion for people with a hearing loss is the embarrassment that comes from not hearing oral instructions, missing key points in a conversation, or not laughing at someone else's joke. Unfortunately, isolation, fear, frustration, and embarrassment may also characterize the everyday life experiences for individuals with a vision loss. Through the visual process, we observe the world around us, and develop an appreciation for the physical environment and a greater understanding of it. Vision is one of our most important avenues for the acquisition and assimilation of knowledge, but we often take it for granted. From the moment we wake up in the morning, our dependence on sight is obvious. We rely on our eyes to guide us around our surroundings, inform us through the written word, and give us pleasure and relaxation.

What if this precious sight were lost or impaired? How would our perceptions of the world change? Losing sight is one of our greatest fears, partly because of the misconception that people with vision loss are helpless and unable to lead satisfying or productive lives. It is not uncommon for people with sight to have little understanding of those with vision loss. People who are sighted may believe that most adults who are blind are likely to live a deprived socioeconomic and cultural existence. Children who have sight may believe that their peers who are blind are incapable of learning many basic skills, such as telling time and using a computer, or of enjoying leisure and recreational activities such as swimming and watching television. Throughout history, some religions have even promoted the belief that blindness is a punishment for sins. As you will see in this chapter, the negative perceptions about people with a hearing or vision loss are often inaccurate and misleading. The vast majority of people with a sensory impairment lead active and productive lives and do not allow their hearing or vision loss to deprive them of the life activities they love and value. They experience joy, fulfillment, and a life of endless possibilities no different from than that experienced by people who can hear or see.

In this chapter, we take a closer look into the lives of people with sensory impairments—those with vision or hearing loss. We begin our journey with the nearby Snapshot of Tamika Catchings, professional basketball player, all-star, and community leader who also happens to be a person with a hearing loss.

FOCUS 1

Describe how sound is transmitted through the human ear.

Hearing Loss

Although Tamika from our opening Snapshot is unable to hear many sounds, her life is one of independence, success, and fulfillment. For Tamika, just as for many people who are deaf or hard of hearing, the obstacles presented by the loss of hearing are not insurmountable.

People with a hearing loss are able to learn about the world around them in any number of ways, such as lip-reading, gestures, pictures, and writing. Some people are able to use their residual hearing with the assistance of a hearing aid. For others, a hearing aid doesn't help because it only makes distorted sounds louder. To express themselves, some people prefer to use their voices; others prefer to use a visual sign language. Most people with a hearing loss use a combination of speech and signing. People with a hearing loss, such as Tamika, may seek and find success in the hearing world. Others seek to be part of a deaf community or deaf culture to share a common language (American Sign Language) and customs. In a deaf culture, those within the community share a common heritage and traditions. People often marry others from within the community. They also have a shared literature and participate in the deaf community's political, business, arts, and sports programs. People in the deaf community do not see the loss of hearing as a disability. From their perspective, being deaf is not an impairment and should not be looked upon as a pathology or disease that requires treatment.

The Hearing Process

To understand hearing loss, we must first understand how normal hearing works. **Audition** is the act or sense of hearing. The auditory process involves the transmission of sound through the vibration of an object to a receiver. The process originates with a vibrator—such as a string, reed, membrane, or column of air—that causes displacement of air particles. To become sound, a vibration must have a medium to carry it. Air is the most common carrier, but vibrations can also be carried by metal, water, and other substances. The displacement of air particles by the vibrator produces a pattern of circular waves that move away from the source.

Audition
The act or sense of hearing.

This movement, which is referred to as a sound wave, can be illustrated by imagining the ripples resulting from a pebble dropped in a pool of water. Sound waves are patterns of pressure that alternately push together and pull apart in a spherical expansion. Sound waves are carried through a medium (e.g., air) to a receiver. The human ear is one of the most sensitive receivers there is; it is capable of being activated by incredibly small amounts of pressure and being able to distinguish more than a half million different sounds. The ear is the mechanism through which sound is collected, processed, and transmitted to an area in the brain that decodes the sensations into meaningful language. The anatomy of the hearing mechanism is discussed in terms of the outer, middle, and inner ears. These structures are illustrated in Figure 13.1.

Figure 13.1 *Structure of the Ear*

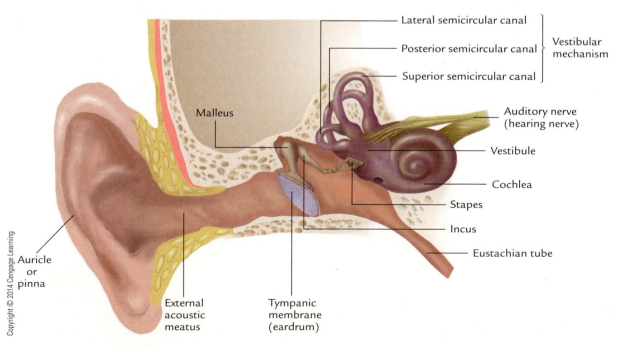

Copyright © 2014 Cengage Learning

Definitions of Hearing Loss

FOCUS 2

Distinguish between the terms *deaf* and *hard of hearing*.

Two terms, *deaf* and *hard of hearing* (or *partial hearing*), are commonly used to indicate the severity of a person's hearing loss. *Deaf* is often overused and misunderstood and is commonly applied to describe a wide spectrum of hearing loss. However, as discussed in this chapter, the term should be used in a more precise fashion.

Hearing loss may be defined according to the degree of hearing impairment, which is determined by assessing a person's sensitivity to loudness (sound intensity) and pitch (sound frequency). The unit used to measure sound intensity is the decibel (dB); the range of human hearing is approximately 0 to 130 dB. Sounds louder than 130 dB (such as those made by jet aircraft at 140 dB) are extremely painful to the ear. Conversational speech registers at 40 to 60 dB, loud thunder at about 120 dB, and a rock concert at about 110 dB.

Hertz (hz)
A unit used to measure the frequency of sound in terms of the number of cycles that vibrating molecules complete per second.

The frequency of sound is determined by measuring the number of cycles that vibrating molecules complete per second. The unit used to measure cycles per second is the **hertz** (Hz). The higher the frequency, the greater the measure in hertz. The human ear can hear sounds ranging from 20 to approximately 13,000 Hz. Speech sounds range in pitch from 300 to 4,000 Hz, whereas the pitches made by a piano keyboard range from 27.5 to 4,186 Hz. Although the human ear can hear sounds at the 13,000 Hz level, the vast majority of sounds in our environment range from 300 to 4,000 Hz.

Deafness

Deafness
A hearing loss greater than 90 dB. Deaf individuals have vision as their primary input and cannot understand speech through the ear.

Deafness describes people whose hearing loss is in the extreme: 90 dB or greater. Even with the use of hearing aids or other forms of amplification, the primary means for developing language and communication for people who are deaf is through the visual channel. **Deafness** as defined by the Individuals with Disabilities Education Act (IDEA) means "a hearing impairment which is so severe that the child is impaired in processing linguistic information through hearing, with or without amplification, which adversely affects educational performance" (IDEA, 34 C.F.R. 300.7).

A person who is deaf is most often described as someone who cannot hear sound. Consequently, the individual is unable to understand human speech. Many people who are deaf have enough residual hearing to recognize sound at certain frequencies, but they still may be unable to determine the meaning of the sound pressure waves.

Hard of Hearing (Partial Hearing)

Hard of hearing
A sense of hearing that is deficient but somewhat functional.

For people defined as **hard of hearing**, audition is deficient but remains somewhat functional. Individuals who are hard of hearing have enough residual hearing that, with the use of a hearing aid, they are able to process human speech auditorily.

The distinction between deaf and hard of hearing, based on the functional use of residual hearing, is not as clear as many traditional definitions imply. New breakthroughs in the development of hearing aids, as well as improved diagnostic procedures, have enabled many children labeled deaf to use their hearing functionally under limited circumstances.

In addition to the individual's sensitivity to loudness and pitch, two other factors are involved in defining deafness and hard of hearing: the age of onset and the anatomical site of the loss.

Prelingual loss
Pertaining to hearing impairments occurring prior to the age of 2, or the time of speech development.

Postlingual loss
Pertaining to hearing impairments occurring at any age following speech development.

Age of Onset Hearing loss may be present at birth (congenital) or acquired at any time during life. **Prelingual loss** occurs prior to the age of 2, or before speech development. **Postlingual loss** occurs at any age following speech acquisition. In nine out of ten children, deafness occurs at birth or prior to the child's learning to speak. The distinction between a congenital and an acquired hearing loss is important. The age of onset will be a critical variable in determining the type and extent of interventions necessary to minimize the effect of the individual's disability. This is particularly true in relation to speech and language development. A person who is born with hearing loss has significantly more challenges, particularly in the areas of communication and social adaptation (Centers for Disease Control, 2012; Correa-Torres, 2008).

Anatomical Site of the Hearing Loss In terms of anatomical location, the two primary types of hearing loss are peripheral problems and central auditory problems. There are three types of peripheral hearing loss: conductive, sensorineural, and mixed. A **conductive hearing loss** results from poor conduction of sound along the passages leading to the sense organ (inner ear). The loss may result from a blockage in the external canal, as well as from an obstruction interfering with the movement of the eardrum or ossicle. The overall effect is a reduction or loss of loudness. A conductive loss can be offset by amplification (hearing aids) and medical intervention. Surgery has been effective in reducing a conductive loss or even in restoring hearing.

A **sensorineural hearing loss** results from an abnormal sense organ and a damaged auditory nerve. A sensorineural loss may distort sound, affecting the clarity of human speech; it cannot presently be treated adequately through medical intervention. A sensorineural loss is generally more severe than a conductive loss and is permanent. Losses of greater than 70 dB are usually sensorineural and involve severe damage to the inner ear. One common way to determine whether a loss is conductive or sensorineural is to administer an air and bone conduction test. An individual with a conductive loss would be unable to hear a vibrating tuning fork held close to the ear, because of blocked air passages to the inner ear, but may be able to hear the same fork applied to the skull just as well as someone with normal hearing would. An individual with a sensorineural loss would not be able to hear the vibrating fork, regardless of its placement. This test is not always accurate, however, and must therefore be used with caution in distinguishing between conductive and sensorineural losses. **Mixed hearing loss**, a combination of conductive and sensorineural problems, can also be assessed through the use of an air and bone conduction test. In the case of a mixed loss, abnormalities are evident in both tests.

Although most hearing losses are peripheral, as are conductive and sensorineural problems, some occur where there is no measurable peripheral loss. This type of loss, which is referred to as a central auditory disorder, occurs when there is a dysfunction in the cerebral cortex. The cerebral cortex, the outer layer of gray matter of the brain, governs thought, reasoning, memory, sensation, and voluntary movement. Consequently, a central auditory problem is not a loss in the ability to hear sound, but a disorder of symbolic processes, including auditory perception, discrimination, comprehension of sound, and language development (expressive and receptive).

Conductive hearing loss A hearing loss resulting from poor conduction of sound along the passages leading to the sense organ.

Sensorineural hearing loss A hearing loss resulting from an abnormal sense organ (inner ear) and a damaged auditory nerve.

Mixed hearing loss A hearing loss resulting from a combination of conductive and sensorineural problems.

Classification of Hearing Loss

Hearing loss may be classified according to the severity of the condition. The symptom severity classification system shown in Table 13.1 presents information relative to a child's ability to understand speech patterns at the various severity levels.

Classification systems based solely on a person's degree of hearing loss should be used with a great deal of caution when determining appropriate services and supports. These systems do not reflect the person's capabilities, background, or experience; they

Table 13.1 Classification of Hearing Loss

Hearing Loss in Decibels (dB)	Classification	Effect on Ability to Understand Speech
0 to 13	Normal hearing	None
16 to 25	Slight hearing loss	Minimal difficulty with soft speech
26 to 40	Mild hearing loss	Difficulty with soft speech
41 to 55	Moderate hearing loss	Frequent difficulty with normal speech
56 to 70	Moderate to severe hearing loss	Occasional difficulty with loud speech
71 to 90	Severe hearing loss	Frequent difficulty with loud speech
> 91	Profound hearing loss	Near total or total loss of hearing

merely suggest parameters for measuring a physical defect in auditory function. As a young child, for example, Tamika from the opening Snapshot was diagnosed as having a hearing loss in both ears, yet throughout her life she successfully adjusted to both school and community experiences. Clearly, many factors beyond the severity of the hearing loss must be assessed when determining an individual's potential. In addition to severity of loss, factors such as general intelligence, emotional stability, scope and quality of early education and training, the family environment, and the occurrence of other disabilities must also be considered.

Prevalence, Causes, and Characteristics of Hearing Loss

FOCUS 3

What are the estimated prevalence, causes, and characteristics of hearing loss?

Hearing loss usually gets worse over time and increases dramatically with age. Estimates of hearing loss in the United States go as high as 28 million people. Of these 28 million, approximately 11 million people have significant irreversible hearing loss, and one million are deaf. Only 5 percent of people with hearing loss are under the age of 17; nearly 43 percent are over the age of 65. Contrast this to the fact that only 12 percent of the general population is over the age of 65 years (Centers for Disease Control, 2012; National Academy on an Aging Society, 2012). Men are more likely than women to have a hearing loss; caucasians are proportionately overrepresented among people with a hearing loss. The prevalence of hearing loss decreases as family income and education increase (National Academy on an Aging Society, 2012).

The U.S. Department of Education (2011) indicated that more than 73,000 students defined as having a hearing impairment and between the ages of 6 and 21 are receiving special education services. These students account for approximately .1 percent of school-age students identified in the United States as having a disability. It is important to note that these figures represent only those students who receive special education services; a number of students with hearing loss who could benefit from additional services do not receive them. Of the students with a hearing loss receiving special education, approximately 49 percent were being served in general education classrooms for at least 80 percent of the school day. Another 39 percent spent at least a part of their day in a general education classroom, 12 percent in separate public/private day schools or residential living facilities for students with a hearing loss (ibid.).

CEC

Standard 2
Development and Characteristics of Learners

Causation

A number of congenital (existing at birth) or acquired factors may result in a hearing loss. Approximately one child in a thousand is born deaf because of factors associated with heredity, maternal rubella or German measles, or drugs taken during pregnancy. Substance abuse, disease, and constant exposure to loud noises are all causes of hearing loss. Loss of hearing is also a normal part of the aging process, beginning as early as the teen years when the high-frequency hearing of childhood starts to diminish.

Heredity Although more than 200 types of deafness have been related to hereditary factors, the cause of 18 percent of prelingual hearing loss remains unknown (Center for Assessment and Demographic Studies, 2012). However, current doctors and researchers do understand some genetic forms of hearing loss and deafness, such as **Connexin 26**. Connexin 26 is a complex genetic disorder that leads to flawed copies of the gap junction protein, beta 2 (GJB2), gene. Everyone has two copies of this gene, but if both birth parents have flawed copies of the GJB2/Connexin 26 gene, they may unknowingly pass the hearing loss on to their newborn child. Because genetic defects that cause hearing loss are usually rare, they are not included in routine prenatal genetic screenings. One of the most common diseases affecting the sense of hearing is **otosclerosis**. The cause of this disease is unknown, but it is generally believed to be hereditary and is manifested most often in early adulthood. About 10 percent of adults have otosclerosis; it can be passed from one generation to the next but not manifest itself for several generations.

Connexin 26
A genetic disorder that leads to flawed copies of the beta 2 gene. If both birth parents have flawed copies of this gene, they may unknowingly pass a hearing loss on to their newborn child.

Otosclerosis
A disease of the ear characterized by destruction of the capsular bone in the middle ear and the growth of a weblike bone that attaches to the stapes. The stapes is restricted and unable to function properly.

The disease is characterized by destruction of the capsular bone in the middle ear and the growth of weblike bone that attaches to the stapes. Hearing loss results in about 13 percent of all cases of otosclerosis and at a rate for females that is twice the rate for males. Victims of otosclerosis suffer from high-pitched throbbing or ringing sounds known as **tinnitus**. There is no specific treatment or any medication that will improve the hearing in people with otosclerosis. Surgery (stapedectomy) may be recommended when the stapes (stirrup) bone is involved.

Tinnitus
High-pitched throbbing or ringing sounds in the ear, associated with disease of the inner ear.

Prenatal Disease

Several conditions, although not inherited, can result in sensorineural loss. The major cause of congenital deafness is infection, of which rubella, cytomegalovirus (CMV), and toxoplasmosis are the most common. The rubella epidemic of 1963 to 1965 dramatically increased the incidence of deafness in the United States. During the 1960s, approximately 10 percent of all congenital deafness was associated with women contracting rubella during pregnancy. For about 40 percent of the individuals who are deaf, the cause is rubella. About 50 percent of all children with rubella incur a severe hearing loss. Most hearing losses caused by rubella are sensorineural, although a small percentage may be mixed. In addition to hearing loss, children who have had rubella sometimes acquire heart disease (50 percent), cataracts or glaucoma (40 percent), and intellectual disabilities (40 percent). Since the advent of the rubella vaccine, the elimination of this disease has become a nationwide campaign, and the incidence of rubella has dramatically decreased.

Congenital cytomegalovirus (CMV) is viral infection that spreads by close contact with another person who is shedding the virus in body secretions. It is also spread by blood transfusions and from a mother to her newborn infant. CMV is the most frequently occurring virus among newborns and is characterized by jaundice, microcephaly, hemolytic anemia, mental retardation, hepatosplenomegaly (enlargement of the liver and spleen), and hearing loss. Although no vaccine is currently available to treat CMV, some preventive measures can be taken—such as ensuring safe blood transfusions, practicing good hygiene, and avoiding contact with people who have the virus. CMV is detectable in utero through amniocentesis.

Congenital cytomegalovirus (CMV)
Viral infection that spreads by close contact with another person who is shedding the virus in body secretions.

Congenital toxoplasmosis infection is characterized by jaundice and anemia, but frequently the disease also results in central nervous system disorders (such as seizures, **hydrocephalus**, and microcephaly). Approximately 13 percent of infants born with this disease are deaf.

Congenital toxoplasmosis infection
Characterized by jaundice and anemia, this disease frequently results in central nervous system disorders.

Hydrocephalus
Condition resulting in excess cerebrospinal fluid in the brain.

Other factors associated with congenital sensorineural hearing loss include maternal Rh-factor incompatibility and the use of ototoxic drugs. Maternal Rh-factor incompatibility does not generally affect a firstborn child, but as antibodies are produced during subsequent pregnancies, multiple problems can result, including deafness. Fortunately, deafness as a result of Rh-factor problems is no longer common. Since the advent of an anti-Rh gamma globulin (RhoGAM) in 1968, the incidence of Rh-factor incompatibility has significantly decreased. If RhoGAM is injected into the mother within the first 72 hours after the birth of the first child, she does not produce antibodies that harm future unborn infants.

A condition known as **atresia** is a major cause of congenital conductive hearing loss. Congenital aural atresia results when the external auditory canal is either malformed or completely absent at birth. A congenital malformation may lead to a blockage of the ear canal through an accumulation of cerumen, which is a wax that hardens and blocks incoming sound waves from being transmitted to the middle ear.

Atresia
The absence of a normal opening or cavity.

Postnatal Disease

One of the most common causes of hearing loss in the postnatal period is infection. Postnatal infections—such as measles, mumps, influenza, typhoid fever, and scarlet fever—are all associated with hearing loss. Meningitis is an inflammation of the membranes that cover the brain and spinal cord and is a cause of severe hearing loss in school-age children. Sight loss, paralysis, and brain damage are further complications of this disease. The incidence of meningitis has significantly declined over the three decades, however, thanks to the development of antibiotics and chemotherapy.

SuperStock

Loud noise is a leading cause of hearing problems. Adolescents are subjected to damaging noise levels when headphones on CD, MP3, or DVD players are turned up too high.

Otitis media
An inflammation of the middle ear.

Another common problem that may result from postnatal infection is **otitis media**, an inflammation of the middle ear. This condition, which results from severe colds that spread from the eustachian tube to the middle ear, is the most common cause of conductive hearing loss in younger children. Otitis media (also called "ear infection") ranks second to the common cold as the most common health problem in preschool children. Three out of every four children have had at least one episode by the age of 3. The disease is difficult to diagnose, especially in infancy, at which time symptoms are often absent. Otitis media has been found to be highly correlated with hearing problems (Moore, 2007; National Institute on Deafness and Other Communication Disorders, 2012c).

Environmental Factors Environmental factors—including extreme changes in air pressure caused by explosions, physical abuse of the cranial area, impact from foreign objects during accidents, and loud music—also contribute to acquired hearing loss. Loud noise is rapidly becoming a major cause of hearing problems; about 30 million people are subjected to dangerous noise levels in everyday life (National Institute on Deafness and Other Communication Disorders, 2012c; Owen, 2007). Most of us are subjected to hazardous noise, such as noise from jet engines and loud music, more often than ever before. With the popularity of headphones and earbuds, such as those used with iPods or MP3 players, many people (particularly adolescents) are subjected to damaging noise levels. Occupational noises (such as those from jackhammers, tractors, and sirens) are now the leading cause of sensorineural hearing loss. Other factors associated with acquired hearing loss include degenerative processes in the ear that may come with aging, cerebral hemorrhages, allergies, and intercranial tumors.

Characteristics

The effects of hearing loss on the learning or social adjustment of individuals are extremely varied, ranging from far-reaching (as in prelingual sensorineural deafness) to quite minimal (as in a mild postlingual conductive loss). Fortunately, prevention, early detection, and intervention have recently been emphasized, resulting in a much improved prognosis for individuals who are deaf or hard of hearing.

Intelligence Research on the intellectual characteristics of children with hearing loss has suggested that the distribution of IQ scores for these individuals is similar to that of hearing children (Marschark, Lang, & Albertini, 2007; Moores, 2008). Findings suggest that intellectual development for people with hearing loss is more a function of language development than of cognitive ability. Any difficulties in performance appear to be closely associated with speaking, reading, and writing the English language, but are not related to level of intelligence. For example, children using sign language have to divide their attention between the signs and the instructional materials. Although the child may seem slower in learning, it may be that the child simply needs more time to process the information.

Speech and English Language Skills Speech and English language skills are the areas of development most severely affected for those with a hearing loss, particularly for children who are born deaf. These children develop speech at a slower pace than their peers with normal hearing; thus, they are at greater risk for emotional difficulties and isolation from their peers and family (Hintermair, 2008; Kaland & Salvatore, 2012; Rathmann, Mann, & Morgan, 2007). The effects of a hearing loss on English language development vary considerably. For children with mild and moderate hearing losses, the effects may be minimal. Even for individuals born with moderate losses, effective communication skills are possible because the voiced sounds of conversational speech remain audible. Although individuals with moderate losses cannot hear unvoiced sounds

CEC

Standard 2
Development and Characteristics of Learners

Standard 3
Individual Learning Differences

(such as a sigh or cough) and distant speech, English language delays can be prevented if the hearing loss is diagnosed and treated early (Hintermair, 2008). The majority of people with hearing loss are able to use speech as the primary mode of English language acquisition.

For the person who is congenitally deaf, most loud speech is inaudible, even with the use of the most sophisticated hearing aids. These people are unable to receive information through speech unless they have learned to lip-read. Sounds produced by people who are deaf may be extremely difficult to understand. Children who are deaf exhibit significant problems in articulation, voice quality, and tone discrimination. Even as early as 8 months of age, babies who are deaf appear to babble less than babies who can hear. One way to assist these babies in developing language is to provide early and specialized training in English language production and comprehension. Another approach is to teach them sign language long before they learn to speak. Since hand-eye coordination develops earlier in infants than verbal skills, signs, such as "yes", "no", "please", "more", "stop", or "milk", can be learned before any speech develops. For the infant or toddler with a hearing loss, it is the ability to communicate with parents, teachers, and caregivers that is critical. Sign language can be a very functional form of communication as exemplified in the situation below.

> *"Languishing in front of the TV, watching a gripping episode of* Teletubbies, *a baby of 10 months waves down Mom and signals for a bottle of the good stuff. No crying, no fuss. He just moves his hands in a pantomime of milking a cow—the international sign for* milk. *Mom smiles, signs back her agreement, and fetches Junior's bottle"* (McKeen, 2012).

Parents of infants with a hearing loss often ask the question, "At what age can I begin to teach sign language?" It is important to remember that a hearing loss is most often not related to cognitive ability. Therefore, infants with a hearing loss can learn cognitive tasks, such as signing, at the same age as their hearing peers (about 8 months). Gestures, such as throwing kisses or waving "bye-bye" are forms of sign language.

Educational Achievement

The educational achievements of students with a hearing loss may be significantly delayed compared with achievements of students who can hear. Students who are deaf or have a partial hearing loss have considerable difficulty succeeding in an educational system that depends primarily on the spoken word and written language to transmit knowledge. Low achievement is characteristic of students who are deaf (Heine & Slone, 2008;

Huntstock/Jupiterimages

Sign language can enhance the communication and language skills of young children with a hearing loss.

Marschark, Lang, & Albertini, 2007); they average three to four years below their age-appropriate grade levels. Reading is the academic area most negatively affected for students with a hearing loss. Any hearing loss, whether mild or profound, appears to have detrimental effects on reading performance (Gallaudet Research Institute, 2012; Narr, 2008). To counteract the difficulty with conventional reading materials, specialized instructional programs have been developed for students with a hearing loss (Marschark & Spencer, 2011; McAnally, Rose, & Quigley, 2005; Poobrasert & Cercone, 2009).

DEBATE FORUM
LIVING IN A DEAF CULTURE

Deaf culture: a cultural group comprised of people who share similar and positive attitudes toward deafness. The "core deaf culture" consists of those people who have a hearing loss and who share a common language, values, experiences, and a common way of interacting with one another. The broader deaf community is made up of individuals (both deaf and hearing) who have positive, accepting attitudes toward deafness that can be seen in their linguistic, social, and political behaviors. People in a deaf culture seek out one another for social interaction and emotional support.

The inability to hear and understand speech may lead an individual to seek community ties and social relationships primarily with other individuals who are deaf. These individuals may choose to isolate themselves from hearing peers and to live, learn, work, and play in a social subculture known as "a deaf culture" or "deaf community."

POINT

The deaf culture is a necessary and important component of life for many people who are deaf. People who are deaf have a great deal of difficulty adjusting to life in a hearing world. Through the deaf culture, they can find other individuals with similar problems, common interests, a common language (American Sign Language), and a common heritage and culture. Membership in the deaf culture is an achieved status that must be earned by the individuals who are deaf. The individuals must demonstrate a strong identification with the deaf world, understand and share experiences that come with being deaf, and be willing to participate actively in the deaf community's educational, cultural, and political activities. The deaf culture gives such people a positive identity that cannot be found among their hearing peers.

COUNTERPOINT

Participation in the deaf culture only serves to isolate people who are deaf from those who hear. A separate subculture unnecessarily accentuates the differences between people who can and who cannot hear. The lives of people who are deaf need not be different from that of anyone else. Children who are deaf can be integrated into general education schools and classrooms. People who are deaf can live side by side with their hearing peers in local communities, sharing common bonds and interests. There is no reason why they cannot participate together in the arts, enjoy sports, and share leisure and recreational interests. Membership in the deaf culture will only further reinforce the idea that people who have disabilities should both grow up and live in a culture away from those who do not. The majority of people who are deaf do not seek membership in the deaf culture. These people are concerned that the existence of such a community makes it all the more difficult for them to assimilate into society at large.

What Do You Think? Please visit the Education CourseMate website for Human Exceptionality, *11th edition, to access and respond to questions related to the Debate Forum.*

Social Development A hearing loss modifies a person's capacity to receive and process auditory stimuli. People who are deaf or have a partial hearing loss receive a reduced amount of auditory information. That information is also distorted, compared with the auditory input received by those with normal hearing. Thus, the perceptions of auditory information by people with a hearing loss, particularly those who are deaf, will differ from those who can hear. Ultimately, this difference in perception has a direct effect on each individual's social adjustment to the hearing world.

Jamie Squire/Getty Images

When 20-year-old Terence Parkin arrived at the Sydney 2000 Olympic Games, his goal was to make his mark for South Africa and show the world what people who are deaf can accomplish. Terence, who was born with a severe hearing disability and uses sign language to communicate with his coach, achieved his goal by swimming to a silver medal in the 200-meter breaststroke. "I think it will confirm that deaf people can do things," he said afterwards. "Other people will hopefully think now that we're just like other people. The only thing deaf people can't do is hear."

Standard 5
Learning Environments and Social Interactions

Deaf culture
A culture where people who are deaf become bonded together by a common language (sign language), customs, and heritage, and rely on each other for social interaction and emotional support.

Reviews of the literature on children's social and psychological development suggest that there are developmental differences between children who are deaf and children who can hear (Kaland & Salvatore, 2012; Scheetz, 2004; Tasker & Schmidt, 2008). Different or delayed language acquisition may lead to more limited opportunities for social interaction. Children who are deaf may have more adjustment challenges when attempting to communicate with children who can hear. However, they appear to be more secure when conversing with peers who have a hearing loss.

For some people who are deaf, social isolation from the hearing world is not considered an adjustment problem. On the contrary, it is a natural state of being where people are bonded together by a common language, customs, and heritage. People in the **deaf culture** seek out one another for social interaction and emotional support. The language of the culture is sign language, where communication occurs through hand signs, body language, and facial expressions. Sign language is not one universal language. American Sign Language (ASL) is different from Russian Sign Language (RSL), which is different from French Sign Language (FSL), and so on. ASL is not a form of English or of any other language. It has its own grammatical structure, which must be mastered in the same way as the grammar of any other language. (American Sign Language is discussed in greater detail later in this chapter.)

In addition to a common language, the deaf culture also has its own unique set of interactive customs. For example, people who are deaf value physical contact with one another even more than people in a hearing community. It is common to see visual and animated expressions of affection, such as hugs and handshakes in both greetings and departures. Regardless of the topic, discussions are frank, and there is no hesitation in getting to the point. Gatherings within the deaf culture may last longer because people like to linger. This may be particularly true at a dinner, where it is perfectly okay to sign (talk) with your mouth full. It will obviously take longer to eat because it is difficult to sign and hold a knife and fork at the same time.

Standard 1
Foundations

Within the deaf community, the social identity of being a person who is deaf is highly valued, and there is a fierce internal loyalty. Everyone is expected to support activities within the deaf culture, whether in sports, arts and literature, or political networks. The internal cohesion among the community's members includes a strong expectation that people will marry within the group. In fact, nine out of ten people in the deaf culture marry others within the same community. This loyalty is so strong that parents who are deaf may hope for a child who is deaf to pass on the heritage and tradition of the deaf culture to their offspring. Although hearing people may be welcomed within the deaf community, they are seldom accepted as full members. (See the nearby Debate Forum, "Living in a Deaf Culture.")

Multidisciplinary Educational Services and Supports for People with a Hearing Loss

FOCUS 4

Identify four approaches to teaching communication skills to people with a hearing loss.

Standard 5
Learning Environments and Social Interactions

Standard 7
Instructional Planning

In the United States, educational programs for children who are deaf or hard of hearing emerged in the early 19th century. The residential school for the deaf was the primary model for delivery of educational services; it was a live-in facility where students were segregated from the family environment. In the latter half of the 19th century, day schools were established in which students lived with their families while attending special schools exclusively for deaf students. As the century drew to a close, some public schools established special classes for children with a hearing loss within general education schools.

The residential school continued to be a model for educational services well into the 20th century. However, with the introduction of electrical amplification, advances in medical treatment, and improved educational technology, more options became available within the public schools. Today, educational programs for students who are deaf or hard of hearing range from the residential school to inclusive education in a general education classroom with support services. For a more in-depth look at the importance of educational supports for students with hearing loss placed in general education settings, see the nearby Case Study, "A Community of Learners."

Research strongly indicates that children with a hearing loss must receive early intervention as soon as possible if they are to learn the language skills necessary for reading and other academic subjects (Gilbertson & Ferre, 2008; Marschark, Lang, & Albertini, 2007; McGowan, Nittrouer, Chenausky, 2008). There is little disagreement that the education of children with a hearing loss must begin at the time of the diagnosis. Educational goals for students with a hearing loss are comparable to those for students who can hear. Students with a hearing loss bring many of the same strengths and weaknesses to the classroom as hearing students. Adjustment to learning experiences is often comparable for both groups, as well. Students with a hearing loss, however, face the formidable problems associated with being unable to communicate effectively with teachers and students who can hear. For more information on interacting with people who have a hearing loss, see this chapter's Inclusion and Collaboration through the Lifespan.

Teaching Communication Skills

The approaches commonly used to teach communication skills to students with a hearing loss include auditory, oral, manual, and total communication. There is a long history of controversy regarding which approach is the most appropriate. However, no single method or combination of methods can meet the individual needs of all children with a hearing loss. Our purpose is not to enter into the controversy regarding these approaches but to present a brief description of each approach.

The Auditory Approach
The auditory approach emphasizes the use of amplified sound and residual hearing to develop oral communication skills. The auditory channel is considered the primary avenue for language development, regardless of the severity or type of hearing loss. The basic principles of the auditory-verbal approach are to:

1. Promote early diagnosis of hearing loss in newborns, infants, toddlers, and young children, followed by immediate audiologic management and auditory-verbal therapy.

2. Recommend immediate assessment and use of appropriate, state-of-the-art hearing technology to obtain maximum benefits of auditory stimulation.

3. Guide and coach parents to help their child use hearing as the primary sensory modality in developing spoken language without the use of sign language or emphasis on lip-reading.

4. Guide and coach parents to become the primary facilitators of their child's listening and spoken language development through active, consistent participation in individualized auditory-verbal therapy.

The Weld County School District 6 has housed the preschool through 12th-grade program for students who are deaf or hard of hearing at University Schools for more than 60 years. During this time, the school district has formed a strong working relationship with the professors from the Deaf Education Program at the University of Northern Colorado. These mutually beneficial relationships have produced several innovative practices. For example, University Schools, in collaboration with the district, has one of a few programs in the United States that serves students who are deaf or hard of hearing using a co-enrollment model. This arrangement enables students who are deaf or hard of hearing to attend general education classrooms all day with their hearing peers. Two teachers—a general education teacher and a teacher of students who are deaf or hard of hearing—plan, teach, and share equal responsibility for the entire class throughout the day.

The two teachers both signed for themselves. There was no interpreter assigned to the classroom, although if interpreters had free time, they would often come into the classroom to help. Teachers conducted instruction using total communication—simultaneous sign and speech. The general education teacher had developed his signing skills by taking classes and by teaching in the co-taught classroom for the past six years.

When the co-taught program began, the school established the philosophy that it would strive to be a community of learners. The teachers knew that to establish such a community, everyone would need the skills to communicate with one another. To help students and teachers develop their signing skills, instruction in sign language was provided for all elementary-level students as a special course (like art, music, physical education, and Spanish). In addition, it has become well known throughout the school that sign and speech are used to communicate in this third- and fourth-grade classroom. Consequently, hearing students who had an interest in signing or who had been in the first- and second-grade co-taught classroom often asked to be placed in this class. The school believes that these actions, as well as interpreting at all school functions and expecting hearing students to sign for themselves, have been important ingredients in the development of a community of learners.

WELD'S TRANSFORMED LITERACY PROGRAM

The first major change implemented was to stop teaching reading, writing, and spelling as separate content areas. The teachers integrated these content areas into a single literacy block. Thus, their literacy philosophy became "Read Like Writers and Write Like Readers." Literacy was taught every day from 7:55 until 11:00 a.m. Although this seemed like a large block of time for students to stay on task, they were often reluctant to stop for lunch. The literacy instructional time was divided into three major components: sustained silent reading followed by student activities and direct instruction with appropriate accommodations:

Sustained Silent Reading. Each morning, students were expected to read silently for 30 minutes. They could read from a variety of materials (fiction and nonfiction books, magazines, poetry, comics, or newspapers). Also during this block of time, teachers had the opportunity to observe students reading or to have reading conferences with individual students or small groups of students.

Student Activities. The teachers used the remainder of the literacy block in a variety of ways. Activities included teacher-directed, whole-group reading, writing, and spelling lessons and time for students to work on individual or small-group projects. The end of the literacy block time was allocated for students to receive peer feedback on unfinished projects, present finished products to the class, reflect on what was learned through journal writing, and discuss what was learned in small- or whole-group settings.

Direct Instruction—with Accommodations. The initial teacher-directed lessons gave an overview of how reading comprehension strategies help readers understand what is being read. Each lesson included accommodations so that students who were deaf or hard of hearing had direct access to the information through graphic representations, closed-captioning, or other aids. The teachers discovered that this practice was beneficial to all students.

APPLICATION QUESTIONS

1. What does "a community of learners" mean in the classrooms at University Schools?

2. Why didn't the school assign interpreters to the classroom?

3. How did the school help students and teachers develop their signing skills?

4. What does the philosophy "Read Like Writers and Write Like Readers" mean to you?

SOURCE: Adapted from Wurst, D., Jones, D., & Luckner, J. (2005, May/June). Promoting literacy development with students who are hard-of-hearing, and hearing. *Teaching Exceptional Children,* 37(5), 56–57.

5. Guide and coach parents to create environments that support listening for the acquisition of spoken language throughout the child's daily activities.

6. Guide and coach parents to help their child integrate listening and spoken language into all aspects of the child's life.

7. Guide and coach parents to use natural developmental patterns of audition, speech, language, cognition, and communication.

8. Guide and coach parents to help their child self-monitor spoken language through listening.

9. Administer ongoing formal and informal diagnostic assessments to develop individualized auditory-verbal treatment plans, to monitor progress, and to evaluate the effectiveness of the plans for the child and family.

10. Promote education in regular schools with peers who have typical hearing and with appropriate services from early childhood onward. (Alexander Graham Bell Academy, 2012)

Standard 4
Instructional Strategies

The auditory approach uses a variety of electroacoustic devices to enhance residual hearing, such as binaural hearing aids, acoustically tuned earmolds, and FM units. FM units employ a behind-the-ear hearing aid connected to a high-powered frequency-modulated radio-frequency (FM-RF) system. These units use a one-way wireless system on radio frequency bands. The student wears the receiver unit (about the size of a deck of cards), and the teacher wears a wireless microphone-transmitter-antenna unit. One advantage of using an FM-RF system is that the teacher can be connected to several students at a time.

The Oral Approach The oral approach to teaching communication skills also relies on the use of amplified sound and residual hearing to develop oral language. This approach emphasizes the need for people with a hearing loss to function in the hearing world. Individuals are encouraged to speak and be spoken to. In addition to electroacoustic amplification, the teacher may employ speech-reading, reading and writing, and motokinesthetic speech training (feeling an individual's face and reproducing breath and voice patterns). **Speech-reading** is the process of understanding another person's speech by watching lip movement and facial and body gestures. This skill is difficult to master, especially for people who have been deaf since an early age and, thus, never acquired speech. Problems with speech-reading include the fact that many sounds are not distinguishable on the lips; readers must attend carefully to every word spoken, a difficult task for preschool and primary-age children. Additionally, speech-readers must be able to see the speaker's mouth at all times.

Speech-reading
The process of understanding another person's speech by watching lip movement and facial and body gestures.

If a severe or profound hearing loss automatically made an individual neurologically and functionally "different" from people with normal hearing, then the oral approach may not be tenable. However, outcome studies show that individuals who have, since early childhood, been taught through the active use of amplified residual hearing are indeed independent, speaking, and contributing members of mainstream society.

The Manual Approach The manual approach to teaching communication skills stresses the use of signs in teaching children who are deaf to communicate. The use of signs is based on the premise that many such children are unable to develop oral language; consequently, they must have some other means of communication. Manual communication systems are divided into two main categories: sign languages and sign systems.

Sign languages
Complex combinations of hand movements that communicate whole words and complete thoughts rather than the individual letters of the alphabet.

Sign languages are systematic and complex combinations of hand movements that communicate whole words and complete thoughts rather than the individual letters of the alphabet. One of the most common sign languages is the **American Sign Language** (ASL) with a vocabulary of more than 6,000 signs. Examples of ASL signs are shown in Figure 13.2.

American Sign Language (ASL)
A type of sign language commonly used by people with hearing impairments. ASL signs represent concepts rather than single words.

ASL is currently the most widely used sign language among many adults who are deaf, because it is easy to master and has historically been the preferred mode of communication. It is a language, but it is not English. Its signs represent concepts rather than single words. The use of ASL in a school setting has been strongly recommended by some advocates for people who are deaf because it is considered their natural language (National Institute on Deafness and Other Communication Disorders, 2012a).

Alabama, Hawaii

Arkansas, Florida, Maine, Kentucky, Louisiana, Virginia, North Carolina, South Carolina

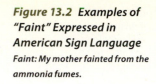

California, Illinois, Utah

Colorado, Texas (1 of 2)

Massachusetts

Michigan, Ohio

Sign systems differ from sign languages in that they attempt to create visual equivalents of oral language through manual gestures. With finger spelling, a form of manual communication that incorporates all 26 letters of the English alphabet, each letter is signed independently on one hand to form words. It is common to see a person who is deaf using finger spelling when there is no ASL sign for a word. The four sign systems used in the United States are Seeing Essential English, Signing Exact English, Linguistics of Visual English, and Signed English.

There is a continuing debate regarding the use of ASL and signing English systems in providing academic instruction to students who are deaf. Should ASL or English be the primary language for instruction? Those advocating a **bicultural–bilingual approach** believe that ASL should be the primary language and English the second language. As the primary language, ASL would then serve as the foundation for the learning of English. The rationale for ASL as the primary language emerges from the values held dear by the deaf community: Children who are deaf must learn academic content in the language of their culture, their natural language. The primary language for children who are deaf is visual, not verbal. Children who are deaf should be considered bilingual students, not students with disabilities. As is true in bilingual education programs for students with differing language backgrounds, there is also the debate about whether ASL should be taught first and then English, or whether both should be taught simultaneously. One side emphasizes the importance of the child's first acquiring the natural language (ASL). The other stresses the need to expose the child to both ASL and English simultaneously and as early as possible. There is little research to support either position.

Total Communication Total communication has roots traceable to the 16th century. Over the past four centuries, many professionals advocated for an instructional system that employed every method possible to teach communication skills: oral, auditory, manual, and written. This approach was known as the combined system or simultaneous method. The methodology of the early combined system was imprecise; essentially, any recognized approach to teaching communication was used as long as it included a manual component. The concept of total communication differs from the older combined system in that it is used not only when the oral method fails or when critical learning periods have long since passed, but also in a much broader sense—as a total communication philosophy, not a system.

Sign systems
Differing from sign languages, sign systems create visual equivalents of oral language through manual gestures. For example, finger spelling uses a separate sign for each letter of the English alphabet.

Bicultural–bilingual approach
Instructional approach advocating ASL as the primary language and English as the second language for students who are deaf.

The philosophy of **total communication** holds that the simultaneous presentation of signs and speech will enhance each person's opportunity to understand and use both systems more effectively.

Total communication programs use residual hearing, amplification, speech-reading, speech training, reading, and writing in combination with manual systems. A method that may be used as an aid to total communication but is not a necessary component of the approach is cued speech. **Cued speech** facilitates the development of oral communication by combining eight different hand signals in four different locations near the person's chin. These hand signals provide additional information about sounds not identifiable by speech-reading. The result is that an individual has access to all sounds in the English language through either the lips or the hands.

Assistive Technology

Educational and leisure opportunities for people with a hearing loss have been greatly expanded through technological advances such as closed-caption television, computers, and the Internet. In this section, we examine 21st-century technology for people with a hearing loss.

Closed-Captioning
Closed-caption television translates dialogue from a television program into printed words (captions or subtitles). These captions are then converted into electronic codes that can be inserted into the television picture on sets specially adapted with decoding devices. The process is called the line-21 system because the caption is inserted into blank line 21 of the picture.

In its first year of operation in 1958, national closed-caption programming was available about 30 hours a week. By 1987, more than 200 hours a week of national programming were captioned in a wide range of topics, from news and information to entertainment and commercials. By 1993, all major broadcast networks were captioning 100 percent of their prime-time broadcasts, national news, and children's programming. With the passage of the Television Decoder Circuitry Act of 1993, the numbers of viewers watching closed-caption television expanded even more dramatically. This act required that all television sets sold in the United States that measure 13 inches or larger be equipped with a decoder that allows captions to be placed anywhere on the television screen. (This prevents captions from interfering with on-screen titles or other information displayed on the TV broadcast.) In 1997, the U.S. Congress passed the Telecommunications Act, which required virtually all new television programming to be captioned by January 2006. The clear intent of the law was to expand access to television for millions of people who are deaf.

Computers, Smartphones, Tablets, and the Internet
Personal computers, electronic tablets, and smartphones add an exciting dimension to information access for people with a hearing loss. These widely used devices place people with a hearing impairment in an interactive setting using Internet applications ("apps") and computer software. Learning can be individualized so that students can gain independence by working at their own pace and level.

Various apps are now available for instructional support across academic subject areas from reading and writing to learning basic sign language. Software is available that will display a person's speech in visual form on the screen to assist in the development of articulation skills. Another innovative computer system is called C-Print, developed by the National Technical Institute for the Deaf. Using a laptop computer equipped with a computer shorthand system and commercially available software packages, C-Print provides real-time translations of the spoken word. C-Print provides a major service to students with a hearing loss as they attend college classes or oral lectures; they typically find note taking an extremely difficult activity, even when an oral interpreter is available (National Technical Institute for the Deaf, 2006).

Through e-mail, texting, interactive chatrooms, smartphones, and the infinite number of websites, the Internet offers people with a hearing loss access to all kinds of visual information through the quickest and most convenient means possible. Harris Communications and the American Sign Language Browser at Michigan State University are just two examples of sites designed specifically for people who are deaf.

Telecommunication Devices A major advance in communication technology for people with a hearing loss is the telecommunication device (TDD). In 1990, the Americans with Disabilities Act renamed these devices **text telephones (TTs)**. TTs send, receive, and print messages through thousands of stations across the United States. People with a hearing loss can now dial an 800 number to set up conference calls, make appointments, or order merchandise or fast food. Anyone who wants to speak with a person using a TT can do so through the use of a standard telephone.

The teletypewriter and printer system (TTY) is another effective use of technology for people who are deaf. It allows them to communicate by phone via a typewriter that converts typed letters into electric signals through a modem. These signals are sent through the phone lines and are then translated into typed messages and printed on a typewriter connected to a phone on the other end. Computer software is now available that can turn a personal computer into a TTY.

Text telephones (TTs)
Telephones that send, receive, and print messages through thousands of stations across the United States.

Health Care for People with a Hearing Loss

Several medical specialists are involved in health care assessment and intervention, including the geneticist, the pediatrician, the family practitioner, the otologist, the neurosurgeon, and the audiologist. Prevention of a hearing loss is a primary concern of genetics specialists. A significant percentage of hearing loss is inherited or occurs during prenatal, perinatal, and postnatal development. Consequently, genetics specialists play an important role in preventing disabilities through family counseling and prenatal screening.

Early detection of a hearing loss can prevent or at least minimize the impact of the disability on the overall development of individuals. Generally, it is the responsibility of the pediatrician or family practitioner to be aware of a problem and to refer the family to an appropriate hearing specialist. This requires that the physician be familiar with family history and conduct a thorough physical examination of the child. The physician must be alert to any symptoms (such as delayed language development) that indicate potential sensory loss.

The **otologist** is a medical specialist who is most concerned with the hearing organ and its diseases. Otology is a component of the larger specialty of diseases of the ear, nose, and throat. The otologist, like the pediatrician, screens for potential hearing problems, but the process is much more specialized and exhaustive. The otologist also conducts an extensive physical examination of the ear to identify syndromes that are associated with conductive or sensorineural loss. This information, in conjunction with family history, provides data used to recommend appropriate medical treatment.

Treatment may involve medical therapy or surgical intervention. Common therapeutic procedures include monitoring aural hygiene (e.g., keeping the external ear free from wax), blowing out the ear (e.g., a process to remove mucus blocking the eustachian tube), and administering antibiotics to treat infections. Surgical techniques may involve the cosmetic and functional restructuring of congenital malformations such as a deformed external ear or closed external canal (atresia). Fenestration is the surgical creation of a new opening in the labyrinth of the ear to restore hearing. A stapedectomy is a surgical process conducted under a microscope whereby a fixed stapes is replaced with a prosthetic device capable of vibrating, thus permitting the transmission of sound waves. A myringoplasty is the surgical reconstruction of a perforated tympanic membrane (eardrum).

Another widely used surgical procedure is the **cochlear implant**. This electronic device is surgically placed under the skin behind the ear. It consists of four parts: (1) a microphone for picking up sound, (2) a speech processor to select and arrange sounds picked up by the microphone, (3) a transmitter and receiver/stimulator to receive signals from the speech processor and convert them into electric impulses, and (4) electrodes to collect the impulses from the stimulator and send them to the brain. The implant does not restore or amplify hearing. Instead, it provides people who are deaf or profoundly hard of hearing with a useful "sense" of sound in the world around them. The implant overcomes "nerve deafness" (sounds blocked

FOCUS 5
Why is early detection of hearing loss so important?

Standard 1
Foundations

Standard 2
Development and Characteristics of Learners

Standard 8
Assessment

Otologist
Specialist involved in the study of the ear and its diseases.

Cochlear implant
Procedure that implants an electronic device under the skin behind the ear to directly stimulate the auditory nerve.

from reaching the auditory nerve) by getting around damage to the tiny hair cells in the inner ear and directly stimulating the auditory nerve. An implant electronically finds useful or meaningful sounds, such as speech, and then sends these sounds to the auditory nerve.

Cochlear implants are becoming more widely used with both adults and children. More than 219,000 children and adults worldwide have had the surgery (National Institute on Deafness and Other Communication Disorders, 2012b). Some adults who were deafened in their later years reported useful hearing following the implant; others still needed speech-reading to understand the spoken word. Most children receive the implants between the ages of 2 and 6 years. Debate continues about which age is optimal for the surgery, but it appears that the earlier, the better. The American Speech Hearing and Language Association (2012) suggests that the younger a child who was born deaf receives an implant, the greater the benefit achieved in the areas of speech perception and speech and language development. The existing research suggests that cochlear implants assist in the learning of speech, language, and social skills, particularly for young children. However, there are still issues to be addressed, such as understanding the risk of possible damage to an ear that has some residual hearing, as well as the risk of infection from the implant (Berg, Ip, Hurst, & Herb, 2007).

Whereas an otologist offers a biological perspective on hearing loss, an **audiologist** emphasizes the functional impact of losing one's hearing. The audiologist first screens the individual for a hearing loss and then determines both the nature and the severity of the condition. Social, educational, and vocational implications of the hearing loss are then discussed and explored. Although audiologists are not specifically trained in the field of medicine, these professionals interact constantly with otologists to provide a comprehensive assessment of hearing.

Working together, audiologists and otologists provide assistance in the selection and use of hearing aids. At one time or another, most people with a hearing loss will probably wear hearing aids. Hearing aids amplify sound, but they do not correct hearing. Hearing aids have been used for centuries. Early acoustic aids included cupping one's hand behind the ear as well as the ear trumpet. Modern electroacoustic aids do not depend on the loudness of the human voice to amplify sound, but utilize batteries to increase volume. Electroacoustic aids come in three main types: body-worn aids, behind-the-ear aids, and in-the-ear aids. Which hearing aid is best for a particular person depends on the degree of hearing loss, the age of the individual, and his or her physical condition.

Body-worn hearing aids are typically worn on the chest, using a harness to secure the unit. The hearing aid is connected by a wire to a transducer, which is worn at ear level and delivers a signal to the ear via an earmold. Body-worn aids are becoming less common because of the disadvantages of them being chest-mounted, the location of the microphone, and inadequate high-frequency response. The behind-the-ear aid (also referred to as an ear-level aid) is a common electroacoustic device for children with a hearing loss. All components of the behind-the-ear aid are fitted in one case behind the outer ear. The case then connects to an earmold that delivers the signal directly to the ear. In addition to their portability, behind-the-ear aids have the advantage of producing the greatest amount of electroacoustic flexibility (amount of amplification across all frequencies). The primary disadvantage is a problem with acoustic feedback. As discussed earlier in this chapter, the behind-the-ear aid may be used with an FM-RF system. These aids may be fitted monaurally (on one ear) or binaurally (on both ears).

The in-the-ear aid fits within the ear canal. All major components (microphone, amplifier, transducer, and battery) are housed in a single case that has been custom-made for the individual user. The advantage of the in-the-ear aid is the close positioning of the microphone to the natural reception of auditory signals in the ear canal. In-the-ear aids are recommended for people with mild hearing losses who do not need frequent changes in earmolds. Accordingly, these aids are not usually recommended for young children.

Although the quality of commercially available hearing aids has improved dramatically in recent years, they have distinct limitations. Commercial hearing aids make sounds louder, but do not necessarily make them more clear and distinct. The criteria for determining the effectiveness of a hearing aid must be based on how well it fits, as well as each individual's communication ability. The stimulation of residual hearing through a hearing aid enables most people with a hearing loss to function as hard of hearing. However, the use of a hearing aid must be implemented as early as possible,

Audiologist
A specialist in the assessment of a person's hearing ability.

In 2010, four Norwegian researchers (Tollefsen, Dale, Berg, & Nordby, 2011) conducted a survey of Norwegian citizens with disabilities, including those with sensory impairments, to better understand their use of social media. The researchers asked specifically about the use of Facebook, Twitter, and Skype, but respondents were free to talk about other forms of social media in their lives. A few highlights of responses from people with hearing and vision loss follow:

> I am severely hard of hearing (hearing aid user) and visually impaired. Facebook has become an extremely important arena for me to keep updated. The social aspects of visual or hearing impairments do not matter here. I use what I have learned on Facebook when I later meet people face to face, and this has made it much easier for me to follow and understand the context of conversations. It has also become much easier to keep in touch with people I otherwise would not have had the resources to keep in contact with. For me, Facebook provides the opportunity for a more active social life out in "real life."

The previous quote . . . suggests that social media actually provide a significant added value in relation to social participation in "real life." A woman who is blind says:

> I use whatever I have found on Facebook when I meet people. For example, others can see that someone is pregnant and ask how it's going. I can't see this, but I have often found out about it on Facebook. Then I can ask!

Questions for Reflection

Why do you think many people with sensory impairments in this survey view social media as a "valued-added" part of their lives? What are the challenges for people with sensory impairments in accessing social media sites?

SOURCE: Tollefsen, M., Dale, Ø., Berg, M, & Nordby, R. (2011). *Connected!: Disabled and use of social media*. Retrieved March 12, 2012, from http://medialt.no/news/en-US/connected-disabled-and-use-of-social-media/737.aspx.

---

before sensory deprivation takes its toll on the child. It is the audiologist's responsibility to weigh all the factors involved (such as convenience, size, and weight) in the selection and use of an aid for the individual. The individual should then be directed to a reputable hearing aid dealer.

Vision Loss

To more fully understand the nature of vision loss within the context of normal sight, we begin with a Snapshot, a personal story about John who is a 9-year-old boy with a vision impairment. We then review the physical components of the visual system and define the terms *blind* and *partially sighted*.

The physical components of the visual system include the eye, the **visual cortex** in the brain, and the **optic nerve**, which connects the eye to the visual cortex. The basic anatomy of the human eye is illustrated in Figure 13.3. The **cornea** is the external covering of the eye, and in the presence of light, it bends or refracts visual stimuli. These light rays pass through the **pupil**, which is an opening in the iris. The pupil dilates or constricts to control the amount of light entering the eye. The **iris**, the colored portion of the eye, consists of membranous tissue and muscles whose function is to adjust the size of the pupil. The **lens**, like the cornea, bends light rays so that they strike the retina directly. As in a camera lens, the lens of the eye reverses the images. The **retina** consists of light-sensitive cells that transmit the image to the brain via the optic nerve. Images from the retina remain upside down until they are neurally flipped over in the visual cortex occipital lobe of the brain.

The visual process is much more complex than suggested by a description of the physical components involved. The process is an important link to the physical world, helping us to gain information beyond the range of other senses, while also helping us to integrate the information acquired primarily through hearing, touch, smell, and taste. For example, our sense of touch can tell us that what we are feeling is furry, soft, and

FOCUS 6
Distinguish between the terms *blind* and *partially sighted*.

Visual cortex
The visual center of the brain, located in the occipital lobe.

Optic nerve
The nerve that connects the eye to the visual center of the brain.

Cornea
The external covering of the eye.

Pupil
The expandable opening in the iris of the eye.

Iris
The colored portion of the eye.

Lens
The clear structure of the eye that bends light rays so they strike the retina directly.

Retina
Light-sensitive cells in the interior of the eye that transmit images to the brain via the optic nerve.

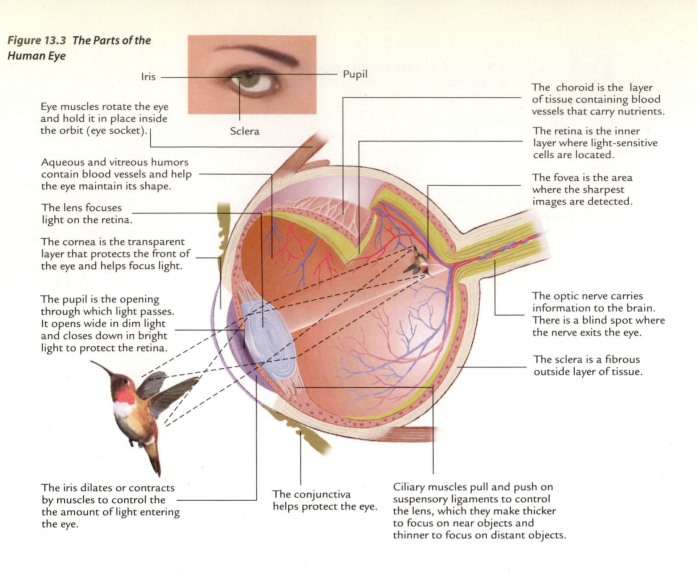

Figure 13.3 The Parts of the Human Eye

Iris

Pupil

Sclera

Eye muscles rotate the eye and hold it in place inside the orbit (eye socket).

Aqueous and vitreous humors contain blood vessels and help the eye maintain its shape.

The lens focuses light on the retina.

The cornea is the transparent layer that protects the front of the eye and helps focus light.

The pupil is the opening through which light passes. It opens wide in dim light and closes down in bright light to protect the retina.

The iris dilates or contracts by muscles to control the the amount of light entering the eye.

The conjunctiva helps protect the eye.

The choroid is the layer of tissue containing blood vessels that carry nutrients.

The retina is the inner layer where light-sensitive cells are located.

The fovea is the area where the sharpest images are detected.

The optic nerve carries information to the brain. There is a blind spot where the nerve exits the eye.

The sclera is a fibrous outside layer of tissue.

Ciliary muscles pull and push on suspensory ligaments to control the lens, which they make thicker to focus on near objects and thinner to focus on distant objects.

warm, but only our eyes must tell that it is a brown rabbit with a white tail and pink eyes. Our nose may perceive something with yeast and spices cooking, but our eyes must confirm that it is a large pepperoni pizza with bubbling mozzarella and green peppers. Our hearing can tell us that a friend sounds angry and upset, but only our vision can register the scowl, clenched jaw, and stiff posture. The way we perceive visual stimuli shapes our interactions with and reactions to the environment, while providing a foundation for the development of a more complex learning structure.

The term *vision loss* encompasses people with a wide range of conditions, including those who have never experienced sight, those who had normal vision prior to becoming partially or totally blind, those who experienced a gradual or sudden loss of acuity across their field of vision, and those with a restricted field of vision. A variety of terms are used to define vision loss; this has created some confusion among professionals in various fields of study. The rationale for the development of multiple definitions is directly related to their intended use. For example, eligibility for income tax exemptions or special assistance from the American Printing House for the Blind requires that individuals with vision loss qualify under one of two general subcategories: **blind** or partially sighted (low vision).

Blindness

The term blindness has many meanings. In fact, there are over 150 citations for blind in an unabridged dictionary. **Legal blindness**, as defined by the Social Security Administration (2012), means either that vision cannot be corrected to better than 20/200 in the better eye or that the visual field is 20 degrees or less, even with a corrective lens. Many people who

Blind
Condition in which central visual acuity does not exceed 20/200 in the better eye with correcting lenses, or in which visual acuity, if better than 20/200, is limited in the central field of vision.

Legal blindness
Visual acuity of 20/200 or worse in the best eye with best correction as measured on the Snellen test, or a visual field of 20 percent or less.

Visual acuity
Sharpness or clearness of vision.

Born prematurely and weighing only 1 pound 13 ounces, John is a child with vision loss. Now 9 years old, John lives with his parents and brother, Michael, none of whom have any visual problems. John loves the latest technology and has several TVs (including one that is 3-D), a computer, smartphone, and digital recorder. He doesn't care for outdoor activities and isn't into sports. He uses braille to read and has a cane to help him find his way through the world:

John: "I really like to be blind, it's a whole lot of fun. The reason I like to be blind is because I can learn my way around real fast and I have a real fast-thinking memory. I can hear things that some people can't hear and smell. Actually, my sense of hearing is the best."

John's parents: "John can do anything he wants to do if he puts his mind to it. He's smart enough, and he loves all kinds of communication [devices]. He talks about being on the radio, on TV, and there's no reason why he can't do that as long as he studies hard in school."

Michael: "I didn't want a blind brother."

John: "Sometimes my brother gets along good and sometimes he comes here in my room and under my desk there's a little power switch that controls all my TVs, scanner, and [digital] recorder. He'll flip that then he'll laugh about it, run and go somewhere, and I'll have to turn it back on, lock my door, and go tell Mom. So that's how he handles it and she puts him in time-out."

John's third-grade teacher: "John is very well adjusted. He has a wonderful, delightful personality. He's intelligent. We were a little worried about his braille until this year. Probably because of his prematurity, [he has] a little trouble with the tactual. Of course, braille is all tactual . . . . But he's pulling out of that and that was his last problem with education. He's very bright. He could do many things. He loves computers."

John: "I'd like to be a few different things, and I'll tell you a few of them. I'd like to be a newscaster, an astronaut, or something down at NASA, and a dispatcher. So that's three of the things out of a whole million or thousand things I'd like to be."

meet the legal definition of blindness still have some sight and may be able to read large print and get around without support (i.e., without a guide dog or a cane).

As we have noted, the definition of legal blindness includes both acuity and field of vision. **Visual acuity** is most often determined by reading letters or numbers on a chart using the **Snellen test** or by using an index that refers to the distance from which an object can be recognized. People with normal eyesight are defined as having 20/20 vision. However, if an individual is able to read at 20 feet what a person with normal vision can read at 200 feet, then his or her visual acuity would be described as 20/200. Most people consider those who are legally blind to have some light perception; only about 20 percent are totally without sight. A person is also considered blind if his or her field of vision is limited at its widest angle to 20 degrees or less (see Figure 13.4). A restricted field is also referred to as **tunnel vision** (or pinhole vision or tubular vision). A restricted field of vision severely limits a person's ability to participate in athletics, read, or drive a car.

Blindness can also be characterized as an educational disability. Educational definitions of blindness focus primarily on students' ability to use vision as an avenue for learning. Children who are unable to use their sight and rely on other senses, such as hearing and touch, are described as functionally blind. Functional blindness, in its simplest form, may be defined in terms of whether vision is used as a primary channel of learning. Regardless of the definition used, the purpose of labeling a child as functionally blind is to ensure that he or she receives an appropriate instructional program. This program must assist the student who is blind in utilizing other senses as a means to succeed in a classroom setting and, in the future, as an independent and productive adult.

Snellen test
A test of visual acuity.

Tunnel vision
A restricted field of vision that is 20 degrees or less at its widest angle.

Figure 13.4 The Field of Vision

(a) 180°
Normal field of vision is about 180°.

(b) 20°
A person with a field of vision of 20° or less is considered blind.

Standard 1
Foundations

Standard 2
Development and Characteristics of Learners

Partially sighted
Visual acuity greater than 20/200 but not greater than 20/70 in the better eye after correction.

Braille
A writing system for the blind that involves combinations of six raised dots punched into paper, which can be read with the fingertips.

Standard 1
Foundations

FOCUS 7

What are the distinctive features of refractive eye problems, muscle disorders of the eye, and receptive eye problems?

Refractive problems
Visual disorders that occur when the refractive structures of the eye fail to properly focus light rays on the retina.

Hyperopia
Farsightedness; a refractive problem wherein the eyeball is excessively short, focusing light rays behind the retina.

Partial Sight (Low Vision)

People with partial sight or low vision have a visual acuity greater than 20/200 but not greater than 20/70 in the best eye after correction. The field of education also distinguishes between being blind and being partially sighted when determining what level and extent of additional support services a student requires. The term **partially sighted** describes students who are able to use vision as a primary source of learning.

A vision specialist often works with students with vision loss to make the best possible use of remaining sight. This includes the elimination of unnecessary glare in the work area, removal of obstacles that could impede mobility, use of large-print books, and use of special lighting to enhance visual opportunities. Although children with low vision often use printed materials and special lighting in learning activities, some use **braille** because they can see only shadows and limited movement. These children require the use of tactile or other sensory channels to gain maximum benefit from learning opportunities (Bishop, 2005; Lund & Troha, 2008; Poon & Ovadia, 2008; Supalo, Malouk, & Rankel, 2008).

There are two very distinct perspectives on individuals who are partially sighted and their use of residual vision. The first suggests that such individuals should make maximal use of their functional residual vision through the use of magnification, illumination, and specialized teaching aids (e.g., large-print books and posters), as well as any exercises that will increase the efficiency of remaining vision. This position is contrary to the more traditional philosophy of sight conservation, or sight saving, which advocates restricted use of the eye. It was once believed that students with vision loss could keep what sight they had much longer if it was used sparingly. However, extended reliance on residual vision in conjunction with visual stimulation training now appears actually to improve a person's ability to use sight as an avenue for learning.

Classifying Vision Loss

Vision loss may be classified according to the anatomical site of the problem. Anatomical disorders include impairment of the refractive structures of the eye, muscle anomalies in the visual system, and problems of the receptive structures of the eye.

Refractive Eye Problems

The most common types of vision loss occur when the refractive structures of the eye (cornea or lens) fail to focus light rays properly on the retina. The four types of **refractive problems** are hyperopia, or farsightedness; myopia, or nearsightedness; astigmatism, or blurred vision; and cataracts.

Hyperopia occurs when the eyeball is excessively short from front to back (has a flat corneal structure), forcing light rays to focus behind the retina. People with hyperopia can clearly visualize objects at a distance but cannot see them at close range. These individuals may require convex lenses so that a clear focus will occur on the retina.

Figure 13.5 Normal, Myopic, and Hyperopic Eyeballs

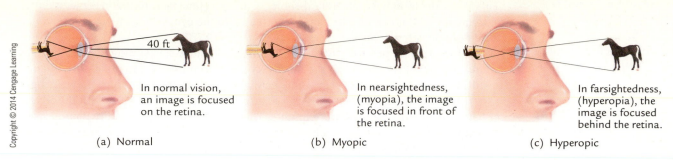

In normal vision, an image is focused on the retina.

In nearsightedness, (myopia), the image is focused in front of the retina.

In farsightedness, (hyperopia), the image is focused behind the retina.

(a) Normal   (b) Myopic   (c) Hyperopic

Myopia occurs when the eyeball is excessively long (has increased curvature of the corneal surface), forcing light rays to focus in front of the retina. People with myopia can view objects at close range clearly but cannot see them from a distance (such as 100 feet). Eyeglasses may be necessary to assist in focusing on distant objects. Figure 13.5 illustrates the myopic and hyperopic eyeballs, and compares them to the normal human eye.

Astigmatism occurs when the curvature or surface of the cornea is uneven, preventing light rays from converging at one point. The rays of light are refracted in different directions, producing unclear, distorted visual images. Astigmatism may occur independently of or in conjunction with myopia or hyperopia.

Cataracts occur when the lens becomes opaque, resulting in severely distorted vision or total blindness. Surgical treatment for cataracts (such as lens implants) has advanced rapidly in recent years, returning most of the vision that was lost.

Muscle Disorders

Muscular defects of the visual system occur when one or more of the major muscles within the eye are weakened in function, resulting in a loss of control and an inability to maintain tension. People with muscle disorders cannot maintain their focus on a given object for even short periods of time. The three types of muscle disorders are **nystagmus** (uncontrolled rapid eye movement), **strabismus** (crossed eyes), and **amblyopia** (an eye that appears normal but does not function properly). Nystagmus is a continuous, involuntary, rapid movement of the eyeballs in either a circular or a side-to-side pattern. Strabismus occurs when the muscles of the eyes are unable to pull equally, thus preventing the eyes from focusing together on the same object. Internal strabismus (**esotropia**) occurs when the eyes are pulled inward toward the nose; external strabismus (**exotropia**) occurs when the eyes are pulled out toward the ears. The eyes may also shift on a vertical plane (up or down), but this condition is rare. Strabismus can be corrected through surgical intervention. People with strabismus often experience a phenomenon known as double vision, because the deviating eye causes two very different pictures to reach the brain. To correct the double vision and reduce visual confusion, the brain attempts to suppress the image in one eye. As a result, the unused eye loses its ability to see. This condition, known as amblyopia, can also be corrected by surgery or by forcing the affected eye into focus by covering the unaffected eye with a patch.

Receptive Eye Problems

Disorders associated with the receptive structures of the eye occur when there is a degeneration of or damage to the retina and the optic nerve. These disorders include optic atrophy, retinitis pigmentosa, retinal detachment, retinopathy of prematurity, and glaucoma. **Optic atrophy** is a degenerative disease that results from the deterioration of nerve fibers connecting the retina to the brain. **Retinitis pigmentosa**, the most common hereditary condition associated with loss of vision, appears initially as night blindness and gradually causes degeneration of the retina. Eventually, it results in total blindness.

Myopia
Nearsightedness; a refractive problem wherein the eyeball is excessively long, focusing light in front of the retina.

Astigmatism
A refractive problem that occurs when the cornea surface is uneven or structurally defective, preventing light rays from converging at one point.

Cataract
A clouding of the eye lens, which becomes opaque, resulting in visual problems.

Nystagmus
Uncontrolled rapid eye movements.

Strabismus
Crossed eyes (internal) or eyes that look outward (external).

Amblyopia
Loss of vision due to an imbalance of eye muscles.

Esotropia
A form of strabismus causing the eyes to be pulled inward toward the nose.

Exotropia
A form of strabismus in which the eyes are pulled outward toward the ears.

Optic atrophy
A degenerative disease caused by deteriorating nerve fibers connecting the retina to the brain.

Retinitis pigmentosa
A hereditary condition resulting from a break in the choroid.

Retinal detachment
A condition that occurs when the retina is separated from the choroid and sclera.

Retinopathy of prematurity
A term now used in place of retrolental fibroplasia.

Retinal detachment occurs when the retina separates from the choroid and the sclera. This detachment may result from disorders such as glaucoma, retinal degeneration, or extreme myopia. It can also be caused by trauma to the eye, such as a boxer receiving a hard right hook to the face.

Retinopathy of prematurity (ROP) is one of the most devastating eye disorders in young children. It occurs when too much oxygen is administered to premature infants, resulting in the formation of scar tissue behind the lens of the eye, which prevents light rays from reaching the retina. ROP gained attention in the early 1940s, with the advent of better incubators for premature infants. These incubators substantially improved the concentration of oxygen available to infants, but resulted in a drastic increase in the number of children with vision loss. The disorder has also been associated with neurological, speech, and behavior problems in children and adolescents. Now that a relationship has been established between increased oxygen levels and blindness, premature infants can be protected by careful control of the amount of oxygen received in the early months of life.

Prevalence, Causes, and Characteristics of Vision Loss

FOCUS 8

What are the estimated prevalence, causes, and characteristics of vision loss?

The prevalence of vision loss is often difficult to determine. For example, although about 20 percent of children and adults in the United States have some vision loss, most of these conditions can be corrected to a level where they do not interfere with everyday tasks (such as reading and driving a car). Approximately 1 in 3,000 U.S. children is considered legally blind (Batshaw, Pellegrino, & Rozien, 2008), while 3 percent of the total population (9 million people) have a significant vision loss that will require some type of specialized services and supports. About 5 percent of U.S. children (approximately 1.2 million) have a serious eye disorder (KidSource, 2012). This figure increases to 20 percent for people over the age of 65. If cataracts are included, nearly 50 percent of people over the age of 65 have a significant vision loss. The U.S. Department of Education (2011) reports that approximately 24,000 students with a visual impairment between the ages of 6 and 21 received specialized services under IDEA in U.S. public schools. This accounts for 0.4 percent of all students with disabilities receiving special education services.

Causation

Vision loss may be associated with both genetic and acquired disorders. A number of genetic conditions can result in vision loss, including:

Albinism
Lack of pigmentation in eyes, skin, and hair.

Photophobia
An intolerance to light.

Retinoblastoma
A malignant tumor in the retina.

Microphthalmia
An abnormally small eyeball.

Anophthalmia
Absence of the eyeball.

Glaucoma
A disorder of the eye, which is characterized by high pressure inside the eyeball.

Buphthalmos
An abnormal distention and enlargement of the eyeball.

- **albinism** (resulting in **photophobia** because of lack of pigmentation in eyes, skin, and hair),
- retinitis pigmentosa (degeneration of the retina),
- **retinoblastoma** (malignant tumor in the retina),
- optic atrophy (loss of function of optic nerve fibers),
- cataracts (opaque lens resulting in severely distorted vision),
- severe myopia associated with retinal detachment,
- lesions of the cornea,
- abnormalities of the iris (coloboma or aniridia),
- **microphthalmia** (abnormally small eyeball),
- hydrocephalus (excess cerebrospinal fluid in the brain) leading to optic atrophy,
- **anophthalmia** (absence of the eyeball), and
- **glaucoma** or **buphthalmos** (abnormal distention and enlargement of the eyeball).

Glaucoma results from increased pressure within the eye that damages the optic nerve if left untreated. It is responsible for about 4 percent of all blindness in children (Batshaw, Pellegrino, & Rozien, 2008). The incidence of glaucoma is highest in people over the age of 40 who have a family history of the disease. Glaucoma is treatable, either through surgery to drain fluids from the eye or through the use of medicated eye drops to reduce pressure.

Acquired disorders associated with vision loss may occur prior to, during, or after birth. Several factors present prior to birth, such as radiation or the introduction of drugs into the fetal system, may result in vision loss. A major cause of blindness in the fetus is infection, which may be due to diseases such as rubella and syphilis. Other diseases that can result in blindness include influenza, mumps, and measles.

One of the leading causes of acquired blindness in children worldwide is vitamin A deficiency (**xerophthalmia**). Xerophthalmia is ranked among the World Health Organization's top ten leading causes of death through disease in developing countries (United Nations World Food Programme, 2012).

Another cause of acquired blindness is retinopathy of prematurity (ROP). As noted earlier, ROP results from administering oxygen over prolonged periods of time to infants with low birth weight. Almost 80 percent of preschool-age blind children lost their sight as a result of ROP during the peak years of the disease (1940s through 1960s).

Vision loss after birth may be due to several factors. Trauma, infections, inflammations, and tumors are all related to loss of sight. **Cortical visual impairment** (CVI) is a leading cause of acquired blindness. CVI, which involves damage to the occipital lobes and/or the visual pathways to the brain, can result from severe trauma, asphyxia, seizures, infections of the central nervous system, drugs, poisons, or other neurological conditions. Most children with CVI have residual vision.

The most common cause of preventable blindness is **trachoma**. This infectious disease affects more than 150 million people worldwide. Trachoma is associated with compromised living standards and hygiene (such as lack of water and unsanitary conditions) within a community. Although the incidence of trachoma has been reduced worldwide, it remains a serious health risk to millions of people in rural areas with significant levels of poverty (Lewallen et al., 2008).

The most common vision problems in adults, particularly those over the age of 60, are caused by **macular degeneration**. This condition is the result of a breakdown of the tissues in the macula (a small area in the middle of the retina). Macular degeneration affects more than 165,000 people each year, and 16,000 of them go blind as a result of the disease. Nearly two million Americans have impaired vision due to macular degeneration. With macular degeneration, central vision becomes distorted and blurry. The individual also has considerable difficulty differentiating colors (Riddering, 2008). New advances in the treatment of macular degeneration include laser surgery and drug therapy.

Characteristics

A vision loss present at birth will have a more significant effect on individual development than one that occurs later in life. Useful visual imagery may disappear if sight is lost prior to the age of 5. If sight is lost after the age of 5, it is possible for the person to retain some visual memories. These memories may be maintained for years to come, assisting the person to better understand newly learned concepts. Total blindness that occurs prior to age 5 has the greatest negative influence on overall functioning. However, many people who are blind from birth or early childhood are able to function at about the same level as sighted people of equal ability.

Intelligence Children with vision loss sometimes base their perceptions of the world on input from senses other than vision. This is particularly true of children who are congenitally blind, whose learning experiences are significantly restricted by the lack of vision. Consequently, everyday learning opportunities that people with sight take for granted, such as reading the morning newspaper or watching television news coverage, may be substantially altered.

Reviews of the literature on intellectual development suggest that children with vision loss differ from children with sight in some areas of intelligence, ranging from understanding spatial concepts to a general knowledge of the world (Batshaw, Pellegrino, & Rozien, 2008; McLinden & McCall, 2006). However, comparing the performances of individuals with and without sight may not be appropriate because those with sight have an advantage. The only valid way to compare the intellectual capabilities of these children must be based on tasks in which vision loss does not interfere with performance.

Standard 2
Development and Characteristics of Learners

Xeropthalmia
Vitamin A deficiency that can lead to a lack of mucous-producing cells (known as dry eye) or blindness.

Cortical visual impairment (CVI)
A leading cause of acquired blindness, which involves damage to the occipital lobes and/or the visual pathways to the brain, resulting from severe trauma, infections, or drug abuse.

Trachoma
Infectious bacterial disease associated with poor living standards and inadequate hygiene. Leads to blindness due to repeated infections causing irritation and scars on the eyelids.

Macular degeneration
An age-related condition in which the macula (tissues within the retina) break down, resulting in distorted and blurred central vision.

Standard 2
Development and Characteristics of Learners

Standard 3
Individual Learning Differences

Speech and Language Skills For children with sight, speech and language development occur primarily through the integration of visual experiences and the symbols of the spoken word. Depending on the degree of loss, children with vision loss are at a distinct disadvantage in developing speech and language skills because they are unable to visually associate words with objects. As a result, such children must rely on hearing or touch for input, and their speech may develop at a slower rate. Once these children have learned speech, however, it is typically fluent.

Preschool-age and school-age children with vision loss may develop a phenomenon known as **verbalisms**, or the excessive use of speech (wordiness), in which individuals may use words that have little meaning to them (e.g., "Crusaders are people of a religious sex" or "Lead us not into Penn Station"). Some research suggests that children with visual impairments may have a restricted oral vocabulary, compared with that of sighted peers, because they lack the visual input necessary to piece together all of the information available in a given experience (Papadopolous, Argyropolous, & Kouroupetroglou, 2008; Sacks & Silberman, 2000).

Verbalisms
Excessive use of speech (wordiness) in which individuals use words that have little meaning to them.

Academic Achievement The academic achievement of students with vision loss may be significantly delayed, compared with that of students with sight. Numerous factors may influence academic achievement for students with vision loss. In the area of written language, these students have more difficulty organizing their thoughts to write a composition because they lack the same opportunities as children with sight to read newspapers and magazines. Decoding in the area of reading may be delayed because students with visual impairments often use braille or large-print books as the media to decode. Decoding is a much slower process when the reader is using these two media. Reading comprehension is also affected because it depends so much on the experiences of the reader. Once again, the experience of students with visual impairments may be much more limited than that of students with sight; therefore these children don't bring as much information to the reading task (Papadopoulos Argyropoulos, & Kouroupedtroglou, 2008).

Other possible reasons for delays in academic achievement range from excessive school absences due to the need for eye surgery or treatment to years of failure in programs that did not meet each student's specialized needs. On the average, children with vision loss lag two years behind sighted children in grade level. Thus, any direct comparisons between students with vision loss and those with sight would indicate significantly delayed academic growth for the visually impaired. However, this might have resulted from children with vision loss entering school at a later age, from frequent absence due to medical problems, or from lack of appropriate school resources and facilities. For more in-depth information about academic learning and children with a vision loss, see the nearby Reflect on This, "Creating and Using Tactile Experience Books for Young Children with Visual Impairments."

Social Development The ability of children with vision loss to adapt to the social environment depends on a number of factors, both hereditary and experiential. It is true that each of us experiences the world in his or her own way, but common bonds provide a foundation on which to build perceptions of the world around us. One such bond is vision. Without vision, perceptions about ourselves and those around us can be drastically distorted.

For people with vision loss, these differences in perception may produce some social-emotional challenges. Children with vision loss are less likely to initiate a social interaction and have fewer opportunities to socialize with other children (Leigh & Barclay, 2000; Steinweg, Griffin, Griffin, & Gingras, 2005). They are often unable to imitate the physical mannerisms of others and, therefore, do not develop one very important component of social communication: body language. Because the subtleties of nonverbal communication can significantly alter the intended meaning of spoken words, people's inability to learn and use visual cues (such as facial expressions and hand gestures) has profound consequences for interpersonal interactions. People with vision loss can neither see the visual cues that accompany the messages received from others nor sense the messages that they may be conveying through body language.

Differences between people with a vision loss and those who are sighted may also result from exclusion of the person with a vision loss from social activities that are integrally related to the use of sight (such as sports and movies). People with vision loss are often excluded from such activities without a second thought, simply because they cannot see. This reinforces the mistaken notion that they do not want to participate and would not enjoy these activities. Social skills can be learned and effectively used by people with vision loss. Excluding them from social experiences more often stems from negative public attitudes than from the individuals' lack of social adjustment skills.

Orientation and Mobility A unique limitation facing people with vision loss is the challenge of moving about from place to place. These individuals may be unable to orient themselves to other people or objects in the environment simply because they cannot see them and therefore do not understand their own relative position in space. Consequently, they may be unable to move in the right direction and may fear getting injured, so they may try to restrict their movements to protect themselves. Parents and professionals may contribute to such fears by overprotecting the individual who has vision loss from the everyday risks of life. Shielding in this way will hinder the person's acquisition of independent mobility skills and create an atmosphere that promotes lifelong overdependence on caregivers.

Author and mountain climber Erik Wiehenmayer didn't let blindness interfere with his life's passion: to scale some of the world's highest mountains.

Didrik Johnck/Corbis

Vision loss can affect fine motor coordination and interfere with the ability to manipulate objects. Poor eye–hand coordination interferes with learning how to use tools related to job skills and daily living skills (such as using eating utensils, a toothbrush, or a screwdriver). Prevention or remediation of fine motor problems may require training in the use of visual aid magnifiers and improvement of basic fine motor skills. This training must begin early and focus directly on experiences that will enhance opportunities for independent living.

Perceptual-Motor Development Perceptual-motor development is essential in the development of locomotion skills, but it is also important in the development of cognition, language, socialization, and personality. Most children with vision loss appear

REFLECT ON THIS CREATING AND USING TACTILE EXPERIENCE BOOKS FOR YOUNG CHILDREN WITH VISUAL IMPAIRMENTS

Very young children with sight learn to read by making a connection between the words they hear on a regular basis and written reading materials. In other words, they observe the functional relationship between real life activities and the written word. However, young children with a vision loss do not have this same opportunity. As suggested by Lewis and Tolla (2003),

Visual impairment can directly interfere with the observation of

symbols and events that are key to the development of early literacy skills. . . . For young children who are blind or who have severe visual impairments, the visual aspects of books written for emergent readers present a significant problem. The obvious solution to this accessibility issue is the use of raised line drawings in conjunction with braille text. Interpretation of raised line drawings, however,

is a far more difficult task than is recognition and identification of pictures. Raised-line drawings attempt to present the three dimensional world in two dimensions. Although we can visually see the relationship, a circle is really very unlike the way a ball feels; the outline of a birthday cake bears no resemblance to its tactile reality. Similarly, the outline of the "Cat in the Hat" holding a fish cannot

Reading is a critical tool for children with a vision loss. While young children with sight learn to read using both auditory and visual cues, those with a vision loss must often rely on tactile materials as well.

© Spencer Grant/Photo Edit

be easily related to the outline of the cat sitting in a chair. The details and constancy that make even abstract illustrations so identifiable visually cannot be reproduced in a tactile form. Books published for young children with vision feature text that is simple and often repetitive. This repetition helps emerging readers to memorize the text, so that attention can be placed on the correspondence between the text and spoken words. This same practice can be used in tactile experience books published for young children with visual impairments. Although it is tempting to write long descriptive passages, young children benefit when there are few words on the page. They also benefit when phrases are repeated, such as "In my bathroom, there is a," or "When we fixed the doorknob, we used. . ." (p. 22, 24).

Questions for Reflection

1. What are some of ways in which children with a vision loss are able to participate in early reading activities?

2. How can educators, parents, and caregivers assure that children with a vision loss have the opportunity to learn to read?

to have perceptual discrimination abilities (such as discriminating texture, weight, and sound) comparable to those of children with sight (Bishop, 2005). Children with vision loss do not perform as well on more complex tasks of perception, including form identification, spatial relations, and perceptual-motor integration (Bouchard & Tetreault, 2000).

A popular misconception regarding the perceptual abilities of people with vision loss is that because of their diminished sight, they develop greater capacity in other sensory areas. For example, people who are blind are supposedly able to hear or smell some things that people with normal vision cannot perceive. This notion has never been empirically validated.

Education Assessment and Instructional Content

FOCUS 9

Describe two content areas that should be included in educational programs for students with vision loss.

When assessing the cognitive ability, academic achievement, language skills, motor performance, and social-emotional functioning of a student with a vision loss, an IEP team must also focus on how the student utilizes any remaining vision (visual efficiency) in conjunction with other senses. The Visual Efficiency Scale (see Barraga & Erin, 2002) assesses the overall visual functioning of individuals to determine how they use sight to acquire information. As suggested by Bishop (2005), if an individual has remaining vision, it is important that professionals and parents promote its use. It is a myth that remaining useful vision will be conserved by not using it.

A functional approach to assessment focuses on a person's visual capacity, attention, and processing. Visual capacity includes both acuity and field of vision; it also encompasses the response of the individual to visual information. The assessment of visual attention involves observing the individual's sensitivity to visual stimuli (alertness), ability to use vision to select information from a variety of sources, attention to a visual stimulus, and ability to process visual information. Visual-processing assessment determines which, if any, of the components of normal visual functioning are impaired.

CEC

Standard 3
Individual Learning Differences

Standard 4
Instructional Strategies

Standard 7
Instructional Planning

The educational needs of students with vision loss are comparable to those of their sighted counterparts. In addition, many instructional methods currently used with students who are sighted are appropriate for students with vision loss. However, educators must be aware that certain content areas that are generally unnecessary for sighted students are essential to the success, in a classroom, of students with vision loss. These areas include mobility and orientation training as well as acquisition of daily living skills.

Guide dogs and electronic mobility devices (such as this global positioning device) assist people who are blind in moving safely, efficiently, and independently through their environment.

The ability to move safely, efficiently, and independently through the environment enhances the individual's opportunities to learn more about the world and, thus, be less dependent on others for survival. Lack of mobility restricts individuals with vision loss in nearly every aspect of educational life. Such students may be unable to orient themselves to physical structures in the classroom (desks, chairs, and aisles), hallways, rest rooms, library, and cafeteria. Whereas people with sight can automatically establish a relative position in space, individuals with vision loss must be taught some means of compensating for a lack of visual input. This may be accomplished in a number of ways. It is important that students with vision loss not only learn the physical structure of their school, but also develop specific techniques to orient themselves to unfamiliar surroundings.

These orientation techniques involve using the other senses. For example, the senses of touch and hearing can help students identify cues that designate where the bathroom is in the school. Although it is not true that people who are blind have superior hearing abilities, they may learn to use their hearing more effectively by focusing on subtle auditory cues that often go unnoticed. The efficient use of hearing, in conjunction with the other senses (including any remaining vision), is the key to independent travel for people with vision loss.

Independent travel with a sighted companion, but without the use of a cane, guide dog, or electronic device, is the most common form of travel for young school-age children. The major challenges for children with low vision in moving independently and safely through their environment include

- knowing where landmarks are throughout the school setting;
- being familiar with the layout of classrooms and common areas, such as the library, gym, and cafeteria;
- knowing where exits, rest rooms, the main office, and other relevant school and classroom areas are located; and
- understanding the school's emergency procedures, such as fire, tornado, or earthquake drills. (Cox & Dykes, 2001)

Other challenges for students with low vision include adapting to changes in lighting, negotiating stairs and curbs, and walking in bad weather.

With the increasing emphasis on instructing young children in orientation at an earlier age, use of the long cane (Kiddie Cane) for young children has become more common. As these children grow older, they may be instructed in the use of a Mowat sensor. The **Mowat sensor**, approximately the size of a flashlight, is a handheld ultrasound travel aid that uses high-frequency sound to detect objects. Vibration frequency increases as objects become closer; the sensor vibrates at different rates to warn of obstacles in front of the individual. The device ignores everything but the closest object within the beam.

Guide dogs or electronic mobility devices may be appropriate for adolescents or adults, because the need to travel independently increases significantly with age. A variety of electronic mobility devices are currently being used for everything from enhancing hearing efficiency to detecting obstacles.

The **Laser Cane** converts infrared light into sound as light beams strike objects in the path of the person who is blind. It uses a range-finding technique with a semiconductor laser and a position-sensitive device (PSD). Proximity to an obstacle is warned by vibration at different levels of frequency.

The **SonicGuide** or Sonic Pathfinder, worn on the head, emits ultrasound and converts reflections from objects into audible noise in such a way that the individual can learn about the structure of objects. For example, loudness indicates size: The louder the noise, the larger the object. To use the SonicGuide effectively, people with low vision should have mobility skills. It is designed for outdoor use in conjunction with a cane, a guide dog, or residual vision.

The acquisition of daily living skills is another content area important to success in the classroom and to overall independence. Most people take for granted many routine events of the day, such as eating, dressing, bathing, and toileting. People with sight learn very early in life the tasks associated with perceptual-motor development, including grasping, lifting, balancing, pouring, and manipulating objects. These daily living tasks become more complex during the school years as children learn personal hygiene, grooming, and social etiquette. Eventually, people with sight acquire many complex daily living skills that later contribute to their independence as adults. Money management, grocery shopping, doing laundry, cooking, cleaning, making minor household repairs, sewing, mowing the lawn, and gardening are all daily tasks associated with adult life and are learned from experiences that are not usually a part of an individual's formal educational program.

For children with vision loss, however, routine daily living skills are not easily learned through everyday experiences. These children must be encouraged and supported as they develop life skills; they must not be overprotected from everyday challenges and risks by family and friends.

Academic Content

Mobility training and daily living skills are components of an educational program that must also include an academic curriculum. The nearby Case Study, "Mike and Josh," illustrates classroom strategies to improve academic learning for three students who have low vision and other disabilities.

Particular emphasis must be placed on developing receptive and expressive language skills. Students with vision loss must learn to listen in order to understand the auditory world more clearly. Finely tuned receptive skills contribute to the development of expressive language, which allows these students to describe their perceptions of the world orally. Some research suggests the use of a language experience approach (LEA) as a means to develop language skills and prepare students for reading (Dorr, 2006; Koenig & Holbrook, 2005). The LEA involves several steps, as described in Figure 13.6.

Oral expression can be expanded to include handwriting as a means of communication. The acquisition of social and instructional language skills opens the door to many areas, including reading and mathematics. Reading can greatly expand the knowledge base for children with vision loss. For people who are partially sighted, various optical aids are available: video systems that magnify print, handheld magnifiers, magnifiers

Figure 13.6 *General Steps in the Language Experience Approach*

1. Arrange for and carry out a special event or activity for the child (or a group of children), such as a visit to the town's post office or a nearby farm. A naturally occurring experience such as a classmate's birthday or a school assembly may also be used, but it is important to continue to expand the child's experiences through unique and special activities (such as attending a circus or riding in a rowboat).Use a multisensory approach and active learning to immerse the child fully in the experience.

2. After the activity, have the child tell a story about what happened. If he or she has trouble getting started, use some brief prompts ("What happened first?"). As the child tells the story, write it down word for word with a braillewriter. Generally, the stories are relatively short at this stage in the student's literacy development. Three important points need to be emphasized:

   • Use a braillewriter (rather than a computer) to write the story so that the child knows that what he or she is saying is being recorded through writing. Have the child follow along with his or her finger just behind the embossing head, if appropriate.

   • Write the story in braille as the child is speaking. It is not instructionally effective to write it in print and later transcribe it into braille. Writing immediately in braille makes the child aware of the natural relationship between spoken and written words.

   • Write down the child's words exactly as he or she says them. Do not fix grammatical errors or attempt to control the vocabulary in any way. One of the goals of using this approach is to build the child's trust. If the child thinks that his or her story needs to be "fixed," then this feeling of trust is interrupted, and the child may be less willing to share his or her experiences and stories in the future.

3. Reread the story immediately with the child, using the shared reading strategy just discussed. The child will remember much of the story and will be able to read along, saying many of the words. Do not stop or pause during this step to have the child sound out or analyze words. The immediate rereading should be a holistic experience recounting the child's story.

4. Continue rereading the story through shared reading on subsequent days. Soon, the child will independently know more of the words and may even begin to recognize some of the words out of context.

5. Arrange contextually appropriate reading-strategy lessons based on the story, especially as the child approaches kindergarten. For example, if the story has several *p* words in it, talk about the initial /*p*/ sound. The child can scan to find the *p* words in the story and make a list, perhaps in a shared writing experience, of other *p* words. A comprehension activity may involve writing a new ending of the story by changing one feature (e.g., "How would your story have ended if . . . ?"). Related art activities or binding the story into a book may also be fun and motivating for the child.

SOURCE: Koenig, A. J., & Holbrook, M. C. (Eds.). (2005). Literacy skills. In *Foundations of education: Volume II, Instructional strategies for teaching children and youths with visual impairments*, 2nd ed. (pp. 276–277). New York: AFB Press.

attached to eyeglasses, and other telescopic aids. Another means to facilitate reading for partially sighted students is the use of large-print books, which are generally available in several print sizes through the American Printing House for the Blind and the Library of Congress. Other factors that must be considered in teaching reading to students who are partially sighted include adequate illumination and the reduction of glare. Advance organizers prepare students by previewing the instructional approach and materials to be used in a lesson. These organizers essentially identify the topics or tasks to be learned, give the student an organizational framework, indicate the concepts to be introduced, list new vocabulary, and state the intended outcomes for the student.

Abstract mathematical concepts may be difficult for students who are blind. These students will probably require additional practice in learning to master symbols, number facts, and higher-level calculations. As concepts become more complex, additional aids may be necessary to facilitate learning. Specially designed talking microcomputers, calculators, rulers, and compasses have been developed to assist students in this area.

MIKE: Mike, a tenth-grader, was born deaf and has recently been diagnosed with Usher syndrome. He has poor night vision and is slowly beginning to lose his visual fields. His visual acuity continues to be 20/20 . . . Mike has been advised to move his head to scan the entire line or page when reading. Mike has special interests in planets and likes to read about the topic . . . The teacher shows pictures of planets, describing each one, and has Mike identify which planet the teacher is referring to by spelling the name of the planet—that is, circling the letters in the letter chart in front of him.

JOSH: Josh is an 8-year-old with cerebral palsy as a result of premature birth. He has excellent verbal skills but has difficulties with fine motor skills and any spatial-related tasks (such as drawing a tall tree on the left side of the house or writing the letter p) . . . Josh is placed in a general education second-grade classroom and possesses basic concepts comparable to that of a second-grader without disabilities . . . Josh is asked to verbally illustrate as he draws a house or writes a letter within the grid or dots. If he has problems, the teacher demonstrates, for example, "drawing a line on the second row between the second and fourth dots, the chimney is sticking out between the third and fourth dots." If Josh is confused with rows and lines of dots, the

© Spencer Grant / Photo Edit

teacher may number the dots so that he can follow the numbers instead of the lines and rows of dots. However, numbered dots should be faded out gradually so that Josh will use spatial concepts rather than numbers.

APPLICATION QUESTIONS

1. Mike, a student who has both a vision loss and was born deaf, is losing his visual fields. What strategies are used to

For children with a vision loss, the use of visual aids in addition to auditory stimuli enhances their ability to learn new concepts.

assist Mike in coping with his emerging field loss?

2. Josh is a child with vision loss and cerebral palsy who has difficulties with fine motor skills and spatial-related tasks. Describe the task that Josh uses to improve his skills in these two areas.

SOURCE: Li, A. (2004). Classroom strategies for improving and enhancing visual skills in students with disabilities. *Teaching Exceptional Children, 36*(6), 38–46.

Standard 4
Instructional Strategies

Standard 7
Instructional Planning

Standard 8
Assessment

Communication Media

For students who are partially sighted, their limited vision remains a means of obtaining information. The use of optical aids in conjunction with auditory and tactile stimuli provides these individuals with an integrated sensory approach to learning. However, this approach is not possible for students who are blind. Because they do not have access to visual stimuli, they may have to compensate through the use of tactile and auditory media. Through these media, children who are blind develop an understanding of themselves and of the world around them. One facet of this development process is the acquisition of language, and one facet of language acquisition is learning to read.

For students who are blind, the tactile sense represents entry into the symbolic world of reading. The most widely used tactile medium for teaching reading is the braille system.

This system, which originated with the work of Louis Braille in 1829, is a code that utilizes a six-dot cell to form 63 different alphabetical, numerical, and grammatical characters. To become a proficient braille reader, a person must learn 263 different configurations, including alphabet letters, punctuation marks, short-form words, and contractions. Braille is not a tactile reproduction of the standard English alphabet, but a separate code for reading and writing.

Braille is composed of from 1 to 6 raised dots depicted in a cell or space that contains room for two vertical rows of three dots each. On the left, the dots are numbered 1, 2, and 3 from top to bottom; on the right the dots are numbered 4, 5, and 6. This makes it easy to describe braille characters. For example, "a" is dot 1, "p" is dots 1, 2, 3, and 4, and "h" is dots 1, 2, and 5.

In braille any letter becomes a capital by putting dot 6 in front of it. For example, if "a" is dot 1, then "A" is dot 6 followed by dot 1, and if "p" is dots 1, 2, 3, and 4, then "P" is dot 6 followed by dots 1, 2, 3, and 4. This sure is easier than print, which requires different configurations for more than half of the capital letters. If "h" is dots 1, 2, and 5, what is "H"? Research has shown that the fastest braille readers use two hands. Using two hands also seems to make it easier for beginning braille readers to stay on the line. Do you think this might have something to do with two points constituting a line as my geometry teacher used to tell us (Pester, 2012)?

Braille is used by about one of every ten students who are blind and is considered by many to be an efficient means for teaching reading and writing. The American Printing House for the Blind produces about 28 million pages in English braille each year (Pester, 2012). Critics of the system argue that most readers who use braille are much slower than those who read from print and that braille materials are bulky and tedious. It can be argued, however, that without braille, people who are blind would be much less independent. Some people who are unable to read braille (such as people with diabetes who have decreased tactile sensitivity) are more dependent on sight readers and recordings. Simple tasks—such as labeling cans, boxes, or cartons in a bathroom or kitchen—become nearly impossible to complete.

Braille writing is accomplished through the use of a slate and stylus. Using this procedure, a student writes a mirror image of the reading code, moving from right to left. The writing process may be facilitated by using a braillewriter, a hand-operated machine with six keys that correspond to each dot in the braille cell.

Innovations for braille readers that reduce some of the problems associated with the medium include the Mountbatten Brailler and the Braille 'n Speak. The Mountbatten Brailler is electronic and, hence, easier to operate than a manual unit. The Mountbatten Brailler weighs about 15 pounds and can be hooked up to a computer keyboard attachment to input information.

The Braille 'n Speak is a pocket-size battery-powered braille note taker with a keyboard for data entry with voice output. The device can translate braille into synthesized speech or print. Files may be printed in formatted text to a printer designed to enable users to input information through a braille keyboard. The Braille 'n Speak has accessories for entering or reading text for a host computer, for reading computer disks, and for sending or receiving a fax.

In regard to educational programs for students who are blind, the U.S. Congress responded to concerns that services for these students were not addressing their unique educational and learning needs, particularly their needs for instruction in reading, writing, and composition. In IDEA, Congress mandated that schools make provision for instruction in braille and the use of braille unless the IEP team determines that such instruction and use are not appropriate to the needs of the student (U.S. Department of Education, 2011).

One tactile device that does not use the braille system is the Optacon scanner. This machine exposes printed material to a camera and then reproduces it on a fingerpad, using a series of vibrating pins that are tactile reproductions of the printed material. Developed by J. C. Bliss, Optacons have been available commercially since 1971, and thousands are currently in use worldwide. Although the Optacon greatly expands access to the printed word, it has drawbacks as well. It requires tactile sensitivity, so reading remains a slow, laborious process. Additionally, considerable training is required for individuals to become skilled users. These drawbacks, along with the development of reading machines, have resulted in the declining use and production of the Optacon scanner.

The Braille'n Speak translates braille into synthesized speech and is so portable that it can be carried anywhere.

© Robin Sachs/Photo Edit

Many of the newer communication systems do not make use of the tactile sense because it is not functional for all people who are blind (many, including some elderly people, do not have tactile sensitivity). Such individuals must rely solely on the auditory sense to acquire information. Specialized auditory media for people who are blind are becoming increasingly available. One example is the reading machine, hailed as a major breakthrough in technology for people with a vision loss. Reading machines convert printed matter into synthetic speech at a rate of 1 to 2.5 pages per minute. They can also convert print to braille. The costs associated with reading machines have decreased substantially in the past few years; most can be purchased with computer accessories for about $1,000. Several advocacy organizations for those with blindness and many banks throughout the United States currently provide low-interest loans for people with vision loss so that they can purchase the device. The first commercial reading machines were invented by Ray Kurzweil in the 1970s, culminating in today's L&H Kurzweil 1000 and 3000 Reading Systems. The Kurzweil 1000 makes any printed or electronic text easily accessible to people with low vision or blindness. The Kurzweil 3000 provides struggling readers the opportunity to learn from the same content and curriculum materials as their peers by facilitating assigned readings, assisting in the learning of critical study skills, and independently completing writing projects and tests (Kurzweil Technologies, 2012).

Reading machines are now readily available and affordable for people with low vision through a number of companies world-wide. The most recent reading machine software and newly developed "apps" can be found in pocket size devices, including smartphones and tablets (i.e., iPad.) in addition to desk top personal computers and laptops. E- readers, such as the Amazon Kindle and Nook, have the capability to increase text size with one touch, thus significantly enhancing availability for people with low vision to all types and forms of text. While printed text is not likely to go away anytime in the foreseeable future, the affordable e-readers and new tablet technologies are clearly changing the face of publishing. Such technologies can only mean good news for people with low vision or blindness. Other auditory aids that assist people who are blind include personal computers, smart phones, electronic tablets, calculators, watches, calendars and e-readers with voice output; digital recorders; and numerous other personal digital assistants (PDAs). For example, the Note Teller is a small, compact machine that can identify denominations of U.S. currency using a voice synthesizer that communicates in either English or Spanish.

Communication media that facilitate participation of people with vision loss in the community include specialized library and newspaper services that offer books in large print, on cassette, and in braille. The *New York Times*, for example, publishes a weekly special edition with type three times the size of its regular type. The sale of large-print books has increased during the past ten years; many have also become available through the Internet or on computer disc (electronic books).

Responding to a human voice, devices known as **personal digital assistants** (PDAs) can look up a telephone number and make a phone call. Using a synthesized voice, some PDAs can read a newspaper delivered over telephone lines, balance a checkbook, turn home appliances on and off, and maintain a daily appointment book.

Closed-Circuit Television

Closed-circuit television (CCTV) systems are another means to enlarge the print from books and other written documents. Initially explored in the 1950s, CCTV systems became more practical in the 1970s, and they are now in wider use than ever before. The components of the CCTV systems include a small television camera with variable zoom lens and focusing capacity, a TV monitor, and a sliding platform table for the printed materials. An individual sits in front of the television monitor to view printed material that can be enhanced up to 60 times its original size through the use of the TV camera and zoom lens. Some CCTVs are also available with split-screen capability to allow near and distant objects to be viewed together. These machines can also accept input directly from a computer as well as printed material.

Educating Students with Vision Loss in the Least Restrictive Environment

More recently, some residential schools have advocated an open system of intervention. These programs are based on the philosophy that children who are blind should have every opportunity to gain the same experiences that would be available if they were growing up in their own communities. Both open and closed residential facilities exist today as alternative intervention modes; they are no longer the primary social or educational systems available to people who are blind. Just like John in one of the chapter Snapshots, the vast majority of people who are blind or partially sighted now live at home, attend local public schools, and interact within the community. For more information about including people with vision loss in family, school, and community, see this chapter's Inclusion and Collaboration through the Lifespan on p. 355.

Educational programs for students with vision loss are based on the principle of flexible placement. Thus, a wide variety of services are available to these students, ranging from general education class placement, with little or no assistance from specialists, to separate residential schools. Between these two placements, the public schools generally offer several alternative classroom structures, including the use of consulting teachers, resource rooms, part-time special classes, or full-time special classes. Placement of students in one of these programs depends on the extent to which the loss of vision affects their overall educational achievement. Many students with vision loss are able to function successfully within inclusive educational programs if the learning environment is adapted to meet their needs.

Some organizations advocating for students who are blind strongly support the concept of flexible placements within a continuum ranging from general education classroom to residential school (American Foundation for the Blind, 2012). The American Foundation for the Blind recommends a full continuum of alternative placements, emphasizing that students who are visually impaired are most likely to succeed in educational systems where appropriate instruction and services are provided in a full array of program options by qualified staff to address each student's unique educational

Personal digital assistants
Handheld computer device that can be programmed to perform multiple functions such as making a phone call, reading a newspaper, or maintaining a daily calendar or address book.

Closed-circuit television (CCTV)
A system that includes a small TV camera with a zoom lens, which allows an individual with vision loss to view printed material enlarged up to 60 times its original size.

Standard 5
Learning Environments and Social Interactions

needs. Whether the student is to be included in the general education classroom or taught in a special class, a vision specialist must be available, either to support the general education classroom teacher or to provide direct instruction to the student. A vision specialist has received concentrated training in the education of students with vision loss. This specialist and the rest of the educational support team have knowledge of appropriate educational assessment techniques, specialized curriculum materials and teaching approaches, and the use of various communication media. Specialized instruction for students who have vision loss may include a major modification in curricula, including teaching concepts that children who are sighted learn incidentally (such as walking down the street, getting from one room to the next in the school building, getting meals in the cafeteria, and using public transportation).

Health Care and Social Services for People with Vision Loss

FOCUS 10

Why is the availability of appropriate health care and social services important for people with vision loss?

CEC

Standard 1
Foundations

Standard 8
Assessment

Health care services for vision loss include initial screenings based on visual acuity; preventive measures such as genetic screening, appropriate prenatal care, and early developmental assessments; and treatment ranging from optical aids to surgery. Some people with vision loss may have social adjustment difficulties, including a lack of self-esteem and general feelings of inferiority. To minimize these problems, social services should be made available as early as possible in the person's life.

Initial screenings for vision loss are usually based on the individual's visual acuity. Visual acuity may be measured through the use of the Snellen test, developed in 1862 by Dutch ophthalmologist Herman Snellen. This visual screening test is used primarily to measure central distance vision. The subject stands 20 feet from a letter chart, or E chart (the standard eye chart for testing vision), and reads each symbol, beginning with the top row. The different sizes of each row or symbol represent what a person with normal vision would see at the various distances indicated on the chart. As indicated earlier in this chapter, a person's visual acuity is then determined via an index that refers to the distance at which an object can be recognized. People with normal eyesight are defined as having 20/20 vision.

Because the Snellen test measures only visual acuity, it must be used primarily as an initial screening device that is supplemented by more in-depth assessments, such as a thorough ophthalmological examination. Parents, physicians, school nurses, and educators

Table 13.2   Warning Signs of Visual Problems

Physical Symptoms	Observable Behavior	Complaints
Eyes are crossed.	Blinks constantly	Frequent dizziness
Eyes are not functioning in unison.	Trips or stumbles frequently	Frequent headaches
Eyelids are swollen and crusted, with red rims.	Covers one eye when reading	Pain in the eyes
Eyes are overly sensitive to light.	Holds reading material either very close or very far away	Itching or burning of the eyes or eyelids
Sties occur frequently.	Distorts the face or frowns when concentrating on something in the distance	Double vision
Eyes are frequently bloodshot.	Walks cautiously	
Pupils are of different sizes.	Fails to see objects that are to one side or the other	
Eyes are constantly in motion.		

must also carefully observe a child's behavior, and document a complete history of possible symptoms of a vision loss. These observable symptoms fall into three categories: appearance, behavior, and complaints. Table 13.2 describes some warning signs of vision loss. The existence of symptoms does not necessarily mean a person has a significant vision loss, but it does indicate that an appropriate specialist should be consulted for further examination.

Prevention

Prevention of vision loss is one of the major goals of the field of medicine. Because some causes of blindness are hereditary, it is important for the family to be aware of genetic services. One purpose of genetic screening is to identify those who are planning to have a family and who may possess certain detrimental genotypes (such as albinism or retinoblastoma) that can be passed on to their descendants. Screening may also be conducted after conception to determine whether an unborn fetus possesses any genetic abnormalities. Following screening, a genetic counselor informs the parents of the test results so that the family can make an informed decision about conceiving a child or carrying a fetus to term.

Adequate prenatal care is another means of preventing problems. Parents must be made aware of the potential hazards associated with poor nutritional habits, the use of drugs, and exposure to radiation (such as X-rays) during pregnancy. One example of preventive care during this period is the use of antibiotics to treat various infections (influenza, measles, and syphilis, for example), thus reducing the risk of infection to the unborn fetus.

Developmental screening is also a widely recognized means of prevention. (It was through early developmental screening that a medical specialist confirmed that John, from a Snapshot in this chapter, had a serious vision loss and would require the assistance of a trained vision specialist.) Early screening of developmental problems enables the family physician to analyze several treatment alternatives and, when necessary, refer the child to an appropriate specialist for a more thorough evaluation of developmental delays.

This screening—which includes examination of hearing, speech, motor, and psychological development—includes attention to vision as well. Early screening involves a medical examination at birth, assessing the physical condition of the newborn, and also obtaining a complete family medical history. The eyes should be carefully examined for any abnormalities, such as infection or trauma.

At 6 weeks of age, visual screening forms part of another general developmental assessment. This examination should include input from the parents about how their child is responding (e.g., smiling and looking at objects or faces). The physician should check eye movement and search for infection, crusting on the eyes, or **epiphora**, an overflow of tears resulting from obstruction of the lachrymal ducts.

Epiphora
An overflow of tears from obstruction of the lachrymal ducts of the eye.

The next examination should occur at about 6 months of age. A defensive blink should be present at this age, and eye movement should be full and coordinated. If any imbalance in eye movements is noted, a more thorough examination should be conducted. Family history is extremely important, because in many cases there is a familial pattern of vision problems.

Between the ages of 1 and 5 years, visual evaluation should be conducted at regular intervals. An important period occurs just prior to the child entering school. Visual problems must not go undetected as children attempt to cope with the new and complex demands of the educational environment.

Treatment

In addition to medicine's emphasis on prevention of vision loss, significant strides have been made in the treatment of these problems. The nature of health care services depends on the type and severity of the loss. For people who are partially sighted, use of an optical aid can vastly improve access to the visual world. Most of these aids take the form of corrective glasses or contact lenses, which are designed to magnify the image on the retina. Some aids magnify the retinal image within the eye, and others clarify the retinal image. Appropriate use of optical aids, in conjunction with regular medical examinations, not only helps correct existing visual problems but may also prevent further deterioration of existing vision.

Atropinization
Treatment for cataracts that involves washing the eye with atropine, permanently dilating the pupil.

Standard 1
Foundations

Standard 5
Learning Environments and Social Interactions

Standard 8
Assessment

Surgery, muscle exercises, and drug therapy have also played important roles in treating people with vision loss. Treatment may range from complex laser surgical procedures and corneal transplants to the process known as **atropinization**.

Social services can begin with infant stimulation programs and counseling for the family. As the child grows older, group counseling can help the family cope with their feelings about blindness and provide guidance in the area of human sexuality (limited vision may distort perception of the physical body). Counseling eventually extends into matters focusing on marriage, family, and adult relationships. For adults with vision loss, special guidance may be necessary in preparation for employment and independent living.

Mobility of people with vision loss can be enhanced in large cities by the use of auditory pedestrian signals known as audible traffic signals (ATS) at crosswalks. The *walk* and *don't walk* signals are indicated by auditory cues, such as actual verbal messages (e.g., "Please do not cross yet"), different bird chirps for each signal, or a Sonalert buzzer. ATS is somewhat controversial among people who are blind and professionals in the field. Those who do not support the use of ATS have two basic concerns. First, the devices promote negative public attitudes, indicating a presumption that such assistance is necessary for people who are blind to be mobile. Second, the devices may actually contribute to unsafe conditions because they mask traffic noise for people who are blind.

Restaurant menus, elevator floor buttons, and signs in buildings (such as rest rooms) can be produced in braille. Telephone credit cards, personal checks, ATM cards, special mailing tubes, and panels for household appliances are also available in braille. Access to community services is greatly enhanced by devices that use synthesized speech for purchasing subway and rail tickets and for obtaining money from automatic teller machines.

Looking Toward a Bright Future

In the United States, nearly 11 million people have an irreversible hearing loss and 9 million people have vision loss that will require some type of specialized services and supports. For these individuals, life in the 21st century is very different than for the generations that came before them. New research on effective education, health care, and social services, as well as advances in new technologies, is enhancing life in school, family, and community every day. Innovations in education, such as described in our earlier Case Study, "A Community of Learners," enable students who are deaf or hard of hearing to be fully included in their neighborhood school and learn side by side with hearing peers. This program strives to create a community of learners where all children share the common language of both spoken English and sign language. Major advances in computer programs are now readily available to assist school-age students with a hearing loss across a variety of academic subject areas, from reading and writing to learning basic sign language. The Internet has created a whole new world for those with a hearing loss as well as their hearing peers through social networking, interactive chat rooms, and an infinite number of websites.

For people with vision loss, print-to-speech reading machines, such as those designed by Ray Kurzweil, have become very small, inexpensive, palm-sized devices that can read books, printed documents, and other real-world texts such as signs and displays. GPS technology has made available user-friendly navigation devices that assist people in getting around; these devices are particularly helpful for those with a vision loss who need to avoid physical obstacles in their path and move easily through their environment (Kurzweil Technologies, 2012). Braille readers can now read their books on the Internet thanks to a historic technological breakthrough by the Library of Congress called Web-Braille. Readers now have access to more than 3,000 electronic braille books recently placed on the Internet. Many hundreds of new titles are added each year. As a result of new computer technology, braille readers may now access Web-Braille digital braille book files with a computer and a refreshable braille display (electronic device that raises or lowers an array of pins to create a line of braille characters) or a braille embosser (Library of Congress, 2012). It is indeed a changing world for those with sensory impairments—a world that holds the promise of a bright future.

EARLY CHILDHOOD YEARS

Tips for the Family

- Orient your family members (children, cousins, and other extended family members) so they have a good understanding about their supportive roles and how they can be understanding, helpful, and encouraging.

- Keep informed about organizations that can provide support to your child with a vision or hearing loss.

- Get in touch with your local health, social services, and education agencies about infant, toddler, and preschool programs for your child.

- Become familiar with the individualized family service plan (IFSP) and how it can serve as a planning tool to support the inclusion of your child in early intervention programs.

- Collaborate with professionals to determine what modes of communication (oral, manual, and/or total communication) will be most effective in developing early language skills with your child with a hearing loss.

- Provide appropriate and multiple sources of input for your child with a vision or hearing loss.

- Help your child with a vision loss to become oriented to the environment by removing all unnecessary obstacles around the home (e.g., shoes left on the floor, partially opened doors, a vacuum cleaner left out).

Tips for the Preschool Teacher

- Focus on developing expressive and receptive communication in the classroom as early as possible in your child with a hearing loss.

- Help classmates interact with the child with a hearing or vision loss in appropriate ways. Parents and other specialists can give you helpful suggestions.

- If the child with a hearing loss doesn't respond to sound, have the hearing children learn to stand in the line of sight.

- Work closely with parents so that early communication and skill development for a young child with a hearing loss are consistent across school and home environments.

- Become very familiar with acoustical devices (e.g., hearing aids) that a young child with a hearing loss may use. Make sure that these devices are worn properly and that they work in the classroom environment.

- Instruction in special mobility techniques should begin as early as possible with a young child who has vision loss.

Tips for Preschool Personnel

- Support the inclusion of young children with a hearing or vision loss in your classrooms and programs.

- Support teachers, staff, and volunteers as they attempt to create successful experiences for young children with a hearing or vision loss in the preschool setting.

- Collaborate with families to keep them informed and active members of the school community.

Tips for Neighbors and Friends

- Collaborate with the family of a young child with a hearing or vision loss to seek opportunities for interactions with peers in neighborhood play settings.

- Focus on the capabilities of the young child with a hearing or vision loss, rather than on the disabilities. Understand how the child with a hearing loss communicates: Orally? Manually? Or both? If the child uses sign language, take the time to learn fundamental signs that will enhance your communication with him or her.

- Help the child with a vision loss to develop a sense of touch and to use hearing to acquire information. The young child may also need assistance in learning to smile and make eye contact with others.

- Help children in the classroom who have sight interact with a child with

vision loss by teaching them to speak directly in a normal tone of voice.

- Become very familiar with both tactile (e.g., braille) and auditory aids (e.g., personal readers) that young children may use to acquire information.

ELEMENTARY YEARS

Tips for the Family

- Learn about your rights as parents of a child with a hearing or vision loss. Actively collaborate with professionals in the development of your child's individualized education program (IEP). Through active participation, establish goals on the IEP that will focus on your child's unique and particular needs.

- Participate in as many school functions for parents as possible (e.g., PTA, parent advisory groups, volunteering) to connect your family to the school.

- Seek information on in-school and extracurricular activities available that will enhance opportunities for your child to interact with school peers.

- Keep the school informed about the medical needs of your child with a hearing loss. If he or she needs or uses acoustical devices to enhance hearing capability, help school personnel understand how these devices work.

- If your child with a vision loss needs or uses specialized mobility devices to enhance access to the environment, help school personnel understand how these devices work.

Tips for the General Education Classroom Teacher

- Outline schoolwork (e.g., the schedule for the day) on paper or the blackboard so the student with a hearing loss can see it.

- Remember that students with hearing loss don't always know how words fit together to make understandable sentences. Help students develop skills by always writing in complete sentences.

- Have the student with a hearing loss sit where he or she can see the rest of the class as easily as possible. Choose a buddy to sit nearby to help the student with a hearing loss stay aware of what is happening within the classroom.

- Don't be surprised to see gaps in learning. Demonstrations of disappointment or shock will make the student feel at fault.

- Be sure to help the student with a hearing or vision loss know what is going on at all times (e.g., pass on announcements made over the intercom).

- Have scripts (or outlines of scripts) for movies and videotapes used in class. Let the student with a hearing loss read the script for the movie.

- When working with an interpreter, remember to:

  - Introduce the interpreter to the class at the beginning of the year, and explain his or her role.

  - Always speak directly to the student, not to the interpreter.

  - Pause when necessary to allow the interpreter to catch up, because he or she may often be a few words behind.

  - Face the class when speaking. (When using a blackboard, write on the board first, then face the class to speak.)

- Include students who are deaf in class activities, and encourage these students to participate in answering questions.

- Introduce the vision specialist to the class. A professional trained in the education of students with vision loss can serve as an effective consultant in several areas (e.g., mobility training, use of special equipment, communication media, and instructional strategies).

- Encourage peer support, an effective tool for learning, in the classroom setting. Peer buddy systems can be established in the school to help a child with initial mobility needs and/or to provide any tutoring that would help him or her succeed in the general education classroom.

Tips for School Personnel

- Integrate school resources as well as children. Wherever possible, help general education classroom teachers access the human and material resources necessary to meet the needs of students with a hearing or vision loss. For example:

  - The audiologist. Keep in close contact with this professional, and seek advice on the student's hearing and the acoustic devices being used.

  - The special education teacher trained in hearing loss. This professional is necessary both as a teacher of students with a hearing loss and as a consultant to general educators. Activities can range from working on the development of effective communication skills to dealing with behavioral difficulties. The general education teacher may even decide to work with the special education teacher on learning sign language, if appropriate.

  - Speech and language specialists. Many students with a hearing loss will need help with speech acquisition and application in the school setting.

  - A vision specialist. A professional trained in the education of students with vision loss can serve as an effective consultant to you and the children in several areas (e.g., mobility training, use of special equipment, communication media, and instructional strategies).

  - An ophthalmologist. Students with a vision loss often have associated medical problems. It is helpful for teachers to understand any related medical needs that can affect a child's educational experience.

Tips for Neighbors and Friends

- Help families with a child with a hearing or vision loss to be an integral part of neighborhood and friendship networks. Seek ways to include the family and the child in neighborhood activities (e.g., outings, barbecues, outdoor yard and street cleanups, crime watches).

SECONDARY AND TRANSITION YEARS

Tips for the Family

- Become familiar with adult services systems (e.g., rehabilitation, Social Security, health care) while your son or daughter is still in high school. Understand the type of vocational or employment training needed prior to graduation.

- Create opportunities outside of school for your son or daughter to participate in activities with same-age hearing peers.

Tips for the General Education Classroom Teacher

- Collaborate with specialists in hearing or vision loss and other school personnel to help students adapt to subject matter in your classroom (e.g., science, math, physical education).

- Become aware of the needs of students with a hearing or vision loss in your classroom and with the resources available for them. Facilitate student learning by establishing peer support systems (e.g., note takers) to help students with a hearing loss be successful.

- Use diagrams, graphs, and visual representations whenever possible when presenting new concepts to a student with a hearing loss.

- Help the student with a hearing or vision loss become involved in extracurricular high school activities. If you are the faculty sponsor of a club or organization, explore whether the student is interested and how he or she could get involved.

- Maintain positive and ongoing contact with the family.

Tips for School Personnel

- Encourage parents of high school–age students with a hearing or vision loss to participate in school activities (such as committees and PTA).

- Parents will be more active when school personnel have general and positive contact with the family.

Tips for Neighbors, Friends, and Potential Employers

- Collaborate with family and school personnel to create opportunities for students with a hearing or vision loss to participate in community activities as much as possible with peers.

- As a potential employer for people with a hearing or vision loss, work with the high school and vocational rehabilitation counselors to locate and establish employment training sites.

ADULT YEARS

Tips for the Family

- Become aware of the supports and services available for your son or daughter in the local community in which they will live as adults. What formal supports are available in the community through government-funded programs or advocacy organizations for people with a hearing loss?

- Explore adult services in the local community in the areas of postsecondary education, employment, and recreation.

Tips for Neighbors, Friends, and Potential Employers

- Seek ways to become part of a community support network for individuals with a hearing or vision loss. Be alert to ways in which these individuals can become and remain actively involved in community employment, neighborhood recreational activities, and local church functions.

- As potential employers in the community, seek out information on employment of people with a hearing or vision loss. Locate programs that focus on establishing employment opportunities for people with a hearing or vision loss, while meeting your needs as an employer.

FOCUS REVIEW

FOCUS 1 Describe how sound is transmitted through the human ear.

- A vibrator—such as a string, reed, or column of air—causes displacement of air particles.
- Vibrations are carried by air, metal, water, or other substances.
- Sound waves are displaced air particles that produce a pattern of auricular waves that move away from the source to a receiver.
- The human ear collects, processes, and transmits sounds to the brain, where they are decoded into meaningful language.

FOCUS 2 Distinguish between the terms *deaf* and *hard of hearing*.

- People who are deaf typically have profound or total loss of auditory sensitivity and very little, if any, auditory perception.
- For people who are deaf, the primary means of information input is through vision; speech received through the ears is not understood.
- People who are hard of hearing (partially hearing) generally have residual hearing through the use of a hearing aid, which is sufficient to process language through the ear successfully.

FOCUS 3 What are the estimated prevalence, causes, and characteristics of hearing loss?

- It has been extremely difficult to determine the prevalence of hearing loss. Estimates of hearing loss in the United States are as high as 28 million people; approximately 11 million people have significant irreversible hearing loss, and one million are deaf.
- More than 71,000 students between the ages of 6 and 21 have a hearing impairment and are receiving special education services in U.S. schools. These students account for approximately 1.5 percent of school-age students identified as having a disability.
- Although more than 200 types of deafness have been related to hereditary factors, the cause of 50 percent of all hearing loss remains unknown.
- A common hereditary disorder is otosclerosis (bone destruction in the middle ear).
- Nonhereditary hearing problems evident at birth may be associated with maternal health problems: infections (e.g., rubella), anemia, jaundice, central nervous system disorders, the use of drugs, sexually transmitted disease, chicken pox, anoxia, and birth trauma.
- Acquired hearing losses are associated with postnatal infections, such as measles, mumps, influenza, typhoid fever, and scarlet fever.
- Environmental factors associated with hearing loss include extreme changes in air pressure caused by explosions, head trauma, foreign objects in the ear, and loud noise. Loud noise is rapidly becoming one of the major causes of hearing problems.
- Intellectual development for people with hearing loss is more a function of language development than of cognitive ability. Any difficulties in performance appear to be closely associated with speaking, reading, and writing the English language but are not related to level of intelligence.
- Speech and English language skills are the areas of development most severely affected for those with a hearing loss. The effects of a hearing loss on English language development vary considerably.
- Most people with a hearing loss are able to use speech as the primary mode for language acquisition. People who are

congenitally deaf are unable to receive information through the speech process unless they have learned to speech-read.

- Reading is the academic area most negatively affected for students with a hearing loss.

- Social and psychological development in children with a hearing loss is different from that in children who can hear. Different or delayed language acquisition may lead to more limited opportunities for social interaction. Children who are deaf may have more adjustment challenges when attempting to communicate with children who can hear, but they appear to be more secure when conversing with children who are also deaf. Some people who are deaf do not consider social isolation from the hearing world an adjustment problem. Rather, it is a natural state of being where people are bonded together by a common language, customs, and heritage.

FOCUS 4 Identify four approaches to teaching communication skills to people with a hearing loss.

- The auditory approach to communication emphasizes the use of amplified sound and residual hearing to develop oral communication skills.

- The oral approach to communication emphasizes the use of amplified sound and residual hearing but may also employ speech-reading, reading and writing, and motokinesthetic speech training.

- The manual approach stresses the use of signs in teaching children who are deaf to communicate.

- Total communication employs the use of residual hearing, amplification, speech-reading, speech training, reading, and writing in combination with manual systems to teach communication skills to children with a hearing loss.

FOCUS 5 Why is early detection of hearing loss so important?

- Early detection of hearing loss can prevent or minimize the impact of the disability on the overall development of an individual.

FOCUS 6 Distinguish between the terms *blind* and *partially sighted*.

- Legal blindness is determined by visual acuity of 20/200 or worse in the best eye after correction or by a field of vision of 20 percent or less.

- Educational definitions of blindness focus primarily on students' inability to use vision as an avenue for learning.

- People who are partially sighted have a visual acuity greater than 20/200 but not greater than 20/70 in the best eye after correction.

- People who are partially sighted can still use vision as a primary means of learning.

FOCUS 7 What are the distinctive features of refractive eye problems, muscle disorders of the eye, and receptive eye problems?

- Refractive eye problems occur when the refractive structures of the eye (cornea or lens) fail to focus light rays properly on the retina. Refractive problems include hyperopia (farsightedness), myopia (nearsightedness), astigmatism (blurred vision), and cataracts.

- Muscle disorders occur when the major muscles within the eye are inadequately developed or atrophic, resulting in a loss of control and an inability to maintain tension. Muscle disorders include nystagmus (uncontrolled rapid eye movement), strabismus (crossed eyes), and amblyopia (loss of vision due to muscle imbalance).

- Receptive eye problems occur when the receptive structures of the eye (retina and optic nerve) degenerate or become damaged. Receptive eye problems include optic atrophy, retinitis pigmentosa, retinal detachment, retinopathy of prematurity, and glaucoma.

FOCUS 8 What are the estimated prevalence, causes, and characteristics of vision loss?

- Approximately 20 percent of all children and adults have some vision loss; 3 percent (9 million people) have a significant vision loss that will require some type of specialized services and supports.

- Fifty percent of people over the age of 65 experience a significant loss of vision (including cataracts).

- Over 26,000 students have visual impairments and receive specialized services in U.S. public schools.

- A number of genetic conditions can result in vision loss, including albinism, retinitis pigmentosa, retinoblastoma, optic atrophy, cataracts, severe myopia associated with retinal detachment, lesions of the cornea, abnormalities of the iris, microphthalmia, hydrocephalus, anophthalmia, and glaucoma.

- Acquired disorders that can lead to vision loss prior to birth include radiation, the introduction of drugs into the fetal system, and infections. Vision loss after birth may be due to several factors, including trauma, infections, inflammations, and tumors.

- The leading cause of acquired blindness in children worldwide is vitamin A deficiency (xerophthalmia). Cortical visual impairment (CVI) is also a leading cause of acquired blindness.

- Performance on tests of intelligence may be negatively affected in areas ranging from spatial concepts to general knowledge of the world.

- Children with vision loss are at a distinct disadvantage in developing speech and language skills because they are unable to visually associate words with objects. They cannot learn speech by visual imitation but must rely on hearing or touch for input. Preschool-age and school-age children with vision loss may develop a phenomenon known as verbalisms, or the excessive use of speech (wordiness), in which individuals may use words that have little meaning to them.

- In the area of written language, students with vision loss have more difficulty organizing thoughts to write a composition. Decoding for reading may be delayed because such students often use braille or large-print books as the media to decode. Decoding is a much slower process with these two media. Reading comprehension is also affected because it depends so much on the experiences of the reader.

- Other factors that may influence the academic achievement include (1) late entry into school; (2) failure in inappropriate school programs; (3) loss of time in school due to illness, treatment, or surgery; (4) lack of opportunity; and (5) slow rate of acquiring information.

- People with vision loss are unable to imitate the physical mannerisms of sighted peers and thus do not develop body language, an important form of social communication. People with sight may misinterpret what people with a vision loss say because the latter's visual cues may not be consistent with the spoken word.
- People with vision loss are often excluded from social activities that are integrally related to the use of vision, thus reinforcing the mistaken idea that they do not want to participate.
- Lack of sight may prevent people from understanding their own relative position in space, and may affect fine motor coordination and interfere with their ability to manipulate objects.
- The perceptual discrimination abilities of people with vision loss in the areas of texture, weight, and sound are comparable to those of sighted peers.
- People who are blind do not perform as well as people with sight on complex tasks of perception, including form identification, spatial relations, and perceptual-motor integration.

FOCUS 9 Describe two content areas that should be included in educational programs for students with vision loss.

- Mobility and orientation training. The ability to move safely, efficiently, and independently through the environment enhances individuals' opportunities to learn more about the world and thus be less dependent on others. Lack of mobility restricts individuals with vision loss in nearly every aspect of educational life.
- The acquisition of daily living skills. For children with a vision loss, routine daily living skills are not easily learned through everyday experiences. These children must be encouraged and supported as they develop life skills, not overprotected from everyday challenges and risks by family and friends.

FOCUS 10 Why is the availability of appropriate health care and social services important for people with vision loss?

- Much vision loss can be prevented through genetic screening and counseling, appropriate prenatal care, and early developmental assessment.
- The development of optical aids, including corrective glasses and contact lenses, has greatly improved access to the sighted world for people with vision loss.
- Medical treatment may range from complex laser surgical procedures and corneal transplants to drug therapy (such as atropinization).
- Social services address issues of self-esteem and feelings of inferiority that may stem from having a vision loss.

Council for Exceptional Children (CEC) Standards to Accompany Chapter 13

 If you are thinking about a career in special education, you should know that many states use national standards developed by the Council for Exceptional Children (CEC) to assess a teacher candidate's knowledge and skills for working with students with disabilities. See a complete listing of the 10 CEC Content Standards on the inside back cover of this text.

1 Foundations
2 Development and Characteristics of Learners
3 Individual Learning Differences
4 Instructional Strategies
5 Learning Environments and Social Interactions
7 Instructional Planning
8 Assessment

Mastery Activities and Assignments

 To master the content within this chapter, complete the following activities and assignments. Online and interactive versions of these activities are also available on the accompanying Education CourseMate website, where you may also access TeachSource videos, chapter web links, interactive quizzes, portfolio activities, flash cards, an integrated eBook, and much more!

1. Complete a written test of the chapter's content. If your instructor requires a written test of your content knowledge for this chapter, keep a copy for your portfolio. A practice test on the information covered in this chapter is available through the *Human Exceptionality* CourseMate website.

2. Review the Case Studies, "A Community of Learners" and "Mike, and Josh," and respond in writing to the Application Questions. Keep a copy of the Case Studies and your written responses for your portfolio.

3. Read the Debate Forum in this chapter and then visit the *Human Exceptionality* CourseMate website to complete the activity "Take a Stand." Keep a copy of this activity for your portfolio.

4. Participate in a community service learning activity. Community service is a valuable way to enhance your learning experience. Visit our CourseMate website for suggested community service learning activities that correspond to the information presented in this chapter. Develop a reflective journal of the service learning experience for your portfolio.

CHAPTER 14

Physical Disabilities and Other Health Disorders

© Richard Hutchings/Photo Edit

FOCUS PREVIEW

As you read the chapter, focus on these key concepts:

1 Identify several disabilities that may accompany cerebral palsy.

2 What is spina bifida myelomeningocele?

3 Identify three things that occur when the spinal cord is bruised or injured.

4 Describe the physical limitations associated with muscular dystrophy.

5 Describe the AIDS disease stages through which individuals with the syndrome move.

6 What are the critical symptoms of asthma in children and youth?

7 Describe the immediate treatment for a person who is experiencing a tonic/clonic seizure.

8 Identify several problems individuals with diabetes may experience later in life without adherence to diet, exercise, and medical regimens.

9 Identify present and future interventions for the treatment of children and youth with cystic fibrosis.

10 Describe the impact on body tissues of the sickling of red blood cells in sickle-cell disease (SCD).

11 Describe the focus of educational interventions for individuals with traumatic brain injuries.

12 What are the current views about the causes of attention deficit/hyperactivity disorder (ADHD)?

I Have Cerebral Palsy . . . It Doesn't Have Me!

Hi! My name is Michael Anwar, and I am a fifth-grade general education student at Evergreen Elementary in the Mead School District in Mead, Washington. I was born with cerebral palsy. The doctors told my mom that I would never be able to do things like most kids. For instance, I would never be able to walk.

There are many different types of cerebral palsy. I have ataxic cerebral palsy, which is characterized by fluctuating muscle tone and uncoordinated movement patterns. My cerebral palsy affects my gross motor skills (balance, posture, functional mobility), fine motor skills (hand skills), and communication skills (articulation and breathing).

When I first started school, I had difficulty walking, talking, singing, maintaining balance to sit at a table, getting on and off the school bus, eating, keeping up with my assignments, managing my clothing and backpack, using the bathroom, and all of the other typical things that preschoolers do (e.g., cutting, coloring, gluing, holding a crayon).

At school, I have an individualized education plan (IEP). This is a legally binding document that defines my education program. My team is comprised of me, my mom and dad, a paraeducator, teacher, education specialist,

Courtesy of Michael Anwar

school psychologist, as well as occupational, physical, and speech therapists. Through the years, they have taught me to be my own self-advocate.

Thanks to a lot of hard work on my part and with my therapist's help, I am now independent in almost everything I do at school. I can independently walk, talk, and sing. I can sit at a regular desk and get on and off the school bus with my neighborhood friends. During lunch, I can carry my own lunch tray, eat with my friends, and play safely on the playground. I am able to keep up with all of my classroom assignments because my teacher and paraeducator support me in using assistive technology. I use a laptop with technology

that allows me to scan in worksheets so I can type on them instead of write. Throughout the school day, I am able to take my coat on and off all by myself. I can also put on my backpack at the end of the day. I am able to use the bathroom all by myself. I can hold a crayon, color, and glue, beautifully. I am also able to be independent in PE, music, and library because my teachers adapt or modify assignments as necessary.

My ability to be independent in school has inspired me to participate in outside activities. My outside interests include wheelchair basketball, football, adapted snowboarding, four-wheeling, weight lifting, playing with my two dogs, and swimming.

In the past, people with cerebral palsy did not have many options. Today, I know that I can accomplish any goal that I set for myself. The reasons that I have been able to overcome many obstacles in my life are because of my great sense of humor, my flexibility, my self-acceptance, and, besides, I am irresistibly cute! I look forward to driving, holding a job, dating, getting married, and raising a family. My disability does not disable ME . . . I disable it!!!!

SOURCE: Adapted from Anwar, M., Boyd, B., & Romesburg, A. M. (2007). I have cerebral palsy . . . it doesn't have me! *Exceptional Parent, 37*(6), 100.

A Changing Era in the Lives of People with Physical Disabilities

Advancements and inventions in many fields are bringing hope to many children, youth, and adults with physical disabilities as well as their families. Physical disabilities may influence a person's ability to move about, to use arms and legs effectively, to swallow food, and/or to breathe independently. Physical disabilities may also affect other primary functions, such as vision, cognition, speech, language, hearing, and bowel and bladder control.

However, as indicated earlier, technologies, inventions, and developments in many fields are improving the lives of young people and adults with physical disabilities.

The degree to which individuals with physical disabilities participate in their neighborhoods and communities is directly related to the quality and timeliness of treatments received from various professionals; the nurturing and encouragement provided by parents, siblings, and teachers; the support and acceptance offered by peers, neighbors, relatives, and other community members; and the careful application of assistive and related technologies.

Developments in assistive technologies, stem cell research, person-specific medications, advanced surgical techniques, transplants, gene therapies, and other preventative and early therapies have and will continue to have lasting and positive impacts on infants, children, youth, and adults with physical disorders.

The Individuals with Disabilities Education Act (IDEA) uses the term **orthopedic impairment** to describe students with **physical disabilities** and the term **other health impaired** to describe students with health disorders.

The discussion of physical disabilities will be limited to a representative sample of physically disabling conditions: cerebral palsy, spina bifida, spinal cord injuries, and muscular dystrophy. We will present important information about definitions, prevalence, causation, and interventions.

Orthopedic impairment
An impairment such as an amputation, the absence of a limb, or a condition associated with cerebral palsy that may affect physical and educational performance.

Physical disabilities
Disabilities that can affect a person's ability to move about, use the arms and legs, and/or breathe independently.

Other health impaired
A category of disability that includes students with limited strength as a consequence of health problems.

FOCUS 1

Identify several disabilities that may accompany cerebral palsy.

Cerebral Palsy

Cerebral palsy (CP) represents a group of chronic conditions that affect muscle coordination and body movement. It is a neuromuscular disorder caused by damage to one or more specific areas of the brain, most often occurring during fetal development usually before birth, but may follow during or shortly after birth. *Cerebral* refers to the brain, and *palsy* speaks to muscle weakness and poor motor control. Secondary conditions may develop with CP, which may improve, worsen, or remain the same (American Academy for Cerebral Palsy and Developmental Medicine, 2011; Parkes & Hill, 2010).

Movement characteristics of individuals with CP include spastic—stiff and difficult movement; athetoid—involuntary and uncontrolled movement; and ataxic—disturbed depth perception and very poor sense of balance. Individuals with spastic CP may experience ongoing challenges with pain (Gorodzinsky, Hainsworth, & Weisman, 2011). There are several categories for cerebral palsy, which depend on the part of parts of the body affected (see Table 14.1).

Individuals with CP are likely to have mild to severe problems in nonmotor areas of functioning, including hearing impairments, speech and language disorders, intellectual deficits, visual impairments, and general perceptual problems. Because of the

Standard 2
Development and Characteristics of Learners

Table 14.1	Topographical Descriptions of Paralytic Conditions
Description	**Affected Area**
Monoplegia	One limb
Paraplegia	Lower body and both legs
Hemiplegia	One side of the body
Triplegia	Three appendages or limbs, usually both legs and one arm
Quadriplegia	All four extremities and usually the trunk
Diplegia	Legs more affected than arms
Double hemiplegia	Both halves of the body, with one side more affected than the other

multifaceted nature of this condition, many individuals with CP are considered people with multiple disabilities. Thus, CP cannot be characterized by any one set of common symptoms or attributes; it is a condition in which a variety of problems may be present in differing degrees of severity.

Prevalence and Causation

About 764,000 individuals in the United States display clinical features of CP. Nearly 10,000 infants are born each year with CP or develop it shortly after birth. The prevalence rate for CP is 3.3 per 1,000, with many more boys affected than girls (4:1) (United Cerebral Palsy, 2012). The fundamental causes of CP are insults to the brain (Mukherjee & Gaebler-Spira, 2007). Seventy percent of these insults take place during the intrauterine period of development (Yamamoto, 2007). Thirty percent of these insults occur during the birthing process. Any condition that can adversely affect the brain can cause CP. Environmental toxins, malnutrition, radiation damage, maternal disease, infections (measles, HIV, syphilis, etc.), prematurity, trauma, multiple births, insufficient oxygen to the brain—all of these and many more are risk factors for the development of CP (United Cerebral Palsy, 2012). Early symptoms of CP include delayed motor development, abnormal muscle tone, and atypical motor functioning.

Interventions

There is no cure for CP; rather, professionals and parents must work to manage the condition and its various manifestations, beginning as soon as the CP is diagnosed. Early and ongoing interventions and therapies center on the child's movement, social and emotional development, learning, language, speech, and hearing.

Effective interventions for the various forms of CP are based on accurate and continuous assessments. Motor deficits and other challenges associated with CP are not unchanging but evolve over time. Continuous assessment allows care providers to adjust treatment programs and select placement options in accordance with the emerging needs of the child, youth, or adult (Parkes & Hill, 2010).

Management of CP is a multifaceted process that involves many medical and human service specialties working in teams (Martin, 2006; United Cerebral Palsy, 2012). These teams, composed of medical experts, physical and occupational therapists, teachers, social workers, volunteers, and family members, join together to help children, youth, and adults with CP realize their potential and self-selected goals. Vital goals of management/therapy may include developing or improving existing skills, decreasing complications of CP, lessening skeletal deformity, improving mobility, and developing communication skills.

The thrust of the management efforts depends on the nature of the problems and strengths presented by the individual child, youth, or adult. More specifically, interventions are directed at

- preventing additional physical deformities;
- decreasing adverse symptoms;
- developing useful posture and movements;
- providing appropriate surgeries when needed;
- dealing with feeding and swallowing problems;
- developing appropriate motor skills;
- securing suitable augmentative communication and other assistive devices;
- prescribing appropriate medications to reduce spasticity, drooling, muscle spasms, seizures, and to aid body control; and
- developing mobility and appropriate independence skills. (Kahn, 2009; United Cerebral Palsy, 2012)

Because of the multifaceted nature of CP, other specialists may also be involved, including ophthalmologists, audiologists, massage therapists, speech and language clinicians, and vocational and rehabilitation specialists.

CEC

Standard 5
Learning Environments and Social Interactions

LEARNING THROUGH SOCIAL MEDIA MY LIFE WITH CEREBRAL PALSY: REMOVING THE FENCE AROUND SOCIAL BARRIERS ONE POST AT A TIME

Laura Forde is a young adult. She has been blogging for several years. As a child, she felt quite lonely and secluded because others her age did not know how to communicate with her. However, as she moved through her schooling, she developed greater independence, becoming a "spunky and determined adult." She now communicates regularly from her blog. What follows is one of her recent postings:

Why I am glad I grew up in the time I did

In coming up with today's post, I found myself in a reflective space. . . . [O]ut my window, the snow is softly falling and the forecast later today looks bleak so I am told. It is this weather that leaves the thought of going out to be an undesired one, and yet I have a strong need: the need for community.

The digital age helps the disabled

I often wonder what my life would be like if I grew up in a different time. The Internet helps to maintain or build a community that I otherwise wouldn't have. The digital age has helped me be less lonely, less aware of my physical limitation. That isn't just because of this blog; it's Facebook, Twitter, AbilityOnline, and the other places online that I frequent.

Why I love blogging and think we all should have a blog

We all have a story worth telling, and I love how the blog for me does not require any adaptation to participate; it simply requires learning and a learning curve and some dedication. But I don't "look" different nor do I do things differently from the next guy that runs a blog. Blogs are about shared experience and I hope you will do me the honor of sharing my blog with your friends and family and your community online. I feel like this blog is helping to reduce social stigma, and without the Internet, this blog wouldn't be here.

SOURCE: Copyright © 2012 by Laura Forde. Laura Forde is a blogger and public speaker from Ontario Canada you can learn more about her at http://lifeofthedifferentlyabled.com

Physical and occupational therapists play significant roles in the lives of children and youth with CP (Martin, 2006). These individuals provide essentially three types of crucial services: (1) assessments to detect deformities and deficits in movement quality; (2) program planning, such as assisting with the writing of IEPs and other treatment plans, selecting adaptive equipment and assistive devices, and developing home and school programs for parents and other family members; and (3) delivery of therapy services.

School-centered services may include indirect treatment provided in the form of consultation, training, and informal monitoring of student performance; direct service through regular treatment sessions in out-of-class settings; and in-class or multisite service delivery to students in general education classrooms, in their homes, or at other community sites (Mukherjee & Gaebler-Spira, 2007).

Recent developments in augmentative communication and computer-centered technologies have had a tremendous impact on children, youth, and adults with CP and other conditions that impair speech and language production (Beukelman & Mirenda, 2005). Many augmentative communication devices are electronic or computer-based. These devices provide symbols or icons that, when pressed or activated with an optical pointer in certain sequences, produce audio output such as "No thank you. I don't like that," and "Do you know what we are having for lunch?"

Selecting augmentative communication devices for a child or youth is a team effort. Teachers, parents, speech and language specialists, physical and occupational therapists, and rehabilitation engineers play important roles in assisting with the selection process. Major benefits of augmentative and alternative communication in general education classrooms include increased interaction of students with disabilities with classroom peers, increased acceptance of students with disabilities, and greater connections with teachers—thus, resulting in improved relationships, greater learning, and better understanding of children with disabilities. As people with CP move into adulthood, they may require various kinds of support, including continuing therapy, personal assistance services, independent living services, vocational training, and counseling.

CEC

Standard 1
Foundations

ASSISTIVE TECHNOLOGY
VGO: THE ULTIMATE SCHOOL-BASED ROBOT

Deanne Fitzmaurice/Sports Illustrated/Getty Images

FOR SOME STUDENTS, ATTENDING SCHOOL ISN'T POSSIBLE

Injuries, extended illnesses, immune deficiencies, and other physical challenges prevent students from physically being able to attend school. School districts try to accommodate these children with special needs by providing online courses, in-home tutors, special busing, videoconferencing, and more. But these are expensive and very limiting because students miss out on the classroom experience and social life that come with attending school. Now, they can participate in classroom discussions and share in the social aspects of locker-side chats, lunch period, and moving from class to class.

VGO ENABLES STUDENTS TO ATTEND SCHOOL FROM A DISTANCE

At VGo, we love putting the spotlight on Lyndon Baty, a high school student in Knox City, Texas, who has an illness that requires him to remain at home because of the risk of physically being in class. He's a perfect example of the type of student who benefits greatly by being able to "attend" school via his VGo—or "BatyBot" as it's affectionately known at Lyndon's school.

From the safety of his home, in the morning, Lyndon gets on his computer instead of the bus. He uses VGo to move around school, interact with teachers, chat with his friends between classes, and spend the lunch period with them without endangering his health.

Lyndon operates his VGo simply with an Internet-connected computer equipped with audio capabilities and a webcam. VGo runs for a full school day before needing to be recharged.

VGo for Remote Students has opened up academic and social environments to other students who are disabled or have immune deficiencies as well. There are no longer boundaries between them and the world that was previously inaccessible.

SOURCE: Adapted from VGo. (2012). VGo Communications, Inc. Retrieved February 22, 2012, from www.vgocom.com/remote-student.

Spina Bifida

"*Spina Bifida* [SB] or *myelodysplasia* is a collective term for malformations of the spinal chord and is the most common NTD [neural tube deficit]. This defect can occur at any level of the spinal cord, although it more commonly affects the lumbar and sacral spine" (Lazzaretti & Pearson, 2010, p. 671). Spina bifida (SB) is characterized by an abnormal opening in the spinal column. It originates in the first days of pregnancy, often before a mother even knows that she is expecting. Through the process of cell division and differentiation, a neural tube forms in the developing fetus. At about 26 to 27 days, this neural tube fails to completely close. This failure results in various forms of spina bifida, frequently causing paralysis of various portions of the body, depending on the location of the opening. It may or may not influence the individual's intellectual functioning. Spina bifida is usually classified as either spina bifida occulta or spina bifida cystica.

Spina bifida occulta is a very mild condition in which a small slit is present in one or more of the vertebral structures. Most people with spina bifida occulta are unaware of its presence unless they have had a spinal X-ray for diagnosis of some other condition. Spina bifida occulta has little, if any, impact on a developing infant.

Spina bifida cystica is a malformation of the spinal column in which a tumorlike sac herniates through an opening or cleft on the infant's back (see Figure 14.1). Spina bifida cystica exists in many forms; however, two prominent forms will receive attention in our discussion: spina bifida meningocele and spina bifida myelomeningocele. In spina bifida meningocele, the sac contains spinal fluid but no nerve tissue. In the myelomeningocele type, the sac contains nerve tissue.

FOCUS 2

What is spina bifida myelomeningocele?

Figure 14.1 *Side Views of the Spine*

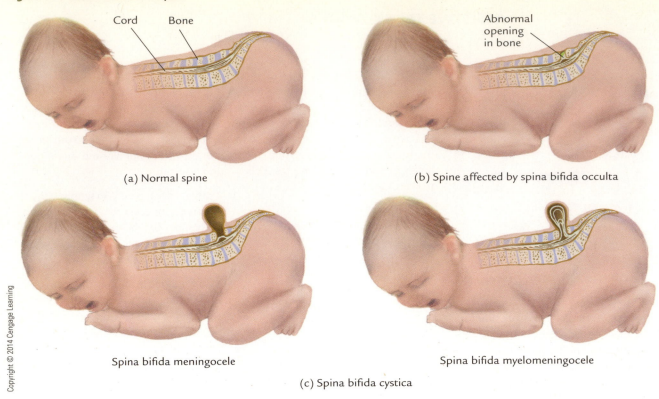

Cord   Bone

(a) Normal spine

Abnormal opening in bone

(b) Spine affected by spina bifida occulta

Spina bifida meningocele

Spina bifida myelomeningocele

(c) Spina bifida cystica

Spina bifida myelomeningocele is the most serious form of neural tube defect (NTD). It generally results in weakness or paralysis in the legs and lower body, an inability to control the bladder or bowel voluntarily, and the presence of other orthopedic problems (club feet, dislocated hip, and so on). There are two types of myelomeningocele. In one, the tumorlike sac is open, revealing the neural tissue; in the other, the sac is closed or covered with a combination of skin and membrane.

Prevalence and Causation

Prevalence figures for all neural tube defects is one in 1,500 births. The highest rates for these defects occur with Hispanic women and the lowest rates appear in Asian and black women (Nehring, 2010). Actually the prevalence of spina bifida (SB) has decreased over time in part because of prenatal screening, increased consumption of folic acid by pregnant mothers, and elective terminations of pregnancies (Law & Davis, 2007).

The exact cause of SB is unknown, although there is a slight tendency for the condition to run in families. In fact, myelomeningocele appears to be transmitted genetically, probably as a function of certain prenatal and environmental factors interacting with genetic predispositions (Nehring, 2010). It is also possible that certain antiseizure medications taken by the mother prior to or at the time of conception, or during the first few days of pregnancy, may be responsible for the defect. Environmental factors such as nutrition and diet also play a role.

Folic acid deficiencies have been implicated strongly in the causation of SB. Pregnant mothers should take particular care to augment their diets with 0.4 mg of folic acid each day. Folic acid is a common water-soluble B vitamin. Intake of this vitamin reduces the probability of neural tube defects in developing infants (Spina Bifida Association of America, 2012). The regular use of vitamin B_{12} may also reduce the incidence of SB and NTDs (Nehring, 2010).

Teratogens
Substances or conditions that cause malformations.

Infant exposure to various **teratogens** may also induce defects in the spine. These include valproic acid, carbamazepine (a seizure control medication), and other agents/drugs.

Other causative factors include radiation, maternal hyperthermia (high fever), and excess glucose. Also, congenital rubella has been implicated in causing SB and NTDs (Nehring, 2010).

Interventions

Several tests are now available to identify babies with myelomeningocele before they are born. One such test involves analysis of the mother's blood for the presence of a specific fetal protein (alpha-fetoprotein, AFT). AFT leaks from the developing child's spine into the amniotic fluid of the uterus and subsequently enters the mother's bloodstream. If blood tests prove positive for this AFT, ultrasonic scanning of the fetus may be performed to confirm the diagnosis. SB may also be detected through an ultrasound of an emerging fetus, potentially revealing a malformation of the spine.

Confirmation of the myelomeningocele creates intense feelings in parents. If the diagnosis is early in the child's intrauterine development, parents are faced with the decision of continuing or discontinuing the pregnancy or subjecting the emerging fetus to intrauterine surgery. There are, however, increased risks associated with this surgery for mothers and infants. These include early labor and delivery, fetal demise, and potential problems with bladder and bowel functioning in affected infants (Nehring, 2010). If parents decide to continue the pregnancy, they have time to process their intense feelings and to prepare for the child's surgery, birth, and care. If the decision is to discontinue the pregnancy, they must deal with the feelings produced by this action as well. If the condition is discovered at the time of the child's birth, it also produces powerful and penetrating feelings, the first of which is generally shock. All members of the health team (physicians, nurses, social workers, and so on), as well as other people (clergy, siblings, parents, and close friends), can help parents cope with the feelings they experience and the decisions that must be made.

Immediate action is often called for when the child with myelomeningocele is born, depending on the nature of the lesion, its position on the spine, and the presence of other related conditions. Decisions regarding medical interventions are extremely difficult to make, for they often entail problems and issues that are not easily or quickly resolved. For example, in 80 percent of children with myelomeningocele, a portion of the spinal cord is exposed, placing them at great risk for developing bacterial meningitis, which has a mortality rate of over 50 percent.

The decision to undertake surgery is often made quickly if the tissue sac is located very low on the infant's back. The purpose of the surgery is to close the spinal opening and lessen the potential for infection.

Another condition that often accompanies myelomeningocele is hydrocephalus, a condition characterized by excessive accumulation of cerebral fluid within the brain. More than 25 percent of children with myelomeningocele exhibit this condition at birth. Moreover, 70 to 90 percent of all children with myelomeningocele develop it after they are born. Surgery may also be performed for this condition in the first days of life. The operation includes inserting a small, soft plastic tube between the ventricles of the brain and connecting this tube with an absorption site in the abdomen. The excessive spinal fluid is diverted from the ventricles of the brain to a thin layer of tissue, the peritoneum, which lines the abdominal cavity (see Figure 14.2).

Children with spina bifida myelomeningocele may have little if any voluntary bowel or bladder control. This condition is directly attributable to the paralysis caused by malformation of the spinal cord and removal of the herniated sac containing nerve tissues. However, children as young as 4 years old can be taught effective procedures to manage bladder problems. As they mature, they can develop effective regimens and procedures for bowel management (Mason, Santoro, & Kaul, 2008).

Physical therapists play a critical role in helping children as they learn to cope with the paralysis caused by myelomeningocele (Harris, 2008). Paralysis obviously limits the children's exploratory activities, so critical to later learning and perceptual–motor performance. With this in mind, many such children are fitted with modified skateboards or other wheeled devices that allow them to explore their surroundings. Utilizing the strength in their arms and hands, they become quite adept in exploring their home and

Standard 5
Learning Environments
and Social Interactions

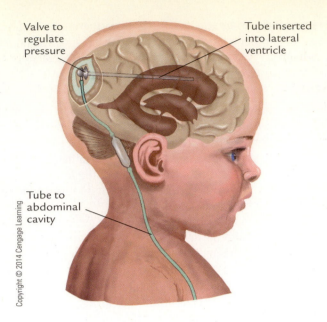

Figure 14.2 Ventriculoperitoneal Shunt

Valve to regulate pressure

Tube inserted into lateral ventricle

Tube to abdominal cavity

Copyright © 2014 Cengage Learning

Standard 5
Learning Environments and Social Interactions

Standard 10
Collaboration

neighborhood environments. Gradually, they move to leg braces, crutches, a wheelchair, or a combination of the three. Some children are ambulatory and do not require the use of a wheelchair.

Education programs for students with serious forms of spina bifida vary according to the needs of each student (Jahns, 2008). The vast majority of students with myelomeningocele are served in general education classrooms. School personnel can contribute to the well-being of these students in several ways: making sure that physical layouts permit students to move effectively with their crutches or wheelchairs through classrooms and other settings; supporting students' efforts in using various bladder and bowel management procedures and ensuring appropriate privacy in using them; requiring these students to be as responsible as anyone else in the class for customary assignments; involving them fully in field trips, physical education, and other school-related activities; and communicating regularly with parents. Additionally, if the student has a shunt, teachers should be alert to signs of its malfunctioning, including fever, irritability, neck pain, headache, vomiting, reduced alertness, and decline in school performance. These symptoms may appear very quickly and may be mistaken for flu-like symptoms. Teachers should take any of these aforementioned symptoms very seriously. As with all physical disabilities, collaboration and cooperation among all caregivers are vitally important to the well-being of each child or youth.

TEACHSOURCE VIDEO
INCLUDING STUDENTS WITH PHYSICAL DISABILITIES: BEST PRACTICES

Please visit the Education CourseMate website for *Human Exceptionality*, 11th edition, at CengageBrain.com to access this chapter's TeachSource Video. In this video, you'll see how second-grade teacher Lisa Kelleher and her classroom aide play a central role in orchestrating the learning and development of MaryAnne, a child with spina bifida.

1. How are Lisa, her aide, and the children in this classroom contributing to the academic and social learning of MaryAnne?

2. What, if any, special training or preparation do you think was needed for MaryAnne's placement and full participation in the class?

3. Are there stellar aspects of the services being provided or are they merely average? Are there any problems with the service delivery?

Spinal Cord Injury

Spinal cord injuries happen without any advanced notice. They are generally a result of some normal activity—driving a car, hiking, skiing, sledding, or diving. About 11,000 spinal cord injuries take place each year in the United States (Miller, 2007). "Spinal cord injury (SCI) is damage to the spinal cord that results in a loss of function such as mobility or feeling. Frequent causes of damage are trauma (car accident, gunshot, falls, etc.) or disease (polio, spina bifida, Friedreich's ataxia, etc.). The spinal cord does not have to be severed in order for a loss of functioning to occur. In fact, in most people with SCIs, the spinal cord is intact, but the damage to it results in loss of functioning" (Spinal Cord Injury Resource Center, 2012).

When the spinal cord is traumatized or severed, **spinal cord injury** (SCI) occurs. Trauma can result through extreme extension or flexing from a fall, an automobile accident, or a sports injury. The cord can also be severed through the same types of accidents, although such occurrences are extremely rare. Usually in such cases, the cord is bruised or otherwise injured, after which swelling and (within hours) bleeding often occurs. Gradually, a self-destructive process ensues, in which the affected area slowly deteriorates and the damage becomes irreversible (Spinal Cord Injury Resource Center, 2012).

The overall impact of injury on an individual depends on the site and nature of the insult. If the injury occurs in the neck or upper back, the resulting paralysis and effects are usually quite extensive. If the injury occurs in the lower back, paralysis is confined to the lower extremities. Similar to individuals with spina bifida, those who sustain spinal cord injuries may experience loss of voluntary bowel and bladder function.

Spinal cord injuries rarely occur without individuals sustaining other serious damage to their bodies. Accompanying injuries may include head trauma, fractures of some portion of the trunk, and significant chest injuries.

The physical characteristics of spinal cord injuries are similar to those of spina bifida myelomeningocele except there is no tendency for the development of hydrocephalus. The terms used to describe the impact of spinal cord injuries are *paraplegia*, *quadriplegia*, and *hemiplegia*. Note, however, that these terms are global descriptions of functioning and are not precise enough to convey accurately an individual's actual level of motor functioning.

Prevalence and Causation

About 450,000 individuals live with SCIs in the United States. Causes include motor vehicle accidents (42 percent); violence—primarily gunshot wounds (15.3 percent); sports-related injuries (7.4 percent); falls (27.1 percent); and other causes (8.1 percent). Significant numbers, nearly 25 percent of the SCIs are alcohol-related (Mayo Clinic, 2012). The average age for SCI injuries is now 38 years (Spinal Cord Injury Resource Center, 2012). About 5 percent of the SCIs occur in children, primarily from automobile-related accidents and falls (Liverman, Altevogt, Joy, & Johnson, 2005).

Interventions

The immediate care rendered to a person with SCI is crucial. The impact of the injury can be magnified if proper procedures are not employed soon after the accident or onset of the condition. Only properly trained personnel should move and transport a child, youth, or adult with a suspected SCI (Huffman, Fontaine, & Price, 2003).

The first phase of treatment provided by a hospital is the management of shock. Quickly thereafter, the individual is immobilized to prevent movement and possible further damage. As a rule, surgical procedures are not undertaken immediately. The major goal of medical treatment at this point is to stabilize the spine, manage swelling, and prevent further complications. Pharmacological interventions are also critical during this phase of treatment. Recent studies support the use of high and frequent doses of methylprednisolone. This medication often reduces damage to nerves cells, decreases swelling near the injury site, and improves the functional outcome for the affected individual, thus reducing secondary damage. Catheterization may be employed to control urine flow, and steps may be taken to reduce swelling and bleeding at the injury site. Traction may be used to stabilize certain portions of the spinal column and cord.

FOCUS 3

Identify three things that occur when the spinal cord is bruised or injured.

CEC

Standard 1
Foundations

Spinal cord injury
An injury derived from the bruising, traumatizing, or severing of the spinal cord, producing bleeding and swelling that often produce irreversible damage resulting in a loss of motor and/or sensory functioning.

Many of us hear news and talk show commentaries about stem cells, related research, and anticipated applications of the research. What follows is a series of questions and linked answers that will help you speak more knowledgeably about this exciting field of study that has profound implications for children, youth, and adults with all kinds of disabilities, diseases, and injuries.

WHAT IS A STEM CELL?

Stem cell is an umbrella term used to categorize a group of cells. Stem cells come in different varieties and might be specific to a particular tissue type.

Usually, when people use the term *stem cell*, they are referring to embryonic stem cells. A stem cell is a cell that is capable of dividing asymmetrically into two daughter cells that are not exactly alike. The overwhelming majority of cells in your body cannot do this.

This may not sound too compelling, but consider that you originated from one cell. The clear cells lining the cornea of your eye and the skin cells gripping this paper originally came from the same cell. A stem cell line can grow and mature into different cell types and tissues.

MEDICALLY, WHAT ARE THE POTENTIAL USES FOR STEM CELLS?

Stem cells can give rise to any tissue. There are types of tissues in adults that do not regrow, or that have the potential to do so very slowly.

Neural (brain and spinal cord) tissue is an example. If scientists can figure out how to trigger neural stem cells to regrow, it may be possible to help paralyzed patients walk again or to treat diseases such as Parkinson's, Alzheimer's, or dementia.

There also exists the possibility of growing tissues for implantation, such as skin for a burn victim or an organ transplant for a cancer patient. The potential uses are numerous and it is likely that more possibilities will come forth once more is known about stem cells.

HOW ARE HUMAN EMBRYONIC STEM CELLS OBTAINED?

Human embryonic stem cells are obtained from the inner cell mass of a blastocyst, an extremely small spherical cluster of cells present about five days after fertilization.

DO SCIENTISTS HAVE TO CREATE NEW EMBRYOS SPECIFICALLY TO DESTROY THEM?

Yes and no. There are already over 400,000 extra embryos that have been created via in-vitro fertilization that will never be implanted into surrogate mothers. Essentially, there are a lot of potential resources.

Questions for Reflection

1. What still puzzles you about the talk and debate about stem cells and stem cell research?

2. Should stem cell research be advanced to help treat individuals who have serious debilitating conditions such as Parkinson's, Alzheimer's, or dementia?

SOURCE: Adapted from Graf, R. (2009). Stem cells for dummies: A few questions answered. New University. Retrieved April 17, 2009, from http://www.newuniversity.org/2007/10/features/stem_cells_for_dummies42/.

Medical treatment of SCIs is lengthy and often tedious. See the nearby Reflect on This, "What Do You Know about Stem Cells?" for answers to questions about new stem cell–related treatments. Once physicians and other medical personnel have successfully stabilized the spine and treated other medical conditions, the rehabilitation process promptly begins. Individuals with SCI are taught to use new muscle combinations and to take advantage of any and all residual muscle strength. They are also taught to use orthopedic equipment, such as hand splints, braces, reachers, headsticks (for typing), and plateguards.

Traumatic SCI is accompanied by various pain syndromes—sometimes phantom pain. Relieving pain is a significant challenge over the lifespan of individuals with SCIs.

Psychiatric and other support personnel are also engaged in rehabilitation activities. Psychological adjustment to SCI and its impact on the individual's functioning can take a great deal of time and effort. The goal of all treatment is to help an injured person become as independent as possible.

As individuals master necessary self-care skills, other educational and career objectives can be pursued with the assistance of the rehabilitation team. The members of this collaborative team change constantly in accordance with the needs of each individual.

We've all seen exoskeletons in some of the most popular science fiction, even if we didn't know that's they were called. Sigourney Weaver used an exoskeleton designed for cargo lifting in outer space to kill the alien queen in Aliens. Tony Stark used a more personalized and hi-tech one to save the world as Iron Man. Believe it or not, paraplegics could be using one sooner rather than later to walk again.

Introducing the personal exoskeleton—the mechanical bodysuit that could get people with spinal cord injuries back on their feet. The military already has them, rehab clinics are using them, and with costs coming down and technology improving, it looks like they're going to be available for personal use in the near future.

When a skiing accident left Amanda Boxtel a T11-12 paraplegic 18 years ago, doctors told her what they have told hundreds of thousands of people with spinal cord injuries: You'll never walk again. Undeterred, she carved out a new life for herself. She started a nonprofit, helped create adaptive skiing programs, and spoke often as a motivational speaker. Still, Boxtel missed the natural feeling of simply standing up and moving around. The closest she felt to natural body movements was when she was on horseback.

That was before she was invited to try the Ekso exoskeleton (earlier called eLegs) in 2010. The Ekso is the signature product of Ekso Bionics, one of the pioneering companies manufacturing exoskeletons. Walking with the aid of the Ekso proved even more natural than horseback riding, according to Boxtel. "I had forgotten how tall I was.

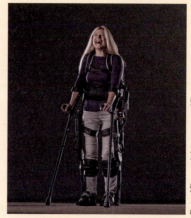

Photo of Ekso exoskeleton courtesy of Ekso Bionics http://eksobionics.com

How it is to look someone eye to eye," says Boxtel, adding, "[Using Ekso] was the most powerful psychological and emotional experience for me."

SOURCE: From Priya Ramachandran, "From Science Fiction to Reality: Exoskeletons." Copyright © 2012 National Spinal Cord Injury Association a program of United Spinal Association. Reprinted with permission.

Education for individuals with spinal cord injuries is similar to that for uninjured children or adults. Teachers must be aware, however, that some individuals with spinal cord injuries will be unable to feel pressure and pain in the lower extremities, so pressure sores and skin breakdown may occur in response to prolonged sitting. Opportunities for repositioning and movement will help prevent these problems. Parents and teachers should be aware of signs of depression that may accompany reentry into school.

Muscular Dystrophy

"The muscular dystrophies (MD) are a group of more than 30 genetic diseases characterized by progressive weakness and degeneration of the skeletal muscles that control movement. Some forms of MD are seen in infancy or childhood, while others may not appear until middle age or later. The disorders differ in terms of the distribution and extent of muscle weakness (some forms of MD also affect cardiac muscle), age of onset, rate of progression, and pattern of inheritance" (National Institute of Neurological Disorders and Strokes, 2012b). The muscles of the heart and some other involuntary muscles are also affected in some forms of muscular dystrophy, and a few forms involve other organs as well. Muscular dystrophy is a progressive disorder that may affect the muscles of the hips, legs, shoulders, and arms, progressively causing these individuals to lose their ability to walk and to use their arms and hands effectively and functionally. The loss of ability is attributable to fatty tissue that gradually replaces healthy muscle tissue. Heart muscle may also be affected, resulting in symptoms of heart failure. The seriousness of the various dystrophies is influenced by heredity, age of onset, the physical location and nature of onset, and the rate at which the condition progresses (National Institute of Neurological Disorders and Strokes, 2012b).

CEC

Standard 1
Foundations

FOCUS 4
Describe the physical limitations associated with muscular dystrophy.

Duchenne-type muscular dystrophy (DMD) is the most common form of childhood muscular dystrophy. DMD generally manifests when children are between the ages of 2 and 6. Early in the second decade of life, individuals with DMD use wheelchairs to move from place to place. By the end of the second decade of life, or early in the third, young adults with DMD die from respiratory insufficiency or cardiac failure (Muscular Dystrophy Association, 2012).

DMD is first seen in the pelvic girdle, although it sometimes begins in the shoulder girdle muscles. With the passage of time, individuals begin to experience a loss of respiratory function and are unable to cough up secretions that may result in pneumonia. Also, severe spinal curvature develops over time with wheelchair use, although this curvature may be prevented with spinal fusion.

Prevalence and Causation

About 200,000 people are affected by muscular dystrophies and related disorders. About one in every 4,700 males is affected by DMD (Dooley, Gordon, Dodds, & MacSween, 2010). Mothers who are carriers transmit this condition to 50 percent of their male offspring. One-third of the cases of DMD arise by mutation in families with no history of the disease.

Abnormalities in muscle protein genes cause muscular dystrophies. Each human cell contains tens of thousands of genes. Each gene is a string of DNA and is the code or recipe for a given protein. If the recipe for a muscle-related protein is lacking or is missing a key ingredient, the results can be tragic. The missing or diminished ingredient is dystrophin, an essential and critical component of healthy muscle fibers (Muscular Dystrophy Association, 2011). Without dystrophin, muscle cells explode and die.

Interventions

There is no known cure for muscular dystrophy. Treatments focus on maintaining or improving the individual's functioning and preserving his or her ambulatory independence for as long as possible. The first phases of maintenance and prevention are handled by physical therapists, who work to prevent or correct contractures (a permanent shortening and thickening of muscle fibers).

Drugs identified as *catabolic steroids* may have significant benefits for children and youth with DMD. The most often prescribed of these drugs is prednisone. It lessens the loss of muscle function or increases muscle strength in individuals with DMD. These drugs may lengthen the period of time in which individuals with DMD may be able to walk and to use their arms—several months to a couple of years (Parent Project Muscular Dystrophy, 2012). However, prednisone also has many potentially damaging side effects, which can be severe over a prolonged period, including loss of bone and muscle tissue, significant weight gain, loss of bone and (ironically) muscle tissue, thinning of the skin, elevated blood pressure and blood sugar, and serious psychological side effects, including depression and sleeping problems.

As DMD becomes more serious, treatment generally includes prescribing supportive devices, such as walkers, braces, night splints, surgical corsets, and hospital beds. Eventually, a person with muscular dystrophy will need to use a wheelchair.

The terminal nature of DMD and other health conditions pose challenging problems to affected individuals, their families, and caregivers. Major symptoms that may be experienced include pain, nausea, vomiting, seizures, convulsions, decreased appetite, mouth sores, fatigue, cough, difficulty swallowing foods, and skin problems.

Fortunately, significant progress has been made in helping individuals with terminal illnesses deal with death. Programs developed for families who have a terminally ill child, youth, or adult serve several purposes. They give children with terminal illnesses opportunities to ask questions about death; to express their concerns through writing, play, or other means; and to work through their feelings.

Programs for parents are designed to help them understand their children's conceptions about death, to suggest ways in which the parents might respond to certain questions or concerns, and to outline the steps they might take in successfully preparing for and responding to the child's death and related events. One such program is Compassionate Friends (Compassionate Friends, 2012). This organization, which is composed of parents who have lost children to death, provides sensitive support and resources to other parents who have lost a child to injury or disease.

At this juncture, you may want to examine the Inclusion and Collaboration through the Lifespan feature toward the end of this chapter. It offers valuable suggestions for interacting with young children, school-age children, youth, and adults with physical disabilities.

A Changing Era in the Lives of People with Health Disorders

As described in IDEA, **health disorders** cause individuals to have "limited strength, vitality, or alertness, due to chronic or acute health problems such as a heart conditions, tuberculosis, rheumatic fever, nephritis, asthma, sickle-cell anemia, hemophilia, epilepsy, lead poisoning, leukemia, or diabetes which adversely affect . . . educational performance" (23 Code of Federal Regulations, Section 300.5 [7]). In recent years, new subgroups have emerged within the health disorders area. They are often referred to as **medically fragile** and/or **technologically dependent** (American Federation of Teachers, 2009). These individuals are at risk for medical emergencies and often require specialized support in the form of ventilators or nutritional supplements. Often children or youth who are medically fragile have progressive diseases such as cancer or AIDS. Other children have episodic conditions that lessen their attentiveness, stamina, or energy.

Health disorders affect children, youth, and adults in a variety of ways. For example, a child with juvenile diabetes who has engaged in a vigorous game of volleyball with classmates may need to drink a little fruit juice or soda pop just before or after an activity to regulate blood sugar levels. An adult with diabetes may need to follow a special diet and regularly receive appropriate doses of insulin. The following health disorders will be reviewed in this section: acquired immune deficiency syndrome (AIDS), asthma, seizure disorders (epilepsy), diabetes, cystic fibrosis (CF), sickle-cell disease (SCD), traumatic brain injury (TBI), and attention deficit/hyperactivity disorder (ADHD).

Again, there is cause for optimism for children, youth, and adults with health disorders. This optimism centers on research and development efforts in many fields that are producing new person-specific medications, gene therapies, assistive devices, new surgical procedures, and a host of other inventions that heighten an individual's capacity to function more fully and to mitigate some of the effects of the health disorders.

Human Immunodeficiency Virus (HIV) and Acquired Immune Deficiency Syndrome (AIDS)

Acquired immunodeficiency syndrome (AIDS) is a set of symptoms and infections in individuals resulting from the specific injury to the **immune system** caused by infection with the human immunodeficiency virus (HIV). AIDS in children and youth is defined by two characteristics: (1) the presence of the **human immunodeficiency virus** (HIV), a virus that attacks certain white blood cells within the body, and/or the presence of antibodies to HIV in the blood or tissues as well as (2) recurrent bacterial diseases (National Center for HIV/AIDS, Viral Hepatitis, STD, and TB Prevention, 2012).

Individuals with AIDS move through a series of disease stages. The first stage is the exposure stage, or the period during which the transmission of the HIV occurs. Young people may be infected with HIV but may not yet exhibit the life-threatening conditions associated with AIDS. The second stage is characterized by the production of antibodies in infected individuals. These antibodies appear about 2 to 12 weeks after the initial transmission of the virus. About 30 percent of individuals experience flu-like symptoms for a few days to several weeks. During stage three, the immune system declines, and the virus

Standard 1
Foundations

Health disorders
Disabling conditions characterized by limited stamina, vitality, or alertness due to chronic or acute health problems.

Medically fragile
A disability category that includes people who are at risk for medical emergencies and often depend on technological support to sustain health or even life.

Technologically dependent
A disability category that includes people who require some technological assistance to meet their essential health needs while participating in daily activities.

Standard 1
Foundations

FOCUS 5
Describe the AIDS disease stages through which individuals with the syndrome move.

Immune system
A system of organs, tissues, cells, and cell products that attack potentially disease-causing organisms or substances.

Human immunodeficiency virus
A class of viruses that infect and destroy helper T cells of the immune system, making the body unable to combat and counter opportunistic infections.

begins to destroy cells of the immune system. However, many individuals with HIV are asymptomatic during this stage. This asymptomatic phase may continue for 3 to 10 years. About half of all individuals with HIV develop AIDS within 10 years.

Most children with HIV infection are diagnosed before the illness manifests itself (Fahrner & Romano, 2010). For children, the onset of AIDS ranges from one to three years. Generally, AIDS manifests itself within two years of the initial infection (Ball & Bindler, 2008). At stage four, individuals begin to manifest symptoms of a damaged immune system, including weight loss, fatigue, skin rashes, diarrhea, and night sweats. In more severe cases, opportunistic diseases appear in individuals with AIDS. At stage five, recurrent and chronic diseases begin to take their toll on individuals. Gradually, the immune system fails and death occurs.

Researchers have identified several patterns of disease development in HIV-infected children. The mean age of onset in exposed children is about 4.1 years. About 33 percent of exposed children remain AIDS-free until up to 13 years of age. Often the most serious symptoms do not appear until these children enter school or begin their adolescent years.

Prevalence and Causation

The Centers for Disease Control and Prevention "estimates 1.2 million people in the United States (US) are living with HIV infection. One in five (20%) of those people are unaware of their infection. Despite increases in the total number of people in the US living with HIV infection in recent years, the annual number of new HIV infections has remained relatively stable. However, new infections continue at far too high of a level, with approximately 50,000 Americans becoming infected with HIV each year" (Centers for Disease Control and Prevention, 2011d, p. 1).

Increasingly, heterosexual adolescents are at greater risk than infants to contract the HIV virus—this is because of unprotected sexual activities. "At least one adolescent in the United States is infected with HIV each hour" (Ricci & Kyle, 2009b, p. 162). Left untreated or undiagnosed, youth may not evidence any symptoms of AIDS until 10 years later as adults.

The cause of AIDS is the human immunodeficiency virus (HIV). This virus is passed from one person to another through various means, including the exchange of bodily fluids, usually semen or vaginal secretions; blood exchange through injection drug use (IDU); and exchange through blood transfusions, perinatal contact, and breast milk. Mothers who are infected with HIV can dramatically reduce the transmission of the virus to their yet-to-be born children by taking zidovudine during pregnancy.

Many children with AIDS do not grow normally, do not make appropriate weight gains, are slow to achieve important motor milestones (crawling, walking, and so on), and evidence neurological damage (Fahrner & Romano, 2010). As HIV turns into AIDS, these children are attacked by life-threatening **opportunistic infections**. Also, many of the children, as indicated earlier, develop more serious neurological problems associated with mental retardation, cerebral palsy, and seizure disorders.

Opportunistic infection
An infection caused by germs that are not usually capable of causing infection in healthy people but can do so given certain changes in the immune system (opportunity).

Interventions

To date, there is no known cure for AIDS. The best cure for AIDS in children and youth is prevention. Treatment is generally provided by an interdisciplinary team composed of medical, educational, and health care professionals.

Much progress has been made in testing and applying new antiretroviral therapies to combat AIDS and in developing agents to treat opportunistic infections. Early diagnosis of infants with HIV is crucial. Early antiviral therapy and prophylactic treatment of opportunistic diseases can contribute significantly to the infected child's well-being and prognosis over time. Some infants benefit significantly from highly active antiretroviral therapy (HAART) (Fahrner & Romano, 2010). The frequency and nature of various treatments depend on the age of onset and the age at which the child develops the first opportunistic infection.

Providing appropriate interventions for infants with AIDS can be challenging. These infants, like infants without AIDS, are totally dependent on others for their care. Many mothers who pass the AIDS virus on to their children are not adequately prepared to care effectively for their infants. Typically, these mothers come from impoverished environments with little access to health care and other appropriate support services. Additionally, these mothers may be intravenous drug users and, therefore, are not reliable or trustworthy caregivers.

Treating adolescents with HIV and AIDS can be challenging. For example, compliance with medical regimens for all age groups is difficult. However, for those who are HIV-positive and have no obvious symptoms, keeping regular medical appointments and taking antiviral medications are not only highly problematic, but also constant reminders of a chronic, if not fatal, disease. Current treatment advances and carefully maintained drug regimes "have turned a disease that used to be a death sentence into a chronic, manageable one for individuals who live in countries where antiretroviral therapy is available" (Ricci & Kyle, 2009b, p. 164). These regimens need to be adhered to with almost perfect precision— otherwise the drug resistance sets in and the outcomes are tragic.

Youth with HIV and AIDS need to learn how to make medical regimens a regular part of their lives to maintain good health and longevity. They also require assistance in dealing with the psychological reactions of anxiety and depression that often accompany the discovery of HIV infection. Finally, they and others benefit significantly from instruction directed at helping them to understand AIDS, to make wise decisions about their sexual and other high-risk behaviors, to use assertiveness skills, and to communicate effectively with others.

Laws regarding the disclosure of AIDS to others vary across states. "Many states and some cities have *partner-notification* laws—meaning that, if you test positive for HIV, you (or your health care provider) may be legally obligated to tell your sex or needle-sharing partner(s). In some states, if you are HIV-positive and don't tell your partner(s), you can be charged with a crime. Some health departments require health care providers to report the name of your sex and needle-sharing partner(s) if they know that information—even if you refuse to report that information yourself.

"Some states also have laws that require clinic staff to notify a 'third party' if they know that person has a significant risk for exposure to HIV from a patient the staff member knows is infected with HIV. This is called 'duty to warn'" (AIDS.gov, 2012).

In many states, neither students with AIDS nor their parents are compelled by law to disclose their HIV medical status to school personnel or child care providers (Child Care Law Center, 2005; Fahrner & Romano, 2010). Nevertheless, the parents or students may share this information with a limited number of school-based personnel if they determine this would benefit their child, including the school nurse, the principal, and the child or youth's teacher(s). This information should be treated with the utmost confidentiality.

"Unfortunately, there is widespread but unwarranted anxiety among parents whose children attend school with a youngster with AIDS, fearing that their own child may contract the disease. The AIDS virus (human immunodeficiency virus, or HIV) is transmitted only through blood, blood products, and sexual contact. Casual physical contact—including touching or holding hands with someone with AIDS, or sharing a drinking glass—will not transfer the AIDS virus" (American Academy of Pediatrics, 2011).

Students with HIV who are on strict medical regimens will need time to take their medications. Missing dosages could seriously jeopardize a student's health. Fatigue is a common occurrence in these students. Ample opportunities should be available for rejuvenation and respite from demanding physical activities.

Essential teacher-related behaviors in working with children and youth with AIDS include working collaboratively with care providers, providing sensitive and nonjudgmental services, heeding the guidelines to prevent blood-borne infections (see Figure 14.3, "Universal Precautions and Their Benefits in School Settings"), helping young people adhere to their medication regimens, modeling appropriate respectful behaviors, and maintaining privacy and confidentiality. Also, teachers, parents, and other community organizations play key roles providing instruction related to preventing AIDS and its transmission.

CEC

Standard 5
Learning Environments and Social Interactions

Figure 14.3 *Universal Precautions and Their Benefits in School Settings*

Universal Precautions

- Thorough hand washing, before and after contacting individuals, objects, or secretions.
- Use of personal protective equipment (barrier protection) (gloves, masks, etc.).
- Application of safe methods of disposing waste, cleaning up spills, and handling laundry.
- Procedures for dealing with accidental exposure to potentially infectious materials.

Benefits of Adhering to Universal Precautions

- They protect infected individuals from further infection.
- They protect the privacy of infected individuals.
- They protect the health of service providers.
- They protect the health of other students.

SOURCE: Adapted from Best, S. J., Heller, K. W., & Bigge, J. L. (2005). *Preventing infectious disease transmission and implementing universal precautions in Chapter 3: Health impairments and infectious diseases in teaching individuals with physical or multiple disabilities.* (p. 79).

Asthma

FOCUS 6

What are the critical symptoms of asthma in children and youth?

CEC

Standard 1
Foundations

Asthma is evidenced by swelling and inflammation of the air passages that transport air from the mouth and nose to the lungs. This swelling within the affected passages causes them to narrow, thus limiting the air entering and exiting the individual. Symptoms can be activated by allergens, drugs, foods, inhalants, or other irritants that are drawn into the lungs, resulting in swollen, constricted, or blocked airways. Symptoms include diminished breathing capacity, coughing, wheezing, tightness in the chest, and excessive sputum (Ratcliffe & Kiechhefer, 2010). In severe cases, asthma can be life-threatening (Asthma and Allergy Foundation of America, 2009d).

Prevalence and Causation

Nearly one in ten children in the United States is affected by asthma. Most recent studies suggest that 8.4 percent of adults and 8.5 percent of children have asthma (American Lung Association, 2012; Centers for Disease Control and Prevention, 2012b).

Asthma is genetic in its origin—it is inherited. However, for asthma to display itself, to be awakened, it must be triggered. Triggers vary greatly across children, youth, and adults (Asthma and Allergy Foundation of America, 2012c). In response to these triggers, the large airways (bronchi) contract into spasm. Swelling soon follows, leading to a further narrowing of the airways and excessive mucus production, which leads to coughing and other breathing difficulties.

Triggers include waste from common household insects (house dust mites, cockroaches, and so on), grass pollens, mold spores, and pet dander. Other triggers involve medications, air pollution (ozone, nitrogen dioxide, sulfur dioxide, and so on), cleaning agents, tobacco smoke, and various chemicals and industrial compounds. Also, some early childhood infections, particularly respiratory infections, set the stage for the potential development of asthma. Emotional stress has also been implicated as a potential trigger or aggravator (Asthma and Allergy Foundation of America, 2012c).

Interventions

Several interventions are useful to children, youth, and adults with asthma. It is important for all age groups with asthma to eliminate or moderate exposure to potential triggers—appropriate actions may prevent or moderate asthma symptoms (Asthma and Allergy Foundation of America, 2012a). Interventions include increasing the anti-inflammatory medication in advance of anticipated exposure to certain triggers, using appropriate bronchodilators for much the same purpose, and limiting the time of exposure to potential or known triggers.

Table 14.2	Contents of an Asthma Management Plan
Brief history of the student's asthma.	

- Asthma symptoms
- Information on how to contact the student's health care provider, parent/guardian
- Physician and parent/guardian signature
- List of factors that make the student's asthma worse
- The student's personal best peak flow reading if the student uses peak flow monitoring
- List of the student's asthma medications
- A description of the student's treatment plan, based on symptoms or peak flow readings, including recommended actions for school personnel to help handle asthma episodes

SOURCE: Adapted from "Asthma and Physical Activity in the School: Asthma Management Plan," http://www.kidneeds.com/diagnostic_categories/articles/asthmaphysicalactiv.htm.

As indicated earlier, medications play a key role in treating and managing asthma. Bronchodilators, appropriately administered, reduce the swelling and inflammation in the affected airways and generally provide short-term reprieves from common symptoms. Other physician-prescribed, anti-inflammatory medications regularly administered contribute significantly to the management of the disease and its symptoms. For moderate to severe cases of asthma, anti-IgE therapy is recommended. This is a relatively new and very expensive therapy (Asthma and Allergy Foundation of America, 2012b).

Generally, the side effects of the asthma-prescribed medications are minimal. However, frequent use of bronchodilators may indicate a need for further medical consultation. Also, some forms of asthma are cold- or exercise-induced. In these cases, parents and other care providers will want to determine the benefits and related risks in having their children engage in activities that may activate asthma and its symptoms.

Like so many other health conditions, teachers and others who have regular and frequent access to children and youth with asthma need to understand the disease and its consequences. Many families will have created an "asthma management plan" with two primary purposes: effectively managing the disease on a daily basis and creating a rescue plan in the event of a severe asthmatic attack. The plan outlines warning signs, identifies rescue medicines, provides steps to take with an attack, and describes conditions that would warrant calling a doctor. The asthma management or action plan is an incredibly helpful tool for school personnel to have on hand (see Table 14.2).

Frequently, the symptoms associated with asthma are more evident during the day when children or youth participate in various school-related activities (recess, physical education, or other physically demanding activities). If there is some likelihood of severe asthmatic attacks, medications should be available within the school, teachers should know how to administer them, and the medications should be adequately stored in a secure cabinet, generally located in the school nurse's office. Communication and collaboration among and between teachers, parents, and other school personnel are vital to the successful treatment of asthma in children and youth.

CEC

Standard 5
Learning Environments and Social Interactions

Standard 10
Collaboration

Seizure Disorders (Epilepsy)

"Epilepsy is a brain disorder in which clusters of nerve cells, or neurons, in the brain sometimes signal abnormally. In epilepsy, the normal pattern of neuronal activity becomes disturbed, causing strange sensations, emotions, and behavior or sometimes convulsions, muscle spasms, and loss of consciousness. . . . Having a seizure does not

FOCUS 7
Describe the immediate treatment for a person who is experiencing a tonic/clonic seizure.

Figure 14.4 *First Aid for Seizures*

1. Cushion the head. 2. Loosen tight necktie or collar. 3. Turn on side. 4. Put nothing in the mouth.

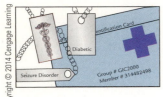

5. Look for identification. 6. Don't hold the person down. 7. Seizure ends. 8. Offer help

CEC

Standard 1
Foundations

necessarily mean that a person has epilepsy. Only when a person has had two or more seizures is he or she considered to have epilepsy. EEGs and brain scans are common diagnostic tests for epilepsy" (National Institute of Neurological Disorders and Stroke, 2012a). Several classification schemes have been employed to describe the various types of seizure disorders. We will briefly discuss two types of seizures: tonic/clonic and absence.

Generalized tonic/clonic seizures, formerly called *grand mal seizures*, affect the entire brain. The tonic phase of these seizures is characterized by a stiffening of the body; the clonic phase is distinguished by repeated muscle contractions and relaxations. Tonic/clonic seizures are often preceded by a warning signal known as an aura, in which the individual senses a unique sound, odor, or physical sensation just prior to the onset of the seizure. In some instances, the seizure is also signaled by a cry or similar sound. The tonic phase of the seizure begins with a loss of consciousness, after which the individual falls to the ground. Initially, the trunk and head become rigid during the tonic phase. The clonic phase follows and consists of involuntary muscle contractions (violent shaking) of the extremities. Irregular breathing, blueness in the lips and face, increased salivation, loss of bladder and bowel control, and perspiration may occur (Epilepsy Foundation, 2009b).

The nature, scope, frequency, and duration of tonic/clonic seizures vary greatly from person to person. Such seizures may last as long as 20 minutes or less than one minute (see Figure 14.4). One of the most dangerous aspects of tonic/clonic seizures is potential injury from falling and striking objects in the environment.

A period of sleepiness and confusion usually follows a tonic/clonic seizure. The individual may exhibit drowsiness, nausea, headache, or a combination of these symptoms. Such symptoms should be treated with appropriate rest, medication, or other therapeutic remedies. The characteristics and aftereffects of seizures vary in many ways and should be treated with this in mind.

"Absence seizure—also known as petit mal—involves a brief, sudden lapse of consciousness. Absence seizures are more common in children than adults. Someone having an absence seizure may look like he or she is staring into space for a few seconds" (Mayo Clinic, 2012a). During these seizures, the brain ceases to function as it normally would. The individual's consciousness is altered in an almost imperceptible manner. Young people with this type of seizure disorder may experience these seizures as often as 100 times a day. Such inattentive behavior may be viewed as daydreaming by teachers or work supervisors, but the episode is really due to momentary bursts of abnormal brain activity that individuals cannot control. The lapses in attention caused by this form of epilepsy can greatly hamper the individual's ability to respond properly to or profit from a teacher's presentations or a supervisor's instructions. Treatment and control of absence seizures are generally achieved through prescribed medications.

Prevalence and Causation

Prevalence figures for seizure disorders vary, in part because of the social stigma associated with them. "In the United States, epilepsy affects more than 326,000 children younger than 15 years of age . . ." (Blair, 2010, p. 487). About 200,000 new cases of epilepsy are diagnosed each year (Epilepsy Foundation, 2012). Half of all of the cases of seizure disorders in children appear before 10 years of age. Unfortunately, large numbers of adults and children have seizure disorders that remain undiagnosed and untreated.

The causes of seizure disorders are many, including perinatal factors, tumors of the brain, complications of head trauma, infections of the central nervous system, vascular diseases, alcoholism, infection, maternal injury or infection, and genetic factors (Blosser & Reider-Demer, 2009; Epilepsy Foundation, 2009a). Also, some seizures are caused by ingestion of street drugs, toxic chemicals, and poisons. Nevertheless, no explicit cause can be found in seven out of ten individuals with seizure disorders (Epilepsy Foundation, 2012).

Researchers are endeavoring to determine what specific biophysical features give rise to seizures. If they can discover the underlying parameters, they may be able to prevent seizures from occurring.

Interventions

The treatment of seizure disorders begins with a careful medical investigation in which the physician develops a thorough health history of the individual and completes an in-depth physical examination. Moreover, it is essential that the physician receive thorough descriptions of the seizure(s). These preliminary diagnostic steps may be followed by other assessment procedures, including blood tests, video capturing of seizure episodes, CT scans or MRIs, cranial ultrasounds, and spinal fluid taps to determine whether or not the individual has meningitis (Ricci & Kyle, 2009a). EEGs (electroencephalograms) may also be performed to confirm the physician's clinical impressions. The electroencephalogram is a test to detect abnormalities in the electrical activity of the brain. However, it should be noted that many seizure disorders are not detectable through electroencephalographic measures. As indicated earlier, accurate diagnoses are essential to providing effective treatments (National Institute of Neurological Disorders and Stroke, 2012a).

Many types of seizures can be treated successfully with precise drug management. Significant headway has been made with the discovery of effective drugs, particularly for children with tonic/clonic and absence seizures. Maintaining regular medication regimens can be very challenging for children or youth and their parents. Anticonvulsant drugs must be chosen very carefully, however. The potential risk and benefit of each medication must be balanced and weighed. Once a drug has been prescribed, families should be educated in its use, in the importance of noting any side effects, and in the need for consistent administration. In some instances, medication may be discontinued after several years of seizure-free behavior. This is particularly true for those young children who do not have some form of underlying brain pathology.

Other treatments for seizure disorders include surgery, stress management, a vagus nerve stimator (an electronic device designed to prevent seizures by sending small bursts of electrical energy to the brain), brain infusion of the chemical muscimol into affected areas of the brain, and diet modifications. The goal of surgery is to remove the precise part of the brain that is damaged and is causing the seizures. Surgery is considered primarily for those individuals with uncontrollable seizures, essentially those who have not responded to anticonvulsant medications. Using a variety of sophisticated scanning procedures, physicians attempt to isolate the damaged area of the brain that corresponds with the seizure activity. The outcomes of surgery for children and youth with well-defined foci of seizure activity are excellent. Of individuals who undergo surgery, 55 to 90 percent experience positive outcomes (National Institute of Neurological Disorders and Stroke, 2012c; 2012d). Obviously, the surgery must be done with great care. Brain tissue, once removed, is gone forever, and the function that the tissue performed is eliminated or only marginally restored.

Stress management is designed to increase a child's or youth's general functioning. Because seizures are often associated with illnesses, inadequate rest, and other stressors, parents and other care providers work at helping children, youth, and adults understand the importance of attending consistently to their medication routines, developing emotional resilience, and maintaining healthful patterns of behavior.

Diet modifications are designed to alter the way the body uses energy from food. Typically, our bodies convert the carbohydrates we consume into glucose (sugar). Several types of seizures can be controlled by instituting a ketogenic diet (National Institute of Neurological Disorders and Stroke, 2012a; 2012c). This diet focuses on consuming fats rather than carbohydrates. Instead of producing glucose, individuals on this diet produce ketones, a special kind of molecule. This change in food consumption causes alterations in the metabolism of the brain that normally uses sugars to "fire" its functions. For reasons that are not completely understood, the brain is less receptive to certain kinds of seizures under this diet. However, the diet is extraordinarily difficult to maintain on a long-term basis and is now rarely used or recommended.

Individuals with seizure disorders need calm and supportive responses from others—teachers, parents, and peers. The treatment efforts of various professionals and family members must be carefully orchestrated to provide these individuals with opportunities to use their abilities and talents. Educators should be aware of the basic fundamentals of seizure disorders and their management. They should also be aware of their critical role in observing seizures that may occur at school. The astute observations of a teacher may be invaluable to a health care team that is developing appropriate medical and other interventions for a child or youth with seizure disorders. Additionally, teachers should have the necessary skills to attend to seizures before, during, and following their occurrence. It is vitally important that teachers and parents be able to accurately and sensitively describe to other children and youth what has happened when a student experiences a seizure in their classroom and what they might do in a similar situation, thus lessening the chances for misunderstanding and the development of stigmas associated with seizure disorders.

CEC

Standard 5
Learning Environments and Social Interactions

Diabetes

CEC

Standard 1
Foundations

FOCUS 8

Identify several problems individuals with diabetes may experience later in life without adherence to diet, exercise, and medical regimens.

Consistent insulin delivery is essential to the wellbeing of young people with diabetes.

The term diabetes mellitus refers to a developmental or hereditary disorder characterized by inadequate secretion or use of insulin, a substance that is produced by the pancreas and used to process carbohydrates. There are two types of diabetes mellitus: insulin-dependent diabetes mellitus (IDDM), commonly known as type 1 or juvenile onset diabetes, and noninsulin-dependent diabetes mellitus (NIDDM), referred to as type 2 or adult-onset diabetes (American Diabetes Association, 2009; Doyle & Grey, 2010).

Glucose—a sugar, one of the end products of digesting carbohydrates—is used by the body for energy. Some glucose is used quickly, whereas some is stored in the liver and muscles for later use. However, muscle and liver cells cannot absorb and store the energy released by glucose without insulin, a hormone produced by the pancreas that converts glucose into energy that body cells use to perform their various functions. Without insulin, glucose accumulates in the blood, causing a condition known as hyperglycemia. Left untreated, this condition can cause serious, immediate problems for people with IDDM, leading to loss of consciousness or to a diabetic coma (American Diabetes Association, 2009).

Typical symptoms associated with glucose buildup in the blood are extreme hunger, thirst, and frequent urination. Although progress has been made in regulating insulin levels, the

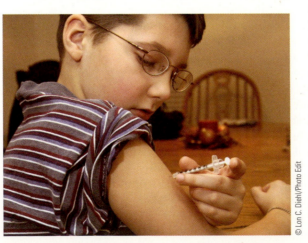

© Lori C. Diehl/Photo Edit

prevention and treatment of the complications that accompany diabetes—blindness, cardiovascular disease, and kidney disease—still pose tremendous challenges for health care specialists and affected individuals.

Consider this revealing description of a 9-year-old who had been diagnosed with type 1 diabetes at age 6: "She had pricked her finger for a blood test 9,000 times and received more than 2,000 insulin shots in the past three years. She typically has four blood checks a day, eats on a relentlessly regular schedule, and may wake up out-of-kilter at night when her blood-sugar level drops. The 'adjustments' necessitated by diabetes—which as far as she knows will be lifelong—are wrenching" (Clark, 2003, p. 6). This brief description helps us sense the challenges that children and youth with diabetes and their families experience.

IDDM, or juvenile-onset diabetes, is particularly troublesome. Compared with the adult form, juvenile-onset diabetes tends to be more severe and progresses more quickly, thus increasing the likelihood of the onset of conditions associated with type 2 diabetes. Generally, the symptoms of type 1 diabetes are easily recognized. The child develops an unusual thirst for water and other liquids. His or her appetite also increases substantially, but listlessness and fatigue occur despite increased food and liquid intake. Young people with type 1 diabetes need insulin to convert starches, sugars, and other foods for vitally important energy. Thus, insulin injections are imperative in managing the disease.

In contrast to type 1 diabetes, with type 2 diabetes, insulin injections are not always necessary because the pancreas is still able to produce insulin, but often it does not make sufficient amounts for cell usage. Type 2 diabetes (NIDDM) is the most common form of diabetes and is often associated with obesity in individuals over age 40. Individuals with this form of diabetes are at less risk for diabetic comas; most individuals with NIDDM can manage the disorder through exercise and dietary restrictions. If these actions fail, insulin therapy may be necessary.

Prevalence and Causation

Almost 9 percent of the U.S. population has diabetes—25.8 million individuals. Of this number, 18.8 million have been diagnosed with the condition. Seven million are undiagnosed, and 70 million are prediabetic. Each year, 1.9 million new cases of diabetes are identified in adults 20 and older (American Diabetes Association, 2012a). Type 2 diabetes has become increasingly common in children—primarily as a result of staggering growth rates in childhood obesity (Science Codex, 2009). According to the Centers for Disease Control and Prevention (2012a), "Childhood obesity has more than tripled in the past 30 years."

The causes of diabetes remain obscure, although considerable research has been conducted on the biochemical mechanisms responsible for it. Diabetes develops gradually in individuals. A combination of genetic dispositions and environmental triggers and conditions give rise to type 1 diabetes. The exact variables that underlie this form of diabetes are still unclear.

Individuals who develop type 2 diabetes incrementally create conditions in their body in which their cells become unresponsive to the effects of insulin. Additionally, the pancreas is unable to make sufficient insulin to overcome this unresponsiveness. Thus, sugars accumulate in the bloodstream with very negative outcomes for affected individuals. Like in type 1 diabetes, genetic and environmental variables play a role in the onset of type 2 diabetes. Interestingly, becoming overweight is strongly linked to the development of type 2 diabetes, although not every individual with type 2 diabetes is overweight (Mayo Clinic, 2012b).

Interventions

Medical treatment centers on the regular administration of insulin, which is essential for children and youth with juvenile diabetes. Several exciting advances have been made in recent years in the monitoring of blood sugar levels and the delivery of insulin to people with diabetes. Also, recent success with pancreas transplants has virtually eliminated the disease for some individuals. Significant progress is also being made in the development of the bioartificial pancreas and gene therapies (Gebel, 2012).

Solid progress has been made in transplanting insulin-producing islet cells to individuals with type 1 diabetes. However, this approach is complicated by shortages in the availability of whole pancreases and by the rejection of these new cells in recipients. Other sources of pancreatic tissue are present in fetal tissue. This controversial approach makes

Sarah, who has juvenile-onset diabetes and is now in sixth grade, migrated from her regular, self-administered shots for her diabetes to an insulin infusion pump several years ago. Sarah, however, believes that the pump makes her look different among her peers and wants to return to the shots. Recently, she "disinstalled" her pump. Her mom is worried about her and her health, knowing that she has played an important role in monitoring Sarah's pump regimens and related insulin doses.

APPLICATION

1. How could you help Sarah with the transition she is making?

2. How could you help Sarah's mother with her concerns about Sarah social and medical well-being?

use of tissues—stem cells derived from aborted or unused fetuses. Also, animal islet cells are currently being investigated, particularly islet cells derived from pigs, whose insulin differs by only one molecule from that of humans. However, transplantation of these cells poses similar rejection problems for recipients.

Hybrid technologies are also being pursued. Perhaps the most promising is the production of artificial beta cells that could be used in an artificial pancreas. This approach entails inserting new genes into naturally occurring cells that would produce insulin and be sensitive to the rise and fall of blood glucose.

Maintaining normal levels of glucose is now achieved in many instances with insulin infusion pumps, which are worn by people with diabetes and are powered by small batteries. The infusion pump operates continuously and delivers the dose of insulin that the physician and the patient determine. This form of treatment is effective only when used in combination with carefully followed diet and exercise programs. These pumps, if carefully monitored and operated, contribute greatly to "controlling" diabetes, thus reducing or slowing the onset and risks for eye disease, nerve damage, and kidney disease.

Juvenile-onset diabetes is a lifelong condition that can have a pronounced effect on the child or youth in a number of areas. Complications for children with long-standing diabetes include blindness, heart attacks, skin disorders, neuropathy (weakness and numbness) in the feet, and kidney problems. Many of these problems can be delayed or prevented by maintaining adequate blood sugar levels with appropriate food intake, exercise, and insulin injections.

Teacher and other care providers need to work carefully with parents and other medical personnel in monitoring treatment and medication regimens, supporting blood sugar monitoring efforts, and being alert to changes in student behavior or performance that may merit immediate action or consultation with medical or other therapeutic personnel. Also, teachers play key roles in helping children and youth embrace and engage in activities and events that enhance their physical well-being, lessening the likelihood of problems with childhood obesity and related conditions. Communication between teachers and parents is essential in caring for and educating children and youth with diabetes.

Cystic Fibrosis

Standard 1
Foundations

FOCUS 9

Identify present and future interventions for the treatment of children and youth with cystic fibrosis.

"Cystic fibrosis is an inherited chronic disease that affects the lungs and digestive system of about 30,000 children and adults in the United States (70,000 worldwide). A defective gene and its protein product cause the body to produce unusually thick, sticky mucus that clogs the lungs and leads to life-threatening lung infections; and obstructs the pancreas and stops natural enzymes from helping the body break down and absorb food" (Cystic Fibrosis Foundation, 2012a). Cystic fibrosis (CF) "is the most common life-shortening genetic illness among white children, adolescents, and young adults" (Hazle, 2010, p. 405). Fortunately, great progress has been made in significantly lengthening the life expectancies of individuals with CF to more than 37 years—some into their 40s (Cystic Fibrosis Foundation, 2012a).

Prevalence and Causation

In the United States, about 30,000 children and adults have cystic fibrosis. More than 10 million individuals—one in every 31 are carriers of the defective CF gene but do not have the disease (Cystic Fibrosis Foundation, 2012b).

CF is a genetically transmitted disease. A child must inherit a defective copy of the CF gene from each parent to develop the disease. The gene for the CF transfer regulator (CFTR) is very large; some 2,000 mutations have already been identified with the disease. CFTR, a protein, produces improper transportation of sodium and salt (chloride) within cells that line organs such as the lungs and pancreas. CFTR prevents chloride from exiting these cells. This blockage affects a broad range of organs and systems in the body, including reproductive organs in men and women, the lungs, sweat glands, and the digestive system.

Interventions

The prognosis for individuals with CF depends on a number of factors. The two most critical are early diagnosis of the condition and the quality of care provided after the diagnosis. If the diagnosis occurs late, irreversible damage may be present. With early diagnosis and appropriate medical care, most individuals with CF can achieve weight and growth gains similar to those of their normal peers. Early diagnosis and improved treatment strategies have lengthened the average lifespan of individuals with CF; more than half now live into their 30s and 40s.

The best and most comprehensive treatment is provided through CF centers located throughout the United States. These centers provide talented medical and support staff (respiratory care personnel, social workers, dieticians, genetic counselors, and psychologists). Moreover, they maintain diagnostic laboratories especially equipped to perform pulmonary function testing and sweat testing. Sweat of children with CF has abnormal concentrations of sodium or chloride; in fact, sweat tests provide the definitive data for a diagnosis of CF in infants and young children.

Interventions for CF are varied and complex and treatment continues throughout the person's lifetime. Consistent and appropriate application of the medical, social, educational, and psychological components of treatment enable these individuals to live longer and with less discomfort and fewer complications than in years past. Treatment of CF is designed to achieve a number of goals. The first is to diagnose the condition before any severe symptoms are exhibited. Other goals include control of chest infection, maintenance of adequate nutrition, education of the child and family regarding the condition, and provision of a suitable education for the child.

Management of respiratory disease caused by CF is critical. If respiratory insufficiency can be prevented or minimized, the individual's life will be greatly enhanced and prolonged. Antibiotic drugs, postural drainage (chest physical therapy), airway clearance systems, and medicated vapors play important roles in the medical management of CF (Alba & Chan, 2007).

Diet management is also essential for children with CF. Generally, children with this condition require more caloric intake than their normal peers. The diet should be high in protein and should be adjusted if a child fails to grow and/or make appropriate weight gains. Individuals with CF benefit significantly from the use of replacement enzymes that assist with food absorption. Also, the intake of vitamins is very important to individuals with digestive system problems.

The major social and psychological problems of children with CF are directly related to chronic coughing, small stature, offensive stools, gas, delayed onset of puberty and secondary sex characteristics, and potentially unsatisfying social relationships. Also, these children and youth may spend significant amounts of time away from school settings for aggressive pulmonary and antibiotic therapies (Brady, 2009). Thus teachers, counselors, and other support personnel play essential roles in helping these students feel at home in school, assisting them in making up past-due work, forming friendships, taking medications including enzyme treatments, providing appropriate privacy for rest and coughing episodes, helping other children and youth understand the condition, and receiving other appropriate school-based care (Hazle, 2010). Collaboration between school personnel,

Standard 2
Development and Characteristics of Learners

Standard 10
Collaboration

parents, and health care providers is essential to the well-being of children and youth with CF. Moreover, support groups play important roles in helping students with CF understand themselves and their disease and develop personal resilience and ongoing friendships.

Sickle-Cell Disease

Standard 1
Foundations

FOCUS 10

Describe the impact on body tissues of the sickling of red blood cells in sickle-cell disease (SCD).

"Sickle-cell disease (SCD) is a group of inherited red blood cell disorders" (Centers for Disease Control and Prevention, 2012g). Sickle-cell disease profoundly affects the structure and functioning of red blood cells. The hemoglobin molecule in the red blood cells of individuals with SCD is abnormal in that it is vulnerable to structural collapse when the blood–oxygen level is significantly diminished. As the blood–oxygen level declines, these blood cells become distorted and form bizarre shapes. This process, which is known as sickling, distorts the normal donut-like shapes of cells into shapes like microscopic sickle blades. Obstructions in the vessels of affected individuals can lead to stroke and to damage of other organs in the body (see Figure 14.5).

Figure 14.5 *Normal and Sickled Red Blood Cells*

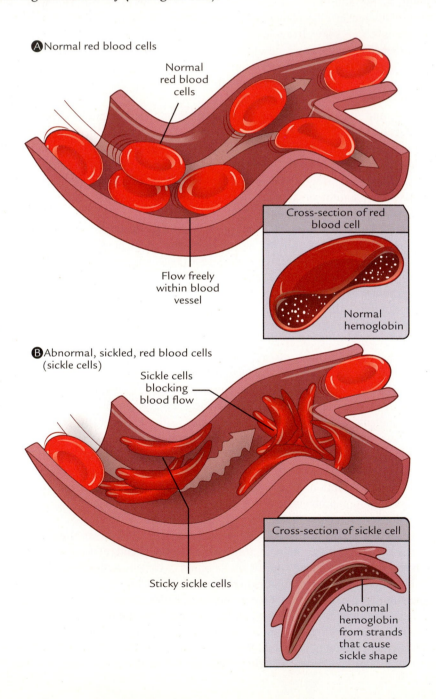

People affected by sickle-cell disease (SCD) may experience unrelenting **anemia**. In some cases, it is tolerated well; in others, the condition is quite debilitating. Another aspect of SCD involves frequent infections and periodic vascular blockages, which occur as sickled cells block microvascular channels. These blockages can often cause severe and chronic pain in the extremities, abdomen, or back. In addition, the disease may affect any organ system of the body. SCD also has a significant negative effect on the physical growth and development of infants and children.

Prevalence and Causation

About 1 in 12 African Americans is a carrier of the sickle-cell gene. *A thousand infants are born with SCD each year.* In the United States, 70,000 to 100,000 individuals are impacted by this disease (Pitts & Record, 2010; Centers for Disease Control and Prevention, 2012g). One in every 1,000 to 1,400 Hispanics is born with SCD (Human Genome Project, 2009).

Sickle-cell disease is caused by various combinations of genes. A child who receives a mutant S-hemoglobin gene from each parent exhibits SCA to one degree or another. The disease usually announces itself at 6 months of age and persists throughout the individual's lifetime.

Interventions

A number of treatments may be employed to deal with the problems caused by sickle-cell disease, but the first step is early diagnosis. Babies—particularly infants who are at risk for this disease—should be screened at birth. Early diagnosis lays the groundwork for the prophylactic use of antibiotics to prevent infections in the first five years of life. This treatment, coupled with appropriate immunizations and nutrition, prevents further complications of the disease. Moreover, these treatments significantly reduce death rates associated with SCD. One of the primary goals of treatment is the prevention of crises and related sickling episodes.

Children, youth, and adults usually learn to adapt to their disease and lead relatively normal lives. When their lives are interrupted by crises, a variety of treatment approaches can be used. For children, comprehensive and timely care is crucial. For example, children with SCD who develop fevers should be treated aggressively. In fact, parents of these children may be taught how to examine the spleen and recognize early signs of potentially serious problems. Hydration is also an important component of treatment. Lastly, pain management may be addressed with narcotic and nonnarcotic drugs.

Several factors predispose individuals to SCD crisis: dehydration from fever, reduced liquid intake, and hypoxia (a result of breathing air that is poor in oxygen content). Those who have a history of SCD crises should avoid stress, fatigue, and exposure to cold temperatures.

Treatment of crises is generally directed at keeping the individual warm, increasing liquid intake, ensuring good blood oxygenation, and administering medication for infection. Assistance can also be provided during crisis periods by partial-exchange blood transfusions with fresh, normal red cells. Transfusions may also be necessary for individuals with SCA who are preparing for surgery or who are pregnant.

Teachers and other care providers may assist with the following: dispensing medications in keeping with school regulations and policies; honoring recommendations for activity restrictions; making referrals to appropriate medical personnel if pain and fever become evident; encouraging affected students to dress warmly during cold weather; and responding immediately in the event of SCA crises. As with all physical and health disorders, collaboration and communication among caregivers are key elements of serving children and youth so affected.

Traumatic Brain Injuries

"Traumatic brain injury (TBI), a form of acquired brain injury, occurs when a sudden trauma causes damage to the brain. TBI can result when the head suddenly and violently hits an object, or when an object pierces the skull and enters brain tissue. Symptoms of a TBI can be mild, moderate, or severe, depending on the extent of the damage to the brain" (National Institute of Neurological Disorders and Stroke, 2012e). TBI injuries happen, for example,

Anemia
Anemia is a condition in the body where the blood is abnormally low in red blood cells or the red cells do not have enough hemoglobin to carry oxygen from the lungs to the other cells of the body.

Standard 10
Collaboration

Standard 1
Foundations

FOCUS 11
Describe the focus of educational interventions for individuals with traumatic brain injuries.

in car accidents when the head hits the windshield and in bicycle accidents when the head hits the ground. The trauma caused by the rapid acceleration or deceleration of the brain may cause the tearing of important nerve fibers in the brain, bruising of the brain itself as it undergoes the impact with the skull, brain stem injuries, and swelling of the brain.

Medical professionals describe two types of brain damage, primary and secondary. *Primary damage* is a direct outcome of the initial impact to the brain. *Secondary damage* develops over time as the brain responds to the initial trauma. For instance, an adolescent who is hit accidentally with a baseball bat may develop a hematoma, an area of internal bleeding within the brain. This may be the primary damage. However, with the passage of time, the brain's response to the initial injury may be pervasive swelling, which may cause additional insult and injury to the brain.

Standard 1
Foundations

In the school context, the Individuals with Disabilities Act (IDEA) defines traumatic brain injury as "an acquired injury to the brain caused by an external physical force, resulting in total or partial functional disability or psychosocial impairment, or both, that adversely affects a child's educational performance. Traumatic brain injury applies to open or closed head injuries resulting in impairments in one or more areas, such as cognition; language; memory; attention; reasoning; abstract thinking; judgment; problem-solving; sensory, perceptual, and motor abilities; psychosocial behavior; physical functions; information processing; and speech. Traumatic brain injury does not apply to brain injuries that are congenital or degenerative, or to brain injuries induced by birth trauma" (U.S. Department of Education, 2012).

Head injures may result in disabilities that adversely and severely affect individuals' information processing, social behaviors, memory capacities, reasoning and thinking, speech and language skills, and sensory and motor abilities.

Prevalence and Causation

The statistics associated with traumatic brain injury are sobering. About 1.7 million people sustain TBIs each year. Of this number, about 52,000 individuals die and 275,000 are hospitalized (Centers for Disease Control and Prevention, 2012d; 2012e). About 475,000 TBIs take place with children (0 to 14 years of age). About 80,000 to 90,000 are permanently disabled from their accidents or injuries. About 180 per 100,000 children under age 15 experience a TBI. Of that number, about 5 to 8 percent experience a severe TBI. More than 5 million individuals in the United States "are living with TBI-related disabilitie[s]" (Centre for Neuro Skills, 2012, p. 1). Also, significant numbers of military personnel, more than 229,000, were diagnosed with a TBI between 2000 and 2011. Tragically, TBI is the signature injury of veterans of the Iraq and Afghanistan wars (Defense and Veterans Brain Injury Center, 2012).

It is now estimated that 5.3 million children and adults in the United States are living with the consequences of sustaining a traumatic brain injury. Of all the head injuries that occur, 40 percent involve children. About 2 to 5 percent of the children and youth who experience a TBI develop severe neurologic complications; others develop lasting behavior problems, and over one-third experience lifelong disabilities.

"The single most preventative risk factor is alcohol usage" (Cifu, Kreutzer, Slater, & Taylor, 2007, p. 1,134). If youth and young adults controlled their alcohol consumption, many TBIs would not occur. Additionally, many TBIs could be prevented with proper use of seat belts, air bags, child restraints, and helmets, and securing guns from accidental discharge and misuse by children. (See the nearby Debate Forum, "Should We Protect Our Children and Youth from Firearm Violence?" for a look at both sides of the gun control issue.)

Standard 5
Learning Environments and Social Interactions

For small children, the most common cause of TBIs is a fall from a short distance. Such children may fall from a tree, playground equipment, their parents' arms, or furniture. Another major cause of injury in young children is physical abuse. These injuries generally come from the shaking or striking of infants, which may cause sheering of brain matter or severe bleeding. Common causes of head injuries in older children include falls from playground swings or climbers, bicycles, or trees; blows to the head from baseball bats, balls, or other sports equipment; gunshot wounds; and pedestrian accidents (Centers for Disease Control and Prevention, 2012f).

DEBATE FORUM
SHOULD WE PROTECT OUR CHILDREN AND YOUTH FROM FIREARM VIOLENCE?

Consider the following facts:

"The latest data from the U.S. Centers for Disease Control and Prevention show that 3,042 children and teens died from gunfire in the United States in 2007—one child or teen every three hours, eight every day, 58 every week.

2,161 were homicide victims
683 committed suicide
198 died in accidental or undetermined circumstances
2,665 were boys
377 were girls
397 were under age 15
154 were under age 10
85 were under age 5

Almost six times as many children and teens—17,523—suffered nonfatal gun injuries." (Children's Defense Fund, 2010)

"After almost two decades of reporting on youth gun violence, CDF's latest installment of *Protect Children, Not Guns* makes clear that our national obsession with guns continues to result in the senseless and unnecessary loss of young lives. The Centers for Disease Control and Prevention (CDC) reports that a total of 3,042 children and teens died by gunfire in 2007—a number nearly equal to the total number of U.S. combat deaths in Iraq and four times the number of American combat fatalities in Afghanistan to date. Another 17,523 children and teens suffered nonfatal gun injuries in 2007 and the emotional aftermath that follows. In each case it was a gun that ended or changed a young life forever" (Children's Defense Fund, 2010, p. 1).

"With over 280 million guns in civilian hands, the terrible truth is that there is no place to hide from gun violence. Children and teens are not safe from gun violence at school, at home, or anywhere else in America. A recent study found that rural and urban children and teens are equally likely to die from firearm injuries. Young people in urban areas are more likely to be homicide victims while rural children and teens are more likely to be victims of suicide or accidental shootings. The CDC estimates that nearly two million children live in homes with loaded and unlocked guns" (Children's Defense Fund, 2010, p. 1).

POINT

Gun control of any kind is repugnant to many individuals, particularly those who have strong feelings about the "right to bear arms." These individuals argue that controlling firearms is a violation of their civil rights. These individuals see any restriction of access to firearms or control of their use as undue government intervention and control.

COUNTERPOINT

As a society, we can no longer ignore the deaths and injuries to children and youth that are caused by firearms. We ought to treat firearms as we treat cars. Cars must have certain safety devices, or they are not available for purchase or use. Likewise, only those licensed to drive may legally get behind the wheel of a car. These governmental measures are directed at enhancing the safety of citizens. The same measures should apply to firearms. The essential goal is prevention, not control.

What Do You Think? Please visit the Education CourseMate website for Human Exceptionality, *11th edition to access and respond to questions related to the Debate Forum.*

Figure 14.6 *Characteristics of Children with Traumatic Brain Injury*

Medical/Neurological Symptoms

- Sensory deficits affecting vision, hearing, taste, smell, or touch
- Decreased motor coordination
- Difficulty breathing
- Dizziness
- Headache
- Impaired balance
- Loss of intellectual capabilities
- Partial to full paralysis
- Poor eye–hand coordination
- Reduced body strength
- Seizure activity (possibly frequent)
- Sleep disorders
- Speech problems (e.g., stuttering, slurring)

Cognitive Symptoms

- Decreased attention
- Decreased organizational skills
- Decreased problem-solving ability
- Difficulties keeping up at school
- Difficulty with abstract reasoning
- Integration problems (e.g., sensory, thought)
- Poor organizational skills
- Memory deficits
- Perceptual problems
- Poor concentration
- Poor judgment
- Rigidity of thought

- Slowed information processing
- Poor short- and long-term memory
- Word-finding difficulty

Behavioral/Emotional Symptoms

- Aggressive behavior
- Denial of deficits
- Depression
- Difficulty accepting and responding to change
- Loss of reduction of inhibitions
- Distractibility
- Feelings of worthlessness
- Flat affect (expressionless, lacking emotion)
- Low frustration level
- Unnecessary or disproportionate guilt
- Helplessness
- Impulsivity
- Inappropriate crying or laughing
- Irritability

Social Skills Development

- Difficulties maintaining relationships with family members and others
- Inability to restrict socially inappropriate behaviors (e.g., disrobing in public)
- Inappropriate responses to the environment (e.g., overreactions to light or sound)
- Insensitivity to others' feelings
- Limited initiation of social interactions
- Social isolation

SOURCE: Adapted from Pierangelo, R., and G. A. Guiliani. (2001). *What every teacher should know about students with special needs: Promoting success in the classroom*, pp. 98–100. Champaign, IL: Research Press. Copyright © 2001 by R. Pierangelo and G. G. Guiliani. Reprinted by permission.

The number of children and others who experience serious head trauma would be significantly reduced if seat belts and other child restraint devices were consistently used. Further reductions in such injuries would be achieved by significantly decreasing accidents due to driving under the influence of alcohol and other mind-altering substances.

Programs directed at reducing the number of individuals who drive while under the influence of alcohol or other substances should be vigorously supported. Likewise, children (and everyone else) should wear helmets when bicycling and should obey safety rules that reduce the probability of serious accidents.

Interventions

Individuals with a TBI present a variety of challenges to families and professionals. The injuries may affect every aspect of an individual's life (see Figure 14.6 for effects on children) (Bullough, 2011). The resulting disabilities also have a profound effect on the individual's family. Often the injuries radically change the individual's capacities for learning and making sense of different kinds of incoming information (verbal, written, nonverbal, visual, and so on).

Generally, individuals with a TBI will need services and supports in several areas: cognition, speech and language, social and behavioral skills, as well as physical functioning. Cognitive problems have an impact on thinking and perception. For example, people who have sustained a brain injury may be unable to remember or retrieve newly learned or processed information. They may be unable to attend or concentrate for appropriate periods of time. Another serious problem is their inability to adjust or respond flexibly to changes in home, school, community, or work environments.

A person with TBI may also struggle with speech, producing unintelligible sounds or indistinguishable words. Speech may be slurred and labored. Individuals with a TBI may know what they want to say, but are unable to express it. Professionals use the term aphasia to describe this condition. Expressive aphasia is an inability to express one's own thoughts and desires.

Language problems may also be evident. For example, a school-age student may be unable to retrieve a desired word or expression, particularly during a "high-demand" instructional session or during an anxiety-producing social situation. Given their difficulties with word retrieval, individuals with a TBI may reduce their overall speech output or use repetitive expressions or word substitutions. Many children with a brain injury express great frustration at knowing an answer to a question, but being unable to retrieve it when called on by teachers.

Social and behavioral problems may present the most challenging aspects of TBI. For many individuals, the injury produces significant changes in their personality, their temperament, their disposition toward certain activities, and their behaviors. These social and behavioral problems may worsen over time, depending on the nature of the injury, the preinjury status of the brain, the preinjury adjustment of the individual and family, the person's age at the time of the injury, and the treatment provided immediately after the injury. Behaviors emanating from a TBI include increased irritability and emotionality, compromised motivation and judgment, an inability to restrict socially inappropriate behaviors, insensitivity to others, and low thresholds for frustration and inconvenience.

Neuromotor and physical disabilities are also characteristic of individuals with a TBI. Neuromotor problems may be exhibited through poor eye–hand coordination. For example, an adolescent may be able to pick up a ball, but be unable to throw it to someone else. In addition, a person with a TBI may have impaired balance, an inability to walk unassisted, significantly reduced stamina, or paralysis. Impaired vision and hearing may also be present. The array and extent of the challenges individuals with brain injuries and their families face can be overwhelming and disheartening. However, with appropriate support and coordinated, interdisciplinary treatment, individuals and their families can move forward with their lives and develop effective coping skills.

Like other people with disabilities, individuals with a TBI significantly benefit from systems of care—collaborative/multidisciplinary approaches and interventions that address unique family and individual needs. Because of the nature and number of the deficits that might ensue as a result of a head injury, many specialists must be involved in a coordinated and carefully orchestrated fashion. Early comprehensive care is vital to the long-term, functional recovery of individuals with a TBI.

Furthermore new medical technologies have revolutionized diagnostic and treatment procedures for TBIs. In previous decades, the vast majority of these individuals died within a short time of their accidents. With the development of **computerized tomography** (CT) scans, intracranial pressure monitors, **magnetic resonance imaging** (MRI), **voxel-based morphometry** (VBM), and the capacity to control bleeding and brain swelling, many individuals with traumatic brain injury survive. Also, CT scans and voxel-based morphometry of individuals without brain injuries now provide physicians and other health care providers with essential, normative information about the extent of the injury to the brain to compare with the uninjured brains of other individuals of the same age and gender. Voxel-based morphometry is a computational method for measuring differences in local concentrations of brain tissue, through comparisons of multiple brain images from individuals with and without injuries.

Head injuries may be described in terms of the nature of the injury. Injuries include concussions, contusions, skull fractures, and epidural and subdural hemorrhages:

- *Concussions*. The most common effects of closed-head injuries, concussions, occur most frequently in children and adolescents through contact sports such as football, hockey, and

CEC

Standard 3
Individual Learning
Differences

CEC

Standard 8
Assessment

Computerized tomography
Computerized tomography (CT) is a method of examining body organs by scanning them with X-rays and using a computer to construct a series of cross-sectional scans of the organs.

Magnetic resonance imaging
Magnetic resonance imaging (MRI) is a medical imaging technique used in radiology to visualize internal structures of the body in detail.

Voxel-based morphometry
Voxel-based morphometry (VBM) is a neuroimaging analysis technique that allows investigation of specific areas of brain anatomy.

Many soldiers who return from the Iraq and Afghanistan Wars experience mild to severe traumatic brain injuries. At least 15-25 percent of returning soldiers experience mild traumatic brain injuries (TBIs), often characterized by chronic and severe headaches, emotional irritability, sleep problems, impaired cognition, and other challenging health issues. What follows are personal reflections of soldiers about the impact of their brain injuries.

You tell yourself that physical injuries always happen to someone else, that it'll never happen to you. It took a long time for me to come to terms with my injury. (Source: Make the Connection: Physical Injury. Retrieved July 20, 2012 from http://maketheconnection.net/events/injury)

I was having trouble seeing. Everything was blurry, the headaches were non-stop, . . . I was confused all the time. All of these were symptoms of a brain injury—we just didn't know it yet (Source: Make the Connection: What are the effects of traumatic brain injury? Retrieved July 20, 2012 from http://maketheconnection.net/conditions/traumatic-brain-injury)

At times, I wish that my spouse would just 'get it' and understand all the things that I am dealing with. What I figured out is that the more honest and up front I am, the more that happens and better things get. We take it one day at a time. (Source: Make the Connection: What can I do about family and relationship issues? Retrieved July 20, 2012 from http://maketheconnection.net/events/family-relationships#1)

I had a short fuse. If you looked at me the wrong way I'd basically walk up to you and say, "You got an issue?" (Source: Make the Connection: If I'm experiencing anger or irritability, what can I do about it right away? Retrieved July 20, 2012 from http://maketheconnection.net/symptoms/anger-irritability/)

I'd say that the biggest thing that I had to deal with was frustration. I didn't know why I was forgetful all the time or always in a bad mood. I didn't know that I had a traumatic brain injury. (Source: Make the Connection: What are the mental health-related effects of TBI that I need to be aware of? Retrieved July 20, 2012 from http://maketheconnection.net/symptoms/anger-irritability/)

It's entirely too easy to get too down, and not want to work on the things to get you back to where you need to be… (Source: Traumatic Brain Injuruty: The Journey Home: Matthew James. Retrieved July 20, 2012 from http://www.traumaticbraininjury-atoz.org/Personal-Journeys.aspx)

You gotta do your part and it's hard. You gotta just reach inside and be the Soldier or Marine that you are, and go forward. (Source: Traumatic Brain Injury: The Journey Home: Michael Welch. Retrieved July 20, 2012 from http://www.traumaticbraininjury-atoz.org/Personal-Journeys.aspx)

…it's very important early on to be realistic about what you're facing. But also, find some hope in that reality. . . . don't give up hope…

(Source: Traumatic Brain Injury: The Journey Home: Ted Wade. Retrieved July 20, 2012 from http://www.traumaticbraininjuryatoz.org/Personal-Journeys.aspx)

I've learned a lot about my own brain over the past years, probably more than the average person would ever want to know, but sadly knowing what's wrong doesn't help fix it. The only thing that does help is repetition and retraining. I know there are still many things that I have to work on, but thankfully I believe there is still hope. (Source: crlynch.com/: Update January 2008. Retrieved July 20, 2012 from http://www.crlynch.com/page19.html)

Some days I can't distinguish the PTSD (post-traumatic stress disorder) from the head injury. . . The PTSD [post traumatic stress disorder] can be cured, but the head injury, I don't know. It's just going to take time. (Source: NM Brain Injury Advisory Council: Charlie. Retrieved July 20, 2012 from http://nmbiac.com/stories.html)

Questions for Reflection

1. If you were a spouse, parent, or sibling of a returning soldier with TBIs, what steps would you take to prepare yourself for assisting with the care and treatment of your loved one?

2. What services would you access?

3. How would you inform yourself?

4. Who would be your most reliable information providers?

martial arts. They are characterized by a temporary loss of consciousness with amnesia. Children who display weakness on one side of the body, exhibit a dilated pupil, or experience vomiting may have a concussion and should be examined immediately by a physician.

- *Contusions.* This kind of injury is characterized by extensive damage to the brain, including laceration of the brain, bleeding, swelling, and bruising. The resulting effect

Figure 14.7 *An Epidural Hematoma*

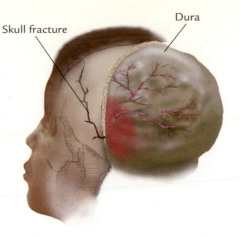

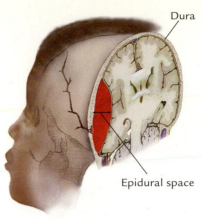

(a) A forceful injury occurs in the temporal area of the brain.

(b) The injury may result in a fractured skull, causing bleeding in the middle meningeal artery. Blood collects between the skull and the dura, a rough membrane covering the brain.

(c) As the blood collects, pressure builds on vital structures within the brain.

of a brain contusion is intense stupor or coma. Individuals with contusions should be hospitalized immediately.

- *Skull fractures.* The consequences of **skull fractures** depend on the location, nature, and seriousness of the fracture. Unfortunately, some fractures are not easily detectable through radiologic examination. Injuries to the lower back part of the head are particularly troublesome and difficult to detect. These basilar skull fractures may set the stage for serious infections of the central nervous system. Immediate medical care is essential for skull fractures to determine the extent of the damage and to develop appropriate interventions.

- *Epidural and subdural hemorrhages.* Hemorrhaging, or bleeding, is the central feature of epidural and subdural hematomas. Hematomas are collections of blood, usually clotted. An epidural hematoma is caused by damage to an artery (a thick-walled blood vessel carrying blood from the heart) between the brain and the skull (see Figure 14.7). If this injury is not treated promptly and appropriately, the affected individual will die. A subdural hematoma is caused by damage to tiny veins that draw blood from the outer layer of the brain (cerebral cortex) to the heart. The aggregation of blood between the brain and its outer covering (dura) produces pressure that adversely affects the brain and its functioning (see Figure 14.8). If the subdural bleeding is left untreated, the result can be death.

Medical treatment of TBI proceeds generally in three stages: acute care, rehabilitation, and community integration. During the acute stage, medical personnel focus on maintaining the child's or youth's life, treating the swelling and bleeding, minimizing complications, reducing the level of coma, and completing the initial neurologic examination. This stage of treatment is often characterized by strained interactions between physicians and parents. Many physicians are unable to respond satisfactorily to the overwhelming psychological needs of parents and family members because of the complex medical demands presented by the injured child or youth. Other trained personnel—including social workers, psychologists, and clergy—play vital roles in supporting parents and other family members. Again, we see the importance of systems of care where talented professionals work together to achieve optimal outcomes for all concerned.

If a child, youth, or adult remains in a coma, medical personnel may use special stimulation techniques to reduce the depth of the coma. If the patient with a TBI becomes agitated by stimuli in the hospital unit, such as visitors' conversations, noises produced by housecleaning staff, obtrusive light, or touching, steps may be taken to control or reduce these problems. As the injured individual comes out of the coma, orienting him or her to the

Skull fractures
Skull fractures are characterized by a break in one or more of the bones in the skull usually occurring as a result of blunt force trauma.

Figure 14.8 A Subdural Hematoma

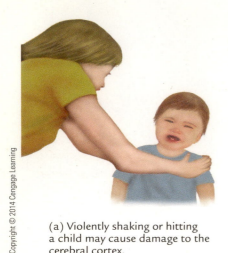

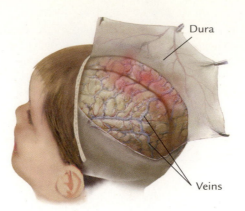

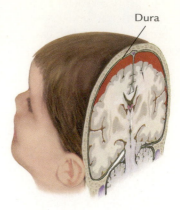

Copyright © 2014 Cengage Learning

(a) Violently shaking or hitting a child may cause damage to the cerebral cortex.

(b) Trauma to the brain results in the rupturing of small veins.

(c) Blood gathers between the dura and the brain, resulting in pressure on vital brain structures.

environment becomes a priority. This may include explaining where the patient is located, introducing care providers, indicating where loved ones are, sharing what has happened since the injury, and responding to the individual's other questions. Many people who have been injured do not remember the accident or the medical interventions administered.

The next stage of treatment is rehabilitation. During this phase, the individual seeks to relearn and adequately perform preinjury skills and behaviors. This treatment may take time—often months—and considerable effort. Children and youth are prepared gradually for return to their homes and appropriate school environments. Their families prepare as well, receiving ongoing support and counseling. Additionally, arrangements are also made for appropriate speech/language, physical, and occupational therapies and for any specialized teaching necessary.

Many individuals return to their homes, schools, or employment settings as vastly different people. These differences often take the shape of unpredictable or extreme expressions of emotion. Furthermore, these individuals may have trouble recognizing and accepting their post-injury challenges and deficits.

The last stage of intervention is community reintegration, focusing on providing counseling and therapy to help individuals cope with their injuries and their residual effects; helping families maintain the gains that have been achieved; terminating specific head injury services; further developing language facility and skills; seeking disability determination; and referring individuals to community agencies, educational programs, and vocational rehabilitation for additional services as needed.

Educational supports focus on environmental changes that facilitate daily living and address critical transition issues that arise in preparing the child's or youth's return to appropriate school settings. Communication and collaboration are absolutely essential to the transition from the hospital/care facility to the school environment. Several groups are involved in ensuring that the care and support are optimal: parents and teachers, professionals within the school, and school professionals working with clinical/medical personnel outside the school. It is essential that educators and health providers work together to blend clinical, educational, and family interventions effectively.

Unfortunately, many children and youth with a TBI leave hospitals or rehabilitation settings without adequate preparation for the demands inherent in returning to home and school environments. Also, many teachers who receive these students are not adequately prepared to respond to their cognitive, academic, and behavioral needs.

Students with traumatic brain injury may return to one of several school placements, depending on their needs. Appropriate teaching activities include establishing high

CEC

Standard 7
Instructional Planning

Standard 10
Collaboration

expectations, reducing stimuli and conditions that elicit challenging behaviors, using appropriate reductive techniques for stopping or significantly reducing aggressive or noncompliant behaviors, eliminating rewards for negative or problematic behaviors, providing precise feedback, giving students strategies for organizing information, and providing many opportunities for practice.

Educational services are tailored to a student's specific needs. Efforts are directed at improving students' general behaviors, such as problem solving, planning, and developing insight. Teaching strategies focus on developing appropriate social behaviors (performing in stressful situations, improving initiative taking, working with others, etc.), building expressive and receptive language skills (word retrieval, event description, understanding instructions, reading nonverbal cues, etc.), and writing skills (sentence development, legibility, etc.; see Figure 14.9). Also, some individuals with a TBI may benefit greatly from

Figure 14.9 *Classroom Strategies for Children and Youth with TBI*

- **Study guide or content outline.** Students may need an outline to follow so they can anticipate content.
- **Pictures or visual cues.** Signals are a good way to alert students that they need to do something differently.
- **Systematic verbal rehearsal.** Students may have to "practice" a verbal cue and what is expected of them.
- **Homework assignment book.** All assignments will need to be written down because of poor short-term memory.
- **Teach memory strategies.** Students may need to learn memory tricks such as mnemonics, pictures, or limericks.
- **Scribe or note taker.** Classmates may want to take turns taking good notes and having them photocopied at the end of class to give to the student. TBI victims often can listen but cannot take notes and listen at the same time.
- **Recognition versus recall.** Do not assume, when students recognize information, that they recall how it fits into the big picture. Check for understanding.
- **Modify work amounts.** Because focusing may be a serious problem, shorten assignments to the minimum necessary. Increase assignments gradually if the students are successful.
- **Alternative forms of expression.** General statements and satire may go right over their heads. Be very specific and to the point.
- **Provide feedback on responses.** Always state that an answer is correct or needs more input. The students may not pick up on a smile or nod that would be affirming.
- **Classroom aides.** It is often necessary to hire a classroom aide to help a student stay on task, organize, and plan homework.
- **Assist with confusion.** Watch for the confused look. These students are not likely to raise their hands and ask questions.
- **Avoid overreactions.** These students may ask the same question over and over because of poor short-term memory. Be patient. Repeat as needed.
- **Accept inconsistencies in performance.** These students may do very well on, say, Tuesday. This raises the bar for expectations. Remember that they may not be able to do this well the rest of the week.
- **Routine and schedule.** Be prepared for problems if there is a late start, a substitute teacher, early dismissal, or shortened classes. Changes do not come easy to students with a TBI.
- **Behavior management strategy.** Have a plan in mind for misbehavior. The regular plan may not work well. Preferably, talk with students ahead of time and let them know how you plan to discipline them.
- **Simple, concrete language.** Use short sentences that are to the point. Try to keep directions down to as few steps as possible.
- **Alert to transitions.** State that the bell is going to ring in five minutes and that they should begin putting things away in an orderly fashion. It may help to state which class is next.
- **Communication book.** While students are given time to do homework at the end of class, it would be good to communicate with parents how things are going in class, to note positives, and to discuss areas that need work.

INCLUSION AND COLLABORATION THROUGH THE LIFESPAN
PEOPLE WITH PHYSICAL DISABILITIES AND OTHER HEALTH DISORDERS

EARLY CHILDHOOD YEARS

Tips for the Family

- Work closely with medical and other health-related personnel to lessen the overall impact of the disorder or injury over time.

- Become familiar with special services available in your community and region for the disability or disorder.

- Learn about simple applications of behavior modification for use in your home environment by completing a parent training class.

- Seek out appropriate assistance through advocacy and support groups.

- Pursue family or individual counseling for persistent relationship-centered problems.

- Develop sensible routines and schedules for the child or youth.

- Communicate with siblings, friends, and relatives; help them become informed about the disability and disorder and their role in the treatment process.

- Join advocacy and support groups that provide the information and assistance you need.

- Do not overprotect your child or youth. Provide them with boundaries, discipline, responsibility, and encouragement.

Tips for the Preschool Teacher

- Communicate and collaborate with parents, special education personnel, and health care providers to develop appropriate expectations, management, and instruction.

- Watch for abrupt changes in the child's behavior. If they occur, notify parents and other professionals immediately.

- Involve socially sophisticated and sensitive peers and other older children in working with the preschooler.

- Become familiar with events that "set off" the child or pose special problems for the child's involvement.

- Be sure that the physical environment in the classroom lends itself to the needs of children who may have physical or health disorders (e.g., aisles in the classroom are sufficiently large for the free movement of a wheelchair).

- Use management procedures that promote appropriate independence, give rise to following instructions, and foster appropriate learning.

Tips for Preschool Personnel

- Participate in team meetings with the preschool teacher.

- Communicate frequently with the student's parents about concerns and promising developments.

- Employ appropriate management strategies used by the parents and the preschool teacher.

- Help other children understand and accept the child with a disability or disorder.

- Become aware of specific needs and potential talents of the child by consulting with parents.

- Be sure that other key personnel in the school who interact directly with the child are informed of his or her needs; collaborate in offering the best services and supports possible.

- Orient all the children in your setting to the needs of the child with a disability or disorder. This could be done by you, the parents or siblings, or other educational personnel in the school. Remember, your behavior toward the child will say more than words will ever convey.

- Be sure to make arrangements for emergency situations. For example, some peers may know exactly what to do if a fellow class member begins to have a seizure or an asthmatic attack. Additionally, classmates should know how they might be helpful in directing and assisting a child during a fire drill or other emergency procedures.

Tips for Neighbors and Friends

- Involve a child with physical disabilities or health disorders and his or her family in holiday gatherings.

- Be sensitive to dietary regimens, opportunities for repositioning, and alternative means for communicating if needed.

- Become aware of the things that you may need to do. For example, you may need to learn what to do if a child with insulin-dependent diabetes shows signs of glucose buildup.

- Offer to become educated about the condition and its impact on the child.

- Become familiar with recommended management procedures for directing the child.

- Teach your own children about the dynamics of the condition; help them understand how to react and respond to variations in behavior.

ELEMENTARY YEARS

Tips for the Family

- Maintain a healthy and ongoing relationship with the care providers who are part of your child's life.

- Acknowledge their efforts and express appreciation for actions that are particularly helpful to you and your child.

- Continue to be involved with advocacy and support groups.

- Stay informed by subscribing to newsletters and magazines disseminated by advocacy organizations.

- Develop and maintain positive relationships with the people who teach and serve your child within the school setting.

- Remember that the transition back to school and family environments requires very explicit planning and preparation.

- Learn about and use management procedures that promote the child's well-being, growth, and learning.

- Establish functional routines and schedules for family activities.

Tips for the General Education Classroom Teacher

- Be informed and willing to learn about the unique needs of a child or youth with disabilities and disorders in your classroom. For example, schedule a conference with the child's parents before the year begins to talk about medications, prosthetic devices, levels of desired physical activities, and so on.

- Remember that teamwork and coordination among caring professionals and parents are essential to the child's success.

- Use socially competent and mature peers to assist you (e.g., providing tutoring, physical assistance, social support in recess activities).

- Be sure that plans have been made and practiced for dealing with emergency situations (e.g., some children may need to be carried out of a building or room).

- If the child's condition is progressive and life-threatening, consult with parents and other professionals to prepare peers and others for the potential death of the child or youth.

Tips for School Personnel

- Become informed; seek to understand the unique characteristics of a disability or disorder.

- Seek to understand and use instructional and management approaches that are well suited to the child's emerging strengths and challenges.

- Use the expertise that is available in the school and school system; collaborate with other specialists.

- Take advantage of opportunities to profit from parent training.

- Be sure that all key personnel in the school setting who interact with the child on a regular basis are informed about treatment regimens, dietary requirements, and signs of potentially problematic conditions such as fevers and irritability.

- Meet periodically as professionals to deal with emergent problems, brainstorm for solutions, and identify suitable actions.

- Institute cross-age tutoring and support. When possible, have a child with a physical or health condition become a tutor.

Tips for Neighbors and Friends

- Adopt an inclusive attitude about family and neighborhood events; invite the child or youth to join in family-centered activities, picnics, and holiday events.

- Learn how to respond effectively and confidently to the common problems that the child or youth may present.

- Communicate concerns and problems immediately to parents in a compassionate and caring fashion.

- Provide parents with respite care.

SECONDARY AND TRANSITION YEARS

Tips for the Family

- Work closely with school and adult services personnel in developing transition plans.

- Develop a thoughtful and comprehensive transition plan that includes education, employment, housing, and use of leisure time.

- Become aware of all the services and resources that are available through state and national adult services programs.

- Remember that for some individuals with physical or health disabilities, the secondary or young adult years may be the most trying, particularly if the student's condition is progressive in nature.

- Begin planning early in the secondary school years for the youth's transition from the public school to the adult world (schooling, work, transportation, independent living, etc.).

- Be sure that you are well informed about the adult services offered in your community and state.

Tips for the General Education Classroom Teacher

- Be sure that appropriate steps have been taken to prepare the youth to return to school, work, and related activities.

- Work closely with members of the multidisciplinary team in developing appropriate schooling and employment experiences.

- Report any subtle changes in behavior immediately to parents and other specialists within the school.

- Continue to be aware of the potential needs for accommodation and adjustment.

- Treat the individual as an adult.

- Realize that the youth's studies or work experiences may be interrupted from time to time for specialized or regular medical treatments or other important health care services.

Tips for School Personnel

- Determine what environmental changes need to be made.

- Employ teaching procedures that best fit the youth's current cognitive status, attention deficits, physical functioning, and academic achievement.

- Be prepared for anger, depression, and rebellion in some youth with a TBI.

- Focus on the youth's current and emerging strengths.

- Acknowledge individuals by name, become familiar with their interests and hobbies, joke with them occasionally, and involve them in meaningful activities such as fund-raisers, community service projects, and decorating for various school events.

- Provide opportunities for all students to receive recognition and be involved in school-related activities.

- Realize that peer assistance and tutoring may be particularly helpful to certain students. Social involvement outside the school setting should be encouraged (e.g., going to movies, attending concerts, etc.).

- Use members of the multidisciplinary team to help with unique problems that surface from time to time. For example, you may want to talk with special educators about management or instructional ideas that may improve a given child's behavior and academic performance in your classroom.

Tips for Neighbors, Friends, and Potential Employers

- Involve the youth in appropriate family, neighborhood, and community activities, particularly youth activities.
- Become informed about the youth's capacities and interests.
- Provide employment explorations and part-time employment.
- Be aware of assistance that you might provide in the event of a youth's gradual deterioration or death.
- Encourage your own teens to volunteer as peer tutors or job coaches.

ADULT YEARS

Tips for the Family

- Begin developing appropriate independence skills throughout the school years.
- Determine early what steps can be taken to prepare the youth for meaningful part-time or full-time employment, or postsecondary training.
- Become thoroughly familiar with postsecondary educational opportunities and adult services for individuals with disabilities.
- Explore various living and housing options early in the youth's secondary school years.
- Work with adult service personnel and advocacy organizations in lining up appropriate housing and related support services.
- Know your rights and how you can qualify your son or daughter for educational or other support services.

Tips for Neighbors, Friends, and Employers

- Create opportunities for the adult to be involved in age-relevant activities, including movies, sports events, going out to dinner, and so on.
- Provide regular opportunities for recognition and informative feedback. Be sure to regularly provide people with physical disabilities or health disorders specific information and feedback about their work performance. Feedback may include candid comments about their punctuality, rate of work completion, and social interaction with others. Withholding information, not making reasonable adjustments, and not expecting these individuals to be responsible for their behaviors are great disservices to them.

Standard 5
Learning Environments and Social Interactions

Standard 10
Collaboration

assistive technology devices that aid in communication, information processing, learning, and recreation. These technologies help individuals with a TBI and other disabilities communicate with others, display what they know, access information, and participate in various learning and recreational activities.

The initial individualized education programs (IEPs) for students with a brain injury should be written for short periods of time, perhaps six to eight weeks. Moreover, these IEPs should be reviewed often to make adjustments based on the progress and growth of students. Often, students improve dramatically in the first year following their injuries. Children and youth with a TBI generally experience the most gains in the first year following the injury, with little progress made thereafter. Flexibility and responsiveness on the part of teachers and other support staff are essential to the well-being of students with a traumatic brain injury.

For students who want to move on to postsecondary education, interdisciplinary team members may contribute significantly to the transition process. Critical factors include the physical accessibility of the campus, living arrangements, support for academic achievement, social and personal support systems, and career/vocational training and placement.

For students who might find it difficult to continue their schooling after high school, transition planning for employment is essential. Prior to leaving high school, students with a TBI should have skills associated with filling out job applications, interviewing for jobs, and participating in supervised work experiences. State vocational agencies also play key roles in assisting young people with a TBI following high school. They provide services related to aptitude assessment, training opportunities after high school, and trial job placements.

Collaboration and cooperation are the key factors in achieving success with individuals who have a traumatic brain injury. A great deal can be accomplished when families, students, and care providers come together, engage in appropriate planning, and work collaboratively.

Attention Deficit/Hyperactivity Disorder

Standard 1
Foundations

FOCUS 12

What are the current views about the causes of attention deficit/hyperactivity disorder (ADHD)?

Attention deficit/hyperactivity disorder (ADHD) is one of the most common mental disorders in children and adolescents. Symptoms include difficulty staying focused and paying attention, difficulty controlling behavior, and very high levels of activity (Goldstein, 2011). "Studies show that the number of children being diagnosed with ADHD is increasing, but it is unclear why" (National Institute of Mental Health, 2012b). ADHD often persists into adulthood, requiring treatment and attention throughout the adult years (Barkley, 2006a; Kelly & Ramundo, 2006; National Institute of Mental Health, 2008). Examine the attendant definition of ADHD found in Figure 14.10.

Children with ADHD—especially boys—often evidence problems in developing school-related academic skills and in achieving satisfactory behavior/emotional adjustment (Daley & Birchwood, 2010). They frequently experience significant challenges with grade retention, expulsions, and suspensions. Left untreated as children and youth, adults with ADHD may encounter serious problems, many related to drug abuse, criminality, and unsatisfactory relationships with others (Barkley, 2006d; Frodl, 2010; Froehlich, Lanphear, Epstein, Barbaresi, Katusic, & Kahn, 2010; Glass, Flory, Martin, & Hankin, 2011; Wilens, et al., 2011).

Three different types of ADHD have been proposed.

- **Predominantly inattentive type:** It is hard for the individual to organize or finish a task, to pay attention to details, or to follow instructions or conversations. The person is easily distracted or forgets details of daily routines.

- **Predominantly hyperactive-impulsive type:** The person fidgets and talks a lot. It is hard to sit still for long (e.g., for a meal or while doing homework). Smaller children may run, jump, or climb constantly. The individual feels restless and has trouble with impulsivity. Someone who is impulsive may interrupt others a lot, grab things from people, or speak at inappropriate times. It is hard for the person to wait his or her turn or listen to directions. A person with impulsiveness may have more accidents and injuries than others.

- **Combined type:** Symptoms of the above two types are equally present in the person. (Centers for Disease Control and Prevention, 2012b)

There is not a single test for ADHD. Licensed professionals collect information about the child, youth, or adult using a variety of approaches, each tailored to the respective age groups and settings in which the behaviors may occur, carefully determining their frequency, function, and impact on the affected individual. These might include behavior rating scales, ongoing structured observations, and diagnostic interviews with individuals who know the child or youth well—parents, coaches, babysitters, and others (Barkley & Edwards, 2006; DuPaul & Kern, 2011a; Efron & Sciberras, 2010; Wright, Shelton, & Wright, 2009).

Standard 8
Assessment

Prevalence and Causation

Research suggests that about 3 to 7 percent of children manifest ADHD. In the United States, nearly 3.8 to 7.45 percent of school-age children manifest ADHD (Barkley, 2006c). Obviously, many "normal" children evidence mild features of the disorder, but are not diagnosed as such. Many more boys than girls are affected by ADHD—five to nine times greater. However, the presenting symptoms in both boys and girls are very similar (Barkley, 2006c).

ADHD is presumed to be a function of a central nervous system disorder. Also, ADHD can co-occur with other disorders, including intellectual disabilities, sensory impairments, and serious emotional and behavior disorders (Harty, Miller, Newcorn, & Halperin, 2009; Selekman, 2010; Thorell & Rydell, 2008; Youngstrom, Arnold, & Frazier, 2010).

The exact causes and precise factors that give rise to ADHD remain unclear. However, there is a clear relationship between ADHD and genetic/environmental factors (Nikolas & Burt, 2011). "The totality of the evidence indicates that neurological and genetic factors play a substantial role in the origins and expressions of this disorder" (Barkley, 2006c, p. 237).

In this regard, magnetic resonance imaging (MRI) is helping researchers uncover some of the neurological factors associated with ADHD. Some children with ADHD appear to be wired differently than their same-age peers without the condition. In some children with

A. Either (1) or (2):

1. Six (or more) of the following symptoms of *inattention* have persisted for at least six months to a degree that is maladaptive and inconsistent with developmental level:

Inattention

  a. Often fails to give close attention to details or makes careless mistakes in schoolwork, work, or other activities

  b. Often has difficulty sustaining attention in tasks or play activities

  c. Often does not seem to listen when spoken to directly

  d. Often does not follow through on instructions and fails to finish schoolwork, chores, or duties in the workplace (not due to oppositional behavior or failure to understand instructions)

  e. Often has difficulty organizing tasks and activities

  f. Often avoids, dislikes, or is reluctant to engage in tasks that require sustained mental effort (such as schoolwork or homework)

  g. Often loses things necessary for tasks or activities (e.g., toys, school assignments, pencils, books, or tools)

  h. Is often easily distracted by extraneous stimuli

  i. Is often forgetful in daily activities

2. Six (or more) of the following symptoms of *hyperactivity-impulsivity* have persisted for at least six months to a degree that is maladaptive and inconsistent with developmental level:

Hyperactivity

  a. Often fidgets with hands or feet or squirms in seat

  b. Often leaves seat in classroom or in other situations in which remaining seated is expected

  c. Often runs about or climbs excessively in situations in which it is inappropriate (in adolescents or adults, may be limited to subjective feelings or restlessness)

  d. Often has difficulty playing or engaging in leisure activities quietly

  e. Is often "on the go" or often acts as if "driven by a motor"

  f. Often talks excessively

Impulsivity

  g. Often blurts out answers before questions have been completed

  h. Often has difficulty awaiting turn

  i. Often interrupts or intrudes on others (e.g., butts into conversations or games)

B. Some hyperactive-impulsive or inattentive symptoms that caused impairment were present before age 7 years.

C. Some impairment from the symptoms is present in two or more settings (e.g., at school [or work] and at home).

D. There must be clear evidence of clinically significant impairment in social, academic, or occupational functioning.

E. The symptoms do not occur exclusively during the course of a pervasive developmental disorder, schizophrenia, or other psychotic disorder and are not better accounted for by another mental disorder (e.g., mood disorder, anxiety disorder, dissociative disorder, or a personality disorder).

Code based on type:
Attention deficit/hyperactivity disorder, combined type: if both Criteria A1 and A2 are met for the past six months
Attention deficit/hyperactivity disorder, predominantly inattentive type: if Criterion A1 is met but Criterion A2 is not met for the past six months
Attention deficit/hyperactivity disorder, predominantly hyperactive-impulsive type: if Criterion A2 is met but Criterion A1 is not met for the past six months
Coding note: For individuals (especially adolescents and adults) who currently have symptoms that no longer meet full criteria, "In Partial Remission" should be specified.

SOURCE: Reprinted with permission from American Psychiatric Association. (2000). *Diagnostic and statistical manual of mental disorders*, 4th ed., text rev. (p. 92). Copyright 2000 American Psychiatric Association.

ADHD, their brain development follows a normal path of development but progresses in a delayed fashion. This delay in development on average is generally three years behind children without the disorder (National Institute of Mental Health, 2012a).

Interventions

Treatments and interventions for individuals with ADHD are centered on reducing symptoms and improving everyday functioning in home, classroom, social, and work settings. ADHD requires multiple interventions that fall into two broad categories: behavioral and medical. As is true in many disability areas, effective treatment involves a multidisciplinary team approach and includes combinations of techniques as determined by individual needs (Pugach & Winn, 2011; Reid & Johnson, 2011; Williamson & McLeskey, 2011).

Standard 5
Learning Environments and
Social Interactions

Children Controlling hyperactive and impulsive behavior in children appears to be most effectively accomplished with medication (often methylphenidate or Ritalin) (Froehlich, McGough, & Stein, 2010; Ryan, Katsiyannis, & Hughes, 2011). Evidence is emerging that pharmacological control of behavioral challenges is more effective than nonmedical interventions, such as behavioral treatment (Powell, Thomsen, & Frydenberg, 2011; Ryan, Katsiyannis, & Hughes, 2011; Stroh, Frankenberger, Cornell-Swanson, Wood, & Pahl, 2008; Vaughan, Roberts, & Needelman, 2009). Research supporting the effectiveness of medication is accumulating, but such medical intervention shows no effect, or very limited influence, on academic performance (DuPaul & Kern, 2011b; Graziano, Geffken, & Lall, 2011; Hale et al., 2011). Current thinking suggests that even though there are clear benefits to the use of medication, it may be overprescribed; side effects and issues of potential abuse need further research (Frodl, 2010; Kalikow, 2011; Lee, Humphreys, Flory, Liu, & Glass, 2011).

Some researchers advise caution in the use of psychostimulants for both theoretical and practical reasons. First, there are concerns regarding side effects, as one would expect. In some cases, it is difficult to distinguish psychological characteristics that may appear to be side effects (such as increased anxiety) from the symptoms of ADHD itself. Additionally, some researchers express uneasiness about appropriate dosage, overprescription, and unhealthy side effects such as increased tobacco and alcohol use. There are also matters of potential for abuse, and issues related to management planning and implementation for children being treated with medication (Comstock, 2011; Rabiner, Anastopoulos, & Costello, 2010).

Children who are young when they begin to receive medication may take it over a very long period; however, it is unclear what the cumulative effects may be on physical or intellectual development (van de Loo-Neus, Rommelse, & Buitelaar, 2011). For preschoolers, there is some evidence that susceptibility to side effects might be greater (DuPaul & Kern, 2011b; Posey, Bassin, & Lewis, 2009). Further investigation in both these areas is certainly warranted. Concerns about medication interventions have been raised in the popular press and continue to arise periodically as the field grapples with the challenges these children and youth present (Higgens, 2009; Shute, 2009).

The hyperactive and impulsive behaviors of many children with ADHD clearly present a significant challenge to parents, teachers, and other school personnel during the elementary school years. Elementary teachers describe these children as fidgety, impulsive, often off-task, and constantly disruptive (DuPaul, Weyandt, & Janusis, 2011; National Institute of Mental Health, 2008). These behaviors are often accompanied by deficits in academic performance (Barnard-Brak, Sulak, & Fearon, 2011; McConaughy, Volpe, & Antshel, 2011).

Nonmedical, school-based interventions can also be effective in improving the classroom behaviors of elementary-age school children with ADHD. In general, targeted behavior modification strategies appear to be more effective for controlling behavioral problems than those that involve cognitive-behavioral or cognitive interventions. Cognitive-behavioral therapies are based on combining behavioral techniques with efforts to change the way a person thinks about his or her behaviors. Research evidence suggests limited beneficial results from cognitive-behavioral interventions for children with ADHD (Levine & Anshel, 2011).

Educators should arrange the classroom setting to enhance the child's ability to respond, attend, and behave in a manner that is conducive to learning. Teachers may have to monitor the directions they give students with ADHD, often cuing them to the fact that a direction or message is about to be delivered. This might be done with a prompt such as "Listen, John" or some other signal that the teacher is comfortable making and is well understood by the student as meaning a directive is to follow (Fowler, 2010; Geng, 2011).

Student learning is enhanced by strategies that involve considerable structure (Reid & Johnson, 2011). Instruction, such as writing lessons, may be more effective if reinforcement is combined with modeling and increased practice (Browder & Spooner, 2011; Hedin, Mason, & Gaffney, 2011). These children often require individualized instruction from a teacher or aide, focused on the specific content area needing attention, such as reading, math, or spelling (Riley, McKevitt, Shriver, & Allen, 2011; van Kraayenoord, Miller, & Moni, 2009).

Multiple treatment approaches (often termed *multimodal treatments*), such as drug and behavior therapies, are more effective than just one kind of treatment for children with ADHD (Jensen, Abikoff, & Brown, 2009; Owens & Fabiano, 2011; Springer & Reddy, 2010). This is important in the case of children with ADHD, because a high proportion receive both medical treatment and school-based instruction. All collaborating parties must pay special attention to facilitating communication among physicians and others providing treatment.

Adolescence and Adulthood Once viewed as a childhood condition, ADHD is now known to have a significant presence beyond those early years and is accompanied by an array of other behaviors and conditions in adolescence and adulthood (Bussing, Mason, & Bell, 2010; Elkins, Malone, Keyes, Iacono, & McGue, 2011; Mao, Babcock, & Brams, 2011; Taylor, Deb, & Unwin, 2011). These include social impairments, greater number of driving-related problems (license suspensions, accidents, and traffic citations), continuing academic challenges, underachievement in work settings, presence of other psychiatric conditions, and inhibition/self-control issues (Barkley, 2006d; Kent, et al., 2011). Current research suggests that ADHD is far more persistent into adulthood than once was thought; it often requires continuing treatment (Bramham, Young, & Bickerdike, 2009; Sprich, Knouse, & Cooper-Vince, 2010). Interventions appropriate for adolescents and adults with ADHD must be reassessed, and where appropriate, modified in an age-appropriate manner (Kraft, 2010, Mao, Babcock, and Brams, 2011; Mitchell, Robertson, Kimbrel, & Nelson-Gray, 2011). However, cognitive challenges such as the impulse control and memory problems found in children with ADHD occur in many adults with ADHD as well (Mitchell et al., 2011; Storm & White, 2010). Further, medication remains an effective treatment for the impulsivity and difficulty in focusing on tasks that continue into the adolescent and adult years for many people with ADHD.

Adolescents and adults with ADHD may not exhibit hyperactivity but may still have considerable difficulty in focusing on tasks, controlling impulses, and using appropriate social skills. Again, medication may be an effective treatment for some of these behaviors as many of the adult/adolescent-prescribed medications enhance the individual's executive function of the brain—the brain's capacity to help an adolescent or adult manage and control his or her behavior and impulses (National Resource Center on ADHD, 2012). There is still much to be learned about the treatment of adults with ADHD. Future research will help us understand the salient aspects of treatment and how they play out in managing the symptoms of ADHD and achieving worthwhile long-term outcomes for adolescents and adults with this disorder.

LOOKING TOWARD A BRIGHT FUTURE

This is so much to be positive about in considering the future for children, youth, and individuals with physical disabilities and health disorders. Consider for a moment the comments made by young Michael Anwar, cited at the outset of the chapter, when he wrote "I have cerebral palsy . . . it doesn't have me!" Michael is proof positive that caring professionals can help children and youth respond with more resilience and optimism in coping with their conditions and grow in uniquely positive ways during the duration of their lives.

Some of our greatest causes for hope center on medical advances in gene therapies, stem cell research, uniquely person-specific medications, early treatment procedures, and highly innovative surgical techniques—too many to describe in great detail. Also, we are benefiting from the talents and skills of highly creative engineers and inventors who are developing new orthotics, highly functional assistive and augmentative devices, artificial limbs, exoskeletons, home and office control systems, and robotics.

Finally, we are becoming more inclusive, spontaneous, and caring in our responses to individuals with physical disabilities, disorders, and injuries—much in part because they are now so much a natural part of all of our daily experiences in our neighborhoods, schools, and communities. We know them. They have been in our classrooms. We feel more comfortable around them because of our own face-to-face interactions with them, their families, and their unique talents and capacities.

FOCUS REVIEW

FOCUS 1 Identify several disabilities that may accompany cerebral palsy.

- Often, individuals with cerebral palsy have several disabilities, including hearing impairments, speech and language disorders, intellectual deficits, visual impairments, and general perceptual problems.

FOCUS 2 What is spina bifida myelomeningocele?

- Spina bifida myelomeningocele is a type of spina bifida cystica that announces itself in the form of a tumorlike sac, on the back of the infant, that contains both spinal fluid and nerve tissue.
- Spina bifida myelomeningocele is also the most serious variety of spina bifida because it generally includes paralysis or partial paralysis of certain body areas, causing lack of bowel and bladder control.

FOCUS 3 Identify three things that occur when the spinal cord is bruised or injured.

- Generally three things occur: swelling, bleeding, and a self-destructive process that gradually ensues, in which the affected area slowly deteriorates and the damage becomes irreversible.

FOCUS 4 Describe the physical limitations associated with muscular dystrophy.

- Individuals with muscular dystrophy progressively lose their ability to walk and use their arms and hands effectively, because fatty tissue begins to replace muscle tissue.

FOCUS 5 Describe the AIDS disease stages through which individuals with the syndrome move.

- The first stage is the exposure stage, or the period during which the transmission of the HIV occurs.
- The second stage is characterized by the production of antibodies in infected individuals. These antibodies appear about 2 to 12 weeks after the initial transmission of the virus.

- During stage three, the immune system declines, and the virus begins to destroy cells of the immune system.

FOCUS 6 What are the critical symptoms of asthma in children and youth?

- Symptoms include diminished breathing capacity, coughing, wheezing, tightness in the chest, and excessive sputum.

FOCUS 7 Describe the immediate treatment for a person who is experiencing a tonic/clonic seizure.

- Cushion the head.
- Loosen any tight necktie or collar.
- Turn the person on his or her side.
- Put nothing in the mouth of the individual.
- Look for identification.
- Don't hold the person down.
- As the seizure ends, offer help.

FOCUS 8 Identify several problems individuals with diabetes may experience later in life without adherence to diet, exercise, and medical regimens.

- Physical complications that occur over time may result in blindness, heart attacks, skin disorders, neuropathy (weakness and numbness) in the feet, and kidney problems.

FOCUS 9 Identify present and future interventions for the treatment of children and youth with cystic fibrosis.

- Drug therapy for prevention and treatment of chest infections
- Diet management, use of replacement enzymes for food absorption, and vitamin intake
- Family education regarding the condition
- Chest physiotherapy and postural drainage
- Inhalation therapy
- Psychological and psychiatric counseling
- Use of mucus-thinning drugs, gene therapy, and lung or lung/heart transplant

FOCUS 10 Describe the impact on body tissues of the sickling of red blood cells in sickle-cell disease (SCD).

- Because sickled cells are more rigid than normal cells, they frequently block microvascular channels.
- The blockage of channels reduces or terminates circulation in these areas, and tissues in need of blood nutrients and oxygen die.
- The brain injury often results in permanent disabilities.

FOCUS 11 Describe the focus of educational interventions for individuals with traumatic brain injuries.

- Educational interventions are directed at improving the general behaviors of the individual, including problem solving, planning, and developing insight; building appropriate social behaviors such as working with others, suppressing inappropriate behaviors, and using appropriate etiquette; developing expressive and receptive language skills, such as retrieving words, describing events, and understanding instructions; and developing writing skills.
- Other academic skills relevant to the students' needs and developmental level of functioning are also taught.
- Transition planning for postsecondary education and training is also essential to the well-being of an individual with traumatic brain injury.

FOCUS 12 What are the current views about the causes of attention deficit/hyperactivity disorder (ADHD)?

- Current evidence suggests that neurological and genetic factors play substantial roles in the causation of ADHD.

Council for Exceptional Children (CEC) Standards to Accompany Chapter 14

 If you are thinking about a career in special education, you should know that many states use national standards developed by the Council for Exceptional Children (CEC) to assess a teacher candidate's knowledge and skills for working with students with disabilities. See a complete listing of the 10 CEC Content Standards on the inside back cover of this text.

1 Foundations
2 Development and Characteristics of Learners
3 Individual Learning Differences
5 Learning Environments and Social Interactions
7 Instructional Planning
8 Assessment
10 Collaboration

Mastery Activities and Assignments

 To master the content within this chapter, complete the following activities and assignments. Online and interactive versions of these activities are also available on the accompanying Education CourseMate website, where you may also access TeachSource videos, chapter web links, interactive quizzes, portfolio activities, flash cards, an integrated eBook, and much more!

1. Complete a written test of the chapter's content. If your instructor requires a written test of your content knowledge for this chapter, keep a copy for your portfolio. A practice test on the information covered in this chapter is available through the premium website.
2. Respond in writing to the Application Questions for the Case Study, "Sarah and the 'Pump.'" Keep a copy of the case study and your written response for your portfolio.
3. Read the Debate Forum, "Should We Protect Our Children and Youth from Firearm Violence?" Then visit the Education CourseMate website to complete the activity, "Take a Stand." Keep a copy of this activity for your portfolio.
4. Participate in a community service learning activity. Community service is a valuable way to enhance your learning experience. Visit the Education CourseMate website for suggested community service learning activities that correspond to the information presented in this chapter. Develop a reflective journal of the service learning experience for your portfolio.

Exceptional Gifts and Talents

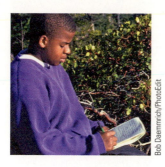

Bob Daemmrich/PhotoEdit

You are about to explore an area of exceptionality that is unlike any other that you have studied to this point. It represents a unique part of the ability/talent spectrum, and it is not generally well understood by educators, policy makers, and parents. For many, it invites little attention. In many states, it is not a vital consideration for funding, supporting, or encouraging. As a nation, we are not committed to these individuals who represent this unique slice of the ability/talent spectrum. Beliefs prevail that these children, youth, and young adults will thrive without any specialized services or supports in developing their intellect, creativity, abilities, gifts, and talents. In contrast, others believe that nurturing these abilities, gifts, and talents is absolutely essential and vital to our collective well-being and our progress as a nation.

With today's press for energy sources, we often speak about capturing and using renewable energy. The energy and capacity evident in these individuals by definition are virtually inexhaustible, unlikely to disappear or run out. However, that energy and capacity must be uncovered, developed, and utilized. This is true of children, youth, and young adults who are gifted and talented or who have the potential for becoming such. In the absence of appropriate development and nurturing, this renewable resource in each generation of young people will be lost, underdeveloped, or not developed at all. This is particularly true of diverse young people who come from challenging economic and social environments—environments that are impoverished and often do not provide the experiences so central to well-being, capacity building, and talent development. Without appropriate support and stimulation, these children and youth languish—never having opportunities to realize their innate talents, to build capacities, and to make valuable contributions—so essential to their well-being and the health and vitality of their families, neighborhoods, communities, and nation. This is also true for those who are *twice exceptional*: young people with disabilities who are also gifted. Now more than ever, we realize that giftedness in its many hues can be present and be developed in all kinds of children, youth, and adults.

PART IV: CHAPTER OVERVIEW

Chapter 15 begins with a brief story about Wayne—an extraordinarily talented jazz pianist and academic who also holds a doctorate in German. As a young child, he was provided with appropriate encouragement and stimulation to develop his talents. On the concert stage, in family gatherings, and in other venues, he would make you marvel at his capacity for improvisation and his penchant for engaging audiences with his music. This Snapshot sets the stage for the remainder of the chapter that provides timely and useful information about the history and conceptions of intelligence and its origins. Additionally, this chapter reveals various definitions of giftedness, identifies characteristics associated with giftedness, speaks to current means for assessing giftedness or identifying potential for such in children and youth, addresses the central role of talent development in nurturing giftedness, describes approaches for nurturing giftedness, and identifies historically neglected groups of gifted individuals.

CHAPTER 15

Gifted, Creative, and Talented

Jose Luis Pelaez Inc/Getty Images

FOCUS PREVIEW

As you read this chapter, focus on these key concepts:

1   Briefly describe several historical developments directly related to the identification and measurement of various types of giftedness.

2   Identify four major components of definitions that have been developed to describe giftedness.

3   Identify four problems inherent in accurately describing the characteristics of individuals who are gifted.

4   Identify three factors that appear to contribute significantly to the emergence of various forms of giftedness.

5   Indicate the range of assessment devices used to identify the various types of giftedness.

6   Identify seven strategies that are utilized to foster the development of gifted children during early childhood.

7   Identify five general approaches that are utilized to foster the development of gifted school-age children and adolescents.

8   Identify four challenges females face in dealing with their giftedness. What five factors are important to recognizing giftedness in individuals with disabilities?

Wayne: Reflections of a Very Talented Jazz Musician

Art historian Bernard Berenson defined *genius* as "the capacity for productive reaction against one's training." Albert Einstein explained himself as having "lived in that solitude which is painful in youth, but delicious in the years of maturity." Wayne has been a translator, an adjunct professor of humanities, a freelance jazz pianist, and has managed commercial and Department of Defense proposals for over 20 years.

Wayne met the usual challenges and pitfalls of being the second born among ten siblings. It helped that his parents encouraged him, approved even of average grades and thought his ordinary progress on the piano exemplified real talent. Wayne attended public schools and grew up in a home with an adequate piano and a library comprising church monthlies, popular-culture magazines, the holy writ, his father's abundant medical library, and an ample collection of Reader's Digest Condensed Books. He started taking piano lessons at age 9 from an uninspired neighborhood teacher who prepared students to play piano for Christian devotionals.

Courtesy of Wayne Egan

At age 12, Wayne quit piano lessons. At age 14, he redirected his aesthetic focus to playing and arranging jazz. By age 16, Wayne became interested in literature and foreign language; he began writing poetry and studying German. Amid the commotion and cultural upheaval of the late 1960s, Wayne spent four years in the U.S. Army, and sought refuge from military life in literature, language study, and jazz piano.

Wayne finally emerged as a man of unusual personal achievement in music and language arts. His synthesis of literature and music became his "productive reaction" against his training and upbringing. As a self-taught jazzer, Wayne internalized hundreds of songs and rhythms, including the "swing" facet that eludes many of the best-trained classical pianists. At a gig, jam session, or in the recording studio, Wayne had to be well prepared, declaring himself ready for almost anything with little or no rehearsal—simultaneously performer, composer, and arranger. His personal harmonic style evolved from intricate exploration of the harmony of Bill Evans and George Shearing. He discovered the colossal advantage of playing the piano—that one instrument on which recurrent harmonic variation is most easily achieved.

Wayne played piano at Nordstrom for 10 years, taught writing and humanities at the University of Phoenix, and currently plays salon piano at an upscale restaurant. He composes ad hoc lyrics and songs to entertain at professional conventions, reunions, and private parties. He lives now amid a clutter of essential books, personal journals, reharmonized jazz standards, and a few obscure songs that deserve to become standards. These artifacts are sources of intermittent happiness for someone whose talent is less a gift than the result of strong personal will and self-direction.

The terms *gifted*, *creative*, and *talented* are associated with children, youth, and adults who have extraordinary abilities in one or more areas of performance. Some believe that gifts and talents are overrated—that outstanding performance in most endeavors comes from consistent and deliberate practice (Colvin, 2008). What do you think? What really gives rise to individuals like Wayne—the talented musician and academic?

The gifted, creative, and talented are a diverse array of individuals. In many cases we admire these specialists, performers, and athletes. Occasionally we are a little envious of their abilities. Their ease in mastering diverse and difficult concepts is impressive. Because of their unusual abilities and skills, educators and policy makers frequently assume that these individuals will reach their full potential without any specialized programs or targeted encouragement.

Standard 1
Foundations

A Changing Era in the Lives of Children, Youth, and Adults Who Are Gifted, Creative, and Talented

Gifted, creative, and talented
Terms applied to individuals with extraordinary abilities or the capacity for developing them.

For years, behavioral scientists described children and youth with exceptionally high intelligence as being **gifted**. Only recently have researchers and practitioners included the adjectives **creative** and **talented**, to suggest domains of performance other than those measured by traditional intelligence tests. Now more than ever, children, youth, and adults with remarkable talents or creative capacities are being identified for participation in programs designed to encourage and nourish their gifts and capacities. No longer are gifted programs solely targeted at those with high IQs. Obviously, not all individuals who achieve high scores on intelligence tests are creative or talented. Capacities associated with creativity include *elaboration* (the ability to embellish or enrich an idea), *transformation* (the ability to construct new meanings or change an idea into something new and novel), and *visualization* (the capacity to manipulate ideas or see images mentally) (Sternberg, Jarvin, & Grigorenko, 2011). Individuals who are talented may display extraordinary skills in mathematics, sports, music, or other performance areas (Sternberg, 2006; Treffinger, 2004). "A child [or individual] may demonstrate gifted behavior at one point in development, but not necessarily at another point in development or may exhibit gifted behavior in one domain, but not necessarily across all domains . . ." (Horowitz, 2009, p. 9). Some individuals soar to exceptional heights in a talent domain, others achieve in intellectual areas, and still others excel in creative endeavors. A select few exhibit remarkable achievement across several domains like Wayne featured in our opening Snapshot.

Historical Developments

FOCUS 1

Briefly describe several historical developments directly related to the identification and measurement of various types of giftedness.

Definitions that describe the unusually able in terms of intelligence quotients and creativity measures are recent phenomena. Not until the beginning of the 20th century was there a suitable method for potentially quantifying or measuring the human attribute of intelligence. The breakthrough occurred in Europe when Alfred Binet, a French psychologist, constructed the first developmental assessment scale for children in the early 1900s. This scale was created by observing children at various ages to identify specific tasks that ordinary children were able to perform at each age. These tasks were then sequenced according to age-appropriate levels. Children who could perform tasks well above that which was normal for their chronological age were identified as being developmentally advanced.

Binet and Simon (1905; 1908) developed the notion of **mental age**. The mental age of a child was derived by matching the tasks (memory, vocabulary, mathematical, and comprehension, etc.) that a child was able to perform according to the age scale (which gave the typical performance of children at various stages). Although this scale was initially developed and used to identify children with mental retardation in the Parisian schools, it eventually became an important means for identifying those who had higher-than-average mental ages as well.

Lewis M. Terman, an American educator and psychologist, expanded the concepts and procedures Binet developed. He was convinced that Binet and Simon had discovered an approach that would be useful for measuring intellectual abilities in all children. This belief prompted him to revise the Binet instrument, adding greater breadth to the scale. In 1916, Terman published the **Stanford-Binet Intelligence Scale** in conjunction with Stanford University. During this period, Terman introduced the term **intelligence quotient**, or **IQ**. The IQ score was obtained by dividing a child's mental age (MA) by his or her chronological age (CA) and multiplying that figure by 100 (MA/CA × 100 = IQ). For example, a child with a mental age of 12 and a chronological age of 8 would have an IQ of 150 (12/8 × 100 = 150). See the nearby Reflect on This, "An IQ of 228: Is That Possible?" for an example of a person with an extraordinary IQ.

Gradually, other researchers became interested in studying the nature and assessment of intelligence. They tended to view intelligence as an underlying ability or capacity that expressed itself in a variety of ways. The unitary IQ scores that were derived from the Stanford-Binet tests were representative of and contributed to this notion.

Mental age (MA)
A score that represents the individual's mental age according to various tasks he or she is able to perform on a given IQ test. Children who are able to complete tasks well beyond their chronological age (CA) will have a higher mental age (MA) and thus a higher-than-average IQ score (MA, 12 years/CA, 8 years × 100 = IQ 150).

Stanford-Binet intelligence scale
A standardized individual intelligence test, originally known as the Binet-Simon scales, which was revised and standardized by Lewis Terman at Stanford University.

Intelligence quotient (IQ)
A score obtained from an intelligence test that reflects the relationship between one's chronological age and one's mental age (MA, 12 years/CA, 8 years × 100 = IQ 150).

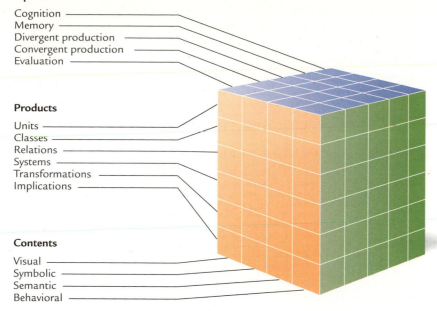

Each little cube represents a unique combination of one kind of operation, one kind of content, and one kind of product—and hence a distinctly different intellectual ability or function.

Figure 15.1 *Guilford's Structure of the Intellect Model*

Operations

Cognition
Memory
Divergent production
Convergent production
Evaluation

Products

Units
Classes
Relations
Systems
Transformations
Implications

Contents

Visual
Symbolic
Semantic
Behavioral

SOURCE: From *Way Beyond the IQ*: *Guide to Improving Intelligence and Creativity* (p. 151), by J. P. Guilford, 1977, Buffalo, NY: Creative Education Foundation. Copyright 1977 by Creative Education Foundation. Reprinted by permission.

Over time, however, other researchers came to believe that intellect was represented by a variety of distinct capacities and abilities (Cattell, 1971; Guilford, 1959). This line of thinking suggested that each distinct, intellectual capacity could be identified and assessed. Several mental abilities were investigated, including memory capacity, divergent thinking, vocabulary usage, and reasoning ability (see Figure 15.1). Gradually, use of the multiple-ability approach outgrew that of the unitary-intelligence notion. Proponents of the multiple-ability approach were convinced that the universe of intellectual functions was extensive and that the intelligence assessment instruments utilized at that time measured a very small portion of an individual's true intellectual capacities (Sternberg, Jarvin, & Grigorenko, 2011).

REFLECT ON THIS
AN IQ OF 228: IS THAT POSSIBLE?

At the age of 10, Marilyn vos Savant answered every question on the Stanford-Binet correctly. At the time, her mental age was "22 years and 11 months," and her calculated IQ was 228. Since that time, she has been listed in the *Guinness Book of World Records* for five years under "Highest IQ" for her childhood and adult scores (Savant, 2012, p. 1). Marilyn currently lives in New York with her husband. She is an executive at Jarvik Heart, Inc., and she writes a regular column for *Parade* magazine, which is a supplement to Sunday newspapers (Knight, 2009).

Question for Reflection

What experiences as a child (in addition to her native endowment) do you think contributed to this test performance at 10 years of age?

SOURCES: Knight, S. (2009). *Is high IQ a burden as much as a blessing?* Retrieved May 15, 2009, from www.ft.com/cms/s/2/4add9230-23d5-11de-996a-00144feabdc0.html; Savant, M. (2012). *About Marilyn*. Retrieved April 10, 2012, from http://marilynvossavant.com/about-marilyn/.

One of the key contributors to the multidimensional theory of intelligence was J. P. Guilford (1950; 1959). He saw intelligence as a diverse range of intellectual and creative abilities. Guilford's work led many researchers to view intelligence more broadly, focusing their scientific efforts on the emerging field of creativity and its various subcomponents, such as divergent thinking, problem solving, and decision making. Gradually, tests or measures of creativity were developed, using the constructs drawn from models Guilford and others created (Treffinger, 2004).

In summary, conceptions of giftedness during the early 1920s were closely tied to the score that an individual obtained on an intelligence test. Thus, a single score—one's IQ—was the index by which one was identified as being gifted. Beginning with the work of Guilford (1950, 1959) and Torrance (1961, 1965, 1968), notions regarding giftedness were greatly expanded. *Giftedness* began to be used to refer not only to those with high IQs, but also to those who demonstrated high aptitude on creativity measures. More recently, the term *talented* has been added to the descriptors associated with giftedness. As a result, individuals who demonstrate remarkable skills in the visual or performing arts or who excel in other areas of performance may be designated as gifted. Figure15.2 reveals how our perspectives on giftedness have changed over time with the acceptance of new, multifaceted definitions of giftedness.

Figure 15.2 *New Perspectives in Gifted Education*

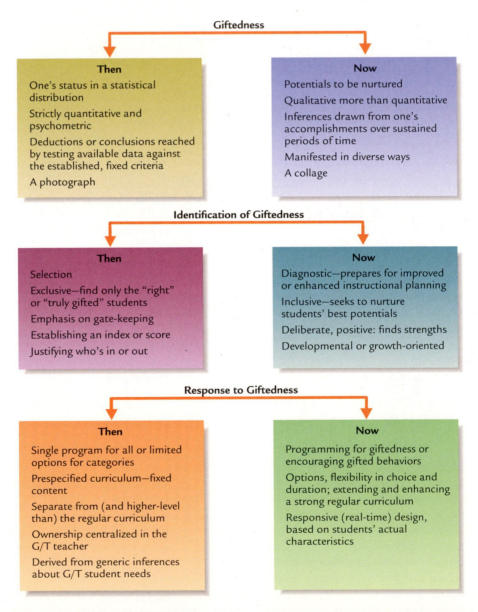

Giftedness

Then
- One's status in a statistical distribution
- Strictly quantitative and psychometric
- Deductions or conclusions reached by testing available data against the established, fixed criteria
- A photograph

Now
- Potentials to be nurtured
- Qualitative more than quantitative
- Inferences drawn from one's accomplishments over sustained periods of time
- Manifested in diverse ways
- A collage

Identification of Giftedness

Then
- Selection
- Exclusive—find only the "right" or "truly gifted" students
- Emphasis on gate-keeping
- Establishing an index or score
- Justifying who's in or out

Now
- Diagnostic—prepares for improved or enhanced instructional planning
- Inclusive—seeks to nurture students' best potentials
- Deliberate, positive: finds strengths
- Developmental or growth-oriented

Response to Giftedness

Then
- Single program for all or limited options for categories
- Prespecified curriculum—fixed content
- Separate from (and higher-level than) the regular curriculum
- Ownership centralized in the G/T teacher
- Derived from generic inferences about G/T student needs

Now
- Programming for giftedness or encouraging gifted behaviors
- Options, flexibility in choice and duration; extending and enhancing a strong regular curriculum
- Responsive (real-time) design, based on students' actual characteristics

SOURCE: Adapted from *New Visions for Gifted Education: Issues and Opportunities*, by D. J. Trettinger (p. 17), copyright © 1989 by the Center for Creative Learning, Sarasota, Florida. Reproduced by permission of the publisher.

Currently, there is no federal mandate in the United States requiring educational services for students identified as gifted, as is the case with other exceptionalities. Only 22 states have mandated programs for gifted students (National Association for Gifted Children, 2012a). The actual funding of services for individuals who are gifted is a state-by-state, local challenge, so there is tremendous variability in the quality and types of programs offered to students in various states (Clark, 2008).

In coming years, we will probably see *talent development* replace gifted education as the guiding concept (Claxton & Meadows, 2009; Hong & Milgram, 2008; Treffinger, Nassab, & Selby, 2009). This description suggests a kind of programming that is directed at all students, not just those identified as gifted, talented, or creative (Clark, 2008; Davis, Rimm, & Siegle, 2011). A "benefit [of this kind of programming] is that the talent development orientation eliminates the awkwardness of the words *gifted* and, by exclusion, *not gifted*" (Davis & Rimm, 2004, p. 28).

Definitions and Prevalence

Capturing the essence of any human condition in a definition can be very perplexing. This is certainly true in defining the human attributes, abilities, and potentialities that constitute giftedness, creativity, and talent (Davis, Rimm, & Siegle, 2011; Matthews & Foster, 2009; Worrell & Erwin, 2011). Throughout this chapter, we will use the terms *gifted* and *giftedness* to represent all forms of talents, capacities, and creativity.

Definitions of giftedness serve several important purposes (Horowitz, 2009; Worrell & Erwin, 2011). For example, definitions may have a profound influence on the number and kinds of students ultimately selected in a school system, on the types of instruments and selection procedures used, on the scores students must obtain to qualify for specialized instruction and/or programs, on the amount of funding required to provide services, and on the types of preparation educators need to teach students who are gifted. Thus, definitions are important from both practical and theoretical perspectives (Moon, 2006).

Definitions of giftedness have been influenced by a variety of knowledgeable individuals (Cattell, 1971; Gardner, 1983; Guilford, 1959; Piirto, 1999; Ramos-Ford & Gardner, 1997; Renzulli & Reis, 2003; Sternberg, 1997; Torrance, 1966). As you will soon discover, there is no universally accepted definition of giftedness (Clark, 2008).

Ross (1993) defined giftedness in the following manner:

Children and youth with outstanding talent perform or show the potential for performing at remarkably high levels of accomplishment when compared with others of their age, experience, or environment. These children and youth exhibit high performance capability in intellectual, creative, and/or artistic areas, possess an unusual leadership capacity, or excel in specific academic fields. They require services or activities not ordinarily provided by the schools. Outstanding talents are present in children and youth from all cultural groups, across all economic strata, and in all areas of human endeavor. (p. 3)

The current definition, a derivative of an earlier government report—the *Marland Report to Congress*, is as follows:

Students, children, or youth who give evidence of high achievement capability in areas such as intellectual, creative, artistic, or leadership capacity, or in specific academic fields, and who need services and activities not ordinarily provided by the school in order to fully develop those capabilities. (National Association for Gifted Children, 2012b)

Definitions like these guide school personnel and others in pursuing several important objectives. These include identifying students across disciplines with diverse talents, using many different kinds of assessment measures to identify gifted students, identifying "achievement capabilities" and not necessarily demonstrated performance in students, searching actively for giftedness in all student populations (cultural, ethnic, economic, etc.), and considering students' drives and passions for achievement in various areas.

Also, new conceptions of giftedness and intelligence have emerged from theoretical and research literature (Esping & Plucker, 2008; Passow, 2004; Ramos-Ford & Gardner, 1997;

CEC

Standard 1
Foundations

FOCUS 2

Identify four major components of definitions that have been developed to describe giftedness.

Figure 15.3 Catalysts for the Development of Gifts and Talents

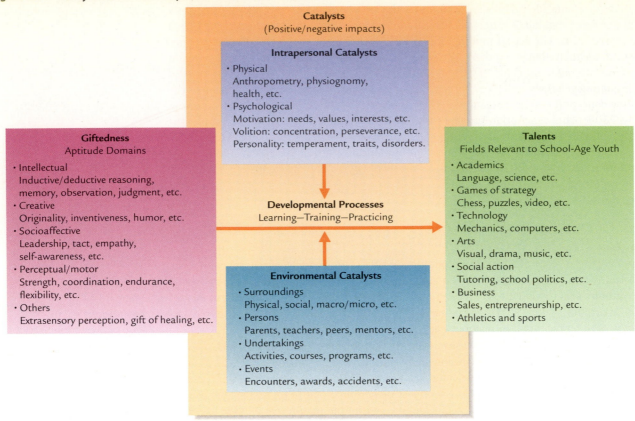

Catalysts
(Positive/negative impacts)

Intrapersonal Catalysts
- Physical
  Anthropometry, physiognomy, health, etc.
- Psychological
  Motivation: needs, values, interests, etc.
  Volition: concentration, perseverance, etc.
  Personality: temperament, traits, disorders.

Giftedness
Aptitude Domains

- Intellectual
  Inductive/deductive reasoning, memory, observation, judgment, etc.
- Creative
  Originality, inventiveness, humor, etc.
- Socioaffective
  Leadership, tact, empathy, self-awareness, etc.
- Perceptual/motor
  Strength, coordination, endurance, flexibility, etc.
- Others
  Extrasensory perception, gift of healing, etc.

Developmental Processes
Learning—Training—Practicing

Environmental Catalysts
- Surroundings
  Physical, social, macro/micro, etc.
- Persons
  Parents, teachers, peers, mentors, etc.
- Undertakings
  Activities, courses, programs, etc.
- Events
  Encounters, awards, accidents, etc.

Talents
Fields Relevant to School-Age Youth

- Academics
  Language, science, etc.
- Games of strategy
  Chess, puzzles, video, etc.
- Technology
  Mechanics, computers, etc.
- Arts
  Visual, drama, music, etc.
- Social action
  Tutoring, school politics, etc.
- Business
  Sales, entrepreneurship, etc.
- Athletics and sports

SOURCE: From "Is There Any Light at the End of the Tunnel?" by F. Gagné, 1999, *Journal of the Education of the Gifted*, 22(2), pp. 191–234. Copyright © 1999 by Sage Publications, Inc. Reprinted with permission.

Sternberg, 1997). One of these approaches is Sternberg's triarchic theory of human intelligence (Sternberg, 1997; Sternberg, Jarvin, & Grigorenko, 2011). In this approach, intellectual performance is divided into three parts: analytic, synthetic, and practical. Analytic intelligence is exhibited by people who perform well on aptitude and intelligence tests. Individuals with synthetic giftedness are unconventional thinkers who are creative, intuitive, and insightful. People with practical intelligence are extraordinarily adept in dealing with problems of everyday life and those that arise in their work environments. Recently, Sternberg (2009) coined the term *WICS*: wisdom, intelligence, creativity, synthesized—a form of giftedness. His premise is that wisdom, intelligence, and creativity are developed and formed—they are not entirely innate, but must be cultivated and nurtured (Sternberg, Jarvin, & Grigorenko, 2011). Gagné (1999) has also identified catalysts that give rise to gifts and talents in young people (see Figure 15.3).

Another view of giftedness has been developed by Ramos-Ford and Gardner (1997). They have defined intelligence or giftedness as "an ability or set of abilities that permit an individual to solve problems or fashion products that are of consequence in a particular cultural setting" (Ramos-Ford & Gardner, 1991, p. 56). This perspective on giftedness is referred to as the theory of multiple intelligences. Intelligence is assumed to manifest itself in linguistic, logical-mathematical, spatial, musical, bodily-kinesthetic, interpersonal, and intrapersonal behaviors (Esping & Plucker, 2008). Table 15.1 provides brief definitions of each of these behaviors, as well as the child and adult roles associated with each type of intelligence.

These and other definitions of giftedness have moved us from unitary measures of IQ to multiple measures of creativity, problem-solving ability, talent, and intelligence. However, despite the movement away from IQ scores and other changes in definitions of giftedness, critics argue that many if not most local, district, and state definitions are elitist in nature and favor the "affluent" and "privileged" (Borland, 2003; Ford, 2003).

Table 15.1	The Seven Intelligences	
Intelligence	**Brief Description**	**Related Child and Adult Roles**
Linguistic	The capacity to express oneself in spoken or written language with great facility	Superb storyteller, creative writer, or inventive speaker: Novelist, lyricist, lawyer
Logical-mathematical	The ability to reason inductively and deductively and to complete complex computations	Thorough counter, calculator, notation maker, or symbol user: Mathematician, physicist, computer scientist
Spatial	The capacity to create, manipulate, and represent spatial configurations	Creative builder, sculptor, artist, or skilled assembler of models: Architect, talented chess player, mechanic, navigator
Bodily-kinesthetic	The ability to perform various complex tasks or activities with one's body or part of the body	Skilled playground game player, emerging athlete or dancer: Surgeon, dancer, professional athlete
Musical	The capacity to discriminate musical pitches, to hear musical themes, and to sense rhythm, timbre, and texture	Good singer, creator of original songs or musical pieces: Musician, composer, director
Interpersonal	The ability to understand others' actions, emotions, and intents and to act effectively in response to verbal and nonverbal behaviors of others	Child organizer or orchestrator, child leader, or a very social child: Teacher, therapist, political social leader
Intrapersonal	The capacity to understand well and respond to one's own thoughts, desires, feelings, and emotions	A sensitive child, a resilient child, or an optimistic child: Social worker, therapist, counselor, hospice worker

The definitions of giftedness are diverse (Clark, 2008; Moon, 2006; Stephens & Karnes, 2000). Each of the definitions we have examined reveals the challenges associated with defining the nature of giftedness (Worrell & Erwin, 2011). In a multicultural, pluralistic society, such as that of the United States, different abilities and capacities are encouraged and valued by different parents, teachers, and communities. Also, definitions of giftedness are often a function of educational, societal, and political priorities at a particular time and place (Phillipson & McCann, 2007; Sternberg, Jarvin, & Grigorenko, 2011).

Prevalence

Determining the number of children who are gifted is a challenge. The complexity of the task is directly related to problems inherent in determining who is gifted and what constitutes giftedness (Gallagher, 2004). The numerous definitions of giftedness range from

TEACHSOURCE VIDEO MULTIPLE INTELLIGENCES: ELEMENTARY SCHOOL INSTRUCTION

Please visit the Education CourseMate website for *Human Exceptionality*, 11th edition, at CengageBrain.com to access this chapter's TeachSource Video. In this video, you will meet teacher Frederick Won Park. At the outset of the video, he makes this statement: "There are many ways to define intelligence." He goes on to speak about intelligence as a means for solving problems. Although his class is not identified as one for gifted students, you can think about what it would be like to be a gifted child in his class. As you watch this video, think about what Mr. Park does to motivate, energize, and engage his students. Also, think about these questions:

1. How does he motivate student thinking and visualization?

2. How does he prime students for writing?

3. Would this class be a good choice for a student who is gifted? Why or why not?

quite restrictive (in terms of the number of children to whom they apply) to very inclusive and broad descriptions. Consequently, the prevalence estimates are highly variable.

Prevalence figures compiled before the 1950s were primarily limited to the intellectually gifted: those identified primarily through intelligence tests. At that time, 2 to 3 percent of the general population was considered gifted. During the 1950s, when professionals in the field advocated an expanded view of giftedness (Conant, 1959; DeHann & Havighurst, 1957), the prevalence figures suggested for program planning were substantially affected. Terms such as *academically talented* were used to refer to the upper 15 to 20 percent of the general school population.

Thus, prevalence estimates have fluctuated, depending on the views of politicians, policy makers, researchers, and professionals during past decades. Currently, 3 to 25 percent of the students in the school population may be identified as gifted, depending on the regulations from state to state and the types of programs offered.

Characteristics

CEC

Standard 2
Development and Characteristics of Learners

FOCUS 3

Identify four problems inherent in accurately describing the characteristics of individuals who are gifted.

People with gifts and talents come from every ethnic, cultural, and socioeconomic background. While some individuals achieve in intellectual endeavors, others excel through athletics.

Accurately identifying the characteristics of gifted people is an enormous task. Different types of studies have generated many characteristics attributed to those who are gifted (see Table 15.2; MacKinnon, 1962; Terman, 1925). Gradually, what emerged from these studies were oversimplified, incomplete views of giftedness.

Unfortunately, much of the initial research related to the characteristics of giftedness was conducted with limited population samples. Generally, the studies did not include adequate samples of females or individuals from various ethnic and cultural groups, nor did early researchers carefully control for factors directly related to socioeconomic status.

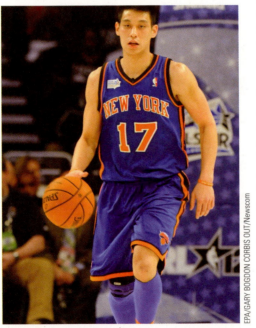

EPA/GARY BOGDON CORBIS OUT/Newscom

Therefore, the characteristics generated from these studies were not representative of gifted individuals as a whole but, rather, reflected the characteristics of gifted individuals from advantaged environments.

Given the present multifaceted definitions of giftedness and emerging views of intelligence, we must conclude that gifted individuals come from all population sectors. Consequently, research findings of the past must be interpreted with great caution as practitioners weigh and assess a particular youth's behaviors, attributes, talents, motivations, and dispositions.

Davis and Rimm (2004) have identified a number of positive and negative characteristics of student who are gifted (see Table 15.2).

Gifted students, who are intellectually able, demonstrate one resounding trait—"they are developmentally advanced in language and thought" (Davis & Rimm, 2004, p. 35). Many learn to speak and read very early. Their mental ages, as revealed in intelligence tests, far exceed their chronological ages. Moreover, their innate curiosity and capacity for asking questions can drive some parents and even teachers to the brink of exhaustion and desperation (Morawska & Sanders, 2009). These students can be unusually tenacious in pursuing ideas, discussing concerns, and raising questions. They may also have interests that would be characteristic of older children and/or adults.

Generally, gifted students are well adjusted and socially adept. There are, of course, exceptions (Reis & Renzulli, 2004). One of the more interesting attributes of gifted children and youth is their penchant for "emotional excitability" and "high sensitivity" (Rimm & Davis, 2004, p. 37). In this regard, their reactions can be more intense—that is, they may

Table 15.2   **Characteristics of Students Who Are Gifted**

Positive Characteristics	General Characteristics	Negative Characteristics
Unusual alertness in infancy and later	Wide interests, interested in new topics	Uneven mental development
Early and rapid learning	High curiosity, explores how and why	Interpersonal difficulties, often due to intellectual differences
Rapid language development as a child	Multiple capabilities (multipotentiality)	Underachievement, especially in uninteresting areas
Superior language ability—verbally fluent, large vocabulary, complex grammar	High care ambitions (desire to be helpful to others)	Nonconformity, sometimes in disturbing directions
Enjoyment of learning	Overexcitability	Perfectionism, which can be extreme
Academic superiority, large knowledge base, sought out as a resource	Emotional intensity and sensitivity	Excessive self-criticism
Superior analytic ability	High alertness and attention	Self-doubt, poor self-image
Keen observation	High intellectual and physical activity level	Variable frustration and anger
Efficient, high-capacity memory	High motivation, concentrates, perseveres, persists, task-oriented	Depression
Superior reasoning, problem solving	Active—shares information, directs, leads, offers help, eager to be involved	
Thinking that is abstract, complex, logical, insightful	Strong empathy, moral thinking, sense of justice, honesty, intellectual honesty	
Insightful, sees "big picture," recognizes patterns, connects topics	Aware of social issues	
Manipulates symbol systems	High concentration, long attention span	
Uses high-level thinking skills, efficient strategies	Strong internal control	
Extrapolates knowledge to new situations, goes beyond what is taught	Independent, self-directed, works alone	
Expanded awareness, greater self-awareness	Inquisitive, asks questions	
Greater metacognition (understanding own thinking)	Excellent sense of humor	
Advanced interests	Imaginative, creative, solves problems	
Needs for logic and accuracy	Preference for novelty	
	Reflectiveness	
	Good self-concept	

SOURCE: Adapted from Davis, G. A., & Rimm, S. B. (2004). *Education of the gifted and talented*, 5th ed. (p. 33). San Francisco: Allyn and Bacon.

feel more joy and also experience greater sadness than age-mates. Table 15.2 lists characteristics often evident in gifted students.

Students who are described as creative share a number of personality attributes and dispositions. They often exhibit high energy and high motivation to succeed or perform. They have a real zest for pursuing tasks and seeking solutions to problems they encounter. Furthermore, they also have a proclivity for risk taking. They love to try new activities,

CEC

Standard 1
Foundations

Table 15.3   Characteristics of Students Who Are Creative

Positive Traits	Approximate Synonyms
Original	Imaginative, resourceful, flexible, unconventional, thinks metaphorically, challenges assumptions, irritated and bored by the obvious, avoids perceptual set, asks "what if?"
Aware of creativeness	Creativity-conscious, values originality, values own creativity
Independent	Self-confident, individualistic, nonconforming, sets own rules, unconcerned with impressing others, resists societal demands
Risk-taking	Not afraid to be different or to try something new, willing to cope with hostility, willing to cope with failure
Motivated	Energetic, adventurous, sensation-seeking, enthusiastic, excitable, spontaneous, impulsive, intrinsically motivated, persevering, works beyond assigned tasks
Curious	Questions norms and assumptions, experiments, inquisitive, wide interests, is a problem finder, asks "why?"
Sense of humor	Playful, plays with ideas, childlike freshness in thinking
Attracted to complexity	Attracted to novelty, asymmetry, the mysterious, theoretical and abstract problems; is a complex person; tolerant of ambiguity, disorder, incongruity
Artistic	Artistic and aesthetic interests, attracted to beauty and order
Open-minded	Receptive to new ideas, other viewpoints, new experiences, and growth; liberal; altruistic
Needs alone time	Reflective, introspective, internally preoccupied, sensitive, may be withdrawn, likes to work alone
Intuitive	Perceptive, sees relationships, finds order in chaos, uses all senses in observing
Intelligent	Verbally fluent, articulate, logical, good decision maker, detects gaps in knowledge, visualizes

SOURCE: Adapted from Davis, G. A., & Rimm, S. B. (2004). *Education of the gifted and talented*, 5th ed. (p. 42). San Francisco: Allyn and Bacon.

to experiment with new behaviors, and to consider novel ways of processing problems or creating things (artistic, mechanical, etc.). Table 15.3 lists characteristics often evident in students described as creative.

No student who is identified as gifted will exhibit all of the characteristics described in this section. However, parents, teachers, coaches, and mentors have an opportunity, as well as an obligation, to encourage these traits, behaviors, proclivities, and dispositions. Again, the collective focus as mentors and encouragers ought to be talent development.

Origins of Giftedness

CEC

Standard 1
Foundations

FOCUS 4

Identify three factors that appear to contribute significantly to the emergence of various forms of giftedness.

Scientists have long been interested in identifying the origins of intelligence. Conclusions have varied greatly. For years, many scientists adhered to a hereditary explanation of intelligence: that people inherit their intellectual capacity at conception. Thus, intelligence was viewed as an innate capacity that remained relatively fixed during an individual's lifetime. The prevailing belief then was that little could be done to enhance or improve intellectual ability.

During the 1920s and 1930s, scientists such as John Watson began to explore the new notion of behavioral psychology, or behaviorism. Like other behaviorists who followed him, Watson believed that the environment played a vitally important role in the development of intelligence as well as personality traits. Initially, Watson largely discounted the role of heredity and its importance in intellectual development. Later, however, he moderated his views, moving toward a theoretical perspective in which both heredity and environment contributed to an individual's intellectual ability.

During the 1930s, many investigators sought to determine the relative influence of heredity and environment on intellectual development. Some proponents of genetics asserted that as much as 70 to 80 percent of an individual's capacity was determined by heredity and the remainder by environmental influences. Environmentalists believed otherwise. The controversy over the relative contributions of heredity and environment to intelligence (known as the **nature versus nurture** controversy) is likely to continue for some time, in part because of the complexity and breadth of the issues involved. For example, studies of identical twins raised in different environments suggest that 44 to 72 percent of their intelligence (general cognitive ability) is inherited. With regard to environmental factors, we are just beginning to understand the dynamic relationships between nature and nurture and how giftedness manifests itself developmentally over time (Horowitz, 2009). Again, "bright children select and are selected by peers and educational programs that foster their abilities. They read and think more. This is the profound meaning of finding genetic influences on measures of the environment. Genes contribute to the experience itself" (Plomin & Price, 2003, p. 120). Plomin and Price (2003) captured it best when they said "it may well be more appropriate to think about [general cognitive ability] as an appetite rather than an aptitude" (p. 121). This appetite allows gifted children and youth to profit more fully from environmental influences over their lifetimes.

Thus far, we have focused on the origins of intelligence rather than on giftedness per se. Many of the theories about the emergence of giftedness have been derived from the study of general intelligence. Few authors have focused directly on the origins of giftedness. Moreover, the ongoing changes in the definitions of giftedness have further complicated the precise investigation of its origins.

The "Star Model" for explaining the causes and antecedents of giftedness is composed of five elements, each of which contributes to gifted behavior (see Figure 15.4). These elements are superior general intellect, distinctive special aptitudes, nonintellective factors, environmental supports, and chance. Associated with each are the descriptors *dynamic* and *static*. The static dimension includes factors that remain relatively constant or unchanged, such as the child's or youth's race and economic status. The dynamic dimension

Nature versus nurture
Controversy concerning how much of a person's ability is related to sociocultural influences (nurture) and how much is due to genetic factors (nature).

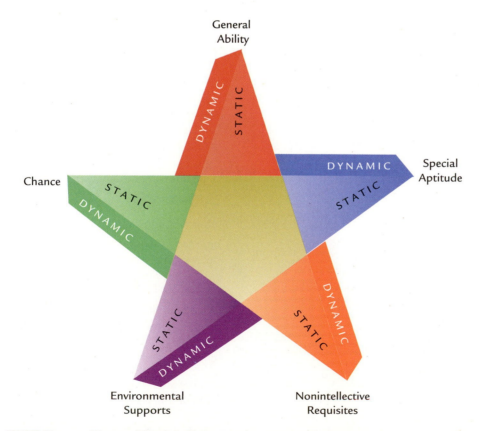

Figure 15.4 *The Star Model: Psychosocial Factors Accounting for Gifted Achievements*

SOURCE: "Nature and Nurture of Giftedness," by A. J. Tannebaum, 2003, in *Handbook on Gifted Education*, edited by N. Colangelo and G. A. Davis (p. 47). Boston, MA: Allyn and Bacon.

includes factors that are fluid and responsive to contextual or environmental changes or interventions. Elaborating on this notion, Hughes (2009) wrote: "Giftedness evolves and factors are developmental: It cannot be definitively fixed or measured. It is grown, not diagnosed" (p. 168). Increasingly, we will move from finding and labeling giftedness to developing it, that is, putting in place the conditions that give rise to talents, creativity, and giftedness.

The abilities associated with superior intelligence are generally factors assessed through intelligence tests (verbal, spatial, and memory capacity). Special abilities are those found, for example, in child prodigies who demonstrate extraordinary musical, mathematical, or other emerging talents. Nonintellective factors are a wide-ranging set of attributes, including, believe it or not, psychopathology and perfectionism. Many gifted artists and writers show clear signs of pathological deviance or emotional distress (Callard-Szulgit, 2003; Reis & Renzulli, 2004). Other, more positive factors associated with this element include motivation, self-concept, and resilience. The influence of environmental support is obvious. "Giftedness requires [a] social context that enables it to mature. . . . Human potential needs nurturance, urgings, encouragement, and even pressures from a world that cares" (Tannenbaum, 2003, p. 54). Last is the element of chance. Often, external factors that coincide with one's preparation and talent development contribute to one's eventual imminence or greatness (Hong & Milgram, 2008; Worrell, 2009). All of these factors come together in a unique fashion to produce various kinds of giftedness.

REFLECT ON THIS STEVE JOBS: "I WILL NEVER FORGET THAT MOMENT."

Like most kids, [Jobs] became infused with the passions of the grown-ups around him. "Most of the dads in the neighborhood did really neat stuff. . . . I grew up in awe of that stuff and asking people about it." The most important of these neighbors, Larry Lang ". . . was my model of what an HP engineer was supposed to be: a big ham radio operator, hard-core electronics guy," Jobs recalled. "He would bring me stuff to play with." As we walked up to Lang's old house, Jobs pointed to the driveway: "He took a carbon microphone and a battery and a speaker, and he put it on this driveway. He had me talk into the carbon mike and it amplified out of the speaker." Jobs had been taught by his father that microphones always required an electronic amplifier. "So I raced home, and I told my dad that he was wrong."

"No, it needs an amplifier," his father assured him. When Steve protested otherwise, his father said he was crazy. "It can't work without an amplifier. There's some trick."

"I kept saying no to my dad, telling him he had to see it, and finally he actually walked down with me and saw it. And he said, 'Well I'll be a bat out of hell.'"

Jobs recalled the incident vividly because it was his first realization that his father did not know everything. Then a more disconcerting discovery began to dawn on him: He was smarter than his parents. He had always admired his father's competence and savvy. "He was not an educated man, but I had always thought he was pretty damn smart. He didn't read much, but he could do a lot. Almost everything mechanical, he could figure it out." Yet the carbon microphone incident, Jobs said, began a jarring process of realizing that he was in fact more clever and quick than his parents. "It was a very big moment that's burned into my mind. When I realized that I was smarter than my parents, I felt tremendous shame for having thought that. I will never forget that moment. . . ."

Another layer of awareness occurred soon after. Not only did he discover that he was brighter than his parents, but he discovered that they knew this. Paul and Clara Jobs were loving parents, and they were willing to adapt their lives to suit a son who was very smart—and also willful. They would go to great lengths to accommodate him. And soon Steve discovered this fact as well. "Both my parents got me. They felt a lot of responsibility once they sensed that I was special. They found ways to keep feeding me stuff and putting me in better schools. They were willing to defer to my needs" (Isaacson, 2011, p. 10–12).

Questions for Reflection

What role did Steve's parents play in nurturing his talents and capacities? How do parents come to know that a child is "special"?

SOURCE: Reprinted with the permission of Simon & Schuster, Inc, from STEVE JOBS by Walter Isaacson. Copyright © 2011 by Walter Isaacson. All rights Reserved.

Finally, Colvin (2008), in his book *Talent Is Overrated: What Really Separates World-Class Performers from Everybody Else*, suggests that many innate or naturally occurring gifts and talents are overvalued—that outstanding performance in most fields of expertise comes from consistent and deliberate practice—even hard work. In the absence of pronounced and persistent practice, giftedness in its various forms is not achieved. Additionally, the significant contributions these individuals could have made never come to light—the artwork, the medical advances, the musical works, the inventions, the artistic performance—all remain dormant and unexpressed.

Assessment

The focus of assessment procedures for identifying giftedness is beginning to change (Sternberg, Jarvin, & Grigorenko, 2011). Elitist definitions and exclusive approaches are being replaced with more defensible, inclusive methods of assessment (Briggs, Reis, Eckert, & Baum, 2006; Davis, Rimm, & Siegle, 2011; Richert, 2003). Tests for identifying people with potential for gifted performance are being more carefully selected; that is, tests are being used with the children for whom they were designed. Children who were once excluded from programs for the gifted because of formal or standard cutoff scores that favored particular groups of students are now being included (Richert, 2003). Multiple sources of information are now collected and reviewed in determining who is potentially gifted (Johnsen, 2008; Worrell & Erwin, 2011). Ideally, the identification process is now directed at identifying needs and potentials rather than merely labeling individuals as gifted. Again, the new thrust is talent development as well as talent identification (Sosniak & Gabelko, 2008; Subotnik & Calderon, 2008; VanTassel-Baska & Stambaugh, 2006).

Several approaches have also been developed to identify children who are disadvantaged and also gifted. Some theorists and practitioners have argued for the adoption of a contextual paradigm or approach. Rather than using information derived solely from typical intelligence tests or other talent assessments, this approach relies on divergent views of giftedness as valued and determined by community members, parents, grandparents, and competent informants. Similar approaches focus on nontraditional measures of giftedness. These approaches use multiple criteria, broader ranges of scores for inclusion in special programs, peer nomination, assessments by people other than educational personnel, and information provided by adaptive behavior assessments. Furthermore, these approaches seek to understand students' motivations, interests, capacities for communication, reasoning abilities, imagination, and humor (Briggs, et al., 2006; Davis, Rimm, & Siegle, 2011; Richert, 2003). For example, if 60 percent of students in a given school population come from a certain cultural minority group and only 2 percent are identified as gifted via traditional measures, the screening committee may want to reexamine and adjust its identification procedures.

Elementary and secondary students who are gifted are identified in a variety of ways. The first step is generally screening (Worrell & Erwin, 2011). During this phase, teachers, psychologists, and other school personnel attempt to select all students who are potentially gifted. A number of procedures are employed in the screening process. Historically, information obtained from group intelligence tests and teacher nominations has been used to select the initial pool of students. However, many other measures and data collection techniques have been instituted since the approach to assessment of giftedness changed from one-dimensional to multidimensional. These techniques may include developmental inventories, classroom observations, parent and peer nominations, achievement tests, creativity tests, motivation assessments, teacher nominations, and evaluations of student projects (Worrell & Erwin, 2011).

Teacher Nomination

Teacher nomination has been an integral part of many screening approaches. This approach is fraught with problems, however. Teachers often favor children who are cooperative,

CEC
Standard 8
Assessment

FOCUS 5
Indicate the range of assessment devices used to identify the various types of giftedness.

well-mannered, and task-oriented. Bright underachievers who are confrontive and/or disruptive may be overlooked. Also, many teachers are unfamiliar with the general traits, behaviors, and dispositions that underlie various forms of giftedness.

Fortunately, some of these problems have been addressed. Several scales, approaches, and guidelines are now available to aid teachers and others who are responsible for making nominations (Davis, Rimm, & Siegle, 2011; Renzulli & Reis, 2003). Teachers who have a thorough understanding of the various kinds of giftedness are in a much better position to provide good information in the nomination, screening, and selection processes (Johnsen, 2008; Johnsen, VanTassel-Baska, & Robinson, 2008).

Intelligence and Achievement Tests

Intelligence testing continues to be a major source of information for screening and identifying general ability or intellectual giftedness in children and adolescents. These tests must be carefully selected. For example, some intelligence tests have low ceilings; that is, they do not allow the participating child or youth to demonstrate their remarkable potential. The same is true of some group-administered intelligence tests. They are not designed to identify students who may have exceptionally high intellectual abilities.

One advantage of intelligence testing is that it often identifies underachievers. Intelligence test scores often reveal students who have wonderful intellectual capacity that may have gone unrecognized because of their pattern of poor school performance.

A serious limitation associated with intelligence tests emerges when they are administered to individuals for whom the tests were not designed. Very few intelligence tests adequately assess the abilities of children and adolescents who are substantially different from the core culture for whom the tests were created. However, some progress is being made in helping educators identify gifted children who are members of minority groups, underachievers, or at risk (Renzulli, 2004).

Similar problems are inherent in achievement tests, which, like intelligence tests, are not generally designed to measure the true achievement of children who are academically gifted. Such individuals are often prevented from demonstrating their unusual prowess because of the restricted range of the test items. These **ceiling effects** prevent youth who are gifted from demonstrating their achievement at higher levels. However, achievement tests do play a very useful role in identifying students with specific academic talents.

Ceiling effects
A restricted range of test questions or problems that does not permit academically gifted students to demonstrate their true capacity or achievement.

Creativity Tests

Tests for creativity serve several purposes. Often they help teachers or practitioners discover capacity that may not be evident in normal classroom interactions and performances. Also, these tests are useful in confirming attributes related to creativity. However, we must realize that creativity tests are difficult to construct. The degree to which they actually measure creativity is often called into question. Because of the nature of creativity and the many forms in which it can be expressed, developing tests to assess its presence and magnitude is a formidable task (Renzulli, 2004; Treffinger, 2004). In spite of these challenges, a number of creativity tests have been formulated (Rimm, 1982; Rimm & Davis, 1983; Torrance, 1966; Williams, 1980). A typical question on a test of divergent thinking might read, "What would happen if your eyes could be adjusted to see things as small as germs?"

Once the screening steps have been completed, the actual identification and selection of students begins. During this phase, each of the previously screened students is carefully evaluated again, using more individualized procedures and assessment tools. Ideally, these techniques should be closely related to the definition of giftedness used by the district and to the program offered to students (Eckert, 2006; Gubbins, 2006; Rogers, 2006).

A series of recommendations and statements that summarize this section on assessment and identification have been identified in Table 15.4. If these recommendations are carefully followed, more appropriate and equitable decisions will be made in identifying and serving children and youth who are gifted or potentially gifted.

Table 15.4	Current Thinking and Recommendations for Identifying Gifted Students

- Adopt a clearly defined but broadened conception of giftedness.
- Avoid using a single cutoff score.
- Use multiple alternative criteria—not multiple required hurdles—from several different sources.
- Use separate instruments or procedures for different areas of giftedness; be sure that tests (including ratings and nominations) are reliable and valid.
- Include authentic assessment (e.g., portfolios, examples of work) and performance-based procedures (e.g., evaluation tasks that elicit problem solving and creativity).
- Be aware that giftedness may appear in different forms in different cultural or socioeconomic groups.
- Repeat assessments over time to identify additional gifted students.
- Use identification data to enhance your understanding of students.

SOURCE: Adapted from Davis, G. A., & Rimm, S. B. (2004). Identifying gifted and talented students. In *Education of the gifted and talented,* 5th ed. (p. 81). San Francisco: Allyn and Bacon.

Services and Supports: Early Childhood

Current research suggests that many young children with high cognitive ability (HCA) can be identified in the middle of the second year of life (Colombo, Shaddy, Blaga, Anderson, & Kannass, 2009). Parents may contribute to HCA and other attributes of their children through a number of pathways (Gottfried, Gottfried, & Guerin, 2009; Horowitz, 2009; Rimm, 2008). During the first 15 months of life, 90 percent of all social interactions with children take place during such activities as feeding, bathing, changing diapers, and dressing. Parents who are interested in advancing social and cognitive development use these occasions for stimulating and talking to their children; providing varied sensory experiences such as bare-skin cuddling, tickling, and smiling; and conveying a sense of trust. Early, concentrated, language-centered involvement with young children gives rise to substantial cognitive, social, and linguistic skills (Horowitz, 2009).

Standard 5
Learning Environments and Social Interactions

Standard 7
Instructional Planning

FOCUS 6
Identify seven strategies that are utilized to foster the development of gifted children during early childhood.

As children progress through the infancy, toddler, and preschool periods, the experiences provided become more varied and uniquely suited to the child's emerging interests and capacities (Subotnik & Calderon, 2008). Language and cognitive development are encouraged by means of stories that are read and told. Children are also urged to make up their own stories. Brief periods are reserved for discussions or spontaneous conversations that arise from events that have momentarily captured their attention. Requests for help in saying or printing a word are promptly fulfilled. Thus, many children who are gifted learn to read before they enter kindergarten or first grade.

Comstock Images/Jupiterimages

Parents play essential roles in nurturing and stimulating children with potential gifts and talents.

During the school years, parents continue to encourage their children's development by providing opportunities that correspond to their strengths and interests. The simple identification games played during the preschool period become more complex and demanding. Discussions frequently take place with peers and other interesting adults in addition to parents. The nature of the discussions and the types of questions asked become more sophisticated. Parents help their children move to higher levels of learning by asking questions that involve analysis (comparing and contrasting ideas), synthesis (integrating and combining ideas into new and novel forms), and evaluation (judging and disputing books, newspaper articles, etc.). Parents can also help by

- furnishing books and reading materials on a broad range of topics.
- providing appropriate equipment as various interests surface (e.g., microscopes, telescopes, chemistry sets).
- providing access to various technologies (computers, sensors, GPS devices, etc.).
- encouraging regular trips to the public libraries and other resource centers.
- providing opportunities for participation in cultural events, lectures, and exhibits.
- encouraging participation in extracurricular and community activities outside the home.
- fostering relationships with potential mentors and other resource people in the community. (Rimm, 2008; Robinson, Shore, & Enersen, 2007)

Preschool Programs

A variety of preschool programs have been developed for young children who are gifted. Some children are involved in traditional programs that focus on activities and curricula devoted primarily to the development of academic skills. Many of the traditional programs emphasize affective and social development as well. The entry criteria for these programs are varied, but the primary considerations are usually the child's IQ and social maturity.

Creativity programs are designed to help children develop their natural endowments in a number of artistic and creative domains (Lubbard, Georgsdottir, & Besançon, 2009; Treffinger, 2004). Another purpose of such programs is to help children discover their own areas of promise. Children in these programs are also prepared for eventual involvement in traditional academic areas of schooling.

Services and Supports: Childhood and Adolescence

FOCUS 7

Identify five general approaches that are utilized to foster the development of gifted school-age children and adolescents.

Giftedness in elementary and secondary students may be nurtured in a variety of ways. A number of service delivery systems and approaches are used in responding to the needs of students who are gifted (Purcell & Eckert, 2006; Robinson, Shore, & Enersen, 2007; VanTassel-Baska & Stambaugh, 2006). The nurturing process has often been referred to as **differentiated education**—that is, an education uniquely and predominantly suited to the natural abilities and interests of individuals who are gifted (Matthews & Foster, 2009; Tomlinson & Hockett, 2008). Programs for children and adolescents are targeted at delivering content more rapidly, using a variety of engaging instructional strategies, delivering more challenging content, examining content in greater depth, pursuing highly specialized content, and/or dealing with more complex and higher levels of subject matter (Caraisco, 2007).

Differentiated education
Instruction and learning activities that are uniquely and predominantly suited to the attributes, capacities, motivations, and interests of gifted students.

Instructional Approaches

Instructional approaches for gifted students are selected on the basis of a variety of factors (Tomlinson & Hockett, 2008). First, the school system must determine what types of giftedness it is capable of serving and supporting. It must also establish identification criteria and related measures that enable it to select qualified students fairly. For example, if the system is primarily interested in enhancing creativity, measures and indices of creativity should be utilized. If the focus of the program is accelerating math

CEC

Standard 7
Instructional Planning

CASE STUDY CALVIN

What follows is a series of cartoon strips from *Calvin and Hobbes*. They depict in part the relationship Calvin has with his dad.

APPLICATION QUESTIONS

1. Is Calvin gifted, creative, and talented? Provide a rationale for your answer.

2. If Calvin's dad asked you how to handle Calvin's "giftedness," what recommendations would you make? Give a rationale for your answers.

3. If Calvin's dad were enrolled in your parenting class and asked for your counsel as the group leader, what would you recommend?

achievement and understanding, instruments that measure mathematical aptitude and achievement should be employed. Second, the school system must select the organizational structures through which children who are gifted are to receive their differentiated education. Third, school personnel must select the instructional approaches to be utilized within each program setting. Fourth, school personnel must select continuous evaluation procedures and techniques that help them assess the overall effectiveness of the program. Data generated from such evaluations can serve as catalysts for making appropriate and meaningful changes (Callahan, 2008). Take a moment to think about Calvin featured in the accompanying case study. What kinds of instructional approaches might be helpful to him in capitalizing on his creativity and great facility for imagining and expressing himself verbally?

CEC

Standard 5
Learning Environments and Social Interactions

Service Delivery Systems

Once the types of giftedness to be emphasized have been selected and appropriate identification procedures have been established, planning must be directed at selecting suitable service delivery systems. Organizational structures for students who are gifted are similar to those found in other areas of special education. Several options have been developed to provide services for students who are gifted (see Figure 15.5). Each of the learning environments in the model has advantages and disadvantages. For example, students who are enrolled in regular education classrooms and are given opportunities to spend time in seminars, resource rooms, special classes, and other novel learning environments profit from these experiences because they are responsive to their interests, talents, and capacities. Furthermore, such pullout activities provide a means for students to interact with one another and to pursue interests for which the usual school curriculum offers little access.

Figure 15.5 Clark's Structuring Gifted Programs

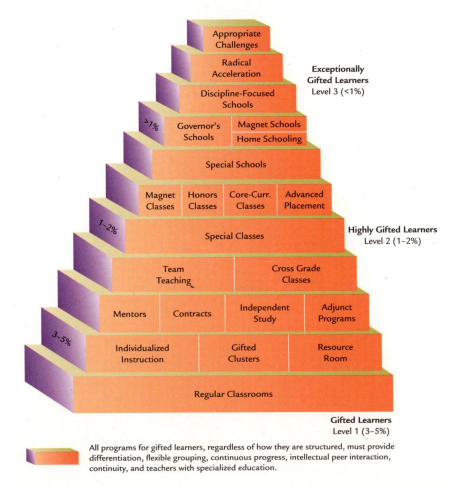

SOURCE: Structuring Gifted Programs by B. Clark, *Growing Up Gifted*, 2008, p. 405, Pearson: Merrill/Prentice Hall.

EARLY CHILDHOOD YEARS

Tips for the Family

- Realize that giftedness is evidenced in many ways (e.g., concentration, memory, pleasure in learning, sense of humor, social skills, task orientation, ability to follow and lead, capacity and desire to compete, information capacity).
- Provide toys that may be used for a variety of activities and purposes.
- Take trips to museums, exhibits, fairs, and other places of interest to your child.
- Talk to the child in ways that foster give-and-take conversation.
- Begin to expose the child to picture books and ask him or her to find certain objects or animals or to respond to age-appropriate questions.
- Avoid unnecessary restrictions.
- Provide play materials that are developmentally appropriate and may be a little challenging.

Tips for the Preschool Teacher

- Look for ways in which various talents and skills may be expressed or developed (e.g., cognitive, artistic, leadership, socialization, motor ability, memory, imagination).
- Capitalize on the child's curiosity. Develop learning activities related to his or her passions and emerging interests.
- Allow the child to experiment with all the elements of language—even written language—as he or she is ready.
- Give the child highly engaging learning experiences.

Tips for Preschool Personnel

- Remember that conversation is critical to the child's development. Do not be reluctant to spend a great deal of time asking the child questions as he or she engages in various activities.
- Become a specialist in looking for and developing gifts and talents across a variety of domains (e.g., artistic, social, cognitive).
- Allow for rapid mastery of concepts, and then allow the child to move on to other, more challenging activities rather than holding him or her back.

Tips for Neighbors and Friends

- Provide preschool opportunities for all children who are potentially gifted to have the necessary environmental ingredients to use their talents or gifts fully—that is, support and encourage talent development.
- Enjoy and sometimes endure the neighborhood child who has chosen your home as his or her lab for various experiments in cooking, painting, and building.
- Collaborate with friends and family in talking about potentially gifted children, considering ways to nurture their development.

ELEMENTARY YEARS

Tips for the Family

- Maintain the search for individual gifts and talents; some qualities may not be evident until the child is older.
- Collaborate with other professionals in providing appropriate experiences and options for gifted learners.
- Provide out-of-school experiences that foster talent or skill development (e.g., artistic, physical, academic, social).
- Enroll the child who is gifted in summer programs offered by universities or colleges.
- Monitor the child's school environment to be sure that adequate steps are being taken to respond to your child's unique skills, interests, and abilities.
- Join an advocacy group for parents in your community and consider taking a parenting class.
- Subscribe to child publications related to your child's current interests.
- Encourage your child's friendships and associations with other children who have like interests and aptitudes.

Tips for the General Education Classroom Teacher

- Provide opportunities for enrichment as well as acceleration.
- Allow students who are gifted to pursue individual or group projects that require sophisticated forms of thinking, production, or problem solving.
- Become involved in professional associations that provide assistance to teachers of students who are gifted.
- Take a course that specifically addresses the instructional strategies that might be helpful children who are gifted.
- Encourage children to become active participants in various events that emphasize particular skills or knowledge areas (e.g., science fairs, music competitions).

Tips for School Personnel

- Develop clubs and programs that enable children who are gifted to pursue their talents.
- Create award programs that encourage talent development across a variety of domains.
- Involve and collaborate with community members (e.g., artists, engineers, writers) in offering enrichment and acceleration activities.
- Foster the use of inclusive procedures for identifying students who are potentially gifted from groups that are culturally diverse, are disadvantaged, or have disabilities.

Tips for Neighbors and Friends

- Contribute to organizations that foster talent development.
- Volunteer to serve as judges for competitive events.
- Be willing to share your talents with young, emergent scholars, musicians, athletes, and artists.

- Become a mentor for someone in your community.

SECONDARY AND TRANSITION YEARS

Tips for the Family

- Continue to provide sources of support for talent development outside of the home.

- Regularly counsel with your child about courses he or she may take—collaborate with counselors and other school personnel.

- Provide access to tools (e.g., computers, video cameras, instruments, brushes and paints) and resources (e.g., magazines, websites, specialists, coaches, mentors) that contribute to your child's development.

- Expect variations in performance from time to time—give your child appropriate breathing room.

- Provide opportunities for relaxation and rest from demanding schedules.

- Continue to encourage involvement with peers who have similar interests and aptitudes.

Tips for the General Education Classroom Teacher

- Provide a range of activities for students with varying abilities.

- Provide opportunities for students who are gifted to deal with real problems or develop actual products.

- Give opportunities for genuine enrichment activities, not just more work—collaborate with professional peers within your discipline and others in making challenging and engaging activities available.

- Remember that giftedness manifests itself in many ways. Determine how various types of giftedness may be expressed in your content domain.

- Help to eliminate the conflicting and confusing signals about career choices and fields of study that are often given to young women who are gifted.

Tips for School Personnel

- Provide, to the degree possible, a variety of curriculum options, activities, clubs, and creative outlets for gifted students.

- Acknowledge and celebrate excellence in a variety of performance areas (e.g., leadership, visual and performing arts, academics).

- Continue to use inclusive procedures in identifying individuals who are potentially gifted and talented.

- Encourage participation in competitive activities in which students are able to use and hone their gifts and talents (e.g., science fairs, debate tournaments, music competitions).

Tips for Neighbors, Friends, and Potential Employers

- Provide opportunities for students to "shadow" talented professionals, artists, and clinicians in your network of employees or friends.

- Volunteer as a professional to work directly with students who are gifted in pursuing a real problem or producing an actual product.

- Become a mentor for a student who is interested in what you do professionally.

- Support the funding of programs for students who are gifted and talented and who come from disadvantaged environments.

- Provide summer internships for students who have a particular interest in your profession, talent domain, or specialty.

- Serve as an adviser for a high school club or other organization that gives students additional opportunities to pursue talent areas.

ADULT YEARS

Tips for the Family

- Continue to nurture appropriate independence.

- Celebrate the individual's accomplishments and provide support for challenges.

- Let go.

Tips for Educational Personnel

- Exhibit behaviors associated with effective mentoring.

- Provide meaningful ways to deal with pressure.

- Allow the individuals to be themselves.

- Provide adequate time for discussion and interaction—unhurried listening.

- Be aware of other demands in the individuals' lives.

Tips for Potential Employers

- Establish appropriately high expectations.

- Be sensitive to changing interests and needs.

- Encourage and support employees who wish to mentor young gifted students on a volunteer basis.

However, the disadvantages of such a program are numerous. Major parts of the school week may be spent doing things that may not be appropriate or engaging for students who are gifted. Also, when gifted students return to general education classes, they are frequently required to make up missed assignments.

As you may recall from Figure 15.5, Clark identified various structures through which gifted children and youth could be served. One of these is assignment to a special class, supplemented with opportunities for course work integrated with regular classes. This may occur at any level of schooling, elementary through high school. This approach has many advantages. Students have the best of both worlds, academically and socially. Directed independent studies, seminars, mentorships, and cooperative studies are possible through this arrangement. Students who are gifted are able to interact in an intensive fashion with other gifted students, as well as with regular students in their integrated classes. This program also has disadvantages, however. A special class requires a well-prepared, competent teacher; many school systems simply do not have sufficient funds to hire specialists in gifted education. Without skilled teachers, special-class instruction or other specialized learning activities may just be more of the general education curriculum.

Implementing service delivery and designing curricula for gifted students are significant but rewarding challenges (Burns, Purcell, & Hertberg, 2006). They demand the availability of sufficient financial and human resources, flexibility in determining student placement and progress, a focus on high-quality achievement and growth, and a climate of excellence characterized by high standards and significant student engagement (Cooper, 2006). Optimally, delivery systems should facilitate the achievement of specific curricular goals, mesh with state standards, correspond with the types of giftedness being nurtured, and prepare students for other experiences yet to come in elementary, secondary, and postsecondary settings (Adams, 2006; Tomlinson, Doubet, & Capper, 2006).

Conditions and strategies associated with successful classrooms and programs for gifted students include teachers who have advanced preparation and knowledge specifically related to gifted education, who relish change, and who enjoy working collaboratively with other professionals. When gifted middle school and high school students were asked to comment about teachers who encouraged them to learn at high levels, they responded with the following: "They personally 'zoom in' on you and your work and help you learn at a different level. They expect a high level of performance from you. They give me stimulating questions to answer and something new to learn. If the teacher is excited and passionate about his or her subject, it makes it much easier for me to put in a lot of effort into whatever I'm doing" (Roberts, 2008, p. 249). Furthermore, effective teachers believe in differentiated instruction and actively implement it, have access to a variety of strategies for delivering this kind of instruction, and have a disposition for leadership and some autonomy in fulfilling their teaching responsibilities (Chuska, 2005; Leppien & Westberg, 2006).

Acceleration

"Acceleration is an intervention that moves students through an education program at rates faster, or at younger ages, than typical. It means matching the level, complexity, and pace of the curriculum to the readiness and motivation of the student" (Colangelo, Assouline, & Gross, 2004a, p. xi). Many forms of acceleration can be pursued and adopted (Colangelo & Assouline, 2009). **Acceleration** enables gifted students to progress more rapidly and learn at a rate commensurate with their abilities. Early entrance to kindergarten or college, part-time grade acceleration, self-paced instruction, curriculum compacting, subject-matter acceleration, and grade skipping are all examples of acceleration (Tomlinson & Hockett, 2008).

Another practice related to grade skipping is telescoped or condensed schooling, which enables students to progress through the content of several grades in a significantly reduced time. An allied practice is allowing students to progress rapidly through a particular course or content offering. Acceleration of this nature provides students with the sequential, basic learning at a pace commensurate with their abilities. School programs that are ungraded are particularly suitable for telescoping. Regardless of their chronological ages, students may progress through a learning or curriculum sequence that is not constricted by artificial grade boundaries.

Other forms of condensed programming found at the high school level include earning credit through examination, enrolling in extra courses for early graduation, reducing or eliminating certain course work, enrolling in intensive summer programs, and taking advanced placement courses while completing high school requirements. Many of these options enable students to enter college early or begin bachelor programs with other advanced students. Many students who are gifted are ready for college-level course work

Standard 7
Instructional Planning

Acceleration
A process whereby students are allowed to achieve at a rate that is consistent with their capacity, achievement, and interests.

I've only been knee-deep in the world of gifted and talented education for three-plus years. Prior to that, my exposure was somewhat minor. I read scores of parenting books (some on gifted children), and we had both girls tested for programming at the Center for Talent Development at Northwestern University. We also considered sending them to Quest Academy in Palatine, Illinois, prior to our move to Colorado. However, it wasn't until this summer that we heard the words about our DD10 (dearest daughter who is 10), "She's an excellent candidate for a grade skip, and she wants to. . . ."

Then, a week or so later, the same scenario repeated itself with my younger daughter at the Gifted Development Center in Denver, Colorado. "She, too, would be a prime candidate for acceleration."

My first reaction was, "Really? Are you serious?" For one, I thought acceleration was primarily geared toward early entrance to kindergarten and profoundly gifted kids entering college. Our two daughters, ages 9 and 10, were smack dab in the middle of elementary school. Did people really grade skip at this juncture? I had loads of questions:

- How will we know if it's the right decision?

- What happens if one skips and the other one doesn't want to?

- What about the fact that one daughter doesn't seem to be particularly fond of school? She's not even getting top marks.

- What about my perfectionist daughter? Will it be too challenging for her?

- What about socially? Are they mature enough to handle a skip?

- Will the school be amenable? How do I even initiate the process of discussing acceleration?

- Should we be concerned that there are equally bright students (perhaps even more advanced) in their current classes? They do have peers. Shouldn't they simply stay where they are?

- Will they feel too much pressure? Is this just a novel idea that will wear off when the work seems harder?

- What about learning gaps? What happens if they don't know what they're supposed to learn about Colorado history and/or certain science requirements?

- What if they start and then hate it?

Thankfully, we got all of these questions answered and then some. Between Dr. Linda Silverman, Barbara ("Bobbie") Jackson Gilman, and Kim Boham at the Gifted Development Center, we not only discussed each question thoroughly, but we also learned an extraordinary amount about research on acceleration, how vital it is for the students (not parents) to initiate the idea, and how to advocate with the school to ensure the best possible outcomes.

We're now several months into the school year, and I must say, the grade skips have had such an extraordinarily positive impact on both girls. We're fortunate that the receiving teachers welcomed the girls with open arms and understanding. The principal, GT [gifted and talented] teacher, GT coordinator, and counselor proved so supportive and insightful. The adjustment has been much smoother than I anticipated. DD10 has confidence navigating the halls of middle school and has made good friends. She even went to her first dance right before Halloween! DD09 has finally gotten comfortable with not immediately knowing the answers in class and is developing much more of a growth mind-set. She says this is her favorite year of school by far.

SOURCE: Adapted from Mersino, Deborah. (2012). How grade skipping changed everything. *Ingenious: Strategic communication, gifted perspective* (blog), Copyright © Deborah Mersino. Reprinted with permission. http://www.ingeniosus.net/archives/category/acceleration

at age 14, 15, or 16—and some even at younger ages. Some students of unusually high abilities are prepared for college-level experiences prior to age 14. See the nearby Debate Forum, "What Would You Do with Jane?" for a discussion of how one gifted student's educational needs could be met with a nontraditional approach.

Some years ago, eminent researchers published a two-volume series entitled *A Nation Deceived: How Schools Hold Back America's Brightest Students* (Colangelo, Assouline, & Gross, 2004a; 2004b). Findings from studies presented in this two-volume series affirmed the value of various forms of acceleration (Colangelo, Assouline, & Gross, 2004b). Consider these prominent findings: Students who experience acceleration are more likely to pursue advanced degrees than those who do not (Kulik, 2004). Virtually all forms of acceleration advance growth in academic achievement (Rogers, 2004). Programs that embrace radical acceleration often produce "extraordinary levels of academic success" (Gross, 2004, p. 94).

Many children who are gifted are prevented from accelerating their growth and learning for fear that they will be hurt emotionally and socially.

Parents' comments such as these are common: She's so young. Won't she miss a great deal if she doesn't go through the fourth and fifth grades? What about her friends? Who will her friends be if she goes to college at such a young age? Will she have the social skills to interact with kids who are much older? If she skips these two grades, won't there be gaps in her learning and social development?

On the other hand, the nature of the questions or comments by parents about acceleration may also be positive: She is young in years only! She will adjust extremely well. Maybe she is emotionally mature enough to handle this type of acceleration. The increased opportunities provided through university training will give her greater chances to develop her talents and capacities. Perhaps the older students with whom she will interact are better suited to her intellectual and social needs.

Consider Jane, a child who is gifted. In third grade, she thrived in school, and just about everything associated with her schooling at that time was positive. Her teacher was responsive and allowed her and others to explore well beyond the usual "read-the-text-then-respond-to-the-ditto-sheet" routine. Much self-pacing was possible, and materials galore were presented for both independent studies and queries.

In the fourth and fifth grades, however, things began to change radically. Jane's teachers were simply unable to provide enough interesting and challenging work for her. It was during the latter part of the fourth grade that she began to view herself as different. Not only did she know, but her classmates also knew that learning came exceptionally easily to her. At this same time, Jane was beginning to change dramatically in her cognitive capacity. Unfortunately, her teachers persisted in unnecessary drills and other mundane assignments, and Jane gradually became bored and lapsed into a type of passive learning. Rather than attacking assignments with vigor, she performed them carelessly, often making many stupid errors. Gradually, what emerged was a child who was very unhappy in school. School had been the most interesting place for her to be before she entered fourth grade. Then it became a source of pain and boredom.

Jane's parents decided that they needed to know more about her capacities and talents. Although it was expensive and quite time-consuming, they visited a nearby university center for psychological services. Jane was tested, and the results were very revealing. For the first time, Jane's parents had some objective information about her capacities. She was, in fact, an unusually bright and talented young lady. Jane's parents then began to consider the educational alternatives available to her.

The counselor who provided the interpretation of the results at the university center strongly recommended that Jane be advanced to the seventh grade in a school that provided services to students who were talented and gifted. This meant that Jane would skip one year of elementary school and have an opportunity to move very rapidly through her junior and senior high school studies. Furthermore, she might be able to enter the university well in advance of her peers.

Jane's parents knew that her performance had diminished significantly in the last year. Moreover, her attitude and disposition about school seemed to be worsening. What would you do as her parents? What factors would you consider important in making the decision? Or is the decision Jane's and hers alone?

POINT

Jane should be allowed to accelerate her educational pace. Moving to the seventh grade will benefit her greatly, intellectually and socially. Most girls develop more rapidly physically and socially than boys do. Skipping one grade will not hinder her social development at all. In fact, she will benefit from the interactions that she will have with other able students, some of whom will also have skipped a grade or two. Additionally, the research regarding the impact of accelerating students is positive, particularly if the students are carefully selected. Jane has been carefully evaluated and deserves to have the opportunity to be excited about learning and achieving again.

COUNTERPOINT

There are some inherent risks in having Jane skip her sixth-grade experience and move on to the seventh grade. Jane is neither socially nor emotionally prepared to deal with the junior high environment. She may be very able intellectually, and her achievement may be superior, but this is not the time to move her into junior high. Socially, she is still quite awkward for her age. This awkwardness would be intensified in the junior high setting. Acceleration for Jane should be considered later on, when she has matured more socially.

She should be able to receive the acceleration that she needs in her present elementary school. Certainly, other able students in her school would benefit from joining together for various activities and learning experiences. The acceleration should take place in her own school, with other students who are gifted and of her own age. Maybe all Jane needs is some time to attend a class or two elsewhere. Using this approach, she could benefit from involvement with her same-age peers and still receive the stimulation that she so desperately needs. Allowing her to skip a grade now would hurt her emotionally and socially in the long run.

What Do You Think? Please visit the Education CourseMate website for Human Exceptionality, *11th edition to access and respond to questions related to the Debate Forum.*

Social-emotional effects of acceleration are not harmful—as a rule, gifted children and youth tend to be more mature socially and emotionally than their same-age peers (Robinson, 2004). Whole-grade acceleration is a "low-risk/high-success intervention for qualified students" (Colangelo, Assouline, & Lupkowski-Shoplik, 2004, p. 85).

Enrichment

Enrichment
Educational experiences for gifted students that enhance their thinking skills and extend their knowledge in various areas.

Experiences tied to **enrichment** extend, deepen, broaden, or enrich a person's knowledge (Tomlinson & Hockett, 2008). Music appreciation, foreign languages, and mythology are enrichment courses that are added to a student's curriculum and are usually not any more difficult than other classes in which the student is involved. Other examples of enrichment involve experiences in which the student develops sophisticated thinking skills (i.e., synthesis, analysis, interpretation, and evaluation), or has opportunities to master advanced concepts in a particular subject area. Some forms of enrichment are actually types of acceleration. A student whose enrichment involves fully pursuing mathematical concepts that are well beyond his or her present grade level is experiencing a form of acceleration. Obviously, the two approaches are interrelated.

Enrichment is the most common administrative approach to serving gifted students. It is also the most abused approach because it is often applied in name only and in a sporadic fashion, without well-delineated objectives or rationale. There are also other problems with the enrichment approach. It is often implemented superficially, as a token response to the demands of parents. Some professionals view enrichment activities as periods devoted to educational trivia or to instruction heavy in student assignments but light in content. Quality enrichment programs are characterized by carefully selected activities, modules, or units; challenging but not overwhelming assignments; and evaluations that are rigorous yet fair. Additionally, good enrichment programs focus on thoughtful and careful plans for student learning and on engaging activities that stress higher-order thinking and application skills. Current enrichment practices make full use of the capacities of the Internet, using wikis, blogs, podcasts, and aggregators for collecting information and completing real-world products and research (Eckstein, 2009). The nearby Assistive Technology feature, "Differentiating Instruction," shows how a specialized database can provide personalized learning options for gifted students.

Enrichment may include such activities as exploring exciting topics not normally pursued in the general curriculum, group-centered activities that focus on cognitive or affective skills and/or processes, and small-group investigations of actual, real-life problems. The keys to these endeavors are high student interest, excellent teaching, and superb mentoring.

There is a paucity of systematic experimental research on enrichment programs. Despite many of the limitations of current and past research, evidence supports the effectiveness of enrichment, particularly when it is delivered to specific ability groups and when the content and rigor of the curriculum coincide with the abilities of the targeted students.

Enrichment activities do not appear to detract from the success students experience on regularly administered achievement tests. Sociometric data on students who are pulled out of general education classrooms for enrichment activities are also positive. Students do not appear to suffer socially from involvement in enrichment programs that take place outside their general education classrooms. Acceleration and enrichment are complementary parts of curricular and service delivery systems for gifted children and youth.

Special Programs and Schools

Programs designed to nurture the talents of individuals in nonacademic and academic areas, such as the visual and performing arts and mathematics, have grown rapidly in recent years (Olszewski-Kubilius & Lee, 2008). Students involved in these programs frequently spend half their school day working in academic subjects and the other half in arts studies. Often an independent institution provides the arts instruction, but some school systems maintain their own separate schools. Most programs provide training in the visual and performing arts, but a few emphasize instruction in creative writing, motion picture and television production, and photography. There are also residential schools for gifted students who specialize in developing stellar academic achievement and growth (Coleman, 2005). Also, distance education is beginning to play a major role in providing challenging, advanced, and stimulating learning experiences to gifted children and youth (Olszewski-Kubilius & Lee, 2008).

So-called governor's schools (distinctive summer programs generally held at university sites), talent identification programs, and specialized residential schools or high schools in various states also provide valuable opportunities for students who are talented and academically gifted (Olszewski-Kubilius & Lee, 2008). Competitively selected students are provided with curricular experiences that are closely tailored to their individual aptitudes and interests. These schools provide unique opportunities for young people to develop strong friendships and support networks that contribute to their social and emotional well-being as well as their talent development (McHugh, 2006). Faculties for these schools are meticulously selected for their competence in various areas and for their ability to stimulate, motivate, and engage students. However, these schools and special programs are few and serve only a small number of the students who would profit from them.

Career Education and Guidance

Career education, career guidance, and counseling are essential components of a comprehensive program for students who are gifted (Liu, Shepherd, Nicpon, 2008; North, 2007; Rimm, 2008; Robinson, Shore, & Enersen, 2007). Ultimately, career education activities and counseling are designed to help students make educational, occupational, and personal decisions. Because of their multipotentiality (their capacity for doing so many things well), it is difficult for some gifted students to make educational and career choices.

Differentiated learning experiences give elementary and middle school students opportunities to investigate and explore (Chuska, 2005). Many of these opportunities are career-related and designed to help students understand what it might be like to be a zoologist, neurosurgeon, or filmmaker. What are the time demands? How stressful is the profession or occupation? Students also become familiar with the preparation and effort necessary for work in these fields. For gifted students in the elementary grades, these explorations often take place on Saturdays or weekends. They help such students understand themselves, their talents, and the essential experiences needed for entry into specific fields of advanced study or practice.

As students mature both cognitively and physically, the scope of their career education activities becomes more sophisticated and varied. In group meetings, gifted students and talented professionals may discuss the factors that influenced a scientist or group of researchers to pursue a given problem or conduct experiments that led to important discoveries or products.

Mentoring

Some students are provided opportunities to work directly with research scientists, artists, musicians, or other professionals. Students may spend as many as three or four hours a day, two days a week, in laboratory facilities, mentored by scientists and professionals. Other students rely on intensive workshops or summer programs in which they are exposed to specialized careers through internships and individually tailored instruction.

The benefits of mentoring for gifted students are numerous. Students have sophisticated learning experiences that are highly motivating and stimulating. They gain invaluable opportunities to explore careers and to confirm their commitment to certain areas of study or reexamine their interests. Mentoring experiences may affirm potential in underachieving students or students with disabilities—potential that was not being tapped through conventional means. Mentoring may also promote the development of self-reliance, specific interpersonal skills, and lifelong, productive friendships.

Career Choices and Challenges

Career interests, values, and dispositions appear to crystallize early in gifted students. In fact, their interests are neither broader nor more restricted than those of their classmates. Some gifted students know quite early what paths they will follow in postsecondary schooling. These paths often lead to careers in engineering, health professions, and physical sciences.

Counseling programs are particularly helpful to adolescents who are gifted. Often they know more about their academic content than they know about themselves. As gifted students come to understand themselves, their capacities, and their interests more fully, they will make better choices in selecting courses of study and professional careers.

Family counseling may also be helpful to parents and other family members. Problems caused by excessive or inappropriate parental expectations may need to be addressed in a family context. Counselors and therapists may help parents develop realistic expectations consistent with their child's abilities, aspirations, and true interests. As with other exceptionalities, counseling services are best provided through interdisciplinary/collaborative efforts.

Problems and Challenges of Giftedness

Students who are gifted must cope with a number of problems. One problem is expectations—the expectations they have of themselves and those expectations that parents, teachers, and others have explicitly and implicitly imposed upon them (Berlin, 2009). Students who are gifted frequently feel an inordinate amount of pressure to achieve high grades or to select particular professions. They often feel obligated or duty-bound to achieve excellence in every area, a syndrome called perfectionism. Sadly, such pressure can foster a kind of conformity and prevent students from selecting avenues of endeavor that truly fit them and reflect their personal interests.

Several social-emotional needs that differentiate students who are gifted from their same-age peers have been identified:

CEC

Standard 1
Foundations

- Understanding how they are different from and how they are similar to their peers
- Appreciating and valuing their own uniqueness as well as that of others

REFLECT ON THIS
WHAT A COLOSSAL LOSS!

He started reading as a toddler, played piano at age 3, and delivered a high school commencement speech in cap and gown when he was just 10—his eyes barely visible over the podium.

Brandenn Bremmer was a child prodigy: He composed and recorded music, won piano competitions, breezed through college courses with an off-the-charts IQ, and mastered everything from archery to photography, hurtling through life precociously.

Then Brandenn was found dead in his Nebraska home from an apparent self-inflicted gunshot wound to his head.

He was just 14. He left no note.

"Sometimes we wonder if maybe the physical, earthly world didn't offer him enough challenges and he felt it was time to move on and do something great," his mother, Patricia, said from the family home in Venango, Nebraska, a few miles from the Colorado border.

Brandenn showed no signs of depression, she said. He had just shown his family the art for the cover of his new CD that was about to be released.

He was, according to his family and teachers, an extraordinary blend of fun-loving child and serious adult. He loved Harry Potter and Mozart. He watched cartoons and enjoyed video games, but gave classical piano concerts for hundreds of people—without a hint of stage fright.

"He wasn't just talented, he was just a really nice young man," said David Wohl, an assistant professor at Colorado State University, where Brandenn studied music after high school. "He had an easy smile. He really was unpretentious."

Patricia Bremmer—who writes mysteries and has long raised dogs with her husband, Martin—said they both knew their son was special from the moment he was born. The brown-haired, blue-eyed boy was reading when he was 15 months old and entering classical piano competitions by age 4.

"He was born an adult," his mother said. "We just watched his body grow bigger."

He scored 178 on one IQ test—a test his mother said he was too bored to finish.

Question for Reflection

What potential steps, if any, could have been taken to prevent this colossal tragedy?

SOURCE: Adapted from Cohen, S. (2005). *Child prodigy's apparent suicide: "He knew he had to leave," mother says.* New York: Associated Press, March 19. Copyright © 2005 Associated Press. Reprinted with permission.

- Understanding and developing relationship skills
- Developing and valuing their high-level sensitivity
- Gaining a realistic understanding of their own abilities and talents
- Identifying ways of nurturing and developing their own abilities and talents
- Adequately distinguishing between the pursuit of excellence and the pursuit of perfection
- Developing behaviors associated with negotiation and compromise (VanTassel-Baska, 1989)

Students who are gifted need ongoing and continual access to adult role models who have interests and abilities that parallel theirs; the importance of these role models cannot be overstated. Role models are particularly important for gifted students who grow up and receive their schooling in rural and remote areas. Such students often complete their public schooling without the benefit of having a mentor or professional person with whom they can talk or discuss various educational and career-related issues. By using the Internet and telementoring, some students who live in rural or remote communities now have access to mentoring at a distance.

Historically Neglected Groups

Standard 1
Foundations

FOCUS 8
Identify four challenges females face in dealing with their giftedness. What five factors are important to recognizing giftedness in individuals with disabilities?

Girls and individuals with disabilities are less likely to be recognized as gifted and talented for a variety of reasons. Some girls wish to hide their giftedness, believing that their social prospects with girls as well as boys will be diminished. Thus, they hide or do not fully use their remarkable capacities or talents. With regard to children and youth with disabilities who are also gifted, who are twice exceptional, we are still uncovering means for assessing and calibrating their giftedness.

Females

Girls usually tend to deny their giftedness and value their academic abilities lower than boys (Robinson, Shore, & Enersen, 2007). Also, the number of girls identified as gifted appears to decline with age. This phenomenon is surprising when we realize that girls tend to walk and talk earlier than their male counterparts; that girls, as a group, read earlier; that girls score higher than boys on IQ tests during the preschool years; and that the grade-point averages of girls during the elementary years are higher than those of boys.

Just exactly what happens to girls? Is the decline in the number of girls identified as gifted related to their socialization? Does some innate physiological or biological mechanism account for this decline? Why do some gifted females fail to realize their potential? To what extent do value conflicts about women's roles contribute to mixed achievement in gifted women? The answers to these and other important questions are gradually emerging.

One of the explanations given for this decline is the gender-specific socialization that girls receive. Behaviors associated with self-efficacy, competitiveness, risk taking, and independence are not generally encouraged in girls. Behaviors that are generally fostered in girls include dependence, cooperation, conformity, and nurturing. One researcher views the elimination of independent behaviors in girls as being the most damaging aspect of their socialization (Silverman, 1986). Rather than delighting in their emerging skills, talents, and capacities, girls tend to mask or hide them from others (Manning & Bestnoy, 2008).

More recent research suggests that girls who develop social self-esteem, "the belief that one has the ability to act effectively and to make decisions independently," are more likely to realize their potential (Davis & Rimm, 2004). Without independence, girls' ability to develop high levels of creativity, achievement, and leadership is severely limited. Overcoming the impact of sociocultural influences requires carefully applied interventions, counseling, and heightened levels of awareness on the part of parents, teachers, and counselors.

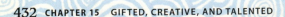

Females who are gifted and talented experience additional problems, including fear of appearing "unfeminine" or unattractive when competing with males; competition between marital and career aspirations; stress induced by traditional, cultural, and societal expectations; and self-imposed and/or culturally imposed restrictions related to educational and occupational choices (Davis, Rimm, & Siegle, 2011). Although many of these problems are far from being resolved at this point, some progress is being made. Women in vastly greater numbers are successfully entering professions men traditionally pursued.

Fortunately, multiple role assignments are emerging in many families, wherein the tasks mothers traditionally performed are shared by all members of the family or are completed by someone outside the family. Cultural expectations are changing; as a result, options for women who are gifted are rapidly expanding.

People with Disabilities: Twice Exceptional

For some time, intellectual giftedness has been largely associated with high IQs and high scores on aptitude tests. These tests, by their very nature and structure, measure a limited range of mental abilities. Because of such limitations, they have not been particularly helpful in identifying people with disabilities who are intellectually or otherwise gifted. However, people with disabilities such as cerebral palsy, learning disabilities, emotional and behavior disorders, and other disabling conditions can be gifted (Montgomery, 2009; Robinson, Shore, & Enersen, 2007; Sternberg, Jarvin, & Grigorenko, 2011). Helen Keller, Vincent van Gogh, and Ludwig van Beethoven are prime examples of individuals with disabilities who were also gifted. Some theorists and practitioners suggest that as many as 2 percent of individuals with disabilities are gifted.

In this context, the twice exceptional are individuals with outstanding ability or potential who achieve high performance despite a physical, emotional, learning, or chronic health disability. Although many challenges are still associated with identifying individuals with disabilities who are gifted, much progress has been made.

Unfortunately, the giftedness of children with disabilities is often invisible to parents and teachers. Factors critical to the recognition of giftedness include environments that elicit signs of talent and capacity, and availability of information about the individual's performance gathered from many sources. With regard to these eliciting environments, it is important that children be given opportunities to perform tasks on which their disabling condition is no impediment. Also, if and when tests of mental ability are used, they must be appropriately adapted, both in administration and scoring. Furthermore, the identification screening should occur at regular intervals. Some children with disabilities change dramatically with appropriate instruction and related assistive technologies. The developmental delays present in children with disabilities and the disabilities themselves pose the greatest challenges to identification efforts (Baum, 2004; Davis & Rimm, 2004).

Stevie Wonder, a twice exceptional individual with remarkable musical talents

Jeff Kravitz/FilmMagic/Getty Images

Differential education for children with disabilities who are gifted is still in its infancy. A great deal of progress has been made, particularly in the adaptive uses of computers and related technologies, but much remains to be done. Additionally, a great deal is still unknown about the service delivery systems and materials that are best suited for these individuals. One of the best approaches parents and teachers can take with gifted children and youth with disabilities is fostering self-confidence, independence, and a sense of personal efficacy—I have what it takes to learn, to succeed, to manage my life, and to realize success (Manning & Bestnoy, 2008).

Children and Youth from Diverse Cultural, Linguistic, Ethnic, and Economic Backgrounds

Rarely are culturally diverse and economically disadvantaged youth identified as gifted (Briggs, Reis, Eckert, & Baum, 2006; Ford, Grantham, & Whiting, 2008; Graham, 2009). These youth are dramatically underrepresented in programs for the gifted and talented (King, Kozleski, & Lansdowne, 2009; Matthews & Shaunessy, 2008; Hong & Milgram, 2008; Spradlin & Parsons, 2008). This underrepresentation is a function of several factors: racism; social and economic inequities; excessive reliance on testing and test scores that may not accurately capture potential and talent in these youth; IQ-based definitions of giftedness; identification practices based on achievement test scores; and a lack of teacher referrals of children for gifted education programs (Bireda, 2011; Center for Comprehensive School Reform and Improvement, 2008; Ford, Grantham, & Whiting, 2008; Warwick & Matthews, 2009). Social and motivational variables also contribute to these diminished numbers, particularly with African American students who are pressured to "act black"—giving a false appearance of not being smart, acting dumb, exhibiting high levels of aggressiveness, being antiauthority, and other related behaviors (Ford, Grantham, & Whiting, 2008; Graham 2009). Some districts are now using a checklist and other appropriate identification measures to help teachers and others look more inclusively and broadly for potentially gifted students (see Figure 15.6) (Hong & Milgram, 2008).

Behaviors that are receiving increased attention in identifying giftedness in diverse children and youth are resilience, acculturation, code switching, and bilingualism. Children who are diverse in some fashion, who maintain positive views of themselves despite challenging problems and environments, may be candidates for gifted programs. The same could be said of children who adjust more quickly, that is, acculturate more rapidly than same-age peers to their surrounding environments. With regard to code switching and bilingualism, children who are adept in their heritage language and who develop another language, and who use both with skill, may be candidates for gifted programs and related activities (Matthews & Shaunessy, 2008). As suggested at the beginning of this chapter, we are now focusing more on inclusive practices in identifying giftedness and are paying more attention to talent development in children and youth who are diverse in some fashion (Harris, Plucker, Rapp, & Marinez, 2009; Hong & Milgram, 2008; Horowitz, 2009; Matthews & Shaunessy, 2008; VanTassel-Baska, 2009).

Effective instructional programs for children and adolescents who are disadvantaged and gifted have several key components. First, the teachers in these programs are well trained in adapting and differentiating instruction for these students, providing culturally responsive teaching and content (Robinson, Shore, & Enersen, 2007; Center for Comprehensive School Reform and Improvement, 2008). These teachers understand learning preferences, how to build and capitalize on students' interests, and how to maximize students' affective, cognitive, and ethical capacities. In addition to providing the typical curricular options for enrichment, acceleration, and talent development, the best programs for these children and youth embrace and celebrate ethnic diversity, provide extracurricular cultural enrichment, attend to differences in learning styles, provide counseling, supply mentoring, create culturally responsive classrooms, foster parent support groups and community connections, provide supportive and stimulating tutoring, and give these children and youth access to significant role models (Bireda, 2011; Sosniak & Gabelko, 2008).

There is general agreement that programs for these children and youth should begin early and should be tailored to the needs and interests of each identified child. They should focus on individual potentialities rather than deficits and should help parents and others understand their roles in fostering giftedness and talent development (Baum, 2004; Sosniak & Gabelko, 2008). Often, the emphasis in the early years is on reading instruction, language development, and foundation skills. Other key components include experiential education that provides children with many opportunities for hands-on learning, activities that foster self-expression, plentiful use of mentors and role models who represent the

Figure 15.6 *Javits Gifted Characteristics Checklist for Underrepresented Populations*

VERBAL ABILITIES
1. Has an expanded vocabulary
2. Asks unusual questions to find out more information
3. Expresses ideas well
4. Elaborates on questions for information

LEARNING CHARACTERISTICS
5. Exhibits quick mastery of skills
6. Has long-term recall of information
7. Has interest in how things work
8. Has the ability to see relationships and make connections
9. Is able to retain more information with less repetition
10. Displays creativeness, originality, putting things and ideas together in novel ways
11. Has a lot of information about one topic
12. Has a questioning attitude
13. Signals perfectionist tendencies
14. Likes to solve puzzles and trick questions
15. Has a wide range of interests
16. Performs well mathematically
17. Stays with a project until it is completed

MOTIVATIONAL CHARACTERISTICS
18. Sets high standards for self
19. Is inquisitive
20. Has a tendency to lose awareness of time/intense concentration
21. Becomes easily impatient with drill-and-routine procedures
22. Is persistent
23. Has keen powers of observation
24. Requires little direction

SOCIAL ABILITIES
25. Tends to dominate peers or situation
26. Has unusual, often highly developed sense of humor
27. Is independent
28. Often finds and corrects own or others' mistakes
29. Is anxious to complete tasks
30. Is often overly sensitive

LEADERSHIP
31. Adapts readily to new situations
32. Is well liked by classmates and demonstrates leadership
33. Carries responsibility well
34. Is self-confident with own age group
35. Is cooperative with teacher and classmates

CREATIVITY
36. Makes up games and activities displaying imagination
37. Expresses original ideas in other ways
38. Demonstrates ability to express feelings and emotions
39. Is articulate in role playing and storytelling
40. Displays a richness in imagery and informal language
41. Demonstrates ability in fine or practical arts

SOURCE: Adapted from Project Bright Horizon, Washington Elementary School District, Glendale, Arizona. Retrieved May 8, 2009, from www.ade.az.gov/asd/gifted/downloads/Project%20 BrightHorizon-GiftedCharacteristicsChecklist.pdf.

child's cultural or ethnic group, involvement of the community, and counseling throughout the school years that gives serious consideration to the cultural values of the family and the child who is gifted.

Looking Toward a Bright Future

In spite of challenging problems in providing all gifted children and youth with appropriate opportunities for talent development, acceleration, and enrichment, there is cause for optimism on several fronts. We are beginning to see concerted efforts in identifying all potentially gifted children and youth. We are broadening the ways in which we seek to identify these children and youth. These efforts are particularly pronounced in recognizing and developing talent and capacity in historically neglected groups: girls, children and youth with disabilities (the twice exceptional), and young people from diverse cultural, linguistic, ethnic, and economic backgrounds.

Recent research is also helping teachers and other professionals understand the underserved and underrepresented gifted populations more thoroughly—recognizing hindrances to talent and capacity development, the vital role of motivation or lack thereof, and cultural factors that contribute to or interfere with talent development. Lastly, we are beginning to understand the trajectory of giftedness over a lifespan, giving us a reasonably complete picture of what it takes to nurture and sustain gifted children, youth, and adults who have the potential to contribute significantly on so many important fronts.

FOCUS REVIEW

FOCUS 1 Briefly describe several historical developments directly related to the identification and measurement of various types of giftedness.

- Alfred Binet developed the first developmental scale for children during the early 1900s. Gradually, the notion of mental age emerged, a representation of what the child was capable of doing compared with age-specific developmental tasks.
- Lewis M. Terman translated the Binet scale and made modifications suitable for children in the United States.
- Gradually, the intelligence quotient, or IQ, became the gauge for determining giftedness.
- Intelligence was long viewed as a unitary structure or underlying ability. But this view gradually changed, and researchers began to believe that intelligence was represented in a variety of distinct capacities and abilities.
- J. P. Guilford and other social scientists began to develop a multidimensional theory of intelligence, which prompted researchers to develop models and assessment devices for examining creativity.
- Programs were gradually developed to foster and develop creativity in young people.
- More recently, V. Ramos-Ford and H. Gardner developed the theory of multiple intelligences, which manifest themselves in linguistic, logical-mathematical, spatial, musical, bodily-kinesthetic, interpersonal, and intrapersonal behaviors.

FOCUS 2 Identify four major components of definitions that have been developed to describe giftedness.

- Children and youth with outstanding talent perform or show the potential for performing at remarkably high levels of accomplishment when compared with others of their age, experience, or environment.
- Gifted children and youth exhibit high performance capability in intellectual, creative, and/or artistic areas, possess an unusual leadership capacity, or excel in specific academic fields.
- Gifted children and youth require services or activities that schools do not ordinarily provide.
- Outstanding talents are present in children and youth from all cultural groups, across all economic strata, and in all areas of human endeavor.

FOCUS 3 Identify four problems inherent in accurately describing the characteristics of individuals who are gifted.

- Individuals who are gifted vary significantly on a variety of characteristics; they are not a homogeneous group.
- Because research on the characteristics of people who are gifted has been conducted with different population groups, the characteristics that have surfaced tend to represent the population studied rather than the gifted population as a whole.
- Many early studies of individuals who are gifted led to a stereotypical view of giftedness.

- Historically, studies on the characteristics of individuals who are gifted have not included adequate samples of females, minority or ethnic groups, or the poor.

FOCUS 4 Identify three factors that appear to contribute significantly to the emergence of various forms of giftedness.

- Genetic endowment certainly contributes to giftedness.
- Environmental stimulation provided by parents, teachers, coaches, tutors, and others contributes significantly to the emergence of giftedness.
- The interaction of innate abilities with environmental influences and encouragement fosters the development and expression of giftedness.

FOCUS 5 Indicate the range of assessment devices used to identify the various types of giftedness.

- Developmental checklists and scales
- Parent and teacher inventories
- Intelligence and achievement tests
- Creativity tests
- Other diverse observational information provided by parents, grandparents, and other knowledgeable adults involved in the gifted child's life

FOCUS 6 Identify seven strategies that are utilized to foster the development of gifted children during early childhood.

- Naturally interacting with and stimulating young children during bathing, feeding, and dressing young children
- Providing appropriate sensory experiences: cuddling, tickling, and touching
- Developing trust: establishing appropriate regimens, providing predictability in schedules and routines, and giving positive support for new experiences and learning
- Lots of language—lots of talking
- Providing experiences with appropriate picture books and other related materials—the reading of stories, talking about stories, having young children make predictions about what will happen next
- Having children tell their own stories and capturing them in print—establishing the rudiments of written language
- Providing many kinds of experiences—visits to different places, making things, engaging in dress-up activities—giving children opportunities for spontaneous and rich play

FOCUS 7 Identify five general approaches that are utilized to foster the development of gifted school-age children and adolescents.

- Differentiated instruction: an approach to gifted education that attends to the natural abilities and interests of children and adolescents
- Enrichment: activities designed to extend, deepen, broaden, or enrich a person's knowledge

- Acceleration: allowing students to move through content and related experiences at a rate that is commensurate with their abilities and capacities
- Governor's schools: highly specialized programs, generally offered at or through universities, to encourage talent development, to give able students opportunities to connect with other talented students, and to work with skilled content specialists and mentors
- Mentoring: allowing gifted students to work with carefully selected specialists or experts who provide ongoing direction and experiences in a given talent or academic domain

FOCUS 8 Identify four challenges females face in dealing with their giftedness. What five factors are important to recognizing giftedness in individuals with disabilities?

- Fear of appearing "unfeminine" or unattractive when competing with males
- Competition between marital and career aspirations
- Stress induced by traditional cultural and societal expectations
- Self-imposed and/or culturally imposed restrictions related to educational and occupational choices
- Provide children and youth with disabilities "eliciting experiences"—experiences that allow them to reveal their talents and capacities.
- Be certain that information gathered about the child or youth with disabilities comes from many sources.
- Adapt measures and assessments of talent, intelligence, or creativity to the child's or youth's capacity—the disabling condition should not be an impediment.
- Consider the use of adaptive technologies to enhance the capacity for expressing talent, creativity, or intelligence.
- Children and youth with disabilities change rapidly—continuously assess for surges in capacity and talent.

Council for Exceptional Children (CEC) Standards to Accompany Chapter 15

 If you are thinking about a career in special education, you should know that many states use national standards developed by the Council for Exceptional Children (CEC) to assess a teacher candidate's knowledge and skills for working with students with disabilities. See a complete listing of the 10 CEC Content Standards on the inside back cover of this text.

1 Foundations
2 Development and Characteristics of Learners
5 Learning Environments and Social Interactions
7 Instructional Planning
8 Assessment

Mastery Activities and Assignments

 To master the content within this chapter, complete the following activities and assignments. Online and interactive versions of these activities are also available on the accompanying Education CourseMate website, where you may also access TeachSource videos, chapter web links, interactive quizzes, portfolio activities, flash cards, an integrated eBook, and much more!

1. Complete a written test of the chapter's content. If your instructor requires a written test of your content knowledge for this chapter, keep a copy for your portfolio. A practice test on the information covered in this chapter is available through the CourseMate website.

2. Respond in writing to the Application Questions for the Case Study, "Calvin." Keep a copy of the case study and your written response for your portfolio.

3. Read the Debate Forum, "What Would You Do with Jane?" And then visit the Education CourseMate website to complete the activity "Take a Stand." Keep a copy of this activity for your portfolio.

4. Participate in a community service learning activity. Community service is a valuable way to enhance your learning experience. Visit the Education CourseMate website for suggested community service learning activities that correspond to the information presented in this chapter. Develop a reflective journal of the service learning experience for your portfolio.

References

Chapter 1

Aristotle. (1941). Politics. In R. McKeon (Ed.), *The basic works of Aristotle (Book 7)* (p. 1,302). New York: Random House.

Baron, R. A., Branscombe, N. R., & Byrne, D. (2008). *Social psychology: Understanding human interaction,* 12th ed. Boston: Allyn and Bacon.

Braddock, D., & Parish, S. L. (2002). An institutional history of disability. In D. Braddock (Ed.), *Disability at the dawn of the 21st century and the state of the states* (pp. 1–61). Washington, D.C.: American Association on Mental Retardation.

Carlson, N. R., Miller, H., Heth, C. D., Donahoe, J. W., & Martin, N. (2009). *Psychology: The science of behavior,* 7th ed. Boston: Allyn and Bacon.

Center on Human Policy at Syracuse University. (2011). A Statement in Support of Families and Their Children. Retrieved August 14, 2011 from http://thechp.syr.edu/famstate.htm.

Dolson, J. (2011). Leveling the playing field: We are differently abled. *Accessites.Org.* Retrieved August 2, 2011 from http://accessites.org/site/2009/03/leveling-the-playing-field-were-all-differently-abled/.

Drew, C. J., & Hardman, M. L. (2007). *Intellectual disabilities across the lifespan,* 9th ed. Columbus, OH: Merrill.

Hardman, M., & McDonnell, J. (2008). Teachers, pedagogy, and curriculum. In M. McLaughlin & L. Florian, *Perspectives and purposes of disability classification systems in research and clinical practice* (pp. 153–169). London: Sage Publishing Co.

Hardman, M. L., & Nagle, K. (2004). Policy issues. In A. McCray, H. Rieth, & P. Sindelar (Eds.), *Contemporary issues in special education: Access, diversity, and accountability* (pp. 277–292). Boston: Allyn and Bacon.

James, W. (1890). *Principles of psychology.* New York: Henry Holt.

Kennedy, J. F. (1963, October 31). *Remarks upon signing Bill for the construction of the Mental Retardation Facilities and Community Mental Health Centers.* Washington, D.C.: The White House.

Kessler Foundation and the National Organization on Disability. (2010). *Survey of the employment of Americans with disabilities.* New York: Author.

Mooney, J. (2007). *The short bus: A journey beyond normal.* New York: H. Holt, 2007.

N.O.D./Harris, L., & Associates (2004). *National Organization on Disability/Harris Survey of Americans with Disability.* New York: Author.

Rock, T., Thead, B. K., Gable, R. A., Hardman, M. L., & Van Acker, R. (2006). In pursuit of excellence: The past as prologue to a bright future for special education. *Focus on Exceptional Children 38*(8), 1–18.

Rosenhan, D. I. (1973). On being sane in insane places. *Science, 179,* 250–258.

Schroeder, S. R., Gerry, M., Gertz, G., & Velazquez, F. (2002). *Usage of the term "mental retardation": Language, image and public education (Final Project Report).* Lawrence, Kansas: University of Kansas Center on Developmental Disabilities and the Center for the Study of Family, Neighborhood and Community Policy.

United States Department of Justice. (2011). A resort community improves access to city programs and services for residents and vacationers. Retrieved August 25, 2011 from www.usdoj.gov/crt/ada/fernstor.htm.

United States Department of Justice, Equal Employment Opportunity Commission (2011). Americans with Disabilities Act: Questions and Answers. Retrieved July 30, 2011 from www.ada.gov/q&aeng02.htm.

United States Holocaust Memorial Museum. (2011). *The quest for racial purity.* Retrieved August 25, 2011 from www.ushmm.org/education/foreducators/resource/.

Wolfensberger, W. (1975). *The origin and nature of our institutional models.* Syracuse, NY: Human Policy Press.

Woolfolk, A. (2009). *Educational psychology,* 11th ed. Upper Saddle River, New Jersey: Prentice-Hall.

Chapter 2

Berry, J. (2009). *Lifespan perspectives on the family and disability.* Austin, TX: Pro-Ed.

Brown v. Topeka, Kansas, Board of Education, 347 U.S. 483 (1954).

Byrnes, M. A. (2011). *Taking sides: Clashing views on controversial issues in special education,* 2nd ed. Guilford, CT: McGraw-Hill Dushkin.

Cassidy, V. M., & Stanton, J. E. (1959). *An investigation of factors involved in the educational placement of mentally retarded children: A study of differences between children in special and regular classes in Ohio.* U.S. Office of Education Cooperative Research Program, Project No. 043. Columbus: Ohio State University.

Drew, C. J., & Hardman, M. L. (2007). *Intellectual disabilities across the lifespan,* 9th ed. Columbus, OH: Merrill.

Florian, L. (2007). Reimagining special education. In L. Florian (Ed.), *The Sage handbook of special education* (pp. 7–20). London: Sage Publications.

Friend, M. P., & Bursuck, W. D. (2012). *Including students with special needs: A practical guide for classroom teachers,* 6th ed. Boston: Pearson.

Hardman, M. L., & Dawson, S. (2008, winter). The impact of federal public policy on curriculum and instruction for students with disabilities in the general classroom. *Preventing School Failure 52*(2), 5–11.

Hardman, M., & Mulder, M. (2004). Critical issues in public education: Federal reform and the impact on students with disabilities. In L. M. Bullock, & R. A. Gable (Eds.), *Quality personnel preparation in emotional/behavior disorders* (pp. 12–36). Dallas, TX: Institute for Behavioral and Learning Differences.

Hehir, T. (2002). IDEA 2002 Reauthorization: An opportunity to improve educational results for students with disabilities. *A timely IDEA: Rethinking federal education programs for children with disabilities*. Washington, D.C.: Center on Educational Policy.

Hendrick Hudson District Board of Education v. Rowley, 458 U.S. 176 (1982).

Huefner, D. S. (2012). *Navigating special education law and policy*. Verona, Wisconsin: Attainment Company.

Johnson, G. O. (1961). *A comparative study of the personal and social adjustment of mentally handicapped children placed in special classes with mentally handicapped children who remain in regular classes*. Syracuse, NY: Syracuse University Research Institute, Office of Research in Special Education and Rehabilitation.

Jordan, A. M., & deCharms, R. (1959). Personal-social traits of mentally handicapped children. In T. G. Thurstone (Ed.), *An evaluation of educating mentally handicapped children in special classes and regular classes*. Chapel Hill, NC: School of Education, University of North Carolina.

McLaughlin, M. J., & Tilstone, C. (2000). Standards and curriculum. The core of educational reform. In M. Rouse & M. J. McLaughlin (Eds.), *Special education and school reform in the United States and Britain* (pp. 38–65). London: Routledge.

Mills v. District of Columbia Board of Education, 348 F. Supp. 866 (D.D.C. 1972).

National Information Center for Children and Youth with Disabilities. (2011). *Questions often asked by parents about special education services*. Washington, D.C.: Author. Retrieved December 23, 2011 from http://nichcy.org/wp-content/uploads/docs/lg1.pdf.

Pennsylvania Association for Retarded Citizens v. Commonwealth of Pennsylvania, 334 F. Supp. (1971).

President's Commission on Excellence in Special Education. (2002). *A new era: Revitalizing special education for children and their families*. Washington, D.C.: Education Publications Center, U.S. Department of Education.

Riddell, S. (2007). A sociology of special education. In L. Florian (Ed.), *The Sage handbook of special education* (pp. 34–54). London: Sage Publications.

Schaller, J., Ynag, N. K., & Chang, S. C. (2004). Contemporary issues in rehabilitation counseling: Interface with and implications for special education. In A. M. Sorrells, H. J. Rieth, & P. T. Sindelar (Eds.), *Critical issues in special education: Access, diversity, and accountability* (pp. 226–242). Boston: Allyn and Bacon.

Sebba, J., Thurlow, M. L., & Goertz, M. (2000). Educational accountability and students with disabilities in the United States and England and Wales. In M. J. McLaughlin & M. Rouse (Eds.), *Special education and school reform in the United States and Britain* (pp. 98–125). New York: Routledge.

Thurstone, T. G. (1959). *An evaluation of educating mentally handicapped children in special classes and regular classes*. U.S. Office of Education, Cooperative Research Project No. OE-SAE 6452. Chapel Hill, NC: University of North Carolina.

United Nations Educational, Scientific, and Cultural Organization (UNESCO). (1994). *World Conference on Special Needs Education: Access and quality*. Salamanca, Spain: Author.

United Nations Educational, Scientific, and Cultural Organization (UNESCO). (2001). *We the children: Meeting the promises of the World Summit for Children*. New York: Author.

U.S. Department of Education. (2011). The Thirtieth Annual Report to Congress on the Implementation of the Individuals with Disabilities Education Act, 2008. Washington, D.C.: U.S. Government Printing Office.

Vaughn, S., Bos, C. S., & Schumm, J. S. (2011). *Teaching students who are exceptional, diverse, and at-risk students in the general education classroom,* 5th ed. Boston: Prentice-Hall.

Wood, J. W. (2006). *Teaching students in inclusive settings: Adapting and accommodating instruction,* 5th ed. Boston: Prentice-Hall.

Zusel, R. (2011). The individualized education program: Getting the most for your child. Retrieved December 23, 2011 from http://blog.friendshipcircle.org/2010/12/20/individualized-education-program-getting-the-best-for-your-child/.

Chapter 3

Arthur-Kelly, M., Foreman, P., Bennette, D., & Pascoe, S. (2008). Interaction, inclusion and students with profound and multiple disabilities: Toward an agenda for research and practice. *Journal of Research in Special Educational Needs, 8*(3), 161–166.

Batshaw, M., Pellegrino, L. & Rozien, N. J. (2008). *Children with disabilities,* 6th ed. Baltimore: Paul H. Brookes.

Bender, W. N. (2008). *Differentiating instruction for students with learning disabilities: Best teaching* practices for general and special educators, 2nd ed. Thousand Oaks, CA: Corwin Press.

Berk, L. E. (2011). *Development through the lifespan,* 2nd ed. Upper Saddle River, NJ: Prentice-Hall.

Berry, J. (2009). *Lifespan perspectives on the family and disability.* Austin, TX: Pro-Ed.

Bierman, K. L., Nix, R. L., Greenberg, M. T., Blair, C., & Domitrovich, C. E. (2008). Executive functions and school readiness intervention: Impact, moderation, and mediation in the Head Start REDI program. *Development and Psychopathology, 20*(3), 821–843.

Bloom, B. S. (1964). *Stability and change in human characteristics*. New York: Wiley & Sons.

Bolt, S. E., & Roach, A. T. (2009). *Inclusive assessment and accountability: A guide to accommodations for students with diverse needs.* New York: Guilford Press.

Center for Applied Special Technology. (2012). *Carnegie Strategy Tutor.* Retrieved January 15, 2012, from www.cast .org/research/projects/ tutor.html (Coyne, P., & Dalton, B., Project Directors).

Crane, J. L., & Winser, A. (2008). Early autism detection: Implications for pediatric practice and public policy. *Journal of Disability Policy Studies, 18*(4), 245–253.

Devore, S., & Hanley-Maxwell, C. (2000). "I wanted to see if we could make it work": Perspectives on inclusive childcare.

Exceptional Children, 66(2), 241–255.

Devore, S., & Russell, S. (2007). Early childhood education and care for children with disabilities: Facilitating inclusive practice. *Early Childhood Education Journal, 35*(2), 189–198.

Division for Early Childhood, Council for Exceptional Children and the National Association for the Education of Young Children. (2012). *Position statement on inclusion.* Retrieved January 10, 2012, from www.dec-sped.org/About_DEC/ Position_Statements_ and_Concept_Papers/ Inclusion.

Dorn, S., & Fuchs, D. (2004). Trends in placement issues. In A. M. Sorrells, H. J. Rieth, & P. T. Sindelar (Eds.), *Critical issues in special education: Access, diversity, and accountability* (pp. 57–72). Boston: Allyn and Bacon.

Drew, C. J., & Hardman, M. L. (2007). *Mental retardation,* 9th ed. Upper Saddle River, NJ: Prentice-Hall.

Dunn, L. M. (1968). Special education for the mildly retarded. Is much of it justifiable? *Exceptional Children, 35*, 229–237.

Eggen, P., & Kauchak, D. (2010). *Educational psychology: Windows on classrooms,* 8th ed. Upper Saddle River, NJ: Merrill Prentice-Hall.

Falvey, M. A., Rosenberg, R. L., Monson, D., & Eschilian, L. (2006). Facilitating and supporting transition. In P. Wehman (Ed.), *Life beyond the classroom: Transition strategies for youth with disabilities*

(pp. 165–181). Baltimore: Paul H. Brookes.

Frankel, E. B., & Gold, S. (2007). Principles and practices of early intervention. In I. Brown & M. Percy (Eds.), *A comprehensive guide to intellectual and developmental disabilities* (pp. 451–466). Baltimore: Paul H. Brookes.

Friend, M. P., & Bursuck, W. D. (2012). *Including students with special needs: A practical guide for classroom teachers,* 5th ed. Boston: Allyn and Bacon.

Friend, M. P., & Cook, L. (2010). *Interactions: Collaboration skills for school professionals,* 6th ed. Upper Saddle River, NJ: Prentice-Hall.

Gargiulo, R., & Metcalf, D. (2013). *Teaching in today's inclusive classrooms: A universal design for learning approach.* Belmont, CA: Wadsworth Cengage Learning.

Gartin, B. C., Murdick, N. L., Imbeau, M., & Perner, D. E. (2002). *How to use differentiated instruction with students with developmental disabilities in the general education classroom.* Alexandria, VA: Council for Exceptional Children.

Gollnick, D., & Chinn, P. C. (2009). *Multicultural education in a diverse society,* 8th ed. Boston: Allyn and Bacon.

Grenier, M., Rogers, R., & Iarusso, K. (2008). Including students with Down syndrome in adventure programming. *Journal of Physical Education, 79*(1), 30–35.

Guralnick, M. J., Neville, B., Hammond, M. A., &

Connor, R. T. (2008). Continuity and change from full inclusion early childhood programs through the early elementary period. *Journal of Early Intervention, 30*(3), 237–250.

Haager, D., & Klinger, J. K. (2005). *Differentiating instruction in inclusive classrooms: The special educator's guide.* Boston: Allyn and Bacon.

Hallahan, D. P. (2002). We need more intensive instruction. In M. Byrnes (Ed.), *Taking sides: Clashing views on controversial issues in special education* (pp. 204–206). Guilford, CT: McGraw-Hill Dushkin.

Hammeken, P. A. (2007). *Inclusion: An essential guide for the paraprofessional,* 2nd ed. Thousand Oaks, CA: Corwin Press.

Hardman, M. L., & Dawson, S. (2008, winter). The impact of federal public policy on curriculum and instruction for students with disabilities in the general classroom. *Preventing School Failure 52*(2), 5–11.

Hardman, M., & McDonnell, J. (2008). Teachers, pedagogy, and curriculum. In M. McLaughlin & L. Florian (Eds.), *Perspectives and purposes of disability classification systems in research and clinical practice* (pp. 153–169). London: Sage Publishing Co.

Hardman, M., & Mulder, M. (2004). Critical issues in public education: Federal reform and the impact on students with disabilities. In L. M. Bullock, & R. A. Gable (Eds.), *Quality personnel preparation* in emotional/behavior disorders (pp. 12–36). Dallas, TX: Institute for Behavioral and Learning Differences.

Harvey, A., Robin, J., Morris, M. E., Graham, H. K., & Baker, R. (2008). A systematic review of measures of activity limitation for children with cerebral palsy. *Developmental Medicine and Child Neurology, 50*(3), 190–198.

Hogansen, J. M., Powers, K., Geenen, S., Gil-Kashiwabara, E., & Powers, L. (2008). Transition goals and experiences of females with disabilities: Youth, parents, and professionals. *Exceptional Children, 74*(2), 225–234.

Hollins, E. R., & Guzman, M. T. (2005). Research on preparing teachers for diverse populations. In M. Cochran-Smith & K. M. Zeichner (Eds.), *Studying teacher education: The report of the AERA panel on research and teacher education* (pp. 477–548). Mahwah, NJ: Lawrence Erlbaum Associates.

Holzberg, C. (2012). *Helping all learners succeed: Special education success stories.* Retrieved January 7, 2012 from www.washington.edu/doit/Press/learning.html. (Originally published in *Technology and Learning,* January 1998).

Horner, R. H., Albin, R. W., Sprague, J. R., & Todd, A. W. (2006). Positive behavior support. In M. E. Snell & F. Brown (Eds.), *Instruction of students with severe disabilities* (pp. 206–250). Baltimore: Paul H. Brookes.

Horner, R. H., Sugai, G., & Anderson, C. M. (2010). Examining the evidence base for school-wide positive behavior support. *Focus on Exceptional Children, 42*(8).

Hosp, M. K., & Hosp, J. L. (2003). Curriculum-based measurement for reading, spelling, and math: How to do it and why. *Preventing School Failure, 48*(1), 10–17.

Howell, K. W., & Nolet, V. (2000). *Curriculum-based evaluation.* Stamford, CT: Wadsworth.

Huefner, D.S. (2012). *Navigating special education law and policy.* Verona, Wisconsin: Attainment Company.

Humphrey, N. (2008). Autistic spectrum and inclusion: Including pupils with autistic spectrum disorders in mainstream schools. *Support Learning, 23*(1), 41–47.

Hunt, J. M. (1961). *Intelligence and experience.* New York: Ronald Press.

Karen, T. J. (2007). *More inclusion strategies that work: Aligning student strengths with standards.* Thousand Oaks, CA: Corwin Press.

Kessler Foundation/National Organization on Disabilities. (2012). *Kessler Foundation/NOD Survey of Americans with Disabilities.* Retrieved January 12, 2012 from www.2010disabilitysurveys.org/indexold.html.

Ketterlin-Geller, L. R. (2008). Testing students with special needs: A model for understanding the interaction between assessment and student characteristics in a universally designed environment. *Educational Measurement: Issues and Practices, 27*(3), 3–16.

Kotering, L., McClannon, T. W., & Braziel, P. M. (2008). Universal design for learning: A look at what algebra and biology students with and without high incidence conditions are saying. *Remedial and Special Education, 29*(6), 352–363.

Lane, H., Hoffmeister, R., & Bahan, B. (2002). Are residential schools the least restrictive environment for deaf children? In M. Byrnes (Ed.), *Taking sides: Clashing views on controversial issues in special education* (pp. 222–228). Guilford, CT: McGraw-Hill Dushkin.

Leafstedt, J. M., Richards, C., Lamonte, M., & Cassidy, D. (2007). Perspectives on co-teaching: Views from high school students with learning disabilities. *Learning Disabilities: A Multidisciplinary Journal, 14*(3), 177–184.

Leppert, M. L., & Rosier, E. M. (2008). In P. J. Accardo (Ed.), *Caput and Accardo's neurodevelopmental disabilities in infancy and childhood: Vol 1: Neurodevelopmental diagnosis and treatment,* 3rd ed. (pp. 395–404). Baltimore: Paul H. Brookes.

Lewis, A., & Norwich, B. (2005). Overview and discussion: Overall conclusions. In A. Lewis & B. Norwich (Eds.), *Special teaching for special children? Pedagogies for inclusion* (pp. 206–221). Berkshire, England: Open University Press.

Lipkin, P. H., & Schertz, M. (2008). Early intervention and efficacy. In P. J. Accardo (Ed.) *Caput and Accardo's neurodevelopmental disabilities in infancy and childhood: Vol 1: Neurodevelopmental diagnosis and treatment,* 3rd ed. (pp. 519–552). Baltimore: Paul H. Brookes.

Lipsky, D. K., & Gartner, A. (2002). Taking inclusion into the future. In M. Byrnes (Ed.), *Taking sides: Clashing views on controversial issues in special education* (pp. 198–203). Guilford, CT: McGraw-Hill Dushkin.

Lund, J. L., & Veal, M. L. (2008). Chapter 4: Measuring pupil learning—How do student teachers assess within instructional models? *Journal of Teaching in Physical Education 27*(4), 487–511.

Mastropieri, M. A., & Scruggs, T. E. (2007). *The inclusive classroom: Strategies for effective instruction.* Upper Saddle River, NJ: Merrill.

Mastropieri, M. A., Scruggs, T. E., & Berkeley S. (2007). Peers helping peers. *Educational Leadership, 64*(5), 54–58.

McDonnell, J. M., & Hardman, M. L. (2009). *Secondary and transition programs for students with intellectual and developmental disabilities.* London: Sage Publishing.

McDonnell, J., Hardman, M., & McDonnell, A. P. (2003). *Introduction to persons with moderate and severe disabilities* (p. 299). Boston: Allyn and Bacon.

McDonnell, J., Hardman, M. L., & McGuire, J. (2007). Teaching and learning in secondary education. In L. Florian (Ed.), *The Handbook of special education* (pp. 378–389). London: Sage Publishing.

Murawksi, W. W. (2008). Five keys to co-teaching in inclusive classrooms. *School Administrator, 65*(8), 29.

National Association for the Education of Young Children. (2012). *NAEYC position statement*. Retrieved January 16, 2012 from www.naeyc.org/files/naeyc/file/positions/PSDAP.pdf.

National Association of School Psychologists. (2012). *Position statement on inclusive programs for students with disabilities*. Retrieved January 15, 2012 from www.nasponline.org/about_nasp/pospaper_ipsd.aspx.

National Organization on Disability (NOD), & Harris Survey. (2004). *National Organization on Disability/Harris Survey of Americans with Disabilities*. New York: Author.

Neal, P. (2008). Are we making a difference? Measurement of family outcomes in early intervention. Chapel Hill, NC: *Dissertation Abstracts International Section A: Humanities and Social Sciences, 68*(7), 2802.

Peterson, J. M., & Hittie, M. M. (2010). *The journey toward effective schools for all learners*. Upper Saddle River, NJ: Prentice-Hall.

Phillips, D. A., & Cabrera, N. J. (2006). *Beyond the blueprint: Directions for research on Head Start families*. Washington, D.C.: National Academies Press.

Piaget, J. (1970). Piaget's theory. In P. H. Mussen (Ed.), *Carmichael's manual of child psychology,* 3rd ed., vol. 1. New York: Wiley.

Pugach, M. C. (2005). Research on preparing general education teachers to work with students with disabilities. In M. Cochran-Smith & K. M. Zeichner (Eds.), *Studying teacher education: The report of the AERA panel on research and teacher education* (pp. 549–590). Mahwah, NJ: Lawrence Erlbaum Associates.

Raver, S. (2010). *Early childhood special education—0 to 8 years: Strategies for positive outcomes.* Upper Saddle River, NJ: Prentice-Hall.

Rose, D. H., & Meyer, A. (2002). *Teaching every student in the digital age: Universal design for learning*. Alexandria, VA: Association for Supervision and Development.

Rosenkoetter, S. E., Whaley, K. T., Hains, A. H., & Pierce, L. (2001). The evolution of transition policy for young children with special needs and their families: Past, present, and future. *Topics in Early Childhood Education, 21,* 3–15.

Sainato, D. M., & Morrison, R. S. (2001). Transition to inclusive environments for young children with disabilities. In M. J. Guralnick (Ed.), *Early childhood inclusion: Focus on change* (pp. 293–306). Baltimore: Paul H. Brookes.

Sapon-Shevin, M. (2008). Learning in an inclusive community. *Educational Leadership, 66*(1), 49–53.

Shapiro-Barnard, S., Tashie, C., Martin, J., Malloy, J., Schuh, M., Piet, J., Lichenstein, S., & Nisbet, J. (2002). Petroglyphs: The writing on the wall. In M. Byrnes (Ed.), *Taking sides: Clashing views on controversial issues in special education* (pp. 210–214). Guilford, CT: McGraw-Hill Dushkin.

Spencer, S. (2005). Lynne Cook and June Downing: The practicalities of collaboration in special education service delivery (Interview). *Intervention in School and Clinic, 40,* 296–300.

Study of Personnel Needs in Special Education. (2006). *General education teachers' role in special education (fact sheet)*. Retrieved July 20, 2006 from http://ferdig.coe.ufl.edu/spense/.

Sugai, G., & Horner, R. (2010). School-wide positive behavior support: Establishing a continuum of evidence-based practices. *Journal of Evidence-Based Practices in Schools, 11*(1), 62–83.

Tan, T. S., & Cheung, W. S. (2008). Effects of computer collaborative group work on peer acceptance of a junior pupil with attention deficit hyperactive disorder. *Computers and Education, 50*(3), 725–741.

Tannock, M. T. (2009). Tangible and intangible elements of collaborative teaching. *Intervention in School and Clinic, 44(3),* 173–178.

U.S. Department of Health and Human Services. (2012). *Head Start Program fact sheet*. Washington, D.C.: Administration on Families and Children. Retrieved January 8, 2012 from www.acf.hhs.gov/programs/ohs/about/fy2010.html.

Vaughn, S., Bos, C. S., & Schumm, J. S. (2011). *Teaching students who are exceptional, diverse, and at-risk students in the general education classroom,* 5th ed. Boston: Prentice-Hall.

Wade, S. E., & Zone, J. (2000). Creating inclusive classrooms: An overview. In S. E. Wade (Ed.), *Inclusive education: A casebook and readings for prospective and practicing teachers* (pp. 1–27). Mahwah, NJ: Lawrence Erlbaum Associates.

White, B. L. (1975). The first three years of life. Englewood Cliffs, NJ: Prentice Hall. *Journal of the Division for Early Childhood Education, 9,* 11–26.

Widerstrom, A. H. (2005). *Achieving learning goals through play: Teaching young children with special needs,* 2nd ed. Baltimore: Paul H. Brookes.

Wood, J. W. (2006). *Teaching students in inclusive settings; Adapting and accommodating instruction,* 5th ed. Boston: Prentice-Hall.

Worrell, J. L. (2008). How secondary schools can avoid the seven deadly sins of inclusion. *American Secondary Education, 36*(2), 43–45.

Chapter 4

Agran, M., Wehmeyer, M. L., Cavin, M., & Palmer,

S. (2008). Promoting student active classroom participation skills through instruction to promote self-regulated learning and self-determination. *Career Development for Exceptional Individuals, 31*(2), 106–114.

Allen, P., Ciancio, J., & Rutkowski, S. (2008). Transitioning students with disabilities into work. *Techniques: Connecting Education and Careers, 83*(2), 22–25.

Babbitt, B. C., & White, C. M. (2002). RU ready? Helping students assess their readiness for postsecondary education. *Teaching Exceptional Children, 35*(2), 62–66.

Bakken, J. P., & Obiakor, F. E. (2008). *Transition planning for students with disabilities: What educators and service providers can do.* Springfield, IL: Charles C. Thomas, Publisher, Ltd.

Bambara, L., Browder, D., & Kroger, X. (2006). Home and community. In M. Snell & F. Brown (Eds.), *Instruction of students with severe disabilities,* 6th ed. (pp. 526–568). Upper Saddle River, NJ: Merrill Publishing/ Prentice Hall.

Bremer, C. D., Kachgal, M., & Schoeller, K. (2003, April). Self-determination: Supporting successful transition. *Research to Practice Brief of the National Center on Secondary Education and Transition, 2*(1), 1–5.

Carter, E. W., Lane, K. L., Pierson, M. R., & Stang, K. K. (2008). Promoting self-determination for transition-age youth: Views of high school

general and special educators. *Exceptional Children, 75*(1), 55–70.

Crockett, M., & Hardman, M. L. (2009). Expected outcomes and emerging values. In J. McDonnell & M. L. Hardman, *Successful transition programs,* 2nd ed. (pp. 25–42). Los Angeles: Sage Publishing.

Drew, C. J., & Hardman, M. L. (2007). *Intellectual disabilities across the lifespan,* 9th ed. Upper Saddle River, NJ: Merrill.

Finn, D., Getzel, E. E., & McManus, S. (2008). Adapting the self-determined learning model for instruction for college students with disabilities. *Career Development for Exceptional Individuals, 31*(2), 85–93.

Friend, M. P., & Bursuck, W. D. (2006). *Including students with special needs: A practical guide for classroom teachers,* 4th ed. Boston: Allyn and Bacon.

Getzel, E. E., & Gugerty, J. J. (2001). Applications for youth with learning disabilities. In P. Wehman (Ed.), *Life beyond the classroom: Transition strategies for young people with disabilities,* 3rd ed.) (pp. 371–398). Baltimore: Paul H. Brookes.

Getzel, E. E., & Thoma, C. A. (2008). Experiences of college students with disabilities and the importance of self-determination in higher education settings. *Career Development for Exceptional Individuals, 31*(2), 77–84.

Hansen, D. L., & Morgan, R. L. (2008). Teaching

grocery store purchasing skills to students with intellectual disabilities using computer-based instruction program. *Education and Training in Developmental Disabilities, 43*(4), 431–442.

Harchik, A., & Ladew, P. (2008). Strategies to help children with special needs enjoy successful community outings. *Exceptional Parent, 38*(12), 75–77.

Hasazi, S. B., Furney, K. S., & Destefano, L. (1999). Implementing the IDEA transition initiatives. *Exceptional Children, 65*(4), 555–566.

Higbee, J. L., & Goff, E. (Eds.). (2008). *Pedagogy and student services for institutional transformation: Implementing universal in higher education.* University of Minnesota: Center for Research on Developmental Education and Urban Literacy.

Joseph, L. M., & Konrad, M. (2009). Have students self-manage their academic performance. *Intervention in School and Clinic, 44*(4), 246–249.

Kessler Foundation and the National Organization on Disability. (2010). *Survey of the Employment of Americans with Disabilities.* New York: Author.

Lock, R. H., & Layton, C. A. (2008). The impact of tutoring attendance on the GPAs of postsecondary students with learning disabilities. *Learning Disabilities: A Multidisciplinary Journal, 15*(2), 55–60.

Manley, K., Collins, B. C., Stenhoff, D. M., & Kleinert, H. (2008). Using a system of least prompts

procedure to teach telephone skills to elementary students with cognitive disabilities. *Journal of Behavioral Education, 17*(3), 221–236.

Margolis, H. S., & Prichard, E. (2008). What to do when your child turns 18. *Exceptional Parent, 38*(11), 24–26.

McDonnell, J. (2009). Curriculum. In J. McDonnell & M. L. Hardman, *Successful transition programs* (pp. 63–80). Los Angeles: Sage Publishing.

McDonnell, J., & Copeland, S. (2011). Teaching academic skills. In M. Snell & F. Brown (Eds.), *Instruction of students with severe disabilities,* 7th ed. (pp. 492–528) Boston: Pearson Group.

McDonnell, J., Hardman, M. L., & McGuire, J. (2007). Teaching and learning in secondary education. In L. Florian (Ed.), *The Handbook of special education* (pp. 378–389) London: Sage Publishing Co.

McDonnell, J. Kiuhara, S., & Collier, P. (2009). Transition to post-secondary education. In J. McDonnell & M. L. Hardman, *Successful transition programs,* 2nd ed. (pp. 320–340). Los Angeles: Sage Publishing.

Muller, E., Schuler, A., & Yates, G. B. (2008). Social challenges and supports from the perspective of individuals with Asperger syndrome and other autism spectrum disabilities. *Autism: The International Journal of Research and Practice, 12*(2), 173–190.

Murawski, W. W., & Dieker, L. A. (2004). Tips and strategies for co-teaching at the secondary level. *Teaching Exceptional Children, 36*(5), 52–58.

Murray, C., Flannery, B. K., & Wren, C. (2008). University staff members' attitudes and knowledge about learning disabilities and disability support services. *Journal of Postsecondary Education and Disability, 21*(2), 73–90.

Murray, C., Wren, C. T., & Keys, C. (2008). University faculty perceptions of students with learning disabilities: Correlates and group differences. *Learning Disability Quarterly, 31*(3).

Payne-Christiansen, E. M., & Sitlington, P. L. (2008). Guardianship: Its role in the transition process for students with developmental disabilities. *Education and Training in Developmental Disabilities, 43*(1), 3–19.

Pierson, M. R., Carter, E. W., Lane, K. L., & Glaeser, B. C. (2008). Factors influencing the self-determination of transition-age youth with high incidence disabilities. *Career Development for Exceptional Individuals, 31*(2), 115–125.

Polychronis, S., & McDonnell, J. (2009). Developing IEPs/-transition plans. In J. McDonnell & M.L. Hardman, *Successful transition programs* (81–100). Los Angeles: Sage Publishing.

Prouty, R. W., Smith, G., & Lakin, K. C. (2001, June). *Residential services for persons with developmental disabilities: Status and trends through 2000.* Minneapolis, MN: University of Minnesota,

College of Education and Human Development, Institute on Community Integration, Research and Training Center on Community Living.

Schnee, E. (2008). "In the real world no one drops their standards for you": Academic rigor in a college worker education program. *Equity & Excellence in Education, 41*(1), 62–80.

Smith, T. L., Beyer, J. F., Polloway, E. A., Smith, D. J., & Patton, J. R. (2008). Ethical considerations in teaching self-determination: Challenges in rural special education. *Rural Special Education Quarterly, 27*(1/2), 30–35.

Steere, D. E., Rose, E., & Cavaiuolo, D. (2007). *Growing up: Transition to adult life for students with disabilities.* Boston: Allyn and Bacon.

Stenhoff, D. M., Davey, B. J., & Lignugaris/Kraft, B. (2008). The effects of choice on assignment completion and percent correct by a high school student with a learning disability. *Education and Treatment of Children, 31*(2), 203–211.

Thurlow, M. L., Sinclair, M. F., & Johnson, D. (2009). Students with disabilities who drop out of school: Implications for policy and practice. *Issues Brief: Examining Current Issues in Secondary Education and Transition.* Retrieved April 11, 2009 from www.ncset.org/publications/viewdesc.asp?id=425.

Tiedemann, C. W. (2008). Finding America's most disability-friendly colleges. *The Exceptional Parent, 38*(9).

University of Illinois at Chicago National Research and Training Center. (2009). *Self-determination framework for people with psychiatric disabilities.* Chicago, IL: Author. Retrieved April 2, 2009 from www.psych.uic.edu/UICNRTC/sdframework.pdf.

U.S. Department of Education (2011). *To assure the free appropriate public education of all children with disabilities: Thirtieth annual report to congress on the implementation of the Individuals with Disabilities Education Act.* Washington, D.C.: U.S. Government Printing Office.

Wagner, M., & Blackorby, J. (1996). Transition from high school to work or college: How special education students fare. In the Center for the Future of Children, *Special education for students with disabilities, 6*(1) 103–120. Los Angeles: The Center for the Future of Children.

Wagner, M., Newman, L., Cameto, R., & Levine, P. (2005). *Changes over time in the early post-school outcomes of youth with disabilities. A report from the National Longitudinal Study (NLTS) and the National Longitudinal Transition Study-2 (NLTS2).* Menlo Park, CA: SRI International.

Wehman, P. (2011). *Essentials of transition planning.* Baltimore: Paul H. Brookes.

Wehmeyer, M. L., Gragoudas, S., & Shogren, K. A. (2006). Self-determination, student involvement, and leadership

development. In P. Wehman, *Life beyond the classroom: Transition strategies for young people with disabilities,* 4th ed. (pp. 41–69). Baltimore: Paul H. Brookes.

Winn, S., & Hay, I. (2009). Transition from school for youths with a disability: Issues and challenges. *Disability & Society, 24*(1), 103–115.

Worrell, J. L. (2008). How secondary schools can avoid the seven deadly school "sins" of inclusion. *American Secondary Education, 36*(2), 43–56.

Chapter 5

Alvarez, H. K. (2007). The impact of teacher preparation on responses to student aggression in the classroom. *Teaching and Teacher Education 23,* 1113–1126.

Arias, M. B., & Morillo-Campbell, M. (2008). Promoting ELL parental involvement: Challenges in contested times. Tempe, AZ: Education Public Interest Center/Education Policy Research Unit; Division of Education Leadership and Policy Studies, Arizona State University. Retrieved from http://epsl.asu.edu/epru/documents/EPSL-0801-250-EPRU.pdf.

Arredondo, P., & Perez, P. (2006). Historical perspectives on the multicultural guidelines and contemporary applications. *Professional Psychology: Research and Practice, 37,* 1–5.

Artiles, A. J., Kozleski, E. B., Trent, S. C., Osher, D., Ortiz, A. (2010). Justifying and explaining disproportionality, 1968–2008: A critique of underlying views of culture. *Exceptional Children 76*(3), 279–299.

August, D., & Shanahan, T. (2006). Introduction and methodology. In D. August & T. Shanahan (Eds.), *Developing literacy in second-language learners: Report of the national literacy panel on language-minority children and youth* (pp. 1–42). Mahwah, NJ: Lawrence Erlbaum Associates Publishers.

Baca, L. M., & Cervantes, H. T. (2004). *The bilingual special education interface,* 4th ed. Columbus, OH: Merrill/Macmillan.

Baldwin, J. R., Faulkner, S. L., & Hecht, M. I. (2006). *Redefining cultures: Perspective across the disciplines*. Mahwah, NJ: Lawrence Erlbaum Associates.

Banks, J. A. (2008). *An introduction to multicultural education,* 4th ed. Boston, MA:Pearson Education, Inc.

Barnum-Martin, L., Mehta, P. D., Fletcher, J. M., Carlson, C. D., Ortiz, A., Carlo, M., & Francis, D. J. (2006). Bilingual phonological awareness: Multilevel construct validation among Spanish-speaking kindergartners in transitional bilingual education classrooms. *Journal of Educational Psychology, 98,* 170–181.

Barranti, C. C. R. (2005). Family health social work practice with Mexican migrant and seasonal farmworking families. In F. K. O. Yuen (Ed.), *Social work practice with children and families* (pp. 117–142).

Binghamton, NY: Haworth Social Work Practice Press.

Barrera, M. (2006). Roles of definitional and assessment models in the identification of new or second language learners of English for special education. *Journal of Learning Disabilities 39,* 142–156.

Berliner, D. (2006). Our impoverished view of educational research. *Teachers College Record, 108,* 949–995.

Blachowicz, C., Fisher, P., & Watts-Taffe, S. (2005). *Integrated vocabulary instruction: Meeting the needs of diverse learners in grades K–5.* Learning Point Associates, North Central Regional Educational Laboratory. Retrieved from www.learningpt.org/pdfs/literacy/vocabulary.pdf.

Bratter, J. L., & Eschbach, K. (2005). Race/ethnic differences in nonspecific psychological distress: Evidence from the National Health Interview Survey. *Social Science Quarterly, 86,* 620–644.

Bruchac, J., (2005). *Code talker.* New York, NY. Penguin Group.

Butcher, J. N., Cabiya, J., Lucio, E., & Garrido, M. (2007). The challenge of assessing clients with different cultural and language backgrounds. In J. N. Butcher, J. Cabiya, E. Lucio, & M. Garrido (Eds.), *Assessing Hispanic clients using the MMPI-2 and MMPI-A* (pp. 3–23). Washington, D.C.: American Psychological Association.

Carpenter, S. Zarate, M. A., & Garza, A. A. (2007). Cultural pluralism and prejudice reduction.

Cultural Diversity and Ethnic Minority Psychology, 13, 83–93.

Chapman, C., Laird, J., & KewalRamani, A. (2010). *Trends in high school dropout and completion rates in the United States: 1972–2008: Compendium Report.* Washington, D.C.: Institute of Education Research; National Center for Education Statistics: U. S. Department of Education.

Clare, M. M., & Garcia, G. (2007). Working with migrant children and their families. In G. B. Esquivel, E. C. Lopez, & S. Nahari (Eds.), *Handbook of multicultural school psychology: An interdisciplinary perspective* (pp. 549–572). Mahwah, NJ: Lawrence Erlbaum Associates Publishers.

Cohen, L. G., & Spenciner, L. J. (2007). *Assessment of children and youth with special needs,* 3rd ed. Boston, MA: Allyn & Bacon.

Coll-Black, S., Bhushan, A., & Fritsch, K. (2007). Integrating poverty and gender into health programs: A sourcebook for health professionals. *Nursing and Health Sciences, 9,* 246–253.

Collier, C. (2004). Including bilingual exceptional children in the general education classroom. In L. M. Baca & H. T. Cervantes (Eds.), *The bilingual special education interface,* 4th ed. (pp. 298–335). Columbus, OH: Merrill/Macmillan.

¡Colorín Colorado! (2011). Bilingualism & English language acquisition. Retrieved from www.colorincolorado.org/article/c184/?sort=title.

Connor, D. J., & Ferri, B. A. (2010). Introduction to DSQ Special Issue: "Why is there learning disabilities?" Revisiting Christine Sleeter's sociopolitical construction of disability two decades on. *Disability Studies Quarterly, 30,* 2. Retrieved from http://dsq-sds.org/article/view/1229/1276.

Cuffe, S. P., McKeown, R. E., Addy, C. L., & Garrison, C. Z. (2005). Family and psychosocial risk factors in a longitudinal epidemiological study of adolescents. *Journal of the American Academy of Child & Adolescent Psychiatry, 44,* 121–129.

Day, J. C. (1995). National population projections; Population profile of the United States. Department of Commerce. Retrieved from www.census.gov/population/www/pop-profile/profile_list.html.

Deaux, K., Reid, A., & Martin, D. (2006). Ideologies of diversity and inequality: Predicting collective action in groups varying in ethnicity and immigrant status. *Political Psychology, 27,* 123–146.

Demee-Benoit, D. (2006). Culturally responsive education: Cultural education through expeditionary learning. Retrieved from www.edutopia,ort/culturally-responsive-education.

Dettmer, P., Thurston, L. P., & Dyck, N. J. (2005). *Consultation, collaboration, and teamwork for students with special needs,* 5th ed. Boston, MA: Allyn & Bacon.

De Von Figueroa-Moseley, C., Ramey, C. T., & Keltner, B. (2006). Variations in Latino parenting practices and their effects on child cognitive developmental outcomes. *Hispanic Journal of Behavioral Sciences, 28,* 102–114.

Diana v. State Board of Education. (1970, 1973). C-70, 37 REP (N.D. Cal., 1970, 1973).

Díaz-Rico, L. T., & Weed, K. Z. (2010). *The cross-cultural, language, and academic development handbook: A complete k-12 reference guide,* 4th ed. Boston, MA: Allyn & Bacon, an imprint of Pearson Education, Inc.

Downing, S. M., & Haladyna, T. M. (2006). *Handbook of test development.* Mahwah, NJ: Lawrence Erlbaum Associates.

Drew, C. J., & Hardman, M. L., (2007). *Intellectual disabilities across the lifespan,* 9th ed. Columbus, OH: Merrill.

Edelsky, C. (2006). *With literacy and justice for all: Rethinking the social in language and education,* 3rd ed. Mahwah, NJ: Lawrence Erlbaum Associates.

Education Week. (2010). Progress on graduation rate stalls: 1.3 million student fail to earn diplomas. *Education Week & Education EPE Research Center,* June. Retrieved from www.edweek.org/media/ew/dc/2010/DC10_PressKit_FINAL.pdf.

Emerson, E., & Hatton, C. (2007). Poverty, socioeconomic position, social capital and the health of children and adolescents with intellectual disabilities in Britain: A replication. *Journal of Intellectual Disability Research, 51,* 866–874.

Epstein, J. L. (2011). *School, family and community partnerships: Preparing educators and improving schools,* 2nd ed. Washington, D.C.: Westview Press, a member of the Perseus Books Group.

Erevelles, N., Kanga, A., & Middleton, R. (2006). How does it feel to be a problem? Race, disability, and exclusion in education al policy. In E. A. Brantlinger (Ed.), *Who benefits from special education? Remediating (fixing other people's children* (pp. 77–99). Mahwah, NJ: Lawrence Erlbaum Associates.

Evans, G. W., & Kim, P. (2007). Childhood poverty and health: Cumulative risk exposure and stress dysregulation. *Psychological Science, 18,* 953–957.

Feldman, S. (2005). The war for children. *Professional Psychology: Research and Practice, 36,* 615–617.

Ferrell, C. B., Beidel, D. C., & Turner, S. M. (2004). Assessments and treatment of socially phobic children: A cross-cultural comparison. *Journal of Clinical Child and Adolescent Psychology, 33,* 260–268.

Ferri, B. A., & Connor, D. J. (2005). Tools of exclusion: Race, disability, and (re)segregated education. *Teachers College Record, 107, Special issue: Brown plus fifty,* 453–374.

Flora, C. B. (2011). *The community capitals framework: A transparent tool for participatory development.* A presentation given at Brigham Young University, English Language Learners Symposium. Retrieved from http://education.byu.edu/ellsymposium/2011/resources.html.

Friend, M., & Cook. L. (2007). *Interventions: Collaboration skills for school professionals,* 5th ed. Boston, MA: Allyn & Bacon.

Fujiki, M., & Brinton, B. (2010). Distinguishing between language difference and language deficit for ELLs. Presentation at Brigham Young University English Language Learners Annual Symposium, 2010. McKay School of Education Vimeo production. Retrieved from http://vimeo.com/13835949.

Gay, G. (2002). Culturally responsive teaching in special education for ethnically diverse students: setting the stage. *Qualitative Studies in Education, 15,* 613–629. DOI:10.1080/0951839022000014349.

Gimbert, B. G., Cristol, D., & Sene, A. M. (2007). The impact of teacher preparation on student achievement in algebra in a "hard-to-staff" urban preK-12-university partnership. *School Effectiveness and Scholl Improvement, 18,* 245–272.

Glimpse, W. (2012). Assessing English language proficiency. Retrieved from http://proximityone.com/elp.htm.

Goldenberg, C. (2008). Teaching English language learners: What the research does—and does not—say. *American Educator, 32*(2), 8–23, 42–44.

Gollnick, D. M., & Chinn, P. C. (2009). *Multicultural education in a pluralistic society,* 8th ed. Upper Saddle River, NJ: Merrill, an imprint of Pearson Education, Inc.

González, N. Moll, L. C., & Amanti, C., Eds. (2005). *Funds of knowledge, theorizing practices in households, communities and classrooms.* Mahwah, NJ. Lawrence Erlbaum Associates, Publishers.

Grant C. A., & Sleeter, C. E. (2009). *Making choices for multicultural education: Five approaches to race, class, and gender,* 6th ed. Danvers, MA: John Wiley & Sons, Inc.

Gregory, R. J. (2007). *Psychological testing: History, principles, and applications,* 5th ed. Boston, MA: Allyn & Bacon.

Hallerod, B., & Larsson, D. (2008). Poverty, welfare problems and social exclusion. *International Journal of Social Welfare, 17,* 15–25.

Harrington, M. M., & Brisk, M. E. (2006). *Bilingual education: From compensatory to quality schooling,* 2nd ed. Mahwah, NJ: Lawrence Erlbaum Associates.

Harry, B. & Klingner, J. (2006). *Why are so many minority students in special education?: Understanding race & disability in schools.* New York, NY: Teachers College Columbia University.

Hauser-Cram, P, Warfield, M. E., Stadler, J., & Sirin, S. R. (2006). School environments and the diverging pathways of students living in poverty. In A. C. Huston and M. N. Ripke (Eds.), *Developmental contexts in middle childhood: Bridges to adolescence and adulthood* (pp. 198–216). New York, NY: Cambridge University Press.

Hays, P. A. (2008). Putting culture to the test: Considerations with standardized testing. In P. A. Hays (Ed.), *Addressing cultural complexities in practice: Assessment, diagnosis, and therapy,* 2nd ed. (pp. 129–151). Washington, D.C.: American Psychological Association.

Hellerman, J., & Vergun, A. (2007). Language which is not taught: The discourse marker use of beginning adult learners of English. *Journal of Pragmatics, 39,* 157–179.

Hendrick, J., & Weissman, P. (2007). *The whole child: Developmental curriculum for the young child,* 7th ed. Upper Saddle River, NJ: Pearson, Prentice Hall.

Hosokawa, B., Mukoyama, Maj. Gen. J. H., Jr., Oshiki, K., Takahashi, M., & Tsutsumida, C. Y., Eds. (2001), *Patriotism, perseverance, posterity; the story of the national Japanese American memorial.* Washington, D.C., National Japanese American Memorial Foundation.

Jimerson, S. R., Burns, M. K., & VanDerHeyden, A. M. (2007). *Handbook of response to intervention: The science and practice of assessment.* New York, NY: Springer Science & Business Media, LLC.

Johnson, J. H. Jr., & Kasarda, J. D. (2011). Six disruptive demographic trends: What census 2010 will reveal. Chapel Hill, NC: *Frank Hawkins Kenan Institute of Private Enterprise, University of North Carolina.* Retrieved from www.kenaninstitute.unc.edu/Census2010Trends/.

Kasperowicz, P. (2011). Republicans push English-only bill, requires language tests. *The Hill,* March. Retrieved from http://thehill.com/blogs/floor-action/ouse/149049-republicans-push-english-only-bill-requiring-language-tests.

Kauffman, J. M., Conroy, M., Gardner, R., & Oswald, D. (2008). Cultural sensitivity in the application of behavior principles to education. *Education and Treatment of Children, 31,* 239–262.

Kishiyama, M. M., Boyce, W. T., Jimenez, A. M., Perry, L. M., & Knight, R. T. (2008). Socioeconomic disparities affect prefrontal function in children. *Massachusetts Institute of Technology, Journal of Cognitive Neuroscience 21*(6), 1106–1115.

Kline, M. V., & Huff, R. M. (2008). *Health promotion in multicultural populations: A handbook for practitioners and students.* Thousand Oaks, CA: Sage Publications.

Krashen, S. (2002, Dec.). *Second language acquisition and second language learning.* Internet Edition. First printed edition 1981 by Pergamon Press Inc.

Larry v Riles. (1972). C-71-2270 US.C, 343 F. Supp. 1306 (N.D. Cal. 1972).

Larry v Riles. (1979). 343 F. Supp. 1306, 502 F. 2d 963 (N.D. Cal. 1979).

Lau v Nicols. (1974). 414, U.S., 562-572 (1974, January 21).

Levin, B. (2006). Schools in challenging circumstances: A reflection on what we know and what we need to know. *School Effectiveness and School Improvement, 17,* 399–407.

Lucchese, F., & Tamis-LeMonda, C. S. (2007). Fostering language development in children from disadvantaged backgrounds. In *Encyclopedia of Language and Literacy Development* (pp. 1–11). London, ON: Canadian Language and Literacy Research Network. Retrieved [insert date] from http://www.literacyencyclopedia.ca/pdfs/topic.php?topId=229

Luykx, A., Okhee, L., Mahotiere, M. Lester, B., L., Hart, J., & Deaktor, R. (2007). Cultural and home language influences on children's responses to science assessments. *Teachers College Record, 109,* 897–926.

Keller-Allen, C. (2008). *The disproportionality of students designated limited English proficient in high incidence disability categories.* Dissertation, George Washington University. Ann Arbor, MI: ProQuest LLC.

MacFarlane, S. B. (2007). Researching health, poverty, and human development. *Critical Public Health, 17,* 191–193.

Marulis, L. M., & Neuman, S. B. (2010). The effects of vocabulary intervention on young children's word learning: A meta-analysis. *Review of Educational Research 80,* 300–335. DOI: 10.3102/0034654310377087.

McDonough, P., Sacker, A., & Wiggins, R. D. (2005). Time on my side? Life course trajectories of poverty and health. *Social Science and Medicine, 61,* 1795–1808.

McMillan, J. H. (2007). *Classroom assessment: Principles and practices for effective standards-based instruction,* 4th ed. Boston, MA: Allyn & Bacon.

Melville, K. (2006). The school drop out crisis: Why one-third of all high school students don't graduate what your community can do about it. *The University of Richmond Pew Partnership for Civic Change.* Retrieved from www.learningtofinish.org.

Merrell, K. W. (2007). *Behavioral, social, and emotional assessment of children and adolescents.* Abingdon, UK: Routledge.

Morrison, G. S. (2007). *Early childhood education today,* 10th ed. Upper Saddle River, NJ: Pearson-Prentice Hall.

Moule, J. (2012). *Cultural competence: A primer for educators,* 2nd ed. Belmont, CA: Wadsworth, Cengage Learning.

Mueller, J. (2011). Authentic assessment toolbox. Retrieved from http://jfmueller.faculty.noctrl.edu/toolbox/whatisit.htm.

Newell, M., & Kratochwill, T. R. (2007). The integration of response to intervention and critical race theory-disability studies: A robust approach to reducing racial discrimination. In S. R. Jimerson, M. K. Burns, & A. M. VanDerHeyden (Eds.), *Handbook of response to intervention: The science and practice of assessment and intervention* (pp. 65–79).

Nippold, M. A. (2006). *Later language development: School age children and young adults,* 3rd ed. Austin, TX: Pro-Ed.

National Center for Education Statistics. (2002). Dropout rates in the United States: 2000. Retrieved from http://nces.ed.gov/pubs2002/droppub_2001/11.asp.

National Center for Education Statistics. (2010). Trends in high school dropout and completion rates in the United States: 1972–2008. *Institute of Education Sciences.* Retrieved from http://nces.ed.gov/programs/digest/d10/tables/dt10_045.asp?referrer=list.

National Center for Education Statistics. (2011). Trends in High School Dropout and Completion Rates in the United States: 1972–2008. *Institute of Education-Sciences.* Retrieved from http://nces.ed.gov/pubs2011/dropout08/tables.asp.

NICHCY (National Dissemination Center for Children with Disabilities). (2010, December). Response to Intervention (RTI). Retrieved from http://nichcy.org/schools-administrators/rti#elements.

Office of Special Education Programs. (2002). Training overheads. Retrieved from www.specialed.us/discoveridea/Training/training.htm.

O'Hara, S., & Pritchard, R. H. (2008). Meeting the challenge of diversity: Professional development for teacher educators. *Teacher Education Quarterly, 35,* 43–61.

Ornstein, E., & Moses, H. (2005). One nation many voices. *School Social Work Journal, 30,* 87–89.

Peoplemovin. (2010). A visualization of migration flows. Retrieved from http://peoplemov.in/.

Perlich, P. (2010). *Coming to our census.* Retrieved from http://education.byu.edu/ellsymposium/2010/.

Pieterse, J.N. (2009). *Globalization and culture: Global mélange.* Lanham, MD: Rowman & Littlefield Publishers, Inc.

Prasad, S. H. (2008). Predicting academic outcomes for at-risk students who are culturally and linguistically divers. *Dissertation Abstracts International Section A: Humanities and Social Sciences, 68,* 2,773.

Ralabate, P. (2007). Truth in labeling: Disproportionality in special education. Washington, D.C.: National Education Association. Retrieved from www.nea.org/assets/docs/HE/EW-TruthInLabeling.pdf.

Reschly, D. J. (2009). Overview document: Prevention of disproportionate special education representation using response to intervention. *National Comprehensive Center for Teacher Quality.* Washington, D.C.: ETS, Learning Point Associates, and Vanderbilt University.

Reynolds, C. R., Livingston, R., & Willson, V. (2006). *Measurement and assessment in education.* Boston, MA: Allyn & Bacon.

Riad, S. (2007). Of mergers and cultures: "What happened to shared values and joint assumptions?" *Journal of Organizational Change Management, 2,* 26–43.

Rodriguez, D. (2005). *A conceptual framework for bilingual special education teacher programs.* Retrieved from www.lingref.com/isb/4/152ISB4.PDF.

Rueda, R., & Yaden, D. B., Jr. (2006). The literacy education of linguistically and culturally diverse young children: An overview of outcomes, assessment, and large-scale interventions. In B. Spodek and O. N. Saracho (Eds.), *Handbook of research on the education of young children,* 2nd ed. (pp. 167–186). Mahwah, NJ: Lawrence Erlbaum Associates.

Salam, R. (2011, February 22). The browning of America: Coming demographic shift is both a success and a challenge. *The Daily Holdings, Inc.* Retrieved from www.thedaily.com/page/2011/02/22/022211-opinions-column-mobility-salam-1-2/.

Salvadore, M. (2012). We are all hyphenated Americans. *Page by Page* blog about reading, *Reading Rockets.* Retrieved from www.readingrockets.org/blog/49695/.

Salvia, J., Ysseldyke, J. E., & Bolt, S. (2007). *Assessment in special education and inclusive education,* 10th ed. Boston, MA: Houghton Mifflin Co.

Skiba, R. J., Poloni-Staudinger, L., & Simmons, A. B. (2005). Unproven links: Can poverty explain ethnic disproportionality in special education: *Journal of Special Education. 39,* 130–144.

Skinner, D., & Weisner T. S. (2007). Sociocultural studies of families of children with intellectual disabilities. *Mental Retardation and Developmental Disabilities Research Reviews, 13,* 302–312. Wiley-Liss, Inc. MRDD Research Reviews. DOI: 10.1002/mrdd.

Skinner, C., Wight, V. R., Aratani, Y, Cooper, J. L., & Thampi, K. (2010). English language proficiency, family economic security, and child development. *National Center for Children in Poverty.* Retrieved from http://nccp.org/publications/pub_948.html.

Sleeter, C. E., & Grant, C. A. (2009). *Turning on learning: Five approaches for multicultural teaching plans for race class, gender, and disability,* 5th ed. Danvers, MA: John Wiley & Sons, Inc.

Smith, P., Lane, E., & Llorente, A. M. (2008). Hispanics and cultural bias: Test development and applications. IN A. M. Llorente (Ed.), *Principles of neuropsychological assessment with Hispanics: Theoretical foundations and clinical practice* (pp. 136–163). New York, NY: Springer Science & Business Media.

Snyder, C. R., Shorey, H. S., & Rand, K. L. (2006). Using hope theory to teaching and mentor academically at-risk students. In W. Buskist and S. F. Davis (Eds.), *Handbook of the teaching of psychology* (pp. 170–174). Malden, MA: Blackwell Publishing.

Solarsh, B., & Alant, E. (2006). The challenge of cross-cultural assessment: The test of ability to explain for Zulu speaking children. *Journal of Communication Disorders, 39,* 109–138.

Spangenberg, E. R., & Sprott, D. E. (2006). Self-monitoring and susceptibility to the influence of self-prophecy. *Journal of Consumer Research, 32,* 550–556.

Spinelli, C. (2006). *Classroom assessment for students in special and general education,* 2nd ed. Upper Saddle River, NJ: Person-Prentice Hall.

Stavans, I. (2002). The browning of America. *The Nation,* May 30. Retrieved from www.thenation.com/article/browning-america.

Stearns, E., & Glennie, E. J. (2006). When and why dropouts leave high school. *Youth and Society, 38,* 29–57.

Sullivan, A. (2011). Disproportionality in special education and placement of English language learners. *Exceptional Children V 77(3),* pp. 317–334. Arlington, VA. Council for Exceptional Children.

Teemant, A., Smith, M. E., & Pinnegar, S. (2003*). Bilingual/ESL endorsement through distance education program: Assessment for linguistically diverse students instruction guide,* 2nd ed. Provo, UT: Brigham Young University.

Trawick-Smith, J. (2006). *Early childhood development: A multicultural perspective,* 4th ed. Upper Saddle River, NJ: Person-Prentice Hall.

Trouilloud, D., Sarrazin, P., & Bressoux, P. (2006). Relation between teachers' early expectations and students' later perceived competence in physical education classes: Autonomy-supportive climate as a moderator. *Journal of Educational Psychology, 98,* 75–86.

U.S. Census Bureau. (2000). Fast Facts for Congress. *U.S. Census Bureau Race Data, Office of Management and Budget.* Retrieved from http://fast-facts.census.gov/servlet/CWSPeople?_event=&geo_id=01000US&_geoContext=01000US&_street=&_county=&_cd=&_cityTown=&_state=&_zip=&_lang=en&_sse=on&ActiveGeoDiv=&_useEV=&pctxt=fph&pgsl=010&_content=&_keyword=&_industry=.

U.S Census Bureau/ (2010a). Revisions to the standards for the classification of federal data on race and ethnicity. *U.S. Census Bureau Race Data, Office of Management and Budget.* Retrieved from www.census.gov/population/www/socdemo/race/Ombdir15.html.

U.S. Census Bureau (2010b). Fact finder. *U.S. Census Bureau, Office of Management and Budget.* Retrieved from http://factfinder2.census.gov/faces/nav/jsf/pages/index.xhtml.

U.S. Census Bureau. (2010c). Quickfacts. Retrieved from http://quickfacts.census.gov/qfd/states/00000.html.

U.S. Census Bureau. (2010d). Poverty. Retrieved from www.census.gov/hhes/www/poverty/data/incpovhlth/2010/tables.html.

U.S. Census Bureau. (2012). The 2012 Statistical Abstract, Table 79. Retrieved from www.census.gov/compendia/statab/cats/births_deaths_marriages_divorces.html.

U.S. Department of Education. (2012). *30th annual report to Congress on the implementation of the Individuals with Disabilities Education Act, 2008.* Washington, D.C.: U.S. Government Printing Office.

Vasquez, M J. R., Lott, V., & Garcia-Vazquez, E. (2006). Personal reflections: Barriers and strategies in increasing diversity in psychology. *American Psychologist, 61,* 157–172.

Vaughn, S., Linan-Thompson, S., Mathes, P. G., Cirino, P. T., Carlson, C. D., Pollard-Durodola, S. D., Gardenas-Hagan, E., & Francis, D. J. (2006). Effectiveness of Spanish intervention for first-grade English language learners at risk for reading difficulties. *Journal of Learning Disabilities, 39,* 56–73.

Waitoller, F. R., Artiles, A. J., Cheney, D. A. (2010). The Miner's Canary: A review of overrepresentation research and explanations. *The Journal of Special Education, 44*(1), 29–49. Austin, TX: Hamill Institute on Disabilities.

Wiese, A. M. (2006). Educational policy in the United States regarding bilinguals in early childhood education. In B. Spodek (Ed.), *Handbook of research on the education of young children,* 2nd ed. Mahwah, NJ: Lawrence Erlbaum Associates.

Wright, R. J. (2007). *Educational assessment: Tests and measurements in the age of accountability.* Thousand Oaks, CA: Sage Publications.

Chapter 6

Abbeduto, L., Seltzer, M. M., Shatuck, P., Krauss, M. W., Orsmond, G., & Murphy, M. M. (2004). Psychological well-being and coping in mothers of youths with autism, Down syndrome, and fragile X syndrome. *American Journal of Mental Retardation, 109*(3), 237–254.

Alonzo, J., Bushey, L., Gardner, D., Hasazi, S., Johnston, C., & Miller, P. (2006). 25 hours in family: How family internships can help school leaders transform from within. *Equity and Excellence in Education, 39*(2), 127–136.

Baker-Ericzén, M. J., Brookman-Frazee, L., & Stahmer, A. (2005). Stress levels and adaptability in parents of toddlers with and without autism spectrum disorders. *Research and Practice for Persons with Severe Disabilities, 30*(4), 194.

Bambara, L. M., & Knoster, T. P. (2009). *Designing positive behavior support plans,* 2nd ed. Washington, D.C.: American Association on Intellectual and Developmental Disabilities.

Banks, M. E. (2003). Disability in the family: A life span perspective. *Cultural Diversity and Ethnic Minority Psychology, 9*(4), 367–384.

Baranowski, M. D., & Schilmoeller, G. L. (1999). Grandparents in the lives of grandchildren with disabilities: Mothers' perceptions. *Education and Treatment of Children, 22,* 427–446.

Baskin, A., & Fawcett, H. (2006). *More than a mom: Living a full and balanced life when your child has special needs.* Bethesda, MD: Woodbine House.

Baxter, C., Cummins, R. A., & Yiolitis, L. (2000). Parental stress attributed to family members with and without disability: A longitudinal study. *Journal of Intellectual & Developmental Disability, 25,* 105–118.

Bertelli, Y., Silverman, J., & Talbot, S. (2009). *My baby rides the short bus.* Oakland California: PM Press.

Blue-Banning, M., Summers, J. A., Frankland, H. C., Nelson, L. L., & Beegle, G. (2004). Dimensions of family and professional partnerships: Constructive guidelines for collaboration. *Council for Exceptional Children, 70*(2), 167–184.

Boscardin, M. L., Brown-Chidsey, R., & Gonzalez-Martinez, J. C. (2001). The essential link for students with disabilities from diverse backgrounds. *Journal of Special Education Leadership, 14*(2), 89–95.

Bosworth, A. S. (2009). Jackpot! In Y. Bertelli, J. Silverman, and S. Talbot (Eds.), *My Baby rides the short bus* (pp. 144-151). Winnipeg, Canada: Fernwood Publishing.

Bree (2011). *Mama tells the whole story.* Retrieved on September 29, 2011 from http://thebuggslife .blogspot.com/2011/02/ buggs-story.html.

Brooke, V., & McDonough, J. T. (2008). The facts ma'am, just the facts: Social Securitdisability benefit programs and work incentives. *Teaching Exceptional Children, 41(1),* 58–65.

Brown, G. (2004). Family-centered care, mothers occupations of caregiving and home therapy programs. In S. A. Esdaile & J. A. Olson (Eds.), *Mothering occupations: Challenge, agency, and participations* (pp. 346–371). Philadelphia: F. A. Davis.

Bruder, M. B. (2000). Family-centered early intervention: Clarifying our values for the new millennium. *Topics in Early Childhood Special Education, 20,* 105–115, 122.

Bui, Y. N., & Turnbull, A. (2003). East meets West: Analysis of person-centered planning in the context of Asian American values. *Education and Training and Mental Retardation and Developmental Disabilities, 38*(1), 18–31.

Buschbacher, P., Fox, L., & Clarke, S. (2004). Recapturing desired family routines: A parent-professional behavioral collaboration. *Research and Practice for Persons with Severe Disabilities, 2*(1), 25–39.

Capitani, J. (2007). What to do with a boy. In K. L. Soper & M. Sears (Eds.), *Gifts: Mothers reflect on how children with Down syndrome enrich their lives* (pp. 10–15). Bethesda, MD: Woodhouse, Inc.

Carpenter, Barry (2000). Sustaining the family: Meeting the needs of families of children with disabilities. *British Journal of Special Education, 27,* 135–144.

Chambers, C. R. (2007). Siblings of individuals with disabilities who enter careers in the disability field. *Teacher Education and Special Education, 30*(3), 115–127.

Chambers, C. R., Hughes, C., & Carter, E. W. (2004). Parent and sibling perspectives on the transition to adulthood. *Education and Training in Developmental Disabilities, 39(2),* 79–94.

Chan, J. B., & Sigafoos, J. (2000). A review of child and family characteristics related to the use of respite care in developmental disability services. *Child and Youth Care Forum, 29,* 27–37.

Chapadjiew, S. (2009). My mama drove the short bus. In Y. Bertelli, J. Silverman, & S. Talbot (Eds.), *My baby rides the short bus: The unabashedly experience of raising kids with disabilities* (pp. 201–211). Oakland, CA: PM Press.

Connors, C., & Stalker, K. (2003). *The views and experiences of disabled children and their siblings: A positive outlook.* London: Jessica Kingsley Publishers.

Correa, I., Hudson, R. F., & Hayes, M. T. (2004). Preparing early childhood special educators to serve culturally and linguistically diverse children and families: Can a multicultural education course make a difference? *Teacher Education and Special Education, 27*(4), 323–341.

Cox, C. (2008), Supporting grandparent-headed families. *The Prevention Researcher, 15,* 14–16.

Darley, S., Porter, J., Werner, J., & Eberly, S. (2002). Families tell us what makes families strong. *Exceptional Parent, 32,* 34–36.

Dempsey, I., & Keen, D. (2008). A review of processes and outcomes in family-centered services for children with a disability. *Topics in Early Childhood Special Education, 28*(1), 42–52.

Dollahite, D.C. (2001, August). Beloved children, faithful fathers: Caring for children with special needs. *Marriage and Families,* 16–21.

Dunlap, G., & Fox, L. (2007). Parent-professional partnerships: A valuable context for addressing challenging behaviors. *International Journal of Development, Disability and Education, 54*(3), 273-285.

Dunst, C. J. (2002). Family-centered practices: Birth through high school. *Journal of Special Education, 36,* 139–147.

Dunst, C. J., & Dempsey, I. (2007). Family–

professional partnerships and parenting competence, confidence, and enjoyment. *International Journal of Disability, Development and Education, 54*(3), 305–318.

Epley, P., Gotto, G. S., Summer, J. A., Brotherson, M. J., Turnbull, A. P., & Friend, A. (2010). Supporting families of young children with disabilities: Examining the role of administrative structures. *Topics in Early Childhood Special Education, 30*(1), 20–31.

Epstein, S. H., & Bessel, A. G. (2002). A parent's determination and a pre-K dream realized. *Exceptional Parent, 32*, 56–60.

Ferguson, Philip M. (2002). A place in the family: An historical interpretation of research on parental reactions to having a child with a disability. *Journal of Special Education, 36*, 124–130.

Fine, M. J., & Nissenbaum, M. S. (2000). The child with disabilities and the family: Implications for professionals. In M. J. Fine & R. L. Simpson (Eds.), *Collaboration with parents and families of children with exceptionalities,* 2nd ed. (pp. 3–26). Austin, TX: PROED.

Fine, M. J., & Simpson, R. L. (2000). *Collaboration with parents and families of children with exceptionalities,* 2nd ed. Austin, TX: PRO-ED.

Fischer, S. (1994). Fathers are caregivers too! *Exceptional Parent, 24*(8), 43.

Fish, M. C. (2000). Children with special needs in nontraditional families. In M. J. Fine & R. L.

Simpson (Eds.), *Collaboration with parents and families of children with exceptionalities,* 2nd ed. (pp. 49–68). Austin, TX: PRO-ED.

Fox, L., & Dunlap, G. (2002). Family-centered practices in positive behavior support. *Beyond Behavior,* 24–26.

Fox, L., Vaughn, B. J., Wyatte, M. L., & Dunlap, G. (2002). "We can't expect other people to understand": Family perspectives on problem behavior. *Exceptional Children, 68*, 437–450.

Frankland, H. C., Edmonson, H., & Turnbull, A. P. (2001). Positive behavioral support: Family, school, and community partnerships. *Beyond Behavior,* 7–9.

Frankland, H. C., Turnbull, A. P., Wehmeyer, M. L., & Blackmountain, L. (2004). An exploration of the self-determination construct and disability as it relates to the Diné (Navajo) culture. *Education and Training in Developmental Disabilities, 39*(3), 191–205.

Friend, M., & Cook, L. (2003). *Interactions: Collaboration skills for school professionals,* 4th ed. Boston: Allyn and Bacon.

Frost, Jennifer. (2002). Sarah syndrome: A mother's view of having a child with no diagnosis. *Exceptional Parent, 32*, 70–71.

Fujiuara, G. T., & Yamaki, K. (2000). Trends in demography of childhood poverty and disability. *Exceptional Children, 66,* 187–199.

Gallagher, G., & Konjoian, P. (2010). *Shut up about*

your perfect kid: A survival guide for ordinary parents of special children. New York: Three Rivers Press.

Gallagher, P. A., Rhodes, C. H., & Darling, S. M. (2004). Parents as professionals in early intervention. *Topics in Early Childhood Special Education, 24* (1), 5–13.

Gaventa, B. (2008). Spiritual and religious supports: What difference to they make? *Exceptional Parent, 38*(3), 66–68.

Geisthardt, C., Brotherson, M., & Cook, C. (2002). Friendships of children with disabilities in the home environment. *Education and Training in Mental Retardation and Developmental Disabilities, 37*, 235–52.

Givens, A. S. (2009). This is what love looks like. In Y. Bertelli, J. Silverman, and S. Talbot (Eds.), *My Baby rides the short bus* (pp. 293–298). Winnipeg, Canada: Fernwood Publishing.

Gorman, J. C. (2004). *Working with challenging parents of students with special needs*. Thousand Oaks, CA: Corwin Press.

Gotto, G. S., Beauchamp, D., & Simpson, M. (2007). Early childhood family supports community of practice . . . Creating knowledge and wisdom through community conversations. *Exceptional Parent, 37*(8), 52–53.

Gray, David E. (2002). Ten years on: A longitudinal study of families of children with autism. *Journal of Intellectual and Developmental Disability, 27*, 215–222.

Griffith, G. M., Hastings, R. P., Oliver, C., Howlin,

P., Moss, J., Petty, J., & Tunnicliffe, P. (2011). Psychological well-being in parents of children with Angelman, Cornelia de Lange and Cri du Chat syndromes. *Journal of Intellectual Disability Research, 55*(4), 397–410.

Grissom, M. O., & Borkowski, J. G. (2002). Self-efficacy in adolescents who have siblings with or without disabilities. *American Journal on Mental Retardation, 107*(2), 79–90.

Harland, P., & Cuskelly, M. (2000). The responsibilities of adult siblings of adults with dual sensory impairments. *International Journal of Disability Development and Education, 47*, 293–307.

Hastings, R. P. (2006). Longitudinal relationships between sibling behavioral adjustment and behavior problems of children with developmental disabilities. *Journal of Autism and Developmental Disorders, 37*, 1,485–1,492.

Hastings, R. P., Daley, D., Burns, C., & Beck, A. (2006). Maternal distress and expressed emotion: Cross-sectional and longitudinal relationships with behavior problems of children with intellectual disabilities. *American Journal on Mental Retardation, 111*(1), 48–61.

Hastings, R. P., & Taunt, H. M. (2002). Positive perceptions in families of children with developmental disabilities. *American Journal on Mental Retardation, 107*, 116–127.

Hauser-Cram, P. (2006). Young children with

developmental disabilities and their families: Needs, policies, and services. In K. M. Thies & J. F. Travers (Eds.), *Handbook of human development for health care professionals* (pp. 287–305). Boston: Jones and Bartlett Publishers.

Hauser-Cram, P., Warfield, M. E., Shonkoff, J. P., Krauss, M. W. (2001). Children with disabilities: A longitudinal study of child development and parent well-being. *Monographs of the Society for Research in Child Development, 66*, 1–114.

Heiman, T., & Berger, O. (2008). Parents of children with Asperger syndrome or with learning disabilities: Family environment and social support. *Research in Developmental Disabilities, 29*(4), 289-300.

Jackson, C. W., & Turnbull, A. (2004). Impact of deafness on family life: A review of the literature. *TECSE, 24*(1), 15–29.

Johnson, C. (2000). What do families need? *Journal of Positive Behavior Interventions, 2*, 115–1

Kazdin, A.E. (2005). Parent management training: Treatment for oppositional, aggressive, and antisocial behavior in children and adolescents. New York: Oxford University Press.

Keen, D. (2007). Parents, families, and partnerships: Issues and considerations. *International Journal of Disability, Development and Education, 54*(3), 339–349.

Knox, M., & Bigby, C. (2007). Moving towards midlife care as negotiated family business:

Accounts of people with intellectual disabilities and their families "Just getting along with their lives together." *International Journal of Disability, Development, and Education, 54*(3), 287–304.

Kolb, S. M., & Hanley-Maxwell, C. (2003). Critical social skills for adolescents with high incidence disabilities: Parental perspectives. *Council for Exceptional Children, 69*, 163–179.

Lach, L.M., Kohen, D. E., Garner, R. E., Brehaut, J. C., Miller, A. R., Klassen, A. F., & Rosenbaum, P. L. (2009). The health and psychological functioning of caregivers of children with neurodevelopmental disorders. *Disability and Rehabilitation, 31*(8), 607–618.

Laman, E., & Shaughnessy, M. F. (2007). An interview with Don Meyer on siblings of individuals with disabilities. *Exceptional Parent, 37*(7), 42–46.

Lamb, M. E., & Meyer, D. J. (1991). Fathers of children with special needs. In M. Seligman (Ed.), *The family with a handicapped child,* 2nd ed. (pp. 151–180). Boston: Allyn and Bacon

Larson, Elizabeth A. (2000). The orchestration of occupation: The dance of mothers. *American Journal of Occupational Therapy, 54*, 269–280.

Lee, A. L., Strauss, L., Wittman, P., Jackson, B., & Carstens, A. (2001). The effects of chronic illness on roles and emotions of caregivers. *Occupational Therapy in Health Care,* 14, 47–60.

Lee, M., & Gardner, J. M. (2010). Grandparents' involvement and support in families with children with disabilities. *Educational Gerontology, 36*(6), 467–499.

Lee, S., Poston, D., & Poston, A. J. (2007). Lessons learned through implementing a positive behavior support intervention at home: A case study on self-management with a student with autism and his mother. *Education and Training in Developmental Disabilities, 42*(4), 418–427.

Levinson, E. M., McKee, L., & DeMatteo, F. J. (2000). The exceptional child grows up: Transition from school to adult life. In M. J. Fine & R. L. Simpson (Eds.), *Collaboration with parents and families of children with exceptionalities,* 2nd ed. (pp. 409–436). Austin, TX: PRO-ED.

Lobato, D. J., Kao, B.T., & Plante, W. (2005). Latina sibling knowledge and adjustment to chronic disability. *Journal of Family Psychology, 19*(4), 625–632.

Luckner, J. L. & Velaski, A. (2004). Healthy families of children who are deaf. *American Annals of the Deaf, 149*(4), 324–335.

Lucyshyn, J. M., Dunlap, G., & Albin, R. W. (2002). *Families and positive behavior support: Addressing problem behavior in family contexts.* Baltimore, MD: Paul H. Brooks Publishing Company.

MacInnes, M. D. (2008). One's enough for now: Children, disability, and the subsequent childbearing of mothers.

Journal of Marriage and Family, 70(3), 758–771.

Mallory, B. L. (2010). An ecocultural perspective on family support in rural special education. *Rural Special Education Quarterly, 29*(2), 12–17.

Mara, M. (2010). Guilt, denial, and videotape. In K. Anderson & V. Foreman (Eds.), *Gravity pulls you in: Perspectives on parenting children with autism spectrum* (p. 11–21). Bethesda, MD: Woodbine House.

Marks, S. U., Matson, A., & Barraza, L. (2005). The impact of siblings with disabilities on their brothers and sisters pursuing a career in special education. *Research and Practice for Persons with Severe Disabilities, 30*(4), 205–218.

Martin, J. E., Van Dycke, J. L., Greene, B. A., Gardner, J. E., Christensen, W. R., Woods, L. L., & Lovett, D. L. (2006). Direct observation of teacher-directed IEP meetings: Establishing the need for student IEP meeting instruction. *Council for Exceptional Children, 72*(2), 187–200.

Matuszny, R. M., Banda, D. R., & Coleman, T. J. (2007). A progressive plan for building collaborative relationships with parents from diverse backgrounds. *Teaching Exceptional Children, 39*(4), 24–31.

McCarthy, A., Cuskelly, M., van Kraayenoord, C. E., & Cohen, J. (2006). Predictors of stress in mothers and fathers of children with fragile X syndrome. *Research in Developmental Disabilities, 27*, 688–704.

McHatton, P. A. (2007). Listening and learning from Mexican and Puerto Rican single mothers of children with disabilities. *Teacher Education and Special Education, 30*(4), 257–248.

McHatton, P.A., & Correa, V. (2005). Stigma and discrimination: Perspectives from Mexican and Puerto Rican mothers of children with special needs. *Topics in Early Childhood Education, 25*(3), 131–142.

McHugh, M. (2003). *Special siblings: Growing up with someone with a disability.* Baltimore: Paul H. Brooks Publishing Company.

McKie, F. (2006). Heather at the neurologist's. *Equity and Excellence in Education, 39*(2), 115–123.

Meyer, D. (Ed.). (2005). *The sibling slam book: What it's really like to have a brother or sister with special needs.* Bethesda, MD: Woodbine House.

Muscott, H. S. (2002). Exceptional partnerships: Listening to the voices of families. *Preventing School Failure, 46*, 66–69.

Nagler, M. (2011). *Finding out your child has a disability: It's not the end of the world.* Retrieved August 19, 2011 from www.allthatwomenwant.com/childdisability.htm.

Neece, C. L., Blacher, J., & Baker, B. L. (2010). Impact on siblings of children with intellectual disability: The role of child behavior problems. *American Journal on Intellectual and Developmental Disabilities, 115*(4), 291–306.

Ong-Dean, C. (2009). *Distinguishing disability.* Chicago, IL: University of Chicago Press.

Orgassa, U. C. (2005). Beyond crisis intervention: Services for families with children with disabilities. In F. K. O. Yuen (Ed.), *Social work practice with children and families: A family health approach* (pp. 73–88). New York: The Haworth Press, Inc.

Orsmond, G.I., Lin, L., & Seltzer, M. M. (2007). Mothers of adolescents and adults with autism: Parenting multiple children with disabilities. *Intellectual and Developmental Disabilities,45*(4), 257–270.

Ortiz, S. O. (2006). Multicultural issues in working with children and families: Responsive intervention in the educational setting. In R. B. Mennuti, A. Freeman, & R. W. Christner (Eds.), *Cognitive-behavioral interventions in educational settings* (pp. 21–36). New York: Routledge Taylor & Francis Group.

Parentlink (2011). *Children with a disability.* Retrieved August 18, 2011 from www.parentlink.act.gov.au/parenting_guides/all_ages/children_with_a_disability.

Parette, H. P., Meadan, H., & Doubet, S. (2010). Fathers of young children with disabilities in the United States: Current status and implications. *Childhood Education, 86*(6), 382–388.

Parish, S. L., Rose, R. A., Grinstein-Weiss, M., Richman, E. L., & Andrews, M. E. (2008). Material hardship in U.S. families raising children with disabilities. *Exceptional Children, 75*, 71–92.

Park, J., Turnbull, A. P., & Turnbull, H. R. (2002). Impacts of poverty on quality of life in families of children with disabilities. *Exceptional Children, 68*(2), 151–170.

Pinkham, B. E. (2010). Is there anything else we should know? In K. Adnerson & V. Forman (Eds.), *Gravity pulls us in: Perspectives on parenting children with autism spectrum* (pp181-188). Bethesda, MD: Woodbine House, Inc.

Pipp-Siegel, S., Sedey, A. L., & Yoshinaga-Itano, C. (2002). Predictors of parental stress in mothers of young children with hearing loss. *Journal of Deaf Studies and Deaf Education, 7*, 1–17.

Poston, D., Turnbull, A., Park, J., Mannan, H., Marquis, J., & Wang, M. (2003). Family quality of life: A qualitative inquiry. *American Association on Mental Health, 41(5)*, 313–328.

Poston, D.J., & Turnbull, A. P. (2004). Role of spirituality and religion in family quality of life for families of children with disabilities. *Education and Training in Developmental Disabilities, 39*(2), 95–108.

Raver, S. A. (2005). Using family-based practices for young children with special needs in preschool programs. *Childhood Education, 82(1)*, 9–13.

Rieger, A., & Scotti, J. (2004). Make it just as normal as possible with humor. *Mental Retardation, 42*(6), 427–444.

Risdal, D., & Singer, G. H. S. (2004). Marital adjustment in parents of children with disabilities: A historical review and meta-analysis. *Research & Practice for Persons with Severe Disabilities, 29*(2), 95–103.

Rivers, Kenyatta O. (2000). Working with caregivers of infants and toddlers with special needs from culturally and linguistically diverse backgrounds. *Infant Toddler Intervention: The Transdisciplinary Journal, 10*, 61–72.

Rummel-Hudson, R. (2008). *Schuyler's monster: A father's journey with his wordless daughter.* New York: St. Martin's Press.

Rupiper, M., & Marvin, C. (2004). Preparing teachers for family centered services: A survey of preservice curriculum content. *Teacher Education and Special Education, 27*(4), 384–395.

Russell, L. M., & Grant, A. E. (2005). *Planning for the future: Providing a meaningful life for a child with a disability after your death.* Palatine, IL: Planning for the Future, Inc.

Sandler, A. G., Warren, S. H., & Raver, S. A. (1995). Grandparents as a source of support for parents of children with disabilities. A brief report. *Mental Retardation, 33*(August), 248–250.

Santelli, B., Ginsberg, C., Sullivan, S., & Niederhauser, (2002). A collaborative study of parent to parent program: Implications for positive behavior support. In J. M. Lucyshyn & G. Dunlap (Eds.), *Families and positive behavior support: Addressing problem behavior in family contexts* (pp. 439–456). Baltimore, MD: Paul H. Brooks Publishing Company.

Scherman, A., Gardner, J. E., & Brown, P. (1995). Grandparents' adjustment to grandchildren with disabilities. *Educational Gerontology, 21*(April/May), 261–273.

Segal, R. (2004). Mother time: The art and skill of scheduling in families of children with attention deficit hyperactivity disorders. In S. A. Esdaile & J. A. Olson (eds.), *Mothering occupations: Challenge, agency, and participations* (pp. 324–345). Philadelphia: F. A. Davis.

Seligman, M., & Darling, R. B. (1989). *Ordinary families, special children.* New York: Guilford Press.

Senal, S. (2010). Sometimes, never. In K. Anderson & V. Foreman (Eds.), *Gravity pulls you in: Perspectives on parenting children with autism spectrum* (p. 49–57). Bethesda, MD: Woodbine House.

Shelden, M. L., & Rush, D. D. (2001). The ten myths about providing early intervention services in natural environments. *Infants and Young Children, 14*, 1–13.

Siklos, S., & Kerns, K. A. (2007). Assessing the diagnostic experiences of a small number of children with autism spectrum disorders. *Research in Developmental Disabilities, 28*, 9–22.

Simmerman, S., Blacher, J., & Baker, B. L. (2001). Fathers' and mothers' perceptions of father involvement in families with young children with a disability. *Journal of Intellectual and Developmental Disability, 26*, 325–338.

Skotko, B., & Levine, S. P. (2009). *Fasten you seatbelt: A crash course on Down syndrome for brothers and sisters.* Bethesda, MD: Woodbine House.

Snow, K. (2001). *Disability is natural: Revolutionary common sense for raising successful children with disabilities.* Woodland Park, CO: BraveHeart Press.

Steeves, P. (2006). Sliding doors—Opening our world. *Equity and Excellence in Education, 39*(2), 105–114.

Stone, J. H. (Ed.). (2005). *Culture and disability: Providing culturally competent services.* In *Multicultural Aspects of Counseling Series 21.* London: Sage Publications.

Stoneman, Z. (2005). Siblings of children with disabilities: Research themes. *Mental Retardation, 43*(5), 339–350.

Stoneman Z. (2007). Examining the Down syndrome advantage: Mothers and fathers of young children with disabilities. *Journal of Intellectual Disability Research, 51*(12), 1,006–1,017.

Stoneman, Z., & Gavidia-Payne, S. (2006). Marital adjustment in families of young children with disabilities: Associations with daily hassles and problem-focused coping. *American Journal of Mental Retardation, 111*(1), 1–14.

Strohm, K. (2005). *Being the other one: Growing up with a brother or sister who has special needs.* Boston: Shambhala Publications, Inc.

Turbiville, Vicki. (1997). *Literature review: Fathers, their children, and disability.* Lawrence, KS: The Beach Center on Families and Disability, The University of Kansas.

Turbiville, V. P., & Marquis, J. G. (2001). Father participation in early education programs. *Topics in Early Childhood Special Education, 21*, 223–231.

Turnbull, A. P., & Turnbull, H. R. (2002). From the old to the new paradigm of disabilities and families: Research to enhance family quality and life outcomes. In J. L. Paul, C. D. Lavely, A. Cranston-Gingras, & E. L. Taylor (Eds.), *Rethinking professional issues in special education.* Westport, CN.

Turner, M. H. (2000). The developmental nature of parent-child relationships: The impact of disabilities. In M. J. Fine & R. L. Simpson (Eds.), *Collaboration with parents and families of children with exceptionalities,* 2nd ed. (pp. 103–130). Austin, TX: PRO-ED.

Tynan, W. D., & Wornian, K. (2002). Parent management training: Efficacy, effectiveness, and barriers to implementation. *Report on Emotional and Behavioral Disorders in Youth, 2*, 57–58, 71–72.

Ulrich, M. E. (2003). Levels of awareness: A closer look at communication between parents and professionals. *TEACHING Exceptional Children, 35*(6), 20–23.

Vacca, J., & Feinberg, E. (2000). Why can't families be more like us?: Henry Higgins confronts Eliza Doolittle in the world of early intervention. *Infants and Young Children, 13*, 40–48.

Verté, S., Hebbrecht, L., & Roeyers, H. (2006). Psychological adjustment of siblings of children who are deaf or hard of hearing. *The Volta Review, 106*(1), 89–110.

Wang, M., Turnbull, A. P., Summers, J. A., Little, T. D., Poston, D. J., Mannan, H., & Turnbull, R. (2004). Severity of disability and income as predictors of parents' satisfaction with their family quality of life during early childhood years. *Research & Practice for Persons with Severe Disabilities, 29*(2), 82–94.

Ward, M. J., Cronin, K. B., Renfro, P. D., Lowman, D. K., & Cooper, P. D. (2000). Oral motor feeding in the neonatal intensive care unit: Exploring perceptions of parents and occupational therapists. *Occupational Therapy in Health Care, 12*, 19–37.

Whitbread, K. M., Bruder, M. B., Fleming, G., & Park, H. J. (2007). Collaboration in special education: Parent-professional training. *Teaching Exceptional Children, 39*(4), 6–14.

Worthington, J., Hernandez, M., Friedman B., & Uzzell, D. (2001). *Systems of care: Promising practices in children's mental health, 2001 Series, Volume 11.* Washington D.C.: Center for Effective Collaboration and Practice, American Institutes for Research.

Young, D. M., & Roopnarine, J. L. (1994). Fathers' childcare involvement with children with and without disabilities.

Topic in Early Childhood Special Education, 14 (Winter), 488–502.

Young, E. L., Calderella, P., Richardson, M. J., and Young K. R. (2011). *Positive behavior support in secondary schools: A practical guide.* New York: Guilford Press.

Zhang, C., & Bennett, T. (2001). Multicultural views of disability: Implications for early intervention professionals. *Infant Toddler Intervention: The Transdisciplinary Journal, 11,* 143–154.

Chapter 7

Aaron, P. G., Joshi, R. M., Gooden, R., & Bentum, K. E. (2008). Diagnosis and treatment of reading disabilities based on the component model of reading: An alternative to the discrepancy model of LD. *Journal of Learning Disabilities, 41*(1), 67–84.

Abbott, L., McConkey, R., & Dobbins, M. (2011). Key players in inclusion: Are we meeting the professional needs of learning support assistants for pupils with complex needs? *European Journal of Special Needs Education, 26*(2), 215–231.

Abreu-Ellis, C., Ellis, J., & Hayes, R. (2009). College preparedness and time of learning disability identification. *Journal of Developmental Education, 32(*3), 28–30, 32, 34–38.

Accardo, P. J. (Ed.). (2008). *Capute and Accardo's neurodevelopmental disabilities in infancy and childhood: Vol 1: Neurodevelopmental diagnosis and treatment,* 3rd ed. Baltimore: Paul H. Brookes Publishing.

Alexander, C. P. (1994). Brain bane: Researchers may have found a cause for dyslexia. *Time, 144(9),* 61.

Algozzine, B., Wang, C., & Violette, A. S. (2011). Re-examining the relationship between academic achievement and social behavior. *Journal of Positive Behavior Interventions, 13*(1), 3–16.

Al-Yagon, M. (2009). Co-morbid LD and ADHD in childhood: Socioemotional and behavioural adjustment and parents' positive and negative affect. *European Journal of Special Needs Education, 24*(4), 371–391.

American Psychiatric Association. (2000). *Diagnostic and statistical manual of mental disorders,* 4th ed., text rev. Washington, D.C.: Author.

American Speech-Language-Hearing Association. (2005). (Central) auditory processing disorders—The role of the audiologist [Position statement]. Available from www.asha.org/policy.

Anderko, L., Braun, J., & Auinger, P. (2010). Contribution of tobacco smoke exposure to learning disabilities. *Journal Of Obstetric, Gynecologic, And Neonatal Nursing: JOGNN / NAACO, 3*9(1), 111–117.

Armbruster, B. B., Lehr, F., & Osborn, J. (2006). *Put reading first: The research building blocks for teaching children to read. Kindergarten through grade 3,* 3rd ed. Jessup, MD: National Institute for Literacy.

Baird, G., Dworzynski, K., Slonims, V., & Simonoff, E. (2010). Memory impairment in children with language impairment. *Developmental Medicine & Child Neurology, 52*(6), 535–540.

Banister, S. (2010). Integrating the iPod Touch in K-12 education: Visions and vices. *Computers in the Schools, 27*(2), 121–131.

Barrera, M., & Liu, K. K. (2010). Challenges of general outcomes measurement in the RTI progress monitoring of linguistically diverse exceptional learners. *Theory Into Practice, 49*(4), 273–280.

Barron, D. A., & Hassiotis, A. (2008). Good practice in transition services for young people with learning disabilities: A review. *Advances in Mental Health and Intellectual Disabilities, 2*(3), 18–24.

Becker, A., McLaughlin, T. M., Weber, K. P., & Gower, J. (2009). The effects of copy, cover and compare with and without additional error drill on multiplication fact fluency and accuracy. *Electronic Journal of Research in Educational Psychology, 7*(2), 747–760.

Beirne-Smith, M., & Riley, T. F. (2009). Spelling assessment of students with disabilities: Formal and informal procedures. *Assessment for Effective Intervention, 34*(3), 170–177.

Bender, W. N. (2008a). *Learning disabilities: Characteristics, identification, and teaching strategies,* 6th ed. Boston: Allyn and Bacon.

Bender, W. N. (2008b). *Differentiating instruction for students with learning disabilities,* 2nd ed. Thousand Oaks, CA: Sage Publications.

Bender, W. N., & Waller, L. (2011). *The teaching revolution: RTI, technology, and differentiation transform teaching for the 21st century.* Thousand Oaks, CA: Corwin.

Berkeley, S., Mastropieri, M. A., & Scruggs, T. E. (2011). Reading comprehension strategy instruction and attribution retraining for secondary students with learning and other mild disabilities. *Journal of Learning Disabilities, 44*(1), 18–32.

Berkeley, S., Scruggs, T. E., & Mastropieri, M. A. (2010). Reading comprehension instruction for students with learning disabilities, 1995–2006: A meta-analysis. *Remedial & Special Education, 31*(6), 423–436.

Berninger, V. W., & May, M. O. (2011). Evidence-based diagnosis and treatment for specific learning disabilities involving impairments in written and/or oral language. *Journal of Learning Disabilities, 44*(2), 167–183.

Bloom, E., & Heath, N. (2010). Recognition, expression, and understanding facial expressions of emotion in adolescents with nonverbal and general learning disabilities. *Journal of Learning Disabilities, 43*(2), 180–192.

Blue, E., & Tirotta, R. (2011). The benefits & drawbacks of integrating cloud computing and interactive whiteboards in teacher preparation. *TechTrends: Linking Research and Practice to Improve Learning, 55*(3), 31–39.

Bock, S. J, Michalak, N., & Brownlee, S. (2011). Collaboration and consultation: The first steps. In C. G. Simpson & J. P. Bakken (Eds.), *Collaboration: A multidisciplinary approach to educating students with disabilities* (pp. 3–15). Waco, TX: Prufrock Press.

Bolt, S. E., Decker, D. M., & Lloyd, M. (2011). Students' perceptions of accommodations in high school and college. *Career Development for Exceptional Individuals, 34*(3), 165–175.

Bond, R. J., & Hurst, J. (2010). How adults with learning disabilities view living independently. *British Journal of Learning Disabilities, 38*(4), 286–292.

Buitelaar, J. K., Wilens, T. E., Shuyu Z., Yu N., & Feldman, P. D. (2009). Comparison of symptomatic versus functional changes in children and adolescents with ADHD during randomized, double-blind treatment with psychostimulants, atomoxetine, or placebo. *Journal of Child Psychology & Psychiatry, 50*(3), 335–342.

Buttner, G., & Hasselhorn, M. (2011). Learning disabilities: Debates on definitions, causes, subtypes, and responses. *International Journal of Disability, Development and Education, 58*(1), 75–87.

Cahill, S. M. (2009). Where does handwriting fit in? Strategies to support academic achievement. *Intervention in School and Clinic, 44*(4), 223–228.

Carnaby, S., Roberts, B., Lang, J., & Nielsen, P. (2011). A flexible response: Person–centered support and social inclusion for people with learning disabilities and challenging behaviour. *British Journal of Learning Disabilities, 39*(1), 39–45.

Carter, E. W., Trainor, A. A., & Ditchman, N. (2011). Community-based summer work experiences of adolescents with high-incidence disabilities. *Journal of Special Education 45*(2), 89–103.

Cerdan, R., Gilabert, R., & Vidal-Abarca, E. (2011). Selecting information to answer questions: Strategic individual differences when searching texts. *Learning and Individual Differences, 21*(2), 201–205.

Cleary, M. J., & Scott, A. J. (2011). Developments in clinical neuropsychology: Implications for school psychological services. *Journal of School Health, 81*(1), 1–7.

Cobb, R. B., & Alwell, M. (2009). Transition planning/coordinating interventions for youth with disabilities: A systematic review. *Career Development for Exceptional Individuals, 32*(2), 70–81.

Cooper, L. L., & Tomayko, M. C. (2011). Understanding place value. *Teaching Children Mathematics, 17*(9), 558–567.

Council for Exceptional Children. (2009). *What every special educator must know: Ethics, standards and guidelines,* 6th ed. Arlington, VA: Author.

Cowden, P. A. (2010a). Social anxiety in children with disabilities. *Journal of Instructional Psychology, 37*(4), 301–305.

Cowden, P. A. (2010b). Preparing college students with moderate learning disabilities with the tools for higher level success. *College Student Journal, 44*(2), 230–233.

Coyne, M. D., Zipoli Jr., R. P., Chard, D. J., Faggella-Luby, M., Ruby, M., Santoro, L. E., & Baker, S. (2009). Direct instruction of comprehension: Instructional examples from intervention research on listening and reading comprehension. *Reading & Writing Quarterly: Overcoming Learning Difficulties, 25*(2–3), 221–245.

Crick. (2011). *WriteOnline.* Westport, CT: Crick . Available at www.cricksoft .com/us/products/tools/ writeonline/default.aspx.

Cumella, S. (2009). Mental health services for people with a learning disability. *Advances in Mental Health and Intellectual Disabilities, 3*(2), 8–14.

DaDeppo, L. M. W. (2009). Integration factors related to the academic success and intent to persist of college students with learning disabilities. *Learning Disabilities Research & Practice, 24*(3), 122–131.

Davis, J. M., & Broitman, J. (2011). *Nonverbal learning disabilities in children: Bridging the gap between science and practice.* New York, NY: Springer Science + Business Media.

Davis, O. S. P., Haworth, C. M. A., & Plomin, R. (2009). Learning abilities and disabilities: Generalist genes in early adolescence. *Cognitive Neuropsychiatry, 14*(4–5), 312–331.

Daviso, A. W., Denney, S. C., & Baer, R. M. (2011). Postschool goals and transition services for students with learning disabilities. *American Secondary Education, 39*(2), 77–93.

Deacon, S. H., Leblanc, D., & Sabourin, C. (2011). When cues collide: Children's sensitivity to letter- and meaning-patterns in spelling words in English. *Journal of Child Language, 38*(4), 809–827.

Dean, V. J., Burns, M. K., & Grialou, T. (2006). Comparison of ecological validity of learning disabilities diagnostic models. *Psychology in the Schools, 43*, 157–168.

Desoete, A., Ceulemans, A., & Roeyers, H. (2009). Subitizing or counting as possible screening variables for learning disabilities in mathematics education or learning. *Educational Research Review, 4*(1), 55–66.

Dettmer, P. A., Knackendoffel, A. J., Thurston, L. P., & Sellberg, N. J. (2009). *Consultation, collaboration, and teamwork for students with special needs,* 6th ed. Boston: Allyn and Bacon.

Devine, M., Taggart, L., & McLornian, P. (2010). Screening for mental health problems in adults with learning disabilities using the Mini PAS-ADD Interview. *British Journal of Learning Disabilities, 38*(4), 252–258.

Dexter, D. D., & Hughes, C. A. (2011). Graphic organizers and students with learning disabilities: A meta-analysis. *Learning Disability Quarterly, 34*(1), 51–72.

Ditterline, J., Banner, D., & Oakland, T. (2008). Adaptive behavior profiles of students with disabilities. *Journal of Applied School Psychology, 24*(2), 191–208.

Dufault, R., Schnoll, R., Lukiw, W. J., Leblanc, B., Cornett, C., Patrick, L., Wallinga, D., Gilbert, S. G., & Crider, R. (2009). Mercury exposure, nutritional deficiencies and metabolic disruptions may affect learning in children. *Behavioral and Brain Functions: BBF 5*, 44.

Dunn, M. W. (2010). Defining learning disability: does IQ have anything significant to say? *Learning Disabilities: A Multidisciplinary Journal, 16*(1), 31–40.

DuPaul, G. J. (2008). Attention deficit hyperactivity disorder. In R. J. Morris & T. R. Kratochwill (eds.), *The practice of child therapy,* 4th ed. (pp. 143–186). Mahwah, NJ: Lawrence Erlbaum Associates Publishers.

Eisenman, L. T., Pleet, Amy M., & Wandry, D. (2011). Voices of special education teachers in an inclusive high school: Redefining responsibilities. *Remedial and Special Education, 32*(2), 91–104.

Elias, M. J., & Leverett, L. (2011). Consultation to urban schools for improvements in academics and behavior: No alibis. No excuses. No exceptions. *Journal of Educational & Psychological Consultation, 21*(1), 28–45.

Farmer, T. W., Hall, C. M., & Weiss, M. P. (2011). The school adjustment of rural adolescents with and without disabilities: Variable and person-centered approaches. *Journal of Child and Family Studies, 20*(1), 78–88.

Fasmer, O. B., Riise, T., Eagan, T. M., Lund, A., Dilsaver, S. C., Hundal, Ø., & Oedegaard, K. J. (2011). Comorbidity of asthma with ADHD. *Journal of Attention Disorders, 15*(7), 564–571.

Ferguson, M., Jarrett, D., & Terras, M. (2011). Inclusion and healthcare choices: The experiences of adults with learning disabilities. *British Journal of Learning Disabilities, 39*(1), 73–83.

Fey, M. E., Richard, G. J., Geffner, D., Kamhi, A. G., Medwetsky, L., Paul, D., Ross-Swain, D., Wallach, G. P., Frymark, T., & Schooling, T. (2011). Auditory processing disorder and auditory/language interventions: An evidence-based systematic review. *Language, Speech, and Hearing Services in Schools, 42*(3), 246–264.

Firth, N., Frydenberg, E., & Greaves, D. (2008). Perceived control and adaptive coping: Programs for adolescent students who have learning disabilities. *Learning Disability Quarterly, 31*(3), 151–165.

Fischer, B., Köngeter, A., & Hartnegg, K. (2008). Effects of daily practice on subitizing, visual counting, and basic arithmetic skills. *Optometry and Vision Development, 39*(1), 30–34.

Friend, A., & Olson, R. K. (2008). Phonological spelling and reading deficits in children with spelling disabilities. *Scientific Studies of Reading, 12*(1), 90–105.

Fuchs, D., Compton, D. L., & Fuchs, L. S. (2011). The construct and predictive validity of a dynamic assessment of young children learning to read: Implications for RTI frameworks. *Journal of Learning Disabilities, 44(*4), 339–347.

Fuchs, L. S., & Fuchs, D. (2011). *Using CBM for progress monitoring in reading.* National Center on Student Progress Monitoring. Available at www.studentprogress.org/.

Gal, E., Schreur, N., & Engel-Yeger, B. (2010). Inclusion of children with disabilities: Teachers' attitudes and requirements for environmental accommodations. *International Journal of Special Education, 25*(2), 89–99.

Gall, M. D., Gall, J. P., & Borg, W. R. (2007). *Educational research: An introduction,* 8th ed. Boston: Allyn and Bacon.

Gardner, T. J. (2011). Disabilities in written expression. *Teaching Children Mathematics, 18*(1), 46–54.

Geary, D. C., Hoard, M. K., Nugent, L., & Bailey, D. H. (2011). Mathematical cognition deficits in children with learning disabilities and persistent low achievement: A five-year prospective study. *Journal of Educational Psychology*, Online First Publication, September 12, 2011. doi: 10.1037/a0025398.

Gelfand, D. M., & Drew, C. J. (2003). *Understanding child behavior disorders,* 4th ed. (p. 238). Belmont, CA: Wadsworth. Used with permission.

Gettinger, M., Schienebeck, C., Seigel, S., & Vollmer, L. (2011). Assessment of classroom environments. In M. A. Bray & T. J. Kehle (Eds.), *The Oxford handbook of school psychology* (pp. 260–283). New York, NY: Oxford University Press.

Goldstein, S. (2011). Learning disabilities in childhood. In S. Goldstein, J. A. Naglieri, & M. DeVries (Eds.), *Learning and attention disorders in adolescence and adulthood: Assessment and treatment,* 2nd ed. (pp. 31–58). Hoboken, NJ: John Wiley & Sons.

Goswami, U. (2008). Reading, dyslexia and the brain. *Educational Research, 50*(2), 135–148.

Graziano, P. A., Geffken, G. R., & Lall, A. S. (2011). Heterogeneity in the pharmacological treatment of children with ADHD: Cognitive, behavioral, and social functioning differences. *Journal of Attention Disorders, 15(*5), 382–391.

Grigal, M., Hart, D., & Migliore, A. (2011). Comparing the transition planning, postsecondary education, and employment outcomes of students with intellectual and other disabilities. *Career Development for Exceptional Individuals, 34*(1), 4–17.

Gronlund, N. E., & Waugh, C. K. (2009). *Assessment of student achievement,* 9th ed. Boston: Allyn and Bacon.

Gross, C. M. (2011). Parenting a child with learning disabilities: A viewpoint for teachers from a teacher and parent. *Issues in Teacher Education, 20*(1), 85–93.

Hackenberg, T. D. (2009). Token reinforcement: A review and analysis. *Journal of the Experimental Analysis of Behavior, 91*(2), 257–286.

Hadley, W. M. (2011). College students with disabilities: A student development perspective. *New Directions for Higher Education, 154,* 77–81.

Hain, L. A., Hale, J. B., & Kendorski, J. G. (2009). The comorbidity of psychopathology in cognitive and academic SLD subtypes. In S. G. Feifer & G. Rattan (Eds.), *Emotional disorders: A neuropsychological, psychopharmacological, and educational perspective* (pp. 199–225). Middletown, MD: School Neuropsych Press.

Harris, M. L., Schumaker, J. B., & Deshler, D. D. (2011). The effects of strategic morphological analysis instruction on the vocabulary performance of secondary students with and without disabilities. *Learning Disability Quarterly, 34*(1), 17–33.

Harrison, J. R., Vannest, K. J., & Reynolds, C. R. (2011). Behaviors that discriminate ADHD in children and adolescents: Primary symptoms, symptoms of comorbid conditions, or indicators of functional impairment? *Journal of Attention Disorders, 15*(2), 147–160.

Haworth, C. M. A., Kovas, Y., Harlaar, N., Hayiou-Thomas, M. E., Petrill, S. A., Dale, P. S., & Plomin, R. (2009). Generalist genes and learning disabilities: A multivariate genetic analysis of low performance in reading, mathematics, language and general cognitive ability in a sample of 8000 12-year-old twins. *Journal of Child Psychology and Psychiatry, 50*(10), 1,318–1,325.

Hills, J. (2011). Meeting the challenges of inclusion. *Primary Science, 117,* 9–11.

Hoekstra, P. J. (2011). Is there potential for the treatment of children with ADHD beyond psychostimulants? *European Child & Adolescent Psychiatry, 20*(9), 431–432.

Hollenbeck, A. F. (2011). Instructional makeover: Supporting the reading comprehension of students with learning disabilities in a discussion-based format. *Intervention in School and Clinic, 46(*4), 211–220.

Holmes, J., Gathercole, S. E., Place, M., Dunning, D. L., Hilton, K. A. & Elliott, J. G. (2010). Working memory deficits can be overcome: Impacts of training and medication on working memory in children with ADHD. *Applied Cognitive Psychology, 24*(6), 827–836.

Holzer, M. L., Madaus, J. W., Bray, M. A., & Kehle, T. J. (2009).The test-taking strategy intervention for college students with learning disabilities. *Learning Disabilities Research & Practice, 24*(1), 44–56.

Hoover, J. J. (2010). Special education eligibility decision making in response to intervention models. *Theory into Practice, 49,* 289–296.

Iseman, J. S., & Naglieri, J. A. (2011). A cognitive strategy instruction to improve math calculation for children with ADHD and LD: A randomized controlled study. *Journal of Learning Disabilities, 44*(2), 184–195.

Jackson, C. (2011). Your students love social media . . . and so can you. *Teaching Tolerance, 39.* Available at www.tolerance.org/magazine/number-39-spring-2011/your-students-love-social-media-and-so-can-you.

Janse, E., de Bree, E., & Brouwer, S. (2010). Decreased sensitivity to phonemic mismatch in spoken word processing in adult developmental dyslexia. *Journal of Psycholinguistic Research, 39*(6), 523–539.

Jenkins, J., & Terjeson, K. J. (2011). Monitoring reading growth: Goal setting, measurement frequency, and methods of evaluation. learning disabilities. *Research & Practice, 26(*1), 28–35.

Jitendra, A. K., & Star, J. R. (2011). Meeting the needs of students with learning disabilities in inclusive mathematics classrooms: The role of schema-based instruction on mathematical problem-solving. *Theory Into Practice, 50*(1), 12–19.

Jitendra, A. K., Burgess, C., & Gajria, M. (2011). Cognitive strategy instruction for improving expository text comprehension of students with learning disabilities: The quality of evidence. *Exceptional Children, 77*(2), 135–159.

Joseph, L. M., & Eveleigh, E. L. (2011). A review of the effects of self-monitoring on reading performance of students with disabilities. *The Journal of Special Education, 45*(1), 43–53.

Judge, S., & Bell, S. M. (2011). Reading achievement trajectories for students with learning disabilities during the elementary school years. *Reading & Writing Quarterly: Overcoming Learning Difficulties, 27*(1–2), 153–178.

Kalikow, K. T. (2011). *Kids on meds: Up-to-date information about the most commonly prescribed psychiatric medications.* New York, NY: W. W. Norton.

Kamawar, D., LeFevre, J., & Bisanz, J. (2010). Knowledge of counting principles: How relevant is order irrelevance? *Journal of Experimental Child Psychology, 105*(1), 138–145.

Kamhia, A. G. (2011). What speech-language pathologists need to know about auditory processing disorder. *Language, Speech, and Hearing Services in Schools, 42*(3), 265–272.

Kaufman, A. S. (2008). Neuropsychology and specific learning disabilities: Lessons from the past as a guide to present controversies and future clinical practice. In E. Fletcher-Janzen & C. R. Reynolds (Eds.), *Neuropsychological* perspectives on learning disabilities in the era of RTI: Recommendations for diagnosis and intervention (pp. 1–13). Hoboken, NJ: John Wiley & Sons.

Kavale, K. A., Spaulding, L. S., & Beam, A. P. (2009). A time to define: Making the specific learning disability definition prescribe specific learning disability. *Learning Disability Quarterly, 32*(1), 39–48.

Kebir, O., Grizenko, N., Sengupta, S., & Joober, R. (2009). Verbal but not performance IQ is highly correlated to externalizing behavior in boys with ADHD carrying both DRD4 and DAT1 risk genotypes. *Progress in Neuro-Psychopharmacology & Biological Psychiatry, 33*(6), 939–944.

Keeley, P. (2011). Formative assessment probes: With a purpose. *Science and Children, 48*(9), 22–25.

Kendall, S., Nino, M., & Stewart, S. (2010). Using the iPhone and iPod Touch@work. *Computers in Libraries, 30*(2), 14–19.

Kibby, M. W. (2009). Why is the school psychologist involved in the evaluation of struggling readers? *Journal of Educational & Psychological Consultation, 19*(3), 248–258.

Kim, T., & Axelrod, S. (2005). Direct instruction: An educators' guide and a plea for action. *The Behavior Analyst Today, 6*(2), 111–120.

King-Sears, M. E., Swanson, C., & Mainzer, L. (2011). TECHnology and literacy for adolescents with disabilities. *Journal*

of *Adolescent & Adult Literacy, 54*(8), 569–578.

Kirby, J. R., Allingham, B. H., Parrila, R., & LaFave, C. B. (2008). Learning strategies and study approaches of postsecondary students with dyslexia. *Journal of Learning Disabilities, 41*, 85–96.

Klingner, J. K., & Edwards, P. A. (2006). Cultural considerations with response to intervention models. *Reading Research Quarterly, 41*, 108–117.

Knowles, T. (2010).The kids behind the label: understanding ADHD [Condensed with permission from *Middle Matters,* 17 (June 2009), 1–3]. *The Education Digest, 76* (3), 59–61.

Kochhar-Bryant, C. A., & Heishman, A. (Cont). (2010). *Effective collaboration for educating the whole child.* Thousand Oaks, CA: Corwin Press.

Koenig, D. (2011). Social media in the schoolhouse. *Teaching Tolerance, 39.* Available at www.tolerance.org/magazine/number-39-spring-2011/social-media-schoolhouse.

Kohnen, S., Nickels, L., & Coltheart, M. (2010). Training rule-of-(E): Further investigation of a previously successful intervention for a spelling rule in developmental mixed dysgraphia. *Journal of Research in Reading, 33*(4), 392–413.

Kovas, Y., & Plomin, R. (2007). Learning abilities and disabilities: Generalist genes, specialist environments. *Current Directions in Psychological Science, 16*(5), 284–288.

Kushki, A., Schwellnus, H., & Ilyas, F. (2011). Changes in kinetics and kinematics of handwriting during a prolonged writing task in children with and without dysgraphia. *Research in Developmental Disabilities: A Multidisciplinary Journal, 32*(3), 1,058–1,064.

Lane, K. L., Menzies, H. M., & Bruhn, A. L. (2010). *Managing challenging behaviors in schools: Research-based strategies that work.* New York, NY: Guilford Press.

Langberg, J. M., Vaughn, A. J., Brinkman, W. B., Froehlich, T., & Epstein, J. N. (2010). Clinical utility of the Vanderbilt ADHD rating scale for ruling out comorbid learning disorders. *Pediatrics, 126*(5), 990–991.

Leichtentritt, J., & Shechtman, Z. (2010). Children with and without learning disabilities: A comparison of processes and outcomes following group counseling. *Journal of Learning Disabilities, 43*(2), 169–179.

Lembke, E. S., Garman, C., Deno, S. L., & Stecker, P. M. (2010). One elementary school's implementation of response to intervention (RTI). *Reading & Writing Quarterly: Overcoming Learning Difficulties, 26*(4), 361–373.

Lenhart, A., Purcell, K., Smith, A., & Zickuhr, K. (2010). *Social media and mobile Internet use among teens and young adults.* Pew Research Center, Pew Internet & American Life Project. Available atwww.pewinternet.org/~/media//Files/Reports/2010/

PIP_Social_Media_and_Young_Adults_Report_Final_with_toplines.pdf.

Lerner, J., & Kline, F. (2006). *Learning disabilities and related disorders,* 10th ed. Boston: Houghton Mifflin.

Lindstrom, J. H., Tuckwiller, E. D., & Hallahan, D. P. (2008). Assessment and eligibility of students with disabilities. In E. L. Grigorenko (Ed.), *Educating individuals with disabilities: IDEIA 2004 and beyond* (pp. 197–225). New York, NY: Springer.

Litvack, M. S., Ritchie, K. C., & Shore, B. M. (2011). High- and average-achieving students' perceptions of disabilities and of students with disabilities in inclusive classrooms. *Exceptional Children, 77*(4), 474–487.

Logan, D. E., Catanese, S. P., & Coakley, R. M. (2007). Chronic pain in the classroom: Teachers' attributions about the causes of chronic pain. *Journal of School Health, 77*(5), 248–256.

Loomis, J. W. (2006). Learning disabilities. In R. T. Ammerman (Ed.), *Comprehensive handbook of personality and psychopathology,* vol. 3 (pp. 272–284). Hoboken, NJ: John Wiley & Sons, Inc.

Lovell, M., & Phillips, L. (2009). Commercial software programs approved for teaching reading and writing in the primary grades: Another sobering reality. *Journal of Research on Technology in Education, 42(*2), 197–216.

Luckner, J. L., & Bowen, S. K. (2010). Teachers'

use and perceptions of progress monitoring. *American Annals of the Deaf, 155*(4), 397–406.

Macaruso, P., & Rodman, A. (2011). Efficacy of computer-assisted instruction for the development of early literacy skills in young children. *Reading Psychology, 32*(2), 172–196.

Machek, G. R., & Nelson, J. M. (2010). School psychologists' perceptions regarding the practice of identifying reading disabilities: Cognitive assessment and response to intervention considerations. *Psychology in the Schools, 47*(3), 230–245.

MacKay, T. (2009). Severe and complex learning difficulties: Issues of definition, classification and prevalence. *Educational and Child Psychology, 26*(4), 9–18.

Maehler, C., & Schuchardt, K. (2009). Working memory functioning in children with learning disabilities: Does intelligence make a difference? *Journal of Intellectual Disability Research, 53*(1), 3–10.

Maehler, C., & Schuchardt, K. (2011). Working memory in children with learning disabilities: rethinking the criterion of discrepancy. *International Journal of Disability, Development and Education, 58*(1), 5–17.

Mahdavi, J. N., & Beebe-Frankenberger, M. E. (2009). Pioneering RTI systems that work: Social validity, collaboration, and context. *TEACHING Exceptional Children, 42*(2), 64–72.

Mammarella, I. C., Lucangeli, D., & Cornoldi, C. (2010). Spatial working memory and arithmetic deficits in children with nonverbal learning difficulties. *Journal of Learning Disabilities, 43*(5), 455–468.

Mangina, C. A., & Beuzeron-Mangina, H. (2009). Similarities and differences between learning abilities, 'pure' learning disabilities, 'pure' ADHD and comorbid ADHD with learning disabilities. *International Journal of Psychophysiology, 73*(2), 170–177.

Marshak, L., Van Wieren, T., & Ferrell, D. R. (2010). Exploring barriers to college student use of disability services and accommodations. *Journal of Postsecondary Education and Disability, 22*(3), 151–165.

Mason, L. H., Harris, K. R., & Graham, S. (2011). Self-regulated strategy development for students with writing difficulties. *Theory Into Practice, 51*(1), 20–27.

McDonald, K. E., Keys, C. B., & Balcazar, F. E. (2009). Living with a learning disability and other marginalized statuses: A multilevel analysis. In Marshall, C. A., Kendall, E., Banks, M. E., & Gover, R. M. S. (Eds.), *Disabilities: Insights from across fields around the world, Vol 1: The experience: definitions, causes, and consequences.* Santa Barbara, CA: Praeger/ABC-CLIO.

McGillivray, J. A., & Baker, K. L. (2009). Effects of comorbid ADHD with learning disabilities on anxiety, depression, and aggression in adults. *Journal of Attention Disorders, 12*(6), 525–531.

McKenzie, R. G. (2009). Obscuring vital distinctions: The oversimplification of learning disabilities within RTI. *Learning Disability Quarterly, 32*(4), 203–215.

McLeskey, J., & Waldron, N. L. (2011). Educational programs for elementary students with learning disabilities: Can they be both effective and inclusive? *Learning Disabilities Research & Practice, 26*(1), 48–57.

McLeskey, J., Landers, E., Hoppey, D., & Willamson, P. (2011). Learning disabilities. *Learning Disabilities Research & Practice, 26*(2), 60-66.

McMaster, K. L., Du, X., & Yeo, S. (2011). Curriculum-based measures of beginning writing: Technical features of the slope. *Exceptional Children, 77*(2), 185–206.

McNamara, J. K., & Willoughby, T. (2010). A longitudinal study of risk-taking behavior in adolescents with learning disabilities. *Learning Disabilities Research & Practice, 25*(1), 11–24.

McNamara, J. K., Scissons, M., & Gutknecht, N. (2011). A longitudinal study of kindergarten children at risk for reading disabilities: The poor really are getting poorer. *Journal of Learning Disabilities, 44*(5), 421–430.

McNamara, J., Vervaeke, S., & Willoughby, T. (2008). Learning disabilities and risk-taking behavior in adolescents: A comparison of those with and without comorbid attention-deficit/hyperactivity disorder. *Journal of Learning Disabilities, 41*(6), 561–574.

Merit. (2011). *Starter paragraph punch*. New York, NY: Merit Software. Available at www.merit-software.com/index.php.

Miller, B., & McCardle, P. (2011). Moving closer to a public health model of language and learning disabilities: The role of genetics and the search for etiologies. *Behavior Genetics, 41*(1), 1–5.

Miller, L. (2009). Informal and qualitative assessment of writing skills in students with disabilities. *Assessment for Effective Intervention, 34*(3), 178–191.

Milsom, A., & Dietz, L. (2009). Defining college readiness for students with learning disabilities: A Delphi study. *Professional School Counseling, 12*(4), 315–323.

Moats, L. C. (2009). Teaching spelling to students with language and learning disabilities. In G. A. Troia (Ed.), *Instruction and assessment for struggling writers: Evidence-based practices* (pp. 269–289). New York, NY: Guilford Press.

Moeller, K., Pixner, S., & Zuber, J. (2011). Early place-value understanding as a precursor for later arithmetic performance—a longitudinal study on numerical development. *Research in Developmental Disabilities: A Multidisciplinary Journal, 32*(5), 1,837–1,851.

Montague, M., Enders, C., & Dietz, S. (2011). Effects of cognitive strategy instruction on math problem solving of middle school students with learning disabilities. *Learning Disability Quarterly, 34*(4), 262–272.

Moore, D. R. (2011). The diagnosis and management of auditory processing disorder. *Language, Speech, and Hearing Services in Schools, 42*(3), 303–308.

Moorman, A., Boon, R. T., & Keller-Bell, Y. (2010). Effects of text-to-speech software on the reading rate and comprehension skills of high school students with specific learning disabilities. *Learning Disabilities: A Multidisciplinary Journal, 16*(1), 41–49.

Morris, D., & Gaffney, M. (2011). Building reading fluency in a learning-disabled middle school reader. *Journal of Adolescent & Adult Literacy, 54*(5), 331–341.

Morris, M. A., Schraufnagel, C. D., Chudnow, R. S., & Weinberg, W. A. (2009). Learning disabilities do not go away: 20- to 25-year study of cognition, academic achievement, and affective illness. *Journal of Child Neurology, 24*(3), 323–332.

Mowat, J. (2009). The inclusion of pupils perceived as having social and emotional behavioural difficulties in mainstream schools: A focus upon learning. *Support for Learning, 24*(4), 159–169.

Murawski, W. W., & Hughes, C. E. (2009). Response to intervention, collaboration, and co-teaching: A logical combination for successful systemic change. *Preventing School Failure, 53*(4), 267–277.

National Center on Response to Intervention. (2010). *Essential components of RTI—A closer look at response to intervention.* Washington, D.C.: Author.

National Joint Committee on Learning Disabilities. (2011a). Learning disabilities: Implications for policy regarding research and practice: A report by the National Joint Committee on Learning Disabilities. *Learning Disability Quarterly, 34*(4), 237–241.

National Joint Committee on Learning Disabilities. (2011b). Comprehensive assessment and evaluation of students with learning disabilities: A paper prepared by the National Joint Committee on Learning Disabilities. *Learning Disability Quarterly, 34*(1), 3–16.

National Reading Panel. (2000). *Teaching children to read: An evidence-based assessment of the scientific research literature on reading and its implications for reading instruction.* Rockville, MD: Author.

National Research Center on Learning Disabilities. (2007). SLD identification overview: General information and tools to get started. Available at www.nrcld.org.

Nelson, J. M., & Harwood, H. (2011a). Learning disabilities and anxiety: A meta-analysis. *Journal of Learning Disabilities, 44*(1), 3–17.

Nelson, J. M., & Harwood, H. R. (2011b). A meta-analysis of parent and teacher reports of depression among students with learning disabilities: Evidence for the importance of multi-informant assessment. *Psychology in the Schools, 48*(4), 371–384.

Northwest Kinematics. (2011). *StoryBuilder.* Salem, OR: Mobile Education. Available at http://mobile-educationstore.com/.

O'Brien, B. A., Wolf, M., & Miller, L. T. (2011). Orthographic processing efficiency in developmental dyslexia: An investigation of age and treatment factors at the sublexical level. *Annals of Dyslexia, 61*(1), 111–135.

O'Brien, G. (2006). Young adults with learning disabilities: A study of psychosocial functioning at transition to adult services. *Developmental Medicine & Child Neurology, 48*, 195–199.

Obrzut, J. E., & Mahoney, E. B. (2011). Use of the dichotic listening technique with learning disabilities. *Brain and Cognition, 76*(2), 323–331.

Obudo, F. (2008). Teaching mathematics to students with learning disabilities: A review of literature. Online Submission. Available at www.eric.ed.gov.erl.lib.byu.edu/PDFS/ED500500.pdf.

O'Connor, M. P. (2009). Service works! Promoting transition success for students with disabilities through participation in service learning. *TEACHING Exceptional Children, 41*(6), 13–17.

Olsen, A., LeMire, S., & Baker, M. (2011). The impact of self-efficacy and peer support on student participation with interactive white boards in the middle school mathematics class. *Journal of Computers in Mathematics and Science Teaching, 30*(2), 163–178.

Overvelde, A., & Hulstijn, W. (2011). Handwriting development in grade 2 and grade 3 primary school children with normal, at risk, or dysgraphic characteristics. *Research in Developmental Disabilities: A Multidisciplinary Journal, 32*(2), 540–548.

Passolunghi, M. C. (2011). Cognitive and emotional factors in children with mathematical learning disabilities. *International Journal of Disability, Development and Education, 58*(1), 61–73.

Pennington, Bruce F. (2009). *Diagnosing learning disabilities: A neuropsychological framework,* 2nd ed. New York, NY: Guilford Press.

Pierangelo, R., & Giuliani, G. A. (2006). *Learning disabilities: A practical approach to foundations, assessment, diagnosis, and teaching.* Boston: Allyn and Bacon.

Pierson, M. R., Carter, E. W., & Lane, K. L. (2008). Factors influencing the self-determination of transition-age youth with high-incidence disabilities. *Career Development for Exceptional Individuals, 31*(2), 115–125.

Porter, J. (2005). Awareness of number in children with severe and profound learning difficulties: Three exploratory case studies. *British Journal of Learning Disabilities, 33*, 97–101.

Powell, S. G., Thomsen, P. H., & Frydenberg, M. (2011). Long- term treatment of ADHD with stimulants:

A large observational study of real-life patients. *Journal of Attention Disorders, 15*(6), 439–451.

Powell, S. R. (2011). Solving word problems using schemas: A review of the literature. *Learning Disabilities Research & Practice, 26*(2), 94–108.

PT Software. (2010). *My writing spot*. Available at www.ptss.net/.

Pugach, M. C., Blanton, L. P., & Correa, V. I. (2011). A historical perspective on the role of collaboration in teacher education reform: Making good on the promise of teaching all students. *Teacher Education and Special Education, 34*(3), 183–200.

Reed, M. J., Kennett, D. J., & Lewis, T. (2011). The relative benefits found for students with and without learning disabilities taking a first-year university preparation course. *Active Learning in Higher Education, 12*(2), 133–142.

Ritchey, K. D. (2011). The first "R": evidence-based reading instruction for students with learning disabilities. *Theory into Practice, 50*(1), 28–34.

Rosenblum, Y., Larochette, A., Harrison, A. G., & Armstrong, I. (2010). The relation between comprehensive assessment procedures and diagnostic stability in school-aged children identified with learning disabilities. *Canadian Journal of School Psychology, 25*(2), 170–188.

Rosenzweig, C., Krawec, J., & Montague, M. (2011). Metacognitive strategy use of eighth-grade students with and without learning disabilities during mathematical problem solving: A think-aloud analysis. *Journal of Learning Disabilities, 44*(6), 508–520.

Rubinsten, O., & Henik, A. (2009). Developmental dyscalculia: Heterogeneity might not mean different mechanisms. *Trends in Cognitive Sciences, 13*(2), 92–99.

Rupley, W. H., Blair, T. R., & Nichols, W. D. (2009). Effective reading instruction for struggling readers: The role of direct/explicit teaching. *Reading & Writing Quarterly: Overcoming Learning Difficulties, 25*(2–3), 125–138.

Sabornie, E. J., Cullinan, D., & Osborne, S. S. (2005). Intellectual, academic, and behavioral functioning of students with high-incidence disabilities: A cross-categorical meta-analysis. *Exceptional Children, 72*, 47–63.

Sayeski, K. L. (2011). Effective spelling instruction for students with learning disabilities. *Intervention in School and Clinic, 47*(2), 75–81.

Scerri, T. S., & Schulte-Körne, G. (2010). Genetics of developmental dyslexia. *European Child & Adolescent Psychiatry, 19*(3), 179–197.

Scheeler, M. C., Macluckie, M., & Albright, K. (2010). Effects of immediate feedback delivered by peer tutors on the oral presentation skills of adolescents with learning disabilities. *Remedial and Special Education, 31*(2), 77–86.

Schmalzl, L., & Nickels, L. (2006). Treatment of irregular word spelling in acquired dysgraphia: Selective benefit from visual mnemonics. *Neuropsychological Rehabilitation, 16*(1), 1–37.

Schneiderman, J. U., Leslie, L. K., & Arnold-Clark, J. S. (2011). Pediatric health assessments of young children in child welfare by placement type. *Child Abuse & Neglect: The International Journal, 35*(1), 29–39.

Searle, M. (2010). *What every school leader needs to know about RTI*. Alexandria, VA: ASCD.

Seethaler, P. M., & Fuchs, L. S. (2011). Using curriculum-based measurement to monitor kindergarteners' mathematics development. *Assessment for Effective Intervention, 36*(4), 219–229.

Semrud-Clikeman, M., Walkowiak, J., Wilkinson, A., & Minne, E. P. (2010). Direct and indirect measures of social perception, behavior, and emotional functioning in children with Asperger's disorder, nonverbal learning disability, or ADHD. *Journal of Abnormal Child Psychology: An official publication of the International Society for Research in Child and Adolescent Psychopathology, 38*(4), 509–519.

Setlik, J., Bond, G. R., & Ho, M. (2009). Adolescent prescription ADHD medication abuse is rising along with prescriptions for these medications. *Pediatrics, 124*(3), 875–880.

Shaw, S. R., & McCabe, P. C. (2007). Hospital-to-school transition for children with chronic illness: Meeting the new challenges of an evolving health care system. *Psychology in the Schools, 45*(1), 74–87.

Sheehy, K. (2009). Teaching word recognition to children with severe learning difficulties: An exploratory comparison of teaching methods. *Educational Research, 51*(3), 379–391.

Shiran, A., & Breznitz, Z. (2011). The effect of cognitive training on recall range and speed of information processing in the working memory of dyslexic and skilled readers. *Journal of Neurolinguistics, 24*(5), 524–537.

Sin, C. H., Francis, R., & Cook, C. (2010). Access to and experience of child and adolescent mental health services: Barriers to children and young people with learning disabilities and their families. *Mental Health Review Journal, 15*(1), 20–28.

Staudt, D. H. (2009). Intensive word study and repeated reading improves reading skills for two students with learning disabilities. *Reading Teacher, 63*(2), 142–151.

Stein, M., Carnine, D., & Dixon, R. (1998). Direct instruction: Integrating curriculum design and effective teaching practice. *Intervention in School and Clinic, 33*(4), 227–233.

Stetter, M. E., & Hughes, M. T. (2010). Using story grammar to assist students with learning disabilities and reading difficulties improve their comprehension. *Education & Treatment of Children (West Virginia University Press)*, p. 115–151.

Stetter, M. E., & Hughes, M. T. (2011). Computer assisted instruction to promote comprehension in students with learning disabilities. *International Journal of Special Education, 26*(1), 88–100.

Stock, P., Desoete, A., & Roeyers, H. (2010). Detecting children with arithmetic disabilities from kindergarten: evidence from a 3-year longitudinal study on the role of preparatory arithmetic abilities. *Journal of Learning Disabilities, 43*(3), 250–268.

Stockard, J. (2010). Promoting reading achievement and countering the "fourth-grade slump": The impact of direct instruction on reading achievement in fifth grade. *Journal of Education for Students Placed at Risk (JESPAR), 15*(3), 218–240.

Stothers, M. E., & Cardy, J. O. (2012). Oral language impairments in developmental disorders characterized by language strengths: A comparison of Asperger syndrome and nonverbal learning disabilities. *Research in Autism Spectrum Disorders, 6(*1), 519–534.

Stothers, M., & Klein, P. D. (2010). Perceptual organization, phonological awareness, and reading comprehension in adults with and without learning disabilities. *Annals of Dyslexia, 60*(2), 209–237.

Swanson, H. L. (2011a). *Learning disabilities: Assessment, identification, and treatment.* New York, NY: Oxford University Press.

Swanson, H. L. (2011b). Dynamic testing, working memory, and reading comprehension growth in children with reading disabilities. *Journal of Learning Disabilities, 44*(4), 358–371.

Swanson, H. L., Jerman, O., & Zheng, X. (2009). Math disabilities and reading disabilities: Can they be separated? *Journal of Psychoeducational Assessment, 27*(3), 175–196.

Swanson, H. L., Kehler, P., & Jerman, O. (2010). Working memory, strategy knowledge, and strategy instruction in children with reading disabilities. *Journal of Learning Disabilities, 43*(1), 24–47.

Sze, S. (2009). Mislabeled reading and learning disabilities: Assessment and treatment for reading difficulties in students with learning disabilities. *College Student Journal, 43*(4), 1,015–1,019.

Taub, M. B. (2011). Review of the literature: Dyslexia. *Journal of Behavioral Optometry, 22*(2), 48–49.

Taylor, H. G., Espy, K. A., & Anderson, P. J. (2009). Mathematics deficiencies in children with very low birth weight or very preterm birth. *Developmental Disabilities Research Reviews, 15*(1), 52–59.

Toland, J., & Boyle, C. (2008). Applying cognitive behavioural methods to retrain children's attributions for success and failure in learning. *School Psychology International, 29*(3), 286–302.

Torgesen, J. K., Wagner, R. K., & Rashotte, C. A. (2010). Computer-assisted instruction to prevent early reading difficulties in students at risk for dyslexia: Outcomes from two instructional approaches. *Annals of Dyslexia, 60*(1), 40–56.

Troia, G. A. (2011). How might pragmatic language skills affect the written expression of students with language learning disabilities? *Topics in Language Disorders, 3*(1), 40–53.

U.S. Department of Education, Office of Special Education Programs. (2008). Annual report to Congress on the implementation of the Individuals with Disabilities Education Act. Washington, DC: Author.

U.S. Department of Education. (2010). *Percentage distribution of students 6 to 21 years old served under Individuals with Disabilities Education Act, Part B, by educational environment and type of disability: Selected years, fall 1989 through fall 2008.* Washington, D.C.: U.S. Department of Education, Office of Special Education Programs, Individuals with Disabilities Education Act (IDEA) database. Retrieved from www.ideadata.org/arc_toc10.asp#partbLRE.

U.S. Department of Education. (2011a). *The 30th annual report to Congress on the implementation of the Individuals with Disabilities Education Act, 2008.* Washington, D.C.: U.S. Government Printing Office.

U. S. Department of Education. (2011b). *Children with disabilities receiving special education under Part B of the Individuals with Disabilities Education Act, 2010.* Washington, D.C.: U. S. Department of Education, Office of Special Education Programs, Data Analysis Systems, OMB #1820-0043. Retrieved from www.ideadata.org.

Viel-Ruma, K., Houchins, D., & Fredrick, L. (2007). Error self-correction and spelling: Improving the spelling accuracy of secondary students with disabilities in written expression. *Journal of Behavioral Education, 16(*3), 291–301.

Viel-Ruma, K., Houchins, D. E., Jolivette, K., Fredrick, L. D., & Gama, R. (2010). Direct instruction in written expression: The effects on English speakers and English language learners with disabilities. *Learning Disabilities Research & Practice, 25*(2), 97–108.

Volpe, R. J., Anastasio, R. J., & DuPaul, G. J. (2011). Classroom and instructional strategies. In S. Goldstein, J. A. Naglieri, J. A., & M. DeVries (Eds.), *Learning and attention disorders in adolescence and adulthood: Assessment and treatment,* 2nd ed. (pp. 467–487). Hoboken, NJ: John Wiley & Sons.

Waber, D. P. (2010). *Rethinking learning disabilities: Understanding children who struggle in school.* New York, NY: Guildford.

Waesche, J. S. B, Schatschneider, C., Maner, J. K., Ahmed, Y., & Wagner, R. K. (2011). Examining agreement and longitudinal stability among traditional and RTI-based definitions of reading disability using the affected-status agreement statistic. *Journal of Learning Disabilities, 44*(3), 296–307.

Wagner, R. K., & Compton, D. L. (2011). Dynamic assessment and its implications for RTI models. *Journal of Learning Disabilities, 44*(4), 311–312.

Walker, S. O., & Plomin, R. (2005). The nature-nurture question: Teachers' perceptions of how genes and the environment influence educationally relevant behaviour. *Educational Psychology, 25*, 509–516.

Waters, J. K. (2010). Enter the iPad (or not?) *T.H.E. Journal, 37*(6), 38–40, 42, 44–45.

Weiser, B., & Mathes, P. (2011). Using encoding instruction to improve the reading and spelling performances of elementary students at risk for literacy difficulties: A best-evidence synthesis. *Review of Educational Research, 81*(2), 170–200.

Wilber, A., & Cushman, T. P. (2006). Selecting effective academic interventions: An example using brief experimental analysis for oral reading. *Psychology in the Schools, 43*, 79–84.

Willcutt, E. G., Betjemann, R. S., McGrath, L. M., Chhabildas, N. A., Olson, R. K., DeFries, J. C., & Pennington, B. F. (2010). Etiology and neuropsychology of comorbidity between RD and ADHD: The case for multiple-deficit models. *Cortex: A Journal Devoted to the Study of the Nervous System and Behavior, 46*(10), 1,345–1,361.

Wixson, K. K., & Valencia, S. W. (2011). Assessment in RTI: What teachers and specialists need to know. *Reading Teacher, 64*(6), 466–469.

Woods, L. L., Sylvester, L., & Martin, J. E. (2010). Student-directed transition planning: Increasing student knowledge and self-efficacy in the transition planning process. *Career Development for Exceptional Individuals, 33*(2), 106–114.

Xin, Y. P., Zhang, D., Park, J. Y., Tom, K., Whipple, A., & Si, L. (2011). A comparison of two mathematics problem-solving strategies: Facilitate algebra-readiness. *The Journal of Educational Research, 104*(6), 381–395.

Yeh, S. S. (2010). Understanding and addressing the achievement gap through individualized instruction and formative assessment. *Assessment in Education: Principles, Policy & Practice, 17*(2), 169–182.

Zigmond, N., Kloo, A., & Volonino, V. (2009). What, where, and how? Special education in the climate of full inclusion. *Exceptionality, 17*(4), 189–204.

Zirkel, P. A., & Thomas, L. B. (2010). State laws and guidelines for implementing RTI. *Teaching Exceptional Children, 43*(1), 60–73.

Chapter 8

Achenbach, L. M., & Rescorla, L. A. *Manual for the ASEBA school-age forms and profiles.* Burlington, VT: University of Vermont, Research Center for Children Youth, and Families.

Adelman, H. S., & Taylor, L. (2006). *The implementation guide to student learning supports in the classroom and school-wide.* Thousand Oaks, CA: Corwin Press.

Algozzine, R., Serna, L., & Patton, J. R. (2001). *Childhood behavior disorders: Applied research & educational practices,* 2nd ed. Austin: Pro-Ed.

Allen-DeBoer, R. A., Malmgren, K. W., & Glass, M. (2006). Reading instruction for youth with emotional and behavioral disorders in a juvenile correctional facility. *Behavioral Disorders: Journal of the Council for Children with Behavioral Disorders, 32*(1), 18.

Arter, P. S. (2007). The positive alternative learning supports program: Collaborating to improve student success. *Council for Exceptional Children, 40*(2), 38.

Barber, B. K., Stolz, H. E., & Olsen, J. A. (2005). Parental control, psychological control, and behavioral control: Assessing relevance across time, culture, and method. *Monographs of the Society for Research in Child Development, 70*(4), 1–137.

Barker, E. D., Oliver, B. R., Viding, E., Salekin, R. T., & Maughan, B. (2011). The impact of prenatal risk, fearless temperament and early parenting on adolescent callous-unemotional traits: A 12-year longitudinal investigation. *Journal of Child Psychology and Psychiatry, 52*(8), 878–888.

Beard, K. Y., & Sugai, G. (2004). First step to success: An early intervention for elementary children at risk for antisocial behavior. *Behavioral Disorders, 29*(4), 396–409.

Benitez, D. T., Lattimore, J., & Wehmeyer, M. L. (2005). Promoting the involvement of students with emotional and behavioral disorders in career and vocational planning and decision-making: The self-determined career development model. *Behavioral Disorders, 30*(4), 431–447.

Benner, G. J., Nelson, J. R., & Epstein, M. H. (2002). Language skills of children with EBD: A literature review. *Journal of Emotional and Behavioral Disorders, 10*, 43–59.

Borg, M. B., & Dalla, M. R. (2005). Treatment of gangs/gang behavior in adolescence. In T. P. Gullotta & G. R. Adams (Eds.), *Handbook of adolescent behavioral problems* (pp. 519–542). New York: Springer Science + Business Media, Inc.

Bower, E. M. (1959). The emotionally handicapped child and the school. *Exceptional Children, 26*, 6–11.

Bradley, R., Henderson, K., & Monfore, D. A. (2004). A national perspective on children with emotional disorders. *Behavioral Disorders, 29*(3), 211–223.

Bullis, M. (2001). Job placement and support considerations in transition programs for adolescents with emotional disabilities. In L. M. Bullock & R. A. Gable (Eds.), *Addressing the* social, academic, and behavioral needs of students with challenging behavior in inclusive and alternative settings (pp. 31–36). Las Vegas, NV: Council for Children with Behavioral Disorders.

Burrell, S., & Warboys, L. (2000, July). Special education and the juvenile justice system. *Juvenile Justice Bulletin*, pp. 1–15.

Burt, S. A. (2009). Rethinking environmental contributions to child and adolescent psychopathology: A meta-analysis of shared environmental influences. *Psychological Bulletin, 135*(4), 608–637.

Burt, S. A., & Neiderhiser, J. M. (2009). Aggressive versus nonaggressive antisocial behavior: distinctive etiological moderation by age, *Developmental Psychology, 45*(4), 1164–1176.

Capaldi, D. M., & Eddy, J. M. (2005). Oppositional defiant disorder and conduct disorder. In T. P. Gullotta & G. R. Adams (Eds.), *Handbook of adolescent behavioral problems* (pp. 283–308). New York: Springer Science + Business Media, Inc.

Carrell, S. E., & Hoekstra, M. L. (2008). Externalities in the classroom: How children exposed to domestic violence affect everyone's kids, Working Paper 14246. Retrieved December 12, 2008, from www.nber.org/papers/w14246.pdf.

Carter, E. W., & Wehby, J. H. (2003). Job performance of transition-age youth with emotional and behavioral disorders. *Council for Exceptional Children, 69*(4), 449–465.

Carter, E. W., Wehby, J. H., Hughes, C., Johnson, S. M., Plank, D. R., Barton-Arwood, S. M., & Lunsford, L. B. (2005). Preparing adolescents with high-incidence disabilities for high-stakes testing with strategy instruction. *Preventing School Failure, 49*(2), 55–62.

Child and Adolescent Bipolar Foundation. (2009). *About pediatric and bipolar disorder.* Retrieved March 25, 2009, from www.bpkids.org/site/PageServer?pagename = lrn_about.

Coleman, M. C., & Webber, J. (2002). *Emotional & behavioral disorders: Theory and practice.* Boston: Allyn & Bacon.

Conroy, M. A., & Brown, W. H. (2004). Early identification, prevention, and early intervention with young children at risk for emotional or behavioral disorders: Issues, trends, and a call for action. *Behavioral Disorders, 29*(3), 224–236.

Conroy, M. A., Hendrickson, J. M., & Hester, P. P. (2004). Early identification and prevention of emotional and behavioral disorders. In R. B. Rutherford, M. M. Quinn, & S. R. Mathur (Eds.), *Handbook of research in emotional and behavioral disorders* (pp. 199–215). New York: Guilford Press.

Crews, S. D., Bender, H., Cook, C. R., Gresham, F. M., Kern, L., & Vanderwood, M. (2007). Rick and protective factors of emotional and/or behavioral disorders in children and adolescents: A mega-analytic synthesis. *Behavioral Disorders: Journal of the Council for Children with Behavioral Disorders, 32*(2), 64–77.

Cross, M. (2004). *Children with emotional and behavioural difficulties and communication problems: There is always a reason.* London, England: Jessica Kingsley Publications.

Crundwell, R. M., & Killu, K. (2007). Understanding and accommodating students with depression in the classroom. *Council for Exceptional Children, 40*(1), 48–54.

Cullinan, D. (2004). Classification and definition of emotional and behavioral disorders. In R. B. Rutherford, M. M. Quinn, & S. R. Mathur (Eds.), *Handbook of research in emotional and behavioral disorders* (pp. 32–53). New York: Guilford Press.

Cunningham, E. M., & O'Neill, R. E. (2007). Agreement of functional behavioral assessment and analysis methods with students with EBD. *Behavioral Disorders: Journal of the Council for Children with Behavioral Disorders, 32*(3), 211–221.

Davis, S. D., Young, E. L., Hardman, S., & Winters, R. (2011). Screening for emotional and behavioral disorders, *Principle Leadership, 11*(9), 12–17.

Dodge, K. A., Dishion, T. J., & Lansford, J. E. (2006). *Deviant peer influence in programs for youth: Problems and solutions.* New York: Guilford Press.

Donovan, S. A., & Nickerson, A. B. (2007). Strength-based versus traditional social-emotional reports: Impact on multidisciplinary team members' perceptions. *Behavioral Disorders: Journal of the Council for Children with Behavioral Disorders, 32*(4), 228–237.

Dunlap, G., Carr, E. G., Horner, R. H., Zarcone, J. R., & Schwartz, I. (2008). Positive behavior support and applied behavior analysis: A familial alliance. *Behavior Modification, 8*(5), 682–697.

Dunlap, G., Strain, P. S., Fox, L., Carta, J. J., Conroy, M., Smith, B. J., et al. (2006). Prevention and intervention with young children's challenging behavior: Perspectives regarding current knowledge. *Behavioral Disorders: Journal of the Council for Children with Behavioral Disorders, 32*(1), 29.

EasyChild Software. (2006). *EasyChild: Encouragement system.* Retrieved June 6, 2006, from www.easychild.com/index.htm.

Eber, L., & Keenan, S. (2004). Collaboration with other agencies: Wraparound and systems of care for children and youths with emotional and behavioral disorders. In R. B. Rutherford, M. M. Quinn, & S. R. Mathur (Eds.), *Handbook of research in emotional and behavioral disorders* (pp. 502–516). New York: Guilford Press.

Eber, L., Breen, K., Rose, J., Unizycki, R. M., & London, T. H. (2008). Wraparound: A tertiary level intervention for students with emotional/behavioral needs, *Teaching Exceptional Children, 40*(6), 18–10.

Eber, L., Hyde, K., & Suter, J. C. (2011). Integrating wraparound into a schoolwide system of positive behavior supports. *Journal of Child and Family Studies, 20*(6), 782–790.

Eber, L., Sugai, G., Smith, C., & Scott, T. (2002). Wraparound and positive behavioral interventions and supports in the schools. *Journal of Emotional and Behavioral Disorders, 10*, 171–180.

Eivers, A. R., Brendgen, M., & Borge, A. I. H. (2010). stability and change in prosocial and antisocial behavior across the transition to school: Teacher and peer perspectives. *Early Education & Development, 21*(6), 843–864.

Ensor, R., Marks, A., Jacobs, L., & Hughes, C. (2010). Trajectories of antisocial behaviour towards siblings predict antisocial behaviour towards peers. *Journal of Child Psychology and Psychiatry, 51*(11), 1208–1216.

Epstein, M. H. (1998). Using strength-based assessment in program with children with emotional and behavior disorders. *Beyond Behavior, 9*(2), 25–27.

Epstein, M. H., & Sharma, J. M. (1997). *Behavior and emotional rating scale.* Austin, TX: PRO-ED.

Essa, E. (2003). *A practical guide to solving preschool behavior problems,* 5th ed. Australia: Thompson/Delmar Learning.

Etscheidt, S. (2006). Behavioral intervention plans: Pedagogical and legal analysis of issues. *Behavioral Disorders: Journal of the Council for Children with Behavioral Disorders, 31*(2), 223–243.

Figlio, D. N., (2007). Boys named sue: Disruptive children and their peers. *Education and Finance Policy, 2*(4), 376–394.

First, M. B., & Tasman, A. (Eds.). (2004). *DSM-IV-TR mental disorders: Diagnosis, etiology, and treatment.* Chichester, England: John Wiley & Sons, Ltd.

Forness, S. R. (2004). Characteristics of emotional and behavioral disorders [Introduction]. In *Handbook of research in emotional and behavioral disorders* (pp. 235–241). New York: Guilford Press.

Forsman, M., Lichtenstein, P., Andershed, H., & Larsson, H. (2010). A longitudinal twin study of the direction of effects between psychopathic personality and antisocial behaviour. *Journal of Child Psychology and Psychiatry 51*:1 (2010), 39–47.

Gable. R. A. (2004). Hard times and an uncertain future: Issues that confront the field of emotional/behavioral disorders. *Education and Treatment of Children, 27*(4), 341–352.

Gallagher, G., & Konjoian, P. (2010). *Shut up about your perfect kid: A survival guide for ordinary parents of special children.* New York: Three Rivers Press.

Goh, D. S. (2004). *Assessment accommodations for diverse learners.* Boston: Allyn & Bacon.

Graczyk, P. A., Connolly, S. D., & Corapci, F. (2005). Anxiety disorders in children and adolescents: Theory, treatment, and prevention. In T. P. Gullotta & G. R. Adams (Eds.), *Handbook of adolescent behavioral problems* (pp. 131–157). New York: Springer Science + Business Media, Inc.

Gresham, F. M., Van, M. B., & Cook, C. R. (2006). Social skills training for teaching replacement behaviors: Remediating acquisition deficits in at-risk students. *Behavioral Disorders: Journal of the Council for Children with Behavioral Disorders, 31*(4), 363.

Griffith, A. K., Trout, A. L., Hagaman, J. L. & Harper, J. (2009). Interventions to improve the literacy functioning of adolescents with emotional and/or behavior disorders: A review of literature between 1965 and 2005. *Behavior Disorders, 33* (3), 124–140.

Guerra, N. G., Boxer, P., & Kim, T. E. (2005). A cognitive-ecological approach to serving students with emotional and behavioral disorders: Application to aggressive behavior. *Behavioral Disorders, 30*(3), 277–288.

Haltigan, J. D., Roisman, G. I., Susman, E. J., Barnett-Walker, K., Monahan, K. C., & The National Institute of Child Health and Human Development Early Child Care Research Network. (2011). Elevated trajectories of externalizing problems are associated with lower awakening cortisol levels in midadolescence. *Developmental Psychology, 47*(2), 472–478.

Hansen, S. D., & Lignugaris-Kraft, B. (2005). Effects of a dependent group contingency on the verbal interactions of middle school students with emotional disturbances. *Behavioral Disorders, 30*(2), 170–184.

Harry, B., Hart, J. E., Klinger, J., & Cramer, E. (2009). Response to Kauffman, Mock, & Simpson (2007): Problems related to under-service of students with emotional or behavioral disorders. *Behavioral Disorders, 34*(3), 164–171.

Heilbrun, A. B. (2004). *Disordered and deviant behavior: Learning gone awry.* Lanham, MD: University Press of America, Inc.

Hester, P. P., Baltodano, H. M., Hendrickson, J. M., Tonelson, S. W., Conroy, M. A., & Gable, R. A. (2004). Lessons learned from research on early intervention: What teachers can do to prevent children's behavior problems. *Preventing School Failure, 49*(1), 5–10.

Howell, J. C., & Egley, A. (2005). Moving risk factors into developmental theories of gang membership. *Youth Violence and Juvenile Justice, 3*(4), 334–354.

Howell, J. C., & Egley, A. (2008). *Frequently asked questions regarding gangs.* Washington, D.C.: National Youth Gang Center.

Ialongo, N., Poduska, J., Werthamer, L., & Kellam, S. (2001). The distal impact of two first-grade preventive interventions on conduct problems and disorder in early adolescence. *Journal of Emotional and Behavioral Disorders, 9*, 146–160.

Jeter, L. V. (2010). Conduct disorders: Are boot camps effective?

Reclaiming Children and Youth: The Journal of Emotional and Behavioral Problems, 19(2), 32–36.

Johnson, C., Eva, A. L., Johnson, L., & Walker, B. (2011). Don't turn away: Empowering teachers to support students' mental health. The Clearing House: A Journal of Educational Strategies, Issues and Ideas, 84(1), 9–14

Johnson, W., McGue, M., & Iacono, W. G. (2009). School performance and genetic and environmental variance in antisocial behavior at the transition from adolescence to adulthood. Developmental Psychology, 45(4), 973–987.

Joseph, G. E., & Strain, P. S. (2003). Comprehensive evidence-based social-emotional curricula for young children: An analysis of efficacious adoption potential. Topics in Early Childhood Special Education, 23(2), 65–76.

Kauffman, J. M. (2005). Characteristics of emotional and behavioral disorders of children and youth. Upper Saddle River, NJ: Prentice-Hall.

Kauffman, J. M., & Landrum, T. J. (2009). Characteristics of emotional and behavioral disorders of children and youth, 9th ed. Upper Saddle River, NJ: Prentice-Hall.

Kauffman, J. M., Bantz, J., & McCullough, J. (2002). Separate and better: A special public school class for students with emotional and behavioral disorders. Exceptionality, 10, 149–170.

Kauffman, J. M., Mock, D. R., & Simpson, R. L. (2007). Forum: Problems related to underservice of students with emotional or behavior disorders. Behavioral Disorders, 33(1), 43–57.

Kauffman, J. M., Simpson, R. L., & Mock, D. R. (2009). Problems related to underservice: A rejoinder. Behavioral Disorders, 34(3), 172–180.

Kendziora, K. T. (2004). Early intervention for emotional and behavioral disorders. In R. B. Rutherford, M. M. Quinn, & S. R. Mathur (Eds.), Handbook of research in emotional and behavioral disorders (pp. 327–351). New York: Guilford Press.

Kendziora, K., Bruns, E., Osher, D., Pacchiano, D., & Mejia, B. (2001). Systems of care: Promising practices in children's mental health, 2001 series, volume I. Washington, D.C.: Center for Effective Collaboration and Practice, American Institutes for Research.

Kennedy, C. H., Long, T., Jolivette, K., Cox, J., Tang, J., & Thompson, T. (2001). Facilitating general education participation for students with behavior problems by linking positive behavior supports and person-centered planning. Journal of Emotional and Behavioral Disorders, 9, 161–171.

Knitzer, J., Steinberg, Z., & Fleisch, B. (1990). At the schoolhouse door: An examination of programs and policies for children with behavioral and emotional problems. New York: Bank Street College of Education.

Konopasek, D. E., & Forness, S. R. (2004). Psychopharmacology in the treatment of emotional and behavioral disorders. In R. B Rutherford, M. M. Quinn, & S. R. Mathur (Eds.), Handbook of research in emotional and behavioral disorders (pp. 352–368). New York: Guilford Press.

Kostewicz, D. E., & Kubina, R. M. (2008). The national reading panel guidepost: A review of reading outcome measures for students with emotional and behavioral disorders. Behavioral Disorders, 33(2), 62–74.

Kurns, S., & Tilly, W. D. (2008). Response to intervention: Blueprints to intervention. Alexandria, VA: National Association of State Directors of Special Education, Inc.

Lane, K. L. (2004). Academic instruction and tutoring interventions for students with emotional and behavioral disorders: 1990 to the present. In R. B. Rutherford, M. M. Quinn, & S. R. Mathur (Eds.), Handbook of research in emotional and behavioral disorders (pp. 462–486). New York: Guilford Press.

Lane, K. L. (2007). Identifying and supporting students at risk for emotional and behavioral disorders within multi-level models: Data driven approaches to conducting secondary interventions with an academic emphasis. Education and Treatment of Children, 30, 135–164.

Lane, K. L., Barton-Arwood, S. M., Nelson, J. R., & Wehby, J. (2008). Academic performance of students with emotional and behavioral disorders served in a self-contained setting. Journal of Behavioral Education, 17(1), 43–62.

Lane, K. L., Kalberg, J. R., & Menzies, H. M. (2009). Developing schoolwide programs to prevent and manage problem behaviors: A step-by-step approach. New York, NY: Guilford.

Lane, K. L., Weisenbach, J. L., Phillips, A., & Wehby, J. H. (2007). Designing, implementing, and evaluating function-based interventions using a systematic, feasible approach. Behavioral Disorders: Journal of the Council for Children with Behavioral Disorders, 32(2), 122–139.

Levitt, J. L., Sansone, R. A., & Cohn, L. (Eds.). (2004). Self-harm behavior and eating disorders: Dynamics, assessment, and treatment. New York: Brunner-Routledge.

Lewis, T. J., Lewis-Palmer, T., Newcomer, L., & Stichter, J. (2004). Applied behavior analysis and the education and treatment of students with emotional and behavioral disorders. In R. B. Rutherford, M. M. Quinn, & S. R. Mathur (Eds.), Handbook of research in emotional and behavioral disorders (pp. 523–545). New York: Guilford Press.

Lopes, J. (2005). Intervention with students with learning, emotional, and behavioral disorders: Why do we take so long to do it? Education and Treatment of Children, 28(4), 345–360.

Maag, J. W. (2006). Social skills training for students with emotional and behavioral disorders: A review of reviews. *Behavioral Disorders, 32*(1), 4–17.

Maag, J. W., & Katsiyannis, A. (2006). Behavioral intervention plans: Legal and practical considerations for students with emotional and behavioral disorders. *Behavioral Disorders, 31*(4), 348–36.

Maag, J. W., & Katsiyannis, A. (2010). Early intervention programs for children with behavior problems and at risk for developing antisocial behaviors: Evidence- and research-based practices, *Remedial and Special Education, 31*(6),464–475.

Mattison, R. E., Hooper, S. R., & Carlson, G. A. (2006). Neuropsychological characteristics of special education students with serious emotional/behavioral disorders. *Behavioral Disorders, 31*(2), 176–188.

Mayer, M., Lochman, J., & Van Acker, R. (2005). Introduction to the special issue: Cognitive-behavioral interventions with students with EBD. *Behavioral Disorders, 30*(3), 197–212.

McCarthy, M. R., & Soodak, L. C. (2007). The politics of discipline: Balancing school safety and rights of students with disabilities. *Exceptional Children, 73*(4), 456–474.

Meadows, N. B., & Stevens, K. B. (2004). Teaching alternative behaviors to students with emotional and behavioral disorders. In R. B. Rutherford, M. M. Quinn, & S. R. Mathur (Eds.), *Handbook of research in emotional and behavioral disorders* (pp. 385–398). New York: Guilford Press.

Menzies, H. M., & Lane, K. L. (2011). Using self-regulation strategies and functional assessment-based interventions to provide academic and behavioral support to students at risk within three-tiered models of prevention, *Preventing School Failure: Alternative Education for Children and Youth, 55*(4), 181–191.

Merrell, K. W., & Walker, H. M. (2004). Deconstructing a definition: Social maladjustment versus emotional disturbance and moving the EBD field forward. *Psychology in the Schools, 41*(8), 899–910.

Miller, M. J., Lane, K. L., & Wehby, J. (2005). Social skills instruction for students with high-incidence disabilities: A school-based intervention to address acquisition deficits. *Preventing School Failure, 49*(2), 27–39.

Murray, J., Irving, B., Farrington, D. P., Colman, I., & Bloxsom, C. A. J. (2010). Very early predictors of conduct problems and crime: Results from a national cohort study. *Journal of Child Psychology and Psychiatry, 51*(11), 1198–1207.

National Center for Children in Poverty. 2010. *Child and youth emergency mental health care (Unclaimed Children Revisited),* Issue Brief No. 1, June 1.

National Center for Education Statistics. (2006). *Table 50. Children 3 to 21 years old served in federally supported programs for the disabled, by type of disability: Selected years, 1976–77 through 2003–04.* Retrieved June 10, 2006 from http://nces.ed.gov/programs/digest/d05/tables/dt05_050.asp.

National Gang Center. (2011a). What community conditions enable gangs to take root? Retrieved December 20, 2011, from www.nationalgangcenter.gov/About/FAQ#q16.

National Gang Center. (2011b). How do youth become involved in and leave gangs. Retrieved December 20, 2011, from www.nationalgangcenter.gov/About/FAQ#q16.

National Institute of Mental Health. (2008). *Bipolar disorder in children and teens.* Retrieved March 25, 2009, from www.nimh.nih.gov/health/publications/bipolar-disorder-in-children-and-teens-easy-to-read/index.shtml.

National Mental Health Information Center. (2006). *National systems of care a promising solution for children with serious emotional disturbances and their families.* Washington, D.C.: Author. Retrieved July 19, 2006, from www.mentalhealth.samhsa.gov/publications/allpubs/Ca-0030/default.asp.

Nelson, J. R., Stage, S., Duppong-Hurley, K., Synhorst, L., & Epstein, M. H. (2007). Risk factors predictive of the problem behavior of children at risk for emotional and behavioral disorders. *Council for Exceptional Children, 73*(3), 367.

Nungesser, N. R., & Watkins, R. V. (2005). Preschool teachers' perceptions and reactions to challenging classroom behavior: Implications for speech-language pathologists. *Language, Speech, and Hearing Services in Schools, 36,* 139–151.

Obiakor, F. E., Enwefa, S. E., Utley, C., Obi, S. O., Gwalla-Ogisi, N., & Enwefa, R. (2004). Serving culturally and linguistically diverse students with emotional and behavioral disorders. In *Meeting the diverse needs of children and youth with EBD: Evidence–based programs and practices.* Arlington, VA: Council for Children with Behavioral Disorders.

Osher, D., Cartledge, G., Oswald, D., Sutherland, K. S., Artiles, A. J., & Coutinho, M. (2004). Cultural and linguistic competency and disproportionate representation. In R. B. Rutherford, M. M. Quinn, & S. R. Mathur (Eds.), *Handbook of research in emotional and behavioral disorders* (pp. 54–77). New York: Guilford Press.

Polsgrove, L., & Smith, S. (2004). Informed practice in teaching students self-control. In Rutherford, R., M. M. Quinn, & Mathur, S. (Eds.), *Research in emotional and behavioral disorders.* New York: The Guilford Press.

Powell, N. P., Boxmeyer, C. L., Baden, R., Stromeyer, S., Minney, J. A., Mushtaq, A., & Lochman, J. E. (2011). Assessing and treating aggression and conduct problems in schools: Implications from the Coping Power Program. *Psychology in the Schools, 48*(3), 233–242.

Quinn, M. M., & Poirier, J. M. (2004). Linking prevention research with policy: Examining the costs and outcomes of the failure to prevent emotional and behavioral disorders. In R. B. Rutherford, M. M. Quinn, & S. R. Mathur (Eds.), *Handbook of research in emotional and behavioral disorders* (pp. 78–97). New York: Guilford Press.

Reinke, W. M., Herman, K. C., & Tucker, C. M. (2006). Building and sustaining communities that prevent mental disorders: Lessons from the field of special education. *Psychology in the Schools, 43*(3), 313–329.

Roberts, C., & Bishop, B. (2005). Depression. In T. P. Gullotta & G. R. Adams (Eds.), *Handbook of adolescent behavioral problems* (pp. 205–230). New York: Springer Science + Business Media, Inc.

Robinson, T. R. (2007). Cognitive behavioral interventions: Strategies to help students make wise behavioral choices. *Beyond Behavior, 17*(1), 7–13.

Rorie, M., Gottfredson, D. C., Cross, A., Wilson, D., & Connell, N, M. (2011). Structure and deviancy training in after-school programs. *Journal of Adolescence, 34*(1), 105–117.

Rosenberg, M. S., Wilson, R., Maheady, L., & Sindelar, P. T. (2004). *Educating students with behavior disorders,* 3rd ed. Boston: Allyn and Bacon.

Rutter, M. (2006). *Genes and behavior: Nature-nurture interplay explained.* Malden, MA: Blackwell Publishing.

Ryan, J. B., Reid, R., & Epstein, M. H. (2004). Peer-mediated intervention studies on academic achievement for students with EBD: A review. *Remedial and Special Education, 25*(6), 330–341.

Ryan, J. B., Pierce, C. D., & Mooney, P. (2008). Evidence-based teaching strategies for students with EBD. *Beyond Behavior, 17*(3), 22–29.

Safran, S. P., & Oswald, K. (2003). Positive behavior supports: Can schools reshape disciplinary practices? *Council for Exceptional Children, 69*(3), 361–373.

Sampers, J., Anderson, K. G., Hartung, C. M., & Scambler, D. J. (2001). Parent training programs for young children with behavior problems. *Infant Toddler Intervention: The Transdisciplinary Journal, 11*, 91–110.

Scott, T. M., & Kamps, D. M. (2007). The future of functional behavioral assessment in school settings. *Behavioral Disorders: Journal of the Council for Children with Behavioral Disorders, 32*(3), 146.

Seifert, K. (2000). Juvenile violence: An overview of risk factors and programs. *Reaching Today's Youth, 4*, 60–71.

Shoenfeld, N. A., & Konopasek, D., (2007). Medicine in the classroom: A review of psychiatric medications for students with emotional or behavioral disorders. *Beyond Behavior, 17*(1), 14–20.

Shores, R. E., & Wehby, J. H. (1999). Analyzing the classroom social behavior of students with EBD. *Journal of Emotional and Behavioral Disorders, 7*(4), 194–199.

Short, J. F., Jr., & Hughes, L. A. (2006). *Studying youth gangs.* Lanham, MD: AltaMira Press.

Shriner, J. G., & Wehby, J. H. (2004). Accountability and assessment for students with emotional and behavioral disorders. In R. B. Rutherford, M. M. Quinn, & S. R. Mathur (Eds.), *Handbook of research in emotional and behavioral disorders* (pp. 216–231). New York: Guilford Press.

Sitlington, P. L., & Neubert, D. A. (2004). Preparing youths with emotional or behavioral disorders for transition to adult life: Can it be done within the standards-based reform movement? *Behavioral Disorders, 29*(3), 279–288.

Smolak, L. (2005). Eating disorders in girls. In D. J. Bell, S. L. Foster, & E. J. Mash (Eds.), *Handbook of behavioral and emotional problems in girls* (pp. 463–487). New York: Kluwer Academic/ Plenum Publishers.

Thornberry, T. P., Krohn, M. D., Lizotte, A. J., Smith, C. A., & Tobin, K. (2003). *Gangs and delinquency in developmental perspective.* Cambridge, UK: Cambridge University Press.

U.S. Department of Education. (2005). *Twenty-fifth annual (2003) report to congress on the implementation of the individuals with disabilities act (vol. 1).* Washington, D.C.: Author.

U.S. Department of Education. (2006). *Federal Register,* August 14, 2006, Part II, 34 CFR Parts 300 and 301. Assistance to states for the education of children with disabilities and preschool grants for children; Final rule. Washington, D.C.: Author.

U.S. Department of Education. (2007). *Twenty-fifth annual (2005) report to congress on the implementation of the individuals with disabilities act (vol. 1).* Washington, D.C.: Author.

U.S. Department of Education. (2010). Twenty-Ninth Annual Report to Congress on the Implementation of the Individuals with Disabilities Education Act, Parts B and C. 2007. Washington, D.C.: Author.

U.S. Department of Education. (2011). Thirtieth annual report to congress on the implementation of the *individuals with disabilities education act, 2008.* Washington, D.C.: Author.

Vazsonyi, A.T. & Huang, L. (2010). Where self-control comes from: On the development of self-control and its relationship to deviance over time. *Developmental Psychology, 46*(1), 245–257.

Vieno, A., Nation, M. Pastore, M., & Santinello, M. (2009). Parenting and antisocial behavior: A model of the relationship between adolescent self-disclosure, parental closeness, parental control, and adolescent antisocial behavior. *Developmental Psychology, 45*(6), 1509–1519.

Vincent, C. G., & Tobin, T.J. (2011). The relationship between implementation of school-wide positive behavior support (sw-pbs) and disciplinary exclusion of students from various ethnic backgrounds with and without disabilities, *Journal of Emotional and Behavioral Disorders, 19*(4), 782–790.

Wagner, M., Kutash, K., Duchnowski, A.J., Epstein, M. H., & Sumi, W. C. (2005). The children and youth we serve: A national picture of the characteristics of students with emotional disturbances receiving special education. *Journal of Emotional and Behavioral Disorders Summer, 13*(2), 79–96.

Walker, H. M., & Severson, H. H. (1992). *Systematic screening for behavior disorders.* Longmont, CO: Sopris West.

Whitted. K.S. (2011). Understanding how social and emotional skill deficits contribute to school failure. *Preventing School Failure: Alternative Education for Children and Youth, 55*(1), 10–16.

Wicks-Nelson, R., & Israel, A. C. (2006). *Behavior disorders of childhood,* 6th ed. Upper Saddle River, NJ: Prentice Hall.

Witt, J. C., Daly, E. M., & Noell, G. (2000). *Functional assessments: A step-by-step guide to solving academic and behavior problems.* Longmont, CO: Sopris West.

Witt, J. C., VanDerHeyden, A. M., & Gilbertson, D.

(2004). Instruction and classroom management. In R. B. Rutherford, M. M. Quinn, & S. R. Mathur (Eds.), *Handbook of research in emotional and behavioral disorders* (pp. 426–445). New York: Guilford Press.

Woodruff, D. W., Osher, D., Hoffman, C. C., Gruner, A., King, M. A., Snow, S. T., & McIntire, J. C. (1999). The role of education in a system of care: Effectively serving children with emotional or behavioral disorders. Systems of Care: Promising Practices in Children's Mental Health, 1998 Series, Vol. III. Washington, D.C.: Center for Effective Collaboration and Practice, American Institutes for Research.

Woolsey, L., & Katz-Leavey, J. (2008). *Transitioning youth with mental health needs to meaningful employment and independent living.* Washington, D.C.: National Clearinghouse on Workforce and Disability for Youth, Institute for Educational Leadership.

Young, E. L., Calderella, P., Richardson, M. J., and Young K. R. (2011). *Positive behavior support in secondary schools: A practical guide.* New York: Guilford Press.

Young, E. L., Sabbah, H. Y., Young, B. J., Reiser, M. L., & Richardson (2010). Gender differences and similarities in a screening process for emotional and behavioral risks in secondary schools, *Journal of Emotional and Behavioral Disorders, 18*(4) 225–235.

Chapter 9

AAIDD (AAMR) Ad Hoc Committee on Terminology and Classification. (2002). Intellecturual disabilities: Definition, classification, and systems of support, 10th ed. (p. 42). Washington, D.C.: American Association on Intellectual and Developmental Disabilities.

AAIDD (AAMR) Ad Hoc Committee on Terminology and Classification. (2009). *Definition of Intellectual Disability.* Washington, D.C.: American Association on Intellectual and Developmental Disabilities (formally known as the American Association on Mental Retardation). Retrieved April 25, 2009, from www.aamr.org/content_100.cfm?navID = 21.

The ARC. (20011a). *Intellectual disability.* Washington, D.C.: The ARC. Retrieved September 14, 2011, from www.thearc.org/page.aspx?pid=2543.

The ARC. (2011b). *Assistive technology for people with intellectual disabilities.* Washington, D.C.: The ARC. Retrieved May 25, 2011, from www.thearc.org/Document.Doc?&id=94.

Batshaw, M., Pellegrino, L., & Rozien, N. J. (2007). *Children with disabilities,* 6th ed. Baltimore: Paul H. Brookes.

Beirne-Smith, M., Patton, J. R., & Hill, S. (2010). *Introduction to intellectual disabilities,* 8th ed. Upper Saddle River, NJ: Merrill.

Berk, L. E. (2005). *Development through the lifespan.* Boston: Allyn and Bacon.

Browder, D. M., Ahlgrim-Delzell, L. A., Courtade-Little, G., & Snell, M. E. (2011). General curriculum access. In M. E. Snell & F. Brown (Eds.), *Introduction to students with severe disabilities,* 7th ed.) (pp. 489–525). Upper Saddle River, NJ: Prentice-Hall.

Browder, D. M., & Spooner, F. (2011). *Teaching students with moderate and severe disabilities.* New York, New York; Guilford Press.

Centers for Disease Control and Prevention. (2011). Tobacco Use and Pregnancy. Retrieved October 14 2011 from www.cdc.gov/reproductivehealth/TobaccoUsePregnancy/index.htm

Children's Defense Fund. (2011). *The state of America's children.* Washington, D.C.: Author.

Corum, S. (2003). Life is short. *Washington Post,* May 18, p. D1.

Crockett, M., & Hardman, M. L. (2009). Expected outcomes and emerging values. In J. McDonnell & M. L. Hardman, *Successful transition programs: Pathways for students with intellectual and developmental disabilities* (pp. 25–42). Los Angeles: Sage Publishing Company.

Dean, J. (2011). Nine-teen year old Riverside teen gleeful about role on new Fox Series. *The Press-Enterprise.* Retrieved September 23, 2011, from www.pe.com/localnews/inland/stories/PE_News_Local_S_glee15.4310398.html.

Drew, C. J., & Hardman, M. L. (2007). *Intellectual disabilities across the* lifespan, 9th ed. Columbus, OH: Merrill.

Gargiulo, R.M. (2011) *Special education in a contemporary society: An Introduction to exceptionality.* London: Sage Publishing.

Guralnick, M. J. (2001). A framework for change in early childhood inclusion. In M. J. Guralnick (Ed.), *Early childhood inclusion: Focus on change* (pp. 3–35). Baltimore: Paul H. Brookes.

Hertzog, J. (2011). The power of language. Retrieved September 24, 2011, from http:// blog.govdelivery.com/ usodep/2010/10/i-just-didnt-know-the-power-of-language.html.

Kaiser, A. P. (2000). Teaching functional communication skills. In M. E. Snell & F. Brown (Eds.), *Instruction of persons with severe disabilities,* 5th ed. (pp. 453–492). Columbus, OH: Merrill.

Katims, D. S. (2000). Literacy instruction for people with mental retardation: Historical highlights and contemporary analysis. *Education and Training in Mental Retardation and Developmental Disabilities, 35*(1), 3–15.

Kittler, P., Krinsky-McHale, S. J., & Devenny, D. A. (2004). Semantic and phonological loop effects on visual working memory in middle-age adults with mental retardation. *American Journal on Mental Retardation, 109*(6), 467–480.

Lakin, C. (2005). Introduction. In K. C. Lakin & A. Turnbull (Eds.), *National goals for people with intellectual and*

developmental disabilities (pp. 1–13). Washington, D.C.: The ARC of the U.S. and the American Association on Intellectual and Developmental Disabilities (formerly AAMR).

Lee, S., Yoo, S., & Bak, S. (2003). Characteristics of friendships among children with and without mild disabilities. *Education and Training in Developmental Disabilities, 38*(2), 157–166.

Maulik, P. K, Mascarenhas, M. N., Mathers, C. D., Dua, T., & Saxena S. (2011, March-April). Prevalence of intellectual disability: a meta-analysis of population-based study. *Research on Developmental Disabilities, 32*(2), 419–436.

Moore, B. J., & Montgomery, J. K. (2008). *Making a difference for America's children: Speech–language pathologists in public schools.* Greenville, SC: Super Duper Publications.

National Organization on Fetal Alcohol Syndrome. (2011). *What is fetal alcohol syndrome?* Retrieved November 2, 2011, from www.nofas. org/faqs.aspx?id=12.

Nirje, B. (1970). The normalization principle and its human management implications. *Journal of Mental Subnormality, 16,* 62–70.

Partnership for Accessible Reading Assessment. (2011). *Reading and Students with Mental Retardation.* University of Minnesota. Retrieved October 8, 2011, from www .readingassessment.info/ resources/publications/ mentalretardation.htm.

Polychronis, S., & McDonnell, J. (2009). Developing IEPs/transition plans. In J. McDonnell & M. L. Hardman, *Successful transition programs: Pathways for students with intellectual and developmental disabilities* (pp. 81–100). Los Angeles: Sage Publishing Company.

President's Committee for People with Intellectual Disabilities. (2011). *Fact Sheet: The Role of the PCPID.* Retrieved October 15, 2011, from www.acf. hhs.gov/programs/pcpid/ pcpid_fact.html.

Sternberg, R. J. (2008). *Cognitive psychology,* 5th ed. Florence, KY: Wadsworth.

U.S. Department of Education. (2007). To assure the free appropriate public education of all children with disabilities. *Twenty-eighth annual report to Congress on the implementation of the Individuals with Disabilities Education Act.* Washington, D.C.: U.S. Government Printing Office.

U.S. Department of Education. (2011). *The Thirtieth Annual Report to Congress on the Implementation of the Individuals with Disabilities Education Act.* Washington, D.C.: U.S. Government Printing Office. Wehman, P. (2011). *Essentials of transition planning.* Baltimore: Paul H. Brookes.

Westling, D., & Fox, L. (2009). *Teaching students with severe disabilities,* 4th ed. Upper Saddle River, NJ: Merrill/ Prentice Hall.

Chapter 10

Aarts, R., Demir, S., & Vallen, T. (2011). Characteristics of academic language register occurring in caretaker-child interaction: Development and validation of a coding scheme. *Language Learning, 61,* 1173–1221.

American Psychiatric Association. (2000). *Diagnostic and statistical manual of mental disorders,* 4th ed. (text rev.). Washington, D.C.: Author.

Anderson, N. B., & Shames, G. H. (2011). *Human communication disorders: An introduction,* 8th ed. Boston: Allyn and Bacon.

Baker, S. E., Hipp, J., & Alessio, H. (2008). Ventilation and speech characteristics during submaximal aerobic exercise. *Journal of Speech, Language, and Hearing Research, 51,* 1203–1214.

Bastiaanse, R., & Thompson, C. K. (2012). *Perspectives on agrammatism.* Hove, East Sussex, UK: Psychology Press.

Battle, D. E. (2009). Language and communication disorders in culturally and linguistically diverse children. In D. K. Bernstein & E. Tiegerman-Farber (Eds.), *Language and communication disorders in children,* 6th ed. (pp. 536–575). Boston: Allyn and Bacon.

Berko Gleason, J., & Bernstein Ratner, N. (2009). *The development of language: International edition,* 7th ed. Boston: Pearson.

Bernstein, D. K. (2009). The nature of language and its disorders. In

D. K. Bernstein & E. Tiegerman-Farber (Eds.), *Language and communication disorders in children,* 6th ed. (pp. 2–27). Boston: Allyn and Bacon.

Bernstein, D. K., & Levey, S. (2009). Language development: A review. In D. K. Bernstein & E. Tiegerman-Farber (Eds.), *Language and communication disorders in children,* 6th ed. (pp. 28–100). Boston: Allyn and Bacon.

Bloodstein, O. & Ratner, N. B. (2008). *A handbook on stuttering,* 6th ed. Florence, KY: Cengage Learning, Inc.

Boone, D. R., McFarlane, S. C., Von Berg, S. L., & Zraick, R. I. (2010). Voice and Voice Therapy: International Edition (8th ed.). Boston: Pearson.

Carey, B., O'Brian, S., Onslow, M., Block, S., Jones, M., & Packman, A. (2010). Randomized controlled non-inferiority trial of a telehealth treatment for chronic stuttering: The Camperdown Program. *The International Journal of Language & Communication Disorders 45,* 108–120.

Chabon, S. S., & Cohn, E. R. (2011). *Communication disorders casebook: Learning by example.* Boston: Pearson.

Chavira, D. A., Garland, A. F., Daley, S., & Hough, R. (2008). The impact of medical comorbidity on mental health and functional health outcomes among children with anxiety disorders. *Journal of Developmental & Behavioral Pediatrics, 29,* 394–402.

Chilosi, A. M., Cipriani, P., Pecini, C., Brizzolara, D., Biagi, L., Montanaro, D., Tosetti, M., et al. (2008). Acquired focal brain lesions in childhood: Effects on development and reorganization of language. *Brain and Language, 106,* 211–225.

Creech, R., & Viggiano, J. (1981). Consumers speak out on the life of the nonspeaker. *ASHA, 23,* 550–552.

DeThorne, L. S., Petrill, S. A., Hart, S. A., Channell, R. W., Campbell, R. J., Deater-Deckerard, K., & Thompson, L. A. (2008). "Genetic effects on children's conversational language use": Erratum. *Journal of Speech, Language, and Hearing Research, 51,* 1381.

Drew, C. J., & Hardman, M. L. (2007). *Intellectual disabilities across the lifespan,* 9th ed. Columbus, OH: Merrill.

Engstrom, E. J. (2008). Cultural and social history of psychiatry. *Current Opinion in Psychiatry, 21,* 585–592.

Faroqi-Shah, Y. (2008). A comparison of two theoretically driven treatments for verb inflection deficits in aphasia. *Neuropsychologia, 46,* 3088–3100.

Ferrand, C. T. (2012). *Voice disorders: Scope of theory and practice.* Boston: Allyn & Bacon.

Fogle, P. T. (2013). *Essentials of communication sciences and disorders.* Florence, KY: Cengage Learning, Inc.

Freed, D. R. (2012). *Motor speech disorders & treatment,* 2nd ed. Florence, KY: Cengage Learning, Inc.

Froemling, K. K., Grice, G. L., & Skinner, J. F. (2011). *Communication: The handbook.* Boston: Pearson.

Gee, J. P. (2008). Game-like learning: An example of situated learning and implications for opportunity to learn. In P. A. Moss, J. P. Gee, & L. J. Jones (Eds.), *Assessment, equity, and opportunity to learn* (pp. 200–221). New York: Cambridge University Press.

Gleason, J. B., & Ratner, N. B. (2009). *The development of language: International edition,* 7th ed. Boston: Pearson.

Greenwood, A., Grassly, J., Hickin, J., & Best, W. (2010). Phonological and orthographic cueing therapy: A case of generalized improvement. *Aphasiology, 24,* 991–1016.

Hardin-Jones, M., & Chapman, K. L. (2008). The impact of early intervention on speech and lexical development for toddlers with cleft palate: A retrospective look at outcome. *Language, Speech, and Hearing Services in Schools, 39,* 89–96.

Hartmann, E. (2008). Phonological awareness in preschoolers with spoken language impairment: Toward a better understanding casual relationships and effective intervention. A constructive comment on Rvachew and Grawburg's (2006) study. *Journal of Speech, Language, and Hearing Research, 51,* 1215–1218.

Johnston, S. S., Reichle, J., Feeley, K. M., Jones, E. A. (2012). *AAC strategies for individuals with moderate to severe disabilities.* Baltimore: Paul H. Brookes Publishing Company.

Justice, L. M., Mashburn, A., Pence, K. L., & Wiggins, A. (2008). Experimental evaluation of a preschool language curriculum: Influence on children's expressive language skills. *Journal of Speech, Language, and Hearing Research, 51,* 983–1001.

Kaderavek, J. N. (2011). *Language disorders in children: Fundamental concepts of assessment and intervention.* Boston: Allyn and Bacon.

Klammler, A., & Schneider, S. (2011). The size and composition of the productive holophrastic lexicon: German-Italian bilingual acquisition vs. Italian monolingual acquisition. *International Journal of Bilingual education and Bilingualism, 14,* 69–88.

Klinto, K., Salameh, E., Svensson, H. & Lohmander, A. (2011). The impact of speech material on speech judgement in children with and without cleft palate. *International Journal of Language & Communication Disorders, 46,* 348–360.

Manning, W. H. (2010). *Clinical decision making in fluency disorders,* 3rd ed. Florence, Ky: Cengage Learning, Inc.

Marion, G., Hussmann, K., Bay, E., Christoph, S., Piefke, M., Willmes, K., & Huber, W. (2008). Basic parameters of spontaneous speech as a sensitive method for measuring change during the course of aphasia. International Journal of Language & Communication Disorders, 43, 408–426.

Martin, N. (2009). The roles of semantic and phonologic processing in short-term memory and learning: Evidence from aphasia. In A. S. C. Thorn & M. P. A. Page (Eds.), *Interactions between short-term and long-term memory in the verbal domain* (pp. 220–243). New York: Psychology Press.

McGowan, M. W., Smith, L. E., Noria, C. W., Culpepper, C., Lanhinrichsen-Rohling, J., Borkowski, J. G., & Turner, L. A. (2008). Intervening with at-risk mothers: Supporting infant language development. *Child & Adolescent Social Work Journal, 25,* 245–254.

Meinzen-Derr, J., Wiley, S. Grether, S., & Choo, D. I. (2011). Children with cochlear implants and developmental disabilities: A language skills study with developmentally matched hearing peers. *Research in Developmental Disabilities, 32,* 757–767.

Moore, B., & Montgomery, J. (2008). *Making a difference for America's children: Speech-language pathologists in public schools,* 2nd ed. Austin, TX: Pro-Ed.

Murdoch, B. E. (2010). *Acquired speech and language disorders,* 2nd ed. New York: Wiley.

Onslow, M., Packman, A., & Payne, P. A. (2007). Clinical identification of early stuttering: Methods, issues, and future directions. Asia Pacific: *Journal of Speech Language and Hearing, 10,* 15–31.

Owens, R. E., Jr. (2010). *Language disorders: A functional approach to assessment and intervention,* 5th ed. Needham Heights, MA: Pearson.

Owens, R. E., Jr. (2008). *Language development: An introduction,* 7th ed. (International ed.). Boston: Pearson.

Owens, R. E., Jr. (2011). Development of communication, language, and speech. In N. B. Anderson & G. H. Shames (Eds.), *Human communication disorders: An introduction,* 8th ed. (pp. 22–58). Boston: Allyn and Bacon.

Owens, R. E., Metz, D. E., & Farinella, K. A. (2011). *Introduction to communication disorders: A lifespan approach,* 4th ed. Boston: Allyn and Bacon.

Payne, K. T. (2011). Multicultural and multilingual considerations. In N. B. Anderson & G. H. Shames (Eds.), *Human communication disorders: An introduction,* 8th ed. (pp. 93–125). Boston: Allyn and Bacon.

Pfeiffer, W. S., & Adkins, K. E. (2012). *Technical communication fundamentals.* Boston: Longman.

Plante, E. M., & Beeson, P. M. (2013). *Communication and communication disorders: A clinical introduction,* 4th ed. Boston: Allyn and Bacon.

Portone, C., Johns, M. M., & Hapner, E. R. (2008). A review of patient adherence to the recommendation for voice therapy. *Journal of Voice, 22,* 192–196.

Radziewicz, C., & Antonellis, S. (2009). Children with hearing loss:

Considerations and implications. In D. K. Bernstein & E. Tiegerman-Farber (Eds.), *Language and communication disorders in children,* 6th ed. (pp. 370–401). Boston: Allyn and Bacon.

Ramig, P. R., & Dodge, D. M. (2010). *The child and adolescent stuttering treatment & activity resource guide,* 2nd ed. Florence, KY: Cengage Learning, Inc.

Raposa, K. A. & Perlman, S. P. (2012). *Treating the dental patient with developmental disorders.* New York: Wiley.

Reed, V. A. (2012). *Introduction to children with language disorders,* 4th ed. Boston: Pearson.

Richardson, L. P., Russo, J. E., Lozano, P., McCauley, E., & Katon, W. (2008). The effect of comorbid anxiety and depressive disorders on health care utilization and costs among adolescents with asthma. *General Hospital Psychiatry, 30,* 398–406.

Robinson, N. B., & Robb, M. P. (2009). Early communication assessment and intervention: A dynamic process. In D. K. Bernstein & E. Tiegerman-Farber (Eds.), *Language and communication disorders in children,* 6th ed. (pp. 102–167). Needham Heights, MA: Allyn and Bacon.

Ryder, N., Leinonen, E., & Schulz, J. (2008). Cognitive approach to assessing pragmatic language comprehension in children with specific language impairment. *International Journal of Language & Communication Disorders, 43,* 427–447.

Schwartz, H. D. (2012). *A primer on communication and communicative disorders.* Boston: Pearson.

Schwartz, R. G. (2009). *Handbook of child language disorders.* London: Psychology Press,

Schwartz, R. G. (2011). Articulatory and phonological disorders In N. B. Anderson & G. H. Shames (Eds.), *Human communication disorders: An introduction,* 8th ed. (pp. 149–182). Boston: Allyn and Bacon.

Seden, J. (2008). Creative connections: Parenting capacity, reading with children and practitioner assessment and intervention. *Child & Family Social Work, 13,* 133–143.

Shapiro, C. J., Prinz, R. J., & Sanders, M. R. (2008). Population-wide parenting intervention training: Initial feasibility. *Journal of Child and Family Studies, 17,* 457–466.

Shaw, M., Heyman, B., Reynolds, L., Davies, J., & Godin, P. (2007). Multidisciplinary teamwork in a UK regional secure mental health unit a matter for negotiation? *Social Theory & Health, 5,* 356–377.

Snowling, M., & Hulme, C. (2012). Interventions for children's language and literacy difficulties. *International Journal of Language & Communication Disorders, 47,* 27–34.

Sweeney, T., & Sell, D. (2008). Relationship between perceptual ratings of nasality and nasometry in children/adolescents with cleft palate and/or velopharyngeal dysfunction. *International Journal of Language & Communication Disorders, 43,* 265–282.

Syrja, R. C. (2011). *How to reach and teach English language learners: Practical strategies to ensure success.* New York: Wiley.

Tiegerman-Farber, E. (2009). The role of the SLP. In D. K. Bernstein & E. Tiegerman-Farber (Eds.), *Language and communication disorders in children,* 6th ed. (pp. 404–435). Boston: Allyn and Bacon.

U.S. Department of Education, Office of Special Education Programs. (2011). The 30th annual report to Congress on the Implementation of the Individuals with Disabilities Education Act. Washington, D.C.: U.S. Government Printing Office.

Van Borsel, J., & Eeckhout, H. (2008). The speech naturalness of people who stutter speaking under delayed auditory feedback as perceived by different groups of listeners. *Journal of Fluency Disorders, 33,* 241–251.

Vinson, B. P. (2012). *Language disorders across the lifespan,* 3rd ed. Florence, KY: Cengage Learning, Inc.

Vukovic, M., Vuksanovic, J., & Vukovic, I. (2008). Comparison of the recovery patterns of language and cognitive functions in patients with post-traumatic language processing deficits and in patients with aphasia following a stroke. *Journal of Communication Disorders, 41,* 531–552.

Weber-Fox, C., & Hampton, A. (2008). Stuttering and natural speech processing semantic and syntactic constraints on verbs. *Journal of Speech, Language, and Hearing Research, 51,* 1058–1071.

Weiss, A. L. (2009). Planning language intervention for young children. In D. K. Bernstein & E. Tiegerman-Farber (Eds.), *Language and communication disorders in children,* 6th ed. (pp. 436–495). Boston: Allyn and Bacon.

Williams, D. F. (2011). *Communication sciences and disorders: An introduction to the professions.* Psychology Press.

Yairi, E., & Seery, C. H. (2011). *Stuttering: Foundations and clinical applications.* Boston: Pearson.

Chapter 11

Abrahams, B. E., & Geschwind, D. H. (2008). Advances in autism genetics: On the threshold of a new neurobiology. *Nature Review Genetics, 9,* 341–356.

American Psychiatric Association. (2000). *Diagnostic and statistical manual of mental disorders* (DSM-IV-TR), 4th ed. (text rev.). Washington, D.C.: Author.

Anckarsater, H. (2006). Central nervous changes in social dysfunction: Autism, aggression, and psychopathology. *Brain Research Bulletin, 69,* 259–265.

Ashbaker, B. Y., Dyches, T. T., Prater, M. A., & Sileo, N. M. (2012). Historical and legal foundations of family involvement in special education. In N. Sileo & M. A. Prater (Eds.), *Working with families of children with special needs: Family and professional partnerships and roles.* (pp. 1-22). Boston: Pearson.

Autism Speaks (2011). *Autism: Should my child take medicine for challenging behavior?: A decision aid for parents of children with autism spectrum disorder.* Autism Speaks Official Blog, September 14th.

Baron-Cohen, S., & Klin, A. (2006). What's so special about Asperger syndrome? *Brain and Cognition, 61,* 1–4.

Bauminger, N., Solomon, M., Aviezer, A., Heung, K., Brown, J., & Rogers, S. J., (2008). Friendship in high-functioning children with autism spectrum disorder: Mixed and non-mixed dyads. *Journal of Autism and Developmental Disorders, 38,* 1211–1229.

Beaumont, R., & Newcombe, P. (2006). Theory of mind and central coherence in adults with high-functioning autism or Asperger syndrome. *Autism, 10,* 365–382.

Bellini, S., & Akullian, J. (2007). A meta-analysis of video modeling and video self-modeling interventions for children and adolescents with autism spectrum disorders. *Exceptional Children, 73,* 264–287.

Bettelheim, B. (1967). *The empty fortress: Infantile autism and the birth of the self.* New York, NY: Free Press.

Billstedt, E., Gillberg, I. C., & Gillberg, C. (2011). Aspects of quality of life in adults diagnosed with autism in childhood: A population-based study. *Autism, 15*(1), 7–20.

Bitterman, A., Daley, T. C., Misra, S., Carlson, E., & Markowitz, J. (2008). A national sample of preschoolers with autism spectrum disorders: Special education services and parent satisfaction. *Journal of Autism and Developmental Disorders, 38,* 1509–1517.

Blacher, J., & McIntyre, L. L. (2006). Syndrome specificity and behavioral disorders in young adults with intellectual disability: Cultural differences in family impact. *Journal of Intellectual Disability Research, 50,* 184–198.

Blakemore S. J., Tavossoli, T., Calo, S., Thomas, R. M., Catmur, C., Frith, U., & Haggard, P. (2006). Tactile sensitivity in Asperger syndrome. *Brain and Cognition, 61,* 5–13.

Blaylock, R. L. (2008). The danger of excessive vaccination during brain development: The case for a link to autism spectrum disorders (ASD). *Medical Veritas, 5,* 1727–1741.

Bondy, A., & Frost, L. (2008). *Autism 24/7: A family guide to learning at home and in the community.* Bethesda, MD: Woodbine House.

Brobst, J. B., Clopton, J. R., & Hendrick, S. S. (2009). Parenting children with autism spectrum disorders: The couple's relationship. *Focus on Autism Other Developmental Disabilities, 24,* 38–49.

Brookman-Frazee, L., Baker-Ericzen, M.,

Stadnick, N., & Taylor, R. (2011). Parent perspectives on community mental health services for children with autism spectrum disorders. *Journal of Child and Family Studies, 14*, 237–257.

Bruns, D. A., & Thompson, S. D. (2012). *Feeding challenges in young children: Strategies and specialized interventions for success.* Baltimore: Paul H. Brookes Publishing Co., Inc.

Cannon, L., Kenworthy, L., Alexander, K. C., Werner, M. A., & Anthony, L. (2011). *Unstuck and on target! An executive function curriculum to improve flexibility for children with autism spectrum disorders, Research edition.* Baltimore: Paul H. Brookes Publishing Co., Inc.

Cappadocia, M., Weiss, J. A., & Pepler, D. (2012). Bullying experiences among children and youth with autism spectrum disorders. *Journal of Autism and Developmental Disorders, 42*(2), 266–277.

Carr, E. G., Dunlap, G., Horner, R. H., Koegel, R.L., Turnbull, A. P., Sailor, W., . . . Fox, L. (2002). Positive behavior support: Evolution of an applied science. *Journal of Positive Behavior Intervention, 4*, 4–16.

Centers for Disease Control and Prevention. (2009). Prevalence of autism spectrum disorders— Autism and Developmental Disabilities Monitoring Network, United States, 2006. *Morbidity and Mortality Weekly Report; Surveillance Summaries 58*(10), 1–20.

Centers for Disease Control and Prevention. (2012). Prevalence of autism spectrum disorders— Autism and Developmental Disabilities Monitoring Network, 14 Sites, United States, 2008. *Morbidity and Mortality Weekly Report: Surveillance Summaries.* 61(3), 1–19.

Cohen, H., Amerine-Dickens, M., & Smith, T. (2006). Early intensive behavioral treatment: Replicaton of the UCLA model in a community setting. *Journal of Developmental & Behavioral Pediatrics, 27*(Suppl 2), S145–S155.

Conroy, M. A., Asmus, J. M., Boyd, B. A., Ladwig, C. N., & Sellers, J. A. (2007). Antecedent classroom factors and disruptive behaviors of children with autism spectrum disorders. *Journal of Early Intervention, 30*, 19–35.

Dale, E., Jahoda, A., & Knott, F. (2006). Mothers' attributions following their child's diagnosis of autistic spectrum disorder: Exploring links with maternal levels of stress, depression and expectations about their child's future. *Autism, 10*, 463–479.

Dillenburger, K., Keenan, M., Doherty, A., Byrne, T., & Gallagher, S. (2010). Living with children diagnosed with autistic spectrum disorder: Parental and professional views. *British Journal of Special Education, 37*(1), 1–11.

Donovan, J. & Zucker, C. (2010, October). Autism's first child. *The Atlantic.* Retrieved February 25, 2012, www.theatlantic.com/magazine/archive/2010/10/autism-8217-s-first-child/8227/.

Dunlap, G., Carr, E. G., Horner, R. H., Zarcone, J. R., & Schwartz, I. (2008). Positive behavior support and applied behavior analysis: A familial alliance. *Behavior Modification, 8*(5), 682–697.

Dyches, T. T. (2010). Educating students with autism and related disorders. In P. Peterson, E. Baker, & B. McGaw (Eds.), *International encyclopedia of education: Special education,* 3rd ed. (pp. 661–668). Oxford, England: Elsevier.

Dyches, T. T., Carter, N., & Prater, M. A. (2011). *A teacher's guide to communicating with parents: Practical strategies for developing successful relationships.* Needham Heights, MA: Pearson/Allyn & Bacon.

Dyches, T. T., Prater, M. A., & Leininger, M. (2009). Juvenile literature and the portrayal of developmental disabilities. *Education and Training in Developmental Disabilities, 44*, 304–317.

Eaton, N. (2008). "I don't know how we coped before": A study of respite care for children in the home and hospice. *Journal of Clinical Nursing, 17*, 3196–3204.

Eaves, L. C., & Ho, H. H. (2008). Young adult outcome of autism spectrum disorders. *Journal of Autism and Developmental Disorders, 38*, 739–747.

Flippin, M., Reszka, S., & Watson, L. R. (2010). Effectiveness of the picture exchange communication system (PECS) on communication and speech for children with autism spectrum disorders: A meta-analysis. *American Journal of Speech-Language Pathology, 19*(2), 178–195.

Fombonne, E. (2009). Epidemiology of pervasive developmental disorders. *Pediatric Research, 65,* 591–598.

Fountain, C., King, M. D., & Bearman, P. S. (2011). Age of diagnosis for autism: Individual and community factors across 10 birth cohorts. *Journal of Epidemiology and Community Health, 65*(6), 503–510.

Freedman, B. H., Kalb, L. G., Zablotsky, B., & Stuart, E. A. (2012). Relationship status among parents of children with autism spectrum disorders: A population-based study. *Journal of Autism and Developmental Disorders, 42*, 539–548.

Gagnon, E. (2001). *The power card strategy: Using special interests to motivate children and youth with Asperger syndrome.* Shawnee Mission, KS: Autism Asperger Publishing Company.

Gau, S. S., Chou, M., Chiang, H., Lee, J., Wong, C., Chou, W., & Wu, Y. (2012). Parental adjustment, marital relationship, and family function in families of children with autism. *Research in Autism Spectrum Disorders, 6,* 263–270.

Giarelli, E., Wiggins, L. D., Rice, C. E., Levy, S. E., Kirby, R. S., Pinto-Martin, J., & Mandell, D. (2010). Sex differences in the evaluation and diagnosis of autism spectrum disorders among children. *Disability and Health Journal, 3,* 107–116.

Gibb, G. S., & Dyches, T. T. (2007). *Guide to writing quality individualized education programs,* 2nd ed. Needham Heights, MA: Allyn & Bacon.

Goin-Kochel, R. P., Mackintosh, V. H., & Myers, B. J. (2006). How many doctors does it take to make an autism spectrum diagnosis? *Autism, 10,* 439–451.

Hall, H. R., & Graff, J. C. (2010). Parenting challenges in families of children with autism: A pilot study. *Issues in Comprehensive Pediatric Nursing, 33,* 187–204.

Harrington, J. W., Patrick, P. A., & Edwards, K. S. (2006). Parental beliefs about autism: Implications for the treating physician. *Autism, 10,* 452–462.

Heaton, P., Williams, K., Cummins, O., & Happe, F. (2008). Autism and pitch processing splinter skills: A group and subgroup analysis. *Autism, 12,* 203–219.

Henault, I. (2006). *Asperger's syndrome and sexuality: From adolescence through adulthood.* London: Jessica Kingsley Publishers.

Hoffman, C. D., Sweeney, D. P., Hodge, D., Lopez-Wagner, M. C., & Looney, L. (2009). Parenting stress and closeness: Mothers of typically developing children and mothers of children with autism. *Focus on Autism and Other Developmental Disabilities, 24,* 178–187.

Hoffman, C. D. Sweeney, D. P., Hodge, D., Nam,

C. Y., & Botts, B. H. (2008). Children with autism: Sleep problems and mothers' stress. *Focus on Autism and Other Developmental Disabilities, 23*(3), 155–165.

Kanai, C., Tani, M., Hashimoto, R., Yamada, T., Ota, H., Watanabe, H., Iwanami, A., & Nobumasa, K. (2012). Cognitive profiles of adults with Asperger's disorder, high-functioning autism, and pervasive developmental disorder not otherwise specified based on the WAIS-III. *Research in Autism Spectrum Disorders, 6,* 58–64.

Kane, M., Connell, J. E., & Pellecchia, M. (2010). A quantitative analysis of language interventions for children with autism. *Behavior Analyst Today, 11*(2), 128–144.

Kanner, L. (1943). Autistic disturbances of affective contact. *Nervous Child, 2,* 217–250.

Karmiloff-Smith, A. (2009). Nativism versus neuroconstructivism: Rethinking the study of developmental disorders. *Developmental Psychology, 45,* 56–63.

Koegel, R. L., & Koegel, L. K. (2012). *The PRT pocket guide: Pivotal response treatment for autism spectrum disorders.* Baltimore: Paul H. Brookes, Publisher, Inc.

Koegel, R. L., & Koegel, L. K. (2006). *Pivotal response treatments for autism: Communication, social, & academic development.* Baltimore: Paul H. Brookes Publishing Company.

Kogan, M. D., Strickland, B. B., Blumberg, S. J.,

Singh, G. K., Perrin, J. M., & van Dyck, P. C. (2008). A national profile of the health care experiences and family impact of autism spectrum disorder among children in the United States, 2005–2006. *Pediatrics, 122,* e1149–e1158.

Ingersoll, B., & Hambrick, D. Z. (2011). The relationship between the broader autism phenotype, child severity, and stress and depression in parents of children with autism spectrum disorders. *Research in Autism Spectrum Disorders, 5*(1), 337–344.

Johnson, N., Frenn, M., Feetham, S., & Simpson, P. (2011). Autism spectrum disorder: Parenting stress, family functioning and health-related quality of life. *Families, Systems, & Health, 29*(3), 232–252.

Jones, C. R. G., Happé, F., Pickles, A., Marsden, A. J. S., Tregay, J., Baird, G., Simonoff, E., & Charman, T. (2011). 'Everyday memory' impairments in autism spectrum disorders. *Journal of Autism and Developmental Disorders, 41,* 455–464.

Lai, M-C., Lombardo, M. V., Pasco, G., Ruigrok, A. N. V., Wheelwright, S. J., Sadek, S. A., Bhismadev Chakrabarti, MRC AIMS Consortium, and Baron-Cohen, S. (2011). A behavioral comparison of male and female adults with high functioning autism spectrum conditions. *PLoS ONE 6*(6): e20835.

Lanou, A., Hough, L., & Powell, E. (2012). Case studies on using strengths and interests

to address the needs of students with autism spectrum disorders. *Intervention in School and Clinic, 47*(3) 175–182.

LeBlanc, L. A. (2010). Using video-based interventions with individuals with autism spectrum disorders: Introduction to the special issue. *Education and Treatment of Children, 33,* p. 333–337.

Legoff, D. B., & Sherman, M. (2006). Long-term outcome of social skills intervention based on interactive LEGO play. *Autism, 10,* 317–329.

Lee, L. C., Harrington, R. B., Louie, B. B., & Newschaffer, C. J. (2008). Children with autism: Quality of life and parental concerns. *Journal of Autism and Development Disorders, 38,* 1147–1160.

Levy, S. E., Giarelli, E., Lee, L. C. Schieve, L. A., Kirby, R. S., Cunniff, C., & Rice, C. E. (2010). Autism spectrum disorder and co-occurring developmental, psychiatric, and medical conditions among children in multiple populations of the United States. *Journal of Developmental and Behavioral Pediatrics, 31*(4), 267–275.

Leininger, M., Dyches, T. T., Prater, M.A., & Heath, M. A. (2010). Teaching students with obsessive-compulsive disorder. *Intervention in School and Clinic, 45*(4), 221–231.

MacFarlane, J. R., & Kanaya, T. (2009). What does it mean to be autistic? Inter-state variation in special education criteria for autism services. *Journal of Child and Family Studies, 18*(6), 662–669.

Mandell, D. S., Ittenbach, R. F., Levy, S. E., & Pinto-Martin, J. A. (2007). Disparities in diagnoses received prior to a diagnosis of autism spectrum disorder. *Journal of Autism and Developmental Disorders, 37*(9), 1795–1802.

Margetts, J. K., LeCouteur, A., & Croom, S. (2006). Families in a state of flux: The experience of grandparents in autism spectrum disorder. *Child: Care, Health and Development, 32*, 565–574.

Matson, J. L. & Wilkins, J. (2008). Nosology and diagnosis of Asperger''s syndrome. *Research in Autism Spectrum Disorders, 2*, 288–300.

Mayes, S., Calhoun, S. L., Murray, M. J., & Zahid, J. (2011). Variables associated with anxiety and depression in children with autism. *Journal of Developmental and Physical Disabilities, 23*(4), 325–337.

McConachie, H., & Robinson, G. (2006). What services do young children with autism spectrum disorder receive? *Child: Care, Health and Development, 32*, 553–557.

Meadan, H., Stoner, J. B., & Angell, M. E. (2010). Review of literature related to the social, emotional, and behavioral adjustment of siblings of individuals with autism spectrum disorder. *Journal of Developmental and Physical Disabilities, 22*(1), 83–100.

Minshew, N. J., & Meyer, J. A. (2006). Autism and related conditions. In M. J. Farah & T. E. Feinberg (Eds.), *Patient-based approaches to cognitive neuroscience,* 2nd ed. (pp. 419–431). Cambridge, MA: The MIT Press.

Montes, G., Halterman, J. S., & Magyar, C. I. (2009). Access to and satisfaction with school and community health services for US children with ASD. *Pediatrics, 124(Suppl.4),* S407–S413.

National Autism Center. (2009). *National Standards Report.* Randolph, MA: National Autism Center.

Nicholas, J. S., Charles, J. M., Carpenter, L. A., King, L. B., Jenner, W., & Spratt, E. G. (2008). Prevalence and characteristics of children with autism spectrum disorders. *Annals of Epidemiology,* 18, 130–136.

Nielson, K. M., Mandleco, B. L., Roper, S. O., Cox, A., Dyches, T. T., Marshall, E. S. (2012). Parental perceptions of sibling relationships in families rearing a child with a chronic condition. *Journal of Pediatric Nursing, 27,* 34–43.

Northey, W. F., Jr. (2009). Effectiveness research: A view from the USA. *Journal of Family Therapy, 31,* 75–84.

Orsmond, G. I., & Seltzer, M. M. (2007). Siblings of individuals with autism spectrum disorders across the life course. *Mental Retardation and Developmental Disabilities Research Reviews, 13*(4), 313–320.

Ozonoff, S., Iosi, A., Baguio, F., Cook, I. C., Hill, M. M., Hutman, T., … & Young, G. S. (2010). A prospective study of the emergence of early behavioral signs of autism. *Journal of the American Academy of Child Adolescent Psychiatry, 49,* 256–266.

Parker, J., Mandleco, B., Roper, S. O., Freeborn, D., & Dyches, T. T. (2011). Religiosity, spirituality, and marital relationships of parents raising a typically developing child or a child with a disability. *Journal of Family Nursing, 17*(1), 82–104.

Parner, E. T., Schendel, D. E., Thorsen, P. (2008). Autism prevalence trends over time in Denmark: Changes in prevalence and age at diagnosis. *Archives of Pediatrics and Adolescent Medicine, 162*(12), 1150–1156

Paul, R., Orlovski, S., Marcinko, H., & Volkmar, F. (2009). Conversational behaviors in youth with high-functioning ASD and Asperger syndrome. *Journal of Autism and Developmental Disorders, 39*(1), 115–125.

Petalas, M. A., Hastings, R. P., Nash, S., Lloyd, T., & Dowey, A. (2009). Emotional and behavioural adjustment in siblings of children with intellectual disability with and without autism. *Autism, 13*(5), 471–483.

Peters-Scheffer, N., Didden, R., Korzilius, H., & Sturmey, P. (2011). A meta-analytic study on the effectiveness of comprehensive ABA-based early intervention programs for children with autism spectrum disorders. *Research in Autism Spectrum Disorders, 5*(1), 60–69.

Perkins, M. R., Dobbinson, S., Boucher, J., Bol, S., & Bloom, P. (2006). Lexical knowledge and lexical use in autism. *Journal of Autism and Developmental Disorders, 36,* 795–805.

Pottie, C. G., & Ingram, K. M. (2008). Daily stress, coping, and well-being in parents of children with autism: A multilevel modeling approach. *Journal of Family Psychology, 22*(6), 855–864.

Rivers, J. W., & Stoneman, Z. (2008). Child temperaments, differential parenting, and the sibling relationships of children with autism spectrum disorder. *Journal of Autism and Developmental Disorders, 38,* 1740–1750.

Rogers, S. J., & Ozonoff, S. (2006). Behavioral, educational, and developmental treatments for autism. In S. O. Moldin & J. L. R. Rubenstein (Eds.), *Understanding autism: From basic neuroscience to treatment* (pp. 443–473). Boca Raton, FL: CRC Press.

Saracino, J., Noseworthy, J., Steiman, M., Reisinger, L., & Fombonne, E. (2010). Diagnostic and assessment issues in autism surveillance and prevalence. *Journal of Developmental and Physical Disabilities, 22*(4), 317–330.

Schaaf, R. C., Toth-Cohen, S., Johnson, S. L., Outten, G., & Benevides, T. W. (2011). The everyday routines of families of children with autism: Examining the impact of sensory processing difficulties on the family. *Autism: The International Journal of Research and Practice, 15*(3), 373–389.

Schlosser, R. W., & Wendt, O. (2008). Effects of augmentative and alternative communication intervention on speech production in children with autism: A systematic review. *American Journal of Speech-Language Pathology, 17,* 212–230.

Shattuck, P. T., Durkin, M., Maenner, M., Newschaffer, C., Mandell, D.S., Wiggins, & Cuniff, C. (2009). Timing of identification among children with an autism spectrum disorder: findings from a population-based surveillance study. *Journal of the American Academy of Child and Adolescent Psychiatry, 48*(5), 474–483.

Smith, L. M. (2007). Parental first-person account to senior author. Retrieved from www.archpediatrics.com. *American Medical Association*, pp. 324–325.

Spek, A., Schatorje, T., Scholte, E., & van Berckerlaer-Onnes, I. (2009). Verbal fluency in adults with high functioning autism or Asperger syndrome. *Neuropsychologia, 47,* 652–656.

Strang, J. F., Kenworthy, L., Daniolos, P., Case, L., Wills, M. C., Martin, A., & Wallace, G. L. (2012). Depression and anxiety symptoms in children and adolescents with autism spectrum disorders without intellectual disability. *Research in Autism Spectrum Disorders, 6*(1), 406–412.

Stuart, M., & McGrew, J. H. (2009). Caregiver burden after receiving a diagnosis of an autism spectrum disorder. *Research in Autism Spectrum Disorders, 3*(1), 86–97.

Tiegerman-Farber, E. (2009). Autism spectrum disorders: Learning to communicate. In D. K. Bernstein & E. Tiegerman-Farber (Eds.), *Language and communication disorders in children,* 6th ed. (pp. 314–369). Boston: Allyn and Bacon.

Toth, K., & King, B. H. (2008). Asperger's syndrome: Diagnosis and treatment. *American Journal of Psychiatry, 165,* 958–963.

Treffert, D. (2009). The savant syndrome: An extraordinary condition. A synopsis: past, present, and future. *Philosophical Transactions of The Royal Society, 364*(1522), 1351–1357.

Treffert, D. A. (2007). The autistic artist, "special faculties," and savant syndrome. *Archives of Pediatric and Adolescent Medicine, 161*(4), 323–234.

U.S. Department of Education, Office of Special Education Programs. (2011). *The 30th annual report to Congress on the Implementation of the Individuals with Disabilities Education Act.* Washington, D.C.: U.S. Government Printing Office.

Volkmar, F. R., & Wiesner, L. A. (2009). *A practical guide to autism: What every parent, family member, and teacher needs to know.* Hoboken, NJ: John Wiley & Sons.

Wallace, G. L. (2008). Neuropsychological studies of savant skills: Can they inform the neuroscience of giftedness? *Roeper Review, 30,* 229–246.

Watson, L. R., Patten E., Baranek, G. T., Poe, M., Boyd, B. A., Freuler, A., & Lorenzia, J. (2011). Differential associations between sensory response patterns and language, social, and communication measures in children with autism or other developmental disabilities. *Journal of Speech, Language & Hearing Research, 54*(6), 1562–1576.

Weismer, S. E., Lord, C., & Esler, A. (2010). Early language patterns of toddlers on the autism spectrum compared to toddlers with developmental delay. *Journal of Autism and Developmental Disorders, 40,* 1259–1273.

White, S. W., Scahill, L., Klin, A., Koenig, K., & Volkmar, F. (2007). Educational placements and service use patterns of individuals with autism spectrum disorders. *Journal of Autism and Developmental Disorders, 37*(8), 1403–1412.

Willis, C. (2009). *Creating inclusive learning environments for young children: What to do on Monday morning.* Thousand Oaks, CA: Corwin Press.

Wolff, J. J., Gu, H., Gerig, G., Elison, J. T., Styner, M., Gouttard, S., Botteron, K. N., Dager, S. R., Dawson, G., Estes, A. M., Evans, A. C., Hazlett, H. C., Kostopoulos, P., McKinstry, R. C., Paterson, S. J., Schultz, R. T., Zwaigenbaum, L., Piven, J., and the IBIS Network. (2012). Differences in white matter fiber tract development present from 6 to 24 months in infants with autism. *American Journal of Psychiatry in Advance,* 1–12. Retrieved from http://ajp.psychiatryonline.org/data/Journals/AJP/PAP/appi.ajp.2011.11091447.pdf.

Zandt, F. (2007). Repetitive behaviour in children with high functioning autism and obsessive compulsive disorder. *Journal of Autism and Developmental Disorders, 37*(2), 251–259.

Chapter 12

Abt Associates (1974). *Assessments of selected resources for severely handicapped children and youth. Vol I: A state-of-the-art paper.* Cambridge, MA: Author (ERIC Document Reproduction Service No. ED 134 614).

The ARC. (2012a). Causes and prevention of intellectual disabilities. Retrieved February 28, 2012, from www.thearc.org/page.aspx?pid=2453.

The ARC. (2012b). *Position statement on education.* Retrieved February 14, 2012, from www.thearc.org/page.aspx?pid=2368.

Batshaw, M., Pellegrino, L. & Rozien, N.J. (2008). *Children with disabilities,* 6th ed. Baltimore: Paul H. Brookes.

Beirne-Smith, M., Patton, J. R., & Hill, S. (2011). *Introduction to intellectual disabilities,* 8th ed. Upper Saddle River, NJ: Prentice-Hall.

Berk, L. E. (2005). *Development through the*

lifespan. Boston: Allyn and Bacon.

Bishop, V. E. (2005). *Teaching visually impaired children,* 3rd ed. Springfield, IL: Charles C. Thomas.

Bremer, C. D., Kachgal, M., & Schoeller, K. (2003, April). Self-determination: Supporting successful transition. *Research to Practice Brief of the National Center on Secondary Education and Transition, 2*(1), 1–5.

Brown, F., & Snell, M. (2011). Measuring student behavior and learning. In M. E. Snell & F. Brown (Eds.), *Instruction for students with severe disabilities,* 7th ed. (pp. 186-223.). Boston: Pearson Group.

Crockett, M., & Hardman, M. L. (2009a). Expected outcomes and emerging values. In J. McDonnell & M. L. Hardman, *Successful transition programs,* 2nd ed. (pp. 25–42). Los Angeles: Sage Publishing.

Crockett, M., & Hardman, M. L. (2009b). The role of secondary education in transition. In J. McDonnell & M. L. Hardman, *Successful transition programs* (p. 44). Los Angeles: Sage Publishing Company.

Drew, C. J., & Hardman, M. L. (2007). *Intellectual disabilities across the lifespan,* 9th ed. Columbus, OH: Merrill.

Ford, A., Davern, L., & Schnorr, R. (2001, July/August). Learners with significant disabilities: Curricular relevance in an era of standards-based reform. *Remedial and Special Education, 22*(4), 214–222.

Giangreco, M. (2011). Educating students with severe disabilities: Foundational concepts and practices. In M. E. Snell & F. Brown (Eds.), *Instruction of students with severe disabilities,* 7th ed. (pp. 1–30). Boston: Pearson Group.

Gollnick, D., & Chinn, P. C. (2012). *Multicultural education in a diverse society,* 9th ed. Boston: Allyn and Bacon.

Hewitt, A., & O'Nell, S. (2009). *I am who I am: A little help from my friends.* Washington, DC: President's Committee on Intellectual Disabilities.

Johnston, S. (2003). Assistive technology. In J. McDonnell, M. Hardman, & A. McDonnell, *Introduction to persons with severe disabilities* (pp. 138–159). Boston: Allyn and Bacon.

Justen, J. (1976). Who are the severely handicapped? A problem in definition. *AAESPH Review,* 1(5), 1–12.

McDonnell, J., Hardman, M., & McDonnell, A. P. (2003). *Introduction to persons with moderate and severe disabilities,* 2nd ed. Boston: Allyn and Bacon.

Meyer, L. H., Peck, C. A., & Brown, L. (1991). Definitions and diagnosis. In L. H. Meyer, C. A. Peck, & L. Brown (Eds.), *Critical issues in the lives of people with disabilities* (p. 17). Baltimore: Paul H. Brookes.

Moore, B. J., & Montgomery, J. K. (2008). *Making a difference for America's children: Speech–language pathologists in public schools.*

Greenville, SC: Super Duper Publications.

Morrison, D. (2010). Social media opens social world to elderly disabled. *Star News Online.* Retrieved March 2, 2012, from www.starnewsonline.com/article/20100126/articles/100129756?p=1&tc=pg.

Quenemoen, R., & Thurlow, M. (2012). *NCEO policy directions: Planning alignment studies for alternate assessments based on alternate achievement standards.* Retrieved February 28, 2012, from www.cehd.umn.edu/NCEO/OnlinePubs/Policy20/PolicyDirections20.pdf.

Rues, J. P., Graff, J. C., Ault, M. M., & Holvoet, J. F. (2006). Special health care procedures. In M. E. Snell & F. Brown (Eds.), *Introduction to students with severe disabilities,* 6th ed. (pp. 251–290). Upper Saddle River, NJ: Merrill.

Sailor, W., & Haring, N. (1977). Some current directions in the education of the severely/multiply handicapped. *AAESPH Review, 2,* 67–86.

Snell, M. E. (1991). Schools are for all kids: The importance of integration for students with severe disabilities and their peers. In J. Lloyd, N. N. Singh, & A. C. Repp (Eds.), *The regular education initiative: Alternative perspectives on concepts, issues, and models* (pp. 133B148). Sycamore, IL: Sycamore.

Snell, M. E., & Brown, F. (2011). Selecting teaching strategies and understanding educational environments.. In M. E.

Snell & F. Brown (Eds.), *Introduction to students with severe disabilities,* 7th ed. (pp. 122-- 185). Boston: Pearson Group. .

TASH. (2012a). *About us.* Retrieved February 19, 2012, from http://tash.org/about/.

TASH. (2012b). *Mission and vision.* Retrieved February 27, 2012, from http://tash.org/about/mission/.

TASH. (2012c). *TASH resolution on life in the community.* Retrieved January 28, 2012, from http://tash.org/advocacy-issues/community-living/.

U.S. Department of Education. (2011). To assure the free appropriate public education of all children with disabilities. *Thirtieth annual report to Congress on the implementation of the Individuals with Disabilities Education Act, 2008.* Washington, D.C.: U.S. Government Printing Office.

Voss, K. S. (2005). *Teaching by design.* Bethesda, MD: Woodbine House.

Wehmeyer, M. L., Gragoudas, S., & Shogren, K. A. (2006). Self-determination, student involvement, and leadership development. In P. Wehman, *Life beyond the classroom: Transition strategies for young people with disabilities,* 4th ed. (pp. 41–69). Baltimore: Paul H. Brookes.

Westling, D., & Fox, L. (2009). *Teaching students with severe disabilities,* 4th ed. Upper Saddle River, NJ: Merrill/Prentice Hall.

Ysseldyke, J. E., & Olsen, K. (2012). *Putting alternate*

assessments into practice: What to measure and possible sources of data. NCEO Synthesis Report 28. Minneapolis: The National Center on Educational Outcomes, University of Minnesota. Retrieved February 1, 2012, from www.cehd. umn.edu/NCEO/Online-Pubs/archive/Synthesis/Synthesis28.htm.

Ysseldyke, J. E., Olsen, K., & Thurlow, M. (2012). Issues and considerations in alternate assessments. NCEO Synthesis Report 27. Minneapolis: The National Center on Educational Outcomes, University of Minnesota. Retrieved January 14, 2012, from www.cehd. umn.edu/NCEO/OnlinePubs/archive/Synthesis/Synthesis27. htm.

Chapter 13

Adams, M. (2003). Elevated: Tamika Catchings will not let her niceness, or her deafness, prevent her from becoming the best player in the W.N.B.A. New York Times Magazine, May 25, pp. 26–29.

Alexander Graham Bell Academy. (2012). Auditory Verbal Principles. Retrieved March 14, 2012, from www.avchears.org/principles.php.

American Foundation for the Blind. (2012). Educating students with visual impairments for inclusion in society: A paper on the inclusion of students with visual impairments. Retrieved January 31, 2009, from www.afb.org/section .aspx?FolderID=3&SectionID=44&TopicID=189&DocumentID=1344.

American Speech Hearing and Language Association (ASHA). (2012). Cochlear implants quick facts. Retrieved March 15, 2012, from www .asha.org/about/news/tipsheets/cochlear_quickfacts.htm.

Barraga, N. C., & Erin, J. N. (2002). Visual impairments and learning, 4th ed. Austin, TX: Pro-Ed.

Batshaw, M., Pellegrino, L. & Rozien, N. J. (2008). Children with disabilities, 6th ed. Baltimore: Paul H. Brookes.

Berg, A. L., Ip, S. C., Hurst, M., & Herb, A. (2007). Cochlear implants in young children: Informed consent as a process and current practices. American Journal of Audiology, 16(1), 13–28.

Bishop, V. E. (2005). Teaching visually impaired children, 3rd ed. Springfield, IL: Charles C. Thomas.

Bouchard, D., & Tetreault, S. (2000). The motor development of sighted children and children with moderate low vision aged 8–13. Journal of Visual Impairments and Blindness, 94, 564–573.

Center for Assessment and Demographic Studies. (2012). Demographic aspects of hearing impairment: Questions and answers, 1994 (Updated 2011). Washington, D.C.: Gallaudet University. Retrieved May 16, 2012, from http://research .gallaudet.edu/Demographics/factsheet .php#Q13.

Centers for Disease Control. (2012). Hearing loss. Retrieved March 4, 2012, from www.cdc.gov/ ncbddd/hearingloss/index.html.

Correa-Torres, S. M. (2008). The nature of the social experiences of students with deaf-blindness who are educated in inclusive settings. Journal of Visual Impairment & Blindness, 102(5), 272–283.

Cox, P. R., & Dykes, M. K. (2001). Effective classroom adaptations for students with visual impairments. Teaching Exceptional Children, 33(6), 68–74.

Dorr, R. E. (2006). Something old is new again: Revisiting language experience. The Reading Teacher, 60(2), 138–146.

Gilbertson, D., & Ferre, S. (2008). Considerations in the identification, assessment, and intervention process for deaf and hard-of-hearing students with reading difficulties. Psychology in the Schools, 45(2), 104–120.

Heine, C., & Slone, M. (2008). The impact of mild central auditory processing disorder on school performance during adolescence. Journal of School Health, 78(7), 405–407.

Hintermair, M. (2008). Self-esteem and satisfaction with life and hard-of-hearing people—a resource-oriented approach to identity work. Journal of Deaf Studies and Deaf Education, 13(2), 278–300.

Kaland, M., & Salvatore, K. (2012). Psychology of hearing loss. Retrieved March 9, 2012, from www.asha .org/Publications/leader/2002/020319/020319d/.

KidSource. (2012). Undetected vision disorders are blinding children: Earlier testing needed to preserve good eyesight. Retrieved January 26, 2012, from www.kidsource.com/kidsource/content/news/vision.html.

Koenig, A. J., & Holbrook, M. C. (2005). Literacy skills. In A. J. Koenig & M. C. Holbrook (Eds.), Foundations of education: Volume II Instructional strategies for teaching children and youths with visual impairments, 2nd ed. (pp. 264–312). New York: AFB Press.

Kurzweil Technologies. (2012). A brief career summary of Ray Kurzweil. Burlington, MA: Lernout & Hauspie. Retrieved March 17, 2012, from www.kurzweiltech .com/aboutray.html.

Leigh, S. A., & Barclay, L. A. (2000). High school braille readers: Achieving academic success. RE: View, 32, 123–131.

Lewallen, S., Massae, P., Tharany, M., Somba, M., Geneau, R., MacArthur, C., & Courtwright, P. (2008). Evaluating a school-based trachoma curriculum in Tanzania. Health Education Research, 23(6), 1068–1073.

Lewis, S., & Tolla, J. (2003). Creating and using tactile experience books for young children with visual impairments. Teaching Exceptional Children, 35(3), 22–25.

Li, A. (2004). Classroom strategies for improving and enhancing visual skills in students with disabilities. Teaching Exceptional Children, 36(6), 38–46.

Library of Congress. (2009). *That all may read*. National Library Service for the Blind and Physically Handicapped (NLS). Retrieved March 2, 2012 from www.loc.gov/nls/.

Library of Congress. (2012). *That all may read*. National Library Service for the Blind and Physically Handicapped (NLS). Retrieved March 2, 2012 from http://www.loc.gov/nls/.

Lund, S. K., & Troha, J. M. (2008). Teaching young people who are blind and have autism to make requests using a variation on the picture exchange communication system with tactile symbols: A preliminary investigation. *Journal of Autism and Developmental Disabilities, 38*(4), 719–730.

Marschark, M., Lang, H. G., & Albertini, J. A. (2007). *Educating deaf students: From research to practice*. New York: Oxford University Press.

Marschark, M., & Spencer, P. E. (2011). *Oxford handbook of deaf studies, language, and education, Volume 2*. New York: Oxford University Press.

McAnally, P. L., Rose, S., & Quigley, S. P. (2005). *Language learning practices with deaf children*, 3rd ed. Austin, TX: Pro Ed.

McGowan, R. S., Nittrouer, S., & Chenausky, K. (2008). Speech production in 12-month-old children with and without hearing loss. *Journal of Speech, Language, and Hearing Research, 51*(4), 879–888.

McKeen, S. (2012). A new language for baby. *The Ottawa Citizen*. Retrieved February 25, 2012, from http://littlesigners.com/article3.html.

McLinden, M., & McCall, S. (2006). *Learning through touch: Supporting children with visual impairments and additional difficulties*. Milton Park Abingdon, UK: David Fulton Publishers.

Moore, D. R. (2007). Auditory processing disorders: Acquisition and treatment. *Journal of Communication Disorders, 40*(4), 295–304.

Moores, D. F. (2008). *Educating the deaf: Psychology, principles and practices plus guide to inclusion,* 5th ed. Boston: Houghton-Mifflin.

Narr, R. F. (2008). Phonological awareness and decoding in deaf/hard-of-hearing students who use visual phonics. *Journal of Deaf Studies and Deaf Education, 13*(3), 405–416.

National Academy on an Aging Society. (2012). *Hearing loss: A growing problem that affects quality of life, 2*, 1–6. Retrieved February 15, 2012, from www.agingsociety.org/agingsociety/pdf/hearing.pdf.

National Institute on Deafness and Other Communication Disorders. (2012a). *American Sign Language. Health information: Hearing and balance*. Retrieved March 2, 2012, from www.nidcd.nih.gov/health/hearing/asl.asp.

National Institute on Deafness and Other Communication Disorders. (2012b). *Cochlear implants.*

Health information: Hearing and balance. Retrieved January 31, 2012, from www.nidcd.nih.gov/health/hearing/coch.asp.

National Institute on Deafness and Other Communication Disorders. (2012c). *Otitis media. Health information: Hearing and balance.* Retrieved March 9, 2012, from www.nidcd.nih.gov/health/hearing/pages/earinfections.aspx.

National Technical Institute for the Deaf. (2006). *Welcome to C-Print*. Rochester, NY: Author.

Official Website of Tamika Catchings. (2012). Retrieved March 12, 2012, from www.catchin24.com/bio/.

Owen, D. T. (2007). Noise-induced hearing loss. *The Instrumentalist, 62*(3), 23–24, 26, 28.

Papadopolous, K., Argyropolous, V. S., & Kouroupetroglou, G. (2008). Discrimination and comprehension of synthetic speech by students with visual impairments: The case of similar acoustic patterns. *Journal of Visual Impairment & Blindness, 102*(7), 420–429.

Pester, P. (2012). *Braille bits*. Louisville, KY: American Printing House for the Blind. Retrieved March 16, 2012, from www.aph.org/edresearch/bits898.htm.

Poobrasert, O., & Cercone, N. (2009). Evaluation of educational multimedia support system for students with deafness. *Journal of Educational Multimedia and Hypermedia, 18*(1), 71–90.

Poon, T., & Ovadia, R. (2008). Using tactile learning aids for students with visual impairments in a first-semester organic chemistry course. *Journal of Chemical Education, 85*(2), 240–242.

Rathmann, C., Mann, W., & Morgan, G. (2007). Narrative structure and narrative development in deaf children. *Deafness and Education International, 9*(4), 187–196.

Riddering, A. T. (2008). Keeping older adults with vision loss safe: Chronic conditions and comorbidities that influence functional mobility. *Journal of Visual Impairment & Blindness, 102*(10), 616–620.

Sacks, S. Z., & Silberman, R. K. (2000). Social skills. In A. J. Koenig & M. C. Holbrook (Eds.), *Foundations of education, Volume II: Instructional strategies for teaching children and youths with visual impairments,* 2nd ed. (pp. 616–652). New York: AFB Press.

Scheetz, N. A. (2004). *Psychosocial aspects of deafness*. Boston: Pearson Education.

Social Security Administration. (2012). *Disability planner: Special rules for people who are blind*. Washington, D.C.: Author. Retrieved March 10, 2012, from www.ssa.gov/dibplan/dqualify8.htm.

Steinweg, S. B., Griffin, H. C., Griffin, L. W., & Gingras, H. (2005). Retinopathy of prematurity. *RE: view: Rehabilitation for blindness and visual impairment, 37*(1), 32.

Supalo, C. A., Malouk, T. E., & Rankel, L. (2008). Low-cost laboratory adaptations for precollege students who are blind or visually impaired. *Journal of Chemical Education, 85*(2), 243–247.

Tasker, S., & Schmidt, L. A. (2008). The "dual usage problem" in the explanations of "joint attention" and children's socioemotional development: A reconceptualization. *Developmental Review, 28*(3), 263–288.

The Official Website of Tamika Catchings. (2012). *Tamika Catchings.* Retrieved March 12, 2012, from www.catchin24.com/bio/.

Tollefsen, M., Dale, Ø, Berg, M, & Nordby, R. (2011). *Connected!: Disabled and use of social media.* Retrieved March 12, 2012, from http://medialt.no/news/en-US/connected-disabled-and-use-of-social-media/737.aspx.

United Nations World Food Programme. (2012). *Hunger.* Retrieved February 1, 2012, from http://www.wfp.org/hunger.

U.S. Department of Education. (2011). To assure the free appropriate public education of all children with disabilities. *Thirtieth annual report to Congress on the implementation of the Individuals with Disabilities Education Act, 2008.* Washington, D.C.: U.S. Government Printing Office.

Wurst, D., Jones, D., & Luckner, J. (2005, May/June). Promoting literacy development with students who are hard-of-hearing, and hearing. *Teaching Exceptional Children, 37*(5) 56–62.

Chapter 14

AIDS.gov. (2012). *Legal disclosure.* Retrieved February 1, 2012, from http://aids.gov/hiv-aids-basics/diagnosed-with-hiv-aids/your-legal-rights/legal-disclosure/.

Alba, A., & Chan, L. (2007). Pulmonary rehabilitation. In R. L. Braddom (Ed.), *Physical medicine & rehabilitation* (pp. 739–751). Philadelphia, PA: Saunders.

American Academy for Cerebral Palsy and Developmental Medicine. (2011). *What is cerebral palsy?* Retrieved on January 11, 2012, from www.aacpdm.org/patients/what_is_cerebral_palsy.php.

American Academy of Pediatrics. (2011). *Contagious health problems in schools: AIDS/HIV infection.* Retrieved February 4, 2012, from www.healthychildren.org/English/ages-stages/gradeschool/school/Pages/Contagious-Health-Problems-in-Schools.aspx?nfstatus=401&nftoken=00000000-0000-0000-0000-000000000000&nfstatusdescription=ERROR%3a+No+local+token.

American Diabetes Association. (2012a). *Diabetes basics: Diabetes statistics.* Retrieved on February 4, 2012, from www.diabetes.org/diabetes-basics/diabetes-statistics/.

American Diabetes Association. (2012b). *Living with diabetes.* Retrieved June 13, 2012, from http://www.diabetes.org/living-with-diabetes/?loc=GlobalNavLWD

American Federation of Teachers. (2009). *The medically fragile child: Caring for children with special healthcare needs in the school setting.* Retrieved January 18, 2011, from www.aft.org/pdfs/healthcare/medically-fragilechild0409.pdf.

American Lung Association. (2012). About asthma. Retrieved February 23, 2012, from www.lung.org/lung-disease/asthma/about-asthma/.

Anwar, M., Boyd, B., & Romesburg, A. M. (2007). I have cerebral palsy . . . it doesn't have me! *Exceptional Parent, 37*(6), 100.

Asthma and Allergy Foundation of American. (2012a). *Prevention.* Retrieved February 12, 2012, from www.aafa.org/display.cfm?id=8&cont=9.

Asthma and Allergy Foundation of American. (2012b). *Treatment.* Retrieved February 12, 2012, from http://www.aafa.org/display.cfm?id=8&cont=8.

Asthma and Allergy Foundation of American. (2012c). *What causes asthma?* Retrieved February 12, 2012, from www.aafa.org/display.cfm?id=8&cont=6.

Asthma and Allergy Foundation of American. (2012d). *What is asthma?* Retrieved February 12, 2012, from http://www.aafa.org/display.cfm?id=8&cont=5.

Ball, J. W., & Bindler, R. C. (2008). Alterations in immune function. In J. W. Ball & R. C. Bindler (Eds.), *Pediatric nursing* (pp. 546–583). Upper Saddle River, NJ: Pearson Education.

Barkley, R. A. (2006a). ADHD in adults: Development course and outcome of children with ADHD and ADHD in clinic-referred adults. In R. A. Barkley, *Attention-deficit hyperactivity disorder,* 3rd ed. (pp. 248–296). New York: Guilford Press.

Barkley, R. A. (2006b). Etiologies. In R. A. Barkley, *Attention-deficit hyperactivity disorder,* 3rd ed. (pp. 219–247). New York: Guilford Press.

Barkley, R. A. (2006c). Primary symptoms, diagnostic criteria, prevalence, and gender differences. In R. A. Barkley, *Attention-deficit hyperactivity disorder,* 3rd ed. (pp. 76–121). New York: Guilford Press.

Barkley, R. A. (2006d). Psychological counseling of adults with ADHD. In R. A. Barkley, *Attention-deficit hyperactivity disorder,* 3rd ed. (pp. 692–703). New York: Guilford Press.

Barkley, R. A., & Edwards, G. (2006). Diagnostic interview, behavior rating scales, and the medical evalution. In R. A. Barkley, *Attention-deficit hyperactivity disorder,* 3rd ed. (pp. 297–334). New York: Guilford Press.

Barnard-Brak, L., Sulak, T. N., & Fearon, D. D. (2011). Coexisting disorders and academic achievement among children with ADHD. *Journal of Attention Disorders, 15*(2), 506–515.

Beena, A place to share. Retrieved April, 16, 2009, from http://tbihome.org/stories/beena2.htm.

Best, S. J., Heller, K. W., & Bigge, J. L. (2004). Teaching Individuals with Physical or Multiple Disabilities, 5th ed. Upper Saddle River, NJ: Prentice Hall.

Beukelman, D. R., & Mirenda, P. (2005). *Augmentative and alternative communication: Supporting children and adults with complex communication needs,* 3rd ed. Baltimore, MD: Paul H. Brookes Publishing Company.

Blair, J. L. (2010). Epilepsy and seizure disorders. In P. J. Allen, J. A. Vessey, & N. A. Shapiro (Eds.), *Child with a chronic condition,* 5th ed., (pp. 486–513). St. Louis, Missouri: Mosby.

Blosser, C. G., & Reider-Demer, M. (2009). Neurologic disorders. In C. E. Burns, A. M. Dunn, M. A. Brady, N. B. Starr, & C. G. Blosser (Eds.), *Pediatric care,* 4th ed.) (pp. 634–672). St. Louis, MO: Sanders.

Brady, M. A. (2009). Respiratory diseases. In C. E. Burns, A. M. Dunn, M. A. Brady, N. B. Starr, & C. G. Blosser (Eds.), *Pediatric care,* 4th ed. (pp. 767–794). St. Louis, MO: Sanders.

Bramham, J., Young, S., & Bickerdike, A. (2009). Evaluation of group cognitive behavioral therapy for adults with ADHD. *Journal of Attention Disorders, 12*(5), 434–441.

Browder, D. M. & Spooner, F. (2011). *Teaching students with moderate and severe disabilities.* New York, NY: Guilford.

Bullough, R. V. (2011). *Adam's fall: Traumatic brain injury, the first 365 days.* Sante Fe, NM: The Sunstone Press.

Bussing, R., Mason, D. M., & Bell, L. (2010). Adolescent outcomes of childhood attention-deficit/hyperactivity disorder in a diverse community sample. *Journal of the American Academy of Child & Adolescent Psychiatry, 49*(6), 595–605.

Centers for Disease Control and Prevention. (2012a). *Adolescent and school health: Childhood obesity facts.* Retrieved February 4, 2012, from www.cdc.gov/healthyyouth/obesity/facts.htm.

Centers for Disease Control and Prevention. (2012b). *Facts about ADHD.* Retrieved February 6, 2012, from www.cdc.gov/ncbddd/adhd/facts.html.

Centers for Disease Control and Prevention. (2012c). *HIV/AID statistics and surveillance: Basic statistics.* Retrieved January 19, 2012, from www.cdc.gov/hiv/topics/surveillance/basic.htm#def.

Centers for Disease Control and Prevention. (2012d). *How many people have TBI?* Retrieved February 6, 2012, from www.cdc.gov/ncipc/pub-res/tbi_in_us_04/tbi_ed.htm.

Centers for Disease Control and Prevention. (2012e). *Injury prevention and control: Traumatic brain injury: How many people have TBI?* Retrieved February 7, 2012, from www.cdc.gov/traumaticbraininjury/statistics.html.

Centers for Disease Control and Prevention. (2012f). *Injury prevention and control: Traumatic brain injury: What are the leading causes of TBI?* Retrieved February 13, 2012, from www.cdc.gov/TraumaticBrainInjury/causes.html.

Centers for Disease Control and Prevention. (2012g). *What you should know about sickle cell disease.* Washington, D.C.: Center for Disease Control and Prevention.

Centre for Neuro Skills. (2012). *Epidemiology of TBI.* Retrieved June 13, 2012, from http://www.neuroskills.com/brain-injury/epidemiology-of-traumatic-brain-injury.php.

Child Care Law Center. (2005). *Caring for children with HIV or AIDS in child care.* San Francisco, CA: Child Care Law Center.

Children's Defense Fund. (2010). *Protect children, not guns 2010.* Washington, D.C.: Children's Defense Fund.

Cifu, D. X., Kreutzer, J. S., Slater, D. N., & Taylor, L. (2007). Rehabilitation after traumatic brain injury. In R. L. Braddom (Ed.), *Physical medicine & rehabilitation* (pp. 1133–1174). Philadelphia, PA: Saunders.

Clark, C. D. (2003). *In sickness and in play: Children coping with chronic illness.* Piscataway, NJ: Rutgers University Press.

Compassionate Friends. (2012). *You need not walk alone.* Retrieved January 18, 2011, from www.compassionatefriends.org/Brochures/you_need_not_walk_alone.aspx.

Comstock, E. J. (2011). The end of drugging children: Toward the genealogy of the ADHD subject. *Journal of The History of The Behavioral Sciences, 47*(1), 44–69.

Cystic Fibrosis Foundation. (2012a). *About cystic fibrosis.* Retrieved February 6, 2012, from www.cff.org/AboutCF/.

Cystic Fibrosis Foundation. (2012b). *Frequently asked questions: Who gets cystic fibrosis?* Retrieved February 6, 2012, from www.cff.org/AboutCF/Faqs/.

Daley, D., & Birchwood, J. (2010). ADHD and academic performance: Why does ADHD impact on academic performance and what can be done to support ADHD children in the classroom? *Child: Care, Health and Development, 36*(4), 455–464.

Defense and Veterans Brain Injury Center. (2012). *TBI numbers by severity—all armed forces.* Retrieved February 2012, from www.dvbic.org/images/pdfs/TBI-Numbers/2010-2011Q3-updates/dod-tbi-2000-2011Q3.

Dooley, J., Gordon, K. E., Dodds, L., & MacSween, J. (2010). Duchenne muscular dystrophy: A 30-year population-based incidence study, *Clinical Pediatrics, 49*(2), 177–179.

Doyle, E. A., & Grey, M. (2010). Diabetes mellitus (Types 1 and 2). In P. J. Allen, J. A. Vessey, & N. A. Shapiro (Eds.), *Child with a chronic condition,* 5th ed. (pp. 427–446). St. Louis, Missouri: Mosby.

DuPaul, G. J., & Kern, L. (2011a). Assessment and identification of attention-deficit/hyperactivity disorder. In *Young children with ADHD: Early identification and intervention* (pp. 23–46). Washington, D.C.: American Psychological Association.

DuPaul, G. J., & Kern, L. (2011b). Psychotropic medication treatment. In *Young children with ADHD: Early identification and intervention* (pp. 149–165). Washington, D.C.: American Psychological Association.

DuPaul, G. J., Weyandt, L. L., & Janusis, G. M. (2011). ADHD in the classroom: Effective intervention strategies. *Theory Into Practice, 50*(1), 35–42.

Efron, D. & Sciberras, E. (2010). The diagnostic outcomes of children with suspected attention deficit hyperactivity disorder following multidisciplinary assessment. *Journal of Paediatrics and Child Health 46*, 392–397.

Elkins, I. J., Malone, S., Keyes, M., Iacono, W. G., & McGue, M. (2011). The impact of attention-deficit/hyperactivity disorder on preadolescent adjustment may be greater for girls than for boys. *Journal of Clinical Child & Adolescent Psychology, 40*(4), 532–545.

Epilepsy Foundation. (2009a). *Understanding epilepsy*. Retrieved April 6, 2009, from www.epilepsyfoundation.org/about/types/causes/index.cfm

Epilepsy Foundation. (2009b). *What is epilepsy?* Retrieved April 6, 2009, from www.epilepsyfoundation.org/about/index.cfm.

Epilepsy Foundation. (2012). *Causes of epilepsy*. Retrieved February 25, 2009, from www.epilepsyfoundation.org/aboutepilepsy/causes/index.cfm.

Fahrner, R., & Romano, S. (2010). HIV infection and AIDS. In P. J. Allen, J. A.Vessey, & N. A., Shapiro (Eds.), *Child with a chronic condition,* 5th ed. (pp. 527–545). St. Louis, Missouri: Mosby.

Fowler, M. (2010). Increasing on-task performance for students with ADHD. *Education Digest: Essential Readings Condensed for Quick Review, 76*(2), 44–50.

Frodl, T. (2010). Comorbidity of ADHD and substance use disorder (SUD): A neuroimaging perspective. *Journal of Attention Disorders, 14*(2), 109–120.

Froehlich, T. E., Lanphear, B. P., Epstein, J. N., Barbaresi, W. J., Katusic, S. K., Kahn, R. S. (2007). Prevalence, recognition, and treatment of attention-deficit/hyperactivity disorder in a national sample of us children. *Archives of Pediatrics & Adolescent Medicine, 161*(9), 857-864.

Froehlich, T. E., McGough, J. J., & Stein, M. A. (2010). Progress and promise of attention-deficit hyperactivity disorder pharmacogenetics. *CNS Drugs, 24*(2), 99–117.

Gebel, E. (2012). *Pushing for diabetes cure*. Retrieved February 4, 2012, from http://forecast.diabetes.org/magazine/features/pushing-a-diabetes-cure.

Geng, G. (2011). Investigation of teachers' verbal and nonverbal strategies for managing attention deficit hyperactivity disorder (ADHD) students' behaviours within a classroom environment. *Australian Journal of Teacher Education, 36*(7), 17–30.

Glass, K., Flory, K., Martin, A., & Hankin, B. L. (2011). ADHD and comorbid conduct problems among adolescents: Associations with self-esteem and substance use. *Attention Deficit and Hyperactivity Disorders, 3*(1), 29–39.

Goldstein, S. (2011). Attention-deficit/hyperactivity disorder. In S. Goldstein & C. R. Reynolds, Eds., *Handbook of neurodevelopmental and genetic disorders in children,* 2nd ed. (pp. 131–150). New York, NY: Guilford Press.

Gorodzinsky, A. Y., Hainsworth, K. R., & Weisman, S. J. (2011). School functioning and chronic pain: A review of methods. *Journal of Pediatric Psychology, 36*(9), 991–1002.

Graf, R. (2009). Stem cells for dummies: A few questions answered. New University. Retrieved April 17, 2009, from http://www.newuniversity.org/2007/10/features/stem_cells_for_dummies42/.

Graziano, P. A., Geffken, G. R., & Lall, A. S. (2011). Heterogeneity in the pharmacological treatment of children with ADHD: Cognitive, behavioral, and social functioning differences. *Journal of Attention Disorders, 15(*5), 382–391.

Hale, J. B., Reddy, L. A., Semrud-Clikeman, M., Hain, L. A., Whitaker, J., Morley, J., Lawrence, K., Smith, A., & Jones, N. (2011). Executive impairment determines ADHD medication response: Implications for academic achievement. *Journal of Learning Disabilities, 44*(2), 196–212.

Harris, J. (2008). Physical therapy. In M. Lutkenhoff (Ed.), *Children with spina bifida: A parents' guide* (pp. 119–150). Bethesda, MD: Woodbine House.

Harty, S. C., Miller, C. J., Newcorn, J. H., & Halperin, J. M., (2009). Adolescents with childhood ADHD and comorbid disruptive behavior disorders: Aggression, anger, and hostility. *Child Psychiatry and Human Development, 40*(1), 85–97.

Hazle, L. A. (2010). *Cystic fibrosis*. In P. J. Allen, J. A. Vessey, & N. A. Shapiro (Eds.), *Child with a chronic condition,* 5th ed. (pp. 405–426). St. Louis, Missouri: Mosby.

Hedin, L. R., Mason, L. H., & Gaffney, J. S. (2011). Comprehension strategy instruction for two students with attention-related disabilities. *Preventing School Failure, 55*(3), 148–157.

Higgens, E. S. (2009, July). Do ADHD drugs take a toll on the brain? *Scientific American.* Retrieved from www.scientificamerican.com/article.

cfm?id=do-adhd-drugs-take-a-toll.

Huffman, D. M., Fontaine, K. L., & Price, B. K. (2003). *Health problems in the classroom 6–12: An a–z reference guide for educators*. Thousand Oaks, CA: Corwin Press, Inc.

Human Genome Project. (2012). *Genetic disease profile: Sickle cell anemia*. Gene Gateway—Exploring Genes and Genetic Disorders. Retrieved June 13, 2012, from www.ornl.gov/sci/techresources/Human_Genome/posters/chromosome/sca.shtml.

Jahns, V. (2008). Educating your child with spina bifida: One size does not fit all. In M. Lutkenhoff (Ed.), *Children with spina bifida: A parents' guide* (pp. 239–262). Bethesda, MD: Woodbine House.

Jensen, P. S., Abikoff, H., & Brown, T. E. (2009). Tailoring treatments for individuals with ADHD and their families. In T. E. Brown (Ed.), *ADHD comorbidities: Handbook for ADHD complications in children and adults* (pp. 415–428). Arlington, VA: American Psychiatric Publishing.

Kahn, A. B. (2009). *Assistive technology for children who have cerebral palsy: augmentation communication devices*. Retrieved March 10, 2009, from www.newhorizons.org/spneeds/inclusion/teaching/kahn.htm.

Kalikow, K. T. (2011). *Kids on meds*. New York: W. W. Norton and Company, Inc.

Kelly, K., & Ramundo, P. (2006). *You mean I'm not lazy, stupid, or crazy?!: The classic self-help book for adults with attention deficit disorder*. New York, New York: Simon and Schuster.

Kent, K. M., Pelham, W. E., Jr., Molina, B. S. G., Sibley, M. H., Waschbusch, D. A., Yu, J., Gnagy, E. M., Biswas, A., Babinski, D. E., & Karch, K. M. (2011). The academic experience of male high school students with ADHD. *Journal of Abnormal Child Psychology, 39*, 451–462.

Kraft, D. P. (2010). Non-medication treatments for adult ADHD: Evaluating impact on daily functioning and well-being. *Journal of American College Health, 59*(1), 57–59.

Law, C., & Davis, R. D. (2007). Rehabilitation concepts in myelominingocele and other spinal dysraphisms. In R. L. Braddom (Ed.), *Physical medicine & rehabilitation* (pp. 1269–1284). Philadelphia, PA: Saunders.

Lazzaretti, C. C., & Pearson, C. (2010). Myelodysplasia. In P. J. Allen, J. A. Vessey, & N. A. Shapiro (Eds.), *Child with a chronic condition,* 5th ed. (pp. 671–685). St. Louis, Missouri: Mosby.

Lee, S. S., Humphreys, K. L., Flory, K., Liu, R., & Glass, K. (2011). Prospective association of childhood attention-deficit/hyperactivity disorder (ADHD) and substance use and abuse/dependence: A meta-analytic review. *Clinical Psychology Review, 31*(3), 328–341.

Levine, E. S., & Anshel, D. J. (2011). "Nothing works!" A case study using cognitive-behavioral interventions to engage parents, educators, and children in the management of attention-deficit/hyperactivity disorder. *Psychology in the Schools, 48*(3), 297–306.

Levy, D. T., Mallonee, S., Miller, T. R., Smith, G. S., Spicer, R. S., Romano, E. O., & Fisher, D. A. (2004). Alcohol involvement in burn, submersion, spinal chord, and brain injuries. *Medical Science Monitor, 10*(1), 17–24.

Liverman, C. T., Altevogt, B. M., Joy, J. E., & Johnson, R. T. (Eds.). (2005). *Spinal cord injury: Progress, promise, and priorities*. Washington, D.C.: National Academies Press.

Mao, A. R., Babcock, T., & Brams, M. (2011). ADHD in adults: Current treatment trends with consideration of abuse potential of medications. *Journal of Psychiatric Practice, 17*(4), 241–250.

Martin, S. (2006). *Teaching motor skills to children with cerebral palsy and similar movement disorders: A guide for parents and professionals*. Bethesda, MD: Woodbine House.

Mason, D. B., Santoro, K., & Kaul, A. (2008). Bowel management. In M. Lutkenhoff (Ed.), *Children with spina bifida: A parents' guide* (pp. 85–104). Bethesda, MD: Woodbine House.

Mayo Clinic. (2012a). *Absence seizure (petit mal seizure): Definition*. Retrieved February 4, 2012, from www.mayoclinic.com/health/petit-mal-seizure/DS00216.

Mayo Clinic. (2012b). Diabetes causes. Retrieved February 25, 2012, from www.mayoclinic.com/health/diabetes/DS01121/DSECTION=causes.

McConaughy, S. H., Volpe, R. J., & Antshel, K. M. (2011). Academic and social impairments of elementary school children with attention deficit hyperactivity disorder. *School Psychology Review, 40*(2), 200–225.

Miller, L. V. (2007). Spinal chord injury. In B. J. Atchinson & D. K. Dirette (Eds.), *Conditions in occupational therapy: Effect on occupational performance* (pp. 311–339). Baltimore, MD: Lippincott, Williams, and Wilkins.

Mitchell, J. T., Robertson, C. D., Kimbrel, N. A., & Nelson-Gray, R. O. (2011). An evaluation of behavioral approach in adults with ADHD. *Journal of Psychopathology and Behavioral Assessment, 33*(4), 430–437.

Mukherjee, S., & Gaebler-Spira, D. J. (2007). *Cerebral palsy*. In R. L. Braddom (Ed.), *Physical medicine & rehabilitation* (pp. 1243–1267). Philadelphia, PA: Saunders.

Muscular Dystrophy Association. (2011). *Facts about Duchenne & Becker muscular dystrophies*. Tucson, AZ: Muscular Dystrophy Association.

Muscular Dystrophy Association. (2012). Diseases: Duchenne muscular dystrophy (DMD). Retrieved on January 18, 2012, from www.mdausa.org/disease/dmd.html.

National Center for HIV/AIDS, Viral Hepatitis, STD, and TB Prevention. (2012). *What are HIV and AIDS?* Retrieved from www.cdc.gov/hiv/topics/basic/index.htm#hiv.

National Institute of Mental Health. (2008). *Attention deficit hyperactivity disorder.* Bethesda, MD: Author.

National Institute of Mental Health. (2012a). *Attention deficit hyperactivity disorder (ADHD):What is attention deficit hyperactivity disorder?* Bethesda, MD: National Institute of Mental Health.

National Institute of Mental Health. (2012b). *Attention deficit hyperactivity disorder in children and adolescents fact sheet.* Bethesda, MD: National Institute of Mental Health.

National Institute of Neurological Disorders and Stroke. (2012a). *NINDS epilepsy information page.* Retrieved February 4, 2012, from http://www.ninds.nih.gov/disorders/epilepsy/epilepsy.htm.

National Institute of Neurological Disorders and Strokes. (2012b). NINDS muscular dystrophy information page: Muscular dystrophy. Retrieved on January 18, 2012, from www.ninds.nih.gov/disorders/md/md.htm.

National Institute of Neurological Disorders and Stroke. (2012c). *Seizures and epilepsy: Hope through research.* Retrieved February 4, 2012, from www.ninds.nih.gov/disorders/epilepsy/detail_epilepsy.htm#192293109.

National Institute of Neurological Disorders and Stroke. (2012d). *Seizures and epilepsy: hope through research.* Retrieved February 13, 2012, from www.ninds.nih.gov/disorders/epilepsy/detail_epilepsy.htm#192443109.

National Institute of Neurological Disorders and Stroke. (2012e). *NINDS traumatic brain injury information page: What is traumatic brain injury?* Retrieved February 6, 2012, from www.ninds.nih.gov/disorders/tbi/tbi.htm.

National Resource Center on ADHD. (2012). *Social skills in adults with ADHD.* Retrieved February 14, 2012, from www.addforums.com/forums/showthread.php?t=16804.

Nehring, W. M. (2010). Cerebral palsy. In P. J. Allen, J. A. Vessey, & N. A. Shapiro (Eds.), *Child with a chronic condition,* 5th ed. (pp. 326–346). St. Louis, Missouri: Mosby.

Nikolas, M. A., & Burt, S. A. (2010). Genetic and environmental influences on ADHD symptom dimensions of inattention and hyperactivity: A meta-analysis. *Journal of Abnormal Psychology, 119* (1), 1–17.

Owens, J. S., & Fabiano, G. A. (2011). School mental health programming for youth with ADHD: Addressing needs across the academic career. *School Mental Health, 3*(3), 111–116.

Parent Project Muscular Dystrophy. (2012). *Steroids/nutritional supplements/antibiotics.* Retrieved January 18, 2012, from www.parentprojectmd.org/site/PageServer?pagename=Care_physical_supplements_options.

Parkes, J., & Hill, N. (2010). The needs of children and young people with cerebral palsy. *Paediatric Nursing, 22*(4), 14–9.

Pitts, R. H., & Record, E. O. (2010). Sickle cell disease. In P. J. Allen, J. A. Vessey, & N. A. Shapiro (Eds.), *Child with a chronic condition,* 5th ed. (pp. 772–794). St. Louis, Missouri: Mosby.

Posey, W. M., Bassin, S. A., & Lewis, A. (2009). Preschool ADHD and medication . . . More study needed?! *Journal of Early Childhood and Infant Psychology, 5,* 57–77.

Powell, S. G., Thomsen, P. H., & Frydenberg, M. (2011). Long-term treatment of ADHD with stimulants: A large observational study of real-life patients. *Journal of Attention Disorders, 15*(6), 439–451.

Pugach, M. C., & Winn, J. A. (2011). Research on co-teaching and teaming: An untapped resource for induction. *Journal of Special Education Leadership, 24*(1), 36–46.

Rabiner, D. L., Anastopoulos, A. D., & Costello, E. J. (2010). Predictors of nonmedical ADHD medication use by college students. *Journal of Attention Disorders, 13*(6), 640–648.

Ramachandran, Priya. (2010). *From science fiction to reality: Exoskeletons.* The National Spinal Cord Injury Association. Retrieved from www.spinalcord.org/from-science-fiction-to-reality-exoskeletons/.

Ratcliffe, M. M., & Kieckhefer, G. M. (2010). Asthma. In P. J. Allen, J. A. Vessey, & N. A. Shapiro (Eds.), *Child with a chronic condition,* 5th ed. (pp. 168–196). St. Louis, Missouri: Mosby.

Reid, R., & Johnson, J. (2011). *Teacher's Guide to ADHD.* What Works for Special-Needs Learners Series. New York, NY: Guilford Publications.

Ricci, S. S., & Kyle, T. (2009a). Nursing care of the child with a neurologic disorder. In S. S. Ricci & T. Kyle, *Maternity and pediatric nursing* (pp. 1138–1186). Philadelphia, PA: Lippincott, Williams, & Wilkins.

Ricci, S. S., & Kyle, T. (2009b). Sexually transmitted infections. In S. S. Ricci & T. Kyle, *Maternity and pediatric nursing* (pp. 141–170). Philadelphia, PA: Lippincott, Williams, & Wilkins.

Riley, J. L., McKevitt, B. C., Shriver, M. D., Allen, K. D. (2011). Increasing on-task behavior using teacher attention delivered on a fixed-time schedule. *Journal of Behavioral Education, 20*(3), 149–162.

Ryan, J. B., Katsiyannis, A., & Hughes, E. M. (2011). Medication treatment for attention deficit hyperactivity disorder. *Theory Into Practice, 50*(1), 52–60.

Science Codex. (2009). *Studies investigate childhood obesity, diabetes* and related conditions. Retrieved April 11, 2009, from http://sciencecodex.com/studies_investigate_childhood_obesity_diabetes_and_related_conditions.

Selekman, J. (2010). Attention-deficit hyperactivity disorder. In P. J. Allen, J. A. Vessey, & N.A. Shapiro (Eds.), *Child with a chronic condition,* 5th ed. (pp. 197–217). St. Louis, Missouri: Mosby.

Shute, N. (2009). ADHD medication: Can your child go without? *U.S News & World Report*. Retrieved from http://health.usnews.com/health-news/family-health/brain-and-behavior/articles/2009/01/14/adhd-medication-can-your-child-go-without_print.html.

Spina Bifida Association of America. (2012) *Fact sheets: Folic acid.* Retrieved January 11, 2012, from www.spinabifidaassociation.org/site/c.liKWL7PLLrF/b.2642343/k.8D2D/Fact_Sheets.htm.

Spinal Cord Injury Resource Center. (2012). *Spinal cord 101*. Retrieved on January 18, 2012, from www.spinalinjury.net/html/_spinal_cord_101.html.

Sprich, S. E., Knouse, L. E., & Cooper-Vince, C. (2010). Description and demonstration of CBT for ADHD in adults. *Cognitive and Behavioral Practice, 17*(1), 9–15.

Springer, C., & Reddy, L. A. (2010). Measuring parental treatment adherence in a multimodal treatment program for children with ADHD: A preliminary investigation. *Child & Family Behavior Therapy, 32*(4), 272–290.

Storm, B. C., & White, H. A. (2010). ADHD and retrieval-induced forgetting: Evidence for a deficit in the inhibitory control of memory. *Memory, 18* (3), 265–271.

Stroh, J., Frankenberger, W., Cornell-Swanson, L., Wood, C., & Pahl, S. (2008). The use of stimulant medication and behavioral interventions for the treatment of attention deficit hyperactivity disorder: A survey of parents' knowledge, attitudes, and experiences. *Journal of Child & Family Studies, 17*(3), 385–401.

Taylor, A., Deb, S., & Unwin, G. (2011). Scales for the identification of adults with attention deficit hyperactivity disorder (ADHD): A systematic review. *Research in Developmental Disabilities, 32*(3), 924–938.

Thorell, L. B., & Rydell, A-M. (2008). Behaviour problems and social competence deficits associated with symptoms of attention-deficit/hyperactivity disorder: effects of age and gender. *Child: Care, Health & Development, 34*(5), 584–595.

United Cerebral Palsy. (2012). *Cerebral palsy information*. Retrieved January 11, 2012, from www.ucp.org/uploads/media_items/cerebral-palsy-fact-sheet.original.pdf.

VGo. (2012). VGo Communications, Inc. Retrieved February 22, 2012, from www.vgocom.com/remote-student.

van de Loo-Neus, G. H. H., Rommelse, N., & Buitelaar, J. K. (2011). To stop or not to stop? How long should medication treatment of attention-deficit hyperactivity disorder be extended? *European Neuropsychopharmacology, 21*(8), 584–599.

van Kraayenoord, C. E., Miller, R., & Moni, K. B. (2009). Teaching writing to students with learning difficulties in inclusive English classrooms: Lessons from an exemplary teacher. *English Teaching: Practice and Critique, 8*(1), 23–51.

Vaughan, B. S., Roberts, H. J., & Needelman, H. (2009). Current medications for the treatment of attention-deficit/hyperactivity disorder. *Psychology in the Schools, 46*(9), 846–856.

Wilens, T. E., Martelon, M., Joshi, G., Bateman, C., Fried, R., Petty, C., & Biederman, J. (2011). Does ADHD predict substance-use disorders? A 10-year follow-up study of young adults with ADHD. *Journal of the American Academy of Child and Adolescent Psychiatry, 50* (6), 543–553.

Williamson, P., & McLeskey, J. (2011). An investigation into the nature of inclusion problem-solving teams. *Teacher Educator, 46*(4), 316–334.

Wright, C., Shelton, D., & Wright, M. (2009). A contemporary review of the assessment, diagnosis and treatment of ADHD. *Australian Journal of Learning Difficulties, 14*(2), 199–214.

Yamamoto, M. S. (2007).

Cerebral palsy. In B. J. Atchinson & D. K. Dirette (Eds.), *Conditions in occupational therapy: Effect on occupational performance* (pp. 9–22). Baltimore, MD: Lippincott, Williams, and Wilkins.

Youngstrom, E. A., Arnold, L. E., & Frazier, T. W. (2010). Bipolar and ADHD comorbidity: Both artifact and outgrowth of shared mechanisms. *Clinical Psychology: Science and Practice, 17*(4), 350–359.

Chapter 15

Adams, C. M. (2006). Articulating gifted education program goals. In J. H. Purcell & R. D. Eckert (Eds.), *Designing services and programs for high-ability learners: A guidebook for gifted education* (pp. 62–72). Thousand Oaks, CA: Corwin Press.

Baum, S. (Ed.). (2004). Introduction to twice-exceptional and special populations of gifted students [Introduction]. In *Twice-exceptional and special populations of gifted students* (pp. xxiii–xxxiii). Thousand Oaks, CA: Corwin Press.

Berlin, J. E. (2009). It's a matter of perspective: Student perceptions of the impact of being labeled gifted and talented. *Roeper Review, 31*(4), 217–223.

Binet, A., & Simon, T. (1905). Methodes nouvelles pour le diagnostique du niveau intellectuel desanomaux. *L'Anee Psychologique, 11,* 196–98.

Binet, A., & Simon, T. (1908). Le development

de intelligence chez les enfants. *L'Anee Psychologique, 14,* 1–94.

Bireda, M. R. (2011). *Schooling for minority children.* Lanham, Maryland: Rowman & Littlefield Education.

Borland, J. H. (2003). Evaluating gifted programs: A broader perspective. In N. Colagnelo & G. A. Davis (Eds.), *Handbook of gifted education* (pp. 293–307). Boston: Pearson Education.

Briggs, C. J., Reis, S. M., Eckert, R. D., & Baum, S. (2006). Providing programs for special populations of gifted and talented students. In J. H. Purcell & R. D. Eckert (Eds.), *Designing services and programs for high-ability learners: A guidebook for gifted education* (pp. 32–48). Thousand Oaks, CA: Corwin Press.

Burns, D. E., Purcell, J. H., & Hertberg, H. L. (2006). Curriculum for gifted education students. In J. H. Purcell & R. D. Eckert (Eds.), *Designing services and programs for high-ability learners: A guidebook for gifted education* (pp. 87–111). Thousand Oaks, CA: Corwin Press.

Callahan, C. M. (2008). Assessing and improving services provided to gifted students: A plan for program evaluation. In F. A. Karnes & K. R. Stephens (Eds.), *Achieving excellence in gifted and talented* (pp. 230–245). Upper Saddle River, NJ: Pearson.

Callard-Szulgit, R. (2003). *Parenting and teaching the gifted.* Lanham, MD: Scarecrow Press.

Caraisco, J. (2007). Overcoming lethargy in gifted and talented education with contract activity packages: "I'm choosing to learn!" *Journal of Educational Strategies, Issues and Ideas, 80*(6), 255–260.

Cattell, R. B. (1971). *Abilities: Their structure, growth, and action.* Boston: Houghton Mifflin.

Center for Comprehensive School Reform and Improvement. (2008). *Issue Brief: Gifted and talented students at risk for underachievement.* Learning Point Associates: Austin, TX.

Chuska, K. R. (2005). *Gifted Learners K-12: A practical guide to effective curriculum and teaching,* 2nd ed. Bloomington, IN: National Educational Service.

Clark, B. (2008). *Growing up gifted,* 7th ed. Columbus, OH: Merrill.

Claxton, G., & Meadows, S. (2009). Brightening up: How children learn to be gifted. In T. Balchin, B. Hymer, & D. J. Matthews (Eds.), *The Routledge international companion to gifted education* (pp. 3–9). New York: Routledge.

Cohen, S. (2005, March 19). *Child prodigy's apparent suicide: "He knew he had to leave," mother says.* New York: Associated Press.

Colangelo, N., & Assouline, S. (2009). Acceleration: Meeting the academic and social needs of students. In T. Balchin, B. Hymer, & D. J. Matthews (Eds.), *The Routledge international companion to gifted education* (pp. 194–202). New York: Routledge.

Colangelo, N., Assouline, S. G., & Gross, M. U. M. (2004a). *A nation deceived: How schools hold back America's brightest students (vol. 1), The Templeton national report on acceleration.* Iowa City, IA: The Connie Belin & Jacqueline N. Blank International Center for Gifted Education and Talent Development.

Colangelo, N., Assouline, S. G., & Gross, M. U. M. (2004b). *A nation deceived: How schools hold back America's brightest students (vol. 2), The Templeton national report on acceleration.* Iowa City, IA: The Connie Belin & Jacqueline N. Blank International Center for Gifted Education and Talent Development.

Colangelo, N., Assouline, S. G., & Lupkowski-Shoplik, A. E. (2004). Whole-grade acceleration. In N. Colangelo, S. G. Assouline, & M. U. M. Gross (Eds.), *A nation deceived: How schools hold back America's brightest students volume II* (pp. 77–76). Carnegie Mellon University: University of Iowa.

Coleman, L. J. (2005). *Nurturing talent in high school: Life in the fast lane.* In *Education and psychology of the gifted series.* New York: Teachers College Press.

Colombo, J., Shaddy, D. J., Blaga, O. M., Anderson, C. J., & Kannass, K. N. (2009). High cognitive ability in infancy and early childhood. In F. E. Horowitz, R. F. Subotnik, & J. J. Matthews (Eds.), *The development of giftedness and talent across the lifespan* (pp. 23–42). Washington, D.C.: American Psychological Association.

Colvin, G. (2008). *Talent is overrated: What really separates world-class performers from everyone else?* New York: Penguin.

Conant, J. B. (1959). *The American high school today.* New York: McGraw-Hill.

Cooper, C. R. (2006). Creating a comprehensive and defensible budget for gifted programs and services. In J. H. Purcell & R. D. Eckert (Eds.), *Designing services and programs for high-ability learners: A guidebook for gifted education* (pp. 125–136). Thousand Oaks, CA: Corwin Press.

Davis, G. A., & Rimm, S. B. (2004). *Education of the gifted and talented,* 5th ed. San Francisco: Allyn and Bacon.

Davis, G. A., Rimm, S. B., & Siegle, D. (2011). *Education of the gifted and talented,* 6th ed. Boston: Pearson.

DeHann, R., & Havighurst, R. J. (1957). *Educating gifted children.* Chicago, IL: University of Chicago Press.

Eckert, R. D. (2006). Developing a mission statement on the educational needs of gifted and talented students. In J. H. Purcell & R. D. Eckert (Eds.), *Designing services and programs for high-ability learners: A guidebook for gifted education* (pp. 15–22). Thousand Oaks, CA: Corwin Press.

Eckstein, M. (2009). Enrichment 2.0: Gifted and talented education for the 21st century. *Gifted Child Today, 32*(1), 59–63.

Esping, A., & Plucker, J. A. (2008). Theories of intelligence. In F. A. Karnes

& K. R. Stephens (Eds.), *Achieving excellence in gifted and talented* (pp. 36–48). Upper Saddle River, NJ: Pearson.

Ford, D. Y. (2003). Equity and excellence: Culturally diverse students in gifted education. In N. Colagnelo & G. A. Davis (Eds.), *Handbook of gifted education,* 3rd ed. (pp. 506–520). Boston: Pearson Education.

Ford, D. Y., Grantham, T. C., & Whiting, G. W. (2008). Another look at the achievement gap: Learning from the experiences of gifted black students. *Urban Education, 43*(2), 216–239.

Gallagher, J. J. (Ed.). (2004). Public policy in gifted education. In *Essential readings in gifted education*. Thousand Oaks, CA: Corwin Press.

Gardner, H. (1983). *Frames of mind: The theory of multiple intelligences*. New York: Basic Books.

Gottfried, A. W., Gottfried, A. E., & Guerin, D. W. (2009). Issues in early prediction and identification of intellectual giftedness. In F. E. Horowitz, R. F. Subotnik, & J. J. Matthews (Eds.), *The development of giftedness and talent across the lifespan* (pp. 43–56). Washington, D.C.: American Psychological Association.

Graham, G. (2009). Giftedness in adolescence: African American gifted youth and their challenges from a motivation perspective. In F. E. Horowitz, R. F. Subotnik, & J. J. Matthews (Eds.), *The development of giftedness and talent across the lifespan* (pp. 109–129). Washington, D.C.: American Psychological Association.

Gross, M. U. M. (2004). Radical acceleration. In N. Colangelo, S. G. Assouline, & M. U. M. Gross (Eds.), *A nation deceived: How schools hold back America's brightest students volume II* (pp. 87–96). University of New South Wales: University of Iowa.

Gubbins, E. J. (2006). Constructing identification procedures. In J. H. Purcell & R. D. Eckert (Eds.), *Designing services and programs for high-ability learners: A guidebook for gifted education* (pp. 49–61). Thousand Oaks, CA: Corwin Press.

Guilford, J. P. (1950). Creativity. *American Psychologist, 5*, 444–454.

Guilford, J. P. (1959). Three faces of intellect. *American Psychologist, 14*, 469–479.

Harris, B., Plucker, J. A., Rapp, K. E., & Marinez, R. S. (2009). Identifying gifted and talented English language learners: A case study. *Journal for the Education of the Gifted, 32* (3), 368–393.

Hong, E., & Milgram, R. M. (2008). *Preventing talent loss.* New York: Routledge.

Horowitz, F. D. (2009). Introduction: A development understanding of giftedness and talent. In F. D. Horowitz, R. F. Subotnik, & D. J. Matthews, (Eds.). *The development of giftedness and talent across the life span* (pp. 3–19). Washington, D.C.: American Psychological Association.

Hughes, J. (2009). Teaching the able child . . . or teaching the child to be able. In T. Balchin, B. Hymer & D. J. Matthews (Eds.), *The Routledge international companion to gifted education* (pp. 161–168). New York: Routledge.

Isaacson, W. (2011). *Steve Jobs*. New York: Simon and Shuster.

Johnsen, S. K. (2008). Identifying gifted and talented learners. In F. A. Karnes & K. R. Stephens (Eds.), *Achieving excellence in gifted and talented* (pp. 135–153). Upper Saddle River, NJ: Pearson.

Johnsen, S. K., VanTassel-Baska, J., & Robinson, A. (2008). *Using the national gifted education standards for university preparation programs*. Thousand Oaks, CA: Corwin Press.

King, K. A., Kozleski, E. B., & Lansdowne, K. (2009, May–June). Where are all the students of color in gifted education? *Principal Magazine*, pp. 17–20.

Knight, S. (2009). *Is high IQ a burden as much as a blessing?* Retrieved May 15, 2009, from www.ft.com/cms/s/2/4add9230-23d5-11de-996a-00144feabdc0.html.

Kulik, J. (2004). Meta-analytic studies of acceleration: Dimensions and issues. In N. Colangelo, S. G. Assouline, & M. U. M. Gross (Eds.), *A nation deceived: How schools hold back America's brightest students volume II* (pp. 13–22). University of Michigan: University of Iowa.

Leppien, J. H., & Westberg, K. L. (2006). Roles, responsibilities, and professional qualifications of key personnel for gifted education services. In J. H. Purcell &R. D. Eckert (Eds.), *Designing services and programs for high-ability learners: A guidebook for gifted education* (pp. 161–182). Thousand Oaks, CA: Corwin Press.

Liu, W. M., Shepherd, S. J., & Nicpon, M. F. (2008). "Boy are tough, not smart": Counseling gifted and talented young and adolescent boys. In M. S. Kiselica, M. Englar-Carlson, & A. M. Horne (Eds.), *Counseling troubled boys: A Guidebook for professionals* (pp. 273–292). New York: Routledge.

Lubbard, T., Georgsdottir, A., & Besançon, M. (2009). The nature of creative giftedness and talent. In T. Balchin, B. Hymer, & D. J. Matthews (Eds.), *The Routledge international companion to gifted education* (pp. 42–49). New York: Routledge.

MacKinnon, D. W. (1962). The nature and nurture of creative talent. *American Psychologist, 17*(7), 484–495.

Manning, S., & Bestnoy, K. D. (2008). Special populations. In F. A. Karnes & K. R. Stephens (Eds.), *Achieving excellence in gifted and talented* (pp. 116–134). Upper Saddle River, NJ: Pearson.

Matthews, D. J., & Foster, J. F. (2009). *Being smart about gifted education: A guidebook for educators and parents*. Scottsdale, AZ: Great Potential Press, Inc.

Matthews, D. J., & Smyth, E. M. (2009). *Encouraging bright girls to keep shining*. Ontario Institute for Studies in Education at the University of Toronto. Retrieved May 16, 2009, from www.hunter.cuny.edu/gifted-ed/-articles/ShiningGirls.shtml.

Matthews, M. S., & Shaunessy, E. (2008). Culturally, linguistically, and economically diverse gifted students. In F. A. Karnes & K. R. Stephens (Eds.), *Achieving excellence in gifted and talented* (pp. 99–115). Upper Saddle River, NJ: Pearson.

McHugh, M. W. (2006). Governor's schools. Fostering the social and emotional well-being of gifted and talented students. *Journal of Secondary Gifted Education, 17*(3), 50–58.

Montgomery, D. (2009). Special educational needs and dual exceptionality. In T. Balchin, B. Hymer, & D. J. Matthews (Eds.), *The Routledge international companion to gifted education* (pp. 218–225). New York: Routledge.

Moon, S. M. (2006). Developing a definition of giftedness. In J. H. Purcell, & R. D. Eckert, R. D. (Eds.), *Designing services and programs for high-ability learners: A guidebook for gifted education* (pp. 23–31). Thousand Oaks, CA: Corwin Press.

Morawska, A., & Sanders, M. R. (2009). Parenting gifted and talented children: Conceptual and empirical foundations. *Gifted Child Quarterly, 53*(3), 163–173.

National Association for Gifted Children. (2012a). *Gifted by state*. Retrieved March 8, 2012, from http://www.nagc.org/DataMapby Stake.aspx.

National Association for Gifted Children. (2012b). Frequently asked questions: Is there a definition of "gifted"? Retrieved March 10, 2012, from www.nagc.org/index2.aspx?id=548.

North, J. (2007). Practical gifted kidkeeping. In L. B. Golden & P. Henderson, (Eds.), *Case studies in school counseling* (pp.223-233). Upper Saddle River, NJ: Pearson.

Olszewski-Kubilius, P., & Lee, S. (2008). Specialized programs serving the gifted. In F. A. Karnes & K. R. Stephens (Eds.), *Achieving excellence: Educating the gifted and talented* (pp. 192–208). Upper Saddle River, NJ: Pearson.

Passow, A. H. (2004). The nature of giftedness and talent. In R. J. Sternberg (Ed.), *Definitions and conceptions of giftedness* (pp. 1–11). Thousand Oaks, CA: Corwin Press.

Phillipson, S. N., & McCann, M. (2007). *Conceptions of giftedness: Sociocultural perspectives*. Mahwah, NJ: Lawrence Erlbaum Associates, Inc., Publishers.

Piirto, J. (1999). *Talented children and adults: Their development and education*. Upper Saddle River, NJ: Prentice-Hall.

Plomin, R., & Price, T. S. (2003). The relationship between genetics and intelligence. In N. Colangelo & G. A. Davis (Eds.), *Handbook of gifted education,* 3rd ed. (pp. 113–123). Boston: Pearson Education.

Purcell, J. H., & Eckert, R. D. (2006). *Designing services and programs for high-ability learners: A guidebook for gifted education*. Thousand Oaks, CA: Corwin Press.

Ramos-Ford, V., & Gardner, H. (1991). Giftedness from a multiple intelligences perspective. In N. Colangelo & G. A. Davis (Eds.), *Handbook of gifted education* (pp. 55–64). Boston: Allyn and Bacon.

Ramos-Ford, V., & Gardner, H. (1997). Giftedness from a multiple intelligences perspective. In N. Colangelo & G. A. Davis (Eds.), *Handbook of gifted education,* 2nd ed. (pp. 54–66). Boston: Allyn and Bacon.

Reis, S. & Renzulli, J. S. (2004). Current research on the social and emotional development of gifted and talented students: Good news and future possibilities. *Psychology in the Schools, 41*(1), 119–130.

Renzulli, J. S. (Ed.). (2004). *Identification of students for gifted and talented programs*. In *Essential readings in gifted education*. Thousand Oaks, CA: Corwin Press.

Renzulli, J. S., & Reis, S. M. (2003). The schoolwide enrichment model: Developing creative and productive giftedness. In N. Colangelo & G. A. Davis (Eds.), *Handbook of gifted education,* 3rd ed. (pp. 184–203). Boston: Pearson Education.

Renzulli Learning (2012). Differentiation engine. Retrieved March 17, 2012, from www.renzullilearning.com/ToolsAndServices/differentiationengine.aspx.

Richert, E. S. (2003). Excellence with justice in identification and programming. In N. Colangelo & G. A. Davis (Eds.), *Handbook of gifted education,* 3rd ed. (pp. 146–161). Boston: Pearson Education.

Rimm, S. (2008). Parenting gifted children. In F. A. Karnes & K. R. Stephens (Eds.), *Achieving excellence in gifted and talented* (pp. 262–277). Upper Saddle River, NJ: Pearson.

Rimm, S. B. (1982). *PRIDE: Preschool and primary interest descriptor*. Watertown, WI: Educational Assessment Service.

Rimm, S. B., & Davis, G. A. (1983, September/October). Identifying creativity, Part II. *G/C/T*, 19–23.

Roberts, J. L. (2008). Teachers of the gifted and talented. In F. A. Karnes & K. R. Stephens (Eds.), *Achieving excellence in gifted and talented* (pp. 246–261). Upper Saddle River, NJ: Pearson.

Robinson, A., Shore, B. M., & Enerson, D. L. (2007). *Best practices in gifted education: an evidenced-based guide*. Waco, TX: Prufrock Press, Inc.

Robinson, N. M. (2004). Effects of academic acceleration on the social-emotional status of gifted students. In N. Colangelo, S. G. Assouline, & M. U. M. Gross (Eds.), *A nation deceived: How schools hold back America's brightest students volume II* (pp. 59–68). Iowa City, Iowa: University of Iowa.

Rogers, K. B. (2004). The academic effects of acceleration. In N. Colangelo, S. G. Assouline, & M. U.

M. Gross (Eds.), *A nation deceived: How schools hold back America's brightest students volume II* (pp. 47–58). Iowa City, Iowa: University of Iowa.

Rogers, K. B. (2006). Connecting program design and district policies. In J. H. Purcell & R. D. Eckert (Eds.), *Designing services and programs for high-ability learners: A guidebook for gifted education* (pp. 207–223). Thousand Oaks, CA: Corwin Press.

Ross, P. O. (1993). *National excellence: A case for developing America's talent*. Washington, D.C.: Office of Educational Research and Improvement, U.S. Department of Education.

Savant, M. (2012). *About Marilyn*. Retrieved April 10, 2012, from http://marilynvossavant.com/about-marilyn/.

Silverman, L. K. (1986). What happens to the gifted girl? In C. J. Maker (Ed.), *Critical issues in gifted education: Defensible programs for the gifted,* Vol. 1 (pp. 43–89). Austin, TX: PRO-ED.

Sosniak, L. A., & Gabelko, N. H. (2008). *Every child's right: Academic talent development by choice, not chance*. New York, New York: Teacher College Press.

Spradlin, L. K., & Parsons, R. D. (2008). *Diversity matters: Understanding diversity in schools*. Belmont, CA: Wadsworth Cengage Learning.

Stephens, K. R., & Karnes, F. A. (2000). State definitions for the gifteandtalented revisited.

Exceptional Children, 66 (2), 219–238.

Sternberg, R. J. (1997). A triarchic view of giftedness: Theory and practice. In N. Colangelo & G. A Davis (Eds.), *Handbook of gifted education,* 2nd ed. (pp. 43–53). Boston: Allyn and Bacon.

Sternberg, R. J. (2006). Creativity is a habit. *Education Week, 25*(24), 64.

Sternberg, R. J. (2009). Wisdom, intelligence, creativity, synthesized: A model of giftedness. In T. Balchin, B. Hymer, & D. J. Matthews (Eds.), *The Routledge international companion to gifted education* (pp. 255–264). New York: Routledge.

Sternberg, R. F., Jarvin, L., & Grigorenko, E. L. (2011). *Explorations in giftedness*. New York, New York: Cambridge University Press.

Subotnik, R. F., & Calderon, J. (2008). Developing giftedness and talent. In F. A. Karnes & K. R. Stephens (Eds.), *Achieving excellence in gifted and talented* (pp. 49–61). Upper Saddle River, NJ: Pearson.

Tannenbaum, A. J. (2003). Nature and nurture of giftedness. In N. Colangelo & G. A Davis (Eds.), *Handbook of gifted education,* 3rd ed. (pp. 45–59). Boston: Allyn and Bacon.

Terman, L. M. (1925). *Genetic studies of genius: Vol. 1. Mental and physical traits of a thousand gifted children*. Stanford, CA: Stanford University Press.

Tomlinson, C. A., & Hockett, J.A. (2008).

Instructional strategies and programming models for gifted learners. In F. A. Karnes & K. R. Stephens (Eds.), *Achieving excellence in gifted and talented* (pp. 154–169). Upper Saddle River, NJ: Pearson.

Tomlinson, C. A., Doubet, K. J., & Capper, M. R. (2006). Aligning gifted education services with general education. In J. H. Purcell & R. D. Eckert (Eds.), *Designing services and programs for high-ability learners: A guidebook for gifted education* (pp. 224–238). Thousand Oaks, CA: Corwin Press.

Torrance, E. P. (1961). Problems of highly creative children. *Gifted Child Quarterly, 5*, 31–34.

Torrance, E. P. (1965). *Gifted children in the classroom*. New York: Macmillan.

Torrance, E. P. (1966). *Torrance tests of creative thinking*. Bensenville, IL: Scholastic Testing Service.

Torrance, E. P. (1968). Finding hidden talent among disadvantaged children. *Gifted and Talented Quarterly, 12*, 131–137.

Treffinger, D. J. (2004). Creativity and giftedness. In S. M. Reis, *Essential readings in gifted education*. Thousand Oaks, CA: Corwin Press.

Treffinger, D., Nassab, C. A., & Selby, E. C. (2009). Programming for talent development: Expanding horizons for gifted education. In T. Balchin, B. Hymer, & D. J. Matthews (Eds.), *The Routledge international companion to gifted education* (pp.

210–217). New York: Routledge.

VanTassel-Baska, J. (2009). The role of gifted education in promoting cultural diversity. In T. Balchin, B. Hymer, & D. J. Matthews (Eds.), *The Routledge international companion to gifted education* (pp. 273–280). New York: Routledge.

VanTassel-Baska, J., & Stambaugh, T. (2006). *Comprehensive curriculum for gifted learners,* 3rd ed. Boston: Person Education. Inc.

Warwick, I., & Matthews, D. J. (2009). Fostering giftedness in urban and diverse communities: Context-sensitive solutions. In T. Balchin, B. Hymer, & D. J. Matthews (Eds.), *The Routledge international companion to gifted education* (pp. 265–272). New York: Routledge.

Williams, F. E. (1980). *Creativity assessment packet*. East Aurora, NY: DOK.

Worrell, F. C. (2009). What does gifted mean? Personal and social identity perspectives on giftedness in adolescents. In F. E. Horowitz, R. F. Subotnik, & J. J. Matthews (Eds.), *The development of giftedness and talent across the lifespan* (pp. 131–152). Washington, D.C.: American Psychological Association.

Worrell, F. C., & Erwin, J. O., (2011). Best practices in identifying students for gifted and talented programs. *Journal of Applied School Psychology, 27*(4), 319–340.

Author Index

Etscheidt, S., 193
Eva, A. L., 182
Evans, A. C., 271
Evans, G. W., 120
Eveleigh, E. L., 170, 172

Fabiano, G. A., 400
Faggella-Luby, M., 170
Fahrner, R., 374, 375
Farinella, K. A., 240, 252, 253, 256, 258, 259
Farmer, T. W., 173
Faroqi-Shah, Y., 248
Farrington, D. P., 187
Fasmer, O. B., 158, 159
Faulkner, S. L., 103
Fawcett, H., 128, 130, 131, 135, 140, 143
Fearon, D. D., 399
Feeley, K. M., 248, 250, 259
Feetham, S., 289
Feinberg, E., 141
Feldman, P. D., 177
Ferguson, M., 173
Ferguson, P. M., 128, 129
Ferrand, C. T., 261, 262, 263
Ferre, S., 328
Ferrell, C. B., 109
Ferrell, D. R., 176
Ferri, C. B., 104, 109
Fey, M. E., 164
Figlio, D. N., 207
Fine, M. J., 130
Finn, D., 91
First, M. B., 189
Firth, N., 167
Fischer, B., 169
Fischer, S., 143
Fish, M. C., 133
Fisher, P., 120, 121
Fleisch, B., 201
Fleming, G., 147
Fletcher, J. M., 106, 274
Flippin, M., 281
Flora, C. B., 103
Flory, K., 397, 399
Fogle, P. T., 241, 243, 248, 250, 251, 252, 253
Fombonne, E., 272, 278
Fontaine, K. L., 369
Ford, A., 303
Ford, D. Y., 410, 434
Forde, Laura, 364
Foreman, P., 79
Forness, S. R., 184, 205
Forsman, M., 187
Foster, J. F., 409, 420

Fountain, C., 272
Fowler, M., 400
Fox, L., 129, 140, 144, 146, 147, 197, 198, 219, 221, 228, 288, 302, 309
Frances, D. J., 106, 108
Francis, R., 173
Frankel, E. B., 63
Frankenberger, W., 399
Frankland, H. C., 132, 143, 144, 146
Frazier, T. W., 397
Fredrick, L., 162, 173
Freeborn, D., 289
Freed, D. R., 243, 245, 246, 252
Freedman, B. H., 290
Frenn, M., 289
Freuler, A., 275
Fried, R., 397
Friedman, B., 146
Friedman, R. M., 197
Friend, A., 161
Friend, M., 31, 53, 56, 73, 110, 113, 132
Frith, U., 271
Fritsch, K., 120
Frodl, T., 397, 399
Froehlich, T., 172, 397, 399
Froemling, K. K., 246, 252, 253, 254
Frost, J., 129
Frost, L., 282
Frydenberg, E., 167
Frydenberg, M., 177, 399
Frymark, T., 164
Fuchs, D., 168, 171
Fuchs, L. S., 166, 168, 171
Fujiki, M., 109, 112
Furney, K. S., 84

Gabelko, N. H., 417, 434
Gable, R. A., 185, 188, 198
Gaebler-Spira, D. J., 363, 364
Gaffney, J. S., 400
Gaffney, M., 160
Gagné, F., 410
Gagnon, E., 285
Gajria, M., 156, 168, 169, 170
Gal, E., 177
Gall, J. P., 156
Gall, M. D., 156
Gallagher, G., 181
Gallagher, J. J., 411
Gallagher, P. A., 141, 142, 147
Gallagher, S., 289
Gallaudet Research Institute, 326

Gama, R., 173
Garcia-Vasquez, E., 103
Garcoa, G., 120
Gardenas-Hagan, E., 108
Gardner, D., 148
Gardner, H., 409, 410
Gardner, J. E., 139, 140, 143
Gardner, R., 116
Gardner, T. J., 161
Gargiulo, R., 74, 224
Garland, A. F., 262
Garman, C., 168
Garner, R. E., 129, 133
Garrido, M., 111
Garrison, C. Z., 109
Gartin, B. C., 78
Gartner, A., 53
Garza, A. A., 102
Gathercole, S. E., 177
Gau, S. S., 289
Gaventa, B., 128
Gavidia-Payne, S., 133
Gay, G., 113
Geary, D. C., 163
Gebel, E., 381
Gee, J. P., 254
Geffken, G. R., 177, 178, 399
Geffner, D., 164
Geisthardt, C., 143
Geneau, R, 341
Geng, G., 400
Georgsdottir, A., 420
Gerig, G., 271
Geschwind, D. H., 276
Gettinger, M., 171
Getzel, E. E., 91
Giangreco, M., 301
Giarelli, E., 271, 272, 275, 276, 278
Gibb, G. S., 280
Gilabert, R., 160
Gilbert, S. G., 165
Gilbertson, D., 193, 328
Gillberg, C., 279
Gillberg, I. C., 279
Gimbert, B. G., 113
Gingras, H., 342
Ginsberg, C., 146
Giulliani, G. A., 156, 165
Glaeser, B. C., 91
Glass, K., 397, 399
Glass, M., 185
Gleason, J. B., 242
Glimpse, W., 106
Gnagy, E. M., 400
Godin, P., 243
Goertz, M., 44

Subject Index

Aristotle, 9

Articulation disorders, 255–259.
    See also Speech disorders
    vs. delayed speech, 254
    functional, 255
    intervention for, 258–259
    treatment of, 255

Articulation problems, **220**

Asperger's syndrome, **51**, **268**, 274
    in early childhood, 271
    social communication and, 273

Assessment
    alternate, **38**, **303**
    authentic, **113**, 303
    for CLD, 108–109, 110–111
    criterion-referenced, 165
    curriculum-based, **79**, **165**
    for EBD, 191–195
    formal, 165–166
    functional, **65**
    for gifted, creative, and talented,
        417–418
    informal, 165–166
    for learning disabilities, 165–167
    for multicultural education, 110–111
    neuropsychological, **18**
    nondiscriminatory, **110**, 111
    norm-referenced, 165
    for severe and multiple disabilities,
        303–304
    strength-based, 194
    techniques, 193–195
    for vision loss, 344–346

Assistive technology, **78**, **232**
    closed-captioning, 332
    computers, 332
    for EBD, 205
    in elementary school, 78
    for functional life skills, 307–309
    for gifted, creative, and talented,
        428–429
    hearing loss, 332–333
    for intellectual disabilities, 231
    Internet, 332
    for language disorders, 249
    for severe and multiple disabilities,
        307–309
    smartphones, 332
    software for writing, 171
    tablets, 332
    telecommunications devices, 333
    VGo for Remote Students, 365

Association for Children with Learn-
    ing Disabilities, 10

Asthma, 376–377
    causes of, 376
    interventions for, 376–377

management plan for, 377*t*
    prevalence of, 376

Astigmatism, **339**

Athetosis, **302**

Atresia, **323**

Attention deficit disorder, 189

Attention deficit-hyperactivity
        disorder (ADHD), 397–401
    in adolescents, 400
    in adults, 400
    causes of, 397–399
    in children, 399–400
    combined type, 397
    diagnostic criteria for, 398*f*
    interventions for, 399–400
    medications for, 399
    multimodal treatments for, 400
    predominantly hyperactive-impulsive
        type, 397
    predominantly inattentive type, 397
    prevalence of, 397–399
    types of, 397

Audible traffic signals (ATS), 354

Audiologist, **334**

Audition, **319**

Auditory approach, in hearing loss
        communication, 328–330

Auditory processing disorder, **164**

Augmentative communication, **249**,
        281, **309**, 364

Aura, 378

Authentic assessment, **113**, **303**

Autism
    apps for, 285
    first diagnosis of, 277
    IDEA and, **268**
    IDEA definition of, 271

Autism Siblings, 290*t*

Autism spectrum disorders (ASD),
        266–295, **268**
    in adult years, 293
    applied behavior analysis for,
        281–282
    behavioral interventions for, 287–289
    caregiving and, 289
    causes of, 278–279
    characteristics of, 271–276
    conditions associated with, 275–276
    creative educational services for, 285
    diagnostic criteria for, 269–271
    diagnostic terms for, 270*t*
    in early childhood, 271, 292
    educational classification for, 271
    educational interventions for, 280
    in elementary school, 292–293
    evaluation of, 268–269
    evidence-based practices for, 280–285

family and, 289–291
    functional skills and, 284
    gender and, 278
    IDEA and, 271
    IEP for, 280
    impairments in, 272
    in mass media, 268
    medications for, 287
    multidisciplinary collaboration for,
        279–293
    parents and, 289–290
    perseveration in, 275
    in preschool, 280, 292
    prevalence of, 278
    repetitive behavioral patterns in,
        273–274
    rituals in, 274–275
    routines in, 274–275
    savant skills in, 276
    in school-aged children, 280
    in secondary and transition years, 293
    social communication and, 272–273
    social interaction skills and, 273
    social relationships and, 284
    therapeutic interventions for, 280
    in toddlers, 280
    treatments for, 281–282*t*
    visual structure/support for, 282–284

Average, 5

Baby talk, 257

Bacterial meningitis, 367

Barrier-free facilities, **20**

Basic interpersonal communication
        skills (BICS), 106

*Behavioral and Emotional Rating
    Scale, Second Edition (BERS-2)*,
    195*f*

Behavioral contract, **172**

Behavioral factors, **224**

Behavioral interventions, 171–172

Behavior disorders, **182**

Behind-the-ear aid, 334

Berenson, Bernard, 405

Bernhardt, Sarah, 8

Best Buddies International, 218

BEZH (Bureau of Education for the
        Handicapped), 27

Bias
    environmental, 7
    measurement, **110**
    test, **110**

Bicultural-bilingual approach, **331**

Bilingual, **106**

Binet, Alfred, 406

Biomedical factors, **222**

Bipolar disorders, 185

Emergency rooms, 203
Emotional and behavioral disorders (EBD), 177, 189–190
  academics and, 185–186
  in adolescents, 205–207
  in adult transition, 200
  assessment of, 191–195
  causes of, 187–188
  characteristics of, 184–186
  classification of, 188–190
  clinically derived classification of, 189–190
  contributing factors, 183
  in early childhood, 197–198
  in elementary school, 198–201
  full inclusion and, **207**
  gangs and, 206
  IDEA definition of, 182–183
  inclusive education and, 207
  intelligence and, 184
  interventions for, 196–207
  multidisciplinary collaboration for, 196–207
  normal behavior and, 183
  PBS for, 192
  prevalence of, 183
  RTI for, 192
  screening for, 191–192
  socialization and, 184–185
  statistically derived classification of, 188–190
  wraparound services for, 201–205
Emotional disorders, **182**
Employment
  ADA and, 14
  of adults with disabilities, 84–85
  assistive technology for, 231
  high school and, 94–95
  intellectual disabilities and, 233–234
  supported, 234
Encephalitis, **225**
English as a second language (ESL), **106**
English language learners (ELL), **105**, 109
Enrichment, **428**
Enuresis, 190
Environmental bias, 7
Environmental context, 215
Epidural hemorrhages, 391
Epilepsy, **302**, 377–380
  ASD and, 276
  causes of, 379
  first aid for, 377*f*
  interventions for, 379–380
  ketogenic diet for, 380
  prevalence of, 379

stress management for, 380
tonic/clonic seizures in, 378
ESEA. *See* Elementary and Secondary Education Act
ESL. *See* English as a second language
Esotropia, **339**
Ethnic diversity, 105–106
Evidence-based early intervention, 62–64
Evidence-based inclusive education, 53–56
  acceptance in, 53
  age-appropriate classrooms in, 55–56
  characteristics of, 53–55
  cultural diversity in, 53
  in elementary school, 70–79
  formal supports in, 53
  general curriculum in, 56
  natural supports in, 53
  neighborhood schools in, 55–56
  in preschool, 67–68
  school-wide support in, 56
Exceptional, **4**
Exoskeleton, 371
Exotropia, **339**
Expressive language disorders, **245**
Extended family, 139–140
Eye, parts of, 336*f. See also* Vision loss

Facebook, 335
Family, 128–149
  autism and, 289–291
  characteristics of, 132–133
  cultures and, 132–133
  diagnosis and, 129–131
  disabilities and, 128–149
  dyadic relationships in, 135–136
  extended, 139–140
  father-child relationships in, 136–137
  grandparents, 139–140
  life cycle of, 140–141
  mother-child relationships in, 135–136
  roles of, 132–133
  sibling relationships in, 137–139
  as social/ecological system, 128–129
  spousal relationships in, 133–135
  support for, 140–143, 144–151
  training for, 147–148
Family-centered support, 141–142
FAPE. *See* Free and appropriate public education
Farsightedness, **228**, 339*f*
FAS. *See* Fetal alcohol syndrome
Father-child relationships, 136–137
Fathers. *See also* Family

preferences of, 137
responses of, 136–137
Feeding disorders, 189
Fernandina Beach, Florida, ADA and, 12
Fetal alcohol effects, 225
Fetal alcohol syndrome (FAS), **224**
Figure-ground discrimination, **163**
Flowers, Vonetta, 239
Fluency disorders, 253–255
Formal supports, **53**
Fragile X syndrome, **223**, 276
Fraternal twins, **165**
Free and appropriate public education (FAPE), 30, 42
French Sign Language (FSL), 327
Friday's Kids Respite, 134
Full inclusion, 52, 54–55, **207**
Functional articulation disorders, **255**
  causes of, 256–257
Functional assessment, **65**
Functional life skills
  assistive technology for, 307–309
  autism and, 284
  high school and, 93–94
  preschool and, 67
  severe and multiple disabilities and, 307
Funds of knowledge, **113**

Galaburda, Albert, 160
Galactosemia, **224**
Gangs, 206
Gastronomy tube feeding, **302**
General curriculum, **33**, 42, 56
General education, 102
General education teachers, 58
Generalization, **219**
Genetic counselor, **17**
Geneticist, **17**
Genetics
  gifted, creative, and talented and, 415
  hearing loss and, 322–323
  intellectual disabilities and, 223
  severe and multiple disabilities and, 301
Genius, 405
Genocide, 9
Gifted, creative, and talented, 404–437, **406**
  acceleration for, 425–428
  in adolescence, 420–432
  in adult transition, 424
  in adult years, 424
  assessment for, 417–418
  assistive technology for, 429
  career choices and challenges for, 430–431

Kinesthetic, **164**
Klippel-Trenaunay-Weber syndrome, 15
Kurzweil, Ray, 350
Kurzweil 1000/3000 Reading System, 350

Labels, 4–5
  effects of, 6
  self-labeling, 6
  separating person and, 7
Language, 240–241
  components of, 240–241
  development of, 241–242
  intellectual disabilities and, 220
  severe and multiple disabilities and, 302
  vision loss and, 342, 346–347
Language acquisition, 116
Language deficits in EBD, 186
Language disorders, 243–250
  acquired, 246
  aphasia, 245–246
  assistive technology for, 249
  augmentative communication for, **249**
  causes of, 246–247
  classification of, 245–246
  definition of, 244–245
  expressive, **245**
  ILP for, 247–248
  receptive, 245
  treatment of, 247–250
Language diversity, 106–108, 111–112
Language experience approach (LEA), 346
Larry P. v. Riles, 110
Laser Cane, **346**
Learned helplessness, **220**
Learning, intellectual disabilities and, 218–219
Learning disabilities, 4, **153–156**.
  See also Intellectual disabilities
  academics and, 159–163, 167
  adaptive skills and, 166–167
  in adolescents, 172–176
  assessment for, 165–167
  behavior interventions for, 171–172
  causes of, 164–165
  characteristics of, 158–164
  classification, 156–157
  cognition and, 163
  college and, 175–176
  criteria for identifying, 155*f*
  definitions of, 154
  discrepancy and, 162
  in elementary school, 167–168
  emotional characteristics of, 164
  environmental factors in, 165

genetic factors in, 165
  hyperactivity and, 164
  information processing and, 163
  instruction and support for, 168–171, 172–173
  intelligence and, 162–163, 166–167
  learning characteristics and, 163–164
  mathematics and, 162, 169
  maturational delay and, 165
  multidisciplinary collaboration for, 176–177
  neurological factors in, 164–165
  prevalence of, 157–158
  reading and, 159–161, 169–171
  reasonable accommodations and, 175
  RTI for, 157, 168
  screening for, 166
  social characteristics of, 164
  spelling and, 161–162
  writing and, 161–162
Learning Disabilities Association, 10
Least restrictive environment (LRE), 33. *See also* individualized education program; special education
  CLD and, 117
  IDEA and, **33**
  for multicultural education, 117
  for special education, 36*t*, 38, 117
  for vision loss, 351–352
Legal blindness, **336**
Leno, Jay, 8
Lens, **335**
Limited English proficiency (LEP), **106**, 112
Line-21 system, 332
Linguistic intelligence, 411*t*
Locke, John, 16
Logical-mathematical intelligence, 411*t*
Low birth weight, **225**
Luvox (drug), 287

Macular degeneration, **341**
Magnetic resonance imaging (MRI), **389**
Mainstreaming, 27, **52**
Malocclusion, **257**
Manual approach, in hearing loss communication, 330–331
Martin, Casey, 15
Maternal infection, **224**
Mathematics
  assessment for, 167
  instruction and support for, 169
  learning disabilities and, 162, 169
Maturational delay, 165
Measurement bias, **110**
Medically fragile, **373**

Medical model, **16**
Memory, intellectual disabilities and, 218–219
Meningitis, 323
Mental age, **406**
Mental health, intellectual disabilities and, 215
Mental health care, emergency rooms for, 203
Mental retardation, 6
Mentoring, 430
Metabolic disorder, **224**
Metabolism, intellectual disabilities and, 224
Methylphenidate, 399
Microphthalmia, **340**
Migrant Education Programs, 120
Migrants, 120
Mills v. Board of Education of the District of Columbia, 11, 28*t*
Mirror writing, **161**
Mixed hearing loss, **321**
Modified cultural pluralism, **103**
Monoplegia, 362*t*
Mood disorders, 185
Morphemes, 240
Morphology, **240**
Mothers. *See also* Family
  dyadic relationships, 135–136
  overprotectiveness by, 136
Motivation, 220
Motor skills, intellectual disabilities and, 227
Mountabatten Braille, 349
Mowat sensor, **346**
MTSS. *See* Multitiered system of support
Multicultural education, **102**
  assessment for, 110–111
  culturally and linguistically responsive teaching in, 113–114
  IEP for, 116
  LRE for, 117
  parents and, 114–116
  process checklist, 120
  professional preparation for, 113
  role of, 102–104
  for severe and multiple disabilities, 305
  special education and, 104–109
Multidisciplinary collaboration, **56**, **109**
  for adolescents, 177, 205–206
  for ASD, 279–293
  childhood and, 177
  for communication disorders, 243
  cooperative learning in, 60
  in early childhood, 60–81, 197–198
  for EBD, 196–207

Special Education Content Standard 6:
COMMUNICATION

Special educators understand **typical and atypical language development** and the ways in which exceptional conditions can interact with an individual's experience with and use of language. Special educators use individualized strategies to **enhance language development** and **teach communication skills** to individuals with ELN. Special educators are familiar with **augmentative, alternative, and assistive technologies** to support and enhance communication of individuals with exceptional needs. Special educators match their communication methods to an individual's language proficiency and cultural and linguistic differences. Special educators provide **effective language models** and they use communication strategies and resources to **facilitate understanding of subject matter for individuals with ELN whose primary language is not English**.

Special Education Content Standard 7:
INSTRUCTIONAL PLANNING

Individualized decision-making and instruction is at the center of special education practice. Special educators develop **long-range individualized instructional plans** anchored in both general and special curricula. In addition, special educators systematically translate these individualized plans into carefully selected **shorter-range goals and objectives**, taking into consideration an individual's abilities and needs, the learning environment, and a myriad of cultural and linguistic factors. Individualized instructional plans emphasize **explicit modeling** and **efficient guided practice** to assure acquisition and fluency through maintenance and generalization. Understanding of these factors, as well as the implications of an individual's exceptional condition, guides the special educator's selection, adaptation, and creation of materials, and the use of powerful instructional variables. Instructional plans are **modified based on ongoing analysis of the individual's learning progress**. Moreover, special educators facilitate this instructional planning in a **collaborative context** including the individuals with exceptionalities, families, professional colleagues, and personnel from other agencies as appropriate. Special educators also develop a variety of **individualized transition plans**, such as transitions from preschool to elementary school and from secondary settings to a variety of postsecondary work and learning contexts. Special educators are comfortable using **appropriate technologies** to support instructional planning and individualized instruction.

Special Education Content Standard 8:
ASSESSMENT

Assessment is integral to the decision-making and teaching of special educators, and special educators use **multiple types of assessment information** for a variety of educational decisions. Special educators use the results of assessments to help identify exceptional learning needs and to develop and implement individualized instructional programs, as well as to adjust instruction in response to ongoing learning progress. Special educators understand the **legal policies and ethical principles of measurement and assessment** related to referral, eligibility, program planning, instruction, and placement for individuals with ELN, including those from culturally and linguistically diverse backgrounds. Special educators understand **measurement theory and practices** for addressing issues of validity, reliability, norms, bias, and interpretation of assessment results. In addition, special educators understand the appropriate **use and limitations** of various types of assessments. Special educators collaborate with families and other colleagues to assure **non-biased, meaningful assessments and decision-making**. Special educators conduct **formal and informal assessments** of behavior, learning, achievement, and environments to design learning experiences that support the growth and development of individuals with ELN. Special educators use assessment information to **identify supports and adaptations** required for individuals with ELN to access the general curriculum and to participate in school-, system-, and statewide assessment programs. Special educators **regularly monitor the progress** of individuals with ELN in general and special curricula. Special educators use **appropriate technologies** to support their assessments.

Special Education Content Standard 9:
PROFESSIONAL AND ETHICAL PRACTICE

Special educators are guided by the profession's ethical and professional practice standards. Special educators practice in multiple roles and complex situations across wide age and developmental ranges. Their practice requires ongoing attention to **legal matters** along with serious professional and **ethical considerations**. Special educators engage in **professional activities** and participate in learning communities that benefit individuals with ELN, their families, colleagues, and their own professional growth. Special educators view themselves as **lifelong learners** and regularly reflect on and adjust their practice. Special educators are aware of how their own and others' attitudes, behaviors, and ways of communicating can influence their practice. Special educators understand that culture and language can interact with exceptionalities, and [they] are **sensitive to the many aspects of diversity** of individuals with ELN and their families. Special educators actively plan and engage in activities that foster their professional growth and keep them **current with evidence-based best practices**. Special educators know their own limits of practice and practice within them.

Special Education Content Standard 10:
COLLABORATION

Special educators routinely and effectively **collaborate with families, other educators, related service providers, and personnel from community agencies in culturally responsive ways**. This collaboration assures that the needs of individuals with ELN are addressed throughout schooling. Moreover, special educators embrace their special role as advocates for individuals with ELN. Special educators promote and advocate the learning and well-being of individuals with ELN across a wide range of settings and a range of different learning experiences. Special educators are viewed as specialists by a myriad of people who actively seek their collaboration to effectively include and teach individuals with ELN. Special educators are a **resource to their colleagues** in understanding the laws and policies relevant to individuals with ELN. Special educators use collaboration to **facilitate the successful transitions** of individuals with ELN across settings and services.

Council for Exceptional Children Standards Correlation Chart

As in the previous edition, the contents of *Human Exceptionality: School Community and Family*, Eleventh Edition, correspond with the Council for Exceptional Children (CEC) Standards. Icons in the margins highlight the relevant CEC Standards. This handy correlation chart provides page numbers for specific CEC standards found in each chapter.

Part/Chapter	Council for Exceptional Children (CEC) Standards
Part I Through the Lifespan	
Chapter 1 **Understanding Exceptionalities in the 21st Century**	1 Foundations, pp. 5, 13 2 Development and Characteristics of Learners, p. 13 5 Learning Environments and Social Interactions, p. 20 9 Professional and Ethical Practice, p. 18
Chapter 2 **Education for All**	1 Foundations, pp. 26, 27, 29, 41 2 Development and Characteristics of Learners, p. 29 3 Individual Learning Differences, pp. 31, 34, 37, 38 7 Instructional Planning, p. 31 8 Assessment, pp. 30, 37 9 Professional and Ethical Practice, p. 3?
Chapter 3 **Inclusion and Collaboration in the Early Childhood and Elementary School Years**	1 Foundations, p. 61 3 Individual Learning Differences, pp. 53, 73 4 Instructional Strategies, p. 59, 64, 77 5 Learning Environments and Social Interactions, pp. 51, 63, 67 7 Instructional Planning, pp. 64, 69 9 Professional and Ethical Practice, p. 53 10 Collaboration, pp. 56, 70
Chapter 4 **Secondary Education and Transition Planning**	1 Foundations, pp. 83, 86 2 Development and Characteristics of Learners, p. 92 3 Individual Learning Differences, p. 91 4 Instructional Strategies, pp. 91, 92, 95 5 Learning Environments and Social Interactions, pp. 84 7 Instructional Planning, pp. 85, 87 9 Professional and Ethical Practice, pp. 83, 88
Part II Perspectives on Diversity and the Family	
Chapter 5 **Cultural and Linguistic Diversity**	1 Foundations, pp. 113, 117 2 Development and Characteristics of Learners, pp. 109, 111 3 Individual Learning Differences, pp. 109, 111 5 Learning Environments and Social Interactions, p. 115 8 Assessment, pp. 110, 113 9 Professional and Ethical Practice, pp. 113, 147
Chapter 6 **Exceptionalities and Families**	1 Foundations, p. 128 3 Individual Learning Differences, p. 135 5 Learning Environments and Social Interactions, pp. 140, 146 9 Professional and Ethical Practice, p. 148 10 Collaboration, p. 143
Section III People Who Are Exceptional	
Chapter 7 **Learning Disabilities**	1 Foundations, p. 154 2 Development and Characteristics of Learners, p. 159 3 Individual Learning Differences, p. 159 5 Learning Environments and Social Interactions, pp. 168, 173 7 Instructional Planning, pp. 168, 173 8 Assessment, pp. 165, 175